Principles of Corporate Finance

Haim Levy
Hebrew University of Jerusalem

With the assistance of
Michael J. Alderson
Saint Louis University

SOUTH-WESTERN College Publishing

An International Thomson Publishing Company

11-9-01

Publisher/Team Director: Ch
Acquisitions Editor: Ch
Development Editor: D
Production Editor: Pegg
Marketing Manager: Lisa L. Lysne
Production House: Pre-Press Company, Inc.
Cover Design: Paul Neff Design
Internal Design: Craig LaGesse Ramsdell

Library of Congress Cataloging-in-Publication Data
Levy, Haim.
    Principles of corporate finance/Haim Levy.
        p.   cm.
    Includes index.
    ISBN 0-538-84741-7
        1. Corporations—Finance.   I. Title.
    HG4026.L474   1997
    658. 15—dc21   97-36159
                                         CIP

2 3 4 5 6 7 8 D1 4 3 2 1 0 9 8

Printed in the United States of America

I(T)P®
International Thomson Publishing
South-Western College Publishing is an ITP Company.
The ITP trademark is used under license.

PREFACE

Financial markets have been changing rapidly over the last decade. New financial instruments have evolved and the task of the firm's chief financial officer (CFO) has changed. *Principles of Corporate Finance* explains recent innovations in capital markets along with the proven theories and techniques of corporate finance. It is designed to help students focus on the foundations of corporate finance and to help them prepare for their duties in their first job. Students who study this book will learn and understand the principles of finance and will be able to discuss them intelligently with supervisors and peers "in their own words."

The text emphasizes the most widely used financial innovations—the ones that occupy most of the CFO's time. To reinforce this point, I have made extensive use of quotes and citations from the financial media. These materials help the student "listen" to corporate finance specialists as they describe the issues they face and how to solve them. The CFO's arguments are woven into the text and provide a bridge between the classroom and the executive suite.

DISTINCTIVE FEATURES

Principles of Corporate Finance includes a number of useful and distinctive features:

1. It provides precise analysis that is relevant to the firm. It avoids financial models of limited usefulness.

2. Arguments are presented logically, then buttressed by intuitive explanations. Numerical and graphical illustrations complement this approach. Mathematical formulas are avoided unless they are necessary; in many cases they are relegated to footnotes or appendices.

3. Every chapter includes at least one application with a complete solution. Such applications—which use actual data or a quote from a CFO—show students the relevance of the key issues studied in that chapter. Knowing that they are dealing with real issues increases students' motivation and enthusiasm.

4. At least one mini–case study (reflecting a real issue described in the financial media or a firm's financial statements) appears at the end of each chapter.

5. Each chapter ends with a large, rich set of problems and exercises. These range from simple numerical problems, to more challenging decision-making exercises, to actual problems taken from the financial media.

6. Applying Theory to Practice boxes, which appear in all chapters, contain additional material from the financial press. They pinpoint the financial issues faced by CFOs and motivate the students to study the issues discussed in the chapter.

7. Many solved problems are interspersed within the chapter text. Reading through the solved problems enhances students' understanding of the issues discussed in the chapter.

8. The Internet is a new and useful source of financial information. Each chapter in this book contains one or more boxes that briefly describe how to use the Internet to enrich the study of finance. In addition, Professor Russ Ray, of the University of Louisville, has contributed an appendix at the end of the book that describes how to use the Internet.

EMPHASIZING RELEVANCE

The following are a few examples of how this book emphasizes relevance:

- Chapter 1 presents excerpts from the daily diary of Ken Matlock, the CFO of Walter Industries. These excerpts give students a flavor of what CFOs actually do.

- Economic Value Added (EVA) and Market Value Added (MVA) are hot ideas among CEOs and CFOs. Because these two ideas are widely employed by practitioners, they are introduced in Chapter 1 and contrasted with the traditional goal of stock value maximization.

- Modern finance advocates using the weighted average cost of capital (WACC) in capital budgeting. Financial executives favor the Economic Value Added principle. Chapter 10 demonstrates that the two ideas amount to basically the same thing.

- Chapter 14 illustrates the decision to "go public" by studying Robert Mondavi, the owner/manager of the famous Napa Valley winery.
- Options and optionlike securities have traditionally been taught in the investments course. Today, however, corporations such as IBM, Merck, and Intel successfully employ options and other derivatives to reduce risk. They can be challenged in court if they do not use derivatives to reduce risk.

    It's beginning to become an expectation that if the capacity to hedge exists and it can be done safely, there will be criticism, and possibly litigation, if advantage isn't taken of that opportunity (Fortune, *25 July 1994*).

    Therefore, Chapter 11 emphasizes derivatives as a tool for the financial executive.

STRUCTURE OF THE BOOK

Principles of Corporate Finance has been designed as a flexible teaching tool. Here is a brief description of what you will find within it:

- Part 1 discusses the financial environment, the goal of the firm, and the task of the CFO. Because many subsequent chapters use accounting concepts, Chapter 3 reviews the basics of financial statement analysis. If you do not wish to teach financial statements early in the course, you can simply discuss the basic accounting definitions and skip most of this chapter.
- Part 2 is devoted to project evaluation with emphasis on the NPV criterion. It shows how proper use of this investment rule helps the firm meet its financial goals.
- Part 3 introduces risk. It reviews the historical record on the mean return and variability of stocks, bonds, and other assets; defines risk; and shows how firms should apply risk measures in capital budgeting. The difference between the project cost of capital, which varies according to the project's unique risk characteristics, and the firm's cost of capital is emphasized.
- Part 4 discusses long-term financing, the economic features of bonds and stocks, and the process of going public.
- Part 5 is devoted to capital structure and dividend policy. It focuses on three important questions: Should a firm finance its projects by debt or equity, is there an optimum mix of financing, and, if so, what economic factors determine this mix?
- Part 6 discusses long- and short-term financial planning.
- The final part, Part 7, deals with short-term financial management, including managing cash asssets, and accounts receivable and inventory.

This text does not contain separate chapters on leasing, mergers, or international finance. Instead, these topics are integrated into the relevant chapters. The lease-versus-buy decision appears as an application in Chapter 7, where students learn how to construct a project's cash flows. After all, the incremental cash flow is the key issue in the lease-buy decision. Mergers and acquisitions are covered in

Chapters 5 and 9. There we see that the economic evaluation of a merger, in principle, is no different from evaluation of any other project.

International finance is crucial as the financial world becomes more and more global. To reflect this growing importance, international financial management issues are integrated throughout the book. For example, *Principles of Corporate Finance* covers such issues as Japanese and American executives' attitudes, responsibilities, and compensation; the price/earnings multiples in various countries; and the cost of capital of firms operating in various countries (in particular, the United States and Japan) and its effect on international competition. The text also shows how firms involved in international trade can use derivatives to hedge the foreign currency risk.

INTENDED AUDIENCE

This text is designed for a first course in finance. No previous course work in finance is assumed. Although the book is self-contained, some basic algebra is helpful. The text is appropriate for majors and nonmajors alike.

SUPPLEMENTARY ITEMS

Experience shows that students really learn the basics of corporate finance by working numerous, realistic problems and exercises. As mentioned, many of the pedagogical features of this text were designed to provide a real-world flavor. The *Solutions Manual* includes worked-out solutions to these problems. In addition, short answers to some of the end-of-chapter problems appear at the end of the text itself. These answers help students see if they are on the right track.

Professor Joseph Vu of DePaul University has written a *Test Bank* that will be useful in devising class examinations. He has also developed a *Study Guide* that provides additional support materials and contains additional problems for students to work on.

Thomson Investor's Network is an Internet-based, online financial service that offers up-to-the-minute financial information. Four-month subscriptions are available with qualified adoptions of this text. Learn more at http://www.thomsoninvest.net.

Professor Steven Wyatt of the University of Cincinnati has developed a CD-ROM that helps students explore financial management in a uniquely interactive way. His *Finance: An Interactive Approach* combines hands-on practice, exercises, simulations, animated exhibits, and a built-in calculator.

REVIEWERS

In writing this text, I have benefited from the helpful comments of many reviewers. I would like to thank the following instructors for taking time to help me improve the book:

Michael Alderson
St. Louis University

Yakov Amihud
New York University

George Aragon
Boston College

Robert Balik
Western Michigan University

Keqian Bi
University of San Francisco

Gerald Bierwag
Florida International University

Arthur Cox
University of Northern Iowa

Charles Cox
Brigham Young University

Shreesh Deshpande
University of San Diego

Jeanette Diamond
University of Nebraska, Omaha

Edward Dyl
University of Arizona

John Ellis
Colorado State University

Daniel Falkowski
Canisius College

Sharon Garrison
East Tennessee University

James Gentry
University of Illinois

Deborah Gregory
Bentley College

Alan Grunewald
Michigan State University

Deborah Gunthorpe
University of Tennessee

Thomas Hamilton
St. Mary's University

John Harris
Clemson University

David Heskel
Bloomsburg University

Ronald Hoffmeister
Arizona State University

James Jackson
Oklahoma State University

Stanley Jacobs
Central Washington University

Vahan Janjigian
Northeastern University

Hazel Johnson
University of Louisville

Michael Keenan
New York University

James Keys
Florida International University

Richard Kish
Lehigh University

Ladd Kochman
Kennesaw State University

Yoram Kroll
Hebrew University

David Kunz
Southeast Missouri State University

John Lightstone
State University of New York, Albany

Jason Lin
Northwest Missouri State University

William McDaniel
Florida Atlantic University

Rita Maldonaldo-Bear
New York University

Ralph May
Southwestern Oklahoma University

Ronald Shrieves
University of Tennessee

Lalatendu Misru
University of Texas, San Antonio

Keith Smith
Purdue University

Karlyn Mitchell
North Carolina State University

Jonathan Sokobin
Southern Methodist University

Joseph Ogden
State University of New York, Buffalo

Jill Wetmore
Saginaw Valley State University

James Pawlukiewicz
Xavier University

Steve Wyatt
University of Cincinnati

Robert Puelz
Southern Methodist University

David Yamoah
Kean College

George Racette
University of Oregon

James Yoder
West Georgia College

Meir Schneller
Virginia Polytechnic Institute

J. Kenton Zumwalt
Colorado State University

I also wish to thank Natalie Elisof, Yael Ben-David, Eitan Goldman, Boaz Libovitz and, in particular, Allon Cohen, who provided excellent research assistance. Mike Alderson made many important contributions to the text and the supplementary items. Thank you, Mike. In addition, I wish to thank Dennis Hanseman, Peggy Buskey, and Ann Torbert, whose many suggestions and skillful handling greatly improved this book.

Finally, I would like to thank Maya Landau, who edited this book in its early stages, and Hyla Berkowitz for an excellent typing job.

Haim Levy

Applying Theory to Practice: List of Applications

Chapter	Application
1	The Economic Value Added (EVA) Principle
2	Service Comes First in the U.S.A.
3	Vehicle with Value: Ford's Finance Unit Could Drive the Stock Higher
4	The $67 Million Ivax Buyout
5	NPV, Market Value Added (MVA), and the Invested Capital
5	Creating Positive NPV by Merger
6	Using the Payback Method: The Americans versus the Japanese
7	The Golden Pond Company
7	Lease-versus-Buy Decisions
8	Firm's Foreign Currency Risk Management: A Portfolio Approach
9	Coca-Cola and PepsiCo: The Gain from Merger
10	Intel's Investment Abroad: Country Risk
10	The Capital Budget of Chrysler Corporation
11	Using Options to Reduce Foreign Risk
12	The Bond Market: Risk and Reward
13	Estimating Meditronic, Inc.'s Cost of Equity
14	IPOs and the Cost of Equity: Boston Chicken
15	Leverage and Regulation: Oklahoma Gas and Electric Corporation
16	Boeing Corporation's Capital Structure
17	Gerber Products' Dividend Policy
18	PACCAR, Inc.'s Pro Forma Statements
19	J.C. Penney's Working Capital Management
20	Cash Assets Management at Toys 'R' Us
21	The Cost of J.C. Penney's Credit Card

Your Turn: Applying Theory to Practice List of Mini–Case Studies

Why study corporate finance? There are several reasons why it is worthwhile. First, finance is a challenging, dynamic profession. Most big financial transactions, mergers, acquisitions, and spinoffs are orchestrated by firms' Chief Financial Officers. Without a good knowledge of corporate finance, it is unlikely that you would be involved in such fascinating transactions.

The excitement—and the rewards—of a career in finance are captured in the following excerpt from a recent *Fortune* article:

Once glorified bookkeepers, the best chief financial officers are now rounded players who orchestrate megadeals, fix troubled companies, and hatch creative ideas. The pantheon encompasses Stephen Bollenbach, an architect of Disney's $19 billion acquisition of Capital Cities/ABC; Judy C. Lewent of Merck, a math wizard with a formula for handicapping R&D projects; and GE's Dennis Dammerman, a master of building businesses for the 21st century . . . .

Disney, for instance, lured Bollenbach with a signing bonus package estimated at $20 million, $7 million more than Deion Sanders pocketed for jumping to the Dallas Cowboys.

One reason companies don't mind paying these millions is that such stars can save millions in fees, especially on big deals. Super-CFOs are nimble, original dealmakers who don't always need Wall Street types to handle acquisitions and spinoffs for them. Bollenbach and his staff, for *instance, conceived and negotiated the Disney acquisition of Cap Cities without the help of a single securities firm, saving their company at least $20 million in fees. The trend worries prominent investment bankers, one of whom complains: "The CFOs absolutely compete with us. That's why our fees are going down."*

"Source: Shawn Tully, "Super CFOs: They Can't Jump . . . ," *Fortune,* 13 November 1995.

Second, a job as a CFO is becoming a springboard to even bigger jobs—in particular, president and CEO of a firm.

Third, no matter whether you are the firm's CFO or CEO, statistics reveal that the reward is very high. For example, in 1994, in a survey of 549 companies, the CFOs earned an average of $898,000 in total annual compensation. Compensation for super CFOs and CEOs is even greater—Michael Eisner of Walt Disney earned more than $200 million in 1993!

Who said no one wants to be a statistic? So, what's the catch? To earn such high salaries, you need corporate finance experience. To get that experience, you need that all-important first job. That's where this course—and this textbook—come in. Their aim is to give you enough knowledge that you can get your first job—even without experience. Pay careful attention to the many examples, applications, and mini-cases. They employ actual examples and actual data and provide a close approximation to the kinds of situations you will encounter on the job.

By studying this book and becoming a CFO, you may soon be part of the salary statistics reported in the financial press.

BRIEF CONTENTS

CONTENTS

PART 2 PROJECT EVALUATION

PART 3   PORTFOLIO AND CAPITAL BUDGET DECISIONS

8 The Gain from Diversification 257

9 Risk and Return 300

PART 4   LONG-TERM FINANCING

PART 5   CAPITAL STRUCTURE AND DIVIDEND POLICY

15 Does Capital Structure Matter?: A Perfect Market   551

PART 6   FINANCIAL PLANNING

18 Long–Term Financial Planning 675

19 Short–Term Financial Planning 705

PART 7   SHORT-TERM FINANCIAL MANAGEMENT

CHAPTER 1

THE ROLE OF THE FINANCIAL MANAGER

LEARNING OBJECTIVES

After reading this chapter, you should understand:

1. Why individuals and firms invest and the concept of reallocation of consumption over time.

2. The concepts of cash flow, time value of money, profitability, and risk.

3. The need to form a business organization to raise capital.

4. The pros and cons of the various forms of business organization.

5. The decision makers of a corporation.

6. The principal duties of the chief financial officer (CFO).

7. The potential areas of conflict among the three principal parties who have a stake in the firm: bondholders, stockholders, and managers.

8. The firm's goal and the economic value added (EVA) principle.

CORPORATE FINANCE IN THE NEWS

CREATING STOCKHOLDER WEALTH

Today's investor looks closely at many different signs to track how a company is doing: return on equity, market capitalization, earnings-per-share growth. But of all these yardsticks, only one—called **market value added,** or MVA—is designed to answer capitalism's most fundamental question: Has management increased or diminished the value of the capital that lenders and shareholders have given it? . . .

A close cousin to MVA is EVA, or **economic value added:** after-tax net operating profit in a given year minus a company's cost of capital in that year.

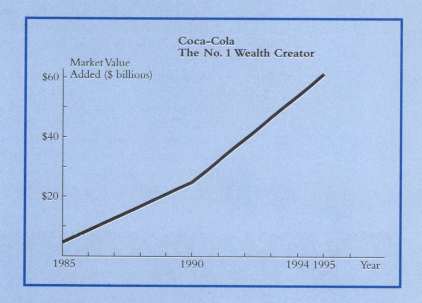

A SERVING OF ADDED VALUE

. . . As a measure of performance, MVA and related techniques are scarcely new. But they have been gaining ground lately as a result of the increased emphasis—in the U.S. and UK at any rate—on the principle of shareholder value.

Sources: Anne B. Fisher, "Creating Stockholder Wealth," *Fortune* 132, no. 12 (December 1995): 105–106. Copyright 1995 Time Inc. All rights reserved. Tony Jackson, "A Serving of Added Value," *Financial Times,* January 13, 1997, p. 8.

1.1 INTRODUCTION AND PREVIEW

The Corporate Finance in the News articles are about managers' ability to create wealth from shareholders' and bondholders' investments. If, for example, shareholders and bondholders invest $100 million in the firm and if the firm's market value increases to $150 million, then $50 million of wealth is created. The firm's goal is to create wealth. By this yardstick, Coca-Cola, which created $60 billion in wealth from 1985 to 1995, had the best financial management. The concepts of EVA and MVA and what investment criteria managers should employ to guarantee wealth creation will be explained in great detail in this book. In this chapter's Applying Theory to Practice, we discuss EVA. We will discuss MVA in Chapter 10 after we have become better acquainted with the cost-of-capital concept.

As you progress through this book, you will probably ask yourself how you can apply the information for your own benefit. For instance, when you read this chapter, you may identify with the chief financial officer (CFO), who controls the firm's financial resources that, when invested in projects, create wealth. You may wonder, "What do I, as a student, have in common with the heads of big corporations or the 'movers and shakers' of Wall Street?" Your present financial situation is more likely to be debt and obligation than a surplus of funds. You may have student loans to repay and rent or car payments to make. However, you have a great deal in common with the financial managers of our largest corporations. They, too, face debt and obligation—but on a larger scale. Indeed, as this book will show, they rely on debt. The main difference between your situation and theirs is that you have yet to acquire the expertise needed to solve your financial problems. So, whether or not you aspire to be a CFO, you will find this book relevant to your concerns in one way or another.

The following *Wall Street Journal* article provides a springboard into our discussion of the CFO's principal concerns. Don't worry if some details in the article seem confusing at this point; they'll become clear as we proceed.

CONNECTING THEORY TO PRACTICE 1.1

KKR'S LUSTER DIMS AS FALL IN RJR STOCK HURTS INVESTORS' TAKE

New York—The record $25 billion buyout of RJR Nabisco made a celebrity of Henry Kravis. But the transaction—once regarded as the deal maker's greatest triumph—now is being tarnished by troubles in the tobacco business that are paring the investment returns of his leveraged-buyout firm, Kohlberg Kravis Roberts & Co.

(continued)

RJR Dwarfs Other KKR Investments Investments from KKR's $5.6 billion 1987 buyout fund; dollar amounts in millions	Company	Investment Date(s)	Amount Invested	Market Value April 23, 1993
	RJR Nabisco	2/9/89, 7/16/90	$3,055	$3,122
	K–III (Media)	Various	380	585[a]
	Duracell	6/24/88	342	1,900
	American Re	9/30/92	300	1,100
	TW Holdings	11/16/92	299	299[b]
	Fleet/Bank of New England	7/10/91	281	530
	Stop & Shop	4/1/88	98	640
	Seaman Furniture	12/15/87	65	0
	KC Cable Associates	9/17/92	36	36[b]
	Granum Communications	12/31/91	19	19[b]
	TOTAL[c]		$4,875	$8,231

[a]As of December 31, 1992.
[b]Valued at cost because held less than one year.
[c]The total includes other investments not listed in this table.

Source: Randall Smith and Eben Shapiro, "KKR's Luster Dims as Fall in RJR Stock Hurts Investors' Take," *Wall Street Journal*, 26 April 1993, sec. A1, 6. Reprinted by permission of *The Wall Street Journal*, © 1993 Dow Jones & Company, Inc. All rights reserved worldwide.

MAKING THE CONNECTION

Kohlberg Kravis Roberts & Co. (KKR) borrowed money and used some of its own resources to purchase other firms in transactions called leveraged buyouts. This article reviews KKR's investments and how they have fared. It shows the various dollar amounts KKR invested over a number of years and the corresponding market value of each investment as of April 1993. Essentially, the article is about KKR's *cash flows*—one important topic in corporate finance. Because cash flow is important, let's examine this concept in more depth.

1.1.1 Cash Flow

When it invests money in a project, a firm expects the project will generate additional funds. The money invested in a project represents a *cash outflow,* and the money the project generates represents a *cash inflow* to the firm. These **cash flows** occur at various times for the project's duration. For example, if a firm pays $10 million cash today to buy a new machine that will result in a cash inflow of $5 million at the end of each of the next three years, the project's cash flow will be as follows:

	Year			
	0	**1**	**2**	**3**
Cash flow	–$10 million	$5 million	$5 million	$5 million

In Connecting Theory to Practice 1.1,[1] we see that from 1987 to 1992 KKR invested \$4,875 million of its own resources (excluding borrowed funds) in various firms. By April 1993 the value of these investments had grown to \$8,231 million. In other words, if KKR had sold all the investments in April 1993, the company's cash inflow would have been \$8,231—almost double its initial investment. However, as we can see, the growth was uneven. Some investments were very profitable. For example, the value of the investment in Duracell increased from \$342 million to \$1,900 million. On the other hand, some investments were not profitable. The value of the investment in Seaman Furniture dropped from \$65 million to zero.

To fully appreciate the information that such investment comparisons provide, you need to become familiar with a number of other basic financial concepts—namely, the *time value of money, risk, financing,* and *project evaluation*.

1.1.2 Time Value of Money

One principal duty of the CFO is to evaluate and compare projects that have different cash flow characteristics. Managers of various departments present to the CFO projects that each believes the company should fund. To choose among these projects, the CFO (and his or her staff) will evaluate each in terms of the cash flows it is expected to generate at different times. In other words, the timing of the cash flows must be considered. To do this properly, financial managers need to know the **time value of money**—the comparison of cash flows occurring at various times. Put simply, the time value of money means that one dollar received today is worth more than one dollar received at some future time. Why? Because today's dollar can be deposited in the bank or invested elsewhere and can earn interest in the interim period. The strength of the preference for one dollar today over one dollar, say, one year from now will depend on the current interest rate.

We are now better equipped to interpret the information in Connecting Theory to Practice 1.1. Suppose that in 1988 you, as KKR's financial manager, were offered an investment in Duracell. Then in 1992 you were offered an investment in American Re, which operates in the reinsurance business and related areas. For simplicity, assume at the time of investment you were certain that the April 1993 Duracell investment value would be \$1,900 million and that the American Re investment value would be \$1,100 million. Which investment would be more profitable? At first glance, Duracell might seem more attractive. However, to enjoy the \$1,900 million from the Duracell project in 1993, you had to make the investment in 1988; whereas to get the \$1,100 million from American Re in 1993, you could have made the investment four years later, in 1992. The superiority of Duracell is not quite so obvious. Duracell provided a larger cash flow in 1993, but your investment was tied up longer—five years as opposed to one year. During the intervening four years, you would have had the \$342 million to use for some other purpose.

Now, consider the profitability of the RJR Nabisco investment. (See the figures given in Connecting Theory to Practice 1.1.) Because the RJR Nabisco investment

---

1. For simplicity, we will assume from here on that the market values reported in Connecting Theory to Practice 1.1 include the dividends obtained from each investment.

grew in value from $3,055 million in 1989–1990 to $3,122 million in 1993, it might seem to have been profitable. However, the $67 million increase in the investment value from 1990 to 1993 may not have been large enough to compensate investors for the time their money was tied up. To be more specific, if KKR borrowed the money to finance this investment and then decided to sell out in 1993, the cash that KKR would obtain from the sale might not be sufficient to cover the interest and the principal to be repaid to the lender. If this were the case, the investment would not be profitable.

These examples show that without a well-defined technique for evaluating cash flows obtained at various dates, we cannot evaluate a project's economic worth or compare it with other competitive projects. The following problem illustrates the importance of the timing of cash flows in determining an investment's profitability.

PRACTICE BOX

Problem

Suppose KKR finances the $3,055 million it needs to invest in RJR Nabisco by borrowing from a bank. The bank charges 15% for the whole period 1989–1993.
a. Is the RJR Nabisco project profitable?
b. How would your answer change if KKR realizes a cash flow of $3,122 million one month after it makes the investment and if the bank charges only 0.5% interest for this month?

Solution

a. In the first case, KKR owes the bank (principal and interest): $3,055 million × 1.15 = $3,513.25 million. Because the market value of RJR Nabisco is $3,122 million, KKR has a net loss of $391.25 million ($3,122 million − $3,513.25 million).
b. In the second case, where KKR realizes a cash flow of $3,122 million one month after its investment, the company realizes a profit of $51.725 million: $3,122 million − ($3,055 million × 1.005) = $3,122 million − $3,070.275 million = $51.725 million.

Developing and applying a well-defined technique to determine the timing of cash flows will be one key topic in this book and in your course. Cash flow evaluation and the time value of money will be discussed in greater detail in Chapters 4 and 5.

1.1.3 Risk

As Connecting Theory to Practice 1.1 showed, some of KKR's investments were very profitable, but others resulted in losses. When a project's future cash flows are uncertain, we say that **uncertainty** or **risk** prevails. One of the financial manager's most difficult tasks is evaluating an investment's risk and, using profit forecasts along with risk assessment, making optimal investment decisions. Risk analysis, the evaluation of uncertain cash flows, and techniques for risk reduction are covered in Chapters 8 through 11.

1.1.4 Financing

Firms need to raise money to finance new investments as well as ongoing projects. KKR raised money to finance its investments by selling stocks to the public—that is, **equity financing**—and by borrowing money—that is, **debt financing.** A firm generally pays interest on its debt, and failure to make required interest payments may cause bankruptcy. A large amount of debt financing may put financial pressure on the company. Should KKR have raised more equity and borrowed less? This is a key issue the firm faces. The optimum mix of equity and debt is discussed in Chapters 15 and 16.

1.1.5 Project Evaluation

In Connecting Theory to Practice 1.1, we read that KKR made many acquisitions in the period 1987–1992. Buying a firm involves taking over all its machinery, buildings, technical know-how, and personnel. Other investments could be cited, such as General Motors opening a new assembly line, a small firm buying a new machine or building, or even an individual investor buying a company's stock or a certificate of deposit from a bank. Criteria to evaluate such investments or projects are needed. As we will see later, the criteria for evaluating either large or small investments are the same. Project evaluation will be discussed in Chapters 5 through 7.

1.2 WHY DO INDIVIDUALS AND FIRMS INVEST?

Joseph Spiers writes:

Something rare and remarkable is going on, as companies buy equipment at fierce rates. The benefit could be enormous.[2]

Spiers goes on to reveal that the growth rate in business equipment investment was 18% in 1993 and 17.5% in 1994, compared to only 6% in 1992 and −3.3% in 1991.

When they provide money to firms to invest, individuals (as stockholders) indirectly invest money in projects. Why do individuals invest? Why don't they simply spend their cash flows on consumption as the cash becomes available? Individuals invest for two main reasons: one is their wish to reallocate consumption over time, and the other is their desire to be wealthy. It's as simple as that.

1.2.1 Reallocation of Consumption

Investors who turn a small amount of cash into a large nest egg are the legends of the investment world. They make an extraordinary profit on their investment.

---

2. Joseph Spiers, "The Most Important Economic Event of the Decade," *Fortune* 131, no. 6 (April 1995):33–40. Copyright © 1995 Time Inc. All rights reserved.

However, people routinely invest a portion of their wealth even without the prospect of an extraordinary return. For instance, individuals and firms invest in riskless assets such as savings accounts and certificates of deposit (CDs), which have fairly certain but relatively low rates of return. **Rate of return** is defined as the percentage change in the investment's value during a given time period, generally one year. Because the rate of return on savings accounts and CDs is low, investors' main motive for using them is their wish to *reallocate consumption over time* rather than their desire to be wealthy.

Let's review two examples of the reallocation of consumption over time. After earning salaries for a given number of years, most people experience a drastic drop in income when they retire. Consider a financial manager who now earns an annual income of $150,000. Due to retire in 10 years, she thereafter will receive a retirement benefit of $30,000 a year. Even if Social Security payments are added, she faces a dramatic drop in her standard of living. Should her co-workers start collecting donations to help support her in her old age? Not really. Remember: She is a financial manager and is well acquainted with that powerful tool called investment. She could, for example, put aside $50,000 a year by reducing consumption today and guarantee a fairly decent level of future consumption.

As a student your annual earnings are probably not $150,000. However, what if an aunt were to bequeath you a million dollars? You could go on a spending spree and live it up for as long as the money lasts. However, such a spending policy would leave little (or nothing) for future consumption. You would do better to invest a substantial part of your wealth to enjoy cash flows for consumption in the years to come. The same is true for investors in general.

Suppose you decide to spend $100,000 the first year, put the remaining $900,000 under your mattress, and withdraw a certain amount each year for consumption. This would constitute a form of investment because it would allow you to reallocate consumption over time, but the *rate of return* on the money held under your mattress would be zero. Why put money under your mattress when you can deposit it in the bank and earn, say, 3% annual interest on it? Moreover, imagine your horror if someone were to find the hidden money and relieve you of your nest egg. Or what if your house were destroyed by fire? Your $900,000 would be a worthless heap of ashes. As before, you would do better to put the money in the bank. In addition to earning interest, U.S. bank deposits are insured up to $100,000 (in which case you could use nine different bank accounts to insure the safety of your entire fortune).

1.2.2 Creating Wealth: The Desire to Be Wealthy

In the previous section we showed how investors can reallocate their wealth across time. However, the amount of wealth we invest today is usually not equal to the amount we will receive from our future investments. If our investments are profitable, the amount we receive in the future will be larger, and sometimes *much* larger, than the amount we invested today. For example, the price of Walt Disney Co. stock in 1985 was about $4 per share (see Connecting Theory to Practice 1.3). An investor with $100,000 could have purchased 25,000 shares. Twelve years later, in August 1997, Disney's price per share surpassed $80. An investor with 25,000 shares would have realized an increase in value to over $2 million. In contrast, if the investor had deposited the $100,000 in a bank account earning 5% annual interest, her wealth in 1997 would have increased to only $179,586.

From this example we can see that the other reason people invest is the desire to be wealthy. A highly profitable investment opportunity may arise, but it may also have a large risk attached. By forfeiting some consumption this year, an investor may enjoy a very large cash flow in the future. Why do people desire to be wealthy? Some see wealth as a means to guarantee security. Some simply enjoy watching their money pile up. Some view wealth as a means to indulge in expensive consumption or to achieve social status and maybe even political power and influence. A few want wealth to provide help to those who are less fortunate.

Investment links the present and the future. By giving up some consumption in the present, individuals and firms can enjoy larger cash flows at later dates. Indeed, most individuals and firms invest a portion of their wealth as a matter of course. Evaluating the alternative investment opportunities available to investors is not a simple task. In fact, it occupies a good deal of the CFO's time. We will devote much attention to this issue in this book.

1.3 RAISING CAPITAL: THE NEED FOR A BUSINESS ORGANIZATION

Suppose you are offered the opportunity to invest in one of two projects: a retail store or a firm that produces computers. The retail outlet requires an initial cash outlay of $10,000, on which you can earn on average 8% annually. The computer firm requires an initial cash outlay of $500 million, on which you can earn on average 15% annually. You prefer the 15% return, but you have only $10,000 to invest. You have two alternatives:

1. Give up the 15% return on the large investment and invest in the retail project earning 8%. In this case you will simply draw the needed money from your savings account and make the investment. Because only one person—you—makes the investment cash outflow, all future cash inflows from the investment will be yours.
2. Approach a large number of investors—say, 50,000—and have each invest $10,000. In this way you have raised the $500 million needed for the large investment, and you can earn 15%. In this case all investors share the investment, the profit, and the risk.

To take advantage of the large profitable investment, an organization of investors is needed. The various ways that investors can form a business organization are discussed next.

1.4 FORMS OF BUSINESS ORGANIZATION

The United States has three main forms of business organization: *sole proprietorships, partnerships,* and *corporations.*

1.4.1 Sole Proprietorship

One person, the proprietor, owns and controls a **sole proprietorship.** Controlling all the business's assets, the proprietor is entitled to all the profits, which are taxed at the personal income tax rate. This form of business is simple to set up and has minimal organization costs. Also, one person makes all business decisions without needing the approval of others.

The disadvantages of a sole proprietorship are as follows:

1. It has *unlimited liability;* that is, creditors can claim the owner's personal assets if the firm's assets are not sufficient to cover creditors' claims.
2. Its life span is limited to the proprietor's lifetime. When the proprietor dies, the proprietorship dissolves.
3. It has a limited capital base. This form of business cannot take on large investments because one person cannot usually generate enough funds.
4. Transferring ownership is difficult. A proprietorship is not traded in a market and has no quoted price.

1.4.2 Partnership

In principle a **partnership** is similar to a proprietorship except that the business has at least two owners—the *partners.* Each partner's share is determined by a partnership agreement, and each partner pays personal income taxes on his or her share of the firm's profits. Compared to a sole proprietorship, a partnership can raise larger sums of money because there is more than one owner.

A partnership has several disadvantages:

1. Partners may disagree about business decisions or operations.
2. Like a proprietorship, it has a limited life span (the lifetime of the partners).
3. It has unlimited liability.
4. It has a limited capital base.
5. Transferring ownership is difficult.

Although a partnership's size is not limited by law, it cannot usually be large because the potential for disagreement increases as the number of partners increases. Both proprietorships and partnerships are usually small and are best suited to medical or legal practices or to businesses requiring relatively low levels of investment.

1.4.3 Corporation

Many major corporations maintain extensive Web sites. Check out Ford's and GM's sites and explore a few of the many links.

http://www.ford.com
http://www.gm.com

A **corporation** is a legal entity formed through articles of incorporation. The owners, or *stockholders,* own shares of the corporation's stock. The greater the number of shares a stockholder holds, the larger his or her ownership in the corporation.

A corporation offers the following advantages:

1. It has *limited liability;* that is, creditors cannot claim the stockholders' personal assets.
2. It has *unlimited life.* Its existence is independent of the stockholders' life spans.
3. It can raise large amounts of capital by selling shares.
4. Transferring ownership is easy. Whenever stockholders buy or sell stocks, transfer of a corporation's ownership occurs.

A corporation also has disadvantages. The main ones are double taxation, agency costs, and organization costs. Each disadvantage is discussed briefly in the following paragraphs.

Double taxation of income is the main disadvantage of a corporation. First the corporation pays taxes on its income. Then the stockholders pay personal income tax on their cash dividends (the corporation's distributed after-tax income) and on their *capital gains* (from selling shares at a profit). The following problem illustrates the effect of double taxation.

PRACTICE BOX

Problem

An investment yields a taxable profit of $100,000. Assume a corporate income tax rate of 35% and a personal income tax rate of 31%.

a. What will be the after-tax *net* income if the money is invested in a corporation?

b. What will be the *net* income if the money is invested in a sole proprietorship?

Solution

a. For simplicity assume you are the sole owner of this firm. If you form a corporation, you face double taxation: First, the firm pays corporate income tax. Its after-tax income will be: $(1 - 0.35) \times \$100,000 = \$65,000$. Then, when you receive your $65,000 dividend, you pay personal income taxes. After you pay all taxes, your income will be

$$(1 - 0.31) \times \$65,000 = \$44,850$$

b. If you form a proprietorship, you pay only personal income tax. Your net income will be

$$(1 - 0.31) \times \$100,000 = \$69,000$$

When it is very large and has many stockholders, a corporation usually hires professional managers to run its business. If the managers' and the stockholders' economic interests do not coincide, the stockholders' interests are likely to suffer.

The losses that stockholders incur when the managers do not act in the stockholders' best interest are called **agency costs.** For example, if a corporation's stock price is $100 per share when management acts in the stockholders' best interest, but is $90 when management does not act in their best interest, stockholders will lose $10 per share. Of course, their total loss will be $10 times the number of shares held. This loss is an agency cost resulting from a conflict of interest between stockholders and management.

The **organization costs** of a corporation are relatively large. Whereas partnerships and proprietorships can begin operations without much paperwork, setting up a corporation generally requires an attorney's services. In addition, corporations usually hire outside accounting firms to compile the quarterly and annual financial statements and tax reports that must be filed with state and federal authorities.

Table 1-1 summarizes the advantages and disadvantages of the three forms of business organization.

Table 1-2 shows the three main forms of business organization in the United States and the magnitude of business each conducts. Although proprietorships far outnumber corporations, the volume of business that proprietorships conduct is relatively small. Indeed, corporations conduct most of the U.S. capital investment. Although most of this book is devoted to corporations, the economic principles presented also apply to the other forms of business organization.[3]

TABLE 1-1 Advantages and Disadvantages of the Three Main Forms of Business Organization	Form of Business		
Characteristics	Proprietorship	Partnership	Corporation
Number of Owners	One	More than one, but not very many	Very large (can be millions)
Liability	Unlimited	Unlimited	Limited
Life Span	Limited to the lifetime of the proprietor	Limited; if one partner withdraws, the firm dissolves	Unlimited
Organization Costs	Negligible	Moderate	Considerable
Taxation	Personal income tax rate	Personal income tax rate(s) of partners	Double taxation: corporate tax and personal income tax rates of stockholders for dividends or capital gains
Ability to Raise Capital	Limited	Moderate	Considerable
Agency Costs	None	Small	Can be very large

3. The *S-corporation* should be mentioned in this context. The income of this business organization is not taxed at the corporate tax rate, rather it is distributed to the owners who pay only personal tax. An S-corporation would seem to enjoy the "best of both worlds"—limited liability and no double taxation. However, the number of shareholders in an S-corporation is limited by law. This permissible roster increased in 1996 to 75 shareholders (see Joseph F. Gelbart, "Taxing Subject," *Barron's,* January 6, 1997, p. 19).

TABLE 1-2 Distribution and Magnitude of Business Conducted by the Main Forms of Business Organization in the United States	Size of Firm by Annual Receipts	Number of Firms (thousands)		
		Proprietorship	Partnership	Corporation
	Total	14,299	1,636	3,628
	Less than $25,000	9,856	1,014	865
	$25,000 to $49,999	1,660	131	241
	$50,000 to $99,999	1,259	142	332
	$100,000 to $499,999	1,334	242	1,145
	$500,000 to $999,999	140	51	415
	Over $1,000,000	50	56	630
		Receipts (billions of dollars)		
	Total	693	465	10,439
	Less than $25,000	66	1	5
	$25,000 to $49,999	60	3	9
	$50,000 to $99,999	89	8	24
	$100,000 to $499,999	276	46	288
	$500,000 to $999,999	96	31	292
	Over $1,000,000	106	376	9,821

Source: U.S. Bureau of the Census, *Statistical Abstract of the United States: 1993,* 113th ed. (Washington, DC: 1993), p. 531.

1.5 WHO ARE THE DECISION MAKERS IN A CORPORATION?

Now online, the Wall Street Journal is read daily by the overwhelming majority of senior executives.

http://www.wsj.com

Figure 1-1 depicts the organizational structure of a typical corporation. By law a corporation must have a board of directors, a chairman (chairperson) of the board, and a president. The stockholders elect the members of the board of directors, who are responsible for safeguarding the stockholders' interest. The board of directors nominates the chairman of the board, who usually fills the position of **chief executive officer (CEO).** The CEO (with board approval) nominates the president, who usually serves as **chief operations officer (COO),** and three vice presidents: the *chief production officer,* the *chief marketing officer,* and the **chief financial officer (CFO).** In small firms the CEO is often also the CFO. However, most large firms have a separate CFO who oversees the activities of both the *treasurer* (responsible for capital budgeting, raising funds, credit policy, inventory, and cash management) and the *controller* (responsible for payroll and tax payments and for the corporation's accounting). The officers' tasks frequently overlap. For example, in small firms the treasurer and controller are usually the same person, and the CFO is often responsible for policy decisions as well as for financial planning.

FIGURE 1-1
Typical Organizational Structure of the Decision Makers in a Corporation

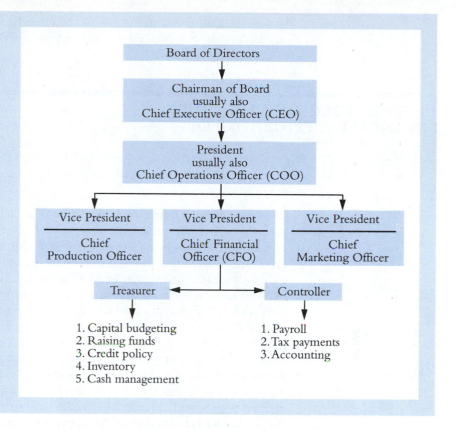

The CEO is the corporation's key decision maker, and no major action can be taken without his or her approval. If the corporation flourishes, the CEO will generally receive the largest bonus; if the firm flounders, he or she will often be the first terminated. The COO is responsible for the corporation's smooth operation and for coordination among its various units. The CFO has responsibility for the corporation's financial planning and policy, such as decisions regarding mergers and acquisitions, dividend policy, pricing of products, and timing and size of stock issues. The CEO, the COO, and the vice presidents work as a team. For example, although the CFO may initiate and manage a merger or a new acquisition, he or she cannot complete such moves without the CEO's involvement and approval.

Although the CEO, the COO, and the vice presidents manage the corporation, the board of directors approves many decisions. For example, the board typically approves dividends, large cash outlays, and the CEO's compensation. The board also discusses the investment strategies that management recommends, but it generally does not make specific management decisions. However, if management does not perform well, the board of directors has the right to dismiss the CEO or any other top manager whom it holds responsible for the failure. For instance, when corporate giants General Motors, IBM, and Kmart lost money in the early 1990s, their respective boards of directors exercised this right and replaced their CEOs.

In this book we focus on the role of the chief financial officer (CFO). Let us take a closer look at the principal areas of activity associated with this position.

1.6 THE ROLE OF THE CHIEF FINANCIAL OFFICER (CFO)

The chief financial officer (CFO)—also referred to as the *financial manager*—is responsible for a wide range of financial decisions. The most important of these decisions are the following:

- *Investment decisions (capital budgeting).* The financial manager needs to know how to evaluate and choose among alternative projects. This task is not particularly difficult if the cash flows can be predicted with certainty. However, it is quite difficult if uncertainty prevails. For instance, consider two one-year projects requiring the same investment of $100 million. One project provides a cash flow of $110 million (earning a profit of $10 million) with certainty; the other has a 50% chance of providing $140 million (a profit of $40 million) and a 50% chance of providing $90 million (a loss of $10 million). Choosing between such projects is probably the most difficult task confronting the financial manager and deals with the area of finance called **capital budgeting.**
- *Financing decisions.* Corporations can issue stock, through which stockholders may purchase a portion of the corporation. Each stockholder has voting rights and is entitled to receive dividends. The corporation may also borrow by issuing bonds. A bondholder is entitled to fixed interest payments but has no voting rights.

    Once a set of projects has been chosen, the financial manager knows how much cash is needed to fund them. Then the manager faces the following dilemmas: Should the corporation issue stock (equity) or bonds (debt) to provide the needed resources? Should the corporation borrow short-term or long-term? These and similar questions are **financing decisions.**

    Making the correct financing decision requires a thorough understanding of the *capital market*—that is, the markets and institutions that specialize in providing financing. The CFO serves as an intermediator between the corporation's operations and the capital markets. The CFO must analyze very carefully the pros and cons of each source of financing. The financing decision determines the corporation's **capital structure**—that is, its mix of financing sources.
- *Dividend policy decisions.* The corporation uses the cash flows generated by the projects that it undertakes to pay its various expenses such as interest (to lenders such as banks and bondholders) and taxes. After paying its expenses, a corporation must decide its *dividend payments.* In this **dividend policy decision,** the financial manager recommends to the board of directors how much of the remaining cash flow should be distributed as dividends and how much of it the corporation should keep to reinvest in new projects.
- *Short-term financial management decisions.* The CFO spends much time making **short-term financial management** decisions—the management of short-

term assets and liabilities such as cash, inventory, and short-term loans. Efficient management of these items and careful scrutiny of cash outflows and inflows may save the corporation a lot of money and may prevent financial distress.

All these decisions are interrelated. For instance, if the corporation undertakes more projects and pays larger dividends, it will have to raise more money to finance new projects. The CFO is also involved—sometimes on a daily basis—in a host of other financial matters, such as deciding on customer credit policy and its effect on the corporation's cash flow or ensuring sufficient cash flow for future payments such as payroll, taxes, and loan repayments.

You may wonder how one person can cope with so many demands. The CFO of a large corporation works very hard, but teams of experts, each responsible for a different aspect of the corporation's financial management, support the CFO. (In fact, if you pursue a career in finance, you will probably begin your career as a member of one of these teams.) The other vice presidents of the corporation also cooperate with the CFO. For example, the production manager provides estimates of how much raw material is needed to guarantee smooth production. The marketing department guides the production department regarding market needs and even recommends the shape of a new product. The CFO employs all these inputs to forecast the corporation's financial needs. Figure 1-2 depicts the principal activities of the financial manager.

The CFO's responsibilities vary from one corporation to another. Generally the larger the firm, the larger the team working with the CFO and the more the CFO

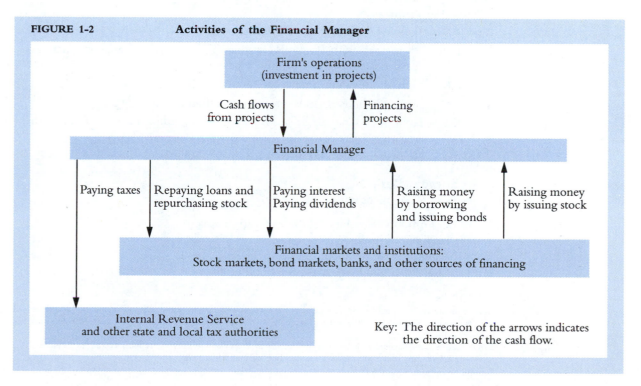

FIGURE 1-2   Activities of the Financial Manager

delegates responsibilities to people working in coordination with and under his or her supervision. Connecting Theory to Practice 1.2 presents a one-week daily diary of Ken Matlock, the CFO of Walter Industries Incorporated ($1.5 billion sales in 1997). Walter Industries is active in home building, financing, and natural resources.[4] The diary, which is reproduced here exactly as obtained from Mr. Matlock, clearly illustrates the CFO's many and varied tasks. Some of the terms used in the diary (such as *proxy, prospectus, underwriting agreement*) may be unfamiliar to you. They will all be explained as we progress through this book.

CONNECTING THEORY TO PRACTICE 1.2

KEN MATLOCK'S DIARY: A TYPICAL WEEK IN THE LIFE OF A CFO

Monday, June 28

8 A.M.   Review revised prospectus draft[5]—reviewed copy to underwriter.[6]

9 A.M.   With Public Relations—return phone calls from three analysts regarding press release on earnings.

10 A.M.   Underwriter's counsel in office.

3 P.M.   Insurance Department and Legal Department—report from . . . Insurance Co. regarding casualty insurance claims/settlements. Discuss two proposed settlements of potentially major claims.

Tuesday, June 29

8 A.M.   Review draft of Annual Report.

9 A.M.   Phone call with Public Relations to . . . , financial analyst with . . . securities company regarding year-end numbers.

10 A.M.   Get Auditor's comments on Annual Report draft.

11 A.M.   With Public Relations—return two financial analyst phone calls.

1 P.M.   Building Manager/Legal Department regarding new contract with outside service company for company cafeteria.

3 P.M.   Analyst from . . . in; meet with Public Relations.

Wednesday, June 30

To New York; meet with underwriters

- Comments regarding 1st draft of prospectus.
- 1st draft of underwriting agreement.
- Revised draft of documents to printer.
- Draft of Rating Agency[7] presentation.

---

4. Walter Industries experienced financial distress in the late 1980s. A weak housing market, a heavy debt load, and asbestos-related lawsuits forced the firm to file for bankruptcy protection in 1989. Later it emerged from bankruptcy, and by 1997 its stock was highly valued.

5. A document containing financial and accounting details that the corporation prepares when it issues securities to the public.

6. Usually an investment banker who handles the security issue and insures its success.

7. Companies such as Standard & Poor's or Moody's that evaluate and rate securities according to the risk involved.

Thursday, July 1

New York

9 A.M.   Meeting with underwriters on financing—finalize Rating Agency presentation.

1 P.M.   Meet with Standard & Poor's (year-end & financing).

3 P.M.   Meet with Moody's (year-end & financing).

Home from New York late.

Friday, July 2

10 A.M.   Building manager regarding proposed changes to telephone system. Review first draft of proxy statement—add officers/directors compensation section. Have outside counsel review compensation section regarding compliance with new SEC[8] rules.

Source: This information was provided to the author by Ken Matlock.

MAKING THE CONNECTION

The CFO's role includes many activities that we will review in detail throughout this book.

This book is devoted to the financial activities of corporations, which are mainly the CFO's responsibility. As just shown, these activities are complex. We will present and clarify the numerous economic factors that a CFO must consider in making decisions. To gain recognition as a knowledgeable manager, you will need to be well versed in all economic factors involved in the decision-making process. However, to be a successful manager requires more than specialized knowledge alone. A background in areas such as politics, history, geography, sociology, psychology, or cultural anthropology will add a valuable dimension to your managerial skills. No matter how well you understand and later apply the financial criteria presented in this book, there will always be room for personal judgments—for example, judgments regarding events such as a possible world oil crisis, the outbreak of a war, the collapse of the Soviet Union, a drought in Florida. Such judgments may well be based on "gut feeling" and intuition—even creative inspiration—rather than on any particular chapter of this (or any other) book.

1.7 CONFLICTS OF INTEREST

A corporation is a complex organization that professional managers, not the owners, operate. Three parties have a stake in the firm: management, bondholders, and stockholders. The goals of these three parties do not necessarily coincide; on the

---

8. Securities and Exchange Commission.

contrary, they may conflict. There are two potential conflicts of interest: those between bondholders and stockholders and those between stockholders and management.

1.7.1 Bondholders versus Stockholders

When a corporation decides to raise money by issuing bonds, it borrows money from its bondholders—the purchasers of the bonds. Bondholders generally receive interest on the money they lend to the corporation, but they do not receive dividends. Should the corporation fail and declare bankruptcy, bondholders could even lose repayment of the "loan's" principal amount and payment of the interest due on it. Bondholders, therefore, have an essentially conservative goal: They want the corporation to at least maintain its financial position. For this reason, bondholders would discourage the corporation from taking on exaggerated risks, or paying overly high dividends, or entering into heavy debt. Indeed, bondholders often attach conditions to their loans that limit managers' freedom in these areas.

The conflicting interests of bondholders and stockholders affect the corporation's choice of equity versus debt financing. From the corporation's point of view, bond financing should be used only if it will benefit the stockholders, because they own the corporation. For example, if the bondholders' constraints on dividends are overly tight and run counter to the stockholders' welfare, the corporation may simply decide not to take on loans (including those created by issuing bonds) but, rather, to finance its projects by issuing only equity. Management has to consider this conflict of interest when deciding on the best debt–equity **financing mix**—one that will maximize the stockholders', not the bondholders', welfare.

1.7.2 Stockholders versus Management

Conflicts of interest between management and stockholders can be major problems in large corporations. These problems usually involve management's actions and compensation.

MANAGEMENT ACTIONS

A manager may prefer a project with large cash flows in the first few years to a project with relatively low cash flows in the first few years followed by very large cash flows in subsequent years, even if the latter project is better for the stockholders. The primary reason for the manager's choice is his or her focus on the short term. If the manager has plans to advance in the corporation (and what manager doesn't?) or to move on to another firm, the cash flows due after he or she leaves will receive less emphasis in the decision-making process—a conflict of interest par excellence. The conflict of interest between managers and stockholders may reduce the corporation's value because of the agency costs associated with management's actions. Also, the corporation may incur additional costs to monitor managers' actions.

To avoid or reduce such conflict, the board of directors may choose to include, as part of top managers' compensation, **stock options**—options to buy stock under favorable conditions. A corporation uses this compensation strategy because it knows that management will be more motivated to increase the corporation's value, which, in turn, will make stockholders more content.

How do stock options work? Suppose that the market price of a firm's stock is $100 and that the manager is given the option to buy the stock at $110. If the stock price increases, say to $140, the manager can exercise the option, buy the stock for $110, and make a $30 profit per share. Managers benefit from the reward only if the stock price increases, and the more it increases, the greater their profit. The following problem demonstrates how a CEO fares when she exercises her stock option.

PRACTICE BOX

Problem

Suppose the CEO of Fine Electronics is awarded an option to buy 100,000 shares of the corporation's stock at $100 per share. The current stock price is $80. The CEO can exercise the option any time she wishes. What is her gain on the option if the stock price rises to $120?

Solution

The CEO can buy the stock for $100 a share and immediately sell it on the market for $120. With a gain of $20 on each option, her total gain is: $20 × 100,000 = $2,000,000.

A CEO's cash flow from an option benefit occurs in the year he or she exercises the stock options. Connecting Theory to Practice 1.3 reports the total compensation of Michael Eisner, Walt Disney's CEO. Note that in 1993, fearing a 1994 hike in income tax for high-income taxpayers, Eisner decided to exercise 5.4 million options worth $202 million before taxes. It's obvious that stock options benefit CEOs who manage their companies well. Do they also benefit stockholders? Consider the price changes of Disney stock: It rose from $3^{49}\!/_{64}$ in 1985 to $42^{5}\!/_{8}$ in 1993. Apparently both Eisner and the stockholders benefited from a well-managed firm. Following the announcement on August 1, 1995, of the second largest merger in U.S. history, in which Disney paid about $19 billion for the acquisition of Capital Cities/ABC, Disney stock jumped 4.9% in one day. By mid 1997, the share price had passed the $80 mark.

CONNECTING THEORY TO PRACTICE 1.3

WHAT MICKEY HAS MADE MICHAEL

With the bulk of his compensation tied to increases in Disney's net income and return on equity, Eisner has bagged a bundle as both exploded over the past decade. He really went off the charts in 1993, when he exercised 5.4 million options worth $202 million before taxes.

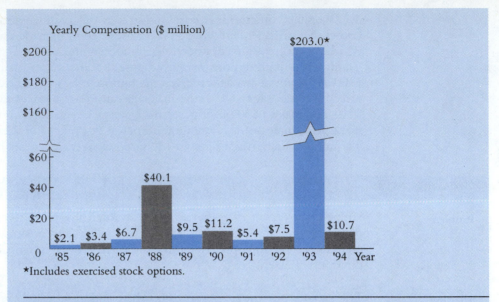

*Includes exercised stock options.

MAKING THE CONNECTION

Mr. Eisner received a lot of money. Was it too much? Not necessarily. Recall that Disney's stock price rose from about $4 in 1985 to over $80 in 1997. If this increase was due to Eisner's excellent management, the compensation may have been well deserved.

MANAGEMENT COMPENSATION

Elected by the stockholders, the board of directors is formally independent of the CEO whom it chooses. The corporation's compensation committee, consisting of board members, determines the CEO's and other top managers' remuneration. These managers, who determine the directors' compensation, can influence the direct or indirect benefits that the board awards them. As a result, the managers and the board do not necessarily act in the stockholders' best interests.

Board members' dependence on management is summarized in a quote from *Forbes* magazine:

Slowly, but steadily, the pay and perks grew, giving boards an incentive to become less vigorous in challenging managements. Many U.S. corporate executives came to believe that stockholder ownership was practically a myth. The prevalent theory was that a modern corporation had many constituents, of which the shareholders were only one relatively unimportant one. If the shareholders didn't like the way management was running the company, they could sell the stock and take their money elsewhere.[9]

9. Dana Wechsler Linden, "Off With Their Perks," *Forbes* 156, no. 13 (December 1995):54–60.

Controversy over management compensation has been mounting, and some firms are beginning to question the size of management compensation packages. For example, in 1992 the board of directors of Kmart decided to hire an outside consultant to study the compensation of Joseph Antonini, Kmart's CEO (who was dismissed in 1995 because of bad financial results).

Also, a movement to tie management compensation to performance is growing. For example, up to 1991 the compensation of Rand Araskog, the CEO of ITT, was not specifically linked to performance. Then institutional stockholders demanded a change in the compensation scheme to increase the association between performance and the CEO's compensation.[10] Charles Sanford, the CFO of Bankers' Trust, suffered a 57% reduction in compensation in 1994 following a drop of 29.9% in the price of the firm's stock. Similarly, Deryck Maughan, the CEO of Salomon Brothers, had a 87% reduction in compensation in 1994 after a 21.1% drop in Salomon's stock price.

Although many corporations have not yet tied executive compensation directly to performance, they are beginning to feel the pressure to do so. Widespread public criticism and stricter SEC disclosure guidelines have prompted some corporations to examine their "executive largesse." Some directors have to sign statements that justify their pay packages. Senior executives are under more pressure to align their interests with those of stockholders. For example, "IBM recently adopted new ownership guidelines that require its senior executives to own company stock equal to two to four times their base salary depending on their position."[11]

Figure 1–3 demonstrates the breakdown of CEOs' compensation for the years 1985 and 1991. We see from this figure that the average compensation "pie" expanded dramatically during this period, from $725,000 a year in 1985 to $1.7 million

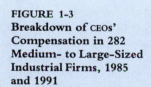

FIGURE 1-3
Breakdown of CEOs'
Compensation in 282
Medium- to Large-Sized
Industrial Firms, 1985
and 1991

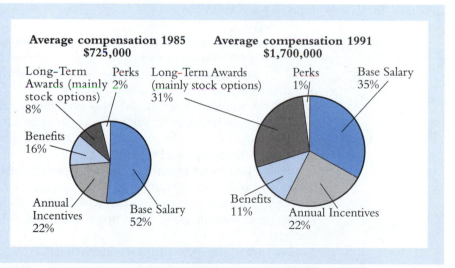

10. Sherman Stratford, "Can You Believe What You See at ITT?" *Fortune* 131, no. 7 (April 1995):109–116.
11. John A. Byrne, "Deliver—Or Else," *Business Week,* March 27, 1995, pp. 36–38.

in 1991. However, during this period the base salary portion of compensation decreased from 52% to 35%—which is more evidence of the trend to tie compensation to performance.

These compensation schemes (and even the more extreme step of replacing managers as a result of poor performance) may not eliminate the conflict of interest between managers and stockholders, but they do reduce it.

1.8 THE CORPORATION'S GOAL: PROFITABILITY VERSUS RISK

Assuming the corporation has significantly reduced conflict of interest between its managers and stockholders, what should be its goal? A common answer is: maximizing its dollar-amount profits or average percentage profit on investment. For instance, if a project requires an initial outlay of $100 and the expected cash flow is $120, the dollar-amount profit will be $20 and the percentage profit will be 20%.

Employing this as the corporation's goal has two drawbacks: one relates to the time value of money; the other, to risk.

Drawback 1. Suppose that a firm is considering two projects, Project A and Project B, which are expected to generate the following cash flows:

	Year			
	0	**1**	**2**	**3**
Project A	−$90 million	$100 million	0	0
Project B	−$90 million	0	0	$120 million

If we assume the corporation can accept only one project, which is better, Project A or Project B? Similar to KKR's various investments (see Connecting Theory to Practice 1.1), the answer to this question is not at all obvious. Project B promises $30 million profit ($120 million − $90 million), and Project A promises only $10 million profit ($100 million − $90 million). However, the cash flow of Project B occurs only in its third year. Because the value of a dollar received today is more than that of a dollar obtained at some future date, profit by itself is not necessarily the best criterion. The firm may prefer Project A.

In a world of certainty, this drawback is not fatal. As will be shown in Chapter 4, some form of *discounting* can be applied to reduce all cash flows to a common time denominator (called the *present value*) to determine which project is more profitable. However, as we will show, this is not a simple task when the future cash flows are uncertain.

Drawback 2. Suppose a firm is considering two projects, Project A and Project B. Project A yields $110 million with certainty; Project B has a 50:50 chance of earning $90 million or $140 million (or a probability of ½ for each of the two outcomes). The initial investment is $100 million for each project. Project B is better "on average" because its *average* income is

$$(\$90 \text{ million} \times \tfrac{1}{2}) + (\$140 \text{ million} \times \tfrac{1}{2}) = \$115 \text{ million}$$

The profit on Project A is $10 million ($110 million − $100 million), and the *average* profit on Project B is $15 million ($115 million − $100 million).

Is it obvious that project B is preferable? To answer this question, suppose the corporation issues bonds and has to pay $100 million in interest to the bondholders. The corporation will finance its interest payment from the cash flow of the project it accepts. If it undertakes Project A, the corporation will have certain cash flow sufficient to cover the interest payment and will assume no risk of bankruptcy. However, if it undertakes Project B, the corporation faces a 50% chance of not meeting its interest obligation and being forced to declare bankruptcy. Project B is more profitable *on average* than Project A, but it is also more risky. Since it is not clear which project should be preferred, average profitability cannot be the corporation's one and only goal. The corporation must also consider *risk*.

Realizing that risk must be considered raises some related questions. Suppose the corporation considers two projects. One is more profitable but also more risky than the other. How do we choose between these two projects? Which factor—profitability or risk—outweighs the other? How can we measure these two factors? Recall that stockholders invest in a corporation to maximize their wealth. They expect the firm's management to select those projects that will achieve this objective. Nevertheless, measuring risk and selecting projects that maximize wealth are not easy tasks. They will be discussed in detail in Chapters 8 through 11.

Any major financial transaction or investment decision will likely affect the current stock price. For example, the publication of information about a government grant to be awarded two years from now, or a contract signed between a defense contractor and a government, or even a transaction to be executed five years from now that today's investors think will be profitable, will affect a corporation's current stock price. With good news on the forthcoming grant, contract, or transaction, the stock will become more attractive, the demand for the stock will increase, and its price will rise. Indeed, one reason that corporations publish their investment plans for the future is so that the market will see the potential in the investment and cause the stock price to rise.

In our example, suppose that the price of the firm's stock is $100 without either Project A or B. In the manager's judgment, the price will increase to, say, $104 if Project A is accepted or to $105 if Project B is accepted. This expectation means that, given the risk involved, the additional average profit of Project B more than compensates stockholders for the extra risk. If Project B is accepted, however, the manager's best judgment is that the stock price will increase, but only to $103, then the firm should opt for Project A.

The decision criterion—maximizing the stock's value—sounds simple. However, in practice, it is difficult to estimate the change in stock price that will result in response to the firm's actions. Moreover, such estimates are generally characterized by uncertainty. This issue will be dealt with in detail in Chapters 8 through 11.

As indicated earlier, management operates the corporation for the stockholders. *The only legitimate criterion in managerial decision making is stockholders' welfare, as measured by their wealth.* The corporation's goal should be to maximize the stockholders' wealth, which is the same as the goal of maximizing the value of the corporation's equity (the stock price times the number of outstanding shares), or simply maximizing the stock price.[12] This goal is consistent with creating stockholder wealth, as discussed in the Corporate Finance in the News article at the beginning of this chapter.

Management should try to maximize the average profit while minimizing risk. However, projects promising a high average profit are generally accompanied by high risk. Managers should accept such projects only if they will induce an increase in the stock price. This trade-off of risk and return is illustrated in Figure 1-4.

Finally, note that when financial managers consider projects with uncertain cash flows spread over a number of years, they must estimate how these future cash flows will affect the *current* stock price. As we shall see in Chapter 13, the current stock price considers the distribution of cash flows across the years as well as the risk involved in these cash flows.

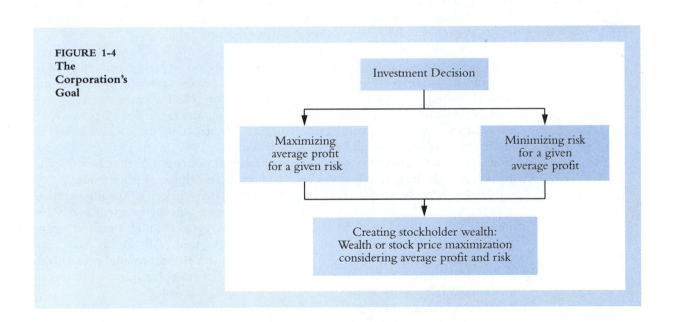

**FIGURE 1-4
The
Corporation's
Goal**

Investment Decision

Maximizing
average profit
for a given risk

Minimizing risk
for a given
average profit

Creating stockholder wealth:
Wealth or stock price maximization
considering average profit and risk

12. Maximizing the stock price, maximizing the value of the equity, and maximizing the value of the firm (the value of the firm's equity plus the value of its liabilities) constitute the same objective. Indeed, in this book we use these three objectives interchangeably. For proof that these three goals are equivalent, see Haim Levy and Marshall Sarnat, "A Pedagogic Note on Alternative Formulations of the Goal of the Firm," *Journal of Business* 50, no. 4 (October 1977):526–528.

1.9 ACHIEVING THE CORPORATION'S GOAL IN PRACTICE: THE ECONOMIC VALUE ADDED (EVA) PRINCIPLE

APPLYING THEORY TO PRACTICE 1.1

THE ECONOMIC VALUE ADDED (EVA) PRINCIPLE

How can the goal of value maximization be achieved in practice? Do managers have any hot new ideas about how to create value? The answer to both questions is something called the **economic value added (EVA) principle,** of which William Smithburg, CEO of Quaker Oats, says, "EVA makes managers act like shareholders. It's the true corporate faith for the 1990s."[13] For more on this "new religion," read on.

EVA®—Economic Value Added—is a financial tool that tells you how much your company is beating the total cost of capital, and what to do about it if you're not.

EVA is also a performance measurement that best accounts for changes in share value. Why? Because what drives a company's share price is the amount by which earnings, properly measured, exceed or fall short of the cost of the capital required to produce those earnings. That's precisely what EVA shows you.

EVA is your company's after tax profits from operations less the cost of all capital employed to produce those profits: not just the cost of debt, but the cost of equity capital as well. When EVA is used as part of a total financial management system, it can help shape every corporate decision, from a company acquisition or divestiture to project budgeting, product development . . . even incentive compensation. . . .

Just measuring EVA isn't enough. You need to adopt it. EVA brings a new kind of financial discipline to companies, it encourages managers to act like owners and boosts shareholder fortunes in the process.

Look at what happens when a company adopts EVA.

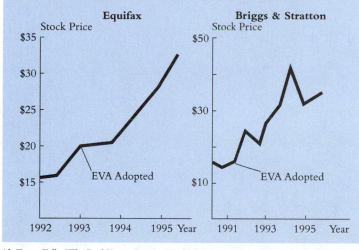

13. Shawn Tully, "The Real Key to Creating Wealth," *Fortune* 128, no. 6 (September 1993):38.

Questions

1. Explain the EVA principle and how it affects stock prices.
2. Suppose Coca-Cola is considering a $1 billion investment in Eastern Europe to be financed by equity only. The annual revenue is estimated to be $200 million, and the production costs (raw materials, wages, etc.) and taxes will be $50 million. The cost of capital mentioned in the article is the minimum dollar amount that must be earned on invested capital. Assume that this is $100 million (or 10% of the investment). What is the EVA?
3. The stock price of Equifax rose from about $20 in 1993 to about $33 in September 1995. What analysis would you perform to ascertain whether adoption of the EVA principle is the main reason for the increase in stock price?

MAKING THE CONNECTION

1. EVA measures a corporation's profit after deducting the correctly measured cost of capital—that is, the total cost of *all* invested capital. If the EVA of the project under consideration is positive, economic value is created, and the corporation's value and stock price increase. The examples of Equifax and Briggs & Stratton are striking. After they adopted EVA, their stock prices skyrocketed.

   The EVA principle emphasizes the accurate measurement of the costs of the corporation's various capital components. This method imposes pressure on managers to employ the invested capital efficiently. (This issue will be discussed in detail in Chapter 10.) If management's compensation is tied to the EVA level, managers will act as if they are the shareholders. Though it does not completely eliminate the conflict of interest between stockholders and managers, the EVA principle at least reduces that conflict, which, in turn, creates economic value. The EVA principle measures the corporation's profit correctly, and the corporation acts in the stockholders' best interest.

2. The EVA is obtained by calculating total costs and subtracting them from revenue:

Revenue		$200 million
Costs		
Production costs and taxes	$ 50 million	
Cost of capital	$100 million	
Total Cost		$150 million
EVA		$ 50 million

   The EVA is positive, and Coca-Cola should accept the project.

3. First, we need to compare Equifax's stock price to the stock prices of similar firms in the same industry during the same period. If we observe similar increases in the stock prices of these other firms and if these firms did not adopt EVA, Equifax's increase in stock price may be due to an increased demand for the products in this industry in general rather than to adoption of EVA.

Second, notice that Equifax's stock price increased even before the firm adopted EVA in 1993. Why? Maybe there are other reasons for the firm's success, such as tying managers' compensation to performance, awarding options to executives, or changing management. In short, the price increase *may* be due to the adoption of EVA principle; but before we draw any conclusion, we should analyze some of the factors mentioned earlier.

*Source: Sterns Stewart & Co., "Forget EPS, ROE and ROI. EVA® Is What Drives Stock Prices," *Fortune* 132, no. 6 (September 1995):10. Copyright © 1995 Time Inc. All rights reserved.

SUMMARY

When individuals invest, they reallocate consumption across time. For relatively small investments, wide-ranging cooperation among many people is not needed. For large investments, some form of business organization is usually needed to raise the needed capital. The three main forms of business organization are *sole proprietorship, partnership,* and *corporation.*

Corporations conduct most U.S. capital investment. The corporation's owners are the stockholders, and its decision makers are the top executives who answer to the board of directors.

In this chapter we have focused on the principal duties of the chief financial officer (CFO). The CFO is responsible for decision making in a number of areas, the most important of which are *capital budgeting, financing, dividend policy,* and *short-term financial management.*

Conflicts of interest may arise between the corporation's owners and the professional managers who run it. However, by devising appropriate compensation schemes, firms can minimize conflicts of interest and can induce managers to create stockholder wealth. These schemes cause managers to act in ways that maximize the stockholders' welfare as measured by the corporation's market value or its stock price. The *economic value added (EVA) principle* coincides with the stockholders' goal—namely, value maximization—and seems to reduce the conflicts of interest between stockholders and management.

CHAPTER AT A GLANCE

1. The reasons people invest:
    a. To reallocate consumption over time
    b. To create wealth (the desire to be wealthy)

2. The forms of business organization:
    a. Sole proprietorship: one owner, personal taxes, unlimited liability
    b. Partnership: at least two owners, personal taxes, unlimited liability
    c. Corporation: many owners, double taxation, limited liability

3. The principal duties of the chief financial officer:
    a. Investment decisions (capital budgeting)
    b. Financing decisions
    c. Dividend policy
    d. Short-term financial management

4. The conflicts of interest in corporations:
   a. Bondholders' wish to minimize risk
   b. Stockholders' wish to maximize the value of equity (stock price)
   c. Managers' wish to maximize their own welfare. Compensation schemes tying remuneration to performance (offering stock options) minimize the conflicts of interest between managers and stockholders.

5. The corporation's goals:
   a. Maximizing the price of stock
   b. Achieving the corporation's goal in practice; managers who employ the economic value added (EVA) principle believe that if a project's EVA is positive, the corporation's value (and its stock price) will increase.

KEY TERMS

Market value added (MVA)
Economic value added (EVA)
Cash flows
Time value of money
Uncertainty
Risk
Equity financing
Debt financing
Rate of return

Sole proprietorship
Partnership
Corporation
Agency costs
Organization costs
Chief executive officer (CEO)
Chief operations officer (COO)
Chief financial officer (CFO)
Capital budgeting

Financing decisions
Capital structure
Dividend policy decision
Short-term financial
   management
Financing mix
Stock options
Economic value added (EVA)
   principle

REVIEW AND PRACTICE

1.1 As an excellent student, you receive a fellowship of $10,000 that you receive in one lump sum. You will not receive more fellowships in the next three years of your study. Would you invest part of this $10,000? Explain.

1.2 List the various forms of business organization and the advantages and disadvantages of each.

1.3 What are the principal duties of the chief financial officer?

1.4 Discuss the concepts of *time value of money* and *risk*.

1.5 You wish to invest $10,000 for one year. You can put it under your mattress or deposit it in the bank. Which investment avenue is more profitable? Which is riskier? Explain.

1.6 Suppose a number of small investments each require an initial outlay of $100,000 and yield a 10% return. Alternatively, one large investment requires an initial outlay of $1 million and yields a 15% return. You have only $100,000. Discuss the various possible actions you might take.

1.7 A corporation raises capital by selling stock and invests $10 million. You participate in this project by investing $1,000. The corporation earns $2 million on its investment and distributes all of its profits to stockholders. What will your dollar return be?

1.8 Suppose the market value of your proprietorship is $1 million. You also have a house valued at $1 million in New York City. You owe the bank $1.5 million, and you file for bankruptcy. How much of your private property will be left after you pay your liability? What would the difference be if you had invested in a corporation rather than in a proprietorship?

1.9 A firm faces two investment choices: Project A, an investment that yields either 20% or −5% with equal probability, or Project B, an investment that yields 2% with certainty. The financial manager and the stockholders prefer Project A. We can say that the average profitability of Project A outweighs its risk. Explain this assertion.

1.10 Suppose the CEO nominates people to the board of directors who, in turn, determine the CEO's financial compensation. How might this situation cause a conflict of interest between stockholders and management? How could the corporation reduce the conflict?

1.11 A corporation's stock price is $100. Its CEO is awarded an option to buy 1 million shares of the stock at $110 per share. If the CEO exercises the stock option, what is his or her profit if the stock price increases to $150?

1.12 Referring to Problem 1.11, would it be better for the stockholders to allow the CEO to buy the stock at $90 regardless of the market price? What about at $200? Discuss the pros and cons of each buying price.

1.13 Suppose a CEO receives a salary of $1 million a year regardless of the corporation's performance. Is this a good or a bad arrangement for the stockholders? Is it better for the corporation to have a one-year renewable contract or a lifetime contract for the CEO?

1.14 A corporation awards its CEO a stock option to buy its stock at $11 per share at any time he or she wishes. The current stock price is $10.
a. Suppose the stock price increases to $12 during the year, and the CEO exercises the option. How much does the CEO make on each share?
b. Suppose the index of all stocks in the industry (or in the economy) increases by 40% during the year. Does the CEO deserve to profit on his or her options? Discuss.

c. Suggest a method to avoid paying the CEO the earnings on the option when the whole stock market drifts upward. (*Hint:* Consider changes in the stock index in the corresponding period.)

1.15 Project A is expected to yield a certain cash flow of $110,000 one year from today. Project B is expected to yield $90,000 or $210,000 with equal probability one year from today. Both require the same initial investment.
a. Which project is more profitable *on average*?
b. Assume the corporation has to pay the bank $100,000 at the end of the year, and that the only available cash is that generated by the project. Which project is riskier?
c. Suppose that if the corporation undertakes Project A, its stock price is estimated to increase by 1%. If it undertakes Project B, the corporation's stock price is estimated to increase by 5%. Which project would the stockholders prefer?
d. Suppose the corporation accepts Project B, which yields only $90,000. As a result, the firm goes bankrupt and fires the CEO. The information is made public, with the consequence that the CEO is unable to find a job in another firm. Which project would the CEO prefer?
e. In light of 1.15c and 1.15d, discuss the concept of agency costs.
f. Suppose the current stock price (before a decision on the projects is made) is $100. One million shares are outstanding. Given the information in 1.15c, calculate the agency costs.

1.16 Suppose Briggs & Stratton replaced its management in 1991 and adopted the EVA principles in the same year. What might account for the increase in the stock price after 1991? (*Hint:* See Applying Theory to Practice 1.1.) Can we definitely conclude that the stock price increase is due to the adoption of the EVA principle?

1.17 William Smithburg, Quaker Oats' CEO, was quoted as saying, "EVA makes managers act like shareholders." Why might this behavior increase a corporation's value? Explain.

INTERNET QUESTION

1.18 The primary goal of a public corporation is maximizing the value of its stock. Visit *Fortune* magazine's Web site and find the Fortune 500 list of firms ranked by total revenue. Which are the top 10? Compare this list to their "Top Performers: Highest Market Value" list. Which is a better measure of corporate success? Why?

http://www.fortune.com

YOUR TURN: APPLYING THEORY TO PRACTICE

OUTCRY OVER CEO PAY

In addition to their regular pay, many executives receive huge grants of stock options and restricted stock that represent real and potential bonanzas. For instance, Leon Hirsch was awarded options for 2.75 million shares of U.S. Surgical stock, and Roberto Goizueta received 1 million shares of restricted Coca-Cola stock.

The average pay of CEOs in the largest companies tops $2 million a year. How do you feel about this? A *USA Today* Investor Panel survey of 360 readers who actively follow their investments reveals the following results:

1. Anger if the company hasn't performed well—50%
2. Anger no matter what the company's performance has been—38%
3. Approval: CEOs work hard for their money—6%

GOODYEAR CHIEF'S PAY APPLAUDED

Stanley Gault, who took over as chairman of Goodyear Tire in June, says he's not doing it for the money. True or not, he's being paid handsomely. In addition to salary and bonus, $776,830 combined, he was awarded stock and stock options now worth $17.9 million.

Analysts say he deserves it. Since he took over, the stock has risen 137%. A peek at his pay:

Stock Options

Last year (1991), Gault was given options to buy 426,000 shares at an average price of $34.42. Thursday, the stock closed at 66⅜. So his paper profit is $13.6 million. He can cash in by exercising the options and selling the stock in two stages starting in June.

This year (1992), Gault also was given options to buy 75,000 shares at $53.75, which can be exercised beginning Jan. 7. Gault's paper profit if exercised at Thursday's close: $946,875.

Stock

Goodyear directors gave Gault shares for 10 cents each in place of a retirement plan. The shares now are worth $3.3 million.

Ralph Whitworth, president of United Shareholders Association, likes the fact that much of Gault's pay was linked to his success in boosting the stock. "That's how it should be," he says. But he doesn't like the stock-for-a-dime deal.

"That means the stock could go down to 11 cents a share and he would still profit," he says.

MEGABUCKS AMID LAYOFFS STOKE OUTRAGE

Michael Whittaker practically spits out the words as he harshly tells how he feels about the mega-pay of top U.S. executives.

"When the little guy is bustin' his b---s working day in and day out, and then a company starts talking about layoffs and wanting the unions to cut here and cut there," says Whittaker, a 36-year-old Marine, "and the guy at the top is pulling in millions of dollars—you wonder where the justice is in that."

A growing number of people are wondering the same thing these days. In recent weeks, a number of CEO pay packages have been revealed to the public—it's the time of year most companies put out their proxy statements, which include executive pay. Some numbers are stunning:

Leon Hirsch, chairman of U.S. Surgical, a medical-instruments company, last year (1991) was awarded options for 2.75 million shares. That would give him a profit of $114 million if he could exercise them all now (he can't till 1996) in addition to his regular pay of $1.8 million last year.

Coca-Cola Chief Executive Roberto Goizueta was granted 1 million shares of restricted stock, which he can sell in 1996. They're worth $82.5 million today. Plus, he raked in pay and bonuses adding up to $4.7 million.

During H.J. Heinz's fiscal year, CEO Anthony O'Reilly cashed in stock options for a $71.5 million profit on top of $3.3 million in salary and bonus. He has options on another 4 million shares, representing a paper profit of $29 million.

The hoopla isn't likely to fizzle soon. More proxies and more pay figures will come out in coming weeks, fueling an issue that has sunk a hook deep into public sentiment. Both *Business Week* and *Fortune* have made executive pay their current cover stories. Congress is threatening to hold hearings, pass legislation, and generally make highly paid CEOs squirm.

But it's workers and individual investors in companies' stock who are really getting steamed. While executive pay is soaring, the unemployment rate has climbed to 7.3%, and many salaried employees are lucky if they get a 5% annual raise. A recent *USA Today* poll showed that 72% of the public believes CEO pay of $1 million or more a year is too much, even if the CEO's company has performed well.

Investors are fed up and want more say in how much a CEO gets paid. A mid-March survey of 360 members of *USA Today*'s Investor Panel found that 88% say they're angry about high CEO pay. And 99% say a CEO should cut his or her pay if the company hits tough times. The panel is made up of *USA Today* readers, including Whittaker, who are active investors.

The public gets particularly peeved at CEOs who get paid a lot of money even as company profits sink. "People who really deserve it and lead their companies to do well, I don't have a problem with that," says Keith Browning, 27, an Investor Panel member and credit analyst for Oscar Mayer. "But I have a problem with CEOs who are not doing well."

Stephen Wolf, chairman of UAL, United Airlines' parent, made $18.3 million in 1990 even though UAL profits plunged 71% that year. Dun & Bradstreet's CEO, Charles Moritz, saw his base pay and bonus climb 63% to $1.6 million from 1987 to 1990. During that time, his company's total return to shareholders—stock price appreciation plus dividends paid—was flat.

The New York City Employees Retirement System, which controls $20 billion in pension funds, is pushing Reebok, one of its investments, to set up an independent committee to decide executives' pay. It says previous committee members had ties to Reebok management.

The next step may be even more shareholder pressure on boards of directors to tighten controls on executive pay. The SEC recently changed its policy to allow shareholder resolutions on executive pay so shareholders can vote to hold pay down. Even corporation-friendly groups such as the National Association of Corporate Directors are suggesting that pay abuses may be curbed.

Thanks to all that plus the threat of congressional action, the furor is being heard by companies, board compensation committees—the groups within a company's hierarchy that set executive pay—and consultants who advise them. Even while some companies complain that the media have sensationalized the abuses, they swear change is coming.

The public outcry "is having a palliative effect on compensation committees," says Gary Hourihan, president of Strategic Compensation Associates, a firm that acts as consultants on executive pay. "The abuses will slowly get curbed."*

Questions

This article provides some information regarding executive pay, performance, and investor attitudes to executive pay. Based on the article as well as on the information in Chapter 1, discuss the following issues:

1. "The larger the CEO's compensation, the smaller the dividends distributed to stockholders, hence the lower the corporation's value." Evaluate this statement. Relate your answer specifically to the pay of Goodyear's CEO.

2. Suppose Coca-Cola's market value is $30 billion and its net income is $3 billion. Calculate the pay of Coca-Cola's CEO as a percentage of these two figures. Should you use the $82.5 million (the value of the shares granted to him), $4.7 million (his annual pay and other bonuses), or both, in your calculation? Which figure is relevant from the investor's point of view: the CEO's pay divided by asset value or the CEO's pay divided by the firm's annual income? Discuss.

Suppose that Coca-Cola's CEO Goizueta increases return on assets by 0.5% more than an alternative, less competent CEO. As a stockholder, do you think the $87.2 million ($82.5 million + $4.7 million) compensation would be justified?

3. A survey shows that 88% of investors are angry about the high level of CEO compensation and that 99% say CEOs should cut their pay if their companies hit tough times. As a member of a board of directors of a large corporation, you believe that high pay attracts the best managers and that the corporation's value will increase far beyond what it would be under a manager who agreed to an average salary. However, a high compensation package might induce angry investors to sell their stock, which would cause the corporation's value to decrease. Would you vote for restrictions on the CEO's pay—for example, that it should be no more than $1 million? Discuss the pros and cons.

Suppose, if the stockholders do not sell their stock in protest, the present CEO increases the stock price by 10%. With an alternative CEO, the stock price would increase by only 9.5%. However, if the $1 million compensation cap is broken, angry stockholders will sell their stock and the corporation's market value will decrease by 10%. Would you keep the present CEO with no compensation cap?

4. Suppose the bonuses awarded to the CFOs of UAL and Dun & Bradstreet are percentages of each firm's *gross revenue*. Would this policy explain why their compensation increased although profit declined (UAL) or was flat (Dun & Bradstreet)? How would you change the compensation schemes to avoid the CEO's pay increasing even when the firm's stock price decreases?

5. Do you believe the action taken by the New York Employees Retirement System, the Securities and Exchange Commission, and Congress to curb CEOs' pay is healthy, or does it contradict the "free economy" concept?

*Source: "Outcry over CEO Pay," USA Today, March 27, 1992, Section B, pp. 1–2. Copyright 1992, USA Today. Reprinted with permission.

CHAPTER 2

THE BUSINESS ENVIRONMENT

LEARNING OBJECTIVES

After reading this chapter,
you should understand:

1. The business environment and how it affects the firm's financial decisions.

2. The capital market and the role of financial intermediaries in the flow of funds between individual investors and firms.

3. The two principal methods firms use to raise capital—stocks (equity) and bonds (debt)—and their risk-return profiles.

4. The growing role of government regulation, environmental protection, and business ethics in corporate America.

5. The relationship between the firm's goal and customer service.

6. How the tax structure affects managerial decision making.

CORPORATE FINANCE IN THE NEWS

SAVING THE FAMILY FACTORY

Taxes are one of the big killers of family businesses. Help may be

on the way. Generally ignored in the clamor over the budget bill

is a huge estate tax break for family-owned private companies.

"For them it's the most important tax change since World War

II," says Jonathan Blattmachr, a partner at New York's Milbank,

Tweed, Hadley & McCloy.

Will the family-business tax cut become law? Its chances are

good.

Source: Laura Saunders, "Saving the Family Factory," *Forbes* 156, no. 13 (December 1995):169.
Reprinted by permission of *Forbes* Magazine © Forbes Inc., 1995.

2.1 INTRODUCTION

A biologist studying a fish must know something about the sea in which that fish swims: the water currents, the tides, the food sources, the competitors for food, and the predators to which this fish may fall prey. All these factors are important in understanding the fish's behavior. Like the biologist who studies fish, we must study the environment in which firms operate to understand them. Sources of money, competitors for these funds, taxes, regulations, and other competing businesses are important factors in the business environment.

The Corporate Finance in the News article illustrates the importance of taxes in the business environment. If a family-business tax cut is enacted, proprietors will have more incentive to form family businesses. In making any decision about their businesses—form of organization, location, and so on—these proprietors consider the economic environment and plan for the future.

The business environment affects the ways that firms raise money. As we know from Chapter 1, one principal duty of a chief financial officer (CFO) is to raise capital for the corporation's projects. Firms use funds, and individual investors supply these funds. These two parties—users and suppliers of funds—are bound by legal financial agreements or "contracts" in the form of the various types of **securities** (such as stocks and bonds) that firms issue.

The supply and demand for capital meet in *capital markets.* The business environment and various other factors operating in the capital market affect firms' investment and financial decisions that, in turn, affect the "contracts" they offer to individual investors. For instance, if the government increases income taxes, it affects the profitability and the relative attractiveness of the available securities. Stocks may become relatively more attractive than bonds, for example. Moreover, the government—federal, state, and local—also raises money in the capital market. These government agencies compete directly with firms for investors' funds and, as a result, affect the price—the interest rate—that firms pay investors for using their money.

In this chapter we discuss the structure of capital markets, the two principal securities traded in the capital market—namely, stocks and bonds—and how the business environment affects firms' financial decisions.

We will also show how the constraints imposed by government regulations and environmental protection, as well as the demand for ethical business practices and improved customer service, may force firms to modify their stockholders' wealth maximization goal (discussed in Chapter 1).

2.2 THE FLOW OF FUNDS

When we discuss long-term or short-term financial transactions, we refer to the *financial markets.* **Financial markets** include **money markets,** those for short-term debt with maturities of less than one year, and **capital markets,** those for long-

http

Our national and over-the-counter stock exchanges support extensive Web sites where they explain themselves, the stock traded there, how to become listed, and so on.
http://www.nyse.com
http://www.amex.com
http://www.nasdaq.com

term debt and equity. Firms generally borrow both short-term and long-term, issue stock, and operate in both money and capital markets.

We may also distinguish between the *primary market,* in which firms and governments raise money by issuing securities, and a *secondary market,* in which existing securities are traded but no new money is raised. We focus on the primary market in this book. However, the secondary market is crucial to how the primary market functions and also gives management an indication of the price at which they can sell new securities.

The *capital market* involves three parties: (1) individual investors; (2) financial institutions such as banks, mutual funds (which pool money from many individuals and invest it in the capital market), and investment banking houses; and (3) firms and government agencies that need capital to finance their projects. Financial institutions are also firms that raise money in the capital market. To distinguish these firms from *production* firms such as General Motors or IBM, we call them **financial institutions** or **financial intermediaries.**

As explained in Chapter 1, one reason why individuals invest is to reallocate consumption over time. They can accomplish this by depositing money in a bank, by directly buying a firm's stocks and bonds, or by buying the stocks and bonds offered by financial institutions that serve as "middlemen" or intermediaries between firms and individual investors. Through financial intermediaries, individuals invest *indirectly* in firms' stocks and bonds. The intermediaries use the cash transferred from individual investors to buy securities (stocks and bonds) or to provide direct loans to firms. The individual investors' cash is finally transferred to the firm's management, which generally uses the funds for capital expenditure.

Let's consider the flow of funds in the financial market, as illustrated in Figure 2-1. Firms compete for the available capital by issuing stocks and bonds. The government (federal, state, and local levels) also competes for funds by borrowing money or by selling bonds. Firms, government agencies, and financial intermediaries attract individual investors by offering dividends (in the case of stocks) or interest (in the case of loans or bonds) on their invested capital. Individual investors, financial institutions, firms, and government agencies are all involved in the financial markets.

2.3 RAISING FUNDS: SECURITIES

As mentioned above, firms issue two main types of securities: common stocks and bonds.[1] The buyers of these securities in the primary markets become the firm's suppliers of funds and can claim some part of the firm's future income. Although many securities other than stocks and bonds are available in the market, we will focus on those issued by firms and on some competing securities issued by government agencies. (For a full description of all the available securities, see any investments text.) Here, we describe the principal characteristics of bonds and

---

1. Another commonly used type of security is preferred stock. Preferred stock has some characteristics of common stock and some characteristics of bonds. We discuss preferred stock in more detail in Chapter 10.

FIGURE 2-1   **Flow of Funds between Individual Investors and Users of Funds (Firms and Government Agencies)**

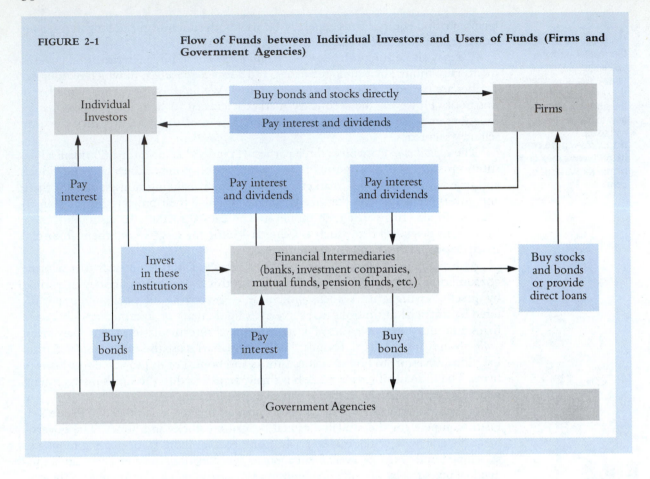

stocks. In Chapters 12 through 14 we will extend the discussion and analysis of these and other securities.

2.3.1 Bonds: Fixed-Income Securities

Firms and government agencies can raise money either by borrowing from a bank or by selling a **bond** to the public, to a bank, or to a financial intermediary. Raising capital by this means is called **debt financing.** You probably know what a bank loan is, but what exactly is a bond? What is the nature of the contract between the firm and the bondholder? An investor who buys a bond—a *corporate bond*—pays the firm cash in return for a piece of paper that entitles the holder to payments at some designated future dates. The payments include the interest and the principal. The interest rate is denominated as a percentage of the bond's principal, also called **par value** or **face value.** The bond's face value—which is the sum transferred to the bondholder at the **maturity date**—is fixed. (This is why some people call bonds *fixed-income securities*.) A bond's face value may (and generally does) differ from its

market value, which is the price at which it can be traded in the market. Depending on supply and demand, the bond's market value may vary daily.

According to *Barron's* (August 4, 1997), IBM had the following bonds listed on the New York Stock Exchange (NYSE):

Interest (%)	Year of Maturity
6⅜	1997
6⅜	2000
7¼	2002
7½	2013
8⅜	2019

Source: "Market Week," *Barron's* 77, no. 31 (August 1997): MW56. Reprinted by permission of *Barron's,* © 1997 Dow Jones & Company, Inc. All rights reserved worldwide.

The last bond, for example, provides 8⅜% interest each year until 2019 when it "matures"; that is, the contract between IBM and the bondholder will expire in 2019. At the maturity date, IBM will repay the **principal** (the bond's face value) to the bondholder. For example, if the bond's face value is $1,000, IBM will pay the bondholder $83.75 ($1,000 × 8⅜%) each year until 2019. In 2019 the bondholder will receive the $1,000 principal as well as the final interest payment.

BONDHOLDERS

The projects that the firm undertakes may result in large cash flows (if they are successful), very small cash flows, or even losses (if they are unsuccessful). Regardless of the projects' success, however, bondholders are entitled to their interest payments *before* the firm can distribute any cash to its owners (stockholders) in the form of dividends. Furthermore, if the firm declares bankruptcy, bondholders have a first-priority claim against any remaining assets. Stockholders cannot sell the assets and take the cash for themselves. It might seem that bondholders have a superior financial position to that of stockholders, but that is not the case. Bonds confer no voting rights. Also, in years of high profit, bondholders do not participate in the "feast"; that is, they receive no more than the fixed interest specified in their contract with the firm.

SPECIAL TYPES OF BONDS

Although in this chapter we are interested mainly in stocks and corporate bonds, we will mention (and later discuss in Chapter 11) other bonds that are available in the market. All bonds compete in the capital market for the same financial resources.

Short-term bonds, called **money market securities,** are usually issued for less than one year. For example, the federal government issues **Treasury bills** (also called **T-bills**) whose maturities range from three months to one year. T-bills are sold at a *discount,* which means that a T-bill might be issued at, say, $95,000 and pay $100,000 when it matures one year later. The interest is the amount of the discount ($100,000 − $95,000 = $5,000) paid at the maturity date. Similarly, firms issue short-term debt in the form of **commercial paper,** which is similar to corporate bonds but has a relatively short maturity. Like T-bills, commercial paper is issued at a discount and pays no interest.

The federal government also issues various types of long-term bonds, called **Treasury notes** and **Treasury bonds,** which generally pay interest semiannually. (The difference between the two, which we'll discuss in a later chapter, has to do with length of maturity.) State and local governments issue **municipal bonds** to finance their operations.

The following problem compares an investment in a T-bill to an investment in a bond.

PRACTICE BOX

Problem

Suppose you can buy a T-bill for $95,000 that matures in one year at $100,000. Alternatively, you can buy a one-year bond with a face value of $100,000 that pays 5% interest at the end of the year. Which investment is more profitable?

Solution

On the T-bill the percentage profit is

$$\frac{\$100,000 - \$95,000}{\$95,000} = 0.0526 \text{ or } 5.26\%$$

On the one-year bond it is

$$\frac{\$105,000 - \$100,000}{\$100,000} = 0.05 \text{ or } 5.00\%$$

The investment in the T-bill is more profitable with a profit of 5.26%. Although you make a $5,000 profit on both investments, you initially invest less in the T-bill.

2.3.2 Stock

When you buy **common stock** (also called *common shares* or *equities*), you will receive a piece of paper as proof of your purchase, as with a bond purchase. This piece of paper documents your partial ownership of the firm. For example, if the firm sells 1 million shares of common stock and you buy 100,000 of them, you own 10% of the firm. Your 10% stake in the firm entitles you to 10% of the total dividends that the firm decides to distribute after paying the fixed interest due to its bondholders. If the firm loses money or if it is not particularly successful, the bondholders may fare better than the stockholders. On the other hand, if the firm realizes a large profit, the opposite will be true: The stockholders may fare better than the bondholders.

For example, up to 1992 IBM paid an annual dividend of about $4 per share. However, when IBM started to lose money, it slashed the dividend drastically to $1 per year, and the stockholders' income was much smaller than the bondholders' income.[2] Fortunately, IBM had retained sufficient earnings from previous years to pay the bondholders their fixed interest *and* to pay the stockholders dividends, albeit smaller than in the past.

The following problem illustrates how bondholders and shareholders fare based on a firm's income.

PRACTICE BOX

Problem

Suppose a firm's income is $500,000. It issues $1 million in bonds that pay 10% annual interest. In addition, the firm issues 80,000 shares of common stock at $100 per share. For simplicity, assume the firm does not pay taxes and distributes all its income (after its interest payments) as dividends.

a. How much of the firm's income do the bondholders receive, and how much do the stockholders receive per share?

b. How would your answer change if the firm's income were $100,000? If it were $1.7 million?

Solution

a. First, 10% of $1 million is $100,000. This is the bondholders' income. The stockholders' income is $400,000; per share, it is

$$\frac{\$400{,}000}{80{,}000 \text{ shares}} = \$5 \text{ per share}$$

b. If the firm's income is only $100,000, all of it goes to the bondholders, and the stockholders receive nothing. If the income is $1.7 million, the bondholders still receive $100,000, but the shareholders now receive $1.6 million, or $20 per share.

As you can see, stockholder income fluctuates with the firm's earnings, whereas bondholder income does not. This is why investors consider bonds to be safer than stocks. However, bondholders stand to lose their money if the firm fails and declares bankruptcy. If no assets are left, bondholders will forfeit both the fixed interest and the principal.

Figure 2–2 sheds some light on the relative sizes of the stock and bond markets. It shows that North America has a larger share of the world bond market than it does of the world stock market.

2. Even so, IBM investors were eventually rewarded. Following a remarkable recovery, IBM's share price more than quadrupled between January 1993 and August 1997.

FIGURE 2-2
The Breakdown of World Stocks and Bonds by Geographic Region

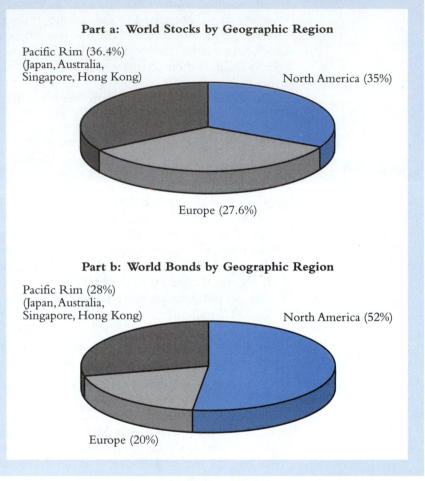

Part a: World Stocks by Geographic Region

Pacific Rim (36.4%)
(Japan, Australia,
Singapore, Hong Kong)

North America (35%)

Europe (27.6%)

Part b: World Bonds by Geographic Region

Pacific Rim (28%)
(Japan, Australia,
Singapore, Hong Kong)

North America (52%)

Europe (20%)

Source: Part a adapted from Morgan Stanley, *Capital International Perspective,* as quoted in Frank J. Fabozzi and Franco Modigliani, *Capital Markets, Institutions, and Instruments* (Engelwood Cliffs, NJ: Prentice Hall, 1992), p. 704. Part b adapted from Salomon Brothers, International Bond Market Analysis, *"How Big Is the World Bond Market?—1990 Update,"* as quoted in Roger G. Ibbotson and Laurence B. Siegel, "The World Bond Market: Market Values, Yields, and Returns," *The Journal of Fixed Income* (June 1991), pp. 91, 92.

2.4 RISK AND RATES OF RETURN ON BONDS AND STOCKS: THE HISTORICAL RECORD

The **rate of return** on an investment is the percentage change in its value over a given period. For example, if an investor buys a share of stock for $100 at the beginning of the year and sells it for $120 at the end of the year, the annual rate of return will be:

$$\frac{\$120 - \$100}{\$100} = 0.2 \text{ or } 20\%$$

If the investor also receives a $5 dividend at the end of the year, the rate of return will be:

$$\frac{\$120 + \$5 - \$100}{\$100} = \frac{\$25}{\$100} = 0.25 \text{ or } 25\%$$

Figure 2-3 shows the average annual rate of return for the period 1926–1996 on various types of securities. The average rate of return on stocks (equity) is much higher than it is on bonds (debt).

Figure 2-3 also shows that the average rate of return on small company stocks has been larger than for large company stocks (17.7% versus 12.7%). Why, then, wouldn't investors always choose small company stocks? The answer is simple: risk. Investment in small firms is generally riskier than investment in large firms because small firms have higher bankruptcy rates and more volatile stock prices. Indeed, Figure 2-3 illustrates one of the most important principles in finance: *the higher the risk, the higher the average rate of return on the investment.* If this were not the case, no one

FIGURE 2-3
Summary Statistics of Annual Total Returns on Basic Securities, 1926–1996

Securities	Average Rate of Return (%)	Standard Deviation (%)	Distribution
Large Company Stocks	12.7	20.3	
Small Company Stocks	17.7	34.1	★
Long-Term Corporate Bonds	6.0	8.7	
Long-Term Government Bonds	5.4	9.2	
Intermediate-Term Government Bonds	5.4	5.8	
U.S. Treasury Bills	3.8	3.3	
Inflation	3.2	4.5	

–90%   0%   90%

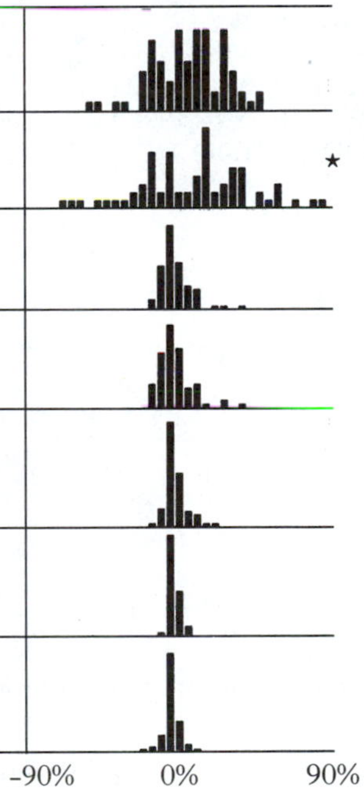

★ The 1933 Small Company Stock Total Return was 142.9%.

Source: Ibbotson Associates, Inc., *Stocks, Bonds, Bills, and Inflation, 1997 Yearbook* (Chicago: Ibbotson Associates, 1997), p. 33.

would invest in risky assets. The difference between the average rates of return on a risky investment and on a riskless investment (such as short-term government bonds and Treasury bills) is the **risk premium,** which can be considered the additional return required to compensate investors for their risk.

We can use the data from Figure 2-3 to calculate the *historical risk premium,* or the difference between the *average* rate of return on an investment and the prevailing riskless interest rate, *r.* When considering future investments, however, the historical risk premium is not as important as the *expected risk premium*. If the proposed investment is riskless, the required rate of return will be the riskless interest rate, *r.* If the investment is risky, the required rate of return will be *k;* and the difference between these two rates, *k − r,* will be the *expected risk premium.* The higher the investment risk, the higher the expected risk premium.

The right-hand side of Figure 2-3 shows the volatility of the rates of return as measured by their standard deviation.[3] As can be seen, the rates of return on equities are more volatile than they are on bonds.

Figure 2-4 illustrates the 1996 value of $1 invested in various securities at the end of 1925. This value is approximately $13 to $34 for bonds, $1,371 for large

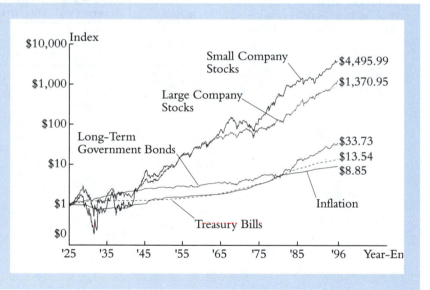

FIGURE 2-4
Wealth Indices of Investments in the U.S. Capital Markets, from 1925 to 1996 (Year-End 1925 = $1.00)

Source: Ibbotson Associates, Inc., *Stocks, Bonds, Bills, and Inflation, 1997 Yearbook* (Chicago: Ibbotson Associates, 1997), p. 28.

3. The standard deviation, σ, is defined as follows:

$$\sigma = \left(\frac{1}{m}\sum_{t=1}^{m}(R_t - \overline{R})^2 \right)^{1/2}$$

where $\overline{R}$ is the average return, m is the number of years, and R_t is the rate of return in year t. In Figure 2.3 the standard deviation is used to measure the volatility of the rates of return across time. For a more detailed discussion of the standard deviation, see Chapter 8.

company stocks, and $4,496 for small company stocks. Note that these are long-term returns. Returns on bonds can be higher than those on stocks in any given year or subperiod.

Figure 2-5 shows the annual rates of return on large company stocks, long-term government bonds, and U.S. Treasury bills from 1926 to 1996. For example, the rate of return on large company stock ranged between 50% and 60% in 1933 and 1954 and between −40% and −50% in 1931. The largest loss on long-term government bonds occurred in 1967; the largest gain, in 1982.

What can we learn from these historical records? First, in most years stocks provide a higher rate of return than bonds. Second, in some years the loss on stocks is relatively large. One thing is sure: "There are no free lunches." Investors who have strong desires to make huge amounts of money will have to assume relatively large risks.

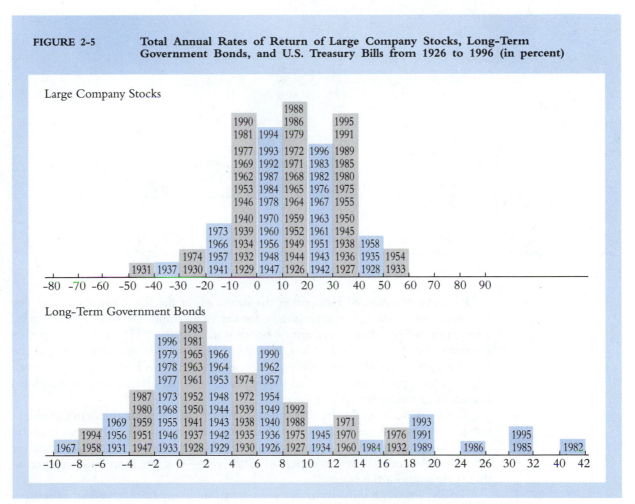

FIGURE 2-5   **Total Annual Rates of Return of Large Company Stocks, Long-Term Government Bonds, and U.S. Treasury Bills from 1926 to 1996 (in percent)**

(Continued)

FIGURE 2-5   (Continued)

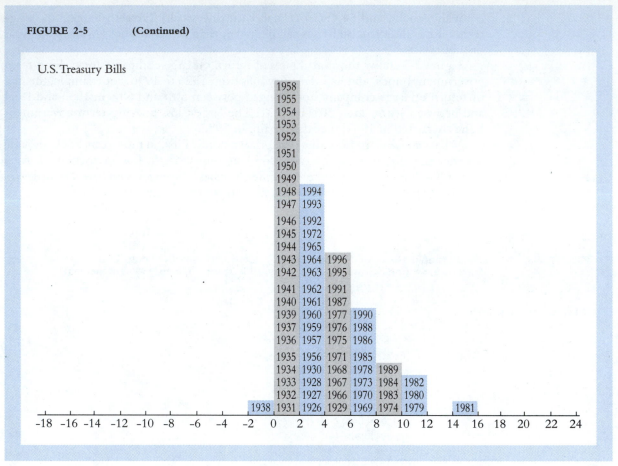

U.S. Treasury Bills

Source: Ibbotson Associates, Inc., *Stocks, Bonds, Bills, and Inflation, 1997 Yearbook* (Chicago: Ibbotson Associates, 1997), pp. 50, 52, 57, 64.

Risk can be analyzed from either the investors' or the firm's point of view. For investors, stocks are riskier than bonds; for the firm, bonds are riskier than stocks. The reason is that interest payment on bonds is mandatory. If the firm cannot pay its interest obligations to bondholders, it may go bankrupt. On the other hand, if the firm issues stock, it may pay dividends but can, especially in lean years, cut or even skip dividend payments. Dividend payments are not mandatory, and stockholders cannot force the firm to pay dividends.

What implications do the data given in Figure 2-3 have for the firm's management? If the firm issues equity, it has to earn on average considerably more than the riskless interest rate on loans; otherwise, stockholders will not be compensated for their risk. As you will see, compensation for risk—risk premium—is a recurring theme throughout this book.

Finally, although long-term investors are more likely to receive higher returns if they invest in stocks rather than in bonds (see Figure 2-4), this is not necessarily the case for short holding periods (of, say, one year), as can be deduced from Figure 2-5.

2.5 THE EFFECTS OF GOVERNMENT AND ENVIRONMENT ON A FIRM'S INVESTMENT DECISIONS

In Chapter 1 we argued that management's primary goal is to select business activities that will maximize stockholders' wealth. However, a firm's activity can be subject to various restrictions. For example, if a firm has monopoly power, government agencies can intervene to protect consumers. One notable government intervention was with American Telephone & Telegraph (AT&T), which held virtual control over most U.S. telephone and telecommunication systems for both long-distance and local calls. Some claimed that AT&T's high market concentration reduced competition and forced customers to pay higher prices than they would had more competition been available. In the early 1970s the U.S. Justice Department filed an antitrust suit against AT&T, which ultimately forced the firm to form its local telephone companies. This spinoff reduced concentration, created more competition, and promoted more efficient production to give customers cost savings.

Business regulation can take many forms. For example, a firm may be forced to spin off some of its businesses, as in the case of AT&T, or regulators may fix the price of a firm's products or services. Also, to comply with environmental regulations, a firm may have to invest more money than anticipated in a project. Given the increasing importance of environmental protection, management's best course is to consider all extraordinary cash outlays and to voluntarily adopt measures to protect the environment. In these cases, business regulation can turn projects initially considered very profitable into financial disaster.

Pension funds, insurance companies, banks, and other financial institutions are also regulated to protect customers. For example, many people invest in pension funds and expect to withdraw their funds after they retire. If a pension fund goes bankrupt as a result of risky investments, its investors will have no retirement funds. For this reason, financial institutions of this kind are heavily regulated and usually have restrictions on the proportion of risky investments they can undertake.

A major regulatory agency is the **Securities and Exchange Commission (SEC),** which supervises the trading of securities, approves new issues, and ensures that insiders (such as members of the board of directors and top management) do not take advantage of information available only to them and not to the public. Using such information to gain an advantage in the securities market is called **insider trading,** and it is illegal.

For example, suppose only the board of directors of Boeing Corporation knows that Boeing will soon sign a profitable contract with the U.S. Navy. If you, as a board member, call your broker and place a buy order for Boeing's stock, your transaction would be illegal. However, after information on the upcoming contract is

http

The government is an important player in financial markets. For one-stop shopping, this site links to scores of government-related Web sites.
http://www.uncle-sam.com

made public in an article published in the *Wall Street Journal* or in a news story on CNN, you would be free to trade in Boeing stock. Your transaction would be considered fair trade because all potential investors will have had access to the information on the upcoming contract. Fair trade requires that all relevant information be available to all potential investors at the same time.

In addition to complying with governmental and environmental regulations, management may face unexpected events that affect investment decisions. Connecting Theory to Practice 2.1 illustrates one such event.

CONNECTING THEORY TO PRACTICE 2.1

CAN TEXACO WIN A BATTLE IF THE LORD IS ON THE OTHER SIDE?

GAS-STATION OWNER SAYS GOD CALLS FOR SABBATH CLOSING, DESPITE COMPANY'S RULES

SALEM, Oregon—Oh, Lord. As if the environmentalists, competitors and the Clinton administration's energy taxes aren't enough, Texaco Corp. has a divinely inspired mess on its hands here these days.

Texaco's troubles began when Barry Davis, a devout Christian fundamentalist who runs three Texaco service stations in Oregon, had a talk with the Almighty. Mr. Davis, 50 years old, credits God for making him Texaco's all-time top pumper—not to mention helping him earn nearly $470,000 last year. Texaco's star says God told him to shut his stations each week for the 24-hour biblical Sabbath—sunset Friday to sunset Saturday. The closings began Jan. 1.

The company says Mr. Davis's uplifting gesture caused a 26% slide in his stations' January sales. Texaco sued Mr. Davis in federal court in Portland, Oregon, last week demanding he pay less attention to the Almighty and more to his contract, which calls for a seven-day-a-week, 24-hour-a-day operation. The company obtained a court order directing Mr. Davis to stay open on the Sabbath.

Mr. Davis, insisting that he can easily make up lost sales during the other six days, ignored the order.

"Bottom line," Mr. Davis says. "I win and God wins."

According to Mitchell Tyner, an attorney for the Seventh Day Adventist Church, "I think a lot has to do with the attitude of the '80s that was more oriented to the free market and less amenable to employees' religious needs."

Indeed, the oil company is clearly perplexed by Mr. Davis's stand. "The defendant has repeatedly claimed he has direct communication with God about his closures," Texaco's attorneys complain in their federal-court filing. The company says it suggested alternatives to shutting down Mr. Davis's stations, such as donating his profits to a religious cause.

"Mr. Davis said he asked God about that and God said it was unacceptable," the company's affidavit says.

But when he announced his decision to shut his pumps for the Sabbath, Mr. Davis says he became a pariah. "For years I was a hero," he says. "Now suddenly they're treating me like the wacko from Waco."

Source: Bill Richards, "Can Texaco Win a Battle If the Lord Is on the Other Side?" Wall Street Journal, 6 May 1993, pp. A1, A8. Reprinted by permission of The Wall Street Journal, © 1993 Dow Jones & Company, Inc. All rights reserved worldwide.

MAKING THE CONNECTION

Firms must consider citizens' civil rights even though those rights may conflict with the goal of maximizing stockholders' wealth. If Mr. Davis has a case and if his case is recognized as involving civil rights, Texaco may lose a great deal of revenue because of Davis's gas stations being closed on the Sabbath.

In summary, when analyzing a project's economic worth, the financial manager must consider more than just the project's cash flow. Government regulations, environmental protection, employees, and various other factors are key to a CFO's decision. Finally, note that regulation and government restrictions are generally known factors and, therefore, can be considered during the project evaluation process. The firm's goal should be maximizing stockholders' wealth subject to these constraints. Lawsuits and actions such as the Davis case are less predictable; when evaluating potential projects, firms should allocate cash reserves for miscellaneous, unforeseeable events, just in case.

Failing to take these factors into account may greatly affect a project's cash flows and the firm's earnings. For example, Archer Daniels Midland reported earnings of $0.35 per share for the six months ended December 31, 1996, compared with $0.70 for the same period in 1995. The reduction in earnings can be explained mainly by a charge of $0.32 per share "for fines and litigation settlements arising out of the United States Department of Justice antitrust investigation of the company's lysine and citric acid products."[4]

2.6 CUSTOMER SERVICE

In maximizing stockholders' wealth, management has to consider government regulations as well as the physical and social environment in which the firm operates. However, not all managers believe the firm's primary goal should be maximizing stockholders' wealth. Some also place high priority on ethical conduct and on employees' and society's needs. As Applying Theory to Practice 2.1 relates, another popular goal in recent years is customer service. Careful analysis of this application leads to this conclusion: For most firms the goal of maximizing stockholders' wealth still holds. However, without satisfied customers, a firm cannot achieve this goal in the long run.

4. "Current Corporate Reports," *Barron's,* 20 January 1997, p. 50.

APPLYING THEORY TO PRACTICE 2.1

SERVICE COMES FIRST IN THE U.S.A.

THE CUTTING EDGE—"YOU'RE NOT IN BUSINESS TO MAKE A PROFIT"

What do the following executives have in common, other than a successful track record: Paul Allair, CEO, Xerox; Edward McCabe, CEO, McCabe and Company; John McConnell, CEO, Worthington Industries; Robert McDermott, CEO, United Services Automobile Association? If you're stumped, here are some clues:

Paul Allair: "I have to change the company substantially to be more market driven. If we do what's right for the customer, our market share and our return on assets will take care of themselves."

Edward McCabe: "You think I want my tombstone to say 'He had 27 offices'? What's important to me is that our company did outstanding advertising. . . . The numbers are not achievements in themselves, but the results of achievements."

John McConnell: "Take care of your customers and take care of your people and the market will take care of you."

Robert McDermott: "The mission and corporate culture of this company are, in one word, service. As a company objective, service comes ahead of either profits or growth. Now, profits and growth do matter . . . but I submit that it's because service comes first at USAA that profits and growth have been so healthy."

Before continuing let me tell you why I developed this little quiz. David Fagiano, president and CEO of AMA, wrote in *Management Review*'s September 1991 "Memo for Members" column that "profit is not the mission of any company that wants to be around for the long haul." He was promptly blasted by irate readers who considered his comments to be worthy of the antichrist. Perhaps he shouldn't have been surprised at the reaction. In 1987, Ernst and Young surveyed 154 CEOs about their top priorities. Profits and growth topped the list; service, for all the lip service it garners, came in 11th. In any event, in the January 1992 issue of *MR,* Fagiano responded to his critics with a column titled "Are We in Business to Make Money?" It should be required reading for every MBA student. . . .

Obviously the desires of shareholders—particularly the large institutional investors that control at least 53 percent of U.S. companies' equity capital—should be a significant concern to any executive. . . .

The problem occurs when profit and shareholder value become the primary goals. The problem also occurs when profit and shareholder value are viewed not as the consequence of effective strategy and policy, but as the raison d'être of the business itself. . . .

Second, managers who focus on the short-term financials are more likely to employ sweeping meat-cleaver approaches to head-count reductions, approaches that often are not carefully thought out and integrated into operational efficiency and long-term competitive strategy, but serve well as quick fixes. It should not be surprising that more than 75 percent of downsizing efforts across American businesses have not yielded any increases in productivity or profitability. . . .

So what is the bottom line of all this? Profits result from good management. They do not define good management. Companies that focus on creating value for their customers yield the highest total returns to investors. The story is the same when it comes to preparing for the future. . . .

And I didn't even mention Warren Phillips, the ex-chairman of Dow Jones & Co. In 1984, he stated his company's philosophy succinctly: "Profit is not the number one goal." What is? Same dull old story: "news content, responsiveness to the customer, and delivery."

Those managers who live by the rule that their top priority is to make profits and enhance shareholder value will achieve precisely the opposite results. Just give them time.

Source: Oren Harari, "You're Not in Business to Make a Profit," *Management Review,* July 1992, pp. 53–55. Reprinted by permission of the publisher from *Management Review* July 1992 © 1992. Oren Harari et al., American Management Association, New York. All rights reserved.

Questions

We have learned that the firm's primary goal is to maximize stockholders' wealth. The questions below assume certainty; hence maximizing profit will also maximize stockholders' wealth. This assumption allows us to properly evaluate the preceding article, which mentions profit and stockholder wealth (or shareholder value) in the same breath. We focus here on "profit" versus "customer service," not on risk analysis.

1. As the manager of an auto manufacturer, you believe customer service comes first and profit comes second. Suppose a car's production cost is $10,000. You decide to sell your cars for $9,000 each. All your customers are happy. Will you continue to manage the firm in the future? Explain.
2. According to Paul Fagiano, profit is not the number one goal. Rather, responsiveness to customers and delivery is. Consider the following two scenarios:
    a. Whether or not you are responsive to customer needs, you sell 10,000 cars a year at $20,000 each. The production cost is $15,000 per car.
    b. If you respond to customer needs, you will sell 10,000 cars per year. However, responsiveness to customers increases the production costs to $16,000 per car. If you do not respond to customer needs, the production costs stay at $15,000 per car, but you lose customers, and your sales drop to 7,000 cars per year. The car's price is $20,000 in all cases.

    Suppose you wish to maximize your profit. In which scenario, 2a or 2b, will you pay more attention to customer needs? Explain.

3. Would you change your answer to Question 2b if 10,000 cars are sold in the first year and it is only thereafter, when customers realize that the firm is not responsive to their needs, that sales drop to 7,000 cars per year?

4. Suppose you can sell 10,000 cars per year at $20,000 per car. In response to customer needs, you added certain options to the car that increased production costs to $16,000 per car. You are now considering cutting these costs to $15,500 by eliminating some of these options. If you do so, you estimate that sales will drop to 9,800 cars a year. Will you cut the costs? What if sales drop to 8,000 cars a year as a result of the cost cut? Discuss.

5. In the article, John McConnell says, "Take care of your customers and take care of your people and the market will take care of you." Is this consistent with the goal of maximizing stockholders' wealth?

6. "If management's goal is to maximize the firm's value in the long run (rather than to obtain a temporary increase in value followed by a sharp decrease), then customer service is actually a means to achieve this goal. Without focusing on customer service, the value maximization cannot be achieved." Discuss this claim.

MAKING THE CONNECTION

1. If production costs are $10,000 and the car's selling price is $9,000, customers will be very happy. However, the firm will lose money, and very shortly it will have to declare bankruptcy. Customer service cannot be the ultimate goal, at least not if you wish to continue managing the firm.

2. a. In this case you succeed in selling 10,000 cars a year at $20,000 each, regardless of responsiveness to customer needs. You will be indifferent to customer service: Your profits will be the same whether you do or do not respond to customer needs.

   b. If you do not respond to customer needs, your profit will be

   $$7{,}000 \text{ cars} \times (\$20{,}000 - \$15{,}000) = \$35 \text{ million}$$

   If you do respond to customer needs, the profit will be

   $$10{,}000 \text{ cars} \times (\$20{,}000 - \$16{,}000) = \$40 \text{ million}$$

   Your profit will be $5 million more if you do respond to customer needs. In this case paying attention to customer needs coincides with profit (or value) maximization.

3. The firm should think long-term and not short-term. As we shall see throughout this book, the firm's value is determined by the present value of all future profits, which should be considered.

4. With the options that customers find attractive, profit is

   $$10{,}000 \text{ cars} \times (\$20{,}000 - \$16{,}000) = \$40 \text{ million}$$

If you eliminate these options, you will sell fewer cars. However, because production costs are lower, your profit will be higher. If sales drop to 9,800 cars, profit will be

$$9{,}800 \text{ cars} \times (\$20{,}000 - \$15{,}500) = \$44.1 \text{ million}$$

If sales drop to 8,000 cars, the profit will be

$$8{,}000 \times (\$20{,}000 - \$15{,}500) = \$36 \text{ million}$$

We see from this example that customer satisfaction is a matter of degree. If you lose sales of only 200 units but your profit increases by $4 million, elimination of the new options is justified. However, the firm should not eliminate the new options if sales drop by 2,000 because the profit will drop by $4 million. Although profit is the ultimate goal, if many customers are dissatisfied and do not buy the product, the firm will not achieve this goal.

5. Taking care of employees may ensure a high level of dedication and may help prevent disruption of production (such as strikes). Although providing for the employees will not yield a direct cash inflow, it may induce value maximization. Customer satisfaction may prove helpful in creating a good image which, in turn, may result in more customers for the firm's product. Ignoring employees and customers may prove disastrous, especially when investors and the general public are involved in the firm's actions.

6. When the firm has competition, as in the motor vehicle industry, this statement is true. If customers are unhappy, say, with Ford cars, they can simply buy another automaker's products. If it pays no attention to customer needs, the firm will not maximize its value in the long run. U.S. automakers are now paying more attention to customer service because of sharp competition among both domestic and foreign automakers. In contrast, when a firm has a monopoly over an essential service or product (such as electricity), this assertion is not correct. Customer service may be very bad, yet the firm can still maximize its value. It is for this reason that such firms are regulated.

2.7 BUSINESS ETHICS

In a country that advocates opportunity for all and also lauds competition, competing businesses and consumers will always be alert to—and ready to denounce—unfair business practices. Such conduct, if not declared illegal, will be condemned as unethical. *Ethics* encompasses society's standards of right and wrong behavior, and **business ethics** applies these moral judgments to business practices. Connecting Theory to Practice 2.2 describes the current status of ethics in the business world and sets the stage for our discussion of business ethics.

Ethics and *fraud* are used rather freely in daily news reporting, but these two words have distinctive meanings. *Fraud* involves breaking the law or not complying with existing regulations, whereas *unethical conduct* involves breaching the ethical codes or deviating from moral norms. The former can be defined objectively, whereas the latter tends to be defined subjectively.

CONNECTING THEORY TO PRACTICE 2.2

THE NEW CRISIS IN BUSINESS ETHICS

To meet goals in these tough times, more managers are cutting ethical corners. The trend hurts both the culprits and their companies, even if they don't get caught.

As this economic slowdown lingers like some stubborn low-grade infection, managers are putting the heat on subordinates. Many of the old rules no longer seem to apply. Says Gary Edwards, president of the Ethics Resource Center, a consulting firm in Washington: "The message out there is, reaching objectives is what matters and how you get there isn't that important."

People lower down on the corporate food chain are telling the boss what they think he wants to hear, and outright lying has become a commonplace at many companies. Michael Josephson, a prominent Los Angeles ethicist who consults for some of America's largest public corporations, says his polls reveal that between 20% and 30% of middle managers have written deceptive internal reports. The Justice Department has become far keener on catching and punishing white-collar criminals since the S&L crisis[5] and the BCCI scandal. Last November tough new sentencing guidelines for corporate crimes went into effect. Warns Josephson: "We are going to see a phenomenal number of business scandals during the 1990s. We are swimming in enough lies to keep the lawyers busy for the next ten years."

Even if you don't land in court, you might find yourself on the front page or the evening news, which could be worse. In the past few years, most media have given much more coverage to business. Newspapers and magazines all over the U.S. now employ investigative reporters with MBAs and business experience to dig into the affairs of companies. The old advice is still the best: Don't do anything on the job you wouldn't want your mother to read about with her morning coffee.

Source: Kenneth Labich, "The New Crisis in Business Ethics," *Fortune* 125, no. 8 (April 1992), pp. 167–176. Copyright © 1992 Time Inc. All rights reserved.

MAKING THE CONNECTION

As unethical behavior is subjective, some actions may be considered unethical by one person but ethical by another person. The best guideline may be that suggested by the preceding article: "Don't do anything on the job you wouldn't want your mother to read about with her morning coffee."

---

5. The S&L crisis refers to the massive defaults of U.S. savings and loan institutions during the late 1980s and early 1990s. These defaults occurred for a variety of reasons, one of which was fraudulent conduct of managers.

In any discussion of business ethics and regulations, the issues tend to become blurred. Many unethical actions are regulated. For example, insider trading is considered unfair and unethical. In the United States, it is also illegal. Anyone involved in insider trading is breaking the law and can be prosecuted. However, creating laws and developing regulations to cover every questionable management action is impossible, and a wide range of actions is unethical but not unlawful.

Consider this scenario. A CEO influences the nomination of board members who, once appointed to the compensation committee, increase the CEO's salary. This maneuver is considered unethical, but it is not unlawful. Because laws and regulations often result from board members' or managers' persistent unethical behavior and from public criticism of their behavior, we may see a law regulating the appointment and composition of compensation committees. If and when such a law is enacted, influencing board nominations or CEO compensations will move from the unethical-conduct category to the unlawful-conduct category.

As we learned in Chapter 1, CEO compensation schemes have been criticized as being unfair and even unethical. Although the CEO's compensation is usually tied to the firm's performance, the firm sometimes awards its CEO an increase in compensation even when it is losing money. Though this practice is not illegal, the financial media criticize it. How can the firm justify an increase in CEO compensation and a generous bonus when it is actually losing money?

Consider yet another hypothetical example. The CEO of Firm A sits on the compensation committee of Firm B, and the CEO of Firm B sits on the compensation committee of Firm A. In this case the well-known adage, "You scratch my back, and I'll scratch yours," may work very well for these two CEOs. Their compensation may increase, even in a year when their firms are losing money. Are these CEOs breaking the law? Probably not. Are they conducting themselves unethically? Yes. Probably the best way to prevent this situation would be for stockholders to ensure that CEO compensation is tied to performance.

Having strong stakes in the firms they own, stockholders are becoming more vocal in their criticism of management's ethical standards. For example, in 1992 two suits were filed against the management of Sprint. One suit claimed that the company misled investors when it reported low midyear earnings, and the other accused Sprint of improperly obtaining information about competitors.

Any attempt to identify cut-and-dried rules regarding ethical and unethical conduct is bound to be controversial. *Webster's Dictionary* defines *ethics* as "a body of moral principles of a particular culture." What is considered unethical conduct varies among cultures.

2.8 THE TAX STRUCTURE

Both individuals and businesses must consider taxation—an overwhelming constraint in the business environment—when planning their investment strategies.

2.8.1 How Taxes Affect Investment Decisions

As we read in the Corporate Finance in the News article, a family-business tax cut may encourage more family businesses. Connecting Theory to Practice 2.3 illustrates some ways that changes in the tax rate on individuals can affect investment decisions. Investing in financial markets generally involves **capital gains** or **capital losses.** For example, if you buy a share of stock for $100 and sell it for $150, you have a capital gain of $50, which is taxed. If you sell the stock for $80, you have a capital loss of $20. If you receive income in the form of dividends or interest, you pay income tax rather than capital gains tax. Connecting Theory to Practice 2.3 reveals the prevailing U.S. income tax and capital gains tax rates.

CONNECTING THEORY TO PRACTICE 2.3

IT'S ALMOST NOW! A TAX CUT FOR CAPITAL GAINS

Few policy proposals put as warm a glow in the hearts of American business leaders, entrepreneurs, and investors as the idea of cutting the tax rates on capital gains. Lower capital gains taxes reduce the cost of capital because they in-

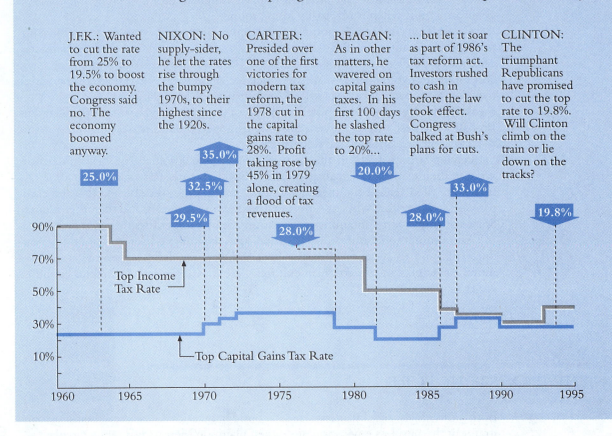

J.F.K.: Wanted to cut the rate from 25% to 19.5% to boost the economy. Congress said no. The economy boomed anyway.

NIXON: No supply-sider, he let the rates rise through the bumpy 1970s, to their highest since the 1920s.

CARTER: Presided over one of the first victories for modern tax reform, the 1978 cut in the capital gains rate to 28%. Profit taking rose by 45% in 1979 alone, creating a flood of tax revenues.

REAGAN: As in other matters, he wavered on capital gains taxes. In his first 100 days he slashed the top rate to 20%...

...but let it soar as part of 1986's tax reform act. Investors rushed to cash in before the law took effect. Congress balked at Bush's plans for cuts.

CLINTON: The triumphant Republicans have promised to cut the top rate to 19.8%. Will Clinton climb on the train or lie down on the tracks?

crease its after-tax return. From this flow all kinds of beneficent effects, including increased national output, more investment, higher asset prices—and, of course, larger profits for investors. James L. Mann, chief executive officer of SunGard Data Systems, a computer service firm with 1994 revenues of $440 million, speaks for the consensus in corporate America when he says, "It's good for the economy, good for my business, and good for me." The view from Wall Street is just as unequivocal. Bullish as his company's trademark Texas longhorns, Merrill Lynch's chief investment strategist Charles Clough states, "Past capital gains cuts have led to investment booms, and presumably there'd be nothing different this time. . . ."

Source: Rob Norton, "It's Almost Now! A Tax Cut for Capital Gains," *Fortune* 131, no. 2 (February 1995): 68–69. Copyright © 1995 Time Inc. All rights reserved.

MAKING THE CONNECTION

The income tax rate varies; at times it has been extremely high or relatively low. Changes in the tax rate, and in the gap between the income tax and the capital gains tax rates, affect an individual's decision to invest in stocks and bonds. These individual decisions, in turn, affect the amount of resources available to firms for investment in projects. Individuals and firms should consider the tax structure when making investment decisions.

As seen in the illustration in Connecting Theory to Practice 2.3, the top income tax rate was as high as 90% in the early 1960s and as low as 28% in the early 1990s. Except for a short time in the early 1990s, the **capital gains tax** rate was always substantially lower than the income tax rate. In 1997, the tax rate was widely expected to be lowered from 28% to 20% (and even to 18.0% for stocks held for at least five years). The article in Connecting Theory to Practice 2.3 claims that the economy will favor a reduction in the capital gains tax rate, which would increase national output, investment, and asset (stock) prices and would decrease the firm's cost of capital. (The relationship between cost of capital and investment will be covered in Chapter 10.) Although Connecting Theory to Practice 2.3 discusses individual tax rates, changes in corporate tax rates would have the same effect on the economy. A tax reduction would reduce the firm's cost of capital.

Financial decisions are not made in a vacuum. In addition to complying with regulatory, environmental, and ethical constraints, we must also pay taxes. In the mid-1990s, a firm paid approximately one-third of its net income as federal taxes. In previous years the amount was even larger—as much as 50%. In addition, individual investors pay both personal income tax on dividends received and capital gains tax on profits from the sale of their stock. Add to this amount the various local and state taxes, and taxes clearly reduce personal income and corporate profits.

Taxation also affects a firm's financial and investment decisions. For example, should the firm issue stocks or bonds? Should the firm buy a machine or lease one? Each decision directly affects the firm's tax burden, and the tax structure is an integral part of the environment in which the firm operates. An astute financial manager will know how to minimize the firm's taxes. For instance, U.S. firms have opened and operated overseas branches in such countries as Mexico, Brazil, China, Taiwan, and Korea. In addition to cheaper labor, these firms also get tax breaks—which create a better business environment for the firms.

How taxes affect an individual project's cash flows will be discussed in detail in Chapter 7. In the remainder of this chapter, we describe the corporate and individual tax structures that prevailed when this book was written—that is, after the changes the Clinton administration introduced in 1993.

2.8.2 Individual and Corporate Income Taxes

As we saw in Connecting Theory to Practice 2.3, personal and corporate income tax rates change over time. This potential for change affects investment planning in a long-term project. Even if the project's future pretax cash flows are certain (they generally are not), the financial manager must realize that the after-tax cash flows will be uncertain because the future tax rate is unknown. For instance, President Bush, reneging on his famous "Read my lips" promise of no tax increase, did raise the tax rates. Then, in 1993, the Clinton administration increased both the personal and the corporate income tax rates.

Table 2-1 presents the 1997 individual and corporate tax rates. Let's look first at the individual income tax rates. Take, for example, the Joint Return column. If you and your spouse have a combined income of $41,200, you will be taxed at 15% and will pay income taxes of $6,180 (15% × $41,200). If your income is just $100 more (i.e., $41,300), you will be taxed at 28% on this additional $100 income ($28). The highest tax rate on individual income in the top income bracket currently stands at 39.6%, as opposed to 28% during the Reagan administration. Until July 1997, the Clinton administration did not change the capital gains tax, which stayed at 28%. For example, if you buy a share of stock for $100 and sell it after two years for $200, you will have a capital gain of $100 and must pay a capital gains tax of $28 (28% × $100 = $28).

Although the Clinton administration kept the top *average* **corporate tax** rate at 35%, it increased the marginal corporate tax rate. The **marginal tax rate** is the rate paid on the additional income earned over a certain amount. To demonstrate the relationship between average and marginal tax rates, consider the $100,000–$335,000 corporate income bracket. The corporate tax rate is $22,250 plus 39% of the *additional income* above $100,000. In other words, a firm pays $22,250 as taxes on its first $100,000 of income and pays 39% on the additional income above $100,000. Thus, the *marginal* corporate tax in this income bracket is 39%. However, at the $335,000 income level, the *average* corporate tax is:

$$\frac{\$22,250 + [(\$335,000 - \$100,000) \times 0.39]}{\$335,000} = \frac{\$22,250 + \$91,650}{\$335,000}$$

$$= \frac{\$113,900}{\$335,000} = 0.34 \text{ or } 34\%$$

TABLE 2-1   U.S. Individual and Corporate Tax Rates

Tax Rates for Individuals, 1997

Tax Rate (%)	Joint Return ($)	Head of Household ($)	Married Filing Separately ($)	Unmarried Individual ($)
15	0–41,200	0–33,050	0–20,600	0–24,650
28	41,200–99,600	33,050–85,350	20,600–49,800	24,650–59,750
31	99,600–151,750	85,350–138,200	49,800–75,875	59,750–124,650
36	151,750–271,050	138,200–271,050	75,875–135,525	124,650–271,050
39.6	Over 271,050	Over 271,050	Over 135,525	Over 271,050

U.S. Corporation Income Tax Rates, 1997

Taxable Income Over ($)	Tax Paid on the Lower Bracket ($)	Plus This % in the Excess over the Lower Bracket (marginal rate) (%)	Average Tax Rate at Top of the Bracket (tax paid divided by income) (%)
0	0		15 15.00
50,000	7,500		25 18.33
75,000	13,750		34 22.25
100,000	22,250		39 34.00
335,000	113,900		34 34.00
10,000,000	3,400,000		35 34.33
15,000,000	5,150,000		38 35.00
18,333,333	6,416,667		35 35.00

Source: Internal Revenue Service, Publication S42, 1997, p. 7.

where the **average tax rate** is defined as the total tax divided by the total income. Although the marginal income tax rate in this range is 39%, the average tax rate in this bracket does not exceed 34%. Calculation of the average tax rate of other income brackets reveals that it never exceeds 35%. From here on we will assume incomes large enough so that the marginal and average corporate tax rates are effectively equal to 35%.

Table 2-2 shows the maximum corporate and individual income tax rates of various countries. A low individual income tax rate may give an individual some incentive to emigrate. However, the corporate income tax rate *may* be an important factor in selecting the location of one's business. It might be worthwhile to live in one country and to conduct business in another if you pay lower corporate income taxes in the foreign country.

TABLE 2-2 Corporate and Individual Taxes: An International Comparison (in Percent)		Maximum Corporate Tax Rate (%)	Maximum (Individual) Income Tax Rate (%)
	U.S.A.	35.0	39.6
	United Kingdom	33.0	40.0
	Japan	37.5	50.0
	Finland	25.0	25.0
	Italy	36.0	51.0
	Germany	45.0	53.0
	France	33.3	56.8
	Netherlands	35.0	60.0
	Norway	28.0	28.0
	Sweden	28.0	30.0

Source: European Taxation Database, IBFD, 1993.

Also worth noting: Whereas the United States, Japan, the United Kingdom, and Sweden impose a capital gains tax on investments in securities, most European countries do not.

SUMMARY

The flow of funds from individual investors to the firm and then back to the investors can be a direct flow or an indirect flow via financial intermediaries (such as pension funds and mutual funds). The firm can raise capital in many ways, but its principal sources are stocks (equities) and bonds (debt). Stocks are riskier for investors, and bonds are riskier for the firm. To compensate them for their exposure to risk, investors in stocks require a higher average rate of return than do investors in bonds.

In Chapter 1 we argued that the firm's primary goal should be maximizing stockholders' wealth.

However, the firm cannot pursue this goal without considering the regulatory, environmental, and ethical constraints in the business environment. Therefore, the firm's goal should be maximizing stockholders' wealth subject to those constraints. Some firms declare that their goals are broader—such as caring for employees and satisfying customers. These goals are commendable, and they may also coincide with maximizing stockholders' wealth in the long run.

CHAPTER AT A GLANCE

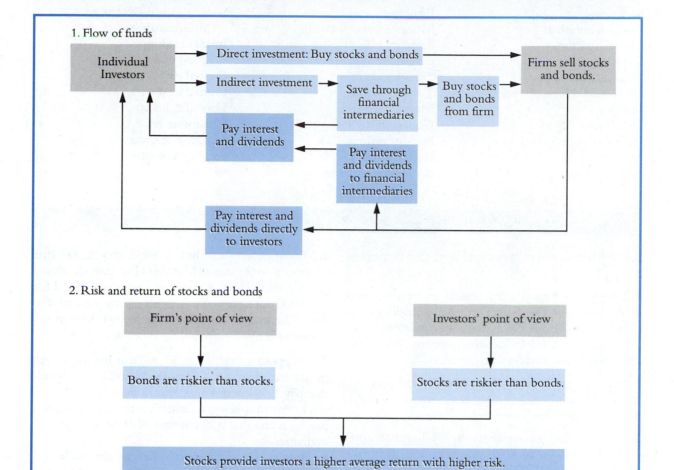

1. Flow of funds

   Individual Investors

   Direct investment: Buy stocks and bonds → Firms sell stocks and bonds.

   Indirect investment → Save through financial intermediaries → Buy stocks and bonds from firm

   Pay interest and dividends

   Pay interest and dividends to financial intermediaries

   Pay interest and dividends directly to investors

2. Risk and return of stocks and bonds

   Firm's point of view

   Investors' point of view

   Bonds are riskier than stocks.

   Stocks are riskier than bonds.

   Stocks provide investors a higher average return with higher risk.

3. Management's consideration of the business environment includes:
   a. Taxes
   b. Government regulations (federal, state, and local)
   c. Environmental protection
   d. Business ethics

KEY TERMS

Securities
Financial markets
Money markets
Capital markets
Financial institutions
Financial intermediaries
Bonds
Debt financing
Par value (face value)
Maturity date
Market value

Principal
Money market securities
Treasury bills (T-bills)
Commercial paper
Treasury notes
Treasury bonds
Municipal bonds
Common stock
Rate of return
Risk premium
Business regulation

Securities and Exchange
   Commission (SEC)
Insider trading
Business ethics
Capital gains
Capital losses
Capital gains tax
Corporate tax
Marginal tax rate
Average tax rate

REVIEW AND PRACTICE

2.1 What are the two principal ways that firms raise money?

2.2 Suppose firms pay 5% annual interest on their debt financing. The federal government decides to issue similar bonds (with the same maturity) that pay 6% interest. How does the government's action affect the firms' financial position?

2.3 Firms pay investors dividends and interest, whereas federal agencies pay only interest. What is the reason for this difference?

2.4 The federal government sells T-bills for $96,000 each. The bills mature in one year and their face value is $100,000. What is the annual rate of return on such an investment?

2.5 Suppose a firm's future income has an equal chance of being $90,000 or $200,000 in any year. The firm is considering whether to finance the projects generating this income by issuing $1 million of equity or by selling $1 million of bonds on which it will be required to pay $50,000 interest at the end of each year.
a. Calculate the two alternative rates of return for the bondholders and for the stockholders.
b. Are bonds or stocks riskier for the firm? Why? How would your answer change if, instead of $90,000, the minimum income was $20,000?
c. Are bonds or stocks riskier for investors?

2.6 Suppose you can buy a T-bill at $96,000 that matures in one year at $100,000 but pays no interest. Alternatively, you can buy a one-year bond for $100,000 that pays 4% interest at the end of the year. The bond's par value is $100,000. Which investment is more profitable?

2.7 Suppose a firm earns $1 million before paying its interest obligations. It issues $1 million in bonds that pay 10% interest and 90,000 shares of common stock. For simplicity, assume that the firm does not pay taxes and that it distributes all of its net earnings as dividends.
a. How much of the firm's income do the bondholders receive, and how much do the stockholders receive per share?
b. How would your answer change if the firm earned an income of $100,000? Of $1.9 million?

2.8 A firm controls 25% of the market of a certain product. Management is considering acquiring another firm that controls 35% of the market of this product. Should regulators intervene? Explain. Distinguish between an essential product (such as public transportation) and a nonessential product (such as plastic geraniums or green lipstick).

2.9 What is the risk involved when a pension fund or an insurance firm invests its assets in high-risk stocks? What type of regulations are typically imposed on such firms? Whom does the regulation protect in such a case, and how?

2.10 Metal Company's earnings and CEO's compensation are as follows

Year	Firm's earnings ($ millions)	CEO compensation ($ millions)
1	150	1.0
2	110	1.2
3	–10	1.4

If you were a member of the firm's ethics committee, what would you have to say about these figures? What would you suspect?

2.11 A firm declares one of its goals is to ensure that its employees' income is fair and that they will have a few recreation hours during the week. "Because this costs money, the firm will not maximize its value." Appraise this claim.

2.12 Suppose the tax rate is a flat 34% on corporation income and 36% on individual income. A firm's revenue is $100 million before taxes. Assume it pays the corporate income tax and then distributes whatever is left as dividends, on which stockholders pay individual income tax. Describe how the $100 million income is divided between the Internal Revenue Service and the stockholders.

2.13 Describe which of these actions is illegal, which is legal and ethical, and which is legal but unethical:

a. Insider trading.
b. As the CEO, you nominate your friend to the board of directors.
c. As the CEO, you use the firm's money to buy a private plane and a vacation resort in Acapulco.
d. Manipulating the accounting figures.
e. Giving your spouse a job in the firm for $250,000 a year.
f. Changing the method the firm uses to calculate profit, with the changes fully explained in the firm's financial statements.
g. As an entrepreneur and expert in the electronics industry, you raise money from investors to start a new firm. After raising the money, you decide to resign.

2.14 As CEO you are considering a profitable project that involves an investment of $1 million today and a return of $2 million one year later. However, the project's construction and operation are likely to pollute a nearby river. Would you undertake the project? What if preventing water pollution means an additional $1 million cash outlay?

2.15 When U.S. airlines were deregulated, the resulting competition caused a price war, and many airlines lost money. Suppose some managers, operating under pressure to cut costs, are allocating reduced funds for airplane maintenance. Would this justify the demand to reimpose price regulations on airlines? Explain.

2.16 Suppose a phone company has a monopoly over telecommunications in a given area. The production cost of the service is $0.10 per unit, and the firm charges the customer $0.80 per unit. Do you think an antitrust suit is justified? Suppose if the firm sold its service for $0.12 per unit, it would make a normal and reasonable profit. How can regulation protect the customers?

2.17 Suppose your firm has a monopoly over a certain product. You can sell 1 million units of the product at $1 per unit or 2 million units at $0.40 per unit. The production costs are $0.20 per unit regardless of the number of units produced. Which price policy would you choose? Explain your answer carefully. How could regulation protect the customer?

I N T E R N E T   Q U E S T I O N

2.18 Visit the Web sites on the New York Stock Exchange, the American Stock Exchange, and NASDAQ. Which one is largest in terms of number of shares traded? In terms of dollar volume?

    http://www.nyse.com
    http://www.amex.com
    http://www.nasdaq.com

GERMAN UNION'S LEADER IS DRAWN INTO TRADING PROBE

FRANKFURT—Franz Steinkuehler, chairman of Germany's IG Metall engineering union, has been drawn into this country's latest insider-trading probe.

This one involves the April 2 announcement by Daimler-Benz AG that it would dissolve its Mercedes AG Holding unit and convert MAH shares 1-for-1 into Daimler-Benz shares at year end.

Because MAH shares at the time were trading about 125 marks ($77.56) below Daimler-Benz's stock price, the deal provided a windfall for MAH holders. One of them, by his own admission, was Mr. Steinkuehler, a labor representative on Daimler-Benz's supervisory board.

The insider-trading commission of the Frankfurt stock exchange launched its investigation because MAH shares began rising days before the announcement. The affair is embarrassing for Daimler-Benz, which this year hopes to list its shares on the New York Stock Exchange. It's also an embarrassment for the IG Metall union, which is in the middle of a huge wage strike across eastern Germany.

Meeting reporters yesterday, Mr. Steinkuehler confirmed news reports that he had bought 2,100 shares of MAH for a total of 998,406 marks just ahead of the April 2 announcement. He made a 106,049-mark profit when he sold off nearly half the holding after MAH's share price soared after April 2, he said.

Mr. Steinkuehler denied any wrongdoing or advance knowledge of the MAH share swap. He said he learned of the deal only on the second day of the company's supervisory board meeting,

on April 2, when management informed directors of its plan.

"The charge that I illegally took advantage of inside information is therefore false and I judge it to be an attempt to discredit my person," he said in a statement to union membership.

Mr. Steinkuehler distributed copies of his reply to bourse investigators in which he laid out MAH stock transactions for himself and his son. These included purchases of 2,100 MAH shares for his accounts at BIG Bank AG at prices ranging from 453 marks to 493 marks between March 18 and April 1. His biggest single order, for 1,000 MAH shares, was made for his son's account on April 1, a day before the Daimler-Benz announcement.*

Additional information: On April 19, the price of an MAH share was 563 marks. In 1993, insider trading was not illegal in Germany, but legislation banning it was under consideration.

*Source: Terence Roth, "German Union's Leader Is Drawn into Trading Probe," *Wall Street Journal,* 18 May 1993, p. A14. Reprinted by permission of *The Wall Street Journal,* © 1993 Dow Jones & Company, Inc. All rights reserved worldwide.

Questions

1. Assume that Mr. Steinkuehler bought all of the 2,100 shares at 493 marks each. What rate of return did he achieve between March 18 and April 19? What was the rate of return on an annual basis?

2. Did Mr. Steinkuehler break the law in Germany? Would his behavior be considered illegal in the United States?

3. Do you believe Mr. Steinkuehler's action was unethical? Why or why not?

LEARNING OBJECTIVES

*After reading this chapter,
you should understand:*

1. The reasons why investors, analysts, lenders, and management rely on financial statement analysis to assess a firm's current and future performance and profitability.

2. The importance and formats of the three principal financial statements: income statement, balance sheet, and statement of cash flows.

3. The reasons why management may sometimes use "window dressing" techniques to improve a firm's financial statements.

4. The three principal market value ratios: price/earnings, market/book value, and dividend yield.

5. The reasons for and advantages of time series and industry financial analyses.

6. The reasons why international comparative financial analysis is difficult to perform.

7. (Appendices) The various ratios to use when performing financial ratio analysis: liquidity, financial leverage, activities, and profitability.

CORPORATE FINANCE IN THE NEWS

INVESTORS MUST DEMAND CLEAR, CLEAN, AND INDEPENDENT FINANCIAL REPORTS

The New York Stock Exchange first asked listed companies to make annual reports in 1886. The Big Board required reports, with earnings statements and balance sheets, starting in 1900. Distribution of reports to shareholders was required in 1909. But the reports did not prevent mismanagement. When businesses went astray, the reports were criticized as vague and misleading.

Since 1977, Congress has required every public company to maintain internal accounting controls sufficient to provide reasonable assurances that transactions are executed in accordance with management's general or specific authorization and that transactions are recorded as necessary to permit preparation of financial statements in conformity with generally accepted accounting principles.

That law, part of the Foreign Corrupt Practices Act, opened the door to the auditor's office and put a government official at the boardroom table. The SEC followed up with a series of rules for accounting standards, becoming in effect the Securities, Exchange, and Accounting Commission. By 1992, the commission could say without even creating controversy that its goal was to put shareholders at the boardroom table so they could "see the company through the eyes of management."

Source: Thomas G. Donalan, "No Accounting for Auditors" (editorial), *Barron's* 42, no. 42 (October 1995):46. Reprinted by permission of *Barron's*, © 1995 Dow Jones & Company, Inc. All rights reserved worldwide.

3.1 INTRODUCTION

http

Financial data on firms (financial statements, ratio analyses, etc.) are available at hundreds of sites, including
http://www. thomsoninvest.net
http://www.hoovers. com
http://www.bloomberg. com

If you have taken an accounting course, you already know that a firm's cash flows do not necessarily correspond to its accounting earnings. Indeed, a firm's financial statements can show a glowing earnings picture even when it has little cash available for ongoing operations or for investments in new projects. In this book we show that cash flows, rather than accounting earnings, should be used to evaluate firms and projects.

If so, why bother with a firm's financial statements? There are three very good reasons for analyzing financial statements:

1. The many transactions that a firm conducts during the year are hard to follow. The financial statements summarize these transactions and allow both managers and shareholders to evaluate—albeit not always in a precise manner—the firm's performance. Managers can use the statements for planning and for evaluating the firm's financial position.

2. Financial analysts base their investment decisions on a firm's financial statements. Remember: The firm's goal is to maximize stockholders' wealth. If the analysts do not like what they see in the firm's financial statements, they may decide to sell their stock or may recommend that their clients do so. In that case, the stock price will decrease and the firm will not achieve its objective.

3. Last, but not least important, reporting to stockholders is mandatory.

Financial statement analysis, an evaluation of the firm based mainly on information contained in its financial statements, uses accounting data to measure the firm's historical performance and forecast its profitability. For example, if the firm's earnings are relatively low and if the firm has a high proportion of debt financing, creditors may believe bankruptcy is imminent and may not lend the firm additional funds. If stockholders see a declining trend in sales and earnings, they may not purchase the firm's stock. Financial statement analysis also has internal purposes. Managers need to detect troublesome signals and to take corrective action. The firm also uses financial statement analysis to help determine its future financial needs.

In this chapter we discuss financial statements and financial statement analysis. We first introduce the statements themselves and show how investors, creditors, and management can use them for various purposes. Some techniques of financial statement analysis will be discussed in this chapter. Others will be discussed later in the book. Appendix 3A presents financial ratio analysis.

3.2 AN OVERVIEW OF THE FIRM'S FINANCIAL STATEMENTS

A firm is required to prepare quarterly and annual financial statements that summarize its financial activities during the period under review. Financial statements contain information on such items as profit (or loss), interest payments, dividends, financing (stock or bond issues, loans), debt repayments, and capital expenditures. So, even though most information they give is not based on cash flows, financial statements do indicate the overall success or failure of the financial decisions the firm has taken during the period. They do not give the full picture, but financial statements do provide a reasonable "rough sketch."

Financial statements contain information for many users: for stockholders (investors), for banks and bondholders (lenders), for the board of directors (in discussing the firm's economic health), for labor unions (in negotiating wage demands), for the Internal Revenue Service (to determine the firm's tax liability), and for the CFO. During the course of his/her work, the CFO is bombarded with figures. The financial statements—and, in particular, the financial ratios derived from them—provide a condensed picture of the firm's financial situation and pinpoint the firm's strengths and weaknesses. The CFO then knows what measures need to be taken to correct undesirable trends.

More than one year's results are usually analyzed. Any sustained decrease or increase in reported earnings indicates real changes or trends occurring in the firm. It is thus no wonder that the stock market reacts favorably to increases and unfavorably to decreases in earnings, even though the accounting figures do not precisely reflect the firm's economic profit or its cash flows.

We focus in this chapter mainly on Ford Motor Company's financial statements. We selected 1992 because it had some special features—a big loss, a change in accounting principles, and a relatively large increase in sales that was not accompanied by an increase in profit. These features allow an interesting analysis of the accounting figures. Later, in Applying Theory to Practice 3.1, we continue an analysis of Ford based on 1994 and 1995 accounting and market data.

A firm's annual financial statements usually begin with the chairperson's "personal" letter to the stockholders. The letter summarizes the important developments and major events of the year, positive and negative, and the "inevitably rosy" future outlook. For example, Harold A. Poling, Chairman of Ford Motor Company, wrote in the 1992 report:

Although 1992 was difficult, we can report a number of positive developments in Ford . . . . [Our achievements, however, were clouded by a record loss of $7.4 billion.] . . . . Although the stockholder's equity was greatly reduced by changes in accounting principles, our cash flow was not affected, and the company's financial structure remains strong.*

The chairperson's letter is usually followed by a series of glossy shots of the firm's latest new products (in Ford's case, new vehicle models) and then by a listing of the board members. Only then are the firm's financial "secrets" revealed to us. These revelations take the form of three **financial statements:** the *income statement,* the *balance sheet,* and the *statement of cash flows.* Positive results are generally reported without explanation, whereas negative results are inevitably accompanied by a host of explanations. (One common observation is that financial reports are generally divided into two groups: those with good results and those with good explanations.)

---

* The Ford Motor Company, *1992 Annual Report.*

Every annual report contains an *auditor's opinion,* a statement prepared by a professional accounting firm as to the reliability and accuracy of the financial statements. The auditor's report comes either before or immediately after the financial statements. The auditors generally write: "In our opinion the financial statements fairly present the firm's financial position in conformity with generally accepted accounting principles."

The goal of financial statement analysis is to assess the firm's financial strength and to forecast its future earnings. We will analyze Ford's financial reports from the standpoint of the outsider who, apart from these published reports, has no other information about the firm. The outsider might be a bank considering whether to lend money to the firm, or an investor considering whether to buy the firm's stock, or another firm considering a takeover. In our analysis of Ford's financial statements, we will identify the main features of the firm's economic development and decide what additional information we would need to better understand Ford's financial position. The statements are presented in Figures 3-1, 3-2, and 3-3 in the order they appeared in Ford's annual financial report.

3.3 THE INCOME STATEMENT

The **income statement** reports the firm's earnings (or losses) during the reported period. We will demonstrate how to read this statement and how to interpret the given information by examining Ford's income statements for 1991 and 1992 (see Figure 3-1). As you can see, Ford Motor Company provides separate income statements for its Automotive Unit and its Financial Services Unit, as well as a *consolidated* statement for both units.

A firm's income is determined as follows:

$$\text{Income} = (\text{Revenue} - \text{Expenses}) + (\text{Gains} - \text{Losses}) \qquad (3.1)$$

from operations   from other activities

Annual reports always provide income statements for at least two consecutive years. The 1991 and 1992 income statements of Ford Motor Company reveal that the firm's sales revenue from its Automotive Unit grew very rapidly, from about $72 billion in 1991 to about $84 billion in 1992, though the unit actually lost money both years. The Financial Services Unit's income increased from about $1.46 billion in 1991 to about $1.82 billion in 1992 despite a small decrease in revenues (from $16.2 billion to $15.7 billion, respectively).

Another item worth noting appears in the Total Company section: a loss of about $6.88 billion in 1992 due to changes in the method of accounting for future retiree health benefits. This item is not a cash flow loss (that is, Ford did not pay

FIGURE 3-1   **Consolidated Statement of Income for Ford Motor Company and Subsidiaries for the Years Ended December 31, 1992 and 1991 (in millions, except amounts per share)**

	1992	1991
AUTOMOTIVE		
Sales (Note 1)	$84,407.2	$72,050.9
Costs and expenses (Note 1)		
Costs of Sales	81,747.7	71,826.6
Selling, administrative, and other expenses	4,434.5	3,993.4
Total costs and expenses	$86,182.2	$75,820.0
Operating (loss)/income	(1,775.0)	(3,769.1)
Interest income	653.3	676.5
Interest expense	860.7	902.6
Net interest (expense)/income	$ (207.4)	$ (226.1)
Equity in net income/(loss) of affiliated companies (Note 1)	15.4	(28.4)
Net revenue/(expense) from transactions with Financial Services (Note 15)	15.4	(28.2)
(Loss)/Income before income taxes and cumulative effects of changes in accounting principles—Automotive	$(1,951.6)	$ (4,051.8)
FINANCIAL SERVICES		
Revenues (Note 1)		
Costs and expenses	15,725.1	16,235.4
Interest expense	7,055.8	8,316.6
Operating and other expenses	2,944.8	2,822.6
Provision for credit and insurance losses (Note 9)	1,795.1	2,159.2
Depreciation (Note 8)	2,089.1	1,500.4
Total costs and expenses	$13,884.8	$14,798.8
Net (expense)/revenue from transactions with Automotive (Note 15)	(15.4)	28.2
Income before income taxes and cumulative effects of changes in accounting principles—Financial Services	1,824.9	1,464.8
TOTAL COMPANY		
(Loss)/Income before income taxes and cumulative effects of changes in accounting principles	$(126.7)	$ (2,587.0)
Provision/(Credit) for income taxes (Note 5)	294.7	(395.4)
(Loss)/Income before minority interests and cumulative effects of changes in accounting principles	(421.4)	(2,191.6)
Minority interests in net income of subsidiaries	80.4	66.4
(Loss)/Income before cumulative effects of changes in accounting principles	$ (501.8)	$ (2,258.0)
Cumulative effects of changes in accounting principles (Notes 2 and 5)	(6,883.2)	—
Net (loss)/income	$ (7,385.0)	$ (2,258.0)
Preferred Stock dividend requirements	209.4	22.0
(Loss)/Income attributable to Common and Class B Stock	$ (7,594.4)	$ (2,280.0)
Average number of shares of Common and Class B Stock outstanding	486.5	475.8

(continued)

FIGURE 3-1   **(Continued)**

**AMOUNTS PER SHARE OF COMMON STOCK AND CLASS B
STOCK AFTER PREFERRED STOCK DIVIDENDS (Note 1)**

(Loss)/Income before cumulative effects of changes in accounting principles	$ (1.46)	$(4.79)
Cumulative effects of changes in accounting principles	(14.15)	—
(Loss)/Income	$(15.61)	$(4.79)
Cash dividends	$ 1.60	$ 1.95

Source: The Ford Motor Company, *1992 Annual Report*.

$6.88 billion in cash). Rather, it is simply an outcome of the change in accounting principles mandated by the Financial Accounting Standards Board (FASB).[1] Yet, even without this item, the loss would have been $501.8 million, which, although not as large as in 1991, is substantial. The bottom lines of the table provide the per-share data—earnings per share (a negative amount) and dividend per share.

Suppose you are a financial analyst and are considering buying Ford's stock (or recommending that a client do so). Or suppose you are the CEO of a large bank that is considering lending money to Ford. Which items in this income statement would you want to analyze in greater depth? What additional information would you need from the firm? What conclusions can you draw regarding Ford's future income?

To answer, we first need to examine the sales figures for the Automotive Unit. Simple calculation reveals that sales grew by about 17% in 1992 (the ≅ sign means "approximately" or that the numbers are rounded):

$$\frac{\$84.4 \text{ billion} - \$72.1 \text{ billion}}{\$72.1 \text{ billion}} \cong 0.171 \text{ or } 17.1\%$$

We would expect such a healthy growth rate to be accompanied by a large profit, but this profit did not materialize. Why not? Could the growth have been due to an aggressive sales promotion involving liberal price discounts? If so, investors and lenders need to consider what may happen if Ford discontinues the discount policy. Ford's market share may fall, and the company may find itself back at square one. (See the lower sales and higher loss in 1991.) Or perhaps the firm changed its product mix to achieve a higher volume of sales on low-profit products. Yet another explanation might be that Ford decided to enter new markets (such as the East European market) and incurred large fixed initial costs. If so, the success or failure of its marketing strategy will be apparent in future financial statements. These tentative explanations for why the figures for sales and profits do not correspond show that it is crucial to know the reason for the growth in sales. Only then can we determine whether this growth is likely to produce a healthy future profit.

1. This change is explained in notes 2 and 5 that accompany Ford's financial statements. These notes are an integral portion of the report and sometimes contain crucial information. For the sake of brevity, we do not provide all of these lengthy notes here.

3.4 THE BALANCE SHEET

The **balance sheet** provides an instant picture of the firm's accounting assets and liabilities on a given date. The balance sheet for Ford Motor Company has two halves: On the left are the firm's assets, and on the right are the firm's liabilities and the stockholders' equity.

The two sides must be balanced by definition.

$$\text{Assets} = \text{Liabilities} + \text{Stockholders' Equity} \qquad (3.2)$$

Alternatively, stockholders' equity is expressed as

$$\text{Stockholders' Equity} = \text{Assets} - \text{Liabilities} \qquad (3.3)$$

The consolidated balance sheet for Ford Motor Company and its subsidiaries (see Figure 3-2) shows that the accounting value of the equity held by Ford's stockholders in 1992 was $14,752.9 million. Recall that creditors have a first-priority claim on both the firm's income and its assets. For this reason, stockholders' equity is generally seen as a residual—the firm's assets minus what the firm owes its creditors.

Ford Motor Company issues common stock and preferred stock.[2] The value of the common stock equity is calculated as follows:

$$\text{Common Stock Equity} = \text{Total Assets} - \text{Liabilities} - \text{Preferred Stock Equity} \qquad (3.4)$$

Ford's common stock equity for 1992 (in millions) is

Common Stock Equity	=	Total Assets	−	Automotive Unit Liabilities	−	Financial Services Liabilities	−	Preferred Stock Equity
↓		↓		↓		↓		↓
$14,752.9	=	$180,545.2 −		$51,392.4	−	$113,317.4	−	$1,082.5

Let us first analyze the firm's various assets.

The Securities and Exchange Commission maintains extensive financial data on publicly traded U.S. firms.
http://www.sec.gov/edgar

3.4.1 Assets

Current assets are those that will be converted into cash within one year by the firm's regular activities. The firm's ability to convert assets into cash on short notice and without incurring a loss is called **liquidity.** The most liquid asset is, of course, *cash* itself. The second most liquid asset is the firm's *marketable securities,* which the firm can sell whenever it wishes without necessarily incurring a loss but, sometimes, at a profit. *Accounts receivable* (or simply *receivables*) represent money not yet collected for the firm's services and goods. The accounts receivable are listed net of *bad debt;* that is, debt that the firm considers uncollectible is subtracted from total accounts receivable before listing them in the balance sheet. *Inventory* consists of the raw materials

---

2. The dividends paid on *preferred stock* are prespecified. Unlike dividends on common stock, dividends on preferred stock do not vary along with the firm's profitability. If the firm loses money, it can skip the dividends on preferred stock.

FIGURE 3-2   Consolidated Balance Sheet for Ford Motor Company and Subsidiaries December 31, 1992 and 1991 (in millions)

ASSETS	1992	1991
Automotive		
Cash and cash equivalents	$ 3,504.0	$ 4,958.0
Marketable securities, at cost and accrued interest (approximates market, Note 19)	5,530.9	4,794.5
Total cash, cash equivalents, and marketable securities	$ 9,034.9	$ 9,752.5
Receivables	2,883.6	3,150.6
Inventories (Note 4)	5,451.3	6,215.3
Deferred income taxes	2,479.7	2,112.0
Other current assets	618.6	529.4
Net current receivable from Financial Services (Note 15)	1,368.0	92.1
Total current assets	$ 21,836.1	$ 21,851.9
Equity in net assets of affiliated companies (Note 1)	2,751.0	2,179.4
Net property (Note 6)	22,160.0	22,522.3
Deferred income taxes	5,014.4	—
Other assets (Notes 1 and 2)	5,339.1	5,780.3
Net noncurrent receivable from Financial Services (Note 15)	69.4	63.5
Total Automotive assets	$ 57,170.0	$ 52,397.4
Financial Services		
Cash and cash equivalents	3,182.1	3,175.2
Investments in securities (Notes 7 and 19)	6,873.9	5,925.2
Net receivables and lease investments (Notes 8, 9, and 19)	106,144.1	105,274.7
Other assets (Note 1)	7,175.1	7,656.9
Total Financial Services assets	$123,375.2	$122,032.0
Total assets	$180,545.2	$174,429.4

LIABILITIES AND STOCKHOLDERS' EQUITY	1992	1991
Automotive		
Trade payables	$ 7,943.9	$ 7,019.9
Other payable	1,631.2	1,912.2
Accrued liabilities (Note 10)	9,983.4	9,910.4
Income taxes payable	317.7	394.7
Debt payable within one year (Note 11)	1,248.7	2,579.6
Total current liabilities	$ 21,124.9	$ 21,816.8
Long-term debt (Note 11)	7,067.9	6,538.7
Other liabilities (Note 10)	21,866.7	8,726.0
Deferred income taxes	1,332.9	1,182.7
Total Automotive liabilities	$ 51,392.4	$ 38,264.2
Financial Services		
Payable	1,513.6	1,364.6
Debt (Note 11)	90,187.8	88,294.7
Deposit accounts (Note 12)	14,030.3	16,882.2
Deferred income taxes	1,616.4	1,647.0
Other liabilities and deferred income	4,531.9	4,330.8
Net payable to Automotive (Note 15)	1,437.4	155.6
Total Financial Services liabilities	$113,317.4	$112,674.9
Preferred stockholders' equity in a subsidiary company (Note 1)	1,082.5	800.0
Stockholders' equity		
Capital stock (Notes 13 and 14)		
Preferred stock, par value $1.00 per share (aggregate liquidation preference of $3.4 billion and $2.3 billion)	0.1	*
Common stock, par value $1.00 per share (454.1 and 447.9 million shares issued)	454.1	447.9
Class B Stock, par value $1.00 per share (35.4 million shares issued)	35.4	35.4
Capital in excess of par value of stock	4,697.6	3,378.8
Foreign currency translation adjustments and other (Note 1)	(62.7)	837.4
Earnings retained for use in business	9,628.4	17,990.8
Total stockholders' equity	$ 14,752.9	$ 22,690.3
Total liabilities and stockholders' equity	$180,545.2	$174,429.4

*Less than $50,000.

Source: The Ford Motor Company, *1992 Annual Report.*

used in production and finished goods (vehicles in Ford's case) not yet sold. *Deferred taxes* result from timing differences between financial statements and tax records. For example, different tax liabilities may be incurred by using different depreciation methods for tax purposes and for preparing financial statements. In our example, Ford can carry its heavy losses forward for seven years for tax purposes. This means that for tax purposes, losses in "lean" years can be added to (thereby reducing) the firm's earnings in "fatter" subsequent years. Ford's deferred tax payments are entered as an asset because the firm will pay less taxes in the future when it offsets these losses against future income. Ford's automotive unit's total current assets in 1992 were about $21.8 billion.

As we continue down the balance sheet, we come to less liquid assets. These noncurrent assets include the stocks of other companies that Ford holds and net property (such as buildings and machinery). These other assets are added to the current assets to arrive at a total of Automotive Unit assets.

We next move to the current assets of the Financial Services Unit. Because the Financial Services Unit is not involved in production, it has no heavy machinery. Rather, it has about $106 billion in the form of receivables and other short-term assets.

Total assets for both units of Ford Motor Company totaled about $180.5 billion in 1992.

3.4.2 Liabilities and Stockholders' Equity

The right-hand side of the balance sheet (Figure 3-2) lists the firm's financing sources. These sources include *liabilities* (money owed to the bank, to suppliers, to bondholders, or others) and *stockholders' equity.*

CURRENT LIABILITIES

Listed first are *current liabilities*—those that are payable within one year or less, including *trade payables.* For example, if Ford buys raw materials on 60 days' credit, then it will have to pay the suppliers within 60 days. *Accrued liabilities* consist mainly of amounts payable to employees (salaries, wages, Social Security). Ford also has *income taxes payable*—outstanding debts to the tax authorities. In addition, any debt due to be repaid within a year is also listed in the current liability section, even though it may have been a long-term debt originally. For example, a 10-year loan taken out 9½ years ago will be listed as a debt in the current liability section. Note that Ford's automotive unit's total current liabilities in 1992 were about $21.1 billion, an amount about the same as its total current assets.

DEBT AND EQUITY

As we continue down the right-hand side of the balance sheet, we see two main items: *debt* and *equity.* The huge debt of the Financial Services Unit in 1992 (about $90 billion) consists mainly of bank loans to finance the credit it provides its customers. This debt is short-term because customer credit is usually short-term and listed under accounts receivable. We say that these loans *stand against* accounts receivable.

Ford Motor Company had about $7.1 billion in long-term debt and about $14.7 billion in equity. In addition, it had about $1 billion worth of preferred stock. The equity is in the form of common stock, preferred stock, and retained earnings. When the firm issues stocks, it records the proceeds from the sale as the **book value** of equity. When the firm earns money on its operations, it may distribute some portion as dividends and may retain some portion in the firm. The retained portion increases the book value of the equity.

3.4.3 Market Value versus Book Value

Especially for long-term assets and liabilities, a sizable gap may exist between market value and book (accounting) value. For example, consider the $22.2 billion net property entry on the assets side. Ford may have bought items included in this asset line over a period of several years. If Ford were to sell these items today, the price they would bring—their **market value**—might be much higher than their accounting value (because of inflation, for example). However, according to accepted accounting rules, we ignore the market value of such assets and report only their **historical value**—that is, original cost minus accumulated depreciation. The gap between market and accounting values may also be due to unrecorded assets. For instance, intangibles such as goodwill (the firm's good reputation or a trademark's value) may represent considerable economic value but have zero accounting value.[3]

Generally, a large gap also exists between the book (accounting) value and the market value of equity. For example, in 1992 the total accounting value of Ford's common stock equity was $14.8 billion. When Ford's 1992 financial statements were published, the market price of Ford's common stock was about $53 per share, and 454.1 million shares were outstanding. This puts the market value of Ford's common stock equity at

$$454.1 \text{ million shares} \times \$53 \cong \$24.07 \text{ billion}$$

That amount is much higher than the $14.8 billion total stockholders' equity recorded in Ford's balance sheet. Similar gaps between market and book values may also exist for debt.

In light of the differences between book and market values, are the data given in the balance sheet useful? It depends. In Ford's case, since the accounting value of the equity severely understates the market value, the equity figures are not very meaningful. For example, if you want to buy the firm or a portion of it, you should examine the market value of the equity because the accounting value is meaningless. The book value of the equity per share was

$$\frac{\$14.8 \text{ billion}}{454.1 \text{ million shares}} \cong \$32.59$$

whereas the share price was $53. Any investor would want to pay the accounting value for Ford's shares, but no one would sell them at that price.

---

3. According to generally accepted accounting procedures, goodwill is recorded in the balance sheet only if the firm purchases it, not if the firm generates it.

On the other hand, the balance sheet data on current assets and current liabilities are very useful. The gap between the market and accounting values of current assets and current liabilities is usually quite small. As we shall see in Chapter 12, the shorter the maturity of the debt, the smaller the gap is. How would you use this information? Suppose as the CEO of a bank, you are considering whether to provide a short-term loan to Ford Motor Company. If Ford's current assets are $10 billion and its current liabilities are $20 billion, you will probably be reluctant to provide the loan. How would the firm pay $20 billion of liabilities within a year with only $10 billion of assets readily convertible into cash? Although Ford might produce more cash by sales, the firm's cash level could decrease even further if it loses money. Given this financial scenario, you would probably deny the loan request.

A firm is normally considered financially weak if it has a *negative* net working capital, where **net working capital** is defined as follows:

$$\text{Net Working Capital} = \text{Current Assets} - \text{Current Liabilities} \qquad (3.5)$$

The 1992 net working capital of Ford's Automotive Unit was

$$\$711.2 \text{ million} = \$21{,}836.1 \text{ million} - \$21{,}124.9 \text{ million}$$

Although this figure is positive, it is not very impressive if we consider the volume of Ford Motor Company's operations.

The following problem demonstrates how to complete a balance sheet when only some figures are known.

PRACTICE BOX

Problem

A firm's net working capital is −$100, its long-term debt is $200, its equity is $100, and its total assets are $1,000. Use these figures to construct the firm's balance sheet.

Solution

First, write the known amounts into the balance sheet format:

Assets		Liabilities	
Current assets	$?	Current liabilities	$?
Fixed assets	$?	Long-term debt	$200
		Equity	$100
Total	$1,000	Total	$1,000

Now perform some computations to fill in the unknown amounts. Because total liabilities are $1,000, the current liabilities are

$$\$1{,}000 - \$200 - \$100 = \$700$$

(continued)

Now use the formula for net working capital to find the amount of current assets:

$$\text{Net Working Capital} = \text{Current Assets} - \text{Current Liabilities}$$
$$-\$100 = \text{Current Assets} - \$700$$

The current assets must be $600, and the fixed assets must be $1,000 − $600 = $400.

3.5 THE STATEMENT OF CASH FLOWS

The firm includes in its statement of cash flows any cash flow it pays or receives. The transactions that appear in the income statement and balance sheet are recorded on an accrual basis rather than on a cash flow basis. For example, suppose the firm purchases a machine on January 1, 1997, for $10 million and pays for it in cash. The firm depreciates the machine evenly over 10 years. The cash outflow is then $10 million, but the income statement will record only the $1 million of depreciation as a cost. In the next year (1998), the firm records an additional $1 million of depreciation as a cost even though no cash outlay occurred.

Revenue is similarly recorded in the income statement on an accrual basis, regardless of whether the sale was for cash or for credit. For example, suppose the firm's sales in 1997 were $100 million. Of this amount, $20 million was in cash, and the remaining $80 million was on credit, payable in March 1998. On its 1997 income statement, the firm records revenue of $100 million as income even though the cash flow was only $20 million. Similarly, when the firm receives a cash flow of $80 million in 1998, it will not record that cash flow as income that year. These two examples illustrate the difference between the *accrual* basis of the income statement and balance sheet and the *cash flow* basis of the statement of cash flows.

The **statement of cash flows** lists all of the firm's cash inflows and cash outflows from operating, investing, and financing activities during the year. For example, if the firm's sales during the year amount to $10 million and the cash obtained from these sales is $4 million ($6 million are credit sales), it records only $4 million as a cash inflow. Of course, the firm records any money collected during the year from previous years' credit sales as a cash inflow.

Ford Motor Company's 1992 statement of cash flows is presented in Figure 3-3. The firm reports cash flows from investing activities and operations separately. A negative cash flow from operations for one year is not necessarily a danger signal. For instance, an aggressive promotional drive or a liberal credit policy may produce results in the next year, and only then will the firm report a positive cash flow. However, a negative cash flow for several consecutive years is not just a danger signal: It spells disaster!

As you can see from Figure 3-3, the Automotive Unit's 1992 cash flow from operations was $5,753.3 million. Note 18 to the statement of cash flows shown in Figure 3-4, shows how Ford obtained this cash flow.

FIGURE 3-3   **Consolidated Statement of Cash Flows of Ford Motor Company and Subsidiaries for the Year Ended December 31, 1992 (in millions)**

	1992–Automotive	1992–Financial Services
Cash and cash equivalents at January 1	$ 4,958.0	$ 3,175.2
Cash flows from operating activities (Note 18)	5,753.3	5,762.4
Cash flows from investing activities		
Capital expenditures	(5,696.6)	(92.9)
Proceeds from sale and leaseback of machinery and equipment	262.7	—
Acquisitions of other companies	0	(461.4)
Proceeds from sales of subsidiaries	52.0	0
Acquisitions of receivables and lease investments	—	(134,619.3)
Collections of receivables and lease investments	—	123,144.3
Purchases of securities	(50,436.6)	(12,877.2)
Sales of securities	49,629.1	12,168.5
Proceeds from sales of receivables	—	6,465.4
Loans originated net of principal payments	—	(937.6)
Investing activity with Financial Services	709.3	—
Other	(492.6)	372.2
Net cash used in investing activities	$ (5,972.7)	$ (6,838.0)
Cash flows from financing activities		
Cash dividends	(977.4)	—
Sale of Preferred Stock	1,104.0	—
Issuance of Common Stock	221.0	—
Changes in short-term debt	(425.5)	2,739.3
Proceeds from issuance of other debt	1,864.5	13,382.1
Principal payments on other debt	(1,597.7)	(13,121.9)
Financing activity with Automotive	—	(709.3)
Changes in customers' deposits, excluding interest credited	—	(3,418.1)
Receipts from annuity contracts	—	703.4
Issuance of subsidiary company preferred stock	—	282.5
Other	79.0	(10.1)
Net cash provided by/(used in) financing activities	267.9	(152.1)
Effect of exchange rate changes on cash	(220.7)	(47.2)
Net transactions with Automotive/Financial Services	(1,281.8)	1,281.8
Net (decrease)/increase in cash and cash equivalents	(1,454.0)	6.9
Cash and cash equivalents at December 31	$ 3,504.0	$ 3,182.1
Total cash and cash equivalents	$6,686.1	

Source: The Ford Motor Company, *1992 Annual Report.*

FIGURE 3-4 **Ford Motor Company's Cash Flow from Operating Activities**
Note 18. Cash flows: A reconciliation of net (loss)/income to cash flows from operating activities for 1992 *(in millions)*

	Automotive	Financial Services
Net (loss)/income	$(8,627.9)	$1,242.9
Adjustments to reconcile net (loss)/income to cash flows from operating activities: Cumulative effects of change in accounting principles	7,094.3	(211.1)
Depreciation and amortization	4,666.6	2,089.1
(Earnings) in excess of dividends remitted/losses of affiliated companies	15.9	51.0
Provision for credit and insurance losses	—	1,795.1
Foreign currency adjustments	(362.0)	—
(Credit)/provision for deferred income taxes	(447.3)	333.2
Changes in assets and liabilities:		
Decrease in accounts receivable and other current assets	103.1	—
Decrease in inventory	380.1	—
Increase/(decrease) in accounts payable and accrued and other liabilities	2,616.7	295.2
Changes in unearned premiums	—	(281.0)
Other	313.8	(113.6)
Cash flows from operating activities	$ 5,753.3	$5,762.4

Source: The Ford Motor Company, *1992 Annual Report.*

As Figure 3-4 shows, the firm's net income from its Automotive Unit was negative—a loss of $8,627.9 million. Does this amount represent the net cash outflow from the unit's operations? Not really, because some of its operations do not involve cash flows. As explained earlier, financial statements are on an accrual basis rather than on a cash basis. To obtain the cash flow from operations, any cost that is not a cash flow is *added* to the net income, and any income that is not cash is *deducted*. For example, the second item listed in Note 18 is a $7,094.3 million cost, which is not a cash outflow. It is a loss due to the change in accounting principles, so it is added to income.

By the same token, **depreciation** is not a cash outflow but an accounting cost. It is an allocation, over an asset's useful life, of the cash outflow on a previous capital expenditure. For instance, suppose the firm bought a plant and some equipment several years ago. At the time of purchase, the amount paid was cash outflow. This year the firm allocates some fraction of that original cash outflow as a cost called depreciation. As depreciation is not a cash outflow, it is added to income.

We also see in Note 18 that the accounts receivable decreased in 1992 by $103.1 million. This amount represents money collected during 1992 in addition to sales. Even if it does not affect 1992 earnings, the decrease in accounts receivable increases Ford's cash flow, and it is added to the cash flow.

Under the accrual method, a firm needs to include the cost of goods sold in the income statement as an expense, even though it is not a cash outflow. Let us illustrate how the cost of goods sold (an accounting figure) is adjusted to obtain cash flow figures. According to accounting rules, cost of goods sold is beginning inventory plus cost of goods manufactured minus inventory at year-end. Suppose a firm enters the cost of goods sold in its income statement as follows:

Inventory, beginning of year	$100 million
Plus: Cost of goods manufactured[4]	+$ 60 million
Minus: Inventory, year-end	–$ 50 million
Cost of goods sold	$110 million

The firm records the $110 million cost of goods sold as a cost in its income statement. However, because the firm's cash outflow (manufacturing costs, which we assume were paid for in cash) was only $60 million, the remaining $50 million is financed, so to speak, by a reduction in the amount recorded for the firm's inventory. Because the $50 million is not a cash outflow, it is added in the statement of cash flows.

This is exactly what Ford Motor Company did on a larger scale. In decreasing its inventory by $380.1 million, Ford increased its 1992 cash flow. Similar corrections were conducted on the other items. For instance, the firm purchased goods (which it recorded as a cost in the income statement) but did not pay for all of them in cash. The $2,616.7 million increase in the accounts payable and other liabilities reflects the additional cash remaining in the firm from the transaction and is a source of cash flow that is added. With these adjustments, we find that although the Automotive Unit's income was –$8,627.9 million, its cash flow was +$5,753.3 million. Thus, Ford had approximately $14 billion difference between income and cash flow from operations. These two figures explain Poling's claim that "although the stockholders' equity was greatly reduced, our cash flow was not affected."

Note 18 to Ford's statement of cash flows provides the details of the cash flow from operations. As you can see from Figure 3–3, cash flow from operations is only one component in Ford's statement of cash flows. The cash Ford automotive held at the beginning of the year was $4,958.0 million. We add to this amount the cash flows from operations in the manner described above. Then we need to add and subtract cash flows that are not from operations. *Cash outflows* (such as making capital expenditures, paying cash dividends, and purchasing securities) are then *deducted* from the cash flow balance. *Cash inflows* to the firm (such as selling of securities and issuing debt) are *added* to the balance of cash flows.[5]

The bottom line of Ford's automotive unit's statement of cash flows (Figure 3–3) reveals that the firm's cash balance decreased during the year. What is the significance

---

4. For a firm whose activity is trade, not production, the "costs of goods manufactured" is "purchase of goods."

5. When it exchanges one asset (or liability) for another with no net cash flow, the firm reports this activity as two transactions, each of which affects cash flow. For example, suppose that the firm exchanges some of its shares for bonds. The firm will enter the bond transaction as cash inflow and the stock transaction as cash outflow, and the net effect on the firm's total cash flow will be zero.

of this figure for readers of the financial statements? If a firm's cash flows from operations are low or negative for several consecutive years, lenders will worry about the firm's declaring bankruptcy. What is more, the firm will have difficulty selling its stock if investors believe it is financially distressed. Why, then, wouldn't a firm take out more loans (or issue additional stock) to increase the cash flows reported at year-end? Some firms do. Such actions might be possible in the short run, but it would be wrong for a firm to adopt them as long-term policy. (As we shall see, taking actions to improve the look of the numbers in the balance sheet would not only be unethical, but also illegal in some cases.)

Readers of financial statements have an obligation to protect themselves. They should realize that the changes in cash flows in a given year may be arbitrary, and careful analysis of cash flows over several consecutive years is more meaningful than examining one year's results. They should scrutinize especially carefully the cash flows generated from operations because these are perhaps the most important indication of a firm's financial strength. Let us review the following example:

Earnings and Cash Flow per Share of Fischer and Porter Corporation (in \$)[6]

Year	1985	1986	1987	1988	1989	1990	1991	1992	1993*	1994*
Earnings per share	1.10	0.40	0.50	−0.84	0.62	−1.61	−4.36	0.31	0.50	0.70
Cash flow per share	1.93	1.27	1.68	0.28	1.85	−0.20	−3.00	1.63	1.70	2.10

* Estimates

Source: *The Value Line Investment Survey* 49, no. 1, Part 3 (September 17, 1993): 141.

These figures show that the firm can maintain a positive cash flow even in a year with negative earnings. However, if it experiences low profitability over several consecutive years, the firm's cash flow is also affected. (See years 1988–1991.)

The following problem demonstrates how to calculate a firm's year-end cash flow.

PRACTICE BOX

Problem

A firm's beginning-of-year cash position was \$10,000. During the year, the following events occurred: The firm sold \$2,000 in stock and \$3,000 in bonds, and it paid \$100 interest and \$250 in dividends. Net proceeds from sales were \$10,000, \$500 was paid in taxes, and depreciation charges were \$7,000. The firm allocated \$2,000 to its employee retirement plan and purchased a fixed asset for \$30,000, paying \$15,000 for it in cash with \$15,000 to be paid one year later. What was the firm's cash position at year-end?

---

6. In 1994 Fischer and Porter was acquired by Elsag Bailey Process Automation, N.V., and changed its name to Bailey-Fischer and Porter.

Solution

We have to include all items involving cash outflow or cash inflow. Depreciation and allocation to the retirement plan are not included because they are not cash flows. Therefore, we have:

Cash position, beginning of year		$ 10,000
Add:		
Stock issue	$ 2,000	
Bond issue	3,000	
Net proceeds from sales	10,000	
Total		$ 15,000
Subtract:		
Dividend payment	$ (250)	
Interest payment	(100)	
Tax payment	(500)	
Fixed asset payment	(15,000)	
Total		$(15,850)

The cash position at year-end = $10,000 + $15,000 − $15,850 = $9,150.

3.6 "WINDOW DRESSING"

Investors in a firm's stock, as well as banks and other lenders, analyze the firm's strength mainly through its financial statements. Particularly when the firm is financially distressed, management may employ a **"window dressing" technique,** which is basically an attempt to show a strong financial statement for the period covered by the financial statements. This technique may mislead investors, who may later sue the firm if they discover the deception. Connecting Theory to Practice 3.1 illustrates such a case.

CONNECTING THEORY TO PRACTICE 3.1

FLORIDA GETS $100 MILLION IN INSURER FAILURE

by Glenn Collins

Merrill Lynch & Company, Coopers & Lybrand and a law firm have agreed to pay the State of Florida $100 million to settle charges involving the biggest failure of an insurance company in Florida's history.

Merrill, the nation's largest brokerage house, will pay $45 million of the settlement. Coopers & Lybrand, the accounting firm, will pay $50 million, and the New York law firm of Shereff, Friedman, Hoffman & Goodman will pay $5 million, Florida officials announced Friday. The three firms will be severed from a trial that is to begin in September.

"This is a major victory for consumers across the nation," said Bill Nelson, the Florida Insurance Commissioner.

A spokesman for Merrill Lynch, Timothy Gilles, said yesterday that "it is relatively less expensive for us to settle this particular case at this price rather than continue to pay the ongoing costs of this litigation."

He added: "Merrill is fully reserved for the amount of this settlement, and it will have no future impact on earnings." Coopers and Shereff could not be reached for comment yesterday.

In the settlement, Merrill and the other firms denied any wrongdoing. "The settlement should not be construed as an admission of guilt," Mr. Gilles said.

The lawsuit, originally asking for $300 million but later increased to $500 million, was brought by Florida regulators in December 1991, and involved the failure of the Guarantee Security Life Insurance Company. The suit followed an investigation of the activities of the insurer's parent, Transmark USA Inc., which was accused of looting the insurer.

Guarantee Security, based in Jacksonville, was seized by Florida insurance regulators in August 1991, after the value of its huge junk-bond investments had collapsed.

The Florida regulators said that officials of Transmark, who were forced out when the insurer was seized, had depleted the company's assets in a series of "phantom trades" between Guarantee and Merrill Lynch. These trades were used to move risky junk bonds off the insurer's books and onto Merrill's books for a few days at the end of several years, from 1984 to 1991, regulators said.

The investigators charged that these trades inflated Guarantee's worth by hundreds of millions of dollars during the periods when the insurer was preparing to report its financial health to regulators. The transfers allowed the company to appear solvent, the regulators asserted, when in fact the company became insolvent in 1985.

The suit contended that Merrill had swapped safer and more liquid Treasury notes with Guarantee Security for its junk bonds. Then, days later, the trades would be reversed, with the junk bonds going back to Guarantee Security and the Treasury notes going back to Merrill, the regulators charged.

The suit said that fraudulent broker-confirmation slips were issued by Merrill, allowing Guarantee Security to misrepresent its financial condition. The regulators said that Coopers and Shereff had also been parties to the transactions. A spokesman for Shereff contended in 1991 that the law firm had represented Transmark, not Guarantee.

Merrill responded that the securities transactions were ethical and legal. "We deny that there was any wrongdoing," Mr. Gilles said yesterday. "We maintain that the year-end transactions were legitimate and there was no wrongdoing on the part of Merrill Lynch."

Merrill came to another settlement last year with the Securities and Exchange Commission, resolving all issues in the Guarantee case, Mr. Gilles said. The out-of-court agreement involved no payment or penalty, but Merrill agreed to alter its record-keeping procedures in the future, Mr. Gilles said.

The settlement brings to a close any Florida state action against Merrill, Coopers and Shereff in the suit against Guarantee Security.

Source: Glenn Collins, "Florida Gets $100 Million in Insurer Failure," *New York Times*, 17 July 1995, D2. © *The New York Times* 1995.

MAKING THE CONNECTION

As the article indicates, Merrill Lynch agreed (for a fee) to buy the junk bonds (very low-quality bonds) from Guarantee Security for a few days only and then to resell them to Guarantee Security. Guarantee Security could then show a relatively strong financial statement even though the firm was financially distressed. Some firms sell assets (such as bonds) that they hold, show a strong cash position on the financial statement publication date, and after a few days rebuy the same assets.

3.7 MARKET VALUE RATIOS

Based on financial statement and market information, investors, creditors, and managers can calculate various ratios that forecast the firm's future prospects. Ratios that are based solely on financial statements are presented in Appendix 3A. Here we focus on ratios that use a combination of financial statement and market data. These are the ratios that the financial media commonly use and quote. For each *market value ratio*, we use one figure from the financial statements and another figure from the market—the firm's stock price.

3.7.1 Price/Earnings Ratio

The **price/earnings (P/E) ratio,** the most widely used ratio in financial analysis, is calculated as follows:

$$\text{Price/Earnings Ratio} = \frac{\text{Price per Share}}{\text{Earnings per Share}}$$

When earnings are zero or negative (as with Ford Motor Company in 1992), the P/E ratio is meaningless. But if, for example, P = $100 and E = $10, the P/E ratio is 10. Loosely speaking, this implies that investors are willing to wait 10 years to cover their investment in the stock. Professional analysts generally recommend investing in firms with low P/E ratios because, on average, such firms represent "bargains." Analysts believe in general that the lower the P/E ratio, the more attractive the investment is. (For a detailed discussion of the pros and cons of the widely used P/E ratio, see Chapter 13.)

3.7.2 Market/Book Value Ratio

The **market/book value ratio** measures the relationship between the accounting value of the firm's assets and the market price of its stock. It is obtained by dividing the stock price per share by the book value of equity:

$$\text{Market/Book Value Ratio} = \frac{\text{Stock Price per Share}}{\text{Book Value of Equity per Share}}$$

Ford's 1992 market/book value ratio was therefore

$$\frac{\$53 \text{ per share}}{\$14{,}752.9 \text{ million}/489.5 \text{ million shares}} \cong 1.76$$

Financial analysts often use this ratio to find "bargains" in the market. Generally speaking, the lower this ratio, the more attractive the stock is considered. However, the ratio should be used carefully. Sometimes a high ratio reflects the firm's expected future growth rather than the expensive price of the stock.

   This ratio is expected to be higher than 1 in firms with a high growth rate of their sales and earnings (called *growth firms*). The reason is that potential future growth in earnings is reflected in the current stock price, whereas the book value of equity per share is based on historical costs and does not consider potential growth. (For more about growth firms, see Chapter 13.)

3.7.3 Dividend Yield Ratio

The **dividend yield ratio,** more commonly referred to as **dividend yield,** measures the relationship between the dividends per share and the stock price, expressed on a percentage basis. It is calculated as follows:

$$\text{Dividend Yield Ratio} = \frac{\text{Dividend per Share}}{\text{Stock Price per Share}}$$

Ford's 1992 dividend yield was

$$\text{Dividend Yield Ratio} = \frac{\$1.60}{\$53} \cong 0.0302 \text{ or } 3.02\%$$

Analysts interpret a low dividend yield ratio (relative to prevailing interest rates) as indicating an overvalued stock that should be sold. A high dividend yield ratio will trigger purchase orders, which will cause the stock price to increase.

APPLYING THEORY TO PRACTICE 3.1

VEHICLE WITH VALUE: FORD'S FINANCE UNIT COULD DRIVE THE STOCK HIGHER

Ford Motor Company has four units: Automotive, Ford Motor Credit, Associates Corp. of North America, and USL Capital. The last two operate autonomously. However, Ford Credit helps in the marketing of Ford's automobiles. Ford Motor Credit, Associates Corp., and USL Capital combined appear in Ford's financial statements as the Financial Services Unit. As the following article indicates, analyst Stephen Girsky saw great potential in Ford's stock because it is undervalued. Mr. Girsky claims that investors who purchase Ford stock pay $29 per share, with $24.54 for Ford's other assets (cash, the Financial Services Unit) and only $4.46 for the automotive or vehicle business. In this application we analyze Girsky's calculations and draw a few conclusions regarding the use and misuse of accounting figures.

After technology, the best-performing major group in the stock market this year has been financial companies, which are up an average of 30%. Auto stocks, on the other hand, rank among the market's big laggards.

This divergence could make for a buying opportunity in the shares of Ford Motor, which has a significant financial-services division whose strong performance has largely gone unrecognized by investors focused on the weakening U.S. car market.

"Ford is undervalued. It's the most attractive of the Big Three," says Stephen Girsky, Morgan Stanley's auto analyst.

Girsky recently broke down the value of Ford's assets and concluded that investors buying Ford at its current price of 29 are paying just $4.46 per share for the company's worldwide automotive business, or a paltry 1.8 times estimated 1995 profits.

The accompanying table shows Girsky's method. He thinks Ford's financial services unit is worth $17.71 per share, roughly 11 times trailing 12-month profits. The Morgan Stanley analyst adds in the value of Ford's stakes in Mazda and Kia, a Korean car concern, plus Ford's huge net cash position of $7 billion, or $5.94 a share, and the company's overfunded pension plan, before subtracting the preferred stock on its balance sheet.

Hidden Value

After the value of Ford's nonvehicle businesses are subtracted from the company's stock price, Wall Street is valuing the core car business at only $4.46 per share. This gives that business an implied price-to-earning ratio of a mere 1.8.

Asset	Value per share
Financial Services	$17.71*
Mazda & Kia Stakes	1.06
Net Cash	5.94
Overfunded Pension Plan	1.21
Less Preferred Stock	−1.38
Total	24.54
Ford Stock Price	29.00
	−24.54
Price Paid for Car Business	4.46

* Estimate.
Source: Morgan, Stanley.

Chrysler, General Motors and Ford all have profitable, captive finance subsidiaries, but Ford alone boasts significant, stand-alone, non-auto finance businesses in the Associates Corp. of North America and USL Capital, a leasing company. Associates, a large consumer-finance firm, is the jewel here. With $35 billion in assets, it should generate $700 million in after-tax profits in 1995, or roughly 65 cents for each of Ford's 1.07 billion shares. Ford bought Associates from Paramount in 1989 for $3.35 billion, and the company is probably worth at least double that price now.

The big question is whether Ford follows Sears, ITT, RJR Nabisco and so many other big companies and goes the spinoff route, with all or part of its financial-services division, in a bid to boost its stock price. "I don't think anything is imminent, but I think a spin-off is a real option for the company down the road," Girsky says. When asked about a potential spinoff at an analysts' meeting in May, Ford CEO Alex Trotman was noncommittal, and a Ford spokesman reiterated that position Friday. Yet Trotman and other Ford executives aren't happy about Ford's stock price. And probably the best way to highlight the asset value in Ford would be some sort of a spinoff.

Girsky concedes that a sale or spinoff of Ford Motor Credit is a long shot, because the captive finance unit is critical to Ford's marketing efforts. It would be much tougher for Ford to craft cut-rate financing deals or attractive leasing terms for auto buyers if Ford Motor Credit were a stand-alone company.

Yet Associates and USL operate autonomously and together are probably worth about $9 per Ford share. If Girsky's numbers were recalculated to exclude Ford Motor Credit from the financial-services division, the result still yields an attractive residual value for the combined auto business and Ford Motor Credit of about $15 per share, or four times projected 1996 earnings.

Girsky admits that many investors are unenthusiastic about Ford, and that some institutional investors are dubious about a spinoff scenario. "The reaction I've gotten about the report is: 'That's a nice analysis, and Ford's a cheap stock, but there's no catalyst to get the stock moving.'"

Investors are worried about Ford's profits, which are getting cramped by the softening auto market and heavy spending on redesigned vehicles, such as the new Ford Taurus and Mercury Sable. Ford is now expected to earn about $4 in 1996, down from year-earlier estimates of $5.50 and last year's $4.81.

Still, Ford has plenty of allure. "It not only has more hidden value than GM and Chrysler, but it's the cheapest of the three based on other valuation measures as well," Girsky asserts, ticking off its price/sales ratio, balance sheet and dividend. Ford shares now yield 4.3%, higher than both GM and Chrysler.

Girsky is betting that Ford's redesigned vehicles prove popular with consumers, and that profits rebound to $4.75 in 1996. Given Ford's valuable assets and earnings power, Girsky thinks its shares have little downside. His 12-month price target: $40 per share.

Source: Andrew Bary, "Vehicle with Value: Ford's Finance Unit Could Drive the Stock Higher," *Barron's, Market Week* (25 August 1995): mw12. Reprinted by permission of *Barron's, Market Week* © 1995 Dow Jones & Company, Inc. All rights reserved worldwide.

Questions

1. Earnings per share (EPS) is the firm's net income divided by the number of outstanding shares. The expected EPS of Ford for 1995 was $4 per share. Using the information given in the article, what is the EPS estimate of the Automotive Unit?

2. Suppose you accept Girsky's accounting technique to obtain the P/E ratio. Do you believe it is meaningful to calculate the P/E ratio for the Automotive Unit alone?

3. Discuss Girsky's method of obtaining the P/E ratio of 1.8. What additional accounting information would you require before buying what the article refers to as an "undervalued" stock?

4. Suppose a firm has only two items in its balance sheet: cash of $10 per share and equity of $10 per share. The stock's market price is $11, and the expected EPS is $1. Use Girsky's method to calculate the P/E ratio. Discuss your results and evaluate Girsky's calculation method.

MAKING THE CONNECTION

1. For the Automotive Unit (Ford's vehicle business), the P/E ratio is 1.8. Because the price paid for this unit (according to Girsky's calculation) is $4.46, we have the relationship:

$$\frac{P}{E} = \frac{\$4.46}{EPS} = 1.8$$

The estimate for 1995 EPS is = $4.46/1.8 \cong $2.47.

2. Ford Motor Credit cannot be separated from the Automotive Unit. Suppose, for example, that Ford adopts a liberal credit policy that drastically increases sales. As a result of this policy, the Automotive Unit records a large profit and Ford Motor Credit records only a slim profit (or even a loss). Because these two units are interrelated and cannot be separated, the Automotive Unit's P/E ratio alone may be meaningless.

3. Ford's stock price on August 1995 was $29. According to the article, the firm has assets not related to the vehicle business totaling $24.54 per share. The article claims that for the Automotive Unit's future earnings only the following amount is paid:

$$\$29.00 - \$24.54 = \$4.46$$

Is this assertion correct? It depends. We need additional accounting information before we can provide a complete answer.

In principle, however, Girsky's method is wrong because it focuses on the firm's assets (one side of the balance sheet) and overlooks liabilities (the other side of the balance sheet). In particular, the firm's debt, accounts payable, and other liabilities should also be included in the calculation. For example, suppose the firm owes the bank $10 per share. In that case, not all assets belong to the stockholders, and in the calculation we should first deduct what the firm owes its creditors. Only then can we divide the net assets (which belong to the stockholders) by the number of shares to obtain per-share values. However, if the firm has no liabilities, the $4.46 is a reasonable figure.

Before accepting the 1.8 P/E figure, we need to know all of the firm's assets (such as accounts receivable) and, in particular, all its liabilities (such as debt and accounts payable). Alternatively, the 1.8 figure implicitly assumes that all other financial items (including accounts receivable, accounts payable, and debt) are zero or that they exactly cancel each other—a very unlikely case.

4. Applying Girsky's method, we may subtract the asset value of $10 per share (cash) from the stock price. For the firm's future earnings per share, we pay only $1:

$$\$11 - \$10 = \$1$$

Because the EPS is $1, the P/E ratio is 1.

This ratio is absurd. The firm needs the cash to create future earnings. By subtracting cash from the market price, we implicitly assume that the firm can distribute cash to the stockholders without affecting future earnings. However, recall that if the firm distributes cash, it will have nothing to invest and will not realize the $1 projected EPS. The true EPS in the example is $11/$1 = 11, not 1.

Using the same argument, Girsky's method of deducting the $5.94 cash per share from the stock price makes no sense. The firm may need this cash for its operations; without its operations the firm's EPS would decline. One may claim that the firm could distribute cash assets to stockholders without affecting its operating profit. Even if this is the case (which it rarely is in practice), we cannot adopt Girsky's calculation method because even free cash earns interest and affects the EPS.

3.8 TIME SERIES AND INDUSTRY FINANCIAL ANALYSES

The best way to interpret and analyze changes in a firm's financial ratios is to identify the reasons for the changes. Unfortunately, the information required for this identification is not usually available to outside analysts. Two highly recommended ways to interpret a firm's financial ratios are (1) to analyze them over time (time series analysis) and (2) to compare them to the ratios of other firms in the same industry (industry analysis).

Analyses based on one-year financial statements are very hard to interpret. For example, suppose a firm's earnings per share in a given year is $5. Is this a good sign or a bad sign? Actually, the figure by itself is meaningless. Meaningful analysis can be obtained only by reviewing the firm's financial statements over several years. This type of analysis is called **time series analysis.** For example, if the EPS is $10, $5, and $4 for three consecutive years, it would seem that the firm has a severe problem of declining profits.

Suppose we do observe a declining trend in a firm's EPS. Does this decline mean that the firm's management is incompetent and should be replaced? Should you avoid business deals with the firm? Not necessarily. The firm's management may be very competent, but a downward trend in the entire industry may have translated to declining profits for all firms for several consecutive years. For example, the oil crisis in the early 1980s depressed stock prices of firms in the auto industry. A firm's management can be considered successful if the firm's EPS declined *less than that of competitors* in the same industry. When you compare a firm's financial position in a given year (or over more than one year) to that firm's competition in the same industry, you perform **industry analysis.**

In this chapter we have reviewed Ford Motor Company's financial statements to analyze its financial position. The firm experienced difficulties during 1991 and 1992. All its profitability measures, including EPS, were negative. Was Ford's management incompetent? To answer this question, we first must answer the following questions: How did Ford do in comparison to the other firms in the same industry? In comparison to foreign auto producers?

Table 3-1 provides EPS data across years and across firms. From this table we see that Ford's negative EPS in 1991 and 1992 actually reflected a trend of declining EPS that started in 1989. Ford was not alone; almost all car-producing firms had declining

TABLE 3-1 Earnings per Share (in $), 1984–1994: Automobile Industry*	Year	Ford	GM	Chrysler	Honda Motors	Nissan Motors	Toyota Motors	Volvo
	1984	5.26	7.11	5.22	1.07	0.30	0.70	4.51
	1985	4.54	6.14	6.25	1.65	0.18	0.92	6.32
	1986	6.16	4.11	6.31	1.12	0.13	1.18	5.59
	1987	9.05	5.03	5.90	1.59	0.26	1.00	8.40
	1988	10.96	6.82	5.08	1.49	0.70	1.27	10.04
	1989	9.13	6.33	1.36	1.06	0.58	1.32	10.35
	1990	1.86	−4.09	0.30	1.10	0.28	1.64	−0.05
	1991	−4.79	−8.85	−2.74	1.00	0.35	1.78	3.70
	1992	−1.46	−4.85	1.38	0.67	−0.38	0.99	−5.26
	1993†	3.30	1.80	5.30	0.40	−0.50	0.89	0
	1994†	5.00	4.25	6.00	0.50	0.25	0.60	3.25

* For the foreign firms, the earnings are per American Depository Receipts (ADRs) rather than per share. An ADR represents one share or a combination of shares traded on U.S. markets.

† Estimates.

Source: *The Value Line Investment Survey* 49, no. 1, Part 3 (September 17, 1993):103–105, 109–112.

EPS in the late 1980s and early 1990s. Automakers were expected to recover in 1994, with Ford's EPS estimated to reach $5.00. Thus, Ford's declining EPS was due not to incompetent management, but rather to macroeconomic factors (such as unemployment and recession) that affected the auto industry as a whole.

In Table 3-1 the EPS projections for 1994 are $5.00 for Ford Motor Company and only $0.50 for Honda Motors. Does this mean that Ford's profitability is superior to Honda's? Not necessarily, because EPS *varies with the number of shares issued.* Were Ford Motor Company to double the number of shares issued (with no change in its operations and earnings), its EPS would drop from $5.00 to $2.50, but its relative profitability would not change.

Table 3-1 also shows that each automaker's EPS fluctuates yearly. To compare the automakers' EPS fluctuations over time, we could use **index analysis,** which would track yearly EPS percentage changes (or growth) relative to a common base year. For example, if Ford's $5.26 EPS in 1984 is set as the base, then Ford's EPS in 1985 will be

$$\frac{\$4.54}{\$5.26} \times 100 \cong 86.3$$

This figure tells us that Ford's 1985 EPS dropped approximately 14%.

When the EPS is negative—for instance, Ford's −$4.79 in 1991—the index will be

$$\frac{-\$4.79}{\$5.26} \times 100 \cong -91.1$$

This tells us that Ford's 1991 EPS was 191.1% lower than its 1984 EPS.

Index analysis allows us to trace the firm's EPS fluctuations regardless of the absolute values of EPS.

The base year's value is usually set to 100 (for example, 100 = $5.26 for Ford), and the EPS of each year is then compared to the 100 base. This method is particularly helpful when comparing the EPS of several different firms. Figure 3-5 compares the EPS index of Ford Motor Company with those of General Motors and Honda. In most years Ford performed better than General Motors. Even though Ford's 1991 EPS shows a severe downturn, it was less severe in percentage terms than the downturn in GM's EPS. Honda, on the other hand, was only slightly affected by the 1991 downturn and fared much better in 1991 and 1992 than either Ford or GM. However, as early as 1993, Ford was expected (by ValueLine) to recover more quickly than Honda.

Industry analysis shows that Ford Motor's record was probably better and certainly no worse than that of other auto producers. The decline in profit reflected a decline in the auto industry, and declining EPS had little to do with the performance of Ford's management.

Although we have used EPS to demonstrate time series and industry analyses, other key financial variables (such as debt/equity ratio and current ratio, explained in Appendix 3A) can also be used just as effectively.

FIGURE 3-5
Performance of the EPS Index in the Automobile Industry, 1984–1994

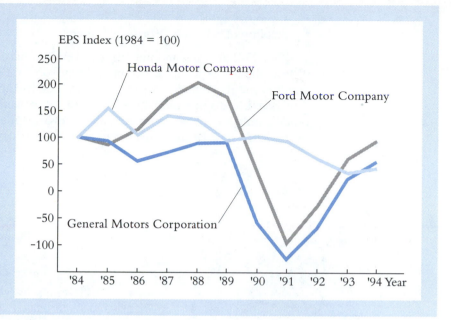

3.9 INTERNATIONAL COMPARATIVE FINANCIAL ANALYSIS

If financial ratio and profitability analyses reveal promising investments abroad, investors have little reason to invest solely in U.S. firms. In fact, investors have easy access to foreign investments, and financial analysts should be able to analyze the financial statements of foreign companies. However, because of differences in accounting practices, comparing financial statements of firms in various countries can be difficult. In some cases, accounting practices among countries are so different that they render such comparisons meaningless.

The major differences in accounting practices among countries are

- Publication of consolidated statements
- Publication of accounts corrected for fiscal distortion
- Treatment of goodwill and intangibles
- Inflation and revaluation accounting
- Depreciation methods
- Existence of "hidden" reserves
- Treatment of pension liabilities
- Research and development
- Currency adjustments and treatment of currency hedging
- Treatment of extraordinary expenses

- Inventory valuation
- Stability of accounting principles used[7]

Table 3-2 provides an international comparison of three financial ratios. To emphasize the danger of international comparisons, we selected a year with large differences among countries. Japan, a clear outlier, had an overall P/E ratio of 56.9 and a market/book value ratio of 4.97. Both ratios were much higher than those of other countries. These ratios do not necessarily mean that Japanese stocks were overpriced. The Japanese use accounting rules that are markedly different from

TABLE 3-2 Financial Ratios: An International Comparison	P/BV	P/E	Yield	
				International Indexes (in U.S. dollars)
	2.53	18.8	2.3	World Index
	3.02	26.0	1.6	Europe, Australia, Far East (EAFE) Index
	1.80	13.0	3.6	Europe Index
				National Indexes (in U.S. dollars)
	1.87	13.3	3.8	Hong Kong
	2.56	33.4	1.6	Norway
	1.91	11.5	4.4	United Kingdom
	1.96	23.6	1.4	Singapore/Malaysia
	1.57	11.3	4.7	Australia
	1.68	12.0	3.2	Canada
	1.94	12.1	3.6	United States of America
	1.10	10.2	5.6	New Zealand
	2.49	15.6	1.9	Sweden
	1.38	10.7	4.3	Netherlands
	1.92	13.2	2.7	France
	4.97	56.9	0.5	Japan
	2.00	14.2	3.9	Belgium
	1.24	15.8	3.6	Spain
	1.50	14.2	2.2	Finland
	1.59	18.1	2.0	Denmark
	1.65	28.1	2.4	Austria
	1.77	15.3	2.6	Italy
	1.51	15.4	2.3	Switzerland
	1.91	15.8	3.6	Germany

P/BV = (market) price/book value ratio; P/E = price/earnings ratio; Yield = dividend yield
Source: Morgan Stanley, "Capital International," February 1989.

7. Bruno Solnik, *International Investment* (Reading, Mass.: Addison Wesley, 1996): 216.

those that other countries, particularly the United States, use. Because accounting principles do not affect market values, comparison of ratios based solely on market values is more meaningful than those based on book values. For example, Japan's dividend yield was only 0.5%, compared to 2% to 4% in other countries.

The financial data presented in Table 3-2 is useful in illustrating the dangers of international comparisons. These ratios change over time. By mid-1997, stock prices in the United States and most other Western countries had reached record highs. For example, in the United States, the Dow-Jones Industrial Average exceeded the 8,250 level. P/E ratios increased and yields fell. The overall P/E ratio rose to 26 and the dividend yield dropped to 1.50% as of August 1, 1997. In the United Kingdom, the average P/E ratio on FTSE shares was 17.47 in mid-1997. Thus, changes in P/E and yield over time are more relevant than comparisons across countries at the same point in time.

3.10 A WORD OF CAUTION

Ratio analysis can be very useful, but it should always be accompanied by in-depth examination of a number of ratios rather than one isolated ratio. For example, suppose a firm's P/E ratio increases from 10 to 15. Is this a good or a bad sign? It could be a good sign if the firm has discovered a new product (say, a new medicine that it patents for a 10-year period). In this case the P/E ratio increase would reflect an increase in forecasted earnings. However, if it is due to a decrease in the firm's earnings per share, the P/E ratio increase could be a bad sign. If the firm's stock is overpriced, a deluge of sale orders may follow.

Relying on one ratio can be meaningless or, worse, misleading. Only by analyzing a *set* of ratios, complementing them with additional data (such as the interest rate or the corresponding ratios of other firms in the same industry), and scrutinizing the financial statements can we meaningfully interpret the firm's financial position. Moreover, the copious notes that often accompany financial statements should not be overlooked. These notes contain important information such as changes in accounting procedures, leasing activities, and outstanding litigation.

SUMMARY

Various parties use a firm's financial statements and financial ratio analyses for various purposes. The main users of a firm's financial statements are the stockholders and financial analysts who are interested in the firm's strength and potential profitability. If used carefully, financial statements can be very helpful in deciding whether to invest in a firm's stock. Creditors also use the information in the financial statements to decide whether to lend money to the firm and to determine the appropriate interest rate to compensate them for the firm's risk of insolvency. In analyzing the firm's trends, management uses the information in financial statements to determine whether appropriate corrective action is needed.

The main financial statements, published quarterly and annually, are the income statement, the balance sheet, and the statement of cash flows. The income statement reports the firm's earnings (or losses) during the reported period. Income (or loss) is calculated as revenue minus expenses. The balance sheet is a picture of the firm's accounting assets and liabilities on a given date. On the balance sheet, assets must equal liabilities plus stockholders' equity. Assets are reported on the balance sheet at their historical (book) value, rather than at market value. The balance sheet also reveals the firm's net working capital. The statement of cash flows lists all cash inflows and outflows from operating, financing, and investing activities during the period. Although all financial statements are audited to ensure their reliability and accuracy, users must be alert to the possibility of "window dressing" that makes financial results look stronger than they really are.

Financial ratios are meaningful only when analyzed over time and among firms in the same industry. When analyzing financial statements of foreign firms, comparisons to U.S. firms can be difficult because of differences in accounting practices.

Financial statements and financial ratio analysis can be misleading and should be used in conjunction with information that does not usually appear in the firm's financial statements, such as market information and information on competing firms in the same industry.

CHAPTER AT A GLANCE

1. A firm's main financial statements are
    a. *Income statement,* which shows the firm's profit (loss) during the reporting period
    b. *Balance sheet,* which provides a picture of the firm's assets and liabilities at the end of the reporting period
    c. *Statement of cash flows,* which depicts cash inflows and outflows during the reporting period

2. The main users of financial statement analysis are
    a. Stockholders and financial analysts
    b. Creditors
    c. Management

3. Financial ratios:

$$\text{Price/Earnings (P/E)} = \frac{\text{Price per Share}}{\text{Earnings per Share}}$$

$$\text{Market/Book Value} = \frac{\text{Stock Price per Share}}{\text{Book Value of Equity per Share}}$$

$$\text{Dividend Yield} = \frac{\text{Dividend per Share}}{\text{Stock Price per Share}}$$

KEY TERMS

Financial statement analysis	Market value	Price/earnings (P/E) ratio
Financial statements	Historical value	Market/book value ratio
Income statement	Net working capital	Dividend yield ratio
Balance sheet	Statement of cash flows	Time series analysis
Liquidity	Depreciation	Industry analysis
Book value	"Window dressing" technique	Index analysis

REVIEW AND PRACTICE

3.1 Why does a firm's management use financial statement analysis?

3.2 Why do creditors use financial statement analysis?

3.3 Why do stockholders use financial statement analysis?

3.4 How can a financial statement constitute "good news" for stockholders and "bad news" for creditors? Give examples.

3.5 What are a firm's most liquid assets? What are its least liquid assets?

3.6 A firm has total assets of $100 million and total liabilities of $80 million. Calculate the firm's equity.

3.7 Use the following data to prepare the income statement (all figures in millions). Assume this list contains all revenues and expenses for the current year.

Sales	$100
Cost of goods sold	60
Operating and administrative expenses	10
Interest expense	10

The corporate tax rate is 35%.

3.8 Use the following data to prepare the income statement (all figures in millions). Assume the information reported here contains all revenues and expenses for the current year.

Cost of goods sold	$ 60
Operating and administrative expenses	10
Interest expense	10

Sales are $100. However, the firm receives only $70 in cash, and the other $30 is an increase in receivables. Assume a tax rate of 35%.

3.9 "If the accounts receivable are equal to the accounts payable, they cancel out. Therefore, total assets and total liabilities and equity in the balance sheet will be unaffected by the size of these accounts." Evaluate this statement.

3.10 An entrepreneur has an annual taxable income of $10 million. She considers borrowing $500 million from the bank at 6% annual interest, and buying $500 million of corporate bonds that pay 6% annual interest. How would these transactions affect her taxable income? Her after-tax rate?

3.11 "Issuing bonds and using the cash proceeds to buy land that does not generate any income and is not depreciable will have no effect on total liabilities and equity in a firm's balance sheet, or on the net income appearing in its income statement." Evaluate this claim.

3.12 You have the following information on Symor Corporation:

Description	($ thousand)
Cash, beginning of year	500
Cash flow from borrowing	1,000
Payment of production costs	40,000
Payment of dividends	200
Payment of taxes	100
Payment for purchases of building	10,000
Proceeds from sales of equity shares	5,000
Proceeds from product sales	50,000

What is Symor's cash position at year-end?

3.13 Use the following data to prepare the firm's balance sheet (all figures in millions). Assume these figures account for all of the firm's assets, liabilities, and equity.

Cash	$10
Machinery	50
Accounts payable	10
Accounts receivable	15
Taxes payable	5
Long-term debt	25
Accumulated retained earnings	27
Common stock (par value $1)	8

3.14 Prepare a balance sheet with the following information (all figures in millions). Assume these figures account for all the firm's assets, liabilities, and equity.

Cash	$10
Marketable securities	8
Receivables	12
Inventory	3
Net property	40
Accounts payable	20
Taxes payable	5
Long-term debt	12
Preferred stock	8
Common stock (par value $1)	20
Accumulated retained earnings	—

3.15 An entrepreneur starts a new business. She borrows $10 million (the principal is due in 5 years) and issues 10 million shares of stock (par value $1 per share) at $2 per share. All the equity she receives above the shares' par value is marked as capital in excess of par value. She buys $5 million of marketable securities and holds the rest in cash for new investment in property. Construct the balance sheet.

3.16 Use all or some of the following data to prepare the firm's income statement:

Description	($ million)
Sales	50
Fixed assets	250
Cost of goods sold	10
Expenses	2
Interest expense	1
Dividends	2
Current liabilities	1
Income tax	10

3.17 Use all or some of the following data to prepare the firm's balance sheet. Calculate the retained earnings.

Description	($ million)
Cash	50
Accounts receivable	20
Inventory	30
Fixed assets (net)	50
Accounts payable	25
Interest payment	5
Dividend payment	3
Debt	10
Common stock	10
Retained earnings	?
Sales	300

3.18 A firm's cash inflow from operations was $800,000 during the year. The cash outflow on capital expenditures was $200,000. The firm collected receivables for $100,000 and repurchased its own stock for $150,000. The firm paid dividends of $10,000 and issued debt for $5,000 and common stock for $15,000. The beginning-of-the-year cash position was $300,000. Prepare the statement of cash flows for the period. What is the firm's year-end cash position?

3.19 How does each of the following activities affect the year-end cash holdings? In your answer, simply say "increase," "decrease," or "does not change."
a. Bought a machine on 2 years' credit
b. Bought a machine for cash

c. Sold marketable securities

d. Paid dividends

e. Repurchased the firm's stock

3.20 The EPS of an oil company increased 25% in a recent year. Do you think that the firm's management should be rewarded for this success? What other analysis would you do before you made your final decision?

3.21 A firm's financial statements, dated December 31, show a long-term loan of $10 million. The firm can repay its loan at any date it wishes. (The interest is calculated for the length of time the loan is outstanding.) The firm repays its loan on January 10 of the following year. Some creditors claim that this was a "window dressing" strategy.

a. Do you agree with them? Explain.

b. Why do you think the firm took out the loan?

3.22 A firm has the following balance sheet (all figures in millions)

	($ million)
Assets	
Current assets	$100
Net fixed assets	200
Total	$300
Liabilities and Stockholders' Equity	
Liabilities	
Current liabilities	$ 20
Long-term debt	30
Equity	
Common stock (at par $4)	50
Accumulated retained earnings	50
Capital in excess of par value (capital surplus)	150
Total	$300

The firm has 100 million shares outstanding. The stock's market price is $1 per share. Calculate the market/book value ratio. Would investment analysts consider this firm's stock attractive?

3.23 Issuing bonds for $100 million at an 8% interest rate and using the proceeds to repay the principal on $100 million in short-term liabilities (on which the firm paid 9% interest) will:

a. Have no effect on the total liabilities and stockholders' equity in the firm's balance sheet.

b. Increase the firm's net income by less than $1 million.

Discuss these two statements. Assume a 35% corporate tax rate.

3.24 A firm increases its receivables by $100,000 and its payables by $50,000. It uses $50,000 of its cash holdings to buy machinery. What effect do these transactions have on the net working capital?

3.25 Consider two firms in the same industry. Firm A discovers a new, profitable product and immediately takes out a patent on it. Firm B does not discover a new product. The P/E ratio of Firm A is 20, and the P/E ratio of Firm B is 10. A financial analyst argues: "Since these two firms are in the same industry, they should have approximately the same P/E ratio. So, sell the stock of Firm A and buy the stock of Firm B." Do you agree with this position? Explain.

INTERNET QUESTIONS

3.26 Visit the Stock Center at Thomson Investor's Network Web site and look at the financial statements and ratios of a Fortune 500 company of your choice. (Look under "Company Reports.") Then, check the consensus buy/sell recommendation by major analysts for that firm. (The recommendation follows the ratios.) Using the ratios, justify or dispute the recommendation.

http://www.thomsoninvest.net

3.27 Using the Interactive Tool Box at the following Web site, perform a complete ratio analysis. Use some of the financial statements presented in this chapter.

http://www.edgeonline.com

CASH IN THE TILL: TRAWLING FOR PROMISING COMPANIES WITH HEFTY CASH FLOW

What's the best way to measure a stock's value? Without hesitation, many investors would say, "Earnings." And earnings are certainly a good place to start. But looking at earnings alone can obscure some virtues and vices among publicly traded companies. That's why some of the world's savviest investors, corporate raiders included, prefer to look at a company's cash flow, a measure that strips away the sometimes-distortive effects of taxes and interest as well as depreciation taken for plant, property and equipment.

"Reported earnings really are an accounting fiction," avers Michael Metz, chief investment strategist at Oppenheimer & Co. "The single most important factor making a company attractive is its ability to generate discretionary cash flow. That is cash flow in excess of what's needed to conduct its business."

Companies with strong cash flow generally don't need to pour huge sums into building new plants or investing new products. That means there is plenty of cash left to reward shareholders through aggressive stock buybacks and higher dividends, which in turn lead to higher stock prices. To find such opportunities, Oppenheimer periodically screens the stock market in search of companies that look attractive on a cash-flow basis. The accompanying table lists 20 of the more than 100 companies that now make the brokerage firm's cut. The pared-down list includes some well-known companies, like **Apple Computer, Dow Chemical, Phelps Dodge,** and UAL, parent of United Airlines, as well as firms in such currently unfashionable industries as chemicals and steel.

To make the nearby Oppenheimer list, a company's cash flow, which Oppenheimer defines as earnings before interest, taxes and depreciation, has to be at least 20% of the company's "adjusted" stock price. Put another way, a company's adjusted stock price can't be more than five times cash flow.

The adjusted stock price is generated by taking the stock price, adding in debt and preferred stock, and then subtracting out cash on the balance sheet. In adjusting the stock price for debt and cash, Oppenheimer looks at companies the way potential buyers do, because a purchaser must assume a company's debts but gains use of any cash in the till. Two companies may have the same stock price, but the one that has less debt and more cash is probably the more attractive of the two.

Oppenheimer also looks at free cash flow, which is cash flow less capital spending. It then generates a ratio of free cash flow to the adjusted stock prices. To make the grade, companies must have a ratio of 15% or better, about double the market average.

Metz thinks free cash is the better of the two valuation methods because it reflects the capital spending needed to keep companies competitive. Oppenheimer uses financial data for the twelve months ended June 30 for most of its calculations.

Oppenheimer's analysis is a bit like screening the stock market for companies with low price/earnings ratios, but Metz points out that many companies with low P/Es don't generate a lot of cash because they need to invest heavily to keep pace with rivals, while some companies with high P/Es have light capital expenditures and heavy depreciation, and therefore are significant cash generators.

Cash Machines

These companies generate hefty cash flow. Stock prices are adjusted by subtracting cash on the balance sheet and adding in debt. The higher the level of free cash flow relative to the adjusted share price, the better.

Company	Recent Price	Adj. Price	Gross Oper. Cash Flow*	Oper. Cash Flow/ Adj. Price	Free Cash Flow*	Free Cash Flow/ Adj. Price
AK Steel Corp	$ 31.00	$ 30.84	$ 13.13	43%	$ 8.59	28%
Amdahl	9.31	3.67	1.79	49	1.15	31
America West	13.75	18.67	4.93	26	2.90	16
Apple Computer	36.63	28.69	7.62	27	6.42	22
Cummins Engine	35.25	38.29	11.87	31	5.80	15
Cyrk	11.00	5.04	2.26	45	1.68	33
Dow Chemical	67.88	74.13	18.44	25	13.12	18
Georgia Gulf	33.50	41.92	10.19	24	8.60	21
Inland Steel	22.75	38.48	9.83	26	7.27	19
McClatchy News	19.50	15.56	3.60	23	2.52	16
Methanex	6.63	7.02	4.29	61	3.45	49
National Presto	41.00	13.42	3.31	25	2.95	22
Phelps Dodge	63.88	66.48	17.88	27	12.33	19
Rexene	9.38	17.58	8.24	47	6.31	36
Sterling Chem	8.13	10.42	5.21	50	4.60	44
Thiokol	34.63	37.49	7.74	21	5.88	16
UAL	177.38	370.82	117.63	32	55.93	15
USG	28.75	48.62	9.74	20	7.54	16
Wellpoint Hlth	31.13	10.08	3.94	39	3.69	37
Western Digital	15.50	9.31	3.56	38	2.45	26

* Per share.

Source: Oppenheimer & Co.

Source: Andrew Bary, "Cash in the Till," *Barron's*, 6, November 1995, p. 17. Reprinted by permission of *Barron's* © 1995 Dow Jones & Company, Inc. All rights reserved worldwide.

The following are selected data taken mainly from Micron Corporation's financial statements for 1995 (in millions of dollars):

Earnings Before Interest and Taxes (operating expenses)	8,239
Depreciation	1,150
Interest payment	1,522
Cash holding ("Cash in the Till")	5,124
Capital spending	2,500
Preferred stocks	0
Outstanding debt	12,000
Additional Information	
Number of outstanding shares	572,003,382
Current stock price (January 1, 1996)	$68

Read the article "Cash in the Till" and answer the following questions:

1. Calculate the following ratios:

a. Operating cash flow/adjusted stock price

b. Free cash flow/adjusted stock price

In your answer, use Oppenheimer's definitions of operating cash flow, free cash flow and adjusted stock price. Would Micron be an attractive stock by Oppenheimer's criteria?

2. Suppose that the capital spending every year is equal to the annual depreciation. Evaluate Michael Metz's assertion that "Reported earnings really are an accounting fiction." In your calculation compare reported earnings to free cash flow.

3. Suppose again that the annual capital spending is roughly equal to the annual depreciation. Also, suppose that in the past 10 years the capital spending was about $2,500 million each year. Assume now that in 1995 the capital spending jumps to $6,150 million rather than the $2,500 million reported above. Recalculate the free cash flow/adjusted stock price ratio. Would Micron be on Oppenheimer's list? Discuss your results.

4. Micron sells for cash only. The management of Micron is considering selling on 90 days' credit because it believes that will boost sales. It is estimated that with the new policy the following changes will occur in its asset composition (in millions of dollars).

	Selling for cash	Selling for credit
Cash	5,124	500
Receivables	0	4,624
Total	5,124	5,124

One board member opposes the move because it will cause Micron's stock to be deleted from Oppenheimer's list. As a result, its value will go down, which contradicts the goal of the firm, which is maximizing the stockholders' wealth. Carry out the relevant calculations and discuss the board member's claim.

5. The board of directors discusses the possibility of using $4,000 million of its cash for a stock repurchase at the market price of $68 per share. A board member claims: "As a result of this operation, the firm will have less cash, which will increase the adjusted stock price, decrease the ratio of free cash flow to adjusted stock price below 15%, and cause the stock to be deleted from the recommended list. Therefore, the stock repurchase is not recommended." Evaluate the board member's claim. Conduct the necessary calculations to support your answer.

Appendix 3A   Financial Ratio Analysis

If you had $2,000 in the bank and owed $1,000, you might mentally note that your assets are twice your liabilities. This simple computation is an example of *financial ratio analysis,* which investors and lenders use to measure a firm's financial health. These ratios serve the financial analyst and the firm's CFO in various ways. Let us introduce these ratios and discuss their applications.

LIQUIDITY RATIOS

Short-term creditors are concerned with the firm's *liquidity* and its ability to repay short-term debt. As their name implies, **liquidity ratios**—the current ratio and the quick ratio—measure a firm's liquidity.

Current Ratio
The **current ratio** is defined as follows:

$$\text{Current Ratio} = \frac{\text{Current Assets}}{\text{Current Liabilities}} \qquad (3.6)$$

If this ratio is higher than 1, the firm probably has sufficient current assets to repay its current liabilities. If it is lower than 1, the firm's CFO will have to take measures to increase it to avoid bankruptcy.

Let's return to Figure 3-2 and calculate Ford Motor Company's current ratio. In 1992 the total current assets of the Automotive Unit were $21,836.1 million. The footnotes to the balance sheet (not shown in the figure) reveal that all the Financial Services Unit's assets were current assets. Therefore, Ford's total current assets were

$$\$21,836.1 \text{ million} + \$123,375.2 \text{ million} = \$145,211.3 \text{ million}$$

The current liabilities of the two units were

$$\$21,124.9 \text{ million} + \$113,317.4 \text{ million} = \$134,442.3 \text{ million}$$

Therefore, Ford's current ratio in 1992 was

$$\frac{\$145,211.3 \text{ million}}{\$134,442.3 \text{ million}} \cong 1.08$$

Since the ratio is higher than 1, Ford Motor Company's current assets were sufficient to pay its current liabilities.

Quick Ratio

Creditors are sometimes suspicious of the current ratio and question the quality of the firm's current assets, particularly inventory. What if the firm has "dead" inventory—that is, inventory that cannot be sold, such as cars with defects or last year's models? If the firm cannot sell its inventory, its current assets will not be sufficient to cover its current liabilities. If investors have no information on the inventory's quality, they prefer another financial ratio, the **quick ratio,** which is defined as follows:

$$\text{Quick Ratio} = \frac{\text{Current Assets} - \text{Inventory}}{\text{Current Liabilities}} \tag{3.7}$$

Quick in the term *quick ratio* refers to the assumption that the assets can be quickly converted into cash. Ford's quick ratio in 1992 was

$$\frac{\$145,211.3 \text{ million} - \$5,451.3 \text{ million}}{\$134,442.3 \text{ million}} = \frac{\$139,760.0 \text{ million}}{\$134,442.3 \text{ million}} \cong 1.04$$

where $5,451.3 million is the inventory's book value. (See Figure 3-2.) Like its current ratio, Ford's quick ratio is higher than 1. So, the quality of Ford's inventory is no real problem for the potential short-term creditor. Even if its inventory value were zero, Ford would still have enough assets to cover its current liabilities.

If its quick ratio is lower than 1 and if its inventory is "dead," a firm may be financially distressed and may have to sell some of its fixed assets (such as production machines, buildings, or land) to repay its current liabilities. Such a sale generally spells trouble. To prevent financial distress, the CFO must plan the firm's financing sources to keep the quick ratio higher than 1.

FINANCIAL LEVERAGE RATIOS

A firm can finance its projects by equity, by debt, or by a combination of the two. Employing debt, called **financial leverage,** enhances or "levers" the profit to stockholders. However, leverage also increases the firm's risk because (unlike dividend payments to stockholders) paying interest and principal to lenders is mandatory. Especially with risky projects, the larger the proportion of debt in the project's financing, the more risk the firm faces. Why? Because uncertain future cash flows may not be sufficient to cover the firm's contractual obligations to its lenders.

A high current or quick ratio does not sufficiently reassure long-term creditors. Rather, they are interested in the firm's long-term repayment capacity and use the following three **financial leverage ratios** to measure the firm's risk: **debt/assets ratio, debt/equity ratio,** and **equity-multiple ratio.** These ratios are calculated as follows:

$$\text{Debt/Assets Ratio} = \frac{\text{Long-Term Debt}}{\text{Total Assets}} \qquad (3.8)$$

$$\text{Debt/Equity Ratio} = \frac{\text{Long-Term Debt}}{\text{Equity}} \qquad (3.9)$$

$$\text{Equity-Multiple Ratio} = \frac{\text{Total Assets}}{\text{Equity}} \qquad (3.10)$$

Generally speaking, if a firm's debt is small relative to its assets, its risk to long-term creditors is minimal. The firm can sell some of its assets, if necessary, to pay the debt. For creditors, the lower the debt/assets ratio and the debt/equity ratio, the safer the firm.

The equity-multiple ratio measures the ratio of the firm's total assets to its equity. The higher this ratio, the riskier the firm is for creditors. A high equity-multiple ratio implies that the firm finances a high proportion of its assets by debt. The larger the proportion of assets financed by debt, the riskier the firm is.

Let us demonstrate these ratios with the Ford Motor Company data. (See Figure 3-2.)

$$\text{Debt/Assets Ratio} = \frac{\$7,067.9 \text{ million}}{\$180,545.2 \text{ million}} \cong 0.039$$

$$\text{Debt/Equity Ratio} = \frac{\$7,067.9 \text{ million}}{\$14,752.9 \text{ million}} \cong 0.48$$

$$\text{Equity-Multiple Ratio} = \frac{\$180,545.2 \text{ million}}{\$14,752.9 \text{ million}} \cong 12.24$$

Since Ford's Financial Services Unit is involved mainly in short-term financing (borrowing money to finance credit sales) and does not affect long-term creditors, we analyze the Automotive Unit (Ford's production unit) separately.

$$\text{Debt/Assets Ratio} = \frac{\$7,067.9 \text{ million}}{\$57,170.0 \text{ million}} \cong 0.12$$

$$\text{Equity-Multiple Ratio} = \frac{\$57,170.0 \text{ million}}{\$14,752.9 \text{ million}} \cong 3.88$$

As before, the debt/equity ratio is 0.48. For the Automotive Unit, the debt amounts to almost half of the equity and almost 12% of the firm's assets; the volume of the firm's assets amounts to about four times its equity.

Which ratio is more relevant—the one with or without the Financial Services Unit data? Generally, in analyzing the financial strength of a firm you should include all units. In this case, however, you should not include the financial service unit in the ratio analysis calculation. To see this claim, note that the Financial Services Unit borrows money and uses it to make loans to customers. Acting as an intermediary between the capital markets and its customers, this unit conducts "back-to-back" transactions. Because most of the Financial Services Unit's activities are "back-to-back" operations, the financial ratios that include the Financial Services Unit are irrelevant to long-term creditors.

This example reveals that we cannot simply "crunch numbers" from the financial statements. Careful scrutiny of the financial statements—and, in particular, the notes attached to these statements—will help us decide which financial ratio to use.

The following problem illustrates how to compute and to compare the debt/equity and equity-multiple ratios for two firms.

PRACTICE BOX

Problem

The following are selected data from the financial statements of Firm A and Firm B. Data are in millions of dollars.

	Firm A ($ million)	Firm B ($ million)
Long-term debt	100	100
Equity	100	100
Current liabilities	800	0
Total liabilities and stockholders' equity	1,000	200

Using the debt/equity ratio and the equity-multiple ratio, which firm is riskier for the long-term creditor?

Solution

The debt/equity ratio is identical for both firms: $\dfrac{\$100}{\$100} = 1$

(continued)

Since the total assets are equal to the total liabilities plus equity, the equity-multiple ratio is \$1,000/\$100 = 10 for Firm A and \$200/\$100 = 2 for Firm B. With no further investigation of the current assets' quality, we see that Firm A is riskier because it has a much higher equity-multiple ratio. Firm A may have current assets to offset the current liabilities, but if there is no information on its current assets, long-term creditors would consider Firm A to be riskier.

Interest Coverage Ratio

Measuring the firm's ability to pay its interest obligations to creditors, the **interest coverage ratio** is defined as follows:

$$\text{Interest Coverage Ratio} = \frac{\text{Earnings Before Interest and Taxes (EBIT)}}{\text{Interest Expenses}} \qquad (3.11)$$

The higher this ratio, the larger are the earnings before interest and taxes relative to interest expenses, and the smaller is the chance that the firm will be unable to pay the interest. So, the higher the firm's interest coverage ratio, the safer are its creditors.[8] For example, if this ratio is equal to 2, creditors will know that a decrease of up to 50% in the firm's EBIT is possible without risking financial distress. A larger decrease in the EBIT would signify that the firm will be unable to pay the interest from its regular activities.

Because Ford lost money, its 1991 and 1992 interest coverage ratios are meaningless. Had Ford no other assets to pay the interest, it could have gone bankrupt. Even with the negative \$1,775.0 million EBIT in the Automotive Unit (see Figure 3-1), Ford did not go bankrupt. While an interest coverage ratio lower than 1 usually signifies financial distress, bankruptcy occurs only if this ratio is lower than 1 for several consecutive years or if the firm has no other assets to fall back on. Ford Motor Company had its Financial Services Unit to fall back on.

Debt Capacity

As we shall see in forthcoming chapters, debt financing has an important advantage for equity holders. Because interest is tax deductible, debt financing reduces the firm's tax burden. However, debt financing has one drawback. It increases the risk of bankruptcy because, as we have seen, the more uncertain the firm's cash flows, the greater is the chance of being unable to make required interest payments. The CFO must weigh the pros and cons of debt financing very carefully to determine the firm's debt/equity ratio. It is no wonder that utility firms, with their very predictable cash flows, generally use relatively large proportions of debt. In contrast, industrial firms, with their relatively uncertain cash flows, generally use less debt. A firm's ability to employ debt and to reduce its tax burden is called its **debt capacity.** Firms that have stable cash flows borrow more and enjoy the tax benefit that comes with

---

8. Repayment of principal is not included in the interest coverage ratio, although, of course, the firm has to repay the principal. If the firm cannot repay the principal, it may have to declare bankruptcy. However, if the firm is a "going concern" (never liquidates its assets), it can issue new debt to refinance the old debt. The firm uses EBIT to pay interest and uses new debt to pay the old debt principal.

borrowing. Indeed, firms with stable cash flows are commonly characterized by their relatively high debt capacity and high debt/equity ratio.

For example, in 1994 Cooper Tire, an industrial firm, had a debt/equity ratio of 0.07, whereas Central LA Electric, a utility, had a debt/equity ratio of 0.93. The utility, with its relatively stable cash flow, could better afford to borrow money without increasing its risk substantially. Central LA Electric thus had a larger debt capacity than Cooper Tire.

From this discussion, we learn that it is meaningless to compare the financial ratios and, in particular, the leverage ratios of firms in different industries. Indeed, we have seen that financial analysts recommend using time series analysis and industry analysis to make meaningful comparisons.

ACTIVITIES RATIOS

Activities ratios report various aspects of the firm's activities: its asset and inventory turnover, the number of days inventory is held, accounts receivable turnover, and the average time to collect accounts receivable. The ratios that measure these activities provide information on the effectiveness of the firm's operations.

Total Assets Turnover Ratio

A firm invests in assets to generate sales and revenue. The **total assets turnover ratio** measures how effectively these assets are used to generate sales and is defined as follows:

$$\text{Total Assets Turnover Ratio} = \frac{\text{Sales}}{\text{Total Assets}} \qquad (3.12)$$

A relatively high ratio indicates that the firm is using its assets effectively. For instance, a ratio of 4 implies that for each $1 of assets, the firm can create $4 of sales. A ratio of 0.1 means that a $10 million investment creates only $1 million of sales a year—a very poor result that, if repeated for several consecutive years, will probably lead to bankruptcy. In such a case the firm is using its assets very ineffectively. Variations of the total assets turnover ratio are obtained by dividing the sales by the *average* total assets, calculated on the basis of the firm's assets at the beginning and at the end of the year.

For Ford Motor Company's Automotive Unit, the 1992 ratio was

$$\text{Total Assets Turnover Ratio} = \frac{\$84,407.2 \text{ million (Figure 3-1)}}{\$57,170.0 \text{ million (Figure 3-2)}} \cong 1.48$$

The 1.48 figure means little by itself. Such ratios should be compared across years, or for the same year across firms in the same industry. For example, if we see that this ratio is higher for Ford than for General Motors, we can say that Ford uses its assets more effectively than General Motors.

Inventory Turnover Ratio

The faster a firm's inventory moves from storeroom to the customers' hands, the better off the firm will be, since a small investment in inventory will generate relatively large sales. The rate at which inventory is converted into sales is measured by the **inventory turnover ratio,** which is computed as follows:

$$\text{Inventory Turnover Ratio} = \frac{\text{Cost of Goods Sold}}{\text{Year-end Inventory of Finished Goods}} \qquad (3.13)$$

The inventory of a manufacturing firm includes three elements: raw materials, goods in process, and finished goods. For simplicity, assume the inventory is composed entirely of finished goods. If the value of the firm's inventory is $350 at the beginning of the year and $100 at year-end and if the manufacturing cost is $50, the *cost of goods sold* will be

Inventory, beginning of year	$350
Cost of goods manufactured	50
Minus: Inventory, year-end	100
Cost of goods sold	$300

The firm has an inventory of $100 at year-end, and its inventory turnover ratio is

$$\text{Inventory Turnover Ratio} = \frac{\$300}{\$100} = 3.0$$

This ratio measures how quickly the firm will sell the inventory it holds at the end of the year. An inventory turnover ratio of 3.0 indicates that the firm turns over its inventory about three times a year. A very low ratio implies that the firm has a great deal of "dead" inventory. To obtain a meaningful measure, we need to compare this ratio to those of other firms in the industry or to the firm's same ratio in other years.

Days in Inventory

Dividing the days in the year (365) by the inventory turnover ratio produces a measure called **days in inventory:**

$$\text{Days in Inventory} = \frac{365 \ (\text{Days in Year})}{\text{Inventory Turnover Ratio}} \qquad (3.14)$$

This measure indicates the number of days, on average, that the firm holds inventory.[9] Using the above example, we obtain

$$\text{Days in Inventory} = \frac{365}{3.0} \cong 121.67 \text{ Days}$$

9. For nonmanufacturing firms, the days in inventory measure is the number of days goods are held in inventory. For manufacturing firms, however, the inventory is a mix of raw materials, goods in process, and finished goods. In this case, each component should be analyzed separately.

Let us demonstrate these ratios with Ford's 1992 data. Assuming that the inventory of Ford's Automotive Unit is composed entirely of finished goods (otherwise, we would have to deduct the other components) and that total costs, including selling and administrative, are the costs of goods sold, we obtain:

$$\text{Inventory Turnover Ratio} = \frac{\text{Cost of Goods Sold}}{\text{Inventory}} = \frac{\$86,182.2 \text{ million}}{\$5,451.3 \text{ million}} \cong 15.81$$

and

$$\text{Days in Inventory} = \frac{365 \text{ Days}}{15.81} \cong 23.09 \text{ Days}$$

If, indeed, the inventory is composed entirely of finished products (vehicles ready for shipment to dealers), they are held an average of 23.1 days in Ford's inventory. In reality, since the inventory includes raw materials and vehicles on the production line, the inventory of finished goods is smaller. This means that Ford holds the finished vehicles for about 23 days and that its inventory is clearly not "dead." However, to evaluate the speed at which the inventory moves, we need to compare this ratio across years or compare it with the corresponding ratio of other firms in the auto industry.

Accounts Receivable Turnover Ratio
Accounts receivable can be used in the same manner as inventory to obtain two measures: the **accounts receivable turnover ratio,** which indicates how many times a year, on average, the firm collects its receivables, and the **average collection period,** which represents the average number of days it takes the firm to collect its accounts. These measures are calculated as follows:[10]

$$\text{Accounts Receivable Turnover Ratio} = \frac{\text{Sales}}{\text{Accounts Receivable}} \qquad (3.15)$$

$$\text{Average Collection Period} = \frac{365 \text{ (Days in Year)}}{\text{Accounts Receivable Turnover Ratio}} \qquad (3.16)$$

For Ford's Automotive Unit, we get

$$\text{Accounts Receivable Turnover Ratio} = \frac{\$84,407.2 \text{ million}}{\$2,883.6 \text{ million}} \cong 29.27$$

and

$$\text{Average Collection Period} = \frac{365 \text{ Days}}{29.27} \cong 12.47 \text{ Days}$$

---

10. Generally, some portion of the firm's sales are for cash. To analyze bad debt and credit policy, it is more appropriate to have only sales for credit in the numerator. We discuss credit policy in Chapter 21.

Ford collects its accounts payable an average of 29.27 times a year, and on average it waits 12.47 days after it makes its sales to receive cash.

PROFITABILITY RATIOS

Managers, investors, and creditors are interested in the firm's profitability. Various ratios can be derived from the financial statements to assess the firm's profitability. The four most commonly used **profitability ratios** are **net profit margin ratio, gross profit margin ratio, return on total assets (ROA) ratio**, and **return on equity (ROE) ratio.** These ratios are defined as follows:

$$\text{Net Profit Margin Ratio} = \frac{\text{Net Income}}{\text{Sales}} \tag{3.17}$$

$$\text{Gross Profit Margin Ratio} = \frac{\text{EBIT}}{\text{Sales}} \tag{3.18}$$

EBIT—earnings before interest and taxes—is also called operating income (loss).

$$\text{Return on Total Assets (ROA) Ratio} = \frac{\text{Net Income}}{\text{Total Assets}} \tag{3.19}$$

$$\text{Return on Equity (ROE) Ratio} = \frac{\text{Net Income}}{\text{Equity}} \tag{3.20}$$

According to accounting practice, to calculate net income, we deduct interest as an expense, but not dividends. The higher the debt, the lower are the net income and the ROA ratio. Since the ROA ratio is affected by the debt/equity financing mix and does not measure only the profitability of the assets, it has a drawback. One way of overcoming this drawback is to use the following profitability ratio:

$$\text{ROA}^* = \frac{\text{EBIT}}{\text{Total Assets}}$$

This version of the ROA ratio shows the profit on productive assets and is not affected by the financing mix.

Applying these ratios to the 1992 data of Ford's Automotive Unit, we obtain:

$$\text{Net Profit Margin Ratio} = \frac{-\$1,951.6 \text{ million}}{\$84,407.2 \text{ million}} \cong -0.023$$

$$\text{Gross Profit Margin Ratio} = \frac{-\$1,755.0 \text{ million}}{\$84,407.2 \text{ million}} \cong -0.021$$

$$\text{Return on Total Assets Ratio} = \frac{-\$1,951.6 \text{ million}}{\$57,170.0 \text{ million}} \cong -0.034$$

$$\text{ROA}^{\star} = \frac{-\$1,755.0 \text{ million}}{\$57,170.0 \text{ million}} \cong -0.031$$

and, finally,

$$\text{Return on Equity Ratio} = \frac{-\$1,951.6 \text{ million}}{\$14,752.9 \text{ million}} \cong -0.132$$

All these ratios are negative, which indicates that 1992 was, indeed, a bad year for Ford. The only consolation is that 1992 was also a bad year for all U.S. auto manufacturing firms as well as for those in Japan and Europe.

Again, one year's information on financial ratios is not sufficient. Although it can give insight on the firm's financial position, one year's analysis cannot tell us whether the firm is improving, nor how it compares to its competitors.

Appendix 3B   The DuPont System

The ratios discussed in Appendix 3A can be used to apply the **DuPont system,** so named because DuPont's management uses it for the firm's financial planning and control. This method helps pinpoint the factors affecting changes in profitability.

The DuPont system analyzes the relationship among various ratios. Before applying the DuPont system, we need to understand some relationships that will be used later. First, note that the return on assets (ROA) ratio can be rewritten as

$$\text{ROA} = \text{Net Profit Margin Ratio} \times \text{Total Assets Turnover Ratio}$$

and as

$$\text{ROA} = \frac{\text{Net Income}}{\text{Total Assets}} = \frac{\text{Net Income}}{\text{Sales}} \times \frac{\text{Sales}}{\text{Total Assets}} \qquad (3.21)$$

Similarly, the return on equity (ROE) ratio can be rewritten as

$$\text{ROE} = \text{Net Profit Margin Ratio} \times \text{Total Assets Turnover Ratio} \\ \times \text{Equity-Multiple Ratio}$$

and as

$$\text{ROE} = \frac{\text{Net Income}}{\text{Equity}} = \frac{\text{Net Income}}{\text{Sales}} \times \frac{\text{Sales}}{\text{Total Assets}} \times \frac{\text{Total Assets}}{\text{Equity}} \qquad (3.22)$$

Now, suppose we have the following figures from a firm's financial statements (in millions of dollars):

	Year 1	Year 2
Equity	100	100
Total assets	500	500
Sales	1,000	2,000
Net income	10	2

In Year 1 the ROE ratio (Net Income/Equity) is:

$$\frac{10}{100} = 0.10 \text{ or } 10\%$$

In Year 2, the ROE ratio is:

$$\frac{2}{100} = 0.02 \text{ or } 2\%$$

Why did the ROE ratio sharply decrease? Did the firm employ more equity? Did its sales drop? The DuPont system helps answer such questions. Using DuPont's equation for ROE, in Year 1 we obtain:

$$\text{ROE} = \left(\frac{10}{1,000}\right) \times \left(\frac{1,000}{500}\right) \times \left(\frac{500}{100}\right) = 0.10 \text{ or } 10\%$$

In Year 2, we obtain:

$$\text{ROE} = \left(\frac{2}{2,000}\right) \times \left(\frac{2,000}{500}\right) \times \left(\frac{500}{100}\right) = 0.02 \text{ or } 2\%$$

These are the same ROE results as in our first calculation, but the expanded equation helps us understand why ROE decreased from 10% in Year 1 to 2% in Year 2. Note that because the equity-multiple ratio did not change, the decreased ROE was not due to changes in the firm's leverage. The asset turnover ratio increased from 2 to 4, and the profit margin ratio dropped from 0.1 to 0.01. Perhaps the firm initiated a more aggressive sales policy in Year 2, or perhaps it promoted sales by offering large discounts or a liberal credit policy. The increase in sales (from $1,000 to $2,000) without an accompanying increase in profit would support this possibility. Such analysis should draw management's attention to its credit policy, which may need revision (avoid bad debt by restricting credit). A change in the firm's credit policy might have positive effects on its profit margin and ROE.

APPENDIX REVIEW AND PRACTICE

A3.1 "If the current ratio is higher than 2, the firm's creditors are relatively safe." Evaluate this claim.

A3.2 "If the quick ratio is higher than 1, both short-term and long-term creditors are safe." Evaluate this claim. If the quick ratio is 20, who will be safer, short-term creditors or long-term creditors?

A3.3 A firm's quick ratio is 1.5, its current ratio is 2, and its current liabilities are $20 million. What is the value of the firm's inventory?

A3.4 You have the following data on a nonmanufacturing firm (in millions of dollars):

Inventory, beginning of year	100
Goods purchased	200
Inventory, year-end	100

What is the inventory turnover ratio?

A3.5 A firm's sales are $100 million, and its accounts receivable are $20 million. What is the firm's average collection period in days?

A3.6 The return on equity (ROE) is 10%, asset turnover is 4, and the equity-multiple ratio is 2.5. What is the net profit margin?

A3.7 The return on total assets (ROA) is 8%, and the net profit margin is 2%. What is the asset turnover?

A3.8 The following data are taken from the financial statements of Helen Corporation (in millions of dollars):

	Year 1	Year 2
Sales	200	80
Total assets	300	300
Net income	30	60
Equity	150	180

The firm adopted a very liberal credit policy for its customers in Year 1. In Year 2 it changed its policy and required all sales to be made in cash only.

a. Use the DuPont system to analyze the changes in the ROA and the ROE.
b. What might explain the changes in the firm's profitability?
c. As the CFO, what would you want to investigate further in this case? Explain.

A3.9 You have the following information on Bush Corporation (in millions of dollars):

Balance Sheet

Assets		Liabilities and Equity	
Cash	?	Accounts payable	300
Accounts receivable	80	Short-term debt	100
		Long-term debt	?
Inventory	?	Equity	?
Fixed assets	?		
Total assets	?	Total liabilities and stockholders' equity	1,000

The net working capital is $200 million, the quick ratio is 1.00, and the equity-multiple ratio is 2.5. Fill in the missing figures in the balance sheet.

A3.10 The revenue from sales is $1,000, and the accounts receivable are $500. What is the average collection period?

A3.11 A firm's policy is to sell its product on 60 days' credit. The price per unit is $100, and the firm's net profit margin is 8%. To shorten the average collection period, the firm announces a new policy: Anyone who pays cash will get a 10% discount (a price of $90 per unit). Do you think this policy is a good one? Explain.

A3.12 A firm sells each unit for P, and the cost of sales per unit is C. The firm has no other costs or taxes. Define net profit margin. Do you think it provides a good measure of the firm's profitability? Of the firm's risk? Give an example.

A3.13 The firm's net profit margin is measured by $Q(P - C)/QP$, where Q is the number of units sold, P is the price per unit, and C is the cost per unit sold.

Suppose there are two firms: Firm A, with a net profit margin of 10%, and Firm B, with a net profit margin of 2%. Firm B is more profitable because it has a larger volume of sales. Because of competition in the market, the price of the products of these two firms drops by 5%.

a. Assuming no other changes (in particular, no change in production cost per unit), which firm is now more profitable?

b. "It seems that the net profit margin is a good index of the firm's risk." Explain this statement.

A3.14 Which firm is likely to have a higher inventory turnover: Boeing Corporation or a bakery? Explain.

APPENDIX KEY TERMS

Liquidity ratios
Current ratio
Quick ratio
Financial leverage
Financial leverage ratios
Debt/assets ratio
Debt/equity ratio
Equity-multiple ratio

Interest coverage ratio
Debt capacity
Activities ratios
Total assets turnover ratio
Inventory turnover ratio
Days in inventory
Accounts receivable turnover
 ratio

Average collection period
Profitability ratios
Net profit margin ratio
Gross profit margin ratio
Return on total assets (ROA) ratio
Return on equity (ROE) ratio
DuPont system

YOUR TURN: APPLYING THEORY TO PRACTICE 3.2

IBM'S FINANCIAL CRISIS

In the early 1990s, IBM suffered severe losses. Here we focus on these interesting years, taking both the creditors' and the stockholders' viewpoints. Later on, with new management, IBM recovered. Its earnings in 1996 were $5.9 billion, and its earnings in the first quarter of 1997 were $1.2 billion. This turnaround caused the firm's stock to reach a high of $107.87 per share in August 1997. The following tables provide IBM's main financial statements for 1991 and 1992.

Comparative Consolidated Income Accounts, Years Ended December 31 (in millions of dollars)		1992	1991
	Revenue		
	Sales	33,755	37,093
	Software	11,103	10,498
	Maintenance	7,635	7,414
	Services	7,352	5,582
	Rentals & financing	4,678	4,179
	Total revenue	64,523	64,766

Comparative Consolidated Income Accounts, Years Ended December 31 (in millions of dollars) *(continued)*		**1992**	**1991**
	Cost		
	Sales	19,698	18,571
	Software	3,924	3,865
	Maintenance	3,430	3,379
	Services	6,051	4,531
	Rentals financing	1,966	1,727
	Total costs	35,069	32,073
	Gross profit	29,454	32,693
	Selling, general, administrative	19,526	21,375
	R&D, engineering	6,522	6,644
	Restructuring charges	11,645	3,735
	Total operating expenses	37,693	31,754
	Operating income	(8,239)	939
	Other income, principally interest	573	602
	Interest expense	1,360	1,423
	Earnings before taxes	(9,026)	118
	Provision for income taxes	(2,161)	716
	Net earnings before accounting change	(6,865)	(598)
	Effect of changes in accounting principles	1,900	(2,263)
	Net earnings	(4,965)	(2,861)

Consolidated Statement of Cash Flows, Years Ended December 31 (in millions of dollars)	**Cash Flow from Operating Activities**	**1992**	**1991**
	Net earnings	(4,965)	(2,861)
	Adjustments to reconcile net income to cash provided from operating activities:		
	Effect of changes in accounting principles	(1,900)	2,263
	Effect of restructuring charges	8,312	2,793
	Depreciation	4,793	4,772
	Amortization of software	1,466	1,564
	(Gain) in disposition of investment assets	54	(94)
	Other changes that provided (used) cash		
	Receivables	1,052	(886)
	Inventories	704	(36)
	Other assets	(3,396)	5
	Accounts payable	(311)	384
	Other liabilities	465	(1,179)
	Net cash provided from operating activities	6,274	6,725

(continued)

Consolidated Statement of Cash Flows, Years Ended December 31 (in millions of dollars) *(continued)*

Cash Flow from Investing Activities	1992	1991
Payments for plant, rental machines, and other property	(4,751)	(6,497)
Proceeds from disposition of plant, rental machines, and other property	633	645
Investment in software	(1,752)	(2,014)
Purchases of marketable securities & other investments	(3,284)	(4,848)
Proceeds from marketable securities & other investments	3,276	5,028
Net cash used in investing activities	(5,878)	(7,686)

Cash Flow from Financing Activities		
Proceeds from new debt	10,045	5,776
Payments to settle debt	(10,735)	(4,184)
Short-term borrowings less than 90 days, net	4,199	2,676
Proceeds from (payments to) employee stock plans, net	(90)	67
Payments to purchase and retire capital stock	—	(196)
Cash dividends paid	(2,765)	(2,771)
Net cash provided from (used in) financing activities	654	1,368
Effect of exchange rate changes on cash & cash equivalents	(549)	(315)
Net change in cash & cash equivalents	501	92
Cash & cash equivalents at Jan. 1	3,945	3,853
Cash & cash equivalents at Dec. 31	4,446	3,945

BALANCE SHEETS: Comparative Consolidated Balance Sheets, as of December 31 (in millions of dollars)

Assets	1992	1991
Cash	1,090	1,171
Cash equivalents	3,356	2,774
Market securities at cost	1,203	1,206
Notes and accounts receivables—trade net of allowances	12,829	15,391
Sales-type leases receivable	7,405	7,435
Other accounts receivable	1,370	1,491
Inventories	8,385	9,844
Prepaid expenses and other current assets	4,054	1,657
Total current assets	39,692	40,969
Plant, rental machinery, and other property, net	21,595	27,578
Software, net[a]	4,119	4,483
Investments and sundry assets	21,299	19,443
Total assets	86,705	92,473

BALANCE SHEETS:
Comparative Consolidated
Balance Sheets, as of
December 31 (in millions of
dollars) *(continued)*

Liabilities	1992	1991
Taxes	979	2,449
Short-term	16,467	13,716
Accounts payable	3,147	3,507
Compensation & benefits	3,476	3,241
Deferred income	3,316	3,472
Other accrued expenses & liabilities	9,352	7,566
Total current liabilities	36,737	33,951
Long-term debt	12,853	13,231
Other liabilities	7,461	6,685
Deferred income taxes	2,030	1,927
Capital stock[b]	6,563	6,531
Retained earnings	19,124	26,983
Translation adjustments	1,962	3,196
Less: Treasury stock, at cost[b]	(25)	(31)
Total stockholders' equity	27,624	36,679
Total liabilities and stockholders' equity	86,705	92,473
Net current assets	2,955	7,018

[a]Accumulated amortization: 1992, $8,531,000,000; 1991, $6,950,000,000.

[b]Shares at cost: 1992, 356,222; 1991, 331,665.

Source: IBM, *1992 Annual Report.*

Questions

1. Use financial ratio analysis to discuss the financial strengths and weaknesses of IBM during this period. In particular, use the DuPont system to analyze changes in ROA and ROE during 1992, and compare with 1991. Discuss the following issues (and any other issues that you think are relevant):
a. IBM's main problems
b. Whether the net profit margin ratio fell
c. Whether the firm had excessive debt
2. Suppose you are an IBM creditor. You loaned the firm money in 1990 at 8% interest. Would you lend IBM more money now (in 1993)? Would you still charge 8% interest? More? Less?

3. In 1992 the yield on IBM's bonds was about 2% higher than the yield on government bonds (with the same maturity date). What can you learn from this information about IBM's chances of declaring bankruptcy?
4. Would you ask more questions about the nature of the "other accounts receivable" and "prepaid expenses and other current assets"? If so, what questions would you ask, and why would they be important?
5. If you were IBM's CEO, what actions would you take?

CHAPTER 4

PRESENT VALUE AND FUTURE VALUE

LEARNING OBJECTIVES

After reading this chapter you should understand:

1. The relationship between present value (PV) and future value (FV) and how to calculate both.

2. How to use the equations and available tables to calculate the PV and FV of cash flows.

3. The power of compounding.

4. How to calculate the PV and FV of an annuity and a perpetuity, with and without growth in the annual cash flows.

5. How to use the PV and FV formulas in real-life financial transactions.

6. The various compounding and discounting methods.

CORPORATE FINANCE IN THE NEWS

START A COLLEGE FUND FOR THE CLASS OF 2107

Money expects overall inflation to stay below 3% in '96, but college costs figure to climb an estimated 6.5% this year and maintain that double-inflation pace well into the next century.

The Chapmans add money to their kids' college funds every year but, as Bob says, "It never seems like enough." No kidding. If current projections hold, in 18 years public university tuition, room and board will average $115,000 for four years, while a private university degree will approach $250,000. So it's never too early to start saving. Just ask Austin Westbrook and Angela Dickens-Westbrook of New Orleans, who began investing $2,500 a year for their firstborn's college education two years ago—even though the baby is not due to arrive until May.

Source: Karen Cheney, "Your Best Move Will Be to Pay Down Debt," *Money* 24, no. 13 (Forecast 1996): 96–99.

4.1 INTRODUCTION

You may have been told not to count your chickens before they hatch, but you should count the yield on your investments in advance. For the Westbrooks in the Corporate Finance in the News article, will their $2,500 annual savings be sufficient to cover a four-year college education? A private university education? It depends on the yield on those savings. Of course, this answer is not as simple as it might first appear. The Westbrooks'—and your—future cash flows will be spread over a number of years, and the value of a dollar today and its value at various times in the future will be different. In this chapter we will learn how to evaluate cash flows obtained at various times.

If you are like most students who have little wealth, you may believe this topic is merely academic. But you probably have a student loan to repay. As a business student, you should consider that debt as representing an investment in yourself and your studies—that is, as debt financing. When you read this chapter, you may learn how to make the best of your loan and how to choose the best way to repay it. CFOs of corporations make these calculations when they borrow; so should you.

Scan any monthly financial magazine, and you will probably find an article advising you to begin saving now for future needs such as a house, children's college tuition, or even retirement. The numbers in those articles are often mind-boggling: "Save $3,000 a month for 20 years to accumulate $5 million." In this example, the $5 million is the *future value* of the $3,000-a-month savings. The key is to set the future amount you want and to calculate back from there. In this chapter we will show how to calculate the future value of savings. After reviewing the concept of time value of money and working with compounding and discounting, you will be able to analyze the relationship between savings and future value and perform other important calculations relating to cash flows received in various years.

As mentioned in Chapter 1, *time value of money* is one of the most important concepts in finance. It means that the value of a dollar received one year from now is not the same as the value of a dollar received today. We are not talking about dollars stashed under mattresses, but about dollars that are invested in some interest- or profit-bearing vehicle. More often than not, potential investors are confused by the many and varied investment alternatives available in the market.

How, then, can we decide among the various investment and savings options? For instance, most people would prefer to receive $1,000 today rather than next year. They could spend it now, or they could keep it under their mattresses and spend it one year from now. Or, even better, they could deposit the money in the bank and earn interest, say 5%, and have $1,050 to spend one year from now. Whether they would prefer $1,000 today or $1,050 next year is a trickier question. To answer it, we would have to convert the $1,000 and the $1,050 to some equivalent basis. Without some kind of "common denominator"—usually a point in time—comparison between alternative investments is impossible. While the common denominator could be today, next year, or any other date, it is usually the present, which in finance we denote as $t = 0$. All of the investment's cash flows are then evaluated at that date.

To demonstrate, suppose you are offered a $10,000 student loan that you can repay with three different schedules: The first requires you to pay $13,000 five years later; the second requires you to pay $15,000 eight years later; and the third requires you to pay $3,000 a year for four years starting at the end of the third year. Which schedule is most worthwhile for you? To decide, you need to determine what calculations you would have to perform to make the best decision. A CFO faces a similar problem. Various competing projects have different cash flows spread over the years, and for comparison a CFO needs a method that brings all these cash flows to a common denominator. We devote this chapter to showing how to make calculations of this kind; in Section 4.4.2 we demonstrate how to make the optimum choice among these three student loan repayment schedules.

4.2 FUTURE VALUE AND PRESENT VALUE: THE ONE-PERIOD CASE

Future value (FV) and present value (PV) calculations adjust all cash flows to dollars at a common date. Let us illustrate the importance of such a date when comparing dollar amounts received at different times.

Most firms sell their products both on credit and for cash. The cash price is generally lower than the credit price; the difference between the two prices is the *price discount*. For instance, suppose a dealer offers you a Ford Escort for $14,000 in cash or $15,000 on credit for one year. Which payment is better for you (the buyer), and which is better for the dealer (the seller)? To answer this question, we need more information on the interest rate. Let us assume an annual interest rate of 10%. At that rate, which option is better for the dealer? The face value of the two cash flows ($14,000 and $15,000) must be stated taking the time value of money into account. A common denominator must be found to compare them. For instance, you can choose either time 0 or time 1 (which stand for the beginning and end of the year, respectively). If you choose to value all cash flows at the end of the year (time 1), you will use **future value (FV)** comparisons; if you choose to value all cash flows at the beginning of the year (time 0), you will use **present value (PV)** comparisons.

4.2.1 Future Value (FV)

Since the car dealer will receive the $15,000 from the credit sale in the future, the amount clearly represents a *future value*. The $14,000 from the cash sale, which the dealer receives immediately, or at time 0, represents a *present value*. How would the dealer convert the $14,000 present value into an equivalent future cash flow? Quite simply, by depositing the money from the cash sale in the bank and earning, say, 10% interest on it. Then, after one year the car dealer can withdraw

$$\$14,000 + (0.10 \times \$14,000) = \$14,000 \times (1.10) = \$15,400$$

Now the comparison is possible. If the dealer sells the car on credit, she receives $15,000 at the end of the year; if she sells for cash and deposits the money in the bank, she receives $15,400 at the end of the year. (Of course, the dealer could put the money in a wall safe and just hold it, but this would not be too smart because the money would not earn interest.) In this example, the car dealer does better financially by selling cars for cash and would probably prefer to sell as many cars as possible for cash rather than for credit.

The $14,000 received for cash sales is cash-in-hand today and is defined as the *present value (PV)* of the sale. It provides $14,000 cash-in-hand for current spending. Money received in the future is the *future value (FV)*. When we talk about future value, we must specify the date in the future for which the FV is calculated. For instance, we may be talking about the FV of $1 today, at the end of Year 1, at the end of Year 2, and so on. From the previous example, we see that the present and future values at the end of one year (or at Year 1) are related as follows:

$$\text{PV}(1 + r) = \text{FV} \tag{4.1}$$

where *r* is the interest rate. In our example:

$$\$14,000 \times 1.1 = \$15,400$$

Or, in words, the future value of $14,000 in cash received today is $15,400 one year later, if the interest rate is 10%. The higher the interest rate that the bank pays on such cash deposits, the higher will be their future value.

4.2.2 Present Value (PV)

Equation 4.1 can be rewritten as

$$\text{PV} = \frac{\text{FV}}{(1 + r)} \tag{4.2}$$

In the previous example, the car dealer will be indifferent between receiving $15,000 at time 1 or FV/(1 + r) = $15,000/1.1 = $13,636.36 at time 0 (where time 0 is today and time 1 is one year from now). If the car dealer needs the cash at time 0 but receives it only at time 1, she can borrow $13,636.36 from the bank at 10% interest and repay the principal and the interest ($13,636.36 × 1.1 = $15,000) one year later, for exactly the amount the car buyer pays on the credit purchase. If the cash price is $13,636.36 and the car dealer needs the cash at time 1 but receives it at time 0, she can deposit the money in the bank, earn 10% interest on it, and receive $15,000 at time 1.

In general, as long as the PV and FV dollar amounts satisfy Equation 4.2, investors will be indifferent between receiving the PV of the money at time 0 or the FV of the money at time 1. However, in our example, since the car dealer can sell the car for $14,000 cash, she will not be indifferent and will prefer the cash sale over the credit sale.

4.3 FUTURE VALUE AND PRESENT VALUE: THE MULTIPERIOD CASE

A West Coast basketball team offers a contract to Charles Tuck, a very talented basketball player. Charles has two options: (1) a down payment of $2 million with an additional $2 million at the end of each of the next 2 years; or (2) a down payment of $1.5 million and an additional $5 million at the end of Year 2. As Charles's financial manager, which offer do you recommend he take? Charles is highly motivated to maximize his earnings, and you are motivated to do your best for your client and, of course, to maximize your commission. Both options will make Charles and you very rich!

Again, comparison between the two options is not possible without a common denominator. Table 4–1 illustrates the cash flows of Charles's two options. We will use this example to show how *multiperiod future value* and *multiperiod present value* are calculated.

4.3.1 Multiperiod Future Value

First, let us calculate all cash flows in terms of their future value at the end of Year 2. Suppose the interest rate is 10%. If Charles chooses the first option, he receives $2 million immediately. If he deposits this money in the bank, its value after one year (end of Year 1) will be

$$\$2 \text{ million} \times (1.1) = \$2.2 \text{ million}$$

Instead of withdrawing the $2.2 million at the end of Year 1, Charles can leave it in the bank for one more year. At the end of the second year, his $2.2 million will have grown to

$$\$2.2 \text{ million} \times (1.1) = \$2.42 \text{ million}$$

The future value two years from today of the $2 million received at time 0 can be rewritten as

$$\$2 \text{ million} \times (1.1)(1.1) = \$2 \text{ million} \times (1.1)^2 = \$2.42 \text{ million}$$

TABLE 4–1 Charles Tuck's Two Options	Cash Flows		
	Time 0 (Cash Flow 1)	Time 1 (Cash Flow 2)	Time 2 (Cash Flow 3)
Option 1	$2,000,000	$2,000,000	$2,000,000
Option 2	$1,500,000	$ 0	$5,000,000

Note that in the first year Charles will receive just the 10% interest on the principal (the original deposit). However, in the second year, he will receive 10% on the $2 million principal and also on the $0.2 million interest earned in the first year. Interest earned on the principal *and* on the accumulated interest is called **compound interest.**

The PV and FV in the two-year case are related as follows:

$$\text{PV}(1 + r)^2 = \text{FV} \qquad\qquad (4.3)$$

In our example, PV = $2 million. Hence:

$$\text{FV} = \$2 \text{ million} \times (1.1)^2 = \$2.42 \text{ million}$$

As part of Option 1, Charles also receives $2 million at the end of Year 1. If he deposits this sum in the bank for one year, then at the end of Year 2 this deposit will yield a future value of

$$\$2 \text{ million} \times (1.1) = \$2.2 \text{ million}$$

Charles's third and last payment in Option 1 is $2 million at the end of the second year, an amount that is already stated in terms of future value dollars. Altogether, the total FV of Option 1 is

$$\$2.42 \text{ million} + \$2.20 \text{ million} + \$2.00 \text{ million} = \$6.62 \text{ million}$$

Now let us turn to Option 2. The computation for this option is much simpler. Charles receives $1.5 million at time 0. The future value of this sum at the end of two years is

$$\$1.5 \text{ million} \times (1.1)^2 = \$1.815 \text{ million}$$

Charles will also receive $5 million at the end of two years, an amount that is already stated in FV terms. The total FV of Option 2 is

$$\$1.815 \text{ million} + \$5.000 \text{ million} = \$6.815 \text{ million}$$

You recommend that Charles choose the second option, and he agrees. Table 4-2 summarizes the FV calculation on these two options.

TABLE 4-2 Calculating the Future Value of Charles's Cash Flows	Future Value of	Option 1	Option 2
	Cash Flow 1	$2,000,000 × (1.1)² = $2,420,000	$1,500,000 × (1.1)² = $1,815,000
	Cash Flow 2	$2,000,000 × (1.1) = $2,200,000	$0 × (1.1) = $0
	Cash Flow 3	$2,000,000	$5,000,000
	Total FV at the end of the second year	$6,620,000	$6,815,000

4.3.2 Multiperiod Present Value

What if you and Charles want to compare the two options in present value rather than in future value terms? We will show that using PV rather than FV does not change the result if the borrowing interest rate is equal to the lending interest rate.

Table 4–3 presents the PV calculation on Charles's two options. The cash flows received at the end of Year 1 are divided by $(1 + r)$; those at the end of Year 2, by $(1 + r)^2$. The division by $(1 + r)$ and $(1 + r)^2$, whereby we find the present value of a future amount, is called **discounting,** and r is the interest rate or **discount rate.** Table 4–3 reveals that PV comparisons and FV comparisons yield the same preference for the second option.

Let's examine more closely what the PV of $5,471,075 for Option 1 means. If Charles receives that amount today, he can deposit some of the money in the bank at the 10% interest rate to have $2,000,000 for consumption every year during the three-year period. Thus, he is indifferent between receiving the PV today or the three annual cash flows suggested to him (see Table 4–2). To be more specific, he can withdraw $2,000,000 at $t = 0$ and invest the remaining $3,471,075 ($5,471,075 − $2,000,000) at $r = 10\%$. At the end of Year 1, this sum will have grown to $3,818,182.50 ($3,471,075 × 1.1). Then, at $t = 1$, Charles can withdraw another $2,000,000, invest the remaining $1,818,182.50 at $r = 10\%$, and have nearly $2,000,000 ($1,818,182.50 × 1.1 $\cong$ $2,000,000) at the end of Year 2. So, if Charles receives the PV of $5,471,075, he can make bank deposits that will ensure three annual $2,000,000 payments. Therefore, Charles Tuck will be indifferent between these annual future payments and the PV. The following problem demonstrates that calculations based on PV and FV give the same result.

PRACTICE BOX

Problem

By choosing the second option rather than the first, in terms of FV, Charles earns an additional income of $0.195 million ($6.815 million − $6.62 million = $0.195 million); whereas in terms of PV, the additional income is $0.161 million ($5.632 million − $5.471 million = $0.161 million). (See Table 4–3.) Evaluate this statement: "Because the additional income is larger with the FV calculation, Charles should make his decision in terms of FV rather than PV."

Solution

This statement is misleading. Although the additional FV income is larger than the additional PV income, if Charles gets the additional cash flow of $0.161 million immediately, he can deposit it in the bank for two years and obtain a FV of

$$\$0.161 \text{ million} \times (1.1)^2 \cong \$0.195 \text{ million}$$

This result is identical to the FV gain from Option 2. Calculations based on PV and FV give the same result.

TABLE 4-3 Calculating the Present Value of Charles's Cash Flows	Present Value of	Option 1	Option 2
	Cash Flow 1	$2,000,000	$1,500,000
	Cash Flow 2	$\dfrac{\$2,000,000}{(1.1)} \cong \$1,818,182$	$\dfrac{\$0}{(1.1)} = \$0$
	Cash Flow 3	$\dfrac{\$2,000,000}{(1.1)^2} \cong \$1,652,893$	$\dfrac{\$5,000,000}{(1.1)^2} \cong \$4,132,231$
	Total (PV)	$5,471,075	$5,632,231

In general, the relationship between PV and FV for T years is given by

$$\text{FV} = \text{PV}(1 + r)^T \tag{4.4}$$

The PV can be written as follows:

$$\text{PV} = \frac{\text{FV}}{(1 + r)^T} \tag{4.5}$$

Charles Tuck and any other investor will be indifferent between PV and FV as long as the dollar amount received today (PV) and the dollar amount received T years from now (FV) comply with Equations 4.4 and 4.5. For example, if $T = 2$ and $r = 10\%$, you will be indifferent between receiving $100 today or $121 at $T = 2$ because $\$121/(1.1)^2 = \$100$. However, if you are offered $110 today or $121 at $T = 2$, you will prefer $110 today. Using Equation 4.4, we find that the FV of $110 at $T = 2$ is $133.10, which is more than the $121 offered to you. Similarly, if you are offered a choice between $100 today or $130 at $T = 2$, you will prefer $130 at $T = 2$. We have $\$130/(1.1)^2 \cong \$107.44 > \$100$. So, with $r = 10\%$ investors will *not* be indifferent between receiving $100 today or $130 two years hence, if $r = 10\%$.

Throughout most of this chapter, we assume that cash flows are certain and use the riskless interest rate, r, as the discount rate. The riskless discount rate is the prevailing rate of return on riskless investments such as U.S. Treasury bills. If future cash flows are certain, then r is the appropriate discount rate. However, as we have already seen (in Chapter 2), the more uncertain the future cash flows, the higher the required rate of return will be. The difference between the required rates of return on risky investments, which we denote by k, and on riskless investments, r, is called the *risk premium*. If cash flows are uncertain, k substitutes for r, but the analysis remains otherwise the same.

4.4 USING FV AND PV TABLES

Present and future values can be calculated by using either available tables or a financial calculator. We'll explain how to use the tables, which have the advantage of providing insight into the various calculations and the relationships among them. However, most financial managers use calculators because most FV and PV tables are not detailed enough (for example, we cannot calculate present value at a discount rate of 7.256%). Although you'll probably use a calculator, you need to understand what the tables show and how to use them.

4.4.1 Future Value Tables

Table A-1 at the end of the book provides the future value of $1 at the end of T periods for various interest rates. For example, a portion of the table looks like this:

Future Value Factor (FVF) for Various Interest Rates

Period	Interest Rate 10%	20%
1	1.1000	1.2000
2	1.2100	1.4400
3	1.3310	1.7280
4	1.4641	2.0736
5	1.6105	2.4883
⋮	⋮	⋮
50	117.3909	9,100.4382

The number in each cell of the future value table represents the value of $1 at the end of year T when invested at r% and is a **future value factor (FVF).** For example, if the interest rate is 10%, the future value of $1 four years from now is $1.4641. If the interest rate is 20%, the future value of $1 at the end of four years is $2.0736. If you deposit $1 for 50 years, it will grow to $117.3909 at 10% interest and to $9,100.4382 at 20% interest. We denote the future value factors by the notation $\text{FVF}_{r\%,T}$ which, in words, reads as "the future value factor corresponding to r% interest for T years." The FV formula used for constructing Table A-1 is

$$\text{FV} = \$1 \times \text{FVF}_{r\%,T} = \$1 \times (1 + r)^T$$

The following problem demonstrates the FV of a $1,000 investment earning 10% interest for four years.

PRACTICE BOX	
Problem	You deposit $1,000 for four years at an interest rate of 10%. What is its future value at the end of four years?
Solution	From Table A-1, each $1 deposited for four years has a FV of $1.4641. Using the FV formula, we get
	$$\$1,000 \times 1.4641 = \$1,464.10$$

4.4.2 Present Value Tables

Table A–2 at the end of the book presents the PV of $1 received T periods from now for various interest rates. For example, a portion of the table looks like this:

Discount Factors (DF) for Various Interest Rates

Period	Interest Rate	
	10%	20%
1	0.9091	0.8333
2	0.8264	0.6944
3	0.7513	0.5787
4	0.6830	0.4823
5	0.6209	0.4019
⋮	⋮	⋮
50	0.0085	0.0001

For the current interest rates on mortgages, leases, car loans, and so on in your area of the country, visit the Financial Services Network.
http://www.mfsn.com

The number in each cell of the present value tables represents the PV of $1 received at the end of year T at an interest rate of $r\%$ and is called the **discount factor (DF).** The table shows that the PV of $1 received one year from now at 10% interest is $0.9091. The PV of $1 received 50 years from now is $0.0085. The discount factor corresponding to $r\%$ discount rate at T years is generally denoted by $DF_{r\%,T}$. We have $DF_{r\%,T} = 1/(1 + r)^T$. For example, $DF_{10\%,2} = 0.8264$.

We now can solve the student loan dilemma presented earlier in this chapter. Recall that you can repay the $10,000 loan with three different schedules: $13,000 after five years, $15,000 after eight years, or $3,000 a year for four years starting at the end of the third year. To decide which schedule is least costly, you can calculate the PV of the repayments and select the repayment schedule with the lowest PV. Suppose the discount rate is $r = 10\%$. We have the following cash flows:

Cash Flows (in $)

Time Line	1	2	3	4	5	6	7	8
Schedule 1					−13,000			
Schedule 2								−15,000
Schedule 3			−3,000	−3,000	−3,000	−3,000		

Let us calculate the PV of the repayments. At the 10% discount rate we have:

$$\text{Schedule 1: } PV = \frac{\$13,000}{(1.1)^5} \cong \$8,071.98$$

$$\text{Schedule 2: } PV = \frac{\$15,000}{(1.1)^8} \cong \$6,997.61$$

$$\text{Schedule 3: } \text{PV} = \frac{\$3,000}{(1.1)^3} + \frac{\$3,000}{(1.1)^4} + \frac{\$3,000}{(1.1)^5} + \frac{\$3,000}{(1.1)^6}$$

$$\cong \$2,253.94 + \$2,049.04 + \$1,862.76 + \$1,693.42 = \$7,859.16$$

Schedule 2 is the best choice because the PV of the payments is the smallest.

When applying PV and FV, we must remember that these calculations assume that money can be loaned or borrowed at a fixed interest rate—10% in our example.

4.4.3 The Power of Compounding

Suppose you deposit $100 in the bank at 10% interest for two years. What is the FV of your deposit? The answer will depend on whether the bank calculates your interest *with compounding* or *without compounding*.

INTEREST WITHOUT COMPOUNDING

Imagine for a moment that the bank calculates interest without compounding. You earn 10% interest on the $100 deposited for the first year. However, in the second year you do *not* receive interest on the interest earned in the previous year. Without compounding, the FV of your $100 after two years will be as follows:

First-year interest	$ 10
Second-year interest	10
Principal	100
FV	$120

INTEREST WITH COMPOUNDING

If the bank calculates interest with compounding, it pays you in the second year 10% on the $10 earned in the first year. (If it doesn't, you should withdraw the $110 at the end of the first year and deposit it in another bank. Or, to show the bank that you know about compounding, redeposit it in the same bank at 10%!) With annual compounding, the FV of your $100 deposit after two years will be as follows:

First-year interest	$ 10
Second-year interest on the principal	10
10% interest on the $10 earned in first year	1
Principal	100
FV	$121

You may be thinking, "Only one dollar difference? Big deal! Is this the *power* of compounding?" The real power of compounding is seen when you invest for many years, and this is when the gap between the two methods of calculating interest can be dramatic. The higher the interest rate, the greater the gap will be.

Table 4–4 shows the FV of $100 deposited at 10% interest calculated with and without compounding for various lengths of time. The FV is the original investment of $100 plus the accumulated interest. For one year the FV is the same by both methods. The $10 earned reflects the first interest payment, and the compounding effect is not yet felt. For two years, without compounding, the accumulated interest is $20; with compounding, $21. By the end of the tenth year, we begin to see more divergence. The calculation without compounding gives you $100 of accumulated interest (10 times the interest of $10 a year), whereas with compounding you will earn:

$$\$100 \times (1.1)^{10} - \$100 \cong \$259.37 - \$100 = \$159.37$$

So, the interest earned is $100 without compounding and $159.37 with compounding.

Figure 4–1 illustrates the FV of $100 deposited at 10% interest with and without compounding. The curve represents the FV of the investment if the interest is calculated with compounding; the straight line represents the FV of the same investment if the interest is calculated without compounding. As you can see, the distance between the straight line and the curve increases dramatically as the number of years increases.

Table 4.4
The Future Value of Interest: Calculated with and without Compounding

	FV of $100 Deposit at 10% Interest	
Year	**Without Compounding**	**With Compounding**
1	$110	$ 110
2	$120	$ 121
3	$130	$ 133.10
.	.	.
5	$150	$ 161.05
.	.	.
10	$200	$ 259.37
.	.	.
.	.	.
50	$600	$11,739.09
60	$700	$30,448.16
70	$800	$78,974.70

THE EFFECTIVE ANNUAL INTEREST RATE

A new bank sends you a notice that it will offer 10% interest payable *semiannually;* that is, you will receive interest equal to 10%/2 = 5% of your principal at the end of each six months. At first glance, this offer seems the same as the 10% interest you've been earning, and you may wonder why the bank bothered to contact you. Is it the same? Should you shift your savings to the new bank? To answer these questions, we

FIGURE 4-1
Future Value Calculated with and without Compounding (r = 10%)

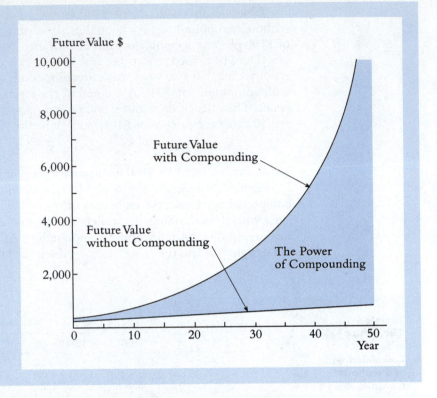

need to calculate the effective annual interest rate. In this case the FV of your deposit will be as follows:

Interest on the principal for the first six months (5% × $100) =	$ 5.00
Interest on the principal for the second six months (5% × $100) =	5.00
Interest on the interest received in the first six months (5% × $5) =	0.25
Principal	$100.00
Total FV	$110.25

By the end of the year, your $100 deposit will grow to $110.25; the $10.25 paid in interest represents, in effect, an annual interest rate of 10.25%. Paying interest more than once a year thus produces an **effective annual interest rate** that differs from the **declared annual interest rate.** In our example, the bank's declared annual interest rate is 10%, but its effective annual interest rate is $(1.05)^2 - 1 = 0.1025$, or 10.25%.

Suppose Bank A offers you an annual interest rate of 10% payable semiannually. Bank B offers an annual rate of 9.96% payable at 2.49% quarterly. To decide where to deposit your money, you will have to calculate the effective annual interest rate.

With Bank A's semiannual compounding, the effective annual interest rate is

$$(1.05) \times (1.05) - 1 = 0.1025 \text{ or } 10.25\%$$

With Bank B's quarterly compounding, it is

$$(1.0249)^4 - 1 \cong 0.10338 \text{ or } 10.338\%$$

Though it might seem that Bank B pays less, it *effectively* pays more.

You can compute the effective annual interest rate by using a calculator or by referring to the PV and FV tables (Tables A-1 through A-5 at the end of the book). For example, to find the FV of $100 deposited in the bank for one year at 10% annual interest paid semiannually, look in the FV table (Table A-1) at $r = 5\%$ and $T = 2$ to obtain FVF = 1.1025. The effective annual interest rate is 10.25%. If a 20% annual interest rate is paid quarterly, look at $r = 5\%$ and $T = 4$ to obtain FVF = 1.2155, for an effective annual interest rate of 21.55%. For elaboration on the relationship between the declared and effective interest rates, and for more details on such calculations, see Appendix 4A.

4.4.4 The Present Value of an Annuity

A series of equal cash flows for a given number of years is called an **annuity.** If the annuity is for an unlimited period (without an end), it is called a **perpetuity.**

How do we calculate the PV of an annuity? Suppose you receive $1 at the end of each year for the next five years. What is the PV of these cash flows? We can find the PV of each payment in Table A-2 and total them, as follows:

Year 1: $DF_{10\%, 1} \times \$1 = 0.9091 \times \$1 = \$0.9091$

Year 2: $DF_{10\%, 2} \times \$1 = 0.8264 \times \$1 = \$0.8264$

Year 3: $DF_{10\%, 3} \times \$1 = 0.7513 \times \$1 = \$0.7513$

Year 4: $DF_{10\%, 4} \times \$1 = 0.6830 \times \$1 = \$0.6830$

Year 5: $DF_{10\%, 5} \times \$1 = 0.6209 \times \$1 = \$0.6209$

Total $\underline{\$3.7907}$

where $DF_{10\%, T}$ is the discount factor corresponding to the 10% discount rate and to year T (as in Table A-2).

But what if you receive $1 in each of the next 20 years? Or 40 years? The calculation would be extremely cumbersome. Fortunately, we can use tables that show the discount factors for annuities. Table A-3 (at the back of the book) gives the PV of a $1 annuity for T years discounted at various interest rates. The figures in Table A-3 are obtained from the figures in Table A-2. To illustrate, let us look at corresponding portions of Tables A-2 and A-3: the discount factors from Table A-2 ($DF_{r\%, T}$) and the discount annuity factors ($DAF_{r\%, T}$) from Table A-3.

Year	10% Interest Rate	
	Discount Factor	Discount Annuity Factor
1	0.9091	0.9091
2	0.8264	1.7355
3	0.7513	2.4869
4	0.6830	3.1699
5	0.6209	3.7908

Note that for $T = 1$, the discount factor is the same as the discount annuity factor. For $T = 2$, the discount annuity factor is the sum of the first two discount factors, as follows:

$$0.9091 + 0.8264 = 1.7355$$

It makes sense. Table A–3 gives us the PV of an annuity, which in the case of $T = 2$ would be

$$\text{PV} = \frac{\$1}{1.1} + \frac{\$1}{(1.1)^2} = \$1 \times \left[\frac{1}{1.1} + \frac{1}{(1.1)^2} \right]$$

$$\cong \$1 \times (0.9091 + 0.8264)$$

$$= \$1 \times (1.7355) = \$1.7355$$

Each discount annuity factor in the right-hand column corresponds to a sum of discount factors from the middle column. For example, for five years at 10% interest, the 3.7908 discount annuity factor is the sum of the five discount factors corresponding to Years 1, 2, 3, 4, and 5. When we total those five figures, we obtain 3.7908. Although the PV of an annuity can be calculated from Table A–2, it is much simpler to use Table A–3 because fewer calculations are required. Of course, if the annuity is $\$C$, rather than $\$1$, we simply multiply the figure in Table A–3 by C. We denote the **discount annuity factors** that appear in Table A–3 by $\text{DAF}_{r\%, T}$, where $r\%$ is the discount rate, T is the number of years, and A stands for "annuity."

The following problem demonstrates that the results from using either Table A–2 or Table A–3 are the same.

PRACTICE BOX

Problem   Suppose you are to receive $1,000 at the end of each of the next three years. Use Tables A–2 and A–3 to calculate the PV at 10% interest. Do you get the same results?

Solution   From Table A–2, we get

$$\text{PV} = (\$1,000 \times 0.9091) + (\$1,000 \times 0.8264) + (\$1,000 \times 0.7513)$$

$$\cong \$909.10 + \$826.40 + \$751.30 = \$2,486.80$$

Using Table A–3, we get

$$\text{PV} = \$1,000 \times \text{DAF}_{10\%, 3}$$

$$= \$1,000 \times 2.4869 = \$2,486.90$$

Thus, we get the same results from using either Table A–2 or Table A–3. (The slight difference is due to rounding of the figures in the tables.)

4.5 THE EQUATIONS

Some financial transactions involved cash flows for 1 year (annuities) and some for an infinite number of years (perpetuities). Some transactions have constant cash flows and some have growing annual cash flows.

Financial managers use several formulas to determine present and future values of annuities and perpetuities with constant or growing annual cash flows. This section discusses and demonstrates some of these equations.

4.5.1 The PV of a Perpetuity

The British government issues bonds, called **consols,** that provide bondholders an endless cash flow stream of £C every year. (£ denotes British pounds sterling; £C is the annual interest that the bondholder receives.) What is the PV of this endless constant annual cash flow? In this case we cannot use Table A–2 because we would have to add an infinite series of figures. We need an equation to calculate the PV of a perpetuity. The present value of a perpetuity of £C (or $\$C$ for that matter) at $r\%$ annual interest is as follows:

$$PV = \frac{C}{1 + r} + \frac{C}{(1 + r)^2} + \frac{C}{(1 + r)^3} + \dots$$

with the dots denoting an endless stream of cash flows. A little algebra shows that the PV can be expressed as[1]

$$PV = \frac{C}{r} \qquad (4.6)$$

The following problem demonstrates how to calculate the interest rate on a perpetuity.

1.

(i) $PV = \dfrac{C}{1 + r} + \dfrac{C}{(1 + r)^2} + \dfrac{C}{(1 + r)^3} + \dots$

Multiplying both sides of this equation by $1/(1 + r)$ we obtain

(ii) $\dfrac{PV}{1 + r} = \dfrac{C}{(1 + r)^2} + \dfrac{C}{(1 + r)^3} + \dfrac{C}{(1 + r)^4} + \dots$

Subtracting equation (ii) from equation (i), we obtain

$$PV - \frac{PV}{(1 + r)} = \frac{C}{(1 + r)}$$

(All other terms on the right-hand side cancel.)
Multiplying all terms by $(1 + r)$, we obtain

$$PV(1 + r) - PV = C$$

and, finally,

$$PV = \frac{C}{r}$$

PRACTICE BOX

Problem

A perpetuity pays $10 a year. The PV of the perpetuity is $200. Calculate the interest rate on this investment.

Solution

Since we are dealing with a perpetuity, we use the following equation:

$$PV = \frac{C}{r}$$

If PV = $200 and C = $10, then

$$\$200 = \frac{\$10}{r}$$

$$r = \frac{\$10}{\$200}$$

$$= 0.05 \text{ or } 5\%$$

4.5.2 The PV and FV of an Annuity

Suppose you own an annuity yielding $$C$ a year for T years. What would its PV be? Of course, you could use Table A-3 to figure the PV. However, an equation provides a shortcut to calculate directly the figures appearing in Table A-3 (without totaling the figures given in Table A-2).

The PV of an annuity is given by the following equation:

$$PV = \frac{C}{1+r} + \frac{C}{(1+r)^2} + \dots \frac{C}{(1+r)^T} = C\left[\frac{1}{r} - \frac{1}{r(1+r)^T}\right] \quad (4.7)$$

where the term in the square brackets is the $DAF_{r\%, T}$.

To see that Equation 4.7 is valid, consider the following three cash flows:

Time Line	1	2	. . .	T	$T+1$	$T+2$ . . .
(a) Perpetuity	C	C	. . .	C	C	C . . .
(b) Perpetual annuity starting at year $T+1$ (you get C from year $T+1$ forward)	0	0	. . .	0	C	C . . .
(c) Annuity for T-years	C	C	. . .	C	0	0 . . .

Cash flow (c) is cash flow (a) minus cash flow (b). Therefore, if we know how to calculate PV(a) and PV(b), we can find PV(c):

$$PV(c) = PV(a) - PV(b)$$

Since cash flow (a) is a perpetuity, we have

$$PV(a) = \frac{C}{r}$$

Cash flow (b) is also a perpetuity that starts at year $T + 1$. Therefore, its value in terms of year T dollars will be C/r, and its PV (in terms of the beginning of the first year, $T = 0$ dollars) will be

$$PV(b) = \frac{C}{r} \times \frac{1}{(1 + r)^T}$$

Subtracting PV(b) from PV(a), we obtain the present value of an annuity for T years:

$$PV(c) = \frac{C}{r} - \left[\frac{C}{r} \times \frac{1}{(1 + r)^T} \right] = C \left[\frac{1}{r} - \frac{1}{r(1 + r)^T} \right]$$

We have thus proved that Equation 4.7 is valid for the calculation of the PV of an annuity.

The relationship between PV and FV is given by Equation 4.4:

$$FV = PV(1 + r)^T$$

Therefore, the FV of an annuity is

$$FV = C \left[\frac{1}{r} - \frac{1}{r(1 + r)^T} \right] \times (1 + r)^T = C \left[\frac{(1 + r)^T}{r} - \frac{1}{r} \right] \qquad (4.7a)$$

Using this equation, we are now able to answer the question posed at the beginning of this chapter: Will the Westbrooks' savings (see Corporate Finance in the News) be sufficient for their firstborn's college education? Their savings of $2,500 per year for 20 years at 8% interest will provide a future value of

$$FV = \$2,500 \left[\frac{(1.08)^{20}}{0.08} - \frac{1}{0.08} \right] \cong \$114,405$$

which will be sufficient for a public university education.

The following problem demonstrates how to use Table A–3 and Equation 4.7 to calculate the PV and FV of an annuity.

PRACTICE BOX

Problem

You receive $100 annually for 10 years. The discount rate is 10%. Use Table A–3 and Equation 4.7 to calculate the PV of this annuity. What is the FV of this annuity?

Solution

First Method:
From Table A–3, we obtain

$$PV = DAF_{10\%,\ 10} \times \$100 = 6.1446 \times \$100 = \$614.46$$

(continued)

where 6.1446 is the discount factor corresponding to 10 years and 10% interest (see Table A–3).

Second Method:
Using Equation 4.7, we have

$$PV = \$100 \left[\frac{1}{0.10} - \frac{1}{0.10 \times (1 + 0.10)^{10}} \right] \cong \$1,000 - [\$1,000 \times 0.38554]$$

where

$$\frac{1}{(1.10)^{10}} = 0.38554$$

Thus

$$PV = \$1,000 - \$385.54 = \$614.46$$

Both methods yield the same PV.
The FV of the annuity is

$$FV = \$614.46 \times (1.1)^{10} \cong \$1,593.75$$

4.5.3 Regular Annuity and Annuity Due

When an annuity's cash payments are made at the end of each period, we have a **regular annuity;** when the cash payments are made at the beginning of each period, we have an **annuity due.** The number of payments is the same in both cases; only the timing of the payments differs.

The difference between these two types of annuity is illustrated in the following chart, where C is the annual cash flow, 0 is the beginning of the first year, 1 is the end of the first year, 2 is the end of the second year, and so on:

Time Line (end of year)	0	1	2	3 ...	$T-1$	T
Regular Annuity	0	C	C	C ...	C	C
Annuity Due	C	C	C	C ...	C	0

In comparing an annuity due to a regular annuity, we see that both have the same cash flows except at dates 0 and T. Thus, we have the following relationship:

$$PV_{AD} = PV_{RA} + C - \frac{C}{(1 + r)^T}$$

where the subscripts AD and RA stand for "annuity due" and "regular annuity," respectively. The last two terms are the PVs of the two cash flows that distinguish between the two types of annuity.

If your calculator or spreadsheet sheet isn't handy, you can always solve future-value and present-value problems by using one of the many time-value calculators available on the Internet. Many also supply colorful graphs of your calculations.
http://www.mount-baker.com/value.html

Thus, if Bank A offered you a loan with annuity due, and Bank B offered an otherwise identical loan with regular annuity, you would prefer to borrow from B because the PV of your payments would be smaller.

Using Equation 4.7 for the regular annuity, we obtain the following relationship:

$$\text{PV}_{AD} = \frac{C}{r}\left[1 - \frac{1}{(1 + r)^T}\right] + C - \frac{C}{(1 + r)^T} = (1 + r)\frac{C}{r}\left[1 - \frac{1}{(1 + r)^T}\right]$$

(To see this, multiply and divide the last two terms on the left hand side by r.)

This relationship can be rewritten (see Equation 4.7) as

$$\text{PV}_{AD} = \text{PV}_{RA}\,(1 + r) \tag{4.8}$$

4.5.4 The PV of a Growing Perpetuity

Suppose you have an endless series of annual cash flows starting at $\$C$ at the end of Year 1 and growing every year by $g\%$. Such a cash flow is a **growing perpetuity,** and its PV is given by the following equation, where the dots represent an endless cash flow stream:

$$\text{PV} = \frac{C}{1 + r} + \frac{C(1 + g)}{(1 + r)^2} + \frac{C(1 + g)^2}{(1 + r)^3} + \cdots$$

This equation can be simplified to[2]

$$\text{PV} = \frac{C}{r - g} \tag{4.9}$$

The following problem demonstrates how to calculate the present value of a growing perpetuity involving dividends.

2. We derive this equation as follows:

$$(\text{i}) \quad \text{PV} = \frac{C}{1 + r} + \frac{C(1 + g)}{(1 + r)^2} + \frac{C(1 + g)^2}{(1 + r)^3} + \cdots$$

Multiplying both sides of this equation by $\dfrac{(1 + g)}{(1 + r)}$, we obtain

$$(\text{ii}) \quad \text{PV} \times \left[\frac{1 + g}{1 + r}\right] = \frac{C(1 + g)}{(1 + r)^2} + \frac{C(1 + g)^2}{(1 + r)^3} + \cdots$$

Subtracting equation (ii) from equation (i), we get

$$(\text{iii}) \quad \text{PV} - \text{PV} \times \left[\frac{1 + g}{1 + r}\right] = \frac{C}{1 + r}$$

(All other terms on the right-hand side cancel.)

Equation (iii) can then be rewritten as

$$\text{PV} \times (r - g) = C$$

or

$$\text{PV} = \frac{C}{r - g}$$

PRACTICE BOX

Problem
A stock will pay a dividend of $4 next year. The dividends will grow at 5% a year forever. If the discount rate, r, is 10%, what is the PV of all future dividends?

Solution
We use the formula for the PV of a growing perpetuity (Equation 4.9):

$$PV = \frac{C}{r - g}$$

Given $C = \$4$, $r = 0.10$, and $g = 0.05$, we get

$$PV = \frac{\$4}{0.10 - 0.05} = \$80$$

The PV of the future dividends is $80.

When the market is in equilibrium, the price of a stock P_0 is equal to the PV of the future dividends. If the future dividends are discounted at the risk-adjusted discount rate, k, Equation 4.8 becomes

$$P_0 = \frac{d_1}{k - g} \tag{4.9a}$$

where d_1 is the first year's dividend. This equation is called the *dividend growth model*. We will discuss this model in Chapters 10 and 12.

4.5.5 The PV and FV of a Growing Annuity

A cash flow may grow for several years, but it may not grow forever. For example, suppose a firm discovers a new product and reasonably assumes that its earnings will grow every year at $g\%$ for a finite number of years. However, the firm realizes this growth will not continue indefinitely. A new, improved product will eventually push the old "new product" out of the market. Or, to take another example, consider the case of a successful 25-year-old professional athlete whose remuneration takes the form of a **growing annuity**—one in which the annual payments increase from year to year. However, after a certain number of years (say, 10), his or her athletic career will probably end, as will the income from playing professional sports.

Calculating the PV and FV of such a growing annuity seems complicated. Fortunately, an equation makes the calculation less complex. When you have a growing cash flow for T years, with the first cash flow C paid at the end of Year 1, the PV is as follows:

$$PV = \frac{C}{1 + r} + \frac{C(1 + g)}{(1 + r)^2} + \ldots + \frac{C(1 + g)^{T-1}}{(1 + r)^T}$$

or

$$PV = C\left[\frac{1}{r-g} - \frac{1}{r-g} \times \frac{(1+g)^T}{(1+r)^T}\right] \qquad (4.10)$$

The FV of the growing annuity is given by multiplying Equation 4.10 by $(1+r)^T$:

$$FV = C\left[\frac{(1+r)^T}{r-g} - \frac{(1+g)^T}{(r-g)}\right] \qquad (4.10a)$$

If the growth rate is zero ($g = 0$), Equations 4.10 and 4.10a reduce to Equations 4.7 and 4.7a.

The following problem compares the present value of a growing annuity to that of a lump sum cash payment.

PRACTICE BOX

Problem   Remember our basketball player Charles Tuck? Suppose he now receives the following two offers:

1. Ten annual payments starting at $1 million and growing at 5% a year. The first payment is made one year from now (at $T = 1$).
2. A lump sum of $7 million to be paid immediately.

The interest rate is 10%. Which offer should he choose?

Solution   Charles should choose the option with the higher PV. Using Equation 4.10, we find that the PV of the growing annuity (Offer 1), where $T = 10$, is

$$PV = \$1,000,000 \times \left[\frac{1}{0.1 - 0.05} - \left(\frac{1}{0.1 - 0.05} \times \frac{(1.05)^{10}}{(1.1)^{10}}\right)\right]$$

$$= \$1,000,000 \times (20 - 20 \times 0.628) \text{ [where } (1.05)^{10}/(1.1)^{10} \cong 0.628]$$

$$= \$1,000,000 \times (20 - 12.56) = \$7.44 \text{ million}$$

The PV of the growing annuity is higher than the $7 million in cash today. The growing annuity is the better option.

4.6 A NOTE ON RISK

In the preceding problem and in most of the previous calculations in this chapter, we have assumed that all cash flows are certain—that is, that they are *riskless*. However,

Charles Tuck may worry about the possibility of the basketball team's losing money or even going bankrupt. As a result, he may consider the future cash flows to be uncertain.

In view of such risk, Charles should discount these average cash flows at a *higher discount rate* to include a risk premium. For instance, he might use a discount rate of 15%. In that case, which of the two options in the preceding problem would Charles prefer? He would prefer to receive the $7 million in cash today because the PV of the growing annuity discounted at $k = 15\%$ is

$$PV = \$1,000,000 \times \left[\frac{1}{0.15 - 0.05} - \left(\frac{1}{0.15 - 0.05} \times \frac{(1.05)^{10}}{(1.15)^{10}} \right) \right]$$

$$\cong \$1,000,000 \times (10 - 10 \times 0.403) = \$5.97 \text{ million}$$

Now that we are familiar with PV and FV concepts and the formulas for calculating various types of cash flow, we can analyze real-life financial transactions. As you will see, it is sometimes difficult to know which of these many equations to use. When we move from textbook to real-life cases, rather than mechanically applying one equation or another, we need to exercise creative insight.

APPLYING THEORY TO PRACTICE 4.1

THE $67 MILLION IVAX BUYOUT

Johnson Products Co., the hair products pioneer, sent a shudder through the [personal-care] industry by agreeing to be acquired by a publicly held company. Ivax Corp., a Miami holding company, proposed acquiring it [Johnson Products] for about $67 million in stock. Johnson shares soared $5.625 [per share], or 30%, on the American Stock Exchange, closing at $24.625; common shares of Ivax, also an Amex-listed stock, closed unchanged at $25.25.

Most of the two dozen or so major players in the personal-care industry, many of whom need additional capital and marketing capabilities, have viewed consolidation as inevitable. Still, the potential for fierce competition from the bigger mainstream companies has remained a major concern.

Johnson's Results on the Rise

The company's results have improved steadily since fiscal 1988, when it lost $2.5 million on slipping sales. In the year ended Aug. 31, Johnson Products earned $3.4 million, or $2.86 a share on sales of $42.9 million.

The agreement with Ivax calls for Mrs. Johnson to remain as chief executive. Each share of Johnson Products common stock will be converted to the right to receive one Ivax common share.

In a prepared statement, Phillip Frost, Ivax chairman and chief executive officer, called the merger "complementary to several of the businesses Ivax is pursuing."

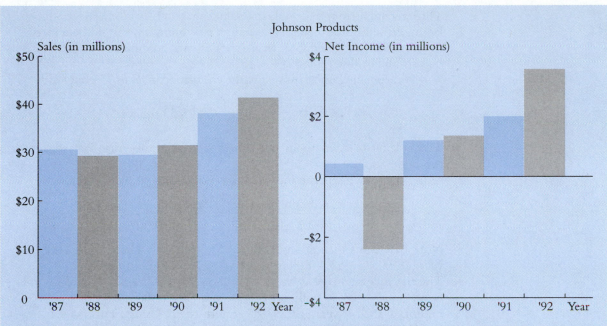

Johnson Products

Source: Brett Pulley, "Johnson Products Agrees to $67 Million Ivax Buyout," *Wall Street Journal*, 15 June 1993, sec. B, p. 2. Reprinted by permission of *The Wall Street Journal*, © 1993 Dow Jones & Company, Inc. All rights reserved worldwide.

Questions

1. Suppose the $3.4 million annual income is a perpetuity. What is the PV of Johnson Products' future incomes calculated at a riskless 7% discount rate?
2. What is the present value of the acquired firm if we add to the riskless interest rate a 5% risk premium?
3. Now assume the income stream is a growing perpetuity beginning at $3.4 million and growing at 8% annually. The discount rate is $k = 12\%$.[3] What is the present value of this perpetuity?
4. The graph in the article shows an income growth rate much greater than 8%. How would your answer to (3) change if the growth rate was 10% for 10 years and 0% thereafter?

MAKING THE CONNECTION

1. Applying the perpetuity formula (Equation 4.6), we obtain the PV of all future earnings:

$$\text{PV} = \frac{C}{r} = \frac{\$3.4 \text{ million}}{0.07} \cong \$48.57 \text{ million}$$

3. A discount rate of 12% is approximately equivalent to the long-term discount rate on U.S. stocks. The discount rate applied to uncertain (or risky) cash flows is called the *cost of capital,* denoted *k*. The larger the risk, the larger the cost of capital. The difference between the cost of capital and the risk-free interest rate is the risk premium. This relationship—cost of capital/risk-free interest rate—is discussed in Chapter 10.

Thus, according to this formula it would seem that Ivax is offering too much.

2. Because the cash flows are uncertain, a risk premium should be added to the discount rate. Therefore, with a modest risk premium of 5%, the earnings should be discounted at $k = 12\%$ (7% + 5%).

Incorporating uncertainty into the calculation gives us an even lower PV:

$$PV = \frac{\$3.4 \text{ million}}{0.12} \cong \$28.33 \text{ million}$$

The risk factor strengthens our previous conclusion—that Ivax's offer is too high.

3. Using the growing perpetuity formula (Equation 4.9), we obtain

$$PV = \frac{C}{k - g} = \frac{\$3.4 \text{ million} \times 1.08}{0.12 - 0.08} = \frac{\$3.672 \text{ million}}{0.04} = \$91.8 \text{ million}$$

Note that Ivax's income in 1992 was $3.4 million. Therefore, in the first year (1993): $C = \$3.4$ million $\times (1.08) = \$3.672$ million.

4. The net income in 1992 was $3.4 million. Therefore, it will be $3.4 million $\times (1.1) = \$3.74$ million in 1993, and $3.4 million $\times (1.1)^{10} \cong \$8.82$ million in the last year of the 10% growth trend. Using Equation 4.10, we find that the PV of these 10 years of income is

$$PV = \$3.74 \text{ million} \left[\frac{1}{0.12 - 0.10} - \frac{1}{0.12 - 0.10} \times \frac{(1.1)^{10}}{(1.12)^{10}} \right]$$

$$= \$3.74 \text{ million} \times [50 - 50 \times 0.8351]$$

$$= \$3.74 \text{ million} \times 8.245$$

$$= \$30.84 \text{ million}$$

All other cash flows obtained from Year 11 on can be totaled by using the perpetuity formula (Equation 4.6).

Accordingly, the PV in terms of Year-10 dollars is

$$\frac{\$8.82 \text{ million}}{0.12} = \$73.50 \text{ million}$$

and the PV in current dollars is

$$\frac{\$73.50 \text{ million}}{(1.12)^{10}} \cong \$23.67 \text{ million}$$

The sum of these two components gives the PV of Johnson Products' cash flow:

$$PV = \$30.84 \text{ million} + \$23.67 \text{ million} = \$54.51 \text{ million}$$

which is less than what Ivax offered.

Ivax's management and its financial advisers were probably familiar with the equations given in this chapter. Nevertheless, they were willing to pay $67 million for Johnson Products. We must conclude that they were better informed than we are and that their growth estimate was higher than ours. Obviously, if Ivax estimated that the 10% growth would continue for a longer time, say 15 years, or that the growth rate would be more than 10%, the PV of the cash flows would be larger.

Epilogue

In the ocean, a small fish that grows fat becomes a candidate to be a tasty meal for a bigger fish. So, too, Ivax, whose share price was 61\frac{1}{16}$ in August 1997, became part of the food chain, as can be seen from the following article.

Could Ivax Get Swallowed?

Insider buying heating up. And takeover whispers getting louder. All that action is fueling a resurgence in the stock of Ivax (IVX), the nation's largest generic drugmaker, making the shares leap from 24 to 29 in recent weeks. What's going on . . . .

Ivax has been talked about as a takeover target all year but it now is starting to appear much closer to doing an actual merger deal, says one investment banker.

Analysts estimate the drugmaker's value at 40 a share on fundamentals alone, based on the company's projected 1996 earnings.

Source: Gene Marshall, "Could IVAX Get Swallowed?" *Business Week,* 2 October 1995, p. 102. Reprinted from October 2, 1995 issue of *Business Week* by special permission, copyright © 1993 by the McGraw-Hill Companies.

We included the Ivax case as a means to apply the various equations studied in this chapter to a real financial transaction. The goal was not to calculate Johnson Products' precise value but, rather, to show what factors should be considered when calculating the PV of cash flows and how to match the various assumptions on growth in earnings with the appropriate equations. More calculations related to the Ivax case are given in the Review and Practice section (Problems 4.20 and 4.21).

SUMMARY

We can compare projects with different cash flow characteristics only if we can establish a "common denominator"—the value of a given dollar amount measured at a specific time. That specific time may be the present, some date in the future, or any other agreed-upon time. With the common denominator established, we can calculate either the present value or the future value of the project's cash flow.

When cash flows are certain, the PV and FV calculations use the riskless interest rate, r, as the discount rate. When cash flows are uncertain, the same techniques and calculations apply. However, a higher discount rate, k, should be used to compensate for the additional risk.

Interest can be calculated with and without compounding. The "power of compounding" becomes evident when the gap between the principal plus interest received with and without compounding increases dramatically over time.

The present and future values of the various cash flows (annuities and perpetuities, with and without growth) can be calculated by using either tables or formulas. The tables and equations provided in the chapter allow us to calculate the following values:

- Future value T years from now of $1 received today
- Present value of $1 received in year T
- Present value of an annuity ($1 received every year for T years)
- Present value of a perpetuity ($1 received every year for an endless number of years)
- Present and future values of a growing perpetuity (an endless stream of cash flows growing each year by $g\%$)
- Present and future values of a growing annuity (a cash flow growing by $g\%$ for a finite number of years)

CHAPTER AT A GLANCE

1. The relationship between FV and PV:

$$FV = PV(1 + r)^T$$

where r is the interest rate and T is the date (year) for which the FV is calculated

2. The PV of a perpetuity:

$$PV = \frac{C}{r}$$

where each cash flow C is received at the end of the corresponding year.

3. The PV and FV values of a regular annuity:

$$PV = \frac{C}{r} - \left[\frac{C}{r} \times \frac{1}{(1 + r)^T}\right]$$

$$FV = C\left[\frac{(1 + r)^T}{r} - \frac{1}{r}\right]$$

where T is the number of equal cash flows, and C is obtained at the end of the corresponding year.

4. The relationship between the PV of a regular annuity (PV_{RA}) and an annuity due (PV_{AD}):

$$PV_{AD} = PV_{RA}(1 + r)$$

where in an annuity due (AD), the cash flows are obtained at the beginning of the corresponding year.

5. The PV of a growing perpetuity:

$$PV = \frac{C}{r - g}$$

where g is the growth rate and $g < r$

6. The PV and FV of a growing annuity:

$$PV = C\left[\frac{1}{r-g} - \frac{1}{r-g} \times \frac{(1+g)^T}{(1+r)^T}\right]$$

$$FV = C\left[\frac{(1+r)^T}{r-g} - \frac{(1+g)^T}{r-g}\right]$$

where T is the number of cash flows

KEY TERMS

Future value (FV)

Present value (PV)

Compound interest

Discounting

Discount rate

Future value factor (FVF)

Discount factor (DF)

Effective annual interest rate

Declared annual interest rate

Annuity

Perpetuity

Discount annuity factors

Consols

Regular annuity

Annuity due

Growing perpetuity

Growing annuity

REVIEW AND PRACTICE

4.1 What is the future value 10 years from now of $1 invested today at an interest rate of 5%?

4.2 Under what conditions will the future value of a series of cash flows be equal to its present value?

4.3 A car dealer can sell a car for $20,000 on one year's credit; that is, the customer pays the $20,000 one year from today. The interest rate is 10%.
a. What should the car's price be in a cash sale if the PV of the credit sale is equal to that of the cash sale?
b. Now assume a credit customer will likely declare bankruptcy or, even worse, leave the country. Would you increase or decrease the car's minimum cash price? Explain.

4.4 You have $10,000 in hand. You are due to receive $5,000 one year from today, and you have no other future income. The annual interest rate is 10%.
a. What is the maximum amount you can spend now?

b. What is the maximum amount you can spend one year from today?

4.5 Would you prefer $10,000 now or $12,000 five years from now? The interest rate is 8%. Does the fact that you need money now or, alternatively, five years from now affect your answer? Explain.

4.6 You have $1,000 now. You know that the FV of this sum will be $1,210 two years from now.
a. What is the annual interest rate?
b. How would your answer change if the $1,210 FV corresponded to four years from now?

4.7 You discover a 100-year bond in your grandfather's bureau. The bond has a face value of $100, and the U.S. Government issued it 100 years ago at 5% annual interest. The principal ($100) and the interest are to be paid at maturity. Assume the annual interest is reinvested at the 5% rate. Suppose you can legally claim payment on the bond. How much would you receive?

4.8 Explain "the power of compounding."

4.9 Consider the following two alternative series cash flows:

Time (Year)	0	1	2	3
Series A	$100	$200	$300	$400
Series B	$250	$250	$250	$250

The interest rate is 10%. Future values are calculated as of the end of the third year.
a. Which series has the higher future value?
b. Which series has the higher present value?
c. Suppose you would now like to compare the value of these cash flows series in terms of dollars at time 1. Which has the higher value? Compare and analyze your results.

4.10 How would your answers to Problem 4.9 change if the interest rate were 1%?

4.11 You deposit $1,000 in the bank for three years at an annual interest rate of 10%. What is the FV of your deposit at the end of the third year calculated with and without compounding? Show the details of your calculations by isolating the "interest on interest" component.

4.12 Gigantica Bank offers you an annual interest rate of 12% without compounding (after two years you get 24% interest), and El Grande Bank offers you 10% interest compounded annually (after two years you get $1.10^2 - 1 = 0.21$, or 21% interest). You want to deposit $10,000 for 10 years. Which bank would you prefer? Would your answer change if you had $1 million to invest?

4.13 Firm ABC sells a machine for $500,000 in cash or for $200,000 in cash plus $350,000 on one year's credit. The risk-free interest rate is 5%. However, because the cash flow from credit sales is risky, the firm's management decides to discount this future cash flow at a higher rate than the risk-free interest rate, such that the PV of the cash flows under the two possible terms of sale will be identical.

a. What discount rate does ABC use?
b. Explain the discount rate ABC uses, given the riskless discount rate of 5%.

4.14 The discount annuity factor (DAF) in Table A–3 for $T = 5$ and $r = 10\%$ is 3.7908. How is this figure related to the series that appears in Table A–2? Show your calculation.

4.15 What is the present value of an annuity where $C = \$1,000$, $T = 50$ years, and $r = 10\%$? What would the PV of this annuity be if the interest rate were zero?

4.16 The PV of an annuity for $T = 10$ years is $100,000. The interest rate, r, is 10%. What is the annual cash flow?

4.17 A client explains this situation: "Our son is 18. We want to make sure he will have $10,000 a year at the end of each of the next three years. We want to deposit money in the bank today such that it will provide him with this *regular annuity* for three years, with the first $10,000 to be withdrawn one year from now and the bank balance to be zero after the three $10,000 withdrawals."
a. How much should your client deposit if the interest rate is 10%?
b. How much should your client deposit if it is an *annuity due*?

4.18 A stock pays a dividend of $1 per share one year from today. Thereafter, the dividend grows at 3% a year forever. The discount rate is 5%.
a. What is the PV of the dividend cash flows?
b. How would your answer change if the dividends were uncertain and the appropriate discount rate were 8% (5% risk-free plus 3% risk premium)?

4.19 A 20-year-old basketball player has a contract for 10 years with annual payments. He receives $1 million in the first year of his contract (paid at the end of the year). The annual payments will grow by 20% a year for the next 10 years. After age 30, his income from basketball will be zero.
a. What is the PV of this growing annuity? (Assume a discount rate $r = 5\%$.)

b. Suppose the athlete wants to consume $200,000 a year. He deposits the rest in the bank at $r = 5\%$. He plans to play professionally for 10 years and then to open a small business that will require an initial investment of $10 million. Will he have enough funds? (*Hint:* Use the growing annuity equation and the relationship between PV and FV.)

4.20 Reread the Ivax buyout case in Applying Theory to Practice 4.1. Suppose now that Ivax assumes a growing annuity for 20 years with a 10% growth rate. After that, the cash flow remains constant forever at $3.4 \times (1.1)^{20}$ million. All other financial data and assumptions are the same. What is the value of Johnson Products?

4.21 Repeat Problem 4.20, assuming a growing annuity for 20 years. After that time, however, Johnson goes bankrupt and receives zero cash flows.

4.22 Which would you prefer, an annuity of $100 for $T = 10$ years or a perpetuity of $50? The discount rate is 10%.

4.23 What is the PV (at Year 0) and the FV (at the end of the fourth year) of the following series of uneven, certain cash flows?

Year	0	1	2	3	4
Cash Flow	$0	$5,000	−$2,000	$1,000	$10,000

Assume a discount rate of $r = 10\%$.

4.24 Repeat Problem 4.23, but assume that the cash flows change to $1,000 in Year 2 and to −$2,000 in Year 3. The cash flows in Years 1 and 4 remain the same. Does the PV increase? Does the FV increase? Explain your results.

4.25 Use the cash flow of Problem 4.23 again. At the beginning of Years 1, 2, and 3, you can lend or deposit money in the bank at $r = 10\%$. At the beginning of Year 4, you can deposit money in the bank at $r = 5\%$. Calculate the PV and FV of these cash flows. Explain your results.

4.26 The following realtor's advertisement, which appeared in December 1993, suggests that home-owners who have mortgages should repay their mortgages and replace them with new ones at lower interest rates. This procedure is called *refinancing*. Moreover, the ad suggests that homeowners should sell their houses and buy newer, bigger ones to take advantage of the lower interest rates.

a. Calculate the monthly payments on the 30-year 10% mortgage and the 30-year 7% mortgage. Are the payments presented in the advertisement correct?
b. Suppose refinancing involves a fixed cost of $10,000. Would you refinance? Assume the appropriate discount rate is 10%.

4.27 Saving $3,000 monthly accumulates to $5 million after 20 years. What is the assumed interest rate?

4.28 Suppose you've just won the lottery—$40,000 annually for 25 years. Visit Stonestreet's Web site and see what each dollar of your winnings will be worth in 15 years. Check their calculations based on what you have learned in this chapter. If you won the lottery, what discount rate would you use to determine the present value of your payout? Why?

http://www.stonestreet.com

YOUR TURN: APPLYING THEORY TO PRACTICE

STUDENT LOANS

The following article provides an excellent opportunity to practice what we have just learned in this chapter. It explains various ways to ease the burden of your student loan repayments. We will analyze the effect of each of the various payment options on the PV of loan payments.

AS GRADS START TO REPAY STUDENT LOANS, HERE'S A PRIMER ON WAYS TO EASE BURDEN

Imagine racking up $15,000 or $20,000 of debt before you even have your first job.

Welcome to the world of new college graduates who took out student loans to finance their education. For some, the tab can be a whole lot higher: as much as $50,000 for those graduating from law or business school and $100,000 for those just out of medical school.

Now with degrees in hand, they have to start paying it all back. And in today's weak economy, many of this spring's graduates are finding that they either don't have a job or aren't making nearly enough to do that.

But while the prospects can seem bleak, there are a variety of ways to get student loans deferred, forgiven, restructured, refinanced or consolidated.

It's not just new grads who can benefit, either. People who still owe money on a school loan, which typically runs for 10 years, can get at least a little financial breathing room if they need it.

"Unlike mortgages, which never have cancellation or deferment options, student loans ac-commodate the needs of people," says Betsy Hicks, coordinator of financial aid for Harvard University.

If you don't have a job, but are actively looking, you may be eligible for a deferment. That means you not only don't have to pay right away, but in some cases the interest meter will be turned off for a while. The government grants deferments on its loans for about a dozen reasons, including returning to school, being pregnant if recently out of school, being temporarily disabled, or serving in the military.

People who can't make ends meet but don't qualify for a deferment may be able to get a forbearance. That suspends principal payments, although interest continues to accrue. Some borrowers can actually get certain loans forgiven if they meet specific conditions, such as teaching in a particular area or going into the military.

Loan Flexibility

For some loans, there's a six-month grace period after graduation before student loan repayments begin. But advisers say it's best to contact your lender as soon as you realize there might be trouble. That's because lenders have a lot of flexibility as long as they are convinced that the borrower intends to pay.

In addition to deferments and forbearances, for example, lenders also offer the option of graduated repayment, featuring low monthly payments that gradually increase. While a $5,000 loan at 8% would normally carry a monthly payment of $60.67, a new graduate opting for graduated repayment would pay only $35.50 a month at first and end up with a final payment of $101.92 after 10 years.

One of the major headaches of managing student loans is the fact that students seldom have just one. Most students put together a portfolio of loans, and can end up writing several checks each month and dealing with a variety of terms and conditions. "A student could graduate with five different loan types, and they could all have different deferment provisions," says Nancy G. Cirone, director of financial aid at Dartmouth Medical School.

That's one reason why some people opt to consolidate their school loans. Under this federal program available through lenders, school loans totaling $7,500 or more can be combined so that the borrower writes only one monthly check. The normal 10-year repayment period can be extended to 20 or even 30 years, making monthly payments much lower.

This can be a good idea for people who can't cover their current monthly payments, but consolidation has a price . . . .

. . . The increased cost comes largely from extending the term of the loan, but also from the 9% minimum interest rate charged on consolidated loans. With some federal loans carrying interest rates as low as 5%, consolidation can increase the cost even if the loan is paid off in 10 years.*

Questions

Assume you are at $t = 0$ (graduation date), and that the first repayment is scheduled for next month, $t = 1$. In all cases, we assume you owe $5,000 at $t = 0$.

1. Suppose the loan will be repaid over 10 years in equal monthly payments. The annual interest rate of 8% starts accumulating from the date of graduation ($t = 0$). Assume the 8% interest rate is the *effective* interest rate; that is, $(1 + r_m)^{12} - 1 = 8\%$, where r_m is the monthly interest rate. At the end of 10 years you will owe nothing. The payments cover the principal ($5,000) and the interest on the outstanding loan. Calculate your

monthly payment. Compare your figure to the figure appearing in the article. If it is different, how do you account for the difference?

2. Repeat Question 1, but assume the monthly interest rate is $(8\%)/12 = 0.667\%$. What is the effective annual interest rate? What is the monthly repayment in this case? Do these figures agree with the information given in the article?

Let us turn now to the four options suggested to ease the loan burden. In all these calculations, use an annual effective interest rate of 8.3%.

3. *Deferment:* If you decide to return to school, you can defer the $5,000 loan payment for five years and the interest meter will be "turned off"; in other words, interest will not accumulate on the $5,000 loan for five years. What is the PV of your loan? Apart from easing the payment pressure, do you stand to gain from this deferment?

4. *Forbearance:* Suppose you postpone the payments for five years, but interest continues to accrue at 8.3% a year. How much will you owe the bank after five years? Do you gain in PV terms? Does it ease the payment pressure? In your answer, analyze two scenarios:

a. You can borrow as much as you need from the bank at the 8.3% annual interest.

b. You have no wealth, your income is low, and the bank refuses to provide the loan.

5. *Consolidation:* Suppose you have educational debt of $30,000, composed of five loans. The interest rates on these loans fall in the range of 5% to 8.3%. The bank offers to consolidate all five loans into one loan. By consolidating the loans, you can extend them by 10 more years, but the interest rate will increase to 10%. Suppose your current income is relatively low.

a. Would you consolidate the loans if you could borrow as much as you wanted from the bank at 8.3%?

b. Would you consider consolidating them if you could not borrow from the bank?

c. Suppose you hold a certificate of deposit yielding 4% interest. How might it affect your consolidation decision?

6. *Graduated Payments:* Instead of paying the regular annuity of $60.67 a month for the next 10 years, you can pay $35.50 in the first month and $101.92 in the last month. This payment plan is a growing annuity. Calculate the monthly growth rate of your payment and the PV of this growing annuity. Assume an effective annual interest rate of 8.3%. You are confident that your future income will increase. Would you prefer the loan with the regular annuity or the loan with the growing annuity?

*Source: Lynn Asinof, "As Grads Start to Repay Student Loans, Here's a Primer on Ways to Ease Burden," *Wall Street Journal,* 17 June 1993, sec. C, p. 1. Reprinted by permission of *The Wall Street Journal* © 1993 Dow Jones & Company, Inc. All rights reserved worldwide.

Appendix 4A   Effective Interest Rate and Continuous Compounding

In all the examples and formulas discussed in this chapter (except for annuity due), we have assumed that each cash flow occurs at the end of a period.

To promote their business, some banks advertise interest on deposits at 5% interest a year compounded quarterly, monthly, or continuously. What do they mean?

Suppose you receive 10% interest compounded semiannually. This means that after six months you receive half of the interest (5%). Then, in the second half of the year, you receive 5% on the principal and also on the interest you earned in the first half of the year. At the end of the year, the value of a $1,000 principal with semiannual compounding will be

$$\text{FV} = \$1,000 \times \left(1 + \frac{0.1}{2}\right) \times \left(1 + \frac{0.1}{2}\right) = \$1,000 \times (1.05)^2 = \$1,102.50$$

The *effective annual interest rate* is defined as the FV of the investment at the end of the year (in this case $1,102.50) divided by the initial investment minus 1. It represents the rate at which wealth accumulates on an annual basis, given the frequency of compounding. In our example,

$$\text{Effective Interest Rate} \ = \frac{\$1,102.50}{\$1,000} - 1 = 0.1025 \text{ or } 10.25\%$$

Obviously, had the interest not been compounded, the effective interest rate would have been equal to the reported interest, or 10%.

If interest is compounded at more frequent intervals, the future value will increase accordingly. For quarterly compounding,

$$\text{FV} = \$1,000 \times \left(1 + \frac{0.1}{4}\right)^4 \cong \$1,103.81$$

$$\text{Effective Interest Rate} \ = \frac{\$1,103.81}{\$1,000} - 1 = 0.10381 \text{ or } 10.381\%$$

For monthly compounding,

$$FV = \$1,000 \times \left(1 + \frac{0.1}{12}\right)^{12} \cong \$1,104.71$$

$$\text{Effective Interest Rate} = \frac{\$1,104.71}{\$1,000} - 1 = 0.10471 \text{ or } 10.471\%$$

In general, when interest is compounded m times during the year, the future value of $1 at the end of the year will be

$$FV = \$1 \times \left(1 + \frac{r}{m}\right)^{m}$$

and the effective interest rate will be

$$\frac{FV}{\$1} - 1 = \left(1 + \frac{r}{m}\right)^{m} - 1$$

When m becomes very large and approaches infinity, we have **continuous compounding,** which is defined as

$$FV = \$1 \times e^{r}$$

where $e \cong 2.718$ (the base of natural logarithms). The corresponding effective interest rate is

$$\text{Effective Interest Rate} = e^{r} - 1$$

At the end of the year, the value of $1 compounded continuously will be $\$e^{r}$. Similarly, at the end of T years, this value will be e^{rT}. Table A–5 at the end of the book provides the value e^{rT}, which is the future value of $1 invested continuously for various values of rT. For example, if $r = 10\%$ and $T = 4.3$ years, then $rT = 0.43$. Look in the left column of Table A–5 at 0.4, then move to the right to column 0.03. At the intersection of the vertical line going down from 0.03 and the horizontal line originating from 0.4, we find 1.537. The future value e^{rT} of $1 invested for 4.3 years at $r = 10\%$ is $1.537.

The following two problems illustrate and compare monthly and continuous compounding.

PRACTICE BOX

Problem

Suppose a bank offers a savings plan with an annual interest rate of 12% compounded monthly.
a. What is the future value of $1 at the end of the year?
b. At the end of two years?
c. What is the effective annual interest rate?   *(continued)*

Solution

a. The value at the end of Year 1 will be

$$\$1 \times \left(1 + \frac{0.12}{12}\right)^{12} \cong \$1.1268$$

b. The value at the end of Year 2 will be

$$\$1 \times \left(1 + \frac{0.12}{12}\right)^{12 \cdot 2} \cong \$1.2697$$

(Note: For two years' savings with monthly compounding we have 24 compounding intervals.)

c. Although the bank offers 12% annual interest for each dollar invested, you get more than $1.12 (1.1268) at the end of the year. The effective interest rate is 12.68%. The result is the same as if the bank had offered you 12.68% interest compounded annually.

PRACTICE BOX

Problem

a. In the previous problem, what is the effective interest rate if the 12% interest rate is compounded continuously?
b. What is the future value of the investment if you invest for one year?
c. For two years?

Solution

a.   Using the continuous compound formula, we have

$$\text{Effective Interest Rate} = e^r - 1 = e^{0.12} - 1 \cong 0.127$$

The effective interest rate is approximately 12.7%. This rate can be found in Table A-5 for $rT = 0.12$ or by using a financial calculator.

b. If you invest for one year, the future value will be

$$\text{FV} = \$1 \times e^r = \$1.127$$

c.   Similarly, for two years,

$$\text{FV} = \$1e^{rT} = \$1 \times 2.718^{0.12 \times 2} \cong \$1.271$$

See Table A-5 under $rT = 0.12 \times 2 = 0.24$.

For a given interest rate, continuous compounding yields a higher effective interest rate (and a larger amount in your account) than an annual interest rate that is compounded semiannually, quarterly, or monthly.

Discounting is the reverse of compounding. Suppose you receive $4,000 one year from now. The annual interest rate is 10%. We can calculate the PV using 10% a year, or (10%)/2 = 5% semiannually, or $(r\%)/m$ per period when there are m periods in a year. The larger m is, the larger is the discount rate used to discount the cash flows, and the smaller their PV is. As m becomes very large, we have **continuous discounting.** The following problem illustrates such calculations.

PRACTICE BOX

Problem

Suppose you are to receive $100,000 one year from now. The interest rate is 10%. What is the PV using annual and continuously compounded interest rates?

Solution

With annual discounting, the PV is

$$\text{PV} = \frac{\$100,000}{1.1} = \$90,909.09$$

With continuous discounting, it is

$$\text{PV} = \frac{\$100,000}{e^r} = \frac{\$100,000}{2.718^{0.1}} = \$100,000 \times 0.9048463 = \$90,484.63$$

If a cash flow is received T years from now, the discount factor is given by e^{-rT}. The figure $1/e^{rt} = e^{-rt}$ can be easily derived from Table A-5 by dividing 1 by the numbers appearing there. For example, $1 received 10 years from now and discounted at 20% continuously compounded is equal to $e^{-0.2 \cdot 10} = e^{-2} = 1/e^2$. From Table A-5 we find that $e^2 = 7.389$. Thus

$$\$1 \times e^{-2} \cong 1/7.389 \cong \$0.135$$

INTEREST RATE CONVERSION

The interest on bank loans can be calculated on an annual basis or on a shorter basis (such as monthly). Suppose you are considering various loans. To know which loan is more expensive, you have to do an **interest rate conversion** to express the interest rates on the same basis (such as annually or monthly). For example, if you pay 1% on a monthly basis, the annual effective interest rate will be

$$(1.01)^{12} - 1 \cong 0.1268 \text{ or } 12.68\%$$

Similarly, if you pay 3% on a quarterly basis, the annual effective interest rate will be

$$(1.03)^4 - 1 \cong 0.1255 \text{ or } 12.55\%$$

By converting all interest rates to the same (annual) basis, we can decide which loan is the most expensive or, conversely, which deposit is the most profitable.

Interest rate conversion is important when you select a bank for your deposits. Suppose Bank A offers an annual rate of 10% (not compounded) and Bank B offers

9.9% a year compounded quarterly. Which rate is better? To decide, we first convert the 9.9% interest into an effective annual interest rate as follows:

$$\text{Effective Interest Rate} = \left(1 + \frac{0.099}{4}\right)^4 - 1 = (1.02475)^4 - 1$$

$$= 0.1027 \text{ or } 10.27\%$$

It then becomes clear that Bank B's 9.9% interest compounded quarterly is better.

APPENDIX KEY TERMS

Continuous compounding   Continuous discounting   Interest rate conversion

APPENDIX REVIEW AND PRACTICE

4A.1 Assume the annual interest rate, r, is 10%. What is the future value 10 years from now of $100 if the interest is compounded
a. Annually?
b. Semiannually?
c. Daily?
d. Continuously?

4A.2 One bank offers a savings plan with an interest rate of 10% compounded annually, and another bank offers an annual rate of 9% compounded continuously.
a. Which bank would you prefer if your investment horizon is 1 year?

b. Which bank would you prefer if your investment horizon is 10 years ($T = 10$)?

4A.3 "If the interest rate is zero, we get the same future value no matter what compounding method we use." Evaluate this statement.

4A.4 You can receive either $994 one year from now or $900 immediately. The annual interest rate is 10%.
a. Which would you prefer if the interest is compounded quarterly?
b. Which would you prefer if it is compounded continuously?

CHAPTER 5

NET PRESENT VALUE AND CREATION OF WEALTH

LEARNING OBJECTIVES

After reading this chapter, you should understand:

1. The concept of creation and destruction of wealth.

2. The net present value (NPV) investment criterion and why positive NPV projects should be accepted and negative NPV projects should be rejected.

3. The validity of the NPV investment criterion for both equity and debt financing.

4. When to use the riskless interest rate and when to use a higher interest rate as a discount rate.

5. The concept of risk premium.

6. How mergers can create a positive NPV.

CORPORATE FINANCE IN THE NEWS

THE CREATION OF WEALTH

Fortune: "How have you gone about creating market value—that is, putting wealth into the hands of shareholders?"

Goizueta: "Back in 1980 we made a study of the returns we were getting from our fountain business. As we found out that we were making much less than our cost of capital, which at that time, with no debt, was about 16% . . . I didn't know anything about EVA or anything, but I knew something very simple, and that is: The way to become richer is to borrow money at a certain rate and invest it at a higher rate and pocket the difference.

So we went very methodically over much of our business . . ."

Source: "A Conversation with Roberto Goizueta and Jack Welch," *Fortune* 132, no. 12 (December 11, 1995): 96–101. Copyright © 1995 Time Inc. All rights reserved.

151

5.1 INTRODUCTION

Roberto Goizueta, CEO of Coca-Cola, and Jack Welch, CEO of General Electric, are known as the most successful wealth creators in the United States.[1] How do they create wealth? What investment rules do they follow?

As Coca-Cola's chief executive, Roberto Goizueta follows a "simple" rule: Get richer by borrowing money at a lower rate, investing it at a higher rate, and pocketing the difference. His rule has worked for Coca-Cola, which with nearly $87.82 billion of wealth in 1996 was the number one U.S. wealth creator. (General Electric was number two with about $80.972 billion.)

Firms create wealth by investing. In this chapter, we introduce the net present value (NPV) investment criterion by which a firm should decide which projects to accept and which to reject. Applying this criterion properly conforms with Goizueta's rule: It guarantees making a profit that exceeds the cost of capital, and thereby creates wealth. Profitable investment is consistent with a firm's goal of maximizing stockholders' wealth.

5.2 DEFINITION AND JUSTIFICATION OF THE NPV RULE: CERTAIN CASH FLOWS

In Chapter 4 we defined present and future values (PV and FV) and showed how they are related. The PV of $1 received one year from now is defined as the amount of money—received today—that is just as attractive as the $1 received in one year. We showed that when cash flows are certain, one can borrow or lend at the riskless interest rate; in this case, the riskless rate, r, is the relevant discount rate. The PV of $1 to be received next year is $1/(1 + r)$, where r is the interest rate. Similarly, when dollars are to be received after t years with certainty, the present value is $1/(1 + r)^t$.

When projects are evaluated, we use the net present value (NPV), which is defined as the PV of all future cash flows less the project's initial outlay. A project's net present value (NPV) is the wealth it creates (or destroys) and equals the sum of the discounted cash flows it generates less the initial investment outlay. The **net present value (NPV)** in the case of certain cash flows is defined as follows:

$$\text{NPV} = \sum_{t=1}^{T} \frac{\text{CF}_t}{(1 + r)^t} - I \tag{5.1}$$

where CF_t denotes the project's cash flow in Year t; I, the initial outlay; T, the project's economic life (in years); and r, the riskless interest rate. Note that since we assume that cash flows are certain, the riskless interest rate is the appropriate discount rate. When we introduce uncertain cash flows, a higher discount rate will be used to compensate for risk.

---

1. See Tony Jackson, "A Serving of Value Added," *Financial Times,* 13 January 1997, p. 8.

The NPV measures the resources a project makes available to the firm today, which the firm can use, for example, to increase dividends. Using NPV as the criterion for making investment decisions gives us the following **NPV rule:**

- If NPV > 0, the project should be accepted.
- If NPV < 0, the project should be rejected.
- If NPV = 0, accepting or rejecting the project is equally attractive.

In Appendix 5A we prove that correctly employing the NPV rule maximizes the stockholders' wealth and the stock price. In the body of this chapter we will show by means of numerical examples that a firm should accept projects with a positive NPV because they create wealth and, therefore, maximize stock price.

Consider the following three projects:

Cash Flows (in millions of dollars)

	$t = 0$	$t = 1$	$t = 2$
Project X	50	0	0
Project Y	−10	0	0
Project Z	−10	5	15

where $t = 0$ is today.

Which of these projects should a firm accept? All stockholders will find Project X attractive. It has zero cash flows at $t = 1$ and $t = 2$ and a positive cash flow of $50 million at $t = 0$. Since the firm can increase its resources by $50 million today, $50 million is the NPV. In the same vein, any rational investor would reject Project Y, with zero cash flows at $t = 1$ and $t = 2$ and a negative cash flow of $10 million at $t = 0$. With its −$10 million NPV, Project Y destroys wealth, and the firm's resources decline by that amount. However, the choice becomes difficult when some cash flows are positive and some are negative, as with Project Z. How do we decide whether to accept or reject Z?

The NPV rule comes to the rescue in such cases. The following examples show how we can rewrite a project like Z so that its cash flows are like those of X or Y, making it easy to reach a decision regarding Project Z.

Before showing how to use the NPV rule in investment decision making, let's first see a simple example of NPV calculations. Suppose a firm is considering the following projects:

Cash Flows (in millions of dollars)

	$t = 0$	$t = 1$	$t = 2$	NPV (at $r = 10\%$)
Project A	−100	0	127.05	5
Project B	−100	104.5	0	−5

where $t = 0$ is today, $t = 1$ is the end of the first year, and $t = 2$ is the end of the second year.

Project A's NPV at a discount rate of $r = 10\%$ is

$$\text{NPV} = \frac{\$127.05 \text{ million}}{(1.1)^2} - \$100 \text{ million} = \$5 \text{ million}$$

Project B's NPV is:

$$\text{NPV} = \frac{\$104.5 \text{ million}}{(1.1)} - \$100 \text{ million} = -\$5 \text{ million}$$

Applying the NPV rule, the CFO would accept Project A (NPV > 0) and would reject Project B (NPV < 0).

Although it is obvious that Project X (in our earlier example) creates wealth, it is not so obvious that Project A creates wealth, because it has negative as well as positive cash flows. However, with an additional transaction in financial markets, we can prove that a project with an overall positive NPV (Project A) creates wealth exactly like a project that has all positive cash flows (Project X). This proof will provide justification for use of the NPV rule and demonstrate its consistency with wealth creation and stock price maximization.

5.2.1 "Banking" a Positive NPV Project

If a firm combines the cash flows of a positive NPV project with a financial transaction (borrowing or lending) to create a cash flow that will be nonnegative every year and positive at $t = 0$ (similar to Project X above), it "banks the project." The combined cash flow is called a "rearranged" cash flow, which does not affect the project's NPV. The higher the NPV, the higher will be the positive cash flow that the firm obtains at $t = 0$ by banking the project. NPV as the optimum investment criterion is justified if when the project's NPV is positive, investors are willing to pay a higher price for the firm's stock.

Let's see how "banking" a project with a positive NPV creates wealth. Suppose the firm in the preceding example is considering the same Projects A and B as before, plus alternative Projects A* and B*, with the following cash flows:

Cash Flows (in millions of dollars)

	$t = 0$	$t = 1$	$t = 2$	NPV (at $r = 10\%$)
Project A	−100	0	127.05	5
Project A*	5	0	0	5
Project B	−100	104.5	0	−5
Project B*	−5	0	0	−5

For illustrative purposes, assume the firm has 100 million outstanding shares, and the value of the stock is $100 million, making the per-share price $1.

Project A* will result in an immediate increase of $5 million in the firm's value with no additional financial outlay. The value of the stock will increase from $100 million to $105 million, and the per-share price will increase from $1 to $1.05. Because the firm makes no additional outlay, stockholders' wealth will also increase by

$5 million. Since Project A* has a positive NPV of $5 million corresponding to its cash flow at $t = 0$, the firm should accept it because Project A* enhances stockholders' wealth and increases the firm's stock price.

By the same logic, the firm should reject project B* because it has a negative NPV of $5 million at $t = 0$ and zero cash flows at $t = 1$ and $t = 2$ (NPV = −$5 million). Accepting Project B* would destroy wealth (in the amount of $5 million) and reduce the stock price to $0.95.

The accept/reject decision is fairly obvious in the previous two cases. Even without a knowledge of finance you could see that the firm should accept Project A* and reject Project B*. The decision regarding Projects A and B is less straightforward. However, if we can show that the cash flows of Project A and Project A* are equivalent and that the cash flows of Project B and Project B* are equivalent (where equivalent means that one project's cash flow can be rearranged so it will be identical to another project's cash flow), then we will know that the firm should accept Project A, just as it should accept Project A*, and that it should reject Project B, just as it should reject Project B*.

If the firm can borrow and lend at the riskless interest rate, any project with a positive NPV will be equivalent to another project with nonnegative cash flows (similar to Project A*). Project A* would create wealth, and any project with a positive NPV will also create wealth. Similarly, any project with a negative NPV will be equivalent to a project with nonpositive cash flows (similar to Project B*). Project B* would destroy wealth, and any project with a negative NPV will also destroy wealth. Therefore, employing the NPV rule in project evaluation will maximize the stockholders' wealth.

We need now to determine whether Projects A and A* are equivalent. If they are, we conclude that Project A will also create $5 million wealth, and the NPV will measure the amount of wealth that Project A creates.

To see why Project A creates wealth amounting to exactly $5 million, let us add a financial transaction with the bank. Assume the firm can borrow and lend at the riskless interest rate. Because the cash flow from the project at $t = 2$ is expected to be $127.05 million, the firm can borrow an amount *today* that will grow to $127.05 million two years from now:

$$\$127.05 \text{ million}/(1.1)^2 = \$105 \text{ million}$$

Thus, the firm borrows $105 million.

Two years later, the firm will have to repay

$$\$105 \text{ million} \times (1.1)^2 = \$127.05 \text{ million}$$

Obviously, this is exactly the amount of Project A's cash flow at $t = 2$. Project A's net cash flow plus the financial transaction in the capital market can be shown as follows:

Cash Flows (in millions of dollars)

	$t = 0$	$t = 1$	$t = 2$
Cash Flow from Project A	−100	0	127.05
Cash Flow from Financial Transaction	105	0	−127.05
Net Cash Flow	5	0	0

Recall that Project A*'s cash flow is $5 million at $t = 0$ and zero in all other years. We can now see the effect of "banking the project." Project A's cash flows combined with the financial transaction's cash flows produce an *identical* net cash flow to that of Project A*. The NPV of projects A and A* are identical—$5 million—and both projects create wealth of $5 million. In other words, by "banking the project" the firm can replicate the cash flows of Project A* for Project A and can make both projects equivalent. Therefore, the firm should accept Project A.

Without access to the capital market, it is impossible to tell whether Project A creates or destroys wealth. Only by borrowing can the firm rearrange Project A's cash flows to produce nonnegative cash flows at $t = 1$ and $t = 2$ and a positive cash flow at $t = 0$. The positive cash flow at $t = 0$ represents the creation of wealth.

Now let's look at Projects B* and B. If they are equivalent, then Project B will also destroy wealth, and as with all projects with a negative NPV, the firm should reject it. We have seen that Project B's NPV is −$5 million, and we need to show that it represents the destruction of $5 million of wealth. Suppose the firm borrows money from the bank such that the project's cash flow minus the amount the firm has to repay the bank at $t = 1$ is exactly zero. Because the project's cash flow at $t = 1$ is $104.5 million, the firm will borrow $95 million ($104.5/1.1 = $95 million) from the bank at 10% interest. One year later it will have to repay

$$\$95 \text{ million} \times 1.1 = \$104.5 \text{ million}$$

This is exactly the amount of Project B's cash flow. Project B's net cash flow plus the financial transaction can be shown as follows:

Cash Flows (in millions of dollars)

	$t = 0$	$t = 1$	$t = 2$
Cash Flow from Project B	−100	104.5	0
Cash Flow from Financial Transaction	95	−104.5	0
Net Cash Flow	−5	0	0

Recall that Project B*'s cash flow is −$5 million at $t = 0$. Since Project B's cash flows produce a net cash flow identical to that of Project B*, the two projects are equivalent. We know that Project B* destroys wealth amounting to $5 million, and since Project B with the financial transaction is identical to Project B*, it will also destroy this amount of wealth. Therefore, the firm should reject Project B.

Because we assume certainty, an alternative use of money is to deposit it in the bank at the interest rate, r. Another way to justify the NPV rule is to compare the project's cash flow to the alternative of depositing in the bank the project's capital outlay. In other words, if instead of investing in Project A, the firm were to deposit $100 million in the bank, it would obtain $121 million ($100 \times (1.1)^2 = $121 million) at $t = 2$. Since this amount is less than the cash flow of Project A at $t = 2$, accepting Project A is a better alternative than depositing the money in the bank. Similarly, if instead of accepting Project B, the firm were to deposit $100 million in the bank, it would obtain $110 million ($100 million $\times 1.1 = $110 million) at $t = 1$. Since this amount is more than the cash flow of Project B at $t = 1$, depositing $100 million in the bank is better than accepting Project B.

When a firm finances a project by borrowing (debt financing), the interest represents an out–of–pocket (financial) cost. A project will be worthwhile only if the present value of its cash flows is larger than the present value of the cash flows repaid to the lender. When a firm finances a project with its own equity (equity financing), it has no out–of–pocket cost. Nevertheless, the profit earned on the project should be at least as much as the interest the firm could earn by depositing the project's initial outlay (the capital investment) in the bank. Otherwise, the firm would do better by rejecting the project and depositing the outlay amount in the bank. The interest forgone as a result of accepting the project rather than depositing the money in the bank is called the **alternative,** or **opportunity, cost.**

"Banking the project" can be generalized to any project. By using the NPV rule, the firm can maximize its stock price regardless of whether it finances the project by equity or by debt. The following problem demonstrates "banking the project" when the firm finances the project by equity rather than by debt. We assume the firm issues stock and then deposits the proceeds from the issue in the bank at interest rate r. When the firm uses the cash deposit to finance the project, we call it equity financing because cash comes from the stock issue rather than from borrowing.

PRACTICE BOX

Problem

A project has the following certain cash flows:

	$t = 0$	$t = 1$	$t = 2$
Cash Flows	−$100	$100	$100

where $t = 0$ is today. The annual interest rate is 10%. The project is financed by the firm's equity.

a. What is the project's NPV?
b. Suppose the firm has cash holdings in the bank yielding 10% annually. Should the firm withdraw money from its bank deposit to invest in the project? In your answer, create zero cash flows ("banking the project") in Years 1 and 2.

Solution

a. The project's NPV is

$$\frac{\$100}{1.1} + \frac{\$100}{(1.1)^2} - \$100 \cong \$73.55$$

The project's NPV is positive. According to the NPV rule, the firm should accept the project.

b. If the firm has the cash to invest and does not need to borrow, a project with a positive NPV still creates wealth. We show below that in financing the project

(continued)

with its own cash holdings and creating zero cash flows from the project in years $t = 1$ and $t = 2$ ("banking the project"), the firm adds $73.55 at $t = 0$. Thus, reducing the bank deposit and financing the project with its own resources, the firm creates wealth amounting to $73.55 (the project's NPV).

If the firm deposits $90.91 ($100/1.1 \cong $90.91) in the bank today, it will receive $100 one year from today. Similarly, if the firm deposits $82.64 ($100/(1.1)^2 \cong $82.64) for two years, it will receive $100 two years from today. By reducing the bank deposit by $173.55 ($90.91 + $82.64 = $173.55), the firm obtains $173.55 cash today, but its future income from the bank is reduced by $100 in each of the next two years. The project's cash flows minus the reduction in the cash flows from the bank will be zero in Years 1 and 2. However, if the firm withdraws $173.55 from the bank today but needs only $100 for the investment, it obtains a $73.55 profit (the positive NPV) from this transaction. This makes the project worthwhile.

5.2.2 A Word of Caution

The interest rate a firm pays on bank loans is usually higher than the interest rate the bank pays on deposits. *The NPV rule is valid only when the interest rates on borrowing and lending are the same.* If the interest rate on borrowing is higher than it is on lending, the NPV rule does not apply. However, since banks generally give large firms preferential treatment, the two rates are usually similar, and any adverse effect as a result of differences in the rates for borrowing and lending will be negligible.

By using the NPV rule, managers can make better investment decisions. The better the decision, the more likely it is that a firm will create wealth and increase its market value. As Connecting Theory to Practice 5.1 relates, the NPV rule also applies to MVA, or market value added.

CONNECTING THEORY TO PRACTICE 5.1

MARKET VALUE ADDED: CREATING STOCKHOLDER WEALTH

Devised by the New York City financial consulting firm Stern Stewart, MVA is much more than just a consultant's whimsy. Top managers at scores of companies—including Coca-Cola, AT&T, Quaker Oats, Eli Lilly, Georgia-Pacific, and Tenneco—have for years kept a close eye on MVA as a way of telling how effectively their strategies make use of the money they invest. An increasing number of investors now use it as a helpful indicator of a stock's future performance.

It is true that some CEOs prefer different performance measures, like return on net assets, and others feel that MVA is just too complicated to bother with. Even so, the number of loyal adherents continues to grow.

Source: Anne B. Fisher, "Creating Stockholder Wealth," *Fortune* 132, no. 12 (December 1995): 105–111.

MAKING THE CONNECTION

EVA and MVA are two related performance measures first introduced in the United States and later enthusiastically accepted by managers and consultants in the United Kingdom. Whereas EVA seeks to measure annual profit, MVA, our focus in this chapter, aims to show the net return in total.

Market value added (MVA) measures the increase in the firm's value as a result of management's actions. MVA is calculated by subtracting total invested capital from the current market value of the firm's debt and equity. For example, if stockholders and bondholders together have invested $100 million and if the firm's value is $150 million, then $50 million of wealth has been created, and MVA is $50 million. Similarly, if the firm invests $100 million provided by its stockholders and bondholders in projects whose NPV is $50 million, the firm's value increases by exactly that amount because $50 million of wealth has been created. In this example, $50 million is the total profit resulting from the $100 million investment.

5.3 NET PRESENT VALUE: UNCERTAIN CASH FLOWS

As mentioned in the preceding section, when a project's cash flows are certain, the appropriate discount rate is the riskless interest rate, r. However, when a project's cash flows are uncertain, the appropriate discount rate, k, will be *higher than* the riskless interest rate to compensate investors for exposure to risk. The difference between k and r represents the *risk premium*. We first encountered this term in Chapter 2; here we examine the meaning of risk premium and show how it is determined.

5.3.1 The Appropriate Discount Rate and the Risk Premium

The rates of return on stocks are more volatile than the rates of return on bonds, and the rates of return on bonds are more volatile than the rates of return on Treasury bills. Investment in stocks is thus considered relatively risky. In Chapter 2 we saw that, in the long run, the average annual rate of return on Treasury bills (T-bills) is about 4% per year and the average rate of return on equity is about 13%. This difference in the average rate of return, 9%, represents the market's (investors') risk premium, whereby investors are compensated for the added risk involved in a given project. For example, by investing in equity for one year, investors may enjoy a 20%

return if the stock price rises or may lose 10% if the stock price falls. Such an investment is considered risky. However, since the return on one-year Treasury bills has
very little deviation, investing in T-bills is less risky. Because investors do not generally like uncertainty, the market prices of two such assets (common stock and T-
bills) will adjust until an *average risk premium* (also called *expected risk premium*) is
obtained on the equity investment.

But how does this market adjustment work in practice? How is the risk premium determined, and what market mechanism determines it? These issues are discussed next.

5.3.2 The Market Mechanism Determining the Risk Premium

Suppose you buy two securities at a cost of $100 each and expect to receive the fol-
lowing cash flows at the end of the year:

Security A (T-bill)		Security B (Stock)	
Cash Flow	Probability	Cash Flow	Probability
$105	1.0	$ 90	½
		$120	½

On average the future cash flows of both assets are $105. Security A yields $105
with certainty (a probability of 100% or 1.0), and the expected cash flow of Security B is $105 ($0.50 \times \$90 + 0.50 \times \$120 = \$45 + \$60 = \$105$).[2] As the initial investment is $100 for both securities, the average rate of return on each asset is 5%
($[\$105 - \$100]/\$100 = 0.05$ or 5%).

Investors who dislike uncertainty will prefer Security A, which yields $105 with
certainty, to Security B, which has an expected but uncertain cash flow of $105.
(Investors will actually realize either $90 or $120.) Because investors generally dislike uncertainty, they will not invest in Security B, and its price will fall, to say $90.
Suppose that at this price, investors are ready to buy exactly the available supply of
the security. At a lower price, investors would wish to buy more than the available
supply; and at a higher price, they wish to buy less than the available supply. When
the security reaches its equilibrium price, investors are indifferent between investing
in Security A (the T-bill) and Security B (the stock), and there will be no more pressure for Security B's price to change. At the $90 equilibrium price, Security B's rate
of return will now be 0%, with a probability of ½, and 33⅓%, with a probability of
½. Security B's average or expected rate of return will be

$$\tfrac{1}{2} \times 0\% + \tfrac{1}{2} \times 33\tfrac{1}{3}\% \cong 16.7\%$$

2. The probability is the chance of obtaining a given result. In our example, there is a 50% chance of obtaining $90 and a 50%
chance of obtaining $120. For instance, if you flip a coin, there is a 50% chance of heads and a 50% chance of tails. If you are
promised $90 for heads and $120 for tails, we say that there is an equal chance—or a 50% probability—of obtaining $90 or $120.
The average cash flow (called also the *mean* or the *expected* value) is defined as the sum of the various possible outcomes multiplied
by their probabilities.

In the text example, we have a rate of return of −10% with a probability of ½, and a return of 20%, also with probability of ½.
The expected rate of return is ½(−10%) + ½(20%) = 5%.

This rate of return (16.7%) called the **required rate of return** is what stockholders require from Security B, given its risk characteristics. Also called the *cost of equity,* or the *cost of capital* if the firm has no debt. The required rate of return is what the firm must earn to compensate its stockholders for their risk exposure. Security A's rate of return will still be 5% because its price did not change. By assumption the market will now be in equilibrium. The **risk premium,** the difference between these two rates of return (16.7% − 5% = 11.7%), is the market's expected rate of return on the risky asset *over and above* the riskless rate of return (which in this case is 5%). If the risk were even greater (for example, cash flows of $80 or $130 with equal probability) or if investors were even more risk averse, the stock price would fall below $90. Consequently, the market would require an even higher risk premium.

The risk premium (in percent) is given by the following equation:

Risk Premium = Expected Rate of Return on Risky Asset − Riskless Interest Rate

The greater the uncertainty regarding an investment's future cash flows, the lower will be the asset's price and the higher will be the expected rate of return on the asset and the risk premium.

The risk premium is not merely a theoretical concept. It works constantly in the market's affairs. The average rate of return on stocks of high-risk firms (such as those in the electronics industry) is much higher than the average rate of return of stocks of low-risk firms (such as utilities). Similarly, the average rate of return on the bonds of high-risk firms (called *junk bonds*) is much higher than it is on government bonds.

We should distinguish between the historical and expected average risk premiums. As discussed in Chapter 2, the *historical risk premium* is the difference between the *average* rate of return on an investment and the riskless interest rate, whereas the *expected risk premium* is the difference between the *required* rate of return on a project being considered by the firm and the riskless interest rate. In this book, unless stated otherwise, *risk premium* refers to the expected risk premium.

In principle the concepts of risk premium and required rate of return are easy to understand. However, in practice the evaluation of risk and the determination of the risk premium are not simple. We know that the risk premium must be positive and that the larger the risk, the larger the risk premium will be. We also know that the larger the risk, the higher will be the discount rate for discounting the expected cash flows and the smaller will be the project's NPV. But how do we measure risk? How do we measure the cost of capital? How do we estimate the project's rate of return? These are probably the most difficult issues in modern finance, and they warrant separate discussion (see Chapters 8, 9, and 10). At this stage we alert you to the facts that most investments are risky and that a discount rate k, called the cost of capital, should be used in calculating their NPV.

5.4 THE PV AND NPV OF BONDS AND STOCKS

Although firms generally invest in physical assets, they also invest in financial assets and even in their own shares (through stock repurchases). Financial assets such as stocks and bonds are evaluated in the same way as physical projects. When using the NPV rule, a firm evaluates a financial asset by estimating its expected (average) future cash flows and discounting them to obtain the PV. If the PV is higher than the asset's current market price, the NPV will be positive, and the firm will consider the asset worthwhile.

Future cash flows received from bonds and stocks are uncertain (or risky). Because the price of these securities (which is one component of the future cash flows) fluctuate, the cash flow from selling them will be uncertain. Moreover, if the firm issuing these securities goes bankrupt, the investment amount will be lost altogether. In evaluating such securities we use a higher discount rate than the riskless interest rate. Let us see how the PV of bonds and stocks is calculated.

5.4.1 The PV of Bonds

A bondholder expects to receive interest of $\$C$ each year plus the return of the principal of $\$B$ when the bond matures at the end of T years. These cash flows are uncertain. If the firm goes bankrupt, the bondholder may receive only partial payments. Given this risk, the appropriate discount rate is k_d where the subscript d stands for debt (also called cost of debt). Then the PV of the bond's cash flows is

$$\text{PV} = \frac{\$C}{1 + k_d} + \frac{\$C}{(1 + k_d)^2} + \ldots + \frac{\$C}{(1 + k_d)^T} + \frac{\$B}{(1 + k_d)^T}$$

If the bond's current price is less than this PV, its NPV is positive, and purchasing the bond creates wealth.

Suppose you consider purchasing a bond that will pay $60 interest at the end of each of the next 10 years (assuming the issuing firm does not go bankrupt). The $1,000 principal will be paid at the end of the tenth year. A bond purchase of this type is similar to lending money for 10 years. Suppose, given the risk of this bond, you believe these cash flows should be discounted at 10%. The bond's market price is $800. Would you buy it? As in project evaluation, the PV of the bond's cash flows is calculated as follows:

$$\text{PV} = \frac{\$60}{1.1} + \frac{\$60}{(1.1)^2} + \ldots + \frac{\$60}{(1.1)^{10}} + \frac{\$1,000}{(1.1)^{10}} \cong \$754.22$$

At a market price of $800, the bond's NPV is negative ($754.22 − $800 = −$45.78), and purchasing the bond is not recommended.

5.4.2 The PV of Stocks

The PV of a share of stock is calculated the same way as the PV of a bond. Suppose that you intend to hold the share for T years. You expect to receive a dividend of $\$d$ at the end of each year, and you expect to sell the share for $\$P$ at the end of the T years. Because stocks are generally riskier than bonds, the appropriate discount rate,

k_e where the subscript e stands for equity (also called the cost of equity), will generally be greater than k_d. The PV of the stock's cash flows is

$$PV = \frac{\$d}{1 + k_e} + \frac{\$d}{(1 + k_e)^2} + \ldots + \frac{\$d}{(1 + k_e)^T} + \frac{\$P}{(1 + k_e)^T}$$

If the current stock price is below this PV, the NPV is positive, and buying the share creates wealth.

We'll use IBM stock to demonstrate how the PV of stocks is evaluated. Suppose the current price of IBM's stock is $40. Let the expected dividend be $6 a year for the next three years and then $8 a year for two years. Suppose you consider purchasing IBM stock, holding it for five years, and then selling it. You estimate that the stock price five years from now will be $60. Since IBM is considered a relatively risky firm, these estimates are highly uncertain, and you believe 20% is the appropriate discount rate. Should you buy the stock?

The PV of the cash flows is calculated as follows:

$$PV = \frac{\$6}{1.2} + \frac{\$6}{(1.2)^2} + \frac{\$6}{(1.2)^3} + \frac{\$8}{(1.2)^4} + \frac{\$8}{(1.2)^5} + \frac{\$60}{(1.2)^5}$$

$$\cong \$5.00 + \$4.17 + \$3.47 + \$3.86 + \$3.22 + \$24.11$$

$$= \$43.83$$

The PV of the stock is higher than the current price, the NPV is positive ($43.83 − $40 = $3.83), and the investment is worthwhile—it creates wealth.

Financial assets should be treated like physical assets for valuation purposes, and the NPV rule should be used to make an investment decision.

Finding the value of bonds and certain other assets is straightforward. But how do you value intellectual property such as books, songs, and software? Visit IPC Group's Web site and learn about the thorny issue in pricing ideas.
http://www.ipcgroup.com

5.5 CREATING WEALTH BY CONTRACTING OR EXPANDING SIZE

In addition to investing in projects or to evaluating their physical and financial assets, some firms have created wealth by contracting or expanding their sizes.

5.5.1 Contracting Size

The business environment is one of fierce competition for market shares. To compete for consumers of their products and services and to remain financially stable, in the early 1990s many firms—large, small, and in-between—had to contract. They have done so by discontinuing unprofitable product lines, by downsizing their staffs, by disposing of or selling unproductive assets, and by selling marginally profitable divisions. Applying Theory to Practice 5.1 relates the effect of IBM's decision to sell its Federal Systems Co. division.

APPLYING THEORY TO PRACTICE 5.1

NPV, MARKET VALUE ADDED (MVA), AND THE INVESTED CAPITAL

IBM IS SELLING FEDERAL SYSTEMS FOR $1.5 BILLION

International Business Machines confirmed that it is selling its Federal Systems Co. division to defense-electronics firm Loral Corp. for $1.5 billion.

IBM Chairman Louis Gerstner cited a rapidly changing market when he commented on his company's sale: it "is in the best long-term interest of IBM and its shareholders." IBM has also been subject to corporate downsizing procedures and has been cutting thousands of jobs to become more profitable and competitive in the computer industry.

Both IBM's and Loral's stock rose to $2.375 and $2.125, respectively, in late trading on the New York Stock Exchange.

Bernard Schwartz stated that he expected a 35 cent increase in per-share earnings for the year ending in March 1995. Mr. Schwartz added that he expected Art Johnson to move to Loral and continue to head up Federal Systems.

Source: Jeff Cole and Laurie Hays, "Loral Tentatively Agrees to Buy IBM's Federal Systems for Nearly $1.5 Billion," *Wall Street Journal*, 13 December 1993, A3.

In addition, we have the following information on IBM as of the selling date:

Market value added (MVA) (in millions)	−$23,722
Invested capital, including Federal Systems (in millions)	$75,287
Invested capital of Federal Systems (in millions)	$1,500
Return on capital	2.7%
Cost of capital	10.2%
Number of outstanding shares (in millions)	572

Source: Data from Laura Walbert, "America's Best Wealth Creators," *Fortune* 128, no. 16 (December 27, 1993): 64. Copyright © 1993 Time Inc. All rights reserved.

Questions

1. What is the NPV of Federal Systems if IBM continues to operate it?
2. Suppose IBM used the $1.5 billion from the sale of Federal Systems to reduce its debt. What would be the effect of the transaction on IBM's market value? Calculate IBM's invested capital, the change in its MVA, and its new MVA after the sale of Federal Systems. (Note: For the purpose of MVA calculation, the invested capital is generally taken from the firm's financial statements.) How would your answer change if IBM holds the $1.5 billion as cash in the bank?
3. Analyze the market reaction to the sale, IBM's cost of capital, and the rate of return on its invested capital.

4. How do you explain Loral's decision to buy Federal Systems in light of your answer to question 1?

MAKING THE CONNECTION

1. If a firm sells an asset that destroys wealth, its stock price will rise. We can use this idea to estimate the NPV of Federal Systems if operated by IBM. Since IBM's stock price increased by $2.375 per share after it sold Federal Systems, the value of this sale to IBM's equity holders is

$$\$2.375 \times 572 \text{ million shares} = \$1,358.5 \text{ million} \cong \$1.36 \text{ billion}$$

The market estimates that if IBM continues to operate Federal Systems, Federal's NPV will be −$1.36 billion.

IBM sold Federal Systems at a price higher than the PV of its cash flows. The negative NPV is avoided, and the value of IBM's equity is increased. Of course, we assume that nothing else occurred in the market to increase the stock price and that the increase represents only the response to the elimination of the negative NPV project.

2. Because of the increase in stock price, the value of IBM's equity increased by about $1.36 billion. If IBM used the $1.5 billion from the sale of Federal Systems to reduce its debt, the change in the debt's value plus the change in the value of equity would be −$0.14 billion ($1.36 billion − $1.5 billion).

The *invested capital* decreases by $1.5 billion (because of the sale of Federal Systems) to $73,787 million ($75,287 million − $1,500 million).

The change in MVA is the change in the market value minus the change in the capital invested:

Change in MVA = Change in Firm's Market Value (Debt + Equity) −
Change in Invested Capital

In our example,

Change in MVA = $1.36 billion = −$0.14 billion − (−$1.5 billion)

If IBM deposits the $1.5 billion in the bank rather than using it to reduce debt, the change in IBM's invested capital is

$$\$1.5 \text{ billion} - \$1.5 \text{ billion} = \$0$$

(Recall that depositing the money in the bank increases the invested capital.) The change in the MVA is as before ($1.36 billion), regardless of what IBM does with the $1.5 billion cash. IBM's MVA after the sale of Federal Systems is

MVA before the Sale + Change in the MVA Due to the Sale
= −$23,722 million + $1,360 million = −$22,362 million

3. IBM's cost of capital is 10.2%, and it earns only 2.7% on its invested capital. These figures imply that many of the firm's projects have a negative NPV and are destroying wealth. Eliminating such projects will increase the firm's value. The rise in the stock price indicates that stockholders expected IBM's rate of return to increase once it sold the negative NPV projects.

4. Why would Loral want to buy Federal Systems? Loral may operate more effectively. A negative NPV project, operated more effectively by another firm, may produce a positive NPV.

5.5.2 Expanding Size

Firms invest in projects to increase their market values. Why not invest in an existing firm rather than in new projects? For example, suppose a firm considers developing marketing channels in Europe. Wouldn't it be preferable to acquire an existing European firm that already has local marketing channels and experience than to start from scratch? Indeed, **acquisitions** of one firm by another or **mergers** of two firms are very common.

Acquisition and mergers can be friendly or unfriendly; the latter are known as *hostile takeovers.* In friendly mergers, the boards of directors of two firms first reach an agreement, and then the respective shareholders are approached and asked to endorse it. In hostile mergers, the *bidding* firm buys the stock of the *target* firm, and the target's board of directors is replaced. Probably one of the best-known recent friendly acquisitions occurred in 1995 between Walt Disney and Capital Cities/ ABC. This acquisition involved a transaction of $19 billion, the second largest in U.S. history.

Several possible sources of gain result from the merging of two firms, creating economic value. One such gain is reduction of duplicate costs between the merged firms. This savings increases the combined firm's ability to compete with other firms, as demonstrated by the Babbage's–Software Etc. Stores merger described in Applying Theory to Practice 5.2.

http

M&A Marketplace bills itself as the largest and most active mergers and acquisitions site on the Internet. At its Web site, you can buy a business, sell a business, find a joint-venture partner, hire an M&A advisor, or obtain M&A funding. http://www.webcom. com/cfnet/welcome. html

APPLYING THEORY TO PRACTICE 5.2

CREATING A POSITIVE NPV BY MERGER

BABBAGE'S, SOFTWARE ETC. STORES TO MERGE IN BID TO COMPETE WITH BIGGER CONCERNS

Babbage's Inc. and Software Etc. Stores Inc. agreed to merge into a specialty software retailer with $500 million in annual revenue and greater clout to compete with mass merchants and computer superstores.

Both companies, which primarily run small, bookstore-like operations in shopping malls, have suffered market-share declines in the past year as bigger retailers have broadened their software offerings. Babbage's and Software Etc. specialize in programs for video game players and home computers.

Shareholders in Dallas-based Babbage's will receive 1.3 shares of the new, as-yet-unnamed holding company for every share of Babbage's stock they own. Shareholders in Minneapolis-based Software Etc. will receive one share in the combined company for each Software Etc. share and will own about 54% of the stock in the new company.

"The combined company will be in a much stronger competitive position," said James B. McCurry, chairman of Babbage's, who will become chairman of the combined firm. "Two plus two will at least equal five."

Better Able to Compete

Mr. McCurry said the new company, which will probably be based in Dallas, will be better able to compete on price by combining administrative and distribution functions and by attaining greater buying leverage. Only 10% of the combined company's 700 stores would overlap in the same shopping mall, he said, and no stores will be closed. Each chain will continue to operate under its existing name.

In Nasdaq Stock Market trading, Babbage's gained $1.25, or 11%, to $13 while Software Etc. added $1, or 11%, to $10. The combined company will have about 15 million shares outstanding, and a market value of about $150 million, based on yesterday's closing prices.

Analysts applauded the merger as a way to regain momentum after a run of declining comparable-store sales and widening losses. "This merger is very astute. There are a lot of economies here," said Lewis H. Alton of L. H. Alton & Co.

Stocks Are Upgraded

Robertson Stephens & Co. analyst Keith Benjamin upgraded both stocks to buy from "market performer" after the merger was announced. "Bigger in this market is going to be better," he said. Next year, with new game-playing platforms coming out and a continued boom in multimedia titles for home computers, "these two companies have a money-making opportunity that's phenomenal," Mr. Benjamin predicted.

The board of the new firm will consist of an equal number of directors from each company. Software Etc. Chairman Leonard Riggio will become chairman of the executive committee of the new company and a director, the companies said. Daniel A. DeMatteo, president of Software Etc., and Gary M. Kusin, president of Babbage's, will continue in their current roles.

The merger, if approved by the boards and shareholders of both companies, is expected to close within 60 days, Mr. McCurry said.

Source: Scott McCartney, "Babbage's, Software Etc. Stores to Merge in Bid to Compete with Bigger Concerns," *Wall Street Journal,* 26 August 1994, B2.

Questions

1. The chairperson of the newly merged firm says, "Two plus two will at least equal five." How is this possible? How does this idea relate to the market value added (MVA) concept? How is a positive NPV created with no increase in the total investment?
2. Software Etc. Stores has about 8.1 million shares and Babbage's has about 5.3 million shares. What is the stockholders' estimate of the change in the MVA of each firm due to the merger? (*Hint:* Analyze the market reaction to the merger announcement.)

MAKING THE CONNECTION

1. The idea that two plus two equals five or that the value of the whole exceeds the sum of its parts is called **synergy.** A merger generates synergy if the market value of the two firms combined increases with no additional investment. The NPV of the existing projects increases because the revenue remains at (at least) the same level and costs decrease (through elimination of duplicative administrative and distribution functions). To sum up, the merged firm's market value increases with no change in the existing investment, the NPVs of the existing projects increase, synergy is generated, and the MVA increases.
2. The share price of Software Etc. Stores increased by $1 to $10, and the price of Babbage's shares increased by $1.25 to $13. The value of the equity of the two firms *before* and *after* the merger announcement is as follows:

Before the Merger Announcement

	Number of shares (millions)	Price per share	Total market value of equity (million $)
Software Etc. Stores	8.1	$ 9	$72.90
Babbage's	5.3	$11.75	$62.28 (rounded)

After the Merger Announcement

	Number of shares (millions)	Price per share	Total market value of equity (million $)
Software Etc. Stores	8.1	$10	$81.0
Babbage's	5.3	$13	$68.9

Assuming no change in the debt's value, the stockholders' estimate of the change in MVA as a result of the merger (mainly as a result of cost cutting) is as follows:

Software Etc. Stores: $81 million – $72.9 million = $8.1 million

Babbage's: $68.9 million – $62.28 million = $6.62 million

Management should always consider the benefits of this type of merger. Instead of purchasing new machines and hiring additional personnel, it is sometimes simply better to acquire an existing firm that already has these machines and personnel. In the rest of the book, when we analyze investment projects, we do not exclude the possibility of acquiring existing firms or merging with them.

SUMMARY

The firm's goal is to maximize stockholders' wealth. When a firm accepts a project, the stockholders' wealth will increase or decrease depending on the project's profitability.

A firm maximizes stockholders' wealth by accepting positive NPV projects and rejecting negative NPV projects. The cash flows of a positive NPV project are equivalent to a stream of nonnegative cash flows with at least one positive cash flow (for example, at $t = 0$). Investors would want the firm to accept such a project because it will increase their wealth. The cash flows of a negative NPV project are equivalent to a stream of nonpositive cash flows with at least one negative cash flow. Accepting such a project would decrease stockholders' wealth, and the firm should reject it. Because it leads to maximization of stockholders' wealth, the NPV rule is the optimum investment criterion.

NPV calculations and investment decisions do not depend on the financing source. When cash flows are certain and the firm finances projects by borrowing, the cost of capital is the interest rate payable to the bank. If the firm finances projects with its own equity, the cost of capital is an opportunity cost and corresponds to the interest rate that would be earned if the firm had deposited the investment outlay in the bank. In the case of certain cash flows, the cost of capital used to discount the project's cash flows is equal to the riskless interest rate. In the case of uncertain cash flows, the firm should discount the project's cash flows at a discount rate, k, that is higher than the riskless interest rate, r. The difference between the two rates is the risk premium investors require to compensate them for the risk involved.

Firms can create wealth by expanding or by contracting. For example, IBM eliminated negative NPV projects and created wealth. When a firm expands, management should always consider the benefits of a merger to cut overlapping costs and to create synergy that will boost the combined firm's value.

CHAPTER AT A GLANCE

1. Net present value:

$$NPV = \sum_{t=1}^{T} \frac{CF_t}{(1 + r)^t} - I$$

2. If positive NPV projects are accepted and negative NPV projects are rejected, the firm's value for the stockholders will be maximized, and the stock price will increase.

KEY TERMS

Net present value (NPV)   Market value added (MVA)   Acquisitions
NPV rule   Required rate of return   Mergers
Alternative/Opportunity cost   Risk premium   Synergy

REVIEW AND PRACTICE

5.1 As CFO you are faced with choosing between Project A and Project B. Both projects require an initial outlay of $100,000. Project A yields $130,000 one year from today, and Project B yields $145,000 two years from today. The average annual rate of return on Project B is the total rate of return divided by 2 ((45%)/2 = 22.5%). The average annual rate of return on project A is 30%. The firm's controller tells you, "Because Project A yields a higher average annual rate of return (30% versus 22.5%), it should be preferred over Project B." Appraise this assertion. (*Hint:* Is there enough information to determine which project is preferable? If not, what other information do you need?)

5.2 Use the data in Problem 5.1 to calculate the NPV of the two projects when the discount rate is 10% and, alternatively, when the discount rate is 20%. Which project has the higher NPV?

5.3 "The larger the firm's market value, the larger is its MVA." Evaluate this assertion.

5.4 A project requires an initial outlay of $1,000 and yields $1,700 at the end of the fifth year. You consider "banking the project" by borrowing $1,000 from the bank. You consider the following two loan strategies: (1) borrowing $1,000 for five years at $r = 10\%$ per year, and (2) borrowing $1,000 for one year, repaying the loan (principal and interest) after the first year, and immediately reborrowing the amount you repaid. You would repeat this procedure four times.
a. If you decide on the first loan strategy, how much will you owe the bank at the end of the fifth year?
b. Which strategy is better: (1) the five-year loan or (2) renewal every year for four years?

5.5 Explain "banking the project" in your own words.

5.6 Define and give an example of the opportunity cost of capital.

5.7 Suppose you have a certain cash flow. Does the financing method affect the project's NPV? In your answer explain the difference between debt financing and equity financing.

5.8 A project has the following certain cash flows:

	$t = 0$	$t = 1$
Cash Flows	−$100	$120

The interest rate is $r = 10\%$. You finance the project by borrowing.
a. Calculate the project's NPV.
b. Show that by "banking the project" you can rearrange these cash flows into the form (+, 0)—a positive flow "today" followed by a zero cash flow at time t.
c. "Because investors like cash flows of the form (+, 0), accepting a project with positive NPV will enhance investors' wealth, which, in turn, is consistent with the firm's goal." Evaluate this assertion.

5.9 Repeat Problem 5.8a and 5.8b, but assume that the firm finances the project with its own equity, withdrawing money from its cash holdings to finance the project.

5.10 Suppose you are offered $200 today with no obligation. You decide to accept the offer. (Who wouldn't?) How does your decision justify the NPV rule for a project whose NPV = $200?

5.11 You are considering the following project that will be financed by borrowing at $r = 10\%$.

	$t = 0$	$t = 1$	$t = 2$
Cash Flows	−$1,000	$800	$600

a. How much do you need to borrow for the project's net cash flow plus the loan to be zero at $t = 1$ as well as at $t = 2$?
b. What is your net profit (or loss) at $t = 0$?
c. Calculate the project's NPV. Compare it to your answer to 5.11b. Explain your results.

5.12 Repeat Problem 5.11, but assume you do not need to borrow. You finance the project by using cash you have in the bank. You reduce the deposit at $t = 0$ such that your income from the bank is reduced by $800 at $t = 1$ and by $600 at $t = 2$. Show the incremental cash flows from the project plus the transaction with the bank.

5.13 A firm has $10,000 in cash. Each of its four stockholders holds 25% of the firm's shares. Management is considering whether to pay the $10,000 as cash dividends or to undertake a project with the following certain future cash flows:

	$t = 0$	$t = 1$	$t = 2$
Cash Flows	−$10,000	$10,000	$3,000

If the firm accepts the project, it will distribute the cash flows received at $t = 1$ and $t = 2$ as dividends. Assume the investors and the firm can borrow and lend at 10%.
a. Investor 1 would prefer to spend all that she can at $t = 0$ (and nothing at $t = 1$ and $t = 2$). Would she want the firm to accept or to reject the project? Explain.
b. Investor 2 would prefer to spend as much as he can at $t = 1$ (and zero at the other dates). Would he want the firm to accept or to reject the project? Explain.
c. Investor 3 would prefer to spend as much as she can at $t = 2$ (and zero at the other dates). Would she want the firm to accept or to reject the project? Explain.
d. Investor 4 would prefer to spread his spending evenly across the two future dates ($t = 1$ and $t = 2$) and spend nothing at $t = 0$. Would he want the firm to accept or to reject the project? Explain.

In your answer, calculate the project's NPV, the cash flows each investor receives (with the investor's financial transaction with the bank), and their corresponding PV.

Do the investors' different spending preferences affect the NPV decision rule? Analyze your results carefully. In particular, compare the total PV of all investors' consumption with and without the project.

5.14 The market value of a firm's equity is $100 million. The firm is considering an investment opportunity that, if it is accepted, will be financed by retained earnings. The project has the following certain cash flows (in millions of dollars):

	$t = 0$	$t = 1$
Cash Flows	−$100	$150

The discount rate is 10%.
a. Calculate the value of the firm's equity if the project is accepted. (*Hint:* A positive NPV increases the value of the firm's equity.)
b. Suppose there are 1 million shares outstanding. Calculate the increase in the stock price as a result of the project.

5.15 Firm A merges with Firm B. Firm A's market value is $100 million, and Firm B's market value is $200 million. After the merger, the combined firm's market value is $350 million. Has synergy been created? Explain the positive change in the MVA even though the combined firm has accepted no new projects.

5.16 A firm is considering four new projects (denoted by 1, 2, 3, and 4) with the following NPVs:

$$NPV_1 = \$100 \text{ million}$$

$$NPV_2 = \$80 \text{ million}$$

$$NPV_3 = \$0$$

$$NPV_4 = -\$20 \text{ million}$$

The firm has 100 million shares outstanding. The stock price before deciding on these projects is $1 per share. Calculate the share price:
a. If the firm accepts Project 1.
b. If the firm accepts Project 1 and Project 2.

c. If the firm accepts Projects 1, 2, and 3.

d. If the firm accepts all four projects.

e. What is the relationship between the NPV rule and the firm's value maximization goal?

5.17 Information on the cash flows of Projects A and B follow:

	$t = 0$	$t = 1$
Project A	−$100	$150
Project B	−$100	$180

a. Which project will stockholders prefer?

b. Does your answer depend on the discount rate?

c. Which project has the higher NPV?

5.18 A project has the following certain cash flows:

	$t = 0$	$t = 1$	$t = 2$
Cash Flows	−$1,000	$800	$700

You have no cash and intend to finance the project by borrowing. The annual interest rate on one-year loans is $r = 10\%$, and the annual interest rate on two-year loans is 15%.

a. You would like a zero net cash flow at $t = 1$ and $t = 2$. How much would you borrow?

b. What is the net cash flow at $t = 0$?

c. What is the project's NPV?

5.19 Repeat problem 5.18, but assume you decide to finance the project using cash currently deposited in the bank. Assume you have enough funds invested in the bank for one year at 10% interest or for two years at 15% annual interest. You finance the project by reducing your deposit in the bank. Make sure the cash flow from the project and the bank transaction (the reduction in the deposit) is zero in all years except $t = 0$.

5.20 Which would you prefer, a certain cash flow of $100 in each of the next three years or $260 today? The annual interest rate is $r = 10\%$.

5.21 Define *risk premium*.

5.22 The return on Asset A one year from today is $110 with certainty. Asset A's current price is $100. The return on Asset B will be either $90 with a probability of ½ or $160 with a probability of ½. The risk premium is 10%. Calculate the equilibrium price of Asset B.

5.23 Suppose a project's cash flow one year from now will be either $100 or $500 with equal probability. The initial investment is $120, and the stockholders' required cost of capital for such risky projects is 20%. If the firm accepts the project, will the stock price increase or decrease? By how much? Assume there are 50 shares outstanding.

5.24 A project has the following certain cash flows:

	$t = 0$	$t = 1$
Cash Flows	−$100	$110

The interest rate for depositing money in the bank is 8%; but when you borrow money, you pay 12% interest.

a. You have a deposit in the bank. Will you accept the project if you have to finance it by withdrawing money from your bank deposit? Show the cash flow you create at $t = 1$ when you create zero net cash flow at $t = 0$ (from the project plus the financial transaction with the bank). Calculate the project's NPV.

b. Suppose you have no resources, and to finance the project you would have to borrow money. Will you accept the project? Again, assume you create a zero cash flow at date $t = 0$ (from the financial transaction and the project's cash flow).

c. Contrast and explain your answers to 5.24a and 5.24b.

5.25 A firm is considering a project with the following certain cash flows:

	$t = 0$	$t = 1$	$t = 2$
Cash Flow	−$100	$0	$121

The interest rate is 10%.

a. Calculate the NPV. Should the firm accept the project?

b. If the firm borrows money from the bank such that the net cash flows at dates $t = 1$ and $t = 2$ (from the financial transaction with the bank and the project) are equal to zero, what will the cash flow be at $t = 0$?

c. In light of your answer to 5.25b, explain the following assertion: "If the project's NPV = 0, the firm will be indifferent between accepting or rejecting it."

INTERNET QUESTIONS

5.26 Assume that you own a small business. Visit BEAR's site and take a snapshot valuation of your business by filling in (hypothetical) cash flows, asset values, etc., and then requesting a "price tag" via e-mail. Using the valuation principles you learned in this chapter, try to determine how BEAR valued your firm.

http://www.bearval.com

5.27 Visit Money Advisor's site and use their Human Life Value Calculator to determine the value of your life. According to their calculations, what is your life worth? Do you agree? Why or why not?

http://www.moneyadvisor.com

YOUR TURN: APPLYING THEORY TO PRACTICE
THE LARGEST WEALTH CREATORS AND WEALTH DESTROYERS

The following data show the five firms with the highest MVA and the five with the lowest MVA of the 1,000 largest U.S. firms in 1995.

Company	MVA Rank	Market Value Added (millions)	Cost of Capital	Invested Capital (millions)
Coca-Cola	1	$60,846	10.0%	$ 8,468
General Electric	2	52,071	12.9%	45,630
Wal-Mart Stores	3	34,996	9.6%	26,559
Merck	4	31,467	12.8%	18,940
Microsoft	5	29,904	14.4%	3,648
Digital Equipment	996	−4,684	12.9%	12,226
International Business Machines	997	−8,864	9.8%	66,268
RJR Nabisco Holdings	998	−11,761	12.9%	33,946
Ford Motor	999	−13,757	12.9%	54,160
General Motors	1,000	−17,803	10.9%	87,065

Source: Anne B. Fisher, "Creating Stockholder Wealth," *Fortune* 132, no. 12 (December 1995): 105–116. Copyright © 1995 Time Inc. All rights reserved.

Questions

1. Suppose a firm invested $10 billion 15 years ago. Today the firm's market value is $20 billion.
a. What is its MVA?
b. Does your answer imply that the firm invested in projects with a very high NPV? (*Hint:* Assume that the firm could earn 7% annual interest at the bank.)
c. How would your answer change if the firm had invested the capital one year ago?
2. For each of the 10 firms listed above, assume constant annual perpetual net cash flows over the

years and that the investment occurred on the publication date of the list. Calculate the average expected annual cash flow that would justify the reported MVA. (*Hint:* Use the firm's cost of capital as reported in the table.)

3. a. How do you explain the variation in cost of capital among the 10 firms?

b. The riskless interest rate is 5%. What is the risk premium of each of these 10 firms?

4. Consider Merck Corporation: Its cost of capital is 12.8%, and the rate of return on its in-vested capital is 19.4%. The interest rate is 5%. Assume these figures will not vary across time.

a. Calculate Merck's annual cash flow and the NPV of its invested capital.

b. Compare these figures to the reported MVA. Calculate what the MVA would be if the cash flows were certain. Assume all capital is invested today and there is no difference between the accounting data and the market value of the invested capital.

Appendix 5A   The NPV Criterion and Wealth Creation: Generalization

In this appendix we demonstrate that the NPV rule guarantees stock price maximization regardless of whether a firm finances the project by debt or equity. We also show that when cash flows are certain, the cost of capital that should be used to discount the future cash flows is the riskless interest rate, r.

Suppose a firm considers a project with an economic life of T years. The cash flow expected in Year t is CF_t ($t = 1, 2, \ldots, T$), and the project's initial outlay at $t = 0$ is I. Should the firm accept the project? The project's NPV is given by Equation 5.1:

$$NPV = \sum_{t=1}^{T} \frac{CF_t}{(1 + r)^t} - I$$

We will show that in this general case a positive NPV project creates wealth and a negative NPV project destroys wealth. Moreover, the wealth a project creates or destroys is exactly equal to its NPV. This result provides economic justification for the NPV as an optimum investment decision rule. We will show this first with debt financing and then with equity financing.

DEBT FINANCING

The project's cash flows are shown in the first row of Table 5A-1. We suggest the following borrowing strategy ("banking the project"), which will create zero cash flows at all dates except for $t = 0$. At $t = 0$, borrow $CF_1/(1 + r)$ for one year. At $t = 1$, repay $(1 + r) \times [CF_1/(1 + r)] = CF_1$. In addition, borrow $CF_2/(1 + r)^2$ at $t = 0$ for two years, and in general borrow $CF_t/(1 + r)^t$ at $t = 0$ for t years.[3] Repay CF_1 at the end of Year 1; CF_2 at the end of Year 2; and in general, repay CF_t at the end of Year t:

---

3. If CF_t is negative, the firm will deposit money in the bank (rather than borrow) to ensure that the net cash flow from the bank and the financial transaction in Year t total zero. If the firm does not have cash to deposit, it can use the borrowed money corresponding to the cash flow amounts produced in other years to deposit against cash flow CF_t.

$$\frac{CF_t}{(1+r)^t} \qquad \times \qquad (1+r)^t \qquad = \qquad CF_t$$

↓		↓		↓
Amount Borrowed for t Years	×	Interest Factor for t Years	=	Repayment to the Bank

If the firm uses this strategy, the project's future cash flows will correspond exactly to the repayments to the bank, and there will be a zero net cash flow at all dates except $t = 0$. How much money will the firm borrow from the bank on these loans? It will receive the following sums:

$$\frac{CF_1}{(1+r)} \quad + \quad \frac{CF_2}{(1+r)^2} \quad + \quad \cdots \quad + \quad \frac{CF_T}{(1+r)^T} \quad = \quad \sum_{t=1}^{T}\frac{CF_t}{(1+r)^t}$$

↓	↓		↓	↓
From 1-Year Loan	From 2-Year Loan		From T-Year Loan	Total Cash Flow from All Loans

Table 5A-1 summarizes the cash flows from the project and from the combined transaction. Note that by using this borrowing strategy, the firm's *net* cash flow (from the bank and the project) will be zero at the end of each year except the beginning of the first year (at $t = 0$). This means that the project is worthwhile *only if the cash flow at the beginning of the first year (t = 0) is positive*—that is, if

$$\sum_{t=1}^{T} CF_t/(1+r)^t \qquad - \qquad I > 0$$

↓		↓
Cash Inflow from Borrowing		Cash Outflow: Project Outlay

TABLE 5A-1   **Cash Flows from the Project and the Financial Transaction: *T*-Year Project with Debt Financing**

Source of Cash	Beginning of First Year	End of First Year	End of Second Year	. . .	End of Tth Year
Project	$-I$	CF_1	CF_2	. . .	CF_T
Borrowing at $t = 0$ from Bank	$\sum_{t=1}^{T} CF_t/(1+r)^t$	$-CF_1$	$-CF_2$	. . .	$-CF_T$
Combined Transaction (Project + Bank)	$\sum_{t=1}^{T} CF_t/(1+r)^t - I$	0	0	. . .	0

$\sum_{t=1}^{T} CF_t/(1 + r)^t - I$ is the project's NPV. Hence, the project creates wealth, and the firm should accept it, only if the NPV is positive when the cash flows are discounted at the riskless interest rate, r. If NPV < 0, the firm should reject the project. The decision rule is

Discount all future certain cash flows at r. *If the NPV is positive, accept the project; if it is negative, reject the project.*

The firm does not actually have to borrow the money as shown in Table 5A-1. That such borrowing *is possible* is sufficient to show that if the NPV > 0, the firm should accept the project. Suppose two members of a board of directors disagree on whether to accept a project. If the NPV > 0, the member in favor of the project can simply cite the borrowing strategy suggested in Table 5A-1 to convince the member who is against borrowing that the project is worthwhile.

EQUITY FINANCING

Suppose the firm issues stock and deposits the proceeds in the bank. Withdrawing money from the bank and using it to finance a project is considered equity financing (because the source of the cash is a stock issue). Does this affect our conclusion regarding the validity of the NPV rule? Not at all. Let us now generalize our NPV results to the case of a T-year project that the firm finances by equity. For this purpose, assume the firm issues stock and has cash holdings. The cash holdings are deposited in the bank, and the firm will have to withdraw them to finance the project.

Table 5A-2 shows the cash flows from such a project as well as the flows generated by withdrawing money from the bank to finance the project. Suppose the firm has money deposited in the bank for one year, for two years, and for T years. If it withdraws $CF_1/(1 + r)$ from the one-year deposit, its cash flow from the bank at $t = 1$ will be reduced by CF_1. (Recall that the money withdrawn can be redeposited in the bank to yield $[CF_1/(1 + r)] \times (1 + r) = CF_1$.) Similarly, the firm withdraws $CF_2/(1 + r)^2$ from the two-year deposit; $CF_3/(1 + r)^3$ from the three-year deposit; and $CF_T/(1 + r)^T$ from the T-year deposit.[4]

By reducing its cash holdings, the firm will reduce its cash flow from the bank by CF_t in Year t ($t = 1, 2, \ldots, T$), but at $t = 0$ the firm will receive the sum of

$$\sum_{t=1}^{T} CF_t/(1 + r)^t$$

Should the firm withdraw its deposits from the bank and use its money to finance the project? Table 5A-2 illustrates that this strategy is recommended *only if the project's NPV is positive.*

The first line of Table 5A-2 shows the project's cash flow. The second line shows the cash flow resulting from withdrawing the $CF_t/(1 + r)^t$ from the t-th year's deposit account. The annual cash flow from the bank in Year t is reduced by $[CF_t/(1 + r)^t] \times (1 + r)^t = CF_t$. In the last line of Table 5A-2, we show the combined cash flows pro-

---

4. If CF_t is negative, the firm borrows $CF_t/(1 + r)^t$ for t years at $t = 0$. This will reduce the equity needed for the project.

TABLE 5A-2	Cash Flows from Project and the Financial Transaction: T-Year Project with Equity Financing					
Source of Cash Flows	**Beginning of First Year**	**End of First Year**	**End of Second Year**	...	**End of Tth Year**	
Project	$-I$	CF_1	CF_2	...	CF_T	
Cash Flows Created by Withdrawals from Deposit in the Bank	$\sum_{t=1}^{T} CF_t/(1+r)^t$	$-CF_1$	$-CF_2$	...	$-CF_T$	
Combined Transaction	$\sum_{t=1}^{T} CF_t/(1+r)^t - I$	0	0	...	0	

duced by withdrawing money from the bank and using it to finance the project. In all years the project's cash flow exactly offsets the reduction in the cash flow from the bank, and so the net cash flow is zero at all dates except $t = 0$. Withdrawing the money from the bank and using it to finance the project is the correct decision if the cash flow at $t = 0$ is positive. However, the net cash flow at $t = 0$ will be positive only if

$$\sum_{t=1}^{T} CF_t/(1+r)^t - I > 0$$

or *only if the project's NPV is positive.*

Whether the firm finances a project by borrowing or by equity, it should discount the future cash flows at the riskless interest rate. (Remember that we assumed certainty.) Borrowed money entails an out-of-pocket expense—namely, the interest paid to the lender. If the firm withdraws money from its bank deposits, the interest rate reflects the *opportunity cost,* or the forgone rate of return that the firm could have earned on the money had it not invested in the project.

Since the financing method does not affect the project's NPV as given by Equation 5.1, the decision whether to accept or reject a project is independent of the financing method. This conclusion holds also for uncertain cash flows and will be discussed in forthcoming chapters. However, when the project's cash flows are uncertain, the cost of capital will be k rather than r, where $k > r$.

APPENDIX REVIEW AND PRACTICE

5A.1 Suppose you have two possible projects, A and B. You can invest in either Project A or Project B, but not in both.

	Today	Year 1	Year 2	Year 3	Year 4
Project A	$-I_A$	CF_{1A}	CF_{2A}	CF_{3A}	CF_{4A}
Project B	$-I_B$	CF_{1B}	CF_{2B}	CF_{3B}	CF_{4B}

Project A has a higher NPV than Project B. Show that by borrowing or lending at the riskless interest rate, r, you can create a cash flow stream for Project A that will dominate the cash flows of Project B. In other words, justify selecting the project with the higher NPV. (*Hint:* Borrow and lend such that by "banking" Project A, you replicate the cash flows of Project B at all dates except $t = 0$.)

5A.2 Suppose a project has the following certain cash flows:

	$t = 0$	$t = 1$	$t = 2$
Cash Flows	−$100,000	$100,000	$100,000

The firm has $500,000 deposited in the bank for one year and $400,000 deposited for two years. The interest rate is $r = 10\%$. If the firm decides to accept the project, it will finance the project by reducing its deposits in the bank.

a. Calculate the project's NPV.

b. "Bank" the project so that the cash flow from the project plus the deposit reduction will be zero at $t = 1$ and $t = 2$. How much wealth does the project create when the firm finances it by equity?

CHAPTER 6

NET PRESENT VALUE VERSUS OTHER INVESTMENT CRITERIA

LEARNING OBJECTIVES

After reading this chapter, you should understand:

1. How to use the following investment decision rules, in addition to net present value (NPV): internal rate of return (IRR), payback period (PBP), accounting rate of return (ARR), profitability index, and discounted payback.

2. The pros and cons of each decision rule and why the NPV rule is superior.

3. Why the NPV and the IRR rules may yield different investment rankings.

4. Why managers use the various decision rules.

CORPORATE FINANCE IN THE NEWS

CORPORATE EXECUTIVES DISCUSS INVESTMENT CRITERIA

In surveying the literature of financial practitioners, we find the following assertions that reflect managers' views on various investment decision criteria:

1. One executive commented, "Your payback could be in two years or twenty, and twenty years scares us to death."[1]

2. A group of practitioners and academics recommended a series of steps for evaluating firms and applied them to Merck Corporation. "Calculate the net present value of the premium. You do this by dividing the premium by an appropriate discount rate, such as the company's cost of capital. Using an arbitrarily chosen 15% discount rate, that yields, for Merck, $11.1 billion."[2]

3. Robert Goizueta, CEO of Coca-Cola, stated, "Back in 1980 we made a study of the returns we were getting from our fountain business. And we found out that we were making much less than our cost of capital which at that time, with no debt, was about 16%."[3]

1. "Harris Conversation for the '90s: A Discussion of a Select Group of Business Executives," *Fortune*, April 20, 1992, p. 254. Copyright © 1992 Times Inc. All rights reserved.
2. Thomas A. Stewart, "Trying to Grasp the Intangible," *Fortune* 132, no. 7 (October 1995):157–158. Copyright © 1995 Time Inc. All rights reserved.
3. "A Conversation with Robert Goizueta and Jack Welch," *Fortune* 132, no. 12 (December 1995):96. Copyright © 1995 Time Inc. All rights reserved.

6.1 INTRODUCTION

The three quotes in Corporate Finance in the News reveal that managers evaluate investments in different ways. The first quote mentions the payback criterion; the second, the net present value; and the third compares return to the cost of capital.

In Chapter 5 we argued that the net present value (NPV) rule produces optimal investment decisions. By accepting projects with positive NPVs and rejecting projects with negative NPVs, managers maximize the value of the firm's stock. However, Table 6-1, as well as the quotes in the Corporate Finance in the News, shows that managers often use other investment criteria. Moreover, Table 6-1 shows that only about 10% of the large multinational firms listed in the *Fortune 500* actually use the NPV rule in making their investment decisions. If the NPV rule produces optimal investment decisions, why do the majority of firms use other investment rules?

In calculating a project's NPV, the CFO needs precise information on the project's risk and on its annual cash flows during the project's life. Unfortunately, the CFO does not always have such precise information. Even though there is strong *theoretical* justification for the NPV rule, we should not be surprised that CFOs use other investment criteria that need less information than the NPV rule.

In this chapter we introduce various alternative investment criteria: *internal rate of return, payback period, accounting rate of return,* and *profitability index.* We discuss their pros and cons and explain why managers use such rules other than NPV in spite of their deficiencies. However, before turning to these other investment criteria, let us summarize the main properties of the NPV rule. Later we will discuss the extent to which the other investment criteria share these properties.

6.2 THE PROPERTIES OF THE NPV RULE

The properties of the NPV rule are as follows:

1. The NPV rule uses the project's cash flows (not its accounting earnings) and considers *all* cash flows during the project's life.

TABLE 6-1 Capital Budgeting Techniques Used as Primary Measures	U.S. firms	Non-U.S. firms	Simple average
Internal rate of return	62.0%	34.0%	48.0%
Net present value	9.0	10.0	9.5
Profitability index	3.0	10.0	6.5
Accounting rate of return	14.0	15.0	14.5
Payback period	12.0	31.0	21.5
Total	100.0%	100.0%	100.0%

Source: Suk H. Kim and Trevor Crick, "Foreign Capital Budgeting Practices Used by the U.S. and Non-U.S. Multinational Companies," *The Engineering Economist* (Spring 1984):207–215.

2. The NPV rule *discounts* the cash flows rather than simply totaling them. In other words, in recognizing that $1 today is worth more than $1 tomorrow, it considers the time value of money.
3. The cost of capital, k, used in the NPV calculation is equal to the riskless interest rate, r, when cash flows are certain. When cash flows are uncertain, the cost of capital is higher than the riskless interest rate. Discounting the project's cash flows at the cost of capital, as we shall see, is unique to the NPV rule.
4. The NPV rule considers the scale or magnitude of the initial investment.
5. The NPV rule is consistent with the firm's goal of maximizing stockholders' wealth as stated in Chapter 1.

The NPV rule is superior because it maximizes wealth. Nevertheless, because firms use investment rules other than the NPV rule, they cannot simply be dismissed. Moreover, it may be useful to understand the practical (as opposed to theoretical) advantages that they may have over the NPV rule.

6.3 THE INTERNAL RATE OF RETURN (IRR) RULE

As Table 6-1 indicates, the main challenger to the NPV rule is the internal rate of return (IRR) rule. We first define the IRR rule, then explain its economic rationale, and finally, contrast it with the NPV rule.

6.3.1 The IRR: Definition

Although the PV of future cash flows can be calculated at any arbitrary discount rate, the NPV rule requires that they be discounted at the cost of capital and that the project's NPV be expressed in dollars. In calculating the project's IRR, we solve for the discount rate (expressed as a percentage) that equates the project's NPV to zero. This specific discount rate is the project's **internal rate of return (IRR).**

The project's IRR is the value of R that satisfies the following equation:

$$\sum_{t=1}^{T} \frac{CF_t}{(1 + R)^t} - I = 0 \tag{6.1}$$

where CF_t is the cash flow in Year t, I is the initial investment, and T is the project's duration in years.

The IRR rule is as follows:[4]

• If $R > k$, the firm should accept the project.
• If $R < k$, the firm should reject the project.

---

4. This rule is valid for most projects with a negative cash flow followed by positive cash flows (- + + + + . . .). If we have cash flows of the form, + - - - - (as in a bank loan), then the rule is reversed; if $R > k$, reject the project; and if $R < k$, accept the project. (See Problem 6.7 at the end of the chapter.)

- If $R = k$, the firm will be indifferent between accepting and rejecting the project.

where k is the relevant cost of capital.

The following problem demonstrates calculation of the IRR for a short-term project.

PRACTICE BOX

Problem

An investment requiring an initial outlay of $1,000 is expected to yield a cash flow of $1,200 at the end of Year 1. What is the project's IRR?

Solution

We solve for the value of the discount rate R that equates the project's NPV to zero. If

$$\text{NPV} = \frac{\$1,200}{1 + R} - \$1,000 = 0$$

then

$$\frac{\$1,200}{1 + R} = \$1,000$$

Therefore,

$$R = \frac{\$1,200}{\$1,000} - 1 = 1.2 - 1 = 0.2 \text{ or } 20\%$$

The project's IRR is 20%.

The preceding problem is a straightforward example of IRR. However, when a project is of longer duration, the calculation of the IRR is less obvious, as shown in the following problem.

PRACTICE BOX

Problem

Suppose a firm is considering the following two-year project:

	Year 0	Year 1	Year 2
Cash flows	−$1,735.54	$1,000	$1,000

What is the project's IRR?   *(continued)*

Solution   By definition, this project's IRR is the value of R that solves the following equation:

$$-\$1,735.54 + \frac{\$1,000}{1 + R} + \frac{\$1,000}{(1 + R)^2} = 0$$

One way of solving this equation is to experiment with various values of R to see which discount rate equates the NPV to zero.

1. Try $R = 0$:

$$\text{NPV} = -\$1,735.54 + \$1,000 + \$1,000 = \$264.46$$

The NPV is positive. So try a higher discount rate.

2. Try $R = 5\%$:

$$\text{NPV} = -\$1,735.54 + \frac{\$1,000}{1.05} + \frac{\$1,000}{(1.05)^2}$$

$$\cong -\$1,735.54 + \$952.38 + \$907.03 = \$123.87$$

The NPV is still positive.

3. Increase the discount rate to $R = 10\%$:

$$\text{NPV} = -\$1,735.54 + \frac{\$1,000}{1.1} + \frac{\$1,000}{(1.1)^2}$$

$$\cong -\$1,735.54 + \$909.09 + \$826.45 = \$0$$

Since the NPV is zero, the project's IRR is 10%.

Additional trial-and-error calculations will sometimes be needed to obtain the discount rate that exactly equates the NPV to zero. However, financial calculators can easily produce the IRR and can make these calculations much easier.

If annual cash flows are constant, as in the preceding problem, financial tables that provide the PV of an annuity can also be used to calculate a project's IRR. See, for example, Table A-3, at the end of the book. The PV of the $1,000 annuity is $1,000 $\times$ DAF($r\%$,2), where DAF($r\%$,2) is the discount annuity factor corresponding to $T = 2$ years and a discount rate of $r\%$. The project's NPV = 0 if

$$\$1,000 \times \text{DAF}_{r\%,2} = \$1,755.54$$

or

$$\text{DAF}_{r\%,2} = \frac{\$1,735.54}{\$1,000} = 1.73554$$

In this example, look at the line corresponding to $T = 2$ (for a two-year project) and move to the right to the number 1.7355. (Only four figures after the decimal are reported in Table A–3, and this produces the slight deviation.) To verify, calculate the PV of the project's cash flows. Because we have a cash flow of $1,000 each year, the PV is

$$\$1,000 \times 1.7355 = \$1,735.50$$

which is equal to the initial investment. (The slight difference is due to rounding of the figures in Table A–3.) Therefore, the NPV = 0. Now move vertically above this figure in the table, and you will find that the associated discount rate is 10%; that is, for the NPV to be zero, the DAF must be 1.7355 and discount rate has to be 10%, and the project's IRR is 10%. However, the tables cannot provide discount rates as precise as, say, 10.23% or 11.2%. In such cases, a financial calculator is not only recommended—it is indispensable! The following problem demonstrates calculation of the IRR for a long-term loan.

PRACTICE BOX

Problem

Suppose that if you take out a $10,000 student loan, you will have to pay $1,627.45 at the end of each of the next 10 years. Use a financial calculator or Table A–3 to compute the loan's IRR from the bank's point of view.

Solution

From the bank's point of view, the IRR is the value of R that solves the equation

$$\$1,627.45 \times \sum_{t=1}^{10} \frac{1}{(1 + R)^t} - \$10,000 = 0$$

or

$$\sum_{t=1}^{10} \frac{1}{(1 + R)^t} = \frac{\$10,000}{\$1,627.45} = 6.1446$$

The term $\sum_{t=1}^{10} \frac{1}{(1 + R)^t}$ is actually the formula for the PV of an annuity. (See Equation (4.7) in Chapter 4.) Therefore, we can use Table A–3.

From the row corresponding to 10 years, we find that the number 6.1446 appears under the discount rate 10%. From the bank's perspective, the IRR of the loan is 10%.

6.3.2 The Economic Rationale for the IRR Rule

The IRR measures a project's profitability in percentage terms. Determining whether that percentage makes the project acceptable depends on how much it will cost the firm to fund the project—that is, on the *cost of capital*. For instance, if the project's IRR is 10% and the cost of capital is less than 10%, the firm should accept the project because its cash flows will sufficiently cover the investment and will result in a profit. To see this relationship, let us return to our two-year project with an initial investment of $1,735.54 and a cash flow of $1,000 in each of the two years. For simplicity, assume certainty; therefore, the cost of capital equals the riskless interest rate. Assume also that the firm finances the project by borrowing the $1,735.54 from the bank. If the project's IRR is 10% and if the firm finances it by borrowing at 10%, the project's cash flows will be *exactly* sufficient to cover the principal and the interest to be paid to the bank. The detailed calculations are shown in Table 6-2, which illustrates project financing by borrowing and the amortization (repayment) of the loan.

Because it finances the project by borrowing, the firm will use the project's $1,000 cash flow at the end of Year 1 to pay $173.55 in interest, and it will use the remaining $826.45 to repay part of the outstanding principal. After the firm pays part of the principal, its outstanding loan will be $909.09 ($1,735.54 − $826.45), and the interest in Year 2 will be only $90.91. The firm will use the $1,000 received in the second year to pay the interest ($90.91), and it will use what is left to repay the outstanding principal ($909.09). This way the project's cash flows plus the financial transaction cash flows will be zero at all dates.

What conclusions can we draw from this example? The IRR measures the percentage profit on a project's investment outlay. An IRR of 10% implies that a firm can borrow at an interest rate of up to 10% and still have a worthwhile project. If a firm borrows at exactly 10%, it will be indifferent between accepting or rejecting the project because the net cash flows will be zero at all dates (see Table 6-2). If the IRR is higher than the interest rate, the firm, in addition to repaying the bank, will make a profit. For instance, in our two-year project, if the cash flows were $1,000 in the

TABLE 6-2 Amortization Table: A Project with IRR = 10% Financed by Borrowing at 10% (figures in $)		Year 0	Year 1	Year 2
	Project cash flows	−1,735.54	1,000.00	1,000.00
		Financial Transaction		
		Year 0	Year 1	Year 2
	Borrow from bank	1,735.54		
	Interest payment (at 10%)		−173.55	−90.91
	Payment of principal		−826.45	−909.09
	Total payment		−1,000.00	−1,000.00
	Loan outstanding	1,735.54	+909.09	0
	Net cash flow from project and bank	0	0	0

first year and $1,100 in the second year, the IRR would be higher than 10% (compute this on a calculator). After repaying the interest and the principal to the bank, the firm would receive the following net cash flows:

	Year 0	Year 1	Year 2
Net cash flows (project and bank)	0	0	$100

where the $100 represents the remaining cash flow. Since the firm would make a $100 profit, it would accept the project because with zero out-of-pocket expense (it financed the project by borrowing) it receives a positive cash flow in Year 2. In other words, if the IRR is higher than the riskless interest rate (which is the cost of capital under certainty), there is a positive net cash flow, and the firm should accept the project. The positive cash flow results because the investment's profitability is greater than the cost of capital, and the project creates an economic value.

Goizueta's quote in Corporate Finance in the News indicates that Coca-Cola uses the IRR rule in investment decisions because the returns (which probably refer to the IRRs) are compared to the cost of capital—exactly as the IRR rule advocates.

6.3.3 Graphical Representation of the IRR Rule

Before we finish explaining the IRR rule, let's look at the graphical relationship among the IRR, the NPV, and the discount rate.

Suppose we have a project with the following cash flows:

	Year 0	Year 1
Cash flows	–$100	$110

The NPV curve shows the NPV of these cash flows for various discount rates. To draw it, we first have to calculate the NPV for various discount rates:

Discount rate (%)	NPV ($)
0	10.00
2	7.84
5	4.76
8	1.85
10	0.00
12	–1.79
20	–8.33

Plotting the NPV ($) on the Y-axis and the discount rate (%) on the X-axis gives us the NPV curve as shown in Figure 6-1. Note that the higher the discount rate, the lower the NPV. At the point where the NPV curve intersects the horizontal axis, the NPV is exactly zero. We define IRR as the discount rate at which NPV = 0. Therefore,

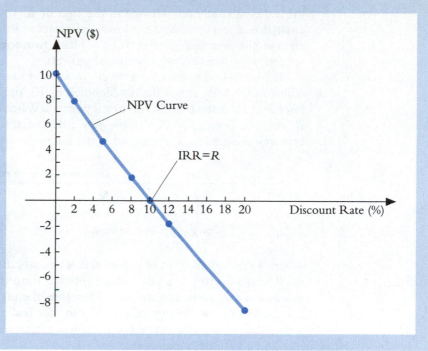

FIGURE 6-1
Graphical Representation of the NPV Curve

it is the point at which the NPV curve intersects the horizontal axis—in this case, 10%.

6.4 THE NPV RULE VERSUS THE IRR RULE

So far, it seems that both the NPV and the IRR rules have economic rationales and that both would be suitable investment criteria. However, the IRR rule can be misleading, depending on whether the projects are *independent* or *mutually exclusive,* as we will now see.

6.4.1 Independent Projects

Most projects have initial outlays followed by positive cash flows, as shown in the following chart:

	Year 0	Year 1	Year 2	Year 3	...
Cash flows	−	+	+	+	...

Projects with only one change in the sign of their cash flows have **conventional cash flows** and are called conventional projects. Projects with more than one sign change (for example, $-+-+++\dots$) have **nonconventional cash flows.** In this section we discuss only conventional projects.

Figure 6-1 illustrates the NPV curve for a conventional project. When the discount rate exactly equals the IRR (denoted by R), the project's NPV is zero. When the discount rate is less than R, the NPV is positive. When the discount rate is higher than R, the NPV is negative. Thus, the NPV rule and the IRR rule lead to the same accept/reject decision, as illustrated in the following chart (see also Figure 6-1):

NPV	IRR	**Decision (by both rules)**
NPV > 0	$R > k$	Accept
NPV = 0	$R = k$	Indifferent
NPV < 0	$R < k$	Reject

where k denotes the cost of capital and R denotes the project's IRR.

The IRR is given as a percentage, which is intuitively better understood than the numerical dollar value of the NPV. Therefore, the IRR rule would seem equivalent, if not preferable, to the NPV rule. Is it? No, not really. As hinted earlier, the issue of which rule is superior depends on projects' characteristics—whether they are independent or mutually exclusive.

Two projects are **independent** if the decision regarding one of them does not affect the decision regarding the other. Put differently, projects are independent if accepting one of them does not rule out the possibility of accepting the other. Independent projects can be analyzed separately, and for independent projects the NPV and the IRR rules lead to the same investment decision.

6.4.2 Mutually Exclusive Projects

However, what if projects are *not independent*—that is, what if they depend on each other? For example, what if a farmer has a piece of land on which he can grow either vegetables or citrus but not both? What if an entrepreneur can invest either in a textile firm or in an oil drilling firm but not both? In such instances, the projects are not independent: Accepting one project means rejecting the other; the projects are **mutually exclusive.** For mutually exclusive projects the NPV and the IRR rules do not necessarily yield the same decision. As we will show, the decision based on the NPV rule is superior. Let us take a closer look at the case of mutually exclusive projects.

Suppose a firm can accept either Project A or Project B but not both. The projects' cash flows are as follows:

	Year 0	Year 1
Project A	−$1,000	$1,200
Project B	−$2,000	$2,360

The projects' IRRS are easy to calculate.

$$\text{Project A:} \quad R = \frac{\$1,200}{\$1,000} - 1 = 0.2 \text{ or } 20\%$$

$$\text{Project B:} \quad R = \frac{\$2,360}{\$2,000} - 1 = 0.18 \text{ or } 18\%$$

Assuming a 10% cost of capital, we can calculate the NPV of each project.

$$\text{Project A:} \quad \text{NPV} = \frac{\$1,200}{1.1} - \$1,000 \cong \$90.91$$

$$\text{Project B:} \quad \text{NPV} = \frac{\$2,360}{1.1} - \$2,000 \cong \$145.45$$

Because the firm can accept only one of these projects, it has a conflict. The NPV rule says to accept Project B because it has the higher NPV; the IRR rule says to accept Project A because it has the higher internal rate of return.

Figure 6-2 shows the NPV curves of these two investments. The two NPV curves intersect at discount rate k_0. If the cost of capital is greater than k_0, there is no conflict between the two rules because

$$\text{NPV}_A > \text{NPV}_B$$

$$\text{IRR}_A > \text{IRR}_B$$

In this case both rules say to choose Project A.

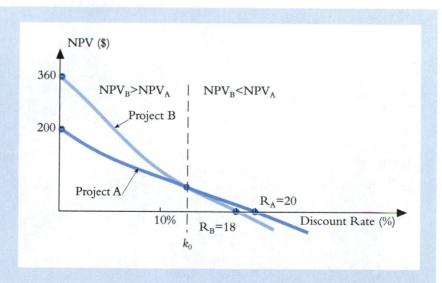

FIGURE 6-2
The NPV Curves of Two Mutually Exclusive Projects

However, in our example, the cost of capital (10%) is smaller than k_0. Therefore,

$$\text{NPV}_\text{B} > \text{NPV}_\text{A}$$

$$\text{IRR}_\text{B} < \text{IRR}_\text{A}$$

which creates a conflict. Which rule leads to the correct investment decision?

We will add a financial transaction to each project to show the superiority of the NPV rule. Under certainty, the firm can carry out a financial transaction with the bank at the 10% interest rate. Under uncertainty, the firm can carry out the financial transaction with its stockholders and bondholders at a higher cost than the riskless interest rate. (The higher discount rate reflects the risk premium that stockholders and bondholders require.) For simplicity, assume certainty and that the firm carries out a financial transaction such that the net cash flow at $t = 1$ is zero. To see the superiority of the NPV rule in this example, let us "bank" the projects—that is, add a borrowing transaction to both projects' cash flows, as depicted in Table 6-3.

As you can see, after "banking" the two projects, Project B provides a larger cash flow at $t = 0$ ($145.45 versus $90.91). Because both projects' net cash flows at $t = 1$ are zero (by construction), the firm will prefer the project with the larger cash flow at $t = 0$.

As this example shows, when the NPV and the IRR rules produce conflicting investment decisions, the NPV rule is superior. Combined with the financial transaction (which by assumption is available), the NPV rule maximizes the cash flow available at $t = 0$ and it also maximizes the stockholders' wealth. This result is consistent with the firm's goal and with the rule that accepting positive NPV projects increases stockholders' wealth (as stated in Chapter 5). We have shown that the higher the NPV, the larger is the increase in stockholders' wealth.

TABLE 6-3 The Cash Flows of Project A and Project B with the Addition of a Financial Transaction	Project A	$t = 0$	$t = 1$
	Cash flow from project	−$1,000	$1,200
	Cash flow from bank	Borrow: $1,090.91	Loan repayment: −$1,200[a]
	Net cash flow	$90.91	$0

	Project B	$t = 0$	$t = 1$
	Cash flow from project	−$2,000	$2,360
	Cash flow from bank	Borrow: $2,145.45	Loan repayment: −$2,360[b]
	Net cash flow	$145.45	$0

[a]$1,090.91 × (1.1) ≅ $1,200

[b]$2,145.45 × (1.1) ≅ $2,360

6.5 THE REASONS FOR THE DIFFERENCES IN PROJECT RANKING BY THE NPV AND THE IRR RULES

Why do the NPV and the IRR rules provide different project rankings? The answer relates to the time value of money. First, note that in discounting the project's cash flows, both rules consider the time value of money. However, the rules' **reinvestment** assumptions consider the time value of money differently, and this is one way in which differences in project ranking may result. The NPV rule assumes that re-investment of the project's interim cash flows are *at the cost of capital,* whereas the IRR rule assumes reinvestment *at the project's IRR.* Another reason for differences in project rankings concerns the scale of investment. The IRR rule does not consider the scale of investment, whereas the NPV rule does. Let us demonstrate how these two factors affect project ranking.

6.5.1 Interim Cash Flow Reinvestment

To see how interim cash flow reinvestment affects project ranking under the NPV and IRR rules, consider the following two projects:

	Year 0 Cash Flow	Year 1 Cash Flow	Year 2 Cash Flow	IRR	PV (at 10% cost of capital)	NPV (at 10% cost of capital)
Project A	−$100	$0	$144	20%	$119.01	$19.01
Project B	−$100	$125	$0	25%	$113.64	$13.64

As you can see, the NPV and the IRR rules yield different rankings. The reason for the difference in this case stems from the different cash flow spread over the two years. Project A provides a cash flow in Year 2, whereas project B provides a cash flow in Year 1.

The initial investments are identical, so we can ignore them and compare either the PV or the FV of the two projects. Both PV and FV should yield the same project ranking as long as the *same cost of capital* is used for discounting and for reinvesting interim cash flows. If we compare present values of the cash flows, Project A is superior. Suppose, though, that we want to compare the two projects in terms of their future values, rather than their present values, and to choose the project with the higher future value. Comparing future values involves reinvestment of interim cash flows.

Let's focus on the reinvestment assumptions inherent in the NPV and IRR criteria. Project A's $144 cash flow is received in Year 2, and because it is already stated in terms of future value, there is no reinvestment. Project B's $125 cash flow is received in Year 1. To compare the two projects, we need to reinvest this interim cash flow for one year. What reinvestment rate should we choose? Reinvesting the $125 cash flow of Year 1 at 25%—Project B's IRR—we receive $156.25 ($125 × 1.25 = $156.25). However, reinvesting the interim cash flow at the *cost of capital,* which in our example is 10%, gives a future value of $137.50 ($125 × 1.1 = $137.50) in Year 2. When we focus on the future values of the projects' cash flows with reinvestment of the interim cash flow at the IRR, Project B looks better because it yields a higher future value ($156.25 versus $144). With reinvestment at the cost of capital (which is used to calculate the project's NPV), Project A looks better because it yields a higher future value ($144 versus $137.50). In summary, FV shows a preference for Project A (with the higher NPV) as long as cash flows are reinvested at the cost of capital. If cash flows are reinvested at the IRR, FV shows a preference for Project B.

Suppose we do wish to work with FV rather than with PV. Which reinvestment rate is relevant? In practice, since the firm can reinvest only at the cost of capital, not at the IRR, the appropriate discount rate is the cost of capital. To illustrate this assertion, suppose that we have certainty and that the discount rate is 10% (investors can borrow or lend money at 10%). The firm can deposit any interim cash flows in the bank at a 10% interest rate. No bank would be willing to pay 25% interest when the prevailing interest rate is 10%. Because the firm borrows and lends at the cost of capital and not at the IRR, the future value calculated with reinvestment of the interim cash flow at the IRR is misleading. Reinvestment of the interim cash flow at the IRR is simply not possible! The firm may have had one extremely profitable project with an IRR of 25%, but this does not mean that the firm will have such projects in the future. Indeed, it would be safe to assume that the interim cash flows will earn 10% but not more than that. The following problem compares the NPVs and IRRs of two projects and then shows how the reinvestment rate can affect project ranking.

PRACTICE BOX

Problem

Consider two mutually exclusive projects with the following cash flows:

	Year 0	Year 1	Year 2
Project A	−$100	$150	$0
Project B	−$100	$0	$200

The cost of capital is 10%.

a. Calculate the NPV and the IRR of these two projects. Do you obtain different rankings?

b. Now reinvest the $150 cash flow of Project A, first at the IRR and then at the cost of capital. How does using these two different rates affect the ranking?

c. Which reinvestment rate is relevant in this case? Why? Which project should be accepted?

Solution

a. Project A's NPV is

$$\frac{\$150}{1.1} - \$100 \cong \$136.36 - \$100 = \$36.36$$

(continued)

Project B's NPV is

$$\frac{\$200}{(1.1)^2} - \$100 \cong \$165.29 - \$100 = \$65.29$$

Project A's IRR is

$$\frac{\$150}{\$100} - 1 = 0.50 \text{ or } 50\%$$

Project B's IRR is given by the value of R that solves the equation

$$\frac{\$200}{(1 + R)^2} = \$100$$

or

$$(1 + R)^2 = 2$$

Thus,

$$R \cong 41.42\%$$

The two rules yield conflicting rankings.

b. Reinvestment of the $150 at the IRR yields $225 ($150 × 1.5 = $225), which is higher than the future value of Project B. If we can reinvest at 50%, Project A is better. However, if we can reinvest only at 10% (the cost of capital), we receive $165 ($150 × 1.1 = $165) in the future, which is less than what we receive on Project B. Therefore, Project B is preferred.

c. Because we can reinvest only at 10%, the NPV ranking is correct, and Project B should be accepted. Note that PV and FV yield the same ranking as long as the reinvestment is at the cost of capital.

6.5.2 The Scale of Investment

As noted previously, differences in project ranking by the NPV and IRR rules may result even without the reinvestment issue. Consider the following two mutually exclusive projects:

	Year 0 Cash Flow	Year 1 Cash Flow	IRR	NPV (at 10% cost of capital)
Project A	−$100	$120	20%	$ 9.09
Project B	−$1,000	$1,150	15%	$45.45

The IRR and NPV rules rank the projects differently. Because it provides higher dollar earnings, the NPV rule gives a ranking that is consistent with the firm's value maximization goal. Although the firm would earn 20% on its initial investment in Project

A and only 15% on its initial investment in Project B, the dollar return on $1,000 ($45.45) is more than the dollar return on $100 ($9.09).

To see why the *dollar profit* is more relevant than the *percentage profit,* assume certainty and that the firm finances the investment by a one-year bank loan at the cost of capital, k = 10%. With Project A, the firm will pay the bank $110 ($100 × 1.1 = $110) at t = 1, and the net future profit will be $10 ($120 − $110 = $10). With Project B, the firm's payment to the bank will be $1,100 ($1,000 × 1.1 = $1,100), and the net future profit will be $50 ($1,150 − $1,100 = $50). Even though the rate of return on the investment is only 15%, Project B produces a larger profit.

This example shows that the IRR rule does not consider the scale of investment: We would get the same IRR of 20% if Project A was in millions of dollars, in dollars, or in cents. The IRR's insensitivity to the scale of investment is a serious drawback. The NPV, on the other hand, does consider the investment scale. If all the figures in the previous example were in millions of dollars, the NPV of Projects A and B would be $9.09 million and $45.45 million, respectively.

6.6 TECHNICAL DRAWBACKS OF THE IRR RULE

So far, we have assumed that all projects have conventional cash flows—cash flows with only one sign reversal (for example, − + + + or + − − −). For nonconventional cash flows—those with more than one sign reversal (for example, + − − + −)—the IRR rule has the following technical drawbacks:

1. There may be no IRR at all.
2. There may be multiple IRRs.
3. The IRR rule may not yield a clear-cut decision when the cost of capital varies over time.

6.6.1 The Case of No IRR

Let's look at why we may have no IRR for nonconventional cash flows. Suppose we have the following cash flows:

	Year 0	Year 1	Year 2
Cash flows (in $ million)	1	−2	1.50

Don't even try to use the calculator to solve the IRR—it simply does not exist![5] If the cost of capital is 0%, the NPV of the cash flows will be

$$\$1 \text{ million} - \$2 \text{ million} + \$1.5 \text{ million} = \$0.5 \text{ million}$$

---

5. Denoting $1/(1 + R) = x$, the IRR can be found by solving for x where $1.5x^2 - 2x + 1 = 0$ (or NPV = 0). This is a quadratic equation, and the solution is given by

$$\frac{2 \pm (4 - 4 \times 1.5 \times 1)^{1/2}}{2 \times 1.5} = \frac{2 \pm (-2)^{1/2}}{3}$$

which has no real solution because $(-2)^{1/2}$ is not a real number.

At a cost of capital of, say, 10%, the NPV will be

$$\$1 \text{ million} - \frac{\$2 \text{ million}}{1.1} + \frac{\$1.5 \text{ million}}{(1.1)^2} \cong \$0.421 \text{ million}$$

At an infinitely large cost of capital (again, hypothetically), the NPV will simply be $1 million because the second- and third-year cash flows vanish.

As you can see in Figure 6-3, the NPV first decreases and then increases; it never intercepts the X-axis. Recall, though, that the project's IRR is *the point at which the NPV curve intersects the X-axis.* In this example, since we have no intersection point, the project has no IRR.

Does having no IRR mean the project is without merit? Not at all. Actually, this project has a positive NPV at any cost of capital, and a firm should accept it. That the project has no IRR simply reflects the IRR rule's technical deficiency when it is applied to nonconventional cash flows; it does not reflect the quality of the project itself.

6.6.2 The Case of Multiple IRRs

The IRR rule's second technical drawback, multiple IRRs, is quite different from its first drawback. With nonconventional cash flows, the number of IRRs can be as great as the number of the cash flow sign reversals.

Suppose you have the following cash flows:

	Year 0	Year 1	Year 2
Cash flows (in $ million)	10	−70	120

Although this cash flow is termed "nonconventional," it is actually very common. For instance, almost every contractual agreement produces a nonconventional cash

FIGURE 6-3
A Project with No Internal Rate of Return (IRR)

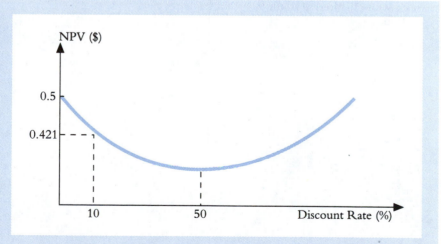

flow. When a firm signs a contract (to supply goods or services), it generally receives an advance ($10 million in our example). Then the firm will invest money (–$70 million), and when it completes the service or delivers the goods, the firm receives final payment ($120 million).

Figure 6-4 depicts the NPV curve of these cash flows. If the cost of capital is zero, the NPV will be

$$\text{NPV} = \$10 - \$70 + \$120 = \$60$$

If the cost of capital is 200%, the NPV will be

$$\$10 \text{ million} - \frac{\$70 \text{ million}}{1 + 2} + \frac{\$120 \text{ million}}{(1 + 2)^2} =$$

$$\$10 \text{ million} - \$23.33 \text{ million} + \$13.33 \text{ million} = \$0$$

and the IRR will be 200%. However, if the cost of capital is 300%, the NPV will again be zero:

$$\$10 \text{ million} - \frac{\$70 \text{ million}}{1 + 3} + \frac{\$120 \text{ million}}{(1 + 3)^2} =$$

$$\$10 \text{ million} - \$17.5 \text{ million} + \$7.5 \text{ million} = \$0$$

in which case we get a second IRR of 300%.[6]

When a project has more than one IRR, the basic rule—that a firm should accept the project if its IRR is greater than the cost of capital—breaks down. In this example, if the cost of capital is greater than 300%, the IRR rule would recommend rejecting the project because $R < k$. However, as we can see from the NPV curve in

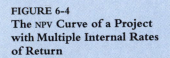

FIGURE 6-4
The NPV Curve of a Project with Multiple Internal Rates of Return

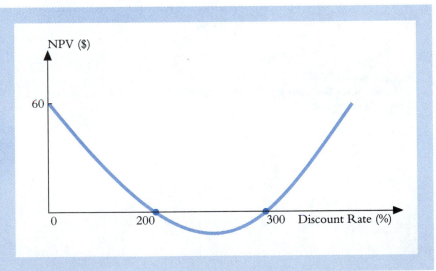

6. Once again, we can use the quadratic equation to solve for the two roots, $R_1 = 200\%$ and $R_2 = 300\%$.

Figure 6-4, a firm should clearly accept the project at any cost of capital over 300% or under 200%.

6.6.3 The Case of Changing Cost of Capital

The cost of capital can change significantly over time, and this causes another technical problem for the IRR rule. Let's see what happens if the cost of capital changes over time. It is easy to demonstrate such a scenario if the cash flows are certain.

Suppose the cost of capital is 5% in Year 1, 10% in Year 2, and 25% in Year 3. Let the project's cash flows be as follows:

	Year 0	**Year 1**	**Year 2**	**Year 3**
Cash flows	−$100	$50	$50	$50

Should a firm accept the project?

By the NPV rule, we have:[7]

$$\text{NPV} = -\$100 + \frac{\$50}{1.05} + \frac{\$50}{1.05 \times 1.10} + \frac{\$50}{1.05 \times 1.10 \times 1.25}$$

$$\cong -\$100 + \$47.62 + \$43.29 + \$34.63 = \$25.54$$

By the NPV rule, a firm should accept the project.

Now let us calculate the IRR. A financial calculator tells us that the IRR is about 23.38%. How do we use the IRR rule in this case? If the IRR is compared to the first or second year's cost of capital (5%, 10%), a firm should accept the project because IRR > 10%. However, if the IRR is compared to the third year's cost of capital, a firm should reject the project because IRR < 25%. When the cost of capital varies, the IRR rule breaks down yet again.

If the IRR rule has numerous deficiencies, why do so many firms use it? The IRR rule has two main advantages over the NPV rule:

1. The IRR is stated in percentage form. When board members learn that a project's profitability is 15%, they can more easily comprehend a percentage figure and can compare it to the rates of return on other investments or to the market interest rate (which are both stated in percentages). The NPV, which is stated in dollar terms (such as $25.54), is harder to compare with other investments and rates.
2. The precise cost of capital is not needed to calculate the IRR. The board of directors may estimate the firm's cost of capital within a range, say 12% to 20%, but it may not be able to tell whether it is 12.5% or 13.75% or any other specific figure within this range. With the IRR, the board can easily make decisions about the most and least profitable projects (such as IRR > 20% and IRR < 12%), without specifying the precise cost of capital.

---

7. Note that the discounted value at the end of the first year of $50 received at the end of the second year is $45.45 ($50/1.1 ≅ $45.45) because the cost of capital corresponding to Year 2 is 10%. The PV of the $45.45 in terms of $t = 0$ is $43.29 ($45.45/1.05 ≅ $43.29) because the cost of capital corresponding to Year 1 is 5%. The $50 received in the third year is discounted in the same manner.

Indeed, many firms use the NPV rule to make their investment decisions (because it is more reliable) and then use the IRR rule to present their cash flow analysis (because it is more easily understood). If firms prefer to use the IRR rule, they should use it in conjunction with the NPV rule.

6.7 THE PAYBACK PERIOD RULE

As we saw in Table 6-1, managers use rules other than the NPV and the IRR to make investment decisions. The **payback period (PBP) rule** is based on the number of years needed to recover the initial investment. The firm may decide, for example, to accept projects that recover their initial investment within two years and to reject projects with a payback period of more than two years. In such cases, we say that two years is the **cutoff period** for accept/reject decisions.

The reciprocal of the payback period provides a percentage figure. For example, if the cutoff period is two years, the *payback reciprocal cutoff rate* is 1 divided by the cutoff period measured in years, or 50%. With a two-year cutoff, the firm will accept projects only if the payback period is two years or less or if the payback reciprocal is 50% or more. If a project's cash flows recover the initial investment in four years, the project's payback period will be four years, and its payback reciprocal will be ¼, or 25%.

To illustrate these concepts, consider the following three projects:

	Year 0 Cash Flows	Year 1 Cash Flows	Year 2 Cash Flows	Year 3 Cash Flows
Project A	−$100	$ 50	$50	$50
Project B	−$100	$100	$50	$50
Project C	−$200	$ 80	$80	$80

If the firm's cutoff period is two years, it will accept Project A because the project's $100 initial investment is recovered in two years. The firm will consider Project B to be even better than Project A because B's initial investment is recovered in one year. Because Project C would take more than two years to pay back the investment, the firm will reject it. In two years Project C's cash flows will still be $40 short of recovering the initial investment. Project C will be rejected.

However, although the PBP rule seems logical, it has a number of serious deficiencies. First, it ignores the time value of money. That is, it simply totals the cash flows without discounting them. Second, it ignores cash flows received *after* the payback period. The following example illustrates these two drawbacks:

	Year 0 Cash Flows	Year 1 Cash Flows	Year 2 Cash Flows	Year 3 Cash Flows
Project A	−$100	$70	$30	$ 50
Project B	−$100	$30	$70	$ 50
Project C	−$100	$40	$40	$1,000

First, compare Projects A and B. If the payback period is two years, Project A and B will be equally attractive because both pay back the initial investment in two years ($70 + $30 = $100 and $30 + $70 = $100). However, as we have already learned, Project A is better because the firm receives its larger cash flow ($70) in Year 1. Because the PBP rule is not based on discounted cash flows, the firm cannot detect the superiority of Project A over Project B. This is the first drawback, which may be overcome by using the discounted payback rule (discussed in Appendix 6A).

Now compare Projects A and C. If the firm's cutoff period is two years, it will accept Project A and reject Project C because Project C's cash flows over two years are only $80 (less than the $100 initial investment). Since the PBP rule ignores all cash flows occurring *after* the two years, it does not consider the $1,000 cash flow in Project C's third year—a clearly unreasonable omission. This is the PBP rule's second drawback: It does not consider *all of the project's cash flows*—that is, cash flows occurring after the cutoff period.

Why, then, do firms use the PBP rule? First, firms usually use it when the annual cash flows are more or less constant over the years. Cash flows of the following type, which are used in textbooks (including this one) to illustrate deficiencies of the PBP rule, rarely exist in the real world:

Year 0 Cash Flow	Year 1 Cash Flow	Year 2 Cash Flow	Year 3 Cash Flow
–$100	$50	$50	$100,000

Second, if the project has a relatively long economic life and the annual cash flows do not vary much across years, the PBP rule will yield a decision similar to that of the IRR rule, which is optimal for *independent* and *conventional* projects. To see this relationship, suppose the project's cash flows take the form of a perpetuity (which can be seen as a project with a very long economic life) of $C per year. In such a case the project's IRR will be the value of R that solves the equation for the perpetuity formula (see Section 4.5.2 for the specific case of PV = I or NPV = 0):

$$I = \frac{C}{R}$$

where I is the initial investment. The IRR is then

$$R = \frac{C}{I}$$

which corresponds to the *reciprocal* of the payback period. For example, if I = $100 and C = $20, then the payback period will be five years, and the reciprocal of the payback will be ⅕ = 0.2 or 20%. For a perpetuity the IRR will be $20/$100 = 0.2 or 20%. *For perpetual cash flows, the IRR is identical to the reciprocal of the payback period.*

In the perpetuity case, using the PBP rule with a cutoff of five years or less is exactly the same as using the IRR rule with a cutoff rate of 20%. Any project that a firm accepts by using the PBP rule (less than five years or a reciprocal higher than 20%) will have an IRR higher than 20%. For example, with a 20% cutoff rate, if the annual perpetual cash flow is C = $25 and I = $100, the payback period will be four years, the payback reciprocal will be 25%, and the IRR will be 25%. With a 20% cutoff rate, the project will be accepted by both the PBP and the IRR rules. Moreover, because the IRR rule leads to the same investment decision as the NPV criterion (for independent and conventional projects) in the case of a perpetuity, the PBP rule will also lead to the same investment decision as the NPV rule. When reviewed in this context, the PBP rule is not as bad as most textbooks claim. When a conventional project's duration is relatively long but not infinite and when its annual cash flows are relatively constant, the payback period reciprocal yields a close, albeit not precise, approximation of the IRR.

Another rationale for using the payback method is the extreme uncertainty of cash flows beyond the cutoff period. Actually, the firm may have no idea whether it will receive any cash flows after the cutoff period. In that case the appropriate risk-adjusted discount rate corresponding to the years beyond the cutoff period will be very high, and the present value of these late cash flows will be negligible.

Last, but not least, is an agency issue. Financial executives are often anxious to recover an investment in a short period of time. If earnings or cash flows are strong in the short run, the executives may well be awarded bonuses or salary hikes. Since they may leave the firm several years down the road, the executives will not be concerned about any lower cash flows at that time. Because the PBP rule emphasizes early cash flows, executives often favor it. As discussed in Chapter 1, this is one instance of conflict of interest between the firm and its managers.

Applying Theory to Practice 6.1 compares U.S. and Japanese CEOs' perspectives on projects with different payback periods.

http

Are you thinking of refinancing your home? Partners Mortgage will calculate the amount of time you must live in your home after refinancing in order to break even. (It's a free calculation—just plug in the numbers.)
http://www.partnersnet.com/calcs/mc_refi.html

APPLYING THEORY TO PRACTICE 6.1

USING THE PAYBACK METHOD: THE AMERICANS VERSUS THE JAPANESE

Fourth executive: Your payback could be in two years or 20, and 20 years scares us to death. Instead, you look at the reasons for the investment. What are the opportunities? What are the threats if we don't do it?

"U.S. companies are doing themselves a terrible disservice with their myopic short-term focus."

Fifth executive: The demand for return is much more severe in this country [the United States] than in others, and that comes out of our tendency to focus on short-term horizons. So in U.S. companies, people start walking away from capital expenditures if the payback is longer than a year. Japanese companies look at a capital investment and see markets penetrated, share captured and dominance achieved, not just a short-term return.

"Why do we put these payback demands on ourselves?"

Sixth executive: I think it has to do with the United States being a country for the individual, with the ideal that if you work hard enough, claw your way to the top, you'll find the streets paved with gold.

In Japan, it's very different. You work together for the common good of your company, your country or whatever.

Our focus on the individual has a great deal of influence on maintaining self-serving short-term horizons.

Source: "Harris Conversation for the '90s: A Discussion of a Select Group of Business Executives," *Fortune,* April 20, 1992, p. 254. Copyright © 1992 Time Inc. All rights reserved.

Questions

1. The fourth executive claims, "Your payback could be in two years or 20, and 20 years scares us to death." Suppose the investment in Project A is $1 million, and the annual cash flow is $500,000 in each of the next two years. Let the initial investment in Project B also be $1 million, and let the annual cash flow, which is a perpetuity, be $50,000. Calculate the payback period and the IRR of each of these two projects. Which project is better? Discuss the fourth executive's claim in light of your results.

2. The fifth executive claims that "people start walking away from capital expenditures if the payback is longer than a year." Suppose a project with an initial investment of $1 million produces an annual cash flow of $500,000 a year forever. According to the fifth executive, a firm would reject the project. Calculate the project's IRR. Discuss the fifth executive's claim in light of your results.

3. Suppose that U.S. executives change their jobs quite often, say every four years, and Japanese executives stay with their firms much longer. The CEO's compensation is determined as some percentage of the value of sales or reported earnings. Can this explain why U.S. CEOs are "myopic" in comparison with their Japanese counterparts?

   Let's be more specific. Consider the following two projects:

Cash Flows (in $ million)

	Year 0	Year 1	Year 2	Year 3	Year 4	Year 5	. . .	Year 10
Project A	−100	50	50	50	50	20	. . .	20
Project B	−100	40	40	40	40	40	. . .	40

The cost of capital is 10%. Suppose the executives' compensation is 10% of the annual cash flow (not including the negative cash outlay on the investment). The U.S. executive leaves the job after four years, whereas the Japanese executive stays for 10 years. Both wish to maximize the PV of their income. Which project will the Japanese executive select? Which will the U.S. executive select? How might your results explain the claims expressed by the quoted executives? Discuss.

MAKING THE CONNECTION

1. The payback periods of Projects A and B are as follows:[8]

$$\text{Project A:} \quad \frac{\$1,000,000}{\$500,000} = 2 \text{ years}$$

---

8. If all cash flows are given at the end of each year, the payback period will be a round number. However, in many cases the cash flow is spread across the whole year (products are sold year-round). In such cases the payback period can be expressed as a fraction.

$$\text{Project B:} \quad \frac{\$1,000,000}{\$50,000} = 20 \text{ years}$$

By the payback method, Project A is preferred.

Project A's IRR is zero because the value of R that solves the following is $R = 0$.

$$\$1,000,000 = \frac{\$500,000}{1 + R} + \frac{\$500,000}{(1 + R)^2}$$

Since Project B is a perpetuity, its IRR is given by

$$\$1,000,000 = \frac{\$500,000}{1 + R} + \frac{\$50,000}{(1 + R)^2} + \ldots = \frac{\$50,000}{R}$$

The value of R that solves the equation is 5%.

In contrast to the payback method, the IRR method indicates a preference for Project B. In general the fourth executive's fear of long payback periods does have a solid economic foundation. A preference for the shorter payback project (Project B) may lead to even worse profitability (IRR = 0). However, the cash flows may become more uncertain (riskier) the longer-term the forecast is, which may explain the preference for short projects.

2. The project's IRR is determined by solving the following equation:

$$\$1,000,000 = \frac{\$500,000}{1 + R} + \frac{\$500,000}{(1 + R)^2} + \ldots$$

The IRR (which is the value of R that solves the above equation) is 50%. However, this project would be rejected because its payback is two years, which is longer than the one-year cutoff period. Once again, rejecting a project with a payback period longer than one year would be a mistake. This would be true even if the $500,000 cash flow repeated itself for only a limited number of years (say, 3–4 years). A one-year payback acceptance policy might be justifiable if the risk and the corresponding cost of capital after the first year were extremely high; then the PV of any later cash flows would be negligible. However, such a policy would be inappropriate in most cases.

3. First, let us calculate the NPV of the two projects:

    At a 10% discount rate,

    $$\text{NPV}_A = \$217.99 \text{ million} - \$100 \text{ million} = \$117.99 \text{ million} \quad \text{and}$$
    $$\text{PV}_A = \$217.99 \text{ million}$$

    $$\text{NPV}_B = \$245.78 \text{ million} - \$100 \text{ million} = \$145.78 \text{ million} \quad \text{and}$$
    $$\text{PV}_B = \$245.78 \text{ million}$$

    Project B should be preferred.

Now let's calculate the PV of the CEOs' compensation. Since the U.S. CEO receives 10% of the cash flow in the first four years, his/her cash flow will be

Cash Flows (in $ million)

	Year 1	Year 2	Year 3	Year 4
Project A	5	5	5	5
Project B	4	4	4	4

No calculation is needed to conclude that the U.S. CEO will prefer Project A with the early cash flows. The Japanese CEO receives 10% of the PV of all cash flows. As the PV of Project B is $245.78 million and the PV of Project A is $217.99 million, the Japanese CEO will prefer Project B.

Discussion
Project A's payback period is two years, whereas Project B's is two and a half years. The greater job mobility of U.S. executives may explain why they are "myopic" and prefer projects with short payback periods and why Japanese executives have longer horizons.[9] A firm's compensation committee should be aware of such possible distortions and should suggest a compensation scheme that will reveal Project B's preference to both the stockholders and the CEO.

6.8 THE ACCOUNTING RATE OF RETURN RULE

As its name implies, the **accounting rate of return (ARR) rule** is based on accounting figures. Although this rule has several drawbacks, it is popular (see Table 6-1) and it deserves our attention.

To illustrate the accounting rate of return, let us consider a project with the following cash flows and accounting figures:

	Year 0	Year 1	Year 2	Year 3
Cash flows	–$1,000	$ 500	$1,000	$500
Net accounting revenue before depreciation		$1,000	$1,000	$ 0
Depreciation		–$ 500	–$ 500	$ 0
Net accounting earnings		$ 500	$ 500	$ 0

9. For this view see M. P. Narayanan, "Managerial Incentives for Short-Term Results," *Journal of Finance* 40 (December 1985):1469–1484.

The project's net revenue from sales is $1,000 for each of the first two years. However, the firm sells on credit, collects only $500 in the first year, and receives the remaining $500 of the first year's sales in Year 2. In Year 2 the firm receives $1,000 in cash ($500 from Year 2 sales and $500 from Year 1 sales). The $500 the firm receives in Year 3 is from Year 2 credit sales.

Accounting earnings are not the same as cash flows. The firm records sales of $1,000 each year as income, regardless of whether it receives the cash during that year or one year later. Moreover, the firm subtracts the depreciation of the initial investment annually.[10]

6.8.1 Two Ways to Calculate ARR

The accounting rate of return can be calculated in two ways. The first way of defining it is

$$ARR_1 = \frac{\text{Annual Accounting Income}}{\text{Investment}} \tag{6.2}$$

where the subscript 1 indicates that this is the first method. For simplicity, assume that apart from depreciation, the firm has no other expenses and no taxes. In our example ARR_1 is

$$ARR_1 = \frac{\$500}{\$1,000} = 0.5 \text{ or } 50\%$$

The firm depreciates the investment during the project's lifetime. For instance, if the investment's book value is $1,000 at the beginning of the project and zero at the end of the project, its average investment is only $500. This investment characteristic is reflected in a variation of the accounting method, whereby the income is divided by the average investment:

$$ARR_2 = \frac{\text{Annual Accounting Income}}{\text{Investment}/2} \tag{6.2a}$$

In our example,

$$ARR_2 = \frac{\$500}{\$1,000/2} = 1 \text{ or } 100\%$$

If the ARR_1 (or ARR_2) is greater than some predetermined critical value, the project should be accepted. Otherwise, it should be rejected.

If accounting income varies across years, the *average* annual income ($150 million in our example) is usually the numerator.

How well does the ARR match the IRR, which are both expressed as percentages? The accounting rate of return may differ from the IRR. For instance, we find (using a

---

10. Assuming a two-year project and straight-line depreciation, the firm depreciates $500 each year. For a detailed discussion of depreciation, see Chapter 7.

calculator), that the above project's IRR is approximately 43.76%, which differs from both the accounting rates of return.

However, for long-term projects in which there is little difference between cash flows and earnings (as when all sales are for cash), the ARRs yield similar decisions to those in which the IRR rule obtains.[11]

6.8.2 Drawbacks of the ARR Rule

The ARR rules have two main drawbacks. First, they are not based on cash flows. As seen in the previous example, cash flows may be very different from accounting earnings. A project with a large accounting profit may actually have *no cash flow* at all for a number of years, and the ARRs do not consider financial situations of this type.

Second, the ARR rules do not recognize the disadvantage of not receiving cash in the early years. If a project earns $100 in the first year and $300 in the second year, the average of $200 is simply taken as the numerator. Even if these were cash flows and not merely accounting earnings, the ARR rule would not distinguish between cash flow patterns such as "100 and 300" versus "300 and 100". The ARR rule completely ignores the time value of money.

If the ARR rule has such serious drawbacks, why do firms use it? The reason is that the firm's accountant has traditionally prepared the figures for the income statement. Accountants predate modern finance and were probably called upon to evaluate projects. Even today, with the modern finance tools available for project evaluation, many large firms still use the ARR rule to support their NPV and IRR calculations. You have little option but to be familiar with this rule.

6.9 THE PROFITABILITY INDEX RULE

Table 6-1 reveals that some firms use the **profitability index (PI) rule** as their principal technique in making investment decisions. The profitability index is the project's PV divided by its initial investment:

$$PI = PV/I \tag{6.3}$$

where I is the investment in the project. If PI > 1, a firm should accept the project; otherwise, the firm should reject it. This investment rule adheres to the principle that cash flows should be discounted at the cost of capital, k. Presenting profitability in percentage form facilitates comparison with other projects.

Although the profitability index has some intuitive appeal, it can be misleading, as the following example will show.

---

11. If the firm depreciates the investment evenly over N years and N is very large, the accounting rate of return will be

$$ARR_1 = \frac{C}{I} - \frac{I/N}{I} = \frac{C}{I} - \frac{1}{N}$$

where C is the constant annual cash flow and I/N is the annual depreciation. If N is very large, then $1/N$ becomes very small, and ARR_1 will be close to the reciprocal of the payback period, which in turn will be close to the IRR. Thus, ARR_1 will be very close to the IRR for long-term projects.

	PV	I	PI
Project A	$100	$ 25	4
Project B	$500	$250	2

Suppose the two projects are mutually exclusive. By the PI rule, the firm will prefer Project A because its PI is higher than that of Project B. However, Project A's NPV is $75 ($100 − $25), whereas Project B's NPV is $250 ($500 − $250). By the NPV rule, the firm should prefer Project B. The PI is helpful only in comparing investments of the same scale or investments that are not mutually exclusive.[12] In such cases it provides a percentage profitability figure that has intuitive appeal and can be used in conjunction with the NPV rule.

SUMMARY

A number of investment criteria were discussed and compared in this chapter.

The *net present value (NPV) rule* is superior to other decision criteria and is consistent with the firm's goal of maximizing stockholders' wealth. The NPV method discounts all cash flows at the cost of capital and considers the scale of investment.

The *internal rate of return (IRR) rule* discounts all the project's cash flows, but the discount rate may differ from the firm's cost of capital. If projects are independent and the cash flows are conventional, the IRR and NPV methods yield the same accept/reject decision. However, when projects are mutually exclusive or cash flows are nonconventional, the IRR method may lead to erroneous decisions. The IRR is expressed as a percentage, which can be easily and intuitively understood.

The *payback period rule (PBP)* is based on the project's cash flows but not on *all* of them. It ignores cash flows received after the cutoff period. Since this method ignores some cash flows and does not discount others, it often yields erroneous results.

The *accounting rate of return rules (ARR)* are based on earnings rather than on cash flows. The earnings are not discounted.

The *profitability index rule (PI)* gives a percentage figure, which managers can easily understand, as with the NPV method, cash flows are discounted at the firm's cost of capital. The profitability index may lead to erroneous decisions when projects are mutually exclusive.

Although the payback and accounting rate of return rules may lead to erroneous decisions, they are quite popular in practice. Firms may legitimately use these methods only under certain conditions—namely, in cases where annual cash flows are constant, where the differences between accounting earnings and cash flows are minimal, and where the economic lives of the projects are relatively long. In such cases these two rules yield results that are similar to those the IRR rule produces. If projects are conventional and not mutually exclusive, the two rules lead to the same decision as the NPV rule.

---

12. Suppose that for two projects denoted by A and B, we have $PI_A > PI_B$, or

$$\frac{PV_A}{I_A} > \frac{PV_B}{I_B}$$

If the two projects have the same scale ($I_A = I_B = I$), this implies that $PV_A > PV_B$, or $PV_A - I > PV_B - I$, or $NPV_A > NPV_B$. In this case the profitability index rule leads to the same decision as the NPV rule.

CHAPTER AT A GLANCE

1. The NPV rule:
   Calculate NPV using the equation

   $$\sum_{t=1}^{T} \frac{CF_t}{(1 + k)^t} - I$$

   where k is the cost of capital.
   If NPV > 0, accept the project.
   If NPV < 0, reject the project.
   If NPV = 0, the firm will be indifferent between accepting and rejecting the project.

2. The IRR rule:
   Determine the value of R that solves the equation

   $$\sum_{t=1}^{T} \frac{CF_t}{(1 + R)^t} - I = 0$$

   If $R > k$, accept the project.
   If $R < k$, reject the project.
   If $R = k$, the firm will be indifferent between accepting and rejecting the project.

3. The payback period rule:
   Calculate the number of years, N, needed to recover the investment.
   If $N <$ cutoff period, accept the project.
   If $N >$ cutoff period, reject the project.
   If $N =$ cutoff period, the firm will be indifferent between accepting or rejecting the project.

4. The accounting rate of return rules:
   Calculate

   $$ARR_1 = \frac{\text{Revenue} - \text{Depreciation}}{\text{Investment}}$$

   or

   $$ARR_2 = \frac{\text{Revenue} - \text{Depreciation}}{\text{Investment}/2}$$

   where Revenue is the average net revenue before depreciation and zero tax is assumed. (Similar criteria can be defined on a posttax basis.)
   If ARR_1 or $ARR_2 >$ critical value, accept the project.
   If ARR_1 or $ARR_2 <$ critical value, reject the project.

5. The profitability index rule:
   Calculate

   $$PI = \frac{PV}{I}$$

   where I is the investment in the project.
   If PI > 1, accept the project.
   If PI < 1, reject the project.

KEY TERMS

Internal rate of return (IRR)
Conventional cash flows
Nonconventional cash flows
Independent projects

Mutually exclusive projects
Reinvestment
Payback period (PBP) rule
Cutoff period

Accounting rate of return (ARR)
  rules
Profitability index (PI) rule

REVIEW AND PRACTICE

6.1 A firm with a current cash flow of $10 million is considering two alternatives. One is to pay the $10 million as a cash dividend to stockholders. The other is to invest it in a security yielding $12 million with certainty one year from now and then pay out the resulting sum as dividends. You hold 5% of the firm's stock. You are about to purchase a $500,000 house on the California coast. You do not wish to sell your shares.
a. Suppose you are unable to take out a cash loan. Which alternative would you prefer the firm to choose?
b. Suppose both you and the firm can borrow and lend at 10%. Which alternative would you prefer now? Discuss your results. Is the NPV rule valid when borrowing and lending are not feasible?

6.2 You are considering whether to invest in a one-year project with the following certain cash flows:

	Year 0	Year 1
Cash flows	−$80,000	$100,000

You can borrow and lend at 10%.
a. Would you invest in this project? Explain.
b. You are now considering a risky project requiring the same initial outlay of $80,000. However, the cash inflow of this project now has an equal probability of being either $80,000 or $120,000. Do you have enough information to use the NPV rule to make your decision? Explain your answer.
c. The risk premium for the project described in (b) is estimated to be 8%. Do you have enough information to calculate the NPV? If so, should you accept the project?

6.3 Calculate the IRR of the following cash flows:

	Year 0	Year 1	Year 2	Year 3
Cash flows	−$100	$50	$50	$50

6.4 The following project is being considered:

	Year 0	Year 1	Year 2
Cash flows	−$1,833.38	$1,000	$1,000

a. Calculate the IRR.
b. Assume that the cash flows are certain and that the discount rate is 10%. You borrow the money to finance the project. Use an amortization table (like Table 6-2) to show whether the project's cash flows are sufficient to return the principal and interest on the borrowed money. Would you accept or reject the project? Explain.

6.5 Repeat Problem 6.4, but use the following cash flows:

	Year 0	Year 1	Year 2
Cash flows	−$1,527.78	$1,000	$1,000

6.6 Assume a project's cash flows are as follows:

	Year 0	Year 1	Year 2
Cash flows	−$38,897	$10,000	$10,000

	Year 3	Year 4	Year 5
Cash flows	$10,000	$10,000	$10,000

Use Table A-3 at the end of the book to calculate the IRR. Explain how you used the table. Use a calculator to verify your results.

6.7 You are offered a student loan with the following cash flows:

	Year 0	Year 1	Year 2	Year 3
Cash flows	$10,000	−$4,000	−$4,000	−$4,000

where $10,000 is the loan amount and the other flows are the loan repayments.

a. Draw the NPV curve for the following discount rates: 0%, 5%, 12%, and 20%.

b. Calculate the IRR on the loan. Suppose your cost of capital is 5%. Would you accept the loan?

c. What are the cash flows for the bank? Draw the bank's NPV curve for the above discount rates and calculate the IRR. Compare and explain your results.

6.8 You have two projects with the following cash flows:

	Year 0	Year 1
Project A	−$ 100	$ 150
Project B	−$1,000	$1,500

a. Draw the NPV curves of these two projects for the following five discount rates: 0%, 5%, 10%, 20%, and 50%.

b. The discount rate is 20%. Calculate the two projects' NPVs. Which would you prefer by the NPV rule? Which would you prefer by the IRR rule?

c. Which rule would you prefer if the projects were mutually exclusive? Why?

6.9 "When two projects are independent and the cash flows are conventional, then the NPV and IRR yield the same accept/reject decision." Evaluate this statement. Defend your answer.

6.10 Define *conventional* and *nonconventional cash flows*. Give one example of each.

6.11 You are 21 years old and have a degree in engineering. You are considering whether to seek employment or to embark on a two-year MBA degree course. Describe (in terms of + or −) the cash flows of investment in an MBA degree.

6.12 You are interested in both law and business administration. You have been accepted at the Whar-

ton Business School in Philadelphia and at Loyola Law School in Chicago. Discuss your investment dilemma. Are these two investments mutually exclusive or independent?

6.13 You have the following cash flows:

	Year 0	Year 1
A	−$1,000	$1,200
B	−$3,000	$3,360

At what discount rate are the NPVs of these two cash flows identical?

6.14 You are considering two projects with the following certain cash flows:

	Year 0	Year 1
Project A	−$100	$170
Project B	−$200	$300

a. Calculate each project's NPV and IRR. Assume a discount rate of 5% and that the projects are mutually exclusive. Which should you accept? In your answers to 6.14b and 6.14c assume you can borrow and lend at 5%. Show your financial transaction with the bank.

b. Suppose you wish to consume only at date $t = 0$. Which project would you choose? Why?

c. Suppose you wish to consume only at date $t = 1$. Which project would you choose? Why?

d. Use your answers to 6.14b and 6.14c to defend the NPV rule.

6.15 You have two mutually exclusive projects with the following cash flows:

	Year 0	Year 1	Year 2
Project A	−$50	$ 0	$75
Project B	−$50	$64	$ 0

The cost of capital is 10%.

a. Calculate each project's NPV and IRR. Which project is better according to the NPV rule? Which is better according to the IRR rule?

b. Reinvest Project B's interim cash flow at the project's IRR. Which project yields a higher future value? Does the assumption of reinvestment at the IRR make sense? Can you defend it?

6.16 Suppose you are considering two mutually exclusive projects with the following cash flows:

	Year 0	Year 1
Project A	–$ 10	$ 14
Project B	–$100	$120

The cost of capital is 10%.

Calculate the IRR and NPV. Is there a conflict between the rankings obtained by the two methods?

6.17 A project has the following cash flows:

	Year 0	Year 1	Year 2
Cash flows	$10	–$20	$20

The cost of capital is 10%.
a. Calculate the project's NPV. Draw the NPV curve for the following discount rates: 5%, 10%, 50%, and 100%.
b. Can you calculate the IRR? Would you accept the project? Explain.

6.18 Now reverse the cash flow signs in Problem 6.17 to obtain the following cash flows:

	Year 0	Year 1	Year 2
Cash flows	–$10	$20	–$20

"We still do not have an IRR, but this time the project should be rejected." Do you agree? Compare your results here to those obtained in Problem 6.17.

6.19 A project has the following cash flows:

	Year 0	Year 1	Year 2
Cash flows	$1	–$5	$4

a. Calculate the project's IRR. Is there more than one IRR?
b. Draw the NPV curve for the following discount rates: 0%, 5%, 10%, 20%, 50%, and 100%. The cost of capital is 10%. Would you accept or reject this project?

6.20 Suppose you have two mutually exclusive projects with the following cash flows:

	Year 0	Year 1
Project A	–$ 100	$ 150
Project B	–$1,000	$1,400

The cost of capital is 10%.
a. Which project does the NPV rule prefer?
b. Which project does the profitability index prefer? In light of this example, what is your verdict on the profitability index?

6.21 A project has the following cash flows:

	Year 0	Year 1	Year 2	Year 3
Cash flows	–$20	$10	$10	$10

The cost of capital is 10% for the first year, 15% for the second year, and 30% for the third year.
a. Calculate the project's NPV and IRR.
b. Would you accept the project according to the ranking that the NPV rule gives? That the IRR rule gives? Discuss your results.

6.22 "When a project's cash flows are constant and its economic life is quite long (as in utility firms), the result obtained by the payback period method will be very close to that obtained by the IRR method." Discuss this claim. Use a numerical example to support your answer.

6.23 Calculate the payback period and the IRR for two projects with the following cash flows:

Year								
	0	1	2	3	4	5	. . .	20
Project A	–$100	$50	$50	$ 0	$ 0	$ 0	. . .	$ 0
Project B	–$100	$50	$50	$50	$50	$50	. . .	$50

For which project does the payback reciprocal yield a closer approximation to the IRR?

6.24 A project with an initial cash outlay of $1 million yields an accounting income before depreciation of $100,000 each year. All sales are in cash. The project's duration is 20 years. Assume an annual depreciation of $50,000 ($1 million/$20 = $50,000) and a discount rate of 10%. Calculate ARR_1, ARR_2, the NPV, and the IRR. Analyze your results.

6.25 "If cash flows are constant over the years, if the before-depreciation accounting income equals the firm's cash flow, and if the project duration is very long, then the accounting rate of return (ARR_1) rule and the payback period rule will yield very similar rankings." Assume an annual depreciation of I/N, where N is the project duration and I is the investment. Discuss the above assertion and demonstrate your answer for $N = 1, 10, 50$, and 100 years. Assume that the annual cash flow is $20 and that $I = 100$. (*Hint:* Use the reciprocal of the payback period.)

INTERNET QUESTIONS

6.26 Take the "MEAD Pop Quiz" on capital budgeting and see how well you understand the concepts of net present value, internal rate of return, and payback. Then grade yourself—the answers are available. How well did you do?
http://160.147.66.30/mead_faq.htm

6.27 The payback method is commonly used to decide whether or not to refinance a home mortgage. (How long would you have to live in a home after refinancing in order for the monthly savings to exceed the financing costs?) Use a major search engine, search for the word "refinancing," and locate a refinancing worksheet. Type in some hypothetical figures to see what a payback period would be.

YOUR TURN: APPLYING THEORY TO PRACTICE

TIMESHARING FOR SALE

NETJETS ALLOWS THRIFTY EXECS TO FLY ON SHORT NOTICE

Owning a jet isn't all it's cracked up to be. Just ask Clark A. Johnson, CEO of Pier 1 Imports Inc. The Fort Worth retailer has operations scattered across 42 states. When executives needed to visit sites in Iowa, Minnesota, North Dakota, and South Dakota, they could hit them all in a day in the company's British Aerospace PLC HS 400. But there was always something. On days when the plane went unused, Pier 1 had to pay the company pilots anyway. Johnson had to fly commercial when the chief pilot got sick, or when the jet went in for maintenance. There was the danger shareholders would complain he was living high on the hog. And it was expensive.

Pier 1 found an alternative. Some years ago, Johnson's former business chum Jack Nicklaus told him about NetJets, a jet-ownership program that lets executives use planes anywhere in the continental U.S. within four hours—for the expense of owning just a piece of a plane. So in 1986, Johnson sold the HS 400 and bought a three-eighths share of a Cessna Citation II, which seats seven. "It is a management tool that enables us to spend more time in the field with a far-flung operation," he says. After signing with NetJets in 1987, he says, Pier 1 cut its aviation costs by nearly 40% over five years, without sacrificing convenience.

No Deadheads

Today, Pier 1 is one among more than 100 companies or individuals that have become NetJets owners. The program is run by Executive Jet Aviation Inc., based in Montvale, N.J., one of the country's largest jet charter and management companies. NetJets offers some major advantages over full-plane ownership. Costs can be significantly lower. Participants pay only for actual flight time—not for the many hours of so-called deadhead time that jet owners or charterers must pay for when jets are traveling empty. NetJets planes also come ready to fly, eliminating the need for maintenance, leasing hangars, or keeping pilots on salary.

And there's another huge advantage: Unlike condo shares, where participants can enjoy the house only when the others are gone, NetJets is arranged so that a company with as little as a one-quarter share can use up to two jets at any time. The trick, says CEO Richard T. Santulli, a mathematician and onetime head of Goldman, Sachs & Co.'s leasing group, was beginning with a core pool of eight unowned jets and combining it with a sophisticated software program that tracks jet movements and keeps them flying as efficiently as possible. NetJets is growing quickly: EJA anticipates revenues of roughly $50 million in 1993, jumping 50% to $75 million by 1994, with NetJets providing 70% of those revenues.

The program has widest appeal among small to midsize companies that aren't large enough to keep a jet in frequent use. But it's also attracting a broad audience beyond that. Many NetJets owners are private investors or retired top executives loath to give up the perks of corporate life. Former Primerica CEO Gerald Tsai Jr., Atlanta Falcons owner Rankin M. Smith, and retired G. D. Searle CEO D. C. Searle all own NetJets shares. NetJets is also gaining fans among large corporations such as Texaco and Sara Lee that use NetJets to supplement corporate fleets.

Now, Santulli is preparing to broaden his audience. To date, NetJets has used mostly Citation IIs, which have a range of only 1,600 nautical miles—New York to Houston. Executive Jet is close to a deal with BAe for 20 BAe 1000s, a midsize jet that carries eight and flies 3,000 miles—coast to coast. The deal hasn't closed, but BAe is so eager to expose its new plane to corporate users that it will offer to guarantee the residual value of the planes after five years, protecting buyers from a downturn in the market.

The concept does more than help corporate purchases look thrifty. It gives jet manufacturers another way to push their wares. Roughly 40% of the companies and individuals buying NetJets

shares are first-time plane owners, Santulli says. "One thing that's been sorely lacking is the industry's ability to attract new people into the marketplace," says Bob Zuskin, a jet analyst at consultant Avitas Inc. "The beauty of NetJets is that is allows people in essence to own jets for a fraction of the cost." Of course it may be less chic to boast, "I own one-eighth of a jet." But then, the zeitgeist of the '90s isn't swank, it's thrift.

Comparing the Costs

Costs	NetJets[a]	Full Ownership
Acquisition cost	$630,000.00	$2,500,000.00
Direct operating (Cost per hour— 200 hours per year)	1,060.00	817.25
Fixed cost	134,580.00	204,528.00
Cost of capital	37,800.00	150,000.00
Depreciation	63,000.00	250,000.00
Total annual costs	447,380.00	767,978.00

[a]Assuming one-quarter jet share

Source: Andrea Rothman, "Timeshare for Sale—In a Corporate Jet," *Business Week,* 14 June 1993, p. 77. Reprinted from June 14, 1993 issue of *Business Week* by special permission. Copyright © 1993 by The McGraw-Hill Companies.

Comments regarding the data that appear in the article:

1. The direct operating costs are what the firm pays NetJets per hour for using the service. If NetJets is not used at all, the payment is zero. In answering the following questions, assume 200 flying hours are used annually.
2. The fixed costs are paid to NetJets regardless of the number of flying hours the firm uses.
3. Assume a cost of capital of $k = 6\%$.
4. Assume that a one-quarter jet share is sufficient for the CEO's flying needs.

Questions

1. The article gives data on costs but not on the project's cash inflows.

a. Discuss the difficulties in calculating the NPV and the IRR (to see whether full ownership of a plane is worthwhile) in the absence of data on the cash inflows. Why is it difficult to measure the profitability of such a project? In what respect is this project different from other projects?

b. How, in your view, can the firm decide whether to acquire full ownership of a plane?

2. The CEO can use commercial airlines, NetJets timesharing, or a company jet. Flying by NetJets or a company jet rather than commercial airlines increases the number of hours that a CEO can devote to the firm. This increase in CEO efficiency translates to additional revenue to the firm of $0.5 million a year. The annual airfare costs on commercial airlines are $100,000.

a. Use the data provided to calculate the NPV, the IRR, the payback period, and the accounting rate of return for the incremental cash flows obtained by transferring from a commercial airline to (i) NetJets timesharing or (ii) full ownership of a plane. Assume the plane is fully depreciated in 10 years and that the project ends after 10 years. Cost of capital is $k = 6\%$, and its payback period is 10 years.

b. Which alternative is best according to each of the investment criteria mentioned above? (*Hint:* Do not overlook the increase in CEO efficiency and the annual airfare on commercial airlines.)

3. You estimate that you need six hours' notice for domestic flights rather than the four hours promised. Thus, with timesharing the CEO may have to wait up to six hours for the plane to become available and may risk missing an important emergency meeting. As a result, although full ownership is estimated to increase the firm's earnings by $0.5 million a year, timesharing would increase revenue by only $300,000 a year. Recalculate all the profitability measures for the timesharing project.

a. Which option would the payback period rule prefer?

b. The accounting rate of return rule?

c. The NPV rule?

d. The IRR rule?

Discuss your results.

Appendix 6A   The Discounted Payback Rule

As explained earlier, the payback period (PBP) rule does not discount cash flows. The discounting problem is partially overcome by the **discounted payback rule,** which is based on the number of years it takes the *discounted cash flows* to recover the initial investment. For instance, consider two projects with the following cash flows:

	Year 0	Year 1	Year 2	Year 3
Project A	−$100	$90	$40	$50
Project B	−$100	$40	$90	$50

If the cutoff period is two years, the conventional payback rule will accept both projects because their cash flows recover the initial investment at most within two years. The third-year cash flows are ignored because the cutoff is two years. According to the discounted payback rule, we first have to discount the cash flows. If the relevant cost of capital is 20%, the discounted cash flows will be as follows:

	Year 0	Year 1	Year 2	Year 3
Project A	−$100	$\frac{\$90}{1.2} = \$75.00$	$\frac{\$40}{(1.2)^2} \cong \$27.78$	$\frac{\$50}{(1.2)^3} \cong \$28.94$
Project B	−$100	$\frac{\$40}{1.2} \cong \$33.33$	$\frac{\$90}{(1.2)^2} = \$62.50$	$\frac{\$50}{(1.2)^3} \cong \$28.94$

The discounted payback rule clearly reveals the superiority of projects that have early cash flows, and it acknowledges the time value of money. Project A's discounted cash flows are more than sufficient to recover the investment in two years ($75.00 + $27.78 = $102.78 > $100). However, this rule with its two-year cutoff would reject Project B because its discounted cash flows do not recover the investment in two years ($33.33 + $62.50 = $95.83 < $100).

Although the discounted payback corrects one drawback of the PBP rule by discounting cash flows, it still ignores cash flows received after the payback period. In other words, even if Project B were to yield $1 million in its third year, the discounted payback rule would still reject it.

APPENDIX KEY TERM

Discounted payback rule

CHAPTER 7

ESTIMATING PROJECT CASH FLOWS

LEARNING OBJECTIVES

After reading this chapter, you should understand:

1. How projects are initiated and how cash flows are estimated.

2. The difference between cash flows and accounting earnings.

3. Why a firm should evaluate new projects based on the incremental cash flow principle, which considers opportunity costs, variable and fixed costs, and side effects.

4. How a firm should treat a new project's net working capital.

5. The cash flows corresponding to lease-versus-buy decisions.

6. How to evaluate the cash flows of projects with unequal economic lives.

7. How to determine the optimal replacement policy.

8. The effect of inflation on cash flows, the cost of capital, and profitability.

CORPORATE FINANCE IN THE NEWS

WHAT'S A LOYAL CUSTOMER WORTH?

Customers are the most important asset a company has. They are the source from which all cash flow flows . . . . How much is a new customer worth? How much should you pay to keep an old one?

. . . First, decide on a meaningful period of time over which to do the calculations. This will vary depending on your planning cycles and your business: A life insurer should track customers for decades, a disposable-diaper maker for just a few years, for example.

Next, calculate the profit (net cash flow) customers generate each year. Track several samples—some newcomers, some old-timers—to find out how much business they gave you each year, and how much it cost to serve them. If possible, segment them by age, income, sales channel, and so on. For the first year, be sure to subtract the cost of acquiring the pool of customers, such as advertising, commissions, back-office costs of setting up a new account. Get specific numbers—profit per customer in year one, year two, etc.—not averages for all customers or all years. Long-term customers tend to buy more, pay more (newcomers are often lured by discounts), and create less bad debt.

Then chart customer "life expectancy," using the samples to find out how much your customer base erodes each year. Again, specific figures are better than an average like "10% a year"; old customers are much less likely to leave than freshmen. In retail banking, 26% of account holders defect in the first year; in the ninth year, the rate drops to 9%.

Once you know the profit per customer per year and the customer-retention figures, it's simple to calculate net present value. Pick a discount rate—if you want a 15% annual return on assets, use that. Apply the rate to each year's profit, adjusted for the likelihood that the customer will leave. In year one, the NPV will be profit $\div 1.15$. Next year, NPV = (year-two profit $\times$ retention rate) $\div 1.15^2$. In year n, the last year in your figures, the NPV is the nth year's adjusted profit $\div 1.15^n$. The sum of years one through n is how much your customer is worth—the net present value of all the profits you can expect from his tenure.

This is invaluable information. You can use it to find out how much to spend to attract new customers, and which ones.

7.1 INTRODUCTION

The preceding Corporate Finance in the News article demonstrates how a project's cash flow is measured. Customer satisfaction is the investment in this specific case. Once its future cash flows are determined, the investment's NPV calculation is straightforward. However, it is not obvious which expenses and income items should be included and which should be excluded. For example, suppose the firm borrows $1 million and spends it on advertising. Should the firm record the interest payment on the loan as a cash outflow? What about the CFO's salary? What about depreciation and taxes? This chapter addresses the principles that provide guidelines regarding which expenses or income should be included and which should be excluded from NPV calculations. We also explain the differences between accounting income and cash flows and the reasons for these differences. We reemphasize that cash flow—not accounting income—is relevant for project evaluation.

7.2 INITIATING A PROJECT AND FORECASTING SALES

Projects do not suddenly appear; someone has to suggest them to the board. Such suggestions can come from the production department, from the marketing department, or from any other department of the firm. Some firms even have research and development departments with research teams working year-round searching for new ideas and new projects. Initiating good projects is not a simple task. Connecting Theory to Practice 7.1, which describes a capital investment scheme in the United Kingdom, emphasizes the difficulty in finding good projects.

CONNECTING THEORY TO PRACTICE 7.1

THE UNITED KINGDOM EXPERIENCE: INVESTORS WARNED OF HIGHER RISKS

Investors are likely to be faced with higher risks under the Budget's venture-capital proposals, according to fund managers in Manchester. Ian Hamilton Fazey writes

"We as an industry invest about £1bn [1 billion British pounds] a year in around 1,000 projects. Less than half is genuine development capital or start-ups. Most are management buy-outs. The problem is not finding money to invest in projects, but in finding good projects to invest it in," Mr. Folkman said.

Mr. Mike Masters, finance director of Trinity International Holdings, the Chester-based regional newspaper publisher and a former senior manager with the Royal Bank of

Scotland, said: "There are not enough worthwhile projects around . . . . There are plenty of projects, but venture capital managers have to look hard to find good ones."

Source: "Investors Warned of Higher Risks," *Financial Times*, 1 December 1994, p. 12.

MAKING THE CONNECTION

The article indicates that many investments are actually management buyouts of existing firms or existing projects rather than start-up projects. The larger problem for managers wanting to record ever-increasing profits is not raising the money, but finding good projects with promising future cash flows.

The highly competitive computer industry provides perhaps the best example of the difficulty firms have in finding good projects with promising future cash flows. For example, consider Apple Computer's product development. The first company to introduce a mass-market computer in 1976, Apple has since introduced many new products, including the Apple II (April 1977); the Macintosh (January 1984); the Newton (August 1993), its first handheld communicator;[1] and the PowerBook (October 1994), its first notebook computer. Apple's projects have been extremely risky, and not all have been successful. Some have failed for technical reasons; some have failed because they were too expensive; and some have failed because they were marketed too late after competitors had introduced similar, perhaps superior, products.

In evaluating projects and calculating their NPVs, a firm discounts future expected cash flows that are based on a set of forecasts. If all project forecasts are precise, the firm will incur no losses; unfortunately, forecasts are not perfectly accurate. Losses—even bankruptcy—may result if forecasted cash flows do not materialize. New products fail in various industries because actual cash flows deviate from the expected cash flows or because management makes strategic mistakes (not considering enough market factors or being overoptimistic about new products).

However, not all firms have products that fail or have unpredictable sales or future cash flows. For example, firms that supply water or electricity or those that sell groceries can predict future sales and future cash flows fairly easily and accurately. Of course, their projects, because they have a high degree of certainty, generally also yield a relatively low rate of return. The riskier firms such as Apple Computer have higher average profits on their projects.

In calculating a project's NPV, the firm must discount the project's cash flows. The higher the risk, the larger the discount rate that the firm should use. In this chapter we focus on the cash flows, not on the cost of capital, but we continue to bear in mind that the cost of capital may, and indeed should, vary with risk (that is, with the uncertainty of the project's cash flow).

1. Kathy Rebello, Russell Mitchell, and Evan I. Schwartz, "Apple's Future: Can New CEO Michael Spindler Bring Back the Glory Days?" *Business Week*, 5 July 1993, pp. 24–25.

Once we have a given project's sales and costs estimates, the next question is, How do we forecast its future cash flows? As we shall see, the cash flow forecast is usually derived from the sales forecast. However, a large volume of sales does not guarantee success. For instance, if the cash flow from such sales is deferred (for example, because of a relaxed credit policy), the firm may have large revenue from sales and large accounting profit, yet actually incur losses. Let's analyze this difference between cash flows and accounting income and show how to derive the cash flow from the accounting figures.

7.3 CASH FLOWS VERSUS ACCOUNTING DATA

In Chapter 3 we explained the difference between the firm's income statement and its statement of cash flows. We emphasized that cash flow figures are more relevant in the investment decision than the accounting figures. However, cash flow figures can be derived from the forecasts of the accounting income statement. In this section we will review two specific examples of differences between accounting statements and cash flow figures: sales versus cash proceeds and the effect of depreciation on taxes owed.

7.3.1 Sales Versus Cash Proceeds: Accounts Receivable

Suppose Boeing Company decides to adopt a liberal credit policy, allowing 50% of its sales in Year 1 to be paid one year later at $t = 2$ and 50% of its sales to be collected for cash at $t = 1$. The firm is considering a project that involves an investment of $500 million at $t = 0$ (beginning of the first year) and sales of $600 million in Year 1. Should Boeing accept the project?

Since standard accounting procedures specify that sales be recorded in the year they are made, we obtain the following differences between the sales figures and the cash receipts:

	Year 1	Year 2
Accounting revenue from sales	$600 million	$0
Cash flow from sales	$300 million	$300 million

With its new credit policy, Boeing will receive a cash flow of $300 million in Year 1, and the remaining $300 million will be accounts receivable. According to the accounting rules, however, Boeing will record $600 million as revenue. Boeing should not base its decision whether to accept this project on the accounting income because the accounting figures do not consider the time value of money.

Let us compare the project's NPV based on the accounting figures with its NPV based on the actual cash flows. Assume that all figures pertain to the end of the year and that Boeing's cost of capital is 15%. Using the accounting figures we obtain (in $ million):

$$\text{NPV} = \frac{\$600}{1.15} - \$500 \cong \$21.74$$

Using the cash flow figures we obtain (in $ million):

$$\text{NPV} = \frac{\$300}{1.15} + \frac{\$300}{(1.15)^2} - \$500 \cong -\$12.29$$

where $500 million is the initial investment. The accounting and cash flow figures produce conflicting results. The accounting figures suggest that Boeing should accept the project, whereas the cash flow figures suggest that Boeing should reject the project. Because the cash flow approach is theoretically superior, the project should be rejected.

7.3.2 Depreciation and Taxes

A firm that invests in machinery and buildings, generally depreciates those assets over a certain number of years. Thus, if $1 million is invested and the asset is depreciated over 10 years, only $100,000 will be recorded as a depreciation expense in each year. As we noted earlier, depreciation causes a difference between accounting and cash flow figures—that is, the systematic allocation of cost over an asset's life.

A firm pays federal, state, and local income taxes. Taxable income is calculated as the gross revenue less costs. Since depreciation is considered a tax-deductible cost, it reduces the firm's tax payment. However, as this section will show, depreciation is not a cash outflow but, rather, an accounting *cost allocation* across years. If there were no taxes, depreciation would not affect a project's cash flow. However, because there are taxes, depreciation does affect the firm's tax payments and, consequently, the project's net cash flow.

To illustrate this claim, suppose a firm is considering a four-year project requiring an initial outlay of $1 million for machinery. All sales and all expenses are in cash. The net revenue from sales is estimated to be $500,000 a year. According to the accounting rules, the firm can deduct from these net proceeds the depreciation on the initial investment. If the firm depreciates the machinery evenly across the four years of the project, the annual depreciation will be $250,000. However, depreciation is not a cash outflow; it is an accounting allocation of the initial investment. The firm will have a cash outflow of $1 million at $t = 0$, but it will have no additional cash outflows on machinery in the future. According to accounting rules, the firm's annual income is $250,000, but its annual cash flow is $500,000. The intuitive explanation for the cash flow's relevance is that the $1 million cash outlay has already been accounted for at $t = 0$. Deducting depreciation would involve a double counting of this expense, as shown in the following table:

	Years				
	0	1	2	3	4
Investment at $t = 0$ and annual income with depreciation deducted ($)	−1,000,000	250,000[a]	250,000[a]	250,000[a]	250,000[a]
Cash flows (without depreciation deducted) ($)	−1,000,000	500,000	500,000	500,000	500,000

[a]($500,000 − $250,000)

Can we conclude that a firm should disregard depreciation in constructing a project's annual cash flows? This conclusion would be justified in a world with no taxes, because depreciation is not a cash flow. However, because taxes do exist, depreciation does affect a project's cash flow. The larger the depreciation, the lower the tax payment, and the more attractive the project will be.

Although depreciation is not cash flow, it affects the tax liability, the project's after-tax cash flow, and its after-tax NPV. The tax saving from depreciation is called the *depreciation tax shelter*. A firm should add $T \times D$ to its annual after-tax cash flow, where T is the corporate tax rate and D is annual depreciation. The importance of depreciation in determining the project's cash flow is illustrated in the following problem.

PRACTICE BOX

Problem

A firm is considering an electronics industry project located in the South of England, and it will spend £1 million (one million pounds sterling) on machinery. The British tax authorities allow depreciation of investments in the electronics industry over two years. However, as an incentive to invest in the North of England, in that region they allow depreciation over one year.

Suppose the firm estimates its sales at £2 million in each of the next two years and its costs (excluding depreciation and taxes) to be $1 million. Let the corporate tax rate be $T = 0.50$. To focus on the effect depreciation has on the cash flow, assume that these sales and costs are all in cash. The investment is considered extremely risky; therefore, the firm's CFO estimates the after-tax cost of capital to be 35%.

Calculate the project's NPV if it is executed in the North of England and in the South of England. Should the firm accept the project? If so, where?

Solution

Cash flow calculations (in £ million) are as follows:

	North of England		South of England	
	Year 1	Year 2	Year 1	Year 2
(1) Sales	2	2	2	2
(2) Costs (excluding depreciation)	1	1	1	1
(3) Net cash inflow before taxes	1	1	1	1
(4) Depreciation	1	0	0.5	0.5
(5) Taxable income	0	1	0.5	0.5
(6) Taxes ($T = 0.50$)	0	0.5	0.25	0.25
(7) Net income	0	0.5	0.25	0.25
(8) = (7) + (4) Net cash flow = Net income + Depreciation	1	0.5	0.75	0.75

(continued)

Before calculating the NPV, let's examine the cash flow figures. We subtract the depreciation from the £1 million annual before–tax cash flow (line 3 minus line 4). If the project is undertaken in the North of England, the depreciation will be £1 million in Year 1 and zero in Year 2. If the project is located in the South of England, depreciation will be £0.5 million in both years. The result—taxable income—is shown on line 5. Then we calculate the tax payment (see line 6) and the net income (see line 7). However, because depreciation is not a cash outflow (we deduct it only to calculate the tax payment), we add it back to the net income (see line 8). The net cash flow for each assumption is shown on line 8.

Another way to obtain this result is as follows:

1. Calculate the after-tax cash flow assuming that depreciated income is not tax-deductible.
2. Add to the cash flows the depreciation tax shelter, which is equal to the tax rate times the amount of depreciation.

For example, for Year 1, if the project is located in the South, we obtain the following figures (in £ million):

1. After-tax cash flow (excluding depreciation):

$$(1 - \text{Tax rate}) \times (\text{Pretax cash flow}) = (1 - 0.5) \times 1 = 0.5$$

2. Depreciation tax shelter:

$$\text{Tax rate} \times \text{Depreciation} = 0.5 \times 0.5 = 0.25$$

The after-tax cash flow with depreciation deducted for tax purposes is 0.75 (0.5 + 0.25 = 0.75), which is the same result as that obtained by the previous method.

Let us now calculate the project's NPV.

In the South (in £ million),

$$\text{NPV} = \frac{0.75}{1.35} + \frac{0.75}{(1.35)^2} - 1 \cong -0.033$$

In the North (in £ million),

$$\text{NPV} = \frac{1}{1.35} + \frac{0.5}{(1.35)^2} - 1 \cong 0.74 + 0.274 - 1 = 0.014$$

The firm should accept this project only if it is located in the North of England.

We learn from the preceding problem that

1. Depreciation does not affect the total after-tax cash flow. It is £1.5 million regardless of the project's location.
2. Depreciation, although not a cash outflow, reduces the tax bill.

3. With accelerated depreciation (as in the North of England), a firm pays lower taxes in the earlier years (Year 1 in the North) and higher taxes in later years (Year 2 in the North). Being familiar with the time value of money, we understand why the ability to defer tax payments to later years will increase a project's NPV.

4. Finally, the total tax payment across the two years is the same (£0.5 million) regardless of the project's location. The only difference is the spread of these tax payments across years.

Federal, state, and local taxes are cash outflows. The lower the tax rates and the more items that are tax-deductible, the lower the tax burden will be. In 1995 public discussion began on replacing the existing U.S. tax system with a flat tax rate (a constant rate, estimated in the range of 17%–19% applied to all income). A flat tax would likely eliminate several deductions (such as interest, foreign tax, and various employee benefits). It is not clear that all industries would prefer the new, lower flat tax rate. Some would lose money as a result of the change to a flat tax rate, as the graph in Connecting Theory to Practice 7.2 shows.

CONNECTING THEORY TO PRACTICE 7.2

FLAT TAX SNAPSHOT*

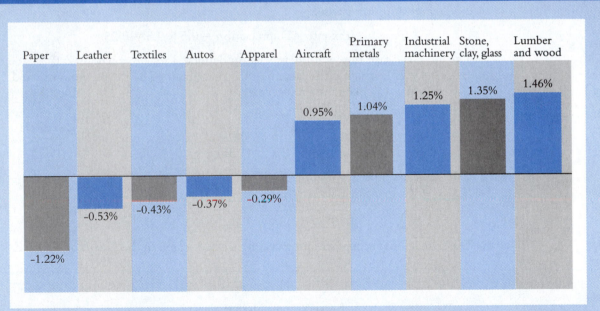

Source: Ann Reilly Dowd, "The Flat Tax Takes a Few Lumps from the Beancounters," *Fortune* 132, no. 7 (October 1995): 42. Copyright © 1995 Time Inc. All rights reserved.

*The differences are expressed as a percent of total sales.

7.4 THE INCREMENTAL CASH FLOW PRINCIPLE

Since a firm may be involved in a number of projects, a new project may affect the cash flows of existing projects. Therefore, a firm should evaluate new projects based on the **incremental cash flow principle.** In other words, the project's cash flows should include all increases or decreases in cash flows to the firm (that is, the incremental change) that result from accepting the new project. Let's elaborate on the incremental cash flow principle by considering several specific issues: sunk costs, opportunity costs, variable and fixed costs, and side effects.

7.4.1 Sunk Costs

Sunk costs are outlays that have already been made and that should not affect future decisions. Suppose you lost $10,000 last year in the stock market. This year you believe that you can make $9,000 in the market. You have sufficient funds available for investment. Should you invest them in the stock market? Last year's loss is a sunk cost and should not affect your decision this year.

Let's return to Apple Computer. Suppose Apple spent $10 million on research and development over five years to develop the Newton. In deciding whether to mass-produce the new model, Apple estimates that it requires a $50 million investment in production facilities. In estimating the Newton's future cash flows and evaluating this project, should Apple include the $10 million spent on research and development as a cash flow? The answer is no. That $10 million is a sunk cost and should not affect Apple's decision whether to produce the project. Apple already considered the $10 million outlay when it made the decision to invest in research and development, and Apple should not incorporate that outlay in its decision whether to start production.

Let's consider some numbers to demonstrate this assertion. For example, suppose the firm's cost of capital is 28%. (Why so high? The risk is very large.) If the firm's estimate of the project's future net cash flows is $25 million in each of the next four years, we have:

	Year				
	0	**1**	**2**	**3**	**4**
Cash flows (in $ million)	−50	25	25	25	25

The NPV at the 28% discount rate is

$$(\$25 \text{ million} \times 2.2410) - \$50 \text{ million} = \$6.025 \text{ million}$$

Since the project creates economic value, the firm should accept it. Conversely, if (mistakenly) Apple were to deduct the R&D expense, the cash flow at $t = 0$ would be −\$60 million, the decision would be reversed, and Apple would reject the Newton project.

Next, let's show that if Apple accepts the Newton project, the firm's *total wealth* will be higher than if it rejects the project. This result will justify the assertion that the \$10 million is a sunk cost that Apple should not include in the project's cash flows. Recall that the firm's total wealth has already changed by −\$10 million as a result of the R&D investment. Since a positive NPV creates value, if Apple accepts the project the firm's total wealth will change by only

$$-\$10 \text{ million} + \$6.025 \text{ million} = -\$3.975 \text{ million}$$

Because the firm's goal is to maximize its value (total wealth), and because a lower reduction in the firm's value is obtained by accepting the project than by rejecting it, Apple fares better with the project. Had Apple included the sunk costs in the cash flow calculation, as we have seen, the firm would have rejected the project and would not have improved its total wealth by \$6.025 million.

For another example of sunk costs, consider the costs of seismographic tests that oil prospecting firms usually conduct before deciding whether to drill a well. Suppose the cost of conducting such a seismographic test is \$1 million. After obtaining the results, a firm estimates the expected NPV from drilling to be \$0.75 million. By the incremental cash flow principle, the firm should accept the project and drill the well. However, if the cost of the test is deducted, the NPV would be negative (−\$0.25 million). This \$1 million cost is a sunk cost. The money has already been spent, and the firm should make its decision whether or not to drill without deducting the sunk cost.

These examples demonstrate that the firm should employ the incremental cash flow principle, which guarantees that the firm's total wealth is maximized.

7.4.2 Opportunity Costs

Suppose Sears, Roebuck & Company is considering whether to open a new department store in Orlando, Florida. The store would require an additional 20,000 cubic feet of storage space in Sears's main Chicago warehouse. Because the warehouse currently has 100,000 cubic feet of unused space, the manager doing the financial analysis does not include storage costs in the incremental cash flows of the Orlando department store project. Is this correct? It depends. If it has no other use for the empty warehouse space, then Sears should treat the storage costs as a sunk cost and should not include them in the cash flow calculation. However, if Sears could rent this space to another firm for, say, \$10 per cubic foot per year, it should charge the new project at

$$\$10 \times 20,000 \text{ cubic feet} = \$200,000 \text{ per year}$$

As we saw in Chapter 5 (see Section 5.2.1), such costs are called *opportunity* or *alternative costs*. In our example, these costs reflect the firm's forgone income (income given up) if it were to use the space for the new project.

Conceptually, the rule regarding opportunity costs is quite clear, but in practice it is sometimes a tough call. For example, suppose Sears cannot currently rent this space but needs it one year later. (For example, a warehouse in another part of the country is flooded, and Sears must store the salvaged inventory from that warehouse somewhere.) In such a case Sears would have to build a new warehouse or rent space from other firms, and the storage costs would be zero in the first year and positive after the first year. A precise procedure for estimating such costs is given in the following section.

7.4.3 Variable Costs Versus Fixed Costs

Whether a firm includes certain costs among its cash flows depends on whether those costs are fixed or variable. **Fixed costs** are those that remain constant for the firm, regardless of whether it accepts a project; **variable costs** are those that are likely to change if the firm accepts the project. According to the incremental cash flow principle, a firm should include variable costs and should exclude fixed costs in the project's cash flows. Although this rule sounds simple, it isn't really. Once again, in practice there are certain gray areas.

Because overhead costs are generally fixed, they should not be included in the project's cash flows. Overhead costs are not directly related to a specific project and are generally allocated among the firm's departments. Examples include the wages of central office employees, the firm's electricity bill, and the CFO's salary. Should the firm include some portion of overhead costs in the project's cash flows? If the electricity costs of the central office are fixed and are not likely to increase as a result of the new project, they should not be included in the project's cash flows. However, if the new project increases electricity and water bills, these costs will be considered variable costs and will be included among the cash flows.

What about the salaries of the CEO and other top executives? If these costs are the same whether or not the firm accepts the new project, they should not be included in the cash flow calculation. However, what if the new project is expected to occupy, say, 10% of the CEO's working time? Because the CEO's time is extremely limited, the firm's acceptance of this project may prevent the executive from handling other projects. In such a case the firm should include 10% of the CEO's salary and compensation in the cash flow calculation as an *opportunity cost*.

To pursue the issue even further, consider the firm's administrative personnel. Initially the firm may have excess administrative capacity and may be able to handle the project at no extra cost. However, at a later stage it may find itself shorthanded and may have to hire additional personnel. As in the Sears warehouse example, the costs will be zero in the short run but positive in the long run; in other words, costs that are fixed in the short run may become variable in the long run. In principle the overhead costs that the financial analyst allocates to each department should not be included in the cash flows of the incremental project. However, in some cases more careful analysis is needed to determine whether some of these costs should be recorded as opportunity costs (as with the CEO's time). The following problem illustrates how costs that are fixed in the short run may not be fixed in the long run.

PRACTICE BOX

Problem

Suppose a firm is considering Project A, which has an NPV of $25,000. The project will employ 20% of the administrative staff's time. This department currently has an overcapacity. The firm records the 20% overhead cost, which has a PV of $40,000, as a fixed cost and does not incorporate it in the project's cash flows.

A few days later the firm reviews Project B. This project also needs an administrative staff costing $40,000 in PV terms. As there is now no overcapacity in administration, the firm would have to hire additional personnel to handle Project B. Project B's NPV is –$10,000 when the PV of the $40,000 incremental administrative cost is included in its cash flows. The firm accepts Project A and rejects Project B. Did the firm reach the best accept/reject decision?

Solution

No, it did not. According to the incremental cash flow principle, if the firm had considered Project B a few days earlier than it did Project A, administrative staff costs would not have been included. In that case the NPV of Project B would have been $30,000 (–$10,000 + $40,000 = $30,000), which is higher than Project A's $25,000 NPV. Furthermore, if the firm had considered Project A a few days later, its NPV would have been –$15,000 ($25,000 – $40,000 = –$15,000), and the firm would have rejected it. The sequence in which the firm considered the projects affected their NPVs. This result indicates that the firm's treatment of administrative overhead was misguided.

The firm should have examined both projects under review and should have given each project an equal chance of having the overhead overcapacity. The NPV of all projects should first be calculated *without* overhead costs to ascertain each project's profitability. In our example, Project A's NPV would be $25,000 and Project B's NPV would be $30,000. Clearly, Project B is preferable. Accordingly, it should be accepted and should have the benefit of the overcapacity. However, if the firm accepts Project B, Project A's NPV will be only –$15,000 ($25,000 – $40,000 = –$15,000) because Project B uses the overcapacity (that is, the incremental cost of $40,000 must be considered in calculating Project A's NPV). Therefore, the firm should accept Project B and reject Project A. Let's look at the firm's incremental NPV under all alternatives to show that this is the best decision.

Decision	NPV
Project A accepted/Project B rejected	$25,000
Project B accepted/Project A rejected	$30,000
Both projects accepted	$25,000 + $30,000 – $40,000 = $15,000
Both projects rejected	$0 *(continued)*

> By accepting only Project B, the firm maximizes its value. This decision agrees with the results obtained by the procedure we have suggested for handling the firm's overcapacity.

The principle described in the preceding problem holds for any overcapacity: storage overcapacity, administrative overcapacity, CEO/CFO time, and so forth. In practice the choices can sometimes be very difficult. For instance, what if Project B had been reviewed one year later and not just a few days after Project A? Clearly, a firm cannot consider all possible future projects, and there is no formula for all possible scenarios. What the firm and the CFO need is a fair share of intuition and some plain good luck!

7.4.4 Side Effects

When acceptance of a particular project affects the cash flows of other projects, the result is a **side effect.** Suppose Ford Motor Company produces a new auto model similar in size to the Escort but more fuel efficient. Suppose the NPV of this project (the new car) without side effects is estimated to be $900 million. When Ford introduces the new car, potential Escort buyers may shift to the new car, in which case the sales and the future cash flows of the Escort will decrease. If the PV of the Escort's reduced cash flow is $500 million, then according to the incremental cash flow principle, the new project's NPV will be only $400 million because Ford should deduct the $500 million PV of the side effect.

One project will sometimes enhance the cash flows of another project. For example, when a department store stocks a new, attractive product, customers who come to the store to buy this product are also likely to purchase other items. Firms often sell certain products at a discount or even at a loss to encourage customers to buy other, nondiscounted products. In such instances the side effect will be positive, and according to the incremental cash flow principle, the firm may not lose even though it appears that way if the side effects are not considered.

In summary, a firm should evaluate each project according to the incremental cash flow principle and should incorporate the positive or negative side effects on other existing projects to make the correct investment decision.

7.5 SEPARATING THE INVESTMENT AND FINANCING DECISIONS

In Chapter 5 we claimed that the financing method—whether equity or debt—did not affect the project's NPV. Some people may question that claim. They may argue that if the firm takes out a loan, the cash outflows incurred by the debt, including the interest expense, will not be zero. The payments of principal and interest represent real cash outflows, not just accounting figures. A firm pays interest to capital suppliers exactly as it pays wages to labor suppliers. On the other hand, these doubters argue, if a firm finances the project by equity, it will have no such interest expense. So, they say, according to the incremental cash flow principle, the project's NPV will depend on the financing method because the net cash flows depend on the financing method.

So does the financing method affect the NPV? No, it doesn't. Based on the argument in Chapter 5, a firm should not deduct interest even if it is an actual cash flow. Perhaps you have guessed (or remembered) the intuitive explanation of that argument. By discounting the project's cash flows, a firm has already considered the time value of money (and has accounted for the interest expense). If it were to deduct the interest, the firm would be double-counting the interest charges. (This double-counting argument is similar to the one regarding depreciation earlier in this chapter.)

Another reason why a firm should not incorporate interest expenses is that its debt (and interest expense) is generally not tied to a specific project but, rather, reflects its long-term financing policy. A firm should not deduct interest charges from each and every specific project under consideration. For example, if the firm decides to have $100 million in debt, this choice will affect its long-term financing policy because the firm will use the $100 million for all its projects and operations. In Chapter 5 we assumed that cash flows are certain and that the riskless interest rate is the relevant discount rate. In practice cash flows are risky, and firms finance their operations by both debt and equity. By a similar argument, since dividends are not tied to a specific project, a firm should not include them in project cash flows. When the firm finances its projects using a mix of equity and debt, the discounting process accounts for both the interest cost and the equity costs. We will discuss how these two components affect the cost of capital in Chapter 10.

In the rest of this book, we will adhere to the incremental cash flow principle, but we will separate the investment and financing decisions. Accordingly, interest charges and dividends should not be deducted from the project's cash flows.

7.6 THE TREATMENT OF WORKING CAPITAL

When we speak of an investment, it is natural to think about machinery, buildings, and land. We sometimes forget that most projects also need cash in the bank and money to finance an inventory of raw materials, products in process, and finished goods. These should also be included as investments when evaluating a project. The firm's credit policy usually determines the amount of investment needed. If the firm sells on credit, it receives cash from sales much later. In the meantime the firm needs money to finance production and to pay wages, utilities, and other expenses. If the firm buys its raw material on credit, it delays its payments and needs less cash to finance a smooth operation.

The investment needed to maintain the cash and inventory necessary to run the project is the required investment in net working capital for the new project. **Net working capital** is defined as current assets less current liabilities. An increase in current assets for the project represents a use of funds, and the firm must finance the current assets. An increase in current liabilities is a source of funds that reduces the needed investment.

Suppose a firm is considering a new project. The initial outlay on machinery and buildings is $10 million. To run the project smoothly, the firm must hold $0.5

million in cash and $2 million in inventory. The firm sells on credit and needs an additional $1 million to finance the receivables. It also buys on credit from its suppliers, who will provide a financing source of $0.2 million. The investment required in net working capital for the project is as follows:

Cash	$0.5 million
+ Inventory	$2.0 million
+ Receivables	$1.0 million
− Payables	−$0.2 million
Increase in net working capital	$3.3 million

The total initial outlay on the project is therefore $13.3 million.

In the treatment of the investment in net working capital, we need to consider two additional factors:

1. When the project is "closed down"—say, after 5 years—we need to add back the net working capital as cash inflow. The firm sells the inventory held and does not have to renew it, and the firm can use the cash in the bank and the money received from customers to pay its suppliers.
2. Because sales fluctuate over time, the investment in net working capital may also fluctuate. For example, if sales increase and receivables are, say, 20% of sales, then receivables also increase. An increase in receivables implies that the investment in working capital increases. Nevertheless, because it is interested in cash flows, not in net working capital, the firm needs to calculate only the net working capital needed initially. Then, in preparing the forecast of future cash flows, any change in sales or in credit policy may affect the future cash flows and the project's NPV. Further, if the firm forecasts that it will need more inventory at some future date, it should add it as cash outflow at that date. In Applying Theory to Practice 7.1, we illustrate the principle that a firm's credit policy affects the timing of a project's cash flow, and hence its NPV.

APPLYING THEORY TO PRACTICE 7.1

THE GOLDEN POND COMPANY

The Golden Pond Company operates in Orlando, Florida. The firm is considering building an additional amusement park that will have a wild-water wave pool, buildings, and restaurants. Since all the firm's sales are for cash, the cash inflow from sales and gross revenue are identical. The firm's variable costs amount to 50% of its revenue, with 60% of these costs paid in cash and 40% paid for on credit for one year. The new investment is $200 million ($100 million in equipment and $100 million in buildings), plus $10 million investment in net working capital (mainly cash). Golden Pond will depreciate the equipment by the accelerated method (by whch relatively high proportions of the asset's values are depreciated in early years) over four years, and the buildings will be depreciated over 31.5 years. The buildings will be placed in service in January. The annual depreciation percentages are as follows (see Appendix 7A):

Year	Equipment	Buildings
1	33.33%	3.042%
2	44.45%	3.175%
3	14.81%	3.175%
4	7.41%	3.175%

Golden Pond estimates annual sales at $400 million for each of the next four years. As a result of the new project, the after-tax cash flows from the firm's other amusement parks will decline by $20 million a year. The firm has already paid $25 million on an after-tax basis for research and development of the new project. The value of buildings in the Orlando area is expected to increase to an estimated $110 million after four years of operation. The value of equipment after four years of use will be zero. Assume that the after-tax cost of capital is 15%, and the corporate tax rate is 34%. The firm uses vacant land for the new attraction, and it has no alternative use for the land for the next four years. Should the company proceed with the project?

MAKING THE CONNECTION

Table 7-1 summarizes this information and shows the project's cash flows. Let's examine the main items affecting the project's cash flow.

Golden Pond will have a capital gain when it sells the buildings. However, it will have to pay taxes on the difference between the revenue from selling the buildings and the depreciated cost of the buildings. The depreciation on the buildings in the first four years is

$$3.042\% + 3.175\% + 3.175\% + 3.175\% \cong 12.57\%$$

Therefore, the net book value of the buildings at $t = 4$ is

$$\$100 \text{ million} \times (1 - 0.1257) = \$87.43 \text{ million}$$

The capital gains tax will be

$$0.34 \times (\$110 \text{ million} - \$87.43 \text{ million}) = \$7.674 \text{ million}$$

The net after-tax cash flow from selling the buildings will be

$$\$110 \text{ million} - \$7.674 \text{ million} = \$102.326 \text{ million}$$

which is $2.326 million more than Golden Pond spent on them.

The side-effect costs of $20 million a year represent the reduction in the after-tax cash flows from the firm's other amusement parks.

TABLE 7-1 Golden Pond's Cash Flows (in $ million)	Year					
	0	1	2	3	4	5
Property	(100)				102.326	
Equipment	(100)					
Net working capital	(10)				10	
Sales revenue (in cash)		400	400	400	400	
Variable costs[a]		(120)	(120) + (80)	(120) + (80)	(120) + (80)	(80)
Side effect[b]		(20)	(20)	(20)	(20)	
Taxes (see figures below)		(55.634)	(51.808)	(61.885)	(64.401)	
Project cash flows	(210)	204.366	128.192	118.115	227.925	(80)

	Income Figures for Tax Purposes (by Year)			
	1	2	3	4
Revenue	400	400	400	400
Operating costs	(200)	(200)	(200)	(200)
Depreciation on equipment	(33.330)	(44.450)	(14.810)	(7.410)
Depreciation on property	(3.042)	(3.175)	(3.175)	(3.175)
Income before tax	163.628	152.375	182.015	189.415
Taxes at 34%	(55.634)	(51.808)	(61.885)	(64.401)

[a]The variable costs are $200 million a year. However, only $120 million is paid in the same year, and the remaining $80 million is paid one year later. The $80 million of variable costs from Year 4 occurs in Year 5.

[b]Reduction in income from other amusement parks.

Golden Pond recovers net working capital (mainly cash) of $10 million at the end of the fourth year. Since the $25 million paid to the research group is a sunk cost, it is not included in the cash flow calculation. Since the land has zero alternative cost, it is not included in the initial outlay. Finally, the firm pays income taxes. The firm is allowed to depreciate its equipment over four years for tax purposes.

Should Golden Pond accept the project? The bottom line of the upper part of Table 7.1 summarizes the firm's cash flows during the five years. The after-tax cash flows are as follows:

	Year					
	0	1	2	3	4	5
Cash flows (in $ million)	−210	204.366	128.192	118.115	227.925	−80

The firm's after-tax cost of capital is 15%. At this discount rate, the project's NPV is

$$
\begin{aligned}
\text{NPV} = &-\$210 \text{ million} + (0.8696 \times \$204.366 \text{ million}) \\
&+ (0.7561 \times \$128.192 \text{ million}) + (0.6575 \times \$118.115 \text{ million}) \\
&+ (0.5718 \times \$227.925 \text{ million}) + (0.4972 \times -\$80 \text{ million}) \cong \$232.855 \text{ million}
\end{aligned}
$$

Thus, Golden Pond should accept the project.

Note that although the accounting figures generally differ from cash flow figures, we use the accounting rules to calculate the tax payments. For example, the equipment may actually depreciate evenly over the four years, but the tax authority allows the firm to use accelerated depreciation, which decreases the tax burden. (See Appendix 7A.) Second, after using the accounting figures to calculate the tax payment, we use the annual cash flow to evaluate the project.

If there were no taxes, we could use the cash flows directly. With taxes, however, we must use the accounting framework to calculate the tax bill, and only then can we shift to the cash flow framework.

7.7 LEASE-VERSUS-BUY DECISIONS

A firm can use leasing to finance a plant, equipment, vehicles, and property. The *lessee* uses the assets and makes payments to the *lessor* who provides the asset. There are two types of lease agreements: an *operating lease* and a *financial lease*. In an operating lease agreement, the lessor is responsible for maintenance of the asset; in a financial lease agreement, the lessee usually pays maintenance costs.

A firm must decide whether to buy an asset or lease it. If it buys the asset, the firm can depreciate its value and will benefit from the depreciation tax shelter. If it leases the asset, the firm's lease payments are tax-deductible. Leasing exempts the firm from the large initial cash outlay involved in purchasing the asset. The firm makes the **lease-versus-buy decision** by examining the incremental cash flows of the two options. If $\text{NPV}_{\text{lease}} > \text{NPV}_{\text{buy}}$, the firm will prefer the lease option. Otherwise, the buy option is better. Because the benefits of using the equipment (the firm's sales) are the same in either case, we focus on the cash outlays and tax savings of these two options. We demonstrate this type of decision with a car-leasing example in Applying Theory to Practice 7.2.

APPLYING THEORY TO PRACTICE 7.2

LEASE-VERSUS-BUY DECISIONS

CBM Inc. is considering whether to lease or buy 20 luxury cars for its executives. The available lease terms are as follows:

$0 **Down Payment** **24-Month Lease**		$429 **Per Month** **24-Month Lease**		$11,462 **One-Time Lease Payment** **24-Month Lease**	
Monthly Payment	$537	Monthly Payment	$429	One-Time Lease Payment	$11,462
Down Payment	$0	Down Payment	$2,450	Refundable Security Deposit	$575
Refundable Security Deposit	$550	Refundable Security Deposit	$450	Cash Due at Signing	$12,037
Cash Due at Signing	$1,087	Cash Due at Signing	$3,329	Cash Outlay Over 24 Months	$12,037

Source: *Wall Street Journal,* 8 August 1994.

The cost of a new Lincoln, including sales tax, is $37,500. If CBM buys the cars, assume it can depreciate each car as follows:

	Year					
	1	**2**	**3**	**4**	**5**	**6**
Depreciation	20%	32%	19%	12%	11%	6%

Assume that the corporate tax rate is 34%, and the riskless interest rate is 6%. Without taxes the discount rate for certain cash flows is 6%; but with taxes the discount rate is lower, 3.96% [$(1 - 0.34) \times 6\% = 3.96\%$] because interest is tax-deductible.[2]

If CBM buys the cars, it will hold them for six years before selling them. For simplicity assume the cars' market value (also called *residual value* or *salvage value*) will be zero in six years' time. If CBM decides to lease the cars, assume it will select the zero down payment option and make a lease payment of $6,444 at the end of each year ($12 \times \$537 = \$6,444$). Assume also that the lease arrangement is guaranteed for six years. Focus only on the option of the zero down payment. Should CBM buy or lease the cars? Conduct all calculations for one car.

MAKING THE CONNECTION

First, we have to list the relevant cash flows. If CBM leases the car, the annual lease payments will be tax-deductible. Therefore, the after-tax cash flow will be only[3]

$$(1 - 0.34) \times \$6,444 \cong \$4,253$$

2. Let's use a simple example to illustrate that the discount rate will be lower because of interest deductibility. Suppose the firm borrows $100 million on which it has to pay 6% interest, or $6 million annually. The firm's taxable income before interest is $200 million. What is the after-tax cost of debt? With no borrowing the firm's income is $132 million [$(1 - 0.34) \times \$200$ million $= \$132$ million]. With borrowing the firm's net income is $128.04 million [$(1 - 0.34) \times (\$200$ million $- \$6$ million) $= \$128.04$ million]. Therefore, the after-tax cost of debt is only $3.96 million ($132 million $- \$128.04$ million $= \$3.96$ million), or 3.96% of the amount borrowed.

3. Although the firm pays $6,444 in cash to the lessor, the fact that the lease expense is tax-deductible reduces the firm's tax payment by $2,191 ($0.34 \times \$6,444 = \$2,191$). The overall cash flow created by the lease is the cash paid to the lessor less the tax shield:

$$(1 \times \$6,444) - (0.34 \times \$6,444) = (1 - 0.34) \times \$6,444 \cong \$4,253$$

Depreciation in the first year is 20%. Therefore, the depreciation tax shelter in Year 1 is \$2,550 ($0.2 \times 0.34 \times \$37,500 = \$2,550$). The depreciation tax shelter for other years is calculated in the same way except that the depreciation rate will vary. The resulting cash flows are as follows:

Cash Flows of Leasing Versus Buying

	Year						
	0	**1**	**2**	**3**	**4**	**5**	**6**
Leasing the Car							
Cash flows	\$ 0	−\$4,253	−\$4,253	−\$4,253	−\$4,253	−\$4,253	−\$4,253
Buying the Car							
Car purchase	−\$37,500						
Depreciation rate (rounded figures)		0.20	0.32	0.19	0.12	0.11	0.06
Depreciation tax shelter (Depreciation rate × 0.34 × \$37,500)[4]		\$2,550	\$4,080	\$2,422.50	\$1,530	\$1,402.50	\$765
Buying the Car Cash flows	−\$37,500	\$2,550	\$4,080	\$2,422.50	\$1,530	\$1,402.50	\$765
Incremental Cash Flows (Leasing Minus Buying)							
Cash flows	\$37,500	−\$6,803	−\$8,333	−\$6,675.5	−\$5,783	−\$5,655.5	−\$5,018

If CBM leases the car, it will save \$37,500 in Year 0 (by not having to pay for the car). The firm will have to make the lease payments in all other years, and will also forfeit the depreciation tax shelter. The decision whether to lease or buy the car will depend on the NPV of the incremental cash flows. Note that the depreciation tax shelter and the lease payments are certain cash flows.[5] The appropriate cost of capital of certain cash flows is the after-tax riskless interest rate. In this example, as we have seen, that rate is 3.96% [$(1 − 0.34) \times 6\% = 3.96\%$]. The NPV of the incremental (leasing minus buying) cash flows at this cost of capital is thus

$$\text{NPV}_{\text{lease}} - \text{NPV}_{\text{buy}} = \$37,500 - [\$6,803/1.0396 + \$8,333/(1.0396)^2 + \$6,675.5/(1.0396)^3 + \$5,783/(1.0396)^4 + \$5,655.5/(1.0396)^5 + \$5,018/(1.0396)^6] = \$37,500 - 33,778.73 \cong \$3,721.27$$

CBM obtains an incremental cash flow with a positive NPV by leasing the cars rather than buying them. Therefore, leasing is better than buying, and

4. It is also equal to $T \times D_t$ where T is the tax rate and D_t the depreciation in Year t.
5. The lease payments are a certain cash flow commitment. The depreciation tax shelter is also certain: If the firm has a positive income, its tax bill will be reduced by the depreciation tax shelter. If the firm loses money and does not pay tax, it can carry the loss forward or backward on its tax returns to benefit from the depreciation tax shelter. Therefore, the depreciation tax shelter is also relatively certain.

CBM Inc. should lease the cars. However, this decision is affected by one of our assumptions: that each car's market value will be zero after six years of use. If a six-year-old car has a positive market value, the decision to lease rather than to buy the cars may be reversed.

7.8 EVALUATING THE CASH FLOWS OF PROJECTS WITH UNEQUAL LIVES

Projects have different life expectancies. For example, some may be expected to run their course in a year or two, whereas others may take ten years to do so. When projects are mutually exclusive, we need to compare their NPVs. However, comparison of the NPV of mutually exclusive projects that have **unequal economic lives** is not straightforward. To evaluate such projects, we must first modify their cash flows to equate their economic lives. For example, consider two projects with the following cash flows (in $ million):

	Year				
	0	**1**	**2**	**3**	**4**
Project A	−100	—	—	—	300
Project B	−100	150	—	—	—

The firm's cost of capital is 15%. Which project should the firm accept?

First we calculate the NPV of each project.

$$\text{Project A: NPV} = (\$300 \text{ million} \times 0.5718) - \$100 \text{ million}$$
$$= \$171.54 \text{ million} - \$100 \text{ million} = \$71.54 \text{ million}$$

$$\text{Project B: NPV} = (\$150 \text{ million} \times 0.8696) - \$100 \text{ million}$$
$$= \$130.44 \text{ million} - \$100 \text{ million} = \$30.44 \text{ million}$$

Here, 0.5718 at 0.8696 are the relevant discount factors.

If the projects are independent, the firm should accept both. The fact that they have unequal lives is not a problem.

However, unequal lives may be a problem if the projects are mutually exclusive. Take the case of a farmer who owns a piece of land. He can plant either a seasonal crop that will yield a return of $150 million at the end of one year (Project B) or, alternatively, an orchard that will produce its first fruit four years later (Project A). Assume identical initial costs of $100 million. After four years the farmer intends to sell the land to a developer, who will pay the same price for the land regardless of its current use. Which mutually exclusive option is better?

If we look at the two projects' NPVs, the orchard is better. But is this a correct comparison? As we shall see, it is not. With the one-year seasonal crop, at the end of the first year the farmer will have vacant land that he can use for another purpose or can sell. Suppose the farmer continues to plant one-year crops for four years. He invests $100 million each year to yield $150 million at the end of the year. The land will thus be occupied for the same time period under both alternatives. The cash flows of Project B (in $ million) repeated four times will be as follows:

	Year				
	0	**1**	**2**	**3**	**4**
Investment	−100	−100	−100	−100	
Cash inflow		150	150	150	150
Net cash flow	−100	50	50	50	150

The NPV of this modified project at 15% cost of capital is

$$\text{NPV} = -\$100 \text{ million} + \$50 \text{ million} \times 2.2832 + \$150 \text{ million} \times 0.5718$$
$$= \$99.93 \text{ million}$$

where 2.2832 and 0.5718 are the relevant discount factors (with a 15% cost of capital) for a three-year annuity and for one payment in the fourth year, respectively. By recording the cash flows properly, we find that Project B is better because it provides a higher NPV. To compare mutually exclusive projects that use the same resource (such as the farmer's land), it is important to equate their economic lives and only then calculate the NPVs of the competing projects.

For simplicity, we ignored the cost of the land and focused on the project's economic life. If the land cost $150 million, this would have to be added as an expense at $t = 0$, and its market resale value would have to be added at the end of Year 4. However, these complicating factors would not affect the calculation, and Project B would still be superior. Even with another alternative, as demonstrated in the following problem, Project B is still the farmer's best choice.

PRACTICE BOX

Problem

Repeat the preceding example, but consider the following additional information:

1. The land cost $150 million, and the farmer can resell it at the end of the fourth year for the same price.
2. The farmer now has a third option (Project C): a two-year crop with an initial investment of $80 million (plus the cost of the land), a zero cash flow in Year 1, and a $180 million cash flow in Year 2.

Assume there are no taxes. Which of the three options is best?

Solution

The NPV of the cash outlay for the purchase of the land is

$$-\$150 \text{ million} + \frac{\$150 \text{ million}}{(1.15)^4} \cong -\$64.24 \text{ million}$$

(continued)

Thus, Project A's NPV is now

$71.54 million (as obtained before) − $64.24 million = $7.3 million

Project B's NPV is

$99.93 million (as obtained before) − $64.24 million = $35.69 million

Now let's examine Project C—the two-year crop option. The cash flows (in $ million) with two repetitions of this project will be as follows:

	Year				
	0	**1**	**2**	**3**	**4**
Cash flows	−80	—	180	—	180
			−80		
Cash flows from land	−150				150
Net cash flows	−230	—	100	—	330

The $150 million is the cash price for the purchase and resale of the land. Project C's NPV will be

$$-\$230 \text{ million} + \frac{\$100 \text{ million}}{(1.15)^2} + \frac{\$330 \text{ million}}{(1.15)^4} \cong \$34.29 \text{ million}$$

The two-year crop (Project C) does not affect the decision; the one-year crop (Project B) with an NPV of $35.69 million is still the best alternative.

7.9 REPLACEMENT DECISIONS

A firm or an individual faces another type of decision: how often to replace a machine (or an automobile). Such **replacement decisions** also require modification of the project's cash flows to obtain equal economic lives. Generally, the longer you keep an asset, the higher will be its annual maintenance costs and the lower will be its resale value. On the other hand, the longer you keep an asset, the longer you save the cost of buying a new one. To illustrate, consider a machine that costs $20,000 and generates annual cash flows (before maintenance expenses) of $25,000 a year for three years. The firm can sell the machine at the end of Year 1, 2, or 3. The maintenance costs and the salvage value of the machine are as follows:

Year	Maintenance costs ($)	Salvage value ($)
1	0	13,000
2	8,000	4,000
3	12,000	0

The firm's cost of capital is 10%. How often should the firm replace the machine? To find the answer, we need to calculate the NPV of the various options. If the firm replaces the machine after one year, the machine's NPV will be

$$NPV_1 = \frac{\$25,000}{1.1} + \frac{\$13,000}{1.1} - \$20,000 \cong \$14,545.45$$

where −$20,000 represents the initial cost of buying a new machine. If the firm replaces the machine after two years, we have

$$NPV_2 = \frac{\$25,000}{1.1} + \frac{\$25,000}{(1.1)^2} - \frac{\$8,000}{(1.1)^2} + \frac{\$4,000}{(1.1)^2} - \$20,000 \cong \$20,082.64$$

If the firm holds the machine for three years, the machine's NPV will be

$$NPV_3 = \frac{\$25,000}{1.1} + \frac{\$25,000}{(1.1)^2} + \frac{\$25,000}{(1.1)^3} - \frac{\$8,000}{(1.1)^2} - \frac{\$12,000}{(1.1)^3} - \$20,000$$

$$\cong \$26,543.95$$

If we compare the NPVs of the three alternatives, we see that NPV_3 is the highest. Therefore, replacing the machine every three years appears to be the best policy.

However, this conclusion may be wrong because we are not comparing equal lives. If the firm replaces it every three years, the machine creates sales of three times $25,000. If it replaces the machine every year, the firm has to incorporate the $25,000 income three times, too; otherwise, we would be assuming that the business closes down after one year. Therefore, the one-year replacement policy has to be repeated three times for correct comparison between the one-year and three-year replacement policy. The one-year replacement policy creates an additional NPV of $14,545.45 in Year 1 and also in Year 2. Since the NPV obtained from the second year of operation is in terms of Year 1 dollars, we discount it by 1.1 to get current dollars. Similarly, since the NPV of the third year of operation is in terms of Year 2 dollars, we discount it by $(1.1)^2$ to get current dollars. By employing the one-year replacement policy three times, we find that the total NPV for three years of operation is

$$NPV = \$14,545.45 + \frac{\$14,545.45}{1.1} + \frac{\$14,545.45}{(1.1)^2} \cong \$39,789.62$$

which is higher than the three-year replacement policy. Therefore, the one-year replacement policy seems preferable to three-year replacement.

Before we accept this answer, though, we should repeat the one-year replacement policy twice to make sure it is better than the two-year replacement policy. For the one-year replacement policy, repeated twice, we obtain the following NPV:

$$NPV = \$14,545.45 + \frac{\$14,545.45}{1.1} \cong \$27,768.59$$

which is higher than the NPV of the two-year replacement policy. Therefore, the optimal decision is to replace the machine every year.

In Appendix 7B we present another technique for comparing projects with unequal lives. Called the *uniform annuity series (UAS)*, this technique produces the same result as that obtained by equating projects' economic lives.

7.10 CASH FLOWS AND CAPITAL BUDGETING IN AN INFLATIONARY ENVIRONMENT

You may have heard some people make comments such as "I remember when you could buy a gallon of gas for 29¢." What they are commenting about is **inflation**—a sustained increase in the general level of prices. In the 1990s the annual inflation rate averaged a relatively low 4% in most countries of the Western world. The 1996 inflation rate was 3.3%. The rate during the 12 months preceding 8/14/97 was 2.2%, and the rate expected for 1998 was 2%–3%. A decade earlier, in the early 1980s, inflation rates surpassing 10% a year were quite common. Does inflation affect a project's cash flows? Its NPV? The discount rate? If so, how? These issues and, in particular, the effect of inflation on project evaluation are discussed next.

7.10.1 Nominal and Real Interest Rates and the Cost of Capital

The interest rates that the financial media publish represent **nominal interest rates,** unless stated otherwise. The financial media also publish information on the inflation rate. The **real interest rate** is calculated on the basis of these two components.

The following example illustrates the difference between the nominal and the real interest rates. Suppose the owner of a sporting goods shop is considering whether to buy an inventory of 100 basketballs at $10 each or to deposit $1,000 in the bank at 10% interest and receive $1,100 for her deposit at the end of the year. At that point she will use the $1,100 to buy basketballs.

Does the shop owner really make a 10% profit by depositing the $1,000 in the bank? Well, it depends. If the price of basketballs changes during the year by less than 10% and if there are no taxes, she does. If at the end of the year the price of each basketball is $10.50 (for simplicity assume the selling price of all goods also increases by 5%), she will be able to buy 104.76 basketballs ($1,100/$10.50) compared to the 100 basketballs she could buy with her money at the beginning of the year.

How much does the shop owner really earn on her deposit? In *nominal* terms she earns 10% because her wealth increases from $1,000 to $1,100. However, in *real* terms (in terms of basketballs) she can buy only 4.76% more basketballs. The reason she cannot buy 110 balls with her 110% amount of money is that inflation (by causing the price of the balls to increase) has eroded her nominal profit.

The 10% interest rate in our example is called the *nominal interest rate;* it does not take inflation into account. The interest rate adjusted for inflation is the *real interest rate.* The nominal interest rate measures the percentage increase on your dollar amount (10% in our example); the real interest rate measures the percentage increase in the goods that you can buy with the same initial wealth (4.76% in our example).

Economist Irving Fisher claimed that inflation does not affect the real interest rate and that the nominal interest rate adjusts itself to the inflation rate.[6] This adjustment in the nominal interest rate is called the **Fisher effect.** Whether the real interest rate remains constant or not, the formal relationship between the historical (in contrast to its expected value) inflation rate and the interest rate is defined as follows:

$$\text{Real interest rate} = \frac{1 + \text{Nominal interest rate}}{1 + \text{Inflation rate}} - 1 \qquad (7.1)$$

The real interest rate in our basketball example is

$$\text{Real interest rate} = \frac{1 + 0.1}{1 + 0.05} - 1 = \frac{1.1}{1.05} - 1 \cong 0.0476 \text{ or } 4.76\%$$

An approximation of the real interest rate can be obtained as follows:

$$\text{Real interest rate} \cong \text{Nominal interest rate} - \text{Inflation rate}$$

In our example,

$$\text{Real interest rate} \cong 10\% - 5\% = 5\%$$

This method gives only an approximation. The lower the interest and inflation rates, the better the approximation will be.

A firm must adjust its cost of capital (which is the minimum required rate of return on investment) for inflation. The higher the expected inflation rate, the higher the nominal cost of capital will be. The increase in the cost of capital represents compensation for inflation. The same relationship as in Equation 7.1 holds for the real and nominal costs of capital:

$$\text{Real cost of capital} = \frac{1 + \text{Nominal cost of capital}}{1 + \text{Inflation rate}} - 1 \qquad (7.2)$$

To illustrate, suppose the firm's minimum required rate of return in the absence of inflation is 15% and the expected inflation rate is 5%. From Equation 7.2 we know that

$$\text{Nominal cost of capital} = (1 + \text{Real cost of capital}) \times (1 + \text{inflation rate}) - 1$$

In our example,

$$\text{Nominal cost of capital} = (1 + 0.15) \times (1 + 0.05) - 1 = 20.75\%$$

With 5% inflation, the firm must earn 20.75% on its investment to guarantee a 15% rate of return in real terms.

7.10.2 Nominal and Real Cash Flows Without Taxes

A nominal cash flow is the actual amount of money received. A real cash flow is the amount of money received, adjusted for inflation. If inflation is absent, the two are equal. To illustrate these concepts—and the NPV calculation when inflation prevails—let's return to our sporting goods example. Suppose the owner of the sport-

6. See Irving Fisher, *The Theory of Interest: Determined by Impatience to Spend Income and Opportunity to Invest It* (New York: Augustus M. Kelley Publishers, 1965). Fisher's original work was published in 1930.

ing goods shop invests $1,000 in an inventory of basketballs at time $t = 0$. She estimates that 50 balls will be sold in Year 1 ($t = 1$) and another 50 will be sold in Year 2 ($t = 2$). Assume that without inflation the selling price would be $15 a ball and that all these cash flows are certain.

Suppose now that there is 5% inflation each year, that all prices, including basketball prices, increase by 5% a year, and that the nominal interest rate is 10%. In this case, since the selling price of a basketball will be $15.75 ($15 × 1.05 = $15.75) in Year 1 and $16.5375 ($15 × 1.05^2 = $16.5375) in Year 2, the **nominal cash flow** will be $787.50 (50 × $15.75 = $787.50) in Year 1 and $826.875 (50 × $16.5375 = $826.875) in Year 2. Because the nominal interest rate is 10% and we assume certainty, the cost of capital will be equal to the interest rate, and the investment's NPV will be

$$\text{NPV} = \frac{\$787.50}{1.1} + \frac{\$826.875}{(1.1)^2} - \$1,000 \cong \$399.28$$

Real cash flows are flows adjusted for inflation. The NPV calculated with real cash flows is also called the NPV calculated in real terms.

The shop owner may wish to conduct all calculations in real terms and completely ignore inflation. Can she? The answer is yes. In this case the annual revenue will be $750 (50 × $15 = $750), which is the real cash flow without the price rise. This represents the cash flow in constant dollar terms. For example, suppose the shop owner wishes to replenish her inventory at the end of the year. Because of the 5% inflation, the $787.50 obtained in Year 1 is worth only $750 ($787.50/1.05 = $750) in constant dollars. The reason is that, by assumption, there is 5% inflation, which means that the purchasing power of $787.50 one year from today is the same as the purchasing power of $750 today. The shop owner can buy the same number of basketballs according to the hypothetical calculation (which ignores inflation) and the calculation that accounts for the actual price (the increased price): $750/$10 = 75 basketballs and $787.50/$10.50 = 75 basketballs, respectively.

However, if *real cash flows* are used, then the *real cost of capital* should be used to discount those cash flows where the real cost of capital is the discount rate adjusted for inflation. In our example the real discount rate is 4.76% (1.10/1.05 − 1 ≅ 4.76%). The NPV of the real cash flow with the real discount rate will be

$$\text{NPV} = \frac{\$750}{1.0476} + \frac{\$750}{(1.0476)^2} - \$1,000 \cong \$399.31$$

We get the same NPV with real calculations as with nominal calculations (the slight difference being due to rounding).

What can we learn from this example? The most important lesson is consistency: If you use nominal cash flows, use the nominal cost of capital to calculate the project's NPV. If you use real cash flows, use the real cost of capital to calculate the NPV. You can choose whichever is more convenient because both methods yield the same NPV. So far we have assumed certainty. If cash flows are uncertain, we obtain the same result, but we must discount the nominal cash flows by the nominal cost of capital, k, or the real cash flows by the real cost of capital as given by Equation 7.2.

If the firm's revenue and costs are expected to increase at a different rate than the general inflation rate, the firm should either (1) adhere to the nominal calculations because the inflation effect in the numerator and the denominator in the PV calculation will not cancel, or (2) take the nominal cash flows of the specific project under consideration, discount them by the general inflation rate to obtain the real cash flows, and then discount the real cash flows by the real cost of capital.

Another reason that inflation should not be ignored in project evaluation is that depreciation is not adjusted to the inflation rate. That is, the firm's after-tax cash flow will not change at exactly the same rate as the inflation rate.

7.10.3 Nominal and Real Cash Flows with Taxes

As we saw in the previous section, once you have estimates of project cash flows, you can use either the nominal or the real cash flows for project evaluation. If all prices increase at the same rate and you use the discount rate properly, you get the same NPV regardless of whether nominal or real values are used.

Is it possible for inflation to have no effect on a project's profitability? Are firms indifferent to inflation? Perhaps in a world without taxes, but not in the real world, where inflation affects tax payments. Recall that firms are allowed to deduct depreciation on assets for tax purposes, thereby decreasing their tax burden. However, depreciation is calculated on the basis of *historical costs* with no adjustment for inflation, and the tax burden increases with inflation. Because revenues are collected in inflated prices while depreciation is based on historical (uninflated) costs, the firm's real economic profit after renewing equipment and inventory (at higher cost) will be lower in comparison to the no–inflation case. A rise in the inflation rate with no increase in allowable depreciation increases tax payments and decreases the project's NPV in real terms. The tax authorities are aware of the distortion that inflation causes and allow firms to deduct accelerated depreciation to compensate for the inflation effect (see Appendix 7A).

Thus, on the one hand, in inflationary periods the project's NPV decreases because depreciation is based on historical costs; on the other hand, it increases because of accelerated depreciation. The net effect of these two factors depends on the inflation rate. At high inflation rates the NPV will decrease; at low rates it will increase.

SUMMARY

Projects do not just appear; someone has to suggest them to the board and provide estimates of the sales volume at various prices, production costs, and other relevant figures. These figures are then used to construct an income statement to calculate the firm's income tax liability, as explained in Applying Theory to Practice 7.1. With information on income tax, accounts receivable, and accounts payable, the cash flows can be estimated and then used in the economic evaluation of the project.

To estimate the cash flows, we use the incremental cash flow principle. Sunk costs are excluded; opportunity costs and variable costs are included. Side-effect costs or benefits are also included. The treatment of fixed costs is tricky because some costs may be fixed in the short run but variable in the long run. The interest expense on debt financing is not included because the cost of debt is already accounted for in the cost of capital when evaluating the project. Mutually exclusive projects with unequal economic lives should be compared only after equating their economic lives.

Cash flows and the cost of capital are affected by inflation. In a world without taxes the nominal framework (using a nominal discount rate and nominal cash flows) and the real framework (real discount rate and real cash flows) yield the same results as long as all prices increase at the same rate.

In the real world, however, inflation does hurt firms because of taxes. Depreciation is based on his-torical costs, not current costs. As a result, the re-ported profit in the firm's financial statements is larger in an inflationary environment, and the firm pays more taxes which, in turn, affect the net cash flows. The real economic profit after renewing equipment (at higher cost) will be lower in compar-ison to the no-inflation case. However, the tax au-thorities allow firms to use accelerated depreciation to alleviate the tax burden.

CHAPTER AT A GLANCE

1. Incremental cash flow principle

Include:

Proceeds from sales
Cash outlay on purchasing goods
Opportunity costs
Variable costs
Working capital
Taxes
Side effects
Initial outlay

Do not include:

Sales
Purchase of goods
Accounts payable
Accounts receivable
Depreciation
Sunk costs
Interest
Dividends

Include fixed costs only if they are likely to become variable at a later stage of the project.

2. Projects with unequal lives

Independent Projects

Calculate the NPV of each project and make a decision by the NPV rule.

Mutually Exclusive Projects

Find common economic life and then calculate the NPV. Make a decision by the NPV rule.

3. Relationship of nominal and real interest rates

Nominal and real interest rates are related by the formula

$$\text{Real interest rate} = \frac{1 + \text{Nominal interest rate}}{1 + \text{Inflation rate}} - 1$$

An approximation of this relationship is

$$\text{Real interest rate} \cong \text{Nominal interest rate} - \text{Inflation rate}$$

4. Nominal and real costs of capital

$$\text{Real cost of capital} = \frac{1 + \text{Nominal cost of capital}}{1 + \text{Inflation rate}} - 1$$

KEY TERMS

Incremental cash flow principle	Net working capital	Real interest rate
Sunk costs	Lease-versus-buy decision	Fisher effect
Fixed costs	Unequal economic lives	Nominal cash flow
Variable costs	Replacement decisions	Real cash flow
Side effect	Inflation	
Opportunity costs	Nominal interest rate	

REVIEW AND PRACTICE

7.1 You have been asked to forecast the future sales of Safeway (supermarkets) and Apple Computer. Which forecast, in your view, is likely to be more accurate? For which firm's expected cash flows will you apply a higher discount rate? Why?

7.2 A firm's annual revenue from sales is $100,000. The firm obtains cash for 30% of its sales and sells 70% on credit for one year. The firm purchases goods for $50,000 a year, paying 50% in cash and 50% on credit for one year. Suppose the firm makes sales and purchases in Years 1, 2, and 3. Calculate the firm's annual cash flows.

7.3 A project requires an initial investment outlay of $100,000, which is depreciated evenly over two years. The cash revenue before deducting depreciation and taxes is $80,000 in each of the two years. The tax rate is 35%.
a. What are the firm's annual after-tax accounting earnings?
b. What are the firm's after-tax annual cash flows?
c. Would you accept the project if the after-tax cost of capital is 10%?

7.4 Repeat your calculation for Problem 7.3, but assume the IRS allows the firm to use accelerated depreciation: 70% of its assets are depreciated in Year 1; 30%, in Year 2.
a. Does the accelerated depreciation affect the firm's after-tax accounting earnings during these two years?
b. Does the accelerated depreciation affect the firm's after-tax cash flow?

c. Does the accelerated depreciation affect the project's NPV? Compare and explain your results in Problems 7.3 and 7.4.

7.5 A firm provides credit for six months to promote sales. However, if customers pay cash, they get a 5% discount. Suppose the firm's annual revenue from sales is $100,000.
a. Calculate the firm's cash flow resulting from one year's sales if all sales are for credit.
b. Calculate the firm's annual cash flow if all sales are for cash.
c. If the annual discount rate is 10%, which alternative is better for the firm? Which alternative is riskier? Why?

7.6 Define and give an example of a *sunk cost*.

7.7 Define and give an example of an *opportunity cost*.

7.8 Define and give an example of a *side effect*.

7.9 A car manufacturer is considering producing a new model. The estimated costs and the net cash flows from this project (in $ million) are as follows:

	Year					
	0	1	2	3	...	10
Cash flows	−800	300	300	300	...	300

This project will create a side effect for the firm: an increase in the demand for spare parts. The net cash flow from the incremental demand for spare parts is expected to be zero in Years 1 and 2 (new cars do not need spare parts), $20 million annually in Years

3 through 6, and $30 million annually in Years 7 through 10. The cost of capital is 10%.

a. What is the project's NPV? Should the firm accept the project?

b. How would your answer change if in Year 2 the firm had to spend an additional $50 million on machinery to produce the spare parts?

7.10 An electronics firm is considering whether to invest in research and development of a new product. The firm estimates there is a 20% chance that the research and development will fail (zero cash inflows will occur) and an 80% chance that a new product will be developed that will generate the following cash flows (in $ million):

	Year 1	Year 2	Year 3
Cash flows	−200	600	600

The cost of the research and development in Year 0 would amount to $100 million, and the investment in machinery in Year 1 would be $200 million.

a. Calculate the project's average annual cash flow.

b. Is the project risky? If so, why?

c. Should the firm invest in the R&D if the cost of capital is 30%?

7.11 How would your answer to Problem 7.10 change if the project's annual cash flows in Years 2 and 3 were $180 million rather than $600 million?

7.12 The Chicago Bulls club owner is planning a basketball game in Europe. The game may be broadcast on local television. If the game is not shown on television, 20,000 fans are expected to show up at the gate, paying an average of $50 per ticket. All income is paid to the Bulls. If the game is broadcast on television, the Bulls will receive $250,000 from the TV station three days before the game, but only 14,900 fans are expected to attend the game. The team's expenses (including flying the club's private plane to Europe) are estimated to be $200,000, payable by the Bulls three days before the team receives revenue from the ticket sale. The annual cost of capital is 20%.

a. Should the club play the game in Europe? Calculate the NPV with and without the broadcast.

b. Should the club agree to have the game broadcast on television? Show the incremental cash flow resulting from the broadcast and calculate its NPV.

c. How would your answer change if the cost of capital was 1% daily? Explain.

7.13 In Problem 7.12 suppose a key player (guess who?) comes down with the flu and cannot play. As a result, the number of fans expected to show up will be 10,000 with no television broadcast and 8,000 with the television broadcast. The club considers hiring Shaquille O'Neal as a guest player, and with O'Neal the number of fans will be 12,000 with no television broadcast and 10,000 with the television broadcast. However, O'Neal wants $40,000 for the game (the $40,000 is to be paid three days before the game with the other expenses).

a. List all the club's options and calculate the cash flow of each one.

b. Calculate the NPV of each option and find the optimal decision. In solving the problem assume a 0.5% daily cost of capital.

7.14 Continuing with the Bulls' European game, now suppose a fire breaks out in the club's private plane while it is parked at the airport in Europe three days before the game. (Relax—no players were on board.) The plane was not insured, and the loss is $30 million. Because of this heavy loss the club's owner decides the game in Europe has a negative NPV; he decides to cancel the game and return to the United States.

a. Would you agree with his decision? Defend your answer. (*Hint:* Consider sunk costs.)

b. What if the fire had happened in Chicago before the team left for Europe? Compare the NPV of cases 7.14a and 7.14b. Use the 0.5% cost of capital. Assume that expenses increase to $250,000 if the team is flown to Europe on a commercial airline. (The stars fly first-class, of course.)

7.15 A firm is considering a new project. The required investment at date $t = 0$ is $5 million ($4 million in machinery and $1 million in buildings). The firm depreciates the buildings over 31.5 years by the straight-line method and depreciates the machinery over four years by the accelerated method. (See Tables 7A-2 and 7A-3 in Appendix 7A for the depreciation rates.) Assume the buildings are placed in service in January of Year 1.

The required investment in net working capital is $0.5 million. The project's economic life is three years. The firm expects the revenue from sales in each of these years to be $6 million, with 60% for cash and 40% on credit for one year. The firm's operating costs (before depreciation, interest, and taxes) are $2 million a year, all in cash. The machinery is fully depreciated in four years, but the value of the buildings at the end of the third year is estimated to be $0.95 million. The firm plans to sell the buildings at the end of the third year. It pays 36% tax on its income and 28% tax on any capital gain from selling the buildings. The firm's cost of capital is 10%.

a. Construct the firm's income statement for the next four years and calculate how much tax it pays in each of these years.

b. Construct the project's cash flows.

c. Calculate the project's NPV. Should the firm accept the project?

d. How would your decision change if the sales were not $6 million with certainty but $10 million with a probability of ½ and $2 million with a probability of ½? Give the direction of possible changes (a nonquantitative answer).

7.16 Suppose you can replace your car every year or every two years. Are these options mutually exclusive, or are they independent? Explain your answer.

7.17 "Given two projects with unequal economic lives, we must (by project repetitions) bring the two projects to the same economic life; otherwise the NPV calculations will be meaningless." Evaluate this statement.

7.18 In the early 1980s investors received 18% on their bank deposits, and the inflation rate was 12%. In the early 1990s the interest rate was 5%, and the inflation rate was 3%.

a. Assuming zero taxes, calculate the real interest rate in these two periods. Employ the precise formula and then the approximation method. Explain your results.

b. Repeat 7.18a assuming a 31% tax on interest.

7.19 Define *nominal* and *real interest rates.* Is the real interest rate always lower than the nominal interest rate?

7.20 The kind of car you want costs $20,000. You have this sum but decide you can wait for the car and deposit the money in the bank for two years at an annual interest of 10%. After two years you realize that the same brand car now will cost you $22,000. Suppose the prices of all goods increase at the same rate as the car.

a. What is the annual inflation rate?

b. What is the real annual interest rate?

c. What is the real after-tax interest rate if you pay a 39.6% marginal tax rate on the interest income? What is the approximate after-tax real interest rate?

7.21 The nominal interest rate is 15%, and the real after-tax interest rate is 8%. You pay 31% income tax on interest. What is the inflation rate?

7.22 Suppose Firm A is considering whether to buy or lease textile machines from Firm B. Does the revenue from the textile sales (which are uncertain) affect the lease-versus-buy decision? If not, can the revenue be ignored altogether?

7.23 A firm can buy a machine for $100,000 and depreciate it under the three-year asset classification. (See Appendix 7A, Tables 7A-1 and 7A-2.) The machine's economic life is three years. If it buys the machine, the firm will assume that the machine's salvage value is zero at the end of three years. If it leases the machine, the firm's annual lease payments will be $48,000. Assume that the tax rate is 34%.

a. What should the riskless interest rate be for the firm to be indifferent between buying or leasing the machine? Now assume that the actual riskless interest rate is 8%. Should the firm lease the machine or buy it?

b. Suppose if it buys the machine, the firm will have additional after-tax transaction costs amounting to $50,000. How might this change your answer? (Assume a riskless interest rate of 8%.)

7.24 Suppose Exxon is considering a one-year project with a certain cash flow of $100 million. Assume no taxes and no depreciation. The real riskless interest rate is 5%, and the initial investment is $96 million.

a. Should Exxon accept the project?

b. How would your answer change if inflation were 10% and if all prices (including the cash flows the project generates) increased at the same rate?

c. How would your answer change if, with inflation, the cash flows from Exxon projects increased by 20% but the general price index increased by only 10%?

7.25 "The nominal and real calculations in Problem 7.24 (which relate to differential inflation) produce the same results." Discuss this claim.

INTERNET QUESTIONS

7.26 Use the Interactive Tool Box in the following Web site to prepare a cash flow statement. You can either fill in hypothetical amounts or use some real data if it is available.

http://www.edgeonline.com

7.27 Visit *Fortune* magazine's Web site and find the top ten firms (ranked by revenue) in their *Fortune 500* list. Then go to the Thomson Investor's Network site and find these companies' cash flows for the past four years. Do you see a relationship between revenues and cash flows? Based on what you know, what *should be* the relationship between revenue and cash flow?

http://www.fortune.com
http://www.thomsoninvest.net

YOUR TURN: APPLYING THEORY TO PRACTICE
PREMIUM CUT FOR PROJECTS WITH HIGH RISK

Background

When a firm sells on credit, its customers may declare bankruptcy, and the firm may lose money. This potential loss cannot occur, of course, if all sales are for cash. When a firm exports its products on credit, it may not be able to collect the cash if the import country has no foreign currency to pay or if the government of the import country decides to freeze payments in foreign currency because of economic stress, war, or other circumstance. All these risks are called *country risk* or *political risk*. To reduce these risks and to encourage exporting, England has established the Export Credits Guarantee Department (ECGD). In exchange for payment of a risk premium, ECGD guarantees the payments to the exporter.[7] This issue is discussed in the following article.

PREMIUMS CUT FOR PROJECTS WITH HIGH RISK

The chancellor yesterday threw further support behind Britain's export drive by announcing improvements in the terms and cover provided by the Export Credits Guarantee Department.

Premiums charged by the ECGD for political risk will be reduced from December 12 by an average of 10 per cent. Rates for some markets that have recently re-established their creditworthiness will be cut even more deeply, and by more than 20 per cent for Argentina, Brazil, the Philippines, Egypt, and Vietnam.

As an example, the government said the premium for a typical project in India would fall from 5 per cent to 3.75 per cent.

---

7. Firms can buy insurance against political risk and currency inconvertibility. For example AIG Global Trade and Political Risk Insurance Company offers insurance for political risks of up to $120 million per project. *Business Week*, 17 January 1997, p. 17.

The government also plans to increase, to £3.5bn in 1997–98, ECGD cover for so-called amber zone markets, where risk is either unusually high or where the ECGD's exposure is most highly concentrated. Amber zone markets include China, India, South Africa, and Indonesia. . . .

"These measures will provide an added incentive for British exporters to play an even greater role in the most successful and rapidly growing economies in the world," Mr. Clarke said.

Mr. Michael Heseltine, trade and industry secretary, said the changes would boost the competitiveness of British exporters . . . .

Exporters have long argued that premiums for high-risk markets were substantially above those charged by export credit agencies in other European countries, though rates for lower risks are generally more competitive.

However, the government warned that ECGD political risk premiums for Mexico, Colombia, Zimbabwe, and Slovakia will rise from the end of March, when temporary rate-capping arrangements introduced for these markets in the last Budget are due to expire.

Source: Guy de Jonquières, "Premiums Cut for Projects with High Risk," *Financial Times,* 30 November 1994, p. 23.

Questions

1. Suppose a British firm is considering an investment of £7 million in a project where all products are exported to India. The firm's annual expenses (including tax payments) are £2 million, which are assumed to occur at the end of each of the next five years. The expenses are all in cash. The project's economic life is five years. Since the firm sells to Indian firms on one year's credit, the sales, which are assumed to take place at the end of each year, are paid at the end of the following year. The annual sales are estimated to be £5 million, and the assets have zero salvage value.

The project is exposed to a country risk, and, therefore, the British firm discounts the average cash flows by 25%. Should the firm accept the project?

2. If the exporter agrees to pay 3.75% of the export in premiums to ECGD, the country risk will be reduced to zero. In that case the appropriate discount rate of the project will be only 15%. Should the exporter insure itself? Assume (a) the tax rate is 42%; (b) the insurance premium is tax-deductible; and (c) the insurance premium is paid in cash for each year's sales at the end of the year in which the sales are made, not when the cash flow from the sales is received.

Appendix 7A   Depreciation Tables

Most assets produce revenue for several years. Accordingly, they are depreciated over their economic lives. Depreciation is the cost of the assets for a given period, as reported in the income statement for that period. Because depreciation is tax-deductible, the earlier the depreciation occurs, the better the firm fares, because it will receive the depreciation tax shelter cash flow sooner. The depreciation permitted for tax purposes is generally different from economic depreciation—that is, the actual reduction in the asset's market value over a given period.

Congress changes the allowed depreciation permitted for tax purposes from time to time. Currently (1997) the **Modified Accelerated Cost Recovery System (MACRS)** is in place. According to the MACRS, different types of assets are assigned to prespecified class life recovery periods, as shown in Tables 7A-1 and 7A-2.

Table 7A-1 provides the recovery periods of various types of assets, and Table 7A-2 provides the corresponding depreciation allowed. For example, automobiles fall in the five-year recovery period. In Table 7A-2, assets with five-year recovery periods are depreciated over six years. Why the one-year difference? The reason is an assumption called the *half-year convention*. This rule states that if an asset is placed in service in the middle of the first year, it will have only half of the depreciation allowed in the first year (relative to the depreciation allowed if the same asset is placed in service at the beginning of the year), and therefore the depreciation period is extended to the sixth year. The depreciation rate will thus vary over the recovery period depending on when during the year the asset is placed in service.

Firms can use either the accelerated depreciation method or the straight-line method (even depreciation across the years). The accelerated method is generally preferred because it decreases the tax payment in the first year. Some assets—residential rental property and commercial real estate (such as buildings)—can be depreciated only by the straight-line method. Table 7A-3 provides the annual depreciation on industrial property as a function of the month in which the property was placed in service.

The market value of a depreciable asset at any time is called its *residual value* or *salvage value*. This value is the amount the firm expects to realize if it sells the asset. If a depreciable asset is sold, the sale price minus the undepreciated book value is added to the firm's income and is taxed at the firm's marginal tax rate.

TABLE 7A-1 Classes and Asset Lives	Class	Type of asset
	3-year	Certain manufacturing tools
	5-year	Trucks, automobiles, computers
	7-year	Most industrial equipment
	10-year	Certain industrial equipment
	15-year	Roads, low income housing
	20-year	Certain long-lived property such as electric and gas utility property
	27.5-year	Residential real property
	31.5-year	Nonresidential real property

TABLE 7A-2   **The Depreciation Rate**
General Depreciation System
Applicable Depreciation Method: 200 or 150 Percent
Declining Balance Switching to Straight Line
Applicable Recovery Periods: 3, 5, 7, 10, 15, 20 Years
Applicable Convention: Half–Year

If the Recovery Year Is:	And the Recovery Period Is:					
	3–year	5–year	7–year	10–year	15–year	20–year
	The Depreciation Rate Is:					
1	33.33	20.00	14.29	10.00	5.00	3.750
2	44.45	32.00	24.49	18.00	9.50	7.219
3	14.81	19.20	17.49	14.40	8.55	6.677
4	7.41	11.52	12.49	11.52	7.70	6.177
5		11.25	8.93	9.22	6.93	5.713
6		5.76	8.92	7.37	6.23	5.285
7			8.93	6.55	5.90	4.888
8			4.46	6.55	5.90	4.522
9				6.56	5.91	4.462
10				6.55	5.90	4.461
11				3.28	5.91	4.462
12					5.90	4.461
13					5.91	4.462
14					5.90	4.461
15					5.91	4.462
16					2.95	4.461
17						4.462
18						4.461
19						4.462
20						4.461
21						2.231

Source: *U.S. Master-Tax Guide, 1994,* 77th ed. (Chicago: Commerce Clearing House, 1993), p. 326.

APPENDIX A KEY TERM

Modified accelerated cost recovery system (MACRS)

TABLE 7A-3   **The Straight–Line Depreciation Rate**
General Depreciation System
Applicable Depreciation Method: Straight Line
Applicable Recovery Period: 31.5 Years
Applicable Convention: Mid–Month

And the Month in the First Recovery Year the Property Is Placed in Service Is:

If the Recovery Year Is	1	2	3	4	5	6	7	8	9	10	11	12
	The Depreciation Rate Is:											
1	3.042	2.778	2.513	2.249	1.984	1.720	1.455	1.190	0.926	0.661	0.397	0.132
2	3.175	3.175	3.175	3.175	3.175	3.175	3.175	3.175	3.175	3.175	3.175	3.175
3	3.175	3.175	3.175	3.175	3.175	3.175	3.175	3.175	3.175	3.175	3.175	3.175
4	3.175	3.175	3.175	3.175	3.175	3.175	3.175	3.175	3.175	3.175	3.175	3.175
5	3.175	3.175	3.175	3.175	3.175	3.175	3.175	3.175	3.175	3.175	3.175	3.175
6	3.175	3.175	3.175	3.175	3.175	3.175	3.175	3.175	3.175	3.175	3.175	3.175
7	3.175	3.175	3.175	3.175	3.175	3.175	3.175	3.175	3.175	3.175	3.175	3.175
8	3.175	3.174	3.175	3.174	3.175	3.174	3.175	3.175	3.175	3.175	3.175	3.175
9	3.174	3.175	3.174	3.175	3.174	3.175	3.174	3.175	3.174	3.175	3.174	3.175
10	3.175	3.174	3.175	3.174	3.175	3.174	3.175	3.174	3.175	3.174	3.175	3.174
11	3.174	3.175	3.174	3.175	3.174	3.175	3.174	3.175	3.174	3.175	3.174	3.175
12	3.175	3.174	3.175	3.174	3.175	3.174	3.175	3.174	3.175	3.174	3.175	3.174
13	3.174	3.175	3.174	3.175	3.174	3.175	3.174	3.175	3.174	3.175	3.174	3.175
14	3.175	3.174	3.175	3.174	3.175	3.175	3.174	3.175	3.174	3.175	3.174	3.175
15	3.174	3.175	3.174	3.175	3.174	3.175	3.174	3.175	3.174	3.175	3.174	3.175
16	3.175	3.174	3.175	3.174	3.175	3.174	3.175	3.174	3.175	3.174	3.175	3.174
17	3.174	3.175	3.174	3.175	3.174	3.175	3.174	3.175	3.174	3.175	3.174	3.175
18	3.175	3.174	3.175	3.174	3.175	3.174	3.175	3.174	3.175	3.174	3.175	3.174
19	3.174	3.175	3.174	3.175	3.174	3.175	3.174	3.175	3.174	3.175	3.174	3.175
20	3.175	3.174	3.175	3.174	3.175	3.174	3.175	3.174	3.175	3.174	3.175	3.174
21	3.174	3.175	3.174	3.175	3.174	3.175	3.174	3.175	3.174	3.175	3.174	3.175
22	3.175	3.174	3.175	3.174	3.175	3.174	3.175	3.174	3.175	3.174	3.175	3.174
23	3.174	3.175	3.174	3.175	3.174	3.175	3.174	3.175	3.174	3.175	3.174	3.175
24	3.175	3.174	3.175	3.174	3.175	3.174	3.175	3.174	3.175	3.174	3.175	3.174
25	3.174	3.175	3.174	3.175	3.174	3.175	3.174	3.175	3.174	3.175	3.174	3.175
26	3.175	3.174	3.175	3.174	3.175	3.174	3.175	3.174	3.175	3.174	3.175	3.174
27	3.174	3.175	3.174	3.175	3.174	3.175	3.174	3.175	3.174	3.175	3.174	3.175
28	3.175	3.174	3.175	3.174	3.175	3.174	3.175	3.174	3.175	3.174	3.175	3.174
29	3.174	3.175	3.174	3.175	3.174	3.175	3.174	3.175	3.174	3.175	3.174	3.175
30	3.175	3.174	3.175	3.174	3.175	3.174	3.175	3.174	3.175	3.174	3.175	3.174
31	3.174	3.175	3.174	3.175	3.174	3.175	3.174	3.175	3.174	3.175	3.174	3.175
32	1.720	1.984	2.249	2.513	2.778	3.042	3.175	3.174	3.175	3.174	3.175	3.174
33	0.000	0.000	0.000	0.000	0.000	0.000	0.132	0.397	0.661	0.9926	1.190	1.455

Source: *U.S. Master-Tax Guide, 1994,* 77th ed. (Chicago: Commerce Clearing House, 1993), p. 329.

Appendix 7B   **Optimal Replacement Decision:**
The Uniform Annuity Series (UAS)

In the text example about machine replacement (see Section 7.9), we had one-, two-, and three-year replacement possibilities. The least common multiple for this example was six years $(1 \times 2 \times 3)$, and in principle we would have had to repeat the one-year replacement policy six times, the two-year replacement policy three times, and the three-year replacement policy two times. However, in our specific case, since the one-year replacement policy was better than the three-year replacement policy, there was no need to compare the two-year replacement policy to the three-year replacement policy.

What would we do if we were dealing with a longer economic life and had to decide whether to replace the machine every one, two, three, . . . or even 15 years? In such cases we would have to repeat each project numerous times to obtain the same economic life for all of the possible alternatives. Such calculations are cumbersome. However, mathematical formulas are available to bring the economic life of all options to infinite life—that is, to repeat all projects an infinite number of times. The formulas are somewhat complicated; fortunately, there is no need to learn them. Instead, we can use the **uniform annuity series (UAS)** method. In this method each project is replaced by a hypothetical series of constant annual cash flow, such that the PV of these cash flows is equal to the project's NPV. The UAS method circumvents the formulas as well as the complicated calculations.

As the UAS is defined as the annuity that yields the same NPV as the NPV of a given project, it is determined as follows:

$$\text{UAS} = \text{NPV} \Big/ \sum_{t=1}^{T} \frac{1}{(1 + k)^t}$$

In the machine replacement example, for a one-year replacement policy we calculate the UAS as the value that solves the following equation:

$$\text{NPV}_1 = \$14{,}545.45 = \frac{\text{UAS}_1}{(1 + k)}$$

Substituting $\text{NPV}_1 = \$14{,}545.45$ and $k = 0.1$, we get

$$\$14{,}545.45 = \frac{\text{UAS}_1}{(1.1)}$$

Therefore:

$$\text{UAS}_1 = \$14{,}545.45 \times 1.1 \cong \$16{,}000$$

The subscript 1 indicates that this is the UAS corresponding to the one-year replacement policy. The firm will be indifferent between receiving the project's actual cash flows or $16,000 at the end of Year 1 because both produce the same NPV.

For the two-year replacement policy, UAS_2 is defined as follows:

$$\text{NPV}_2 = \$20{,}082.64 = \frac{\text{UAS}_2}{(1 + k)} + \frac{\text{UAS}_2}{(1 + k)^2}$$

$$\$20{,}082.64 = \text{UAS}_2 \left[\frac{1}{1.1} + \frac{1}{(1.1)^2} \right]$$

Therefore,

$$\text{UAS}_2 \cong \$11{,}571.42$$

Finally, for the three-year replacement policy,

$$\text{NPV}_3 = \$26{,}543.95 = \frac{\text{UAS}_3}{1 + k} + \frac{\text{UAS}_3}{(1 + k)^2} + \frac{\text{UAS}_3}{(1 + k)^3}$$

$$\$26{,}543.95 = \text{UAS}_3 \left[\frac{1}{1.1} + \frac{1}{(1.1)^2} + \frac{1}{(1.1)^3} \right]$$

Therefore,

$$\text{UAS}_3 \cong \$10{,}673.72$$

The UAS cash flows of the three replacement policies can be written in the form of annuities as follows:

	Year 1	Year 2	Year 3
One-year replacement policy	$16,000.00		
Two-year replacement policy	$11,571.42	$11,571.42	
Three-year replacement policy	$10,673.72	$10,673.72	$10,673.72

By construction, the PV of each UAS is exactly equal to the project's NPV under the corresponding replacement policy. For example, the PV of the two-year policy is exactly as obtained before:

$$\frac{\$11{,}571.42}{1.1} + \frac{\$11{,}571.42}{(1.1)^2} = \$20{,}082.64 = \text{NPV}_2$$

In other words, the investor will be indifferent between obtaining this UAS or the original cash flow because both yield the same NPV.

However, because each replacement policy can be repeated indefinitely, these uniform annuity series can be continued for an infinite number of years. For example, if we replace the project at the end of Year 1, in Year 2 we again get the NPV resulting from the next one-year replacement, and the UAS is, once again, $16,000. With infinite replacement we get the following UAS for the three replacement policies:

	Year 1	Year 2	Year 3	. . .
One-year replacement policy	$16,000.00	$16,000.00	$16,000.00	. . .
Two-year replacement policy	$11,571.42	$11,571.42	$11,571.42	. . .
Three-year replacement policy	$10,673.73	$10,673.73	$10,673.73	. . .

Because these cash flows are perpetual, there is no need to find common duration for all projects. By construction, each policy yields the same cash flow every year. We select the policy that yields the highest annual cash flow, which, as before, is the one-year replacement policy. Recall that because we have a perpetuity, the option with the highest annual cash flow will also have the highest NPV.

Finally, note that the project does not have to be repeated an infinite number of times. It is enough to choose the replacement policy with the highest UAS. We know that this UAS can be repeated as many times as we wish. By definition, the option with the highest UAS also yields the highest NPV.

The following problem demonstrates how to apply the UAS method when deciding to replace an automobile.

PRACTICE BOX

Problem

Bob Levy bought a Honda Civic for $15,000. The maintenance costs and the price of used Hondas are as follows:

Year	Maintenance costs ($)	Price of used Hondas ($)
1	100	10,000
2	500	8,000
3	1,500	7,000
4	3,000	5,000

Assume Bob likes driving a Honda Civic but wonders what is the best replacement strategy and wants to keep driving it. Use the UAS to determine Bob's best car replacement policy. Assume a 10% cost of capital.

Solution

First, recall that we have no revenue here. The revenue is, so to speak, the pleasure derived from driving the car, saving time, not having to rely on public transportation, and other intangible benefits. Still, the principle remains the same: Bob should select the car replacement policy with the highest NPV—which in the case of no dollar revenue is the policy with the lowest NPV of costs.

The NPV of the first-year replacement is

$$\text{NPV}_1 = \frac{+\$10{,}000}{1.1} - \frac{\$100}{1.1} - \$15{,}000 = -\$6{,}000$$

UAS_1 is

$$-\$6{,}000 = \frac{\text{UAS}_1}{1.1}$$

Thus,

$$\text{UAS}_1 = -\$6{,}600$$

(continued)

The NPV of the second-year replacement is

$$NPV_2 = \frac{\$8,000}{(1.1)^2} - \frac{\$100}{1.1} - \frac{\$500}{(1.1)^2} - \$15,000 \cong -\$8,892.56$$

UAS$_2$ is

$$NPV_2 = UAS_2\left(\frac{1}{1.1} \times \frac{1}{(1.1)^2}\right) \cong UAS_2 \times 1.7355$$

$$-\$8,892.56 = UAS_2(1.7355)$$

Thus,

$$UAS_2 \cong -\$5,123.92$$

The NPV for the three-year replacement is

$$NPV_3 = \frac{\$7,000}{(1.1)^3} - \frac{\$100}{1.1} - \frac{\$500}{(1.1)^2} - \frac{\$1,500}{(1.1)^3} - \$15,000 = -\$11,371.90$$

UAS$_3$ is

$$-\$11,371.90 = UAS_3\left(\frac{1}{1.1} + \frac{1}{(1.1)^2} + \frac{1}{(1.1)^3}\right) \cong UAS_3 \times 2.4869$$

Thus,

$$UAS_3 = -\$4,572.72$$

Finally, the NPV for the four-year replacement is

$$NPV_4 = \frac{\$5,000}{(1.1)^4} - \frac{\$100}{1.1} - \frac{\$500}{(1.1)^2} - \frac{\$1,500}{(1.1)^3} - \frac{\$3,000}{(1.1)^4} - \$15,000$$

$$\cong -\$15,265.08$$

UAS$_4$ is

$$UAS_4 = NPV_4 / \left(\frac{1}{1.1} + \frac{1}{(1.1)^2} + \frac{1}{(1.1)^3} + \frac{1}{(1.1)^4}\right) \cong -\$15,265.08/0.31699$$

$$\cong -\$4,815.63$$

Bob Levy should choose the replacement policy with the lowest NPV of costs. He should replace the Honda every three years.

APPENDIX KEY TERM

Uniform annuity series (UAS)

APPENDIX B REVIEW AND PRACTICE

7B.1 Define *uniform annuity series (UAS)*. How do you use the UAS? Give an example.

7B.2 You own a great new car and definitely will not sell it after a year. After the second year, however, you may be forced to replace it because of maintenance costs. The following table shows data on the price of used cars (the same brand as yours) and their maintenance costs:

Year	Maintenance Costs ($)	Price of Used Cars ($)
1	0	15,000
2	500	13,000
3	1,000	12,000
4	2,500	11,000
5	4,000	11,000

How often should you plan to replace your car? Assume a new car costs $20,000 and the cost of capital is 10%. Also assume the maintenance costs are paid at the end of each year. (*Hint:* Use either the same economic life for all strategies or the UAS, whichever is easier for you.)

CHAPTER 8

THE GAIN FROM DIVERSIFICATION

LEARNING OBJECTIVES

After reading this chapter,
you should understand:

1. Why portfolio diversification is important for both financial managers and investors.

2. How to calculate and interpret an individual asset's mean rate of return and standard deviation.

3. How to calculate a portfolio's mean rate of return and standard deviation.

4. The role of correlation in determining the standard deviation of a portfolio's rate of return.

5. How to derive the mean standard deviation frontier and the mean standard deviation efficient set.

CORPORATE FINANCE IN THE NEWS

"TWO APPROACHES TO DIVERSIFICATION"

Fortune: You both are strong advocates of the kind of business you're in: GE, the diversified portfolio; Coke, the one-trick pony. Why?

Goizueta [the CEO of Coca-Cola]: Our return on capital is almost 33%, about three times our cost of capital.

Welch [the CEO of General Electric]: All our industries don't grow at the same rate. Our plastics business might be more like Roberto's business in terms of top-line growth. But in our other businesses, it allows us enormous staying power.

If one of the businesses is going to be weak, and it's a great business but it's in a difficult moment, I can support it. If I'm a single product guy in a weak business like that, in a business that cycles dramatically, I get whacked. So the staying power that our businesses have allows us to stay for the long haul.

Goizueta: To G.E., it is different businesses. In our case the hedge comes from different geographies. Different countries.

8.1 INTRODUCTION

Coca-Cola focuses on one product whereas General Electric (GE) has a diversified portfolio of products. Both firms are very successful and both hedge their risk: Coca-Cola by selling its products in different geographical areas and GE by diversifying in many different products so that stronger ones can support weaker ones. Both the portfolio of activities (projects) that a firm selects and the portfolio of securities that an individual investor selects have one thing in common: hedging or reducing risk by diversification. We have already noted that when cash flows are risky, the discount rate has to be adjusted; a higher discount rate should be used. Second, the larger the risk, the higher the appropriate discount rate. In this and the next two chapters, we discuss how risk is measured, how to reduce risk, and more about the relationship between risk and the discount rate.

We begin by discussing how the standard deviation of an asset's rate of return measures its uncertainty (risk) and why investors dislike uncertainty. Investors generally hold a combination of assets, called a **portfolio**, rather than a single asset. We show how the portfolio's standard deviation measures the risk and then show how each asset included in the portfolio affects the portfolio's risk. Furthermore, we show that the higher the contribution of a given asset to the portfolio's risk, the higher this asset's required expected return.

A CFO has two good reasons to be interested in risk and rates of return on financial assets.

First, investors can reduce their risk by investing in the stocks of a number of firms to create a well-diversified portfolio. However, because transaction costs force them to confine investment to a relatively small number of assets, many investors may be willing to pay a higher price for the stock of a firm that has well-diversified projects. Moreover, if many investors believe the firm has accepted a project that is overly risky in relation to its expected rate of return, they may decide to sell their stock. As a result, the stock price—and the market value of the firm's equity—will decrease. The risk-return characteristics of projects that the firm accepts affect both the risk-return characteristics of its stock and the market value of its equity. By understanding stockholders' attitudes toward risk, a CFO will be better positioned to select projects that maximize the firm's stock value. Diversification among projects increases the firm's value because it lowers the risk of bankruptcy and lowers the interest rate payable on its debt.

Second, a firm should undertake investments in physical assets only if, for a given level of risk, those assets provide a higher expected rate of return than investments in the financial market. A firm sometimes buys other firms' securities or repurchases some of its own stock because doing so is more profitable than investing in new physical assets. To make optimal investment decisions, a CFO has to know how to evaluate the risk and rates of return of these financial securities and how to compare them to the risk and return on other available investments in physical projects.

8.2 UNCERTAINTY OF RETURNS: THE SOURCE OF RISK

As we have seen, investors are concerned with expected return and risk. Scan any financial magazine or newspaper and you will find advertisements that attract investors to financial products based on some combination of risk and return. Ads that tout high rates of return are understandable: everyone likes high returns. However, as we have seen elsewhere, high returns usually have a price—exposure to increased risk.

8.2.1 Volatility

If the return on an investment can be predicted precisely (as with short-term government bonds or Treasury bills), we say that the return is certain or that the asset is riskless. If the rate of return cannot be predicted with certainty and if the investment's value fluctuates (as with stocks), we say that **volatility** exists. Most investors do not like uncertainty or volatility. If an asset's future value is unknown, we say that its value is uncertain, or that its value is volatile, or that it is a risky investment. Both practitioners and academicians use *uncertainty*, *volatility*, and *risk* interchangeably. In this chapter we define a quantitative measure of risk that is directly related to the volatility of the rate of return and show why firms and individual investors should consider both rate of return and risk when making their investment decisions.

8.2.2 Probability Distribution

The rate of return on financial assets such as stocks and bonds is calculated similarly to the internal rate of return (IRR) on projects. (See Chapter 6, Section 6.3.) To see this, suppose you buy a stock for $80, hold it for one year, and then sell it for $90. Assume no dividends are paid. The IRR of your investment will be the value of R that satisfies the equation:

$$\$80 = \frac{\$90}{1 + R}$$

$$R = \frac{\$90}{\$80} - 1 = 0.125 \text{ or } 12.5\%$$

If the stock also pays a $5 dividend at the end of the year, the IRR will be

$$\$80 = \frac{\$90 + \$5}{1 + R}$$

$$R = \frac{\$95}{\$80} - 1 = 0.1875 \text{ or } 18.75\%$$

If you plan to invest in a stock for, say, one year, you will know its current price, but you will not know its price at the end of the year. If you estimate a range of $65 to $120, you will be exposed to risk. That is, you may know the range of the rates of return, but you will not know the actual rate of return until one year from now. If you estimate a smaller range of $70 to $90, the investment is still risky. However, because the stock price volatility is smaller, the risk is smaller. The listing of all possible outcomes (such as a price range of $65–$120 or $70–$90 in the example above) together with the probability (chance) attached to each outcome is called the **probability distribution** (or, simply, the *distribution*) of the rates of return.[1]

Let's first examine the risk of a single-asset investment. (We will discuss the more complex case of portfolio investment later.) Suppose you invest in a one-year, zero-coupon[2] government bond, which is assumed to be riskless.[3] Its current market price is $90, and its face value (principal) is $100. What is the rate of return on this investment?

Simple calculation reveals that the bond's rate of return is:

$$R = \$100/\$90 - 1 \cong 0.111 \text{ or } 11.1\%$$

In this example, since the $100 will be obtained *with certainty* one year from now, 11.1% represents a *certain* or *riskless* rate of return.

Now suppose that instead of buying the bond, you purchase one share of IBM stock for $90. The value of the stock one year from now is uncertain because its price at that time will depend on the state of the economy. Consider the following scenarios:

State of the Economy	Probability	Stock Price	Rate of Return (No Dividends Are Paid)
Expansion	1/2	$ 130	$= (\$130/\$90) - 1 \cong 0.444$ or 44.4%
Recession	1/2	$ 80	$= (\$80/\$90) - 1 = -0.111$ or −11.1%

The listing of all possible outcomes (in this case, 44.4% and −11.1%), along with the associated probabilities, is the probability distribution of the investment in the IBM stock.

A distribution of rates of return is commonly characterized by its *expected rate of return* and its *standard deviation*. The expected rate of return measures the average rate of return, and the standard deviation measures the volatility (or the dispersion or uncertainty) of the rates of return around the expected rate of return. We shall see below that the higher the standard deviation, the riskier the investment.

8.2.3 The Expected Rate of Return

Suppose you play a game in Las Vegas and roll a die. You receive the dollar value of the number that shows up. The expected value of the prize you receive is defined as

1. For instance, when you roll a die, the chance (probability) of each of the numbers 1, 2, 3, 4, 5, or 6 showing up is 1/6. The set of possible results and their respective probabilities is the probability distribution of the outcomes. Before the die is rolled, the results will be uncertain. After the die is rolled, the result is known. The same principle applies when you invest in a financial asset. On the investment date there will be a range of possible results, but only one rate of return will be realized when the asset is sold. When we say an investment in a stock is risky, we mean that the future rate of return is not known with certainty.

2. The holder of a zero-coupon bond receives the bond's face value at maturity but no interim payments.

3. For simplicity we assume no inflation. Otherwise, the bond would be risky in real terms.

$$\text{Expected prize} = (1/6 \times \$1) + (1/6 \times \$2) + (1/6 \times \$3) + (1/6 \times \$4)$$
$$+ (1/6 \times \$5) + (1/6 \times \$6) = \$3.50$$

where 1/6 is the probability of each outcome. You can calculate the expected rate of return on a financial asset in the same way.

The expected rate of return, which we denote by $\bar{R}$ (read as "R bar"), is defined as follows:

$$\bar{R} = \sum_{i=1}^{m} P_i R_i \qquad (8.1)$$

where R_i is the ith possible outcome (rate of return), P_i is the probability corresponding to R_i, and m is the number of possible outcomes (or possible values of R). Note that the sum of the probabilities $\sum_{i=1}^{m} P_i$ equal 1. In words, the definition of expected rate of return reads as:

Expected rate of return = Sum of {Probability multiplied by the corresponding rate of return}

The expected rate of return is the rate of return that should be expected *on average*. To illustrate the meaning of this average, let's consider once again a game of dice. If you play this game many times, your prize on average will be about $3.50. If you play the game a great many times your average prize will be exactly $3.50. Note that the *realized* rate of return in each game is usually different from the *expected* rate of return.

In the previous IBM stock example, the expected rate of return is

$$(\tfrac{1}{2} \times 44.4\%) + (\tfrac{1}{2} \times -11.1\%) = 16.65\%$$

and the realized return is either 44.4% or −11.1%. The following problem further demonstrates calculation of the expected rate of return.

PRACTICE BOX

Problem

Calculate the expected rates of return on Stocks A and B, assuming equal probability for each of the following rates of return:

Probability	Stock A	Stock B
¼	7%	8%
¼	−5%	4%
¼	12%	9%
¼	6%	7%

(continued)

Solution	From equation (8.1) we have Stock A's expected return

$$\bar{R} = \tfrac{1}{4}(7\%) + \tfrac{1}{4}(-5\%) + \tfrac{1}{4}(12\%) + \tfrac{1}{4}(6\%) = 5\%$$

and Stock B's expected return

$$\bar{R} = \tfrac{1}{4}(8\%) + \tfrac{1}{4}(4\%) + \tfrac{1}{4}(9\%) + \tfrac{1}{4}(7\%) = 7\%$$

Now that we know how to calculate the expected rate of return, let's see how to use that information to make financial decisions. Review the rates of return and the corresponding probabilities of three alternative assets provided in Table 8-1. Is Asset C, with the highest expected rate of return, the best investment? No, not necessarily, because the realized rate of return may fall short of the expected value and may even reflect a loss for the investor. One cannot rely solely on the expected rate of return in selecting among the various investments because the risk of losing money is not identical across the three assets.

Investors may be reluctant to invest in Asset C. To demonstrate this, consider the case of Bill, a business student. Bill has an initial wealth of $10,000. He will need a minimum of $9,000 for tuition and living expenses next year. Because he will not need this sum until next year, he plans to invest the money for one year in either Asset A, B, or C. Bill could earn a certain 6% rate of return by investing the money in Asset A, but he would prefer to earn more than 6%. If Bill chooses Asset B, he may well earn more than the rate of return on Asset A. Even if the lowest rate of return occurred, Bill would still have the $9,000 minimum amount at the end of the year:

$$\$10,000 \times [1 + (-0.1)] = \$10,000 \times 0.9 = \$9,000$$

TABLE 8-1   **Possible Rates of Return (in percent) on Three Assets**

Asset A		Asset B		Asset C	
Rate of Return (%)	Probability	Rate of Return (%)	Probability	Rate of Return (%)	Probability
6	1	−10	¼	−20	¼
		0	¼	10	½
		20	½	40	¼
		Expected Rate of Return			
6%		7.5%		10%	

If Bill chooses Asset C, he could earn 40%. However, if the worst outcome occurred, he would end up with

$$\$10,000 \times [1 + (-0.2)] = \$10,000 \times (0.8) = \$8,000$$

Since Bill would *not* have the $9,000 minimum required for the coming school year, he decides to avoid Asset C (with the highest expected profit) because it would put his career at risk.

Now let's consider a business decision that is similar to Bill's but on a larger scale: A loss may lead to declaring bankruptcy rather than dropping out of school. Suppose Michael Gordon, the owner of a Nike store in Chicago, has a $9 million bank loan to repay one year from now. Michael currently has $10 million to invest for one year and is considering the three assets presented in Table 8-1. If the return on his investment falls short of $9 million, Michael will go bankrupt. Therefore, he will probably not select Asset C, even though it has the highest expected return, because realizing a −20% rate of return would force him to declare bankruptcy. As for the other assets, even if the lowest outcomes occurred, the future income would be sufficient to cover the $9 million loan repayment.

In a nutshell, Asset C has the advantage of the highest possible rate of return and the highest expected rate of return, but it also has the disadvantage of the lowest possible rate of return of −20%. Like Bill and Michael, many investors will prefer Asset B (or even Asset A) over Asset C. These two examples show that you cannot rely solely on the expected rate of return in selecting an investment. You must also consider the risk of losing money. Empirical evidence shows that, in general, investments (projects or portfolios of securities) with relatively large potential losses have relatively large expected returns. The reason is explained in the next section.

8.3 RISK AVERSION AND THE RISK PREMIUM

Investors should consider both the expected rate of return and risk. In this section we discuss the risk involved in an investment.

8.3.1 Risk Aversion

Table 8-2 shows the distribution of the rates of return for two assets whose expected returns are identical, $120, thereby allowing us to focus on risk. The return on Asset A is certain ($120 with a probability of 1), whereas the return on Asset B is uncertain ($110 with a probability of ½ and $130 with a probability of ½). Which investment would you prefer?

Empirical evidence and data taken from the stock market suggest that most investors would prefer Asset A. These investors, called **risk averters**—and most investors are risk averters—dislike volatility. If the expected returns on two investments are identical, risk averters will always prefer the one with the lower volatility.

TABLE 8-2		Asset A		Asset B	
Distribution of Rate of Return on Two Assets (Current Price = $100)		**Return**	**Probability**	**Return**	**Probability**
		$120	1	$110	½
				$130	½
	Expected return[a]	$120		$120	
	Variance	0		100[b]	
	Standard deviation	$0		10%[c]	

[a]In percentage terms, the expected rate of return is $120/$100 − 1 = 20%

[b]Variance = (½) × ($110 − $120)^2 + (½) × ($130 − $120)^2 = 100. See Equation (8.3) in Section 8.4.

[c]Standard deviation = (100)$^{1/2}$ = 10. In percentage terms, it is $10/$100 = 10%

To convince risk averters to buy Asset B rather than Asset A, we would have to entice them with a higher expected rate of return.

8.3.2 Asset Price and the Risk Premium

We now show how preference for certain income (or aversion to risk) affects an asset's current price and expected rate of return. Review again the example given in Table 8-2, where Assets A and B have the same expected return of $120, but now assume that *initially* both Assets A and B have a price of $100. Asset A yields $120 with certainty at the end of the year, and Asset B yields either $110 or $130 with equal probability. The expected rate of return on both assets is 20%. If *all* investors in the market were risk averters, they would all buy riskless Asset A. No one would buy risky Asset B.

Is such a scenario possible? No, it isn't. Someone must be buying Asset B; otherwise, it would simply disappear. Market dynamics work to change prices and, at a sufficiently low price, most assets eventually find purchasers. For simplicity assume that Asset A's price remains unchanged and that Asset B's price falls to, say, $95 because there is no demand for it at $100. Since the future cash flows of either $110 and $130 are unchanged, the distribution of Asset B's rate of return at the lower price will be

$$R = (\$110/\$95) - 1 \cong 0.158 \text{ or } 15.8\%, \text{ with probability } ½$$

and

$$R = (\$130/\$95) - 1 \cong 0.368 \text{ or } 36.8\%, \text{ with probability } ½$$

Therefore, Asset B's expected rate of return will be

$$R_B = (½ \times 15.8\%) + (½ \times 36.8\%) = 26.3\%$$

Asset A's expected rate of return will remain unchanged at 20%.

If the market is in equilibrium (in other words, there is neither excess demand nor excess supply at these prices and investors have bought all available assets), then the difference between the expected rates of return on these two assets will be 6.3%. This difference represents the **risk premium** that investors required as compensation for the risk involved in Asset B.

The more risk averse the investors, the lower Asset B's equilibrium price, the larger the expected rate of return, and the larger the risk premium. If investors are even more risk averse and if Asset B's equilibrium price is $90, the two possible rates of return will be 22.2% [($110/$90) − 1 = 22.2%] and 44.4% [($130/$90) − 1 ≅ 44.4%], respectively. The expected rate of return will be 33.3% [R = 0.5(22.2%) + 0.5(44.4%) = 33.3%], and the risk premium will be 13.3%. The expected rate of return on risky assets can be expressed as

> Expected rate of return on risky asset = Rate of return on riskless asset   (8.2)
>   + Risk premium

The following problem demonstrates calculation of the expected rate of return and the risk premium of a risky asset.

PRACTICE BOX

Problem

The market is in equilibrium. Investment C yields a 10% rate of return with certainty. Investment D yields −10% with a probability of ½ and 40% with a probability of ½. Calculate the risk premium.

Solution

From Equation 8.2 we can determine that the risk premium equals the expected rate of return on the risky asset minus the rate of return on the riskless asset. The expected rate of return on the risky Asset D is:

$$\text{Expected rate of return} = (\tfrac{1}{2} \times -10\%) + (\tfrac{1}{2} \times 40\%) = 15\%$$

$$\text{Risk premium} = 15\% - 10\% = 5\%$$

8.4 STANDARD DEVIATION AS A MEASURE OF RISK

Just as there are techniques that measure return, there are also techniques that measure risk. The most commonly used index with which to measure risk is the *standard deviation*. To explain this index, we first need to define the *variance* of the rates of return. The variance of possible outcomes, denoted by σ^2, is calculated as

$$\sigma^2 = \sum_{i=1}^{m} P_i(R_i - \bar{R})^2 \tag{8.3}$$

Here R_i is the ith possible return on the asset, P_i is the probability of outcome i, m is the number of possible outcomes, and $\overline{R}$ is the expected rate of return. In words, variance is expressed as:

> **Variance** = Sum {Probability multiplied by the squared deviation of the rate of return from the expected rate of return}

The **standard deviation,** denoted by σ, is simply the square root of σ^2.

The standard deviation, like the variance, measures the average deviation of the various outcomes from the expected rate of return: The larger the deviations, the larger the variance and the standard deviation. To demonstrate the calculation of the variance and standard deviation, consider an investment that yields a rate of return of 0% with a probability of ½ or a rate of return of 30% with a probability of ½. The expected rate of return is

$$\overline{R} = (\tfrac{1}{2} \times 0\%) + (\tfrac{1}{2} \times 30\%) = 15\%$$

The variance is

$$\sigma^2 = P_1 \times (R_1 - \overline{R})^2 + P_2 \times (R_2 - \overline{R})^2$$
$$= \tfrac{1}{2}\,(0\% - 15\%)^2 + \tfrac{1}{2}\,(30\% - 15\%)^2 = (225\%)^2$$

Note that we square the deviations. If the rates of return are expressed in percentages, the variance will be expressed in terms of "percent squared"; if the returns are in dollar figures, the variance will be expressed in terms of "dollars squared." Because such units are hard to interpret, the standard deviation is generally used. The standard deviation is expressed in percents, dollars, and so on. For instance, in the preceding example, since the variance was 225 percent squared, the standard deviation is

$$\sigma = \sqrt{225\%^2} = 15\%$$

Note, that if one investment has a higher variance than the other, the former will also have a higher standard deviation. Therefore both variance and standard deviation may be used interchangeably as measures of risk. The standard deviation measures the volatility of the rates of return around the expected rate of return: the greater the volatility, the larger the standard deviation. Table 8-3 illustrates the relationship between volatility of rates of return and the standard deviation for three projects, X, Y, and Z. The initial investment in each asset is $100. The dispersion of the return, as well as the standard deviation, is greatest for Asset Z. The probability distribution of the returns of these three assets is shown in Figure 8-1.

Suppose that X, Y, and Z are the only three assets available in the market and an investor chooses to invest in only one of them. (Portfolio considerations will be discussed in the next section.) Let's compare the dollar returns on each of these three assets. Asset Y can be considered identical to Asset X plus $10 and -$10 with an equal probability. Asset Z is identical to Asset X plus $20 and -$20 with equal probability. Risk averters do not like such changes (of ± $10) because the satisfaction they might derive from the gain if they realize the higher return (an extra $10 on

TABLE 8-3   **Variance of the Rate of Return on Three Assets (per $100 Investment)**

	Asset X		Asset Y		Asset Z	
	Return	**Probability**	**Return**	**Probability**	**Return**	**Probability**
	$130	1	$120	½	$110	½
			$140	½	$150	½
Expected return ($)	130		130[a]		130[b]	
Variance, σ^2	0		100[c]		400[d]	
Standard deviation, σ($)	0		10		20	

[a]$(½) \times 120 + (½) \times 140 = 130$

[b]$(½) \times 110 + (½) \times 150 = 130$

[c]$(½) \times (120 - 130)^2 + (½) \times (140 - 130)^2 = 100$

[d]$(½) \times (110 - 130)^2 + (½) \times (150 - 130)^2 = 400$

FIGURE 8-1
The Set of Outcomes of Investment in Three Assets Accompanied by the Probabilities of These Outcomes

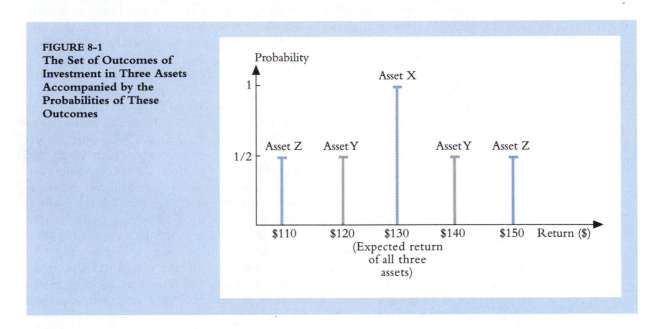

Asset Y or $20 on Asset Z) is not tempting enough to offset the loss if they realize the lower income ($10 less on Asset Y or $20 less on Asset Z). Risk averters prefer to avoid the "honey in the beehive" not because they dislike honey, but because they know there is a chance of getting stung (lower return). Risk averters prefer Asset X over Asset Y and Asset Y over Asset Z. For a given expected return, *the higher the standard deviation, the less attractive the asset.*

Table 8–3 compares three assets with the *same expected return.* We see that as the standard deviation increases, the volatility of the probability distribution around the expected value also increases. Therefore, the standard deviation measures the risk involved with the investment. Since risk averters will avoid Assets Y and Z, the market prices of these two assets will fall until some investors would buy them. When this occurs, the three assets will no longer have identical expected rates of return. For example, if Asset X's price remains at $100, if Asset Y's price falls to, say, $95, and if Asset Z's price falls to, say, $90, their expected rates of return will be

$$\text{Asset X: } \frac{\$130}{\$100} - 1 = 0.3 \text{ or } 30.00\%$$

$$\text{Asset Y: } \frac{\$130}{\$95} - 1 = 0.3684 \text{ or } 36.84\%$$

$$\text{Asset Z: } \frac{\$130}{\$90} - 1 = 0.4444 \text{ or } 44.44\%$$

Risk aversion affects asset prices that, in turn, affect the expected rates of return. This example shows that *the higher the volatility, the higher the standard deviation.* Because volatility is identified with risk, we can assert that *the higher the standard deviation (risk), the higher the risk premium.*

Although the risk–return relationship and the risk premium are theoretical concepts, they have many practical implications. In Figure 2–3, which presents historical rates of return, we see that the larger the standard deviation of the rate of return, the higher the *historical* mean rate of return. For example, since the annual mean rate of return for the period 1926–1996 is 12.7% on stocks and 3.8% on T-bills, the historical risk premium is 8.9% {12.7% − 3.8% = 8.9%}. Stocks are riskier than T-bills, and the 8.9% difference between the mean rates of return reflects the compensation that investors require by investors for their exposure to risk. If some change in the economy caused stocks to become even riskier than indicated in Figure 2–3, what would determine the risk premium? The market mechanism would work exactly as explained before: Investors would sell stocks, stock prices would decrease, the expected rates of return would increase, and as a result, the risk premium would increase.

So far we have seen that the standard deviation of rates of return helps determine the required risk premium when each asset is considered in isolation. However, for diversified portfolios that consist of a number of assets, including risky ones, additional factors must be considered.

8.5 DIVERSIFICATION

Diversification is summed up in the adage, "Don't put all your eggs in one basket." Such advice makes sense because if the basket is dropped or tipped, all the eggs could be broken. Similar to not keeping all eggs in one basket, investors prefer not to place all their holdings in any one investment. If the investment fails, their holdings are gone. Investors hedge their risk with **diversification,** which spreads their risk by investing in a number of assets with different risk-return characteristics. Diversification applies to a firm's choices in project selection, as well as to the choices of financial assets that a firm or an individual buys. Connecting Theory to Practice 8.1 addresses Americans' diversification of wealth through investments in real estate (homes), stocks, bonds, and mutual funds.[4]

CONNECTING THEORY TO PRACTICE 8.1

DO AMERICAN HOUSEHOLDS HAVE TOO MANY EGGS IN THE MARKET BASKET?

Watch Out! Your biggest investment. For years, that meant just one thing to American families: their homes. Home was not only where the heart was but also where most wealth resided. But no more.

For the first time in nearly a quarter century, Americans have more of their wealth tied up in stocks, bonds, and mutual funds than in residential real estate, according to data compiled by the Federal Reserve Board.

One nagging concern: What happens to the average American family when the long-running bull market falls flat? Accumulating wealth in stocks, bonds and mutual funds is a wonderful development, but the flip side is that households now are assuming for themselves risks that were previously borne by banks, insurance companies, and pension funds.

The stampede into mutual funds has been triggered by the propagation of a convincing factoid, namely, that stocks have returned 10% a year for the past seven decades. This year's 20% gain in popular benchmarks such as the Dow Jones Industrial Average has done nothing to shake families' growing confidence in the stock market.

Yet, not so many years ago, the public also thought double-digit annual returns were the norm for what were then their two biggest investments: their homes and so-called "cash equivalents," meaning certificates of deposit and money-market mutual funds.

Source: Randall W. Forsyth and Sandra Ward, "Do American Households Have Too Many Eggs in the Market Basket?" *Barron's* 75, no. 36 (September 1995): 25. Reprinted by permission of *Barron's,* © 1995 Dow Jones & Company, Inc. All Rights Reserved Worldwide.

MAKING THE CONNECTION

Even if returns are in the range of 10–20% a year, investors with most of their money in stocks, bonds, and mutual funds may be in trouble if the "bull

---

4. *Mutual funds* are investment companies that sell shares of the company to the public and use the proceeds to invest in a professionally-managed, diversified portfolio of financial assets. One of the key advantages of mutual funds is pooled diversification. Small investors can generally obtain more diversification by being part of a fund than they could if they invested their money directly in stocks or bonds. In 1995 there were more than 6,000 publicly traded mutual funds with more than $2 trillion in assets under management.

market falls flat." Investing a large fraction of wealth in a single security is similar to putting too many eggs in one basket. That wealth is not diversified among enough assets.

To demonstrate the benefit of diversification, let us simplify and assume only two assets are available: IBM stock and General Motors (GM) stock. An investor considers whether to buy only IBM stock, only GM stock, or a portfolio composed of both stocks. Can the investor reduce the risk by owning both stocks?

Using actual rates of return from the two stocks' prices, Figure 8–2 shows the results of the investor's three alternatives. The rates of return on the portfolio composed of both stocks are much more stable than the rate of return on either stock separately. Indeed, the portfolio's standard deviation is 12.59%, while IBM's and GM's standard deviations are 22.28% and 17.39%, respectively.[5] In diversifying between the two stocks, the investor reduces the uncertainty. Generally speaking, the larger the number of assets over which wealth is diversified, the lower the risk exposure.

FIGURE 8-2   **Annual Rates of Return on IBM and GM Stocks and on a Portfolio Composed of 50% of Each Asset**

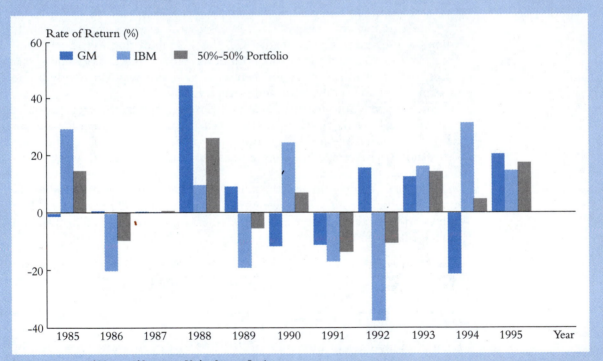

Source: CRISP tapes and Money and Investment Update Internet Service.

---

5. This effect occurs because bad years for GM are not necessarily bad years for IBM and vice versa. The portfolio's volatility is relatively small because, on average, a low return in bad years for one firm may be offset by higher returns for the other. This point is discussed in more detail in the following section.

8.6 RISK IN A PORTFOLIO CONTEXT

We have seen that an asset's standard deviation measures its risk. Does the standard deviation of the asset's returns always indicate the risk on that asset? For a portfolio consisting of *only* that asset, the answer is yes. However, if an investor holds more than one risky asset in an investment portfolio, the answer is no. In such case the individual asset's risk will depend on the standard deviation of its own rate of return *and* on the *correlation* of its rate of return with the rates of return on other assets held in the portfolio.

At this stage in the chapter we regard **correlation** as a measure of the degree to which the rate of return on one asset moves in relation to the rate of return on another asset. If the rates of return on two assets tend to increase and decrease together, we say they are *positively correlated*. If the return on one asset tends to increase when the other one decreases, we say that they are *negatively correlated*.

To understand the relationship between an asset's required risk premium and the correlation of its rate of return with those of other assets held in a portfolio, suppose an investor holds a portfolio composed of two stocks, A and B. The two stocks may be positively correlated. That is, Asset A's rate of return is relatively high when Asset B's rate of return is relatively high and vice versa. Or the stocks may be negatively correlated. That is, Asset A's rate of return is relatively high when Asset B's rate of return is relatively low and vice versa. The correlation between two stocks is denoted by ρ (read as "rho"): $\rho = 1$ when there is a perfect positive correlation; $\rho = -1$ when there is a perfect negative correlation; and $\rho = 0$ if the two assets are uncorrelated or independent (if there is no relationship between the assets' returns). Thus, ρ can be in the range $-1 \leq \rho \leq +1$; and the larger ρ is (in absolute value), the stronger the degree of association between the two assets.

Table 8-4 shows the rates of return on Assets A and B, and Table 8-5 shows the rates of return on a portfolio with 50% of total investment in each of these two

TABLE 8-4	Rates of Return on Stock A and Stock B Held Separately			
	Return on Stock A		**Return on Stock B**	
	Rate of Return (R_A)	**Probability**	**Rate of return (R_B)**	**Probability**
	40%	½	40%	½
	−20%	½	−20%	½
Expected rate of return (%)[a]	10		10	
Variance[b] σ^2	900		900	
Standard deviation σ (%)	30		30	

[a]Mean = (½ × 40%) + (½ × −20%) = 10%

[b]Variance = (½) × (40% − 10%)² + (½) × (−20% − 10%)² = 900

assets and under the three different assumptions about the correlation between the probability distributions of their returns. If you invest proportion w_A in Asset A and w_B in Asset B (where $w_A + w_B = 1$), the portfolio's rate of return is $w_A R_A + w_B R_B$, where R_A and R_B are the returns on Assets A and B, respectively. The left-hand column of Table 8.5 assumes *perfect positive correlation* between the assets' returns. Thus, if a 40% rate of return is realized on Stock A, then a 40% rate of return will also be realized on Stock B. The portfolio rate of return will also be 40% ($\frac{1}{2} \times 40\% + \frac{1}{2} \times 40\%$, where $w_A = \frac{1}{2}$ and $w_B = \frac{1}{2}$) with probability of $\frac{1}{2}$. Similarly, if the lower outcome occurs for Stock A (−20%), then the lower outcome will also be realized on Stock B. In that case the portfolio's rate of return is −20% with probability of $\frac{1}{2}$.

The right-hand column of Table 8-5 represents a distribution in which there is *perfect negative correlation* between the two assets' returns. Accordingly, if a 40% rate of return occurs on Stock A, then a −20% rate of return will occur on Stock B, and the portfolio will earn a total of 10% [$\frac{1}{2} \times (40\%) + \frac{1}{2} \times (-20\%)$]. Similarly, if a −20% rate of return is realized on Stock A, then a 40% rate of return will be earned on Stock B. Again, the portfolio will have a 10% rate of return. No matter what the outcome, the total return obtained on the two assets will be 10%—that is, you will receive 10% on your investment with a probability of 1 (i.e., with certainty).

Finally, the middle column of Table 8-5 reports the intermediate case of *zero correlation* (there is no association, either positive or negative, between the two assets' returns). Because the probability of each possible rate of return is $\frac{1}{2}$, the probability of receiving 40% on Stock A *and* 40% on Stock B is given by the product of their probabilities (i.e., $\frac{1}{2} \times \frac{1}{2}$). Thus, you get 40% on Stock A with probability $\frac{1}{2}$ and 40% on Stock B with probability $\frac{1}{2}$, or 40% on your portfolio with a probability of

TABLE 8-5   **Rates of Return on a Portfolio Composed of Stock A and Stock B (Portfolio's Return = $\frac{1}{2}R_A + \frac{1}{2}R_B$)**

	Perfect Positive Correlation ($\rho = 1$)		Zero Correlation ($\rho = 0$)		Perfect Negative Correlation ($\rho = -1$)	
	Rate of Return	Probability	Rate of Return	Probability	Rate of Return	Probability
	40%	$\frac{1}{2}$	40%	$\frac{1}{4}$	10%	1
	−20%	$\frac{1}{2}$	10%	$\frac{1}{2}$		
			−20%	$\frac{1}{4}$		
Expected rate of return (%)	10		10		10	
Variance σ^2	900[a]		450[b]		0	
Standard deviation σ (%)	30		21.21		0	

[a]Variance = $(\frac{1}{2}) \times (40\% - 10\%)^2 + (\frac{1}{2}) \times (-20\% - 10\%)^2 = 900$

[b]Variance = $(\frac{1}{4}) \times (40\% - 10\%)^2 + (\frac{1}{2}) \times (10\% - 10\%)^2 + (\frac{1}{4}) \times (-20\% - 10\%)^2 = 450$

¼ [(½ × ½) = ¼]. Similarly, you get −20% with probability of ¼ (both stocks decrease). Note, however, that 10% is obtained with a probability of ½ because it encompasses two events: 40% on Stock A and −20% on Stock B, and −20% on Stock A and 40% on Stock B. Each of these two events has a probability of ¼, so you will earn 10% with a probability of ½.[6]

Table 8-5 indicates that the expected rate of return on each portfolio is 10% regardless of the degree of correlation between the two assets' returns. However, the variance of the portfolio's return will vary with the degree of correlation between the two stocks' returns. In the case of perfect negative correlation between the rates of return, a portfolio consisting of these two assets with $w_A = w_B = $ ½ will guarantee a certain income. No risk premium will be required.

The important conclusion from this example relates to the perfect negative correlation case; although each asset is risky when held *separately* (with a standard deviation of 30%), they are riskless when held together in a portfolio. The perfect negative correlation between the two assets' returns completely eliminates uncertainty. Thus, an individual asset's standard deviation represents risk *only when the asset is held in isolation*. This principle also holds (albeit to a lesser degree) even if the correlation is not −1, as long as it is not +1. When the asset is held in a portfolio with other assets, the correlation between asset rates of returns has to be incorporated into the risk measure.[7]

We turn now to the relationship between a portfolio's expected rate of return and its standard deviation. We see how the portfolio's expected rate of return and its standard deviation are calculated and the importance of correlation in calculating a portfolio's standard deviation.

8.7 EXPECTED RATE OF RETURN AND STANDARD DEVIATION ON A PORTFOLIO OF ASSETS

Since most investors hold a portfolio rather than a single asset, we need to calculate the expected value and the standard deviation of the portfolio's rates of return.

In comparing various investment strategies, we find it convenient to denote the total amount of investment by 100% and then to analyze the various combinations produced by diversifying this 100% among assets. In their portfolios, investors will diversify their wealth in n assets where w_1 is the proportion (or weight) allocated to Asset 1, w_2 is the weight allocated to Asset 2, and so on. In general, w_i is the weight allocated to Asset i. The weights represent the proportions of wealth invested in each available asset, and the sum of the weights must equal 1 (or in percentage terms, 100%).

---

6. If the rate of return on one asset is determined independently of that on the other asset, we say that the two assets are independent. In such case the probability of one rate of return occurring in Asset A and another one occurring in Asset B is simply the product of these two probabilities, or ½ × ½ = ¼. Since we may have −20% on A and 40% on B, or the other way around, the total probability is ¼ + ¼ = ½.

7. To emphasize this point further, suppose that you have two assets, A and B, with standard deviations $\sigma_A = 20\%$ and $\sigma_B = 10\%$, respectively. Is Asset A riskier than Asset B? If the two assets are held separately, then Asset A is riskier than Asset B. However, if the two assets are held in a portfolio with other assets, the answer will depend on the correlation between the rates of return on Assets A and B and on those of the other assets held in the portfolio. The more negative these correlations, the less risky the portfolio.

8.7.1 The Portfolio's Expected Rate of Return

A portfolio's expected rate of return, denoted by $\bar{R}_p$, is calculated by summing all the expected rates of returns on the assets comprising the portfolio, multiplied by their corresponding weights. This gives us the *weighted average* of the expected rates of return for all the assets held in the portfolio.

The portfolio's expected rate of return is expressed as

$$\bar{R}_p = \sum_{i=1}^{n} w_i \bar{R}_i$$

where w_i is the proportion of the portfolio invested in Asset i, R_i is the mean rate of return on Asset i, and n is the number of assets in the portfolio. In words, a portfolio's expected rate of return reads:

$$\bar{R}_p = \text{Sum of \{the weight of the asset in the portfolio multiplied} \quad (8.4)$$
$$\text{by its expected rate of return\}}$$

For example, if the portfolio has only two assets, if the expected rates of return are 10% on the first asset and 20% on the second, and if $w_1 = \frac{1}{2}$ and $w_2 = \frac{1}{2}$, we have

$$\bar{R}_p = (w_1 \times \bar{R}_1) + (w_2 \times \bar{R}_2) = (\tfrac{1}{2} \times 10\%) + (\tfrac{1}{2} \times 20\%) = 15\%$$

If we change the investment proportions, the portfolio's expected rate of return will change, too. For example, if $w_1 = \frac{1}{4}$ and $w_2 = \frac{3}{4}$, we have

$$\bar{R}_p = (\tfrac{1}{4} \times 10\%) + (\tfrac{3}{4} \times 20\%) = 17.5\%$$

8.7.2 Covariance and Correlation

The standard deviation measures the variability of a given asset's rates of return, and *correlation* measures the degree to which the rates of return on any given pair of assets *move together*.

For example, Table 8-6 gives the historical rates of return on two stocks over a four-year period. There is a positive correlation between the two stocks' rates of return. When one stock does well, the other tends to do well; and when one does poorly, so does the other. Figure 8-3 graphically demonstrates this positive comovement.

In Figure 8-3 the vertical axis shows Stock 1's rates of return, and the horizontal axis shows Stock 2's rates of return. For example, in year 2, Stock 1's rate of return was 15% and Stock 2's was 20%. Connecting all points in Figure 8-3 shows that the graph slopes upward from left to right. This upward-sloping curve represents positive correlation.

TABLE 8-6 Rates of Return (in percent) on Two Stocks over a Four-Year Period	Year	Rate of Return (%)	
		Stock 1	Stock 2
	1	5	10
	2	15	20
	3	−5	−10
	4	25	60

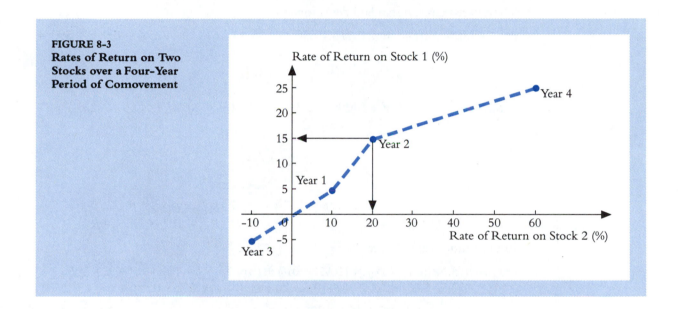

FIGURE 8-3
Rates of Return on Two Stocks over a Four-Year Period of Comovement

In this example it is clear that a positive correlation exists between the two stocks' returns. However, in some cases the picture is not so clear, and we need to define correlation more precisely.

The correlation coefficient between Stocks 1 and 2, denoted by $\rho_{1,2}$, is given by

$$\text{Correlation coefficient} = \rho_{1,2} = \frac{\sigma_{1,2}}{\sigma_1 \sigma_2} \tag{8.5}$$

where $\sigma_{1,2}$ is the **covariance** between the two stocks, defined as

$$\sigma_{1,2} = \sum_{t=1}^{m} P_t (R_{1,t} - \bar{R}_1)(R_{2,t} - \bar{R}_2) \tag{8.6}$$

Here $R_{1,t}$ and $R_{2,t}$ are the rates of return on Stocks 1 and 2, respectively, in period t; P_t is the probability of occurrence of a specific pair of outcomes corresponding to year t; and $\bar{R}_1$ and $\bar{R}_2$ are the expected rates of return on Stocks 1 and 2, respectively.

Suppose the historical rates of return for the four years given in Table 8-6 are good estimates of the future rates of return, and the probability of each pair of returns occurring is ¼. For example, the joint probability of the outcome pair (5%, 10%) is ¼, and it is also ¼ for the two other outcome pairs. We may use Equation 8.5 to calculate the two stocks' correlation. The expected rates of return are

$$\bar{R}_1 = (¼ \times 5\%) + (¼ \times 15\%) + (¼ \times -5\%) + (¼ \times 25\%) = 10\%$$

$$\bar{R}_2 = (¼ \times 10\%)^2 + (¼ \times 20\%) + (¼ \times -10\%) + (¼ \times 60\%) = 20\%$$

Their variances and standard deviations are

$$\sigma^2_{R_1} = ¼(5\% - 10\%)^2 + ¼(15\% - 10\%)^2 + ¼(-5\% - 10\%)^2 + ¼(25\% - 10\%)^2 = 500/4$$

hence

$$\sigma_{R_1} = \sqrt{125}$$

$$\sigma^2_{R_2} = ¼(10\% - 20\%)^2 + ¼(20\% - 20\%)^2 + ¼(-10\% - 20\%)^2 + ¼(60\% - 20\%)^2$$
$$= 2,600/4$$

hence

$$\sigma_{R_2} = \sqrt{650}$$

The covariance is given by

$$\sigma_{1,2} = P_1 \times (R_{1,1} - \bar{R}_1) \times (R_{2,1} - \bar{R}_2) + P_2 \times (R_{1,2} - \bar{R}_1) \times (R_{2,2} - \bar{R}_2) +$$
$$P_3 \times (R_{1,3} - \bar{R}_1) \times (R_{2,3} - \bar{R}_2) + P_4 \times (R_{1,4} - \bar{R}_1) \times (R_{2,4} - \bar{R}_2)$$

In our numerical example:

$$\sigma_{1,2} = (¼) \times (5\% - 10\%) \times (10\% - 20\%) + (¼) \times (15\% - 10\%) \times (20\% - 20\%) +$$
$$(¼) \times (-5\% - 10\%) \times (-10\% - 20\%) + (¼) \times (25\% - 10\%) \times (60\% - 20\%)$$

$$= 12.5 + 0 + 112.5 + 150 = 275$$

Therefore, the correlation, $\rho_{1,2}$, is

$$\rho_{1,2} = \frac{275}{\sqrt{125}\sqrt{680}} \cong \frac{275}{11.18 \times 25.50} \cong 0.96$$

We see that the correlation is positive, as suggested by Figure 8-3.

8.7.3 The Portfolio's Standard Deviation

To find a portfolio's standard deviation, we first need to calculate its variance. The portfolio's variance can be calculated in two ways: by directly using the portfolio's rate of return or by using the individual assets' variances and covariances. Given the portfolio's rate of return, we can calculate the portfolio's variance directly as follows:[8]

---

8. The formula for the portfolio's variance is the same as Equation 8.3, except that R_p (portfolio returns) substitutes for R (individual asset returns).

Portfolio variance = Sum of {probabilities multiplied by the squared deviation of the portfolio's rate of return from its expected rate of return}

Table 8-7 demonstrates the calculation of the variance and standard deviation of two portfolios, as described next:

Portfolio 1: ½B + ½C

$$\sigma_p^2 = P_1 \times (R_{p,1} - \bar{R}_p)^2 + P_2 \times (R_{p,2} - \bar{R}_p)^2 + P_3 \times (R_{p,3} - \bar{R}_p)^2$$

where

$$P_1 = P_2 = P_3 = \tfrac{1}{3}$$

Therefore,

$$\sigma_p^2 = \frac{(20\% - 15\%)^2}{3} + \frac{(10\% - 15\%)^2}{3} + \frac{(15\% - 15\%)^2}{3} = \frac{50}{3}$$

and

$$\sigma_p = \sqrt{\frac{50}{3}}$$

Portfolio 2: (½)A + (¼)B + (¼)C

$$\sigma_p^2 = P_1 \times (R_{p,1} - \bar{R}_p)^2 + P_2 \times (R_{p,2} - \bar{R}_p)^2 + P_3 \times (R_{p,3} - \bar{R}_p)^2$$

Hence,

$$\sigma_p^2 = \frac{(12.5\% - 10\%)^2}{3} + \frac{(7.5\% - 10\%)^2}{3} + \frac{(10\% - 10\%)^2}{3} = \frac{12.5}{3} = \frac{25}{6}$$

and

$$\sigma_p = \sqrt{\frac{25}{6}}$$

TABLE 8-7		Expected Rates of Return, Variances, and Standard Deviations (in percent) of Three Assets and Two Portfolios				
		Rate of Return (%)				
State of the Economy	**Probability**	**Asset A**	**Asset B**	**Asset C**	**Portfolio 1** (½) B + (½) C	**Portfolio 2** (½) A + (¼) B + (¾) C
Boom	⅓	5	10	30	20	12.5
Normal	⅓	5	5	15	10	7.5
Recession	⅓	5	15	15	15	10
Expected rate of return		5	10	20	15	10
Variance σ^2		0	50/3	150/3	50/3	25/6
Standard deviation σ		0	$\sqrt{50/3}$	$\sqrt{150/3}$	$\sqrt{50/3}$	$\sqrt{25/6}$

Calculating portfolio standard deviation by this direct method is fairly straight-forward because we treat the portfolio as an asset. Once we have a series of rates of return on a portfolio and their corresponding probabilities, we can easily calculate the variance. However, this simple method does not provide us with clues as to the relationship between the portfolio's standard deviation, and its individual assets' standard deviations and the role of correlation. As we shall see below, the mathematical computation of the portfolio's variance does shed light on the relationship between the correlations and the portfolio's variance.

8.7.4 Employing Correlation to Calculate Portfolio Standard Deviation: The Two–Asset Case

To find the portfolio's standard deviation, we need to calculate its variance and then take the square root of that variance. In this section we use data from Table 8-8 to illustrate how portfolio variance is related to correlation among the assets' returns. The table provides the expected rates of return and the standard deviations of Assets A and B and three possible portfolios.

To better understand the components of a portfolio's variance, we first calculate the correlation of the returns on Assets A and B, denoted by $\rho_{A,B}$, which is demonstrated in Table 8-9. The table shows the correlation to be $\rho_{A,B} = 0.7559$.

Using the information in Tables 8-8 and 8-9, we now can show that when the portfolio is composed of Assets A and B, the portfolio's variance σ^2 can be calculated by the following formula:[9]

$$\sigma_p^2 = w_A^2 \sigma_A^2 + w_B^2 \sigma_B^2 + 2 w_A w_B \sigma_A \sigma_B \rho_{A,B} \tag{8.7}$$

where w_A and w_B are the proportions of Assets A and B in the portfolio, respectively. The portfolio's standard deviation is the square root, σ_p.

Table 8-10 demonstrates that the formula is valid for the three portfolios given in Table 8-8. Whether we calculate the variance directly from the portfolio's rate of return (as in Table 8-8) or by applying Equation 8.7 (as in Table 8-10), we get the same results. To see this, compare σ in Tables 8-8 and 8-10.

For example, direct calculation of Portfolio 1's variance (composed of equal weights of Asset A and Asset B) is given by

$$\sigma_p^2 = \frac{(7.5\% - 12.5\%)^2 + (7.5\% - 12.5\%)^2 + (22.5\% - 12.5\%)^2}{3} = 50$$

and

$$\sigma_p = \sqrt{50} = 7.07$$

---

9. Since $\rho_{A,B} = \sigma_{A,B}/\sigma_A \sigma_B$, Equation 8.7 can be rewritten in terms of the covariance rather than the correlation as follows: $\sigma^2 = w_A \sigma_A + w_B \sigma_B + 2 w_A w_B \sigma_{A,B}$.

TABLE 8-8   **Rates of Return (in percent) on Assets A and B and on Three Portfolios (in percent)**

State of the Economy	Probability	Individual Assets		Portfolios		
		A	B	1	2	3
				½A + ½B	⅓A + ⅔B	⅔A + ⅓B
Recession	⅓	5	10	7.5	6	9
Normal	⅓	10	5	7.5	6	9
Expansion	⅓	15	30	22.5	27	18
Expected rate of return		10	15	12.5	14	11
Variance, σ^2		50/3	350/3	50	258/3	78/3
Standard deviation, σ		$\sqrt{50/3}$	$\sqrt{350/3}$	$\sqrt{50}$	$\sqrt{258/3}$	$\sqrt{78/3}$

TABLE 8-9   **Correlation Between the Rates of Return on Assets A and B**

State of the Economy	Probability	Asset A		Asset B		Product of the Deviations $(R_A - \bar{R}_A) \times (R_B - \bar{R}_B)$
		Rate of Return (%) R_A	Deviation from Mean (%) $R_A - \bar{R}_A$	Rate of Return (%) R_B	Deviation from Mean (%) $R_B - \bar{R}_B$	
Recession	⅓	5	$5 - 10 = -5$	10	$10 - 15 = -5$	$(-5) \times (-5) = 25$
Normal	⅓	10	$10 - 10 = 0$	5	$5 - 15 = -10$	$0 \times (-10) = 0$
Expansion	⅓	15	$15 - 10 = 5$	30	$30 - 15 = 15$	$5 \times 15 = 75$
Expected rate of return		10		15		

Covariance, $\sigma_{A,B}$

$$\frac{(25 + 0 + 75)}{3}$$

$$= \frac{100}{3}$$

Correlation $\rho_{A,B} = \sigma_{A,B}/\sigma_A\sigma_B$

$$\frac{\dfrac{100}{3}}{\sqrt{50/3} \times \sqrt{350/3}}$$

$$\cong \frac{100}{7.07 \times 18.71}$$

$$\cong 0.7559$$

TABLE 8-10   **Portfolio Variance of Portfolios 1, 2, and 3 Given in Table 8-8**

		Portfolio Variance Components			Portfolio Variance
Portfolio	Allocation Strategy	$w_A^2 \sigma_A^2$	$w_B^2 \sigma_B^2$	$2 w_A w_B \rho_{AB} \sigma_A \sigma_B$	σ_p^2
1	½A + ½B	$(½)^2 \times 50/3$	$(½)^2 \times 350/3$	$2 \times (½) \times (½) \times 0.7559$ $\times (50/3)^{1/2} (350/3)^{1/2}$	50
2	⅓A + ⅔B	$(⅓)^2 \times 50/3$	$(⅔)^2 \times 350/3$	$2 \times (⅓) \times (⅔) \times 0.7559$ $\times (50/3)^{1/2} (350/3)^{1/2}$	258/3
3	⅔A + ⅓B	$(⅔)^2 \times 50/3$	$(⅓)^2 \times 350/3$	$2 \times (⅔) \times (⅓) \times 0.7559$ $\times (50/3)^{1/2} (350/3)^{1/2}$	78/3

The same result is obtained when we use Equation 8.7:

$$\sigma_p^2 = \left(\frac{1}{2}\right)^2\left(\frac{50}{3}\right) + \left(\frac{1}{2}\right)^2\left(\frac{350}{3}\right) + 2\left(\frac{1}{2}\right)\left(\frac{1}{2}\right)0.7559\left(\frac{50}{3}\right)^{1/2}\left(\frac{350}{3}\right)^{1/2} \cong 50$$

and

$$\sigma_p = \sqrt{50}$$

8.7.5 Employing Correlation to Calculate Portfolio Standard Deviation: The *n*-Asset Case

The variance of the returns of a portfolio composed of n assets is given by summing all the weighted variances as well as all the weighted covariances (of all pairs of assets), where the weights are the corresponding investment proportions. Although in principle this is a simple extension of Equation 8.7 for the two-asset case, counting all possible covariances can be cumbersome. Therefore, we need a systematic method to keep track of all possible terms.

To understand the logic of the systematic method we use, imagine a square as described by Figure 8-4a. On the diagonal we have the variance terms, $w_i^2\sigma_i^2$, for $i = 1, .., n$ and in the off-diagonal boxes we have the covariance terms, $w_i \, w_j \, \sigma_{i,j}$, where i denotes the ith row of the square and j denotes the jth column. For example, in Row 3 and Column 2, the term $w_3 \, w_2 \, \sigma_{3,2}$ is the covariance between Assets 3 and 2 $(\sigma_{3,2})$ multiplied by their respective investment weights, w_3 and w_2. Note that this table is symmetrical. If we look at Row 2 and Column 3, we get $w_2 \, w_3 \, \sigma_{2,3}$, which is equal to $w_3 \, w_2 \, \sigma_{3,2}$ because $\sigma_{2,3} = \sigma_{3,2}$. The covariance between Assets 2 and 3, $\sigma_{2,3}$, is the same as the covariance between Assets 3 and 2, $\sigma_{3,2}$. Thus, the boxes contain all variance components as well as all covariances multiplied by the respective portfolio weights. Summing all terms in all boxes yields the *portfolio variance*.

Substituting $\rho_{ij}\sigma_i\sigma_j$ for σ_{ij}, the portfolio variance is given by the formula

$$\sigma_p^2 = \sum_{i=1}^{n} w_i^2 \sigma_i^2 + 2\sum_{i=1}^{n} \sum_{\substack{j=1 \\ j>i}}^{n} w_i w_j \rho_{ij} \sigma_i \sigma_j \qquad (8.8)$$

Each variance is multiplied by its squared investment weight $(w)^2$, and then we count twice[10] each contribution $w_i w_j \rho_{i,j} \sigma_i \sigma_j$. On the diagonal, we have terms $w_i^2 \sigma_i^2$ and on the off-diagonal, we have $w_i w_j \sigma_{i,j}$.

When we have only two assets, the square described by Figure 8-4b will contain only four cells. In that case, when Assets A and B are denoted by 1 and 2, respectively, Equation 8.8 reduces to the simpler Equation 8.7.

The following problem demonstrates calculation of a portfolio variance.

FIGURE 8-4A The Components of Portfolio Variance: The *n*-Asset Case	Asset	1	2	3	.	.	.	*n*
	1	$w_1^2\sigma_1^2$	$w_1 w_2 \sigma_{1,2}$	$w_1 w_3 \sigma_{1,3}$	.	.	.	$w_1 w_n \sigma_{1,n}$
	2	$w_2 w_1 \sigma_{2,1}$	$w_2^2\sigma_2^2$	$w_2 w_3 \sigma_{2,3}$	.	.	.	$w_2 w_n \sigma_{2,n}$
	3	$w_3 w_1 \sigma_{3,1}$	$w_3 w_2 \sigma_{3,2}$	$w_3^2\sigma_3^2$	.	.	.	$w_3 w_n \sigma_{3,n}$
	.	.	.	.	.	.	.	.
	.	.	.	.	.	.	.	.
	.	.	.	.	.	.	.	.
	n	$w_n w_1 \sigma_{n,1}$	$w_n w_2 \sigma_{n,2}$	$w_n w_3 \sigma_{n,3}$	.	.	.	$w_n^2\sigma_n^2$

FIGURE 8.4B The Components of Portfolio Variance: The Two-Asset Case	Asset	1	2
	1	$w_1^2\sigma_1^2$	$w_1 w_2 \sigma_{1,2}$
	2	$w_2 w_1 \sigma_{2,1}$	$w_2^2\sigma_2^2$

10. The restriction $j > i$ avoids double counting some terms. For example, $w_1 w_2 \rho_{1,2} \sigma_1 \sigma_2$ is counted but $w_2 w_1 \rho_{2,1} \sigma_2 \sigma_1$ is not (because here $j > i$). Thus, the multiplication by 2 already accounts for these two terms.

PRACTICE BOX

Problem   You have three securities with $\sigma_1 = 0.1$, $\sigma_2 = 0.2$, and $\sigma_3 = 0.3$. Assume $\rho_{1,2} = \frac{1}{2}$, $\rho_{1,3} = \frac{1}{4}$, and $\rho_{2,3} = -\frac{1}{2}$. You invest equally among these three assets. What is the portfolio variance?

Solution   As $w_i = \frac{1}{3}$ for all three securities, we have:

$$\sigma = (\tfrac{1}{3})^2 \, (0.1)^2 + (\tfrac{1}{3})^2 \, (0.2)^2 + (\tfrac{1}{3})^2 \, (0.3)^2$$

$$+ \, 2 \times \tfrac{1}{3} \times \tfrac{1}{3} \times \tfrac{1}{2} \times 0.1 \times 0.2$$

$$+ \, 2 \times \tfrac{1}{3} \times \tfrac{1}{3} \times \tfrac{1}{4} \times 0.1 \times 0.3$$

$$+ \, 2 \times \tfrac{1}{3} \times \tfrac{1}{3} \times (-\tfrac{1}{2}) \times 0.2 \times 0.3 \cong 0.0128$$

8.8 INVESTMENT STRATEGIES

The allocation of wealth among the assets in a portfolio is called an **investment strategy.** As we shall see below, the correlation coefficient plays a central role in determining the investment strategy.

8.8.1 Diversifying Across Unrelated Industries

Portfolio managers generally agree that investors should diversify among assets, although they often disagree on the number of assets that investors need to be adequately diversified. Most concur, however, that diversification across "unrelated industries" is more important than the actual number of stocks held in the portfolio, as Connecting Theory to Practice 8.2 indicates.

CONNECTING THEORY TO PRACTICE 8.2

HOW TO BUILD A STOCK PORTFOLIO EVEN IF YOU AREN'T A MONEYBAGS

"You don't want more than one company in an industry, and you don't want companies in related industries," says Mr. Lipson [president of Horizon Financial Advisers]. For example, an auto manufacturer and a steel company that supplies auto manufacturers will move together. Further, "you also don't want industries that respond to the economic cycle the same way, such as trucking and basic manufacturing," he says.

While Mr. Lipson believes that investors need at least 15 stocks to be adequately diversified, other advisers are comfortable with a smaller number. "It's not so much the number of names that make you diversified, but how you spread them out," says George Vanderheiden, who heads the equity growth group for Fidelity Investments.

Source: Ellen E. Schultz, "How to Build a Stock Portfolio Even If You Aren't a Moneybags," *Wall Street Journal*, 10 April 1992, pp. C1, C13. Reprinted by permission of *The Wall Street Journal*, © 1992 Dow Jones & Company, Inc. All Rights Reserved Worldwide.

MAKING THE CONNECTION

The notion of "related" or "unrelated" stocks pertains to the correlation between the various stocks' rates of return. The gain from diversification depends on the correlation among the rates of return. If the correlation is zero, we say the stocks are unrelated, and risk reduction can be achieved by diversification. If the correlation is positive and large, only limited risk reduction can be achieved. Pairs of stocks with negatively correlated rates of return are preferable to stocks with positively correlated rates because risk reduction is enhanced when the returns move in opposite directions. However, because it is difficult to find negatively correlated stocks, the experts recommend "unrelated" stocks—that is, stocks with zero correlation between their rates of return.

8.8.2 Efficient and Inefficient Investment Strategies

Throughout most of this chapter we have assumed similar expected rates of return on assets. We did this to focus on the impact of diversification on the variance of the portfolio's rate of return. We have seen that, in general, the larger the number of assets in the portfolio and the lower the correlations among the rates of return, the smaller the portfolio's risk.

In practice, since individual assets will rarely have equal expected rates of return, any change in the investment weights of a diversified portfolio will change both the portfolio's expected rate of return and its variance. Indeed, various portfolio combinations should be examined very carefully to identify efficient and inefficient combinations of assets. An investment strategy is *efficient* if either of the following holds:

1. There is no other investment strategy with a higher expected rate of return and an equal or smaller standard deviation.
2. There is no other investment strategy with a smaller standard deviation and an equal or higher expected rate of return.

If there is an investment strategy (or portfolio) such that either (1) or (2) does not hold, we say that it is an *inefficient* strategy. Investors who are risk averse (who dislike volatility) will never select an investment strategy that is not efficient.

8.8.3 The Expected Rate of Return— Standard Deviation Frontier

The group of all efficient investment strategies (portfolios and individual assets alike) forms a subgroup of all possible investments. Efficient investment strategies constitute the **mean standard deviation (E–σ) efficient set,** where *mean* is another name for expected rate of return. Every investment strategy that is efficient by the mean-standard deviation criterion is also efficient by the mean-variance criterion. So the terms "mean-standard deviation efficient set" and "mean-variance efficient set" are used interchangeably. In this section we demonstrate the efficient set, first with portfolios composed of two assets and then with portfolios of more than two assets.

Table 8-11 demonstrates a portfolio's expected rate of return and standard deviation for various investment strategies and for various assumed correlation coefficients. In general, the larger the correlation coefficient, the smaller the gain from

TABLE 8-11   **Mean Rate of Return and Standard Deviation on a Two-Asset Portfolio for Various Levels of Correlation**

Part a: Basic Inputs—Mean Rate of Return and Variance of the Two Assets

	Asset A	Asset B
Mean rate of return (in %)	10	20
Variance	10	15

Part b: Portfolio's Expected Rate of Return (E)[a] and Standard Deviation (σ)[b] for Various Weights and Correlations Between the Two Assets

Invested Weights		Correlation, $\rho = -1$		Correlation, $\rho = -\frac{1}{2}$		Correlation, $\rho = \frac{1}{2}$		Correlation, $\rho = 1$	
w_A	$w_B = 1 - w_A$	E (%)	σ	E (%)	σ	E (%)	σ	E (%)	σ
1	0	10.0	3.16	10.0	3.16	10.0	3.16	10.0	3.16
0.9	0.1	11.0	2.46	11.0	2.67	11.0	3.06	11.0	3.23
0.8	0.2	12.0	1.75	12.0	2.24	12.0	2.99	12.0	3.30
0.7	0.3	13.0	1.05	13.0	1.92	13.0	2.97	13.0	3.37
0.6	0.4	14.0	0.35	14.0	1.75	14.0	2.99	14.0	3.45
0.55	0.45	14.5	0	14.5	1.74	14.5	3.01	14.5	3.48
0.5	0.5	15.0	0.36	15.0	1.79	15.0	3.05	15.0	3.52
0.4	0.6	16.0	1.06	16.0	2.01	16.0	3.15	16.0	3.59
0.3	0.7	17.0	1.76	17.0	2.38	17.0	3.29	17.0	3.66
0.2	0.8	18.0	2.47	18.0	2.84	18.0	3.46	18.0	3.73
0.1	0.9	19.0	3.17	19.0	3.34	19.0	3.65	19.0	3.80
0	1	20.0	3.87	20.0	3.87	20.0	3.87	20.0	3.87

[a]The expected value is given by: $E = w_A 10 + (1 - w_A)20$

[b]The variance is given by

$$\sigma_p^2 = u_A^2 10 + (1 - w_A)^2\, 15 + 2w_A\,(1 - w_A)\rho\sqrt{10}\sqrt{15}$$

where ρ is the assumed correlation, and 10 and 15 are the variances of the two assets, respectively.

diversification. For example, a portfolio with a 12% expected rate of return and with weights of 0.8 and 0.2 invested in Assets A and B, respectively, has a standard deviation of 1.75% if the correlation coefficient is −1; 2.24% if the correlation coefficient is −½; 2.99% if the correlation coefficient is ½; and 3.3% if the correlation is 1.

We can use the portfolio's expected rate of return (E) and standard deviation (σ) given in Table 8-11 to diagram all the resulting portfolios in Figure 8-5. The curves *AB, AaB, AbB,* and *AMB* correspond to the correlation coefficients of 1, ½, −½, and −1, respectively, given in Table 8-11. For perfect positive correlations of returns, all portfolios lie on the straight line *AB.*

For perfect negative correlation $\rho_{A,B} = -1$, all available portfolios lie on the two line segments *MB* and *MA.* By changing the investment proportions, investors can shift among the different portfolios on these two lines. For any portfolio on line *MA,* there will be a better portfolio on line *MB.* For example, Portfolio K′ is better than Portfolio K because K′ has the same risk (σ) but a higher expected rate of return.

As we can see from Table 8-11, for $\rho = -1$ there is an investment strategy that brings the portfolio's standard deviation to zero (point *M* touches the vertical axis). In our example this occurs for $w_A = 0.55$. Drawing all resulting portfolios for $\rho = -½$ and $\rho = ½$, we obtain the curves *AbB* and *AaB,* respectively, which describes all the (E, σ) combinations resulting from various diversification strategies. As we can see

FIGURE 8-5

Impact of the Correlation Coefficient on the E-σ Frontier and on the E-σ Efficient Set

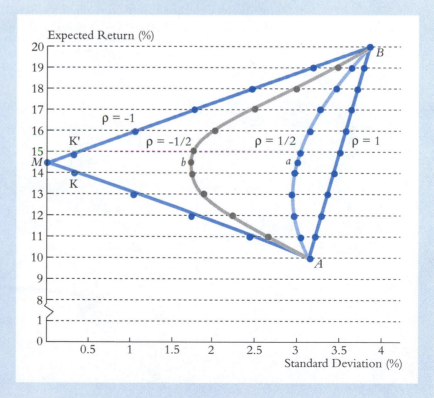

from Figure 8-5 the lower the correlation, the further the curve bulges to the left, signifying larger risk reduction due to diversification.

While the various curves and lines in Figure 8-5 describe the available portfolios (for various correlation coefficients), investors will never select many of them because they are *inefficient portfolios*. For example, any portfolio lying on line *MA* is inefficient because, for the case $\rho = -1$, there is a better portfolio on line *MB* (compare Portfolios K and K′). The set of portfolios lying on line *MB* is called the *efficient set*. By the same argument, the efficient set for $\rho = -\frac{1}{2}$ is *bB*; for $\rho = \frac{1}{2}$, *aB*. For $\rho = 1$ all portfolios are efficient (line *AB*). Because we move from *A* to *B*, both the expected value and the standard deviation increase, and no portfolio dominates the other. According to their individual preferences, investors will select a portfolio from the efficient set.

When a portfolio includes more than two stocks, the analysis changes slightly. To illustrate, suppose there are five stocks, labeled A, B, C, D, and E in Figure 8-6. Investors can select a portfolio composed of only two stocks (some of these curves are marked "2") or a portfolio composed of three stocks, four stocks, or five stocks. Not all portfolios are efficient. For example, both Portfolios P and P″ are inefficient because Portfolio P′ dominates them. The set of *all* portfolios such that, for a given expected rate of return, the standard deviation is minimized in the **E–σ frontier,** as given by *EMA* in Figure 8-6. The efficient set is *MA*.

Generally, the larger the number of available assets and the lower the correlations among them, the more to the left the efficient frontier shifts. For a given expected rate of return, the portfolio's risk is reduced. Investors should follow these steps:

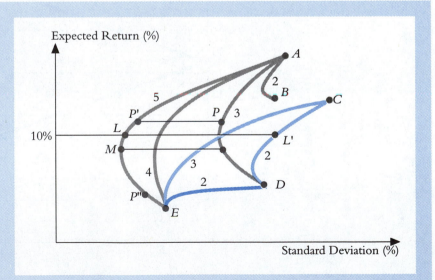

FIGURE 8-6
The Mean Standard Deviation Frontier of Portfolios Composed of Two to Five Assets

1. Find the $E-\sigma$ frontier.
2. Identify the efficient set of portfolios on the frontier.
3. Select the optimum portfolio that fits their risk-return preferences from the mean variance efficient set.

Identifying the efficient set has two benefits. First, it helps ensure that investors will not mistakenly select an inefficient portfolio. Second, when we add a riskless asset and allow investors to mix it with a portfolio taken from the efficient set, we can establish a risk index for each individual asset that accounts for the stock's own variance as well as all the correlations with the other assets in the portfolio. Using the risk index, we can estimate the firm's cost of equity. These topics are developed in the next two chapters.

APPLYING THEORY TO PRACTICE 8.1

FIRM'S FOREIGN CURRENCY RISK MANAGEMENT: A PORTFOLIO APPROACH

BUYING ISSUES DENOMINATED IN JAPAN'S CURRENCY SHIFTS FOREIGN-EXCHANGE RISKS

TOKYO—Japan's big investors are shoveling cash into foreign bonds at record rates again. But most are choosier this time than during the 1980s: They want yen-based bonds, which force overseas borrowers to shoulder currency risks that Japanese once typically held.

Japanese investors bought a net $20.2 billion in foreign bonds in June, the government said, a record for any month and double what they bought in the year-earlier month. But while the government doesn't specify the currency of those investments, analysts in Tokyo say roughly half were in so-called Euroyen bonds, which are denominated in yen but issued in European markets. That was more than went into any other sector.

"We are putting money in domestic bonds and Euroyen bonds instead of increasing our (holdings of) foreign-currency-denominated bonds," says Osamu Nagase, a fund manager at Sumitomo Marine & Fire Insurance Co. "We are very nervous about currency risks."

Transfer of Risk

Or consider Sumitomo Marine & Fire. To diversify risk, insurance companies here hold a certain portion of their huge portfolios outside Japan. So Sumitomo has bought yen bonds issued by the Italian government and by a New Zealand electric utility, says Mr. Nagase. "We haven't put new money in foreign-currency-denominated bonds since last May," he says.

By borrowing in yen, foreign entities take over many of the risks associated with currency fluctuations. To raise the yen they owe, many foreign borrowers must use complex currency derivatives, leaving them dependent on unrelated parties for their streams of yen. Borrowers also risk seeing their debts balloon if the yen soars against their own currencies. China and Indonesia, both big recipients of yen-denominated loans in recent years, have already seen their debts soar on the yen's strength.

Nonetheless, many foreign borrowers are eagerly indulging Japanese investors' fears of foreign currency. Non-Japanese entities from around the world issued 23.1 billion yen of Euroyen bonds between April and June this year, more than triple the amount issued during the same period in 1994. Recently, Lehman Brothers Japan Inc. has received "a number of serious inquiries" from U.S. companies wanting to borrow in yen, says Russell Jones, the firm's chief economist in Tokyo.

ADDITIONAL INFORMATION

The foreign exchange rate is 100 yen per dollar. The interest rate Japanese lenders receive on yen-dominated bonds is 3%; on dollar-denominated bonds, 7%.

QUESTIONS

1. Suppose a Japanese lender who wishes to lend $100 million for one year expects it equally likely that the exchange rate one year from now will be 85 yen per dollar or 115 yen per dollar. Calculate the rates of return to the Japanese lender under three alternatives:
   a. Lending in yen
   b. Lending in dollars
   c. Lending half in yen and half in dollars
   Describe graphically the resulting expected return and risk on a set of E–σ axes.

2. In light of your results in Question 1, discuss the assertion: "But while the government doesn't specify the currency of those investments, analysts in Tokyo say roughly half were in so-called Euroyen bonds, which are denominated in yen."

3. Now consider Sumitomo Marine & Fire Insurance Company. The firm plans to invest $100 million abroad for one year. It has insured many non-Japanese, and from the firm's past experience the CFO estimates it will need to pay $53.5 million to insured Americans at the end of the year. (Assume this payment is certain.)
   a. Use the information regarding the foreign exchange rate given in Question 1 to calculate the expected rate of return and the standard deviation of the three lending alternatives cited in Question 1. In your calculation, add the profit (or subtract the loss) due to the possible foreign exchange fluctuations on the $53.5 million, to the return from lending the $100 million.

   b. Draw the three portfolios on a graph, as done in Question 1.

   c. Discuss your results.

MAKING THE CONNECTION

1. a. Lending in yen yields 3% with certainty. Thus, $E = 3\%$ and $\sigma = 0$.

    b. If the Japanese firm lends in dollars, the investment at the current exchange rate is: \$100 million $\times$ 100 yen per dollar = 10,000 million yen or 10 billion yen.

        One year from now, the lender will receive \$107 million [\$100 million $\times$ (1.07) = \$107 million]. When exchanging it for yen at the end of the year, the lender will receive either:

$$\$107 \text{ million} \times 85 \text{ yen per dollar} = 9.095 \text{ billion yen}$$

or

$$\$107 \text{ million} \times 115 \text{ yen per dollar} = 12.305 \text{ billion yen}$$

Therefore, the rate of return will be either:

$$R_1 = \frac{9.095 \text{ billion yen}}{10 \text{ billion yen}} - 1 = -0.0905 \text{ or } -9.05\%$$

or

$$R_2 = \frac{12.305 \text{ billion yen}}{10 \text{ billion yen}} - 1 = 0.2305 \text{ or } 23.05\%$$

Since there is an equal probability of each of these two rates of return occurring, we have the following expected value and standard deviation:

$$\overline{R} = \tfrac{1}{2} \times (-9.05\%) + \tfrac{1}{2} \times 23.05\% = 7\%$$

$$\sigma^2 = \tfrac{1}{2}(-9.05\% - 7\%)^2 + \tfrac{1}{2}(23.05\% - 7\%)^2 \cong 257.603$$

Thus, $\sigma = 16.05\%$.

    c. If half of the money is loaned in yen and half in dollars, we obtain a portfolio with

$$\overline{R} = \tfrac{1}{2} \times 3\% + \tfrac{1}{2} \times 7\% = 5\%$$

Note that the variance of lending in yen is zero, and the correlation of this certain return with return on the dollar loan is zero. In that case, and using Equation 8.7, we find that

$$\sigma^2 = (\tfrac{1}{2})^2 \times (16.05)^2 \cong 64.401$$

and

$$\sigma \cong 8.025\%.$$

The three portfolios are drawn on $E-\sigma$ axes as shown in the following diagram:

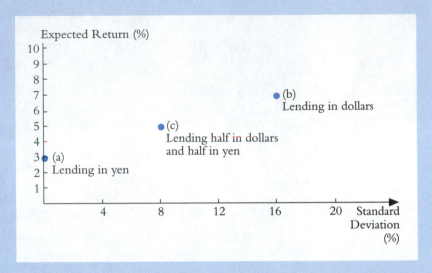

2. As we can see from the figure, no portfolio dominates any other. In spite of the foreign exchange risk and in spite of being "nervous about currency risk," some Japanese investors prefer to take the risk and receive the high interest rate involved with lending in dollars rather than in yen. This is the reason why only roughly half of the investments are in yen. It is possible that the Japanese investors diversify and invest in a portfolio like Portfolio c in the figure, or it is possible that some invest in Portfolio a and some in b such that when we sum all the investments, about half are in yen.

3. a. Let us first calculate $\bar{R}$ and σ for a loan denominated in dollars. The firm receives $107 million on the $100 million loan. Let us first calculate the gain or loss due to the $53.5 million payments to the American clients.

   The current exchange rate is 100 yen per dollar; therefore, if the exchange rate rises to 115 yen per dollar, Sumitomo will have to pay more yen to convert the money needed to pay the insured Americans. The loss will be

   $53.5 million $\times$ (115 yen/dollar $-$ 100 yen/dollar)
   = 802.5 million yen

Similarly, if the yen trades at 85 yen per dollar, the profit will be

   $53.5 million $\times$ (100 yen/dollar $-$ 85 yen/dollar)
   = 802.5 million yen.

Therefore, if the exchange rate turns out to be 115 yen per dollar, the rate of return will be

$$R_1 = \frac{12.305 \text{ billion yen} - 0.8025 \text{ billion yen}}{10 \text{ billion yen}} - 1$$

$$\cong 0.1503 \text{ or } 15.03\%$$

Alternatively, if the exchange rate turns out to be 85 yen per dollar, the rate of return will be

$$\frac{9.095 \text{ billion yen} + 0.8025 \text{ billion yen}}{10 \text{ billion yen}} - 1$$

$$\cong -0.0103 \text{ or } -1.03\%$$

The expected rate of return is

$$\overline{R} = \tfrac{1}{2}(-1.03\%) + \tfrac{1}{2} \times 15.03\% = 7\%$$

and the variance is

$$\sigma^2 = \tfrac{1}{2}(-1.03\% - 7\%)^2 + \tfrac{1}{2}(15.03\% - 7\%)^2 \cong 64.48$$

Thus, $\sigma \cong 8.03\%$.

Now let us turn to the policy of lending half in yen and half in dollars. The firm invests 10 billion yen: 5 billion yen in yen–dominated bonds and 5 billion yen in purchasing $50 billion dollar-denominated bonds. Thus, at the end of the year it receives in return for its portfolio loan:

$$5 \text{ billion yen} \times 1.03 = 5.15 \text{ billion yen}$$

plus

$$\$50 \text{ million} \times 1.07 = \$53.50 \text{ million}$$

If the exchange rate at the end of the year is 115 yen per dollar, the rate of return will be

$$\frac{5.15 \text{ billion yen} + (\$53.50 \text{ million} \times 115) - 0.8025 \text{ billion yen}}{10 \text{ billion yen}} - 1$$

$$= 0.05 \text{ or } 5\%$$

If the exchange rate is 85 yen per dollar, the rate of return will be

$$\frac{5.15 \text{ billion yen} + (\$53.50 \text{ million} \times 85) + 0.8025 \text{ billion yen}}{10 \text{ billion yen}} - 1$$

$$= 0.05 \text{ or } 5\%$$

(when the loss or gain on the \$53.5 million paid to the insured Americans is calculated as before and is equal to 0.8025 billion yen). Thus, the expected rate of return is 5% and the variance is zero.

Finally, if all lending is in yen, the firm's rate of return will be as follows for the two exchange rates:

If the exchange rate is 115 yen per dollar:

$$\frac{10 \text{ billion yen} \times 1.03 - 0.8025 \text{ billion yen}}{10 \text{ billion yen}} - 1$$

$$= -0.05025 \text{ or } -5.025\%$$

If the exchange rate is 85 yen per dollar:

$$\frac{10 \text{ billion yen} \times 1.03 + 0.8025 \text{ billion yen}}{10 \text{ billion yen}} - 1$$

$$= 0.11025 \text{ or } 11.025\%$$

The expected value is

$$\overline{R} = \tfrac{1}{2}(-5.025\%) + \tfrac{1}{2} \times 11.025\% = 3\%$$

and the variance is

$$\sigma^2 = \tfrac{1}{2}(-5.025\% - 3\%)^2 + \tfrac{1}{2}(11.025\% - 3\%)^2 = 64.40$$

Thus, $\sigma \cong 8.025\%$.

b. A graph of the resulting three portfolios for the Sumitomo Marine & Fire Insurance Co. on a set of $E-\sigma$ axes is as follows:

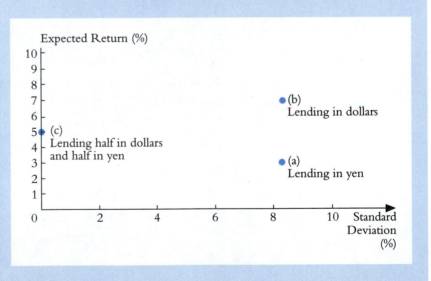

c. *Discussion*. For the Japanese investors the safest policy is lending in yen, thus transferring the currency risk to the borrowers. However, all strategies are efficient as seen in the graph for Question 1. For a firm that must make future payments in dollars, lending in dollars may be safer than lending in yen because the loss or gain due to foreign exchange fluctuations on the lending transaction and on the needed payments in dollars may cancel each other. Indeed, we see that for Sumitomo Marine & Fire Insurance Co., lending half in dollars and half in yen is the safest strategy. It even dominates what is considered the safest strategy in Question 1; namely, lending 100% in yen.

This strategy has implications for any firm involved in exports and imports. Holding foreign currencies may be safer than holding local currency if the firm needs to make future payments in this foreign currency.

SUMMARY

Risk analysis is important for both investors and management. A CFO must understand the risk-return relationship and the concept of risk premium in order to maximize the firm's value. The CFO can apply the same principle of risk reduction by diversification when selecting physical projects.

An asset's profitability is measured by its expected rate of return. Its risk is measured by the standard deviation of the rates of return. However, when an asset is held in a portfolio with other assets, the standard deviation of the rates of return on the individual asset may be a misleading measure of risk. If the asset is negatively correlated with other assets in the portfolio, it may be considered low-risk in a portfolio context even though it has a relatively large standard deviation.

Generally, the larger the number of the assets and the lower the correlations among the assets, the larger the gain from diversification. Investors should diversify across stocks from different, preferably unrelated industries. In constructing a portfolio, investors should select a strategy that minimizes the standard deviation of the portfolio's rate of return for a given expected return. By using this principle, we obtain the $E-\sigma$ frontier, which can be divided into the mean-variance efficient set and a set of inefficient portfolios.

Diversification, however, should not be undertaken at any price. A firm with expertise in one area of business may have no special advantage in other areas. Hence diversification, though reducing risk, may also reduce the expected rate of return. Indeed, George Fisher, who was elected in 1993 to direct Kodak, claims that the firm failed in the past because it "committed huge resources to diversification: drugs, clinical diagnostic machines and batteries. Meanwhile, they neglected huge new opportunities in photography . . ." [Subrata N. Chakravarty, "How an Outsider's View Saved Kodak," *Forbes* (13 January 1997) p. 45]. Diversification has an advantage—reduced risk—but that goal should not be achieved at any price. If the expected rate of return is drastically reduced, it may be better to avoid diversification.

CHAPTER AT A GLANCE

1. For an individual asset:

    a. Expected rate of return: $\bar{R} = \sum_{i=1}^{m} P_i \bar{R}_i$

    b. Variance: $\sigma^2 = \sum_{i=1}^{m} P_i (R_i - \bar{R})^2$

    where P_i = probability of outcome i, R_i = ith return on the asset, m = the number of observations, and $\bar{R}$ = the mean rate of return on the asset.

2. For two–asset portfolios:

    a. Expected rate of return: $\bar{R}_p = w_1 \bar{R}_1 + w_2 \bar{R}_2$
    where w_i (i = 1, 2) is the weight of the ith asset in the portfolio.

    b. Covariance: $\sigma_{1,2} = \sum_{i=1}^{m} P_i (R_{1,i} - \bar{R}_1)(R_{2,i} - \bar{R}_2)$

    where P_i is the probability that the pair $(R_{1,i}, R_{2,i})$ occurs.

    c. Correlation coefficient: $\rho_{i,j} = \sigma_{i,j} / (\sigma_i \sigma_j)$

    d. Variance: $\sigma_p^2 = w_1^2 \sigma_1^2 + w_2^2 \sigma_2^2 + 2 w_1 w_2 \rho_{1,2} \sigma_1 \sigma_2$

3. For n–asset portfolios:

    a. Expected rate of return: $\bar{R}_p = \sum_{i=1}^{n} W_i \bar{R}_i$

    b. Variance: $\sigma_p^2 = \sum_{i=1}^{n} w_i^2 \sigma_i^2 + 2 \sum_{i=1}^{n} \sum_{\substack{j=1 \\ i>j}}^{n} w_i w_j \rho_{ij} \sigma_i \sigma_j$

KEY TERMS

Portfolio	Risk premium	Covariance
Volatility	Variance	Investment strategy
Probability distribution	Standard deviation	Mean-standard deviation (E–σ)
Expected rate of return	Diversification	efficient set
Risk averters	Correlation	E–σ frontier

REVIEW AND PRACTICE

8.1 "The rates of return and the risk of investment portfolios are irrelevant to the firm's financial manager because he or she deals with physical projects, not with stocks." Evaluate this claim. (*Hint*: Review the Corporate Finance in the News article at the beginning of the chapter.)

8.2 "If an investment has more than one possible rate of return, it is considered an uncertain or risky investment." Explain this statement. Give an example of a certain and an uncertain investment.

8.3 The return on Stock A one year from now will be $140 with a probability of ½ or $80 with a probability of ½. The current stock price is $100. The riskless interest rate is 5%. Calculate the risk premium.

8.4 By playing a roulette wheel, you may win $1,000 with a probability of ½ or lose $1,000 with a probability of ½.

   Would you play this roulette wheel? Are you a risk averter?

8.5 "If the covariance $\sigma_{1,2}$ is positive, then the correlation $\rho_{1,2}$ will also be positive." Do you agree? Provide the proof of your answer.

8.6 Suppose you are given the following information regarding the rates of return (in percent) on three assets:

		Rate of Return		
State of the Economy	Probability	Asset A	Asset B	Asset C
Expansion	⅓	5	10	30
Recession	⅓	5	5	15
Normal	⅓	5	15	15

Calculate the expected rate of return and standard deviation for each asset as well as the covariance and correlation coefficient for each possible pair of assets.

8.7 Can a covariance be greater than 1? Can a correlation coefficient be greater than 1? Explain.

8.8 Suppose you invest 30% of your wealth in Asset A, which has a realized rate of return of 40%; 25% of your wealth in Asset B, which has a realized rate of return of −10%; and 45% of your wealth in Asset C, which has a realized rate of return of 15%. What is the realized rate of return on the portfolio?

8.9 Now plan your investment for next year. Repeat Problem 8.8 but instead of *realized* rates of return, you believe that for each asset each of the corresponding returns has a probability of ½ and that there is a probability of ½ of receiving a zero return on each asset. Calculate the expected rate of return on this portfolio.

8.10 "The existence of less than perfect correlation does not really reduce portfolio risk because the risky components in the portfolio remain risky." Evaluate this statement and defend your answer using a port-

folio consisting of equal proportions of two securities, each with a standard deviation of 30%.

8.11 Calculate the variance of a portfolio divided equally among four uncorrelated assets with standard deviations of 10%, 20%, 30%, and 40%, respectively.

8.12 The following are the rates of return (in percent) on Assets A and B:

State of the Economy	Rate of Return (%)	
	Asset A	Asset B
1	−10	10
2	20	17
3	−2	0
4	4	8
5	12	19

a. Calculate the rate of return on a portfolio in State 4 of the economy if $w_A = \frac{1}{5}$ and $w_B = \frac{4}{5}$. How would your answer change if the investment weights were $w_A = \frac{1}{2}$ and $w_B = \frac{1}{2}$?
b. Calculate the portfolio's mean rate of return and variance if $w_A = \frac{1}{2}$ and $w_B = \frac{1}{2}$. Assume each state of the economy has a probability of 1/5 of occurring.
c. Now assume that the probability of State 1 of the economy is 6/10 and that the probability of each of the other four states is 1/10. Calculate the portfolio's mean rate of return and variance for weights $w_A = w_B = \frac{1}{2}$.

8.13 You have two stocks with the following rates of return:

State of the Economy	Rate of Return (%)	
	R_A	R_B
1	10	10
2	−5	−5
3	15	15

The probability of each state of the economy is ⅓.
a. Calculate the correlation between Stock A and Stock B.
b. Calculate the variance of a portfolio composed of $w_A = \frac{1}{2}$ and $w_B = \frac{1}{2}$.

c. Calculate the variance of a portfolio composed of $w_A = \frac{1}{3}$ and $w_B = \frac{2}{3}$. Explain your results.

8.14 Suppose you have three stocks with the following parameters:

$$\sigma_1 = 1; \sigma_2 = 2; \sigma_3 = 3$$

$$\sigma_{1,2} = 0; \sigma_{1,3} = 1; \sigma_{2,3} = 5$$

Your portfolio consists of equal proportions of each of these stocks.
a. Calculate the portfolio variance.
b. How would your results change if all of the covariances were zero?

8.15 What is the E–σ *frontier* and how does it differ from the E–σ *efficient set*?

8.16 Consider the two sets of E–σ frontiers derived by investing in Assets A and B, as depicted below. Which line represents the lower correlation? Why?

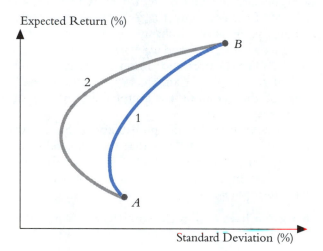

8.17 Suppose $\sigma_A = 30\%$, $\sigma_B = 20\%$, and $\rho_{A,B} = -\frac{3}{4}$. The investment weights are $w_A = 0.30$ and $w_B = 0.70$. What is the portfolio's standard deviation?

8.18 "You don't want more than one company in an industry, and you don't want companies in related industries." Use Equation 8.7 to explain this statement.

8.19 Assume the returns on two securities are perfectly negatively correlated. Derive the investment

weights that will ensure zero portfolio variance. Formalize these investment proportions in terms of the variances of the individual assets. Illustrate your solution for $\sigma_1 = 10\%$ and $\sigma_2 = 20\%$.

8.20 Demonstrate graphically how a reduction in the correlation between two assets, each with a mean rate of return of 10%, and a standard deviation of 10%, decreases the portfolio risk. Start at the point where $\rho_{1,2} = 1$ and reduce $\rho_{1,2}$.

8.21 Suppose you are hired as a consultant for a mutual fund that invests in the stocks of 100 different companies located in Canada. Interestingly, all 100 stock prices are strongly correlated with weather conditions. What would you recommend regarding the number of assets to include in a portfolio?

8.22 The following table lists the rates of return for 10 years on Chevron and Mobil (both energy firms) and on Sears and United States Steel (USX) (unrelated areas of business).

Year	Rate of Return (%)			
	Chevron	**Mobil**	**Sears**	USX
1	74.9	53.7	−7.3	47.8
2	−6.1	−42.3	16.4	30.8
3	−15.8	14.9	75.9	−22.9
4	16.5	22.8	30.1	43.5
5	−0.4	7.4	−8.6	−7.6
6	27.5	19.3	28.3	8.0
7	26.7	37.3	11.2	−4.5
8	−2.2	8.8	−3.7	45.3
9	22.0	21.6	27.1	4.9
10	46.4	38.2	−0.7	25.2

Assume the rates of return corresponding to each year have an equal possibility of 1/10 of reoccurring. Calculate the correlation and portfolio variance when $w_A = w_B = \frac{1}{2}$ for a portfolio consisting of
a. Chevron and Mobil
b. Sears and USX
Explain your results.

8.23 "For every portfolio on the E–σ efficient set, there is another portfolio with an identical standard deviation that is $E-\sigma$ inefficient." Evaluate this statement.

8.24 Suppose we have two securities, A and B. Illustrate graphically the change in the $E-\sigma$ efficient frontier as the correlation coefficient moves from 1 to −1.

8.25 The following table gives the rates of return over 10 years for six major U.S. companies:

Rate of Return (%)

Year	AT&T	Coca-Cola	Dow	Du Pont	GE	GM
1	31.1	12.2	−1.0	−2.5	0.3	−7.0
2	11.8	50.2	10.9	5.9	57.9	57.7
3	14.6	9.9	35.0	44.6	27.1	23.9
4	28.3	20.9	−9.5	3.0	1.3	15.7
5	32.8	36.8	47.2	38.3	31.5	0.3
6	8.7	35.4	41.3	28.0	22.1	3.3
7	15.7	7.1	55.9	14.5	10.9	8.3
8	12.5	21.3	2.8	7.6	6.2	39.5
9	52.3	60.4	26.7	39.4	43.0	9.8
10	−33.4	24.3	−31.0	−3.8	−5.9	−10.8

Assume the historical rates of return are the best estimates of the future rates of return. There is a probability of 1/10 of each year's outcome reoccurring.

a. Calculate the expected rate of return and standard deviation for each security.

b. Rank the securities in ascending order by their standard deviation of returns. Compute the standard deviations for investment portfolios consisting of $n = 2, 3, 4, 5$, and 6, where a portfolio with $n = 2$ refers to the two securities with the two lowest standard deviations, a portfolio with $n = 3$ refers to the three securities with the three lowest standard deviations, and so forth. Assume equal weighting of securities in each portfolio. Discuss your results.

8.26 Visit the Stock Center at Thomson Investor's Network and construct a portfolio of five of the riskiest stocks you would like to invest in. Then, track the stocks for three weeks and compare your portfolio's return to the individual returns of each stock. What can you conclude about diversification? http://www.thomsoninvest.net

8.27 Use the credit card calculator at the following Web site to analyze your credit card situation and risks. Based on what you found, what changes (if any) should you make in your credit card usage? http://www.moneyadvisor.com

---

YOUR TURN: APPLYING THEORY TO PRACTICE
AND THE WINNER IS . . . STOCKS, BY SEVERAL LENGTHS

All investors are asset allocators. The mega-investors like DeWitt Bowman, chief investment officer of California Public Employees' Retirement System, invest to increase their firms' equities. A 5% increase in equity of a $79 billion firm means a substantial amount of money and makes Bowman's investment decision even more difficult when the stock market reaches unexplored heights.

Welcome to the world of asset allocation. Whether we realize it or not, we are all asset allo-

cators—from mega-investors such as Bowman to employees moving money around their 401(k) plans or retirees pulling money out of banks to seek higher returns. Some allocators do it with a pencil and pocket calculator, others with supercomputers. But they're all driving at the same thing: to create a mix of assets that will hit the sweet spot where the investor gets the most return for the least risk.

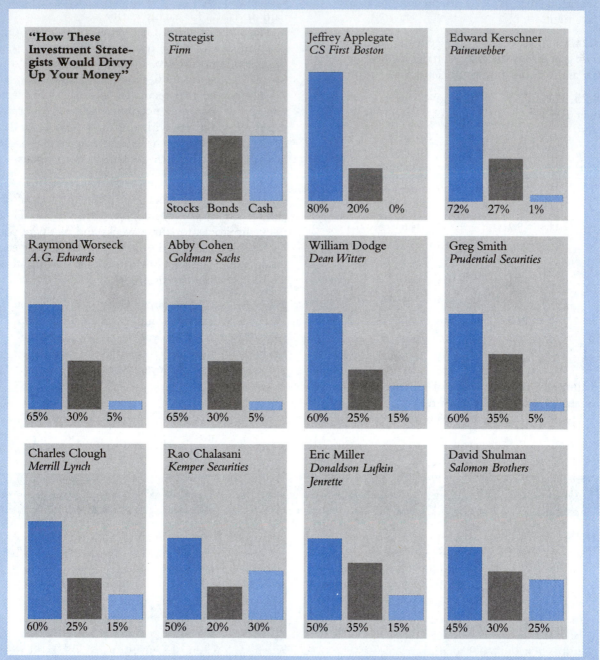

"How These Investment Strategists Would Divvy Up Your Money"

Strategist / Firm	Stocks	Bonds	Cash
Jeffrey Applegate / CS First Boston	80%	20%	0%
Edward Kerschner / Painewebber	72%	27%	1%
Raymond Worseck / A.G. Edwards	65%	30%	5%
Abby Cohen / Goldman Sachs	65%	30%	5%
William Dodge / Dean Witter	60%	25%	15%
Greg Smith / Prudential Securities	60%	35%	5%
Charles Clough / Merrill Lynch	60%	25%	15%
Rao Chalasani / Kemper Securities	50%	20%	30%
Eric Miller / Donaldson Lufkin Jenrette	50%	35%	15%
David Shulman / Salomon Brothers	45%	30%	25%

Source: Jeffrey Laderman, "And the Winner Is . . . Stocks, by Several Lengths," *Business Week*, no 3352 (27 December 1993): 48–49. Reprinted by special permission, © 1993 by the McGraw-Hill Companies, Inc.

Additional Information

Assume the following long-run annual data regarding bonds and stocks:

	Mean Rate of Return (%)	Standard Deviation (%)
Common stocks	12.0	21.1
Long-term corporate bonds	5.2	8.5

The correlation between these returns is 0.19. The return on cash is 3%, is certain, and has zero correlation with the returns on bonds and stocks.

Questions

1. For each of the ten investment strategies suggested in figure accompanying the article, calculate the portfolio's expected rate of return and variance. Plot your results, with the portfolio mean rate of return on the vertical axis and its standard deviation on the horizontal axis. Are there any inefficient strategies among these ten strategies?

2. From the results you obtain in Question 1, is Jeffrey Applegate or David Shulman more optimistic regarding the stock market? Explain your answer.

3. Repeat your calculations in Question 1, but assume the expected rate of return on bonds is only 4%, the rate of return on cash is 2%, and the standard deviations and correlations remain the same. Compare these results to those in Question 1. Given the new expected rate of return estimates, would you recommend that more be invested in stock than the article's investment strategies recommend? Plot the portfolios' expected rates of return and variances of Question 1 and Question 3 on the same graph.

4. Suppose now that the correlation between stocks and bonds is −0.5. All other parameters remain the same. The fund managers are considering shifting all their cash holdings into bonds. Would you support such a move? Plot your results—with and without such a shift—on an expected value-variance diagram. Explain your conclusions.

5. Suppose the mean rate of return on Xerox's stock is 10.64 and its variance is 300. As the portfolio corresponding to the investment strategy of First Boston dominates Xerox's stock by the mean-variance rule, your partner wants to recommend to Xerox's management that it invest in Portfolio 1 (First Boston), rather than in physical projects, to reach a better mean-variance profile. Discuss this recommendation.

So far, we have referred to asset allocation in securities. The next two questions consider asset allocation among projects.

6. In the Corporate Finance in the News article, the CEO of Coca-Cola asserts . . . "the hedge comes from different geographies. Different countries." Suppose Coca-Cola's sales are divided equally among three countries. If a *local* competitor introduces a new soft drink, Coca-Cola will lose 10% of its revenue in the corresponding country. The chance of a local competitor introducing a new soft drink is 10%, and the chances of local competitors introducing new soft drinks in the three countries are independent. That is, new soft drinks will affect Coca-Cola's revenue only in the local country where a new soft drink is introduced. What is the probability distribution of the percentage revenue lost? What would be the distribution of the percentage revenue loss if Coca-Cola's sales were in only one country? In light of your results, discuss the CEO's assertion of hedging risk across countries.

7. Suppose that if GE's sales drop by 20% or more it will go bankrupt. Explain GE's assertion that diversification among different projects "allows us enormous staying power." (See Corporate Finance in the News at the beginning of the chapter.)

CHAPTER 9

RISK AND RETURN

BETA MANIA

Risk management has grown into a multi-billion-dollar industry. Full-page ads stressing the need for this service appear from large measurement organizations. Mutual funds trumpet themselves as low risk—stick with us and you won't be badly hurt in a downturn.

If you knew Beta, you could forget about the fundamentals like working capital, debt load, cash flow and the like. If you bought stocks with low Betas, you would very likely stay high and dry when the deluge came. It is on this volatility argument that most risk measurement rests.

Source: David Dreman, "Beta Mania," *Forbes* 156, no. 8 (October 1995): 138. Reprinted by Permission of FORBES Magazine © Forbes Inc., 1995.

LEARNING OBJECTIVES

After reading this chapter,
you should understand:

1. How to derive the efficient frontier when borrowing and lending are possible.

2. The risk–return relationship for efficient portfolios given by the capital market line.

3. The relevance of the risk–return relationship to a firm's management.

4. The definition of beta as a measure of risk and how to calculate beta.

5. The risk–return relationship of individual assets and portfolios given by the capital asset pricing model.

6. How a merger or acquisition can increase a firm's value.

7. Why management can increase a firm's stock price by diversification among projects.

9.1 INTRODUCTION

As explained in Chapter 1, the firm's goal is to maximize its stockholders' wealth, which is equivalent to maximizing its stock price. The expected profit and the risk on investment determine the stock price. According to the Corporate Finance in the News article, the index of that risk is beta.

Individual investors commonly hold a portfolio of assets rather than just one asset. Similarly, a firm invests in a portfolio of projects rather than in one project. Such diversification reduces risk.

When we consider risk, we soon ask the following questions: What is the appropriate measure of an individual asset's risk when it is held in a portfolio with other assets? What is the relationship between an asset's required rate of return and its risk? And more important, why is it crucial for management to know how investors in the capital market evaluate risk? In particular, what is the relationship between the cost of equity and a stock's (or project's) risk?

In Chapter 8 we measured an asset's risk by the standard deviation of its rate of return. Because it ignores the effect of correlations among the assets in a portfolio, the standard deviation is *not* the appropriate risk measure of an individual asset within that portfolio. Is there a simple yet accurate method that considers all possible correlations in measuring the risk of each individual asset included in a portfolio? Indeed, there is. We show in this chapter that a very useful index called *beta* can measure the risk of each individual asset in a portfolio. Both investors and management often use beta to measure their risk.

In this chapter we discuss the risk–return relationship of individual assets and portfolios. We define beta, demonstrate how to calculate it, and show that it measures an individual asset's contribution to the portfolio's risk.

9.2 RISK AND THE RATE OF RETURN ON EFFICIENT PORTFOLIOS: THE CAPITAL MARKET LINE

First, let's examine the relationship between risk and return of efficient portfolios. By diversifying among all available risky assets, investors obtain the mean-standard deviation frontier such as the one described by the curve *ALA'* in Figure 9-1. As we learned in Chapter 8, segment *LA'* represents the *efficient frontier,* and L is the portfolio with the least possible standard deviation. Accordingly, investors will select their portfolios from segment *LA'*.

But how does an investor choose an optimum portfolio from segment *LA'*? The individual investor's attitude to risk will influence his or her optimum portfolio. An investor who is highly risk averse will choose from the lower part of the efficient frontier (that is, points close to *L*), thereby sacrificing some return in order to decrease risk. In contrast, an investor who is less risk averse will choose from the upper part of the efficient frontier (that is, points close to *A'*).

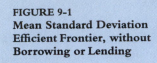

FIGURE 9-1
Mean Standard Deviation Efficient Frontier, without Borrowing or Lending

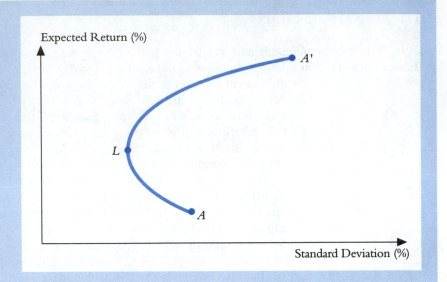

However, since stockholders have diverse preferences, it seems we can say little about their diversification strategies without knowing their preferences. We shall see that this is not the case. It is possible to identify the optimum portfolio of risky assets without knowing the investors' preferences. Assuming that they can borrow or lend at the riskless interest rate, *all investors,* regardless of their attitude toward risk, will choose the same portfolio of risky assets. This is a very important result because it allows us to measure risk and to derive the firm's cost of equity.

9.2.1 The Mean Standard Deviation Efficient Frontier with a Riskless Asset

If they can borrow and lend money at the riskless interest rate, *r*, all investors (regardless of their attitude to risk) will choose the same portfolio of risky assets, Portfolio m, to combine with the riskless asset. (See Figure 9-2.) In this case, the efficient frontier is given by line *ra*, which we also call the **capital market line (CML)**. Although the riskless asset can be combined with any risky asset to create a new portfolio, all investors fare better by mixing the riskless asset with Portfolio m, which is the point on the curve *LA′* that produces the highest possible slope of the straight line rising from point *r* on the vertical axis (see Figure 9.2).

Why will all investors choose to mix Portfolio m with the riskless asset? Because by doing so they maximize their expected rate of return for a given level of risk. Although they can mix the riskless asset with other risky assets, any other diversification strategy will be inferior to diversifying between the riskless asset *r* and Portfolio m. To demonstrate, consider an investor who mixes Portfolio m with the riskless

FIGURE 9-2
**Mean Standard Deviation
Efficient Frontier with
Borrowing and Lending of a
Riskless Asset**

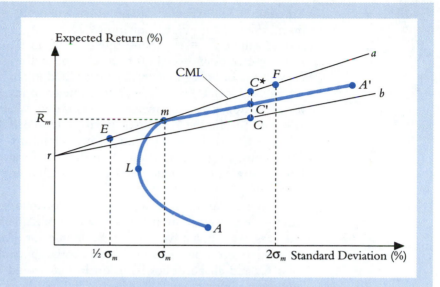

asset to obtain a new portfolio, P. The return on this portfolio is $R_p = w \times r + (1 - w) \times R_m$, with expected rate of return, $\bar{R}_p$, as follows:

$$\bar{R}_p = wr + (1 - w)\bar{R}_m \qquad (9.1)$$

Because r is certain (riskless), Portfolio P's standard deviation will be:[1]

$$\sigma_p = (1 - w)\sigma_m \qquad (9.2)$$

Substituting w from Equation 9.2 into Equation 9.1, we obtain the CML:[2]

$$\bar{R}_p = r + \frac{\bar{R}_m - r}{\sigma_m}\sigma_p \qquad (9.3)$$

Equation 9.3 represents a straight line with an intercept at r and a slope of $(\bar{R}_m - r)/\sigma_m$. What is the economic meaning of this straight line? It represents all possible combinations of Portfolio m and the riskless asset. For example, to attain point r, simply invest $w = 1$ (or 100%) in the riskless asset. Because the rate of return is certain, your portfolio's standard deviation will be zero ($\sigma_p = 0$), and by

1. The rate of return on the portfolio is $wr + (1 - w)R_m$. Since r is certain, it has zero variance, and the portfolio's variance is $(1 - w)^2\sigma_m^2$, with a standard deviation of $(1 - w)\sigma_m$.
2. Note that $1 - w = \sigma_p/\sigma_m$ and that $w = 1 - \sigma_p/\sigma_m$. Substituting w and $(1 - w)$ in Equation 9.1 yields Equation 9.3:

$$\bar{R}_p = (1 - \sigma_p/\sigma_m)r + \bar{R}_m\sigma_p/\sigma_m \qquad \text{or} \qquad \bar{R}_p = r + \frac{\bar{R}_m - r}{\sigma_m}\sigma_p$$

Equation 9.3 its expected rate of return will be $\bar{R}_p = r$. If you invest only in Portfolio m, then $w = 0$ and, by Equation 9.2, $\sigma_p = \sigma_m$. In this case your expected rate of return will be $\bar{R}_p = \bar{R}_m$. (Substitute $\sigma_p = \sigma_m$ in Equation 9.3 to obtain this result.) For any investment weight $0 < w < 1$, you will mix Portfolio m with lending because some of your money will be deposited in the bank yielding the riskless interest rate, r. Finally, you may borrow money and invest it in Portfolio m. If $w = -1$, for every dollar that you invest from your own wealth, you will borrow $1 and invest your $1 plus the $1 that you borrowed in Portfolio m. In this case, by Equation 9.2, $\sigma_p = (1 - (-1)) \times \sigma_m = 2\sigma_m$. This portfolio is represented by point F on the CML. Thus, all points (portfolios) on the CML located to the left of point m reflect lending strategies (or bond purchases), and all points to the right of point m reflect borrowing strategies.

In the above examples we combined Portfolio m with the riskless asset. Why is this the best diversification policy? Can we mix the riskless asset with other risky assets? Yes, we can, but we would have an inferior diversification policy. For instance, the riskless asset could be mixed with another portfolio of risky assets, such as Portfolio C, and all portfolios lying on line rb would be attainable (see Figure 9-2). However, for each portfolio lying on line rb, there would be a better portfolio on the CML (compare Portfolios C and C*). Therefore, all investors will prefer to mix the riskless asset with Portfolio m. Note that this assertion holds even though Portfolio m itself does not dominate Portfolio C. The capital market line CML is the line with the highest attainable slope among those connecting point r with the efficient frontier, with Lmb'. All portfolios located on the CML will be *efficient*. That is, for each portfolio lying on this line, there will be *no other portfolio* with the same expected rate of return and a lower standard deviation or with the same standard deviation and a higher expected rate of return. In contrast, all portfolios located below the CML will be *inefficient*. That is, for any portfolio below the CML, there will be a portfolio located on the CML that dominates it. Regardless of their attitude toward risk, investors will choose an efficient portfolio located on the CML. Because all portfolios on the CML are efficient and all portfolios below the CML are inefficient, the CML describes a linear relationship between the risk and the expected rate of return of *all* and *only* efficient portfolios.

As a result, the availability of a riskless asset helps determine which portfolio of risky assets is optimal without knowing individual investors' attitude to risk. However, we do need to know investors' risk preferences to determine the optimal location of their portfolios on the CML—that is, to determine the optimal lending or borrowing strategy.[3]

The following problem demonstrates alternative investment diversification strategies.

---

3. The investment decision can be separated into two steps: (1) selecting the optimal portfolio of risky assets (Portfolio m) and (2) selecting the optimal borrowing and lending policy. All investors, regardless of their risk preference, will select Portfolio m in Step 1. This property, which is called the *separation theorem* or *separation property*, is helpful in deriving the CAPM, as we'll see in Section 9.5.

PRACTICE BOX

Problem

The expected rate of return on Portfolio m is $\bar{R}_m = 15\%$, and the standard deviation is $\sigma_m = 10\%$. The riskless interest rate is $r = 5\%$.

a. Find the expected rate of return and the standard deviation corresponding to the following alternative investment diversification strategies: $w = 1$, $w = \frac{1}{2}$, $w = 0$, where w is the investment weight in the riskless asset. Are these three points located on the same straight line?
b. Now suppose that for each dollar you invest from your own wealth, you borrow \$2 (i.e., $w = -2$). Find the mean rate of return and the standard deviation for $w = -2$. Is the new portfolio on the CML?

Solution

a. When $w = 1$, we get

$$\bar{R}_{p_1} = r = 5\% \text{ and } \sigma_{p_1} = 0.$$

When $w = \frac{1}{2}$ we get

$$\bar{R}_{p_2} = (\frac{1}{2} \times 5\%) + (\frac{1}{2} \times 15\%) = 10\%$$

$$\sigma_{p_2} = (1 - \frac{1}{2})\sigma_m = \frac{1}{2} \times 10\% = 5\%$$

When $w = 0$, we get

$$\bar{R}_{p_3} = \bar{R}_m = 15\% \text{ and } \sigma_{p_3} = \sigma_m = 10\%$$

The subscripts 1, 2, and 3 denote the portfolios corresponding to the above three investment strategies.

We obtain the following three portfolios:

Diversification Strategy	Expected Rate of Return (%)	Standard Deviation (%)
$w = 1$	5	0
$w = \frac{1}{2}$	10	5
$w = 0$	15	10

The slope of the CML in this example is:

$$\frac{10\% - 5\%}{5\% - 0\%} = \frac{15\% - 10\%}{10\% - 5\%} = 1$$

Because the slope is 1.0 everywhere, the three points must lie on a straight line. The line starts at r, so the CML equation corresponding to this specific example is:

$$\bar{R}_p = 5\% + 1 \times \sigma_p \qquad \textit{(continued)}$$

b. When $w = -2$, you borrow $2 for each $1 invested from your own wealth and invest $3 in Portfolio m. Note that, as required, the sum of all the investment weights is 1 ($-2 + 3 = 1$). Therefore, we get:

$$\overline{R}_p = (-2 \times r) + (3 \times \overline{R}_m) = (-2 \times 5\%) + (3 \times 15\%) = -10\% + 45\% = 35\%$$
$$\sigma_p = 3 \times \sigma_m = 3 \times 10\% = 30\%$$

where $\overline{R}_p$ is the expected rate of return and σ_p is the standard deviation on the portfolio with borrowing. Note that -10% is the interest rate paid on the $2 borrowed.

When $w = -2$, the portfolio's expected rate of return is 35%, and its standard deviation is 30%. Because the slope of the line is 1 and the intercept is at $r = 5\%$ (see Question a., above), this portfolio will be located on the CML: ($35\% = 5\% + 1 \times 30\%$).

9.2.2 The Market Portfolio

Portfolio m, which all investors hold, is called the **market portfolio.** Suppose there are n risky assets and the market value weight of the ith asset is w_i, where $\Sigma\, w_i = 1$. For example, if IBM's market value is 1% of the total value of all available assets, then the w corresponding to IBM is 0.01. The portfolio composed of n assets, weighted according to their market values, is the market portfolio.

We have seen in Section 9.2 that regardless of their preferences, all investors should hold the same portfolio. Because of this, it must be the market portfolio; otherwise, the market will not be in equilibrium. For example, if IBM stock accounts for 1% of the total market value and all investors wish to hold 2% of their assets in IBM stock, there is no equilibrium—investors wish to hold more stock than there is available. The price of IBM stock will rise until the proportion of IBM stock held in investors' portfolios equals the proportion of IBM stock in the market. If investors select stock in the manner described in Section 9.2, then they must hold the market portfolio in equilibrium.

In practice, due to transaction costs and other market imperfections, investors may not hold the market portfolio. Nevertheless, for the analysis in this chapter we assume that individuals do hold the market portfolio.

It is often convenient to use a proxy for the market portfolio that does not include all available assets, such as the Standard & Poor's 500 Index or the Dow Jones Industrial Average. When we provide numerical examples, we will use such a proxy.

9.3 RISK AND THE RATE OF RETURN ON INDIVIDUAL ASSETS

We now turn attention to the relationship between risk and return on individual assets. From material covered in Chapter 8 and Section 9.2 of this chapter, we can make the following four observations:

1. Regardless of a portfolio's size and whether or not it is optimal, the standard deviation of returns will be the relevant measure of portfolio risk.

2. A portfolio composed of only one stock will not be optimal. Generally, the larger the number of assets included in the portfolio, the better the investor fares.

3. An investor should select the optimal portfolio from portfolios located on the capital market line.

4. The risk index of each stock held in a portfolio is *not* measured by its standard deviation because all correlations with the returns on the portfolio's other stocks must be considered.

In this section we show that *beta*, rather than standard deviation, measures the risk of an individual stock in a portfolio composed of a large number of assets.

9.3.1 What Is Beta?

As noted in the chapter introduction, **beta** measures the risk of an individual stock in a portfolio. As a risk index, beta accounts for not only the stock's own standard deviation, but also for all the correlations among other securities available in the market. (You may be saying to yourself at this point, "Please don't do this to me—I finally understand standard deviation as a measure of risk, and I am perfectly happy with it . . . . Why complicate matters?" But bear with us; the benefit from understanding this concept will become apparent.) Beta is calculated using historical rates of return on the individual asset and the market portfolio. It measures the volatility of the asset's rate of return relative to the market portfolio's rate of return. If the volatility of the asset's returns is larger than the market portfolio's volatility, we say the stock is riskier than the market portfolio. Similarly, if the asset's rate of return fluctuates less than the market portfolio's, the stock is considered less risky than the market portfolio.

Connecting Theory to Practice Box 9.1 and Section 9.3.2 explain more precisely how beta is calculated and what it means as a measure of risk.

CONNECTING THEORY TO PRACTICE 9.1

WHAT BETA MEASURES

Commonly associated with measuring volatility of individual stocks, beta tracks how closely a fund follows the ups and downs of the stock market. It's calculated by looking at the month-to-month fluctuation of a fund's total return over a three-year period, compared with similar movements of the S&P 500 stock index. For purposes of comparison, the S&P 500 is assigned a beta of 1.00. A fund with a beta of less than 1.00 is less volatile than the broader market. A figure higher than 1.00 means a fund is more volatile, and thus its risk—and potential reward—is higher.

Source: John Meehan, "How Savvy Fund Investors Tally the Risk," *Business Week*, no. 3126 (October 1989): 118. Reprinted by special permission, ©1989 by The McGraw-Hill Companies, Inc.

MAKING THE CONNECTION

We see that stocks are classified by their beta, where beta measures volatility in the stock price relative to the volatility of some proxy for the market portfolio. Beta is meaningful only if an investor holds a well-diversified portfolio—the market portfolio.

Would you completely eliminate risk if you held the market portfolio? Not really. No matter how well-diversified your portfolio, you cannot completely eliminate risk. It is impossible to avoid volatility caused by macroeconomic factors. For instance, an oil crisis will cause the stock market to take a nose dive; and a peace treaty or a decrease in interest rates will usually cause a rise in the stock market. Diversification cannot eliminate the ups and downs in stock prices due to such factors. You have probably heard about the 1987 stock market crash, in which the overall stock values decreased by more than 20% in one day. No matter how well-diversified a portfolio may have been on October 19, 1987, an investor would not have avoided loss because the entire stock market decreased. Similarly, in a recession the market will decrease; and although investors can diversify, they cannot completely eliminate risk.

Macroeconomic factors such as the trade balance, the budget deficit, changes in interest rates, or wars are sources of market volatility and can affect market rates of return. Market volatility cannot be diversified away because most stocks are affected in the same direction. However, stock prices do not increase or decrease at a uniform rate in response to a given macroeconomic factor, and a stock's beta measures its sensitivity to such unavoidable market fluctuations. Actually, as we shall see, it measures the individual stock's contribution to a portfolio's overall risk. The higher a given stock's contribution to a portfolio's risk, the higher that stock's expected rate of return will have to be. Otherwise, investors will not hold the stock, and its price will fall.

The risk of an individual asset held in a portfolio is measured by the asset's rate of return sensitivity to fluctuations in the market portfolio's rate of return. This is exactly what beta measures. For Stock i, if beta equals 2 ($b_i = 2$), then when the market portfolio's price rises by 1%, the stock's price is expected to increase by 2%. Conversely, if market prices decrease by 1%, the change in Stock i's price is expected to be –2%. If b_i is greater than 1 (as in our example), the stock is considered an **aggressive stock,** which means it is riskier than the market portfolio, because it fluctuates more sharply than the market itself.

Similarly, if b_i is smaller than 1, the stock will fluctuate less than the market and, therefore, is considered relatively safe—a **defensive stock**. Such stock will "defend" the investor from big losses, but it will not provide large gains.

Finally, if $b_i = 1$, the movement of the stock price is expected to be the same as price movements in the market as a whole. Such stock is **neutral stock;** and is located between aggressive and defensive stocks.

Figure 9-3 depicts three lines, called **characteristic lines,** describing the three types of stock in terms of the relationship between their rates of return and the market portfolio's rate of return. The steeper the line, the more sensitive the stock to market fluctuations.[4]

The stocks of technology firms such as Apple Computer and Microsoft are considered aggressive because if the market increases (or decreases) by $x\%$, in most cases, these stocks will increase (or decrease) on average by more than $x\%$. The stocks of utilities such as Florida Gas Corporation or Florida Power and Light are considered defensive because if the market increases by $x\%$, utility firms' stock prices will increase, on average, by less than $x\%$.

In summary, fluctuations in a stock's rate of return may be larger or smaller than the fluctuations in the market portfolio's rate of return. The larger the average fluctuation in an individual stock's rate of return relative to changes in the market portfolio's rate of return, the larger the beta. When an individual stock is held in a portfolio, beta is the risk measure of that stock. The larger the beta, the riskier the stock. We will now see a formal definition of beta and how it is calculated.

FIGURE 9-3
Characteristic Line of Aggressive, Defensive, and Neutral Stocks

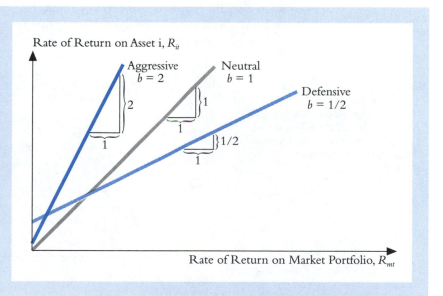

4. The intercept of the characteristic lines with the horizontal axis may vary from one stock to another and can even be negative.

9.3.2 How Is Beta Measured?

The beta of Firm i is defined as follows:

$$b_i = \frac{\sigma_{i,m}}{\sigma_m^2} \tag{9.4}$$

where $\sigma_{i,m}$ is the covariance between the rates of return on Asset i and on the market portfolio, and σ_m^2 is the variance of the market portfolio's rate of return. Equation 9.4 accounts for all correlations of the i-th asset with other assets in the portfolio. Equation 9.3 is the slope of the characteristic line in Figure 9-3, which has the form $R_{it} = a_i + (b_i \times R_{mt}) + e_{it}$, where R_{it} and R_{mt} are the rates of return on Stock i and on the market portfolio at time t respectively; and a_i is the intercept of the line with the vertical axis. The term e_{it} denotes the vertical deviation of observation t from this straight line (See Figure 9-4.) The larger the beta, the steeper the slope and the larger the individual asset's risk. The numerator in Equation 9.4 is $Cov(R_i, R_m)$. Because $R_m = \sum_{j=1}^{n} w_j R_j$ (the weighted average of all rates of return), $\sigma_{i,m}$ can be rewritten as

$$\sigma_{i,m} = Cov\left(R_i, \sum_{j=1}^{n} w_j R_j\right) = w_i \sigma_i^2 + \sum_{\substack{j=1 \\ i \neq j}}^{n} w_j Cov(R_i, R_j)$$

But $Cov(R_i, R_j) = \rho_{ij} \times \sigma_i \times \sigma_j$, so b_i accounts for security i's variance as well as for its correlations with other assets. Note that a_i, the intercept of the line with the vertical

FIGURE 9-4
Regression Line Describing the Linear Relation Between Apple Computer's Stock and the Market Portfolio

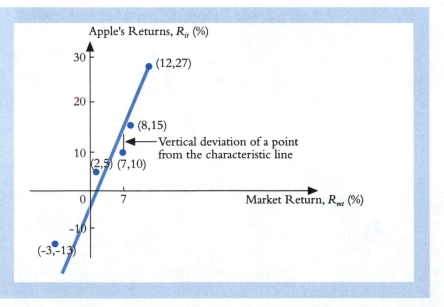

axis, varies among stocks and can be negative. It is equal to $a_i = \bar{R}_i - b_i \bar{R}_m$. It depends on b_i and, therefore, it varies among stocks.

EXAMPLE: CALCULATING BETA FOR APPLE COMPUTER

To measure a stock's risk (beta), we need to know the stock's and market portfolio's *future* or *ex-ante* rates of return. Since this information is almost never available, we use *historical* or *ex-post* rates of return to estimate beta. To be more specific, to calculate beta, we need to know the market portfolio's rates of return. That means that we first need to identify the market portfolio. Because the number of assets that comprise the market portfolio is quite large, we generally use some proxy such as the Standard & Poor's (S&P) 500 Composite Index for the market portfolio.

In the following table, Columns (1) and (2) give the rates of return on Apple Computer (R_{it}) and on the market portfolio (R_{mt}) for five years. The remaining columns—(3), (4), (5), and (6)—are calculated from Columns (1) and (2).

Year I	(1) R_{it} Apple	(2) R_{mt} Market	(3) $(R_{it} - \bar{R}_i)$	(4) $(R_{mt} - \bar{R}_m)$	(5) $(R_{mt} - \bar{R}_m)^2$	(6) = (3)×(4) $(R_{it} - \bar{R}_i) \times (R_{mt} - \bar{R}_m)$
1	−13	−3	−21.8	−8.2	67.24	178.76
2	5	2	−3.8	−3.2	10.24	12.16
3	15	8	6.2	2.8	7.84	17.36
4	27	12	18.2	6.8	46.24	123.76
5	10	7	1.2	1.8	3.24	2.16
Sum	44	26	0	0	134.8	334.2
Mean return	8.8	5.2				
Market variance (σ_m^2)					$\dfrac{134.8}{5} = 26.96$	
Covariance $(\sigma_{i,m})$						334.2/5 = 66.84

We assume that the outcomes corresponding to each year have an equal chance of recurring and that this probability is equal to ⅕. We use this ex-post data as an estimate of ex-ante rates of return. Using Equation 9.4, we get

$$b_i = \frac{\sigma_{i,m}}{\sigma_m^2} = \frac{66.84}{26.96} \cong 2.479$$

where

$$66.84 = \frac{1}{5}\sum_{t=1}^{5}(R_{it} - \bar{R}_i)(R_{mt} - \bar{R}_m) = \sigma_{i,m}$$

and

$$26.96 = \frac{1}{5}\sum_{t=1}^{5}(R_{mt} - \bar{R}_m)^2 = \sigma_m^2.$$

To review the academic literature on risk, visit the Financial Economists Network and look at some of the articles there.
http://www.ssrn.com

With a beta of 2.479, Apple's stock is volatile; its fluctuations are, on average, much larger than the market portfolio's fluctuations.

Does Apple Computer's large beta make any difference to an investor? Does it make any difference to Apple's CFO? It definitely does! The larger the beta, the riskier the stock. Investors will be reluctant to hold Apple's stock unless it provides them with a high mean rate of return to compensate them for the high risk.

9.3.3 Why Is Beta Relevant to the CFO?

Beta conveys information that is crucial to the CFO for four reasons:

1. The higher the stock's beta, the higher the rate of return that stockholders require. To accommodate that rate of return, the CFO must carefully evaluate projects and accept only those with an adequate expected rate of return. Otherwise, investors will sell the stock, its price will fall, and the firm will not achieve its value maximization goal.[5]

2. The firm can affect the beta of its stock. In particular, the risk characteristics of the firm's projects affect the risk characteristics of its cash flows that, in turn, influence the stocks' price fluctuations and the firm's beta. For example, an oil company may reduce its very large beta by acquiring a retail clothing chain or a fast-food chain whose cash flows are more predictable. Similarly, financing an investment mainly by debt, rather than by equity, increases beta.

    We do not advocate that the firm should act to decrease its beta (because the expected return will also decrease). Rather, we advocate that the firm should know the *consequence* of its actions on its beta. If a planned action is expected to change beta, the CFO should check whether the accompanying change in the expected rate of return would be satisfactory. If not, the firm should avoid this action.

3. If a firm holds a given percentage of its assets in securities, it should obtain information on the betas and expected rates of return of these securities to ensure that it selects the desired risk–return investment profile.

4. If it has enough cash on hand and if management believes its stock is undervalued, the firm may decide to repurchase some of its shares.

    How might the CFO conclude that the firm's stock is undervalued? Beta measures the stock's risk, which is related to the stock's required rate of return. The larger the beta, the larger the required rate of return. Suppose, given beta, the required rate of return is 20%. If management believes the stock will earn an average rate of return of 30%, the stock is considered undervalued. Information regarding the stock's beta is crucial for stock buyback decisions.

---

5. In Chapter 10 we show that beta is used to estimate the firm's cost of equity. This cost of equity is then used to calculate the firm's cost of capital that, in turn, determines which projects the firm should accept and which it should reject.

9.3.4 Which Is the Correct Measure of Risk: Standard Deviation or Beta?

We now know that both beta and standard deviation measure risk. Which is better, and how can we decide which to use? The question should really be: When should we use beta, and when should we use the standard deviation?

Because both the standard deviation and beta measure fluctuations in the rate of return, it might be tempting to believe that these two risk indexes produce the same risk ranking. While this is true for efficient portfolios—those located on the CML—it is not the case for inefficient portfolios or for individual stocks. Consider the following data regarding the rates of return of Stock A, Stock B, and the market portfolio for three years:

Year	Rate of Return (%)		
	Stock A	Stock B	Market Portfolio
1	5	5	5
2	10	15	10
3	15	10	15

The expected rate of return of each of these assets is 10%, and the variances are identical for all three assets:

$$\sigma_A^2 = \sigma_B^2 = \sigma_m^2 = \frac{(5 - 10)^2 + (10 - 10)^2 + (15 - 10)^2}{3} = 50/3$$

Hence the standard deviation is 4.08%.

The betas of Stocks A and B are calculated as in the Apple Computer example. Thus:

$$b_A = \frac{[(5 - 10)(5 - 10) + (10 - 10)(10 - 10) + (15 - 10)(15 - 10)]}{50/3}$$

$$= \frac{50/3}{50/3} = 1$$

$$b_B = \frac{[(5 - 10)(5 - 10) + (15 - 10)(10 - 10) + (10 - 10)(15 - 10)]}{50/3}$$

$$= \frac{25/3}{50/3} = \frac{1}{2}$$

This example shows that beta and the standard deviation are not identical risk measures. Stocks A and B have the same standard deviation, but A has a beta of 1 and B has a beta of 0.5. The difference is this: The standard deviation measures the fluctuations of the stocks' rates of return while beta measures these fluctuations *relative* to the market fluctuations. Although Stocks A and B have the same standard deviation, Stock B tends to offset the market portfolio's fluctuations. Holding Stock B along with the market portfolio is, therefore, less risky than holding Stock A with the market portfolio.

Now let's turn to a real-life example: The betas and standard deviations of AT&T and General Electric, based on their monthly rates of return for ten years, are as follows:

	Beta	Standard Deviation
AT&T	0.91	9.52%
General Electric	1.19	6.49%

Which stock is riskier? As you can see, beta and standard deviation rank these two firms' risk differently. So the answer depends on the risk measure we select.

The main question is: Which risk measure is more relevant? It depends. If we want to measure the *market portfolio's* or *any other efficient portfolio's risk, both* the standard deviation and beta will be appropriate. That is, both will produce the same risk ranking.[6] However, if we want to measure an *individual asset's risk, beta* will be the appropriate risk measure. In such cases, the standard deviation of the asset's returns would be misleading. In the preceding example, for instance, Stock B is less risky than Stock A because it has a lower beta. The CFO is interested in the firm's risk (the risk of one asset), not in the efficient portfolio's risk. Therefore, beta, rather than standard deviation, is of interest to the firm.

Let us see why beta measures an individual asset's contribution to the portfolio's risk.

Suppose the investment proportion of Asset i in the market portfolio is w_i and there are n assets. The market portfolio's rate of return is $R_m = \Sigma\, w_i\, R_i$. The market portfolio's beta is $b_m = \text{Cov}(R_m, R_m)/\sigma_m^2 = 1$. Substituting $\Sigma\, w_i\, R_i$ for R_m yields $b_m = \text{Cov}(\Sigma\, w_i\, R_i, R_m)/\sigma_m^2 = \Sigma\, w_i\, \text{Cov}(R_i, R_m)/\sigma_m^2 = \Sigma\, w_i\, b_i = 1$. Accordingly, the beta of the market portfolio, which is composed of n risky assets, is equal to 1, it is the weighted average of the individual assets' betas. Since b_m is the market portfolio's percentage change when it changes by $x\%$, b_m must be equal to 1 (the market portfolio's sensitivity to itself). Thus, $w_i b_i$ is Asset i's percentage contribution to the portfolio's beta. Since investors hold an efficient portfolio and determine the investment proportions w_i, the higher b_i, the riskier the stock. For a given investment weight, w_i, the more it will contribute to the market portfolio's beta.[7]

---

6. The rate of return of a portfolio located on the CML is given by $R_p = wr + (1 - w)\, R_m$ where w is the investment proportion in the riskless asset.

The standard deviation of portfolio R_p is $\sigma_p = (1 - w)\, \sigma_m$ and its beta is

$$b_p = \text{Cov}[wr + (1 - w)R_m, R_m]/\sigma_m^2 = (1 - w)\, \sigma_m^2/\sigma_m^2 = 1 - w$$

When w decreases, both σ_p and b_p increase. If the beta of one efficient portfolio is larger than the beta of another, the same must hold regarding their standard deviations. Therefore, for portfolios located on the CML, both the standard deviation and beta can be used as risk measures.

7. In proving that $b_m = \Sigma\, w_i b_i$, we use the following rules: $\text{Cov}(X + Y, Z) = \text{Cov}(X, Z) + \text{Cov}(Y, Z)$ and $\text{Cov}(aX, Z) = a\text{Cov}(X, Z)$, where a is a constant.

The following problem demonstrates the calculation and comparison of two portfolio stocks.

PRACTICE BOX

Problem

Suppose there are only two stocks in the market—A and B. Let w_A and w_B denote the weights of Stock A and Stock B, respectively, and let b_A and b_B be their respective betas. Assume $w_A = w_B = \frac{1}{2}$, and $b_A = 1.5$.

What is b_B? Which stock contributes more to the market portfolio's beta?

Solution

First note that: $w_A b_A + w_B b_B = 1$.
Therefore, $(\frac{1}{2} \times 1.5) + (\frac{1}{2} \times b_B) = 1$.   So, $b_B = 0.5$.

Stock A's contribution to the portfolio's beta is 0.75 ($w_A b_A = 0.75$). Stock B's contribution is 0.25 ($w_B b_B = 0.25$). Since Stock A contributes more to the market portfolio beta than Stock B, it is considered to be riskier than Stock B, as indicated by their betas.

Table 9-1 provides the betas of eight firms in a recent year. As you can see, Gerber Products is a neutral stock with $b = 1$. All stocks appearing above Gerber Products in the table are aggressive, and all stocks appearing below it are defensive. Prices of the aggressive stocks are likely to be more volatile than the market as a whole, and prices of the defensive stocks are likely to be less volatile. Thus, Micropolis has to accept projects with higher expected rates of return than does Central L.A. Electricity to compensate investors for the risk of its aggressive stock.

TABLE 9-1 Betas of a Sample of Firms		
	Micropolis	1.75
	Hewlett-Packard	1.35
	Ben & Jerry's	1.15
	Gerber Products	1.00
	Heinz	0.95
	Bank of Montreal	0.80
	Centerior Energy	0.60
	Central L.A. Electricity	0.50

Source: *Value Line Investment Survey*, various issues. (Value Line Publishing, New York, N.Y.)

9.4 UNIQUE RISK AND MARKET RISK

The risk of the individual stocks forming the market portfolio can be separated into two components:

1. **Unique risk**, also called **nonsystematic risk** or **diversifiable risk**, is the risk peculiar to the stock under consideration.
2. **Market risk**, also called **systematic risk** or **nondiversifiable risk**, is the risk stemming from general market fluctuations.

The characteristic line (see Figure 9-3) is given by:

$$R_{it} = a_i + b_i R_{mt} + e_{it}$$

where R_{it} and R_{mt} are the rates of return on stock i and on the market portfolio in period t; a_i and b_i are the intercept and slope (beta) of the line, respectively; and e_{it} is the deviation from the line. Historical data are commonly used to estimate this so-called regression line of R_{it} on R_{mt}.

Taking the variance of both sides yields[8]

$$\sigma_i^2 = b_i^2 \sigma_m^2 + s_{e_i}^2$$

we see that the variance of the rate of return on the i-th asset can be decomposed into two components. The first—σ_m^2—depends upon market fluctuations. The other—$s_{e_i}^2$—is specific to the firm and is called *unique risk*. If all points (R_{it}, R_{mt}) are located on the characteristic line, $e_{it} = 0$ in every period and $\sigma_i^2 = b_i^2 \sigma_m^2$—i.e., all risk is systematic. If $b_i = 0$ (a horizontal characteristic line) and $\sigma_i^2 = s_{e_i}^2$ and all risk is nonsystematic.

Unique risk can be eliminated by diversification with other assets. The firm's unique risk reflects deviations over and above what is expected for a given fluctuation in the market portfolio. For example, for a stock whose beta is 0.5, if the market decreases by 10%, then we would expect the firm's stock to decrease by 5%. If the firm's stock actually decreases by 7%, the extra 2% decline in the stock price may be due to firm-specific factors (for example, a reaction to the CFO's resignation). All deviations from the *expected* change in the rate of return on the stock (corresponding to a given beta) are considered unique risk. If a large portfolio is held, the effect of firm-specific events will tend to cancel each other, and we can ignore unique risk. In a large portfolio, beta is the only relevant measure of risk.

Can we also ignore market risk if, for one reason or another, investors hold a portfolio composed of a small number of assets—say, two assets—rather than Portfolio m? *Beta will be irrelevant* for such investors. Instead, the standard deviation of the two-asset portfolio will be a more appropriate risk measure.[9] In such a scenario we would advise the investor to switch to the market portfolio. With a portfolio composed of only a few stocks, nonsystematic fluctuations most likely *will not cancel each other,* and investors will not be compensated for this unique risk.

An investor who cannot switch to the market portfolio should know that he or she is exposed to a risk for which no risk premium is paid. Let us elaborate. Figure 9-5

---

8. The term $2cov(R_{it}, R_{mt}) = 0$ by the way the regression line is constructed.

9. In the extreme case of a one-stock portfolio, the stock's standard deviation, rather than its beta, will be the appropriate risk measure.

demonstrates the relationship between the appropriate risk measure and portfolio size. Consider three groups of stocks:

1.   Group A: All stocks have $b = 1.0$.
2.   Group B: All stocks have $b = 0.5$.
3.   Group C: All stocks have $b = 2.0$.

Assume the market portfolio's standard deviation is $\sigma_m = 10\%$ and each stock's standard deviation is $\sigma = 30\%$. Figure 9-5 provides (on the vertical axis) the portfolio's standard deviation for these three groups. As the number of stocks included in the portfolio increases, the portfolio's standard deviation, σ_p, decreases.[10]

Let's focus first on Part a, corresponding to Group A. Note that if only *one* stock is held in the portfolio, $\sigma_p = 30\%$. When the number of assets included in the portfolio become very large, the portfolio's standard deviation approaches the market portfolio's standard deviation, σ_m.[11] No further reduction in standard deviation is possible because the market portfolio's fluctuations are due to macroeconomic factors, which diversification cannot eliminate. In Group A, since $b = 1.0$ for all stocks, the portfolio's beta is also 1.0. Thus, the portfolio will fluctuate, on average, the same way as the market portfolio. We also see from Figure 9-5 that σ_p approaches σ_m as the number of assets included in the portfolio increases. The shaded area represents the portfolio's diversifiable risk, which can be eliminated by holding a large portfolio.

Part b is similar to Part a except that the beta of each stock in Group B is 0.5. Therefore, σ_p fluctuates at half the market portfolio's rate. Thus, when the number of stocks included in the portfolio becomes very large, $\sigma_p = 0.5 \times \sigma_m = 5\%$. Finally, since Group C includes stocks with $b = 2.0$, σ_p approaches twice σ_m, or 20%.

What can we learn from this figure? First, if you hold a small portfolio (e.g., only one stock), you cannot ignore the unique risk. It will affect your portfolio risk. Second, if you hold a very large portfolio, you can ignore the unique risk, so beta is the appropriate measure of risk for individual assets in the portfolio. The higher the beta, the higher the standard deviation of the portfolio held. (Compare the three parts of Figure 9-5.)

We know that the higher an asset's risk, the higher its expected rate of return. Are investors paid risk premiums on the unique risk? Suppose an investor plans to hold only one asset in a portfolio with a standard deviation of 30%. This investor would love to receive a risk premium to compensate for the relatively large risk. However, no one will pay a large premium on the asset. The expected return on a risky asset is its future expected value divided by its current price. The higher the current price for a given expected future value, the lower the expected return. The more sophisticated investors will be holding a large portfolio, and when that same asset is held in a large portfolio, its risk will be much smaller. Realizing its relatively low risk, more sophisticated investors will bid up the price of the asset, causing its expected rate of return to fall. As a result, an investor planning to hold only one asset will be forced to buy

---

10. If all covariances within each group are identical, the decrease in σ_p is smooth as shown in Figure 9-5. If they are not, we may have some spikes, but the general form of the curve remains the same.

11. The portfolio's beta is $b_p = \Sigma \, w_i b_i$. By assumption, all $b_i = 1$. Therefore, $b_p = 1$. The portfolio rate of return is $R_{pt} = a_p + b_p R_{mt} + e_{it}$ and $\sigma_p^2 = b_p^2 \sigma_m^2 + s_{ei}^2$. If a large number of assets are held, unique risk approaches zero, and $\sigma_p^2 = b_p^2 \sigma_m^2$. In Group A, $b = 1$; hence, $\sigma_p = \sigma_m$. In Group B, $b = 0.5$; hence $\sigma_p = 0.5\sigma_m$. In Group C, $b = 2$; hence, $\sigma_p = 2\sigma_m$.

FIGURE 9-5
The Standard Deviation of the Portfolio Rate of Return on a Portfolio as a Function of the Number of Assets in the Portfolio: Diversifiable Risk

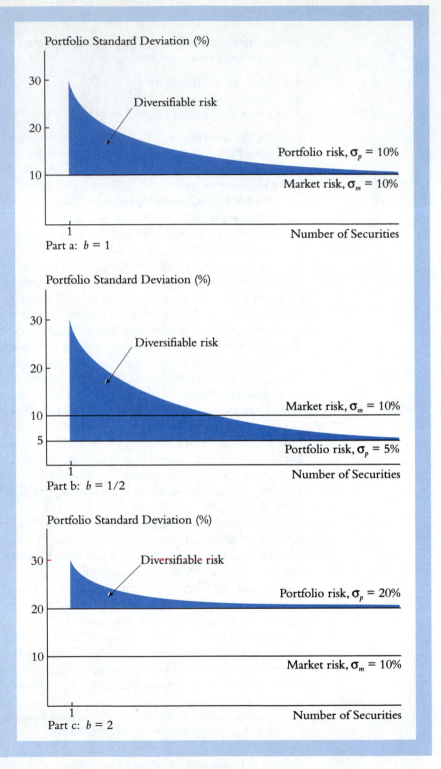

the asset at a relatively high price and will not be compensated for that asset's unique risk component simply because no one will pay a premium for risk that diversification can eliminate. The same is true if one holds a small number of assets in a portfolio. In a large portfolio, on the other hand, since beta measures the individual assets's contribution to portfolio risk, the risk premium will be directly related to beta, not to the unique risk that is completely eliminated.

The question is, then, what is the precise relationship between expected rate of return and beta? We turn to this next.

9.5 THE SECURITY MARKET LINE AND THE CAPITAL ASSET PRICING MODEL

By now you should be convinced that investors should hold a large portfolio and that each individual asset's risk should be measured by its beta. Therefore, the higher the asset's beta, the higher its expected rate of return. But what is the precise relationship between the expected rate of return and beta? To answer that, we return to the capital market line and then turn to a concept called the *security market line* (SML).

9.5.1 The Security Market Line

The CML provides a linear relationship between the expected rate of return and the standard deviation of an efficient portfolio. The SML provides a linear relationship between the expected return and beta for all assets—efficient portfolios, inefficient portfolios, and individual assets. We first derive the SML for efficient portfolios and then show that all other assets must be on the same line.

From our CML discussion in Section 9.2, we know that it is optimal to invest (1) in Portfolio m, (2) in the riskless asset, or (3) to diversify across Portfolio m and the riskless asset. How does the CML help us find an individual asset's risk-return relationship? To see how we can use the CML information, note that the riskless asset's beta is zero and the market portfolio's beta is 1.0. Since we know there are no free lunches in the market, we expect Asset m with the higher risk (as evidenced by a higher beta) to have a higher expected rate of return than the riskless asset (i.e., $\bar{R}_m > r$) as demonstrated in Figure 9-6. Any combination of riskless assets and m will create a new efficient portfolio p_1 with:

Expected rate of return: $\bar{R}_p = wr + (1 - w)\bar{R}_m$

Beta: $b_p = (1 - w)b_m = 1 - w$

where w is the investment proportion in the riskless asset.[12] The subscript p denotes a portfolio composed of Asset m and the riskless asset. For a given investment proportion w, we obtain $(\bar{R}_p, b_p)$, which is a point on the SML.

---

12. Using Equation 9.4, we get:

$$b_p = \text{Cov}(wr + (1 - w)R_m, R_m)/\sigma_m^2$$
$$= [\text{Cov}(wr, R_m) + \text{Cov}((1 - w)R_m, R_m)]/\sigma_m^2$$
$$= [0 + (1 - w)\sigma_m^2]/\sigma_m^2 = 1 - w$$

The first term is zero because r is constant.

FIGURE 9-6
Linear Relationship Between
Expected Rate of Return and
Beta: The Security Market
Line (SML)

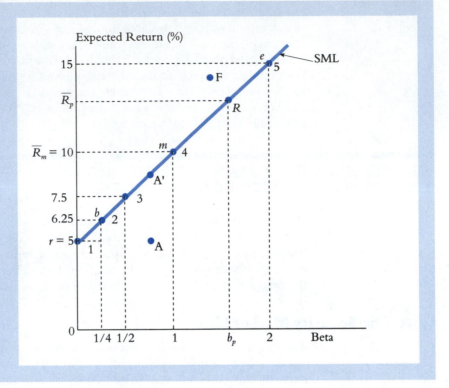

By changing the investment proportion in the riskless asset, investors create new port-folios composed of Asset m and the riskless asset. In the following problem we show that for such combinations the portfolio's beta and its expected return are located on a straight line called the **security market line (SML),** which describes the linear rela-tionship between the assets' mean rates of return and their corresponding betas.

PRACTICE BOX

Problem

Suppose $r = 5\%$, $\overline{R}_m = 10\%$, and $\sigma_m = 20\%$.

a. Calculate the expected rate of return on an efficient portfolio with the fol-lowing investment proportions: $w = 1$, $w = \frac{3}{4}$, $w = \frac{1}{2}$, $w = 0$, and $w = -1$ in the riskless asset. We denote these portfolios as 1, 2, 3, 4, and 5, respectively.

b. Are all of these portfolios located on the same line? What is the slope of this line?

c. What is its intercept with the vertical axis?

Solution

a. The expected rate of return and the betas of the efficient portfolios can be calculated using the formulas $\overline{R}_p = wr + (1 - w)\overline{R}_m$ and $b_p = 1 - w$. These re-

(continued)

sults are shown in the table below. For example, for Portfolio 2 where $w = \frac{3}{4}$, the portfolio's expected rate of return is 6.25% [$\frac{3}{4} \times 5\% + \frac{1}{4} \times 10\% = 6.25\%$], and its beta is $\frac{1}{4}$ {$b_p = 1 - w = 1 - \frac{3}{4} = \frac{1}{4}$}. If w is negative, the investor will borrow money and will invest in Portfolio m his/her own money plus the borrowed money. For example, if $w = -1$, the investor will borrow $1 for each $1 invested from his/her own wealth, and the new portfolio's expected rate of return will be

$$w \times r \qquad + \qquad (1-w)\overline{R}_m \qquad = \qquad \overline{R}_p$$

$$\downarrow \qquad\qquad\qquad \downarrow \qquad\qquad\qquad \downarrow$$

$$-1 \times 5\% \qquad + \qquad (1-(-1)) \times 10\% \qquad = \qquad 15\%$$

$$\downarrow \qquad\qquad\qquad \downarrow \qquad\qquad\qquad \downarrow$$

| Interest payment on borrowed $1 | Expected rate of return on $2 investment in Portfolio m | Total portfolio expected rate of return |

Similarly, we obtain the following expected rates of return and betas for all five portfolios:

Portfolio	Investment Weight in the Riskless Asset	Portfolio Expected Rate of Return, $\overline{R}_p$ (%)	Portfolio Beta ($b_p = 1 - w$)
1	$w = 1$	5	0
2	$w = \frac{3}{4}$	6.25	$\frac{1}{4}$
3	$w = \frac{1}{2}$	7.5	$\frac{1}{2}$
4	$w = 0$	10	1
5	$w = -1$	15	2

  b. Are all these portfolios located on the same line? They are. To see this, we calculate the slope of the line by examining the location of each portfolio relative to point r. For example, for $w = \frac{3}{4}$, we have a slope of

$$\frac{6.25\% - 5\%}{\frac{1}{4} - 0} = \frac{1.25\%}{\frac{1}{4}} = 5\%$$

For Portfolio 5, with $w = -1$, we have a slope of 5 [$(15\% - 5\%)/2 = 5$]. Calculating the slope of the line created by connecting each portfolio with r for all other points reveals that the slope is 5% for all portfolios. Therefore, all portfolios must be located on the same line. As the riskless asset is also on the line (for $w = 1$), we find that all portfolios are located on the same straight line. (See Figure 9-6.)

  c. This line has an intercept of $r = 5\%$.

In the preceding problem we demonstrated the straight line with five portfolios. By changing w, we can create additional portfolios, all sharing the same property. They will all be located on the same straight line, the security market line.

The Risk-Return Ratio

We can draw two main conclusions regarding portfolios located on the SML:

1. The higher the risk, b, the higher the expected rate of return.
2. The slope of the line rising from point r and passing through a portfolio is the ratio of the risk premium, $\overline{R}_p - r$, to the portfolio's beta, b_p. Connecting each portfolio with the point r corresponding to the interest rate on the riskless Asset creates a line with the given slope. We shall see that all risky assets located on the SML have the same ratio of risk premium to beta. This property is used in the derivation of the capital asset pricing model, as we will also see below.

9.5.2 The Capital Asset Pricing Model

On the basis of Harry Markowitz's breakthrough mean-standard deviation diversification analysis (see Chapter 8), Sharpe and Lintner developed the capital asset pricing model (CAPM),[13] one of the most important contributions to financial analysis. The *capital asset pricing model (CAPM)* describes the precise linear equilibrium relationship between the expected rate of return and the beta of individual assets and portfolios.

The following steps provide a simple way to see how the CAPM can be derived:

1. As the CML analysis in Section 9.2 showed, all investors, regardless of their preference, will diversify between the market portfolio and the riskless asset.
2. The slope of the SML for the market portfolio and riskless interest rate, r, is given by $(\overline{R}_m - r)/b_m = (\overline{R}_m - r)/1 = \overline{R}_m - r$, because $b_m = 1$.
3. The intercept of the SML with the vertical axis is given by point r. (See Figure 9-6.)
4. By combining R_m and r, we have an efficient portfolio located on the SML whose expected return is $\overline{R}_p$ at beta b_p. By having the slope and the intercept, we have the formula for a straight line. Therefore, the formula for the SML for efficient portfolios is given by $\overline{R}_p = r + (\overline{R}_m - r) b_p$, where $\overline{R}_p$ is the expected rate of return and b_p is the beta of the portfolio that is located on the SML.

    In the numerical example given in Section 9.5.1, we saw that all combinations of Asset m and riskless Asset r must be located on the SML.

    According to the CAPM, not only is any combination of Assets m and r located on the SML (as shown above), but it is impossible to have assets in the market (individual assets or a portfolio of assets) that are not located on the SML. Thus, $\overline{R}_i = r + (\overline{R}_m - r)b_i$ for *each* Asset i available in the market. This is quite different from the claim in Step 4—and much stronger.
5. The CAPM relies on three assumptions:

---

13. For the capital asset pricing model: William F. Sharpe, "Capital Asset Prices: A Theory of Market Equilibrium," *Journal of Finance* (September 1964): 425–442; and John Lintner, "Security Prices, Risk and Maximal Gains from Diversification," *Journal of Finance* (December 1965): 587–615. For the mean-variance analysis, see Harry M. Markowitz, "Portfolio Selection," *Journal of Finance* (March 1952): 77–91.

a. All investors have homogeneous (identical) expectations regarding assets' rates of returns.
b. Investors can borrow and lend at the same interest rate.
c. There are no transaction costs.

The CAPM's main claim is that when these three assumptions hold, all assets (individual assets as well as portfolios) must have the same risk premium/risk ratio, which is given by

$$(\overline{R}_m - r)/b_m = (\overline{R}_m - r)/1 = \overline{R}_m - r$$

If there are assets with different ratios, investors will sell those with a low ratio and will buy others with a high risk-return ratio. In equilibrium, all assets will have the same risk-return ratio, which will be equal to the SML's slope. Thus, for Asset i we must have

$$\overline{R}_i = r + (\overline{R}_m - r)b_i \qquad (9.5)$$

The relationship given by Equation 9.5 holds not only for efficient portfolios that are created by combinations of Assets m and r, but it also holds for any asset available in the market, regardless of whether it is efficient or inefficient.

Why do we need the three assumptions to derive the CAPM? The derivation relies on the premise that all investors hold the same portfolio of risky assets, Portfolio m. This means that the mean-standard deviation efficient frontier (Figure 9-2) is the same for all investors, and this is possible *only if* they all have homogeneous expectations regarding mean rates of return, variance, and covariance. Finally, to select the same optimum portfolio, m, from the CML, investors have to be able to borrow and lend at the same interest rate. The three assumptions, Steps 1–4, and the process that leads to equilibrium asset prices and to the linear risk-return relationship given in Equation 9.5, are together known as the capital asset pricing model (CAPM).

Why is it impossible for an asset to be located above or below the SML as the CAPM claims? Knowing that beta is the appropriate risk measure, the proof is straightforward. Suppose Asset A is located below the SML. (See Figure 9-6.) First, recall that by mixing m with riskless Asset r, we obtain the straight line $\overline{R}_p = r + (\overline{R}_m - r)b_p$ for efficient portfolios. Thus, by changing the investment proportion of assets m and r, an efficient portfolio A' can be created on the SML with the same beta as Asset A but with a higher expected rate of return (Step 4). Portfolio A' will dominate Asset A because A' has a higher expected rate of return for the same level of risk, expressed by beta. Because Asset A' dominates A, investors will sell Asset A and will buy Portfolio A' with the proceeds.[14] This selling process will cause a decrease in Asset A's price, its expected rate of return will increase, and equilibrium will be restored with Asset A located on the SML. When this occurs, all assets' risk-return ratios will be the same, and the selling of Asset A will stop.

14. Note that Portfolio A' includes some proportion of Portfolio m, and Portfolio m which includes all assets available in the market in some proportion. However, if we eliminate, say, $1 of Asset A and add $1 of Portfolio A', we reduce the amount invested in Asset A. This process will continue as long as Portfolio A' dominates Asset A. As a result of selling Asset A and buying Portfolio A', all asset prices may change, and the line SML given in Figure 9-6 may also change. These changes are expected to continue as long as there are assets that do not lie on the straight line as given in Figure 9-6.

Similarly, according to the CAPM, no asset can be located above the SML. If there is such an asset, like Asset F in Figure 9-6, all investors will prefer to diversify between Asset F and the riskless Asset r, thereby creating a line higher than the SML. In such case no one will hold the market portfolio m. This state would contradict our CML analysis, according to which all investors mix the market portfolio m with the riskless asset. In such a case the prices of assets will change until the market portfolio, when connected with Asset r, creates the largest possible slope.

9.5.3 The Risk Premium and Asset Pricing

Although we do not see asset prices in Equation 9.5, the model is called the capital *asset pricing* model because the expected rate of return, $\bar{R}_i$, determines the asset's price. To see this, suppose $(\bar{R}_m - r) = 0.10$, $r = 0.05$, and beta $= 1$. Suppose also that investors expect the stock price to be \$115 at the end of the year (including all reinvested dividends). What is the current equilibrium stock price as the CAPM implies? As $\bar{R}_i = 0.05 + 0.10 \times 1 = 0.15$ (see Equation 9.5), the current stock price, P_0, must satisfy the condition:

$$\frac{\$115 - P_0}{P_0} = 0.15 \quad \text{or} \quad 1.15 \times P_0 = \$115$$

Therefore, $P_0 = \$100$.

Suppose now that the firm becomes riskier but that the expected stock price at the end of the year is unchanged. To be more specific, suppose beta is now equal to 1.5. Then, by Equation 9.5 we have:

$$\bar{R}_i = 0.05 + (0.10 \times 1.5) = 0.20$$

and the current stock price, P_0, will be

$$\frac{\$115 - P_0}{P_0} = 0.20 \quad \text{or} \quad 1.20 \times P_0 = \$115$$

Therefore, the price will fall to

$$P_0 = \frac{\$115}{1.20} \cong \$95.83$$

CAPM implies Equation 9.5, and Equation 9.5 determines the expected rate of return, $\bar{R}_i$, which, in turn, determines the current stock price, P_0.

We can see from this example that the current stock price (as the CAPM implies) and the risk premium $(\bar{R}_i - r)$ are determined simultaneously. When stock risk increases (beta rises from 1 to 1.5), the risk premium rises from 10% to 15%, and the price falls from \$100 to \$95.83.

9.5.4 The Equal Percentage Contribution Rule of the CAPM

The CML tells us that investors should diversify between the market portfolio and the riskless asset. This leads to the CAPM, which tells us that there is a linear relationship between the expected rate of return, $\bar{R}_i$, and risk, b_i.

As explained above, all investors hold Portfolio m (with the riskless asset). The portfolio risk premium is $\overline{R}_m - r$, and the portfolio risk is $\Sigma\ w_i b_i = 1$ (see Footnote 11). If Asset i has a weight of w_i in the portfolio, it contributes $w_i\ (\overline{R}_i - r)$ to the portfolio risk premium and $w_i b_i$ to the portfolio risk. The CAPM implies that, in equilibrium, each asset contributes the same *percentage* to the portfolio risk premium and to its risk. For instance, if AT&T contributes 1% to the portfolio risk premium, it must also contribute 1% to the portfolio risk. If IBM contributes 5% to the portfolio risk premium, it must also contribute 5% to the portfolio risk. Each asset included in a portfolio works equally hard. If it were otherwise, there would be no equilibrium, which would imply that assets are located below or above the SML in Figure 9-6. Thus, in equilibrium, the CAPM implies the **equal percentage contribution rule** (EPCOR).

To see that the CAPM implies the EPCOR, note that Asset i's *percentage* contribution to the market portfolio risk premium, $\overline{R}_m - r$, is $w_i \times (\overline{R}_i - r)/(\overline{R}_m - r)$.[15] Asset i's percentage contribution to the portfolio risk is $w_i b_i / b_m = w_i b_i$ (because $\Sigma\ w_i b_i = b_m$, $= 1$ where w_i is Asset i's weight in the market portfolio).

When the EPCOR holds, we have

$$w_i(\overline{R}_i - r)/(\overline{R}_m - r)w_i b_i$$

If the CAPM holds, then EPCOR holds (and vice versa). To see this, recall that according to the CAPM, we have

$$\overline{R}_i = r + (\overline{R}_m - r)b_i$$

Subtract r from both sides and then divide both sides by $\overline{R}_m - r$ to obtain:

$$(\overline{R}_i - r)/(\overline{R}_m - r) = b_i$$

Finally, multiply by w_i to obtain the EPCOR:

$$w_i(\overline{R}_i - r)/(\overline{R}_m - r) = w_i b_i$$

If a given asset does not contribute the same *percentage* to the portfolio risk premium and to its risk, we do not have equilibrium, and some assets must be located either below or above the SML.

An intuitive explanation of the EPCOR is: Suppose there are only two stocks, A and B (so that the market portfolio is composed of these two stocks). If Stock A contributes 90% to the portfolio risk premium and only 10% to the portfolio risk, then Stock B must contribute 10% to the risk premium and 90% to the portfolio risk. Is this the best portfolio? No, it isn't, because an investor has an incentive to increase the investment weight in Stock A and to decrease the investment weight in Stock B. Since Stock A has a better return–risk ratio in that its contribution to the expected rate of return is relatively high and its contribution to the risk is relatively low, investors will sell Stock B and buy Stock A. Consequently, the prices and the return–risk ratios of these two assets will change. After the changes, if Stock A contributes, say, 70% to the risk premium and 70% to the portfolio risk, and if Stock B contributes 30% to the risk premium and 30% to the portfolio risk, the EPCOR will hold, the CAPM will hold, and there will be no further incentive to change the portfolio's composition. Both

15. Note that $\Sigma\ w_i(\overline{R}_i - r) = \Sigma\ w_i\overline{R}_i - \Sigma\ w_i r = \overline{R}_m - r$. Then $w_i(\overline{R}_i - r)/(\overline{R}_m - r)$ is the percentage contribution of Asset i to the risk premium.

assets will be located on the SML. If all assets are located on the SML, they will be neither overpriced nor underpriced, and the market will be in equilibrium.

According to the CAPM, investors hold the market portfolio. If so, does it pay for a firm to diversify among projects? Does it pay for two firms to merge? (The value of U.S. mergers grew from about $100 billion in 1991 to more than $600 billion in 1996.) Do such mergers offer investors something they could not otherwise obtain? Consider the following: On December 15, 1996, the largest merger in aviation history was announced. Boeing Corporation merged with McDonnell Douglas. On December 16, Boeing's stock rose from $96.75 per share to $100.75, and McDonnell's rose from $52 to $62.50. How can we explain this favorable market reaction?

Applying Theory to Practice 9.1 illustrates how a merger affects a portfolio's expected rate of return and investors' risk–return profiles.

APPLYING THEORY TO PRACTICE 9.1

COCA-COLA AND PEPSICO: THE GAIN FROM MERGER

Suppose Coca-Cola and PepsiCo are considering a merger. The following table provides summary data on the two firms:

	Coca-Cola	PepsiCo
Beta	1.1	1.2
Net 1994 earnings ($ million, estimated)	2,555	1,920
Total sales ($ million)	16,700	27,300
Advertising costs as percent of sales	8.5%	5.4%
Recent stock price ($)	44	43
Number of shares outstanding (in millions)	1,303	790
Tax rate	35%	35%

Source: *Value Line Investment Survey*, 10th ed. (New York: Value Line Publishing, 1993), pp. 1535, 1537. The figures for 1994 are estimates.

Questions
1. Assume that the market portfolio's expected rate of return is 14% and the riskless interest rate is 4%. What are the expected rates of return on Coca-Cola and PepsiCo stocks?
2. Assuming the CAPM is valid, what would the beta be if the above two firms merged? Would the investor gain from such a merger? Would the merger offer the investor a new risk-return profile that was previously unavailable?
3. Management believes that after the merger and because of reduced competition, advertising costs can be reduced to 4% of total sales of the merged companies without affecting sales. Use the CAPM framework to describe the market reaction to such a merger. Do investors gain?

4. Suppose that, due to transaction costs, some investors with relatively small capital (called "small investors") can hold only one stock along with the riskless asset. Other ("large") investors hold both Coca-Cola and PepsiCo. (For simplicity assume these are the only two stocks available.) Ignoring the cost saving given in Question 3 above, do the investors benefit from the merger? Demonstrate your answer graphically. Consider and discuss market and unique risks.

5. In light of your answers to Questions 2 and 4, should the firm diversify across projects taken from various industries and countries, or should it ignore such diversification because investors can achieve it directly by holding a well-diversified portfolio? (Assume there are no cost savings as in Question 3.)

MAKING THE CONNECTION

1. Using the CAPM and the above information, the expected rates of return are estimated to be:

$$\text{Coca-Cola: } \bar{R} = 4\% + (14\% - 4\%) \times 1.1 = 15\%$$
$$\text{PepsiCo: } \quad \bar{R} = 4\% + (14\% - 4\%) \times 1.2 = 16\%$$

2. The beta of any portfolio is $\Sigma\, w_i\, b_i$. When two firms with market value of equity V_1 and V_2 merge, holding the merged firm's stock is similar to holding a portfolio of the two firms' stocks where the portfolio weights are as follows:

$$w_1 = \frac{V_1}{V_1 + V_2} \quad \text{and} \quad w_2 = \frac{V_2}{V_1 + V_2}$$

The merged firm's beta is given by the weighted average of the individual betas, with the relative market value of the firms' equity serving as weights. First, let us calculate these weights, which we denote by w_1 and w_2 (where $w_1 + w_2 = 1$):

$$\text{Coca-Cola's market value} = \$44 \times 1,303 \text{ million shares}$$
$$= \$57,332 \text{ million}$$

$$\text{PepsiCo's market value} = \$43 \times 790 \text{ million shares}$$
$$= \$33,970 \text{ million}$$

Therefore, $w_1 \cong 0.63$ and $w_2 \cong 0.37$.
The merged firm's beta would be

$$(0.63 \times 1.1) + (0.37 \times 1.2) = 1.137$$

If the CAPM holds, the merged firm's expected rate of return would be

$$\bar{R} = 4\% + (14\% - 4\%) \times 1.137 = 15.37\%$$

Suppose an investor holds a well-diversified portfolio and invests $K of that total portfolio in Coca-Cola and PepsiCo, with $K allocated such that 63% is in Coca-Cola and 37% is in PepsiCo. Let's focus on the investment of this $K, ignoring the investor's other assets. Then, without the merger, the Coca-Cola/PepsiCo "portfolio" has a beta of 1.137. Such a portfolio's mean rate of return would be

$$(0.63 \times 15\%) + (0.37 \times 16\%) = 15.37\%$$

which is exactly the same expected return as would be achieved *after the merger* by investing $K in the merged firm.

Therefore, in a perfect market where investors can diversify directly among all the available stocks, the merger would not be beneficial because the investor can achieve the merged firm's mean rate of return and beta by direct diversification between the two stocks. The merger does not offer a risk-return profile that was unavailable before.

3. The analysis changes when the merger induces cost savings. In our case the total cost of advertising without the merger is

$$(8.5\% \times \$16,700 \text{ million}) + (5.4\% \times \$27,300 \text{ million})$$
$$= \$2,893.7 \text{ million}$$

The merged firm could save on advertising without affecting sales. The total cost of advertising would be

$$4\% \times (\$16,700 \text{ million} + \$27,300 \text{ million}) = \$1,760 \text{ million}$$

Therefore, the savings would be $1,133.7 million.

However, since the advertising costs are tax-deductible, the net savings would be lower, as follows:

$$\text{Net savings} = (1 - \text{tax rate}) \times \text{before-tax savings}$$

$$= (1 - 0.35) \times \$1,133.7 \text{ million} \cong \$736.91 \text{ million}$$

Net earnings would be expected to grow. The expected rate of return on the merged firm's stock would be located above the SML. Demand would increase for the merged firm's stock, its price would increase, and the mean rate of return would decrease until, in equilibrium, the merged firm's stock would once again be located on the SML. The net effect would be an increase in the merged firm's total value. Thus, by the merger, the firm's value increases, and the firm can achieve its goal as stated in Chapters 1 and 2.

Let's go back to the Boeing–McDonnell Douglas merger. There was no reduction in risk because an investor could have held a portfolio of the two firms' stocks before the merger. However, Boeing's CEO, Phil Condit, announced that about $1 billion will be saved through streamlined operations. These cost savings explain the market reaction to this merger.

4. Suppose we have the following figure for Coca-Cola and PepsiCo:

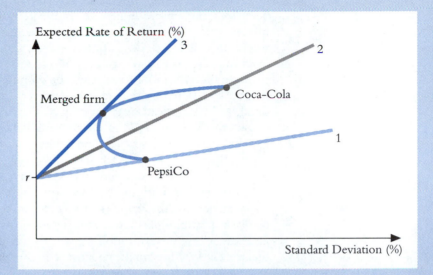

Some investors will hold only Coca-Cola stock and will be on line 2 in the above figure. Assuming the expected rates of return and standard deviation are as in the figure, small investors who hold only one stock will not invest in PepsiCo because line 1 is below line 2. Large investors who hold the market portfolio will diversify between the two stocks. Investors who hold only one stock are exposed to unique risk and are not compensated for it (because large investors determine the market prices). After the merger, those small investors (who can only hold one stock) fare better because they move from line 2 to line 3.

To summarize, if there are no cost savings, mergers do not increase the stock price. When there are cost savings, a merger benefits investors because the stock price increases. If the market is imperfect (due to transaction costs) and not all investors hold the market portfolio, a merger may increase the firms' value even without cost savings.

5. In a perfect market we have seen that a merger of Coca-Cola and PepsiCo does not provide any added value because the merged firm's new risk and return can be achieved directly by holding a portfolio of these two stocks. A similar argument holds regarding diversification across projects. In a perfect market the firm should not attempt to reduce risk by diversifying across projects. By holding a portfolio of stocks of various firms, each specialized in one industry, investors achieve the desired diversification across projects, and the firm has no gain from diversification across projects. Why then does the CEO of General Electric emphasize the importance of diversification across projects and the CEO of Coca-Cola emphasize the importance of

diversification across countries as hedges for risk? Here are two explanations why such diversification is important in practice:

a. Securities markets are imperfect. Transaction costs do exist, and some investors hold portfolios composed of a relatively small number of stocks. In such a case diversification across projects or mergers provide investors a better risk-return portfolio (compare line 3 to line 2 in the graph to Question 4). Investors will be willing to pay a higher price for the stock of a firm with diversified projects (or the stock of a merged firm), and diversification across projects may increase the stock price— a result that does not hold in a perfect market with no transaction costs.

b. Relying on one industry (or one country) may create a risk of bankruptcy. By holding projects taken from different industries, during a temporary bad period in one industry, the cash flow from other industries supports the firm until the bad period ends. This is a long-run survival consideration for the firm's management, in contrast to short-run (say, one year) portfolio decision making by investors. Indeed, this is the main justification for diversification across projects that the CEO of General Electric gives in the Corporate Finance in the News article of Chapter 8.

9.6 A WORD OF CAUTION

The CAPM and beta (in particular) as measures of risk assume that all investors have homogeneous expectations regarding assets' rates of return and that they will choose to invest in the risky Portfolio m, called the market portfolio. The model also assumes no transaction costs and extensive diversification. Finally, the model assumes that investors can borrow and lend at the same riskless interest rate. In practice these assumptions do not hold, and investors may not hold very large portfolios. In such a case neither the security's beta nor its standard deviation will be the correct measure of the risk. Beta takes account of all correlations (including those with assets not held in the portfolio) and the standard deviation ignores all correlations (including those with assets held in the portfolio). Alternative models that consider limited diversification are beyond the scope of this book.[16] In a perfect market with no transaction costs and in the absence of possible bankruptcy, diversification across projects does not create value. In an imperfect market with transaction costs, diversification across projects, as well as mergers, may create value.

Whether the CAPM explains stock-price behavior well and whether beta is the correct measure of risk (and, in particular, whether Equation 9.5 holds) are empirical questions. Numerous empirical studies have tested the CAPM. While most studies show

16. If investors do not hold the same market portfolio, the general capital asset pricing model (GCAPM) substitutes for the CAPM. For more details on the GCAPM see Harry M. Markowitz, "Risk Adjustment," *Journal of Accounting, Auditing and Finance* (Spring 1990): 213–225; Robert C. Merton, "A Simple Model of Capital Market Equilibrium with Incomplete Information," *Journal of Finance* 42 (1987): 483–510; W. F. Sharpe, "Capital Asset Prices With and Without Negative Holdings," *Journal of Finance* 46 (June 1991): 489–510; and H. Levy, "Equilibrium in an Imperfect Market: A Constraint on the Number of Securities in a Portfolio," *American Economic Review* 68 (1978): 643–658.

a positive relationship between average rate of return and risk supporting—at least partially—the CAPM, Fama and French claim that there is no support for beta as a means of risk. Other studies refute the Fama and French conclusions. Thus, the results of the empirical test of the CAPM remain inconclusive. Alternative models that consider the limited diversification—but are beyond the scope of this book—are needed.[17]

In following chapters we show how the CAPM and beta can be used to estimate the cost of equity.

SUMMARY

Investors choose their optimal portfolio from the mean-standard deviation efficient set. Generally, a portfolio's composition will depend on the investor's risk-return preference. However, if investors are able to borrow and lend at the riskless interest rate, all of them will select the same mix of risky assets called the market portfolio. This is portfolio m which maximized the slope of the CML. By changing the investment proportions in the market portfolio and the riskless asset, investors can switch from one efficient portfolio to another, and all these portfolios will be located on the capital market line that represents the linear risk-return relationship of efficient portfolios.

A given portfolio's risk measure is the standard deviation of its rates of return. If investors hold only one asset in the portfolio, that asset's standard deviation is the correct measure of the portfolio's risk. However, it is better to hold a well-diversified portfolio and thereby reduce the portfolio's standard deviation without reducing its expected rate of return. The risk index of an individual asset held in a well-diversified portfolio will be beta, not the standard deviation. However, the portfolio's risk will still be given by the standard deviation of its rates of return.

Beta is defined as the covariance of the individual asset's rate of return and the market portfolio's rate of return divided by the variance of the market portfolio's rate of return. It measures the sensitivity of the individual asset's rate of return to changes in the market portfolio's rate of return.

Any combination of the market portfolio and the riskless asset produces an efficient portfolio whose expected rate of return and beta are located on a straight line called the security market line. However, according to the capital asset pricing model, all other assets (e.g., individual stocks, mutual funds) must also be located on the SML.

A CFO is mainly interested in his or her firm's stock and, therefore, will be interested in the SML rather than the CML. However, the SML results are

The University of Iowa maintains an interesting finance Web site. You can participate in Fidelity's Guess the Dow, their Investment Challenge, and PAWWS' Portfolio Challenge.
http://www.biz.iowa.edu

For a glossary of terms describing financial risks of any type, visit this Web site. You've heard about beta, arbitrage, CAPM, systematic risk, and the efficient frontier; but do you know what deltas, collars, leptokurtosis, swaptions, and inverse floaters are?
http://www.contingencyanalysis.com/glossary.htm#

17. For studies supporting—at least partially—the CAPM, see for example, F. Black, M. C. Jensen, and M. Scholes, "The Capital Asset Pricing Model: Some Empirical Tests" in M. C. Jensen, ed., *Studies in the Theory of Capital Markets* (New York, 1972), pp. 79–121; M. Miller and M. Scholes, "Rates of Return in Relation to Risk: A Reexamination of Some Recent Findings," in Michael C. Jensen, ed., *Studies in the Theory of Capital Markets* (New York, 1972), pp. 47–78. For a recent paper that completely refutes the CAPM, see E. Fama and K. French, "The Cross Section of Expected Stock Returns," *Journal of Finance* 47 (1992): 427–466. After Fama and French, the following papers dispute their results and support the CAPM: Y. Amihud, B. J. Christensen, and H. Mendelson, "Further Evidence on the Risk-Return Relationship" (working paper, Stanford University, 1992); Ravi Jagannathan and Zhenyu Wang, "The CAPM is Alive and Well," *Federal Reserve Bank of Minneapolis*, Staff Report 1965, November 1993; H. Levy, "Risk and Return: An Experimental Analysis," *International Economic Review*, February 1997.

based on the fact that all investors choose a portfolio located on the CML. Therefore, these two lines are related. We need the CML to understand the SML.

Management and financial analysts may use beta as a measure of risk. Using beta and the SML, a CFO can estimate investors' minimum required rate of return from the firm's stock. Projects should be selected to provide earnings that will satisfy this market requirement. Otherwise, investors will sell the stock, its price will decrease, and the firm will not achieve stock-price maximization.

Bankruptcy and bankruptcy costs will be discussed in Chapter 16. However, even if we ignore the possibility of bankruptcy, the firm's stock price may increase after diversification in projects undertaken by the firm. In a perfect market with no transaction costs, the stock price will not increase, and management should not bother with such diversification.

CHAPTER AT A GLANCE

1. The capital market line (CML):

$$\bar{R}_p = r + \frac{\bar{R}_m - r}{\sigma_m}\sigma_p \tag{9.3}$$

holds only for efficient portfolios.

2. The security market line (SML):

$$\bar{R}_i = r + (\bar{R}_m - r)b_i \tag{9.5}$$

holds for individual assets, as well as for portfolios, where $b_i = \sigma_{i,m}/\sigma_m^2$ is the risk index, beta σ_m^2 is the variance of the market portfolio, and $\sigma_{i,m}$ is the covariance between Security i and the market portfolio.

3. The capital asset pricing model (CAPM):
   a. Asserts that the risk-return relationship given by the SML holds for all assets in the market and that in equilibrium, all assets (individual assets and portfolios alike) must be located on the SML.
   b. Assumes homogeneous expectations regarding rates of return, no transaction costs, and borrowing and lending at the same interest rate.

4. Total risk can be decomposed as follows:

$$\sigma_i^2 \qquad = \qquad b_i^2\sigma_m^2 \qquad + \qquad s_{e_i}^2$$

Total risk   =   Market risk   +   Unique risk

Under CAPM, risk premium paid only for market risk.
Unique risk eliminated by diversification, and hence not priced.

KEY TERMS

Capital market line (CML)
Beta
Market portfolio
Aggressive stock
Defensive stock
Neutral stock

Characteristic lines
Unique risk (nonsystematic risk or diversifiable risk)
Market risk (systematic risk or nondiversifiable risk)
Security market line (SML)

Capital asset pricing model (CAPM)
Equal percentage contribution rule (EPCOR)

REVIEW AND PRACTICE

9.1 How does the shape of the mean–standard deviation efficient frontier change if both borrowing and lending can take place at the riskless interest rate? What is this new line called? Is it possible for an inefficient portfolio to be located on this line?

9.2 Describe graphically the mean–standard deviation efficient frontier when there are risky assets and when borrowing is possible at 10% and lending is possible at 5%.

9.3 The rates of return on General Motors' stock and on the market portfolio, R_m, for four years were as follows:

	Rates of Return (%)	
Year	General Motors	R_m
1	−5	10
2	20	15
3	−2	−6
4	30	25

a. Calculate beta.
b. Calculate the market and unique risks.

9.4 $R_m = 10\%$, $\sigma_m = 10\%$, and $r = 5\%$. Draw the CML.

9.5 By the CML we have:

$$\bar{R}_p = r + \frac{(\bar{R}_m - r)}{\sigma_m}\sigma_p$$

which holds for efficient portfolios.
By the SML we have:

$$\bar{R}_i = r + (\bar{R}_m - r)bi$$

which holds for efficient portfolios as well as for inefficient portfolios and individual assets.
Show that these two formulas are equivalent (i.e., that no contradiction arises) for efficient portfolios.

9.6 You have the following information about a stock:
1. It is an aggressive stock.

2. The systematic risk is 0.016.
3. The market portfolio has the following possible rates of return:

Probability	Rate of Return
⅓	0.05
⅓	0.2
⅓	0.1

Calculate the stock's beta.

9.7 You have the following monthly rates of return:

Month	J.C. Penney	Kodak	Exxon	GE	IBM	Market
1	3.65	10.51	6.00	3.49	4.78	6.80
2	−2.07	2.98	1.28	4.05	6.55	1.39
3	0.00	5.95	−1.86	4.05	2.17	2.33
4	−8.63	6.08	−1.90	−0.39	2.71	−2.74
5	−0.79	6.81	7.40	8.35	11.20	8.82
6	6.35	−6.99	−0.26	0.54	−2.08	−0.60
7	−3.05	−9.83	8.36	3.43	−5.11	−0.43
8	−3.15	−18.64	−2.46	−13.44	−7.55	−8.74
9	−3.66	−5.60	−2.00	−11.34	4.42	−4.90
10	13.85	7.37	0.00	−4.59	−0.94	−1.00
11	3.42	10.45	4.68	5.29	8.98	6.31
12	4.41	4.11	2.22	5.73	−0.55	2.81
Mean	0.8608	1.1	1.7883	0.4308	2.0483	0.8375

Source: CRIS tapes.

a. Calculate the betas for these stocks.
b. Plot the characteristic lines. Discuss your results.

9.8 Use the data in Problem 9.7. The monthly riskless interest rate for this period is 0.42%. Calculate the monthly risk premium, $\bar{R}_i - r$, for each security. Explain your results.

9.9 Use the data in Problem 9.7 and the monthly riskless interest rate of 0.42% to draw the security market line and to plot each security on the graph. Assuming the betas are correct, what are the stock's expected rates of return? Locate these points on the SML.

9.10 You have the following information on the ex-post rates of return for CBM Corporation and the market portfolio:

	Rates of Return (%)	
Year	CBM	Market Portfolio
1	10	12
2	0	8
3	−5	4
4	40	15

a. Is the CBM stock aggressive, defensive, or neutral?
b. Is the market portfolio aggressive, defensive, or neutral?
c. Calculate the beta of CBM stock.
d. If the rate of return on the market portfolio in Year 5 is 20%, what would be your best estimate of CBM's rate of return?
e. Calculate the systematic and nonsystematic risk.

9.11 Suppose you hold a portfolio composed of four stocks where $b_1 = 1$, $b_2 = 1.5$, $b_3 = 2$, and $b_4 = 2.4$. You invest equally in these four stocks. What is your portfolio's beta?

9.12 A stock offers an expected rate of return of 15%. Its beta is 2. The market portfolio's expected rate of return is 10%. Assume the cost of equity (which is defined as the expected rate of return by stockholders) can be estimated by the CAPM as follows: $k_i = r + (R − r)\, b_i$. What should the riskless interest rate be for the stock's NPV to be exactly zero?

9.13 Suppose that risky assets are in the market and that investors can borrow and lend at a nominal rate of 6%. We also have inflation, but the future inflation rate, h, is unknown. The real interest rate is $[1.06/(1 + h)] − 1$.
a. Are both lending and borrowing riskless? Explain.
b. How does inflation affect the efficient frontier? The CAPM?
c. It is suggested that borrowing and lending be linked to the cost of living index (a procedure called *indexation*). The interest rate actually paid is $(1 + r)(1 + h) − 1$, where r is a predetermined interest rate, say 2%. Will the CAPM be valid with indexation?

9.14 Suppose the market is composed of two risky assets, A and B, and one riskless asset. You have the following information:

	Mean Rate of Return (%)	Standard Deviation (%)
Asset A	15	8
Asset B	20	10

The correlation between the two assets' rates of return is 0.6, and the riskless interest rate is 5%.
a. Calculate the portfolio's mean rates of return and standard deviations for the following weights:

$$w_A = 0 \qquad w_B = 1$$
$$w_A = 0.1 \qquad w_B = 0.9$$
$$w_A = 0.5 \qquad w_B = 0.5$$
$$w_A = 0.9 \qquad w_B = 0.1$$

b. Suppose you are restricted to choosing only one of the above risky portfolios, but you can borrow and lend at 5%. What portfolio would you choose? Show graphically the capital market line of all the possible mean-standard deviation combinations.
c. How would your results change if the interest rate were 12%?

9.15 Firms A and B merge. Before the merger, the following information is available:

	Mean rate of return (%)	Beta
Firm A	25	2.0
Firm B	10	0.5

The market portfolio's expected rate of return is 15%.
a. Assume the CAPM holds. What is the riskless interest rate?
b. After the merger, the newly merged firm's beta is 1.25. What were the relative sizes of these two firms before the merger? Explain.

9.16 The CFO of AT&T estimates the firm's cost of capital to be 12%. However, in reviewing the AT&T balance sheet, we find that AT&T holds several million dollars of U.S. Treasury bills on which the annual rate of return is 3%.

a. If the future cash flows from the Treasury bill investment are discounted at 12%, will you receive a positive, zero, or negative NPV on the investment in Treasury bills?

b. Can the CAPM be used to justify investment in securities with such a low rate of return? Explain.

9.17 Two shares of stock are purchased for $100 each at the beginning of a year. The expected values of Stock A and Stock B one year from now are $120 and $150, respectively. The market is in equilibrium, and the riskless interest rate is 5%. The market portfolio's mean rate of return is 15%.

a. Calculate the beta of each of these two stocks.

b. Assume that $\bar{R}_i$ given by Equation 9.5 is the cost of equity which is the expected rate of return by stockholders. What is the PV of the investment in each of these two stocks? What is the NPV?

c. Suppose you hold a portfolio composed of one share of each stock. Calculate your portfolio's beta. Calculate this portfolio's PV and NPV.

9.18 "If two portfolios of risky assets are both located on the CML, their rates of return must be perfectly positively correlated." Evaluate this claim.

9.19 Two stocks, A and B, each have a beta equal to 2. However, Stock A's variance is twice as large as Stock B's variance.

a. Which stock is more risky?

b. Which stock provides a higher expected rate of return?

9.20 The beta of Honda Motors stock is 1.5. The firm's CEO is considering whether to purchase Toyland, a toy manufacturer whose beta is 0.8. Toyland is one-fourth the size of Honda. At a stockholders' meeting, some investors raise objections to the purchase of Toyland, claiming that it will decrease Honda's mean rate of return and, therefore, "We will all be worse off." Assume the CAPM holds and the market is in equilibrium.

a. Do you agree with the claim that after the purchase the mean rate of return will fall?

b. Do you agree that Honda's stockholders will be worse off?

c. Given that $\bar{R}_m = 10\%$ and $r = 5\%$, what is Honda Motors's mean rate of return? What is Toyland's? What is the new firm's rate of return after the purchase? What would be the new firm's beta?

9.21 Security i's percentage contribution to the portfolio's risk premium is $w_i (\bar{R}_i - r)/(\bar{R}_m - r)$, and its percentage contribution to the portfolio's beta is $w_i b_i / b_m = w_i b_i$. It is claimed that in CAPM equilibrium the percentage contribution to the portfolio risk premium must be equal to the percentage contribution to the portfolio's beta. Do you agree? Discuss your results and describe the economic factors that would cause these percentage contributions to be equal.

9.22 It is given that $b_1 = 1$, and that $\bar{R}_1 - r = 10\%$ and $\bar{R}_2 = 20\%$ (b_2 is unknown). Stocks 1 and 2 are the only two in the market. Both firms' market value are equal. What must the riskless interest be if we are to have CAPM equilibrium? (*Hint:* Check the percentage contribution to the risk premium and variance.)

9.23 There are three stocks in the market: A, B and C. Stock A contributes 30% to the portfolio's risk premium and 70% to the portfolio's risk. Stock B contributes 20% to the portfolio's risk premium and 20% to the portfolio's risk.

a. What are Stock C's corresponding contributions to the risk premium and risk?

b. Does the equal percentage contribution rule hold?

c. Does the CAPM hold?

d. Plot the three stocks on a diagram. Let the vertical axis denote the contribution to the portfolio's risk premium; and the horizontal axis, the contribution to the portfolio's risk.

e. Suggest economic factors that might act in the market to restore equilibrium.

9.24 Berkshire Hathaway, Inc. is a diversified company with operations primarily in property/casualty insurance, newspaper publication, retail of home furnishings, and fine jewelry.

The following is taken from the president's letter to the stockholders in the firm's 1993 financial statements:

The strategy we've adopted precludes our following standard diversification dogma. Many pundits would therefore say the strategy must be riskier than that employed by more conventional investors. We disagree. We believe that a policy of portfolio concentration may well decrease risk if it raises, as it should, the intensity with which an investor thinks about characteristics before buying into it.[18]

The president believes that "concentration" of the investment may well reduce risk. Discuss his arguments justifying this assertion. Do these arguments contradict the principles of diversification as the CAPM implies? Explain.

9.25 In Applying Theory to Practice 9.1, we discussed the gain from mergers in the CAPM framework. In 1995 AT&T announced a breakup of its business into three firms, each with its own board of directors. AT&T's stock price jumped by 11% within hours of announcement. This translated to a $10 billion increase in market value of the equity. In *Fortune* magazine John Wyatt explained the market reaction:

Much of that lift comes from the altered dynamics of spun-off businesses and their parents. Freed from internal conflicts that often afflict conglomerates, managers in spun-off companies have the authority to get on with the pressing task at hand: making money.[19]

Explain Mr. Wyatt's argument on a spunoff firm's gains in the CAPM framework.

INTERNET QUESTIONS

9.26 Visit the "Mutual Fund Center" at Thomson Investor's Network. Pick out some low-risk funds based first on the standard deviation of returns, and then on beta. Then, look at the 1-, 3-, and 5-year returns on those funds. Next, do the same things with some high-risk funds. Show, using your findings, how return is related to risk.

http://www.thomsoninvest.net

9.27 At Thomson Investor's Network, find the average ROEs of several major industries. Discuss whether these ROEs make sense given the industries' riskiness.

http://www.thomsoninvest.net

---

18. President's letter, Financial Statements of Berkshire Hathaway, Inc., 1993.

19. John Wyatt, "Why Spinoffs Work for Investors," *Fortune* 132, no. 8 (October 1995): 90. Copyright © 1995, Time Inc. All rights reserved.

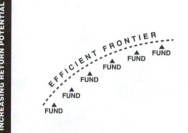

Questions

You are considering whether to invest in one of the funds T. Rowe Price offers or to diversify directly in the stock market. Many securities are available in the market, and you have the *ex-post* mean-standard deviation frontier based on those securities.

1. Suppose you have the ex-post rates of return on T. Rowe Price funds for the last ten years. How would you decide whether the funds' ex-post performance was good or bad? (*Hint:* Use the efficient frontier concept that T. Rowe Price employs.)

2. Suppose you have $50,000 to invest. If you invest directly in stocks, you will diversify equally among five stocks that you select. Assume the ex-post distribution of the rates of return on assets available in the market represents the ex-ante rates of return.

a. What calculation would you conduct in deciding whether to invest directly in the stock market or to invest in a mutual fund?

b. How would your answer change if you invested in five stocks but did not limit yourself to an equally weighted portfolio? Show your analysis graphically.

c. Is the efficient set derived from many stocks relevant for an investor with $50,000 to invest? Discuss.

3. How would your answer to Question 2 change if you had $50 million to invest and you could diversify in many stocks?

4. Suppose all the mutual funds are located on the SML. Would you recommend investing in one of them? Explain. If your answer is yes, which one would you choose?

5. The advertisement claims that investors "have a wide variety of needs, based on different levels of risk tolerance and different time horizons." Two employees, one aged 40 and the other aged 60, would like to invest for their retirement at age 65. They can revise their portfolios every year. Would their efficient frontiers be the same? How would the investment horizon affect their diversification between stocks and bonds?

6. How would you "translate personal attitudes about money into an understanding of risk?" Compose a set of questions to help an investor answer the question: "What kind of investor am I?"

7. In your opinion, are there any factors missing in the T. Rowe Price advertisement regarding the investor characteristics that might significantly influence an investor's asset allocation preference and risk tolerance? (*Hint:* Suppose you have a $1 million beach house!)

8. Suppose you have only $50,000 to invest but can borrow *and* lend at $r = 5\%$.

a. How would this affect your choice between investing in mutual funds or diversifying directly in stocks? Demonstrate your answer graphically.

b. Which framework is better suited to your investment choice, the SML or the CML?

9. Suppose all mutual funds are located on the CML. Would it be beneficial to diversify your investment across all these funds? Explain.

10. Delek is a firm specializing in oil products. Suppose you calculate Delek stock's mean rate of return and price volatility (variance) and find that it is located well to the right of the efficient frontier. It is claimed that this result is due to Delek's CFO having accepted projects with negative NPVs, and some stockholders are calling for the CFO's resignation. Discuss this complaint.

CHAPTER 10

COST OF CAPITAL, RISK, AND THE OPTIMAL CAPITAL BUDGET

LEARNING OBJECTIVES

After reading this chapter you should understand

1. The difference between the firm's cost of capital and a project's cost of capital.

2. How the CAPM can be used to estimate the cost of equity.

3. The weighted average cost of capital and its relationship to the marginal cost of capital.

4. How the firm's optimal capital budget is determined.

5. The relationship between the cost of equity and the price-earnings (P/E) ratio.

CORPORATE FINANCE IN THE NEWS

THE IMPORTANCE OF COST OF CAPITAL

The best CFOs play investor's advocate, weighing whether today's investments will boost tomorrow's share price. One standard they use is the cost of capital. For years companies ignored the price of money by investing in a host of subpar projects. CFOs are restoring the cost of capital as an essential yardstick. "We set the hurdle rate at 18%," says David Devonshire, CFO of Owens-Corning Fiberglas, the building supplies manufacturer. "I'm here to challenge anyone—even the CEO—who gets emotionally attached to a project that doesn't reach our benchmark."

CFOs also act as the company's bridge to its investors, a role that requires sophisticated schmoozing in constant meetings with analysts and wooing of institutional shareholders. Says ITT president and former finance chief Robert Bowman: "The CFO communicates with the people who vote every day on whether value is created."

Source: Shawn Tully, "Super CFOs: They Can't Jump . . . ," *Fortune* 132, no. 10 (November 1995): 160. © 1995, Time Inc. All rights reserved.

In Chapters 1 and 5 we introduced EVA and MVA as two investment criteria that have gained popularity in the U.S. and U.K. These criteria rely heavily on the concept of cost of capital: "EVA takes the year's profit figure . . . and subtracts the notional cost of capital, including equity."[1] Thus, the cost of capital is a key factor in the accept-reject decision for new projects.

1. See Tony Jackson, "A Serving of Added Value," *Financial Times,* 13 January 1997, p. 12. © Financial Times, 1997.

10.1 INTRODUCTION

The Corporate Finance in the News article makes several important points. First, CFOs conduct investment strategy with the objective of "boosting" share prices and stockholders' wealth. Second, the cost of capital is an essential yardstick in the firm's decision whether to accept or reject a project. Third, when the firm ignores the "price of money" (or the cost of capital), investments in subpar projects destroy wealth.

In our discussion of capital budgeting, we assumed either that projects' cash flows were certain and discounted them at the riskless interest rate or, alternatively, that projects' cash flows were uncertain and discounted their *expected* annual cash flows at a discount rate higher than the riskless rate. As we saw in Chapter 5, the *cost of capital* is the minimum required expected return on an investment. When cash flows are certain, the cost of capital represents the interest rate the firm would pay if it had to borrow the money to finance the investment. When cash flows are uncertain, the cost of capital represents the minimum rate of return that stockholders and bondholders require. If a firm's managers do not produce rates of returns that exceed the cost of capital—by executing projects with positive NPVs—they do not create wealth for the firm. Therefore, the cost of capital is a key criterion in project evaluation.

In this chapter we will review various aspects of the cost of capital: how cost of capital is determined; variations of cost of capital in different countries and implications of those variations for a firm's capital expenditures in those countries; relationship among the risk index, beta, and the firm's cost of capital; and finally, whether the firm should use the same cost of capital for all its projects.

10.2 THE COST OF CAPITAL FOR FIRMS AND PROJECTS: A GENERAL RULE FOR PROJECT EVALUATION

As the minimum required expected rate of return from an investment, the cost of capital is the "hurdle rate" that the project must exceed. If its return exceeds this hurdle rate, the investment creates wealth, and the firm should undertake it. Generally, the riskier the project under consideration, the higher its cost of capital because investors require compensation for their risk exposure. Determining the investment risk and the implied cost of capital corresponding to that risk is crucial to the firm.

In determining the cost of capital, management faces two principal issues:

1. *Project risk.* How is a project's cost of capital determined, how does it vary from one project to another, and how is it related to the firm's cost of capital?
2. *Financing risk.* For a given set of projects that the firm undertakes, how do the costs of equity and debt financing affect the firm's cost of capital?

Since the risks of the various projects a firm undertakes are not necessarily the same, the cost of capital used to discount cash flows may vary from one project to another. We must distinguish between the firm's cost of capital and the individual project's cost of capital. These two costs are defined as follows:

- The **firm's cost of capital** (FCC) is the risk-adjusted discount rate at which the firm's total cash flow should be discounted.
- A **project's cost of capital** (PCC) is the risk-adjusted discount rate at which the individual project's cash flow should be discounted.

When they purchase a firm's stock, stockholders buy a portion of the *firm's* total cash flow produced by all of its accepted projects. The FCC will then be the discount rate that stockholders should use to calculate the present value of the firm's expected cash flow. For example, when Boeing acquired McDonnell Douglas for $14 billion in 1996, the FCC of McDonnell Douglas was relevant for discounting the acquired firm's expected cash flow. For mergers and acquisitions, the FCC of the *acquired* firm is relevant because an entire firm is purchased.[2]

When a firm evaluates individual projects, the project discount rate (PCC) may vary from one project to another because risk may vary. To illustrate, suppose a U.S. firm is considering two investments: an electronics project located in South America and a food store chain located in U.S. midwestern states. The electronics firm's PCC is expected to be larger than the food chain store's PCC because of the larger risk associated with the location and the volatility of the industry.

Although the FCC and the PCC are generally different, they are related to each other in this way: Accepting a relatively large, risky project that has a very large PCC may affect the firm's risk and, therefore, its FCC. For example, Walt Disney Co.'s FCC most likely changed following its acquisition of Capital Cities/ABC. In this section we discuss the relationship between the PCC and the FCC and the conditions under which they are equal. For simplicity we first assume a firm that is financed entirely by the sale of stock—that is, an all-equity firm—and focus on the association between the FCC and the PCC of such a firm.[3] In later sections we introduce borrowing—that is, debt financing—and discuss how the costs of debt, equity, and other financing sources determine the FCC. We also discuss methods for estimating the FCC and PCC.

A firm that is fully financed by equity is called an unlevered firm; one that is partially financed by equity and partially by debt is called a levered firm. We begin with an unlevered firm whose market value is V_0 and whose expected annual cash flow is $\overline{X}$. Since the firm has no intention of liquidating its assets, the cash flow is considered a perpetuity.[4] The relationship among the firm's market value, its expected cash flow, and its FCC is given by:[5]

$$V_0 = \frac{\overline{X}}{1 + k} + \frac{\overline{X}}{(1 + k)^2} + \ldots = \frac{\overline{X}}{k}$$

2. Note that for the purchaser, acquiring another firm is similar to accepting a new large project. For the *acquiring firm*, the FCC of the target firm is the PCC of this project. It should not be confused with the FCC of the acquiring firm itself.

3. Alternatively, we can assume a levered firm, but the proportions of bonds and stocks must be fixed. In such cases, we analyze the effect of a newly accepted project on the firm's total value without distinguishing the separate effects on the values of the firm's stocks and bonds.

4. For the definition of a perpetuity, see Chapter 4 Section 4.5. Similar results are obtained if the firm operates for a given number of years and then liquidates its assets or if the expected cash flow, $\overline{X}$, varies over time.

5. If the expected cash flows change over time, they are simply discounted to obtain the firm's value. For simplicity we assume constant expected cash flows. For a discussion of the procedure for discounting growing cash flows, see Chapter 4.

where k is the discount rate of the firm's expected total annual cash flow and therefore, by definition, is the FCC. For a given expected annual cash flow produced by *all* projects ($\bar{X}$) and a given observed value of the firm, V_0, it is easy to solve for FCC. That discount rate is $k = \bar{X}/V_0$. Investors determine the value k in the marketplace. For example, if the firm's cash flow becomes riskier, without a change in the expected value of the cash flow, $\bar{X}$, stockholders will sell their shares, V_0 will decline, and k will increase. The increase in the FCC reflects the additional compensation required in the market for the increase in risk. Thus, we have

$$k = \bar{X}/V_0 = \text{FCC} \tag{10.1}$$

Suppose the firm is now considering a new stock issue to raise $\$I$ to finance a new project. The expected additional annual perpetual cash flow that this project will generate is denoted $\bar{X}_I$. The firm's risk may change due to the new project; if so, the firm's cost of capital will also change. Suppose with the new project the FCC is $k_1 = k + k_I$, where k_I is the *change* in the FCC due to the new project.[6] Should the firm accept the project? What discount rate should the firm use to capitalize the new project's expected cash flow, $\bar{X}_I$? To answer these questions we need to first examine the new project's effect on the firm's value.

By accepting the new project, the firm's value will generally change. The firm's value with the new project will be V_1:

$$V_1 = \frac{\bar{X}_1}{k_1} = \frac{\bar{X} + \bar{X}_I}{k + k_I}$$

where $\bar{X}_1$ is the firm's expected annual cash flow if it accepts the project, $\bar{X}_I$ is the additional expected cash flow of the new project, k_1 is the firm's *new* discount rate or cost of capital, and $\bar{X}$ and k are the corresponding values without the new project.

Economic value is created, and the firm should accept the project only if the NPV is positive—that is, if the firm's value increases by more than the cash outlay on the new investment.

$$\text{NPV} = (V_1 - V_0) - I > 0$$

where $V_1 - V_0$ is the present value of the *incremental* cash flow (or the change in the firm's value), and I is the investment outlay the firm raises to finance the new project.

To illustrate, suppose the firm's value, V_0, is $\$10,000$ and it considers a new investment requiring an initial outlay of $\$1,000$. The firm plans to issue more stock to raise the $\$1,000$ needed. Only if the firm's value is expected to increase by more than $\$1,000$ (if $V_1 > \$11,000$) should the firm accept the project. In that case the project is expected to have a positive NPV because it will add more than the $\$1,000$ investment outlay to the firm's value. This evaluation procedure corresponds to the NPV rule *stated in terms of the firm's value*. Thus, by the NPV rule, the firm should accept the project only if

$$V_1 = \frac{\bar{X} + \bar{X}_I}{k + k_I} > V_0 + I$$

6. If the incremental project has no effect on the FCC, we simply have $k_I = 0$.

Recalling that $\bar{X}_I/I$ is the project's IRR[7] and conducting a few algebraic manipulations, we find that the firm should accept the project only if[8]

$$\text{IRR} > k + k_I + V_0\frac{k_I}{I} \tag{10.2}$$

Equation 10.2 is a formal way of saying what the CFO of Owens-Corning says in Corporate Finance in the News. The right-hand side of the equation is the project's hurdle rate, or cost of capital, while the left-hand side is its profitability. Equation 10.2 implies that economic value is created only if the project's IRR is greater than the hurdle rate on the right-hand side of the equation.[9] We saw in Chapter 6 Section 6.3 that the firm should accept a project only if its IRR is greater than the project's cost of capital. Therefore, the hurdle rate by definition is equal to the PCC. The general rule for project evaluation is that the firm should accept the project only if IRR > PCC.

Accept if $\qquad\qquad \text{IRR} > k + k_I + V_0\frac{k_I}{I} = \text{PCC} \tag{10.2a}$

Equations 10.2 and 10.2a are general in that they do not rely on any assumptions regarding the nature of the risk index. If the project earns more than the PCC, it *creates economic value* and is considered worthwhile. For example, if, given the project's risk, the firm's management requires, say, 18% from a project and its estimated IRR is, say, 20%, the project creates wealth and should be accepted. Finally, note that if the project does not change the firm's risk, $k_I = 0$ and PCC = FCC. Compare Equations 10.1 and 10.2a.

Generally, since a project's future cash flows are uncertain, the IRR is also uncertain. The firm must base its accept-reject decision only on *expectations* of project return, and the cost of capital it uses to evaluate projects will be the minimum required expected rate of return. To simplify our presentation in this chapter, we will refer to the cost of capital as the minimum required rate of return, keeping in mind that if cash flows are uncertain, the cost of capital is the minimum required expected rate of return. We demonstrate how PCC is calculated in the following problem.

7. For a perpetuity we have

$$I = \frac{\bar{X}_I}{1 + R} + \frac{\bar{X}_I}{(1 + R)^2} + \ldots = \frac{\bar{X}_I}{R}$$

Thus, the IRR is

$$R = \frac{\bar{X}_I}{I}$$

8. Cross-multiply to find that the firm should accept the project only if

$$\bar{X} + \bar{X}_I > V_0 k + V_0 k_I + Ik + Ik_I$$

But $V_0 = \bar{X}/k$, and, therefore, $\bar{X} = V_0 k$. We can subtract this term from both sides of the equation. After dividing all remaining terms by I, we find that the project has a positive NPV and should be accepted only if

$$\bar{X}_I/I > k + k_I + V_0 k_I/I$$

when $\bar{X}_I/I$ is the project's IRR.

9. In this chapter and for simplicity only, we assume conventional projects because nonconventional projects may have no IRR or multiple IRRs. Because projects are also assumed not to be mutually exclusive, the IRR rule can be safely used. If these assumptions do not hold, the discussion will be in terms of NPV rather than IRR; this will affect the presentation but not the results.

PRACTICE BOX

Problem

Suppose Metals Corporation's expected annual cash flow (perpetuity) is $10,000 and its market value is $100,000. Thus, by Equation 10.1, the FCC is $k = 10\%$.

The firm is considering a new project requiring an outlay of $10,000. The new project involves a plant located in another country and, therefore, is exposed to relatively high risk. The CFO estimates that the new discount rate of the firm's cash flows will increase by 1%. Thus, the new FCC will be 11%.

a.   What is the new project's minimum required rate of return (PCC)?

b.   Suppose the expected annual incremental cash flow due to the new project (a perpetuity) is $3,000. Should Metals accept the project?

Solution

a.   Denoting the expected additional cash flow by $\bar{X}_I$, we find that economic value is created only if

$$V_1 = \frac{\bar{X} + \bar{X}_I}{k_1} = \frac{\$10,000 + \bar{X}_I}{0.11} > \cdot V_0 + I = \$100,000 + \$10,000$$

$$= \$110,000$$

Therefore, economic value is created only if the firm's average earnings on the new project are at least

$$\bar{X}_I > (\$110,000 \times 0.11) - \$10,000 = \$2,100$$

The additional investment is $10,000, so the minimum required rate of return from the new project (PCC) is

$$\text{PCC} = \frac{\$2,100}{\$10,000} = 0.21 \text{ or } 21\%$$

The same result is obtained by using Equation 10.2a directly and substituting 0.1 for k, 0.01 for k_I, $10,000 for I, and $10,000 for V_0. We determine that the project's cost of capital is

$$\text{PCC} = k + k_I + V_0 \frac{k_I}{I}$$

$$= 0.1 + 0.01 + \$100,000 \frac{0.01}{\$10,000}$$

$$= 0.21 \text{ or } 21\%$$

b.   With $\bar{X}_I = \$3,000$ and PCC $= 0.21$, we obtain

$$\text{NPV} = \frac{\$3,000}{0.21} - \$10,000 \cong \$14,285.71 - \$10,000 = \$4,285.71$$

Since the NPV is positive, Metals should accept the project. This is not surprising because the project's IRR is 30% ($3,000/$10,000) and the PCC is only 21%.

The PCC is usually different from the FCC, and usually also varies from one project to another. Is the incremental project's PCC usually larger than k, which is the firm's FCC before it accepts or rejects the project? Not necessarily. The PCC can be smaller if the project's risk is relatively small. For instance, suppose a firm in the electronics industry (which is very risky) decides to acquire a food store chain (which is less risky), or General Motors decides to invest in short-term government bonds (which are riskless). In such cases the incremental project's risk will probably be smaller than the risk of the firms' existing projects. Therefore, k_I will be negative, which will lower the FCC.

In the rest of the book we use the terms *cost of capital, hurdle rate, minimum required rate of return, risk-adjusted discount rate,* and, simply, *discount rate* interchangeably. Always bear in mind that each project has its unique cost of capital that depends on the risk of its cash flows. Similarly, each firm has a unique cost of capital that depends on the risk of its total cash flows.

Finally, we should stress that estimating an existing firm's FCC is much easier than estimating a new project's PCC. The FCC can be based on the firm's actual cash flows and on the volatility of these cash flows. We can use beta to measure the firm's risk. Because estimating risk is more difficult for a new project, the FCC is commonly used as a benchmark and then some percentage is added or subtracted to obtain the PCC. However, such an adjustment is subjective and will depend on a project's estimated risk. Even so, the firm's management should use the principles expressed in Equation 10.2 in making such subjective PCC estimates.

In Applying Theory to Practice 10.1, Intel decided on an additional risk premium of $k_I = 2\%$. Actually, Intel's management faced the problem of determining the project's risk and estimating the required change in the firm's discount rate. There are several ways to analyze a project's risk, all of which are based on its cash flow characteristics. In the next section we show how the CAPM can be used to estimate the cost of capital for both the firm and for individual projects.

APPLYING THEORY TO PRACTICE 10.1

INTEL'S INVESTMENT ABROAD: COUNTRY RISK

In 1992 Intel Corporation was ranked first among the top ten computer chip makers in the world, after climbing from eighth in 1982. Intel is a growing company with revenues of $11.5 billion in 1994, $16.2 billion in 1995, and $20.9 billion in 1996.

Intel's management knows that to stay at the top, aggressive investments are needed. In 1993 the firm announced a plan to invest $1.5 billion in Israel, a country with a plentiful supply of skilled workers. Israel is also an attractive investment proposition due to government incentives aimed at stimulating the economy. Intel will receive a grant amounting to 38% of the investment.

Investing abroad is riskier than investing in the United States due to *country risk* (the possibility of war, different regulations, etc.) and *foreign exchange risk* (fluctuations in the foreign currency relative to the domestic one—in this case, the U.S. dollar). Given the size of the required investment and the Israeli grant, Intel's CFO decides to increase the risk premium of the project to $k_I = 2\%$.

Additional information:

1. Intel's average cash flow (excluding the new project) divided by V_0 (the current market value in 1993) was estimated to be $\bar{X}/V_0 = 15\%$.
2. Intel's market value at the time the decision was made was $V_0 = \$10$ billion.

QUESTIONS

1. What is the minimum required rate of return (the PCC) on the investment in Israel? (Assume a perpetuity and ignore taxes.)

2. What minimum expected cash flow $\bar{X}_I$ is required for Intel to accept the new project?

MAKING THE CONNECTION

In analyzing Intel's new investment, we must first calculate the project's discount rate, PCC. Remember: Although the total project cost is $1.5 billion, Intel will receive a government grant and will actually invest less than this amount. Since it receives a 38% grant, Intel's investment in Israel will be $930 million (0.62 × $1,500 million).

1. What is the PCC of the new investment in Israel? Using Equation 10.2, we obtain the following:

$$\text{PCC} = k + k_I + \frac{V_0}{I}k_I$$

$$= 15\% + 2\% + \frac{\$10 \text{ billion}}{\$0.93 \text{ billion}} \times 2\%$$

$$= 15\% + 2\% + (10.753 \times 2\%)$$

$$\cong 38.51\%$$

2. The minimum required expected cash flow of the new project to be accepted is $\bar{X}_I$ given by

$$\text{IRR} = \frac{\bar{X}_I}{I} = \frac{\bar{X}_I}{\$930 \text{ million}} = 0.3851 \text{ or } 38.51\%$$

The minimum required expected annual cash flow from the new project is $\bar{X}_I = \$930$ million × 0.3851 = $358.143 million. The new project would have to earn on average about $360 million a year to be profitable and to create wealth.

Remarks
In September 1995 Israel's Minister of Finance announced that the grant to Intel had been approved. Intel accepted the project a month later. By 1997, construction was under way and the plant was expected to be operational in 1998.

10.3 USING BETA TO ESTIMATE THE COST OF CAPITAL: AN ALL-EQUITY FIRM

One difficult problem that a CFO faces is estimating the cost of capital. The CFO can use intuition or rules of thumb. However, even if she uses intuition, it is a good idea to use a formal model as a benchmark. Then the CFO can use subjective beliefs, intuition, and experience to complement the estimate the formal model gives. A convenient formal model for estimating the cost of capital is the *capital asset pricing model (CAPM)*. To simplify the explanation of how to use the CAPM to estimate the cost of capital, we assume an all-equity firm. The firm's cost of capital is the minimum rate of return that the firm's investors require. Since an all-equity firm has no bondholders, the FCC is the minimum rate of return that stockholders require.

In Chapter 9 we saw that, in equilibrium, an asset's expected rate of return is related to its risk (beta) as follows:

$$\bar{R}_i = r + (\bar{R}_m - r)b_i$$

The CAPM tells us that the stockholders' minimum expected rate of return required from Stock i is $\bar{R}_i$ where b_i is Stock i's beta, $\bar{R}_m$ is the market portfolio's expected rate of return, and r is the riskless interest rate. The larger the risk, b_i, the larger the stock's required expected rate of return, $\bar{R}_i$.

Since $\bar{R}_i$ is the stockholders' minimum required rate of return, it can be used as the firm's cost of equity. Because we assumed (for the time being) an all-equity firm, $\bar{R}_i$ will be the firm's cost of capital, FCC. Denoting as before the cost of capital by k and the firm's beta by b, we obtain an estimate of the firm's cost of capital from the following equation:

$$k = r + (\bar{R}_m - r)b \qquad (10.3)$$

Because b is the firm's beta, the value of k given by Equation 10.3 is the FCC, not the PCC. However, if the incremental project has the same risk as the firm's existing projects, then PCC = FCC, and k can be used to discount the project's and the firm's expected cash flows. If the NPV discounted at k is positive, the project will be worthwhile. To illustrate, consider a one-year investment whose initial outlay is $100,000 and whose cash flow expected at the end of the year is $120,000. The project's expected rate of return is $\bar{R} = 20\%$. If the cost of capital given by Equation 10.3 is 15%, the firm should accept the project because $\bar{R} > k$. Indeed, the firm should accept the project because its NPV is positive ($\$120,000/1.15 - \$100,000 \cong \$4,347.83$).

Equation 10.3 can also be used for project evaluation when the FCC and PCC differ. However, in that case, the project's beta, rather than the firm's beta, is the proper input to Equation 10.3. If the new project's risk is larger than the average risk of the firm's existing projects, its beta will be larger than the firm's beta without the new project. In such cases we use a higher discount rate to discount the project's average cash flows.

10.3.1 The Effect of a New Project on the FCC: Copper Corporation's Expansion

We learned in Applying Theory to Practice 10.1 that the firm needs to know both its cost of capital and the project's cost of capital. We show in the following example how the firm can use the CAPM to estimate these two values and how they are related.

Assume Copper Corporation's beta is 1.2, $\bar{R}_m = 12\%$, and $r = 4\%$. Using Equation 10.3, we find that the firm's cost of capital will be:

$$k_{FCC} = 4\% + (12\% - 4\%) \times 1.2$$

$$= 4\% + (8\% \times 1.2)$$

$$= 4\% + 9.6\%$$

$$= 13.6\%$$

Suppose Copper Corporation is considering a new project whose beta is 2. Obviously, this project will increase the firm's risk, but by how much? To answer that question, we need to do some calculations, beginning with the new project's PCC. Employing the CAPM, where k_{PCC} is the new project's minimum required rate of return, we get the following:

$$k_{PCC} = 4\% + (12\% - 4\%) \times 2$$

$$= 20\%$$

Suppose that the project under consideration is conventional and independent of all other projects, then if the project's IRR is greater than k_{PCC}, the NPV will be positive, and Copper should accept the project.

Because it is different from existing projects' risk, the new project's risk affects the firm's risk. With this project, the firm's stock will have a beta that is larger than the original value of 1.2. How much larger depends on the size of the new project relative to the firm's existing value. The firm's beta *with* the new project will be the *weighted* average of its beta *without* the new project and the project's beta. The relative size of the firm and the size of the project outlay will determine the weightings used in calculating the new beta. Suppose, for example, that Copper Corporation's value is $100 million and that its new project involves acquiring a firm of similar size. We would assign a weight of ½ to each beta, because the firm's value and the project's value (each $100 million) are each half of the total investment. The firm's new beta after the acquisition would be the weighted average of the firm's original beta and the project's beta:[10]

$$b_{after} = (\tfrac{1}{2} \times 1.2) + (\tfrac{1}{2} \times 2) = 1.6$$

The firm's cost of capital after the new investment is accepted will be

$$k_{after} = 4\% + (12\% - 4\%) \times 1.6 = 16.8\%$$

Thus, 16.8% is the expected rate of return on the firm's stock after acquiring the new firm.[11]

Figure 10-1 illustrates the evaluation of new projects using the CAPM. The horizontal axis measures the project's beta and the firm's beta; the vertical axis, the project's expected rate of return (given by its IRR). For simplicity we assume conventional projects that are not mutually exclusive, and the firm can base its investment decision on the IRR. The *SML* line in the figure is the *security market line*, which depicts the

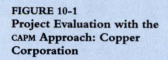

FIGURE 10-1
Project Evaluation with the CAPM Approach: Copper Corporation

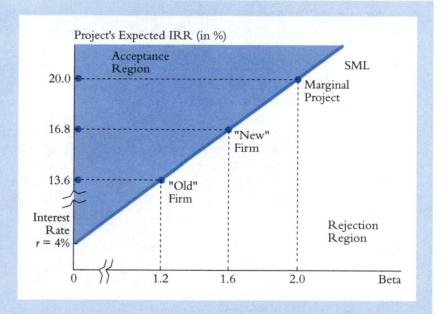

10. Note that the beta of a portfolio with a rate of return of $w_1R_1 + w_2R_2$ is just $w_1b_1 + w_2b_2$ where R_1 and R_2 are uncertain rates of return, w_1 and w_2 are the weights, and b_1 and b_2 are the betas of R_1 and R_2, respectively (see Chapter 9).
11. For another way to look at this, suppose the firm's value before the project is accepted is $100 million and the outlay for the new project is $100 million. Because the firm's expected rate of return is 13.6% on the old investment and 20% on the new investment, the expected cash flow on the total investment will be $33.6 million ($13.6 million + $20 million = $33.6 million). The expected rate of return on the total investment will be 16.8% ($33.6 million/$200 million = 0.168 or 16.8%), which is consistent with the FCC figure given above.

minimum required rate of return for a given level of risk. In other words, all points on the SML provide the minimum required IRR for a given beta. If the project's expected rate of return is higher than this minimum, then the firm should accept the project.

For Copper Corporation the costs of capital of the "old" firm (before the project is accepted), the "new" firm (after the project is accepted), and the project itself (the "marginal project") are located on the SML. Because CAPM estimates the new project's minimum *required* rate of return of 20% and if the project's expected IRR is 20%, the NPV will be zero and the firm will be indifferent between accepting or rejecting the new project. According to the CAPM, a firm should accept projects whose IRRs are located *above* the SML because their IRR is higher than the corresponding PCC (and, therefore, their NPV will be positive). The firm should reject all projects located *below* the SML because their NPV will be negative. Because all projects located exactly on the SML have zero NPV, Copper Corporation will be indifferent between accepting and rejecting such projects.

The following problem demonstrates how another firm considers an investment.

PRACTICE BOX

Problem

Strong Steel, an all-equity firm, is considering a new project with a perpetual cash flow. The initial outlay is $100,000, and the project's beta is 3. The estimate of the market portfolio's expected rate of return, $\overline{R}_m$, is 14%, and the riskless interest rate, r, is 3.5%.

a.   What is the project's minimum required rate of return?
b.   Suppose the project's expected annual cash flow is $40,000. Should Strong Steel accept the project? What is the project's IRR?
c.   Suppose Strong Steel's value before taking the project is $1 million and its beta is 2. The firm finances the project by selling stock and distributes the NPV of the new project as cash dividends. What is Strong Steel's beta with the new project?

Solution

a.   Applying the CAPM, the project's minimum required rate of return is

$$k = 3.5\% + (14\% - 3.5\%) \times 3 = 35\%$$

The PCC is 35%.

b.   With a perpetual expected annual cash flow of $40,000, we have the following:

$$\text{NPV} = \frac{\$40,000}{0.35} - \$100,000 \cong \$14,285.71$$

The NPV is positive, and Strong Steel should accept the project.

This result is not surprising because this project's IRR is 40%, given by the value R that solves the equation for a perpetuity: *(continued)*

$$\$100,000 = \frac{\$40,000}{1 + R} + \frac{\$40,000}{(1 + R)^2} + \ldots = \frac{\$40,000}{R}$$

$R = 40\%$, and because this is larger than the minimum required rate of return of 35%, the project's NPV is positive.

c. Because the NPV is distributed to stockholders, Strong Steel's value if it accepts the project is $1,100,000. With the new project Strong Steel's beta is the weighted average:

$$\left(\frac{\$100,000}{\$1,100,000} \times 3\right) + \left(\frac{\$1,000,000}{\$1,100,000} \times 2\right) \cong 2.09$$

In concluding our discussion of a new project's effect on the firm's cost of capital, we need to clarify a limitation the CAPM imposes. To calculate the cost of capital using the CAPM, we need to know the values of r, $\bar{R}_m$, and b. The riskless interest rate, r, poses no problem since the interest rate on short-term U.S. Treasury bills is generally used. A good estimate of $\bar{R}_m$, the market portfolio's expected rate of return, is the historical average rate of return on an index of stocks such as the S&P 500 Index.

Finally, we need estimates of beta for both the firm and the project. To measure the firm's beta, historic rates of return are commonly used, and these estimates are published in the financial media. Estimating the project's beta is the only difficult task. Because the project under consideration generally has no record of prices or rates of return, it is difficult to estimate its beta. In such cases the firm's management will have to make a subjective estimate. However, when one firm acquires another firm whose shares *are* listed in the stock market, which occurred in some of the large mergers and acquisitions in the 1980s and 1990s, rates of return and, therefore, betas are available. This makes the application of the CAPM easier.

For example, when Boeing merged with McDonnell Douglas in December, 1996, it could estimate McDonnell's beta by using historical data. Using market prices for the previous five years, one could calculate Boeing's beta as 0.51 and Mc-Donnell Douglas's as 0.23. Boeing's market value before the merger was about $33 billion whereas McDonnell Douglas's was about $13 billion. Therefore the beta for the combined firm was

$$b_{combined} = \frac{\$33 \text{ billion}}{\$13 \text{ billion} + \$33 \text{ billion}} \times 0.51 + \frac{\$13 \text{ billion}}{\$13 \text{ billion} + \$33 \text{ billion}} \times 0.23$$

$$\cong 0.431$$

Because the average monthly rate of return on the market for these five years was about 1.1% and the monthly yield on Treasury bills was about 0.3%, we can estimate the monthly cost of equity of the combined firm as

$$k_{combined} = 0.3\% + (1.1\% - 0.3\%) \times 0.431 \cong 0.64\%$$

which gives a yearly cost of capital of

$$k_{yearly} = (1.0064)^{12} - 1 \cong 7.96\%$$

10.3.2 The CAPM as a Specific Case of a General Rule for Measuring the Cost of Capital

In this section, we've presented two formulas for measuring the project's cost of capital. According to the right-hand side of Equation 10.2a, the PCC for an all-equity firm is

$$\text{PCC} = k + k_I + V_0\frac{k_I}{I}$$

According to Equation 10.3, the project's cost of capital (for an all-equity firm) as implied by the CAPM is

$$\text{PCC} = r + (\overline{R}_m - r)b$$

where b is the beta of the project under consideration.

The fact that there are two formulas raises several questions. Do they yield the same results? How are they different? Which is better? In fact, both methods do yield the same results. The difference between the two is that the CAPM formula represents a specific case of the general formula. If management can estimate k_I, the general formula is better because it does not rely on the CAPM assumptions. However when estimating k_I is difficult, the CAPM provides a formula for such an estimation; this is particularly useful when one firm acquires another whose beta is known. The CAPM, rather than replacing the general formula, complements it by suggesting a way to estimate k_I, as demonstrated in the following problem.

PRACTICE BOX

Problem

Suppose Gerber Products' beta is 1.5, $\overline{R}_m = 10\%$, $r = 3\%$, and the firm's value, V_0, is $100 billion. Gerber is considering acquiring Food Lion, whose beta is 0.8. The investment outlay is $50 billion. Assume Gerber's value after the acquisition would be $150 billion.

a. Calculate Gerber's beta if it undertakes the project.
b. What is the PCC estimated by using the CAPM? What is the PCC given by the general formula (Equation 10.2) using the CAPM estimate for k_I?

Solution

a. We first calculate the new project's effect on Gerber's FCC. Before undertaking the new project, Gerber's FCC is as follows:

$$\text{FCC} = r + (\overline{R}_m - r)b_{\text{before}} = 3\% + (10\% - 3\%) \times 1.5 = 13.5\%$$

Gerber's beta after the acquisition is the weighted average of the two betas:

$$b_{\text{after}} = \left(\frac{\$100 \text{ billion}}{\$150 \text{ billion}} \times 1.5\right) + \left(\frac{\$50 \text{ billion}}{\$150 \text{ billion}} \times 0.8\right)$$

$$= (\tfrac{2}{3} \times 1.5) + (\tfrac{1}{3} \times 0.8) \cong 1.2667 \qquad \textit{(continued)}$$

Using the CAPM, we find Gerber's cost of capital after the acquisition is as follows:

$$FCC_{after} - 3\% + (10\% - 3\%) \times 1.2667 = 11.8669\%$$

The new investment would cause a decrease in the FCC from 13.5% to 11.8669%, and a change in the cost of capital, $k_I = -1.6331\%$.

b. We turn now to the calculating the PCC by two methods. Using the CAPM:

$$PCC = 3\% + (10\% - 3\%) \times 0.8 = 8.60\%$$

Using general formula (10.2a), where $k_I = -1.6331\%$ (as estimated by the CAPM):

$$PCC = 13.5\% - 1.6331\% + \frac{\$100 \text{ billion}}{\$50 \text{ billion}} \times (-1.6331\%) \cong 8.60\%$$

We see that the two methods yield consistent results: a PCC of 8.60%.

From the discussion and examples we can conclude that Equation 10.2 is the more general formula and is always valid. The CAPM is a specific case of this general formula and provides a formula for estimating the crucial value of k_I. Using the CAPM is easy when one firm acquires another because this new acquisition's beta is generally known. When the new project's beta cannot be estimated using market data, the CAPM is more difficult to use.

Management may sometimes doubt the validity of the estimate of k_I obtained by the CAPM. The firm may then use its preferred method for estimating the new project's effect on the firm's risk. Alternatively, the firm may decide to use the CAPM as a benchmark but may adjust it, say, by adding 1% to the k_I estimate as a margin of error. We illustrate this procedure in the following problem.

PRACTICE BOX

Problem

Let us return to the previous problem, but this time suppose Gerber Products' management adds a 1% confidence margin to the CAPM's estimate of the change in the cost of capital, k_I. What is the new project's minimum required rate of return?

Solution

Previously we saw that, by the CAPM, Gerber's cost of capital decreases by −1.6331%. Now we add the 1% confidence margin to k_I to obtain the following:

$$-1.6331\% + 1\% = -0.6331\%$$

We can use this confidence margin with Equation 10.2 to obtain the project's cost of capital:

$$PCC = 13.5\% - 0.6331\% + \frac{\$100 \text{ billion}}{\$50 \text{ billion}} \times (-0.6331\%) \cong 11.6\%$$

(continued)

If Gerber is likely to earn 11.6% or more on Food Lion, the firm should accept the investment. Otherwise, Gerber should reject it.

Thus far we have assumed an all–equity firm. We turn now to the more realistic case of firms financed by both equity *and* debt to see how the various financing sources affect the FCC. We will later extend the result to include financing by preferred stock.

10.4 WEIGHTED AVERAGE COST OF CAPITAL: DEBT AND EQUITY FINANCING

Thus far we have assumed an all-equity firm and have focused on project risk. In this section we broaden our assumptions about the firm's sources of capital to analyze the costs of debt and equity and their effects on the FCC. The uncertainty of the project's cash flows and the way the firm finances its projects affect the uncertainty of cash flows to stockholders. Now we assume all projects have identical risk, so $k_I = 0$, which allows us to focus on how various financing policies affect the cost of capital. Specifically, we assume PCC = FCC for all projects and discuss the effect of financing methods on the cost of capital.

Earlier we saw that the cost of equity is equal to the FCC for an all-equity firm. Now that we are introducing debt financing, also called *financial leverage*, this relationship no longer holds, and we must distinguish between the cost of equity, k_e, and the FCC, denoted by k. We will first assume a world without corporate taxes before we discuss the cost of capital in the more realistic world with taxes.

10.4.1 Without Taxes

A firm usually finances its operations by some mix of debt and equity. For the time being, assume the firm finances all projects by a fixed financing mix of the firm's choosing. We want to determine two things: What is the firm's cost of capital? How do the specific costs of debt and equity affect its cost of capital? We demonstrate below (and prove in Appendix 10A) that the firm's cost of capital is a *weighted average* of the specific costs of debt and equity, where the weights are the proportions of debt and equity in the firm's financing. In this section we analyze the various costs and their relationship to the weighted average cost of capital.[12] The first step in this analysis is to define the specific costs of debt and equity.

COST OF DEBT

The **cost of debt**, denoted by k_d, is the interest rate the firm pays when it issues debt. For example, if the firm borrows $1,000 and pays annual interest of $50, the cost of debt is 5%.

---

12. For now, we ignore flotation costs. These will be discussed in detail in Chapter 14.

What is relevant in calculating the cost of debt is the *current* interest rate at which the firm can issue new debt.

COST OF EQUITY

The **cost of equity**, denoted by k_e, is the minimum expected rate of return that the firm's stockholders require. The cost of equity can be measured by two methods:

1. By using the CAPM formula with beta calculated from the rates of return on the stock and on the market portfolio, as explained in Chapter 9.
2. By the expected rate of return to stockholders implied by the market. If the firm's equity market value is $\$E_L$ and if the firm issues debt of $\$B$ on which it pays interest of $\$rB$, where r is the interest rate, the expected rate of return to the stockholders is $k_e = (\bar{X} - rB)/E_L$, where $\bar{X}$ is the firm's expected annual cash flow.[13]

Each method requires a different estimate: an estimate of beta in Method 1 and an estimate of $\bar{X}$ in Method 2.[14]

THE WEIGHTED AVERAGE COST OF CAPITAL

The **weighted average cost of capital (WACC)** is just what its name implies: the average of the costs of the firm's debt and equity weighted by their proportions in the firm's capital structure. It is calculated as:

$$\text{WACC} = w_e k_e + w_d k_d \tag{10.4}$$

where k_e is the cost of equity, k_d is the cost of debt, and w_e and w_d are the proportions of the debt and equity financing.

We claim that the WACC should be used as the discount rate for project evaluation. In this section, we have assumed that all projects have the same risk. Therefore, the claim is equivalent to saying that the WACC is equal to the project's cost of capital as well as to the firm's cost of capital (FCC). From this point on we will use the term *WACC*, which is more familiar in finance.

Using the WACC as a hurdle rate guarantees the creation of wealth. Any project that has a positive NPV when its cash flows are discounted at the WACC will create wealth, and any project with a negative NPV will destroy wealth. To demonstrate that the WACC is the appropriate discount rate to use in project evaluation, we show that if a project's NPV discounted at the WACC is positive, it generates enough expected cash flows to pay the costs of debt and of equity with some (expected) cash flow left over. Therefore, any project whose NPV when discounted at the WACC is positive creates wealth.

Suppose that Leedo Corporation's cost of debt, k_d, is 5%, and its cost of equity, k_e, is 25%. The firm is financed 40% by debt and 60% by equity. Therefore:

$$\text{WACC} = 5\% \times (0.40) + 25\% \times (0.60) = 2\% + 15\% = 17\%$$

13. The cost of equity can also be inferred using dividend models, which will be discussed in detail in Chapter 13. This method relies on an estimate of the growth rate of the firm's dividends.
14. Note that, by the CAPM, we have $k_e = \bar{R}_i = r + (\bar{R}_m - r)b$ and by definition (2) we have $k_e = \bar{R}_i = (\bar{X} - rB)/E_L$. In one method we need to estimate b; in the other, $\bar{X}$. If the firm's risk increases, b will increase, and the stock price and E_L will decrease. Thus, both methods will detect an increase in the cost of equity and are consistent with one another.

Furthermore, suppose Leedo considers a project whose initial investment is $10 million. For simplicity assume it is a one-year project and the expected cash flow at the end of the year is $12 million. The project's IRR is 20% and its WACC is 17%. We show below that because IRR > WACC the project should be accepted. The WACC is the cutoff rate that should be employed.

The project's NPV, using 17% as the cost of capital, is as follows:

$$\text{NPV} = \frac{\$12 \text{ million}}{1.17} - \$10 \text{ million} \cong \$0.256 \text{ million}$$

If we can show that the project creates $0.256 million of new wealth, we can confirm that a WACC of 17% is the appropriate discount rate. Table 10-1 summarizes the cash flows involved. Employing the 40% debt and 60% equity financing policy, Leedo borrows $4 million for one year. It promises to return to the bondholders $4.2 million ($4 million × (1.05) = $4.2 million) one year from now. Leedo also issues $6 million of equity. To understand the cost of the equity, we'll assume something quite unlikely: that Leedo liquidates itself after a year, returning to the stockholders their initial investment plus at least the 25% minimum required rate of return—namely, $7.5 million ($6 million × 1.25 = $7.5 million).

Table 10-1 demonstrates that Leedo's *net* cash flow at time $t = 0$ is zero because the firm finances the $10 million needed for the project by $6 million new equity and $4 million new debt. Leedo expects to receive $12 million from the project at $t = 1$ and is expected to pay a minimum of $7.5 million to its stockholders and $4.2 million to its bondholders. The project's expected cash flow is sufficient to repay the stockholders and the bondholders their initial investment as well as their required costs (25% and 4%, respectively). Moreover, an excess positive cash flow of $0.3 million is left at the end of the year ($t = 1$), which belongs to the shareholders.

Because the $0.3 million positive cash flow is received at the end of the year, the profit's PV is

$$\frac{\$0.3 \text{ million}}{1 + \text{WACC}} = \frac{\$0.3 \text{ million}}{1.17} \cong \$0.256 \text{ million}$$

where 17% is the WACC.[15]

TABLE 10-1		$t = 0$	$t = 1$
Net Cash Flow from Projects, Stockholders, and Bondholders (in $ million)	(1) Project's cash flows	−10	12
	(2) Firm–stockholders' cash flow	6	−6 × (1.25) = −7.5
	(3) Firm–bondholders' cash flow	4	−4 × (1.05) = −4.2
	(4) = (1) + (2) + (3)		
	Net cash flow to the firm	0	0.3

15. Another way, which directly shows that the wealth increases by $0.256 million at $t = 0$, is as follows: The firm raises $$I$ such that it will pay the stockholders and the bondholders at $t = 1$ all of the $12 million the project creates. We have: $0.6 \times I \times (1.25) + 0.4 \times I \times (1.04) = \$12$ million, where $(0.6 \times I)$ is raised by equity and $(0.4 \times I)$ by debt. The net cash flow at $t = 1$ is zero. However, at $t = 0$ the firm raises the following amount:

$$I = \frac{\$12 \text{ million}}{0.6 \times 1.25 + 0.4 \times 1.04} \cong \$10.256 \text{ million}$$

Because the project's cash outlay is only $10 million, it creates a wealth of $0.256 million.

By recording the direct cash flows involved with this investment, we confirm that $0.256 million of wealth is created—which is exactly the result determined by a direct NPV calculation—with WACC serving as the discount rate. Similar calculations can show that if its IRR is less than 17%, the project destroys wealth because the future cash flow is not sufficient to pay the expected costs. Therefore, we conclude that the WACC is the right figure to use as a discount rate in project evaluation.

AN INTUITIVE JUSTIFICATION OF THE WACC

The cost of debt is generally lower than the cost of equity. The question, then, is why doesn't a firm increase its proportion of debt financing and, thereby, reduce the WACC? As the debt proportion increases, the stockholders' risk will increase because the firm will have to commit to larger future repayments of debt. That is, k_e will increase as the firm becomes riskier, and the WACC may also increase in spite of using debt whose cost is lower. The firm should seek the debt–equity mix that minimizes the WACC. In this chapter we merely assume that such a financing mix exists; in Chapters 15 and 16 we analyze the factors that determine the best financing mix.

Although the firm may have a long-run optimal debt-equity ratio, it does not necessarily finance all projects with this mix. For example, although the firm's optimal mix might be 30% debt and 70% equity, it may have some projects entirely financed by debt, just as it may have some entirely financed by equity. This deviation from the optimal financing mix is due to transaction costs. Issuing securities every year would be expensive, so the firm may decide to space its issues. Also, when the interest rate is relatively high, the firm may decide to issue stock and then wait for the interest rate to decline before issuing bonds. Nevertheless, even if a project is fully financed by debt (which has a lower cost than equity), the firm still should use the WACC, not the cost of debt, as a discount rate.

To illustrate this point, suppose a firm decides to fully finance Project A by debt. The cost of debt is 5%, the WACC is 15%, and the project's IRR is 10%. If discounted at the cost of debt, Project A would be accepted because IRR = 10%, which is greater than the 5% cost of debt. Suppose that after one month the firm considers project B, whose IRR is 14%. To restore the long-run debt-equity ratio, the firm decides to finance this project by equity. If discounted at the cost of equity, Project B would be rejected because k_e = 15% > IRR = 14%. That is, the firm would accept a project whose IRR is 10% but reject a project whose IRR is 14%.

To avoid this absurdity, the firm should discount all projects at the same WACC regardless of the source of financing of the project under consideration. In that way each project "enjoys" the lower cost of debt. Discounting all projects by the WACC, the firm avoids an arbitrary decision based solely on how it finances a project. Therefore, in the rest of the book we ignore the particular mix at which a project is financed. The long-run optimal debt-equity mix will always be used in calculating the cost of capital.

10.4.2 With Taxes

We used the pretax analysis in the preceding section to introduce the concept of WACC. In reality, though, taxes do exist, and *only the after-tax cost of capital is relevant.*

From this point on all costs are after-tax costs, although we do not change our notation: The after-tax cost of equity will be denoted by k_e; the cost of debt, by k_d.

The after-tax cost of equity is the required rate of return *after corporate taxes are paid*. Using the CAPM to estimate the cost of equity is automatically done on an after-tax basis because rates of return in the market, which are used to calculate beta, also reflect the firm's after-tax profit.[16] Here we demonstrate the after-tax cost of equity using Method 2 of the cost of equity (see Section 10.4) because it shows more explicitly how taxation affects the cost of equity. Using Method 2, the cost of equity is the after-tax expected rate of return to the equity holders:

$$k_e = \frac{(1 - T)(\overline{X} - rB)}{E_L}$$

where T is the average corporate tax rate (assumed constant), $(1 - T)(\overline{X} - rB)$ is the stockholders' after-tax expected cash flow, and E_L is the market value of the levered firm's equity.

The bondholders' minimum required rate of return is r, yet the firm's after-tax cost of debt is lower—$(1 - T)r$—because interest is tax-deductible. In effect, the firm pays the bondholders only a portion of r; and the Internal Revenue Service (IRS), so to speak, pays the rest. To demonstrate this point, suppose an all-equity firm's before-tax earnings are $100 million. With $T = 35\%$, the corporate tax payment is $35 million, and the after-tax earnings will be $65 million. Now suppose the firm borrowed $200 million at $r = 10\%$. Because the interest is tax-deductible, the taxable income is $80 million [$100 million − (0.10 × $200 million) = $80 million], the tax payment is $28 million (0.35 × $80 million), and the after-tax earnings will therefore be $52 million (0.65 × $80 million). Debt financing reduces the tax payment from $35 million to $28 million and saves the firm $7 million in taxes. The firm's net income is $65 million without the debt financing and $52 million with debt financing. Although bondholders receive a 10% interest rate, the firm pays only $13 million of interest, which implies an after-tax cost of 6.5% ($13 million/$200 million). This confirms the formula for the after-tax cost of debt: $(1 - T)r = (1 - 0.35) \times 0.10 = 0.65$ or 6.5%.

The firm's after-tax cost of capital, k, as a weighted average of the various after-tax costs, is as follows:

$$k = \text{FCC} = \text{WACC} = w_e k_e + w_d (1 - T)r = w_e k_e + w_d k_d \qquad (10.5)$$

where k_e and k_d are the *after-tax* specific costs. We emphasize that the after-tax cost of debt is $(1 - T)r$, rather than r.

The following problem demonstrates calculation of a firm's after-tax cost of equity, after-tax cost of debt, and after-tax weighted average cost of capital.

---

16. When we later use the dividend models, cost of equity is automatically calculated on an after-tax basis because the firm pays dividends only after it pays corporate tax.

PRACTICE BOX

Problem

Airbus finances its total investment in all projects using 40% equity and 60% debt. The interest rate is $r = 5\%$; the tax rate, $T = 35\%$. Airbus's total value is $100 million. The expected annual pretax cash flow is $15 million.

a. What is the after-tax cost of equity?
b. What is the after-tax cost of debt?
c. What is the after-tax weighted average cost of capital?

Solution

Airbus's $100 million total value is divided between $40 million of equity and $60 million of debt.

a. The after-tax cost of equity is

$$k_e = \frac{(1 - T)(\bar{X} - rB)}{E_L}$$

$$= \frac{(1 - 0.35)(\$15 \text{ million} - 0.05 \times \$60 \text{ million})}{\$40 \text{ million}}$$

$$= 0.65 \times \frac{\$12 \text{ million}}{\$40 \text{ million}} = 0.195 \text{ or } 19.5\%$$

b. The after-tax cost of debt is

$$(1 - 0.35) \times 5\% = 3.25\%$$

c. The weighted average cost of capital is

$$\text{WACC} = 0.40 \times 19.5\% + 0.60 \times 3.25\%$$
$$= 7.8\% + 1.95\% = 9.75\%$$

10.4.3 The Weighted Average Cost of All Financing Sources

Thus far we have limited our discussion to equity and debt because they are the principal financing sources. However, in practice other financing sources are available, and the most noteworthy is preferred stock.

Preferred stock, a class of equity security, has characteristics of both bonds and stocks. As its name implies, preferred stock has preference over common stock, in terms of payment of dividends. The holders of **preferred stock** are paid a *total* fixed-dollar dividend of $\$D_p$ that on a *per-share* basis is $\$d_p$. However, the holder of preferred stock has no claim on a firm's additional profit even in a very prosperous year. If a firm has a bad year, failure to pay preferred dividends does not cause bankruptcy. In that respect preferred stock is similar to common stock. All earnings remaining after the firm pays interest, rB, and dividends on the preferred stock, D_p, belong to the holders of common stock. If the price of the preferred stock is P_p, the dividend yield on preferred stocks is defined as follows:[17]

$$k_p = \frac{d_p}{P_p}$$

where k_p, which is the dividend yield, is also called the cost of capital of the preferred stock.

Because dividends on preferred stock are *not* tax-deductible, k_p is an after-tax cost. When a firm finances an investment by debt, equity, and preferred stock, its cost of capital is the weighted average of *all these sources combined*. Therefore, the firm's cost of capital, k, is still the weighted average cost of *all* its sources of financing:

$$k = \text{FCC} = \text{WACC} = w_e k_e + w_d k_d + w_p k_p \tag{10.6}$$

where w_e, w_d, and w_p are the weights of the three sources of financing in the firm's budget (with p denoting preferred stock).

10.5 THE OPTIMAL CAPITAL BUDGET

Every year the firm's management must decide the volume of its capital expenditure and then prepare a capital budget. A firm that accepts positive NPV projects and rejects negative NPV projects has achieved an **optimal capital budget** because its stock price has been maximized. Connecting Theory to Practice 10.1 demonstrates the relationship between capital budget and cost of capital.

CONNECTING THEORY TO PRACTICE 10.1

THE MOST IMPORTANT ECONOMIC EVENT OF THE DECADE: U.S. COMPANIES BUY EQUIPMENT AT FIERCE RATES

Boom! Don't look now, but U.S. companies are shelling out for capital equipment more furiously than at any time since the heady 1960s—back when the dollar was as good as gold, and America was undefeated master of the economic universe. Investment in everything from steel mill machinery to office computer networks has soared 47% in the past three years, providing much of the power behind the overall economic expansion, and more is on the way.

"In the long run, the ability of the U.S. to invest substantial amounts is related to how much we save," says Richard Rippe, chief economist at Prudential Securities. Greater saving would lower interest rates and increase stock prices, reducing the cost of capital for companies that buy plant and equipment.

---

17. This definition is analogous to the definition of the regular dividend yield, d/P, in Chapter 3. Here we deal with the dividend (d_p) and price (P_p) of preferred stock.

10.5.1 The Optimal Capital Budget with Independent Projects

To facilitate the discussion of the firm's optimal capital budget, we need to introduce the concept of the **investment schedule (IS)**, which is a curve that describes all the firm's available projects ranked by their profitability. To illustrate the IS, suppose the firm is considering the following three projects—A, B, and C:

	Initial Investment ($)	IRR (%)
Project A	100,000	20
Project B	500,000	12
Project C	200,000	8

For simplicity we assume all three projects have some risk. Their cash flows should be discounted at the WACC. Figure 10-2 illustrates the investment schedule (IS) of these three projects. The vertical axis of the IS shows each project's IRR, and the horizontal axis shows each project's capital expenditure. The cost of capital is depicted by the horizontal line labeled *WACC*, which in this example is assumed to be 10%. The three projects are ranked according to their IRRs. Project A has an IRR of 20% and requires an investment of $100,000. Project B's IRR is 12% and it requires an additional $500,000. Finally, Project C has an IRR of 8% and requires an additional $200,000 investment.

We can use the investment schedule to identify the firm's optimal capital budget, which is determined at the point where the *WACC* line crosses the *IS*. In our example the firm's optimal capital budget is $600,000. Projects A and B, each with an IRR

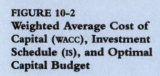

FIGURE 10-2
Weighted Average Cost of Capital (WACC), Investment Schedule (IS), and Optimal Capital Budget

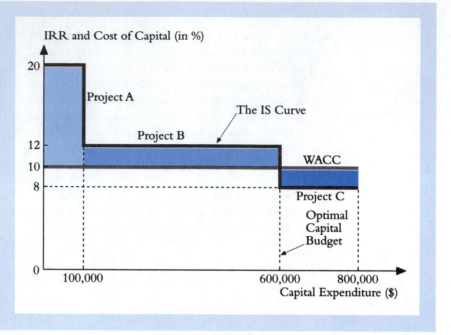

larger than the WACC, create wealth, and the firm should accept them. In contrast, the firm should reject Project C, with an IRR smaller than the WACC. We use the same principle in the rest of this chapter: The intersection point of the *IS* and the cost of capital curve determines a firm's optimum level of capital expenditure.

10.5.2 The Optimal Capital Budget with Mutually Exclusive Projects

In Figure 10-2 we ranked all projects by their IRRs. However, ranking by IRR is permissible *only if the projects are independent.*[18] If some of the projects are mutually exclusive, the IRR ranking may be misleading, as we saw in Chapter 6. However, if the WACC is constant (as in Figure 10-2), it is easy to overcome this difficulty. In such case we first calculate the NPV of the mutually exclusive projects and then select the project with the highest NPV to include on the IS. Once the mutually exclusive project with the highest NPV is included in the investment schedule, the procedure discussed in regard to Figure 10-2 can be used to determine the optimal capital budget.

To illustrate, suppose that in addition to Projects A, B, and C, the firm also considers Project A★, which is mutually exclusive of Project A. Suppose we have the following information regarding Projects A and A★:

---

18. We also assume that projects are conventional; otherwise, the IRR may not be defined, or there may be multiple IRRs.

Project	Initial Investment ($)	IRR (%)	NPV ($, calculated at 10% cost of capital)
A	100,000	20	50,000
A★	300,000	15	80,000

Since Project A★ has a higher NPV, it dominates Project A. The firm will accept Projects A★ and B, which will require a total capital budget of

$$\$300,000 + \$500,000 = \$800,000$$

10.6 THE COST OF EQUITY AND THE PRICE/EARNINGS RATIO: AN INTERNATIONAL COMPARISON

The cost of equity, as discussed before, is the expected rate of return on equity; that is:

$$k_e = \frac{(1 - T)(\bar{X} - rB)}{E_L}$$

The numerator is the expected net cash flow to the stockholders, and the denominator is the market value of the firm's equity.

Professional investors commonly estimate the numerator on the basis of the firm's *net income* appearing in this firm's latest financial statements. (See Chapter 3.) This amount will be only an estimate because the firm's net current income does not necessarily coincide with its net cash flow and because net income represents the *previous* year's income (or the average income over several years), not future expected income. However, because this estimation method is commonly used and because the cost of equity relying on this estimate is published in the financial media, we cannot ignore it.

An estimate of the cost of equity based on accounting net income is as follows:

$$
\text{Cost of equity} = \frac{\text{Net income of previous year}}{\text{Market value of equity}}
$$

$$
= \frac{\text{Income per share} \times \text{Number of shares}}{\text{Price per share} \times \text{Number of shares}}
$$

$$
= \frac{E}{P}
$$

where E is the net income per share and P is the stock price. This E/P ratio is used to estimate the firm's cost of equity. Its reciprocal, the P/E ratio, is called the *price/earnings multiplier*.

Now we have all the tools to analyze some often-heard claims about international business competition, summarized in Connecting Theory to Practice 10.2.

CONNECTING THEORY TO PRACTICE 10.2

THE SIMPLE TRUTH ABOUT INTERNATIONAL COMPETITION: A DISCUSSION WITH A SELECT GROUP OF BUSINESS EXECUTIVES

A group of forward-looking senior executives met recently at the Harris Bank to discuss the challenges and complexities of international competition . . . . Excerpts from their conversation follow:

First Executive: [One] issue is that the cost of capital is substantially lower in other countries than it is here.

Second Executive: Japanese public companies can get much different multiples on earnings, so they can raise public money incrementally at a much lower effective cost in terms of earning averages . . . . Lower capital costs mean the Japanese can take a completely different view on returns.

Third Executive: We're in a 50/50 joint venture with a Japanese company. Our Japanese partner's cost of capital is *one-quarter of ours*. Given the time value of money, we must make a higher return *up front*. There's no way to catch up if a project goes beyond six or seven years with an 18 percent rate. We've created these short-term pressures and accepted a short-term view. So it's a tough, tough cycle to stop.

Seventh Executive: We're never going to be able to compete with the Japanese *cost of capital*.

Source: "Harris Conversation for the '90s: A Discussion of a Select Group of Business Executives," *Fortune* (April 20, 1992): 252. Copyright © 1992, Time Inc. All rights reserved.

MAKING THE CONNECTION

The claim that U.S. firms cannot compete with the high Japanese multipliers can be restated as: "U.S. firms cannot compete with the low E/P ratio or low cost of equity that their Japanese counterparts have."

TABLE 10-2 European Price/Earnings Ratios: An International Comparison	1991	1992	1993 [a]	1994 [a]
Britain	18.0	17.8	17.8	14.2
Germany	19.3	22.8	24.4	21.6
France	13.5	19.5	27.8	22.0
Italy	18.7	34.2	85.4	69.3
Spain	10.6	11.5	13.7	11.8
Netherlands	11.3	13.0	14.4	12.6

[a] Estimated

Before we can make a conclusion similar to that of the U.S. executives in Connecting Theory to Practice 10.2, a word of caution is needed. The earnings used to calculate the P/E ratio are taken from income statements. If inflation differs among countries and if the earnings are not adjusted for inflation, or if different accounting principles are used, such a comparison could be meaningless. Table 10-2 provides the P/E ratio for several European countries. As we can see, the range of ratios is quite wide. In the early 1990s the representative P/E ratios, not reported in the table, for the United States and for Japan were about 23 and 60, respectively. The high P/E ratio observed in Italy (69.3) in the 1994 estimate can hardly be compared with the low P/E ratio in the Netherlands (12.6) because Italy had a much higher inflation rate. Although the reciprocal of the P/E ratio may in some cases be used to estimate the firm's cost of equity, it may be very misleading in international comparisons.[19]

Applying Theory to Practice 10.2 addresses and analyzes a major U.S. automaker's capital expenditure policy in relation to its earnings per share (EPS) and its cash flow per share.

APPLYING THEORY TO PRACTICE 10.2

THE CAPITAL BUDGET OF CHRYSLER CORPORATION

Capital expenditures, earnings, and cash flows fluctuate over time and a change in capital expenditure usually affects earnings and cash flows. In this application we analyze the change in capital expenditure Chrysler Corporation undertook in 1993 (using information available at that time).

The following data regarding Chrysler Corporation were available:

Year	Capital Spending per Share ($)	Earnings per Share ($)	Cash Flow per Share ($)
1994[a]	5.70	6.00	10.55
1993[a]	5.45	5.30	9.30
1992	7.74	1.38	6.82
1991	7.74	-2.74	2.74
1990	8.00	0.30	6.53
1989	7.33	1.36	7.42
1988	7.01	5.08	9.88
1987	5.79	5.90	7.93
1986	6.06	6.31	7.57
1985	4.58	6.25	8.34

[a] Estimates

Source: *The Value Line Investment Survey*, 1st ed. (New York: Value Line Publishing, 1993), p. 103.

19. Using the P/E ratio yields a reasonable estimate when the firm's earnings do not grow aggressively over time. The current year's earnings do not serve as a good estimate of the future (or expected) earnings for rapid growth firms. The treatment of cost of equity for firms with aggressive growth (or supergrowth) is deferred until Chapter 13. For instance, if the whole Japanese market is a supergrowth market and if the U.S. market is a normal-growth market, the P/E comparison across these two countries will be meaningless. In such a case the U.S. executives' claim may be invalid.

Additional information:

1. Chrysler's earnings per share in the first half of 1995 was $1.8 in comparison to $4.64 per share in the first half of 1994.
2. As we can see from the table, capital spending was $8.00 per share in 1990 and $5.70 per share in 1994. On the other hand, since 1991 there has been an increasing trend in earnings per share and in cash flow per share.

QUESTIONS

Use IS–WACC curves to analyze Chrysler's capital expenditure policy and its relationship to the observed earnings per share. Analyze the various possible explanations for the increase in EPS, in particular in 1991–1994, in spite of the decline in the capital expenditure per share in this period. In your answer consider the impact of the following factors on the firm's EPS:

a. A possible time lag between the capital expenditure and its effect on the EPS.
b. A possible decrease in available profitable investment projects (i.e., a shift in the IS curve) or a possible increase in WACC. Demonstrate your analysis graphically.
c. A possible decrease in the capital expenditure due to the elimination of negative NPV projects. Demonstrate your analysis graphically.

MAKING THE CONNECTION

There are several possible explanations for the observed financial results:

a. A time lag exists between the investment date and the realized earnings date. Therefore, the high earnings in 1993 and 1994 could reflect the large capital expenditures in earlier years, in particular in 1990. If this is the case, Chrysler is in very bad shape because its low capital spending in 1993 and 1994 was likely to result in low future earnings. The sharp decline in the earnings per share in the first half of 1995 conforms with this explanation.
b. Another possibility is that in 1993 and 1994 either the IS shifted downwards (i.e., fewer profitable projects were available) or the WACC increased. This would have resulted in a decrease in the optimum capital expenditure. When the IS curve drops from IS_0 to IS_1, the optimum capital expenditure drops from B_0 to B_1 (see Figure 10-3a). When the WACC increases from $WACC_0$ to $WACC_1$, the optimum capital budget also decreases (see Figure 10-3b). In either case, the firm's situation deteriorates, and its future earnings can be expected to decline.
c. Another possibility is that Chrysler reduced its capital expenditure by eliminating negative NPV projects. In such cases capital expenditure may decrease and EPS may increase simultaneously (though some time lag may

FIGURE 10-3
Possible Explanations for the Reduction in Chrysler's Capital Expenditures

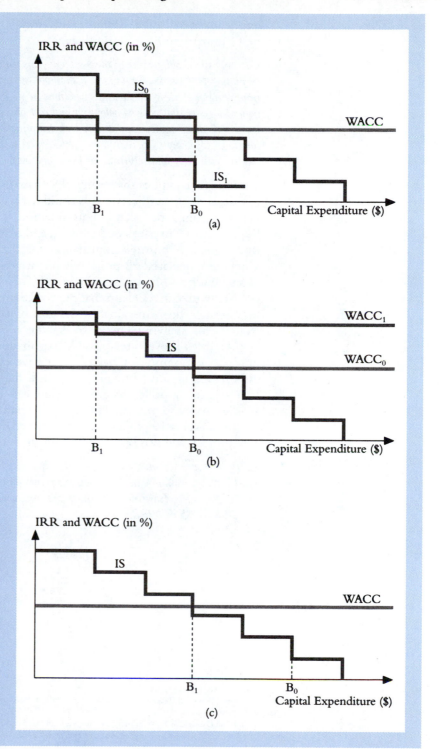

exist, depending on the type of investment). This *possible* explanation is best summarized by John Rutledge:

Creating shareholder value in the next few years isn't going to be easy . . . . My advice to managers: Give your company a thorough return-on-capital scan, identifying and improving or excising the specific operations in your company that destroy shareholder value by generating returns below normal cost of capital levels. . . . Easy-to-get bank loans and cheap equity capital may look tempting but may be a trap. Even at today's low rates, for many U.S. companies the cheapest source of capital is still their in-house bank—extracting low-return assets from their own balance sheet.[20]

Rutledge implies that many U.S. firms are overinvesting. By eliminating negative NPV projects, firms could decrease capital expenditure and increase earnings per share. This situation is illustrated in Figure 10-3c. Suppose that Chrysler's budget is B_0, and negative NPV projects were being undertaken. A possible explanation for the increase in earnings is that Chrysler eliminated all projects with negative NPVs, thereby reducing its capital budget to B_1 and simultaneously increasing its earnings.

Many executives claim that many U.S. firms accept negative NPV projects because they miscalculate the cost of equity. For an elaboration, see Your Turn: Applying Theory to Practice at the end of this chapter.

We listed above three possible explanations; they are not mutually exclusive. For example, Chrysler may have cut its capital expenditure by eliminating negative NPV projects, but it may have also used a less aggressive investment policy to produce new cars (with a positive NPV) and lost market share and reduced EPS in the first half of 1995.

By October 1995 Chrysler was satisfied that it had cut enough negative NPV projects and was optimistic about the future.

Chrysler Corp has made clear that it believes it has become a lean, mean fighting machine that would be hard pressed to squeeze much more out of its $50 billion balance sheet . . . . Earnings per share are forecasted at $7.62 in 1996, $8.23 in 1997, $10.15 in 1998.[21]

20. John Rutledge, "Beware of Bankers Bearing Gifts," *Forbes* 151, no. 9 (April 1993): 48. Reprinted By Permission of FORBES Magazine © Forbes Inc., 1993.
21. Steven Lipin and Gabriella Stern. "Chrysler Plans Suggest Firm Has Ample Cash, Even for a Downturn," *Wall Street Journal* 20 (October 1995), p. A1. Reprinted by permission of *The Wall Street Journal*, © 1995 Dow Jones & Company, Inc. All Rights Reserved Worldwide.

SUMMARY

The cost of capital is the minimum rate of return required from an investment. The greater an investment's risk, the larger the project's cost of capital. We distinguish between the firm's cost of capital and a project's cost of capital.

To calculate the firm's value, the FCC should be used as the relevant discount rate. However, to evaluate a new project, the PCC should be used as a discount rate. If the firm's risk does not vary with the new project and if the FCC is constant, then the PCC will equal the FCC.

Estimating a new project's risk is difficult. It is suggested that the CAPM be used to estimate a new project's required rate of return, with the new project's beta serving as its risk measure. Although this method is excellent when one firm acquires another firm whose beta is known, it is difficult to measure a new project's beta when it is a physical asset.

Holding the project's risk constant, we next focused on how the sources of financing affect the cost of capital. When some portion of the firm is financed by debt and some by equity, the cost of capital is a weighted average of the various costs—thus the name, weighted average cost of capital (WACC). The intersection point of the WACC line with the investment schedule determines the optimal capital budget.

CHAPTER AT A GLANCE

1. All-equity firm—no corporate tax:
   a. Firm's cost of capital (FCC):

$$\text{FCC} = k = \frac{\overline{X}}{V_0}$$

   where $\overline{X}$ is the firm's expected annual cash flow and V is the firm's market value.
   b. Project's cost of capital (PCC):

$$\text{PCC} = k + k_I + \frac{V_0}{I}k_I$$

   where k is the firm's cost of capital (FCC) without the project; k_I is the firm's change in the discount rate due to the new project; V_0 is the firm's value without the project; and I is the new project's outlay. (If all projects have the same risk, $k_I = 0$ and PCC = FCC.)

2. Levered firm with corporate tax:
   a. Cost of debt:

$$k_d = (1 - T)r$$

   b. Cost of equity:

$$k_e = (1 - T)\frac{\overline{X} - rB}{E_L}$$

   c. Cost of preferred stock:

$$k_p = \frac{d_p}{P_p}$$

3. After-tax WACC with debt, preferred stock, and equity financing:

$$\text{WACC} = w_e k_e + w_d k_d + w_p k_p$$

where w_e, w_d, and w_p are the proportions of equity, debt, and preferred stock, respectively.

4. Relationship between PCC, FCC, and WACC:
   a. For all firms, WACC = FCC; for all-equity firms, FCC = cost of equity.
   b. WACC used as a discount rate if whole firm is purchased.
   c. PCC used as a discount rate for project evaluation when risk varies across projects. (If all projects have the same risk, then PCC = WACC.)

KEY TERMS

Firm's cost of capital (FCC)

Project's cost of capital (PCC)

Cost of debt

Cost of equity

Weighted average cost of capital (WACC)

Preferred stock

Optimal capital budget

Investment schedule (IS)

REVIEW AND PRACTICE

10.1 Define a project's *cost of capital*.

10.2 Explain the relationship between the creation of economic value, cost of capital, and a project's IRR. Evaluate the following statement: "For economic value to be created, the IRR must be higher than the project's cost of capital." In your answer distinguish between conventional and nonconventional projects.

10.3 A firm's value is $V = \$100$ million. A project requiring an initial outlay of $10 million has a cash flow of $8 million in each of the next two years. The PCC is 10%. Does the project create economic value if the firm accepts it?

10.4 Suppose a project's risk differs from the firm's average risk. It is given that $k_I = 1\%$. In such case the larger the project's initial outlay relative to the firm's value, the larger the difference between the FCC and the PCC. Do you agree? Explain.

10.5 Suppose the cost of the funds raised to finance each incremental project is larger than the cost of financing the previously accepted projects. This implies that the discount rate, k, used in the equation $V = \bar{X}/k$ increases as the capital budget increases. Do you agree? Discuss your answer.

10.6 The firm's value is $V = \$10$ million. The average annual (perpetual) cash flow is $\bar{X} = \$1$ million. Calculate the firm's cost of capital.

10.7 A firm is considering a project requiring an initial outlay of $1 million and providing a perpetual annual cash flow of $\$\bar{X}$. Without the project, the firm's value, V_0, is $15 million and the cost of capital, k, is 10%. It is also known that the new project will increase the firm's cost of capital by $k_I = 5\%$. What is the PCC? What is the minimum required value of $\bar{X}_I$ for the project to be accepted?

10.8 A firm's value is $V_0 = \$100,000$, and its cost of capital is $k = 10\%$. The firm is considering an additional $100,000 investment in riskless bonds with a 5% yield. What is this investment's minimum required rate of return (PCC)? Calculate the firm's cost of capital $k_1 = k + k_I$ where k_1 refers to the firm's new cost of capital if it accepts the investment. (Assume no taxes.)

10.9 A firm's stock has a beta of 1.5. The market portfolio's mean rate of return is $\bar{R}_m = 12\%$, and the riskless interest rate is $r = 4\%$. The firm employs 40% debt and 60% equity. The interest rate on the debt is 4%. Assume no corporate taxes. What is the firm's WACC?

10.10 The stock of an all-equity firm has a beta of 1.5. Because of market conditions the firm is considering a new stock issue and investing the $10 million proceeds in riskless bonds. The investment is for one year, after which the firm plans to sell the bond and use the proceeds for other investments. The market portfolio's mean rate of return is $\bar{R}_m = 12\%$, and the riskless interest rate, r, is 8%.
a. What is the firm's cost of equity before it issues the stock?
b. What is the proposed investment's marginal cost of capital?
c. Suppose the firm's market value before issuing the stock is $5 million. Calculate the firm's cost of capital after it issues the stock and invests the proceeds in bonds.

10.11 A project requires an initial outlay of $60,000 and is expected to yield an annual cash flow of $\bar{X} = \$10,000$. The cash flow is a perpetuity. The project's beta is 2, the market portfolio's mean rate of return is $\bar{R}_m = 15\%$, and the riskless interest rate, r, is 4%. The firm is an all-equity firm. Should the firm accept the project? What is the project's NPV?

10.12 The value of a firm's equity, E_L, is $100 million. The value of its debt is $50 million on which 5% interest is payable. The pretax average cash flow is $\bar{X} = \$15$ million, and the marginal corporate tax rate, T, is 0.35.
a. What is the firm's after-tax cost of equity?
b. What is the firm's after-tax cost of debt?
c. What is the after-tax WACC?

10.13 Define the cost of equity as estimated by the CAPM. Can the cost of equity be equal to the riskless interest rate? Explain and exemplify your answer.

10.14 Suppose a firm is considering the following projects, all with one-year maturity and with the same risk:

Project	Investment at $t = 0$ (in $)	Expected Cash Flow at $t = 1$ (in $)
A	1,000	1,100
B	5,000	6,000
C	1,000	2,000
D	6,000	9,000
E	7,000	7,100

a. The firm's WACC is 15%. Draw the investment schedule and the WACC line and find the optimal capital budget. Which investments should the firm undertake? How much wealth do the executed projects create?
b. How would you change your answer if Project B has a larger risk than the other projects and, therefore, has PCC = 25%?

10.15 Define the after-tax cost of equity, the after-tax cost of debt, and the after-tax weighted average cost of capital.

10.16 It is given that the cost of equity is

$$k_e = \frac{(1 - T)(\bar{X} - rB)}{E_L} = 15\%$$

The same cost of equity is obtained by using the CAPM. It is given that $\bar{R}_m = 12\%$ and $r = 5\%$.
a. Calculate the firm's beta.
b. Suppose the firm's beta has been changed to 2 and all other values, apart from the stock price, remain the same. By how much should the stock price fall so that the two methods for estimating the cost of equity still yield the same result?

10.17 The firm's cost of equity is $k_e = 15\%$, the interest rate is $r = 10\%$, and the corporate tax rate is $T = 0.35$. The firm finances its operation by 50% debt and 50% equity.
a. Calculate the after-tax cost of debt.

372

Part 3   Portfolio and Capital Budget Decisions

b. Suppose that the interest rate falls to $r = 5\%$ and the firm decides to double its debt. As a result of the drop in the interest rate and the change in the debt-equity ratio, the stock price increases by 10%. All other factors remain the same. What is the firm's new cost of equity?

c. Will the decrease in interest rate and the increase in stock price induce an increase or decrease in the firm's capital budget?

10.18 An all-equity firm has annual cash flow of $\overline{X}$ = $1 million for the next 5 years and $\overline{X}$ = $2 million from Year 6 forever. The FCC is 10%. What is the firm's value? (Ignore taxes.)

10.19 A firm is considering the following independent and conventional projects:

Project	Investment (in $ million)	IRR
A	500	30%
B	300	20%
C	200	15%
D	400	12%
E	1,000	10%

The WACC curve is flat at 14%.

a. Plot the WACC curve and the investment schedule.

b. What is the optimal capital budget? What are the NPVs of all accepted projects?

10.20 Suppose that when Walt Disney considered acquiring Capital Cities/ABC, it had the following data: Walt Disney's market value is $45 billion, and its perpetual annual cash flow is $5.5 billion. Walt Disney agreed to pay $19 billion for Capital Cities/ABC. (Assume that at this price, the NPV of the acquisition was zero.) It is estimated that acquiring Capital Cities/ABC will increase Walt Disney's cost of capital by k_I = 1%. Assume Walt Disney used the PCC rule to evaluate the acquisition. What PCC did Walt Disney use in this evaluation?

10.21 Use the following data in your decision whether to accept or reject the following project:

Project:	Initial outlay	$1 million
	Annual perpetual posttax cash flow	$150,000
Firm:	Price per preferred shares	$P_p = \$50$
	Preferred dividend per share	$d_p = \$4$
	Number of preferred shares	10 million
	Common stock price	$P = \$100$
	Number of common shares	50 million
	Market value of bonds	$2 billion
	Interest rate on bonds	$r = 10\%$
	Corporate tax rate	$T = 35\%$
	Beta of stock	$b = 2$
	Market portfolio mean return	$\overline{R}_m = 15\%$

10.22 "The more equity the firm employs, the higher the reported earnings in the firm's income statement." Do you agree with this claim? Does it provide an incentive for the CFO to use equity rather than debt? Suppose the firm issues equity and reduces its debt. What will be the effect on the earnings per share?

10.23 A firm issued stock at $100 per share 10 years ago. The firm's cost of equity $[k_e = (1 - T)(\overline{X} - rB)/E_L]$ at the time the stock was issued was 20%. Due to an increase in the interest rate, the stock price fell to $50. Assume there are no changes in $\overline{X}$, T, rB, and the number of shares outstanding. Calculate the cost of equity with the new stock price. Assuming the firm does not need to raise more money, which cost of equity is relevant for project evaluation: 20% or the new cost of capital you calculate? Defend your answer.

10.24 Ford Motor Company's beta is 1.15, and Honda Motor Company's beta is 0.75. The market value of Ford's equity is twice as large as that of Honda. The market portfolio's average rate of return is $\overline{R}_m$ = 12%, and the riskless interest rate, r, is 3%.

a. Calculate the cost of equity of each of these two firms.

b. Suppose these firms merge. What would be the new firm's cost of equity?

10.25 The weighted average cost of capital is FCC = WACC = 15%. The firm considers two mutually exclusive projects: Project A in the electronics industry and Project B in the food industry. The project in the electronics industry is riskier than the other projects that the firm accepted and it will increase the firm's cost of capital by 1%. The project in the food industry, which is less risky than the other projects, will decrease the FCC by 2%. Use the following information to calculate each project's cost of capital, IRR, and NPV. Which project should the firm undertake?

Additional information:

Value of the firm without the project	$V = \$100$ million
Initial outlay on Project A	$I_A = \$10$ million
Initial outlay on Project B	$I_B = \$50$ million
Annual perpetual expected cash flow of Project A	$X_A = \$5.2$ million
Annual perpetual expected cash flow of Project B	$X_B = \$3.6$ million

INTERNET   QUESTIONS

10.26 Read the sample issue of the *Cost of Capital Quarterly* at Ibbotson's Web site. Find the median cost of equity capital for normal-sized firms and compare it to the cost of small capitalization firms. Does the difference seem excessive? Why? Justify this in terms of risk.

http://www.ibbotson.com/ccq2_sam.htm

10.27 Use the Interactive Tool Box at the following Web site to find some capital resources (debt capital, venture capital, etc.) for a business you would like to start. Then look at various types of venture capital (seed funding, first-round funding, etc.). Which type of venture capital do you think would be most costly? Least costly? Why?

http://www.edgeonline.com

YOUR TURN: APPLYING THEORY TO PRACTICE
COMPETITION WITH THE JAPANESE

Most of the information needed for this case is given in Connecting Theory to Practice 10.2. We add the following information:

In the early 1990s the Japanese multiplier on earnings was on average P/E = 60, while the U.S. multiplier on earnings was on average P/E = 23. Assume the earnings multiplier can be used to estimate the whole economy's cost of equity. U.S. firms can borrow on average at 8%, and the inflation rate in the United States is 4%. Japanese firms can borrow on average at 3%, and the inflation rate in Japan is 2%.

Questions
1. Assume all-equity firms. Calculate the cost of capital of an average Japanese and an average U.S. firm. How do you use the earnings multiplier to calculate the cost of equity?
2. Calculate the cost of capital for a Japanese and a U.S. firm financed by 50% debt and 50% equity. Assume 35% corporate tax in both countries. An executive claims: "Our Japanese partner's cost of capital is one-quarter of ours." Evaluate this claim in light of your calculations.
3. Refer now only to pure equity firms. Suppose a U.S. firm and a Japanese firm are considering the following investments. Each project requires an initial outlay of $100 million. What is the optimal capital budget of the U.S. and the Japanese firms?

Project	IRR (%)	Project	IRR (%)
1	15	9	7
2	14	10	6
3	13	11	5
4	12	12	4
5	11	13	3
6	10	14	2
7	9	15	1
8	8	16	−2

4. What is each firm's total dollar profit on investment? What is the average profit of the projects that are accepted?

5. Suppose both firms produce the same product. Which firm will be able to offer its product at a lower price? Which firm will be able to survive an economic recession? (*Hint:* The lower the cost of capital, and the higher the NPV, the more easily the firm can handle a decline in profit without going bankrupt.)

6. What might be the reason for the lower WACC in Japan? (*Hint:* The Japanese save a larger proportion of their incomes than their American counterparts.)

7. What can the U.S. government do to help U.S. firms compete with the Japanese?

Appendix 10A   The After-Tax Weighted Average Cost of Capital

We learned in Chapter 7 that interest payments are not included in cash flow in project evaluation. We use the same method here: We treat the whole firm as a project (that is, the whole firm is a candidate for acquisition) and ignore interest payments. The levered firm's value, V_L, is

$$V_L = \frac{(1 - T)\overline{X}}{k}$$

The levered firm's cost of capital is

$$k = \frac{(1 - T)\overline{X}}{V_L} \tag{10.7}$$

where $\overline{X}$ is the expected cash flow and T is the tax rate. Now suppose the firm pays interest of $\$rB$ and preferred dividends of $\$D_p$. Adding and subtracting $(1 - T)rB$ and D_p in the numerator of Equation 10.7, we can rewrite it as follows:

$$k = \frac{(1 - T)\overline{X}}{V_L} = \frac{(1 - T)(\overline{X} - rB) - D_p}{V_L} + \frac{(1 - T)rB}{V_L} + \frac{D_p}{V_L}$$

This can further be rewritten as

$$k = \frac{(1 - T)(\overline{X} - rB) - D_p}{E_L} \times \frac{E_L}{V_L} + (1 - T)r\frac{B}{V_L} + \frac{D_p}{E_p} \times \frac{E_p}{V_L}$$

where E_p is the preferred stock's value.

Because $(1 - T)(\overline{X} - rB) - D_p$ is the expected after-tax cash flow to the stockholders and E_L is the market value of the equity, $[(1 - T)(\overline{X} - rB) - D_p]/E_L$ is the stockholders' expected rate of return, which by definition is the cost of equity. The cost of preferred stock is D_p/E_p, and the cost of debt is $(1 - T)r$. Hence we obtain

$$k = \text{WACC} = k_e\frac{E_L}{V_L} + (1 - T)r\frac{B}{V_L} + k_p\frac{E_p}{V_L}$$

E_L/V_L, B/V_L, and E_p/V_L are the weights of the various financing sources, so we find that the levered firm's cost of capital is the weighted average cost of capital of the various specific after-tax costs:

$$k = \text{WACC} = w_e k_e + w_d k_d + w_p k_p \qquad (10.8)$$

Because interest is tax-deductible, the cost of debt component is $(1 - T)r$, not r. This lowers the cost of debt, which lowers the WACC and increases the firm's value as well as the NPV of projects under consideration. If interest were not tax-deductible, the cost of debt component would be r, and the firm's value would decrease.

Finally, note that $k = \text{WACC}$ is the firm's cost of capital. If all projects have the same risk, it is also the PCC.

Appendix 10B The Cost of Capital under Capital Rationing

Thus far we have assumed the firm can raise as much money as it needs at a given cost. In practice, the firm may raise money in such a way that the cost increases with the amount of money raised. In that case we say the firm faces an increasing **marginal cost of capital (MCC)**. The principles underlying stock price maximization are that the firm should raise money and accept incremental projects only if the marginal cost of capital (MCC) is smaller than the marginal project's rate of return. Sometimes, however, other constraints such as limited funds or limited time needed to train personnel may influence a firm's decision, and the firm may be forced to slow down its expansion. In such case the firm needs to employ **capital rationing,** which means the firm must choose among acceptable projects and reject some profitable ones.

Although a policy of capital rationing is most often attributed to lack of funds, a firm might also adopt it for other reasons. For example, if a CFO insists on being in charge of all projects, this will limit the number of projects that the firm can undertake. Or stockholders might adopt capital rationing to regain or maintain control of their firm. To illustrate, consider a small firm whose principal owners are members of the same family. These owners know they could expand the firm if they raised money by issuing stocks and bonds. However, by doing so, the family would lose its majority voting rights and forfeit control of the firm. In such case the family may decide to deviate from the goal of value maximization. They will not raise the money and will, therefore, be forced to reject profitable projects to safeguard control of the firm. The decision is not necessarily irrational because the family's benefit derives not only from wealth, but also from controlling a firm passed from one generation to the next.

To illustrate the impact of capital rationing on the firm's investment decision, suppose Safe Toys is considering five projects: A, B, C, D, and E, whose investment schedule is presented in Figure 10B-1. The firm's MCC increases up to a point, say, $500,000; then, due to capital rationing, the MCC curve becomes vertical. This happens because the firm decides not to expand its investment beyond $500,000,

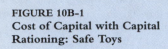

FIGURE 10B-1
Cost of Capital with Capital
Rationing: Safe Toys

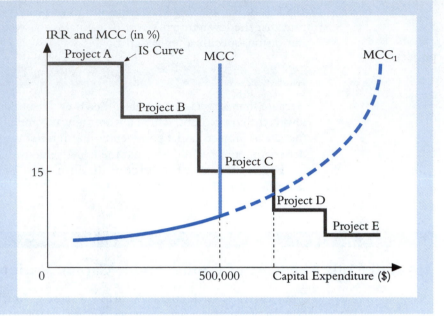

regardless of the available projects' profitability. Thus, we obtain a vertical MCC line. The intersection point of the IS with the MCC line, which in our example occurs at 15%, determines the firm's MCC with the capital budget constraint. Accordingly, the firm would accept Projects A and B and would reject the other three projects. Even though Project C has a 15% IRR, it still would be rejected because it would force the firm to raise more than the $500,000 upper limit of the capital budget.

The dashed MCC curve (denoted by MCC_1) shows the hypothetical MCC if the firm were to raise more money and accept Project C, whose NPV would be positive. The constraint on the capital budget expenditure reduces the firm's value by the NPV of Project C.[22]

APPENDIX KEY TERMS

Marginal cost of capital (MCC)   Capital rationing

22. Real-life calculations are more complicated because firms have multiperiod cash flows, and the project's annual cash flow may ease the constraints in certain years. Accordingly, the cost of capital may vary from year to year due to various annual capital budget constraints and the project's annual cash flow. Some problems of this kind can be solved by linear programming with the help of computer programs that are available for this purpose.

APPENDIX REVIEW AND PRACTICE

A firm is considering the following conventional projects:

Project	Investment (in $ million)	IRR
A	100	30%
B	200	25%
C	400	24%
D	500	23%
E	100	20%
F	1,000	10%

The WACC is flat at 20%. All cash flows are perpetuities.

a. Assuming the projects are independent, what is the optimal capital budget? Which projects should the firm accept? What are the NPVs of the projects that are accepted?

b. Suppose the firm's CFO can examine only four projects a year, and insists on being involved in the evaluation of all those projects. Draw the cost of capital curve on the assumption that Projects A, B, C, and D are accepted.

c. What is the best choice of projects under this capital rationing condition? What is the firm's cost of capital?

CHAPTER 11

HEDGING MACROECONOMIC RISK WITH DERIVATIVES

LEARNING OBJECTIVES

After reading this chapter, you should understand:

1. How management can use derivative assets to reduce a firm's risk.

2. How forward and futures contracts can be used to reduce risk.

3. The basic characteristics of put and call options.

4. How to determine upper and lower bounds on and the value of options.

5. How a firm hedges risk with swap contracts.

6. How misusing derivatives can cause problems.

7. How to use the Black-Scholes option pricing formula.

CORPORATE FINANCE IN THE NEWS

MONEY AND MARKETS

CEO Poll: Derivatives Are Here to Stay

Most major companies use derivatives, and despite huge losses by some, CEOs say they are happy with internal controls. But they are split over how much shareholders need to be told about these instruments, finds a poll of 200 Fortune 500 CEOs, conducted May 31 through June 7 by Clark Martire & Bartolomeo.

Are you satisfied with the way your derivatives have performed?

Yes	83%
No	6%
No answer	11%

Do you plan to use derivatives more in the future or less? Or do you plan no change?

Use more	6%
Use less	2%
No change	92%

Does your treasury/finance department use over-the-counter derivatives?

Yes	35%
No	60%
Not sure	5%

Why does your company use derivatives?

Hedge interest rate risk	19%
Minimize risk overall	14%
Hedge exchange-rate risk	13%
Hedge raw materials costs	5%
Manage assets/liabilities	2%
Other	47%

Do you plan to change your internal controls in the next 12 months?

No	88%
Yes	11%
Not sure	1%

Do you feel companies provide shareholders with enough information about their use of derivatives?

Yes	39%
No	40%
No answer	21%

What information should a company provide to shareholders about derivatives?

How risky its derivatives are	22%
What kinds it uses and how much	21%
Full disclosure if it is speculating	11%
Reasons it uses them	11%
None if it uses them for hedging	6%
Investors don't need to know	6%
Other	23%

11.1 INTRODUCTION

http

Numa Financial Services maintains a one-stop Web site for everything you want to know regarding derivatives: definitions, FAQS, courses, conferences, journals, software, calculators, links, bookstores, and trading. Their site also contains a link to their Global Investor Web site. **http://www.numa.com /index.htm**

Derivatives are financial instruments that can be used to reduce risk. As we see from Corporate Finance in the News, more than half of the firms participating in the poll use derivatives to hedge interest rate risk, to minimize risk overall, to hedge exchange rate risk, and to hedge the risk of increases in raw materials costs. A 1995 *Fortune* article summarizes the characteristics of derivatives: "These financial innovations both warm and burn . . . . Love them or hate them, they're all here to stay." Because derivatives are here to stay, management must know them and how to use them to reduce risk.

A firm undertakes projects with uncertain cash flows and faces *business risk*. Since business risk is under management's control, it can be eliminated. However, totally eliminating this risk is not recommended because doing so would also totally eliminate profitability. In the extreme case the firm's management could invest all its resources in Treasury bills, which yield a low return and have almost zero risk. However, by doing so the firm practically would cease to exist. Stockholders could, instead, invest directly in Treasury bills and avoid the firm's corporate tax and business costs.

In contrast to business risks, *macroeconomic risks* such as changes in interest rates, oil crises, and changes in foreign exchange rates are not under management's control. The firm would like to reduce its exposure to macroeconomic risks; if it doesn't, it may run its operation very efficiently but lose money, for example, due to a drastic change in the foreign currency rate. By using financial instruments called *derivative assets,* or **derivatives**, the firm can reduce its risk exposure and, therefore, its cost of equity. Derivatives are so named because they *derive* their value from an underlying asset's price behavior. For example, an option to buy Intel stock at a predetermined price of $140 per share is a derivative asset. On January 5, 1997, Intel's stock traded at $138⅜. If the price rises above $140, say, to $160, the option's value increases. In this example the option is the derivative asset, and the stock is the underlying asset. Risk reduction using derivatives is called *hedging*. These days stockholders expect firms to hedge macroeconomic risks. In this chapter we focus on the firm's use of derivatives.

The following examples will give you an idea of how a firm can use derivatives to reduce risk:

1. A firm has issued a long-term bond at a fixed interest of 9%. The CFO believes there is a substantial chance that the interest rate will fall in the future. By buying options on the interest rate, the firm can insure itself against losses due to the decline in the interest rate. As we shall see, when the interest rate falls, the option price rises, creating a capital gain for the firm. This capital gain will offset the losses incurred by having to pay 9% interest on its bond when the market interest rate is lower.

2. A firm engaged in international trade can purchase *forward contracts* or options on foreign currency to eliminate or hedge foreign exchange risk. We will see how Ciba Group (a Swiss pharmaceutical firm) uses forward contracts and options for this purpose.

3. A textile firm is planning a new investment. A substantial portion of the firm's cash outlay one year from now will be in the form of investment in cotton, the

raw material needed for the project. The price of cotton fluctuates greatly. If it increases by more than 10%, the project's NPV will turn negative. By buying *futures contracts* that give the firm the right to purchase cotton in the future at a predetermined price, management can hedge the risk of a possible price increase.

Aside from using derivatives to hedge macroeconomic risk, management can also use them for a wide range of other purposes. The remainder of this list provides a few examples:

4. When a firm plans to issue new securities, it runs the risk of not being able to see those securities at a sufficiently high price. Most firms transfer the risk of failing to sell the issue to an investment bank; that is, they use the bank's underwriting of a stock or bond issue to hedge the new issue's risk of failure. How much should the firm pay for this underwriting agreement? We will show that a firm can use a *put option* to evaluate the economic value of such an agreement.
5. When an airline insures its fleet, the insurance serves to hedge the risk of disaster. We will show that a firm can use a put option to determine the fair cost of such insurance.
6. A firm is considering whether to lease cars for its executives with the option of buying the cars at a predetermined price within a specified period. What is this option's economic value?
7. The manager of an investment company or pension fund wants to protect customers against heavy losses in a declining stock market. We will show that the manager can use put options to hedge this risk and to protect the company's clients.
8. Investment in options can be used for speculative purposes. However, a speculator may discover that such investment can be dangerous. In 1995, for example, the British bank Barings lost more than $1 billion due to speculative transactions in derivatives. The Japanese bank Daiwa incurred similar losses in late 1995.
9. Finally, if managers are offered options to buy some of the firm's shares at a relatively low price as part of their remuneration, they will want to know these options' economic value.

Do not be misled by the term "option." Such a derivative is not an "optional" part of corporate finance. Use of options—or, at least, a good understanding of their special features—has become a "must" today. Without basic knowledge of this financial vehicle, a firm risks losing a lot of money. Indeed, as shown in Connecting Theory to Practice 11.1 shows, options and futures are now very crucial management tools, particularly in reducing risk.

CONNECTING THEORY TO PRACTICE 11.1

LEARNING TO LIVE WITH DERIVATIVES

They're here, they're weird, and they're not going away. Yes, these beasties bite, but companies that tame them have a competitive edge.

The Rubicon was in Cincinnati last March. Even as Procter & Gamble was piling up a pretax loss of $157 million by trading in derivatives, it was becoming blazingly clear that despite all their built-in perils, these otherworldly financial instruments had thoroughly insinuated themselves into the heart of business. As the huge size of the market—over $12 trillion—attests, corporations have found plenty of uses for derivatives. Intel, Merck, and others successfully employ them to manage the risks of fluctuating interest and exchange rates. For now, such expertise may represent a competitive edge. But soon, understanding how even the most complex derivatives work will be a competitive necessity. Accordingly, 92% of the CEOs from 200 of America's biggest companies say they plan to continue to use derivatives, a new *Fortune* poll indicates.

All this activity swivels the floodlight onto the hitherto low-profile corporate treasurer. It used to be that these men and women kept quiet track of a company's finances. Now they have metamorphosed into high-stakes "risk managers." Given the fact that the die is cast and derivatives are here to stay, the question is, How should treasurers be *using* them? . . .

Wall Street analysts also are demanding expertise in derivatives management. For example, Deborah Bronston of Prudential Securities knocked her earnings estimate for Cone Mills, a textile company in Greensboro, North Carolina, down 5 cents to $1.90 because she believes that the company hasn't sufficiently hedged its exposure to changing cotton prices. Says Philip McBride Johnson, a partner specializing in derivative products in the Washington law offices of Skadden Arps Slate Meagher & Flom: "It's beginning to become an expectation that if the capacity to hedge exists and it can be done safely, there will be criticism and possibly litigation if advantage isn't taken of that opportunity."

Hedging is invariably cited by critics and advocates alike as the best use of derivatives. Companies put on hedges not to generate profits but to fix what are usually variable costs like foreign-exchange transaction. Thus a U.S. company with contracts to sell products in Germany might buy derivatives that will rise in value if the dollar falls against the mark during the waiting period before the deals close. This provides predictable profits. Banks will often extend more favorable financing terms to such companies because loan officers feel that their more stable earnings make for more reliable credits. Theoretically, hedging also allows the managers of a company to concentrate on their core business and not worry about the forces roiling the currency markets or driving interest rates up and down.

MAKING THE CONNECTION

As the *Fortune* article indicates, corporate treasurers have also become risk managers. If they do not use derivatives, they can expect criticism and possibly even litigation! Despite the near necessity of using derivatives, though, hedging risk costs money. That is why financial professionals do not recommend eliminating all types of risks. However, a firm should hedge risk exposure due to macroeconomic factors that have nothing to do with its specific activity.

The derivatives market is very colorful. There are options, futures, and options on futures. There are options on commodities, on interest rates, on foreign currencies, on indexes of stocks, and more. In this chapter we show how a firm can use derivative assets to hedge risk. But let's first learn about the basic characteristics of options, the nature of the option contract agreement, and the cash flows involved. We start with the simple hedging tool: the *forward contract*. Understanding forward contracts and their limitations will set the stage for understanding *futures contracts*, which firms more commonly use.

11.2 FORWARD CONTRACTS

In conducting a cash transaction, a buyer pays cash when the seller delivers goods. In contrast, when engaging in a **forward contract,** the buyer and the seller agree to exchange goods for cash at some future date (say, January 1 of the next year), at a predetermined price. While various forward contracts can be made, the most common are foreign exchange forward contracts. Let us first define what the terms of these contracts are.

Table 11-1 reports data on forward contracts. For example, on January 6, 1997, one U.S. dollar could be traded for 1.5671 German marks (DM). That was the *current exchange rate* for cash transactions, also called the *spot rate*. The *forward exchange rate*—or, simply, the *forward rate*—between these two currencies depended on the delivery date. If you wished to buy or sell dollars for a delivery one month later on February 6, 1997, you could close a deal for 1.5640 DM per dollar. If you wished a delivery date six months later (July 6, 1997), the forward rate was 1.5484 DM per dollar.

In the following problem we demonstrate how forward contracts can be used to hedge foreign currency risk.

TABLE 11-1 Spot and Forward Exchange Rates Against the Dollar	Closing	One Month	Three Months	Six Months
Germany (DM)	1.5671	1.5640	1.5580	1.5484
Japan (Y)	116.35	118.84	114.87	113.41

Source: *Barron's* (January 6, 1997): MW55. Reprinted by permission of *Barron's Market Week*, © 1997 Dow Jones & Company, Inc. All Rights Reserved Worldwide.

PRACTICE BOX

Problem

A U.S. marketing firm buys agricultural machinery in the United States for $1 million and sells it to a Japanese firm. The U.S. firm pays in cash but sells the machines to the Japanese on six months' credit terms. The sale is for 120 million yen.

a.   The annual discount rate is 10% so the discount rate is 5% for the six-month period. What would be the NPV if the future exchange rate remains 116.35 yen per dollar?

b.   What will be the NPV if the exchange rate six months from now is 80 yen per dollar? If it is 120 yen per dollar?

c.   Use Table 11-1 to show how the U.S. firm can guarantee a positive NPV by using a forward contract.

Solution

a.   The firm will receive 120 million yen six months from now at the exchange rate of 116.35 yen per dollar. The firm will receive $1.031 million (120 million yen/116.35).

If the firm invests $1 million today, the NPV of this transaction is as follows:

$$\frac{\$1.031 \text{ million}}{1.05} - \$1 \text{ million} \cong -\$18,095.24$$

b.   If the exchange rate six months from now is 80 yen per dollar, the firm will receive $1.5 million (120 million yen/80 yen per dollar = $1.5 million).

The NPV is:

$$\frac{\$1.5 \text{ million}}{1.05} - \$1 \text{ million} \cong \$428,571$$

If the exchange rate is 120 yen per dollar, the firm will receive $1 million (120 million yen/120 yen per dollar = $1 million).

The NPV is

$$\frac{\$1 \text{ million}}{1.05} - \$1 \text{ million} \cong -\$47,619$$

With no hedging the firm may profit but also may lose ($47,619) if there are adverse changes in the foreign currency exchange rate.

c.   The firm cannot know the future exchange rate. Moreover, the firm's management does not want macroeconomic factors such as international trade and government monetary policy to interfere with its operation. Therefore, the firm can hedge the risk by buying a forward contract to sell yen at a predetermined price one year from now.

Suppose the firm buys a contract to sell 120 million yen at 113.41 yen per dollar six months from now (see Table 11-1). The firm will receive $1,058,108 (120 million yen/113.41 yen per dollar).

(continued)

> The NPV is
>
> $$\frac{\$1,058,108}{1.05} - \$1 \text{ million} \cong \$7,721.67$$
>
> If it uses a forward contract, the firm eliminates foreign currency risk.

The preceding problem demonstrates how a firm can completely eliminate foreign exchange risk by using forward contracts. In this specific case the U.S. firm's profits may even increase in comparison with a transaction at the current exchange rate. However, if the forward rate were higher, say 118 yen per dollar, the firm's profit would decline relative to a transaction at the current exchange rate.

Who is taking this risk? You buy a forward contract from your bank. Does this mean that the bank is exposed to the risk? No. The bank is operating as a mediator. It finds another customer (say a Japanese firm that exports to the U.S. on credit) who wishes to sell dollars one year from now. Both sides eliminate risk through the transaction. This risk reduction is intact as long as one of the parties does not default.

Forward contracts have a major deficiency. If prices fall sharply, one party has a strong incentive to default. For example, suppose Cone Mills has a forward contract to buy cotton from Cotton Corporation in July at 76.4 cents per pound. Suppose the current price of cotton is 75 cents per pound but falls in July to 40 cents per pound. Cone Mills can buy cotton in July at 40 cents in the market, but it is committed to pay 76.4 cents per pound to Cotton Corporation. Cone Mills has a strong incentive to default—to walk away from this transaction. Firms and institutions that know and trust each other engage in forward transactions. When such trust does not exist, a firm needs a financial tool that minimizes the incentive to default—this is exactly what a futures contract, to which we turn next, does.

11.3 FUTURES CONTRACTS

Futures contracts exist on a wide variety of items: agriculture products (corn, oats, wheat, livestock and meat, coffee, orange juice, cotton, sugar), metals and petroleum (gold, silver, crude oil), and financial assets (various currencies, Treasury bonds, various stock indices). Like a forward contract, a **futures contract** can be used to hedge risk. Both contracts commit buyer and seller to exchange goods for cash at some future date at a predetermined price. The futures contract, however, has the following differences: It is traded on a financial exchange, it offers more flexibility in its delivery date, and its cash flows differ.

Since futures contracts are traded on organized exchanges, whereas forward contracts are not, prices of futures contracts are reported daily in the financial media, as shown in Table 11-2. Because they have an organized market, futures contracts are more liquid than forward contracts, and a buyer of futures contracts can

TABLE 11-2 Futures Contracts for Cotton[a] (Cotton 2: 50,000 lbs; cents per lb)	Season's			Weeks			Net Chg.	Open Int.
	High	Low	Month	High	Low	Sett		
	85.15	72.00	Mar 97	75.90	74.00	74.08	−0.99	22,623
	85.40	73.10	May 97	76.75	75.35	75.43	−0.95	13,157
	85.40	73.75	Jul 97	77.60	76.35	76.40	−0.80	7,200
	81.30	74.60	Oct 97	77.50	76.75	76.60	−0.80	1,294
	80.10	74.30	Dec 97	77.00	76.25	76.28	−0.69	9,874
	81.00	75.50	Mar 98	77.85	77.25	77.25	−0.75	453
	81.00	76.25	May 98	78.45	78.45	77.80	−0.65	320

Fri. to Thurs. sales 23,657.

Total open interest 58,702

[a]Each contract is for 50,000 outstanding pounds of cotton.

Source: *Barron's* (January 6, 1997): MW95. Reprinted by permission of *Barron's Market Week*, © 1997 Dow Jones & Company, Inc. All Rights Reserved Worldwide.

"net out" his or her position by *selling* a similar futures contract. For example, the buyer who has a July contract to buy cotton and a July contract to sell cotton would not have to make a delivery of cotton.

The second difference between forward and futures contracts relates to delivery dates. Forward contracts specify precise delivery dates. With futures contracts the seller can choose any delivery date during the specified *delivery month*. If the seller of a July cotton futures contract notifies the exchange clearinghouse that he will deliver the cotton on July 15, the *clearinghouse* notifies one of the contract buyers to be ready to receive the cotton in a few days. (The clearinghouse selects one of the many July buyers at random.) Choosing the delivery date at any day during the month gives the seller some flexibility.

Third, the cash flows of forward and futures contracts are much different. With forward contracts one party delivers the product and the other pays cash for it on the delivery date. Futures contracts are marked to market on a daily basis. **Mark to market** means that cash flows in and out on a daily basis whenever there are changes in the futures contract prices. As will be explained below, this mark-to-market daily cash settlement drastically reduces the risk of default. We noted earlier that forward contracts should be conducted between "friends" who trust each other. In contrast, futures contracts can be executed between strangers because the incentive to default is relatively small. This feature makes futures contracts the better financial tool.

Table 11–3 demonstrates the cash flows to the buyer and the seller of a futures contract. Suppose that on January 6, 1997 Cone Mills buys a July 1997 futures contract at 76.40 cents per pound. If it had been a forward contract, then on July 16 the buyer would pay $38,200 (76.40 cents per pound × 50,000 pounds) per contract. Instead, with a futures contract, cash flows are involved each time the price changes. For simplicity assume the price changes only twice. (In reality the price is likely to

TABLE 11-3   **Cash Flows to Buyer and Seller of Cotton Futures Contracts: Mark-to-Market Daily Cash Settlements**

Closing price (cents per pound)	January 6 76.40	March 1 77.40	May 1 76.32	July 16 76.32
Buyer	Buyer purchases cotton futures contracts at 76.40 cents per pound.	Buyer receives one cent per pound from the clearinghouse within one business day.	Buyer must pay the clearinghouse 1.08 cents per pound within one business day.	Buyer pays 76.32 cents per pound and receives the cotton.
Seller	Seller sells futures contracts at 76.40 cents per pound.	Seller pays the clearinghouse one cent per pound within one business day.	Seller receives from the clearinghouse 1.08 cents per pound within one business day.	Seller receives 76.32 cents per pound of cotton and delivers the cotton to the buyer within one business day.
Buyer's cash flow per 50,000-pounds contract	—	1 cent per pound $\times$ 50,000 pounds = $500	1.08 cents per pound $\times$ 50,000 pounds = –$540	–76.32 cents per pound $\times$ 50,000 pounds = –$38,160
Seller's cash flow per 50,000-pounds contract	—	–$500	$540	$38,160

change daily, and the same technique for determining the cash flow would be used on a daily basis.) Suppose that on March 1 the price rises to 77.40 cents. The seller, who loses from such an increase (because she or he is committed to sell at a lower price), must pay 1 cent per pound to a clearinghouse that, in turn, pays the sum to the buyer. Then, on May 1, the price drops to 76.32 cents, and the buyer pays the clearinghouse 1.08 cents per pound, which is passed along to the seller. Assuming no further changes in price, the buyer pays the seller 76.32 cents per pound on July 16 and the seller delivers the cotton. The total cash flow to the buyer for all dates is $38,200 ($500 – $540 – $38,160 = –$38,200). This amount is exactly what the buyer would have paid in a forward contract. Similarly, the seller receives $38,200, just as he or she would have received in a forward contract.

However, there are two differences between the cash flows of forward and futures contracts. The first is that in futures contracts the interim cash flows cannot be ignored, and the PV of interim cash flows in a futures contract may be different from the PV of cash flows in a forward contract. The more important factor is that the incentive to default is lower with futures contracts because the daily losses are not very large. With forward contracts all losses are accumulated to one payment on the delivery date, producing a stronger incentive to default.

On top of these cash flows, each trader establishes a margin account of 15% of the contract value. The margin is a security account consisting of near-cash securities to ensure that traders are able to satisfy their obligations under futures contracts. Because both parties are exposed to possible losses, both must post a margin. But because the margin is in terms of interest-earning securities, it does not impose a substantial cost on the traders.

Continuing with our previous example, Cone Mills has hedged its risk against an increase in the price of cotton by buying a futures contract at 76.4 cents per pound. But what happens if the price of a pound of cotton falls to 40 cents? Cone Mills is locked into this transaction and must pay 76.4 cents per pound. Is there a way for Cone Mills to hedge possible increases in the cotton price while also enjoying the lower price of cotton if the price falls? As we shall see below, options can provide Cone Mills a hedge against price increases and a benefit if the price falls. However, since there are no free lunches in the market, these options cost money. We devote most of the remaining chapter to options, their characteristics, their usages, and their pricing.

11.4 THE BASIC CHARACTERISTICS OF OPTIONS

An **option** is a contract that gives its holder the *right* but not the *obligation* to buy or sell a well-defined asset (usually a stock) at a predetermined price within a specified period of time. Investment strategies in the options market are based on two fundamental types of options—put options and call options. A **call option** gives the holder the right to *buy* an asset at a predetermined price within a specified period of time. A **put option** is the opposite: It gives the holder the right to *sell* the asset at a predetermined price within a predetermined period.

Originally, put and call options were simply traded between two individuals. Now that a well-developed market for puts and calls has emerged, options are traded in that market and have market prices. Options are traded on several exchanges, the most active being the Chicago Board Options Exchange (CBOE). Options exchanges ensure that the contracts are fulfilled and that the cash flows are transferred daily from one party to another.

11.4.1 The Nature of the Option Contract

Entering the world of options, we encounter a new language. Before going any further, let's define some of the basic terms connected with options:

- **Underlying asset**. The asset on which the option contract is written.
- **Striking price** (or **exercise price**). The fixed, predetermined price at which the holder of the option can buy or sell the underlying asset.
- **Option premium**. The price paid for the option.
- **Expiration date**. The last day on which the option can be exercised. All options listed on the CBOE expire on the third Friday of the month designated in the contract.

- **European option**. An option that can be exercised only on the expiration date itself.
- **American option**. An option that can be exercised at any time up to and including the expiration date. In this chapter we focus on American options.

For every buyer of an option, there must be a seller. We say the seller "**writes**" **an option**. If you buy an option, we say you have a **long position** in the option; and when you write an option, we say you have a **short position** in the option.

11.4.2 Example: IBM's Call Option

Let's illustrate the basic characteristics of options, the option contract, and the cash flows arising from options by studying an option on IBM stock. *Barron's* (January 6, 1997) provides the following information regarding the IBM call option:

Price of call option	$10⅛
Expiration date	Feb 1997
Striking price	$155
Current stock price	$159⅛

These figures tell us that a holder of an IBM call option had the right to buy IBM stock at $155 per share, that this right was valid up to February 1997, and that the holder could **exercise an option** at any time before the third Friday of February 1997. (All options expire on the third Friday of the month.) If a holder exercised this right on January 6, 1997 (the date of the newspaper announcement just mentioned) and immediately sold the stock in the market, he or she would have received $4⅛ ($159⅛ − $155 = $4⅛).

The net cash flow on this transaction would have been $4⅛ per option held. However, there are no free lunches, and the investor did not get this call option for free. The market price of IBM's call option was $10⅛. Note that this option price is higher than the profit from exercising the option immediately. The difference reflects the possibility that IBM's stock price will rise before the third Friday of February, in which case the option holder's profit will be more than $4⅛ per option.

It should be stressed that the trading in options on its stock did not affect IBM's cash flows. An option is a contract between a buyer and a seller. The two parties, in effect, "bet" on the price of some underlying asset (in our example, on the IBM stock); the company itself does not get involved.

Let's summarize what we have learned thus far. If you hold a call option on a stock, you have the *right* (or the option) but not the *obligation* to buy that stock at the striking price. If IBM's stock price suddenly falls and stays below $155 up to the third week of February 1997, the call option will expire worthless. No one will buy the stock for $155 if he or she can purchase it in the market for less than $155. Since the owner of the option is not obligated to buy the stock, the option's value is zero.

Thus far we have discussed call options. Another commonly used derivative is the *put* option. If you hold a put option, you have the *right* but not the *obligation* to sell the underlying asset to the put seller at the striking price. For example, if you hold a put option on IBM stock with a striking price of $160 and the stock price drops to $150, you may sell the stock to the put writer for $160 (and the writer must buy it). You will obtain a cash flow of $10 per share if you immediately repurchase the stock in the market. If the stock price rises above $160, the put option expires worthless.

11.5 STOCK OPTION QUOTATIONS

Now let's examine how the financial media quote stock options. Table 11-4 lists seven options on General Electric stock: four calls and three puts. The first column gives the expiration date; the second column, the striking price (the letter P is added for a put option; otherwise, it is a call option); and the last column, the price of the option.

What does this information tell us? Let's look at the January 1997 call option with a $40 striking price. The buyer of the option pays $61⅞ for it. The striking price was below the current stock price of $99⅛. So the holder could have benefited from an immediate exercise. The benefit from an immediate exercise is $99⅛ − $40 = $59⅛. Would anyone want to buy such an option for $61⅞? Yes, someone who believed that GE stock might rise above $101⅞ by the third Friday of January 1997 may buy it. If the stock behaved as anticipated, the call option holder would benefit from exercising the option.

Now, let's look at the January put option with the $95 striking price. The price quoted for this option is $¾. The put option gives the holder the right to sell the stock at $95 per share. Because the current stock price is $99⅛, an option holder will not benefit by exercising the put option immediately. Whenever a positive cash flow can be obtained by exercising the option immediately, as in the case of the call option with a $40 striking price, we say the option is **in the money**. Otherwise, as in the case of the put option, it is **out of the money.** The following problem demonstrates which of the seven GE options are in the money.

TABLE 11-4 Put and Call Options on General Electric Stock (Current Stock Price = $99⅛)	Expiration Date	Striking Price ($)	Last Price of Option ($)
	January '97	40	61⅞
	January '97	90 P	¼
	January '97	90	9½
	January '97	95 P	¾
	January '97	95	5¼
	January '97	100	2⅛
	January '97	105	¾

PRACTICE BOX

Problem   Which of the seven options given in Table 11-4 are in the money? Which are out of the money?

Solution   Whenever its striking price is *below* the current stock price, a call option is in the money. In the table the *call options* with striking prices of $40, $90, and $95 are in the money.

Whenever its striking price is *above* the current stock price, a put option is in the money. In our example, both put options are out of the money.

Note that in all these examples we have ignored transaction costs. In practice these costs would reduce the cash flows from the transactions described.

In practice, trading in options takes place in *round lots* of 100 shares per contract. Suppose you wish to buy one contract on General Electric's January 1997 $95 call option. You will pay $525 ($5¼ × 100) per contract, where $5¼ is the price of the call option on each share. The option writer will receive the premium of $525. In this chapter we use per-share data. Multiplying by 100 gives the cash flow per 100-share contract.

11.6 THE CASH FLOWS OF STOCK OPTIONS

Options trading is similar to a bet in which one side's gain is the other side's loss. Why do investors buy and sell options? The buyer of a call option hopes to profit from a rise in the underlying stock's price. The seller of a call option does not expect the stock price to rise and hopes to obtain the *premium* from the option's sale without having to pay the buyer. The main motivation for transactions in options lies in the different hopes and expectations prevailing in the market with regard to the underlying asset's future price.

Table 11-5 illustrates the cash flows to the buyers and sellers of puts and calls at the transaction and expiration dates. In this illustration we assume a striking price of $50, a current stock price of $45, a call price of $11, and a put price of $15. We show the cash flows for three possible stock prices at the expiration date. The different hopes of the parties involved in options trading and the cash flows at the option purchase date and at the expiration date are summarized graphically in Figure 11-1.

Note that whatever one side gains, the other side loses; and the total cash flow balances to zero. The call buyer and the put writer are *optimistic* regarding the stock's future price. If the stock price rises, they stand to gain from the transaction. Conversely, the call writer and the put buyer are *pessimistic* and hope to see low stock prices in the future. The lower the stock price at the expiration date, the larger their profit.

TABLE 11-5   **Cash Flows to the Buyer and Seller of Puts and Calls with $50 Striking Price**

	Cash Flow at Transaction Date ($)	Stock Price at Expiration Date ($)		
		30	50	70
Call option ($)				
Cash flow to the call buyer	−11	0	0	70 − 50 = 20
Cash flow to the call writer	11	0	0	50 − 70 = −20
Total cash flow	0	0	0	0
Put option ($)				
Cash flow to the put buyer	−15	50 − 30 = 20	0	0
Cash flow to the put writer	15	30 − 50 = −20	0	0
Total cash flow	0	0	0	0

11.6.1 Value of a Call Option at Various Prices of the Underlying Asset

We can now analyze the cash flows produced by option transactions in greater detail and demonstrate the call option's value for various hypothetical underlying asset prices. Table 11-6 shows the cash flows for a January $95 call option holder at the expiration date for various possible prices of GE stock at that date. The call price is 5¼. At any stock price below the striking price, the cash flow is zero. The right to buy the stock for $95 is worthless if a buyer can purchase the stock in the market for less than $95. If the stock price is higher than $95, say $100, the call option holder

FIGURE 11-1
Hopes and Expectations of Option Traders and Results "at the End of the Day"

	Put buyer and call writer	Put writer and call buyer
If the stock price is above the striking price	Hopes unfulfilled	Hopes fulfilled
If the stock price is below the striking price	Hopes fulfilled	Hopes unfulfilled

TABLE 11-6 Cash Flow to a GE Call Option Holder at Expiration Date	Possible GE Stock Price ($)	Striking Price ($)	Transfer of Cash to Holder ($)
	80	95	0
	85	95	0
	90	95	0
	95	95	0
	100	95	5
	105	95	10
	110	95	15

has the right to buy stock for $95 and then sell it immediately for $100, thereby obtaining a cash flow of $5 per share (or $500 per contract).

The buyer of a call option hopes that the stock's price will rise, so that he or she can cover the cost of buying the option and make a profit. Conversely, the call option writer hopes that the stock price will fall and that he or she will earn the premium without paying the option holder anything. Figure 11-2 shows how the call option's value at the expiration date is related to the underlying stock's value. When the stock price is below the striking price, the option's value is zero. When the stock price is above the striking price, the option's value equals the stock price minus the striking price.

FIGURE 11-2
Call Option's Value at Expiration Date with a Striking Price of $95

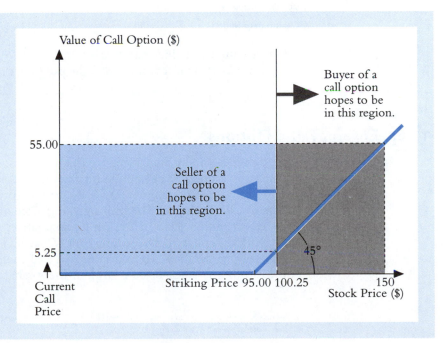

If the stock price is $100¼, the option holder has the right to buy the stock for $95, and his or her cash flow is $5¼, which is the premium paid to the option seller. In this case the buyer and seller of the option come out even.[1] For any price above $100¼, the call option buyer gains because the cash flow from exercising the option is larger than the premium. The option writer loses because he or she pays more than the premium received. The opposite holds if the stock price falls below $100¼.

If the stock price is below $95, the call option expires worthless. The line describing the call option's value coincides with the horizontal axis below $95. If the stock price is above $95, the call option's value equals the stock price minus the striking price. For each $1 increase in the stock price, the call option's value increases by $1 and is described by the 45° line.

The following problem demonstrates a put buyer's cash flows for stock prices at the expiration date.

PRACTICE BOX

Problem

Consider GE's January $90 put option (see Table 11-4). Calculate the option buyer's cash flows for the following hypothetical prices of GE stock at the expiration date: $85, $90, $100, and $105.

Solution

The buyer of this put pays $¼ (see Table 11-4); this is the immediate cash flow transferred from the buyer to the seller of the option. At the expiration date the buyer receives one of the following cash flows:

GE stock price ($)	85	90	100	105
Cash transferred ($)	(90 − 85) = 5	(90 − 90) = 0	0	0

Note that the put holder has the right to sell at $90. He or she hopes for a low stock price because if it is above $90 the put buyer receives nothing.

11.6.2 Leverage and Options

Although they can be used to reduce risk, options can also serve to increase risk. For example, investing in a call option is riskier than holding the underlying asset.

To illustrate this, suppose a stock is currently priced at $100 and the call option on the stock is traded for $10 with a striking price of $92. Further suppose the stock price can be either $115 or $90 on the expiration date. An investor who buys the stock will either earn 15% or lose 10%. What if, instead of investing $100 in the stock, the investor buys 10 call options at $10 each? In this case the investment is also $100. If the stock price is $115 at the expiration date, the value of each call

---

1. For simplicity we ignore the time value of money. However, it should be noted that the buyer pays $5¼ on the purchase date and receives it later at the expiration date.

option will be \$23 (\$115 − \$92 = \$23) and the value of the 10 call options is \$230; this amounts to a 130% rate of return. If the stock price is \$90, the options will be out of the money at the expiration date. Their price will be zero, which implies a 100% loss. By buying the option rather than the underlying stock, the fluctuations in the rates of return are magnified; this is why options traders commonly use the term "leverage effect."

Many people believe that options are highly speculative. However, as we shall see in the next section, if options are used properly, this is not so. On the contrary, a firm may use options to reduce its risk.

11.7 OPTION VALUES

We have seen how the option's value *at the expiration date* is determined. However, potential investors need to know the option's value *prior to the expiration date*. We turn to that topic next.

11.7.1 Upper and Lower Bounds on Call Option Values

A call option's value, which is measured by its current price, C_0, has two components:

1. **Intrinsic value**. This is the value resulting from immediate exercise of the option. If the current stock price, S_0, is below the striking price, E, the intrinsic value is zero. If the current stock price is above the striking price, the intrinsic value is $S_0 - E$. The option holder has the right but not the obligation to exercise the option; therefore, the intrinsic value will always be nonnegative.
2. **Time value**. This is the value based on the possibility that the stock price will rise prior to the expiration date. It, therefore, represents the source of potential future profit.

Consider, for example, the IBM February call option discussed in Section 11.4.2. The striking price was \$155, IBM's stock price was \$159⅛, and the option price was \$10⅛. This option's intrinsic value is the \$4⅛ that a holder can immediately obtain by exercising it. The \$6 difference between the option's price and its intrinsic value is due to the option's time value, based on the hope that the stock price will rise further.

The call option holder pays for these two economic values. The call option's current value cannot be lower than its intrinsic value because this is what the call option holder can obtain immediately by exercising the option in the market—that is, the intrinsic value sets a **lower bound** on the option's price.

A call option also has an upper bound. For a given stock price the call option's value cannot be higher than the current stock price. How much would you pay today for the right to buy the stock in the future? Certainly not more than the stock's current price. Otherwise, it would be better to simply buy the stock in the market. Therefore, the **upper bound** on the call option's value is the current stock price. Figure 11-3

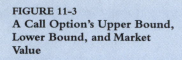

FIGURE 11-3
A Call Option's Upper Bound,
Lower Bound, and Market
Value

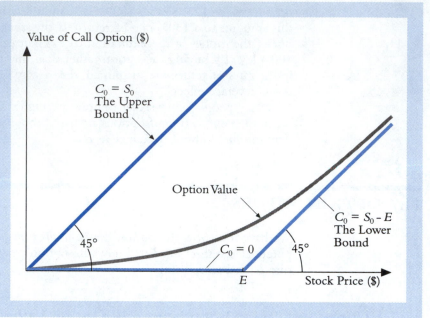

demonstrates a call option's upper and lower bounds. The horizontal axis measures various hypothetical values of the current stock price, S_0.

To elaborate on the two bounds:

1. The upper-bound line is described by a 45° line along which $C_0 = S_0$. For every $1 increase in S_0, the upper bound of C_0 increases by $1, which is described by a 45° line.

2. When the stock price is below E, the lower bound of C_0 is zero because there is no benefit from immediate exercise of the call option.

3. For any $1 stock price increase above E, the lower bound of C_0 also increases by $1. Returning to the IBM call option example, if the stock price is $156 and the striking price is $155, the call option can be exercised immediately, and the holder can receive $1 in cash. When the stock price is $157, the holder can receive $2 immediately. The lower bound of C_0 when the stock price is above E is also described by a 45° line.

4. The call option price must be above (or equal to) the lower bound and below (or equal to) the upper bound. The investor would be ready to pay a price higher than the lower bound because of the option's time value as explained above. The call option's current market price, as a function of the current stock price, can be described by the curve labeled "Option Value" in Figure 11-3. The figure illustrates a typical call option's value curve. For a very low stock price, the call option price is very close to the horizontal axis (the option is worth very lit-

tle); for a very high stock price, the call option price is very close to the lower bound line.

11.7.2 The Pricing of Options

The upper and lower bounds on a call option's value can be easily determined. However, in most cases these bounds are not very useful because they are too far apart. For example, if the stock price is $159⅛ and the call option's striking price is $155, the call option lower bound is

$$S_0 - E = \$159\tfrac{1}{8} - \$155 = \$4\tfrac{1}{8}$$

Therefore, $\$4\tfrac{1}{8} \leq C_0 \leq \$159\tfrac{1}{8}$ (and, indeed, the call price is $10⅛, which falls in this range).

This range is wide and probably not very useful. A CFO who considers purchasing a call option to hedge the firm's risk will want to know whether an option is overpriced or underpriced, and the $4⅛ to $159⅛ range will not be helpful in making a decision. Users of call options will want to know the *exact* call value *prior to the expiration date*; this is a more complex task.

Under what conditions can an option's exact value be determined before the expiration date? To answer this question, we turn to the concept of arbitrage, which is very important in option pricing. **Arbitrage** is a transaction whereby a certain positive cash flow is produced in the future on an investment requiring zero outlay today. Put differently, if $0 invested today produces a positive inflow with certainty in the future, we have an arbitrage transaction.

In equilibrium, arbitrage transactions are not possible. To see this, suppose you can buy a stock for $100 today and obtain $120 *with certainty* one year from now. If you can borrow at 10%, you have a *money machine*. You could borrow $100, buy the stock, and make a certain profit of $10 [$120 − ($100 × 1.1) = $10]. Everyone would want this money machine. The increased demand for this stock will push its market price up until equilibrium is restored when the current stock price fulfills the following condition:

$$S_0 = \frac{\$120}{1.1} \cong \$109.09$$

The stock's certain rate of return must be equal to the riskless interest rate, so that no excess profit can be made by borrowing and investing the borrowed money in the stock. At price S_0, the possibility of arbitrage vanishes. In equilibrium, arbitrage transactions are not available because market forces will have eliminated them.

With options one can create a portfolio composed of the option and the underlying stock such that this portfolio's return is certain. Let us first assume that such a portfolio can be created and show how the option price is determined. We demonstrate this with the use of call options and then show that put option prices can be determined from the call option's price. For example, suppose we create a portfolio by buying one share of stock and writing (selling) two call options on that stock.

This portfolio's total investment will be $I = S_0 - 2C_0$ at $t = 0$. When you write a call, you receive C_0, which decreases the portfolio's initial outlay. If the return on this portfolio at date $t = 1$ is \$K *with certainty*, then by the no-arbitrage argument in equilibrium, we must have

$$\frac{K}{I} = \frac{K}{S_0 - 2C_0} = 1 + r$$

where r is the riskless interest rate corresponding to the investment period—the time interval between $t = 1$ and $t = 0$. If we know K, S_0, and r, then C_0 can be determined—which is the call option's equilibrium price. Any deviation from this value implies that arbitrage transactions are available. We demonstrate this claim in the following problem. Furthermore, we show that if the future stock price can take on only two possible values, a portfolio with a certain future value can be created. Hence the call option price can be determined.

PRACTICE BOX

Problem

Suppose that for each share of IBM stock held, you write n call options. Assume the stock is currently selling for $S_0 = \$100$, and its price will be either \$80 or \$120 at the expiration date. The striking price is $E = \$100$, and the interest rate for the relevant period (from the current date through to the expiration date) is $r = 5\%$.

a. How many call options should you write to guarantee a certain future cash flow? That is, what should be the value of n to ensure a *certain* cash flow in the future? Calculate the cash flow.

b. What is the call option's equilibrium price? How much larger is it than the intrinsic value?

c. What is the NPV on the investment in a portfolio composed of one share of IBM and n call options?

d. What investment strategy would provide an arbitrage profit if the call option price were $C_0 = \$15$?

e. At what price does no arbitrage profit exist?

Solution

a. If we write a call option with a \$100 striking price, we will have to pay nothing if the stock price is \$80 at the expiration date and pay \$20 if it is \$120 at the expiration date. Therefore, if we write n call options for each share held, the portfolio's total future value will be:

If the stock price is \$80: $\$80 - (\$0 \times n)$
If the stock price is \$120: $\$120 - (\$20 \times n)$

To ensure a certain cash flow in the future, regardless of the stock price at the expiration date, we must have

$$\$80 - (n \times \$0) = \$120 - (n \times \$20)$$

(continued)

Therefore:

$$\$120 - \$80 = n \times \$20, \text{ so } n = 2$$

Thus, if we write two call options for each share, the future cash flow will be $80 with certainty.

b. If we write two call options, we receive $2C_0$, which will reduce the portfolio's initial outlay. Therefore, by the no-arbitrage argument we must have

$$\frac{K}{I} = \frac{80}{100 - 2C_0} = 1.05$$

where I is the investment and $80 is the certain return.
Therefore:

$$\$80 = (1.05 \times \$100) - (1.05 \times 2C_0)$$

and

$$C_0 = \frac{\$105 - \$80}{2 \times 1.05} = \frac{\$25}{2.10} \cong \$11.90$$

The call option's intrinsic value is $S_0 - E = \$100 - \$100 = \$0$. Thus, the call option's price will be $11.90 higher than the intrinsic value. The $11.90 is the option's time value and is paid in return for the possibility of future profit.

c. The investment in such a portfolio is

$$S_0 - 2C_0 = \$100 - (2 \times \$11.90) = \$76.20$$

The investment's NPV is

$$\text{NPV} = \frac{\$80}{1.05} - \$76.20 \cong \$0$$

These results shouldn't be surprising. The portfolio's future income is certain. If there is to be no arbitrage profit, the NPV must be zero. If the NPV were positive, investors would buy this portfolio, the price would increase, and the NPV would decrease until it reaches zero.

d. If $C_0 = \$15$, the portfolio's total investment would be

$$S_0 - 2C_0 = \$100 - (2 \times \$15) = \$70$$

The portfolio's internal rate of return is the value of R that satisfies:

$$\frac{\$80}{\$70} = (1 + R) \cong 1.143$$

The rate of return would be 14.3%. Because this rate of return is certain, you could borrow at 5%, invest in the portfolio, and make a certain profit of 9.3%.

(continued)

The investment would be a money machine. People would borrow money and invest in this portfolio, its price would increase until its rate of return fulfills the condition $R = 5\%$, and the arbitrage profit would vanish.

e. We have seen that the call option price cannot be more than $11.90. By a similar argument it cannot be less than $11.90; that is, only at price $11.90 will there be no arbitrage profit.[2]

From this problem we see that if we create a portfolio composed of an option and an underlying asset producing a certain future cash flow, we can determine the option's price before the expiration date. The crucial question is: Is it possible to create a *zero-variance* (or certain return) *portfolio* of this type? If the answer is yes, under what conditions can this be achieved?

In general a riskless portfolio can be created whenever there is perfect correlation (positive or negative) between the returns on two assets. Let us focus on call options, and then use the put-call parity to solve for the put option value. Stocks and call options can be combined in a portfolio to produce a certain return in the following two cases:

1. *The stock price at the expiration date can take on only one of two values.* When the stock price at the expiration date can take on *only two* values (e.g., $80 and $120), no matter what the probabilities of these two values, there will be perfect positive correlation between the call option's and the stock's rates of return. When there are only two possible values, we determine the option value by what is called the *binomial model of option valuation.* Although this is not a very realistic scenario, we consider the binomial model because it helps demonstrate the role of perfect correlation in determining option price. Also, it can be used to derive the well-known Black–Scholes option valuation formula discussed in Appendix 11A.

   To see that perfect correlation exists in such a case, plot a graph with the underlying asset's future value on the horizontal axis and the call option's future value on the vertical axis. Because the stock price can take on only two values, the call option at the expiration date can also have only two values; therefore, there can be only two points on this graph. These two points can be connected by a straight line, indicating a perfect correlation between the two assets' prices.[3] If there are more than two possible prices (i.e., $80, $100, and $180), there will

---

2. To see this claim, we need to introduce the concept of short sales. The investor can borrow one share from a broker, sell it, and receive a cash flow. Thereafter, the investor repurchases the share and returns it to the broker. Such a transaction is called *short selling.*

Let us turn now to our example. If the call option's price is lower than $C_0 = \$11.90$, say $8, then the portfolio's initial investment will be $84 ($S_0 - 2C_0 = \$100 - 2 \times \$8 = \$84$). In such case you could "short" the portfolio to obtain the $84 and deposit it at 5%. The deposit's value at the end of period will be $88.20 ($\$84 \times 1.05 = \$88.20$). You pay $80 when you repurchase the portfolio (recall the portfolio's future value is $80 with certainty) and gain $8.20. When you sell the portfolio short, you sell the share and buy calls, which increases the call price. Any deviation from $11.90 creates an arbitrage opportunity.

3. Suppose we have a straight line of the form $y = a + bx$, where y and x are the stock's and the call option's rates of return, respectively, and b is positive. Then the correlation between y and x will be +1. To see this use Equation 8.5 for the correlation:

$$\rho_{x,\,y} = \frac{\text{Cov}(x,\,y)}{\sigma_x \sigma_y} = \frac{\text{Cov}(x,\,a\,+\,bx)}{\sigma_x \sigma_y} = \frac{b\sigma_x^2}{\sigma_x |b| \sigma_x} = 1$$

where $\text{Cov}(a,x) = 0$, $\text{Cov}(x,bx) = b\sigma_x^2$ and $\sigma_y = |b|\,\sigma_x$ where $|b|$ is the absolute value of b. When we consider a stock and a put option returns, $b < 0$ and $\rho_{x,y} > -1$.

be three points that may or may not lie on one straight line. Deviations from a straight line would mean that there is less than perfect correlation ($\rho < 1$). In this case there is no guarantee that a portfolio with a certain cash flow can be created.

2. *The portfolio can be revised at short time intervals.* In reality the stock price may take many possible values. However, if we add the assumption that the portfolio can be revised at short time intervals, the option price can be determined. Fischer Black and Myron Scholes derived a formula to value options when the stock price takes many values and the portfolio can be revised continuously.[4] The Black-Scholes option pricing formula implicitly assumes perfect correlation between the rate of return on the option and the rate of return on the stock for any short investment interval. More details on the Black–Scholes formula are given in Appendix 11A.

11.7.3 Put-Call Parity

The values of a call option and a put option on the same stock with the same striking price and the same maturity are related by a simple formula called **put-call parity**.

To derive this formula, we consider two possible portfolios. Table 11-7 demonstrates the cash flows on these portfolios—one consisting of a share of stock and a put option financed by borrowing the strike price (Portfolio A) and the other composed of a single call option (Portfolio B). The two portfolios have the same future cash flow, $S_1 - E$, if the stock price at the expiration date is larger than the exercise price and zero otherwise. Two assets with the same future cash flow in each event ($S_1 > E$ or $S_1 < E$) must have the same current price. Therefore, the following expression must hold:

$$C_0 = S_0 + P_0 - \frac{E}{(1 + r)}$$

where C_0 and P_0 are the respective equilibrium prices of the call option and the put option at time $t = 0$, E is the striking price, and r is the riskless interest rate over the period left to the option's expiration. This formula, which relates the put and call prices, is called the *put-call parity*. If S_0 and C_0 are known, the value of P_0 can be determined.

TABLE 11-7 Cash Flows from Two Alternative Portfolios			$t = 0$	Future Cash Flow	
	Investment			If $S_1 > E$	If $S_1 \leq E$
	Portfolio A	Buy stock.	$-S_0$	S_1	S_1
		Buy put.	$-P_0$	0	$E - S_1$
		Borrow at interest rate r.	$E/(1 + r)$	$-E$	$-E$
		Total	$-S_0 - P_0 + E/(1 + r)$	$S_1 - E$	0
	Portfolio B	Buy call.	$-C_0$	$S_1 - E$	0

4. See Fischer Black and Myron Scholes, "The Pricing of Options and Corporate Liabilities," *Journal of Political Economy* 81, no. 3 (May–June 1973): 637.

11.8 HOW FIRMS USE OPTIONS

In the past, options were used mainly by individual investors and by fund managers. Indeed, speculative investors who believe they can predict market movements often use options. Today corporate managers also use options. Option pricing can be applied to a wide range of a firm's operations because many business transactions have option-like features. For instance, firms can use options to hedge risk. We saw in Connecting Theory to Practice 11.1 that financial analysts and investors may penalize managers who do not make use of the available financial tools to hedge risk. In this section we describe some of the ways that management can make good use of options.

11.8.1 Stocks and Bonds as Options

Stocks, bonds, and many other financial transactions can be evaluated using the option valuation model, which provides a tool to estimate whether a given financial transaction is worthwhile. Let's see, first, how the option valuation model can be used to evaluate stock. Suppose you would like to determine whether a levered firm's stock is over- or undervalued. You could use any of several models for that evaluation. In this section we show that the future cash flows to shareholders are identical to a call option's future cash flows when the underlying asset is the firm's total assets. Therefore, we can use the option evaluation formula to evaluate stock.

Suppose a firm has issued both stocks and bonds. Although the stockholders are traditionally considered the firm's owners, the stockholders and bondholders have reversed roles with options—that is, the bondholders are viewed as owners of the firm's assets who sell call options on the firm's assets to the stockholders. Why? Because in a levered firm we can view the stockholders' future cash flow as equal to the cash flow of a call option on the firm's assets. We show next that issuing bonds is equivalent to the stockholders selling the firm's assets to the bondholders but leaving themselves with a call option on the firm's assets. This does not mean that call options on the firm's assets actually exist in the market. However, if stockholders' cash flows are identical to the cash flows on a call option, we can use the formula in Appendix 11A to evaluate those flows. In our specific case, the call value must be equal to the stock value. This provides a way to determine how much the firm's stock is worth.

Management can use this model in several ways. For example, suppose a stock's market price is $105 per share and the valuation model yields a price of $120 per share. Management may decide that the stock is undervalued and repurchase it.

Table 11-8 shows the cash flows to the stockholders and to the holders of a hypothetical call option on the firm's assets. Suppose the market value of the firm's assets at the expiration date is as given in the left-hand column of the table. For example, if the value is $15,000, that means the firm can liquidate its assets and receive a cash flow of $15,000. In that case, if you hold a call option on the firm's assets with a $6,000 striking price, you will receive nothing as long as the asset value is below $6,000. For asset values above $6,000, you will receive the asset value minus the striking price.

Now, instead of holding a call option on the firm's assets, suppose you buy the firm's stock. Suppose further that this firm's leverage consists of debt with a par value of $6,000.[5] If the asset value at the expiration date is below $6,000, the stockholders will receive nothing. If the asset value is greater than $6,000, the cash flow to the stockholders will equal the asset value minus what the firm pays to the bondholders. Because the future cash flow to a levered firm's stockholders equals the cash flow to the holder of a hypothetical call option on the firm's assets at a striking price of $6,000, the market value of a levered firm's stock must be equal to the market value of a call option on the firm's assets.

11.8.2 Bonds, Limited Liability, and Put Options

Continuing the previous example, if no risk of bankruptcy exists and the riskless interest rate is 5%, the bondholders will receive a certain future cash flow. Therefore, the bond's current market value is the discounted value:

$$\frac{\$6,000}{1.05} \cong \$5,714.29$$

where $6,000 is the bond's face value. In this section we show how to use the value of a put option on the firm's assets to estimate by how much the discount rate should be raised to evaluate bonds in case of possible bankruptcy. We do not claim that such a put option exists. However, management can use a hypothetical put to determine the appropriate discount rate.

Suppose the firm's CFO is planning to issue this bond, and the underwriter tells the CFO that the bond can be sold for $5,000. The cost of debt is higher than 5%

TABLE 11-8 Cash Flow on a Levered Firm's Stocks and on a Call Option on the Firm's Assets	Value of the Firm's Assets ($)	(a) Holding a Call Option on the Firm's Assets		(b) Holding the Firm's Stock	
		Striking Price ($)	Call Option Holders' Cash Flow ($)	Debt ($)	Stockholders' Cash Flow ($)
	4,000	6,000	0	6,000	0
	5,000	6,000	0	6,000	0
	6,000	6,000	0	6,000	0
	7,000	6,000	1,000	6,000	1,000
	8,000	6,000	2,000	6,000	2,000
	9,000	6,000	3,000	6,000	3,000
	10,000	6,000	4,000	6,000	4,000
	15,000	6,000	9,000	6,000	9,000

5. For simplicity assume the $6,000 represents the principal as well as the interest paid to bondholders at the expiration date. This type of bond is called a *zero-coupon bond* and will be discussed in Chapter 12.

Do you know what LEAPS are? How about a naked writer? What's the difference between an American option and a European option? You can find the definitions of these terms (and a lot of other terms) in the options glossary maintained by the Chicago Board Options Exchange.
http://www.cboe.com/intro/glossary.html

because of bankruptcy risk. The question the CFO faces is whether $5,000 is the right price for the firm's bond. Should the CFO agree to issue the bond for $5,000?[6] Once again, the CFO can use the option valuation model to decide whether such a price is justified and whether the cost of debt is 20% as the underwriter's suggested price implies. Let's elaborate on the factors that might explain the difference between the $5,714.29 and $5,000 figures.

Because bonds are risky, bondholders may not recover their $6,000 at the expiration date. Therefore, a higher discount rate should be used, and a lower value for the bond will be obtained. But by how much should the discount rate rise to reflect the bond's risk?

The option valuation model can help answer this question. To see this, note that stockholders are protected by the firm's *limited liability* feature. The most they can lose is their investment in the firm. In case of bankruptcy the bondholders cannot claim the stockholder's personal assets. If the bondholders could dig into stockholders' private assets and if the stockholders had enough assets, then the bonds could be considered riskless and their market value would be $5,714.29. However, because of the stock's limited liability feature, the bonds are risky, and their value will be lower than $5,714.29.

The limited liability feature can be seen as a hypothetical put option. The stockholders issue bonds, and bondholders, in effect, give the stockholders a put option on the firm's assets with a striking price of $6,000. If the firm's asset value falls below $6,000, the stockholders will exercise the put option, sell the assets to the bondholders at $6,000, and use that amount to repay the $6,000 debt to bondholders. The net cash flow to stockholders from such a transaction would be zero. In exercising the put option, the assets are simply transferred to the bondholders with no further claim from the stockholders. Bondholders lose the difference between $6,000 and the value of the assets. When the bondholders transfer this put option to the stockholders, they will agree to pay less than $5,714.29 for the bonds because the put has an economic value. The risky bond's value can be expressed as follows:

$$\text{Value of risky bond} = \text{Value of riskless bond} - \text{Value of put option}$$

In our example, if the riskless bond value is $5,714.29 and the put option's value is estimated by the underwriter at, say, $714.29, then the risky bond's value will be $5,000 ($5,714.29 − $714.29 = $5,000). It is reasonable for the firm to receive less than $5,714.29 because it is protected by the limited liability feature. The bond's low price reflects this feature. So, should the firm agree to issue the bond for $5,000? The firm's CFO can use the option valuation model to estimate the value of the hypothetical put option. If the put option's value is $714.29, then $5,000 should be considered a fair price. If it is more than $714.29, then $5,000 is a bargain for the firm.

Evaluating risky bonds and the cost of debt is difficult. The option valuation model provides an explicit method. It is used to evaluate put options that, in turn,

---

6. For simplicity we ignore the underwriter's fee.

enable the risky bond's value to be determined. If, indeed, $5,000 is the correct price of a risky bond, then the cost of the risky debt is 20%.

11.8.3 Insurance and Put Options

As indicated at the beginning of the chapter, managers can use option pricing in making all sorts of business decisions. Here we review the logic behind using put options to price such disparate business transactions as fire insurance, underwriting costs, and portfolio insurance.

FIRE INSURANCE

Firms own property. If there is a fire, the property's value will decline. To avoid the effects of such a disaster, firms purchase insurance. Suppose the insurance agreement stipulates that if fire damage occurs, the insurance company will pay the sum required to restore the value of the firm's assets to their $1 million current value. For example, if the remaining assets' value after a fire is $400,000, the insurance company will pay the firm $600,000 for the loss.

Receiving money in this case is like selling what remains of the assets to the insurance company for $1 million. Accordingly, the firm can be thought of as having a put option on its assets with a $1 million striking price. The option valuation model can be applied to determine whether the premium the insurance company charges is reasonable.

UNDERWRITING COSTS

In Chapter 14 we will see that when it issues a stock or other security, the firm works with a financial institution called an *underwriter*. Suppose the two parties agree that the underwriter will pay the firm $10 for each share of stock issued, even if the stock price drops below $10. How much should the firm pay the underwriter for such an agreement? In essence, the underwriter can be seen as selling a put option to the issuing firm with a striking price of $10. This put option's value can be determined using the option valuation model.

PORTFOLIO INSURANCE

Many portfolio managers protect their clients' investments from large losses by buying put options on market portfolios such as the Standard & Poor's 500 index. Suppose the S&P index's current price is $240. The portfolio manager might buy a put option on the S&P index with a striking price of, say, $220 to protect the value of the portfolio at this striking price.

Thus, the portfolio manager will have a bound on the losses incurred on the portfolio held. If the S&P drops to say, $180, the portfolio manager will exercise the put, and the profit of $40 ($220 − $180) will cover *some* of the losses on the portfolio. Holding a put option with a portfolio of assets reduces the combined portfolio's risk. This option application is called *portfolio insurance*.

Although portfolio insurance is used mainly by portfolio managers, a firm can also use it. A firm that holds a portfolio of assets such as employee pension or retirement funds often has put options on the portfolio to protect its value. Generally, no options are traded on the specific portfolio that a firm, individual investor, or institutional investor holds. However, options are traded on similar portfolios, and one can buy such options to obtain the needed portfolio insurance.

11.8.4 International Trade and Options

Firms involved in international trade can hedge foreign currency risk by using forward contracts, by buying swap contracts (discussed in Section 11.9), or by buying options. In this section we focus on the role of options in reducing foreign currency risk.

Suppose a U.S. firm exports a product to Germany for 100 million German marks (DM). If the current exchange rate is 1.6 DM per dollar or $0.625 per DM, the firm should receive $62.5 million (100 million DM/1.6 = $62.5 million). Suppose the U.S. firm's production costs are $55 million. If it sells the product for cash, the U.S. firm's net profit will be $7.5 million.

If most sales are made on, say, 30 days' credit, the German firm will not have to pay the U.S. firm 100 million DM immediately. As we know, foreign exchange rates fluctuate. The actual profit on this export transaction depends on the exchange rate at the time payment is made. If the exchange rate is 2 DM per dollar in 30 days, the U.S. firm will receive only $50 million (100 million DM/2 = $50 million). In this case the U.S. firm will lose $5 million. However, the CFO can protect the firm from adverse foreign exchange fluctuations by—you guessed it—buying a put option on the exchange rate.

The financial media publish put option prices on foreign currencies. For example, assume that the price of a one-month put option on the DM was 0.43 cents with a striking price of 62.5 cents per DM. At this price, the CFO could buy puts for 100 million DM, which would cost $430,000 ($0.43 per DM × 100 million DM). With a put option, the firm has the right to sell the 100 million DM at 62.5 cents per DM in the future to receive $62.5 million ($0.625 per DM × 100 million DM).

If each DM is worth more than 62.5 cents, the put option will expire worthless, and the firm will lose the $430,000 premium. This would still leave the firm with a large profit. If, on the other hand, the mark is worth less than 62.5 cents, the put option allows the firm to sell each DM for 62.5 cents. Because the firm's profit will be $7.07 million ($62.5 million − $0.43 million premium − $55 million costs), it will not lose money on its export transaction.

11.8.5 Hedging Interest Rate Risk with Options

Suppose a firm has issued bonds that pay an interest rate of 10% and 10 years left to maturity. The CFO believes the market interest rate may drop to 8% in the near future. If this happens, the firm will suffer an opportunity loss because it will still have to pay 10% interest on its bonds. The firm can hedge interest rate risk by buying a call option, called an **interest rate option**, on the bonds. To see how this works, consider the following interest rate option listed in *Barron's* on January 6, 1997:

Interest Rate Option

Bond	Expiration Date	Striking Price	Option Price	N.Y. Close Price
5-year Treasury note	March '97	$65	$1¾₁₆	$62

By paying $1¾₁₆ per option on January 6, 1997, the firm has the right to buy a Treasury note at $65 at any time before March 1997. If the market interest rate decreases, the bond price will increase and the firm will have a capital gain by exercising the call option. This gain will offset the firm's losses due to the higher interest rate on its bonds (10%). Interest rate options can hedge the risk of adverse interest rate fluctuations.

In Applying Theory to Practice 11.1, we see how a firm uses options to hedge foreign exchange and interest rate risks.

APPLYING THEORY TO PRACTICE 11.1

USING OPTIONS TO REDUCE FOREIGN RISK

Ciba Group, a Swiss pharmaceutical firm, is heavily involved in international trade with subsidiaries and associated companies in more than 60 countries around the world.[7] In 1993 the firm's total sales amounted to 22,647 million SF (Swiss francs).

The following extracts are taken from Ciba's 1993 financial statements:

1. Hedged currency situation. An active currency hedging program is followed
   • To minimize transaction losses on foreign currency positions.
   • To cover the downward risks of future cash flows by hedging satisfactory currency rates.
   • Utilizing mainly option-based instruments.
     The strengthening Swiss franc caused unfavorable currency effects in 1993. The impact was significantly reduced by active hedging.
2. Financial instruments. The group enters into forward exchange and option contracts, interest rate and currency swaps, and other financial instruments in order to hedge interest rate and currency risk to enhance the return on liquid funds. The group restricts its exposure to credit risk by entering into such financial instrument contracts only with parties that have an adequate credit rating.
     The return from financial instruments designed to hedge foreign currency movements is included in the profit and loss statement under

7. In December 1996, Ciba merged with Sandoz to create a new firm called Novartis. Its stock trades on the Swiss stock exchange.

"currency and hedging transaction gains(losses)." Returns from financial instruments designed to hedge interest rates or enhance the return on liquid funds are included under "financial income" or "financial expense."

3. Short-term debt in various currencies. The short-term debt (excluding current portion of long-term debt) is denominated in the following currencies and bears interest at the following average rates:

	Short-Term Debt (Stated in SF millions)	Average Interest Rate (%)
Swiss Francs	981	5.3
U.S. Dollars	864	4.0
Pounds Sterling	327	6.1
Deutsche Marks	9	8.5
French Francs	158	6.9
Japanese Yen	75	2.8
Other	843	8.1
Total	3,257	5.8

Source: Ciba Group's 1993 financial statements.

Additional information:
The following is selected data taken from *Barron's*:

Foreign Currency Options[8] (Swiss Francs—cents per unit)	Sales (100s)	Last	N.Y. Close
SFranc May 70½	2	0.52	70.76
SFranc May 70½ P	15	0.36	70.76
SFranc May 71 P	2	0.65	70.76
SFranc May 71½	2	0.37	70.76
SFranc May 76	10	0	70.76
SFranc Jun 70½	1	0.81	70.76
SFranc Dec 68 P	2	1.15	70.76

Source: *Barron's* 74, no. 19 (May 1994): MW89. Reprinted by permission of *Barron's Market Week,* © 1994 Dow Jones & Company, Inc. All Rights Reserved Worldwide.

Questions

1. If Ciba's financial statements were stated in another currency, would the rate of return on the investment be different? Use the information that the Swiss franc (SF) has become stronger relative to the U.S. dollar to demonstrate your answer.

8. Note that the underlying asset is the foreign currency. For example, note the "SFranc May 70½ P" entry. The price of such an option is 0.36 cents, and the current exchange rate is 70.76 cents per franc.

2. The financial statements indicate that Ciba uses options and forward contracts to reduce risk. Explain the difference between these two financial instruments. Should Ciba buy call or put options to reduce its risk? Explain.

3. Ciba uses financial instruments to hedge interest rate risk. Explain interest rate risk and how the firm can eliminate it with interest rate options. Should Ciba buy put or call options on the interest rate? Explain.

4. Let us focus now on Extract 3 and the data taken from *Barron's* reported previously. The firm had a short-term debt denominated in dollars whose value at the end of 1993 was 864 million SF.
   a. Suppose Ciba had to pay the debt in U.S. dollars in May 1994. How many francs will Ciba have paid if the exchange rate on the maturity date of the debt is 65 cents per SF?
   b. Suppose in accounting for the exchange rate and the accumulated interest, Ciba needed to pay the U.S. lender $611.37 million in May 1994. How much in SF would Ciba have paid if it bought a May put option with a striking price of 70½ cents per SF? What would the cost have been in comparison to the unprotected debt suggested in 4a? (Recall that the underlying asset is the SF, and it was assumed the exchange rate in May would fall to 65 U.S. cents for each SF.)

MAKING THE CONNECTION

1. The reported income per share depends on the currency in which these earnings are stated due to the time gap between the investment date and the date at which the sales are made. Since the exchange rate may differ between these dates, reported profit may also change. To illustrate, let us see how a strengthening of the SF affects the firm's earnings. Suppose the firm invested 1 million SF at the beginning of the year and generated sales of 2 million SF at the end of the year. Since Ciba had no other expenses, its net income would be 1 million SF, and the rate of return would be

$$\frac{2 \text{ million SF}}{1 \text{ million SF}} - 1 = 1 \text{ or } 100\%$$

Let us now turn to U.S. dollar calculations. Assume an exchange rate of 2 SF per U.S. dollar at the beginning of the year and 1 SF per U.S. dollar at the end of the year. The investment is $500,000, and the cash flow at the end of the year is $2 million. The reported income would be $1.5 million ($2 million − $0.5 million = $1.5), and the rate of return would be

$$\frac{\$2 \text{ million}}{\$0.5 \text{ million}} - 1 = 3 \text{ or } 300\%$$

The currency used greatly affects the investment's reported profit.

2. The difference between forward contracts and options is that forward contracts (on the exchange rate) specify the exchange rate the investor will

receive at a future date. These contracts must be fulfilled whether the exchange rate increases or decreases; they entail an obligation. Options, on the other hand, promise the investor a bound on the future exchange rate. If, for example, you buy a put option on the exchange rate (to sell SF and receive U.S. dollars) and the exchange rate increases, you will let the option expire and sell the currency (SF) at the higher market rate. However, if the exchange rate decreases, you will exercise your option to sell foreign currency at the striking exchange rate.

Because Ciba is a Swiss firm, it reports its income in SF. However, it has debt in foreign currencies. To hedge the exchange rate risk of its U.S. dollar debt, Ciba should buy put options that guarantee the right to exchange each SF for U.S. dollars at a predetermined rate.

Recall that the higher the exchange rate, the better it is for Ciba. Suppose the put option gives the holder the right to sell each SF for 70 U.S. cents. If the exchange rate in the future is, say, 75 cents per SF, the option will expire worthless. However, if the future exchange rate is 60 cents per SF, the put option will be exercised and the debt will have an upper bound in terms of SF. With these options each SF will be sold for at least 70 U.S. cents.

3. Interest rate risk arises because the firm has long- or short-term debt involving r_0 percent interest to the bondholder, even if the market interest rate falls below r_0 percent. If the rate does fall, the firm loses money in the sense that it loses the opportunity to raise money at the lower interest rate. This risk can be eliminated by buying a call option on a bond of similar maturity to that of the firm's liabilities.

The hedging works as follows: If the interest rate increases, the bond price will fall, and the call option will expire worthless. In such case the firm's debt, which was issued at a lower interest rate, will be preferred to new debt available in the market, and the firm will be satisfied. However, if the interest rate decreases, the bond price will increase. In this event the firm will exercise the call option to buy the bond, say at an exercise price of $900 when the market price is $1,100, and it will realize a capital gain of $200. This capital gain offsets the *opportunity loss* to the firm from issuing the old debt at the former higher interest rate. Ciba, like all firms with long-term debt, may buy call options on interest (actually these are call options on bonds) to reduce its risk.

4. a. The amount of debt payable in U.S. dollars is 864 million SF. Because the current exchange rate is 70.76 cents/franc (see the table from *Barron's*), the debt in dollar terms is $611.37 million (864 million SF × 0.7076 ≅ $611.37 million). Assuming a 65 cent/SF exchange rate on the maturity date, Ciba will need 940.57 ($611.37 million/0.65) million SF to pay its debt. Adverse foreign currency fluctuations lead to losses.

   b. Because Ciba owes $611.37 million and receives $0.705 for each SF when the put option is exercised, it needs to buy 867.2 million

($611.37 million/$0.705) put options (where each put sells 1 SF for $0.705).

Assuming the debt matures in May, the options needed are the May 70½ put options that cost 0.36 U.S. cents each. The total investment in these options will be 4.412 million SF (867.2 million options × $0.0036/0.7076).

If the exchange rate falls to 65 cents per SF, Ciba will exercise its options at $0.705 per SF. All together, Ciba will have $611.38 million (867.2 million put options × $0.705 ≅ $611.38 million), which equals the firm's short-term debt denominated in U.S. dollars (the slight difference is due to rounding).

The total expense of this hedging procedure, including the debt repayments, amounts to 871.61 million SF [4.412 million SF (payment for the options) plus 867.2 million SF (selling the SF when the options are exercised)]. This total is much lower than the 940.57 million SF needed when hedging is not used. In this case (where the exchange rate is 65 cents per SF) hedging the foreign currency risk is beneficial.

11.8.6 Hedging Risk Using Options on Futures

As noted earlier, buying a futures contract entails an obligation, whereas buying an option on a futures contract gives the holder the right but not the obligation to exercise the transaction. Both of these financial instruments have a price, and the firm has to weigh the benefits and costs of each.

For instance, on January 6, 1997, *Barron's* quoted the following price for cotton futures: May 1997, 74.08 cents per pound. This means that on January 6, 1997, a textile firm could buy a contract for cotton to be delivered in May 1997 at a fixed price of 74.08 cents per pound. If in March 1997 the price had jumped to, say, 95 cents per pound, the textile firm would still get the cotton for 74.08 cents per pound. In this way the firm could hedge the risk of an increase in the price of cotton.

Suppose, though, the price of cotton declines to, say, 60 cents per pound, and the firm does not wish to commit itself to 74.08 cents per pound. In that case the firm should have bought a May 1997 *call option on the futures contract*. This complicated-sounding asset would work like this: On January 6, 1997, *Barron's* quoted a call option on a cotton futures contract, with a striking price of 77 cents per pound, at 4.3 cents per pound. If the price of the cotton futures increased above 77 cents, the firm would exercise the option and pay 77 cents to purchase the cotton futures. Similarly, if the price of cotton rose and, as a result, the price of the futures contract also rose to, say, 100 cents per pound, the firm will buy the futures contract for 77 cents per pound even though futures contracts for cotton are traded for 100 cents per pound. The total cost to the firm is 81.3 cents per pound (77 cents per pound + 4.3 cents for the option). However, if the price of the cotton futures contract fell below 77 cents per pound to, say, 70 cents per pound, the firm would enjoy the lower price of cotton and would not exercise the option. Thus, an option on the futures contract, unlike a futures contract itself, does not entail an obligation to complete the transaction. In such case the option expires worthless, and the firm buys the cotton in the market for 70 cents per pound. However, since the firm also bought the option for 4.3 cents per pound, its total cost is 74.3 cents per pound of cotton.

11.9 HEDGING RISK WITH SWAP CONTRACTS

A firm is sometimes involved in transactions that seem very profitable but entail risk that the firm cannot control. To reduce this risk, a firm may use a **swap contract**, which is made between two counterparties who agree to exchange payments based on one asset's value compared to a payment based on another asset's value. A simplified example would be two bondholders agreeing to exchange coupon payments over the life of the bonds. The two sides of a swap are referred to as *counterparties*.

The three principal types of swaps are: interest rate, currency, and commodity. The exchange of cash payments is based on the interest rate levels for interest rate swaps, on foreign exchange rate levels for currency rate swaps, and on commodity price levels for commodity swaps. Let us elaborate on the various swap contracts.

11.9.1 Interest Rate Swaps

In an **interest rate swap** the counterparties exchange interest payments. For example, suppose one counterparty has an outstanding loan on which it is obligated to make interest payments at a fixed rate, and the other counterparty has a loan on which it must make interest payments at a rate that changes periodically. The counterparties decide to exchange the fixed-rate interest payments for the floating-rate interest payments. This is called a *fixed-for-floating swap*. The two parties in a fixed-for-floating swap are the *receive-fixed counterparty* and the *receive-floating counterparty*. The receive-fixed counterparty receives payments based on the fixed rate and makes payments based on the floating rate. Conversely, the receive-floating counterparty receives payments based on the floating rate and makes payments based on the fixed rate. In practice the two parties pay each other only the difference between the cash flows. They can do this through a mediator, or they can pay directly to other parties as explained in Connecting Theory to Practice 11.2.

What is the benefit of such a swap? Connecting Theory to Practice 11.2 describes the parties involved in one interest rate swap and demonstrates their motivation for entering into a swap contract.

> **CONNECTING THEORY TO PRACTICE 11.2**
>
> **LET'S SWAP**
>
> A hamburger franchisee gets his capital from a commercial bank in Chicago, where he can borrow only at a floating rate (say, prime plus 1%) because the

bank simply can't risk loading up its balance sheet with any assets of longer duration than 90 days. Why? Because the bank's liabilities—checking accounts, for example—are of very short duration. A checking customer does not want to be told that he has to wait five years for his paycheck to clear.

The restaurateur, meanwhile, would much prefer the safety of a fixed rate over the next five years, even though the longer-term loan will cost him plenty . . . . He's willing to pay the extra points of interest to avoid the risk that the prime will spike up to 15% and bankrupt him.

Now add two more players to the drama: a bond issuer and an insurance company.

The bond issuer might be the Export-Import Bank of Japan ["Exim"]. Its size and prime credit quality give it access to a credit market the restaurant owner doesn't have, namely, publicly traded seven-year notes. The notes are fixed-rate because that's what Exim Japan lenders—pension funds and insurance companies, for the most part—want. Exim Japan's treasurer, however, is willing to take a chance on floating rates. After all, this company [Exim] is not going to be bankrupted by a sudden jump in the prime, and the yield curve[9] is so abnormally steep that borrowing at the short end is irresistible for borrowers who can stomach the risk.

Solution: rate swaps, mediated by banks or securities firms. In a rate swap, no principal changes hands, just exposures to the yield curve. The hamburger outlet, in effect, picks up Exim Japan's obligation to pay a fixed rate over seven years, while Exim Japan assumes the hamburger outlet's floating-rate exposure. No risk of principal is involved since the players are swapping only streams of interest.

Source: Robert Lenzner and William Heuslein, "The Age of Digital Capitalism," *Forbes* 151, no. 7 (March 1993): 62–72. Reprinted By Permission of FORBES Magazine © Forbes Inc. 1993.

MAKING THE CONNECTION

We see that the restaurateur wants a fixed-interest loan but cannot get one at a reasonable rate. Exim Japan issues fixed-rate bonds because this is what it can sell the insurance company. However, Exim Japan would prefer to issue bonds with floating rates. A swap contract solves the problem. The hamburger outlet picks up Exim Japan's obligation to pay the fixed rate over seven years, and Exim Japan assumes the hamburger outlet's floating-rate exposure. Both parties benefit from the swap.

11.9.2 Currency Swaps

A **currency swap** requires the exchange of different currencies. The first currency swap occurred in August 1981 between IBM and the World Bank. The details of a

9. A yield curve is a graph that relates the number of years until a bond matures (on the horizontal axis) and the annual interest rate called the yield to maturity (on the vertical axis).

currency swap are similar to an interest rate swap except that the exchanges are of different currencies.

For example, suppose British Petroleum (BP) expects to receive $900 million from U.S. sales each quarter for the next two years. BP would like to hedge this foreign exchange exposure, but exchange-traded futures contracts do not extend two years into the future. BP might find a company like PepsiCo that has sales in the United Kingdom but is headquartered in the United States. PepsiCo would like to convert its British pounds into U.S. dollars. A currency swap could hedge the foreign exchange risk for both parties. Specifically, based on current foreign exchange market conditions, a currency swap could be developed where BP agrees to swap $900 million to PepsiCo for £600,000 each quarter for the next two years. Both British Petroleum and PepsiCo would have locked in an exchange rate of $1.5/£.

McDonald's recently engineered a foreign currency swap that company treasurer Carleton Pearl claims saved as much as 3% of the cost of funds. McDonald's issued notes denominated in New Zealand dollars at a 16¾% interest rate. McDonald's managers considered the interest rate of 16¾% relatively low if the NZ dollar depreciates substantially relative to the U.S. dollar—but there is a risk that depreciation may not take place. To avoid this risk, McDonald's conducted a currency swap by which it paid U.S. dollars and received NZ dollars that were used to pay the interest denominated in NZ dollars. By issuing notes in NZ dollars and then conducting a swap transaction at a predetermined exchange rate, McDonald's borrowed money at a relatively low rate and simultaneously eliminated the foreign currency risk.

11.9.3 Commodity Swaps

A **commodity swap**, which protects the firm from changes in the price of commodities, requires the exchange of cash based on a specific commodity's value at specified points in the future. For example, a three-year crude oil swap with quarterly payments would have 12 cash exchanges. If the contract price was $20 per barrel, then the cash exchange would be the difference between the current price of crude oil and $20. If crude oil was selling for $25 per barrel at a quarterly payment, then one counterparty would receive $5 per barrel from the other.

Another example is the jet fuel price risk that airlines face. When fuel prices rise, an airline has a lag in passing along this higher cost to passengers in higher ticket prices. Airlines need an instrument that will help manage future fuel purchases, and commodity swaps fill this need. Airlines may use jet fuel swaps to lock in their future purchase price of fuel, providing stability to their costs. Because commodity swaps allow them to lock in a fixed sale price, fuel suppliers like them. This transaction is similar to an interest rate swap. The buyer of jet fuel has to pay a (variable) price in the future, which is similar to a floating interest rate. The seller of jet fuel prefers a fixed price (like a fixed interest rate). Both parties obtain a fixed price through the swap. One counterparty pays the other the difference between the market price of jet fuel and the fixed price.

11.10 MISUSE OF DERIVATIVES

What happens if a firm uses derivatives as a speculative tool rather than as a means to hedge risk? What if a firm treats the options market like a casino and gambles in the hope of hitting the jackpot? Such behavior must be considered irresponsible. A firm is answerable to its suppliers of funds—its stockholders and bondholders. A firm is expected to use financial tools such as options to hedge risk but not to increase risk by gambling on risky investments. Such behavior can lead to massive losses and financial disaster. Connecting Theory to Practice 11.3 lists a number of such financial disasters.

CONNECTING THEORY TO PRACTICE 11.3

MILESTONES OF THE YEAR

cs First Boston fesses up to having reimbursed a money market client for unauthorized derivatives trades in its account. Two other reimbursements follow. Total cost to the firm: about $40 million.

Gibson Greetings reports that it has suffered $20 million of losses on a derivatives contract.

Procter & Gamble announces $157 million of losses on leveraged derivatives.

Federal Paper Board says it has switched to mark-to-market accounting for certain leveraged derivatives, and taken a second-quarter $11 million charge. Subsequently it restated and lowered earnings for several accounting periods.

Filing a quarterly report, Air Products & Chemicals discloses it had recently absorbed $122 million in derivatives losses.

In connection with a tender for $4.8 billion of debt, Eastman Kodak unwinds numerous swaps and options at a cost of $220 million.

Orange County, California, goes bankrupt.

Bankers Trust is fined and censured by its regulators for defrauding Gibson Greetings in derivatives transactions.

Chemical Bank discloses that unauthorized Mexican peso trades by one of its employees cost it $70 million.

Sued because of derivatives losses in a government-securities mutual fund it ran, Piper Jaffray settles for $70 million.

Source: Carol J. Loomis, "Untangling the Derivatives Mess," *Fortune* 131, no. 5 (March 1995): 50. © 1995, Time Inc. All rights reserved.

MAKING THE CONNECTION

As we can see from the *Fortune* article, these "beasts" can bite when they are not used properly. A firm should use derivatives for risk reduction, not for gambling.

The most dramatic loss due to gambling in the derivative market is not listed in Connecting Theory to Practice 11.3. In 1995 Barings, the long-established and highly reputable British banking house, lost $1.3 billion in the Asian futures market. The revelation sent shockwaves around the financial world.

Over a three-week period Barings trader Nicholas Leeson bought futures and option contracts to the tune of $27 billion. He may have acted on the assumption that the destruction caused by the 1995 Kobe earthquake would stimulate the economy and push up the Nikkei (the Japanese stock market). However, the stock market turned down, and this record bet led to record losses—a total of about $1.3 billion. The Japanese Daiwa bank suffered a loss of approximately $1 billion in 1995 in a case quite similar to that of Baring's.

What can we learn from cases such as these? Nicholson Leeson's actions were illegal. However, because investors were left "high and dry," the trust of investors in the banking system was undermined. Good faith constitutes the foundation of the relationship among users of funds, suppliers of funds, and intermediaries such as banks. Clearly, to restore the trust of all parties involved, the trade in derivatives needs to be governed by tighter rules. If options and other derivatives are used properly, they reduce risk and allow management to focus on managing the firm's operations efficiently. Individuals with an irresistible urge to gamble should do so with their own money. Warren E. Buffett, chairman of Berkshire Hathaway, suggested that the annual reports of corporations be required to include the CEO's affirmation stating that he or she understands each derivative contract into which his or her company has entered. Such a declaration in annual reports, according to Mr. Buffett, will fix "just about every problem that exists."[10]

SUMMARY

Since firms undertake risky projects, management must have expertise in evaluating the risks it takes. However, some macroeconomic risks such as changes in the interest rate or in the foreign exchange rate are not specific to the firm's operation. A firm may operate very efficiently, yet lose money due to factors such as a sudden drop in the foreign exchange rate, political unrest, war, and so on.

Management may reduce or eliminate macroeconomic risk by using derivatives, which are special financial instruments. Options, futures, options on futures, and swaps are important examples. Financial managers must understand and know how to use derivatives.

Although these derivative assets are known for their speculative features, they can be used to re-

duce risk. For example, a firm can reduce its risk by: (1) buying or selling forward contracts on foreign currency; (2) buying future contracts or call options on futures that allow it to buy raw materials in the future at a predetermined price; (3) selling futures contracts on the firm's products to guarantee its income from each unit sold; (4) buying futures contracts or options on foreign currency to reduce the risk of foreign exchange fluctuations; and (5) buying options on interest rates to protect the firm from fluctuations in the interest rate.

Managers can also use option valuation models to analyze various transactions in the capital market and the firm's routine business transactions.

10. Carol J. Loomis, "Untangling the Derivatives Mess," *Fortune* 131, no. 5 (March 1995): 50. © 1995, Time Inc. All rights reserved.

CHAPTER AT A GLANCE

1. Value of a call option at the expiration date:
   If $S_t > E$: value of the call option $= S_t - E$
   If $S_t \leq E$: value of the call option $= 0$
   where S_t is the stock price at the expiration date t and E is the striking price.

2. Value of a put option at the expiration date:
   If $S_t > E$: value of a put option $= 0$
   If $S_t \leq E$: value of a put option $= E - S_t$

3. Upper and lower bounds on a call option, C_0, satisfy the following condition:

$$\max [S_0 - E, 0] \leq C_0 \leq S_0$$

   where S_0 is the current stock price.

4. Exact option price:
   a. When prices of an option and a stock perfectly correlate, portfolio of the stock and the option can be created with zero variance (i.e., with a certain future cash flow of $\$K$).
   b. By no-arbitrage argument:

$$\frac{K}{S_0 - nC_0} = (1 + r)$$

   where n is the number of calls written for each share held in the portfolio such that the portfolio's variance is zero. Given K, S_0, n, and r, C_0 can determine the call option's price.

5. Put–call parity:

$$C_0 = S_0 + P_0 - \frac{E}{(1 + r)}$$

   where C_0 and P_0 are the call option's and put option's current prices, respectively, on the same underlying asset with the same striking price, E, and the same expiration date; and r is the riskless interest rate applying in the time left to the option's expiration date.

KEY TERMS

Derivatives	Expiration date	Time value (option)
Forward contract	European option	Lower bound (option)
Futures contract	American option	Upper bound (option)
Mark to market	Writing an option	Arbitrage
Option	Long position (buying)	Put–call parity
Call option	Short position (selling or writing)	Interest rate option
Put option	Exercise an option	Swap contract
Underlying asset	In the money	Interest rate swap
Striking price (exercise price)	Out of the money	Currency swap
Option premium	Intrinsic value (option)	Commodity swap

REVIEW AND PRACTICE

11.1 You lease a car with the option to buy it after three years for $10,000. Is this a put option or a call option on the car?

11.2 As the CFO of your firm you are awarded an option to buy 1 million of its shares at $50 each. Is this a call option transaction as defined in this chapter?

11.3 Your car's value is $20,000. The probability that it will be stolen during the year is 1/1,000. What kind of option do you need on your car? What should the striking price be if you wish to replace a stolen car with an identical model?

11.4 The following table is taken from *Barron's*:

Chicago Board

Expire Date	Strike Price	Week's Sales	High	Low	Price	Net Chg.	N.Y. Close
Jan 95	35	1338	14¼	13¼	13¼	–½	48¼
Jan 95	40	220	10	8½	9	–¼	48¼
Jan 95	40 P	207	⅝	⅜	½	–⅛	48¼
Jan 95	45	122	6	5¼	5⅜	–⅛	48¼
Jan 95	50	210	3⅛	2½	2¾		48¼
Jan 96	40	127	12	11½	11½	–¼	48¼
Jan 96	60	444	2¾	2⅜	2½		48¼

Source: *Barron's* 74, no. 24 (June 1994): MW86. Reprinted by permission of *Barron's Market Week,* © 1994 Dow Jones & Company, Inc. All Rights Reserved Worldwide.

Using the first option given in the table above, identify the underlying asset, the striking price, the expiration date, and the premium.

11.5 Which of the options in the table in Problem 11.4 are in the money and which are out of the money? Which call option is *deepest* in the money?

11.6   Use the options in the table in Problem 11.4 to answer the following questions.
a. Explain the difference between the prices of Boeing's January 1995 40 put and call options.

b. Calculate the upper and lower bounds on all of Boeing's call options' values.

11.7 Focus on the first option in the table in Problem 11.4.
a. Calculate the cash flows for the call writer and call holder at $t = 0$ and at the expiration date for the following Boeing stock prices: $25, $30, $40, $60.
b. Plot a graph. Show the cash flow to the call holder at the expiration date. In which region does each side hope to be?

11.8 Refer to Problem 11.4.
a. Prepare the cash flows at $t = 0$ and $t = 1$ for the Boeing put option at the expiration date for the following possible stock prices: $25, $40, $60.
b. Plot a graph showing the put value at the expiration date as a function of the stock price. In which regions do the put writer and the put buyer hope to be?

11.9 Review once again the first call option in Problem 11.4.
a. Suppose you wish to invest $100 in either the call option or the underlying stock. How many options or how many shares of stock do you buy?
b. Suppose the stock price is $60 at the expiration date. Calculate the rate of return on each of these two alternate investments.
c. Repeat 11.9b but let the stock price at the expiration date be $30. Discuss the leverage effect of investing in options.

11.10 Suppose the stock price one year from now will be either $80 or $120. The current stock price is $75. You can borrow at the riskless interest rate $r = 5\%$.
a. Is there an arbitrage opportunity?
b. Calculate the maximum interest rate at which an arbitrage transaction is possible.

11.11 A U.S. firm imports luxury cars from Germany and sells them in Japan. Purchasing the cars in Germany on one-month's credit, the U.S. firm sells them in Japan with three-months' credit. The purchase price in Germany is 30,000 DM. The selling price in Japan is 5 million yen. Assume a cost of capital of 15%. Use Table 11-1 to show how the U.S. firm can create a positive NPV in dollars without interest rate risk. Describe the cash flows in dollars, German marks, and yen.

11.12 In October 1997 Polgat Fabrics purchased an October 1998 futures contract on 50,000 pounds of cotton at 79.40 cents per pound. The price remains unchanged until it rises to 90 cents per pound on January 1, 1998. On September 1 the price rises again to 100 cents per pound, and finally in October it reaches 110 cents per pound. Polgat's cost of capital is 10%.
a. Describe Polgat's cash flows between October 1997 and October 1998. Ignoring the cost of capital, how much did Polgat pay for the cotton?
b. What would the cash flow have been if Polgat had bought a *forward* contract at 79.40 cents per pound?
c. What is the PV of the payments on the futures contract? What is the PV of the payments on the forward contract?

11.13 Suppose you create a portfolio by buying one share of stock and writing three calls. You hold the portfolio for one year, and it generates a certain return of $100. The stock price is $110, and the riskless interest rate is 5%. What is the call option's equilibrium price?

11.14 The current stock price is $100, but at expiration date the stock price can be either $90 or $110. The striking price is $95. The riskless interest rate for the relevant period is 5%.
a. How many call options should you write to guarantee a certain cash flow on the portfolio at the expiration date? What is that certain cash flow?
b. What is the call option's equilibrium price?
c. Suppose the market call option price is $2 below what you found in 11.14b. What arbitrage transaction would you conduct? What is your profit?
d. Repeat 11.14c on the assumption that the call option price is $2 above what you found in 11.14b.

11.15 Use the data in Problem 11.14.
a. What is the call price at the expiration date corresponding to each of the two possible stock prices?
b. Suppose the current call price is $C_0 = \$8$. Calculate the call option's and the stock's possible rates of return.
c. Assume each possible stock price has a probability of ½. Calculate the correlation between the call option's and stock's rates of return.
d. How would your results change if the current call price were $C_0 = \$10$?
e. How would the correlation change if the probabilities of the stock price being $90 is ¼ and of it increasing to $110 is ¾? Discuss your results.

11.16 Repeat Problems 11.15a, b, and c, but assume the stock price at the expiration date could be $90, $110, and $150 with equal probability. Can the call option's equilibrium price be determined in such a case? Discuss your results and compare them to those of Problem 11.15.

11.17 You are offered the choice of buying either a futures contract or a forward contract, both having the same price and delivery date. Which would you prefer if you expect the price to grow steadily? Which would you prefer if you expect the price to fall steadily? Give a numerical example to illustrate your results. (*Hint:* Consider the time value of money.)

11.18 Suppose the correlation between an investment in the put option and the underlying asset is −1. The current stock price is $100, and at the expiration date the price will be either $90 or $120 with equal probability. The striking price is $110.
a. You hold one share. How many puts should you buy to guarantee a certain income at the expiration date?
b. The riskless interest rate for the relevant period is 10%. What is the put option's equilibrium price?

11.19 A firm issues stocks and pure discount bonds (they pay no annual interest). The bond's face value is $10,000, and they mature in one year. The riskless interest rate is 5%, and the bond's current market value is $9,000.

a. Calculate the discount rate to be applied to the bonds. Why is it higher than 5%?

b. What is the value of the put option held by the stockholders according to the stock's limited liability feature?

11.20 A restaurant borrows from a bank at a floating interest rate. A very large conglomerate borrows from a pension fund at a fixed interest rate. The restaurant and the conglomerate decide to perform an interest rate swap. Describe the flow of funds among the four parties when each interest payment is due.

11.21 The following options prices on interest rates are taken from *Barron's*:

Interest Rate Options, Chicago Board

Option	Sales (100s)	Interest Rate High	Low	Last	N.Y. Close
IRX Jun 40		$2\frac{1}{8}$	$2\frac{1}{16}$	$2\frac{1}{16}$	41
IRX Jun 40 P		$\frac{1}{16}$	$\frac{1}{16}$	$\frac{1}{16}$	41
IRX Dec 55		$2\frac{5}{8}$	$2\frac{1}{8}$	$2\frac{5}{8}$	41

Option	Sales (100s)	Yields High	Low	Last	N.Y. Close
5yrTN Jun 62½	33	$\frac{1}{8}$	$\frac{1}{8}$	$\frac{1}{8}$	65
5yrTN Jun 65 P		$\frac{5}{8}$	$\frac{5}{8}$	$\frac{5}{8}$	65
5yrTN Jun 70 P	70	$4\frac{7}{8}$	$4\frac{7}{8}$	$4\frac{7}{8}$	65
5yrTN Jul 67½		$\frac{11}{16}$	$\frac{11}{16}$	$\frac{11}{16}$	65

Source: *Barron's* 74, no. 24 (June 1994): MW86. Reprinted by permission of *Barron's Market Week*, © 1994 Dow Jones & Company, Inc. All Rights Reserved Worldwide.

The Treasury notes (TN) pay no interim annual interest (i.e., they are pure discount bonds).

a. Suppose that a firm issues five-year bonds with an interest rate of 10%. If the interest rate in July (just before the expiration date) falls to 5%, will the firm gain or lose?

b. What if the interest rate increase to 15%?

c. Suppose that for each dollar of debt the firm issues it also buys June 70 put options on the interest rate. Suppose that the interest rate on the Treasury note as well as on the firm's debt drops. Describe the firm's gains or losses, with and without the put options. Can the firm protect itself with the put options? How much does such protection cost?

d. Would you recommend that the firm buy a call option on the interest rate? Explain.

11.22 The following table is taken from *Barron's*:

Foreign Currency Options, Philadelphia Exchange

German Marks (cents per unit)

Option	Sales (100s)	High	Low	Last	Net Chg.	N.Y. Close
Dmark Jun 57	4	3.00	3.00	3.00	−0.75	59.99
Dmark Jun 58½ P	3	0.01	0.01	0.01		59.99

Source: *Barron's* 74, no. 24 (July 1994): MW86. Reprinted by permission of *Barron's Market Week*, © 1994 Dow Jones & Company, Inc. All Rights Reserved Worldwide.

a. What is the cash flow to call option holders at $t = 0$ and at the expiration date? Suppose you buy one DM June 57 call option. The exchange rate at the expiration date is 70 cents per DM. What is the realized IRR on such an investment?

b. Repeat 11.22a for a buyer of the June put option.

11.23 A U.S. firm sells to a German firm on credit. The German firm pays 10,000 DM in June.

a. What is the U.S. firm's future cash flow on the transaction if the exchange rate in June is 59.99 cents per DM?

b. What is the U.S. firm's cash flow in June if the exchange rate changes to 50 cents per DM?

c. Assume the transaction is conducted in 1994. Use the data in Problem 11.22 to explain how the U.S. firm can protect itself against adverse foreign currency fluctuations. How much will the insurance cost the firm? Compare the cash flow with and without the protection when the foreign currency rate in June 1994 is 70 cents per DM.

11.24 The following is taken from *Barron's*:

Index Options, Chicago Board

Expiration Date Strike Price	Sales	Week's High	Low	Close	Net Chg.	S&P Close
SP100 Jun 400 *P*	7445	⅜	⅛	³⁄₁₆	−⅛	424.04
SP100 Jun 405	4076	24	18¾	20	−2½	424.04
SP100 Jun 405 *P*	21736	½	³⁄₁₆	¼	−³⁄₁₆	424.04
SP100 Jun 410	10039	19	13⅝	15¼	−2⅜	424.04

Source: *Barron's* 74, no. 24 (June 1994): MW83. Reprinted by permission of *Barron's Market Week*, © 1994 Dow Jones & Company, Inc. All Rights Reserved Worldwide.

Suppose you are the manager of General Motors' employee pension fund. The fund is composed of the same stocks that are contained in the S&P 100 index. In all the calculations assume the pension fund holds one unit of the index at a current market price of $424.04. Conduct all the calculations on this one unit. Ignore the time value of the cash used to purchase the option.
a. What is the investor's rate of return in your pension fund if in June the index is $500? $350?
b. You want to ensure that General Motors' employees will not lose more than 10% of their investment. You buy June 400 put options. Describe the pension fund's rates of return (for the above two prices of the index—$500 and $350) with and without the portfolio insurance.
c. What would be the rate of return if you buy the June 410 call option rather than the put option?

11.25 You are considering the following two portfolios:
(1) Portfolio A—Buy one call option, and buy $E/(1 + r)$ bonds on which you earn the interest rate r.
(2) Portfolio B—Buy one share of the underlying stock.
a. Show that Portfolio A's cash flow at the expiration date is either identical to or higher than Portfolio B's cash flow when the option expires.
b. The current stock price is S_0. Show that the following must hold where C_0 is the current call option price:

$$C_0 \geq \max\ [0,\ S_0 - E/(1 + r)]$$

(*Note:* The value $S_0 - E/(1 + r)$ is greater than the value $S_0 - E$, discussed in the text.)

11.26 You are considering two portfolios:
(1) Portfolio A—Buy one share and one put on a particular stock and borrow $E/(1 + r)$ at r.
(2) Portfolio B—Buy one call on the stock.
a. Show that the cash flows on these two portfolios at the expiration date must be identical.
b. Given the current stock price, S_0, the current call price, C_0, and the current put price, P_0, show that to avoid arbitrage, the put–call parity must hold:

$$C_0 = S_0 + P_0 - E/(1 + r)$$

I N T E R N E T   Q U E S T I O N S

11.27 Take the virtual tour of the Chicago Board Options Exchange. Then describe, for someone who has never visited the site, what you "saw."
    http://www.cboe.com/index.html

11.28 Overall, are derivatives good for the economy? Visit the following Web site and prepare a memo documenting (using their figures) why derivatives are "good" for our markets.
    http://www.fortitude.com/volatil.htm

YOUR TURN: APPLYING THEORY TO PRACTICE

GAO TERMS "DERIVATIVE" MARKET RISK

A two-year government study warns that derivatives, the complex and largely unregulated financial instruments that have grown into a $12 trillion market, pose new and enormous risks to the global financial system.

Derivatives are so named because their value is "derived" from such things as stocks or interest rates. The most basic derivative is an "interest rate swap," in which a company converts its fixed-rate debt into debt that has a floating rate.

Sudden changes in interest rates, like those this year, can turn complex hedges such as these into bad debts, depending on the options embedded in the instrument.

The hazards have become more apparent recently as more major corporations report losses tied in some way to derivatives, among them Procter & Gamble Co., Air Products and Chemicals Inc., Atlantic Richfield Co. and Mead Corp.

The biggest brokers and banks have traditionally made handsome fees selling derivatives. But this year some dealers—such as Bankers Trust New York Corp. and J.P. Morgan & Co.—have lost money trading for their own accounts using a strategy that depends in part on derivatives.

General Electric's Kidder, Peabody & Co. brokerage subsidiary lost nearly half of its capital this year because of questionable derivatives trading that is being investigated by the Securities and Exchange Commission.

The 193-page GAO study acknowledges that in a world of volatile financial markets, derivative deals can help corporations and investors insure themselves against unwanted risks such as rising interest rates or a falling U.S. dollar.

But it warns that if a large dealer of derivatives "failed, the failure could pose risks to other firms—including federally insured depository institutions—and the financial system as a whole."

The report says that derivatives are especially "difficult" to manage because of their "complexity" and place special burdens on corporate executives and boards of directors. It warns that what may appear to be a prudent hedge today can become a bad bet tomorrow.

Of the areas cited for increased regulation, however, official sources said there is growing support among regulators for only some of the recommendations: improved accounting and public disclosure of derivatives holdings; better risk management procedures at companies active in derivatives; and more stringent capital standards for derivatives dealers, whether they be banks, brokerages or insurance companies.

The report calls for comprehensive international supervision of derivatives, which trade largely beyond the reach of regulators. The investigation recommends that "Congress require federal regulation of the safety and soundness of all major U.S. . . . derivatives dealers."

While only somewhat critical of the state of bank regulation of derivatives, the report still sees room for regulatory improvement in the area of securities firms and insurance companies. Bank regulators have substantially more authority to examine and supervise banks that are derivatives dealers than the SEC has . . . .

Source: Brett D. Fromson, "GAO Calls 'Derivatives' Market Risk," *Washington Post,* 18 May 1996, pp. A1, A8.

Questions

1. Suppose a bank uses a large proportion of its resources to buy call options on the S&P index or to write put options on the S&P index. In your view, which of these strategies is more dangerous? Explain why derivatives might endanger the global financial system. As a regulator would you prohibit banks from buying puts or calls?

2. Would the risk of bankruptcy be reduced if banks' involvement in derivatives were limited to no more than 5% of their equity? In your answer distinguish between puts and calls and between writing and buying these options.

3. A firm issues a 5% fixed interest bond for 30 years. It then carries out an interest rate swap, so that it pays a floating rate that is adjusted once a year. Suppose inflation sets in and is expected to remain high for 30 years. The interest rate increases to 10% and is likely to remain at that level. Describe the firm's loss due to the swap.

4. Chemical Inc. invests $100 million in buying out of the money put options on the S&P index. The S&P index fluctuates only mildly and remains above the option's striking price up to the maturity date. What is the effect on Chemical Inc.'s profit? In your view, would Chemical Inc.'s holding of options make it more difficult for the stockholders to estimate the firm's future earnings?

5. Suppose J.P. Morgan & Co. earns a commission on each security transaction it makes for its customers. It also trades securities on its account. Recently the company traded on its own account and wrote a call option on IBM. IBM's stock price increased. How does this affect Morgan's profit? Its stability? If you held an investment account at this firm, would you worry? As a taxpayer should you worry?

6. The GAO study cited previously claims that if a large dealer of derivatives "failed, the failure could pose risks to other firms—including feder-ally insured depository institutions—and the financial system as a whole." Explain this claim. Why should the public be concerned if insured depository institutions fail? (After all, the depositors are insured.)

7. The article states that because of their complexity, derivatives "place special burdens on corporate executives and boards of directors." Suppose, as the CFO of a U.S. firm, you buy raw materials from Germany and export to Japan. All sales and purchases are on three months' credit. You also issue bonds in Japan, on which you pay interest in Japanese yen. Explain the "complexity" that you face. Show that it is difficult to use derivatives, but by using them properly, you can decrease your firm's risk.

8. A U.S. firm invests $100 million in a German firm. The U.S. firm estimates that the following year's profit on its investment will be 20 million DM. To hedge its foreign currency risk, the U.S. firm buys put options to convert 20 million DM into U.S. dollars. At the end of the year it discovers its profit in DM is only 10 million. Explain why "what may appear to be a prudent hedge today can become a bad bet tomorrow."

9. In view of the pros and cons of regulating the trade in derivative assets, which of the following firms would you regulate: banks, insurance firms, Xerox Corporation? Explain your answer. What would be the effect of prohibiting derivatives altogether? Suggest to Congress a regulation scheme for derivatives trading.

Appendix 11A   Black–Scholes Option Pricing Formula

Fischer Black and Myron Scholes derived an option pricing formula for the case where the stock price can have more than two values. In this case the option value and the stock price are related as described by the curve in Figure 11–3 labeled "Option value." Because this is not a straight line, there can be no perfect correlation between the option's and underlying asset's prices. However, the **Black-Scholes option pricing formula** allows the investor to make frequent, periodic revisions of a portfolio. For a very short investment period, the change in the stock price will be very small. We focus on a small segment of the curve in Figure 11-3, and any small segment of the curve is approximately linear. Therefore, for a very short investment period, we can have perfect correlation between the two asset prices, and a portfolio with a certain income can be created. Once we have a perfect correlation, the option price can be derived.

Black and Scholes showed that with continuous portfolio revision, the call option's value is given by the formula:

$$C_0 = S_0 N(d_1) - Ee^{-rt}N(d_2)$$

where

$$d_1 = \frac{\ln(S_0/E) + (r + 1/2\sigma^2)t}{\sigma\sqrt{t}}$$

$$d_2 = d_1 - \sigma\sqrt{t}$$

and

S_0 = the current stock price

E = the exercise (or striking) price

r = the annualized riskless rate of return

σ^2 = the annualized variance of the return on the stock

t = time (in years) to expiration date

$N(d_i)$ = probability that a normally distributed random variable with an expected value of zero and a variance of 1 will be less than or equal to d_i

$\ln$ = the natural logarithm function

where e denotes the base of the natural logarithm and is equal to 2.7183.

Let us illustrate this formula with an example: Suppose we have the following parameters:

$$S_0 = \$100$$

$$E = \$120$$

$$r = 10\%$$

$$\sigma = 0.8$$

$$t = \tfrac{1}{2} \text{ (6 months to expiration date)}$$

According to the formula:

$$d_1 = \frac{\ln(S_0/E) + (r + (1/2)\sigma^2)t}{\sigma\sqrt{t}}$$

$$= \frac{\ln(100/120) + (0.10 + (1/2)(0.8)^2) \times 0.5}{0.8\sqrt{0.5}} = 0.0489 \cong 0.05$$

$$d_2 = d_1 - \sigma\sqrt{t} = 0.0489 - 0.8\sqrt{0.5} = -0.5168 \cong -0.52$$

The area under the cumulative distribution for various values of Z can be obtained from Table 11A-1. For example, for a value of $Z = 1.64$, the corresponding cumulative area can be found at the intersection of the row labeled "1.6" and the column labeled "0.04" ($1.64 = 1.6 + 0.04$). That value is 0.4495. To find the probability that a standard normal random variable, Z, will be smaller than 1.64, we need to add 0.5 to the number obtained from the table. Hence, the probability is 0.9495.

In our case we must substitute the figure we found, $d_1 = 0.05$, for Z. Doing so, we find from Table 11A-1 that

$$N(d_1) = N(0.05) = 0.5199$$

and

$$N(d_2) = N(-0.52) = 1 - N(0.52) = 1 - 0.6985 = 0.3015$$

Therefore:

$$C_0 = S_0 N(d_1) - Ee^{-rt}N(d_2)$$

$$= \$100 \times 0.5199 - \$120e^{-(0.10)(0.5)}(0.3015) = \$17.57$$

APPENDIX KEY TERM

Black-Scholes option pricing formula

APPENDIX REVIEW AND PRACTICE

11A.1 The current stock price is $S_0 = \$100$. The riskless interest rate is $r = 5\%$, and the standard deviation of the compounded annual return is $\sigma = 0.6$. A call option with an exercise price of $E = \$120$ and six months remaining to expiration is written on this stock. Use the Black-Scholes option pricing formula to calculate the call option's value.

11A.2 Use the data given in Problem 11A.1 to analyze how each of the following changes affects the call option's value:

a. r increases to 10%.
b. σ increases to $\sigma = 0.9$.
c. The time to expiration increases to one year.
d. The current stock price rises to $120.
e. The exercise price drops to $110.

TABLE 11A-1   Table Areas for Standard Normal Probability Distributions

Z	0.00	0.01	0.02	0.03	0.04	0.05	0.06	0.07	0.08	0.09
0.0	0.0000	0.0040	0.0080	0.0120	0.0160	0.0199	0.0239	0.0279	0.0319	0.0359
0.1	0.0398	0.0438	0.0478	0.0517	0.0557	0.0596	0.0636	0.0675	0.0714	0.0753
0.2	0.0793	0.0832	0.0871	0.0910	0.0948	0.0987	0.1026	0.1064	0.1103	0.1141
0.3	0.1179	0.1217	0.1255	0.1293	0.1331	0.1368	0.1406	0.1443	0.1480	0.1517
0.4	0.1554	0.1591	0.1628	0.1664	0.1700	0.1736	0.1772	0.1808	0.1844	0.1879
0.5	0.1915	0.1950	0.1985	0.2019	0.2054	0.2088	0.2123	0.2157	0.2190	0.2224
0.6	0.2257	0.2291	0.2324	0.2357	0.2389	0.2422	0.2454	0.2486	0.2518	0.2549
0.7	0.2580	0.2612	0.2642	0.2673	0.2704	0.2734	0.2764	0.2794	0.2823	0.2852
0.8	0.2881	0.2910	0.2939	0.2967	0.2995	0.3023	0.3051	0.3078	0.3106	0.3133
0.9	0.3159	0.3186	0.3212	0.3238	0.3264	0.3289	0.3315	0.3340	0.3365	0.3389
1.0	0.3413	0.3438	0.3461	0.3485	0.3508	0.3531	0.3554	0.3577	0.3599	0.3621
1.1	0.3643	0.3665	0.3686	0.3708	0.3729	0.3749	0.3770	0.3790	0.3810	0.3830
1.2	0.3849	0.3869	0.3888	0.3907	0.3925	0.3944	0.3962	0.3980	0.3997	0.4015
1.3	0.4032	0.4049	0.4066	0.4082	0.4099	0.4115	0.4131	0.4147	0.4162	0.4177
1.4	0.4192	0.4207	0.4222	0.4236	0.4251	0.4265	0.4279	0.4292	0.4306	0.4319
1.5	0.4332	0.4345	0.4357	0.4370	0.4382	0.4394	0.4406	0.4418	0.4429	0.4441
1.6	0.4452	0.4463	0.4474	0.4484	0.4495	0.4505	0.4515	0.4525	0.4535	0.4545
1.7	0.4554	0.4564	0.4573	0.4582	0.4591	0.4599	0.4608	0.4616	0.4625	0.4633
1.8	0.4641	0.4649	0.4656	0.4664	0.4671	0.4678	0.4686	0.4693	0.4699	0.4706
1.9	0.4713	0.4719	0.4726	0.4732	0.4738	0.4744	0.4750	0.4756	0.4761	0.4767
2.0	0.4772	0.4778	0.4783	0.4788	0.4793	0.4798	0.4803	0.4808	0.4812	0.4817
2.1	0.4821	0.4826	0.4830	0.4834	0.4838	0.4842	0.4846	0.4850	0.4854	0.4857
2.2	0.4861	0.4864	0.4868	0.4871	0.4875	0.4878	0.4881	0.4884	0.4887	0.4890
2.3	0.4893	0.4896	0.4898	0.4901	0.4904	0.4906	0.4909	0.4911	0.4913	0.4916
2.4	0.4918	0.4920	0.4922	0.4925	0.4927	0.4929	0.4931	0.4932	0.4934	0.4936
2.5	0.4938	0.4940	0.4941	0.4943	0.4945	0.4946	0.4948	0.4949	0.4951	0.4952
2.6	0.4953	0.4955	0.4956	0.4957	0.4959	0.4960	0.4961	0.4962	0.4963	0.4964
2.7	0.4965	0.4966	0.4967	0.4968	0.4969	0.4970	0.4971	0.4972	0.4973	0.4974
2.8	0.4974	0.4975	0.4976	0.4977	0.4977	0.4978	0.4979	0.4979	0.4980	0.4981
2.9	0.4981	0.4982	0.4982	0.4983	0.4984	0.4984	0.4985	0.4985	0.4986	0.4986
3.0	0.49865	0.4987	0.4987	0.4988	0.4988	0.4989	0.4989	0.4989	0.4990	0.4990
4.0	0.4999683									

Illustration: For $Z = 1.93$, shaded area is 0.4732 out of total area of 1.

Source: From John Neter, William Wasserman, and George A. Whitmore, *Fundamental Statistics for Business and Economics,* 4th ed. (Boston: Allyn and Bacon, 1973). Copyright © 1973 by Allyn and Bacon, Inc., Boston.

CHAPTER 12

LONG-TERM DEBT

LEARNING OBJECTIVES

After reading this chapter,
you should understand:

1. Why management should be acquainted with the characteristics of various types of bonds.

2. Why the interest rate paid on bonds varies over time and across countries.

3. That the yield on bonds measures the firm's cost of debt and, therefore, is relevant for the firm's investment decisions.

4. The various types of risk on bonds: interest rate risk, inflation risk, country and political risk, foreign exchange risk, and bankruptcy risk.

5. Why different types of bonds may have different yields to maturity.

6. How to calculate a bond's yield to maturity and yield to call.

7. The relationship between changes in the yield to maturity and holding period returns.

8. How bonds are classified by their special features, tax obligation, and risk of default.

9. How bondholders' interests are protected.

CORPORATE FINANCE IN THE NEWS

Some of Kmart Corp.'s debt was lowered to junk-bond status by Moody's Investors Service Inc., but the rating service indicated it held a favorable long-term outlook for the discount retailer by taking its debt off review . . . .

Still, (fixed income analyst) Ms. Canella said, Kmart will probably have to pay higher interest rates if it issues any form of debt because of the junk-bond ratings. Most analysts say Kmart, which has been haunted by rumors that it will file for federal bankruptcy-court protection, a rumor the company has staunchly denied, is far from out of the woods. "We don't have enough information yet to judge," said Terrance McEvoy, an analyst for Janney Montgomery Scott Inc.

Source: Robert Berner, "Some of Kmart's Debt Is Lowered to Junk-Bond Status by Moody's," *Wall Street Journal*, 5 February 1996, p. B4. Reprinted by permission of *The Wall Street Journal*, © 1996 Dow Jones & Company, Inc. All Rights Reserved Worldwide.

12.1 INTRODUCTION

We learned in Chapter 10 that the interest rate a firm pays to its bondholders measures its cost of debt. In reviewing Corporate Finance in the News, we learn that Kmart's debt was downgraded to junk-bond status, indicating Kmart's financial distress. Such a downgrading generally leads to a lower market price of bonds and a higher required interest rate by bondholders. The analysts quoted in this article believe that Kmart will have to pay a higher interest rate on new debt issues. In that case, its cost of debt and weighted average cost of capital will probably increase.

In this and the next two chapters we discuss the two principal forms of long-term financing—namely bonds (debt) and stocks (equity). We will see how these forms of financing affect a firm's cash flows, profitability, risk of bankruptcy, cost of debt, and cost of equity. This chapter is devoted to bonds.

When a firm issues bonds, it borrows money. As you learned in Chapter 2, the lender (bondholder) holds a bond, which serves as evidence of the firm's debt and generally contains information on the details of the loan. These details include the periodic interest the firm will pay the bondholder; the *maturity date* at which the firm will repay the loan; and the sum that the firm will repay at the maturity date, called the *principal*, *face value*, or *par value*.

From the firm's viewpoint, the lower the interest rate it pays, the lower its cost of debt and the better the firm fares financially. One main factor affecting the interest rate is the firm's risk of bankruptcy; generally, the higher this risk, the higher the required interest rate on the firm's bonds. If investors consider a particular bond to be risky, the issuing firm will have to pay a higher interest rate to compensate bondholders for their exposure to risk.

The CFO needs to be acquainted with the various types of bonds available in the market, how to measure their rates of return and risk, and what type of economic factors affects these two crucial variables. For example, if the U.S. government issues a bond paying 8% annual interest, the firm's bond will have to offer an interest rate of at least 8%, and probably more. If the firm offers a lower interest rate, investors will buy the higher rate (and lower risk) government bonds; and the firm will not meet its financing needs. Similarly, if the interest rate on government bonds increases, this will also affect the interest rate at which firms can borrow money. A firm does not operate in a vacuum, and the better the CFO's knowledge and understanding of the bond market, the better the firm's debt management and the lower its cost of debt. Our aim in this chapter is to make sure that you, like the CFO, have a good understanding of the bond market.

Most corporate bonds are issued for less than 30 years. However, there are a few exceptions. One well-known exception is the Walt Disney bond issued in 1993 with a maturity of 100 years. Connecting Theory to Practice 12.1 discusses another long-maturity bond that the Santa Fe railroad issued in 1881 and that matured in 1995.

CONNECTING THEORY TO PRACTICE 12.1

AFTER 114 YEARS, IT'S PAYDAY: PATIENCE IS REWARDED MEAGERLY AS INFLATION ERODES 1881 BONDS

It's been 114 years in coming, but there is good news for those who lent money to the Santa Fe railroad in 1881. They are about to be paid back. Checks for part of the loan will go out today. Lenders will have to be patient a little while longer, though, until October, to get the rest.

The seemingly endless Santa Fe story illustrates almost everything that can go wrong for a lender, short of a complete failure to pay. Those who lent the money—or perhaps their great-grandchildren—are about to get dollars that are each worth less than seven 1881 cents. Along the way, lenders have suffered

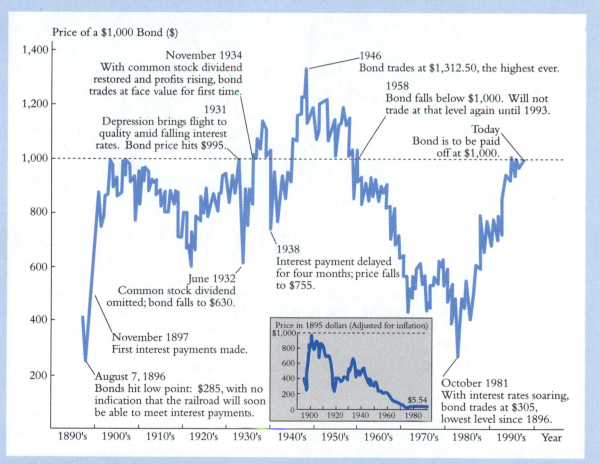

Price of a $1,000 Bond ($)

November 1934
With common stock dividend restored and profits rising, bond trades at face value for first time.

1946
Bond trades at $1,312.50, the highest ever.

1931
Depression brings flight to quality amid falling interest rates. Bond price hits $995.

1958
Bond falls below $1,000. Will not trade at that level again until 1993.

Today
Bond is to be paid off at $1,000.

1938
Interest payment delayed for four months; price falls to $755.

June 1932
Common stock dividend omitted; bond falls to $630.

November 1897
First interest payments made.

August 7, 1896
Bonds hit low point: $285, with no indication that the railroad will soon be able to meet interest payments.

October 1981
With interest rates soaring, bond trades at $305, lowest level since 1896.

Price in 1895 dollars (Adjusted for inflation)
$5.54

Sources: New York Stock Exchange, Commercial and Financial Chronicle, Standard & Poor's (prices); Commerce Department (inflation); "History of the Atchison, Topeka & Santa Fe Railway" by Keith L. Bryant Jr. (Macmillan, 1974).

through corporate reorganizations, fraudulent accounting and foolish business plans. They have been buffeted by volatile interest rates and by worries over credit quality. And they even lost their protection against inflation when Congress and the Supreme Court teamed up against them in the 1930's.

The money being paid back now is for a debt dating to 1881 that ultimately was turned into two issues of 100-year bonds during the railway's 1895 reorganization. The first of those bonds, the one maturing today, was intended to be of lower quality, and the history of the prices it has fetched—ranging from $285 to more than $1,300 for bonds with a face value of $1,000—provides a graphic description of the financial history of the last century. As it happens, the bonds are maturing after the company, now known as the Santa Fe Pacific Corporation, has agreed to be acquired by Burlington Northern Inc., ending its long tradition of independence.

Source: Floyd Norris, "After 114 Years, It's Payday," *New York Times*, 1 July 1995, p. 33. Copyright © 1995 by The New York Times Co. Reprinted by Permission.

MAKING THE CONNECTION

The Santa Fe railroad bond issue raises several interesting questions:

1. Does a bond with a very long maturity necessarily involve losses to the bondholders?
2. Why did the price of the Santa Fe railroad bond fluctuate over time, and why in 1995 did the price approach the bond's $1,000 face value?
3. What roles do inflation, interest rates, and risk of bankruptcy play in determining the bond's price?
4. Do changes in a bond's price affect the firm's cost of debt?

We will answer these and similar questions in this chapter.

Before we proceed, we must understand why management is interested in such issues as Connecting Theory to Practice 12.1 raises. Clearly, management should be involved in production. Management also has several good reasons to be well versed in the characteristics of bonds and how the bond market operates:

1. A firm can issue various types of bonds. Management should be able to measure each type of bond's cost of debt and to decide which is the least costly and which is the best suited to the firm's purposes.
2. Management should be able to judge which type of bond will impose the fewest constraints on the firm's activities and will minimize the risks of financial distress and bankruptcy.
3. A firm can issue bonds that, under certain conditions, can be converted into other financial instruments before maturity. Management should be alert to the effect of a bond's conversion and, if the bond is *callable* (able to be redeemed prior to maturity), the conditions under which it should be recalled. Such provisions affect the firm's cash flow and its tax payments as well as its risk exposure.

4. Bonds are rated for safety. The safer the bonds, the lower the interest rate the firm must pay. Management must find ways of improving the firm's rating to reduce its cost of debt.

5. Management must be acquainted with other bonds available in the market such as government and tax-free bonds. These other bonds compete for investors' funds and provide benchmarks for the interest that should be paid on the firm's bonds.

6. Finally, management must determine the terms of a bond issue—including the maturity date. The terms should be realistic to ensure demand for such a bond; otherwise, the firm will be unable to sell it.

12.2 THE TERMS OF A BOND AND ITS CASH FLOWS

Various kinds of bonds are traded—including corporate bonds, government bonds, and municipal bonds—and the features of these bonds vary. Some of the terms used to describe these features follow, as they would be applied to a hypothetical bond. (We will discuss these terms in more detail throughout the chapter.)

Term	Example	Explanation
Date of issue	1/1/1997	The date on which the firm issues the bond
Principal (also face value, or par value)	$1,000	The amount, stated on the bond certificate, that is paid to the bondholder on the maturity date
Maturity date	1/1/2017	The date on which the principal is paid to the bond-holder
Annual coupon rate (expressed as a percent of face value)	8.50%	The annual interest rate paid on the bond's face value (8.50% $\times$ $1,000 = $85 per year)
Date of coupon	6/30, 12/31	The dates on which the interest (coupon) payments are made (two biannual payments of $85/2 = $42.50)
Offer price (expressed as a percent of face value)	95%	The price of the bond when issued; i.e., 95% of $1,000 = $950
Market price		The bond's current price, which fluctuates over time as a result of changes in demand and supply
Yield to maturity	8.7%	The IRR of the bond's cash flows if the bond is held to maturity (It may fluctuate due to changes in the bond's market price.)

The bond's terms and the price at which it is issued determine the firm's cash flows. For simplicity we will illustrate this using a bond that pays a coupon once a year. Suppose a firm sells 100,000 such bonds. Each bond matures in 10 years, and each sells for $1,000. The firm will receive a cash flow of $100 million (100,000 $\times$ $1,000 = $100 million). What are the firm's financial obligations to its bondholders? First, it must make **coupon** payments as specified in the bond's terms. The bond's face value and the coupon rate determine these interest payments. For example, if the face value is $1,000 and the annual coupon rate is 5%, the firm will have to pay $50 annual interest (0.05 × $1,000 = $50) on each bond and $5 million ($50 × 100,000 = $5 million) to all its bondholders every year. At the bond's *maturity*, in 10 years, the firm will also have to repay the amount stated on the face of the loan—called, alternatively, the *principal*, *face value*, or *par value*—on $1,000 per bond. The firm's cash flows from the bond issue will be as follows:

Cash Flows (in million $)

Year	0	1	2	. . .	9	10
Cash inflow	100					
Cash outflow		−5	−5	. . .	−5	−105
Net cash flow to the firm	100	−5	−5	. . .	−5	−105

The cash flows will be the same for bondholders; however, the signs will be reversed. Bondholders will pay $100 million today, and they will receive $5 million in each of the next nine years and $105 million in the tenth year.

12.3 HOW THE INTEREST RATE IS DETERMINED IN THE MARKET

When a firm or a government agency decides to borrow money, it issues bonds that investors then purchase. Bondholders are a firm's money lenders. The interest rate paid on such financial transactions varies over time and across countries. What economic factors determine the interest rate? Why does the interest rate vary?

A firm issues bonds to finance its projects. The more profitable the available projects, the higher the interest rate that a firm will be able to pay on the borrowed money. To illustrate this point, assume the IRRs of the following four projects are certain. Because these projects are conventional and not mutually exclusive, they can be ranked according to their IRRs:

Project	A	B	C	D
Investment outlay (in million $)	100	100	200	400
IRR (%)	8	10	16	20

The firm makes a profit only if a project's IRR is greater than the interest rate paid on borrowed money. If the interest rate is 25%, the firm will not borrow because the highest IRR is only 20%. If the interest rate is 18%, the firm will borrow $400 million and accept Project D; if 15%, the firm will borrow $600 million and accept Projects C and D; if 9%, it will borrow $700 million and accept Projects B, C, and D. If the interest rate is below 8%, the firm will borrow $800 million and accept all four projects.

If all projects available to all firms were ranked by their IRRs, we would obtain the *aggregate* demand for money by *all* firms. The demand function for borrowed money is described by Curve D in Figure 12-1. As you can see, the lower the interest rate, the larger the amount of money that the firm will be willing to borrow.

A bond offers the purchaser a way to save. Generally, the higher the interest rate, the more the purchaser will wish to save. Curve S in Figure 12-1 describes the savers' supply function of funds. Thus, Figure 12-1 describes the two functions—the demand and supply curves—of funds. The intersection point of D and S determines the market interest rate, r, as well as the amount of borrowed money (and money saved by bondholders), denoted by B.

Thus far we have described the demand for money by firms. In practice we have to add to it governmental agencies' demand for money. Governmental agencies are not usually involved in profit-making projects, so their monetary needs reflect only their budgetary deficits.

Interest rates vary because supply and demand curves change over time due to variation in governmental agency deficits and variation in the profitability (IRR) of available projects. To illustrate, suppose that due to successful research and development or to new possibilities for investing abroad, three new, additional projects, denoted by E, F, and G, become available:

Additional Projects	E	F	G
Investment outlay (in million $)	200	300	500
IRR (%)	20	17	14

With these additional projects, the demand function for borrowed funds will shift from D to D' in Figure 12-1, which will increase the interest rate from r to r_1. On the other hand, in a recession the number of profitable projects declines, and the firm's demand for debt declines as well. In that case, Curve D will shift to the

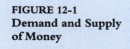

**FIGURE 12-1
Demand and Supply
of Money**

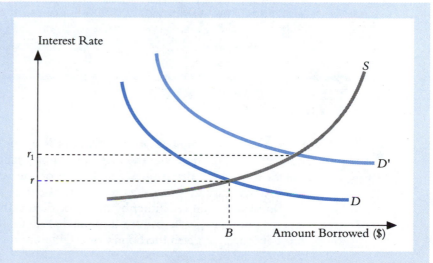

left, and the interest rate will fall. Similarly, when the supply curve, *S*, shifts, the interest rate changes. Demand and supply functions, which may vary across time and among countries, determine the interest rate.

Connecting Theory to Practice 12.2 demonstrates the relationship among saving, the interest rate, and the level of investment.

CONNECTING THEORY TO PRACTICE 12.2

GREATER SAVING WOULD LOWER INTEREST RATES

Economists aren't completely down on the role of public policy. But they tend to favor incentives that they think could spur saving—such as a capital gains tax cut. "In the long run, the ability of the U.S. to invest substantial amounts is related to how much we save," says Richard Rippe, chief economist at Prudential Securities. Greater saving would lower interest rates and increase stock prices, reducing the cost of capital for companies that buy plant and equipment.

Source: Joseph Spiers, "The Most Important Economic Event of the Decade," *Fortune* 131, no. 6 (April 1995):33. Copyright © 1995, Time Inc. All rights reserved.

MAKING THE CONNECTION

As the *Fortune* article implies, a cut in the capital gains tax rate will move the supply curve to the right, causing the interest rate to decrease. As a result, the firm's cost of debt would decrease.

Thus far we have assumed riskless bonds. In practice most bonds have some risk, and various firms will pay different interest rates, which reflect their different risks. In general, as we will see in Section 12.5, the lower the bond's quality, the higher the interest rate that a firm must pay. First, though, we will consider how market price, coupon rate, and the maturity date determine a bond's yield to maturity.

12.4 THE YIELD TO MATURITY AND COST OF DEBT

One of a bond's most important features is its *yield to maturity*. From the bondholder's point of view, yield to maturity is important because it measures an investment's IRR, which determines whether he or she will buy the bond. To the firm, yield to maturity measures the pretax cost of debt.

Bonds are evaluated either by the PV of their cash flows or by their IRR. In calculating a bond's PV, each investor uses the discount rate that he or she considers to be most appropriate given the bond's risk. Different investors may obtain different PVs for the same bond.

For example, consider a one-year bond currently priced at $980, paying a $100 coupon and returning a $1,000 principal one year from now. Suppose there are two investors: The first investor thinks that the bond's cash flow should be discounted at 10%; the second investor perceives this bond to be more risky and considers 15% as the appropriate discount rate. The PV from the first investor's point of view will be

$$PV = \frac{\$100 + \$1,000}{1.1} = \frac{\$1,100}{1.1} = \$1,000$$

For the second investor, the PV will be

$$PV = \frac{\$100 + \$1,000}{1.15} \cong \$956.52$$

At the bond's market price of $980, the first investor will buy the bond but the second investor will not.

Investors may disagree regarding the bond's PV; but, given the market price, they do not disagree regarding the IRR. As in project valuation, IRR is the one value upon which all investors agree. In our example the IRR is given by the value of R that solves the following equation:

$$\$980 = \frac{\$100 + \$1,000}{1 + R}$$

So:

$$R = \frac{\$1,100}{\$980} - 1 \cong 0.1224 \text{ or } 12.24\%$$

Given the coupon, face value, maturity, and current bond price, the IRR can be calculated.

A bond's IRR is called its **yield to maturity,** denoted as y. From the bondholder's point of view, yield to maturity measures the investment's annual rate of return on the investment when the investor holds the bond up to the maturity date.

The general formula for determining the bond's price and its yield to maturity is as follows:

$$P_B = \sum_{t=1}^{T} \frac{C_t}{(1 + y)^t} + \frac{F}{(1 + y)^T} \tag{12.1}$$

where P_B is the bond's market price, C_t is the annual coupon, F is the face value, and y is the yield to maturity. All you need to calculate y is the bond's price, its annual coupon payment, and its maturity.

The PV of the bond's payments is given by

$$PV = \sum_{t=1}^{T} \frac{C_t}{(1 + r)^t} + \frac{F}{(1 + r)^T} \tag{12.2}$$

If $PV = P_B$, the two formulas coincide, and the yield to maturity equals the discount rate. In the rest of the chapter, assume equilibrium. So, we'll use y and r interchangeably.

The yield to maturity is also called the *market interest rate* or simply the *interest rate*. It should not be confused with the coupon rate, which is the rate by which we multiply the par value when calculating the dollar interest to be paid to the bondholders. The following problem demonstrates calculation of a bond's yield to maturity.

PRACTICE BOX

Problem   A corporate bond sells for $900. It pays an annual coupon of $50 at the end of each of the next 30 years. The bond's face value is $1,000. Calculate the yield to maturity.

Solution   Using a calculator, we solve for y, the bond's yield to maturity:

$$\$900 = \frac{\$50}{(1 + y)} + \frac{\$50}{(1 + y)^2} + \ldots + \frac{\$50}{(1 + y)^{30}} + \frac{\$1,000}{(1 + y)^{30}}$$

We find that $y = 5.704\%$.

Investors in the market determine the bond's price. If the coupon and the face value are given, the yield to maturity is determined by Equation 12.1. Generally, the higher the risk of bankruptcy and default, the lower the bond's market price and the higher its yield to maturity. Since investors determine yield to maturity, y represents their expected *required* rate of return on the firm's bond. This required yield represents the firm's pretax cost of debt.[1]

The yield to maturity varies over time if the bond's market price varies over time. Does this mean that the firm's cost of debt will vary accordingly? Suppose a bond's face value and its market price are both $1,000 and the bank pays an annual coupon of $100. Its yield to maturity (and thus the cost of debt) is 10%. If the bond's market price decreases, the yield to maturity will increase.[2] If it increases to 15%, does the firm's cost of debt also increase to 15%, or does it remain at 10%? The answer is that the cost of debt increases to 15%, too.

There are several reasons why 15%, rather than 10%, will be the cost of debt:

1. Suppose the firm needs to raise more capital to finance new projects. Because the current yield to maturity of its bond is 15%, the firm will not be able to issue new bonds at 10%. In other words, investors will be unwilling to buy a bond with an IRR of 10% when other similar bonds are available with IRRs of 15%. Therefore, 15% will be the firm's marginal cost of debt. Although the firm's cost

---

1. It is the pretax cost because since interest is tax-deductible, the after-tax cost of debt is lower.
2. For example, in the preceding Practice Box, the yield to maturity is 5.704%. However, if the market price had been $1,000, the yield to maturity would have been 5%.

of debt was originally 10%, this cost is historical and is irrelevant in making future investment decisions.

2. Assuming (for simplicity only) that all assets are financed by debt, the cost of debt is the firm's minimum required rate of return on its projects. If the firm cannot earn at least 15% on physical projects, it will fare better by repurchasing its own bonds and earning the 15% yield. The firm will buy back its bonds as long as there are no available projects whose rates of return are at least 15%. Thus, 15% is the *minimum* required rate of return on projects, and the *current* 15% yield to maturity will be the firm's (pretax) cost of debt.

The risk involved in investing in the bond affects the bond's price *and* the cost of debt. Now let's review the various types of risks involved in bond investment.

12.5 TYPES OF RISK AFFECTING BONDS

Issuing bonds involves a risk to the two parties. The firm's risk is being unable to pay the interest and principal and facing bankruptcy. The bondholders' risk is losing part or all of their principal and interest if the firm declares bankruptcy. Even if the firm does not go bankrupt, its financial distress could change the interest rate. The higher the bondholders' risk, the higher will be the required yield on bonds. The CFO has two main tasks: issuing bonds whose cash flows fit the firm's needs (which will minimize the risk of bankruptcy) and ensuring that bondholders' risk is minimal, thus reducing the firm's cost of debt.

Investors in bonds are exposed to five main types of risk: interest rate, inflation, country and political, foreign exchange, and bankruptcy. Generally speaking, the higher the risk, the higher the yield to maturity and the higher the firm's cost of debt. A firm's CFO can take actions to minimize some of these risks. In this section we define each type of risk and discuss which of them the firm can control.

12.5.1 Interest Rate Risk

Interest rate risk is defined as the change in a bond's price due to possible changes in the interest rate. The bigger the change in the price for a given change in the interest rate, the larger the bond's interest rate risk. Is investment in a government bond risky? You might think that because government bonds are default-free, they must be riskless. However, this is not the case. Government bonds are also exposed to interest rate risk. When the market interest rate fluctuates, government bond prices also fluctuate.

For example, consider a one-year U.S. Treasury bond with a face value of $1,000 paying an annual coupon of $100 (i.e., a coupon rate of 10%). The market interest rate is also 10%. Using Equation 12.1, we find that the bond's market price at the time of purchase will be

$$P_B = \frac{\$100 + \$1,000}{1.1} = \$1,000$$

The bond's market value will equal its par or face value. Now, if the interest rate decreases to 8%, the bond's market value will increase to

$$P_B = \frac{\$100 + \$1,000}{1.08} \cong \$1,018.52$$

On the other hand, if the interest rate increases to 12%, the market price will decrease to

$$P_B = \frac{\$100 + \$1,000}{1.12} \cong \$982.14$$

Why do changes in the market interest rate affect the price of bonds? What are the economic factors that cause such fluctuations? To answer these questions, consider the Treasury bond we have just been discussing. If the market interest rate decreases to 8%, the government will be able to issue similar one-year bonds at 8%. At this new market interest rate, the bonds paying 10% interest will become real bargain; any astute investor will want to buy them. Consequently, their price will increase and their yield will decrease. This process will stop when all similar bonds have the same yield—in this case 8%—and the yield will equal the new prevailing interest rate. Similarly, if the interest rate increases to 12%, an astute investor will sell the 10% bonds and buy the 12% bonds. However, if the investor is to sell the 10% bonds, their price will have to decrease. At the new equilibrium, the yield on all similar bonds will be 12%.

In summary, when the interest rate increases, bond prices decrease; and when the interest rate decreases, bond prices increase. The strength of the bond price's response to changes in the interest rate is determined by two principal factors: (1) the distribution of payments across years (for a given maturity) and (2) the time to maturity.

Examining the first of these two factors, we show that for a given maturity, the later the cash flows, the greater the sensitivity of the bond price to changes in the market interest rate. To see this, suppose the interest rate is 10% and think about the two bonds, each with a par value of $1,000:

Date (Year)	Today's ($t = 0$) Market Price	End of Year 1 Coupon	End of Year 2 Coupon and Principal
Bond A	P_A = $1,000	$100	$100 + $1,000
Bond B	P_B = $1,000	—	$210 + $1,000

Bond A pays a $100 coupon at the end of both Year 1 and Year 2; Bond B pays $210 coupon at the end of the second year. Both bonds return the principal of $1,000 at the end of Year 2. Each bond has a yield to maturity of 10% (check with your calculator). Both bonds have a maturity of two years, but the spread of their respective cash flows across the two years is different.

If held to maturity, both bonds guarantee a 10% yield. But what if a bondholder suddenly needs the money and decides to sell the bond? Do these two bonds have the same interest rate risk? No, they don't. To see why, suppose the interest rate at

$t = 0$ suddenly jumps to 20% and stays there. Which bond will suffer a sharper decrease in price? Bond A's market price will be

$$P_A = \frac{\$100}{(1.2)} + \frac{\$1,100}{(1.2)^2} \cong \$847.22$$

Bond B's market price will be

$$P_B = \frac{\$1,210}{(1.2)^2} \cong \$840.28$$

As you can see, the two bonds do not have the same capital loss. Bond B's price falls more sharply than Bond A's price. Why? Because Bond A produces a cash flow in Year 1, the investor can reinvest the amount received in Year 1 at the new, higher interest rate (20%). An investor holding Bond B does not have this opportunity, does not receive an interim cash flow and, therefore, cannot take advantage of alternative bond investments yielding 20%. The Bond B investor has the larger loss.

Now suppose the market interest rate declines, say, to 5%. In this case the Bond B holder will fare better because all of his or her money is locked into the "good" investment yielding an interest rate higher than the interest rate currently available on other bonds. The Bond A investor will not fare as well because the interim cash flow can now be reinvested at only 5%.

To sum, the distribution of a bond's cash flows over time affects its price volatility in response to changes in the interest rate. The lower the interim payments, the greater the volatility.

PRACTICE BOX

Problem   Calculate the market prices of Bond A and Bond B in the preceding example if the interest rate decreases to 5% at $t = 0$ and stays there.

Solution   For Bond A

$$P_A = \frac{\$100}{(1.05)} + \frac{\$1,100}{(1.05)^2} \cong \$1,092.97$$

For Bond B

$$P_B = \frac{\$1,210}{(1.05)^2} \cong \$1,097.51$$

The price increase due to the decline in the market interest rate is larger for Bond B. If bondholders decide to sell their bonds, Bond B investors will receive a larger gain.

This example illustrates our previous conclusion: For a given maturity, bonds that pay *no* interim interest before maturity fluctuate more sharply in price than bonds that pay an identical coupon every period. This principle was illustrated in the example for the two-year bond (Bond B). As the length of the bond's maturity increases, the effect of the spread of cash flow across years becomes even more marked. A bond that pays no interim interest before its maturity date is a **zero-coupon bond.**[3] A bond that pays an identical coupon every year is a **level-coupon bond.** Prices of zero-coupon bonds fluctuate more sharply than those of level-coupon bonds. More generally, the greater the concentration of cash flows close to the bond's maturity, the greater the fluctuation in the bond's market price.

The second factor that determines the sensitivity of the bond price to changes in the market interest rate is the time remaining until maturity. The longer the time remaining, the greater the sensitivity of the bond's market price to changes in the interest rate. The longer the bondholder is "locked in," the more sensitive the bond's market price to changes in the market interest rate. To see this, consider two zero-coupon bonds, one with a one-year maturity and the other with a 30-year maturity. Both have a face value of $1,000, and their yield to maturity, before changes in the market interest rate take place, is 10%. Table 12-1 shows the bonds' prices for various market interest rates. As explained previously, a bond's yield to maturity will change until it equals the new prevailing interest rate. Therefore the interest rate will equal the yield to maturity ($r = y$). The bond price is again calculated by Equation 12.2:[4]

$$P_B = \frac{F}{(1 + -r)^T}$$

where $T = 1$ for the short-maturity bond and $T = 30$ for the long-maturity bond. Because both bonds have the same face value and the same yield to maturity, but different time spans, the two bonds' market prices must differ. Table 12-1 shows that for the 10% base interest rate, the current market prices to be about $909.09 for the short-maturity bond and $57.31 for the long-maturity bond. The table suggests that the longer the time until maturity, the more sensitive the bond's price to fluctuations in the interest rate. For the longer maturity bond, if the interest rate decreases from 10% to 1%, the price increases from $57.31 to $741.92; if the interest rate increases to 30%, the bond's price decreases to $0.38. The price of the shorter-maturity bond is more stable.

The Price Change column shows the percentage change in the bond price resulting from changes in the interest rate. Take the 30-year bond: If the interest rate increases from 10% to 15%, the bond's price decreases from $57.31 to $15.10, for a loss of 73.7%.

Figure 12-2 provides a graphic illustration of the sensitivity of bond prices to changes in the interest rate for the two bonds. As you can see, if the interest rate stays at 10%, there is no price fluctuation and, therefore, no loss. The curve depicting the one-year bond is relatively flat, and the curve of the 30-year bond is relatively steep. The shorter the maturity, the smaller the price fluctuations—this is the

---

3. A firm may sell a bond for $800 with a face value of $1,000. The firm will make no periodic interest payments. The profit to the purchaser of the zero-interest bond is the difference between $1,000 and the $800.

4. In equilibrium the PV of the bond's payments will equal its price. Either Equation 12.1 or 12.2 can be used. Equation 12.2 simplifies to $P_B = \dfrac{F}{(1 + r)^T}$ in the case of a zero-coupon bond.

TABLE 12-1	1	2	3	4	5
Bond Price for Various Interest Rates: Zero-Coupon Bonds	Interest rate, r (%)	Short-Maturity (one-year) $P_B = \dfrac{\$1,000}{(1+y)}$	Price Change (in %)	Long-Maturity (30-year) $P_B = \dfrac{\$1,000}{(1+y)^{30}}$	Price Change (in %)
	1	$990.10	8.9	$741.92	1,195
	2	980.39	7.8	552.07	863
	3	970.87	6.8	411.99	619
	4	961.54	5.8	308.32	438
	5	952.38	4.8	231.38	304
	10	909.09	0	57.31	0
	15	869.57	−4.3	15.10	−74
	20	833.33	−8.3	4.21	−93

FIGURE 12-2
Percentage Change in Bond Price Resulting from Changes in the Market Interest Rate: Short-versus Long-Maturity Bond

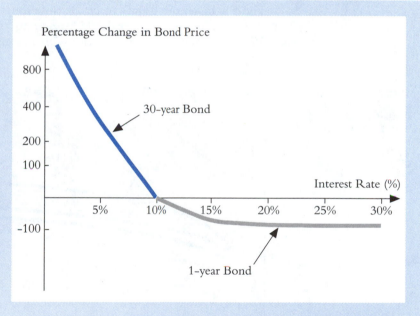

reason why short–term Treasury bills are virtually riskless and are often used as a proxy for a riskless asset.

To summarize, we have shown that in response to changes in the market interest rate,

1. For a given maturity, the closer the cash flows to the maturity date, the greater the fluctuations in the bond's market price when interest rates fluctuate.
2. The longer the maturity, the larger the price fluctuations.

The magnitude of a bond's price fluctuation is determined both by the spread of the bond's cash flows over time and the time remaining until maturity. The financial community considers bonds with relatively long maturity and relatively low interim annual payments to be relatively risky.

Figure 12-3 demonstrates the market yield on U.S. treasury bonds for various maturities. The curve describing the relationship between the yield and the time to maturity is called the **yield curve**. As we can see, in 1997 the U.S. government could borrow at about 5.5% for one year, but it needed to pay higher rates when selling 30-year bonds. The yield curve may shift over time, as indicated by the different curves for 1994 through 1997.

12.5.2 Inflation Risk

The purchasing power of a bond's cash flows depends on expected future inflation rates. The higher the expected future inflation rates, the lower the cash flows' present value and the lower the bond's price. Because future inflation is uncertain, the cash flows are uncertain in real terms. The resulting risk exposure is called **inflation risk.** We can demonstrate inflation risk with an example.

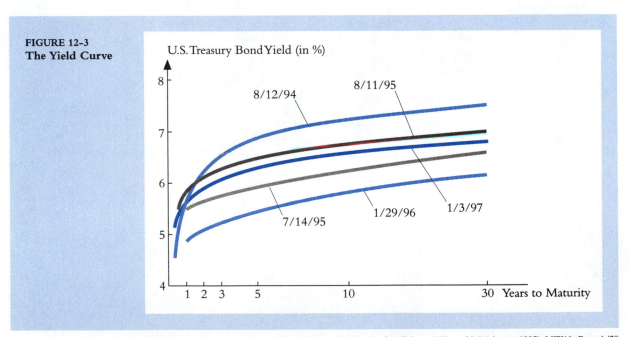

**FIGURE 12-3
The Yield Curve**

Bond payments are usually fixed in dollar terms. Suppose you buy a bond for $1,000 that offers an annual coupon of $50 and the return of $1,000 principal at maturity. Suppose only one year is left to maturity. The yield to maturity is the value of y that satisfies

$$\$1,000 = \frac{\$50 + \$1,000}{1 + y}$$

Therefore $y = 0.05$ or 5%.

If there is no inflation, this represents the real yield to maturity. Now suppose inflation begins immediately after you buy the bond, and the expected annual inflation rate is 3%. The value of your $1,050 at the end of the year in real terms—that is, the purchasing power of your $1,050—will be only $1,019.42 ($1,050/1.03 $\cong$ $1,019.42). The higher the inflation rate, the lower the purchasing power of your $1,050.

If the real interest rate is still 5%, the bond's market value (which is obtained by discounting the real cash flow by the real interest rate), will decrease to $970.88 ($1,019.42/1.05 $\cong$ $970.88). The capital loss (in real terms) to the bondholder will be $29.12.

Alternatively, the analysis can be conducted in nominal terms by discounting the nominal cash flows by the nominal interest. If the analysis is conducted in nominal terms, rather than in real terms, inflation risk can be seen as a special case of interest rate risk. To be more specific, if, due to inflation, the nominal interest rate rises to[5]

$$[(1.05) \times (1.03)] - 1 = 0.0815 \text{ or } 8.15\%$$

then analysis in nominal terms reveals, as before, that the bond price decreases to $970.87 ($1,050/1.0815 $\cong$ $970.87).

Fluctuations in bond prices may be due to changes in the *real* interest rate (even in the absence of inflation) or to changes in the *nominal* interest rate (due to inflation), even if the real interest rate remains unchanged. Some countries eliminate inflation risk by issuing *indexed-linked bonds* that link the coupon and the principal to a cost-of-living index. In January 1997, for the first time in U.S. history, the federal government issued 10-year bonds with interest payments linked to the cost-of-living index. At the end of the first trading day, the real yield to maturity on these bonds was 3.39%. On August 11, 1997 the real yield to maturity on these bonds was 3.375%.

12.5.3 Country and Political Risk

Suppose you buy a dollar-denominated bond from a foreign government or firm. If that foreign country does not have sufficient dollar reserves or if the private firm cannot pay you because of exchange restrictions, you risk losing your investment. Such risk based on events or circumstances in a foreign country is termed **country risk.** You also risk losing your investment if you invest in the bonds of a politically

---

5. As discussed in Chapter 7, the general formula is as follows:

(1 + Real interest rate) $\times$ (1 + Inflation rate) = (1 + Nominal interest rate)

http

Ernst & Young maintains an excellent tutorial on international finance, covering all the major topics: exchange rates, interest rate parity, purchasing power parity, the International Fisher Effect, and much more. If you visit, follow the link "Ernst & Young International."
http://www.trinidad. net/egbudget/ econexch.htm

unstable government. If a revolution occurred in such a country, a new ruler may refuse to honor the previous regime's obligations. Risk caused by political changes in a country is **political risk.**

The U.S. government has never defaulted on its debt in U.S. dollars. If the government does not have enough money to pay its debt, it can always raise taxes or print more money. Treasury bonds are, therefore, considered default-free—this is not the case for external debt that foreign governments issue. Over the years the United States has lost billions of dollars on loans to foreign nations that were unable to repay their debts. For foreign debt denominated in U.S. dollars, it is not surprising to see yields to maturity reaching as high as 30%. These high yields are paid to compensate for country and political risks.

12.5.4 Foreign Exchange Risk

Bonds denominated in foreign currency, even those from a politically stable country, expose U.S. investors to **foreign exchange risk.** Similarly, if a U.S. firm issues dollar-denominated bonds, say, in Germany, German bond purchasers are exposed to exchange rate risk. Suppose, for instance, a U.S. citizen invests in a one-year bond denominated in German marks (DM). Let the bond's price be 1,000 DM and the annual coupon be 100 DM. If the exchange rate at the time the bond is purchased is $1 = 1.8 DM, our U.S. bondholder will invest $555.56. If the exchange rate does not change, one year from now he or she will receive $611.11 (1,100 DM/(1.8 DM/$1) and the investment's rate of return will be 10%.

However, the exchange rate at the end of the year may not be 1.8 DM = $1. Suppose it is 2.5 DM = $1. Then, in dollar terms the U.S. investor will receive only $440 (1,100 DM/(2.5 DM/$1)) and the rate of return will be negative— −20.8%.

Of course, the situation can also go the other way—that is, if the exchange rate falls, the U.S. investor will receive more dollars for his or her 1,100 DM, and the favorable change in the exchange rate will enhance the rate of return. Because it is difficult to predict changes in foreign exchange rates, these potential fluctuations add to the variance of the bondholders' realized future return. Therefore, they are a source of risk.

For U.S. firms *issuing* bonds denominated in German marks, the fixed payments are in German marks. If the dollar depreciates (making each dollar worth fewer marks), then when the firm pays the coupon and the principal, it will have to pay more in dollar terms. Fluctuations in the foreign exchange rate are also a source of risk for the firm that issues bonds.

Nevertheless, U.S. firms have two main reasons for issuing bonds denominated in foreign currencies:

1. In spite of foreign exchange risk, the interest rate on bonds denominated in another currency can be relatively low, therefore, the yield (or cost of debt) may be low as well.

2. A firm that operates internationally generally expects to receive revenue in foreign currency. Issuing bonds in that currency reduces the firm's risk, because the firm can use cash flows from operations, which are in the foreign currency, to pay the bondholders. Paying the bondholders in their domestic currency eliminates foreign exchange risk.

If this second reason is not relevant to the firm, then taking a loan in foreign currency can be very risky. To demonstrate, in 1993 $1 was traded for 125 yen. By April 1995 the exchange rate had fallen to 82 yen to the dollar, and it then rose to 117 yen in January 1997. Thus, borrowing or lending in yen (or other foreign currency) may prove very risky. For example, suppose a U.S. firm borrowed 500 million yen at a 2% annual interest rate when the exchange rate was 125 yen per dollar. The firm received $4 million (500 million yen/125). Suppose that after two years, the firm must repay the loan when the exchange rate is 82 yen per dollar. The U.S. firm must pay 520.2 million yen and must spend $6.34 million (520.2 million yen/82) to purchase them. The firm pays 59% interest rate ($6.34 million/$4 million − 1 ≅ 0.59 or 59%) for the two years—or about 26% a year rather than 2% a year. The big loss is due to the dramatic change in the foreign exchange rate, which the firm did not foresee when it made the loan.

Global Investor maintains a comprehensive Web site for international investors. They track the world's major markets, provide a Global Investor Directory, and provide links to international financial Web sites. They also maintain FINANCEnetWATCH, which tracks financial developments in cyberspace. http://www.numa.com/Index.htm

12.5.5 Bankruptcy Risk and Bond Ratings

Corporate Finance in the News mentioned that Kmart's bonds were rated as junk bonds because of the firm's chance of bankruptcy. This kind of risk of losing interest or principal is called **bankruptcy risk**.

A firm in financial distress may be unable to meet its financial obligations and may declare bankruptcy. In such cases bondholders may lose part—or even all—of their investment.

The risk of bankruptcy can be evaluated by studying a firm's financial reports and its bond ratings. In fact, firms actually pay to have their debt rated. Generally, the higher the risk of bankruptcy, the lower the firm's bond rating, the lower the bond's market price, and the higher its yield to maturity. The high yield on risky bonds incorporates a risk premium to compensate bondholders for the high risk of bankruptcy. The lower the rating, the higher the premium.

The leading bond-rating firms are Standard & Poor's and Moody's. In rating the safety of a firm's debt, these agencies rely primarily on the firm's financial statements. The lower the risk of default and the more protected the bondholders in the case of default, the higher the firm's rating.

Table 12-2 lists various bond ratings that Moody's and s&p give. As we can see, the two agencies use different notations. However, in most cases a high degree of consistency exists between them regarding bond ratings and changes in these ratings over time. In most cases a bond's rating is fairly accurate and a change in that rating can substantially affect a firm's cost of debt and a bondholder's capital gain, as demonstrated in the following problem.

TABLE 12-2   **Bond Ratings***

Moody's	S&P's	Description
Aaa	AAA	Very high quality: No problem paying the interest and principal.
Aa	AA	High quality: Very strong financial position.
A	A	Relatively high quality: High capacity to pay interest and principal but more sensitive to the economic condition of the market.
Baa	BBB	Medium quality: Adequate capacity to pay interest and principal. The strength may change with economic conditions.

Junk Bonds

Ba	BB	Low quality: These bonds provide a high yield but are very speculative.
B	B	The price fluctuations are relatively large.
Caa	CCC	Low quality: Very speculative bonds. High yield accompanied by very high fluctuations.
C	C	Very poor quality: No interest is being paid.
D	D	Very poor: Debt that is in default.

*+ and − may be added to these ratings.

PRACTICE BOX

Problem   Suppose Chrysler Corporation improves its financial position and S&P raises the rating of its bond from B to BBB. As a result, the bond's market price increases from $800 to $900. Assume the bond has a five years to maturity, pays a coupon of $60 annually, and has a face value of $1,000.

a. Calculate the pretax cost of debt before and after the rating change, and the change in the cost of debt. Assume there are no taxes.
b. Calculate the bondholders' percentage capital gain due to the rating change.

Solution   a. The pretax cost of debt is measured by the yield to maturity. The yield to maturity before the change in the rating is given by the value of y_1 that solves the following equation:

$$\$800 = \frac{\$60}{(1 + y_1)} + \frac{\$60}{(1 + y_1)^2} + \ldots + \frac{\$60}{(1 + y_1)^5} + \frac{\$1,000}{(1 + y_1)^5}$$

Thus $y_1 = 11.48\%$.   (continued)

After the rating change the yield to maturity, y_2, is given as follows:

$$\$900 = \frac{\$60}{(1 + y_2)} + \frac{\$60}{(1 + y_2)^2} + \ldots + \frac{\$60}{(1 + y_2)^5} + \frac{\$1,000}{(1 + y_2)^5}$$

Thus $y_2 = 8.54\%$.
The change in the cost of debt is 2.94%.

b. The capital gain due to the rating change is

$$\frac{\$900 - \$800}{\$800} = 0.125 \text{ or } 12.5\%$$

For a given maturity, the lower the bond's rating, the higher its yield to maturity. Figure 12-4 demonstrates this principle: The yield on five-year government bonds is assumed to be 5%. The risk of default of these bonds is zero. As we move to the right on the horizontal axis, the risk of default increases and the yield increases. For example, for corporate bonds rated B, the yield to maturity is 12%, and their default risk premium is 7% (12% − 5% = 7%).

Low-grade bonds provide opportunity for large profits—albeit at high risk. Low-grade bonds that are rated Ba or below by Moody's or BB or below by S&P are **junk bonds**. Investing in low-grade bonds is not necessarily a bad strategy. Table 12-3

FIGURE 12-4
Yield as a Function of the Risk of Default

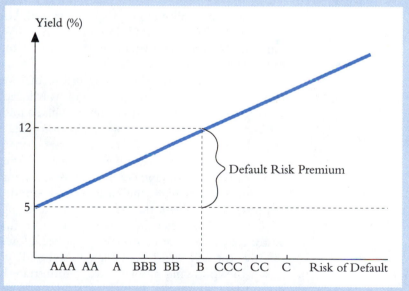

TABLE 12-3 Annual Rates of Return on Junk Bonds, Ten-Year Treasury and S&P 500 Stocks 1982 through 1995	Year	Junk bonds*	10-year Treasuries	S&P 500 stocks
	1982	36.6% ✓	32.0%	21.6%
	1983	13.9	3.5	22.6 ✓
	1984	10.7	12.9 ✓	6.2
	1985	24.9	26.3	31.7 ✓
	1986	15.6	19.9 ✓	18.7
	1987	6.5 ✓	−1.9	5.2
	1988	13.7	6.1	16.4 ✓
	1989	0.4	16.6	31.5 ✓
	1990	−6.4	6.8 ✓	−3.1
	1991	43.8 ✓	16.5	30.5
	1992	16.7 ✓	6.5	7.6
	1993	18.9 ✓	11.9	10.1
	1994	−1.0	−6.1	1.3 ✓
	1995	10.8	15.3	20.2

✓ indicates best-performing of the three markets that year

*CS First Boston high-yield bond index 1995 data through June 30

Source: *Los Angeles Times* 10 July 1995, p. D4. Copyright, 1995, *Los Angeles Times*. Reprinted with permission. Data from CS First Boston Corp.

shows that the realized rate of return on junk bonds was higher than the rate of return on U.S. Treasury bonds in 8 out of the 14 years covered in the table; returns on junk bonds were also higher than the rate of return on the S&P 500 Stock Index in 6 out of the 13 years.

Some professional investors specialize in investing in junk bonds. Probably the name most associated with junk bonds is Michael Milken, the financial adviser who worked for Drexel Burnham Lambert. Milken initially engineered junk bond offerings for financially troubled and high-tech companies. Larger, more established firms were later able to raise money for takeover operations by issuing huge amounts of debt in operations known as *leveraged-buyouts* (LBOs). After Milken's conviction for securities fraud, the market for junk bonds quieted down, but junk bonds still exist in the market.

The relatively high yield of low-grade bonds reflects their higher risk of default. Suppose the yield on the bond of a firm facing bankruptcy is relatively high, say 15%. Does that mean the bondholder will actually earn 15%? Not really. The investor may lose all or part of the principal. However, if the firm avoids bankruptcy, the investor will earn 15%, which is the bond's yield to maturity.

In the following problem, we demonstrate how to calculate the probability of default by making the simplifying assumption that the expected rates of return on all alternative bond investments are equal.

PRACTICE BOX

Problem   The yield to maturity on five-year government bonds is 5%. If the bondholders hold the bond to maturity, they will receive a 5% rate of return. The yield to maturity on otherwise similar AAA bonds is 5.8%, and the yield on B-rated bonds is 9.8%. Suppose the bondholder's expected rate of return on all of these bonds is the same.

What is the implied probability of default of each of these three bonds:
a.   The government bonds?
b.   The AAA-rated bonds?
c.   The B-rated bonds?

Assume that in case of default bondholders lose all of their investment in the bond (i.e., they receive a −100% rate of return).

Solution   Investors require a higher rate of return as compensation for the higher probability of default.
a.   Government bonds are default-free.
b.   The AAA-rated bonds' expected rate of return is

$$P \times (-100\%) + (1 - P) \times 5.8\%$$

where P is the probability of default.

Equating this expected yield to 5%, which is the default-free rate of return, we obtain

$$P \times (-100\%) + (1 - P) \times 5.8\% = 5\%$$

Therefore:

$$P = \frac{-0.8\%}{-105.8\%} \cong 0.00756 \text{ or } 0.756\%$$

c.   A similar calculation gives the B-rated bonds' probability of default

$$P = \frac{-4.8\%}{-109.8\%} \cong 0.0437 \text{ or } 4.37\%$$

We see that because the quality of B-rated bonds is lower than that of AAA-rated bonds, B-rated bonds' rate of return is higher to compensate for the higher probability of default.

Figure 12-5 and Connecting Theory to Practice 12.3 demonstrate how various risk factors affect the yield to maturity. Figure 12-5 demonstrates the yield to maturity on high-quality Aaa bonds, on low-quality Baa bonds, and on U.S. Treasury

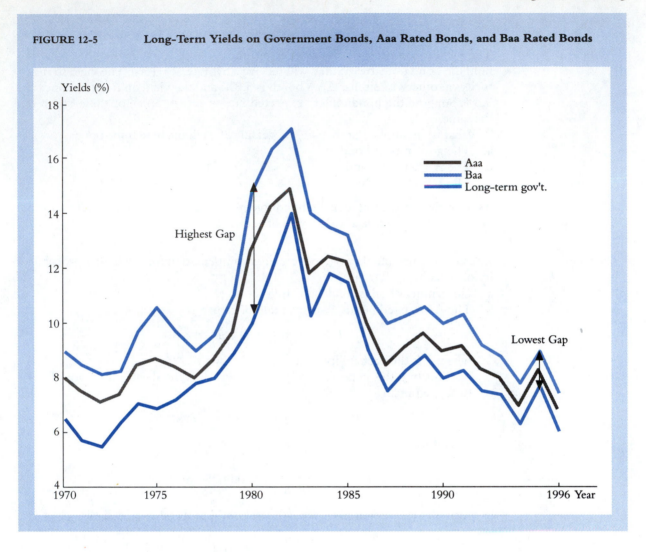

FIGURE 12-5   **Long–Term Yields on Government Bonds, Aaa Rated Bonds, and Baa Rated Bonds**

bonds. As we can see, the yield to maturity on U.S. Treasury bonds is always the lowest, reflecting the lowest risk; and the yield on Baa bonds is the highest. The gap between the yields, reflecting the risk premium, varies over time. The highest risk premium prevailed in 1981 and was approximately 4.5%; the lowest, in 1995, was approximately 1.5%. Treasury bonds are exposed to interest rate risk and inflation risk. The longer their maturity, the greater their risk. Corporate bonds are exposed to one more additional risk: risk of bankruptcy.

CONNECTING THEORY TO PRACTICE 12.3

THE YIELD TO MATURITY: COUNTRY RISK, INFLATION RISK, AND RISK OF BANKRUPTCY

PRICES & YIELDS OF ACTIVE JUNK-BOND ISSUES

Issuer	Cpn.	Maturity	Bid	Ask	Wk. Chg.	%Bid/Yld
American Std.	9⅞	6/1/01	108.250	108.750	+0.000	7.94
Grand Union	12	9/1/04	80.000	80.500	+3.500	16.41
Gulf States Steel	13½	4/15/03	88.250	88.750	-0.250	16.31
Acme Metals	12½	8/1/02	102.250	102.750	-0.250	11.98
Comcast	9⅜	5/15/05	104.875	105.375	-0.125	8.59
LenFest	8⅜	11/1/05	99.500	100.000	-1.250	8.44
Southland	5	12/15/03	83.000	83.500	-0.250	7.94
Stone Container	9⅞	2/1/01	96.250	96.750	-1.000	10.86
Unisys	13½	7/1/97	100.250	100.750	-0.500	13.25
Westpoint Stevens	8¾	12/15/01	100.625	101.125	-1.125	8.60

Source: Lehman Brothers.

J.P. MORGAN OVERSEAS GOVERNMENT BOND INDEX

January 25, 1996

Country	——Local Currency——			——U.S. Dollar——			——Yield——	
	Index	Wkly Chg	YTD Chg	Index	Wkly Chg	YTD Chg	%	YTD Chg
Australia	274.53	0.85	1.16	280.35	0.56	0.26	7.83	-0.13
Belgium	213.13	0.08	2.44	231.50	-0.40	-0.68	5.77	-0.39
Canada	233.60	-0.47	0.54	220.55	-1.46	-0.39	6.97	-0.02
Denmark	240.15	-0.38	1.90	255.31	-0.77	-1.09	6.28	-0.30
France	230.06	-0.07	2.40	240.99	-1.01	-1.34	5.95	-0.38
Germany	180.96	-0.17	1.52	192.29	-0.62	-1.57	5.17	-0.23
Italy	287.45	-0.36	3.04	209.35	-1.04	2.70	9.82	-0.61
Japan	167.07	-0.28	-0.25	189.92	-1.39	-3.36	2.88	0.06
Netherlands	190.66	-0.26	1.78	203.50	-0.72	-1.32	5.46	-0.24
Spain	266.07	-0.33	1.94	228.47	-1.08	-1.03	8.95	-0.33
Sweden	250.67	-2.36	0.83	210.70	-4.89	-2.83	8.08	-0.06
U.K.	233.51	-0.56	0.72	187.54	-1.02	-1.74	7.33	-0.04
U.S.	204.16	-0.51	0.02	204.16	-0.51	0.02	5.73	0.07
Non-U.S.	200.68	-0.30	1.26	193.66	-1.09	-1.53	5.53	-0.13
Global	205.24	-0.38	0.77	203.32	-0.86	-0.93	5.60	-0.06

YTD-Year to date. Yields-Semi-annual. Dec. 31, 1987 = 100. Source: J.P. Morgan Government Bond Index

Source: *Barron's* 76, no. 5 (January 29, 1996): MW100. Reprinted by permission of *Barron's Market Week*, © 1996 Dow Jones & Company, Inc. All Rights Reserved Worldwide.

MAKING THE CONNECTION

The yields on junk bonds and on bonds of different countries, as measured by the J.P. Morgan Overseas Government Bond Index, are shown. Compare the yields on U.S. government bonds (5.73%) and on Grand Union's junk bonds (16.41%). The difference is due mainly to the risk of a Grand Union bankruptcy. Because its pretax cost of debt is 16.41%, Grand Union must earn on average a relatively high rate of return on its projects, compared to firms such as AT&T that have high-quality bonds and lower rates of returns. However, the firm's management can control bankruptcy risk. By not issuing too much debt, by not paying dividends, and by not taking very risky projects, a firm may keep its risk of bankruptcy low. Although management can control this risk, they should not eliminate it entirely because by doing so they may also eliminate the firm's profit.

We now have all the tools we need to answer the questions Connecting Theory to Practice 12.1 raised regarding the Santa Fe railroad bonds. Questions 3 and 4 are general and have already been discussed. Questions 1 and 2 relate specifically to Santa Fe's bonds.

Buying a very long maturity bond is not necessarily bad. If the inflation rate remains low and if interest rates are expected to decrease, the longer the bond's time to maturity, the greater the capital gain on the bond. Investors in the Santa Fe railroad bonds simply underestimated the future inflation and interest rates; and because both turned out to be relatively high, the bond's price decreased. In such a case the longer the maturity, the greater the loss. However, a very long maturity bond does not necessarily involve a loss to bondholders. At the bond's maturity, its price always approaches its face value (in this case, $1,000).

The bond's price can be above or below its face value, as demonstrated with Santa Fe bonds. The bond's price may fluctuate due to changes in the interest rate and in the risk of bankruptcy. If its market price is below its par value, we say the bond is a **discount bond,** or "sells at a discount." If it is traded above par, we say it is a **premium bond,** or "sells at a premium." Any bond can be sold at a premium or at a discount. However, as the bond approaches maturity, its price approaches its par value. The only exception occurs when a firm goes bankrupt and is uncertain that it can pay the bondholders the principal. In such case the bond's price can fall below its face value, even close to the maturity date.

12.5.6 Controlling the Risk on Bonds

We have now discussed five types of risk: interest rate risk, inflation risk, country risk, political risk, and foreign exchange risk. Although a firm cannot directly control these risks, it may minimize its exposure to them. For example, by issuing bonds denominated in U.S. dollars, the firm may eliminate foreign exchange risk. However, foreign investors who purchase such bonds are exposed to foreign exchange risk. As a result, they may demand a higher yield, which would translate into a higher cost of debt for the firm.

Changes in interest rates are a source of risk, but the firm can protect itself from this type of risk by issuing callable bonds (discussed in Section 12.6.1) or by purchasing options on interest rates, discussed in Chapter 11.

Of all the risks a firm faces, it can best control bankruptcy risk. The firm may decide to invest in very risky projects or in less risky ones; it may hedge its risk with options, or it may speculate with options; and it may use a little debt or a lot of debt. To minimize bankruptcy risk, the CFO should try to match interest payments with cash inflows from operations. If the firm expects to receive large cash inflows in the near future, it can issue short-term bonds. If cash inflows are not expected soon, the firm would fare better by issuing long-term debt.

The firm sometimes needs to issue long-term bonds because they best fit its pattern of cash flows. However, since bondholders view such bonds as relatively risky, management faces a conflict between two objectives. The goal, then, is to minimize the cost of debt, whole accounting for both bankruptcy risk and interest rate risk. In Applying Theory to Practice 12.1, you see how the bond market can affect a firm's risk and its reward.

APPLYING THEORY TO PRACTICE 12.1

THE BOND MARKET: RISK AND REWARD

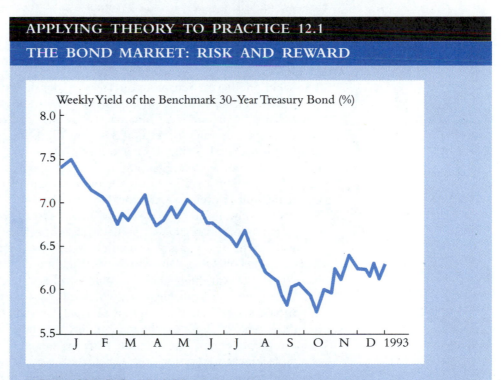

Weekly Yield of the Benchmark 30-Year Treasury Bond (%)

HOW LOW DID IT GO?
The 30-year bond yield dropped as low as 5.79%, the lowest yield since the Treasury began regular auctions of the bond in 1977. Rates rose to 6.34% by year end but were still far below the 7.39% at the end of 1992.

Those investors holding long-term securities, especially those holding highly volatile 30-year Treasury zero-coupon bonds, did extraordinarily well. A zero-coupon bond pays no interest and is sold at a deep discount to face value.

Last year many investors—humming along with bonds they may have bought just a year or two ago—suddenly found themselves holding a load of cash. That's because companies, cities and states, and homeowners rushed to replace higher-yielding debt with lower-yielding debt. The result was a frenzied search for higher yields by investors that sparked a flood of new junk-bond issuance from the lowest-rated issuers since the late 1980s, a handful of 50-year and 100-year corporate bond issues, and a daring plunge by many U.S. investors into the uncharted but higher-yielding waters of bonds of developing nations. People who once bought investment-grade bonds plunged into junk, and veteran junk bond buyers plunged into things like Mexican and Argentine government bonds. . . .

Source: Thomas T. Vogel, Jr., "Bond Investors May Have to Stretch to Repeat Their Double-Digit Returns," *Wall Street Journal*, 3 January 1994, p. R6. Reprinted by permission of *The Wall Street Journal*, © 1994 Dow Jones & Company, Inc. All Rights Reserved Worldwide.

QUESTIONS
1. The yield on 30-year zero-coupon Treasury bonds decreased from 7.39% at the end of 1992 to 5.79% in October 1993. To simplify calculations assume that 29 years are left to maturity. Calculate the capital gain on this bond with a face value of $1,000. Do you think the yield on corporate bonds also declined during this period? Explain.
2. How would your answer regarding the bond's capital gain change if it pays an annual coupon of $73.90 on October 1 each year starting in 1994? Compare your answers to Questions 1 and 2.
3. Firms sometimes issue *callable bonds*, which they can require bondholders to redeem before maturity at a predetermined price. These bonds will be discussed in the next section. The article states that companies "rushed" to replace higher-yielding debt with lower-yielding debt. Suppose the yield on a firm's 30-year, high-grade, callable bond with an annual coupon of $73.90 is 7.39%. The callable price, which is the price the firm must pay its bondholders to redeem the bonds, is $1,100. The yield decreased in October 1993 to 5.79%. Suppose the relevant discount rate for the cash saved by the bond replacement is 6% and the firm has a fixed cost of $50 per bond as a replacement transaction cost. Calculate the PV of the firm's saving by the bond replacement. Should the firm replace the bond if only five years are left until maturity? Explain.
4. The yield on a 30-year corporate bond paying a coupon of $73.90 is 7.39%. The corporate tax rate is 35%. Calculate the firm's after-tax cost of debt. Suppose the yield on the bond decreases to 5.79%. Analyze how the drop in the yield affects the after-tax cost of debt.

MAKING THE CONNECTION

1. The price of the 29-year zero-coupon bond with a 7.39% yield and a $1,000 face value is $1,000/(1.0739)^{29} \cong $126.49. After the yield decreases to 5.79%, the price is $1,000/(1.0579)^{29} \cong $195.48. The capital gain is $68.99; in percentage terms, it is 54.54%.

    Generally, when the yield on Treasury bonds changes, the yield on corporate bonds also changes. Although usually in the same direction, the change is not necessarily of the same magnitude. For example, if investors expect the inflation rate to decline, the yield on all bonds will tend to decline.

2. In this case some of the money is paid before the maturity date. Based on what we know about the timing of cash flows and their effect on bond prices, we should expect the change in the yield to have a smaller effect on the percentage capital gain. Let us elaborate. First, note that if the annual coupon is $73.90, the bond's face value is $1,000, and the yield to maturity is 7.39%, the bond's current price must be $1,000. On October 1, 1993, the yield decreased to 5.79%, but the bond will still pay a $73.90 coupon each year for the next 28 years, plus $1,000 principal and $73.90 interest at the end of the last year. The bond's current market price is as follows:

$$\$1,222.32 = \$73.90/(1.0579) + \$73.90/(1.0579)^2 + \dots$$
$$+ \$73.90/(1.0579)^{28} + \$1,073.90/(1.0579)^{29}$$

    The capital gain in this case is $222.32, compared to the $68.99 gain in Question 1.

    However, the percentage gain, which is relevant because the investor can buy as many bonds as he or she wishes, is lower: $222.32/$1,000 = 0.2223 or 22.23%.

3. Let's look at the two alternatives: If the firm stays with its current bonds, its cash outflows will be as follows:

Year	1993	1994	1995	1996	. . .	2022
Cash flows	$0	$73.90	$73.90	$73.90	. . .	$1,073.90

On the other hand, if the firm calls the bonds, the cash outflows per bond will be as follows:

Year	1993	1994	1995	1996	. . .	2022
Cash flows	$150	$57.90	$57.90	$57.90	. . .	$1,057.90

where the $150 in 1993 is the call price of the old bonds ($1,100) plus the issue cost of the new bonds ($50) minus the selling price of the new bond ($1,000). The difference between these two cash flows represents the firm's cash savings:

Year	1993	1994	1995	1996	. . .	2022
Cash flows	–$150	$16	$16	$16	. . .	$16

Because the discount rate for the firm's future savings is 6%, the present value of this incremental cash inflow is $67.46. By replacing its debt, the firm earns $67.46 per bond in 1993 dollars. In this case the firm should definitely replace the bond.

If only five years are left until maturity, the incremental cash flow will be as follows:

Year	1993	1994	1995	1996	1997	1998
Cash flows	−$150	$16	$16	$16	$16	$16

Using a discount rate of 6%, the present value will be −$82.61, and the savings on the transaction will be negative. In this case the firm should not replace the bond.

The replacement decision is reversed for the shorter maturity bond because the gain from the replacement is received for only five years, whereas the loss from the replacement is $150, as before.

4. Since the coupon payments are tax-deductible, the firm's after-tax cost of debt is calculated by replacing the coupon payment of $73.90 with a payment of $48.035 [0.65 × $73.90]. The after-tax cost of debt is the IRR of the following cash flows:

Year:	0	1	2	. . .	30
Cash flows	−$1,000	$48.035	$48.035	. . .	$1,048.035

Using a financial calculator, we find that IRR = 4.8035%—this shows that if the bond sells at par, the after-tax cost of debt is simply 4.8035%.

If the yield decreases to 5.79%, the after-tax cost of debt of new bond issues will be

$$(1 - T) \times 5.79\% = 0.65 \times 5.79\% = 3.764\%.$$

If the bond is not sold at par, we must use the yield to maturity to determine the after-tax cost of debt.

12.6 CLASSIFICATION OF BONDS BY SPECIAL FEATURES

Bonds can be classified according to their special features. As we shall see, some of these special features are quite sophisticated and provide the CFO with flexible sources of financing.

12.6.1 Callable Bonds

The issuing firm can redeem a **callable bond** prior to its maturity date under certain terms specified in the bond contract.

Suppose the firm issues a 20-year bond at par ($1,000), the coupon rate is 10%, and the annual coupon is $100. If the market interest rate decreases, say, to 8%, the firm may wish to redeem the bonds and issue new ones at the now lower interest rate. However, it can do so only if the bonds are callable. Most corporate bonds are callable. For instance, the firm may be entitled to recall its bonds after the end of the third year at a prespecified price, say $1,100. Thus, if the interest rate falls sharply, the firm will recall the bonds. The bondholder gains $100, which is the difference between the call price and the price paid for the bond. It may seem that the bondholder loses from the callability feature, but this is not the case. Without callability the bond price would be higher, and the gain would be larger. The firm benefits because it can issue new bonds at a lower interest rate and lower its cost of debt.

The **yield-to-call** is the bond's yield calculated on the assumption that it will be recalled. The formula for the yield-to-call is

$$P_B = \sum_{t=1}^{n} \frac{C_t}{(1+y)^t} + \frac{P_c}{(1+y)^n} \qquad (12.3)$$

where n is the number of years until the firm is allowed to recall its bond and P_c is the callable price. For example, if a bond can be called after three years, then the yield-to-call is calculated with $n = 3$.

12.6.2 Convertible Bonds

Most bonds pay both coupon and principal, and neither the firm nor the bondholder can change the cash flows involved. Such bonds are termed **straight bonds.** On the other hand, **convertible bonds** can be converted into shares of stock at a predetermined rate at the bondholder's discretion. Although convertible bonds have a lower yield than straight bonds, investors in convertible bonds may realize a higher cash flow if and when they decide to convert.

To illustrate, suppose a firm issues a convertible bond yielding 8%. The bondholders have the right to convert the bond into stock at a **conversion ratio** of, say, 1 to 25, meaning that they can convert 1 bond into 25 shares. The conversion ratio determines the **conversion price**. If the convertible bond's face value is $1,000, the conversion price will be $1,000/25 shares = $40.

Convertible bonds have two principal advantages for their issuers. First, the firm may be reluctant to sell stock if it believes the stock price is temporarily depressed. Instead, the firm may decide to issue convertible bonds to encourage bondholders to convert their bonds into stock when the stock price increases. For this to occur, however, the conversion price has to be higher than the current stock price. For example, if the current stock price is $15 and management believes that it will be at least $40 in four years' time, the firm will set the conversion price at, say, $40. If the current stock price is $40, the firm will prefer to issue stock rather than bonds. Converting the bonds at the $40 conversion price is similar to issuing stock at $40 a share. Why doesn't the firm wait until the price increases to $40 and then issue stock? A firm that needs cash immediately cannot afford to wait. A convertible bond is a compromise between the firm's immediate need for cash and its preference for equity.

The second advantage of convertible bonds concerns the coupon rate. Convertible bonds generally have lower coupon rates than straight bonds, and the firm saves money by issuing convertible bonds.

Issuing convertible bonds also has two disadvantages. First, if bondholders expect the stock price to continue to increase above the conversion price (in our example $40), they may not immediately convert their bonds into stock. For example, if they convert their bonds only when the stock price is $60, they receive the stock at $40 per share when its market price is $60. This situation works against the interest of the existing shareholders. There is one way to overcome this difficulty: Attach a **call provision** to the convertible bond. If the firm can recall the bond at, say, $1,125, the bondholders, aware of the call provision, will convert their bonds when the stock price is just a little above $45. By attaching a call provision to the convertible bonds, the firm forces conversion at what it considers a reasonable price.

The second disadvantage of issuing convertible bonds concerns potential debt; that is, if its forecast is not realized and the stock price does not increase, the firm will be stuck with debt, in spite of its original intention to issue stock.

12.6.3 Bonds with Warrants Attached

Firms sometimes attach warrants to their bonds. A **warrant** is the right to buy the firm's stock at a prespecified price and within a prespecified period. Thereafter, the warrant expires. For example, suppose a firm can issue a bond at a coupon rate of 10%. The firm might "sweeten" the bond by attaching 20 warrants to each bond, with each warrant entitling its holder to buy one share at $40. Warrants are generally valid for a fairly long period of time, typically four to five years. They allow the firm to issue the bond at a lower coupon rate than it would otherwise.

Warrants are *detachable*, which means the holder can trade them separately in the market. If the stock price is, say, $50 at the expiration date and if, according to the terms of the warrant, the holder can buy the share at $40, the warrant's value at expiration will be $10. However, if the stock's market price is below $40, the warrant will expire worthless.

12.6.4 Floating-Rate Debt and Indexed Bonds

In the 1980s the United States and Europe experienced double-digit inflation rates. As a result, market interest rates rose and bondholders lost money. Indeed, lenders' risk increased so dramatically in the 1980s that many investors refused to lend money at any fixed interest rate. To attract investors back to the bond market, corporations introduced **floating rate debt**—long-term bonds with interest rates subject to adjustment every few months—and linked it to other going interest rates (such as the U.S. Treasury interest rate or the London Interbank Offered Rate, LIBOR). Some of these bonds set upper and lower limits, called *caps* and *collars*, on the interest rates.

Firms in countries experiencing high levels of inflation can also overcome this difficulty by issuing **indexed bonds**, whereby both the coupons and the principal are adjusted to the inflation rate. For example, if the inflation rate is 20%, after two years the bond's face value will change from $1,000 to $1,000 $\times (1.2)^2 = \$1,440$. Some companies also index their debt to their products' prices. They do this to reduce the risk of default if their products' prices drop sharply. However, if their products' prices increase, so do their interest payments. In effect, by issuing such debt companies share their success with the bondholders.

12.6.5 Foreign Bonds and Eurobonds

Although most U.S. investors buy bonds denominated in U.S. dollars, electronic communication makes it easy for them to buy foreign bonds denominated in local currencies (such as German marks or British pounds). In the early 1990s U.S. government bonds yielded 6%, while German government bonds yielded 9%. Why didn't all investors shift their money to Germany to enjoy the higher yield? Such bonds expose investors to the foreign exchange risk discussed earlier. U.S. investors may lose money when they convert a cash flow denominated in German marks into U.S. dollars.

Corporations and governments issue **Eurobonds** that are traded simultaneously in a number of countries. Denominated in one currency—usually the U.S. dollar, the Japanese yen, or the German mark—Eurobonds are traded mainly in London. For example, on November 29, 1994, Walt Disney made a successful appearance in the Eurobond market with a $300 million issue of three-year bonds offering an 8% yield. Mainly Swiss banks and some European institutional investors bought these bonds. Following the Disney offering, PepsiCo issued $250 million, three-year Eurobonds, also with a yield to maturity of about 8%.

http

The International Trade Desk Manual is a comprehensive reference source for almost anything related to international finance.
http://www.island-metro.com

12.7 CLASSIFICATION OF BONDS BY TAX OBLIGATION AND RISK OF DEFAULT

Bonds may also be classified according to their risk of default and whether their cash flows are taxable. For instance, the main differences among corporate bonds, government bonds, and municipal bonds can be summarized as follows:

Class	Risk of default	Taxable
Corporate bonds	Yes	Yes
U.S. government (Treasury) bonds	No	Yes
Municipal bonds	Yes	No

The bankruptcy risk of corporate and municipal bonds varies according to the issuer's financial strength. The bonds of firms with a high risk of bankruptcy are the junk bonds discussed before.

The interest and capital gains earned on U.S. government bonds are taxable, while interest on municipal bonds is tax-free at the federal level. However, the capital gain is taxable. Also, municipal bonds are tax-free at the state level for purchasers who live in the issuing state. The availability of tax-free bonds influences the CFO's decision regarding the terms of a bond issue. We demonstrate this in the next problem.

PRACTICE BOX

Problem

You are considering whether to invest in a one-year corporate bond or a one-year municipal bond. Both have the same risk of bankruptcy and the current price of each is $1,000. The municipal bond pays an annual coupon of $60 and the corporate bond pays an annual coupon of $90. Calculate the rate of return on the two bonds under two assumptions:
a. A zero tax rate.
b. A 39.6% tax rate.

Solution

a. Municipal bonds are tax-free. Therefore, regardless of the tax rate, their rate of return will be

$$\frac{\$1,000 + \$60 - \$1,000}{\$1,000} = 0.06 \text{ or } 6\%$$

With a zero tax rate, the corporate bond's rate of return would be

$$\frac{\$1,000 + \$90 - \$1,000}{\$1,000} = 0.09 \text{ or } 9\%$$

b. With a 39.6% tax rate, the corporate bond's after-tax rate of return will be

$$\frac{\$1,000 + (1 - 0.396)\$90 - \$1,000}{\$1,000} = \frac{\$54.36}{\$1,000} = 0.05436 \text{ or } 5.436\%$$

We obtain the following after-tax rates of return:

Tax rate (%)	Corporate Bond (%)	Municipal Bond (%)
Zero	9	6
39.6	5.436	6

From this result, we see that investors in low tax brackets would do better buying the corporate bond, while investors in the 39.6% tax bracket would do better investing in the municipal bond. We have a *clientele effect*: different investors focus on different types of bonds. If most investors who are candidates to purchase the bonds are in the 39.6% tax bracket, the CFO must raise the pre-tax yield above 9.93%; otherwise, he or she will be unable to sell the bond issue.

12.8 SAFEGUARDING THE INTERESTS OF BONDHOLDERS: THE INDENTURE

Bonds can be short-term (with a maturity of two years or less), intermediate-term (up to 10 years), or long-term (more than 10 years). A firm usually issues debt for relatively long terms. How can the bondholder be assured that after the firm issues debt, it will not adopt policies that favor stockholders at the expense of the bondholders? For example, suppose management thinks the stockholders will benefit if the firm issues more debt. If the firm does issue the debt and uses the proceeds to repurchase its stock, the risk to the *existing* bondholders will increase. Because the firm now has additional fixed interest payments, it faces an increased risk of bankruptcy if it cannot make the payments on time. Therefore, its bond price will decrease. Or, if the firm increases its dividends dramatically, thereby leaving fewer assets in the firm, the bondholders' risk exposure will increase.

An **indenture,** a legal document, spells out the "contract" between the bondholders and the corporation and is used to protect the bondholders' rights. A *trustee*—usually a bank—is appointed to represent the bondholders and to safeguard their legal rights. As protection for the bondholders, the indenture contains restrictive covenants. For example, restrictions may include the level of dividends that the firm may distribute to its stockholders, how much additional debt it may issue, or the minimum current ratio.

Many bonds have a **sinking fund provision** whereby after a grace period the firm is required to retire some portion of its debt every year. This arrangement facilitates repayment of the bond issue. Since regular debt repayment is mandatory, failure to do so may lead to bankruptcy. The bondholders may require that the money be deposited with a trustee who accumulates the yearly payments, invests the transferred money, and pays it as a lump sum to the bondholders at maturity. This is a rare arrangement, however. The more common arrangement is one of the following:

1. The firm or the trustee can use a lottery technique to redeem a given percentage of the bonds every year at their par value.
2. If the bond's market price is below par, the firm can buy some portion of the bonds and transfer them to the trustee to satisfy the sinking fund requirement.

Finally, if the bonds are convertible or callable, the indenture delineates the terms of these provisions.

SUMMARY

Many different types of bonds are available. They may be classified by their cash flows, their tax status, their risk-return profile, and their special provisions.

Firms can borrow directly from banks, or they can sell bonds. The CFO has to decide on the terms of the debt and its maturity (short-, intermediate-, or long-term). The firm can sell its bonds at a discount with a zero or very low coupon, or it can issue level-coupon bonds at the going interest rate. Bonds can be callable, convertible, or have warrants attached to them. Finally, the firm can issue bonds in U.S. dollars or in various currencies.

Callable bonds are issued at a higher interest rate than noncallable bonds, and convertible bonds are sold at a lower yield than nonconvertible bonds. In general, there are no free lunches, so each additional provision has its economic price tag. Each firm will select the type of bond most suited to its needs.

Since the yield to maturity measures the firm's (pretax) cost of debt, it is relevant for the firm's management. The yield to maturity is determined by various types of risk, some of which the firm's management can control and some of which it cannot control. The principal risk factors of bonds are:

(1) interest rate risk, (2) inflation risk, (3) country and political risk, (4) foreign exchange risk, and (5) bankruptcy risk.

The yield-risk profile of bonds is relevant for investors as well as for the firm. The firm can issue short-term bonds, which investors generally deem relatively safe and which have relatively low yields. However, this policy may prove risky to the firm, in particular when it uses money raised to invest in long-term projects that generate cash flows only several years after the initial investment. The CFO should try to find the type of bond that, on the one hand, minimizes the cost of debt and, on the other hand, fits the firm's cash flow from the projects this debt finances. However, in most cases the two goals cannot be achieved simultaneously, and the CFO will have to seek terms that are optimal for the firm.

CHAPTER AT A GLANCE

1. Types of bonds

	Government Bond	Corporate Bond	Municipal Bond
Taxable	Yes	Yes	No
Risk of bankruptcy	No	Yes	Yes
Risk of changes in interest rate	Yes	Yes	Yes
Risk of inflation	Yes	Yes	Yes

2. Valuation formulas
  a. PV of cash flows:

$$\text{PV} = \sum_{t=1}^{T} \frac{C_t}{(1+y)^t} + \frac{F}{(1+y)^T}$$

where C_t is the annual coupon, F is the face value, T is the time to maturity, and r is the appropriate discount rate.
  b. yield to maturity:
  The value of y that solves

$$P_B = \sum_{t=1}^{T} \frac{C_t}{(1+y)^t} + \frac{F}{(1+y)^T}$$

where P_B is the bond's market price.

c. Yield to call:
   The value of y that solves

$$P_B = \sum_{t=1}^{n} \frac{C_t}{(1+y)^t} + \frac{P_c}{(1+y)^n}$$

where P_c is the call price and n is number of years until the bond can be called.

3. Types of risks affecting bonds
   a. Interest rate risk
   b. Inflation risk
   c. Country and political risk
   d. Foreign exchange risk
   e. Bankruptcy risk

KEY TERMS

Coupon	Foreign exchange risk	Conversion ratio
Yield to maturity	Bankruptcy risk	Conversion price
Interest rate risk	Junk bond	Call provision
Zero-coupon bond	Discount bond	Warrant
Level-coupon bond	Premium bond	Floating-rate debt
Yield curve	Callable bond	Indexed bond
Inflation risk	Yield to call	Eurobond
Country risk	Straight bond	Indenture
Political risk	Convertible bond	Sinking fund provision

REVIEW AND PRACTICE

12.1 Suppose that due to a new international agreement, additional highly profitable projects become available. How will the new agreement affect the interest rate? Illustrate your answer graphically.

12.2 A zero-coupon bond's face value is $1,000, the appropriate discount rate is 5%, and there are five years to maturity. What is the bond's PV?

12.3 What is the PV of a bond that pays an annual coupon of $100 and has a face value of $1,000? The appropriate discount rate is 10%.

12.4 The PV of a zero-coupon bond with five years left to maturity is $800. The face value is $1,000. What is the discount rate?

12.5 Prove that for a level-coupon bond with a PV equal to its face value, the following must hold:

$$\frac{C}{F} = r$$

where C is the coupon, F is the face value, and r is the interest rate.

12.6 Instead of paying an annual coupon of $100, a firm decides to pay $50 semiannually. The annual interest rate is 10% and the par value is $1,000. The maturity is five years. Calculate the cash flows' PV before and after the change in the coupon payments. (Note: The semiannual interest rate is $(1.1)^{1/2} - 1 = 0.0488$ or 4.88%.)

12.7 The Japanese government issues bonds in Europe denominated in U.S. dollars and other bonds denominated in yen. Both are issued in London and have the same maturity. The yen-denominated bond's yield is 3.24% and the dollar-denominated bond's yield is 5.48%. How do you account for this difference?

12.8 A bond's face value is $1,000, the coupon is $50 a year, the market price is $800, and the maturity is 15 years. Calculate the yield to maturity. What is the yield to maturity if the coupon is paid semiannually?

12.9 Which of the following statements is correct? Explain.
a. The price of a discount bond must increase at some point during the years left to maturity.
b. The price of a discount bond must increase as the number of years to maturity decrease. Thus, the shorter the maturity, the higher the bond's price.

12.10 A bond currently priced at $900 will mature five years from now at $1,000. The yield to maturity is 8% and a coupon is paid at the end of each year. What is the value of the bond's coupon?

12.11 The yield on a five-year U.S. Treasury bond is 6%. A five-year junk bond is traded at a yield of 12%. Both are zero-coupon bonds with a face value of $1,000. Do you agree with the following assertion? "A two-point drop in the yield (from 6% to 4% and from 12% to 10%, respectively) will produce the same percentage capital gain." Prove and discuss your results.

12.12 You have both a zero-coupon bond and a level-coupon bond paying an annual coupon of $100. Both have five years left to maturity, a face value of $1,000, and a yield to maturity of 10%.
a. Estimate the bonds' current market prices.
b. Assume the yield to maturity increases to 12%. Determine the bonds' market prices and the percentage capital loss on each of these two bonds.
c. Repeat problem 12.12b on the assumption that the yield to maturity on both decreases to 8%. Explain your results.

12.13 A firm is considering whether to issue a zero-coupon bond for 30 years with a yield to maturity of 10% or a level-coupon bond for 30 years with a yield to maturity of 9%. In both cases the face value is $1,000. Since the firm's operating income fluctuates sharply over time, it does not have access to the bond market whenever it wishes. The firm decides to issue the zero-coupon bond.
a. Ignoring taxes, calculate the cost of debt of each of these two bonds. What is the zero-coupon bond's market price?
b. Give reasons for issuing the more expensive bond.

12.14 The yield to maturity on 10-year zero-coupon bonds is 7%, and the face value is $1,000. The expected annual inflation rate is 3%.
a. What is the yield to maturity in real terms?
b. What will the bond's market price be if the real yield to maturity decreases by 1%?
c. What will the bond's market price be if the inflation rate falls to 2% with no change in the real yield?
d. What will the bond's market price be if the real yield decreases by 1% and the inflation rate decreases to 2%? Calculate the capital gain or loss that would result from each of the changes in problems 12.14b, 12.14c, and 12.14d.

12.15 On August 14, 1995, *Barron's* published the following data:

Country	Yield on Government Bonds
Italy	11.11%
Japan	3.03%

The Japanese government has been advised to issue bonds, use the proceeds to buy Italian bonds, and pocket the difference in yields. Analyze this strategy. Under what future scenario might this be a good idea? (Be precise!)

12.16 Assume a maturity of one year and the following bond yields:

U.S. Treasury	4%
AAA-rated bond	5%
B-rated bond	6%

All the bonds are sold at par ($1,000) and there are no taxes. Bondholders lose all of their investment in case of bankruptcy. The coupon is paid at the end of the year. Assume identical expected rates of return on these investments.

a. Calculate the default probability for each of these bonds.

b. Repeat your calculation on the assumption that in case of default bondholders recover 50% of the value of their investment at the end of the year.

12.17 A bond with 10 years to maturity is traded for $950; the annual coupon is $150. The bond is callable at $1,200 after three years. Calculate the yield to maturity and the yield to call on the assumption the bond will be called three years from now.

12.18 The following announcement regarding Kroger bonds appeared in the *Wall Street Journal* on September 30, 1993:

Kroger to Redeem Debentures

CINCINNATI — Kroger Co. said it will redeem its 15½% [bonds] due in 2008. The grocery store operator will pay 100% of the principal amount. Kroger said $500 million of the bonds is outstanding.

a. Assume the Kroger bond traded for $900 in 1992 and $1,000 in 1993. The bond is callable at $1,000. The coupon rate is 15½%. Calculate Kroger's pretax cost of debt in 1992 and 1993.

b. Suppose Kroger's cash flow increases and its bond rating improves. The CFO believes Kroger can issue a bond at a yield of 12% that will mature in the year 2008. Given this information, what will Kroger's new cost of debt be? What would be the price of Kroger's old bond if it were not callable?

12.19 The following graphs illustrate the yield curves in four countries:

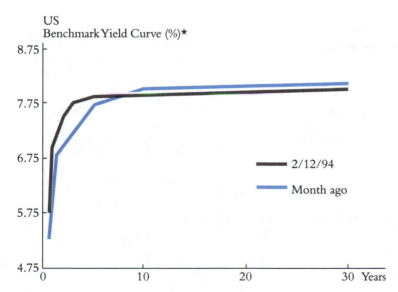

US
Benchmark Yield Curve (%)★

— 2/12/94

— Month ago

★All yields are market convention.
Source: Merrill Lynch

UK
Benchmark Yield Curve (%)★

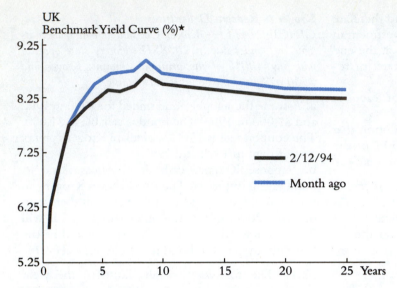

★All yields are market convention.
Source: Merrill Lynch

Germany
Benchmark Yield Curve (%)★

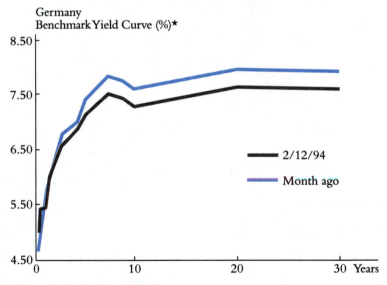

★All yields are market convention.
Source: Merrill Lynch

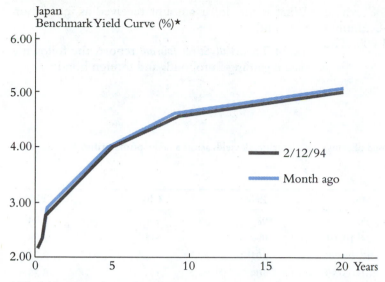

Japan
Benchmark Yield Curve (%)★

★All yields are market convention.
Source: Merrill Lynch

Source: *Financial Times*, 5 December 1994, p. 22. © *Financial Times* 1994.

Suppose the inflation rate in Japan is 1% and is expected to remain 1% in the future.

a. Draw the Japanese real yield to maturity curve—one with the *real* yield on the vertical axis.

b. Suppose the real yield to maturity curves for Germany, the U.K., and the U.S. are the same as in Japan, the only difference being their higher inflation rates. What can we learn about the expected inflation rates from these three graphs? Are the inflation rates in Germany, the U.K., and the U.S. expected to rise?

12.20 A firm issues a convertible bond with a conversion ratio of 10. The bond's par value is $1,000. What is the conversion price?

12.21 A firm has 1,000 shares outstanding and the current price of each share is $100. The firm issues 100 straight bonds at $1,000 each. The bonds pay a $50 annual coupon, and the yield to maturity on the issuing date is 5%. The maturity is 15 years. The yield on 15–year maturity government bonds is 4%.

a. Is there a danger of the firm going bankrupt? Explain.

b. What will be the bond's maximum price if the firm's value suddenly increases and the bondholder thinks there is a zero probability of bankruptcy?

c. Suppose the firm's market value decreases and the risk of bankruptcy becomes substantial. What will be the bond's current price if the yield on the bonds increases to 50%?

d. If the bond is convertible and the conversion ratio is 10:1, calculate the total value of the stock obtained by converting one bond, for the following stock prices: $0, $50, $75, $100, and $200.

e. Suppose if the stock price is $100, there is a 10% chance that it will increase; if it is $200, the probability of it increasing beyond $200 is zero. Analyze the difference between the bond value and the total value of the stock obtained by converting one bond in these two cases.

12.22 A corporate bond pays an annual coupon of $50 and a municipal bond pays an annual coupon of $40. There are no capital gains or losses. At what marginal income tax rate would an investor be indifferent between these two bonds?

12.23 A firm issues a bond at "LIBOR + ½%" where the LIBOR interest rate is quoted at the beginning of each year. The bond's face value is $1,000. The LIBOR rate in each of the three years is:

Year	1	2	3
LIBOR (%)	5	6	4

What is the dollar amount received as interest on the bond?

12.24 The *Wall Street Journal* reports the following data regarding Eurobonds and foreign bonds:

The following is a selected list of actively traded bond offerings with benchmark yields across a range of maturities.

Eurodollar Bonds

Issuer	Cpn. %	Mat.	Price	Chg.	Yld. %
Province of Alberta	7⅛	05/11/98	98 2/16	+2/16	8.04
Kgdom of Belgium	8⅛	24/10/01	99 6/16	+4/16	8.08
Kgdom of Belgium	8¾	17/04/98	101 8/16	−1/16	8.02
Br. Petroleum Amer	9¾	01/03/99	104 6/16	+2/16	8.26
Br. Telecom Fin.	8¾	11/08/99	101 15/16	+2/16	8.04
Caisse Centl Econ	9¼	01/03/95	100 3/16	nc	6.88
Daimier-Benz Amer.	8¼	23/05/96	100 5/16	nc	7.77
Kgdom of Denmark	9¼	21/03/95	100 5/16	nc	6.61
Dupont de Nemours	8½	25/06/98	100 9/16	−1/16	8.11
Energie Beh. Ned.	9	17/10/95	101 5/16	nc	6.82
Eur. Invt. Bank	7½	26/09/96	99 8/16	nc	7.64
Eur. Invt. Bank	8¾	15/07/98	101 15/16	−1/16	7.89
Eur. Invt. Bank	9⅛	02/08/00	104 1/16	+4/16	8.00
Eur. Invt. Bank	9¼	15/11/97	103	−1/16	7.83
Exp. Imp. Bk Japan	9¾	19/05/99	105 8/16	+2/16	8.01
Exxon Cap Corp.	8	02/10/98	99 9/16	−1/16	7.96
Republic of Finland	9	30/05/96	101 6/16	nc	7.69
Ford Capital BV	9½	09/08/00	103 5/16	+4/16	8.51
Ford Capital BV	9¾	05/06/97	102 12/16	−1/16	8.20
Gen. Elec. CR Co.	8⅝	12/03/98	100 15/16	−1/16	8.10
Genl Mfrs Accept Co	9⅛	13/03/96	101 1/16	nc	7.91
Guinness Fin. BV	9	08/01/96	101 2/16	nc	7.55
Int. Amer. Dev Bk	9½	11/01/00	105 6/16	+4/16	8.02
Int. Finance Co.	8¼	18/03/98	100 6/16	−1/16	7.94
Int. Bk Rec & Dev	8½	26/06/16	100 2/16	−4/16	8.30
Int. Bk Rec & Dev	7¼	10/10/96	100 2/16	nc	7.17
Int. Bk Rec & Dev	8⅛	01/03/01	100 15/16	+4/16	7.92
Int. Bk Rec & Dev	8⅜	01/10/99	101 12/16	+2/16	7.91
Int. Bk Rec & Dev	8⅝	01/10/95	101 2/16	nc	6.80
Int. Bk Rec & Dev	8¾	01/03/97	102 4/16	nc	7.56
Int. Fin. Corp	9¼	07/06/95	100 12/16	nc	6.67

Issuer	Cpn. %	Mat.	Price	Chg.	Yld. %
Japan Hway Publ. Co	8⅝	26/06/01	101 14/16	+4/16	8.06
Kansal Elec. Power	10	30/03/96	102 8/16	nc	7.52
Kansal Int. Airport	8½	09/07/98	100 13/16	–3/16	8.03
Kansal Int. Airport	9½	26/09/97	102 11/16	–1/16	8.12
KFW Int. Fin. Inc.	9¼	12/06/95	100 12/16	nc	6.70
Kimberly Clark Co.	9¾	15/06/95	101 13/16	nc	4.63
Oestereich KBank	8¼	15/07/96	100 8/16	nc	7.65
Oestereich KBank	8½	06/03/01	101 7/16	+4/16	8.03
Ontario Hydro	8¼	21/11/01	98 9/16	+4/16	8.35
Philip Morris Inc.	8⅝	09/07/96	100 10/16	nc	7.92
Province of Quebec	9⅛	22/08/01	101 7/16	+4/16	8.68
Republic of Italy	8¾	08/02/01	100 4/16	+4/16	8.51
Republic of Italy	9⅜	03/04/97	102 1/16	nc	8.12
Republic of Italy	9½	14/11/95	101 10/16	nc	7.04
Republic of Italy	9⅝	01/03/99	103 5/16	+2/16	8.44
Tokyo Elec.Power	8¾	28/08/98	101 10/16	–1/16	8.01
Unilever Cap Co.	9¼	29/03/00	104 2/16	+4/16	8.06
World Bank	9	29/06/04	105 8/16	–2/16	7.97
World Bank	9⅝	01/02/99	105	+3/16	7.96

Source: Salomon Brothers International Ltd., London.

Deutsche Mark Eurobonds

U.K.	7⅛	28/10/97	100.90	+.05	6.74
Denmark	6⅛	15/04/98	97.65	+.05	6.95
IBRD Global	7¼	13/10/99	100.25	nc	7.17
E.I.B.	7½	04/11/02	99.50	+.05	7.58
K.F.W.	7¾	06/10/04	99.95	nc	7.75

Source: Westdeutsche Landesbank Girozentrale, Duesseldorf.

Euroyen Bonds

IBRD	6	18/10/96	104.98	nc	2.98
Norway	5⅜	14/02/97	104.35	nc	3.15
IBRD Global	4½	22/12/97	102.75	nc	3.52
Sweden	4⅛	04/02/98	102.48	nc	3.74
Belgium	6	16/12/98	107.30	— .10	3.93
JDB	5	01/10/99	103.70	— .07	4.11
EIB	6⅛	15/03/00	110.30	— .05	4.34
IBRD Global	4½	20/06/00	101.15	— .05	4.30
Italy	3½	20/06/01	92.78	— .05	4.88

The table provides the coupon, the maturity date, the bond price, the daily change in the bond price, and the yield to maturity. Under the heading "Eurodollar Bonds," the table lists selected Eurobonds denominated in dollars. Under the heading "Euroyen Bonds," it lists Eurobonds denominated in yen. For example, JDB issued bonds denominated in yen with a coupon rate of 5% and a maturity date of 01/10/1999. The bond's price is 103.70 (or 1,037 yen per 1,000 yen par value bond) and the yield to maturity is 4.11%.

a. Calculate the yield to maturity of a European Investment Bank (EIB) Eurodollar bond that matures in November 1997. Compare your results to the published yield.

b. Calculate the yield to maturity of the EIB bond in the yen-denominated bond market. Why are the results in problems 12.24a and 12.24b different? In your answer explain the difference between Euroyen bonds and Eurodollar bonds.

c. Suppose U.S. exports are mainly to Japan. Would it be wise from the U.S. viewpoint to raise money in the Euroyen market rather than in the Eurodollar market? Explain.

12.25 The following data are taken from the *Wall Street Journal* of September 30, 1993:

Bonds	Close
AMR zr06	46¾
ANR 13¼97	101⅛
Actava 9⅞97	100⅞
AlskAr 6⅞14	82¼

Note: "zr" denotes zero–coupon bond.

Assume zero corporate tax and calculate the cost of debt of each of these firms. Can the yield to maturity on convertible bonds be used as the cost of debt? Discuss.

INTERNET QUESTIONS

12.26 Using the currency calculator at the following Web site, calculate the foreign currency equivalent of US$100 in terms of British pounds, French francs, German deutschemarks, and Japanese yen.

http://www.moneyadvisor.com

12.27 Using the Global Investor service, determine the percent increase or decrease in a major stock index in each of the "Group of Five" nations. Explain the differences you found based on your knowledge of current events.

http://www.numa.com/index.htm

YOUR TURN: APPLYING THEORY TO PRACTICE

YIELD AND RISK: THE INTERNATIONAL BOND MARKET BASKS IN THE BEST OF ALL WORLDS

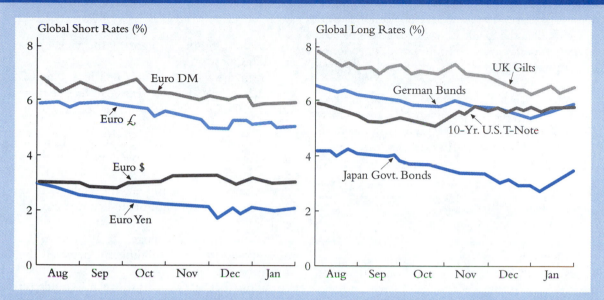

Neither rain nor snow nor steamy economic data seem to deter the bond market these days.

While the weather outside was frightful, the market thinks the economy is delightful. Robust growth poses no threat to interest rates so long as inflation is in check, investors in their wisdom apparently concluded . . . .

The Japanese bond market, the standout performer in 1993, has taken a severe hit so far in 1994. While the market's reverse has claimed some victims . . . the sell-off may have run its course.

Japanese government bonds, or JGBs, generated total returns in the mid-20% range last year for dollar-based investors, largely owing to the yen's sharp appreciation. Yen-based investors also enjoyed strong price gains last year as the yield on the benchmark 10-year JGBs plunged under 3% by year's end from about 4½% at 1993's outset.

The case for JGBs appeared unassailable: The worse things got in Japan, both economically and politically, the better for the bond market.

Right now the severe Japanese recession is causing deflation and unemployment, which are being exacerbated by a vastly overvalued yen. Monetary and fiscal stimuli have been necessary but not forthcoming. The ongoing political crisis, exemplified by the defeat of political reforms by the upper house of the Diet, has staved off fiscal measures. That left lower interest rates as the only way out.

And if that meant a weaker yen, global bond players such as hedge funds didn't care. Hedging their yen exposure back into dollars or any other currency actually increased their yields because of low Japanese money-market rates, around 2%. (The cost of hedging one currency into another is the difference between their respective short-term rates; the investor pays the rate of the currency he's short and earns the rate of the one he's long.) It was a no-lose situation.

Whither now? Tokai Bank Europe, which had been an early bear on the JGB market, now thinks the slide is within a few points of bottoming.

With the yield on the benchmark 10–year having moved back to 3½% in this year's sell-off, with other similar maturity JGBs near 4%, Tokai thinks value has returned to the market. Salomon Brothers adds that the Bank of Japan is likely to ease monetary policy amid continuing weak economic conditions, pushing the benchmark 10–year JGB back to 3¼%.

But the Tokai's European arm doesn't recommend a head–long plunge back into the market. The current quarter is a seasonally weak one for JGBs as Japanese institutions approach fiscal year-end, it notes.

Source: Randall W. Forsyth, "Current Yield," *Barron's* 74, no. 5 (January 1994):58. Reprinted by permission of *Barron's*, © 1994 Dow Jones & Company, Inc. All Rights Reserved Worldwide.

Questions

Questions 1–4 refer to the right-hand figure on page 471. Assume we are dealing with a long-term bond with the same maturity as reported in the figure. In all questions in this case assume zero-coupon bonds, with a face value of $1,000 or 1,000 yen, for bonds denominated in dollars and yen, respectively. Also, for simplicity assume no taxes.

1. The yields on long-term corporate bonds in January 1994 were as follows:

Yield (%)	
U.S. firms (U.S. dollar bonds)	8
Japanese firms (yen bonds)	5

Explain these yields in light of the yields on Japanese government bonds and Treasury notes presented in the previous figure.

2. In January 1994 the yield for bonds issued by U.S. firms but denominated in yen was 5%. (Note: The 8% yield for U.S. corporate bonds given in Question 1 was for dollar-denominated bonds.) Thus, we have the following:

Yield (%)	
U.S. firms (yen bonds)	5
Japanese firms (yen bonds)	5

Explain these figures in light of the yields presented in Question 1.

"From the data given in Questions 1 and 2 we conclude that the U.S. firms can reduce their cost of debt by issuing bonds denominated in yens." Do you agree? Discuss.

3. IBM is considering issuing a 10-year bond in the Eurobond market, to be denominated either in Japanese yen or in U.S. dollars. If the bond is denominated in yen, the yield will be 5%; if the bond is denominated in dollars, the yield will be 8%.

a. What yen/dollar exchange rate 10 years in the future would make IBM indifferent between the two denomination methods?

b. Suppose that IBM exports to Japan. Would you recommend issuing bonds denominated in yen? Explain.

c. How would your answer change if IBM imported rather than exported from Japan?

4. Suppose 10 years from now, a Japanese bank agrees to sell yen to IBM at 95 yen = $1. The current exchange rate is 100 yen = $1. Should IBM issue the bonds in dollars or in yen? If IBM issues the bonds in yen, by how much can it reduce its cost of debt relative to issuing dollar-denominated bonds?

5. Suppose you buy a U.S. 10-year Treasury note, which is a government bond of a particular size and maturity. Assume it is a zero-coupon bond. The yield is 5.8%. You hold the bond for one year and then sell it. Suppose there is no change in the yield and there are no taxes.

a. What is your nominal holding period rate of return?

b. What is the real rate of return if annual inflation is predicted to be 1.3%?

6. It is suggested that if you borrow in Japan at 3.5% and lend in the U.K. at 6.5%, you will make a sure arbitrage profit. Assume there is no difference between the borrowing and lending rates within each country and the relevant yield represents this rate. Do you think you can make a sure profit by such a transaction?

7. The yield on zero–coupon, 10–year Japanese bonds plunged during the year from 4½% to 3%. A U.S. investor who bought the Japanese bonds and held them for one year earned a 25% rate of return.

a. What is the annual rate of return to Japanese investors who bought these bonds?

b. How do you explain the difference between the rate of return to Japanese investors and to U.S. investors? In light of the 25% rate of return to a U.S. investor, calculate the corresponding change of the yen value versus the dollar.

8. Suppose Salomon Brothers is correct in its estimates and the yield on 10–year Japanese bonds decreases from 3½% to 3¼%. Suppose this decrease occurs within a very short period, say one week.

a. Calculate the capital gain on this bond in yen.

b. Calculate the capital gain or loss to a U.S. investor on the assumption that the yen depreciates by about 2% relative to the dollar.

9. We see from the figure accompanying the article that the short-term bond has a lower yield than the long-term bond. Would you recommend raising money by issuing short-term bonds, thus lowering the cost of debt?

LEARNING OBJECTIVES

After reading this chapter, you should understand:

1. How and why management, investors, and underwriters use valuation formulas to value stocks.

2. That stock prices are based on discounted cash flows regardless of the assumed holding period.

3. How to apply the constant dividend growth model to evaluate a firm's growth and to estimate its cost of equity.

4. The difference between normal-growth and supergrowth firms.

5. That under certain conditions, the price/earnings ratio serves as an index of a stock's profitability.

6. The relationship between the CAPM equilibrium prices and the discounted dividend formula.

7. The various forms of market efficiency.

8. That, if the market is efficient, a stock's price will equal the PV of its cash dividends and that all stocks will be located on the security market line.

CORPORATE FINANCE IN THE NEWS

WARREN BUFFETT LIKES COKE

Over the years, especially in the 1980s and 1990s, Buffett [Warren Buffett is the CEO of Berkshire Hathaway] has moved closer to the concept of one-decision growth stocks—buy 'em and hold 'em forever, or at least until their fundamentals deteriorate.

Coca-Cola wasn't cheap by conventional standards when Berkshire Hathaway first bought it in 1988. On the street it was regarded as an excellent but fully valued stock. Coca-Cola has since appreciated by close to 600%, or a compound annual rate of return of some 25%, but Berkshire has taken not a penny in profits and has sold not a single share.

Source: Robert Lenzner and David S. Fondiller, "The Not-So-Silent Partner," *Forbes* 157, no. 2 (January 1996): 78. Reprinted By Permission of FORBES Magazine © Forbes Inc., 1996.

13.1 INTRODUCTION

What are "growth stocks"? What is a "fully valued stock"? Does a stock's value depend on the assumed holding period? Does it make a difference if you "buy 'em and hold 'em forever" or hold them for one year only? If no one holds a stock forever, can we still evaluate it as if it were going to be held forever?

In the previous chapter we discussed debt financing, bond valuation, and the cost of debt. In this chapter we discuss the other main source of long-term financing: common stocks. We will learn how a stock's observed market price can be used to estimate the firm's cost of equity. We will discuss valuation models for nongrowth and growth stocks, define *fully valued stocks,* and discuss how the assumed holding period affects stock valuation.

13.2 COST OF EQUITY AND COST OF DEBT: THE HISTORICAL RECORD

We have claimed throughout the book, and in particular in Chapter 10, that the cost of equity is higher than the cost of debt.[1] The *cost of debt* and the *cost of equity* are defined as the minimum expected rate of return that bondholders and stockholders require, respectively. If our assertion regarding the cost of debt and cost of equity is correct, we expect that stockholders have earned on average more than bondholders. Connecting Theory to Practice 13.1 suggests that this is indeed the case.

CONNECTING THEORY TO PRACTICE 13.1

HISTORY LESSON

Mutual funds and stock salesmen love a particular chart. They often use it. It shows stocks outperforming bonds by five percentage points per year from 1926 to 1992.

Think about this, they like to say: Thanks to the power of compounding at those rates, $10,000 invested in Standard & Poor's composite stock index in 1926, when good dividend data for the index begin, would have climbed to a mountainous $7.3 million by the end of last year.

Bonds? The same investment in long-term Treasurys would have inched up to a mere $237,000. . . .

. . . Siegel [Jeremy Siegel is professor of finance at the Wharton School of Business, University of Pennsylvania] has studied the relative returns of stocks and bonds over a far longer period—from 1802 to the present. .

---

1. In Chapters 15 and 16 we will explain why firms do not finance their operations mainly by debt, although such financing is cheaper, but instead use an optimum debt-equity mix.

Consider this: The 1926–92 period was one of exceptional economic instability. Just before World War II, for example, it was unclear that the country would ever really pull out of the Great Depression. It was by no means clear that the democracies would triumph over fascism. In subsequent decades it wasn't certain that capitalism would triumph over socialism.

Times being highly uncertain, investors demanded—and got—higher nominal returns for the risks inherent in ownership or part ownership of businesses. And, when the uncertainties were strongest—in the 1930s, 1940s and 1950s, for example—stock prices were relatively low, leaving lots of room for the appreciation that took place in the 1960s and 1980s . . . .

Siegel predicts that for the indefinite future stocks will continue to beat bonds, but by a considerably smaller margin than they have over the past half-century or so . . . .

He figures stocks will deliver a total real return of 5% to 6% a year over the next decade, while bonds will return 3% to 4%. And he says that for very long holding periods, say 30 years, stocks are in a way less risky: They don't suffer the same hazard of runaway inflation . . . .

Source: Jason Zweig, "History Lesson," *Forbes* 151, no. 13 (June 1993): 148. Reprinted By Permission of FORBES Magazine © Forbes Inc., 1993.

MAKING THE CONNECTION

Stocks have historically produced better returns than bonds: From 1926 to 1996, stocks outperformed bonds, on average, by 5.6 percentage points per year. We saw in Chapter 10 that the expected rates of return required by stockholders and bondholders are the cost of equity and the cost of debt, respectively. The *Forbes* article reveals several important points. The cost of equity has historically been greater than the cost of debt. Also, in periods of increased uncertainty, stockholders demand and receive higher returns. When uncertainty increases, the cost of equity increases.

http

The New York Stock Exchange has an excellent tutorial on stocks. It covers the history of stocks, how stocks are bought and sold, how a stock exchange works, why stock prices go up and down, regulation, strategies, and much more. It also has lots of pictures and a comprehensive glossary of financial terms.

http://www.nyse.com/public

Are stock valuation models and stockholders' rates of return relevant to a firm's management? Yes, they are, and for several important reasons. To facilitate the discussion in this chapter, we focus on the problem of raising money by selling stock. For an all-equity firm, the cost of equity, k_e, equals the cost of capital, k. If the firm finances its operations with a mix of debt and equity, the cost of equity will differ from k.

13.3 WHY IS IT IMPORTANT TO UNDERSTAND HOW STOCKS ARE VALUED?

Since stock valuation formulas and procedures are very important to potential investors, it might seem more appropriate to discuss them in an investment course rather than in a corporate finance course. However, stock valuation models are also very important to the firm. A number of management goals and decisions depend on the value of stocks, and understanding how to value stocks and considering what factors affect their value are important to managers.

13.3.1 Stock Price Maximization

The firm's goal is to maximize its stock price. Management has the duty to achieve this goal. By understanding relevant economic factors, the firm can affect these factors and through them the stock price. For example, suppose that if the firm issues more debt, investors who use a certain valuation model would consider the firm's risk of bankruptcy to increase substantially. Consequently, these investors would sell their stock, causing its price to decrease. By understanding the effect of its proposed action on the valuation models stockholders use, management would then not try to sell too much debt, and would avoid the decrease in the stock price.

13.3.2 Mergers and Acquisitions

On July 31, 1995, Walt Disney Co. agreed to pay $19 billion for Capital Cities/ABC—one of the largest corporate acquisitions ever. The PV of the expected cash flows from Capital Cities/ABC must have exceeded $19 billion; otherwise, Disney would not have offered this large a sum for the acquisition. Determining the PV of expected cash flow is possible by using various valuation models to help fix the price tags for mergers and acquisitions.

13.3.3 Stock Repurchases

A firm sometimes invests in other firms' securities or acquires other firms outright. Also, a firm frequently "repurchases" or "buys back" its own stock. For example, American Standard announced in January, 1997 that it would buy back its existing shares. When a firm repurchases its stock, it is usually because management considers the stock to be undervalued. That is, the present value of the stock's future expected cash flow is larger than its market price. To reach such a conclusion, management uses valuation models to determine the PV of the expected cash flows.

13.3.4 New Common Stock Issue

Stock valuation methods are essential when a firm goes public. Suppose you own a family firm that is so successful that you wish to expand it. Unfortunately, you lack sufficient financial resources to undertake all your chosen projects. You decide to "go public" by selling stock to outside investors. Because this is an initial public offering (IPO), you do not yet have a market price for your shares and you want to know at what price to offer your stock. You can use a valuation method to put a price tag on your firm's equity.

Witcapital is a New York City start-up company that persuaded the SEC to allow an Internet IPO. It's since grown into a very active cyber investment bank. http://www.witcap. com

Other parties to the initial public offering—the underwriter, who insures the new issue, and potential investors—will also use a valuation formula to verify the reasonableness of the stock price. For example, Redhook Ale Brewery issued stock in an IPO on August 16, 1995, at $17 per share. Trading in the stock opened at $27 the following day and reached $35 in just a few days. This example shows that either a valuation model was used improperly or that the underwriter pressured the issuing firm to sell at a very low price. In retrospect, the firm would have fared better by selling its stock at a higher price. The market would still have easily absorbed the IPO at, say, $20 or even $30.

13.3.5 Estimating the Cost of Equity

Stock valuation models also are useful in estimating the firm's cost of capital. When evaluating projects, management needs to know the weighted average cost of capital. The required rate of return on equity is an essential ingredient in determining the firm's cost of capital. Assuming the stock is correctly priced, stock valuation formulas can be used to estimate the required rate of return on equity. In Chapter 10 we used the CAPM to estimate the cost of equity. In this chapter we add one more approach, one that relies on the present value of dividends, to estimate the cost of equity.

13.3.6 Understanding the Financial Media

Finally, the financial media vocabulary is replete with terms such as "growth rate," "supergrowth firms," and "price-earnings ratio," all of which relate to stock valuation models. To understand these terms, you must be well versed in the valuation methods themselves.

Now that you've seen the various uses of stock valuation models, let's examine what they are and how they work.

13.4 STOCK VALUATION: THE DISCOUNTED CASH FLOW PRINCIPLE

In Chapter 12 we saw that a bond's value is the present value of all its future cash flows (coupons plus principal). We will use a similar discounted cash flow procedure to evaluate stocks—that is, a stock's value is the discounted value of all its future cash flows.

13.4.1 Who Will Sell and Who Will Buy a Firm's Stock?

Unlike bonds, stocks pay dividends rather than interest, and have no maturity date. To illustrate, suppose you believe that Intel will pay a $4 dividend per share at the end of next year and a $5 dividend per share at the end of the following year. You estimate you can sell Intel stock two years from now at $130 per share.

Since these are only estimates, they are uncertain, and as with any uncertain cash flow stream, you discount the cash flows at a discount rate that is the sum of the riskless interest rate and a risk premium. Suppose you decide to use a discount rate of 15%. The current stock price is listed in the *Wall Street Journal* at $P = \$100$. Should you buy the Intel stock? As in performing any other project evaluation, you should use the following discounted cash flow rule, where PV is the present value of the expected cash flows:

- If PV > P, you should buy the stock.
- If PV < P, you should not buy the stock (and you should sell any of the stock that you hold).
- If PV = P, you should be indifferent between buying and not buying the stock.

If PV = P, we say the stock is *fully valued* and not considered a bargain. If many investors believe that PV > P, the excess demand for the stock will increase its price and will create a capital gain. The excess demand for the stock will vanish only when PV = P. This new price will be the stock's equilibrium price.

Case A in Table 13-1 illustrates the PV calculation for Intel stock. Recall that we have assumed a discount rate of 15%. The PV of the $4 dividend paid in the first year is $3.48. At the end of the second year, a $5 dividend is paid and the expected stock price is $130, bringing the total expected cash flow to $135 with a discounted value

Along with other information, the LBO Page lists companies purchased through LBOS, such as RJR Nabisco, Revlon, Safeway, Montgomery Ward, and Dr. Pepper.
http://www.iagi.net/~tt/l

TABLE 13-1 The Present Value of Intel's Expected Dividend and Stock Price

Case A: $d_1 = \$4$, $d_2 = \$5$, and $P_2 = \$130$

	Beginning of First Year	End of First Year	End of Second Year
Expected dividend		$4	$5
Expected stock price			$130
Total expected cash flow		$4	$135
Discount factor (15%)		1/(1.15)	$1/(1.15)^2$
Contribution to the PV		$4/(1.15) \cong \$3.48$	$135/(1.15)^2 \cong \$102.08$
PV of the two years' cash flows		$3.48 + $102.08 = $105.56	

Case B: $d_1 = \$4$, $d_2 = \$5$, and $P_2 = \$120$

	Beginning of First Year	End of First Year	End of Second Year
Expected dividend		$4	$5
Expected stock price			$120
Total expected cash flow		$4	$125
Discount factor (15%)		1/(1.15)	$1/(1.15)^2$
Contribution to the PV		$4/(1.15) \cong \$3.48$	$125/(1.15)^2 \cong \$94.52$
PV of the two years' cash flows		$3.48 + $94.52 = $98.00	

of $102.08. The PV of all the cash flows is $105.56, which is higher than the current stock price of $100. Therefore, the net present value is positive:

$$\text{NPV} = \text{PV} - P = \$105.56 - \$100 = \$5.56$$

Any investor who believes in these expected cash flows will not hesitate to buy the Intel stock.

Given these calculations, who would be inclined to sell Intel stock? Other investors in the market may hold different beliefs regarding the stock. Suppose an investor believes the dividends will be $4 next year and $5 two years from now. This investor also believes Intel stock will be selling at only $120 per share at the end of the second year. If so, the cash flows and the PV of these cash flows will be only $98, as demonstrated by Case B in Table 13-1. An investor who believes the PV is $98 will be inclined to sell the stock for $100 and increase the PV of his or her cash flows by $2.

This situation is typical of the day-to-day transactions in the stock market. Investors who believe a stock is undervalued ($P < \text{PV}$) will buy it, and investors who believe a stock is overvalued ($P > \text{PV}$) will sell it. The discounted cash flow method of stock valuation is relevant for buyer and seller alike, as demonstrated in the following problem.

PRACTICE BOX

Problem

Dan and Ruth are two investors. Both hold Ford Motor Company stock in their portfolios, and both expect Ford to pay a $2 per share dividend one year from now. They also agree that the *expected* price per share one year from now will be $55. However, Dan believes it will be either $50 or $60 with equal probability, and Ruth believes it will be either $45 or $65 with equal probability. The current market price of Ford stock is $49. Dan applies a discount rate of 12%. Ruth considers the stock to be riskier and, therefore, applies a 20% discount rate. Will these two investors trade Ford Motor's stock? If so, who will sell and who will buy?

Solution

Dan applies a discount rate of 12% and, therefore, believes the stock's PV to be

$$\text{PV} = \frac{\$2 + \$55}{1.12} = \frac{\$57}{1.12} \cong \$50.89$$

At the stock's current market price of $49, Dan would do well to keep the shares he has and buy more of the stock.

Ruth applies a higher discount rate (20%). Accordingly, she believes the stock's PV to be

$$\text{PV} = \frac{\$2 + \$55}{1.2} = \frac{\$57}{1.2} = \$47.50$$

At the stock's current market price of $49, Ruth will prefer to sell the stock. The two different beliefs regarding the stock's risk serve as an incentive for a transaction between the two parties.

13.4.2 Does the Assumed Investment Holding Period Affect the Current Market Price?

According to Corporate Finance in the News, Warren Buffett identifies stocks with a high growth rate, buys them, and holds them forever. Would a stock's value be different if the purchaser intended to hold it for only a short while, say a year? Let's examine the value of a stock that is held for one year.

Suppose you invest in a stock for one year. The dividend expected at the end of the year is d_1, and the stock price expected at the end of the year is P_1. By the **discounted cash flow (DCF) principle**, your estimate of the stock's current value is

$$P_0 = \frac{d_1}{1 + k_e} + \frac{P_1}{1 + k_e} \qquad (13.1)$$

where k_e is the cost of equity.

The stock valuation formulas introduced in this chapter, like Equation (13.1), are all based on the discounted value of the future cash flows to stockholders. Most stocks provide annual cash flows forever, although an investor may decide to hold the stock for only a relatively few number of years. Should we, then, consider the ongoing perpetual cash dividends when using stock valuation formulas? As we shall see, stock valuation models assume that investors hold the stock for a very long time, sometimes indefinitely. But what about investors who hold a stock for a relatively short period such as a year? Are the valuation models based on perpetual dividends worthless? No. We show in this section that the assumed holding period is irrelevant in determining the stock's value.

One principal difference between project valuation and stock valuation is the assumed holding period. Projects generally have a well-defined economic life and are valued accordingly, whereas a stock's economic life is undefined. Some investors hold a stock for only one year and others for five or 10 years, or even longer. Suppose no "bargains" are in the market—that is, the present value of the future cash flows exactly equals the stock price. Does how long the investor plans to hold the stock affect the stock's price? We show below that assumed holding period *does not affect* the current stock price.

Suppose investors expect that dividends will be paid at the end of Years 1 and 2 and that the stock price will be P_1 and P_2 at those points in time. Investor A wishes to hold the stock for one year. After receiving dividend d_1, he hopes to sell the stock for P_1 at the end of the first year. Investor B expects to hold the stock for two years, receive dividends d_1 and d_2, and sell the stock at the end of the second year for P_2. Does the planned holding period affect the current stock price, P_0? Can the same price, P_0, represent the discounted value of d_1 and P_1, as well as of d_1, d_2, and P_2? We will see that P_0 represents the discounted cash flow (DCF) regardless of the number of years of the investment.

The PV of future cash flows for a one–year holding period is given by Equation (13.1). For her two–year holding period, Investor B receives dividend d_1 at the end of the first year, d_2 at the end of the second year, and expects to sell the stock for P_2 at the end of the second year. By the DCF principle and using the same discount rate, we get

$$P_0^* = \frac{d_1}{1 + k_e} + \frac{d_2}{(1 + k_e)^2} + \frac{P_2}{(1 + k_e)^2} \qquad (13.1a)$$

where P_0^* is the current price of the stock corresponding to the two-year cash flow.

Does the value P_0^* differ from the value P_0 given in Equation (13.1)? No. Actually, no matter how many years are incorporated in the DCF, the stock's present value is the same. To see this, consider the price P_1 at the end of the first year. An investor who buys the stock *at the end of the first year* and holds it for one year invests P_1, receives dividend d_2 at the end of the second year, and expects to sell the stock at the end of the second year for P_2. By the DCF principle, the price at the end of the first year should be

$$P_1 = \frac{d_2}{1 + k_e} + \frac{P_2}{1 + k_e} \qquad (13.2)$$

Substituting P_1 from Equation (13.2) into Equation (13.1), we obtain

$$P_0 = \frac{d_1}{1 + k_e} + \left[\frac{d_2}{1 + k_e} + \frac{P_2}{1 + k_e} \right] / (1 + k_e)$$

which can be simplified to

$$P_0 = \frac{d_1}{1 + k} + \frac{d_2}{(1 + k)^2} + \frac{P_2}{(1 + k)^2} \qquad (13.3)$$

Because the DCF on the right-hand side of Equation (13.3) is identical to the right-hand side of Equation (13.1a), we can conclude that $P_0^* = P$. Thus, we get the same DCF *irrespective of the number of annual dividends discounted.* We can conclude that whether the stock is held for one year or for two years, the current stock price, which is the PV of the two alternative cash flows given by Equations (13.1) and (13.3), remains the same at P_0. The following problem further demonstrates our conclusion.

PRACTICE BOX

Problem

Suppose the dividend on Combo's stock is expected to be $5 one year from now and $6 two years from now. The stock's market price two years from now is estimated to be $50. The discount rate is 10%.
a.   Estimate the stock price, P_1, one year from now.
b.   What is the current stock price, P_0?

Solution

a.   One year from now the stock price, P_1, will be

$$P_1 = \frac{\$6 + \$50}{1.1} \cong \$50.91$$

(continued)

b. The current stock price, P_0, can be calculated in two ways:
Two-year investment:

$$P_0 = \frac{\$5}{1.1} + \frac{\$6 + \$50}{(1.1)^2} \cong \$4.55 + \$46.28 = \$50.83$$

One-year investment:

$$P_0 = \frac{\$5}{1.1} + \frac{\$50.91}{1.1} \cong \$4.55 + \$46.28 = \$50.83$$

We get the same P_0, regardless of the assumed holding period.

Note that by substituting P_1 from Equation (13.2) into Equation (13.1), we get the discounted value of two annual dividends rather than one. Similarly, the discounted value of d_3 and P_3 can be substituted for P_2 in Equation (13.3). Then, P_4 can be substituted for P_3, and so forth. The general formula for a holding period of n years is given by

$$P_0 = \sum_{t=1}^{n} \frac{d_t}{(1 + k_e)^t} + \frac{P_n}{(1 + k_e)^n} \tag{13.4}$$

If we continue this process indefinitely, each such substitution will add more dividends to the cash flow until we finally obtain Equation (13.5), which shows that stock price P_0 is the DCF of *all future dividends:*[2]

$$P_0 = \frac{d_1}{1 + k_e} + \frac{d_2}{(1 + k_e)^2} + \frac{d_3}{(1 + k_e)^3} + \ldots = \sum_{t=1}^{\infty} \frac{d_t}{(1 + k_e)^t} \tag{13.5}$$

Here d_t is the dividend paid at the end of year t. The same value for the discounted cash flows, P_0, is obtained irrespective of whether Equation (13.1), (13.4), or (13.5) is used.

Of course, investors do not hold a stock for an infinite number of years. Most hold a stock for only a few years. As we have just seen, Equation (13.1), which assumes a holding period of one year, and Equation (13.4), which assumes a finite holding period, yield the same result as the discount formula that relies on an infinite stream of dividends [Equation (13.5)]. Thus, Equation (13.5) can be used for stock valuation even if the stock is to be held for only a short period. From now on, when no bargains are available, we simply assume the stock price corresponds to the PV of all future dividends and use either Equation (13.5), which assumes an infinite holding period, or Equation (13.4), which assumes any finite number of dividends plus the discounted value of the stock price at the end of the holding period.

Figure 13-1 illustrates the PV of a stock's cash flows as a function of various holding periods. We assume the firm pays a dividend of $10 per share each year and the

2. This growth rate, g, must be smaller than the discount rate; otherwise, the stock price would become infinite.

FIGURE 13-1
PV of the Stock's Cash Flows as a Function of Various Holding Periods

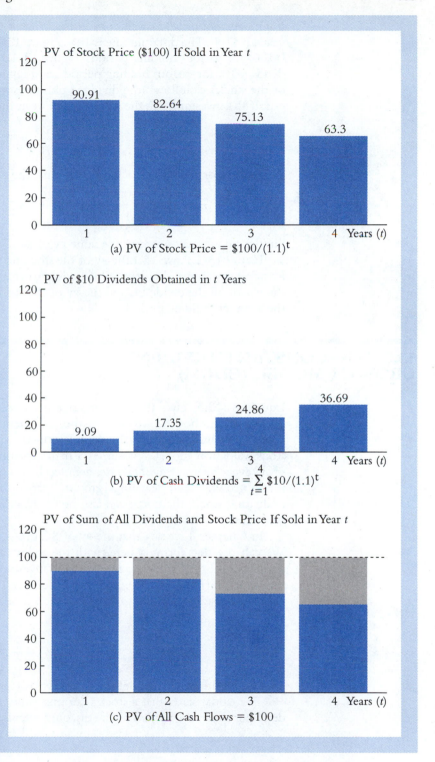

PV of Stock Price ($100) If Sold in Year *t*

(a) PV of Stock Price = $100/(1.1)^t

PV of $10 Dividends Obtained in *t* Years

(b) PV of Cash Dividends = $\sum_{t=1}^{4} \$10/(1.1)^t$

PV of Sum of All Dividends and Stock Price If Sold in Year *t*

(c) PV of All Cash Flows = $100

stock's current price, as well as its future price at the end of each of the subsequent years, is $100. The discount rate is 10%. Figure 13-1A shows the PV of the stock price ($100) for various holding periods. Figure 13-1B shows the PV of the annual dividends ($10) for various holding periods, and Figure 13-1C shows the PV of the *sum* of the stock's cash flows (the dividend plus the stock price) for various holding periods. If the investor holds the stock for one year, the PV of the cash flow will be

$$\frac{\$10}{1.1} + \frac{\$100}{1.1} = \$100$$

If the investor holds the stock for two years, the PV of the cash flow will be

$$\left[\frac{\$10}{1.1} + \frac{\$10}{(1.1)^2}\right] + \frac{\$100}{(1.1)^2} \cong [\$9.09 + \$8.26] + \$82.64 = \$99.99 \cong \$100$$

Similar calculations produce the same PV of $100 for any holding period.

Figure 13-1 shows that the PV of the stock price decreases over time and that the PV of all the annual dividends obtained up to year T increases over time. The *sum* of the PVs of all the dividends and the PV of the stock price remains $100 regardless of the assumed holding period.

13.5 THE CONSTANT DIVIDEND GROWTH MODEL (CDGM)

Equation (13.5) gives the current stock price as the discounted value of all future dividends. But how do we estimate those dividends? In most cases we do so with the **constant dividend growth model (CDGM)**, which is probably the most popular stock valuation model. It assumes a firm's earnings and dividends are expected to grow every year at a *constant* rate, denoted by g, and that's why the expressions "dividend growth" and "earnings growth" can be used interchangeably. Apart from evaluating stock, the CDGM can also be used to evaluate the firm's cost of equity (as we will see in Section 13.9).

In Chapter 4 we saw that the PV of $\$C$ growing at g percent a year is $\$C/(r-g)$. We can use that formula here, with the following substitutions: d_1, the first year's dividend, substitutes for C; and (because investment in stocks is risky) the discount rate appropriate to equity, k_e, substitutes for r. In making these substitutions, we obtain the constant dividend growth valuation model, which is

$$P_0 = \frac{d_1}{k_e - g} \tag{13.6}$$

This dividend growth model is also known as *Gordon's dividend model*.[3]

The CDGM states that a stock's current value, P_0, is given by the first year's dividend per share, d_1, divided by the discount rate, k_e, minus the annual dividend's con-

---

3. See Myron J. Gordon, *The Investment, Financing and Valuation of the Corporation* (Homewood, IL: Irwin, 1962).

stant growth rate, g. The larger the growth rate, the larger the future dividends to be discounted, and the higher the stock price.

By the CDGM, the stock price also grows by g percent a year. To see this, note that after one year the dividend will be $d_2 = d_1 (1 + g)$. The stock price after one year will be

$$P_1 = \frac{d_2}{k_e - g} = \frac{d_1(1 + g)}{k_e - g} = P_0(1 + g) \tag{13.7}$$

This formula is valid only when the growth rate is smaller than the discount factor.

13.5.1 Does an Increase in the Dividend Growth Rate Imply an Increase in the Current Stock Price?

In Corporate Finance in the News, we learned that Warren Buffett favors "growth stocks" such as Coca-Cola. We shall see below that the value of any stock is expected to grow as long as the firm retains and reinvests some portion of its earnings. When practitioners discuss growth stocks, they usually are referring to what we will call "supergrowth stocks." The distinction will now be defined more clearly.

We see almost daily in the financial media that firms change their dividend per share. For example, *Barron's* reported on January 13, 1997 that Brenton Banks increased its dividend per share from 13 cents to 19 cents. Should that 46% growth in dividends affect the stock price? Is Brenton Banks a growth firm? Not necessarily. To answer these questions, we need to examine more closely the *source* of the growth in the dividends per share.

13.5.2 Sources of Growth

Two principal factors contribute to the firm's growth: (1) reinvestment of retained earnings in projects with zero NPVs and (2) reinvestment of retained earnings in projects with positive NPVs. Let's elaborate on these two sources of growth. To focus on the issue of the growth rate of dividends and projects' profitability, we will temporarily assume an all-equity firm. Under this simplistic assumption, the cost of equity is equal to the cost of capital.[4]

1. *Case A: Reinvestment of retained earnings in projects with zero NPVs.* Suppose a firm reinvests its retained earnings in projects such that the *average* IRR on the invested capital exactly equals the cost of capital. In this case the NPVs of that set of projects will be zero and any growth will be the result of the invested retained earnings. Retaining a higher proportion of the earnings will lead to higher growth rates for both earnings *and* dividends. To see this, suppose annual earnings per share is $10 and all earnings are paid out as dividends, which means the dividend per share is $10 and the dividend growth rate is zero. Suppose the firm now

---

4. If the firm is financed by debt as well as by equity, we need to define each project's NPV to the stockholders. To do this, we discount the cash flows to stockholders (after paying interest to bondholders) at k_e. To calculate the NPV we subtract from the PV of these cash flows only the portion of the investment financed by equity.

decides to pay out only $5 per share as dividends and to reinvest the other $5. Since this reinvested $5 per share will lead to additional earnings, both earnings per share and dividends per share will grow. By changing the proportion of earnings paid out as dividends, the firm can provide its stockholders with different combinations of current dividend levels and growth. The more earnings the firm retains, the higher the growth rate of annual dividends.

In the Brenton Banks example, the 13 cents per share dividend Brenton Banks paid in 1996 may have represented the firm's decision to pay a lower dividend to boost future dividend growth. That is, the firm may have retained more of its earnings in 1996, enabling it to produce a 46% boost in the dividends per share in 1997.

2. *Case B: Reinvestment of retained earnings in projects with positive NPVs.* Suppose a firm has the opportunity to invest in projects with positive NPVs. When the firm reinvests its retained earnings in projects yielding more than the rate of return that stockholders require, the extra profit on these projects will cause extra growth in the firm's earnings and dividends. Note that since the firm's profit has increased with *no change* in risk, the rate of return that investors require remains unchanged. In such case the growth rate of the firm's earnings and dividends may increase, even if the proportion of earnings paid out as dividend does not change. For example, if the firm accepts a project with an NPV of $1 million in a given year and another project with an NPV of $2 million in the following year, the EPS and the dividend per share will increase even though the proportion of earnings paid out as dividends stays the same. That's because the "pot" of earnings is larger.

The firms described in Case A are **normal-growth firms** and the firms described in Case B are **supergrowth firms**. The criterion for classifying firms is the *source* of growth, and not the *actual* growth rate. Indeed, one firm may reinvest, say, 90% of its earnings at the required rate of return in zero-NPV projects, and its dividends will grow at, say, 10%. Another firm may reinvest only 20% of its earnings in projects with positive NPVs, and its dividends will grow at only 8%. Because the second firm invested a relatively low proportion of its retained earnings, it had a relatively low growth rate. However, the firm with a 10% growth rate will be classified as a normal-growth firm, while the firm with an 8% growth rate is classified as a supergrowth firm. Regardless of its actual dividend growth rate, *any firm whose projects, on average, yield an IRR greater than* k *is defined as a supergrowth firm.* In practice most supergrowth is due to two factors: a high proportion of retained earnings and the availability of positive NPV projects. Table 13-2 illustrates these two sources of growth: Firms A and B are normal-growth firms; C and D, supergrowth firms. Let's first discuss the normal-growth firms. Firms A and B reinvest their retained earnings in projects with a rate of return equal to the cost of capital, $k = 10\%$. The only difference between these two firms is that Firm A reinvests 50% of its retained earnings, whereas B reinvests 90% of its retained earnings. Therefore, B's dividend growth rate is larger than A's, even though both firms earn the same rate of return on reinvested earnings. In these two cases the source of dividend growth is the reinvestment of retained earnings in projects with zero NPVs. Therefore, both firms are normal-growth firms.

**TABLE 13-2
Dividends,
Earnings, and
Stock Prices for
Various Growth
Rates and at
Various First-
Year Dividends:
Normal-Growth
and Supergrowth
Firms**

Firm A: Normal-growth: $g = 5\%$; first-year dividend, $d_1 = \$5$; and reinvestment at rate of return of 10%.

Year	Earnings per share ($)	Dividends per share ($)	Stock Price ($)
1	10	5	100
2	10.50	5.25	$100 \times (1.05)$
3	11.03	5.51	$100 \times (1.05)^2$
⋮	⋮	⋮	⋮

Firm B: Normal-growth: $g = 9\%$; \$1 first-year dividend, $d_1 = \$1$; and reinvestment at 10%.

Year	Earnings per share ($)	Dividends per share ($)	Stock Price ($)
1	10	1	100
2	10.90	1.09	$100 \times (1.09)$
3	11.88	1.19	$100 \times (1.09)^2$
⋮	⋮	⋮	⋮

Firm C: Supergrowth: $g = 9\%$; first-year dividend, $d_1 = \$5$; and reinvestment at 18%.

Year	Earnings per share ($)	Dividends per share ($)	Stock Price ($)
1	10	5	500
2	10.90	5.45	$500 \times (1.09)$
3	11.88	5.94	$500 \times (1.09)^2$
⋮	⋮	⋮	⋮

Firm D: Supergrowth: $g_1 = 9\%$ for the first year and $g_2 = 5\%$ thereafter; first-year dividend $d_1 = \$5$; and reinvestment at 18% in the first year and at 10% thereafter.

Year	Earnings per share ($)	Dividends per share ($)	Stock Price ($)
1	10	5	103.64
2	10.90	5.45	$103.64 \times (1.09)$
3	11.45	5.72	$103.64 \times (1.09)(1.05)$
⋮	⋮	⋮	⋮

Let's see how the figures in Table 13-2 are calculated, focusing first on Firm A. Assume that earnings per share in the first year is $10 and the firm pays a $5 per share dividend that year (and retains $5 per share). Also assume the firm earns 10% on its investments and the stockholders' required cost of equity is 10%. In the second year the EPS grow to $10.50 because the firm did not pay out as a dividend the $5 per share earned in the first year. Instead, the firm reinvested it at 10%, yielding an additional $5 \times 0.1 = \$0.50$ EPS. Because the firm distributes 50% of its earnings as dividends, it pays a dividend of $5.25 per share in the second year. The earnings, dividends, and the firm's stock price [see Equation (13.7)] grow by 5% from the first year to the second year—and, in this same way, are expected to continue to grow by 5% in all future years.

Using Equation (13.6), we find Firm A's current stock price:

$$P_0 = \frac{d_1}{k_e - g} = \frac{\$5}{0.10 - 0.05} = \frac{\$5}{0.05} = \$100$$

According to Equation (13.7), the stock price also grows by 5% a year. Now let's turn to Firm B. It is also a normal-growth firm that reinvests its retained earnings in projects yielding 10%. The only difference between Firm B and Firm A is that Firm B distributes only $1 as a cash dividend and reinvests its retained earnings of $9 per share in projects yielding 10%. Thus, the dollar return on this level of reinvestment of the retained earnings is $0.90 per share. Firm B repeats this strategy in the second year; 10% of the EPS (0.1 × $10.90 = $1.09) is paid out as a dividend and the remainder is reinvested at 10%. With a growth rate of 9% for all years, the firm's EPS in the third year will be $11.88 (10.90 × 1.09) and the dividend will be about $1.19 ($1.09 × 1.09). This growth rate is assumed to continue indefinitely.

By paying out a lower proportion of earnings as dividends, Firm B has more money left to reinvest, and, therefore, the growth rate of its earnings and dividends is higher than that of Firm A (9% versus 5%). Also, by Equation (13.7), Firm B's stock price, P_1, at the end of the first year should be 9% higher. Note that the increase in the stock price in Year 1 is not due to the availability of projects with an extraordinary profit. On average the firm reinvests as before in projects yielding 10%. However, by paying a dividend per share of $1, rather than $5, Firm B increases its dollar volume of investment in projects, which results in a larger growth rate in its future dividends and stock price.

Does Firm B's higher growth rate and the future increase in its stock price affect the *current* stock price? To answer this question, we can apply Equation (13.6) to Firm B:

$$P_0 = \frac{d_1}{k_e - g} = \frac{\$9}{0.10 - 0.09} = \frac{\$1}{0.01} = \$100$$

Comparing Firms A and B clearly indicates that Firm B's larger dividend growth rate does not lead to a higher current stock price. It is true that Firm B's dividends grow at a faster rate than those of Firm A. But for the higher growth case (9%), we also had a lower dividend base: a first-year dividend of $1 for Firm B as opposed to a first-year dividend of $5 for lower-growth Firm A. These two factors—dividend base and dividend growth—cancel each other, and the stock price remains unchanged at $P_0 = \$100$.

The trade-off between current dividends and growth in dividends has no effect on the current stock price as long as the firm reinvests the retained earnings at the cost of capital. As long as the firm undertakes zero-NPV projects, the dividend growth rate does not affect its current stock price.

Let us now turn our attention to the supergrowth firms, C and D.

13.6 SUPERGROWTH FIRMS

Firms C and D reinvest their retained earnings at a rate of return of 18%, which is higher than the cost of capital of 10%. By definition, then, Firms C and D are supergrowth firms.

First review Firm C in Table 13-2, whose source of change in the growth rate is the availability of projects yielding extraordinary profit (positive NPVs). To be more specific, assume stockholders still require $k = 10\%$ but the firm can invest its retained earnings at 18%. Suppose, like Firm A, Firm C pays a cash dividend of $5 per share in the first year and reinvests $5 per share at 18%. In this case, Firm C's EPS in the second year will be $10 + (\$5 \times 0.18) = \$10.90$.

The second-year dividend, assuming as before that Firm C pays out 50% of its EPS as dividends, will be $\frac{1}{2} \times \$10.90 = \$5.45$. Similarly, the EPS and the dividend per share, DPS, will grow at 9% in all other years.[5]

Applying Equation (13.6) to this specific case, we find that Firm C's current stock price is $500:

$$P_0 = \frac{d_1}{k_e - g} = \frac{\$5}{0.10 - 0.09} = \frac{\$5}{0.01} = \$500$$

Comparison of Firms A and C reveals a dramatic jump in the stock price from $P_0 = \$100$ to $P_0 = \$500$. In comparing Firms A and B, we saw that the source of the difference in their growth rates is their different dividend policies. By reducing the dividend from $5 to $1 and reinvesting a higher proportion of its earnings in projects (at 10%), Firm B increases the growth rate from 5% to 9% but does not achieve a gain in the current stock price because of the lower dividend base. However, comparing Firms A and C, we see that the growth rate increases from 5% to 9% with *no reduction* in the dividend base, which is kept at $d_1 = \$5$. The jump in the growth rate is due to the increase in project profitability (from 10% to 18%) with no change in the firm's risk. This constitutes a real economic gain. The increase in the stock price from $100 to $500 reflects the investors' reaction to the profitable projects, not the increase in the number of dollars reinvested in the firm.

To summarize, the current stock price is not affected by changes in the proportion of earnings paid as dividends, as long as the firm reinvests its retained earnings at k_e. On the other hand, changes in the growth rate that are caused by the availability of positive NPV projects *do* affect the current stock price.

Firms A and B are normal-growth firms that differ only with regard to their dividend policies. Firm C is a supergrowth firm that reinvests money at a rate of return higher than the minimum rate that the stockholders require. Firm D is yet another variation of a supergrowth firm, which we'll consider in the next section.

---

5. Reinvestment at 18% of 50% of the EPS implies a dividend growth rate of $0.18 \times 0.50 = 0.09$. If the firm were to invest 100% of the EPS at 18%, the growth rate would also be 18%.

13.7 SUPERGROWTH FOR A LIMITED TIME PERIOD

Did the dramatic increase in stock price from $100 to $500 surprise you? It really is an impressive jump, which hardly seems justified by the 8% increase in the average profitability of Firm C's projects. However, recall that by the CDGM, this extra profit is assumed to continue indefinitely. Since the present value of the extra 8% profit on all future retained earnings is $400, the stock price increased from $100 to $500.

Does it make sense for a firm to reinvest its earnings at 18% when investors require only 10% on their investment? Maybe so. To see this, suppose a firm discovers and patents a new drug. As a result, it enjoys an 18% rate of return rather than the 10% it would make without the new drug. If the firm's riskiness does not change, the required rate of return will also remain unchanged at 10%. Because the firm is making 18% on its investments, investors will buy the stock, and the stock price will increase until the rate of return equals 10%, consistent with the firm's risk.

As explained earlier, a firm like Firm C, with projects that yield an extraordinary profit, is defined as a supergrowth firm. Can supergrowth continue indefinitely as Equation (13.6) assumes? Probably not, because of competition. When a firm is observed making an extraordinary profit on a given product, competitors will attempt to penetrate the market. If their attempts are successful, both the product's price and its profitability inevitably decrease. For instance, the firm with a newly discovered drug will probably enjoy supergrowth for a limited time, say, for the duration of the patent. After this limited period, competitors will start manufacturing and distributing the drug, and the original producer will revert to being a normal-growth firm until it discovers other new drugs.

Another good example of limited supergrowth is the computer industry. The price of computers was initially very high. IBM, which was known as *the* supergrowth firm in the United States, enjoyed extraordinary profits for many years. Competitors attracted to this profitable business eventually penetrated the market. The prices of computers—and, in particular, of personal computers—decreased dramatically, and IBM's extraordinary profits disappeared. In such case we say that the firm is a supergrowth firm for a limited number of years, after which the growth levels off. Earnings and dividends grow at a normal rate thereafter. In IBM's case, competitors succeeded not only in curtailing IBM's supergrowth, but also in cutting IBM's profit so badly that in the early 1990s it suffered losses. In 1993 IBM's stock price crashed from about $100 a share to about $40 a share. With a new CEO, IBM made a strong recovery in 1995, mainly due to reorganization and cost savings, and greatly improved its growth rate. This is demonstrated in the following problem.

PRACTICE BOX

Problem
a. IBM stock traded for $100 per share in 1991. The dividend per share was $4.84, and the discount rate was estimated to be 15%. If the dividends were a growing perpetuity, what was the estimated growth rate? *(continued)*

b. The firm suffered financial distress in 1992. The dividend was maintained at $4.84, but the stock price decreased to $44. Given the $44 price, what is the new estimate of IBM's long-term growth rate?

c. Due to reorganization and cost savings in 1995, IBM's stock price increased, reaching $164⅝ on January 15, 1997. However, the annual dividend was only $1.40. What was IBM's estimated growth rate in 1997?

Solution

a. Before the crash in IBM stock:

$$\$100 = \frac{\$4.84}{0.15 - g}$$

Thus: $\$15 - \$100g = \$4.84$ or $\$10.16 = \$100g$

$$g = \frac{\$10.16}{\$100} = 0.1016 \text{ or } 10.16\%$$

b. After the fall of IBM's stock price:

$$\$44 = \frac{\$4.84}{0.15 - g}$$

Thus, $g = 4\%$.

c. To find the estimated growth rate after the stock price rebound and the change in dividend, we solve for

$$\$164.625 = \frac{\$1.40}{0.15 - g}$$

Therefore:

$$g = \frac{\$164.625 \times 0.15 - \$1.40}{\$164.625} \cong 0.1415 \text{ or } 14.15\%$$

We illustrate limited supergrowth first by using the example of Firm D in Table 13-2 and then by providing a formula to evaluate a stock that has this type of growth. Suppose the firm pays a dividend of $5 per share in the first year and reinvests its retained earnings in positive NPV projects. The retained earnings in all subsequent years are invested at the normal profit rate for this firm (NPV = 0). In this case the supergrowth lasts only one year, and the dividend growth rate will not be constant. Because Equation (13.6) is appropriate *only* for constant dividend growth, it cannot be used to evaluate the price of this firm's stock. Therefore, we use Equation (13.1) to find the price:

$$P_0 = \frac{d_1}{1 + k_e} + \frac{P_1}{1 + k_e}$$

Let us use Firm D's figures (Table 13-2), which involve supergrowth for one year. In this example, we assume the firm reinvests at an 18% rate of return for one year. With 50% of its earnings paid out as dividends, Firm D's first-year growth rate is 9%. Thereafter, earnings and dividends grow at the normal growth rate of 5% a year. Therefore, if d_1 = $5, then d_2 = $5 $\times$ (1.09) = $5.45, and d_3 = $5.45 $\times$ (1.05) $\cong$ $5.72, and all subsequent future dividends will also grow at 5%. As d_1 = $5 and k = 10% (by assumption), if we know the value of P_1, the stock price at the end of the first year, we can easily solve for P_0. P_1 can be determined by the CDGM because after the first year the dividends will grow at a normal, constant rate. By Equation (13.7) we have

$$P_1 = \frac{d_2}{k_e - g} = \frac{\$5.45}{0.1 - 0.05} = \frac{\$5.45}{0.05} = \$109$$

where d_2 = $5.45. Recall that P_1 corresponds to the PV of all dividends obtained from the second year on. Therefore:

$$P_0 = \frac{d_1}{1 + k_e} + \frac{P_1}{1 + k_e} = \frac{\$5}{1.1} + \frac{\$109}{1.1} \cong \$4.55 + \$99.09 = \$103.64$$

Due to the one-year supergrowth, Firm D's current stock price is $103.64, if the extraordinary rate of return of 18% and annual dividend growth of 9% continued indefinitely. From this example we can conclude that the larger the number of years of extraordinary profit, the bigger the jump in the stock price due to the availability of profitable projects.

Let's now generalize the valuation formula for a stock that enjoys supergrowth for n years and normal growth thereafter. For example, if a firm has a product that is protected by patent for n years, it will have supergrowth for n years. Thereafter, when competitors enter the market, profits will decline and the firm will step into a period of normal growth. In this case the stock price is given by

$$P_0 = \frac{d_1}{k_e - g_1}\left[1 - \frac{(1 + g_1)^n}{(1 + k_e)^n}\right] + \frac{1}{(1 + k_e)^n}\frac{d_1(1 + g_1)^n}{k_e - g_2} \qquad (13.8)$$

where g_1 is the supergrowth rate for n years and g_2 is the normal growth rate. [The derivation of Equation (13.8) is given in Appendix 13A.]

For firm D in Table 13-2, we have n = 1, g_1 = 0.09, g_2 = 0.05, d_1 = $5, and k_e = 0.10. Therefore:

$$P_0 = \frac{\$5}{0.10 - 0.09}\left[1 - \frac{1.09}{1.10}\right] + \frac{1}{1.1}\frac{\$5(1.09)}{0.10 - 0.05} \cong \$103.64$$

Direct calculation gives the same result.

13.8 STOCK VALUATION WHEN ALL EARNINGS ARE PAID OUT AS CASH DIVIDENDS

Occasionally a normal-growth firm decides to distribute all of its earnings as dividends. In that case, if the expected earnings are constant over time, the current stock price is the PV of a perpetuity discounted at k_e%. Using the general assumptions from our example in Table 13-2, let's assume a fifth firm, called E, whose EPS is $10 and whose dividend, d_1, is also $10. Since the firm distributes all of its earnings as dividends, they will not grow over time: The following years' earnings and dividend per share will remain constant at $10. In this case we have a perpetuity, and the PV, which equals the stock price, is given by

$$P_0 = \frac{d_1}{1 + k_e} + \frac{d_1}{(1 + k_e)^2} + \ldots = \sum_{t=1}^{\infty} \frac{d_1}{(1 + k_e)^t} = \frac{d_1}{k_e} \qquad (13.9)$$

For this firm, at a discount rate of 10% as given in Table 13-2, we find that P_0 equals $100.

$$P_0 = \frac{\$10}{0.1} = \$100$$

Figure 13-2 summarizes our discussion by illustrating the dividend stream for four alternate situations. Curves 1 and 2 describe normal-growth firms, and Curves 3 and 4 depict supergrowth firms. Curve 1 presents the case of Firm E—where the EPS is $10, all of which is distributed as a dividend. When a firm does not retain its earnings, the dividend remains constant at $10; the "curve" is a horizontal line. Curve 2 describes Firm A's case—where 50% of the EPS is retained and 50% is paid out as a cash dividend. Accordingly, the first year's dividend is only $5, but the dividend grows because the firm invested the retained earnings at g% per year (5% in our example). As we can see, Curves 1 and 2 intersect. This means that after 15 years, dividends of a firm (Firm A) that reinvests half of its earnings will be larger than those of a firm (Firm E) that distributes all of its earning as dividends.

Curve 3 describes Firm C—a supergrowth firm with a reinvestment rate greater than k—under the *unreasonable* assumption that supergrowth will continue indefinitely. Note that Curve 3 is above Curve 2, reflecting the higher dividends along Curve 3. Therefore, the stock price corresponding to Curve 3 is relatively high (in our example, $P_0 = \$500$). Finally, the more *realistic* case of a supergrowth firm is described by Curve 4, which corresponds to Firm D. Initially, owing to an extraordinary investment opportunity, the earnings and dividends grow at a rapid rate exactly as in Curve 3. However, after a few years the rapid growth ends and the dividends increase at the same rate as that of Curve 2.

The future cash flows for normal-growth firms depend on the proportion of earnings retained and the first-year dividend, d_1. All combinations of d_1 and growth rate g lead to the same stock value, P_0. Increasing the growth rate by decreasing the dividends will not boost the stock price. However, other things equal, a supergrowth

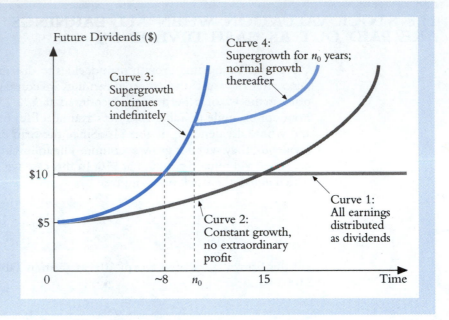

FIGURE 13-2
Increase in Dividend Level by Type of Growth

Future Dividends ($)

Curve 4:
Supergrowth for n_0 years;
normal growth
thereafter

Curve 3:
Supergrowth
continues
indefinitely

Curve 1:
All earnings
distributed
as dividends

$10

$5

Curve 2:
Constant growth,
no extraordinary
profit

0   ~8 n_0 15   Time

stock's value is greater than a normal-growth stock's value because the supergrowth firm invests some of its earnings in positive NPV projects.

13.9 USING THE CDGM TO ESTIMATE THE FIRM'S COST OF EQUITY

Thus far we have used the various stock valuation formulas to calculate the PV of all future cash flows. We have seen that if a stock's PV is higher than its current market price, the stock is a good investment. These valuation formulas can also be used to estimate the cost of equity, k_e. If we assume stocks are "fully valued," then no "bargains" are available in the market (that is, the NPV of all assets is zero). That implies that the observed stock price equals the PV of all future cash flows. With this assumption, we can estimate the cost of equity. Let us elaborate:

By the CDGM, we have

$$P_0 = \frac{d_1}{k_e - g}$$

which can be rewritten as

$$k_e = \frac{d_1}{P_0} + g \qquad\qquad (13.10)$$

If d_1 and P_0 are known and if the expected growth rate, g, can be estimated, we can solve for the stockholders' required cost of equity. In our example, which corresponds to the case of Firm A in Table 13-2, we have $d_1 = \$5$, $P_0 = \$100$, and $g = 5\%$. Thus:

$$k_e = \frac{\$5}{\$100} + g\% = 5\% + 5\% = 10\%$$

which is the firm's cost of equity and the investors' expected rate of return. Management as well as investors can use the valuation formulas discussed earlier in this chapter to estimate the firm's cost of equity. In Appendix 13B we discuss several techniques for estimating the growth rate using historical data. In Applying Theory to Practice 13.1, we demonstrate how actual data can be used to estimate Meditronic, Inc.'s cost of equity.

APPLYING THEORY TO PRACTICE 13.1

ESTIMATING MEDITRONIC, INC.'S COST OF EQUITY

The following table contains selected data from Meditronic, Inc.'s financial statements for the years 1985 through 1996. The firm's stock price at the end of 1995 was $54.

Year	1985	1986	1987	1988	1989	1990	1991
Earnings per share ($)	0.27	0.33	0.40	0.44	0.50	0.58	0.68
Dividends per share ($)	0.05	0.05	0.06	0.08	0.09	0.10	0.12
Dividends/ Net profit ($)	19	17	16	17	17	17	18

Year	1992	1993	1994	1995*	1996*		
Earnings per share ($)	0.83	1.01	1.28	1.80	2.15		
Dividends per share ($)	0.14	0.17	0.21	0.26	0.32		
Dividends/ Net profit ($)	17	17	18	14	15		

*Estimate

Source: *Value Line Investment Survey* various issues. (Value Line Publishing, New York, NY).

Questions

1. Use the above data and the CDGM to estimate the firm's cost of equity at the *beginning* of 1996.

2. How would your answer change if beginning in 1995 the firm began paying
    out 100% of its earnings as dividends and continued to do so thereafter? (The
    dividend per share in 1995 would then be $1.80.) Can you use the CDGM to
    evaluate the cost of capital when the dividend policy is not stable over time?

MAKING THE CONNECTION

1. We use the 1985 through 1995 data to estimate the dividend's annual
    growth rate.

Year	Dividends per Share ($)	Annual Growth Rate of Dividends (%)	Annual Dividend Growth Rate
1985	0.05	—	—
1986	0.05	0.0	0.0
1987	0.06	20.0	20.0
1988	0.08	33.3	33.3
1989	0.09	12.5	12.5
1990	0.10	11.1	11.1
1991	0.12	20.0	20.0
1992	0.14	16.7	16.7
1993	0.17	21.4	21.4
1994	0.21	23.5	23.5
1995	0.26	23.8	757.1[a]
Average annual dividend growth rate		18.2	91.6

[a] Assuming a change in the dividend policy, the dividend growth rate in 1995 is obtained as follows:

$$\frac{\$1.80}{\$0.21} - 1 \cong 7.571 \text{ or } 757.1\%$$

Because this is not an all–equity firm, we denote the cost of equity by
k_e. We use the CDGM to estimate the cost of equity as follows:

$$k_e = \frac{d_1}{P_0} + g$$

Thus:

$$k_e = \frac{\$0.32}{\$54} + 0.182 \cong 0.1879 \text{ or } 18.79\%$$

where d_1 = $0.32, which is the following year's (1996) dividend and P_0 = $54.

2. This problem illustrates the inaccuracies that arise from using the CDGM when there are sharp changes in the dividend policy. To see why, let's use Equation (13.10) with the new average growth rate. If Meditronic, Inc. were to pay out 100% of its earnings as dividends in 1995, the dividend would be $1.80, and the dividend growth rate for 1995 would be ($1.80/$0.21) − 1 or 757.1%. The right-hand column of the table shows that with this change in dividend policy, the average annual growth rate in the dividend would be 91.6%, and the resulting cost of equity would be

$$k_e = \frac{d_1}{P_0} + g = \frac{\$2.15}{\$54} + 0.916 \cong 0.956 \text{ or } 95.6\%$$

where $2.15 is the 1996 dividend with the new dividend policy.

Is it possible for the cost of equity to increase so substantially as a result of a change in the dividend policy? No, it isn't. The CDGM implicitly assumes that the proportion of earnings paid out as dividends—the payout ratio—is more or less constant across years. However, since Meditronic, Inc. changed its payout ratio dramatically in 1995, this model would not be applicable, and the 95.6% figure is irrelevant.

13.10 PV OF DIVIDENDS AND THE PRICE-EARNINGS RATIO

In Chapter 10 we discussed the P/E ratio, whose reciprocal may be used to estimate the cost of equity. We will now elaborate on the P/E ratio, showing how investors use it and discussing the possible errors that may occur if the ratio is not used cautiously.

The financial press regularly publishes *price-earnings (P/E) ratios* of firms, also called *multipliers*, as shown in Table 13-3. The P/E ratio often serves as an investment criterion. It suggests which stocks are "expensive" and which are relatively "inexpensive." The lower the P/E ratio, the less expensive the stock. We discuss here instances where making investment decisions and estimating the cost of capital based on the P/E ratio is justified.

The price/earnings (P/E) ratio is the stock's current price divided by the last reported EPS (denoted by E in the term P/E). For example, if the stock price is $P = $100 and the EPS is $10, then the P/E ratio = 10. Intuitively, the meaning of the P/E ratio in this example is that you have to wait 10 years to recover your $100 investment. Similarly, if P/E = 5, you have to wait five years to recover your investment.

TABLE 13-3 **Reported Stock Data**

Mkt. Sym	52-Weeks High	52-Weeks Low	Company Name	Tick Sym	Div Amt	Vol 100's	Div Yld	Earn P/E	High	Week's Low	Last	Net Chg.	EARNINGS Interim or Fiscal Year	EARNINGS Year ago	DIVIDENDS Latest divs.	DIVIDENDS Record date	DIVIDENDS Payment date
	12	10¼	AmStratill	CSP	1.28	3844	11.8	. . .	11	10¾	10⅞	. . .	. . . .	. . .	M.10⅜	12-29	1-11
	13¾	11⅜	AmStratInco	ASP	1.50a	1113	12.8	. . .	12	11¼	11¼	– ⅛	. . . .	. . .	.10	12-29	1-11
	5⅝	1⅛	AmWasteSvc	AW		3587	. . .	dd	2½	2¼	2⅜	– ⅛	Sep9mDL.18	.04	. . . .	. . . .	. . . .
x	40½	27¼	AmWaterWks	AWK	1.40f	1756	3.8	14	38⅛	36¾	37¼	– ¼	Sep12mX2.65	2.27	q.35	1-26	2-15
	21½	17	AmWaterWks pf		1.25	z2730	6.2	. . .	21½	19¼	20¼	+ ⅜	. . .	. . .	q.31¼	2-9	3-1
	19⅝	17	AmWater pf		1.25	5	6.8	. . .	18½	18½	18½	. . .	. . .	. . .	q.31¼	2-9	3-1
	3⅝	2⅞	AmHotel	AHR	.50c	323	. . .	. . .	3⅜	3¼	3¼	– ⅛	Sep9m.08	.04	c.50	. . . .	3-6-95
	16¼	5¾	AmeriCredit	ACF		3930	. . .	12	13	12⅛	12⅝	+ ⅛	Dec6m.26	.13	. . . .	. . . .	. . . .
	7½	6¼	Americusinc	XUS	.75	2183	10.3	. . .	7⅜	7⅛	7¼	+ ½	. . . .	. . . .	M.05¼	12-29	1-11
	14⅛	6⅞	AmeriData	ADA		4485	. . .	12	8⅞	8¼	8¾	+ ⅜	Sep9m.56	.58	. . . .	. . . .	. . . .
n	25⅛	21¼	Amerigas	APU	1.00e	2262	4.1	. . .	24⅞	24	24⅜	+ ⅛	Sep23wD1.12	. . . .	.55	11-10-95	11-18-95
	3¼	⅝	Ameriquest	AQS		2068	. . .	dd	15/16	13/16	15/16	+ ⅛	Sep3mD.30	D.10	. . . .	. . . .	. . . .
	60⅞	40¾	Ameritech	AIT	2.12f	35648	3.6	16	59⅝	56⅞	59⅜	+1⅞	95DecX3.63	L2.13	q.53	12-29	2-1
x	39	31⅝	Ameron	AMN	1.28	218	3.4	12	38	37½	37⅞	+ ½	Aug9m2.20	1.86	q.32	1-25	2-20
	19½	15¾	Ametek	AME	.24	2284	1.4	10	17¾	17	17	– ⅝	95Dec1.31	.99	q.06	12-8	12-22
	72⅞	56⅜	Amoco	AN	2.60f	45165	3.7	19	70¼	67½	70	+ ⅝	95DecL3.76	X3.60	q.65	2-7	3-10
	11⅜	7¾	AmpcoPgh	AP	.10a	248	1.0	13	11	10½	10½	– ½	Sep9m.61	X.49	q.025+.05	1-15	1-31
	30⅜	18¾	Amphenol	APH		13293	. . .	16	22⅞	21	21	– ⅝	95Dec1.33	.91	. . . .	. . . .	. . . .
	16¾	3⅛	AMRE	AMM	.09j	4323	. . .	cc	16½	15⅛	16½	+ ⅞	Sep9mD.39	D.02	Y	. . . .	7-21-95
	7¾	5⅜	AMREP	AXR		201	. . .	9	5¾	5½	5½	. . .	Oct6m.28	.24	. . . .	. . . .	. . . .
	21⅝	11¼	Amscolnt	ASZ		6512	. . .	18	14⅜	13½	14	+ ⅛	Oct39wL.54	L.27	. . . .	. . . .	. . . .
	41⅜	27	AmSouthBcp	ASO	1.60f	3401	4.2	13	38⅝	37½	38⅜	+ ⅞	95Dec3.00	2.25	q.40	12-8	1-2
	12⅞	9½	AmvstrFnl	AMV	.08e	401	.7	9	11½	11	11¼	– ⅛	Sep9m1.05	.90	.07½	3-18-95	4-13-95
x	45¾	28½	AmwayAsia	AAP	.72f	824	2.1	. . .	34½	32⅞	34⅛	+1½	Nov3m.40	.39	.18	1-25-96	2-14-96
	23½	13¾	AmwayJpn	AJL	.95e	1537	4.1	. . .	23½	22⅝	23⅛	– ⅛	ADRNov3m.27	.19	.3961	8-30-95	12-11-95
	54⅛	37½	AnadrkPete	APC	.30	13027	.6	cc	50	46¾	46¾	–3¼	Sep9m.24	.66	q.07½	12-13	12-27
s	26 95/256	13 95/256	AnalogDevcs	ADI		34834	. . .	22	23	21⅛	22¼	– ¼	950ct1.00	.64	. . . .	. . . .	. . . .
x	39⅝	19¾	Andina	AKO	.35e	3408	1.0	. . .	37	34⅜	34⅜	–1	. . . .	. . . .	.0677	1-24-96	. . . .
	27½	19⅜	Angelica	AGL	.96	1982	4.7	16	20⅝	19¾	20½	+ ¼	Oct39w.98	1.16	q.24	12-15	1-1
	70⅝	53⅛	AnheuserB	BUD	1.76	22537	2.5	17	70⅝	68¾	69⅛	– ¾	Sep9m3.43	3.23	q.44	2-9	3-8
s	22⅛	16⅝	AnixterIntl	AXE		1659	. . .	dd	19⅝	17½	19⅛	+1½	Sep9mL.52	X.47	. . . .	. . . .	. . . .
	38	9¼	AnnTaylor	ANN		22002	. . .	. . .	13⅜	10⅜	10⅞	–1¾	Oct9m.02	1.05	. . . .	. . . .	. . . .
	23¼	15¼	AnthonyInd	ANT	.44	1126	2.1	16	22	20⅜	20½	–1½	Sep9m1.09	.84	q.11	12-28	1-3
	53⅜	32⅜	AonCp	AOC	1.36	12069	2.6	15	52⅝	51¼	52⅝	+ ⅝	Sep9m2.68	2.40	q.34	2-8	2-22
	65½	47	AonCp pf		3.13	17	4.8	. . .	65½	65	65½	. . .	. . . .	. . . .	q.78⅛	1-18	2-1
	26⅜	23⅜	AonCp pfA		2.00	2316	7.7	. . .	26	25½	26	+ ¼	. . . .	. . . .	q.50	1-18	2-1
	31	**22½**	**ApacheCp**	**APA**	**.28**	**13863**	**1.1**	**62**	**26¼**	**25⅝**	**26**	**– ¼**	**Sep9mL.17**	**.48**	**q.07**	**12-29**	**1-31**
	21¼	17¼	Apartmtlnv	AIV	1.66	1959	8.1	22	20⅝	20	20⅜	. . .	Sep9m.65	. . . .	.41½	11-7-95	11-14-95

Source: *Barron's* 76, no. 5 (January 1996): MW20.

Similar to using the payback method in project valuation, if the investor is will-ing to wait, say, seven years to recover his or her investment and the stock's payback is five years, he or she should buy the stock. Conversely, if the stock's payback is longer than seven years, the investor should not buy the stock. When investment an-alysts recommend stock purchases, they talk about a relatively low *multiplier*, mean-ing a low P/E ratio, which is, presumably, a favorable indicator. The lower the P/E ratio, the quicker the stock's payback.

The P/E ratio has two severe limitations. First, it is based on past, rather than on future, earnings per share; and, second, it is based on earnings reported in the firm's financial statements, not on cash flows. These two deficiencies are strong enough to reject the P/E ratio as an investment criterion. However, since practitioners and managers widely use it, the P/E ratio cannot be dismissed without discussion.

A low P/E indicates the stock may be a "bargain" that is not fully priced. How-ever, sometimes there are good reasons for a low P/E. For example, a significant probability of bankruptcy may exist. It is always a good idea to check a firm's funda-mentals before investing in its stock.

The reciprocal of the P/E ratio, E/P, measures the investor's expected annual re-turn. For example, if $P = \$100$ and $E = \$20$, then the expected rate of return on eq-uity is $\$20/\$100$, or 20 percent. We learned in Chapter 10 that the required expected rate of return is the firm's cost of equity. A firm can use E/P to measure this cost. However, the ratio (or its reciprocal) may be meaningful and consistent with the DCF principle under certain conditions:

1. In the case of constant earnings per share, when all earnings are distributed as cash dividends. If so, the most recent year's EPS will equal the future EPS and will represent the cash flow to stockholders.
2. In the case of constant growth in earnings and dividends, as long as the firm is normal-growth and pays out a *fixed* proportion of its earnings as dividends every year.

If either of these conditions hold, then there is no need to examine the firm's other fundamentals because the P/E ratio reflects all of them.

Case 1 is described by Curve 1 in Figure 13-2. The EPS and the DPS are constant at $10. The stock price is $P_0 = \$100$. Thus:

$$\frac{E}{P_0} = \frac{d}{P_0} = \frac{\$10}{\$100} = 0.1 \text{ or } 10\%$$

The IRR of an investment in this stock is 10%. Also, since we have a perpetuity, we know (by the DCF principle) that

$$P_0 = \frac{d}{k_e} = \frac{E}{k_e} \quad \text{and} \quad k_e = \frac{d}{P_0} = \frac{E}{P_0} = 10\%$$

The reciprocal of the P/E ratio and the IRR yield the same expected profitability of 10%. In this case the E/P measures the investment's IRR. This is a trivial case, how-ever. Since the past earnings (and dividends) equal their future values, no harm is done by looking at *past* earnings rather than at *future* dividends. Case 2, where only a portion of the EPS is distributed as dividends, is more common than cases where *all* earnings are distributed as dividends.

Let us estimate the cost of equity by examining Curves 2 (normal-growth) and 3 (supergrowth) in Figure 13-3. The correct cost of equity is calculated as follows:

Curve 2:

$$k_e = \frac{d_1}{P_0} + g = \frac{\$5}{\$100} + 0.05 = 0.1 \text{ or } 10\%$$

Curve 3:

$$k_e = \frac{d_1}{P_0} + g = \frac{\$5}{\$500} + 0.09 = 0.1 \text{ or } 10\%$$

The cost of equity is 10% in both cases. Now, if we use the E/P criterion to measure the cost of equity, we get the following.

For a normal-growth firm:

$$\frac{E}{P_0} = \frac{\$10}{\$100} = 0.1 \text{ or } 10\%$$

For a supergrowth firm:

$$\frac{E}{P_0} = \frac{\$10}{\$500} = 0.02 \text{ or } 2\%$$

where the $10 is the last reported EPS (the figure normally used in calculating the E/P ratio).

According to the discounted cash flow (DCF) method—the correct way to estimate the firm's cost of equity—the cost of equity is 10% for both normal-growth and supergrowth firms. Practitioners, however, often use E/P as an estimate of the cost of equity. Is this justified? The E/P ratio could also be used. From our calculation we see that the E/P method gives a correct figure (10%) for normal-growth firms, but a distorted figure for supergrowth firms. Although we get the same cost of equity for both firms, we make a serious error if we use E/P as an indicator of profitability for a supergrowth firm.

The conclusions are based on a specific numerical example, but they carry over to the general case. The E/P ratio equals the cost of equity, k_e, only for normal-growth firms. E/P is lower than k_e for supergrowth firms. (A formal proof of this assertion is given in Appendix 13C.)

In practice the E/P ratio may also be misleading if the previous year's earnings differ from average earnings. To see the possible distortions, review Apache Corporation's P/E in Table 13-3. Apache's P/E is 62, so the E/P = $\frac{1}{62}$ or about 1.6%. Does this mean that the investors' required rate of return on equity is only 1.6%? No, it doesn't. There are two possible explanations:

1. The firm is enjoying supergrowth, so the P/E is misleading.
2. The reported EPS is low and does not represent the future average EPS.

Any random deviation in the EPS in a given year will produce a distorted P/E ratio.

Only by carefully studying the firm's income statements can we know which of these two explanations is correct.

Finally, the P/E ratio has a technical drawback. When EPS is negative, the P/E ratio is undefined. This is the case for a number of the firms appearing in Table 13-3.

To summarize, one should always rely on the DCF stock valuation method that takes the discounted future dividends into account. The P/E ratio can be used to estimate the average rate of return and cost of equity when $d = E$ is constant over time and when the earnings and dividends grow at a normal rate. In practice the P/E ratio may give a distorted figure for individual firms. However, on average for the whole economy or for a specific industrial sector, the risk of distortion is relatively low, and the ratio can safely be used.

13.11 STOCK MARKET EQUILIBRIUM: HOW STOCK PRICES RESPOND TO NEW INFORMATION

Let us now see how the CAPM and the DCF principle can be used together to identify stocks that are not fully priced.

To use the DCF principle to evaluate the PV of all future dividends, we need to know the approximate cost of equity, k_e. We can use the CAPM to estimate the required rate of return, which is the same as the cost of equity.

In Chapter 9 we learned that in equilibrium, all risky assets will be located on the security market line (SML):

$$\overline{R}_i = r + (\overline{R}_m - r)b_i$$

The value $\overline{R}_i$ corresponds to Firm i's cost of equity because it represents the required expected rate of return, given risk b_i. We, therefore, can use the CAPM to estimate Firm i's cost of equity, $k_{e,i}$, as follows:

$$k_{e,i} = r + (\overline{R}_m - r)b_i$$

We can use market data to estimate b_i and $\overline{R}_m$ (See Chapter 9). With r also observed in the market (as the market interest rate on short-term Treasury bills), we can use this equation to calculate $k_{e,i}$. Then, by the CDGM, $k_{e,i}$ can be used to calculate the PV of the stock's expected future dividends. If the PV is larger or smaller than the observed market price, the market is not in equilibrium, and "bargains" will be available. If the PV equals the stock price for all firms, all stocks will be located on the SML and the market will be in equilibrium.

By Equation (13.6), a stock's value depends on the observed dividend (d_1), the cost of equity, and the expected growth rate of dividends (g). If investors become pessimistic and the growth rate falls, the stock price will decrease. Indeed, the stock prices do change—sometimes very rapidly. October 19, 1987 provides an excellent example of this. In one day the Dow Jones average dropped by about 23%, and the S&P index dropped by almost 22%. Other indexes around the world dropped even more dramatically: 45.8% in Hong Kong, 44.9% in Australia, and 41.6% in Singapore. All these losses occurred on a single day!

What was the explanation for these dramatic changes? Generally speaking, even if all stocks are located on the SML, any new information in the market affects investors' expectations regarding future profit and dividends. They may then start buying and selling frantically, and this, in turn, can cause drastic changes in stock prices. What happened on that October day in 1987 was an extreme example, in a compressed time period, of the stock market's general tendency to move up and down in reaction to new information.

New information may be firm-specific or macroeconomic. For example, a drop in the interest rate (a macroeconomic factor) is generally followed by a surge in the stock market. A change in a given firm's reported profit is a firm-specific factor. For example, in the early 1990s IBM lost money (a firm-specific factor) and cut its dividends. As a result, IBM's stock price plunged from $100 to $40. Investors revised their estimates of future dividends and the dividend growth rate. Since the stock price is very sensitive to changes in the estimate of the dividend growth rate, when both that rate and dividends decreased, the share price declined sharply. In 1996 the opposite situation occurred: IBM's earnings per share and growth rate increased, the dividend was increased, and the stock price promptly followed suit.

Table 13-4 shows how changes in a firm's growth rate affect the stock price. In the table, $d_1 = \$4$ and $k_e = 15\%$. As we can see from the table, the stock price is very sensitive to changes in the dividend growth rate. For example, if $g = 11\%$ and investors revise their estimate only slightly, say, to $g = 10\%$, the stock price will decrease from $100 to $80. For IBM a revision in the estimate of the growth rate from $g = 11\%$ to 5% would be sufficient to explain the decrease in price from $100 to $40.

TABLE 13-4 Relationship Between Stock Price and Dividend Growth Rate (for $d_1 = \$4$, $k_e = 0.15$, and valuation formula, $P_0 = d_1/(k_e - g)$)	Stock Price ($)	Growth Rate, g (%)
	26.67	0
	28.57	1
	33.33	3
	36.36	4
	40.00	5
	44.44	6
	50.00	7
	57.14	8
	66.67	9
	80.00	10
	100.00	11
	133.33	12
	200.00	13
	400.00	14

When new information becomes available, the stock market generally adjusts very rapidly. Some people claim that the market is *efficient*. This means that by the time the new information reaches you or me via the *Wall Street Journal*, we may call our broker only to find that the stock market has already reacted to the information. In this sense the market is *very* efficient. If the market is efficient, there are no bargains, all stocks are fully priced, and PV always equals P_0.

As we shall see in the next section, not everyone agrees that the market is efficient. Many people make their living looking for "bargains" in the capital market.

13.12 THE EFFICIENT MARKET HYPOTHESIS: ARE THERE UNDERVALUED STOCKS?

We've seen that stock prices are sensitive to new market information. Must investors incessantly read the financial news, listen to the radio, watch TV, search the Web, and then exploit new information as soon as it is released in order to ensure a profit? Should they try to predict future information even before it arrives on the market? Could this be the recipe for getting rich? If you had predicted the drastic decrease in IBM's growth rate, you could have sold your IBM stock short and made a lot of money.[6] Or if you knew that Intel's growth rate was about to increase, you could buy the stock now, sell it later at a higher price, and enjoy a profit on your investment.

A large number of academic studies claim that this recipe for becoming rich is not a good one. You cannot "beat the market," they say. The argument is that the market is efficient and in an efficient market, no abnormal profit is available. The **efficient market hypothesis (EMH)** distinguishes among three levels of efficiency: weak, semistrong, and strong.

The *weak form* of the EMH asserts that past price information cannot be used to make an extraordinary profit on stocks. Stock price changes behave according to a *random walk*; that is, day-to-day stock price changes are random.[7] Just because the stock price may have increased in the past does not change the probability of a subsequent increase or a decrease. It is similar to flipping a coin. Assuming you have a balanced coin, the probability of a head showing up equals ½. Suppose you get three heads in three consecutive tosses. What is the probability of a head showing up in the next toss? It is still ½. Because three heads showed up in a row does not change the probability of a head showing up in the next toss. The weak form of the EMH claims that the stock market behaves similarly to the tossing of a coin, and that it has "no memory" of past outcomes. Analyzing past stock price changes in hope of making an extraordinary profit is a waste of time.[8]

---

6. Recall that short selling is borrowing stock from a broker, selling it in the market, and later buying it back and returning it to the broker. If the stock price decreases during this period, the investor can make a profit. By selling short prior to IBM's stock price decrease from $100 to about $40, a short seller would have made a profit of $60 per share!

7. Changes in stock prices are statistically independent.

8. Even if on average the stock market has shown an upward trend and it seems justified to say the probability of a stock-price increase is slightly more likely than a decrease (say a probability of 0.6 for an increase and 0.4 for a decline), the 0.6 probability of a stock price increase will still be independent of the observed outcome of the preceding price changes.

The *semistrong form* of the EMH states that a stock's current market price reflects all publicly available information, including the firm's EPS, its financial statements, and the stock's past prices. If this is true, any analysis of these figures aimed at predicting the future price changes will be worthless—a waste of time and money.

The *strong form* of the EMH states that the current stock price reflects all publicly and privately held information. Accordingly, even insiders (e.g., the firm's directors) who have information that is not yet public, cannot make an abnormal profit by using this information.

The EMH is controversial. Although many might believe in the EMH's weak form, support wanes as we move to the semistrong form and, in particular, to the strong form. As Connecting Theory to Practice 13.2 indicates, after being strongly supported by academics for many years, the EMH has started to lose ground.

CONNECTING THEORY TO PRACTICE 13.2

THE WHEEL TURNS

But the world turns. And today the academic world has been turned upside down. The hottest topics the professors are examining now are the ones they hooted at for years. For investors there are some important lessons here. No longer trying to argue that it is impossible to beat the market except by taking extraordinary risks, the professors are busy trying to figure out why some people consistently do beat the market.

And so the research backing the low-P/E strategy I began advocating in the 1970s and have presented in this column since 1980 is now showing up in some of the same academic journals that rejected the concept when I offered it to them a decade and a half ago.

But it is not only the low-P/E approach that the professors have discovered. Other value yardsticks, notably high cash flow to market price (*Forbes,* June 16, 1986) and high book value to market price, have also been shown to provide superior returns. Two of the most important papers verifying these strategies are about market price to book (1991), written by Eugene Fama and Kenneth French, and another, soon to be published, on low P/E, price to book and price to cash flow, by Josef Lakonishok et al.

The serious investor can now document from many academic sources that there *are* ways to consistently beat the market. So why don't more people beat the market?

The answer is simple. They lack discipline. They won't, or can't, stick to a single line of action, and get pulled hither and yon by whatever happens to be the hot fad. Investors love to follow the crowd. When the crowd rushes after a group of stocks, inevitably that group becomes overpriced and other less fashionable groups become underpriced. This is the overwhelming reason contrarian strategies work so consistently.

When they join the crowd, people almost always are persuaded that they have seen clearly into the future. In spite of powerful evidence to the contrary . . . people believe they can pinpoint the earnings and outlooks for companies years far into the future. Most of the time they prove wrong and it costs heavily. Conversely, people just as consistently underestimate the prospects of out-of-favor stocks.

Crowd-following is also the reason folks drive initial public offerings and exciting groups like the bio-techs to prices bordering on the insane. The pattern is repeated time and again. It has little to do with economics and everything to do with psychology, human nature.

That's why discipline matters so much. You must have the strength of character not to get carried away and instead to do unpopular, unfashionable things.

Not that value investing is infallible. But it's a bit like playing a giant roulette wheel with many more reds than blacks. So play red—you won't win every time, but if you keep at it, the odds are stacked heavily in your favor over time.

Source: David Dreman, "The Wheel Turns," *Forbes* 152, no. 6 (September 1993): 258. Reprinted By Permission of FORBES Magazine © Forbes Inc., 1993.

MAKING THE CONNECTION

Beating the market means using financial analysis to find stocks that are undervalued. In an efficient market this is impossible. The article indicates that some practitioners and some academics believe the market is not efficient.

Both academics and professional investors have lately doubted the efficient market hypothesis. As a matter of fact, key players in the capital market who proved to be very successful (and very rich) do not believe that the market is efficient. In their words:

What do Sequoia Fund's William Ruane, Berkshire Hathaway's Charles Munger and Warren Buffett, and money manager Walter Schloss have in common? They don't believe in efficient markets. Says Buffett: "I'd be a bum on the street with a tin cup if the market were efficient."[9]

The thousands of *chartists* (people who examine price and volume charts) and technicians who try to predict the market by reviewing past data do not believe in the EMH. Such technical analysis is based on the assumption that "bargains" are available in the market. Moreover, firms that employ chartists and technicians indicate their doubt of the EMH by paying for their technical services.

However, these experts may well be the very people who make the market efficient. They may be able to predict the company's earnings before they are published. This does not mean that they are always right. However, those who believe in these experts' work say the experts can predict better on average than nonexperts can. Once the information is printed in the morning newspaper, it

9. Terence P. Paré, "Yes, You Can Beat the Market," *Fortune* 131, no. 6 (April 1995): 68. © 1995, Time Inc. All rights reserved.

is too late; these experts make money by discovering "bargains" first. It is they who push the stock prices in the direction of the stock's new equilibrium price.

Most investors do not work on Wall Street and do not have the skills and the access to information that top managers and finance professionals do. The market is pretty much efficient for most investors. If this is true, what are the EMH implications for investment strategy? In practice there are two implications:

1. According to the EMH, all stocks are correctly priced. If so, there is no way to beat the market.
2. According to the EMH, you must select an efficient portfolio, as recommended in Chapters 8 and 9. Failure to do so will result in losses. For example, if a stock has a beta of 0.2, the average earnings on the stock will be $\bar{R} = 5\% + [(12\% - 5\%) \times 0.2] = 6.4\%$ where we use the CAPM and assume that $r = 5\%$ and $\bar{R}_m = 12\%$. Thus by the EMH, if $b = 0.2$, you cannot make more than 6.4%, an average, on this stock.

This is a relatively low mean rate of return that is due to the very low beta, which means this stock has relatively low covariance with other stocks. Therefore, including this stock in a portfolio will stabilize the portfolio's variability, which is why investors will be willing to accept a return of only 6.4%. However, if your portfolio consists only of this stock, you will lose: You will obtain a relatively low rate of return without the benefit of low portfolio variability. Investors who hold large portfolios that include this stock will enjoy stable portfolio returns.

To summarize, those who do not believe in the EMH should find stocks whose $PV > P_0$ and construct a portfolio of risky assets, as recommended in Chapters 8 and 9. Those who believe in the EMH should seek an optimum portfolio, taking all prices as equilibrium prices ($PV = P_0$) and focusing on selecting the optimum proportion of each asset to be included in their portfolio.

SUMMARY

A firm's management and potential investors use valuation models for stocks. Although the stock valuation formulas discount all future dividends, the same present value of the stock's cash flows is also obtained when the stock is held for a finite number of years n. In such case the stock price is the PV of n years' expected cash dividends plus the PV of the stock if sold after n years.

The most popular stock valuation method is the *constant dividend growth model* (CDGM), which assumes

that a firm pays a constant percentage of its earnings as dividends every year and retains the rest. If the observed price is assumed to be the equilibrium price, then the CDGM formula can be used to estimate the firm's cost of equity, which is also the stock's expected rate of return.

Although the CDGM can be used for both normal-growth and supergrowth firms, supergrowth cannot continue indefinitely. A more reasonable assumption is that the supergrowth will last for only a fixed number of years, after which growth will slow to a normal rate. Nevertheless, whether we have normal growth, supergrowth, or supergrowth for a limited number of years, stock valuation is always based on the discounted value of future dividends.

The popular price/earnings (P/E) ratio is sometimes used in selecting stock and in estimating a firm's cost of equity. The lower the P/E, the higher the stock's expected rate of return and the higher the firm's cost of equity. The P/E rule yields the same profitability estimate as the internal rate of return, and the E/P provides the correct cost of equity when: (a) the firm pays out all earnings as cash divi-

dends and these dividends are constant through time, or (b) the firm pays out some constant percent of the earnings as a cash dividend every year, and the dividend grows at a constant and normal-growth rate.

The fact that most firms fall into these two categories explains the widespread use of the P/E ratio. For supergrowth firms, however, the P/E produces misleading and sometimes absurd results.

If the market is efficient, the PV of future cash flows will equal the stock price, and no "bargains" will be available in the market (NPV = 0).

CHAPTER AT A GLANCE

1. **Stock valuation formulas**
   a. Holding the stock for n years and then selling it

   $\downarrow$

   $$P_0 = \sum_{t=1}^{n} \frac{d_t}{(1 + k)^t} + \frac{P_n}{(1 + k)^n}$$

   $\downarrow$

   b. Holding the stock for an infinite number of years

   $\downarrow$

   $$P_0 = \sum_{t=1}^{\infty} \frac{d_t}{(1 + k)^t}$$

   $\downarrow$

   Both lead to the same stock price, P_0.

2. **Valuation by the CDGM and cost of equity:**
   a. For normal-growth or supergrowth firms

   $$P_0 = \frac{d_1}{k - g} \text{ (and } g < k)$$

   b. Cost of equity is

   $$k_e = \frac{d_1}{P_0} + g$$

3. **Valuation for a nonconstant dividend growth model**
   Supergrowth for n years at g_1 followed by normal growth at g_2:

   $$P_0 = \frac{d_1}{k_e - g_1} \left[1 - \frac{(1 + g_1)^n}{(1 + k_e)^n} \right] + \frac{1}{(1 + k_e)^n} \times \frac{d_1(1 + g_1)^n}{k_e - g_2}$$

4. **Valuation by the E/P ratio with normal growth rate, g**

   $$\frac{E}{P} = \frac{d_1}{P_0} + g$$

KEY TERMS

Discounted cash flow (DCF)   Normal–growth firms
  principle   Supergrowth firms
Constant dividend growth model   Efficient market hypothesis
  (CDGM)   (EMH)

REVIEW AND PRACTICE

13.1 The PV of a firm's cash dividends is $100. The stock price is $P_0 = \$90$. Would you recommend this stock to an investor?

13.2 For what purposes do firms use stock valuation formulas?

13.3 An underwriter at an investment bank is considering guaranteeing an initial public offering (IPO). If the public is unwilling to buy all of the shares at a predetermined price, the underwriter would then have to buy them. After observing the risk of other similar firms, the underwriter decides the discount rate should be 15%.
a. What should be the initial public offering's maximum price if the firm has paid a constant dividend of $5 per share to its private owners over the last 10 years on its stock and the dividend equals the earnings per share?
b. How would your answer change for a normal-growth firm whose current dividend of $5 amounted to only 50% of the earnings?

13.4 Next year a firm will pay a dividend of $1, which will grow in following years by $g = 5\%$ annually. Mr. Smith believes the discount rate should be 10%. Mrs. Jones believes the discount rate should be 12%. Both now have the stock in their portfolios. Will they conduct a transaction? If so, at what price?

13.5 Suppose the expected stock price three years from now is $P_3 = \$150$. You estimate the dividends in the next three years will be $5, $7, and $4, respectively. The appropriate discount rate is 15%.
a. Calculate the stock's expected prices, P_1 and P_2, one and two years from now, as well as the current stock price, P_0.

b. Show that investors who plan to hold the stock one, two, or three years obtain the same value for P_0.
c. What will P_0 be if investors hold the stock indefinitely?

13.6 Next year's dividend is expected to be $d_1 = \$5$. The growth rate is 10% and the discount rate is 15%. What should the stock price, P_0, be?

13.7 A firm's policy is to distribute 40% of its earnings as dividends. The current EPS is $10. The discount rate is 10%.
a. What is the current share price, P_0, if the firm reinvests its retained earnings at 10%?
b. What is the P_0 if the firm reinvests retained earnings at 15%? At 5%?
c. Calculate P_0 if the retained earnings remain idle in the firm's balance sheet (that is, are not used).
d. What is the P_0 if the CFO uses all the retained earnings to buy a yacht?
e. Calculate the stock price, P_1, one year from now for each of the above four cases.

13.8 A firm pays out 50% of its earnings as dividends. The retained earnings are deposited in a bank at the riskless interest rate, $r = 5\%$. Will the firm's dividends grow? If so, what will be the growth rate?

13.9 A firm's EPS is currently $10 and it distributes 20% of those earnings as dividends. The firm reinvests the retained earnings at 15%.
a. Calculate the dividend growth rate, g.
b. What is the growth rate if the firm changes its dividend policy and distributes 60% of its earnings as dividends?
c. What is the current stock price in parts a and b if the discount rate is 15%?

d. How would you change your answer to part c if the discount rate were 10%? Contrast and explain your results to parts c and d.

13.10 A firm's expected annual earnings per share is $5. The firm pays out all of its earnings as dividends. The discount rate is 15%.
a. What is the stock price, P_0?
b. Suppose the riskless interest rate is 15%. Is the market in equilibrium? (*Hint:* The firm's earnings are uncertain.)
c. How would your answer to 13.10b change if the dividends were "certain" rather than "expected"?

13.11 Firms A and B are all-equity firms in the same industry; both have the same business risk. For both firms the expected dividend for next year is $1 per share, the discount rate is 10%, and the growth rate is 5%.
a. Calculate the current stock price for both firms.
b. Suppose Firm B issues more shares and increases its investment in zero-NPV projects. All projects have the same business risk and the firm does not plan to change the dividend/earnings ratio. How will this affect the discount rate, the dividend, the growth rate, and the current stock price? Discuss your results.

13.12 Two firms have the same current EPS of $10. Firm A pays out all of its earnings as dividends. Firm B pays out only 10% of its earnings as dividends and reinvests the retained earnings at 10%. How many years will it take for Firm B's dividend to become larger than Firm A's dividend?

13.13 In the early 1970s IBM's P/E ratio was about 50. How can you explain this high P/E ratio?

13.14 Suppose that you measure the profitability of investment in a stock by the IRR. Under what conditions does the reciprocal of the P/E ratio measure the IRR? Explain your answer.

13.15 Two stocks with P/E ratios of 11 and 15, respectively, are traded. Which is a better buy? Under what conditions, if any, might the stock with the larger P/E ratio be a better buy?

13.16 A firm's beta is 1.5. The market portfolio's expected rate of return is $\bar{R}_m$ = 15%. The riskless

interest rate is 5%. Next year's dividend will be d_1 = $5 and the constant dividend growth rate is 5%. The stock price is P_0 = $60. Is the stock located on the security market line?

13.17 You have the following information regarding Stocks A, B, and C:

Stock	Beta	Annual Dividend Growth Rate (%)	Next Year's Dividend, d_1 ($)
A	1	5	1
B	2	10	4
C	2.5	8	3

The market portfolio's mean rate of return is $\bar{R}_m$ = 15% and the riskless interest rate is r = 5%. The market is efficient and all stocks are located on the SML. Use this information to calculate the stock prices P_A, P_B, and P_C, and to plot the three stocks on the SML.

13.18 A stock's price behaves as follows:

Day	1	2	3	4	5
Price ($)	100	101	102	103	?

a. What is the estimated stock price on Day 5 if the price follows a random walk with an equal probability of changing by $1 or –$1?
b. Given the random walk feature described in 13.18a, what is the probability of obtaining the price series realized in the first four days?

13.19 Suppose a chartist who specializes in Xerox Corporation claims to have developed a buy-sell rule that will ensure an extraordinary profit. She makes a $5 profit on an investment of $100 after one month of trading.
a. The beta of Xerox stock is b = 3. The monthly mean rate of return on the market portfolio is $\bar{R}_m$ = 1% and the monthly riskless interest rate is r = 0.3%. Did the chartist make abnormal returns on Xerox?
b. Suppose the same results obtained for Xerox are obtained for the other 20 stocks the chartist selected during the year. Is the market efficient? Explain.

13.20 In October 1987 the stock market crashed. No significant new information was announced on that day. Does the crash contradict the notion of market efficiency? If so, why?

13.21 Eugene Fama and Kenneth French claim that investors in stocks of small firms and firms with low market-to-book-value ratios earn abnormal (or excess) returns.[10] Which forms of market efficiency are negated by evidence of this type? Explain how you would use the SML to determine whether such a strategy of buying such stocks might yield an abnormal return.

13.22 Textile South pays a dividend of $10 per share and is expected to continue to pay $10 per share in the future. However, the firm also pays a 5% stock dividend every year. A *stock dividend* does not involve a cash transfer; rather, it is a payment in the form of additional shares of stock. For example, if you hold 100 shares and the firm pays a 5% stock dividend, you will receive five of the firm's shares, giving you a total of 105 shares. The firm's cost of equity is $k = 12\%$. What should the stock price be?

13.23 Happy Mill pays a $10 dividend per share. The expected growth rate in the dividend per share is 15%. The expected annual inflation rate is 10%. The current stock price is $75. What are the stock's nominal and real expected rates of return?

13.24 Using the CAPM to estimate the cost of equity, we have

$$k_e = r + (\overline{R}_m - r)b$$

Using the CDGM to estimate the cost of equity, we have

$$k_e = \frac{d_1}{P_0} + g$$

"Because the CAPM estimate depends on the interest rate and the constant dividend growth model does not, the two methods will yield different results." Evaluate and discuss this claim.

13.25 The following chart taken from *Fortune* magazine shows that when the S&P 500 P/E ratio and the yield on bonds are low, investors should favor stocks. When those measures are high, bonds should be preferred.

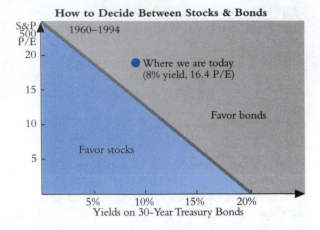

How to Decide Between Stocks & Bonds

This model suggests that when bond yields are 8%, the stock market deserves a P/E of 14. With stocks now at 16.4, bonds appear to be a better buy.

a. Explain in your own words the investment strategy recommended by the *Fortune* chart.
b. Suppose the yield on 30-year Treasury bonds increases from 8% to 10% with no change in the earnings of the companies listed on the S&P 500. By approximately how much do you expect the S&P index to fall if the intersection of P/E ratio and yield lies exactly on the line in the chart?
c. Assume investors select their investment using the above chart. Do you think the point at which yield = 8% and P/E = 16.4 can remain in equilibrium?

INTERNET QUESTION

13.26 The American Association of Individual Investors has assembled a list of stock-picking techniques that "stand the test of time." Given what you now know, what is your opinion of these techniques? http://www.aaii.com

---

10. Eugene Fama and Kenneth French, "The Cross-Section of Expected Stock Returns," *Journal of Finance* 47 (1992): 427–465.

YOUR TURN: APPLYING THEORY TO PRACTICE
STOCK VALUATION, INFLATION, AND STOCK MULTIPLIERS

LYNCH TIES BULL MARKET TO NORMAL EARNINGS

NEW YORK—The stock market has been flashing warning signals since last year. But Peter Lynch says a little math will go a long way toward soothing nervous investors.

Lynch, the former manager of Fidelity's Magellan fund, is famous for his practical approach to investing. He briefly roiled the market Tuesday when reports incorrectly had him predicting an imminent decline in stock prices. In fact, he says, there is a strong case for stocks moving higher. And even some bears say they can't argue with his reasoning.

Simply, Lynch says a 15% increase in revenue over two years coupled with a return to normal earnings would produce earnings gains of more than 50% over these years. If at the same time the basic measure of stock prices relative to earnings—the price-earnings ratio, or P/E—shrank to a normal level, the Dow Jones industrial average still would shoot to 4300 from 3512 Wednesday.

"I hope he's right," Arnold Kaufman, editor of Standard & Poor's *Outlook*, says. "My guess is the next big move is down. But (his scenario) is conceivable. In this economy, his assumptions are reasonable." Here's how the math works:

Over two years, corporate revenue rises roughly 15%—5% more sales and 2% higher prices this year, 5% more sales and 3% higher prices next year. Those price increases easily are in line with expected inflation. The sales increases are conservative in an economy that is growing.

Using those numbers, a company with $100 million in revenue would grow to $115 million. At last year's average 3.1% net profit margin, net income would grow 15% from $3.1 million to just less than $3.6 million. That likely would have something less than a spectacular impact on stocks. But if the profit margin improved to 4.3%,

which is the average for the industrial stocks since 1980, net income would improve to nearly $5 million—a 60% pop that, if repeated throughout the market, would at least sustain stock prices where they are and probably fuel a rise.

Here's why: That kind of earnings gain would drive down the price-earnings ratio of the S&P 500, based on trailing 12-month earnings, from 23 today to 14.5—assuming no change in stock prices. That would leave plenty of room for the P/E to rise to a fairly typical 17 or 18 and for stocks to go up accordingly 10% or more each of the next two years. "People don't understand how low profits are right now," Lynch says. "You don't have to get the best earnings ever. You just need normal earnings."

Lynch cautions that he is not predicting a rally any more than he predicted a rout early this week. But he says investors focusing on low interest rates are looking in the wrong place. "That's an old story," Lynch says of the money fleeing low-yielding bank deposits for stocks. "Earnings are the key to being bullish now."

Speaking of rates: Lehman Bros. strategist Elaine Garzarelli, a famous bull, pegs fair value of the Dow at 4316 by the end of 1994—remarkably close to the Lynch scenario outlined above. She tracks interest rates and says a P/E of 17.8 is just right. The rates on three-month Treasury bills have been edging higher lately. But at Wednesday's 3.11%, they still are well below the 3.77% she flags as a trouble spot.

Epilogue: The Dow-Jones Average rose from 3516 in June 1993 (the date of the article) to 3834 in December 1994, 5117 in December 1995, and 6442 in January 1997. The 12-month earnings rose by 73% from June to December 1993, by 75% in 1993, by 21% in 1994, and by 9% from December 1994 to September 1995. The P/E ratio was about 17 in early 1997. Here, Mr. Lynch was right in his predictions. Moreover, he even

Back to Normal?

Net profit margins of S&P 400 companies plunged to the lowest in 30 years in 1991. A return to normal margins of about 4.5% could propel stocks higher.

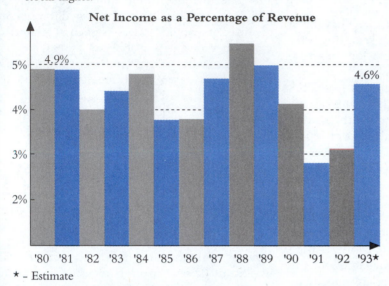

Net Income as a Percentage of Revenue

★ – Estimate

underestimated the growth rates of earnings and of the Dow-Jones Industrial Average.

Source: "Lynch Ties Bull Market to Normal Earnings," *USA Today*, 10 June 1993, p. 3B. Copyright 1993, USA TODAY. Reprinted with permission.

Questions

1. Discuss the pros and cons of the P/E ratio as a measure of future profit. How does it compare with the $k_e = d_1/P_0 + g$ measure? Which is better? Why? Do you think the P/E ratio is a better proxy for individual firms' true profitability or for the whole industry's average profitability?

2. Give the detailed calculation of how Peter Lynch derived the 4300 figure for the Dow Jones Index.

3. Lynch claimed that money fleeing low-yielding bank deposits for stocks is an old story. "Earnings are the key to being bullish now."

a. Explain why low interest rates might stimulate a bullish market.

b. Explain why high earnings might stimulate a bullish market.

4. Suppose net income had grown as predicted and the net profit margin also grows, reaching stability at 4.3%. Revenue will also be stable after two years of growth. The average stock price is $54 and the average EPS is $3; the P/E ratio is 18. On average the firm pays 60% of its earnings as dividends and the average growth rate of the EPS is 7%. Calculate the firm's expected rate of return on equity.

5. Assume the interest rate decreases from 5% to 3%. As a result, the market portfolio's required rate of return, $\bar{R}_m$, decreases from 12% to 10%.

Three stocks have the following characteristics:

Stock	Beta ($)	Dividend Growth Rate (%)	Next Year's Dividend
A	5	4	½
B	5	6	1
C	5	8	2

Use the CAPM and the CDGM to calculate the stock prices before and after the interest rate decrease. Do your findings explain the concept of money fleeing from low-yielding bank deposits to the stock market?

6. How would your results to Question 5 change if $\bar{R}_m$ decreased from 12% to 11%?

Appendix 13A   A Valuation Formula for Supergrowth Stocks

Suppose the dividend at the end of the first year is d_1, that the dividend experiences supergrowth at g_1 for the next n years, and from then on, grows at g_2 (normal growth). The dividends in this case are given as follows:

End of year	1	2	3	$\cdots$	n
Dividends	d_1	$d_1(1 + g_1)$	$d_1(1 + g_1)^2$	$\cdots$	$d_1(1 + g_1)^{n-1}$

Supergrowth period

End of year	$n + 1$	$n + 2$	$n + 3 \ldots$
Dividends	d_{n+1}	$d_{n+1}(1 + g_2)$	$d_{n+1}(1 + g_2)^2 \ldots$

Normal-growth period

Note that d_{n+1} is the same as $d_1(1 + g_1)^n$; that is, the dividend increases at an annual growth rate of g_1 for n years and then at an annual growth rate of g_2.

To calculate the present value of the first n terms, we use the growing annuity formula (from Chapter 4) as follows:

$$PV_{\text{growing annuity}} = \frac{d_1}{k - g_1}\left[1 - \frac{(1 - g_1)^n}{(1 - k)^n}\right]$$

The PV of the dividends corresponding to the normal-growth period is given by

$$\frac{d_{n+1}}{(1 + k_e)^{n+1}} + \frac{d_{n+1}(1 + g_2)}{(1 + k_e)^{n+2}} + \frac{d_{n+1}(1 + g_2)^2}{(1 + k_e)^{n+3}} \cdots$$

$$= \frac{1}{(1 + k_e)^n}\left[\frac{d_{n+1}}{1 + k_e} + \frac{d_{n+1}(1 + g_2)}{(1 + k_e)^2} + \frac{d_{n+1}(1 + g_2)^2}{(1 + k_e)^3} \cdots +\right]$$

Using the formula for a growing perpetuity (see Chapter 4), we obtain the following:

$$PV_{\text{perpetuity}} = \frac{1}{(1 + k)^n} \frac{d_{n+1}}{k - g_2}$$

Combining these two PV components and recalling that $d_{n+1} = d_1(1 + g_1)^n$, we get

$$P_0 = \frac{d_1}{k_e - g_1}\left[1 - \frac{(1 + g_1)^n}{(1 + k_e)^n}\right] + \frac{1}{(1 + k_e)^n} \frac{d_1(1 + g_1)^n}{k - g_2}$$

This is the valuation formula for a stock with supergrowth for n years and normal growth thereafter.

Finally, note that if $g_1 = g_2$, Equation (13.8) reduces to the constant dividend growth formula given by Equation (13.6).

APPENDIX REVIEW AND PRACTICE

13A.1 Next year's dividend per share will be $1, and the growth rate will be $g_1 = 20\%$ for five years. Thereafter, the growth rate will be $g_2 = 5\%$ each year. The discount rate is 10%.
a. Calculate the current market price of the stock.
b. What would be the current price if g_1 lasted for 20 years rather than for 5 years?

13A.2 Assume a stock pays a dividend of $d_1 = \$1$ at the end of the first year, and thereafter the dividend grows at 20% a year for the next n years. From year $n + 1$ on the dividend grows at only 5% a year. The cost of equity is 10%. Prepare a table showing the stock's value as a function of 20% supergrowth for n years. Solve for the stock's value under the following alternate assumptions: $n = 1, 2, 5, 10,$ and 20.

13A.3 Show that when $g_1 = g_2$, Equation (13.8) reduces to the formula for constant dividend growth [Equation (13.6)].

Appendix 13B   Estimating the Dividend Growth Rate in Practice

Suppose a firm pays a dividend amounting to d_t per share in year t. The growth rate of dividends can be estimated in several ways:

1. Review the firm's past dividends and make a subjective estimate based on available information regarding the firm's future operations.
2. Compute the ratio $d_t/d_{t-1} = 1 + g_t$ for each year over, say, the last 10 years and then use the average value of g as an estimate of the future growth rate.
3. If there is a constant growth rate, we have

$$d_n = d_1 (1 + g)^{n-1}$$

where 1 is the first year and n is the number of years of constant dividend growth. Then

$$g = (d_n/d_1)^{1/(n-1)} - 1$$

is the annual growth rate estimate for the n years.

4. Use a regression technique. The dividends in Year t and Year 1 are related as follows:

$$d_t = d_1 (1 + g)^{t-1}$$

Take the logarithm of both sides:

$$\log d_t = \log d_1 + (t - 1) \log (1 + g)$$

This is a linear relationship and we can use a standard regression technique to estimate $\log (1 + g)$, which is the slope of the line. From this value, we can isolate g.

Each of the four methods has its pros and cons. Method 1 is subjective and less scientific than the other methods. However, the opinion of experts is sometimes better than past data because experts may be able to extract information about future dividends from past data. Method 3 relies on two extreme values, d_n and d_1, and may be misleading. Methods 2 and 4 seem to be the best for stable firms—namely, for firms where the past is expected, more or less, to repeat itself in the future. However, if the firm's growth changes drastically (as happened with IBM in the early 1990s), the past will represent a completely irrelevant period. In such cases, Method 1 is recommended.

Appendix 13C   Using E/P as the Cost of Equity for a Normal-Growth Firm

A normal-growth firm is one that accepts projects with zero NPVs. For such project IRR equals the cost of equity, k_e. In this appendix we show that E/P does indeed measure k_e even if the last reported EPS does not represent future cash flow to stockholders. We assume the stock is evaluated at the end of the year, so that E is known.

The following notation will be useful:

P_0 = the current stock price. The stock is assumed to be fully priced, so that P_0 equals the PV of all future dividends.

E = last year's earnings per share.

w = the proportion of earnings the firm retains. Therefore, the current dividend per share is $d = (1 - w)E$.

R = the IRR on the retained earnings that the firm invests.

We assume that all cash flows from the investment are perpetuities.

At the end of each year, the firm pays out a constant proportion of its earnings as dividends. Next year's dividend will be $d_1 = (1 - w)E_1$ where E_1 is next year's earnings per share.

But $E_1 = E + wER$ because wER is the additional earnings due to the reinvestment of wE at the beginning of the first year. Therefore, $d_1 = (1 - w)E(1 + wR)$. Similarly, the second year's EPS is $E_2 = E_1 + wE_1R = E(1 + wR)^2$. The dividend in the second year is $d_2 = (1 - w)E_2 = (1 - w)E(1 + wR)^2$.

We continue this process to determine that each year's dividend is $(1 + wR)$ times the previous year's dividend. Therefore, by the DCF principle:

$$P_0 = \frac{(1 - w)E(1 + wR)}{1 + k_e} + \frac{(1 - w)E(1 + wR)^2}{(1 + k_e)^2} + \ldots$$

where E is current earnings per share. Using Chapter 4's formula for a growing perpetuity, we have

$$P_0 = \frac{(1 - w)E}{k_e - wR} \quad \text{or} \quad k_e = \frac{(1 - w)E}{P_0} + wR$$

where wR is the dividend growth rate, commonly denoted by g.

For a normal-growth firm, $R = k_e$. Substituting, we find that for normal-growth firms:

$$P_0 = \frac{(1 - w)E}{k_e - wk_e} = \frac{(1 - w)E}{(1 - w)k_e} \quad \text{so} \quad k_e = \frac{E}{P_0}$$

E/P_0 measures a normal–growth firm's cost of equity as suggested by the DCF principle—this explains the popularity of the P/E ratio even if it is not directly based on the discounted cash flow model.

For supergrowth firms with positive NPVs projects, $R > k_e$, and we have

$$\frac{E}{P_0} = \frac{k_e - wR}{1 - w} < k_e \quad \text{(because } R > k_e\text{)}$$

E/P_0 underestimates a supergrowth firm's cost of equity.

CHAPTER 14

GOING PUBLIC: WHY AND HOW?

LEARNING OBJECTIVES

*After reading this chapter,
you should understand:*

1. Why a firm decides to go public.

2. How a new issue of stock affects a firm's equity account.

3. The types of securities that a firm can issue to raise money and the rights of its stockholders and bond-holders.

4. The investment bank's role in preparing and underwriting a new issue.

5. Why an initial public offering (IPO) is difficult to price.

6. How a rights offering works.

7. Flotation costs and their effect on the firm's cost of capital.

CORPORATE FINANCE IN THE NEWS

GOING PUBLIC: MONDAVI WINERY

Robert Mondavi began to worry when his knees could no longer support him after a lifetime in the vineyards and on the road . . . .

Surgically implanted artificial joints have restored Mondavi's stride. At 80, he is astonishingly fit, a living testimony to what he calls the "healthful benefits of wine." Far less clear these days is the condition of the wine empire he built with sons Michael, 50, and Tim, 41.

After selling stock to the public in June, the Mondavis raised the cash to pay off a big chunk of their $126 million debt and replant vineyards ravaged by phylloxera, a bug eating its way through the roots of California's grapevines . . . .

The family spent three years agonizing over whether to go public—a process that brought Tim, the wine-maker, and Michael, the company's marketing chief, much closer, their father says. The Mondavis had hoped to raise $53.65 million by selling 3.7 million shares at $14.50 each. Instead, they got about $50 million—$34 million for Robert Mondavi Corp. And $12.5 million for the family, after expenses. They kept 72% ownership of the company and 95% voting control, leaving room to settle Robert's estate by selling more shares without giving up control. Mondavi says the deal will keep the winery in the family for three or four more generations.

Source: James Cox, "Toast of the Wine Industry," *USA Today*, 23 July 1993, pp. 1B–2B. Copyright 1993, USA TODAY. Reprinted with permission.

14.1 INTRODUCTION

When it decides to sell stock to the public for the first time, we say a firm is "going public." In this chapter we discuss the reasons why a firm may decide to go public, the various types of securities that a firm can issue to raise money for its operations, the procedures involved in issuing such securities, and the effect of the flotation costs on the firm's cost of capital.

Like the Mondavi Winery, most firms that go public in the United States begin as relatively small businesses or family firms. These firms are generally "closely held," which means that a small group of people, often family members, hold the shares. As partnerships or small-scale proprietorships, such firms are limited to raising money from family members or from partners in the firm or to borrowing from banks to finance their operations. The names of these firms will not be listed on the New York Stock Exchange or on any other major stock exchange. However, at some stage of their economic lives, they may decide to go public by selling stock to the public to raise money. These firms have various reasons to go public: ambitious growth plans, cashing in on success, or financial distress.

For an example of ambitious growth, suppose a relatively small private firm is considering a very large project that requires an initial investment of $100 million. Such a firm is unlikely to have this amount of money at its disposal, nor can it realistically hope to raise such a sum from family or other private resources. By issuing stock, though, the firm can recruit a large number of investors and produce the needed cash. This firm's main reason for going public is its desire to undertake a project requiring a large investment. Although the firm could finance the large project by issuing bonds or taking out a bank loan, debt financing would increase its risk of bankruptcy. Therefore, equity financing may be more appropriate for the firm.

A firm that goes public generally explains to potential investors how it intends to use the proceeds from the stock issue. This information may explain the firm's reasons for going public. Connecting Theory to Practice 14.1, for example, reveals that Redhook Ale Brewing went public in 1995 with the goal of being number one in the brewing industry.

CONNECTING THEORY TO PRACTICE 14.1
GOING PUBLIC: REDHOOK ALE BREWERY

. . . So it was that a 14-year-old Seattle outfit named Redhook Ale Brewery, which makes Redhook Extra Special Bitter, Ballard Bitter India Pale Ale, and a host of other brands, last month discovered a thirsty audience on Wall Street. Redhook's initial public offering, priced at $17 a share on August 16, opened at 27 the following day. The stock shot up to 35 in the next several days before settling back last week to close at 33¼, giving the company's 8.6 million shares a market cap of $285 million.

BUDDING RELATIONSHIP

Redhook has allocated all offering proceeds to reducing debt for prior plant expansion and for new additions. And it has ambitious growth plans. Using a 10-month-old alliance with Anheuser-Busch, the nation's biggest beer producer, one of its largest distributors and the new owner of some 25% of Redhook (another 10% is owned by GE Capital and 23% by executives and directors), the company aims to become the nation's largest craft brewer. It would thus unseat Boston Beer, whose sales of Samuel Adams brews climbed to $115 million in 1994 . . . .

Source: Thomas N. Cochran and Leslie P. Norton, "Frothy Brews," *Barron's* (September 4, 1995): 30. Reprinted by permission of *Barron's,* © 1995 Dow Jones & Company, Inc. All Rights Reserved Worldwide.

MAKING THE CONNECTION

Redhook Ale Brewery used its stock proceeds to reduce its debt for prior plant expansion and for new additions. Going public enabled it to pursue its goal of becoming the nation's largest craft brewer. Stockholders showed confidence in the brewery's ability to grow, causing the stock price to more than double in just two days!

A small firm may also go public to cash in on the success it has already achieved. Consider the case of a small, family-owned firm with an herbal remedy that may have cancer-fighting properties. The owners may decide to go public in the hope of selling the firm's stock at a relatively high price and earning a high return on its R&D investment. Suppose each share was estimated to be worth $10 before the firm discovered the new remedy. (Only after a firm goes public will the market determine the precise stock price.) After announcing the lab results on the herbal remedy, the firm may be able to sell each share for $50. By selling shares at $50, the owners will realize a sizable profit. Or, the owners may decide not to go public and to produce and market the new remedy on their own. If the owners' specialization is mainly in research and development, they will fare better by going public and forging ahead to discover more new products in their area of expertise.

Another reason why a firm goes public is financial distress, such as heavy debt or damage to a source of income as at the Mondavi vineyards. Apart from Mondavi Winery's financial stress, its founder had turned 80, and new management was needed.

14.2 THE STOCKHOLDERS' EQUITY ACCOUNT

A new stock issue usually affects the firm's earnings per share. The direction and the magnitude of the effect will depend on the new issue's price and how effectively the firm uses the proceeds. Let us consider how a new issue affects the stockholders' equity account, the EPS, and the dividends per share (DPS).

The firm lists the proceeds from the sale of stock as two separate items on its balance sheet: *par value* and **capital surplus.**[1] A security's par value is its face value. Par value is very important for bonds and preferred stocks because interest and preferred dividends are calculated based on par value. For example, an 8% preferred stock with a par value of $1,000 pays $80 per share in dividends. Less important with common stocks, par value is used to calculate common stock value as it appears in the firm's balance sheet. Most states prohibit a firm from distributing the par value to stockholders except upon liquidation. On the other hand, a firm can distribute its capital surplus to stockholders in the form of a cash dividend. If a stock's price is higher than its par value, we say the stock is being sold at a *premium*. The amount of capital surplus is the premium that the stock purchasers pay.

When a firm issues equity, a distinction is made between the stock's par value and the market value. For example, suppose Band Group, Inc. has been authorized to issue 100 million shares with a par value of $1. In 1993, the firm sells 50 million shares at their $1 par value. In 1994, after a successful and profitable year, the firm offers 10 million more shares for sale to the public at $2 a share; in 1997 the firm sells an additional 10 million shares at $3 a share. Of 100 million authorized shares, Band Group sells 70 million to the public. The firm's equity may change due to new issues of stock and retained earnings (or losses). A firm's **equity account** describes the changes in the firm's equity over the years and the various factors contributing to these changes. Band Group's earnings and dividends are reported in Part A of Table 14–1; its equity account, in Part B.

Let us analyze the information provided in Table 14–1. Assume Band Group had no retained earnings up to 1993 when its earnings were $10 million. Of this amount, Band Group distributed $5 million as cash dividends, and kept $5 million in the firm as retained earnings. In 1994 the firm retained an additional $7 million ($15 million − $8 million), thereby accumulating $12 million in the form of retained earnings. A firm's retained earnings will either grow or decline over the years, depending on the success of its operations.

The other source of growth in the firm's equity stems from new issues of common stock. This source is divided into the two components we already mentioned briefly: the stock's par value and the capital surplus. For example, in 1993 Band Group sold $50 million shares. There was no capital surplus. Thus, we know that there was no premium—the shares were sold at their par value. In 1994, the number of shares already issued was 60 million; this means that Band Group sold 10 million additional shares that year to the public at double their par value (i.e., at $2 per share). The premium (or additional capital surplus) in 1994 is calculated as $10 million [10 million shares × ($2 − $1) = $10 million].

Similarly, the additional capital surplus that the 1997 stock issue contributed is calculated as $20 million [10 million shares × ($3 − $1) = $20 million]. Therefore, the total accumulated capital surplus in 1997 is $30 million ($10 million + $20 million = $30 million).

---

1. A firm often lists capital surplus as *additional paid-in capital* on its balance sheet.

TABLE 14–1
Band Group, Inc., 1993–1997

Part A: Earnings and Dividends

Year	1997	1996	1995	1994	1993
Earnings (in $ million)	15	20	20	15	10
Dividends (in $ million)	8	10	12	8	5

Part B: Equity Account

Year	1997	1996	1995	1994	1993
(1) Common stock at par value (100 million authorized shares) ($ million)	70	60	60	60	50
(2) Retained earnings ($ million)	37	30	20	12	5
(3) Capital surplus (or additional paid-in capital) ($ million)	30	10	10	10	0
(4) Total common stockholders' equity ($ million) [= (1) + (2) + (3)]	137	100	90	82	55
(5) Number of shares issued (millions)	70	60	60	60	50
(6) Book value per share ($ per share) = Total equity/Number of shares outstanding [= (4)/(5)]	1.96	1.67	1.50	1.37	1.1

The total common stockholders' equity is the sum of the values of the common stock issued at par, the retained earnings, and the capital surplus. Total common stockholders' equity divided by the number of outstanding shares provides the **book value per share.** Because book value per share is based on historical costs rather than on market values, it might not seem meaningful. However, professional investors and financial analysts do examine it. If the ratio of book value per share to market value per share ratio is relatively high, they will consider the firm underpriced and a possible candidate for takeover. If this ratio is relatively low, practitioners claim that a stock price decrease is likely.

14.3 THE LEGAL RIGHTS OF STOCKHOLDERS

We've said throughout this book that stockholders own the firms in which they hold shares. Here, we review what rights of ownership stockholders have: to receive any dividends the firm declares; to vote on other important matters such as mergers; to vote for the firm's board of directors; and to sell their ownership at a fair market price. These rights vary somewhat, depending on whether the firm has issued more than one type of common stock. While preferred shares convey the right to a pre-determined dividend, they generally involve no voting rights. Most preferred stock is *cumulative*; that is, if for some reason the firm does not pay dividends in a given year, the dividends accumulate and the firm must pay them before any common dividends. *Participating preferred stock* entitles the owner to a share of the firm's profit over and above the predetermined dividend paid to common shareholders.

14.3.1 When There Is One Type of Common Stock

Most firms offer only one type of common stock, with all stockholders entitled to the same dividend and the same voting rights per share and to the right to sell their shares.

DIVIDEND RIGHTS

After the firm has paid its creditors and met its other financial obligations, the board of directors decides what portion of the firm's profit for the year will be distributed to stockholders in the form of dividends. As we saw in earlier chapters, dividends may be in the form of cash payments or additional stock, although cash payments are more usual. The firm makes the dividend distribution on a per-share basis to the common stockholders.

VOTING RIGHTS

When a firm issues only one type of common stock, all shareholders have voting rights. Typically, each share of stock has one vote. With their votes stockholders make decisions affecting the firm's management and elect the board of directors, who elect the firm's officers including, most importantly, the firm's CEO. The election of directors takes place annually at the general stockholders' meeting. Although stockholders can vote in person, they usually transfer their voting rights to other parties by a procedure known as **proxy,** and these other parties may vote as they wish. If stockholders are unhappy with the firm's management and if they succeed in accumulating a large enough number of proxies, they can replace the board, the CEO and any other top officer. This is known as a *proxy fight*.

Directors are generally elected for three years with one-third of them replaced every year. The firm's directors or, in the case of a takeover, the new directors, can directly replace the CEO. Generally holding a very small proportion of the votes, the CEO will usually do all that is in his or her power to stay in office. For instance, the CEO may succeed in having the board of directors pass a resolution making takeovers more difficult. Or, a CEO may propose a rule requiring 75% rather than 51% of the votes to approve a merger.

The most famous technique used to protect the firm (and its management) is a **poison pill provision.** We all know about the cyanide pill that secret agents in spy movies are supposed to swallow to avoid being captured alive. Firms use a similar idea. To avoid being captured in a takeover, the firm may offer some of its existing stockholders and bondholders the right to purchase stock at a sizable discount in the event of a takeover; this will dilute the firm's value for those who might be trying to acquire it and will reduce the chance of a takeover.

Any measure a firm takes to make it less attractive to an acquirer is called a poison pill. For example, if a stock's price is $100, the poison pill provision might stipulate that if any given investor holds more than 25% of the firm's shares, the firm's bondholders will have the right to buy the firm's shares at $40. Anyone who tries to acquire the firm at $100 per share will be at a considerable disadvantage, and the takeover may be avoided. In that case the stockholders lose and the bondholders gain.

Stockholders are not necessarily "poisoned" by such antitakeover strategies. For example, in 1993 Dr. Pepper/Seven Up Corp. fought Cadbury Schweppes' takeover attempt by adopting the following strategy: If Cadbury obtained 26% or more of Dr. Pepper's outstanding shares, Dr. Pepper would offer its shareholders—except for Cadbury—the right to acquire additional shares at a 50% discount. This kind of strategy does not hurt existing stockholders but does make the firm less attractive as a takeover target. Poison pills do not always prevent a takeover. In some cases, the acquiring firm is willing to "swallow" the poison pill in order to complete the acquisition. In other cases, the acquiring firm may raise its bid until agreement is reached. For example, Cadbury Schweppes eventually paid $1.7 billion to purchase Dr. Pepper in 1995.

Poison pill provisions may protect the firm's management from a takeover. However, if the CEO's action is not in the stockholders' best interest or if the firm sustained poor performance, stockholders generally pressure the directors to replace the CEO. For instance, when General Motors and IBM found themselves deeply in the red in the early 1990s, the CEOs of these two corporate giants had no option but to resign. Kmart's CEO also had to resign as chairperson in 1995 for similar reasons, as did Apple's in 1996. Connecting Theory to Practice 14.2 provides an example of how directors who are expected to act in stockholders' best interest, can respond to bad management.

CONNECTING THEORY TO PRACTICE 14.2

KODAK SEEKS OUTSIDER TO BE CHAIRMAN, CEO

SEARCH FOR SAVVY MARKETER, COST CUTTER FOLLOWS DISMISSAL OF WHITMORE

Eastman Kodak Co. directors, who announced their ouster of Chairman and Chief Executive Officer Kay R. Whitmore Friday, are now searching for an outsider who won't need prodding to make massive cost cuts.

Although Mr. Whitmore won't step down until his successor is in place, Kodak stock surged $3.25, or 5.9%, on the news Friday, to close at $58.625 in heavy New York Stock Exchange composite trading.

The ouster took place at a special board meeting at Kodak headquarters July 23 but wasn't announced until Friday because Kodak said it needed time to communicate with customers, suppliers, and business partners. Mr. Whitmore declined to speak with reporters.

At the meeting, the nine outside directors asked Mr. Whitmore and the three other insiders to leave the room, and then voted unanimously to replace him. Board members said the vote was the culmination of years of frustration with Mr. Whitmore, who has been chairman and chief executive since June 1990 and was president for seven years before that. "We've been unanimous on this for two years," said director Roberto C. Goizueta, chairman of Coca-Cola Co. But the board said it delayed its decision, to give Mr. Whitmore a chance to turn the company around.

Source: Joan E. Rigdon and Joann S. Lublin, "Kodak Seeks Outsider to Be Chairman, CEO," *The Wall Street Journal,* 9 August 1993, p. A3. Reprinted by permission of *The Wall Street Journal,* © 1993 Dow Jones & Company, Inc. All Rights Reserved Worldwide.

MAKING THE CONNECTION

Kodak has 12 directors—3 insiders and 9 outsiders. The outsiders, who are not dependent on the CEO, could make the decision to oust him by themselves because they had a majority on the board. Thus, voting rights are very important, because it is the board of directors that directs the firm to act in the best interests of the stockholders.

RIGHT TO A FAIR TRADE IN THE STOCK

Finally, stockholders have the right to sell the stock they own at any time at a fair market price. Stockholders sometimes need protection to make sure that others, particularly insiders, do not manipulate the trade in stock. The **Securities and Exchange Commission (SEC)** is the governmental body responsible for enforcing the rules and regulations governing the trading in securities and for ensuring that a firm's stock is traded fairly. The federal regulations governing new securities issues are established in the Securities Act of 1933, and the Securities Act of 1934 regulates securities already being traded in the market. The SEC oversees the various organized stock exchanges in their daily trading activities. Any violation of trading rules involves penalties, and some violations are subject to fines. Other, more serious violations such as insider trading or using private information are punishable by more severe sentences such as imprisonment.

14.3.2 When There Is More Than One Type of Common Stock

We've said that most firms offer only one type of common stock, with all stockholders entitled to the same dividend and voting rights per share. However, owners of small firms that go public are usually interested in retaining control of the firm. They accomplish this by having the firm issue more than one class of stock. When a firm issues **classified common stock,** all stockholders are generally entitled to the same dividend per share but, depending on the class of share held, not to the same voting power. For example, the firm may attach voting rights to Class A stock but not to Class B stock. Class A shares that have voting rights are called *founder shares.* Alternatively, the firm may entitle holders of Class A stock to 10 votes per share and the holders of Class B stock to only 1 vote per share. In this way the owners can maintain control over the firm at a relatively small cost. Indeed, as seen in Corporate Finance in the News, the Mondavi family "kept 72% ownership of the company and 95% voting control" after going public. This allowed them to engage in estate planning by selling a relatively large number of shares without giving up control.

Most firms listed on the New York Stock Exchange offer only one class of common stock. However, in other countries—in Europe and Canada, for instance—stocks with differential voting rights are widespread. When there are two types of shares, each entitling the owner to the same dividends but different voting rights, the market price of stock with the inferior voting rights is usually lower than the price of stock with augmented voting rights. The percentage difference in the price of the two classes of stock is called the **voting right premium.**

Only in recent years has the New York Stock Exchange allowed listing of nonvoting stock. When General Motors acquired Hughes Aircraft, it paid for the purchase by issuing Class H stock (denoting it "GMH" to distinguish it from General Motors' stock, which is denoted "GM"). GMH stock is devoid of voting rights, and the level of GMH dividends is tied to Hughes Aircraft's performance. For example, on August 13, 1997, *Barron's* reported prices of $60¾ for GM, and $63⅝ for GMH.

Media moguls Steven Spielberg, Jeffrey Katzenberg, and David Geffen recently formed a business entity that planned to raise $900 million in a stock offering with an extreme profit–voting–capital-contribution structure. For 10% capital contribution, S.K.&G. will get 67% of the profit and 100% voting control.

14.4 THE LEGAL RIGHTS OF BONDHOLDERS

A firm can raise money by issuing stock, by issuing bonds, or by borrowing from a bank. When a firm issues bonds, it is actually borrowing money from the public or from investment institutions that buy the bonds.

Bondholders have no voting rights. However, they are entitled to interest and the principal as stated on the bond. Bondholders have *priority claim* on the firm's revenues in the sense that the firm must pay its contractual entitlements before it can pay any dividend to stockholders. For example, a $1,000 bond paying an annual coupon rate of 8% and maturing in the year 2005 entitles the bondholder to $80 each year and repayment of the $1,000 principal in 2005.

If the firm defaults on these payments, the bondholders have the right to demand that the firm initiate liquidation procedures. However, in practice a firm usually negotiates with its bondholders. About half of firms undergo a financial restructuring procedure involving a private agreement worked out with the bondholders. Most of the others complete a financial reorganization under Chapter 11 of the U.S. Bankruptcy Code. Thus, the firm's inability to pay interest or principal does not automatically lead to liquidation.[2] However, if the firm does liquidate its

---

2. For more details on financial restructuring, see Kose John and Larry N.P. Lang, "Troubled Debt Restructuring: An Empirical Study of Private Reorganization of Firms in Defaults," *Journal of Financial Economics* 27 (1990).

assets in a bankruptcy, it will use the proceeds to pay part or all of its obligations to the bondholders, who have a priority claim to those assets in the case of liquidation. Preferred stockholders are next in line. Only thereafter will the firm distribute the remaining proceeds from the liquidation among stockholders, if at all.

The various types of available bonds do not all have the same priority claim to the firm's assets in the case of financial distress. **Mortgage bonds,** for instance, are secured by specific assets that the firm owns. For example, a firm may issue $50 million mortgage bonds, with its Manhattan headquarters serving as mortgage. The **indenture** that delineates the agreement between the firm and the bondholders may specify a limit to the firm's future debt issues or may require the firm's equity-to-debt ratio be no smaller than, say, 2.5. The indenture may also restrict the firm regarding increased dividends to stockholders. The constraints written into the bonds' indentures are known as its **restrictive covenants.**

The firm may also issue *unsecured* bonds called **debentures** and **subordinated debentures.** Mortgage bonds are the most highly secured bonds; then come the debentures. Finally, the firm pays subordinated debentures only after it settles the other, senior bonds. Even the least secure bondholder has priority over stockholders in the case of a liquidation.

The market is aware of these differences in bond security. Therefore, the lower the bond's protection in case of bankruptcy, the higher the bond's yield-to-maturity.

14.5 PREPARING TO ISSUE SECURITIES

A firm wishing to raise money in the securities market must first decide what type of security (common stock, preferred stock, bonds) to issue. Its second decision concerns the size of the issue, which will be based on how much money the firm needs. Once the board of directors approves these decisions, the firm will select an **investment bank** and negotiate its role in the new issue. Investment banks play an important role in implementing a stock or bond issue. You are probably already familiar with the names of the largest U.S. investment banks: Merrill Lynch, Goldman Sachs, First Boston, Salomon Brothers, Lehman Brothers.

Once the issuing firm and the investment bank agree on the terms of the issue (size, type of security, and so on), they will prepare and file two documents with the Securities and Exchange Commission: a registration statement and a preliminary prospectus. The **registration statement** provides financial and legal information on the firm, and the **prospectus** summarizes this information for potential buyers of the security. The SEC's financial analysts, accountants, and lawyers then examine these documents to ensure that the information they contain is adequate and in no way misleading. The SEC normally takes 20 days to approve an issue. The twentieth day after filing with the SEC is considered the issue's *effective registration date*. If the SEC considers the information to be inadequate or misleading, it may delay or halt the public offering by sending a *letter of comment* that specifies the required changes. The time required for SEC approval is known as the *waiting period*, during which the firm can distribute a preliminary prospectus to potential buyers. The preliminary prospectus is commonly known as a *red herring* because of the bold red letters printed on its cover. While the firm can receive oral offers for its securities during the waiting period, it cannot sell them until the effective registration date.

The registration statement filed with the SEC does not quote an offering price for the new issue. Note that the par value, which is determined in the early stages of preparing the issue, is usually different from the offering price and is irrelevant in measuring the issue's success or failure. The **offering price,** the price at which the security is offered to the public, is usually determined toward the end of the waiting period. The new issue's success or failure is measured in terms of the security's market price relative to its offering price. If the firm succeeds in selling all of the planned issue at the offering price, the issue will be considered successful.

Near the end of the waiting period the firm files a price amendment, noting the offering price, and the registration becomes effective. Generally one day after the offering price is determined, the firm prepares a final prospectus, and selling efforts move full speed ahead. This does not mean that the firm makes no sales efforts before the effective date of registration. A firm generally advertises its public offering before that date by what is called the **tombstone.** Connecting Theory to Practice 14.3 illustrates such a tombstone, which is a frequent sight in the financial media.

CONNECTING THEORY TO PRACTICE 14.3

TOMBSTONE ANNOUNCEMENT OF A NEW STOCK ISSUE BY SECURITY CAPITAL U.S. REALTY

These securities have not been registered under the Securities Act of 1933 and may not be offered or sold in the United States except in accordance with the resale restrictions applicable thereto. These securities having been previously sold, this announcement appears as a matter of record only.

U.S. $300,000,000

SECURITY CAPITAL U.S. REALTY

Offering of
24,115,805 Shares

The undersigned acted as placing agents in connection with the offering of certain of these securities outside of the United States.

Goldman Sachs International
Commerzbank Aktiengesellschaft   **J.P. Morgan Securities Ltd.**

The undersigned acted as placing agents in connection with the offering of certain of these securities in the United States in private offerings under the Securities Act of 1933.

Goldman, Sachs & Co.
Commerzbank Capital Markets Corporation   **J.P. Morgan & Co.**

January 1997

Source: *The Economist* (18 January 1997): 72. Permission, Goldman, Sachs & Co.

Once it issues the securities, the firm can list them on a major exchange such as the New York Stock Exchange or the American Stock Exchange. Small firms may list the security on a regional exchange such as those located in Chicago, Philadelphia, Cincinnati, and Los Angeles. The exchange will list, for a modest fee, the stock price and other information about the firm in the news bulletin it publishes. Listing also serves to advertise the firm's stock.

Some firms consider the 20-day waiting period too long between filing with the SEC and offering the stock for sale. Changes in economic conditions during this period may adversely affect the stock price. To overcome this problem, many large firms file a **master registration statement** with the SEC and then update it with a **short-form statement** prior to each public offering. In this way the firm puts its stocks "on the shelf," so to speak, which is why this procedure is commonly called **shelf registration.** The firm then has the option of offering the securities for sale when it believes the time is right without waiting until the 20-day approval period.

14.6 THE ROLE OF THE INVESTMENT BANK

The investment bank may prepare the security issue and market it, or it can assume the risk of floating the issue. If it chooses to assume the risk, the investment bank is said to "underwrite the issue" and is termed an **underwriter.** Let us demonstrate the underwriter's role with a stock issue. (The scenario will be similar for other types of securities such as bonds and preferred stock.) For example, suppose the investment bank in its capacity as underwriter reaches an agreement with the firm to place a new stock issue on the market at an offering price of $100 per share. If at the effective registration date demand for the new issue is strong, investors will compete to pay more than $100 per share. The investment bank must still sell the stock at the agreed-upon offering price. However, the demand may be so weak that the underwriter can sell only part of the new issue. Suppose the stock's market price immediately after issue is $90 per share. Whoever assumes the risk of such an unsuccessful new issue depends on the agreement between the investment bank and the firm. There are two basic arrangements: best-efforts and firm-commitment.

Under a **best-efforts arrangement,** the investment bank helps market the new issue but does not guarantee the issue or assume risk. The investment bank will charge a fee of, say, $2 per share. If the stock is sold for $100 per share, the firm will receive $98 per share and the investment bank will receive the $2 difference, which is called the *spread*. However, the underwriter may be unable to sell the new issue at $100 per share as planned. In that case the firm will not receive all the cash proceeds it had planned.

Under a **firm-commitment arrangement,** the investment bank underwrites the issue and guarantees the firm a certain amount per share regardless of market price fluctuations. If it cannot sell the issue at $100 per share, the underwriter will purchase whatever shares it could not sell. An investment bank that assumes such risk will demand a larger spread. For example, suppose the investment bank guarantees the firm $95 per share. In this case the $5 spread may represent the $2 fee plus $3 as compensation for risk exposure. If the shares are sold at $100 each, the investment bank will receive the full $5. However, if it can sell the issue for only say, $80 a share, the investment bank transfers $95 per share to the firm (as agreed) and assumes the $15 difference (plus expenses) as a loss.

The issuing firm and the investment bank negotiate the offering price. If the issue is a best-efforts arrangement, no conflict of interest will exist between the two parties because the investment bank is not exposed to risk. However, if the issue is sold under a firm-commitment arrangement, the investment bank will want a relatively low offering price to decrease its chance of loss. The issuing firm will want the price as high as possible because, that will maximize its proceeds. Negotiations of this kind are not conducted in a vacuum. Valuation models as advocated in Chapter 13 are sometimes used to arrive at a "fair" price for the stock. In determining the offering price, both parties consider the firm's recent stock price and its fluctuations. If the issue is an initial public offering, the prices of similar stocks in the market are examined. The investment bank can protect itself against large losses by agreeing on the offering price as close as possible to the issuing date.

Even with such protection, the underwriter assumes real risk and sometimes incurs heavy losses. A classic example was IBM's $1 billion debt issue in 1979, the largest in U.S. corporate history. It involved $500 million of seven-year notes and $500 million of 25-year long-term bonds. The offering prices of the notes and bonds were determined on October 3; prices were fixed assuming the yield would be 9.62% on the notes and 9.41% on the bonds. Sales began one day later on October 4. However, changes that would affect the prices of the IBM debt occurred in the financial markets. On the afternoon of October 3, the yield on Treasury bonds increased. On October 6 the Federal Reserve Board announced an increase in the discount rate from 11% to 12% and an additional increase three days later. The price of IBM bonds and notes decreased, causing an increase in the yields to 10.65% on the notes and 10.09% on the bonds. About one-third of the $1 billion issue had to be sold at the lower price and higher yield. The underwriters who had guaranteed the prices suffered substantial losses. Investment banks know that even if the offering price is set as close as possible to the issuing date, underwriting can be very risky, and they charge a premium accordingly.

The difference between the gross proceeds and the net proceeds paid to the firm from security issues is the **flotation cost,** which is generally measured as a percentage of the gross proceeds. Flotation costs vary mainly as a function of the underwriter's risk exposure, which is determined by the following related variables:

1. *Type of security.* Flotation costs are relatively low for bonds and relatively high for common stocks, with preferred stocks in the middle.
2. *Risk of the security.* The greater the security's volatility, the larger the investment bank's risk, and the higher the flotation costs.
3. *State of the economy.* Since the chance of failure is larger in a recession than in an expanding economy, higher flotation costs are expected during an economic downturn.
4. *Size of the issue.* Such costs as prospectus and accounting preparation are fixed and independent of the issue's size. Consequently, flotation costs as a percentage of the gross proceeds will be relatively high for smaller issues. In addition, small firms typically float small issues. Since small firms are generally riskier than large firms, investment banks will usually demand a higher premium in underwriting the issues of small firms.

Flotation costs may reach 15% for bonds and up to 25% for stocks if the issue is relatively small (less than $1 million). For a large issue, say, $100 million or more, they are about 1% for bonds and 3% for common stock. Flotation costs can be quite substantial and should not be overlooked. In Section 14.9 we will see how these costs affect the firm's cost of capital.

In light of substantial flotation costs, why do firms pay investment banks to assume the risk of issuing a new security? The reason is that the consequences of pricing misjudgment, or the failure to sell an issue at the predetermined price, may have severe repercussions on the firm's continuing operations. For example, consider a firm that issues stock to fund new machinery. Before ordering the machinery, the firm may have to invest a certain amount of money to prepare for its installation (such as modifying its facilities or training employees). If the issue fails, the firm will have invested and lost these preparation costs. Instead, the firm may choose to shift the risk to an investment bank.

If the new issue's risk is large, the investment bank may form an **underwriting syndicate,** in which one investment bank initiates the deal and serves as the *lead* or *managing underwriter* and other investment banks join in to share the risk and profit of underwriting the new issue. Other banks may also join as part of the *selling group*, and their participation in the new public offering will be limited to marketing the issue. Besides spreading the new issue's risk, the syndicate will offer the new issue to their customers. An underwriting syndicate may also be formed when the issue is too large for one underwriter to handle, or when an issue is to be offered simultaneously in several markets that require specialized knowledge.

14.7 THE INITIAL PUBLIC OFFERING

When a firm first decides to go public, its first stock issue is an **initial public offering (IPO).**[3] Because no market price serves as a benchmark, the investment bank and the firm often have a tough task negotiating the offer price. Indeed, the margin of error can be quite large.

Sometimes, as in the case of Netscape's IPO, the underwriter and the firm's management underestimate demand for the firm's stock by a wide margin. Netscape's offering price was $28, but demand was such that the market price jumped to over $70 the same day. Two weeks later, the market price was $53¾, still way above the offering price. In an IPO if the owners sell all the firm's shares in one issue and grossly underestimate the market value, they lose money because they sell their shares at a relatively low price. However, Netscape's chairman offered only a relatively small fraction of the firm's stock in the IPO. Since he held many of the firm's shares, he made $500 million on the first day.[4] When a firm is unsure how the market will receive its IPO, it should begin with a relatively small IPO, see how the market reacts, let the market set the stock's price, and later issue more stock priced accordingly. As demonstrated in Applying Theory to Practice 14.1, not all negotiations with investment banks are successful.

http

Capital Markets, Inc., is an emerging cybercompany. Its specialty is IPOS. Virtually anything you want to know about IPOS is available at their Web site, including how to do a complete IPO over the Internet.
http://capmarkets. com/index.html

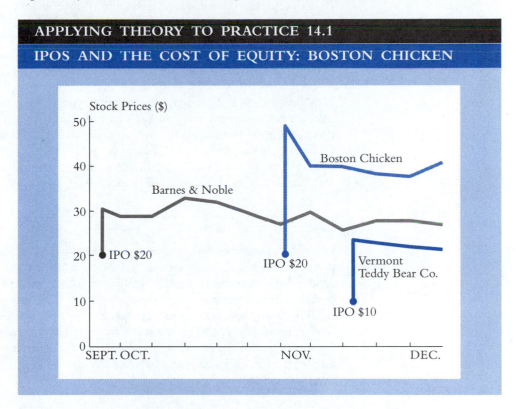

APPLYING THEORY TO PRACTICE 14.1

IPOS AND THE COST OF EQUITY: BOSTON CHICKEN

3. If the firm already has stock traded in the market, an additional stock issue is called a **seasoned new issue**.
4. A. E. S., "Further Fallout from Last Week's Nutty Netscape IPO," *Fortune* (4 September 1995): 21. © 1995, Time Inc. All rights reserved.

Is the initial public offerings market cooling off? Not yet, if the reception accorded Pactel Corp., a wireless communications spin-off from Pacific Telesis, is any indication. Issued on Dec. 6, Pactel Corp. climbed to $25.50 in its first day of trading, 11% above its $23 offering price. But is it a buy? Maybe not. Other recent IPOs, including Barnes & Noble, Boston Chicken, and Vermont Teddy Bear, all soared during their first day on the market, only to languish later.

Source: "How Three Hot IPOs Have Fared," *Business Week* (December 20, 1993): 33. Reprinted by special permission, © 1993 by The McGraw-Hill Companies, Inc.

Questions
Using the preceding figures and assuming a guaranteed price for the stock, analyze these IPOs with special emphasis on the following issues:

1. Were the negotiations with the investment banks successful for the firms?
2. Did the investment banks make money on these IPOs? Did investors in the IPOs make money?
3. Would you expect the same price behavior (i.e., a dramatic price increase on the offering date) on a seasoned new issue?
4. Boston Chicken's stock was offered to the public at $20 per share. Suppose the net proceeds to the firm amounted to $18 per share, and that the stock price on the first day of trade increased to about $50 and then stabilized at $40 per share. Assume Boston Chicken's cost of equity was 15% at $40 per share and the firm pays a cash dividend of $4 per share. Use the constant dividend growth model (CDGM) to calculate the firm's implied growth rate. Use the $4 dividend per share and the dividend growth rate that you have just determined to calculate the IPO's cost of equity. In other words, what is the minimum required rate of return from the projects in which Boston Chicken invested the proceeds from the IPO?
5. What strategy would you recommend for firms such as Boston Chicken to minimize their loss on mispriced IPOs?

MAKING THE CONNECTION

1. No, the negotiations most certainly were not successful for the firms. Suppose the investment banks guaranteed the firm $20 a share. If the new issue cannot be sold at this price, the investment banks will lose money. In these IPOs the new issue's market price jumped far above its offering price.

   The investment banks probably pushed for a relatively low selling price to minimize their risk. The lower the IPO's predetermined selling price, the lower the risk to the investment banks. If so, the firms lost money. For example, Boston Chicken could have sold its stock for at least $40 per share, but received only $20 per share.

2. The price behavior of these IPOs indicates that the investment banks suf-
    fered no losses on these issues; therefore, the risk premium that they charged
    represents their profit. Many investors who subscribed to the IPOs made a
    large amount of money in one day. However, not all investors could make
    such a high rate of return—the winners were only those to whom the in-
    vestment banks sold the stock by an agreement reached before the issuing
    date or before the investment bank decided how to allocate the new issue.

3. When a firm has a stock listed and already trading in the market, the
    chance of error in valuing the firm's new shares is very small. For example,
    on August 4, 1997, Ford Motor's stock was trading for $40\frac{5}{8}$. If Ford had
    chosen to issue new stock, the new issue would have sold at about $40\frac{5}{8}$,
    or a little less, to provide an incentive to potential buyers. Therefore, in the
    case of seasoned issues, we do not expect the type of price behavior we
    saw with the IPOs.

4. By the constant growth dividend model, the cost of equity is given by

$$k_e = \frac{d_1}{P_0} + g$$

Therefore,

$$\frac{d_1}{\$40} + g = \frac{\$4}{\$40} + g = 0.15$$

Solving for g, we get $g = 5\%$.

Currently, given the risk of the firm and a stock price of $40, the cost
of equity is 15%. If the firm obtains a lower price per share of $18 ($20 less
$2 flotation costs), it will have to earn more on its invested capital to meet
the 15% return required by stockholders. Let P denote the offering price
and F the flotation costs. Therefore, the firm's cost of equity at the lower
price per share is

$$\frac{d}{P - F} + g = \frac{\$4}{\$20 - \$2} + 0.05 = \frac{\$4}{\$18} + 0.05 \cong 0.2722 \ \text{ or } \ 27.22\%$$

Thus, to maintain the $4 dividend as well as the 5% dividend growth rate,
the firm will have to earn 27.22% on its investment rather than the 15%
obtained before.

5. If the firm's estimate of the value of the stock is much higher than the in-
    vestment bank's estimate, the best way for the firm's managers to prove that
    their estimate is right is to issue a relatively small IPO on the investment
    bank's terms. Then, after the stock price jumps say, to $40, the firm will
    offer another issue at, say, $38 per share. The cash inflow to the firm will

increase, the cost of equity will decrease, and the wealth of the existing stockholders will increase. For example, Netscape issued the IPO at $28 a share. At a price of $37⅝ on August 4, 1997, it could have on this date another seasoned issue for almost $37 a share.

14.8 THE RIGHTS OFFERING

When a corporation is about to issue additional stock, it is customary to offer the stock first to its existing shareholders at special rates; this is called a **rights offering.** In this arrangement, each shareholder is offered an option to buy a specified number of the new shares at a specified price within a specified time period. The price at which stockholders can buy the new shares is called the **subscription price.** Because the subscription price is generally far below the market price, it seems that stockholders benefit from the rights offering. This is not the case. Because the subscription price is at a discount, the price of the existing shares falls, so their total wealth is unaffected, as long as the stockholders either sell the rights or exercise them. Rights offerings have economic value, and if stockholders ignore them, their wealth will decrease. Let us elaborate. Stockholders have three alternative courses of action:

1. *Exercise the right to buy more shares.* This implies that stockholders will increase their investment in the firm. However, if they wish to, stockholders can sell some of the shares they already own, even one day later, to finance the new purchase. In this way stockholders can exercise the right without increasing their investment in the firm. Remember, however, that the sale of stocks will incur transaction costs.
2. *Trade the rights.* To obtain the economic benefit of the rights, stockholders can trade them in the market by selling them to other investors.
3. *Ignore the rights.* If they ignore the rights, stockholders forfeit the opportunity to make a profit on them and their wealth will decrease.

If they sell their rights, stockholders will decrease their ownership interest in the firm. In fact, one reason for the rights offering is to provide stockholders the opportunity to maintain their investment proportion.

We will show later that investors fare neither better nor worse by exercising their rights. They may choose to sell their shares rather than to exercise them, and equilibrium will be reached when the stock price is such that investors are indifferent between exercising the rights and selling them in the market.

Let's review how a rights offering works with an example. Intex, Inc. has 1 million shares trading at $30 per share. The firm would like to issue 500,000 more shares in a rights offering. For each two shares held, current shareholders will have the right to buy one new share at a subscription price of $20 a share. The stock price is expected to fall after the rights offering because the 500,000 shares are sold at the lower price. The average price is expected to decrease to:

$$\frac{\text{Total market value of equity}}{\text{Number of shares}} = \frac{(1,000,000 \times \$30) + (500,000 \times \$20)}{1,500,000}$$

$$= \frac{\$40,000,000}{1,500,000} \cong \$26.67$$

However, the decrease in price from $30 to $26.67 does not mean that the stockholders lose money. When they purchase shares in the rights offering, their wealth does not change. Before the transaction, each investor holding two shares had a wealth of $60 (2 × $30 = $60). After the transaction, the investor holds three shares, and his or her wealth is $80 (3 × $26.67 = $80). Because the investor paid the firm the subscription price of $20 for the new share, the wealth corresponding to the old investment (after deducting the new investment) is $60, as before. The investor fares neither better nor worse with the rights offering.

Rights detached from the shares may be sold separately in the stock market. The right's market price is quoted as "per right given to one share." In our example the investor can buy two rights,[5] add $20, and buy one share from the new issue. What is the right's value? Due to the rights offering, the price of each share decreases from $30 to $26.67. Because the investor fares neither better nor worse by the rights offering, the value of the right attached to each stock is $3.33 ($30 − $26.67 = $3.33).

The market price of a right attached to each stock should not deviate too much from this $3.33 figure. If the investor decides to sell the right in the market, his or her wealth will be $60[(2 × $26.67) + (2 × $3.33) = $60], which equals the value of two shares before the rights offering.

If the stockholder ignores the rights and lets them expire, his or her wealth after the expiration date will be reduced from $60 to $53.34 (2 × $26.67 = $53.34). Ignoring the rights offering is unwise.

What happens if the stock price falls below the subscription price? In our example, if the stock price falls below $20, the value of the right to buy the stock at $20 is zero.

Rights offerings are typically issued under a **standby underwriting arrangement,** whereby the investment bank guarantees the firm a certain price per share. The underwriter's risk exposure in a rights offering is relatively low, and the subscription price can be set low enough that the probability of the market price falling below that price is relatively small. Thus the underwriting fees for a rights offering are generally lower than those for a seasoned public offering and much lower than those for an IPO.

So far we have discussed public offerings and rights offerings. An alternative way of issuing securities is to sell them in large blocks to institutions, generally at some discount from the market price. This procedure, which requires no investment bank services, is a **private placement.** The firm can also sell the securities in an **auction,** although the proceeds from such a sale will be uncertain. Table 14-2 summarizes the various ways that securities can be issued.

---

5. The rights offering gives shareholders the right to buy one new share for each two shares of existing stock held.

TABLE 14-2		Various Arrangements Between Firms and Investment Banks	
Method of Issue	**Type**	**Description**	**Spread**
Public offering	Firm-commitment	The investment bank assumes risk	Large
	Best-efforts	The investment bank does not assume risk	Small
Rights offering	Direct offer	Direct offer is made to stockholders	Very small
	Standby offer	The investment bank assumes risk	Smaller than public issue but larger than direct offer
Shelf registration	With or without underwriting	Master registration statement is shelved with option of offering the security for sale at short notice	Small
Auction	No underwriting	The firm receives the best price in an auction	Small
Private placement	No underwriting	Securities are sold to institutions	Small

14.9 FLOTATION COSTS AND THE FIRM'S COST OF CAPITAL

Table 14-3 provides a breakdown of the components of flotation cost for registered issues of common stock. As we can see, flotation costs on a new issue can be substantial. Note that the flotation costs of bonds are generally smaller than those of stocks.

Do flotation costs affect the firm's cost of capital? Do they affect the investment decision? We will show in the next subsection that the higher the flotation costs as a proportion of a new issue's proceeds, the lower the firm's tendency to issue securities and to accept new projects.

Before we analyze how flotation costs affect the costs of debt and equity, recall that the firm uses the issue's proceeds to invest in projects. The cost of each component of the firm's capital is the minimum rate of return needed to create enough cash to pay the suppliers of funds (bondholders, stockholders, or both). The firm is generally financed by debt, equity and preferred stock. A project should be accepted only if the cash flow it creates is sufficient to cover the required rate of return by all these financing sources. In what follows we assume first a firm financed fully to one source (e.g., debt, equity) and then consider the combined effect in a firm financed by more than one source. For example, if bondholders require $k_d = 8\%$, then 8% is the cost of debt, and if a firm is fully financed by debt the project must earn at least that much to be accepted. In what follows we measure the cost of capital by the project's minimum required IRR.

TABLE 14-3   Issue Costs as a Percent of Proceeds for Registered Issues of Common Stock, 1971–1975

| Size of Issue ($ million) | General Underwritten Cash Offers | | | Underwritten Rights Issues | | | Nonunder- written Rights Issues |
	Underwriters' Compensation (percent of proceeds)	Other Expenses (%)	Total Cost (%)	Underwriters' Compensation (%)	Other Expenses (%)	Total Cost (%)	Total Cost (%)
Under 0.50	. . .	. . .	. . .	. . .	. . .	. . .	9.0
0.50–0.99	7.0	6.8	13.7	3.4	4.8	8.2	4.6
1.00–1.99	10.4	4.9	15.3	6.4	4.2	10.5	4.9
2.00–4.99	6.6	2.9	9.5	5.2	2.9	8.1	2.9
5.00–9.99	5.5	1.5	7.0	3.9	2.2	6.1	1.4
10.00–19.99	4.8	0.7	5.6	4.1	1.2	5.4	0.7
20.00–49.99	4.3	0.4	4.7	3.8	0.9	4.7	0.5
50.00–99.99	4.0	0.2	4.2	4.0	0.7	4.7	0.2
100–500.00	3.8	0.1	4.0	3.5	0.5	4.0	0.1
Average	5.0	1.2	6.2	4.3	1.7	6.1	2.5

Source: C. W. Smith, "Alternative Methods for Raising Capital Rights versus Underwritten Offerings," *Journal of Financial Economics* 5 (December 1977): 273–307, Table 1, p. 27.

14.9.1 Flotation Costs and the Cost of Debt

A firm that is fully financed by debt is considering a 10-year project with an IRR of 10%. Suppose the firm decides to finance this project by issuing bonds with a maturity of 10 years. (For simplicity assume certainty and zero taxes.) Should the firm accept the project? We have learned the yield to maturity is the cost of debt. If the interest rate paid to bondholders is 10%, the firm will pay exactly what it earns on the project and will be indifferent between accepting or rejecting the project.

Now suppose flotation costs amount to 5%. The yield to maturity is still 10%; bondholders demand this rate of return. In this case the firm's cost of debt will be greater than 10%. For every $1,000 it issues, the firm will receive only $950; $50 will go to the investment bank. However, the firm still has to pay bondholders 10%—an annual coupon of $100 for each $1,000 bond—as well as the principal in Year 10. The $950 that the firm invests must be sufficient to pay bondholders their interest and principal. Otherwise, the firm should reject the project. As less money is available for investment ($950 in our example), if the IRR on this smaller investment is 10%, the money generated will not be sufficient to pay the bondholders. That is, the project will now have to earn more than 10% in order to be accepted. The firm should accept a project with an initial outlay of $950 and an economic life of 10 years only if its IRR is greater than or equal to the value of R that solves the following equation:

$$\$950 = \sum_{t=1}^{10} \frac{\$100}{(1+R)^t} + \frac{\$1,000}{(1+R)^{10}}$$

The value of R that solves the equation is 10.84%, and if the firm earns a 10.84% IRR on the $950 it has invested, the project will generate enough cash to pay the bondholders $100 annual interest and return the $1,000 principal. Because 10.84% is the project's minimum required rate of return, the firm's cost of debt with flotation costs is 10.84%.

If the firm issues the bonds for a very long period and if the flotation costs are spread over many years, the effect on the firm's cost of debt will be smaller. In the extreme case of infinite maturity, the bondholders receive a perpetuity of $100, and we have

$$\$950 = \frac{\$100}{R}$$

The firm's cost of debt is

$$R = \frac{\$100}{\$950} \cong 0.1053 \ \text{ or } \ 10.53\%$$

At the other extreme, if the firm issues one-year bonds, its cost of debt will be

$$\$950 = \frac{\$100 + \$1,000}{1+R}$$

and

$$R = \frac{\$1,100}{\$950} - 1 \cong 0.1579 \ \text{ or } \ 15.79\%$$

which is much larger than the 10% cost of debt. A firm that plans to raise new debt must account for flotation costs.

14.9.2 Flotation Costs and the Cost of Equity

Let's now assume a firm that is fully financed by equity. Without flotation costs the cost of equity is the same whether the source of equity is a stock issue, a rights offering, or retained earnings. In practice, however, flotation costs do exist and affect the various components of equity. We can demonstrate how flotation costs affect the firm's cost of equity by using the CDGM. The firm's cost of equity is obtained by the CDGM as follows:

$$k_e = \frac{d_1}{P_0} + g$$

where d_1 is the first year's dividend, P is the price per share, and g is the dividend growth rate. Retained earnings involve no flotation costs, so their cost is simply k_e. However, for each share sold in a new issue, the firm receives only $P_0 - F$ where F denotes flotation costs per share.

Only $(P_0 - F)$ dollars are available for project investment (per share issued) and stockholders will receive d_1 at the end of the first year, $d_1(1 + g)$ at the end of the second year, and so on. Therefore, to provide the same dividends per share, the firm should earn on the proceeds from the new issue at least the value of R that satisfies

$$P_0 - F = \frac{d}{1 + R} + \frac{d(1 + g)}{(1 + R)^2} + \frac{d(1 + g)^2}{(1 + R)^3} + \ldots = \frac{d}{R - g}$$

Recalling that R is the cost of equity, k_e, we solve the above equation to obtain

$$k_e = \frac{d_1}{P_0 - F} + g$$

which is larger than the $d_1/P_0 + g$ obtained in the absence of flotation costs. For example, if $d_1 = \$8$, $P_0 = \$100$, and $g = 5\%$, then $k_e = d_1/P_0 + g = 13\%$. With $\$10$ per share flotation costs, we obtain

$$k_e = \frac{\$8}{\$100 - \$10} + 0.05 \cong 0.1389 \ \text{ or } \ 13.89\%$$

Flotation costs increase the cost of equity.

However, in spite of the relatively large flotation costs, the cost of equity increases only slightly. In spreading the flotation costs of equity financing over many years, the firm minimizes their effect. The firm can also finance its project from retained earnings, which is also a form of equity financing. Since retained earnings do not incur flotation costs, it is commonly said that retained earnings are "cheaper" than new stock issues.

Now suppose that the firm is fully financed by preferred stock.[6] Preferred stock entitles holders to a certain predetermined dividend (8% of the par value) before the firm pays dividends on its common stock. The cost of capital of preferred stock with no flotation costs is

$$k_p = \frac{d_p}{P_p}$$

where d_p is the dividend per preferred share and P_p is the price of a preferred share. With flotation costs it is

$$k_p = \frac{d_p}{P_p - F}$$

Once again, the effect is generally not too large.

---

6. A firm must have some common stock before it decides to issue preferred stock. In this example, we assume 100% preferred stock in order to isolate the effect of that stock on the cost of capital.

Thus far, we have assumed that a firm can have only one source of financing. In practice, most firms have multiple sources of funds. If so, as we've seen in Chapter 10, a project should be accepted only if its IRR exceeds the WACC. In the next problem we demonstrate how the WACC is calculated with corporate tax and with flotation costs.

PRACTICE BOX

Problem

Suppose Clear Waters, Inc. finances itself by 40% common stock, 20% retained earnings, 10% preferred stock, and 30% long-term debt. The common stock price is $100, the dividend is $4 per share, and the dividend growth rate is 6%. The preferred stock's price is $70, and the dividend paid on it is $6 per share. The bond's price is $1,000; the annual coupon is $60; and the maturity is 10 years. The corporate tax rate is 36%.

The flotation costs are $15 per share on equity, $5 per share on preferred stock, and $50 per bond. No flotation costs are on retained earnings; its cost is given by the firm's cost of equity with no flotation costs.
a.   What is the firm's weighted average cost of capital without flotation costs?
b.   What is its WACC with flotation costs?
c.   Clear Waters is considering a project whose after-tax IRR is 9%. Should this project be accepted?

Solution

a.   Without flotation costs the cost of capital is as follows:

	Common Stock	Retained Earnings	Preferred Stock	Debt
Cost	$\frac{d_1}{P_0} + g$	10%	$\frac{d_1}{P_0} = \frac{\$6}{\$70}$	$(1 - T)\, 6\%$
	$= \frac{\$4}{\$100} + 0.06 = 10\%$		$\cong 8.57$	$\times\, 6\% = 3.84\%$
Weight	0.40	0.20	0.10	0.30

Note that the cost of common stock is the same as the cost of retained earnings without flotation costs. The cost of debt, k_d, is given by the value that solves the equation:

$$\$1,000 = \sum_{t=1}^{10} \frac{(1 - T)\$60}{(1 + k_d)^t} + \frac{\$1,000}{(1 + k_d)^{10}}$$

The value of k_d that solves this equation is 3.84%. It is also given by $k_d = (1 - T) \times 6\% = 3.84\%$, where $T = 0.36$ is the corporate tax rate and 6% is the bond's yield to maturity.

Therefore, the weighted average cost of capital is

$$(10\% \times 0.4) + (10\% \times 0.2) + (8.57\% \times 0.10) + (3.84\% \times 0.30)$$

$$= 4\% + 2\% + 0.857\% + 1.152\% = 8.009\%$$

b. With flotation costs the cost of retained earnings remains 10%, whereas the cost of equity is

$$k_e = \frac{d_1}{P_0 - F} + g = \frac{\$4}{\$100 - \$15} + 0.06 \cong 0.107 \ \text{ or } \ 10.7\%$$

Therefore, it is cheaper to use retained earnings than to issue stock.
The cost of the preferred stock is

$$k_p = \frac{d_1}{P_0 - F} = \frac{\$6}{\$70 - \$5} = \frac{\$6}{\$65} = 0.0923 \ \text{ or } \ 9.23\%$$

The cost of debt is the value of k_d that solves the equation:

$$\$950 = \sum_{t=1}^{10} \frac{(1 - T)\$60}{(1 + k_d)^t} + \frac{\$1,000}{(1 + k_d)^{10}}$$

which is $k_d = 4.5\%$.
The after-flotation weighted average cost of capital is therefore:

WACC = (10.7% × 0.4) + (10% × 0.2) + (9.23% × 0.1) + (4.5% × 0.3)
    = 8.553%

Flotation costs cause the WACC to increase from 8.009% to 8.553%.
c. Even though there are flotation costs, the IRR of 9% is higher than the WACC of 8.553%, so the project should be accepted.

SUMMARY

A firm may raise money by selling common stock, bonds, or preferred stock. Stock may be issued through a rights issue, in which existing shareholders purchase additional shares at a low price, or by selling shares directly to the public. A firm goes public by selling stock to the public for the first time in an initial public offering (IPO).

Common stockholders have voting rights and are entitled to dividends. Preferred shareholders are entitled to a predetermined fixed dividend, but they generally have no voting rights. Bondholders have no voting rights, but are entitled to fixed interest payments and have priority over stockholders in case of bankruptcy and liquidation of the firm's assets.

In most cases a firm uses an investment bank to handle a new issue of securities (i.e., stocks, bonds,

and preferred stock). For a fee that covers expenses and includes a profit, the investment bank will handle the technical details of the new issue and market the securities. In most cases the investment bank will also assume the role of underwriter. The investment bank thereby guarantees the firm a pre-specified amount per share or per bond sold, irrespective of whether the issue is a success or a failure. As underwriter the investment bank assumes the risk involved with the new issue and charges an extra fee for its risk.

The new issue's costs are called flotation costs, which can be substantial. They affect the firm's cost of capital, and projects that might otherwise be accepted may be rejected due to these costs.

CHAPTER AT A GLANCE

Financing Operations by Issuing New Securities and Retained Earnings

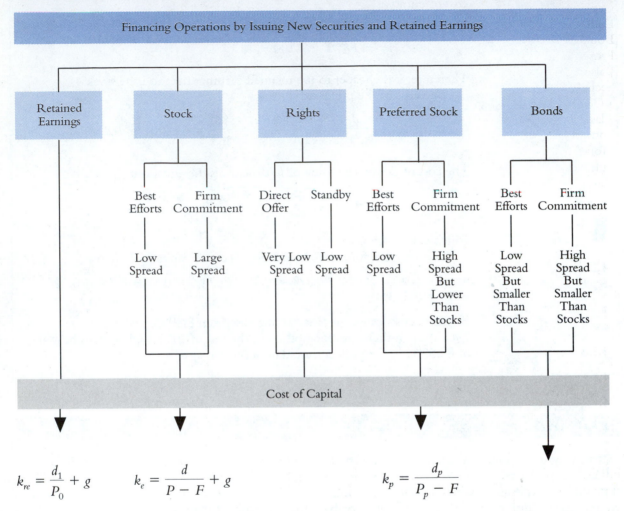

Retained Earnings	Stock	Rights	Preferred Stock	Bonds
	Best Efforts / Firm Commitment	Direct Offer / Standby	Best Efforts / Firm Commitment	Best Efforts / Firm Commitment
	Low Spread / Large Spread	Very Low Spread / Low Spread	Low Spread / High Spread But Lower Than Stocks	Low Spread But Smaller Than Stocks / High Spread But Smaller Than Stocks

Cost of Capital

$$k_{re} = \frac{d_1}{P_0} + g \qquad k_e = \frac{d}{P - F} + g \qquad k_p = \frac{d_p}{P_p - F}$$

k_d that solves:

$$P_b - F = \sum_{t=1}^{n} \frac{(1 - T)C}{(1 + k_d)^t} + \frac{P_F}{(1 + k_d)^n}$$

where P is a common share's price; P_p is a preferred share's price; P_b is each bond's price; P_F is the bond's face value; k_e is the cost of equity; k_p is the preferred stock's cost; k_d is the cost of debt; d_1 is the common stock's dividend in the first year; d_p is the preferred stock's dividend in the first year; $k_{re} = (d_1/P_0) + g$ is the cost of retained earnings; T is the corporate tax rate; C is the bond's annual coupon; F is the flotation cost (which varies from one type of security to another); and g is the dividend growth rate.

KEY TERMS

Capital surplus
Equity account
Book value per share (stock)
Proxy
Poison pill provision
Securities and Exchange
   Commission (SEC)
Classified common stock
Voting right premium
Mortgage bonds
Indenture
Restrictive covenants

Debentures
Subordinated debentures
Investment bank
Registration statement
Prospectus
Offering price
Tombstone
Master registration statement
Short-form statement
Shelf registration
Underwriter
Best-efforts arrangement

Firm-commitment arrangement
Flotation cost
Underwriting syndicate
Initial public offering (IPO)
Seasoned new issue
Rights offering
Subscription price
Standby underwriting
   arrangement
Private placement
Auction

REVIEW AND PRACTICE

14.1 What are the main reasons why a firm may decide to go public?

14.2 Why would a family firm issue more than one class of stock?

14.3 What are the legal rights of stockholders?

14.4 What are the legal rights of bondholders?

14.5 What are *mortgage bonds*?

14.6 What is an *indenture?*

14.7 Define the *spread* in a stock issue. Is it larger or smaller than the spread in a bond issue? Explain?

14.8 "Flotation costs reduce the cost of capital." Do you agree with this statement? Explain.

14.9 A firm has two classes of stock. Class A stock carries five voting rights per share, and Class B stock carries one voting right per share. There are 1 million shares of each. The market prices of Class A stock and Class B stock are $12 and $10, respectively.
a. Calculate the voting right premium.
b. If you wish to hold more than 50% of the votes, what proportion of the firm's capital must you hold if you invest only in Class A stock?
c. How would your answer change if you invested only in Class B stock?

14.10 A firm issues 100 million shares in 1997 at $1 per share. The stock's par value is also $1 per share. In 1998 the firm earns $10 million, distributes $6 million as dividends, and issues 10 million shares at $12 per share. Prepare the stockholders' equity account.

14.11 A firm goes bankrupt. The liquidated assets provide $100 million net of all expenses. The firm is liable for $40 million in mortgage bonds and $20 million in debentures, and it has $100 million in common stock. How will the money from the liquidated assets be distributed?

14.12 A firm issues 10 million shares at $14 per share. An investment bank guarantees the firm $10 per share. What is the spread?

14.13 A stock's current price is $15 per share. An investment bank estimates that the stock's price on the issue date will have the following distribution:

Price	$10	$11	$12	$15	$20
Probability	1/5	1/5	1/5	1/5	1/5

The investment bank that underwrites the issue guarantees the firm $13 per share.
a. What is the spread?
b. What is the investment bank's maximum possible loss?
c. What is the expected loss (or profit)?

14.14 A firm is planning a rights offering at a subscription price of $10 and a ratio of one new share for five shares held. The stock price before the rights offering is $20.
a. What is a right's expected price?
b. Calculate a stockholder's total wealth after the rights offering. Assume she held five shares before the offering.
c. What will the investor's wealth be if she lets the right expire unused?

14.15 A 20-year bond is issued at a yield of 10%. The annual coupon is $100. An investment bank guarantees the firm $950 for each $1,000 bond. What is the investment bank's loss if the yield on the issuing date increases to 12%?

14.16 A firm is planning a rights offering at a subscription price of $100 per share and a ratio of one new share for four shares held. The stock price is $120. The underwriter exerts pressure to decrease the subscription price to $80.
a. Will the firm necessarily lose from a reduction in the price? Suppose the firm decides to decrease the subscription price. What can the firm do to keep the proceeds from the rights offering unchanged?
b. Will the investment bank benefit from a reduction in the subscription price?

14.17 A preferred stock is sold for $100 per share. The dividend is $7 per share. What is the preferred stock's cost of capital if the flotation costs are $10 per share?

14.18 A bond sold to the public at $1,000 pays an annual coupon of $80 a year. The flotation costs are $100 per bond. Assume no taxes.
a. What is the cost of debt if the maturity is one year?
b. What is the cost of debt if the maturity is infinity?
c. What is the cost of debt if the maturity is five years?

14.19 The price of a firm's common stock is $15; the dividend is $3 per share; the dividend growth rate is 8%; and the flotation costs are $2 per share.
a. What is the common stock's cost of capital?
b. What is the retained earnings' cost of capital?

14.20 A firm plans to finance a project by 5% retained earnings, 45% common stock, 25% preferred stock, and 25% bonds. The common stock's price is $100, and its annual dividend is $5. The dividend growth rate is 5%. The preferred stock's price is $100, and its annual dividend is $7 per share. The bond's maturity is one year; its price and face value are $1,000 each; and its annual coupon is $100. The corporate tax rate is 36%. The flotation costs are as follows:

Security	Flotation Cost
Common stock	$10 per share
Preferred stock	$5 per share
Bond	$50 per bond

Calculate the WACC before and after the flotation costs are taken into account.

14.21 Show graphically why a firm's capital expenditure decreases due to flotation costs. (Hint: Draw an investment schedule and WACC line as described in Section 10.5.1, Figure 10.2.)

14.22 A firm's cost of equity with no flotation costs is 10%. The dividend growth rate is 5%. The flotation costs are 20% of the stock price. What is the cost of equity after flotation costs?

14.23 A firm is considering an investment of $100 million with a net annual after-tax cash flow of $10 million for the next 50 years. The firm's capital structure is composed of 50% equity and 50% debt. The price of each bond is $1,000, and the annual coupon before tax is $50. The bond matures in 50 years. The corporate tax rate is 36%. The dividend on equity is $5 per share; the stock price is $100; and the dividend growth rate is 10%. The flotation costs are $100 per bond and $15 per share of common stock.
a. Should the firm accept or reject the project?
b. What is the project's NPV?

14.24 In 1993 Cadbury first attempted to acquire Dr. Pepper. To protect its existing shareholders, Dr. Pepper announced that if Cadbury were to hold more than 26% of its shares it would offer all shareholders except Cadbury the opportunity to buy an additional share at a 50% discount for each share they held. Assume the price of Dr. Pepper was $50 a share. There were 25 million shares outstanding. Cadbury held 25.9% of the shares. Suppose Cadbury had bought an additional 24.2% of the shares at $50 a share, thereby gaining control of the firm (50.1% of the shares).

a. What would the market value of Cadbury's shares have been if the protective provision was not implemented?

b. What would the market value have been if, for each share held, the holders of the remaining shares had the right to buy one share at $25? Calculate the loss to Cadbury due to this protective measure.

14.25

New Offerings Are Hot

Feb. 10	General Magic	+90%
Feb. 9	Information Storage	+82%
Feb. 2	Semitool	+31%
Feb. 2	Brooks Automation	+20%

First-day gain over offering price of initial public offerings

MAGIC OR MANIA?

Just when you thought the initial public offering market was dead, up leaps evidence of speculative fervor that just won't quit. These days, that emotion is in technology . . . .

That promise is what people were looking at Friday. General Magic went public at $14 a share . . . . Everybody knew it would be hot, and those with the pull to get in on the deal did so. Only 5.5 million shares were sold in the offering, but so many of them were promptly flipped that reported volume on Nasdaq came to 6.8 million shares. A lot of powerful investors evidently decided to take the money and run. The shares began trading in the open market at $32, but fell back to $26.625 by Friday's close.[7]

a. Suppose General Magic raises the money and invests it in a new product. The firm's dividend per share is $1, and the dividend growth rate is 12%. What is the minimum IRR that the firm should earn on the new project? Is $14 or $26.625 relevant for the cost of equity calculation? Assume General Magic is an all-equity firm.

b. Given the first-day gain over the initial public offering price of the four issues listed in the table, which of the four underwriting contracts, in your view, was the most profitable for the investment bank? Explain.

INTERNET QUESTION

14.26 Assume that your small company is ready to go public, and you have considered an Internet IPO. Using a search engine, find an investment bank that would underwrite your IPO in cyberspace. What is the best "deal" you can find?

YOUR TURN: APPLYING THEORY TO PRACTICE

NEW BREED OF PREFERRED ISSUES OFFERS TAX BREAKS

On Friday, GTE became the latest company to float a newly popular type of preferred stock that has twofold appeal: It gives issuers a special tax break and offers investors unusually rich yields—around 9%, in fact. More than 30 such preferred offers have been made since October 1993, when Texaco pioneered the technique. Last year, this new class accounted for more than half of all preferred stock issued. Since inception, proceeds total $6.5 billion. The target for

---

7. Floyd Norris, "Is It Magic or Mania for Tech Stocks?" *New York Times*, 12 February 1995, p. 1F.

these new securities has been retail investors, rather than institutions. To lure individuals, issuers have been offering yields that run as much as ¾ of a percentage point above regular preferred stock, and 1¼–1½ points more than the yield on long-term government bonds. GTE, for instance, sold its $450 million issue of the new preferred Friday with a dividend yield of 8.75%, versus an 8% yield on its outstanding preferred and 7.5% for 30-year Treasury bonds.

The new preferred shares, known as Monthly Income Preferred Securities, or MIPS, have other features designed to appeal to individuals. As the accompanying table shows, issuers usually are recognizable companies like Aetna, ConAgra, GTE, Texaco and Transamerica. MIPS are offered initially at $25 apiece to encourage the purchase of "round lots" of 100 shares. They are listed along with regular preferred shares on the New York Stock Exchange. . . .

Investors should also know that MIPS, like regular preferred stock, don't have the security of corporate bonds. If MIPS issuers get into financial trouble, they can defer interest payments for up to five years.

Like other fixed-income securities, the prices of MIPS go up and down with the bond market. Investors who bought MIPS in late 1994 and early 1995 are sitting with nice profits because of the bond market's recent rally, but those who bought the first deals in late 1993 are showing losses. Unfortunately, the downside potential of MIPS is greater than the upside because issuers typically can redeem the securities in five years. This redemption feature caps the shares' appreciation potential but doesn't guarantee any minimum repurchase price . . . .

But you can bet that corporations will keep issuing MIPS, and brokers will surely keep trying to peddle them. In fact, the rush to issue this new type of preferred stock has created intense jockeying among Wall Street underwriters. One reason is that MIPS represent one of the few hot products in corporate finance these days. The

New Breed

• In the past year or so, U.S. companies have been selling a new kind of preferred stock that allows issuers to deduct dividend payments for tax purposes and gives holders richer yields. Issuers duck taxes by floating their new preferred through special-purpose subsidiaries, which in turn take cash from investors and lend it back to the parent company. On $100 million of preferred a company can save as much as $3 million a year in interest costs compared with traditional preferred. The latest deal came Friday from GTE and yielded 8.75%.

Issuer	Date	Amount (millions)	Rating (s&p)	Original Yield	Recent Price	Current Yield
Texaco	10/27/93	$350	A-plus	6.875%	21¾	7.9%
Enron	11/04/93	214	BBB-minus	8.0	22¾	8.9
USX	02/24/94	250	BB-minus	8.75	23½	9.3
PECO Energy	07/20/94	221	Triple-B	9.0	25¾	8.7
Torchmark	09/30/94	200	Single-A	9.13	25⅝	9.0
GTE	10/06/94	489	BBB-plus	9.25	26	8.9
Transamerica	10/18/94	200	A-minus	9.125	25½	8.9
Aetna	11/15/94	275	Single-A	9.5	26⅝	8.8
ConAgra	01/27/95	250	BBB-minus	9.375	26⅝	8.8
GTE	02/24/95	450	BBB-plus	8.75	25	8.75

Preferred Vehicle

Since being introduced in late '93, Monthly Income Preferred Securities have come to dominate the preferred market. The trend is expected to continue this year, with yield-hungry retail customers snapping up all the newly issued shares.

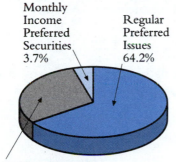

1993
Total Issuance: $15 billion

Monthly Income Preferred Securities 3.7%

Regular Preferred Issues 64.2%

Preferred Issues by Foreign Companies 32.1%

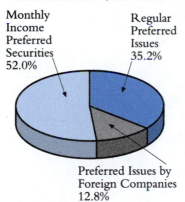

1994
Total Issuance: $6.8 billion

Monthly Income Preferred Securities 52.0%

Regular Preferred Issues 35.2%

Preferred Issues by Foreign Companies 12.8%

"We don't have a preferred-stock market anymore, we have a MIPS market, where we occasionally see a regular preferred deal," says Chris Hogg, a Goldman Sachs vice president, who invented the securities . . . .

Wall Street firms can be counted on to hype just about any new instrument as a breakthough, but MIPS do in fact amount to a true innovation: a security that corporations can treat as debt for tax purposes but one that qualifies as equity in the eyes of the credit-rating agencies like Moody's and Standard & Poor's. In other words, MIPS keep the cost of funds down and keep a firm's debt ratios down, too . . . .

For corporations in the 35% federal bracket, the cost savings from MIPS are significant. Compared to traditional preferred, a MIPS issue can save $3 million in annual interest costs for every $100 million outstanding.

"We were able to get an after-tax interest rate of under 6% on a security with a 9% yield," says Jack Keane, treasurer at Northeast Utilities, whose Connecticut Light & Power unit sold $100 million of MIPS in January. "We were able to lower our costs and improve our overall credit ratings."

The tax break is made possible because the MIPS are issued by a special-purpose partnership, which then lends the proceeds to its corporate parent. The parent, be it Texaco or GTE, is obligated to pay interest to the partnership, which then passes the money on to investors in the form of dividends.

Though MIPS might appear to be a tax dodge, so far the Internal Revenue Service hasn't nixed them. "The IRS seems to be comfortable with the whole thing," says Robert Willens, a tax expert at Lehman Brothers. "They haven't said so directly, but they've made it pretty clear that they approve this kind of technique."

clear leader in the field is their creator, Goldman Sachs, which boasts an 85% market share. Goldman was lead manager for Friday's GTE offering.

Source: Andrew Bary, "What a Deal: New Breed of Preferred Issues Helps Everybody But the Tax Man," *Barron's* (27 February 1995): 17–18. Reprinted by permission of *Barron's*, © 1995 Dow Jones & Company, Inc. All Rights Reserved Worldwide.

Questions

1. Explain in your own words the pros and cons of issuing MIPS.

2. a. Suppose GTE issues $100 million of 8% preferred stocks at par. The firm's pretax earning is $12.308 million. Show how this sum is distributed among the firm's common stockholders, the IRS, and the preferred stockholders. Assume a 35% corporate tax and all net earnings are distributed to the common stockholders.

b. Repeat part a but assume the firm issues $100 million of 8.75% MIPS.

3. Suppose GTE can issue $450 million of 8% bonds or $450 million of 8.75% MIPS.

a. Compare the after-tax cost of each of these two securities. Assume a corporate tax rate of 35%.

b. Suppose GTE is sure that the pretax earnings will be greater than $50 million in each of the next few years. Which issue will be preferred?

c. How would your answer to part b change if the earnings were $10 million or $50 million with an equal probability every year?

4. Which is more relevant in calculating the after-tax cost of Aetna's MIPS: the original yield or the current yield? Explain your answer.

5. Explain the difference between the current yields of USX and Texaco.

6. Suppose a special partnership issues $450 million of 8.75% MIPS and then lends the money to GTE, its corporate parent. Assume 35% corporate tax rate.

a. Describe the cash flow to all parties involved, including the IRS.

b. How will the MIPS issue affect the debt-equity ratio of the consolidated firm?

CHAPTER 15

DOES CAPITAL STRUCTURE MATTER?: A PERFECT MARKET

LEARNING OBJECTIVES

After reading this chapter, you should understand:

1. How leverage affects the stockholders' rate of return under certainty and uncertainty.

2. How a firm uses break-even analysis to assess the effect of leverage on profitability.

3. Modigliani and Miller's claim that capital structure does not matter in a perfect market with no corporate taxes.

4. That in a perfect market stockholders can use "homemade" leverage to avoid paying a premium on a levered firm.

5. That in a perfect market stockholders can "undo" leverage by investing in riskless bonds and, thereby, avoid paying a premium on an unlevered firm.

6. How the firm's capital structure affects stockholders' risk exposure and cost of equity.

7. That in a perfect market the WACC remains constant even though the cost of equity increases with leverage.

CORPORATE FINANCE IN THE NEWS

TODAY'S HOT CONCEPT, TOMORROW'S FOREST FIRE

The steady increase in debt that companies took on to grease the merger machines also reflected a new scientific theory being drummed into business school graduates. During the late 1950s and early 1960s, academics Merton Miller and Franco Modigliani and others had set a revolution in motion with scholarly treatises on capital structure, dividends, and a host of related financial topics, which led to Nobel Prizes for the authors. One hugely important idea to emerge from the classroom, says Carliss Baldwin, professor of finance at the Harvard Business School, was the blurring of the distinction between debt and equity. Previously companies relied on rules of thumb or gut instinct to determine a capital structure. And most firms felt a Depression-bred aversion to being in debt. GE, for instance, had no long-term debt for the first half of the 1950s. (Then, in May 1956, it issued $300 million of 20-year bonds with a coupon of an almost quaint 3.5%.) But Miller and Modigliani showed that, at least theoretically, how much debt a company carries doesn't matter as long as the business generates sufficient cash flow to make it likely that it will meet its interest obligation.

15.1 INTRODUCTION

When General Electric first issued $300 million of bonds in 1956, did abandoning its strategy of all-equity and issuing bonds affect the firm's stock price? Franco Modigliani and Merton Miller (or M & M) claim that (under certain conditions) issuing debt rather than equity "does not matter"—that is, the financing mix that a firm selects will not affect its stock price or its value.

Whether a firm's **capital structure,** its mix of debt and equity, affects its stock price is not purely academic; it also has practical implications. If capital structure does not matter, then management should not devote much time to choosing the firm's financing strategy. But if it does matter, then management should seek the *optimal capital structure*, the one that maximizes the firm's value. Does capital structure matter? To answer this question we distinguish between a "perfect" and an "imperfect" capital market. In this chapter we show that in a **perfect market**—one that has no taxes, transaction costs, bankruptcy costs, or agency costs, and one where individuals and firms can borrow and lend at the same interest rate—capital structure does not matter. However, this case may not be relevant since capital markets are not perfect in the real world. For example, firms and individuals cannot borrow and lend at the same interest rate.

Nevertheless, a thorough review of perfect capital market assumptions and results is crucial for understanding the relationship between capital structure and the firm's value. We will see that in a perfect capital market the cost of equity and stockholders' risk exposure increase as the proportion of debt in the capital structure increases, and that this also applies to imperfect capital markets. The perfect market case, which is the focus of this chapter, pinpoints the crucial factors that may affect firm value. Chapter 16 covers the imperfect market case and how each market imperfection affects capital structure.

In this and the next chapter, we assume that the firm's capital expenditures are fixed; that is, the firm has already chosen which projects to undertake. The firm has only one remaining question: How will it finance the projects?

15.2 SOME PRELIMINARY DEFINITIONS

We begin our study of the perfect capital market with some necessary definitions—some old, some new.

- *Financial leverage*   When a firm finances a portion of its operations by debt, we say that the firm employs financial leverage or that it is a **levered firm.** If a firm does not employ debt, we say that it is an all-equity firm and has no leverage.
- *Financial leverage ratios*   The amount of debt that a firm employs is measured by two ratios: the debt/equity ratio and debt as a fraction of value of the firm.[1]

---

1. Although financial leverage ratios are generally defined in market value terms, book values are sometimes used as estimates of market values, especially in the case of debt. When book values are used, then total assets (from the balance sheet) are used as an estimate of the firm's value.

These financial leverage ratios are used to measure a firm's risk; this is because **financial leverage,** or the use of debt, enhances or "levers" on average a firm's profit to its stockholders, but also increases its risk.

The *debt/equity ratio* is expressed as

$$\text{Debt/equity ratio} = \frac{\text{Market value of long–term debt}}{\text{Market value of equity}}$$

The debt/equity ratio can be larger than 1 for a firm that employs a high level of debt.

The *debt/value of the firm ratio* is expressed as

$$\text{Debt/value of firm ratio} = \frac{\text{Market value of long–term debt}}{\text{Market value of debt and equity}}$$

This ratio cannot be larger than 1.

We will also refer to these two ratios as the firm's *capital structure ratios*.

- *Value of the firm*   Assume a firm issues long-term debt, denoted by B, and equity, denoted by E. The firm's total market value, denoted by V, is the value of all its assets, which belong to bondholders and stockholders together. V is the sum of the market values of components B and E:

$$V = B + E \tag{15.1}$$

- *All-equity firm*   If a firm issues no debt, it is an **unlevered firm** (also called an *all-equity* or a *debt-free* firm). In an all-equity firm, $B = 0$ and $V = E$.
- *Net operating income (NOI)*   NOI is the firm's earnings before it distributes any of its income as interest (to bondholders and banks), as dividends (to stockholders), or as taxes (to the government). Because it is measured before any interest is deducted, NOI is determined by the firm's investments, not by its financial leverage (which indicates how those investments were financed). The NOI is also called EBIT, Earnings Before Interest and Taxes.
- *Optimal financial leverage*   The firm's goal is to maximize its value. For a given invested capital and a given number of shares outstanding, this goal is equivalent to maximizing the firm's stock price. Suppose a firm raises $1,000 by issuing 100 shares of stock at $10 per share. In this case the firm's market value will be $1,000. Suppose, alternatively, that the firm finances its operations by issuing $500 of debt and 50 shares of stock. If the market prefers this financial mix to all-equity, the firm may be able to sell the stock for a higher price, say, $11 per share. In this case the firm's value will be $1,050 [$500 debt + (50 shares × $11) = $1,050]. The firm's value (as well as the stock's value) increases. This example illustrates that when the value of the firm increases, so does the stock price. Therefore, when the value of the firm is maximized, so is the stock price. The level of financial leverage that maximizes the firm's market value is the **optimal financial leverage** or the **optimal capital structure.** The following problem illustrates how one firm's optimal capital structure affects its value and its stock price.

PRACTICE BOX

Problem

Cone Mills Corporation needs $100 million for investment. If the firm uses equity only, Cone Mills will issue 10 million shares at $10 a share. Alternatively, if the firm issues a combination of debt and equity, it will reduce the number of shares issued proportionately to the amount of debt issued. For example, if Cone Mills employs $50 million of debt, it will reduce the number of shares issued by 50% to 5 million. Cone Mills estimates that its shares will be sold at the following prices:

Debt Issue ($ million)	Number of Shares Issued (millions)	Stock Price Estimate ($)
20	8	11
50	5	12
70	3	9

What is Cone Mills's optimal capital structure? What is the firm's corresponding value? What is the corresponding stock price?

Solution

If it raises $20 million of debt, Cone Mills will issue 8 million shares at $11. The firm's value will be

$$\$20 \text{ million} + (8 \text{ million shares} \times \$11) = \$108 \text{ million}$$

For the other levels of debt, we have

$$\$50 \text{ million} + (5 \text{ million shares} \times \$12) = \$110 \text{ million}$$

and

$$\$70 \text{ million} + (3 \text{ million shares} \times \$9) = \$97 \text{ million}$$

Thus, the firm's optimal policy is to issue $50 million of debt. With this capital structure, the firm's value will be $110 million, and its stock price will be $12.

In analyzing the optimal capital structure, we hold investment in physical assets constant and focus on how the financing mix affects the firm's value. In the above problem, the firm obtains more cash ($110 million) than it needs for the investment ($100 million). To keep the investment and the NOI constant, the firm could issue fewer shares or, alternatively, distribute the extra $10 million as dividends and thereby maintain a debt/equity ratio of 1 ($50 million debt/$50 million equity = 1).[2]

15.3 LEVERAGE AND THE RATE OF RETURN ON EQUITY

In employing leverage, a firm affects its rate of return on equity when cash flows are either certain or uncertain. First, we consider certain cash flows.

2. When it distributes extra cash or sells new shares, a firm may affect its stock price. Therefore, a firm may need to use the trial and error method when determining how much it should reduce the number of shares issued.

15.3.1 Certain Cash Flows

Let us start with the simpler case of an all-equity firm, Utopia Industries, which has 100 outstanding shares with a market price of $10 per share. In this case the firm's value equals its equity's value: $V = E = \$1,000$. Let us also assume perfect certainty; that is, Utopia knows its cash flow (NOI) in advance.

Table 15-1 presents Utopia's basic financial data and profitability. The market value of the firm's equity is $1,000. For simplicity we also assume a tax-free world. Since Utopia knows its $150 NOI with certainty, the rate of return on the firm's equity is 15% ($150/$1,000).

Now suppose Utopia is considering a mix of 25% debt and 75% equity such that the total amount of money raised remains constant at $1,000. This financing mix would change the capital structure. However, since the total investment would remain constant, the firm's investment plans and its NOI would be unaffected. Would the change in the capital structure increase the rate of return on the firm's equity?

TABLE 15-1 Utopia Industries: Financial Data		
Market value of equity		$1,000
Debt		$0
NOI		$150
Rate of return on equity		15%

TABLE 15-2 Utopia Industries: Rate of Return on Equity for Various Interest Rates	Interest Rate	Before the Change in Capital Structure	After the Change in Capital Structure (75% equity, 25% debt)
Basic Data			
Market value of equity		$1,000	$ 750
Market value of debt		$ 0	$ 250
Total capital		$1,000	$1,000
NOI		$ 150	$ 150
Interest			
a. 10%		$ 0	$ 25
b. 15%		$ 0	$ 37.50
c. 20%		$ 0	$ 50
Stockholder's Income			
a. 10%		$ 150	$ 125
b. 15%		$ 150	$ 112.50
c. 20%		$ 150	$ 100
Rate of Return on Equity			
a. 10%		15%	16.67%
b. 15%		15%	15%
c. 20%		15%	13.33%

Table 15–2 shows that the answer to this question depends on the interest rate that the firm would have to pay on the debt. In the table the rate of return on equity is calculated for three alternative interest rates: 10%, 15%, and 20%. When the interest rate on debt is below 15%, the rate of return on equity increases after the change in the capital structure. The reason is that the firm earns 15% on the investment but pays a lower interest rate, 10%, on its debt financing. The extra 5% is the stockholders' additional rate of return. When the interest rate is above 15%, the rate of return on equity decreases; but when the interest rate is exactly 15%, the return on equity is unaffected by the change in capital structure.

Let's see how the figures in Table 15–2 were obtained: When the interest rate on debt ($B = \$250$) is $r = 10\%$, the stockholders' net income is $125 [NOI $- rB = \$150 - (0.10 \times \$250) = \$125$]. Stockholders invested $750 in equity; therefore, the rate of return as a percentage of the invested equity is approximately 16.67% ($\$125/\$750 \cong 0.1667$ or 16.67%). When the interest rate on debt is 15%, the stockholders' net income is $112.50 [NOI $- rB = \$150 - (0.15 \times \$250) = \$112.50$], and the rate of return on equity is 15% ($\$112.50/\$750 = 0.15$ or 15%). When the interest rate is 20%, the stockholders' net income is $100 [NOI $- rB = \$150 - (0.2 \times \$250) = \$100$], and the rate of return on equity is approximately 13.33% ($\$100/\$750 \cong 0.1333$ or 13.33%).

What can we learn from this example? Financing part of a firm's operations by debt is similar to having a partner who is entitled to a fixed interest rate on his or her investment. If such a "silent" partner (who has no voting rights) charges less than the firm's rate of return on its operations (in our example less than 15%), the profit after paying this interest bill will enhance the rate of return on equity. This is why we say a firm "levers" or enhances the rate of return on equity when it issues debt. If the partner's charge exactly equals the interest rate, the rate of return on equity will not be affected. Finally, if the partner charges more than the firm's rate of return on its invested equity, the rate of return on the equity will decline. As Table 15–2 illustrates, the effect of Utopia's leverage on the rate of return on equity can be positive (if interest is below 15%), negative (if interest is above 15%), or neutral (if interest is exactly 15%).

Since Utopia would know the interest rate its bondholders (or the bank) charges, the firm's decision should be simple: If the market interest rate is above 15%, Utopia should not issue debt; if it is below 15%, Utopia should exploit this opportunity by issuing debt to enhance ("lever") the profit on its invested equity.

The question remaining for Utopia is: How much debt should it issue? Should it be 25% of total investment? 50%? or more? To answer the question, assume Utopia pays a 10% interest rate on its debt. Table 15–3 shows the rates of return on equity for various proportions of leverage: 0%, 25%, 50%, and 75%. To understand the calculations, look at the last column of Table 15–3. With debt of $750, the interest is $75 ($\$750 \times 0.10 = \$75$), and the shareholders' net income is $75 ($\$150 - \$75 = \$75$). Dividing this net income by the invested equity of $250, we obtain a rate of return on equity of 30%. Other figures in the table are calculated in the same manner. The rate of return on equity increases from 15% in the case of no leverage, to 16.67% for 25% leverage, to 20% for 50% leverage, and to 30% for 75% leverage. In the certainty case the solution of the optimal capital structure question is straight-

TABLE 15-3 Utopia Industries: Rates of Return on Equity for Various Capital Structures	Capital Structure		0%	25%	50%	75%
	Data					
	Market value of equity	$	1,000	750	500	250
	Market value of debt	$	0	250	500	750
	Total value of the firm	$	1,000	1,000	1,000	1,000
	NOI	$	150	150	150	150
	Interest (at 10%)	$	0	25	50	75
	Net income (NOI − Interest)	$	150	125	100	75
	Rate of return on equity	%	15	16.67	20	30

forward: As long as the interest rate is below the rate of return on invested assets (15% in our example), the more leverage the firm employs and the better its shareholders fare, because the rate of return on their investment increases.

The following problem demonstrates the formulas for rates of return on equity for various debt/equity ratios.

PRACTICE BOX

Problem

Safeway Corporation's certain NOI is $100 and the total investment needed to create this income is $1,000. The interest rate is 5%.

a. Write the formula for the rate of return on equity for various debt/equity ratios (B/E). Solve it for $B/E = 1$.

b. Given the assumption of certainty, what economic forces would eliminate the excess profit on the firm's equity?

Solution

a. Paying rB on debt (where $r = 5\%$), leaves (NOI $- rB$) for the stockholders. The rate of return on equity is given by:

$$\frac{\text{NOI} - rB}{V - B}$$

Because $V - B = E$, we get

$$\text{Rate of return on equity} = \frac{\text{NOI} - rB}{E} = \frac{\text{NOI}}{E} - r\left(\frac{B}{E}\right)$$

Therefore, for $B/E = 1$, $E = \$500$, and $B = \$500$, we obtain

$$\text{Rate of return on equity} = \frac{\$100}{\$500} - 0.05 \times (1) = 0.15 \text{ or } 15\%$$

(continued)

b. In equilibrium all certain assets must yield the same rate of return. Because we assume certainty, all investors will rush to buy this stock and its price will increase. In equilibrium if the NOI is certain, the rate of return on equity must equal the riskless interest rate (i.e., 5%).

A firm like Utopia simply does not exist. A real-world firm would have more difficulty choosing the optimal capital structure because it would not know the NOI with certainty. NOI depends on the firm's success. Leverage can enhance the rate of return on equity in good years, but it can have the opposite effect in bad years. We shall now turn from Utopia Industries to Realistic Industries, where we will analyze the impact of leverage in the more relevant case of uncertain future cash flows.

15.3.2 Uncertain Cash Flows

Our next question is: How does leverage affect the rate of return on equity in the case of uncertain cash flows? Connecting Theory to Practice 15.1 suggests the effect of leverage in such real-world situations.

CONNECTING THEORY TO PRACTICE 15.1

WITH CORPORATE DEBT HANGOVER EASING, LEVERAGED FIRMS' SHARES ARE TAKING OFF

Corporate America is starting to recover from the debt binge of the 1980s. And the stock market is starting to take notice.

With the economy on the mend and junk-bond prices rallying, stocks of heavily indebted companies are outperforming the market as a whole. Last year, an index of 200 leveraged stocks compiled by Shearson Lehman Brothers rose 39.2% in price compared with 26.3% for the Standard & Poor's 500-stock index.

Source: Randall Smith, "With Corporate Debt Hangover Easing, Leveraged Firms' Shares Are Taking Off," *Wall Street Journal,* 28 April 1992, p. C1. Reprinted by permission of *The Wall Street Journal,* © 1992 Dow Jones & Company, Inc. All Rights Reserved Worldwide.

MAKING THE CONNECTION

Firms with substantial debt in their capital structure show a higher than average rate of return on equity. Does this mean that firms should rush to issue more debt? Should we be surprised by the high rate of return for firms operating with a high debt/equity ratio? We will see in this section that this result is exactly what the theory predicts: When the market booms, levered firms should outperform unlevered firms; in a recession the opposite holds.

It is realistic to assume that a firm's NOI will be high during an expanding economy and low, or even negative, during a recession. Because a firm has to pay a fixed
interest rate on its debt, the actual rate of return on equity may be enhanced in years
of prosperity but may decline in recession years. Depending on market conditions,
leverage can have a positive or a negative effect. Moreover, the more leverage a firm
employs, the stronger the leverage effect.

To illustrate the leverage effect when NOI is uncertain, we use Utopia's basic data
but change the firm's name to Realistic Industries. The relevant figures are given in
Table 15-4. Note that for simplicity we assume only three possible NOIs: $80 with a
probability of ⅓; $100 with a probability of ⅓; and $150 with a probability of ⅓.
This simple example is sufficient to illustrate the point.

First, let us review some of the calculations in Table 15-4. Consider, for example, the recession scenario when NOI = $80. If Realistic Industries employs no lever-
age (the firm finances its $1,000 investment completely by equity), it pays no
interest and the rate of return on equity is 8% ($80/$1,000 = 0.08 or 8%). When
the firm employs 25% leverage, it issues $250 debt at 10% interest, and the total in-
vested capital is, as before, $1,000. Since the interest is $25 (0.10 × $250 = $25),
Realistic has only $55 ($80 − $25 = $55) left to distribute among the stockholders.
Realistic's rate of return on equity is approximately 7.33% ($55/$750 ≅ 0.0733 or
7.33%). Other figures in Table 15-4 are calculated in the same manner.

The main results of Table 15-4, which allow for uncertain NOI, are as follows:

1. First, we see that leverage affects the rate of return on equity. Generally speaking, the higher the leverage, the greater its effect on the rate of return on equity.
   For example, at 25% leverage the rate of return on equity falls in the range of
   7.33% to 16.67%; while for 50% leverage, the range widens to 6% to 20%.

2. When the rate of return on investment equals the interest rate, the selected
   leverage, regardless of its magnitude, does not affect the rate of return on equity.
   Indeed, we see that in our example corresponding to a normal economy, the
   rate of return on equity is equal to our assumed 10% interest rate, regardless of
   the leverage employed.

3. Since the rate of return on investment is higher than the interest rate in an expanding economy the leverage effect is positive. Moreover, the larger the leverage, the stronger the positive leverage effect. In our example, when the rate of
   return on the investment is 15%, the rate of return on equity increases to
   16.67% with 25% leverage and to 20% with 50% leverage. Beyond 50% leverage
   the rate of return on equity increases even more.

4. During a recession, the opposite holds: The rate of return on equity declines
   from 8% with no leverage, to 7.33% with 25% leverage, and to 6% with 50%
   leverage.

Leverage is commonly called a "double-edged sword": it can help, but it can also
harm. The larger a firm's leverage, the larger its potential profit or loss.

Let's now return to Connecting Theory to Practice 15.1. The *Wall Street Journal*
excerpt claims that the return for levered firms was higher than the average return

TABLE 15-4 Realistic Industries: Leverage Effect on the Rate of Return on Equity When NOI Is Uncertain

	Economic Scenario		
	Recession	Normal	Expansion
NOI	$80	$100	$150
Probability	⅓	⅓	⅓
Zero leverage			
Equity	$1,000	$1,000	$1,000
Debt	0	0	0
Rate of return on investment	8%	10%	15%
25% debt			
Equity	$ 750	$ 750	$ 750
Debt	250	250	250
Interest (at 10%)	25	25	25
Net income	55	75	125
Rate of return on equity	7.33%	10%	16.67%
50% debt			
Equity	$ 500	$ 500	$ 500
Debt	500	500	500
Interest (at 10%)	50	50	50
Net income	30	50	100
Rate of return on equity	6%	10%	20%

	Per-Share Data[a]		
Unlevered firm			
Number of shares	100	100	100
EPS: Distribution U[b]	$ 0.80	$ 1.00	$ 1.50
Levered firm with 50% debt			
Number of shares	50	50	50
EPS: Distribution L[b]	$ 0.60	$ 1.00	$ 2.00

[a]The EPS is the net income divided by the number of outstanding shares. Note: EPS is measured in dollars.

[b]We will discuss these two distributions in Section 15.5.1.

on the S&P index in 1992. In light of the above analysis, these findings are not surprising. The year under consideration was a "boom" year, and as shown in Table 15-4, the greater the leverage, the higher the rate of return on the corresponding stock.

However, a firm should not rush into the bond market during a boom year simply to increase its leverage; a recession or a slowdown in the economy one year later may occur and cause a reversal of these results. In fact, when a CFO selects the firm's optimal capital structure, he or she knows that in a boom economy the larger the leverage, the higher the return on equity. Yet most CFOs do not rush to issue bonds.

The following problem demonstrates the effect of a leverage decision during an expansion and during a recession.

PRACTICE BOX

Problem

Perfect Binder Corporation needs $10 million for investment. It expects to earn an NOI of $3 million in an expanding economy but only $250,000 in a recession. The CFO is considering whether to finance the investment with no debt or, alternatively, with debt of $5 million at 5% interest and $5 million equity. Assuming that this is the only investment undertaken by the firm, calculate the rate of return on equity for these two proportions of debt.

Solution

We obtain the following results:

	Debt Level	
Economic Scenario	B = $0	B = $5 million
Expansion		
NOI	$3 million	$3 million
Interest	$0	$0.25 million (0.05 × $5 million)
Net income	$3 million	$2.75 million
Equity	$10 million	$5 million
Rate of return on equity	30% ($3 million/ $10 million)	55% ($2.75 million/$5 million)
Recession		
NOI	$0.25 million	$0.25 million
Interest	$0	$0.25 million
Net income	$0.25 million	$0 million
Equity	$10 million	$5 million
Rate of return on equity	2.5%	0%

In an expanding economy the rate of return on equity increases from 30% to 55% due to leverage. In a recession the rate of return on equity drops from 2.5% to zero due to leverage.

Leverage affects earnings per share similarly to how it affects the rate of return on equity. The only differences are that EPS is measured in dollars, rather than in percentages, and that its magnitude depends on the number of shares issued.[3] However, changes in the number of shares do not affect the percentage rate of return on equity, and therefore percentage rates are more meaningful in financial leverage analysis. Nevertheless, firms use the EPS in their financial statements, and the financial

3. We explore the details more fully in a later section of this chapter.

media uses EPS as a convenient benchmark for profitability. The analysis of the leverage effect on EPS is discussed next.

15.4 LEVERAGE AND EARNINGS PER SHARE: BREAK-EVEN ANALYSIS

We have seen that leverage affects the rate of return on equity. **Break-even analysis (BEA)** examines the leverage effect on earnings per share (EPS) in dollar terms. To simplify the break-even analysis, we make the assumption that leverage does not affect stock price.

If a firm finances 50% of its investment by debt, its number of shares decreases proportionally to 50%. We adopt such an assumption in the following discussion, but the analysis would be similar if the stock price varies with leverage.[4] We will first illustrate break-even analysis through a numerical example and then discuss the break-even analysis formulas.

15.4.1 A Numerical Example

We will use the basic data of Table 15-4 to illustrate the effect of leverage on the firm's EPS when NOI varies. Figure 15-1 is based on these data and on the assumptions

FIGURE 15-1
EPS and NOI of Realistic Industries.

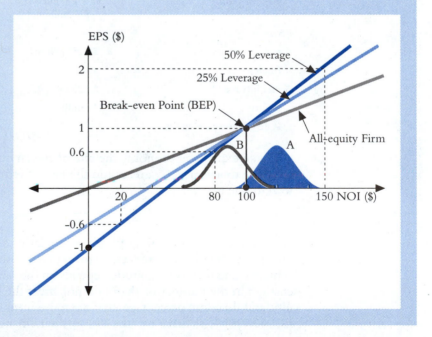

4. As we will later see, Modigliani and Miller claim that in a perfect market leverage does not affect stock price. However, if leverage does affect the price, it is impossible to calculate EPS without knowing the exact relationship between leverage and stock price.

that leverage does not affect the stock price. EPS is measured on the vertical, and NOI, on the horizontal axis. Without leverage Realistic Industries issues 100 shares at $10 per share. With 25% leverage, Realistic issues 75 shares at $10 a share; with 50% leverage, 50 shares at $10 a share. The straight lines show how EPS changes as a result of changes in NOI. Each line corresponds to a different proportion of leverage. These lines are drawn on the assumption that the interest rate on debt is 10%. For example, if the NOI is $150 and Realistic employs 50% leverage, the firm pays $50 (0.10 × $500 = $50) as interest, and the EPS is $2 [($150 − $50)/50 = $2]. We show later on that EPS is a linear function of NOI and that the larger the leverage, the steeper the line.

The line labeled "All-equity" passes through the origin, indicating that when NOI = $0, EPS = $0. Lines labeled "25% leverage" and "50% leverage" show negative figures for EPS when NOI is zero; this makes sense because Realistic still must pay interest. If NOI = $0, the net income after paying interest and the EPS will be negative. Several interesting conclusions can be drawn from Figure 15-1:

1. When NOI = $100, the rate of return on equity of the unlevered firm is 10% ($100/$1,000 = 10%). Because the interest rate is assumed to be 10%, no matter what proportion of leverage Realistic employs, EPS remains unchanged at $1 per share. The point where NOI = $100 is called the **break–even point (BEP).** At the BEP an all–equity firm's rate of return equals the interest rate. In our specific example NOI/$1,000 = 0.1, so the NOI at the break-even point is $100. Any point to the right induces a *positive financial leverage effect*; any point to its left, a *negative financial leverage effect.*

2. The larger the leverage, the steeper the line. Consequently, the larger the leverage, the stronger the leverage effect. This result implies that the EPS of a firm with a high debt/equity ratio is more sensitive to changes in NOI relative to a firm with a relatively low debt/equity ratio.

3. Even if NOI is positive, EPS may be negative because of leverage. For example, if NOI = $20 and the firm employs 50% leverage, net earnings will be negative:

$$\$20 - (0.10 \times \$500) = \$20 - \$50 = -\$30$$

and the EPS will be −$0.60 (−$30/50 = −$0.60). This occurs when the firm's interest expense is larger than its earnings. However, if the firm employs zero leverage, this cannot occur. The following problem demonstrates the relationship between one firm's EPS and NOI.

PRACTICE BOX

Problem

Spring Water's investment is $1,000, with 50 shares at $10 per share and $500 debt. The interest rate is 10%. What is the formula for the straight line that describes the relationship between EPS and NOI? Calculate the break-even point and the rate of return on equity at that point.

a. What is the EPS if NOI = $0?
b. What is the EPS if NOI = $200?

(continued)

Solution   EPS (in dollars) is given by

$$\text{EPS} = \frac{\text{NOI} - (0.10 \times \$500)}{50} = \frac{\text{NOI}}{50} - \$1$$

Therefore the formula for the line is EPS = $-\$1 + (\frac{1}{50})$ NOI. EPS is a linear function (straight line) of the NOI. In our example, the slope of the line is $\frac{1}{50}$, and the intercept is -1 (see Figure 15.4).

The BEP corresponds to the NOI where leverage has no effect on the EPS. This situation is obtained at the point where the EPS of an all-equity firm equals the EPS of a levered firm:

$$\frac{\text{NOI}}{100} = \frac{\text{NOI}}{50} - \$1$$

Multiply all terms by 100 to get

$$\text{NOI} = 2 \times \text{NOI} - \$100$$

At the BEP we have

$$\text{NOI} = \$100$$

If the NOI is $100, the rate of return on equity will be

$$\$100/\$1{,}000 = 10\%$$

which equals the interest rate. As expected, for a 10% rate of return on equity, leverage has no effect on EPS.

a. For NOI = $0, we obtain

$$\text{EPS} = \frac{\$0}{\$50} - \$1 = -\$1$$

b. For NOI = $200, we obtain

$$\text{EPS} = \frac{\$200}{\$50} - \$1 = \$3$$

15.4.2 The Formulas

Thus far we have used examples to demonstrate the effect of leverage on EPS. In this section we provide a general formula for the straight line that appears in the break-even analysis and a formula for determining the break-even point (see Figure 15–1).

Suppose an all-equity firm (which has already decided which projects to undertake) issues n shares and the firm's value is V. Because it has already determined capital expenditure, if the firm decides to employ leverage by issuing debt, B, it should issue less equity. Otherwise, it will have more cash than it needs for its capital expenditures. Because we assume that leverage has no effect on the stock price, a levered firm's number of shares should be reduced to $n_L = n(E/V)$, where E/V is the proportion of equity when leverage is applied.

The EPS of an unlevered firm (EPS_U) is

$$\text{EPS}_U = \frac{\text{NOI}}{n}$$

The EPS of the levered firm (EPS_L) is

$$\text{EPS}_L = \frac{\text{NOI} - rB}{n_L} = \frac{\text{NOI} - rB}{n(E/V)}$$

which can be rewritten as

$$\text{EPS}_L = \frac{\text{NOI}}{n} \times \frac{V}{E} - \frac{rB}{n(E/V)}$$

or

$$\text{EPS}_L = a + b\,\text{NOI} \tag{15.2}$$

where

$$a = \frac{-rB}{n(E/V)} \quad \text{and} \quad b = \frac{V}{nE}$$

A linear relationship exists between the EPS of the levered firm (EPS_L) and its NOI, with a negative intercept, a. The larger the proportion of debt, the larger V/E (that is, the steeper the slope of the line). When $B = 0$ (unlevered firm), $a = 0$ and the line intersects the origin. These results were used in plotting the lines in Figure 15-1.

The break-even point is the NOI level where all the lines in Figure 15-1 intersect. At this point the EPS of the levered firm (EPS_L) equals the EPS of the unlevered firm (EPS_U). This condition can be written as

$$\text{EPS}_L = \frac{\text{NOI} - rB}{n(E/V)} = \frac{\text{NOI}}{n} = \text{EPS}_U$$

Multiplying by nE/V, we get

$$\text{NOI} - rB = \text{NOI}\,(E/V)$$

or

$$\text{NOI}\,[1 - (E/V)] = rB$$

which can be written as

$$\text{NOI}\left[\frac{V - E}{V}\right] = rB$$

However, $V - E = B$. Therefore,

$$\text{NOI} \times B = rVB$$

Dividing by B, we find that the BEP is the point where $\text{NOI} = rV$. Thus,

$$\text{BEP:}\quad \text{NOI} = rV \qquad\qquad (15.3)$$

This says that if the firm's percentage earnings, as measured by NOI/V, exactly equal the interest paid on its bonds, then no matter how much leverage the firm employs, the EPS will be unaffected. That is why all lines cross at the same point, regardless of the proportion of the leverage employed.

Note that taxes do not affect Equation (15.3) because the break-even point is given by the NOI, which solves the equation:

$$\text{EPS}_L = \frac{(1 - T)(\text{NOI} - rB)}{n(E/V)} = \frac{(1 - T)\text{NOI}}{n} = \text{EPS}_U$$

and $(1 - T)$ cancels out, yielding the same break-even point as with the no-tax case.

If the firm knows with certainty that its NOI is above the break-even point, leverage will always increase its earnings per share. However, the firm will not always know when NOI is above the break-even point, and management can only speculate as to the likely distribution of its NOI. For example, consider two firms, A and B, with BEPs of $100. Their NOI distributions are shown in Figure 15-1. Firm A will be inclined to employ more leverage because its chance of having a positive leverage effect is much higher than Firm B's chance of having a positive leverage effect.

In some circumstances, even though the leverage effect may have a very high probability of being positive, a CFO may be against increasing the leverage. This is demonstrated next.

APPLYING THEORY TO PRACTICE 15.1

LEVERAGE AND REGULATION: OKLAHOMA GAS AND ELECTRIC CORPORATION

Oklahoma Gas and Electric Corporation (OG&E), a utility company with monopoly power, is regulated by the Oklahoma Corporations Commission. Generally, the regulator controls the rates the utility charges its customers. If the firm earns too much on its equity, it will be pressured to decrease the rates. In 1993 the firm earned too high a rate of return on equity, and in 1994 the board of directors discussed the possibility of changing the firm's debt level.

The following data were taken from the firm's financial statements and were available to the board of directors in 1994 when they discussed financial leverage:

Year	NOI (or EBIT)[a] ($ million)	Book Value per Share ($)	EPS ($)
1985	148.4	18.89	2.30
1986	177.5	20.43	2.75
1987	167.8	20.11	2.60
1988	206.5	21.01	3.20
1989	196.8	21.28	3.05
1990	218.1	21.92	3.38
1991	211.0	22.60	3.27
1992	156.2	22.35	2.42
1993	174.3	22.60	2.70
1994[b]	167.8	23.40	2.60

[a]The figures were calculated by using the EPS data supplied by *Value Line*. *Value Line Investment Survey* (New York: Value Line Publishing). The tax rate is assumed to be 37.5% (the 1994 level).

[b]Estimates.

In 1994 the firm had a long-term debt of $838.4 million and a total debt of $961.2 million. The interest on the long-term debt was $70.4 million. The firm had 40,327,790 outstanding common shares, valued at $37 a share.

At a board of directors meeting, some members suggested increasing the firm's debt and decreasing its equity. The CFO objected, arguing that in a world of uncertain earnings, leverage could be a double-edged sword. He also quoted the following news item:

A preliminary commission ruling on regulatory issues suggests that Oklahoma Gas and Electric will have to absorb a sizeable blow. Two and a half years ago, the former director of the Public Utility Division of the Oklahoma Corporation Commission alleged that og&e was over earning its allowed return on equity. The occ wound up ruling that og&e rates would be cut to reflect a 12% roe [return on equity].[5]

Additional information
Assume the following:

1. The interest rate paid on the long-term debt is the same as that paid on the total debt.
2. The book value of debt equals its market value.
3. The future distribution of the NOI is the same as that of the previous 10 years. (That is, each value of the NOI listed in the previous table has a ¹⁄₁₀ chance of occurring in the future.)

5. *Value Line* (September 1993): 732.

Analyze the issues raised at the board of directors' meeting. In particular, answer the following questions:

1. What was OG&E's debt/equity ratio in 1994?
2. Given the assumed probability distribution of NOI and the 1994 debt/equity ratio, what was the probability of OG&E having a negative leverage effect?
3. What was the maximum debt level before OG&E obtained a positive probability of a negative leverage effect?
4. Calculate OG&E's ROE (EPS/book value per share) for each of the previous 10 years.
5. In light of your findings, why do you think OG&E decided against increasing its leverage?
6. Suppose ROE rose above 12% in 1995 and 1996 and the Oklahoma commissioner forced the firm to decrease the rates it charged its customers. *Value Line* (January 12, 1996) reported the following values:

Year	EPS ($)	Book Value per Share ($)	ROE (%)
1995	3.07	23.25	13.20
1996[a]	3.20	23.75	13.47

[a] Estimate

Suppose OG&E's long-term debt was $845.2 million in 1995 and 1996, on which it paid $69.7 million in interest annually. Total debt was $903.1 million. If OG&E had issued stock in 1995 and used the proceeds to repurchase all its debt, would the Oklahoma commissioner decrease rates in 1997? Additional information: Suppose net operating income was $125 million in 1995 and $130 million in 1996, and the tax rate was 37% in both years.

MAKING THE CONNECTION

1. Leverage is measured by the ratio of the long-term debt to equity. OG&E's long-term debt/equity ratio in 1994 was

$$\frac{\$838.4 \text{ million}}{40,327,790 \times \$37} \cong 0.562 \text{ or } 56.2\%$$

2. The interest rate OG&E paid on its long-term debt was

$$\frac{\$70.4 \text{ million}}{\$838.4 \text{ million}} \cong 0.0840 \text{ or } 8.40\%$$

Assuming this rate equals the rate OG&E paid on its other debt, the total interest expense was

$$0.0840 \times \$961.2 \text{ million} \cong \$80.74 \text{ million}$$

Because the minimum NOI of the probability distribution was $148.4 million, the probability of a negative leverage effect was zero; this was true in spite of the NOI's uncertainty. Thus, more leverage would have been beneficial.

3. The leverage effect is positive as long as the NOI is greater than rB. Therefore, OG&E could have had debt of B such that

$$0.084 \times B = \$148.4 \text{ million}$$

and

$$B = \$148.4 \text{ million}/0.084 \cong \$1,766.67 \text{ million}$$

Thus, the firm could have increased its leverage substantially. Only if B had exceeded $1,766.67 million would there have been a positive probability of a negative leverage effect.

4. ROE is calculated by dividing the EPS by the book value per share:

Year:	1985	1986	1987	1988	1989	1990	1991	1992	1993	1994
ROE (%):	12.18	13.46	12.93	15.23	14.33	15.42	14.47	10.83	11.95	11.11

5. The firm was regulated. In the quoted news item, it seems that the regulator did not allow the firm to earn more than 12% on its equity. Actually, the article said OG&E might even "absorb a sizeable blow" because of its high earnings in previous years. In most years OG&E's ROE was above 12%. By employing more leverage at 8.4% interest, the firm would have surpassed the 12% ROE ceiling, would have been forced to cut its rates, and would have forfeited the benefit. Beyond a certain point the firm would not have enjoyed the positive effect of the leverage.

    Moreover, if the NOI is below the BEP, a very large leverage would have increased a negative leverage effect. It is true that with negative earnings and a low ROE, the regulator may have allowed the utility firm to charge higher rates. However, the CEO preferred not to have his name associated with failure and preferred not to increase leverage.

6. The number of shares in 1994 was 40,327,790. To redeem all its long-term debt, the firm would have needed to raise $903.1 million by issuing 24,408,108 shares ($903.1 million/$37 $\cong$ 24,408,108 shares). Total shares outstanding would have then been 64,735,898.

    To calculate net profit under the 1995 and 1996 hypothetical capital structure, we use the following definition of net profit:

    Net profit = $(1 - T) \times$ (Net operating income − Interest payment)

If we add $(1 - T)$ multiplied by the interest payment to the levered firm's reported profit, we obtain $(1 - T)$ multiplied by net operating income. Since the interest on long-term debt was about 8.25% ($69.7 million/$845.2 million), the interest on total debt was about $74.51 million (0.0825 × $903.1 million). Therefore,

Year	Net Operating Income (in $ million)
1995	$125 + (1 - 0.37)$74.51 = $171.941
1996	$130 + (1 - 0.37)$74.51 = $176.941

With 64,735,898 shares outstanding, the EPS for an all-equity firm would be as follows:

Year	EPS
1995	$2.66
1996	$2.73

To calculate the ROE, we need to calculate book value per share for an all-equity firm. For 1995 it is

$$\frac{\text{Book value of all-equity firm}}{\text{Number of shares with new issue}}$$

$$= \frac{\$23.25 \times 40{,}327{,}790 + \$903.1 \text{ million}}{64{,}735{,}898} \cong \$28.43$$

In this calculation, $23.25 is the book value per share for a levered firm, and $903.1 million is the new equity raised.

Similar calculations for 1996 yield a book value per share of

$$\frac{\$23.75 \times 40{,}327{,}790 + \$903.1 \text{ million}}{64{,}735{,}898} \cong \$28.75$$

ROE, which is EPS divided by book value per share, is as follows:

Year	ROE
1995	$2.66/$28.43 ≅ 0.0936 or 9.36%
1996	$2.73/$28.75 ≅ 0.0950 or 9.50%

Thus, with a change of capital structure, ROE will be below 12%, and the commissioner will not request a decrease in utility rates.

Most firms operate without the type of regulation described in Applying Theory to Practice 15.1. Leverage is likely to be a double-edged sword for Realistic Industries. How can a firm know whether employing leverage is good or bad? To answer this question, a firm needs to know what effect leverage has on its value. Leverage can be beneficial if it increases the firm's value. We turn our attention to this issue in the next section.

15.5 MODIGLIANI AND MILLER (M & M)

15.5.1 Why Do Modigliani and Miller Claim That Capital Structure Is Irrelevant?

It is impossible to analyze the leverage issue without referring to the work of Nobel Prize winners Franco Modigliani and Merton H. Miller (M & M). Their break-through article, published in 1958, analyzed the effect of leverage on the firm's value and on the cost of capital.[6]

Modigliani and Miller claim that in a perfect market capital structure does not matter. However, as we shall see in Chapter 16, most CFOs believe that capital structure does matter because markets are imperfect. We will first illustrate M & M's argument and then discuss its explicit and implicit perfect-market assumptions. In Chapter 16 we will consider the market imperfections that form the basis of most CFOs' beliefs and behavior.

The discussion of M & M's claim in this and the next chapter is based on the **principle of no arbitrage profit:** If two perfectly-correlated alternative invest-ments yield exactly the same distribution of future rates of return, their current market prices will be identical. This principle is also called the **law of one price.** If the prices are not identical, it is possible to make a certain profit by selling the in-vestment with the higher price and by buying the investment with the lower price. If such a situation exists, the market is not in equilibrium, and an **arbitrage profit** is available. The law of one price is used in comparing the rates of return of levered and unlevered firms throughout this chapter.

To illustrate M & M's claim that capital structure is irrelevant, let us once again re-view the figures presented in Table 15-4 (see Section 15.3.2). In this example the rate of return on equity for an all-equity firm is 8%, 10%, or 15%, each with a prob-ability of ⅓. As before, let us assume the all-equity firm issues 100 shares at $10 per share. Therefore, the EPS will be $0.8, $1, and $1.50 with an equal probability of ⅓. The stock price, by assumption, is $10. Now suppose a similar firm (with the same NOI) issues 50 shares at $10 a share and then complements the investment by issuing $500 of debt. With this 50% leverage, the rates of return on equity will be 6%, 10%, and 20%, respectively. In this case the EPS will be $0.60, $1, or $2, respectively.

M & M claim that in a perfect market the stock prices of any two such similar firms, one levered and one unlevered, will be equal. If differences in prices are ob-served in the market, arbitragers will restore the equilibrium.

Suppose two such firms are in the market. Stockholders will face both probability distributions of EPS denoted by U (unlevered) and L (levered). Let's take the extreme case and assume all investors prefer the levered firm's probability distribution. Will that firm's stock price be higher than the unlevered firm's stock price? The issue is whether investors will be willing to pay more than $10 for a share of the levered

---

6. See F. Modigliani and M. Miller, "The Cost of Capital, Corporation Finance and the Theory of Investment," *American Economic Review* (June 1958): 261–97.

firm. M & M claim that the stock prices of the two firms will be identical. Otherwise, an **arbitrage profit** would exist and the market would not be in equilibrium.

If the unlevered firm's stock price is $10, it is impossible to have a higher price for the levered firm's stock. Why? Because, according to M & M, no rational investor will pay more for the levered firm's stock than for the unlevered firm's stock. Even if investors do prefer probability distribution L to U, a price differential cannot be maintained in the long run. The reason is that investors can create their own leverage by selling the levered firm's stock and taking out a loan to buy the unlevered firm's stock. (We will explain the details of this transaction further on.) In that way, they can obtain the desired leverage at the lower price. Investors who hold the levered firm's stock will sell it, pushing down its price until the market prices of the levered and unlevered firms' stock are identical.

Table 15-5 illustrates these financial transactions. For simplicity we assume the unlevered firm's stock price remains $10. If the levered firm's price is higher, say $11, M & M recommend that investors sell the levered firm's "expensive" stock for $11 and borrow $10 at 10% (the interest rate in our example). They then will have $21 to invest. Putting aside $1 (the certain profit from the transaction), investors can then buy two shares of the unlevered firm at $10 each. The cash flows from this transaction are shown in the right-hand column of the table. For example, if the unlevered firm's EPS is $0.80, then investors will earn $1.60 when they buy two shares of the unlevered firm. However, since they must pay 10% interest on the $10 borrowed, investors will be left with

$$(2 \times \$0.80) - (0.10 \times \$10) = \$1.60 - \$1 = \$0.60$$

This amount is exactly what investors would have earned with one share in the levered firm. Table 15-5 shows that by adopting this borrowing strategy, investors replicate the desired cash flow that they would receive by holding one share of the levered firm, and gain $1 which they put aside.

TABLE 15-5   **Earnings per Share on Levered and Unlevered Firms**[a]

Economic Scenario	Probability	Earnings per Share ($)		Cash Flows from Arbitrage Transaction
		Unlevered Firm	Levered Firm[b]	
Recession	⅓	0.80	0.60	$(2 \times \$0.80) - (0.10 \times \$10) = 0.60$
Normal	⅓	1.00	1.00	$(2 \times \$1.00) - (0.10 \times \$10) = 1.00$
Expansion	⅓	1.50	2.00	$(2 \times \$1.50) - (0.10 \times \$10) = 2.00$
Stock price		$10	$11: Is it possible?	

[a] Figures taken from Table 15-4 (see Section 15.3.2).

[b] 50% leverage is assumed.

This process will continue as long as the levered firm's stock price is higher than that of the unlevered firm. However, selling the levered firm's stock will push its price down, and profit from the transaction will decrease: If the levered firm's share price drops to $10.50, selling will continue, and the transaction will yield a certain profit of $0.50. If the price drops to $10.30, the profit from the transaction will be $0.30. This process will stop when the levered stock and unlevered stock prices are identical. Thus, according to M & M's argument, in equilibrium, the levered firm's stock price cannot be higher than the unlevered stock's price.

An **arbitrage transaction** allows investors to switch from one investment to another without changing the distribution of returns and while earning a certain profit. When investors sell the levered firm's stock and buy the unlevered stock with borrowing, they replace the firm's borrowing with their personal borrowing. This procedure is **homemade leverage.** In M & M's argument homemade leverage is assumed a perfect substitute for the firm's leverage. If so, the firm's leverage has no effect on the stock price, and capital structure is irrelevant. The reason is: Even if all prefer the levered firm's distribution of rates of return, investors will not pay a premium because they can use homemade leverage and achieve the desired distribution.

This arbitrage process conforms with the law of one price. Because the two distributions corresponding to the levered firm and arbitrage transaction given in the left two columns of Table 15-5 are identical, the net investment on each investment must be identical—$10 per share. To see this, recall that the net investment in the levered firm is $10. The net investment in the unlevered firm is $2P_U - \$10$, which is the price investors pay for two shares of the unlevered firm $(2P_U)$ less the $10 loan. By the law of one price we must have, in equilibrium, an equal price for assets that yield identical returns. We, therefore, have

$$2P_U - \$10 = \$10 \quad \text{hence} \quad P_U = \$10$$

Thus far we have seen that the return on the levered firm's stock can be replicated by investing in the unlevered firm plus borrowing. No one will pay a higher price for the levered firm and, therefore, the price cannot exceed $10. But what about the opposite situation? If all investors prefer the unlevered firm's return over that of the levered firm, will they be willing to pay more for the unlevered firm's stock? If the price of the levered firm's share is $10, is it possible for the unlevered firm's price to be higher, say $11? This would constitute paying a premium to the firm without leverage, or penalizing the firm with leverage.

Such a scenario can easily be shown as impossible. If the levered firm's price is $10 per share and the unlevered firm's price is higher, say $11, investors can conduct an arbitrage transaction, obtain the same distribution as before the arbitrage, and make a certain profit. To see this, suppose you hold two shares in the unlevered firm. Your return will be

$$2 \times \$0.80 = \$1.60; \quad 2 \times \$1 = \$2; \quad \text{or} \quad 2 \times \$1.50 = \$3$$

with a probability of ⅓ for each possible outcome. (See Table 15-5.) Your investment is $22 ($11 × 2 = $22) because, by assumption, you hold two shares and the unlevered firm's stock price is $11 per share. M & M would suggest that you conduct the following transaction: Sell your two shares to receive $22; put aside $2; and with the remaining $20, buy one share of the levered firm and invest $10 in riskless bonds. The return on this transaction will be as follows:

Return on the Stock		Return on the Bond	Total Return on a Portfolio of Stocks and Bonds
$0.60	+	0.10 × $10	= $1.60 with a probability of ⅓
$1.00	+	0.10 × $10	= $2.00 with a probability of ⅓
$2.00	+	0.10 × $10	= $3.00 with a probability of ⅓

In this way, you not only replicate the distribution of income that you had before the arbitrage transaction, but you also save $2.

This kind of arbitrage transaction is very attractive. Indeed, all investors offered this opportunity would sell the unlevered firm's stock, and its price would drop until it equaled the levered firm's stock price. By selling the unlevered firm's stock, buying the levered firm's stock, and lending at 10% (investing in a riskless bond), investors could **"undo" the leverage** because the bond they hold cancels the leverage effect of the levered firm's stock. Once again, investors end up with the same return on the two investment strategies. By the law of one price, the initial investment corresponding to these two investment strategies must be identical—in our case $20: two shares at $10 a share by one strategy, and $10 in the stock and $10 in the bond by the other strategy. Thus, the levered firm's stock price can be neither higher nor lower than the unlevered firm's stock price.

Using this argument, M & M claim that a firm cannot increase its value by changing its leverage; that is, capital structure is irrelevant. In equilibrium two firms identical in all respects, except their capital structure, will have the same value.

$$V_L = V_U \tag{15.4}$$

The firm's goal is to select the capital structure that maximizes its value. Irrelevance of capital structure implies that one capital structure is as good as another and that the firm's value will be the same, regardless of the selected capital structure. This argument has been based on a number of assumptions—some explicit and some implicit—that M & M made in devising the arbitrage transaction. Let's review these to be sure we understand the foundation on which the conclusion rests.

First, M & M assume the two firms are identical, except for their capital structures. In particular, their NOI distributions are identical. This assumption is not crucial, and M & M's argument is valid even if the assumption is relaxed.

However, M & M did make the following crucial assumptions characterizing a perfect market:

1. Only one interest rate exists at which both individuals and firms can both borrow and lend. The traditional approach to capital structure claims that using leverage increases the firm's value. To refute this claim, M & M need to assume that individual investors and firms can borrow at the same interest rate. Homemade leverage serves as a perfect substitute for the firm's leverage; that is, if in-

vestors like leverage, they can borrow themselves. For this reason leverage does not increase the firm's value. Without the ability for firms and individuals to borrow and lend at the same rate, the whole argument collapses.

2. No transaction costs exist. Investors pay no commission when they conduct an arbitrage transaction.
3. No taxes are assessed or paid. All earnings are tax-free.
4. The possibility of bankruptcy does not exist. Because they borrow at the riskless interest rate, firms and individuals cannot claim bankruptcy. (Otherwise, the higher the risk of bankruptcy, the higher the interest rate.)

Assumptions 1, 2, and 3 are explicit in the arbitrage transaction, whereas assumption 4 is implicit. In the arbitrage transaction we use the riskless interest rate on borrowing, which implies no risk of bankruptcy. (We elaborate on this assumption in Chapter 16 and show that bankruptcy is costly. Therefore this assumption is critical for M & M's results.)

Finally, M & M do not assume that investors either like or dislike leverage. Actually, M & M provide no information on investor preference. They claim that investors will not pay a premium for a firm's leverage because those investors can create leverage by borrowing on their personal account. Similarly, investors will not pay a premium on unlevered firms when they can buy the levered firm's stock and undo the leverage by buying bonds.

15.5.2 Do Modigliani and Miller Ignore Risk?

According to M & M, the capital structure a firm selects has no effect on its value. One might then be tempted to conclude that leverage has no effect on the distribution of rates of return to stockholders. This is not the case. Actually, $V_L = V_U$ implies that an increase in leverage has the following effects:

1. The cost of equity (expected rate of return) increases.
2. Stockholders' risk exposure increases.
3. The weighted-average cost of capital (WACC) remains unchanged.

M & M do not ignore risk. On the contrary, they recognize that leverage increases stockholders' risk and that the cost of equity must increase to compensate for that additional risk. Moreover, they can determine by exactly how much risk and the cost of equity will increase with an increase in leverage.

We discuss the general formula and demonstrate the effect of leverage on rates of return by using the numerical example of Table 15-4, which involves an unlevered firm and a 50% levered firm.

THE EFFECT OF LEVERAGE ON THE FIRM'S COST OF EQUITY

Stockholders' expected rate of return on equity is the firm's cost of equity. (See Chapter 10, Section 10.4.) We show how capital structure irrelevance implies that the larger the leverage, the higher the cost of equity. To see this, denote the expected value of the firm's NOI by $\overline{\text{NOI}}$. Without leverage, the rate of return on equity is R_U = NOI$/V_U$ where NOI is uncertain. The cost of equity is the expected rate of return:

$$k_U = \bar{R}_U = \frac{\overline{\text{NOI}}}{V_U}$$

(The bar denotes expected value.) The rate of return on the levered firm's equity is

$$R_L = \frac{\text{NOI} - rB}{E_L} = \frac{\text{NOI}}{V_U} \times \frac{V_U}{E_L} - \frac{rB}{E_L}$$

It follows that the levered firm's cost of equity is

$$k_L = \bar{R}_L = \frac{\overline{\text{NOI}} - rB}{E_L} = \left(\frac{\overline{\text{NOI}}}{V_U} \times \frac{V_U}{E_L}\right) - \frac{rB}{E_L}$$

where rB is the interest and E_L is the levered firm's equity. The subscript L distinguishes E_L from the unleveraged firm's equity, E.[7] Note that we multiply the first term by V_U/V_U, which changes nothing. However, if capital structure is irrelevant, $V_U = V_L$ and, by definition, $V_L = E_L + B$ (the levered firm's total value is the sum of its equity and debt). Substituting $E_L + B$ for V_U, we can rewrite the rate of return on the levered firm's equity as

$$R_L = \left(\frac{\text{NOI}}{V_U} \times \frac{E_L + B}{E_L}\right) - \frac{rB}{E_L} = \frac{\text{NOI}}{V_U} + \left(\frac{\text{NOI}}{V_U} - r\right)\frac{B}{E_L}$$

Using the definitions of R_U and R_L we obtain Equation (15.5), which gives the relationship between rates of return on levered and unlevered firms' shares:

$$R_L = R_U + (R_U - r)\frac{B}{E_L} \qquad (15.5)$$

Taking expected values of both sides, we obtain the relationship between levered and unlevered firms' costs of equity:

$$k_L = k_U + (k_U - r)\frac{B}{E_L} \qquad (15.6)$$

Or, in words:

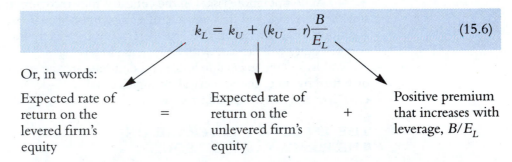

| Expected rate of return on the levered firm's equity | = | Expected rate of return on the unlevered firm's equity | + | Positive premium that increases with leverage, B/E_L |

---

7. With the other variables, this subscript does not need to be added because it is obvious that B corresponds to the levered firm.

From Equation (15.5) we see that the realized leverage effect may be positive or negative in a given year. In a good year, $R_U > r$, and the leverage effect is positive. In a recession when $R_U < r$, the leverage effect is negative because $R_L < R_U$; this is consistent with the break-even analysis discussed in Section 15.4. However, Equation (15.6) shows that the cost of equity increases with leverage when $k_U > r$; otherwise, the firm does not receive a risk premium for its business risk.[8]

Let's return to the numerical example of Table 15-4 and investigate the effect of leverage on the rate of return and cost of equity. First, note that in a recession (NOI = $80), the rate of return on an all-equity firm is 8% and the rate of return on a 50% levered firm is only 6%. Equation (15.5) confirms this result:

$$R_L = R_U + (R_U - r) \frac{B}{E_L}$$

For a 50%-leveraged firm, $B/E_L = 1$, and we obtain

$$R_L = 8\% + (8\% - 10\%) \times 1 = 6\%$$

exactly as obtained in the direct calculation.

When the economy expands:

$$R_L = 15\% + (15\% - 10\%) \times 1 = 20\%$$

as before. These are the same results we obtained in the break-even analysis, confirming the assertion that leverage is a double-edged sword.

The unlevered firm's cost of equity (or expected rate of return) is

$$k_U = \frac{1}{3} \times 8\% + \frac{1}{3} \times 10\% + \frac{1}{3} \times 15\% = 11\%$$

For a 50%-levered firm it is

$$k_L = \frac{1}{3} \times 6\% + \frac{1}{3} \times 10\% + \frac{1}{3} \times 20\% = 12\%$$

Equation (15.6) confirms this direct calculation since

$$k_L = k_U + (k_U - r) \times \frac{B}{E_L} = 11\% + (11\% - 10\%) \times 1 = 12\%$$

Figure 15-2 illustrates the relationship among an unlevered firm's cost of equity (11%), the interest rate (10%), and a levered firm's cost of equity. For example, take the point L_1 where $B/E_L = 1$. The levered firm's cost of equity at this point is 12%. Now take the point denoted by L_2, where $B/E_L = 3$. At this point, the levered firm's cost of equity will be 14% [11% + (11% – 10%) × 3]. Thus, the higher the leverage, the higher the levered firm's cost of equity. Equation (15.5) is used to determine the

8. We assume $k_U = \overline{\text{NOI}}/V_U > r$. In other words, in equilibrium, the unlevered firm should earn, on average, more than the market interest rate. The cost of equity is greater than the cost of debt, r. Otherwise, the firm would fare better by closing the business and depositing the money in the bank, thereby obtaining more expected profit with less risk.

FIGURE 15-2
Cost of Equity and Leverage

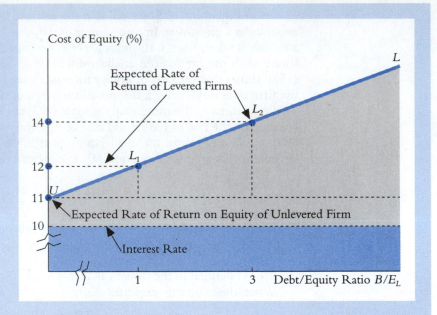

straight line, *UL*, that describes the relationship between the expected rate of return with leverage and the debt/equity ratio.

As stated previously, M & M are not oblivious to risk. On the contrary, they claim that the higher the leverage, the riskier the investment in the stock and the higher the expected cost of equity. Technically, M & M's results imply that the stockholders' expected EPS and the discount rate employed to evaluate this EPS increase at the same pace when leverage is employed. The stock price, which is simply the discounted value of the future expected cash flows, will be the same regardless of the firm's capital structure.

To demonstrate this notion, recall first that the cost of equity increases from 11% for the unlevered firm to 12% for a levered firm with 50% debt. The cost of equity used to evaluate the stock increases by approximately 9.09% (12%/11% − 1). Returning to the figures presented in Table 15-4, the unlevered and levered firms' expected EPS are:

Unlevered firm:

$$\overline{EPS}_U = (\$0.80 \times \tfrac{1}{3}) + (\$1 \times \tfrac{1}{3}) + (\$1.50 \times \tfrac{1}{3}) = \$1.10$$

Levered firm with 50% debt:

$$\overline{EPS}_L = (\$0.60 \times \tfrac{1}{3}) + (\$1 \times \tfrac{1}{3}) + (\$2 \times \tfrac{1}{3}) = \$1.20$$

The expected EPS also increases by approximately 9.09% ($1.20/$1.10 − 1 ≅ 0.0909 or 9.09%). Because the expected EPS and the cost of equity increase at the same rate when leverage is employed, the firm's capital structure does not affect the stock price. Indeed, using the above results, we find that the stock price is as follows:

Unlevered firm:

$$P_U = \frac{\overline{EPS}_U}{k_U} = \frac{\$1.10}{0.11} = \$10 \text{ per share}$$

Levered firm with 50% debt:

$$P_L = \frac{\overline{EPS}_L}{k_L} = \frac{\$1.20}{0.12} = \$10 \text{ per share}$$

Therefore, the price is the same regardless of the capital structure, just as M & M claimed.

Why does the cost of equity increase with leverage? It increases because stockholders are exposed to more risk as leverage increases. We shall see next that both beta and the standard deviation of returns increase as leverage increases.

THE EFFECT OF LEVERAGE ON THE STANDARD DEVIATION OF RETURNS

Rewriting Equation (15.5), we obtain

$$R_L = R_U\left(1 + \frac{B}{E_L}\right) - r\frac{B}{E_L} = R_U\left(\frac{E_L + B}{E_L}\right) - r\frac{B}{E_L}$$

Since $V_L = V_U$ and $E_L + B = V_L$, we have

$$R_L = R_U \times \frac{V_U}{E_L} - r\frac{B}{E_L}$$

Because rB/E_L is constant, the variance is[9]

$$\sigma_L^2 = \left(\frac{V_U}{E_L}\right)^2\sigma_U^2$$

where σ_U^2 is the variance of returns on the unlevered firm.
The standard deviation is

$$\sigma_L = \frac{V_U}{E_L}\sigma_U \qquad\qquad (15.7)$$

Because $V_U/E_L > 1$, $\sigma_L > \sigma_U$, so that leverage increases the standard deviation of the rate of return. Let us demonstrate Equation (15.7) with the numerical data from Table 15-4. The variances of the rate of return for the unlevered and 50%-levered firms are as follows:

---

9. The only uncertain factor in this expression is R_U. We use the rule that $\text{Var}(aX + b) = a^2\text{Var}(X)$, where a and b are constants. In our case, b equals rB/E_L, a equals V_U/E_L, and X equals R_U.

Unlevered firm:

$$\sigma_U^2 = \frac{1}{3} \times (8\% - 11\%)^2 + \frac{1}{3} \times (10\% - 11\%)^2 + \frac{1}{3} \times (15\% - 11\%)^2 \cong 8.67$$

Thus,

$$\sigma_U = (8.67)^{1/2} \cong 2.94\%$$

Levered firm with 50% debt:

$$\sigma_L^2 = \frac{1}{3}(6\% - 12\%)^2 + \frac{1}{3}(10\% - 12\%)^2 + \frac{1}{3}(20\% - 12\%)^2 \cong 34.67$$

Thus,

$$\sigma_L = (34.67)^{1/2} \cong 5.89\%$$

Using Equation (15.7) and $V_U/V_L = 2$ (by assumption), we obtain

$$\sigma_L = \frac{V_U}{E_L} \times \sigma_U = 2 \times 2.94\% = 5.88\%$$

as in the direct calculation.

Figure 15-3 illustrates the distributions of the rates of return on a levered and an unlevered firm's equity. The figure shows that leverage increases both the expected rate of return (the shift to the right in the distribution) and the dispersion of the rates of return (the distribution of the levered firm is flatter than that of the unlevered firm).

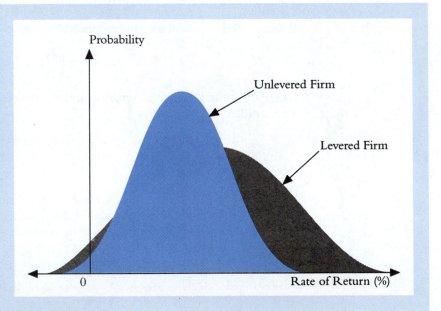

FIGURE 15-3
Distributions of the Rate of Return on Equity of a Levered Firm and an Unlevered Firm

The following problem demonstrates how leverage affects the rate of return.

PRACTICE BOX

Problem

In Connecting Theory to Practice 15.1, the rate of return on the Standard & Poor's index in 1992 was 26.3%. For highly levered firms, the average rate of return was 39.2%. Suppose that the rate of return on all-equity firms was 20% and the riskless interest rate was 6%.

a. What is your estimate of the average leverage of firms included in the S&P index?
b. What is the estimated average leverage of firms with a 39.2% rate of return?

Solution

Because we refer to a given year's rate of return and not to an expected rate of return, we should use Equation (15.5) rather than (15.6).

a. According to Equation (15.5):

$$R_L = R_U + (R_U - r)\frac{B}{E_L}$$

Using the data corresponding to the S&P index we obtain

$$26.3\% = 20\% + (20\% - 6\%)\frac{B}{E_L}$$

or

$$\frac{26.3\% - 20\%}{20\% - 6\%} = \frac{6.3\%}{14\%} = 0.45 = \frac{B}{E_L}$$

The average debt/equity ratio of the firms included in the S&P index is 0.45.

b. For levered firms with a 39.2% rate of return, we have

$$39.2\% = 20\% + (20\% - 6\%)\frac{B}{E_L}$$

Thus

$$\frac{39.2\% - 20\%}{14\%} \cong 1.37 = \frac{B}{E_L}$$

These firms are highly levered; their debt/equity ratio is 1.37.

THE EFFECT OF LEVERAGE ON BETA

Denoting the rates of return on unlevered and levered firms by R_U and R_L, an unlevered firm's beta is $b_U = \text{Cov}(R_U, R_m)/\sigma_m^2$. Similarly, a levered firm's beta is $b_L = \text{Cov}(R_L, R_m)/\sigma_m^2$. Using Equation (15.5), we can rewrite the levered firm's rate of return as

$$R_L = R_U \frac{V_U}{E_L} - r\frac{B}{E_L}$$

Therefore,

$$b_L = \text{Cov}\left(R_U\frac{V_U}{E_L} - \frac{rB}{E_L}, R_m\right)/\sigma_m^2$$

Since rB/E_L is a constant, its covariance with R_m is zero. V_U/E_L is also a constant; therefore, we get[10]

$$b_L = \frac{V_U}{E_L}\text{Cov}(R_U, R_m)/\sigma_m^2$$

or

$$b_L = \frac{V_U}{E_L}b_U \qquad\qquad (15.8)$$

Because $V_U = V_L = E_L + B$ it must be that $V_U > E_L$ or $V_U/E_L > 1$. The levered firm's beta is larger than the unlevered firm's beta; and the higher the leverage, the higher the beta. Using the numerical example of Table 15-4 with b_U assumed to equal 1 and with 50% leverage, $V_U/E_L = 2$. Therefore, $b_L = 2 \times 1 = 2$.

15.6 LEVERAGE AND THE FIRM'S WEIGHTED AVERAGE COST OF CAPITAL

As leverage increases, the proportions of debt and equity as sources of financing change: Debt increases and equity decreases. An all-equity firm's cost of capital is greater than the riskless interest rate. Otherwise, the firm would fare better by investing all its funds in the riskless asset. The difference, $k_U - r$, is compensation for business risk. According to Equation (15.6), $k_L > k_U$ and therefore k_L is also greater than r. We conclude that equity is a more expensive source of financing than debt. Therefore, a reasonable question is: What effect does leverage have on the firm's weighted average cost of capital? We shall see next that leverage does not affect the WACC. The reason, simply stated, is: Although the cost of equity increases with leverage, the proportion of this "expensive" source of financing decreases as leverage increases and the WACC remains constant. We show this first in M & M's framework and then in the CAPM framework.

15.6.1 M & M's Framework

The levered firm's cost of equity is k_L, whereas the unlevered firm's cost of equity or cost of capital is k_U. By Equation (15.6), we have

$$k_L = k_U + (k_U - r)\frac{B}{E_L}$$

---

10. We use the rule asserting that for any two constants a and b, we have $\text{Cov}(ax + b, y) = a\,\text{Cov}(x, y)$.

where r denotes the cost of debt. The levered firm's WACC is

$$\text{WACC} = \frac{E_L}{V_L} k_L + \frac{B}{V_L} \times r$$

where E_L/V_L and B/V_L are the weights of equity and debt in the firm's financing, respectively.

Using Equation (15.6), we have

$$\frac{E_L}{V_L}\left[k_U + (k_U - r)\frac{B}{E_L}\right] + \frac{B}{V_L}r = \frac{E_L}{V_L}k_U + \frac{B}{V_L}k_U - \frac{B}{V_L}r + \frac{B}{V_L}r$$

$$= k_U \frac{E_L + B}{V_L} = k_U$$

(Recall that $E_L + B = V_L$.) Thus, leverage has no effect on the levered firm's WACC; it remains equal to the unlevered firm's cost of capital.

Using the numerical example of Table 15-4, we see that $k_L = 12\%$ $k_U = 11\%$. The WACC is, therefore, 11% [0.5(12%) + 0.5(10%) = 11%]. The WACC is the same for levered and unlevered firms, regardless of the degree of leverage.

15.6.2 CAPM Framework

According to the CAPM, the unlevered firm's cost of equity is: $k_U = r + (\overline{R}_m - r) \times b_U$; and the levered firm's cost of equity is: $k_L = r + (\overline{R}_m - r)\, b_L$. However, because $b_L = (V_U/E_L)b_U$, the levered firm's cost of equity can be rewritten as follows:

$$k_L = r + (\overline{R}_m - r)\frac{V_U}{E_L}b_U$$

The levered firm's WACC is

$$\text{WACC} = \frac{E_L}{V_L}k_L + \frac{B}{V_L}r$$

Substituting for k_L, the WACC becomes

$$\frac{E_L}{V_L}\left[r + (\overline{R}_m - r)\frac{V_U}{E_L}b_U\right] + \frac{B}{V_L}r$$

Rearranging, we get

$$\text{WACC} = \frac{E_L}{V_L}r + \frac{B}{V_L}r + \frac{V_U}{V_L}\overline{R}_m b_U - \frac{V_U}{V_L}r b_U$$

Because

$$\frac{E_L}{V_L}r + \frac{B}{V_L}r = \frac{E_L + B}{V_L}r = \frac{V_L}{V_L}r = r \qquad \text{and} \qquad V_U = V_L$$

We finally get WACC $= r + (\overline{R}_m - r)b_U$, which equals the unlevered firm's cost of equity. Therefore, WACC $= k_U$.

In the CAPM framework, as in the M & M framework, the WACC equals the all-equity firm's cost of capital; this means that leverage does not affect the firm's cost of capital.

SUMMARY

In this chapter we examined how leverage affects the distribution of rates of return to the stockholders and the firm's value. We found that increasing leverage serves to increase the cost of equity as well as the stockholders' risk exposure.

In a perfect market—a market in which firms and individuals can borrow at the same interest rate and in a tax-free world with no transaction costs—the levered firm's value will be identical to that of the unlevered firm. Even though leverage changes the distribution of the rates of return, the share price will remain unchanged. Modigliani and Miller (M & M) reached three main conclusions:

1. Leverage has no effect on the firm's value.
2. The cost of equity increases with leverage.
3. Leverage has no effect on the WACC.

This does not mean that investors will be indifferent between the distribution of returns on levered and unlevered firms. Rather, it means that investors will not pay a premium for the levered firm's stock because they can shift from one distribution to another, free of costs. For example, if they prefer leverage, they can take out a personal loan and create homemade leverage. Similarly, if they do not prefer leverage, they can undo it by investing in riskless bonds.

In a perfect market any financial mix will be optimal. So why do firms struggle with the issue of an optimal capital structure? They do so because the capital market is far from perfect. The optimal capital structure in an imperfect market is the topic of the next chapter.

CHAPTER AT A GLANCE

1. M & M show that:

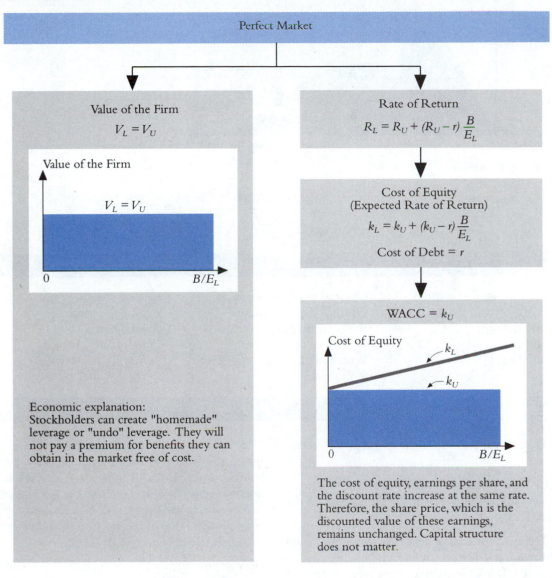

Perfect Market

Value of the Firm

$$V_L = V_U$$

Value of the Firm

$$V_L = V_U$$

0 B/E_L

Economic explanation:
Stockholders can create "homemade" leverage or "undo" leverage. They will not pay a premium for benefits they can obtain in the market free of cost.

Rate of Return

$$R_L = R_U + (R_U - r)\frac{B}{E_L}$$

Cost of Equity
(Expected Rate of Return)

$$k_L = k_U + (k_U - r)\frac{B}{E_L}$$

Cost of Debt $= r$

WACC $= k_U$

Cost of Equity

k_L

k_U

0 B/E_L

The cost of equity, earnings per share, and the discount rate increase at the same rate. Therefore, the share price, which is the discounted value of these earnings, remains unchanged. Capital structure does not matter.

2. Rate of return on equity:

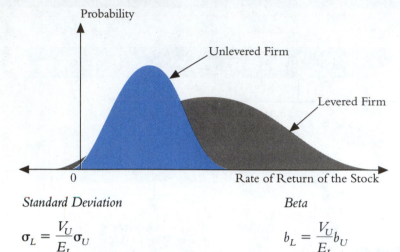

Standard Deviation

$$\sigma_L = \frac{V_U}{E_L}\sigma_U$$

Beta

$$b_L = \frac{V_U}{E_L}b_U$$

KEY TERMS

Capital structure	Optimal financial leverage	Law of one price
Perfect market	Optimal capital structure	Arbitrage profit
Financial leverage	Break-even analysis (BEA)	Arbitrage transaction
Levered firm	Break-even point (BEP)	Homemade leverage
Unlevered firm	Principle of no arbitrage profit	"Undo" the leverage

REVIEW AND PRACTICE

15.1 Define capital structure and optimal capital structure.

15.2 In 1992 General Motors issued $2.9 billion of common stock. The price of the GM stock increased. Explain this market reaction.

15.3 Define homemade leverage. Suppose a firm can borrow at 6% and an individual investor can borrow at 7%. Will homemade leverage be a perfect substitute for the firm's leverage?

15.4 Explain what it means to "undo" leverage. What kind of transaction would you have to conduct to undo leverage?

15.5 Assume zero taxes. An unlevered firm's average NOI is $\overline{NOI}$ = $100,000. The firm's value is $1 million, and the interest rate is r = 5%. What is the firm's average rate of return? What is the average rate of return on the equity of a levered firm that employs $500,000 of debt? How would your results change if the debt were $750,000?

15.6 A new firm needs $10 million for an investment. It is considering issuing 1 million shares of stock at $10 a share. It is also considering issuing some debt. If the firm uses debt financing, the number of shares issued will be reduced proportionally. For example, if it issues $2 million of debt, the firm will issue only 0.8 million shares; if it issues $5 million of debt, the firm will issue only 0.5 million shares, and so on. The firm's founder estimates that the following stock prices will be obtained for various levels of debt:

Debt Issue (in $ million)	Stock Price ($)
1	10
2	10.50
3	11
4	12
5	10

a. What is the firm's optimal capital structure?
b. What is the firm's value and the stock price at this optimal point?

15.7 Assume no taxes and $V_L = V_U$. The firm's NOI is uncertain given by the following:

State of the Economy	Probability	NOI (in $ million)
Expansion	¼	10
Normal	½	5
Recession	¼	−2

It is given that $V_U = \$50$ million.
a. Calculate the mean and variance of the rate of return on the firm's equity.
b. What would be the mean and variance of the rate of return on equity for a capital structure composed of $25 million equity and $25 million debt at 5% interest?
c. Plot the distribution of the rates of return corresponding to the levered and unlevered firms.

15.8 Assume no taxes and that an unlevered firm's stock is priced at $10. The stock price of an otherwise identical levered firm is $15. The interest rate is 5%. The unlevered and levered firms' NOI is $50 million, $100 million, and $200 million with equal probability. The unlevered firm has 100 million shares outstanding and the levered firm has 50 million. The levered firm's debt is $500 million. Show

the arbitrage transaction that investors can conduct. Calculate the profit from such a transaction. Are the probabilities important in arriving at your answer? Explain.

15.9 Repeat Problem 15.8, but this time assume the unlevered firm's stock price is $15 and the levered firm's stock price is $10.

15.10 Assume a firm can borrow and lend at 5%, while individuals can borrow at 6% and lend at 3%. In this economy neither individuals nor firms pay taxes. An unlevered firm issues 100 shares at $1 per share. The NOI is $5 or $25 with equal probability.
a. Another firm is similar except that it has 50% leverage. Will the levered firm's value necessarily be $V_L = \$100$?
b. What can we say about the levered firm's maximum and minimum values?
c. Which of M & M's assumptions do not hold in this case?

15.11 "If there are no taxes and $NOI/V_U = r$, then the rate of return on a levered firm's equity will equal r, irrespective of the debt/equity ratio." Prove this statement.

15.12 Two firms are identical in all respects except that one is levered and the other is not. Suppose there are no taxes and the all-equity firm's cost of capital is $k_U = 10\%$. The interest rate is 8%. Now assume the interest rate falls to 6% and business risk increases so that the unlevered firm's cost of equity remains 10%.
a. What is the rate of return on the levered firm's equity before and after the drop in the interest rate? Assume the debt/equity ratio is 2.
b. Does the levered firm's value change with the reduction in interest rate? Explain.
c. Does the levered firm's cost of equity change? Explain.
d. Does the levered firm's WACC change? Explain.

15.13 Suppose that there are two firms, with NOI_A and NOI_B, respectively. It is known that $NOI_A = -0.5 \times NOI_B$. The two firms merge.

a. Will the merged firm's NOI be more or less stable than the NOI of the separate firms? In your answer assume NOI_B equals –$50 or $300 with equal probability.
b. Suppose these two firms are all–equity firms and $V_{U(B)}$ = $1,000, $V_{U(A)}$ = $500. Is it possible for an investor to construct a portfolio consisting of the stock of these two firms with zero variance? Calculate the mean rate of return on such a portfolio. Are $V_{U(A)}$ and $V_{U(B)}$ equilibrium values? Additional information: The riskless interest rate is 10%.

15.14 Two firms are identical in all respects except for their capital structure. Their NOI is as follows:

- –$500 with a probability of ¼
- $1,000 with a probability of ½
- $2,000 with a probability of ¼

The unlevered firm issues 10,000 shares at $1 per share. The levered firm issues $5,000 debt at 3% and 5,000 shares. You observe that the levered firm's stock price jumps to $1.50.
a. Suppose you hold 1,000 shares of the levered firm. What is the distribution of the rate of return on your investment?
b. What arbitrage transaction would you perform? Show the distribution of income after the transaction.
c. Suppose you invest the money saved in the arbitrage transaction at an interest rate of 3%. What is the distribution of income when you include the return on your savings?
d. How would your answer change if you had to pay a 0.5% transaction cost on the volume of sales and volume of stock purchase?

15.15 Repeat parts a, b, and c of Problem 15.14, but this time assume the firm can borrow at 3% and individual investors can borrow at 4%.

15.16 A firm's NOI will be –$50 or $250 with equal probability. An unlevered firm's value is V_U = $1,000. An otherwise identical levered firm issues $500 debt at 5%.
a. Calculate the mean and variance of the levered firm's and the unlevered firm's rate of return on equity.

b. Suppose now that r = 6%. Does the change in the interest rate affect the mean rates of return? The variance? Explain your results.

15.17 A firm's NOI can be –$10, $0, $3, $40, or $50 with equal probability. The riskless interest rate is 5%. An unlevered firm's value is V_U = $100, and a levered firm issues $B debt. There are no taxes and no transaction costs.
a. What is the probability of a negative leverage effect if B = $50?
b. What is the probability of a negative leverage effect if B = $70?
c. What is the probability of a negative leverage effect if B = $50 and r = 10%?
d. Discuss your results.

15.18 "In the absence of taxes, if B/E_L = 1 and r = 0, the rate of return on a levered firm's equity will be twice as high as that of an unlevered firm." Prove this assertion.

15.19 A firm's NOI = $1,000; its value is V_L = $10,000, and B_L = $2,000. A corresponding unlevered firm issues 1,000 shares. The riskless interest rate is r = 5%. Write the formula for the straight line describing the relationship between EPS and NOI.

15.20 An unlevered firm's value is $100,000. The firm issues 1,000 shares. An otherwise identical levered firm issues $50,000 debt and 1,000 shares. Using M & M's results, what should be the stock price of the levered and unlevered firms? Are your results in accord with M & M's proposition? Explain.

15.21 Suppose individual investors can borrow at 5% and firms can borrow at a higher rate of 6%. An unlevered firm's value is $100 million. What will be a levered firm's value if the firm employs $50 million debt? Can we say that homemade leverage is a perfect substitute for the firm's leverage in this case?

15.22 Define break-even point.

15.23 A firm has the following NOI (in $ million)

NOI	Probability
−10	⅕
0	⅕
10	⅕
20	⅕
50	⅕

The unlevered firm's value is 50, and the interest rate is 5%. Assume zero taxes. The firm issues 50 million shares.

a. Calculate the break-even point.

b. Draw the break-even chart for 50% debt financing.

c. What is the probability of the leverage effect being positive? How would your answer change for 75% debt?

15.24 "The slope of the line used in the break-even analysis of an all-equity firm is 1." Evaluate this assertion.

15.25 If a firm can borrow at $r = 0$, which of the following assertions is wrong? Explain.

a. "All lines used in break-even analysis will pass through the origin."

b. "All these lines will have a slope of 1."

INTERNET QUESTIONS

15.26 Visit *Fortune*'s Web site and find the ten largest firms in their *Fortune* 500 list, as ranked by total revenue. Then, go to the Stock Center at Thomson Investor's Network and find betas for these firms. Is there any relationship between revenue and beta? Why or why not?

http://www.fortune.com

http://www.thomsoninvest.net

15.27 Use the sensitivity analysis calculator maintained by Cybersolve to perform a sensitivity analysis of a hypothetical firm—that is, one with hypothetical fixed costs, etc.

http://www.cybersolve.com/breakeven.
html#voc

YOUR TURN: APPLYING THEORY TO PRACTICE

INTEL CORPORATION: COMPANY LEVERAGE AND HOMEMADE LEVERAGE

Intel is a leading producer of computer chips. The following data are from its financial statements.

Financial Summary: Intel Corporation (in $ thousands)

Year	Total Assets	Long-Term Debt[a]	Operating Income (Loss)
1996	23,735,000	1,003,000	7,553,000
1995	17,504,000	1,105,000	5,252,000
1994	13,816,000	1,136,000	3,387,000
1993	11,344,000	1,113,000	3,392,000
1992	8,088,588	621,778	1,490,046
1991	6,292,104	502,529	1,079,940
1990	5,376,308	344,605	858,335
1989	3,993,983	412,480	557,314
1988	3,549,736	479,273	594,313
1987	2,498,784	298,062	245,936
1986	1,977,352	286,600	(195,259)

[a] Includes put warrants

The operating income (loss) data are used to estimate future operating income. Assume each operating income figure that appears in the table has an equal chance (of ¹⁄₁₁) of occurring in the future. The total assets represent Intel's total investment. Also assume there are no taxes, that total assets equal the firm's total market value, that long-term debt represents the market value of debt, and that total assets minus the long-term debt equals the market value of the equity.

Intel's board of directors is considering changing its capital structure by increasing the debt/equity ratio to 1. One board member claims that this is undesirable because the stockholders' risk exposure will increase substantially. Another board member claims that though such an increase is possible, it will not affect the stock price.

Questions

Intel hires you as a consultant on this issue. Conduct the following calculations, which will form the base for your recommendation:

1. Calculate the distribution of NOI as a percentage of the total assets. Calculate the mean and variance of this distribution. Draw the distribution of the rates of return. What does this distribution represent?

2. Suppose Intel pays 8% interest on its debt. Calculate the rate of return on equity and plot the distribution of the rates of return. Calculate the mean rate of return and the variance of the return on the equity.

3. To check the claim that an increase in debt increases risk, calculate a hypothetical distribution of the rates of return on equity if Intel were to finance 50% of its assets in each of the 11 years with 8% debt. Calculate the corresponding mean rate of return and variance of the rates of return.

4. Compare and analyze the distributions given in Questions 1, 2, and 3. Would you recommend that Intel employ more debt than it currently employs? In a perfect market what would M & M's stand be on this issue? Explain.

5. Suppose a stockholder prefers the distribution of returns induced by 50% debt as given in Question 4. The stockholder invests $10,000 in the equity of such a firm with 50% leverage. Calculate the annual rate of return distribution on that investment. Is it true that risk increases, as one board member claimed?

6. Suppose now that Intel is an all-equity firm. An investor borrows $10,000 and invests $20,000 in Intel equity ($10,000 plus the borrowed money). The investor borrows at 8% interest. Calculate the distribution of the rate of return on the investment after the payment of interest on the borrowed money. Is the desired high risk-return distribution achieved? Compare the distribution to that obtained in Question 5. How does this transaction relate to M & M's homemade leverage argument?

7. Which distribution would a stockholder prefer—the distribution obtained with the actual debt, or the one obtained with 50% debt—if she were to invest in Intel for one year selected at random from the 1986–1996 distribution?

8. Considering all of the previous analyses (and assuming a perfect market with no taxes), would you recommend that Intel increase its debt? Prepare a report supporting your recommendation to the board of directors.

CHAPTER 16

DOES CAPITAL STRUCTURE MATTER?: AN IMPERFECT MARKET

LEARNING OBJECTIVES

After reading this chapter, you should understand:

1. That the capital market is imperfect and, therefore, capital structure does matter.

2. That the principal market imperfections are corporate taxes, bankruptcy costs, and agency costs.

3. That agency costs exist. To safeguard their jobs, managers may choose a capital structure that is less than optimal.

4. That no clear-cut formula exists for finding the optimal capital structure.

CORPORATE FINANCE IN THE NEWS

BOND RALLY STALLS BUT MORE LARGE COMPANIES SCRAMBLE TO ISSUE DEBT AMID DECLINES IN RATES[1]

. . . Lured by recent declines in borrowing costs, more big companies are rushing to raise money in the bond markets. For example, Coca-Cola yesterday sold $150 million of 6% notes due in 10 years. Those notes were priced at $99.809 to yield 6.026%, which was only 0.32 percentage points above comparable Treasury notes.

Hoping for further declines in interest rates, some corporate treasurers are delaying bond issues, investment bankers say. Bankers expect the borrowing pace to increase if Treasury Bond yields sink below the psychologically important 6.5% level.

But other companies are striking now, while bond markets are hot, and a few corporations are selling unusually long-term debt issues . . . .

DOUBLY DELICIOUS TREAT FROM HEINZ[2]

" . . . Heinz is a company with an exceptional and diverse portfolio of brands and businesses with the potential to deliver double-digit earnings growth with relatively low risk," (CEO) O'Reilly asserted in a statement accompanying the dividend announcement. "Our attitude is, we've made the big dispositions, we've acquired the companies we want to. At the moment, the thrust of our companies is to reduce debt . . . one of the quickest ways we can add cents per share to our earnings."

1. *Wall Street Journal*, 16 July 1993. Reprinted by permission of *The Wall Street Journal*, © 1993 Dow Jones & Company. All Rights Reserved Worldwide.
2. Shirley A. Lazo, *Barron's* (September 18, 1995): 45. Reprinted by permission of *Barron's* © 1995 Dow Jones & Company, Inc. All Rights Reserved Worldwide.

16.1 INTRODUCTION

From the first excerpt in Corporate Finance in the News, we learn that when interest rates fall, a firm may rush to the capital market to raise debt, presumably believing that doing so creates wealth. According to the second excerpt, Heinz's CEO O'Reilly believes that reducing debt will increase earnings per share and will presumably create wealth.

In Chapter 15 we learned that capital structure does not affect firm value in a perfect capital market. However, the two Corporate Finance in the News excerpts reveal that capital structure does matter in the real world. The excerpts also suggest that optimal capital structure may vary as market conditions (such as prevailing interest rates) change. Finally, firm-specific factors may determine the optimal capital structure: What is good for Coca-Cola may be bad for Heinz.

Some of the most important and most controversial issues in finance concern a firm's *optimal capital structure*. Does an optimal capital structure exist? If so, what factors determine it? Any capital structure is as good as any other structure in a perfect capital market. Does this also apply to imperfect markets?

An **imperfect capital market** has transaction costs, taxes, possible bankruptcy (which involves bankruptcy costs and causes the interest rate to vary directly with risk), and possible conflicts of interest among stockholders, bondholders, and management (giving rise to agency costs). These factors are enough to destroy Modigliani and Miller's conclusion that capital structure does not matter. To determine its optimal capital structure, a firm must consider taxes, bankruptcy costs, and agency costs.

We used an arbitrage argument in Chapter 15 to show that whenever $V_L \neq V_U$, a financial transaction that guarantees a certain profit can be made. Such transaction will continue to be available until in equilibrium $V_L = V_U$. In practice, however, these transactions involve costs that reduce the profit from arbitrage. This implies that V_L should not be expected to equal V_U in equilibrium, but does not tell us what factors determine the "best" capital structure.

Another reason why the Modigliani-Miller arbitrage argument does not hold is that the interest rate relevant for borrowing is typically greater than the one for lending. Your local bank pays a lower interest rate on a savings account than it charges on a loan. The two principal reasons why the rates differ between borrowing and lending are as follows:

1. The bank operates as an intermediary; that is, it obtains money from savers and channels it to borrowers. To make a profit on such deals, the bank must charge a higher rate on the loans it makes than the rate it pays on savings accounts. If the borrowing and lending rates were equal, and ignoring expenses, the bank's profit would be zero.
2. Any lending institution, including a bank, must consider the possibility that the borrower will go bankrupt. The higher the probability of bankruptcy, the higher the interest rate the bank must charge to compensate for this risk. If a firm and an individual have different bankruptcy risks, they will be able to bor-

row at different interest rates; in most cases, a firm can borrow at a lower interest rate than an individual can.

How are interest rates relevant to the capital structure issue?

As discussed in Chapter 15, if $V_L > V_U$, a person could sell a levered firm's shares, buy an unlevered firm's shares, and borrow on personal account to create *homemade leverage*. However, if a firm can borrow at, say, 8% while an individual can only borrow at 10%, homemade leverage is not a perfect substitute for the firm's leverage. Therefore V_L can exceed V_U in equilibrium.

Similarly, V_U can exceed V_L. In Chapter 15 we argued that an individual could sell unlevered firm's shares, buy levered firm's shares, and lend money or buy bonds; that would undo the *firm's leverage*. However, if the interest rate at which an individual can lend money is lower than the rate at which the levered firm borrows money, the individual may not be able to make an arbitrage profit; this is why it is possible that $V_U > V_L$ in equilibrium.

So, contrary to the assumptions in Chapter 15, the interest rate can be different for borrowing and for lending and can differ among borrowers to reflect different bankruptcy risks. For example, *Barron's* reported the following interest rates (August 4, 1997):

Instrument	Yield
One-year Treasury bills	5.26%
Midwest Savings Bank one-year CDs	6.10%
Sears bonds	9.00%
Prime rate	8.50%

All four rates are for one year. If you loaned money to the U.S. government by purchasing a Treasury bill, you would have earned 5.26%. If you were a very good customer, a bank would charge you 8.50% for a loan. The 3.24% difference between borrowing and lending rates is one reason why the M & M arbitrage argument is not valid for an imperfect market.

This discussion makes two suggestions:

1. Because borrowing and lending interest rates differ, no arbitrage transactions may be available. So V_L and V_U may differ in equilibrium.
2. The borrowing interest rate increases with the risk of bankruptcy. (For example, compare *Barron's* reported Sears' rate with the U.S. Treasury's rate.)

Capital structure does matter and is one of the most important issues confronting a firm's CFO. In practice the capital market is far from perfect: Transaction costs exist, taxes exist, and the interest rates for borrowing and lending are not identical. A firm can generally borrow at a lower interest rate than an individual, and homemade leverage is not a perfect substitute for the leverage that a firm can obtain. Bankruptcies occur and are costly. In addition, professional managers, not owners, usually manage a firm, and managers' interests may run counter to those of the stockholders. Factors such as these render the capital structure very relevant. In this chapter we discuss the

major imperfections in the capital market and how they affect the firm's capital structure. We start with corporate tax, which makes it cheaper for a firm to borrow relative
to the individual investor. Then we discuss bankruptcy costs and agency costs.

16.2 CORPORATE TAXES AND FIRM DISTRESS

In Chapter 15 we assumed a tax-free world. Let us now consider the real world in
which governments levy taxes. In this section we discuss how corporate taxes affect
the firm's value and capital structure. M & M's argument that capital structure is irrelevant relies on the assumption that both a levered and an unleveled firm have the
same expected net operating income (NOI). This may well be true on a pretax basis.
However, M & M show that a levered firm enjoys tax advantages because tax laws
permit it to deduct any interest paid as an expense for tax purposes. This tax advantage increases the levered firm's average cash flow. Capital structure, therefore, is relevant because, other things being equal, the more leverage a firm employs, the
higher the firm's value.[3]

To illustrate how corporate income tax affects the firm's value, let us review the
example given in Table 16-1, which shows the after-tax incomes of a levered and an
unleveled firm. The NOI is assumed to be $150, the interest rate is 10%, the unleveled
firm has $1,000 equity, and the levered firm has $500 debt and $500 equity. The NOI
produced by the total investment is the same for both firms.[4] From Table 16-1, we
see that bondholders' and stockholders' total income increases with leverage.

TABLE 16-1 After-Tax Income of a Levered and an Unlevered Firm (in dollars)		Unlevered Firm ($)	Levered Firm ($)
	NOI	150	150
	Interest	0	50
	Net income before tax	150	100
	Taxes (assumed rate = 40%)	60	40
	Stockholders' after-tax income	90	60
	Bondholders' after-tax income	0	50
	Total after-tax income of stockholders and bondholders	90	110

3. The impact of corporate taxes on the firm's value is discussed in F. Modigliani and M. Miller, "Corporate Income Taxes and the
Cost of Capital: A Correction," *American Economic Review* (June 1963): 433–443. M & M show that with corporate taxes, capital
structure is relevant. However, in a later paper, Miller claims that when corporate as well as personal taxes are taken into account,
capital structure again becomes irrelevant. Miller's controversial argument hinges on the relationship among the marginal personal
income tax rate, the corporate tax rate, and the capital gains tax rate. For more details, see Appendix 16A and M. Miller, "Debt and
Taxes," *Journal of Finance* (May 1977): 261–275. For a discussion of Miller's results see H. Levy and M. Sarnat, *Capital Investment and
Financial Decisions*, 5th ed. (New York: Prentice-Hall, 1994), pp. 382–87.
4. This is not the case if the firm can issue stock at a higher price as a result of employing leverage. In such case we can assume that
the firm will either issue fewer shares to keep the total investment at the $1,000 level or will distribute a cash dividend (i.e., distrib-
ute all extra cash beyond the $1,000 needed for investment).

Figure 16-1 illustrates the division of two hypothetical firms' income among the shareholders, bondholders, and the IRS (Internal Revenue Service). The interesting features of Table 16-1 and Figure 16-1 are: With leverage the tax liability is lower for the levered firm ($40, as opposed to $60 for the unlevered firm), and the tax saving is distributed to the shareholders. The levered firm's total cash flow to shareholders and bondholders is $110, compared to only $90 for the all-equity firm. The $20 difference represents the tax saving due to the interest deduction.

Do not think that the levered firm's shareholders fare worse because they receive only $60 rather than the $90 that the unlevered firm's shareholders receive. In this example the $60 income is based on a much lower investment by the stockholders because half of the levered firm is financed by debt. The reason the unlevered firm's stockholders fare better is that the IRS takes a smaller slice of their income (i.e., the firm's tax burden is reduced through leverage). Indeed, the rate of return to stockholders is 9% ($90/$1,000 = 0.09 or 9%) for an unlevered firm and 12% ($60/$500 = 0.12 or 12%) for a levered firm.

Suppose one investor holds all the firm's securities (bonds and stocks). Because total income from equity and debt would be larger than the income of a similar but a pure equity firm, the investor would prefer leverage. Then, why not increase the proportion of debt and thereby increase the tax saving even more? We will discuss the limits of such a strategy later in this chapter.

16.2.1 The Interest Tax Shield

The tax saving due to leverage is the **interest tax shield.** In the example given in Table 16-1, the interest expense is $50 ($rB = 0.10 \times \$500 = \$50$). Since this is tax-deductible, T percent (the average income tax rate) of this $50 is saved. The tax saving, or the interest tax shield, is given by

$$\text{Interest tax shield} = TrB \tag{16.1}$$

FIGURE 16-1
Division of Income Among Stockholders, Bondholders, and the Internal Revenue Service (IRS) of a Levered Firm and an Unlevered Firm with the Same NOI

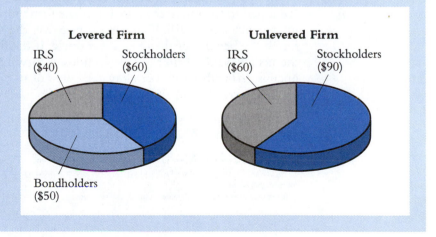

To analyze how leverage affects the firm's value, we first examine the unlevered firm's cash flows and then turn to the levered firm's flows. For an unlevered firm the after-tax cash flow will be

$$(1 - T) \times \text{NOI}$$

For a levered firm with the same capital investment, business risk,[5] and NOI, the total cash flow (to stockholders and bondholders) will be

$$(1 - T) \times (\text{NOI} - rB) + rB = (1 - T) \times \text{NOI} + TrB$$

Recall that we are interested in studying how leverage affects the firm's net income (i.e., bondholders' and stockholders' total net income combined). Therefore, the interest rB is first deducted, which reduces the firm's tax burden, and then is added back to show the cash flow to bondholders.

In our example for the unlevered firm we obtain

$$(1 - T) \times \text{NOI} = (1 - 0.4) \times \$150 = \$90$$

For the levered firm we obtain

$$(1 - T) \times (\text{NOI} - rB) + rB = (1 - 0.4)\,(\$150 - \$50) + \$50$$

$$= 0.6 \times \$100 + \$50 = \$110.$$

After-tax income increases by \$20 [$TrB = 0.4(0.1)\$500 = \$20$] due to leverage. Thus, \$20 is the interest tax shield.

Let the appropriate discount rate for the uncertain cash flow, $(1 - T) \times \text{NOI}$, be denoted by k. The value of the unlevered firm (assuming a perpetuity) will be $V_U = \dfrac{(1 - T)\overline{\text{NOI}}}{k}$, where $\overline{\text{NOI}}$ is the NOI's expected value.[6] The expected value of the levered firm's cash flow has two components: $(1 - T)\overline{\text{NOI}}$ and TrB. Since the first component is identical to that of the levered firm, by the law of one price, its value must be V_U. Also, since the interest tax shield, TrB, is assumed to be certain, it is discounted at the riskless interest rate, r, and therefore its PV is TB.

Why is TrB treated as a certain cash flow? Because as long as it is solvent the firm is entitled to the interest tax shield.[7] If the firm's income is positive, it will enjoy the interest tax shield, TrB. If income is negative, the firm pays no taxes but does not forfeit the benefits of the interest tax shield. If the firm loses money in a given year, the IRS allows the firm to carry such losses forward and backward. Thus, the firm obtains TrB with virtual certainty, regardless of its taxable income in a given year.

The levered firm's value will be V_L:

$$V_L = V_U + TB \qquad\qquad (16.2)$$

---

5. Business risk is the risk inherent in the projects selected and is not due to the way the projects are financed.

6. We distinguish between NOI, which is uncertain value and its $\overline{\text{NOI}}$, which has a fixed value. In PV calculations, $\overline{\text{NOI}}$ should be discounted. (See Chapter 5.)

7. If the firm goes bankrupt, the interest tax shield is forfeited.

$$\text{Value of levered firm} = \text{Value of unlevered firm} \qquad (16.2a)$$
$$+ \text{pv of the interest tax shield}$$

where *TB* is the gain due to leverage.

Figure 16-2 illustrates the value of two firms with the same NOI as a function of debt level, *B*. For zero debt both firms are unlevered and have the same value. As one firm's debt level increases, the gap between the two firms' values grows. This gap represents the PV of the levered firm's interest tax shield. The higher the proportion of debt in the firm's capital structure, the larger the firm's value. Other things being equal, extreme debt financing would be recommended.

Equation (16.2) implies that the more debt the firm employs, the greater its tax benefit and the greater its value. Do managers really behave according to Equation (16.2) and employ extreme levels of debt? If not, why not? A small sample of firms shows they employ various levels of long-term debt relative to their total assets:

Colgate–Palmolive	50%
Intel	4.1%
Coca–Cola	72.2%
Microsoft	0%

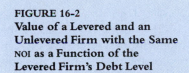
FIGURE 16-2
Value of a Levered and an Unlevered Firm with the Same NOI as a Function of the Levered Firm's Debt Level

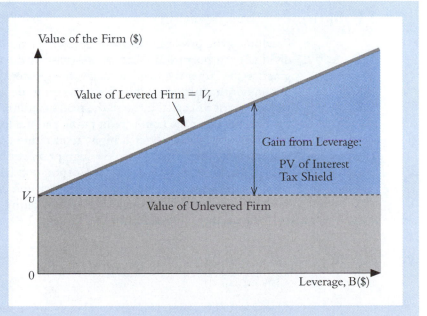

An international study[8] showed average ratios of debt to total assets as follows:

United States	31%
Japan	35%
Germany	20%
France	26%
Italy	28%
United Kingdom	21%

These figures suggest that managers tend not to employ the extreme levels of debt suggested by Equation (16.2). Many firms issue very little or no debt. What is the explanation for this? If CFOs had to answer this question, they would probably say, "We reject the extreme leverage recommendation because there are many real-world factors not considered in M & M's analysis."

Indeed, a number of crucial economic factors are not taken into account in M & M's analysis. Once these factors are incorporated, a firm's optimal capital structure may deviate considerably from the structure that Equation (16.2) implies. Moreover, the optimal capital structure may vary from one firm to another. We shall now relax some of M & M's assumptions, incorporate some of these economic factors into our analysis, and show that the firm's adopted leverage policy may be quite different from the extreme capital structure that Equation (16.2) implies.

16.2.2 Bankruptcy Considerations

Precluding the possibility of bankruptcy, Equation (16.2) assumes that firms and individuals can borrow as much as they wish at the riskless interest rate. However, in practice the larger the firm's leverage, the greater the probability of bankruptcy and the higher the interest rate the firm pays on its debt. The risk of bankruptcy finds its way into cost of capital through the firm's credit rating: The lower the risk of bankruptcy, the better the firm's credit rating and the lower the interest rate at which the firm can borrow. To obtain a high credit rating and to pay a relatively low interest rate on debt, a firm should avoid a high proportion of debt in its capital structure.

For example, in 1991 Chrysler Corporation had lost an investment-grade credit rating. In response, the automaker sold stock and cut its dividend in half to decrease its debt/equity ratio and upgrade its credit rating. Connecting Theory to Practice 16.1 reveals that Chrysler's plan was successful.

---

8. Raghuram G. Rajan and Luigi Zingales, "What Do We Know About Capital Structure? Some Evidence from International Data," *Journal of Finance* 50 (December 1995): 1421–1460.

CONNECTING THEORY TO PRACTICE 16.1

MOODY'S RAISES DEBT RATINGS FOR CHRYSLER

MOVE HELPS COMPANY'S BID TO CUT BORROWING COSTS; S&P AWAITS LABOR TALKS

Moody's Investors Service Inc. upgraded Chrysler Corp.'s debt rating to investment grade, moving the No. 3 U.S. automaker halfway toward its goal of cutting its borrowing costs significantly.

The other half depends on whether Standard & Poor's Corp. does the same thing.

Still, Moody's action late yesterday is a giant step toward getting Chrysler paper out of the junk-bond category and could set the stage for a dividend increase. Both of the big credit-rating concerns downgraded Chrysler debt to junk status in February 1991 for the first time since the automaker's brush with insolvency in the late 1970s. Smaller Fitch Investors Service Inc. promoted Chrysler to investment grade two months ago. About $13 billion of long-term debt was affected by Moody's action.

A Chrysler spokesman said, "Moody's action is good news" and "we are optimistic that S&P will do the same."

Moody's upgrade of Chrysler's debt to investment grade from two notches below investment grade was felt immediately.

"It cut our interest rate payments by a half of a point, or $5 million annually," on the company's $1.1 billion of variable-rate bonds issued to finance a new technical center in suburban Detroit, a Chrysler spokesman said.

An investment-grade credit rating from S&P could further reduce the Highland Park, Mich., automaker's borrowing costs. Thomas P. Capo, Chrysler's treasurer, said this summer that an upgrade by both credit concerns would cut annual costs by at least $33 million.

The upgrade could have a long-term impact as well, solidifying Chrysler's comeback in financial markets. And Robert J. Eaton, chairman and chief executive officer, said at Chrysler's annual meeting that an upgrade was "somewhat of a prerequisite" to a dividend increase.

Source: *Wall Street Journal*, 8 September 1993, p. A3. Reprinted by permission of *The Wall Street Journal,* © 1993 Dow Jones & Company, Inc. All Rights Reserved Worldwide.

MAKING THE CONNECTION

The Chrysler case demonstrates that capital structure, the interest rate on debt, and the firm's value are interrelated. In practice firms do not adopt the extreme debt policy that Equation (16.2) implies because the higher the proportion of debt, the higher the risk of bankruptcy.

Does the absence of debt mean that a firm can avoid bankruptcy? Not really. An unlevered firm that undertakes a risky investment may not be successful. A firm will generally go bankrupt if it cannot meet its financial obligations such as payments to suppliers or employees. Thus, a firm can go bankrupt even in the absence of debt. However, when a firm is levered, the obligation to pay interest significantly increases the probability of bankruptcy.

The inability to pay interest and principal does not automatically lead to formal bankruptcy, however. A firm can often enter a financial agreement, known as a *workout*, with its creditors and reschedule its debt payments. However, if the creditors do not agree to the firm's financial arrangement, the firm can take its case to the federal bankruptcy court where one of the following decisions may be reached:

1. Chapter 7 liquidation, whereby the court decides that the firm has no chance of recovering and appoints a trustee to liquidate the firm's assets and distributes the proceeds to the creditors.
2. Chapter 11 reorganization, whereby the court decides that the firm has a chance of recovering but orders basic reorganization. The provisions of Chapter 11 allow the CEO to continue to manage the firm.

BANKRUPTCY COSTS

Connecting Theory to Practice 16.2 illustrates the costs of **financial distress** and bankruptcy.

CONNECTING THEORY TO PRACTICE 16.2

THE "SURVIVAL OF THE UNFITTEST"

Lots of people are using bankruptcy to hang onto a sizable slice of their wealth while sidestepping a pile of debt. They are the most visible distortion in a larger system in need of an overhaul. Bankruptcy proceedings can drag on for years, allowing debtors to stiff creditors and avoid settlement as long as possible . . . .

Corporate bankruptcies, especially, can turn into marathons, often enriching armies of lawyers and accountants at the expense of creditors . . . . Often the delays help the companies in bankruptcy, but sometimes they have the opposite effect, ensnaring managers of troubled companies in court proceedings instead of giving them time to run the business. That can make it even harder for the companies to get a fresh start, as the law intended . . . .

Bankruptcies have exploded since a 1978 revision of the bankruptcy law made it easier to wipe out debts in court. Last year, bankruptcy filings totaled 971,517, up 178% from 10 years earlier. The 900,874 personal bankruptcies accounted for most of them and cost creditors $21.5 billion last year, Visa estimates. Corporate bankruptcies totaled 70,643, up sharply over 10 years though down from the peak in 1987.

"Bankruptcy has become an acceptable strategy for dealing with various economic problems," says Norman Owen, the vice president for credit management at Levi Strauss & Co.

Source: "Creditor Backlash," *Wall Street Journal*, 17 June 1993, p. A1. Reprinted by permission of *The Wall Street Journal*, © 1993 Dow Jones & Company, Inc. All Rights Reserved Worldwide.

MAKING THE CONNECTION

The number of personal and corporate bankruptcies has increased significantly over the past two decades. Since bankruptcy proceedings are costly and long-term, a firm has a hard time getting a "fresh start."

Apart from having to pay an army of lawyers and accountants, financial distress usually means losing customers, which makes the distress worse. Retaining customers becomes a real problem for such a firm. For example, in 1995, TWA, the nation's seventh largest airline, filed for Chapter 11 bankruptcy (the second time within four years). Creditors agreed to a rescue package that involved forgiving $500 million of the airline's $1.7 billion debt. Financial distress caused TWA a lot of direct and indirect costs: disruptive executive turnover, loss of customers, and having to pay travel agents higher commissions to persuade them to remain loyal to TWA.

Bankruptcies are costly. A firm incurs both direct and indirect bankruptcy costs. For example, cash payments to bankruptcy professionals are direct bankruptcy costs. Other types of costs are indirect bankruptcy costs (or the indirect costs of financial distress—e.g., executive turnover) because they are (difficult-to-measure) opportunity costs incurred as a result of the firm's financial condition. A financially distressed firm or a firm in bankruptcy process may have the following costs:

1. Payments to lawyers and accountants means a reduced cash flow.
2. Since managers spend time in court proceedings, they have less time and energy to run the business.
3. A firm in financial distress quite commonly suffers disruptive executive turnover and management missteps.
4. Customers who know about the financial distress are afraid to do business with the firm.

A wealth of evidence is available on the magnitude of bankruptcy costs. Jerold Warner examined a sample of railroad company bankruptcies and found that direct bankruptcy costs are relatively low, ranging from 1% to 5% of the firm's market value. Lawrence Wiess's broader study estimated the direct costs to be 3.1% of the firm's value.[9] In general, the larger the firm, the lower the direct bankruptcy costs as a percentage of the firm's value.

Edward Altman examined both direct and indirect costs just discussed. His results showed these costs totaled in the range of 11% to 17% of firm value. Opler and Titman reached similar conclusions.[10] Evidence from specific cases reveals significant differences in bankruptcy costs across firms, however. Cutler and Summers estimated the indirect cost of Texaco's 1987 bankruptcy to be 9%, while Kaplan, who studies Campeau's distress, found the indirect cost to be negligible.[11]

The greater the chance of bankruptcy, the greater the chance that the firm will have to incur all of these costs and the lower its value will become. Since both bondholders and stockholders may lose because of these costs, we expect the market value of both the firm's bonds and stocks to decrease when the risk of bankruptcy increases.

In sum, financial distress can be costly. In view of these costs, the greater the firm's risk of bankruptcy, the less investors will be willing to pay for its stocks and bonds. Keeping in mind that the firm's goal is to maximize its stock price, financial distress costs help explain why firms do not adopt the extreme level of debt that M & M's model implies.

We now incorporate the cost of financial distress into M & M's theoretical post-tax argument as expressed by Equation (16.2). Figure 16-3 is similar to Figure 16-2 but is modified to incorporate the PV of the costs of financial distress. For example, if a firm employs debt B_1, the firm's value with the interest tax shield advantage, but before deducting the costs of financial distress, will be V_1. After deducting the PV of the expected costs of financial distress, the levered firm's value will drop to V_2; that is, $V_1 - V_2$ is the cost of financial distress associated with leverage level B_1.

For a given investment plan, the more leverage a firm employs, the higher its probability of not meeting its obligations. Therefore, the costs of financial distress will increase along with leverage. In Figure 16-3 these costs are assumed to be zero for moderate leverage (up to B_0), thereafter increasing in an accelerated fashion as shown by the expansion of the shaded area. In the case illustrated in the figure, $B^\star$ is the firm's optimal level of debt—the one at which value reaches its maximum. Therefore, Equation (16.2) no longer holds with bankruptcy costs, and the optimal capital structure is given by point $B^\star$ (corresponding to value $V^\star$).

The levered firm's value with bankruptcy costs can be written as

$$V_L = V_U + TB - FD \tag{16.3}$$

where FD is the PV of the costs of financial distress.

9. J. B. Warner, "Bankruptcy Costs: Some Evidence," *Journal of Finance* (May 1977): 337–348, and Lawrence Wiess, "Bankruptcy Resolution: Direct Costs and Violation of Priority Claims," *Journal of Financial Economics* 27 (1993).

10. E. I. Altman, "A Further Investigation of the Bankruptcy Cost Question," *Journal of Finance* (September 1987): 1067–1089. T. Opler and S. Titman, "Financial Distress Costs and Capital Structure," *Journal of Finance* (July 1994): 1015–1042.

11. David M. Cutler and Lawrence H. Summers, "The Cost of Conflict Resolution and Financial Distress: Evidence from the Texaco-Pennzoil Litigation," *Rand Journal of Economics* (1988), and Steven N. Kaplan, "Campeau's Acquisition of Federated: Value Added or Destroyed," *Journal of Financial Economics* (1989).

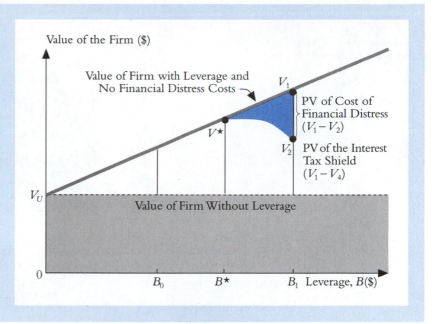

FIGURE 16-3
Value of Two Firms with the Same NOI as a Function of Their Debt Level and the PV of Their Cost of Financial Distress

BUSINESS RISK AND OPTIMAL LEVERAGE

Does an optimal degree of leverage apply to all firms? The answer to this question is no, for two reasons. First, as mentioned above, the larger the firm, the lower the costs of financial distress as a percentage of its value. The direct costs of financial distress differ across firms, and firms' optimal capital structures will differ accordingly. Second, and even more important, two firms that are similar in size and, therefore, have similar financial distress costs as a percentage of value, may be characterized by different **business risk**. The riskier the business, the higher the probability of financial distress, and the lower the optimal leverage.

Business risk is measured by the variability of the firm's NOI, which is caused by fluctuations in sales and revenue. Because the variability of NOI may change as the firm's size changes, NOI is a meaningful measure of business risk when comparing firms of approximately the same size. In this chapter, for convenience, we compare the business risk of firms of the same size.

Figure 16-4 demonstrates the NOI probability distributions of two firms, Firm I and Firm II. Both have the same average NOI. However, since Firm I is in a riskier line of business than Firm II, its NOI probability distribution has a larger variance. We say that Firm I has a larger *business risk*. Should these two firms select the same level of debt in their capital structures?

Firm II can take advantage of the tax benefit of debt because its NOI, although uncertain, is stable. Additional debt financing (at least at a moderate level) will not materially add to Firm II's risk of financial distress. The scenario is different for Firm I; it

FIGURE 16-4
Business Risk of Two Firms with the Same Average NOI

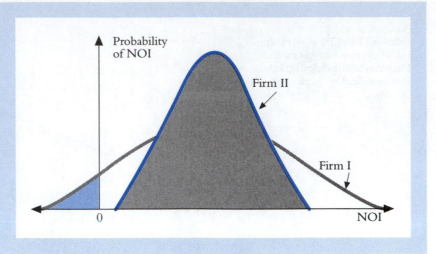

has a substantial probability of a negative NOI. However, even for Firm I, with a possible negative NOI and a relatively low level of debt, the tax advantage of employing leverage may outweigh the cost of financial distress. However, beyond a certain critical level, the advantage would disappear.

As we have seen, the higher the business risk, the smaller the financial leverage the firm should employ. There is a trade-off between these two risks. For example, Eastman Kodak, prior to 1993, had a relatively small business risk achieved by diversification among drugs, diagnostic machines, batteries, and so on. Investing in businesses other than photography reduced the firm's profits and led to the dismissal of the CEO. In 1993, George Fisher, the new CEO, decided to put the focus back on photography. This increased business risk. To compensate, Kodak used the proceeds from selling off assets—more than $8 billion—to reduce its debt. This move turned out to be the correct one, allowing the firm to obtain a better risk–return combination for its shareholders.

Figure 16-5 demonstrates the relationship between business risk and optimal capital structure.[12] First, note that the horizontal line V_{II} is above line V_I. Although the two firms have the same expected NOI, Firm II has less business risk, its average NOI is discounted at a lower cost of capital, and its value is higher. The two rising lines labeled I and II, representing the interest tax shield advantage, have the same slope. Finally, the curves V_I and V_{II} show the two firms' values with the interest tax advantage as well as the cost of financial distress. Firm I is riskier than Firm II, so its financial distress starts growing at a lower level of debt. $B_I^\star$ is the optimal leverage for

---

12. Appendix 16A discusses capital structure and leverage when both personal and corporate taxes are taken into account. Merton Miller's model leads to the conclusion that capital structure is irrelevant. However, DeAngelo and Masulis extend Miller's model and show that capital structure is relevant and that an optimal capital structure exists similar to the one presented in Figure 16-5.

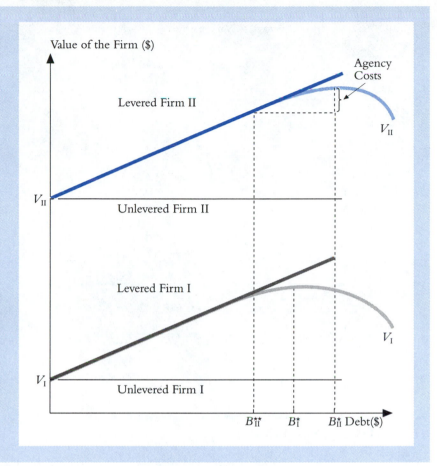

FIGURE 16-5
Value and Optimum Leverage of Two Firms with the Same Expected NOI but Different Business Risk

Firm I and $B_{II}^{\star}$ is the optimal leverage for Firm II. The higher the firm's business risk, the lower the leverage that it should employ. This analysis explains why industries with high business risk employ relatively low leverage.

Table 16-2 shows the capital structure (in percent) of various industries. Column 7 of this table provides the debt/equity ratio based on long-term debt.[13] As we can see, the debt/equity ratio is as low as 0.07 for the electronic computers industries (which have relatively high business risk) and as high as 1.15 for utilities (which have relatively low business risk).[14]

---

13. Short-term debt is not included in the debt/equity ratio because short-term assets usually offset it.

14. The ratio for the motor vehicle industry is actually much lower than the reported figure in Table 16-3. However, as many of the loans in this industry are slightly over 12 months (and the firms have corresponding debt of slightly more than 12 months), much of the short-term debt is included in the long-term debt category.

TABLE 16-2   **Leverage of Various Industries (percent)**

Industry	Common Equity (1)	Preferred Stock (2)	Total Debt (3)	Total (4)	Long-Term Debt (5)	Short-Term Debt (6)	Long-Term Debt/Equity Ratio (7)
Electronic computers	81.6	0.2	18.2	100	6.1	12.1	0.07
Computers and software wholesale	56.8	0.0	43.2	100	24.9	18.3	0.44
Commercial banks	28.4	3.0	68.6	100	30.9	37.7	1.09
Metal mining	37.4	14.5	48.1	100	41.6	6.5	1.12
Drug and proprietary—wholesale	48.2	6.3	45.5	100	39.4	6.1	0.82
Crude petroleum and natural gas	48.6	4.0	47.4	100	45.2	2.2	0.93
Utilities	40.9	6.3	52.8	100	47.2	5.6	1.15
Motor vehicle and car bodies	35.2	0.6	64.2	100	35.5	28.7	1.01
Composite of all industries	35.0	2.9	62.1	100	36.0	26.1	1.03

Source: *Standard and Poor's Compustat Industrial Tapes,* 1994. Reprinted by permission of McGraw-Hill Companies, Inc.

16.3 AGENCY COSTS

Another set of market imperfections that make the mix of debt and equity relevant to the firm's value is agency costs. **Agency costs** arise when the interests of stockholders conflict with those of the bondholders or the managers. The agency costs are the reduction in the value of the firm due to this conflict. These conflicts were assumed not to exist in Modigliani's and Miller's perfect market environment. Similar to the interest tax shield, agency costs that are generated by these conflicts of interest cause a firm's capital structure to affect its total value.

Some agency costs are actually reduced by using debt, while others are magnified at high debt levels. In contrast to corporate taxes, which strictly favor the increased use of debt, different types of agency costs exert opposite influences on corporate capital structures. Focusing on this factor only, the firm's objective is to select a capital structure that, other things being equal, minimizes total agency costs.

16.3.1 Agency Costs That Encourage the Use of Debt

The separation of ownership and control within publicly-held corporations causes various conflicts of interest between the firm's equityholders and managers. These conflicts can be controlled through the effective application of debt claims in the capital structure. In the following discussion, we show that agency costs may encourage the use of debt.

Consumption of *management perks* occurs when managers use corporate resources to acquire goods and services for their personal benefit. Examples of such goods and services include excessive travel, plush offices, use of corporate jets, and luxury hotel accommodations.

A 100% owner-manager has an incentive to use perquisites only when they create value for the firm. In contrast, the manager of a large, publicly-held corporation typically owns a small percentage of the common equity and has an incentive to engage in excessive use of perquisites, because the personal utility these perks provide comes largely at other equityholders' expense.

Suppose that repurchasing stock with borrowed funds moves the debt/equity ratio to 2.0 will increase the manager's proportion of shares from 10% to 30%. Since every dollar of perquisites consumed now costs the manager three times what it did before the capital structure change, the manager has less tendency to overindulge. Debt helps control perquisite consumption by better aligning the interests of managers and equityholders.

A firm can also use debt to control its overinvestment problem. *Overinvestment* occurs when managers reinvest excess cash flows in projects with negative net present values. Motivations to overinvest are driven by "empire building" ambitions or size-based compensation arrangements. During the 1980s financial leverage was often used to force unwieldly conglomerates to eliminate overinvestment by divesting unprofitable lines of business and by cutting costs. Connecting Theory to Practice 16.3 relates how RJR Nabisco used leverage to influence investment policy.

CONNECTING THEORY TO PRACTICE 16.3

RUNNING THE BIGGEST LBO

Taking the toughest job in Corporate America, Louis Gerstner, CEO of RJR Nabisco, slimmed down and revitalized the $17 billion food-and-tobacco giant that had $26 billion of debt when he assumed the position. Living with this kind of leverage, however, appealed to Gerstner. He auctioned more than $3.5 billion of assets, issued $4 billion in junk bonds, hired a management team, discontinued sales of a "smokeless" cigarette, moved corporate headquarters to New York, and ordered cost cuts. Things moved so quickly under Gerstner's direction that RJR Nabisco established a separate department to restate sales, profits, and other key accounts that reflected the company's status.

Source: Judith H. Dobrzynski, "Running the Biggest LBO," *Business Week* (2 October 1980): 72–79.

MAKING THE CONNECTION

CEO Louis Gerstner initiated a series of actions in response to the heavy debt load facing RJR Nabisco. Because Kohlberg, Kravis and Roberts Co. (KKR) purchased RJR with a large amount of borrowed money (a leveraged buyout), the company was forced to sell assets and to cut costs to meet its debt obligations. Gerstner's actions provide an example of how debt reduces agency costs by forcing a firm to operate more efficiently and to eliminate overinvestment.

RJR Nabisco conducted such comprehensive restructuring because the company had spent billions of dollars on unproductive projects (such as a private airport for company executives) that needed disposal. The unusual changes at RJR make it easier to understand how, even in the normal course of business, financial leverage helps control the overinvestment problem by reducing the amount of cash flow available for discretionary investment. Instead of relying on managers to accept only value-creating projects and to pay the residual cash flow as a dividend, shareholders can use debt to commit the firm to a fixed schedule of cash outflows, thereby restricting the amount of surplus cash available to managers. According to Jensen, agency theory suggests that industries such as broadcasting, brewing, chemicals, paper products, and steel were ideal candidates for high debt levels during the 1980s.[15]

16.3.2 Agency Costs That Discourage the Use of Debt

The separation of ownership and control in publicly held corporations can also cause conflicts of interest between stockholders and bondholders and among various types of creditors. Some of these conflicts occur in the ordinary course of business; others are present only when the firm is in financial distress. In the following discussion, we explain the nature of these conflicts and show how the firm can augment its total value by selecting the appropriate type and level of debt obligations.

ASSET SUBSTITUTION

The potential gains and losses available to stockholders and bondholders are very different. Because their fixed claim is not guaranteed, bondholders can lose their entire investment, but their maximum available return is limited to the full payment of interest and principal as scheduled. In contrast, stockholders hold a claim on a firm's residual profits and have limited liability—this means that creditors cannot claim the stockholders' personal assets.

Given these different return distributions, stockholders can alter the firm's collection of assets to benefit themselves at bondholders' expense. By substituting riskier assets of equivalent value for those currently in place, stockholders can lay claim to any additional profits from the change, while bondholders incur any resulting losses. Although the value of a firm's assets remains unchanged, the value of its common

---

15. Michael C. Jensen, "Eclipse of the Public Corporation," *Harvard Business Review* (September–October, 1989): 61–74.

equity will increase and the value of its bonds will decrease. This transfer of wealth occurs because stockholders receive the gains from this rearrangement, while bondholders absorb any losses.

The transfer of wealth from asset substitution represents an agency cost to the firm because (absent formal protection) bondholders will increase the required yield on the debt to reflect the likelihood that equityholders will engage in risk-shifting behavior. Since equityholders will bear the agency costs of asset substitution, they have an incentive to reduce these costs either by limiting the total amount of borrowing, by using secured debt, or by adopting bond covenants that restrict the firm's ability to engage in asset substitution.

UNDERINVESTMENT

Risk-shifting through asset substitution can occur at any level of financial strength or weakness. In contrast, a financially distressed firm incurs a different source of agency costs related to the firm's investment policy. These agency costs are due to *underinvestment*.

Underinvestment occurs because the equityholders are unwilling to fund a project of a financially distressed firm because it would primarily benefit the bondholders. Given their priority claim in the capital structure, bondholders will benefit first from any increase in the value of the financially distressed firm's assets. With their limited liability, shareholders will be unwilling to contribute capital to the firm because the bondholders will have a claim on the amount invested.

To illustrate the underinvestment problem, consider a financially distressed firm that must repay a $1,000 note (originally issued on a discounted basis) at the end of the year. The firm's assets have a market value of only $500; so its equity is zero because the bondholders have first claim to the firm's assets. Just to keep things simple, assume the value of the firm's existing assets will also be $500 at the end of the year.

Now suppose this same firm encounters an extremely profitable investment opportunity. The project would require a $200 initial outlay and would return $400 at the end of the period. Because the firm is financially distressed, it cannot borrow any more money, but it can always sell $200 of additional shares. In this case, unfortunately, the stockholders would not be willing to buy any of these shares because doing so would only enrich the bondholders.

Here's why: Investing in the project will increase the firm's value at the end of the year to $900, all of which it must pay to the bondholders to partially satisfy their $1,000 claim. The bondholders will be quite happy; they will receive $400 more than they otherwise would if the firm didn't invest. However, the bondholders' gain will be at the entire expense of the shareholders, who will receive nothing in return for their additional $200 investment. As such, because it will forgo an otherwise profitable project, the firm incurs an agency cost (the loss of a positive NPV project) related to underinvestment.

A firm usually limits its borrowing when underinvestment is likely to be a problem during financial distress. A firm whose assets' values are very sensitive to its financial condition has more potential for underinvestment. Examples of such assets include those that either are highly specialized or intangible. Because of the underinvestment problem, financial economists expect a linkage between the characteristics of a firm's assets and its capital structure.

MANAGERIAL RISK AVERSION

When it experiences financial distress, a firm may dismiss the CEO and other top managers. For example, large firms such as IBM, General Motors, Kodak, Kmart and Apple Computer replaced their managers when the firms experienced financial distress in the 1990s. Thus a CEO may be reluctant to take on a high-risk but very profitable project or to increase the firm's debt/equity ratio even if the tax advantage outweighs the cost of financial distress. By not accepting a high-risk situation, the CEO avoids the risk of dismissal if the project fails or if the leverage effect is negative. In Chapters 1 and 2 we assumed that the goal of managers as agents of the stockholders is to maximize the firm's value.

In practice, although value maximization might require, say, an optimal capital structure of 50% debt, a firm's managers may employ only, say, 20% debt. Accepting relatively risky projects adds to the firm's business risk, and employing a high debt/equity ratio adds to its financial risk. Management has to consider both. We focus here only on the leverage effect. Leverage can increase the firm's profit and, consequently, the manager's bonus. However, from the manager's viewpoint the payoffs are not symmetrical: Losing one's job is more detrimental than a bonus is beneficial.

16.3.3 Agency Costs and Capital Structure Decisions

The loss of value from excessive perquisite consumption, overinvestment, underinvestment, risk-shifting, and managerial risk-aversion totals the amount of agency costs that a firm incurs. A levered firm's value with both financial distress costs and agency costs can be written as

$$V_L = V_U + TB - FD - AC \qquad (16.4)$$

where FD and AC are the PV of the financial distress costs and agency costs, respectively. This loss is expressed graphically in Figure 16-5. Although the optimal leverage of firm II is $B_{II}^{\star}$, management may choose to employ a different leverage level of $B_{II}^{\star\star}$. The difference between the value of the firm at $B_{II}^{\star}$ and $B_{II}^{\star\star}$ is the agency cost incurred. Note also that this loss is incurred both when management shifts the leverage level above the optimal level, and when the shift is to a leverage level below the optimal level. The following problem demonstrates how to calculate agency costs associated with one firm's capital structure decision.

PRACTICE BOX	
Problem	Morton International Inc.'s balance sheet shows debt of $222.6 million. Assume this amount is also the market value of its debt. The firm has 49 million outstanding shares, and the market price of each share is $85.
	a. Use the above information to calculate the firm's debt/equity ratio. What is the firm's market value?
	b. Suppose Morton is considering issuing $1,000 million more debt to raise its total debt to $1,222.6 million. The firm plans to use the additional cash to reduce its equity by repurchasing stock. Management estimates that the stock price will jump to $100 per share as a result of the change in the capital structure and that after the change, Morton will have an optimal capital structure. Therefore, the firm repurchases $1,000 million/$100 = 10 million shares. What is the firm's market value if the leverage is increased? Does the firm's NOI change?
	c. Suppose that in spite of the information given in Item b, the firm's CEO decides *not* to increase the debt. What agency costs will Morton International incur?
Solution	a. The debt/equity ratio is

$$\$222.6 \text{ million}/(49 \text{ million} \times \$85) \cong 0.0534 \text{ or } 5.34\%$$

The firm's market value is

$$V_L = E_L + B = (49 \text{ million} \times \$85) + \$222.6 \text{ million} = \$4,387.6 \text{ million}$$

b. The firm's market value with the larger leverage is

$$V_L\star = (39 \text{ million} \times \$100) + \$1,222.6 \text{ million} = \$5,122.6 \text{ million}$$

Note that there are now 39 million shares at $100 each and $1,222.6 million of debt. The firm's production level does not change because all the proceeds from the additional debt are used to repurchase stock. Thus, the firm's total investment does not change and, therefore, neither does the firm's NOI.

c. If the firm does not increase its debt, the value lost will be:

$$V_L\star - V_L = \$5,122.6 \text{ million} - \$4,387.6 \text{ million} = \$735.0 \text{ million}$$

This sum constitutes the *agency costs* that Morton incurred.

16.4 A FINAL PERSPECTIVE ON CAPITAL STRUCTURE

Although empirical evidence suggests that several factors affect a firm's mix of debt and equity, managers have no clear-cut formula to use in determining the firm's optimal capital structure. In the following section we briefly review some empirical studies and then cover some guidelines for seeking that optimal mix of debt and equity.

16.4.1 Empirical Evidence

Financial economists have examined how the mix of debt and equity varies across different firms. Describing each study would fill several textbooks; fortunately, the main results of these studies and their overall implications can be summarized in far less space.[16]

Careful examination of capital structures in large samples of firms suggests that the factors listed next influence the mix of debt and equity.

1. *Amount of business risk.* Just as theories based on corporate taxes and bankruptcy costs would predict, firms with more volatile operating earnings use less debt in their capital structures. The value of the interest tax shield is lower for these firms because taxable income may sometimes be insufficient to offset a high level of interest expense. In addition, higher borrowing increases the probability of financial distress and bankruptcy when operating income varies over a wide range, giving prospective direct and indirect bankruptcy costs a greater weight in the decision.

2. *Characteristics of a firm's assets.* Firms with greater amounts of fixed assets tend to have more debt; conversely, firms with more intangible assets, or assets that require higher expenditures on advertising or on research and development, tend to borrow less. Firms that make very unique products also use less debt. For example, drug and electronics industries consistently have less financial leverage, while electric and gas utilities use high amounts of financial leverage. These findings are consistent with theories that suggest the costs of financial distress, as well as the agency costs related to underinvestment, limit corporate borrowing.

3. *Amount of cash flow.* Everything else being equal, firms with greater amounts of cash flow (funds from operating profits) use higher amounts of leverage. This finding is consistent with agency theories of capital structure that suggest debt is useful in controlling overinvestment.

4. *Profitability of the firm.* Studies consistently show that more profitable firms use less leverage. This finding contrasts sharply with what would be expected if firms selected a debt-equity mix based on a trade-off between tax benefits and bankruptcy costs. Stuart Myers pointed out that this result is consistent with a *pecking order* theory of capital structure.[17] Under the pecking order theory, firms prefer internal to external sources of funds. Empirical evidence on pecking order behavior is inconclusive; however, the issue reminds us that our understanding of capital structure formation is far from complete.

---

16. Interested readers are referred to a (very readable) article that reviews the recent literature in capital structure: M. Harris A. Raviv, "The Theory of Capital Structure," *Journal of Finance* (March 1991): 297–356.

17. S. C. Myers, "The Capital Structure Puzzle," *Journal of Finance* (July 1984): 575–592. Under the pecking order theory, firms prefer internal sources of finances because significant transaction costs are related to obtaining external funds. These transaction costs result largely from the fact that managers have more information about the company than investors do. The possibility of "hidden information" causes investors to discount the value of any securities that a firm brings to the market. Securities such as common equity whose value is most sensitive to hidden information will receive the largest discount.

16.4.2 There Is No Formula for the Optimal Capital Structure

Does capital structure matter? Regardless of the academic controversy surrounding this issue, if the interest tax shield, the costs of financial distress, and the agency costs are accounted for, capital structure does matter. A firm should seek an optimal financial mix, which will not ordinarily consist entirely of debt.

However, it is difficult to provide a formula to help financial managers find the optimal capital structure. In this chapter we have discussed some factors that managers must consider when selecting the optimal leverage:

1. PV of the interest tax shield
2. Costs of financial distress and bankruptcy
3. Business risk (i.e., the variability of the NOI)
4. Agency costs

Financial theorists have examined other factors such as hidden information, product market strategies, and threats of hostile takeovers that may influence the capital structure decision. But for simplicity suppose the stockholders exert pressure on management to select the capital structure that maximizes the firm's value with respect to only the four factors (interest tax shield, bankruptcy costs, business risk, and agency costs) just listed. How can management use these factors to determine the optimal capital structure? There is no clear-cut answer. The best we can do is to provide guidelines for seeking the optimal capital structure.

First, management can safely measure the interest tax shield. Similarly, a manager can fairly easily estimate the variability of the NOI (the firm's business risk). However, estimating the costs of financial distress and, in particular, translating an increase in the probability of financial distress into market values are quite difficult. For example, suppose a firm decides to issue an additional $100 million of debt at a 10% interest rate and use the proceeds to repurchase stock. The annual tax shield can be easily calculated:

$$0.10 \times \$100 \text{ million} \times T$$

where T is the corporate tax rate. If $T = 0.4$, the interest tax shield will be $4 million ($10 million $\times$ 0.4 = $4 million). Assuming a perpetuity, the tax shield's PV will be (at 10% discount rate)

$$\frac{TB_r}{r} = \frac{\$4 \text{ million}}{0.1} = \$40 \text{ million}$$

If the probability of financial distress does not change, the firm's market value should increase by $40 million. Management, however, knows that the risk of bankruptcy increases with increased debt financing. The question is: By how much? Suppose management estimates the PV of the cost of financial distress to be only $30 million and, therefore, decides to issue the $100 million debt in the hope that the firm's market value will increase by $10 million ($40 million – $30 million). Investors may have a different view of the cost of financial distress and may react unfavorably. Should the firm's market value decline, the additional debt will have been a financial mistake. However, because knowing the market reaction to the debt issue in advance is impossible, the manager can only use judgment based on experience.

This example contains the ingredients (but not the exact recipe) for seeking the optimal capital structure:

1. First, use the best subjective estimate of the PV of the various factors affecting the optimum capital structure to choose a debt/equity ratio that you consider optimal. You would do well to study the capital structure of experienced (and successful) firms in the same industry.

2. You may or may not have hit the bull's-eye—the optimum capital structure. How will you know? Simply by the results. For instance, in the next capital issue you might decide to raise only debt. If the stock price increases you were not at the optimal leverage before and the stockholders perhaps desire even more debt. Continue this process until the stock price starts to fall. At that point, more debt would harm rather than help. This process may not lead to an exact optimal capital structure, but you will be fairly close to it. Indeed, a firm often experiments with its capital structure in this manner. It is common to issue debt, to use the proceeds to repurchase a portion of the shares in the market (thereby raising the debt/equity ratio), and then to observe the market reaction. This procedure is repeated as long as the firm's market value increases.

3. Finally, recall that the market is dynamic: Interest rates change, business risk changes, and tax rates change. Even the interest tax shield is not certain. Indeed, the optimal capital structure is likely to change repeatedly over time.

While optimal capital structure is conceptually well-defined, measuring the economic value of its various components and identifying it in practice are an art. The theoretical considerations delineated in this chapter can serve as a guide in seeking the optimal capital structure, but they do not constitute a magic formula for finding it. This makes life more difficult but, at the same time, surely more interesting! Let's apply what we know to Boeing Corporation's capital structure.

APPLYING THEORY TO PRACTICE 16.1

BOEING CORPORATION'S CAPITAL STRUCTURE

In early 1993 Boeing's management decided to review its capital structure. Many large firms were turning to the bond market and management wondered whether Boeing, too, should issue more debt.

The following table provides selected financial data for Boeing Corporation for the years 1988–1992, as well as for 1993–1995. In noticing that the debt/equity ratio and earnings tended to grow simultaneously in the period 1988–1992 the board of directors concluded that leverage had helped boost the firm's profits.

Five-Year Summary: Boeing Corporation (in $ million)				
Years before Decision Regarding Long-Term Debt				
	1992	**1991**	**1990**	**1989**	**1988**
Total sales	16,692	30,184	29,314	27,595	20,276
Net earnings	1,554	1,567	1,385	675	614
Long-term debt	1,772	1,313	311	275	251
Stockholders' equity	8,056	8,093	6,973	6,131	5,404

Years after the Decision Regarding Long-Term Debt		
	1995	**1994**	**1993**
Total sales	19,515	21,924	25,438
Net income	393	856	1,244

Prior years have been restated to conform with the presentation used in 1992. Additional information:

1. In 1992 the firm had 349,256,796 shares outstanding. The market price was $37 a share.
2. The EBIT in 1992 was $2,040 million.

Suppose in 1992 the board of directors had hired you to analyze the firm's financial development over the period 1988–1992. In particular, the board would have liked you to assess the effect of introducing extreme changes in the firm's debt/equity ratio on its rate of return on equity and on its risk. If leverage was so beneficial in the past, the members wondered, why not increase it further? In the various calculations that you conduct in Questions 1, 2, and 3 assume the accounting figures for debt and equity reported in the table are good proxies for the market figures. In Questions 4 and 5, assume the accounting figure for debt is a good proxy for the market value of debt but use the market value of equity.

Eventually, Boeing decided not to raise much more debt. The financial data regarding years 1993–1995, included in the table, will be used to analyze whether, in retrospect, the firm's decision was correct.

Questions

1. What were the changes in the firm's capital structure in 1988–1992? In the 1990s, the interest rate in the U.S. fell. Can this explain the observed changes in this ratio?
2. Assume the firm pays 9% interest on its long-term debt and the corporate tax rate is 34%. In the absence of bankruptcy and agency costs [that is, Equation (16.2) holds] estimate what the firm's value would have been each year if it had not employed leverage (i.e., zero leverage firm). Calculate the gain due to the actual leverage employed in each year. When the firm employs leverage, it has more resources to invest because $V_L > V_U$. Are the

firm's investment and NOI the same with and without leverage? What measure can be taken to guarantee the same NOI distribution regardless of the leverage?

3. One board member suggested increasing the debt to $10 billion. What is your estimate of the firm's value in 1992 if it had financed its operations by $10 billion of debt (assuming no change in capital expenditure)? If the firm changes its capital structure but wants to keep the capital expenditure (and NOI) at the same level as in 1992, by how much should it increase dividends? Why didn't Boeing increase its leverage? Suppose $10 billion debt is optimal in the absence of agency costs. Estimate the agency costs.

In answering Questions 4 and 5, use the market values of equity and debt in 1992. The firm's market value is $14,694.5 million, which is the sum of ($37 × 349,256,796 shares + $1,772 million = $12,922.5 million of equity + $1,772 million of debt = $14,694.5 million).

4. Calculate the rate of return on equity for 1994 under two alternate assumptions:
   a. The long-term debt is the same as in 1992.
   b. The long-term debt increases to $10 billion.

   Using the data in the table and other information given in the text, calculate the NOI for 1994. Without performing any more calculations, do you think the leverage effect with $10 billion debt would be positive or negative for 1993?

5. In 1995 the firm's revenue was $19,515 million. Boeing delivered 206 planes, a reduction from 270 planes in 1994. Net income was $393 million (down from $856 million in 1994). What would be the effect of the hypothetical $10 billion leverage in 1995?

MAKING THE CONNECTION

1. To answer these questions, we calculate the debt/equity ratio, using accounting figures, by dividing the long-term debt by the equity. For example, for 1992 we have:

   Debt/Equity = $1,772 million/$8,056 million ≅ 0.2200 or 22.00%

   We obtain the following ratios for the five years:

	1992	1991	1990	1989	1988
Debt/equity ratio	22.00%	16.22%	4.46%	4.49%	4.64%

   We observe a dramatic increase in the debt/equity ratio from 4.46% in 1990 to 16.22% in 1991.

   A decline in the real interest rate in the early 1990s might explain the preference for debt in the capital structure. Similar to many other firms, Boeing took advantage of the low interest rate by issuing debt.

2. Let us employ the data contained in the table to calculate $V_U = V_L - TB$ (in $ million):

	1992	1991	1990	1989	1988
Debt, B	1,772	1,313	311	275	251
Equity, E_L	8,056	8,093	6,973	6,131	5,404
$V_L = E_L + B$	9,828	9,406	7,284	6,406	5,655
$TB(T = 0.34)$	602	446	106	94	85
Value of the unlevered firm					
$V_U = V_L - TB$	9,226	8,960	7,178	6,312	5,570

Up to 1990 the difference between V_U and V_L was very small. The capital structure had very little debt, and the increase in the value of the firm with leverage relatively to the hypothetical case of zero leverage was small. A more significant difference was obtained in 1991 and 1992 when the debt/equity ratio increased.

Note that the firm's value with leverage is larger than its value without leverage. With leverage the firm has more resources to invest. Therefore, the NOI in the levered and unlevered cases are not identical. To analyze the leverage effect, we must hold NOI constant. We have two methods to hold the NOI constant: (1) The extra value in the levered case is distributed as dividends, or (2) more shares are issued in the unlevered case. In both cases we can guarantee the same investment or capital expenditures, which allows us to assume identical NOI probability distributions.

3. We assume here that the value of the firm represents the resources available for investment. The firm's value with the actual debt employed in 1992 was $9,828 million. Thus, the firm's actual total investment made in 1992 was $9,828 million. The hypothetical value of the firm if it would be unlevered is

$$V_U = \$9,226 \text{ million}$$

(See the above calculations.) If the firm employs $10 billion debt, its levered value would be

$$V_L = \$9,226 \text{ million} + (0.34 \times \$10 \text{ billion})$$

$$= \$9,226 \text{ million} + \$3,400 \text{ million} = \$12,626 \text{ million}$$

To keep the capital expenditure unchanged, the firm should distribute as dividends the difference between its levered value and its value before the hypothetical increase in debt, or $2,798 million ($12,626 million − $9,828 million = $2,798 million).

Why didn't Boeing adopt such a debt/equity policy with a relatively high level of debt ($10 billion)? One possible answer is that with such a large debt, the fixed interest expense would be large and might increase the risk of bankruptcy. In 1992 the firm would have had to pay interest of $900 million (0.09 × $10 billion = $900 million). Net earnings in 1992 were much larger, and this level of debt would not have constituted a bankruptcy threat. However, a slight slowdown in the economy might have caused financial distress. Another explanation could be management's fear of being replaced if the firm encountered financial distress. In such a case the lower increase in the firm's value would constitute agency costs.

To summarize, it appears that the firm's relatively low debt/equity ratio is due to the chance of financial distress and agency costs. Assuming the $10 billion debt is optimal without agency costs, this cost is given by the value lost due to the fact that the firm's leverage is less than optimal:

$$\$12{,}626 \text{ million} - \$9{,}828 \text{ million} = \$2{,}798 \text{ million}$$

4. With $856 million annual earnings, the firm will still feel the positive effect of leverage, and an increase of the debt to $10 billion will still be beneficial.

With $856 million annual earnings, the rate of return on equity with the current debt/equity ratio will be

$$\frac{\$856 \text{ million}}{\$12{,}922.5 \text{ million}} \cong 0.0662 \text{ or } 6.62\%$$

To analyze the effect of $10 billion debt on the rate of return on equity, let us first calculate NOI for 1994 given the $1,772 million debt component in the capital structure. We have the following relationship:

$$\text{Net earnings} = (1 - T)\,(\text{NOI} - \text{Interest})$$

Therefore:

$$\$856 \text{ million} = (1 - 0.34)\,[\text{NOI} - (0.09 \times \$1{,}772 \text{ million})]$$

Hence:

$$\text{NOI} = \frac{\$856 \text{ million}}{(1 - 0.34)} + (0.09 \times \$1{,}772 \text{ million}) \cong \$1{,}456.45 \text{ million}$$

With NOI of $1,456.45 million and debt of $10 billion, the firm's earnings will be

$$(1 - 0.34) \times [\$1{,}456.45 \text{ million} - (0.09 \times \$10 \text{ billion})]$$

$$= 0.66 \times (\$1{,}456.45 \text{ million} - \$900 \text{ million})$$

$$= 0.66 \times 556.45 \text{ million} \cong \$367.26 \text{ million}$$

The value of the firm's equity will be

$$\$14{,}694.5 \text{ million} - \$10 \text{ billion} = \$4{,}694.5 \text{ million}$$

(Note: We hold the firm's total value constant; otherwise, the capital expenditure would change. The firm's value is $14,694.5 million, and the equity's value is the firm's value less the $10 billion of debt.)

In 1994 the rate of return on equity would be

$$\frac{\$367.26 \text{ million}}{\$4,694.5 \text{ million}} \cong 0.0782 \text{ or } 7.82\%$$

Thus, employing $10 billion debt will increase the rate of return on equity in 1994. The leverage effect is also positive for 1993 because the earnings were larger than they were in 1994.

5. The pretax operating income is

$$\text{NOI} = \frac{\$393 \text{ million}}{1 - 0.34} + (0.09 \times \$1,772 \text{ million}) \cong \$755 \text{ million}$$

Using the same type of calculation as in Question 4, we find that with $10 billion debt, the return on equity is

$$\frac{(1 - 0.34)(\$755 \text{ million} - \$900 \text{ million})}{\$4,694.5 \text{ million}} \cong -2.01\%$$

With the current level of debt, we have

$$\frac{\$393 \text{ million}}{\$12,922.5 \text{ million}} \cong 3.04\%$$

The firm fares better with the 1992 level of debt; in 1995 the leverage effect is negative.

Final note: In fact, Boeing increased its debt only slightly to $2,348 million on June 30, 1995. This restraint was a smart decision because, otherwise, Boeing would have been in financial distress in 1995. The slowdown in Boeing sales continued. In 1995 the firm announced further job cuts due to diminishing demand for planes in the United States and abroad. Increasing the debt to $10 billion could have led to financial disaster. By not taking on the debt, Boeing survived the slowdown and began growing again when sales rebounded in 1996.

SUMMARY

Transaction costs and differing borrowing and lending interest rates make Modigliani's and Miller's arguments invalid in an imperfect capital market. Accounting for these factors still does not provide a systematic guide to determining the firm's optimal capital structure. However, corporate taxes, bankruptcy risk, and agency costs guide us regarding optimal capital structure.

The interest expense on the debt component of the firm's capital structure is tax-deductible. Because of the interest tax shield, leverage increases the firm's value. However, such results lead to the unrealistic recommendation of extremely high levels of leverage. Contrary to the results of Equation (16.2), firms do not finance themselves exclusively with debt. Economic factors such as business risk, financial distress, and agency costs affect the firm's optimal capital structure.

A firm that is financially distressed faces direct costs as well as indirect costs. Therefore, firms try to avoid such distress by avoiding a high degree of leverage. The greater the firm's business risk, the lower its optimal borrowing and the lower its op-timal degree of leverage. Agency costs may lead managers to employ even less leverage than stock-holders desire. There is no formula that will guaran-tee success in selecting the optimal capital structure. Similar to the chef who perfects recipes, the suc-cessful CFO has to carefully blend all factors to achieve the optimal capital structure.

CHAPTER AT A GLANCE

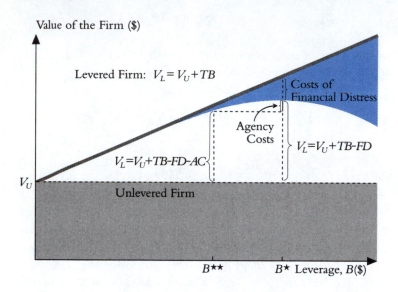

1. In a perfect market, $V_L = V_U$, and capital structure does not matter.

2. When corporate taxes are added, $V_L = V_U + TB$, extreme borrowing is optimal because the larger the debt level, the larger the firm's value.

3. When the costs of financial distress are introduced,

$$V_L = V_U + TB - FD$$

where FD is the PV of the costs of financial distress. The optimum leverage is the value of B at which V_L is maximized.

4. When agency costs are incorporated, we obtain

$$V_L = V_U + TB - FD - AC$$

where AC is the PV of the agency costs. Agency costs are the loss in value arising from conflicts of in-terest among stockholders, bondholders, and management.

KEY TERMS

Imperfect capital market   Financial distress   Agency costs
Interest tax shield   Business risk

REVIEW AND PRACTICE

16.1 Give an example of a bankruptcy cost.

16.2 Give an example of an agency cost.

16.3 What is an *interest tax shield*? Would an increase in the corporate tax rate cause an increase or a decrease in the interest tax shield?

16.4 An unlevered firm's NOI could be $50, $100, or $150, with equal probabilities. The firm issues 10 shares, and the cost of capital is 10%. Use Equation (16.2) to answer the following questions:
a. What would the firm's value be if it were levered? Assume the corporate tax rate is 35%, the interest rate is 5%, and debt is $20.
b. What would the levered firm's stock price be if it had issued 40 shares? What would the firm's value be if it had issued 100 shares? Does the number of shares issued affect the gain from leverage? Does it affect the levered firm's value?

16.5 A firm pays $1 million interest on debt each year for 10 years. It then liquidates its assets.
a. What is the PV of the interest tax shield when $r = 5\%$ and $T = 35\%$?
b. How would your answer change if the interest tax shield remains unchanged indefinitely?

16.6 A firm has the following NOI (in million $):

Year	1	2	3	4
NOI	100	0	0	300

The interest tax shield is $TrB = \$35$ million in each year. The interest rate is 5%.
a. Calculate the PV of the interest tax shield on the assumption that it is $35 million in each of the four years.
b. Does the firm obtain the $35 million in years 2 and 3? (Hint: recall the carry-forward provision, see bottom of pg. 596.)

c. What is the PV of the interest tax shield with the carry-forward provision?
d. Calculate the firm's net income in each of the four years if $T = 35\%$.

16.7 Suppose M & M's formula with taxes holds; namely,

$$V_L = V_U + TB$$

Now add bankruptcy costs (assuming bankruptcy occurs) amounting to 10% of an unlevered firm's value where $V_U = \$1$ million. The tax rate is 35%. The probability of bankruptcy is as follows:

Debt/Equity Ratio	Probability of Bankruptcy
0	0.1
0.1	0.2
0.2	0.3
0.3	0.4
0.4	0.5
0.5	0.5
0.6	0.8
0.7	1

a. Use M & M's results to derive the firm's optimal capital structure in the case of no bankruptcy.
b. What is the firm's optimal capital structure if the average bankruptcy costs are taken into account?

16.8 Firms A and B have the following NOI distributions (in $ million):

Firm A		Firm B	
NOI	Probability	NOI	Probability
$50	½	$125	½
$250	½	$175	½

A NOI lower than the interest rate on debt will result in bankruptcy.

a. Calculate the probability of bankruptcy in these two firms for the following levels of debt: $200, $300, $400, $500, $600, $700, $800, $900, $1,000, and $2,000. The interest rate is 10%.

b. The corporate income tax is $T = 35\%$. Which firm will employ more debt? Explain.

16.9 An unlevered firm's value is $100 million. The interest rate is 10% and the corporate tax rate is 35%. In each year NOI will be either $5 million or $25 million with equal probability. The firm's CEO earns $1 million a year plus 10% of the net cash flow before interest payments, which is defined as $(1 - T) \times (\text{NOI} - rB) + rB$. In the event of bankruptcy, the CEO will be dismissed, and his income will be zero. The CEO's goal is to avoid bankruptcy with certainty. Assume no bankruptcy costs. The stockholders decide that their investment in the firm's equity should be no less than $10 million.

a. What is the firm's optimal capital structure from the stockholders' viewpoint? What is the firm's value with that capital structure?

b. Given that the CEO wants to avoid bankruptcy with certainty, he maximizes the PV of all his future income. The CEO's expected income is discounted at 10%. What is the optimum capital structure from the CEO's viewpoint? What is the PV of his income if he expects to stay with the firm for four years?

c. Calculate the agency costs in Problem 16.9b.

16.10 Using the data in Problem 16.9, this time assume just one cash flow period. If the net income is positive, the CEO will get $1 million plus 10% of the cash flow before interest payments; if the net income is negative, the CEO will get $500,000 but no bonus. Assume the CEO wishes to maximize his average end-of-year income.

a. What is the optimal capital structure from the stockholders' viewpoint?

b. What is the optimum capital structure from the CEO's viewpoint?

c. Calculate the agency costs.

16.11 With no financial distress $V_L = V_U + TB$. Assume the following additional information:

- Expected bankruptcy expenses amount to 1% of the levered firm's value (before financial distress costs) up to a debt level of $10 million, 4% between $10 million and $20 million, and 100% beyond $20 million.
- Agency costs are zero up to $10 million debt, $2 million for $10 to $20 million debt, and $0 beyond $20 million. The firm's value if it is unlevered is $100 million.
- The tax rate is 35%.

a. What is the optimal capital structure with bankruptcy costs but with no agency costs?

b. What is the optimal capital structure with both bankruptcy and agency costs?

c. Calculate the cost of financial distress using the optimal capital structure you found in Problem 16.11b.

16.12 A utility firm and an industrial firm have the following NOI (in $ million):

Utility Firm		Industrial Firm	
NOI	Probability	NOI	Probability
20	½	5	½
40	½	80	½

The interest rate on debt is 10%. The cost of financial distress is estimated to be

($300 million + TB)
    × Probability of bankruptcy in a given year

If the firms did not employ leverage, the value of both would be $V_U = \$1,000$ million. Assume $T = 35\%$.

a. What is the optimal capital structure of each firm?

b. In light of your results, explain why firms with large business risk tend to issue relatively low levels of debt.

16.13 "When the corporate tax rate rises, the levered firm's value rises because $V_L = V_U + TB$." Do you agree? Discuss your answer.

16.14 To minimize agency costs, firms commonly include shares, or options to buy these shares, as part of the CEO's compensation. Explain why this practice might serve to reduce agency costs. How would this affect the capital structure that the CEO selects?

16.15 An unlevered firm's value is $1,000. The firm borrows $500 at $r = 10\%$. The tax rate is 35%.
a. What is the PV of the interest tax shield?
b. What is the PV of the interest tax shield when for three years $T = 35\%$, but from Year 4 on $T = 50\%$?
c. Does the firm's value increase when the tax rate rises?

16.16 Suppose a firm takes on debt with a perpetual interest bill that begins at $5 million a year and increases by 1% every year. The tax rate is 35%. The riskless interest rate is 5%. What is the PV of the firm's interest tax shield?

16.17 "Owing to fixed bankruptcy costs, large firms would be expected, other things being equal, to employ more leverage than small firms." Evaluate this statement.

16.18 The NOI of small firms is generally more volatile than that of large firms. Which of the two will include a larger proportion of debt in their capital structure? Explain.

16.19 A board of directors adopts the following policy: "Whenever EPS is negative two years in a row, the CEO will be replaced."
a. How will this policy affect the business risk (i.e., the project risk) that the CEO accepts?
b. How will this policy affect the debt/equity ratio the CEO selects?

16.20 Suppose an American investor purchases a German firm. The firm owes a German bank 1 million DM. "Because the riskless interest rate in the United States is 5%, the interest tax shield from the American viewpoint is the dollar equivalent of $T \times 1$ million DM $\times 0.05 = T \times 50,000$ DM."
a. Do you agree with this statement?
b. How would you calculate the interest tax shield in this case? Is the cash flow certain?

16.21 A firm's interest tax shield is $10 million. The nominal riskless interest rate is 5%. The future inflation rate is uncertain with a mean of 2% and a stan-

dard deviation of 5%. What is the maximum interest tax shield? Why is it a maximum and not a minimum tax shield?

16.22 When a firm goes through Chapter 11 bankruptcy or reschedules its debt, the senior bondholders reach an agreement in which they lose money to the other parties (junior bondholders, stockholders). The following figure shows the loss to senior creditors and the gain to the other parties:

The Bankruptcy Game
Distribution of Gains* and Losses in Rescue Deals, 1983–1990

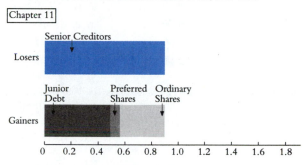

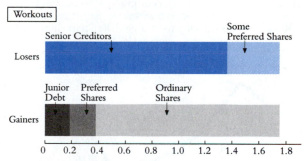

*Benefits from senior creditors giving up more priority rights
Source: London Business School UCLA

Source: "The Bankruptcy Game," *The Economist Year Book*, concise ed. (New York: Addison Wesley, 1992), p. 242. © 1991 The Economist Newspaper Group, Inc. Reprinted with permission. Further reproduction prohibited.

a. Why might senior creditors agree to lose part of their money? Explain your results (Hint: According to Chapter 11, the firm can continue to operate).

b. If you were a shareholder, which would you prefer—a "workout" deal or a Chapter 11 procedure? Why?

16.23 The EPS of Ford Motor Co. and American Telephone and Telegraph (AT&T) were as follows:

Year	Ford ($)	AT&T ($)
1984	5.26	1.25
1985	4.54	1.43
1986	6.16	1.64
1987	9.05	1.88
1988	10.96	2.11
1989	9.13	2.50
1990	1.86	2.51
1991	−4.79	0.40
1992	−1.46	2.86
1993	3.30	3.15
1994	5.00	3.35

Source: *Value Line Investment Survey* (New York: Value Line Publishing) various issues.

In your view, which of these two firms should employ more leverage? Explain.

16.24 The figure below illustrates the monthly volume of sales of powdered-drink mixes and canned soup.

These figures represent average sales. Future sales in each month are expected to deviate only slightly from the average figures for the corresponding month. Suppose two firms, one producing drink mixes and the other producing canned soup, merge.
a. What can you say about the merged firm's business risk relative to the business risk of the separate firms?
b. How will the merger affect the optimal capital structure? Demonstrate your answer graphically. (Let the horizontal axis stand for debt; the vertical axis, for the firm's value.) Plot the separate firms' and the merged firm's values on the same graph.

At the Checkout. Marketers of highly seasonal products such as canned soup and powdered-drink mixes find it difficult to sell their products off-season. Some marketers, including Campbell Soup and Kraft General Foods, maker of Kool-Aid, are working to change that. Chart shows volume sales, in millions of units.

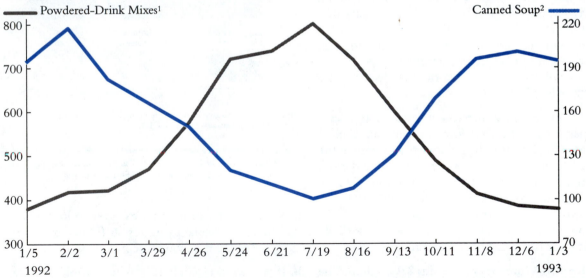

Seasonal Sales

¹ Powered–drink unit volume=reconstituted pints

² Soup unit volume=16-ounce cans

Source: From Eben Shapiro, "Food Firms Seek a Plan for All Seasons," *Wall Street Journal*, 29 July 1993, p. B1. Reprinted by permission of *The Wall Street Journal*, © 1993 Dow Jones & Company, Inc. All Rights Reserved Worldwide.

16.25 The average ratio of total debt to total value for nonfinancial firms in various countries in the early 1990s was estimated as follows:

United States	45%
Canada	50%
United Kingdom	58%
Germany	60%
France	64%
Japan	82%

Source: *OECD Financial Statistics*, various issues.

What factors might explain the variability of this ratio across countries? Discuss.

INTERNET QUESTIONS

16.26 Visit the Stock Center at Thomson Investor's Network and calculate the debt ratio of a major auto manufacturer. Then, calculate the ratio for a major service company, such as Merill Lynch. Based on what you learned about leverage, what would account for the difference in the ratios?

http://www.thomsoninvest.net

16.27 Visit the following Web site and compare the ten firms with the highest debt/equity ratios to the ten firms with the lowest ratios. What conclusions can you derive from this comparison?

http://www.pbpost.com/top50/chart17.htm

YOUR TURN: APPLYING THEORY TO PRACTICE

ARCHER DANIELS MIDLAND COMPANY: LEVERAGE AND EARNINGS PER SHARE

Operating, Financial and Other Data (in thousands, except per-share data)

	1994	1993	1992	1991
Operating				
Net sales and other operating income	$11,374,372	$8,811,362	$9,231,502	$8,468,198
Earnings before extraordinary loss	$484,069	$534,509	$503,757	$466,678
Per common share	$0.93	$0.99	$1.54	$1.42
Financial				
Long-term debt	$2,021,417	$2,039,143	$1,562,491	$980,273
Shareholders' equity	$5,045,421	$4,883,251	$4,492,353	$3,922,295
Weighted average shares outstanding (000's)	520,300	539,900	327,326	328,460

Operating, Financial and Other Data (in thousands, except per-share data)

	1990	1989	1988	1987	1986	1985
Operating						
Net sales and other operating income	$7,751,341	$7,928,836	$6,798,394	$5,774,621	$5,335,975	$4,738,767
Earnings before extraordinary loss	$483,522	$424,673	$353,058	$265,355	$239,373	$163,908
Per common share	$1.48	$1.31	$1.07	$0.81	$0.74	$0.51
Financial						
Long-term debt	$750,901	$690,052	$692,878	$657,465	$570,248	$569,323
Shareholders' equity	$3,573,228	$3,033,503	$2,630,529	$2,367,673	$2,075,887	$1,803,394
Weighted average shares outstanding (000's)	327,010	324,259	329,902	329,484	324,602	320,770

Use the data to analyze how leverage affects the firm's profit and its EPS. Assume the accounting values equal the market values and the firm's total assets are the sum of its long-term debt and shareholders' equity.

Questions

1. Calculate the debt/total assets ratio for each year from 1985 to 1994. Assume the formula $V_L = V_U + TB$ holds and that $T = 35\%$. What would be the firm's value in each year if it were an all-equity firm? In your answer, assume the operating income does not change with the change in the capital structure. (This can be the case if with leverage the firm first issues equity and then repurchases some of its stock and finances the repurchases by debt. In such case the firm's value increases without affecting its physical activity.)

2. Assume the firm paid 35% corporate tax each year and the interest rate on long-term debt was 10%. Use the above figures to calculate the NOI for each year. Calculate the EPS the firm would have had if it had been an all-equity firm. In which year was the leverage effect negative? In which was it positive?

3. Using the 1994 data, calculate the break-even point (in terms of NOI) and the EPS analysis line. (In your answer rely on Section 15.4 of the previous chapter.) What is the slope of this line? What is its intercept? (Hint: Assume $V_L = E_L + B$ where E_L is the levered firm's equity, B is the long-term debt, and V_L is the total assets of the firm, $r = 10\%$, and corporate tax is 35%.)

4. Calculate the break-even point for each of the ten years and compare it to the actual NOI. In light of your analysis, do you think the firm should take on more debt? Should it take on less debt? Explain your results carefully.

5. In light of your results in Question 4, does the firm have agency costs? If so, why?

Appendix 16A   Corporate Taxes, Personal Taxes, and Leverage

The maximum personal tax rate has changed dramatically over time, from 70% in 1980 to 28% under the Reagan Administration. In 1996 it stood at 39.6%. As of early 1997, the capital gains tax was expected to be reduced from 28% to about 20%. Do personal taxes, capital gains taxes, and their variation over time affect the firm's capital structure decision?

To analyze the role of personal taxes on the firm's value, let us assume the simpler case first: These rates are fixed and do not change with the individual investor's taxable income. We will consider three types of tax rates:

1. T = corporate income tax rate
2. T_g = personal capital gains tax rate
3. T_p = personal income tax rate (the rate applicable to dividends and interest)

Figure 16A-1 illustrates the tax burden and the net income in debt and equity financing scenarios after personal and corporate tax on each dollar of operating income. If the firm pays its operating income to bondholders as interest, it pays no corporate tax. However, the investor who receives the interest pays T_p. Earnings on investment financed by equity are taxable: A firm pays T as corporate tax, and then its

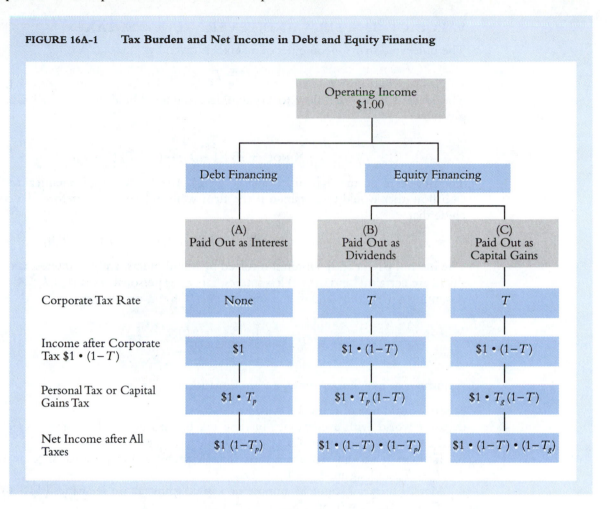

FIGURE 16A-1   Tax Burden and Net Income in Debt and Equity Financing

Operating Income
$1.00

Debt Financing

Equity Financing

(A)
Paid Out as Interest

(B)
Paid Out as
Dividends

(C)
Paid Out as
Capital Gains

	Debt Financing (A)	Equity (B)	Financing (C)
Corporate Tax Rate	None	T	T
Income after Corporate Tax $\$1 \cdot (1-T)$	$\$1$	$\$1 \cdot (1-T)$	$\$1 \cdot (1-T)$
Personal Tax or Capital Gains Tax	$\$1 \cdot T_p$	$\$1 \cdot T_p(1-T)$	$\$1 \cdot T_g(1-T)$
Net Income after All Taxes	$\$1 (1-T_p)$	$\$1 \cdot (1-T) \cdot (1-T_p)$	$\$1 \cdot (1-T) \cdot (1-T_g)$

stockholders pay T_g or T_p on the net income depending on whether the investors realize earnings on capital gains or they receive dividends and pay personal income tax.

If you consider either lending a firm money or investing in its shares, which would you prefer? You would look for the avenue that provides the higher cash flow. If $T_p > T_g$ (which is the case in most European countries as well as in the United States), then Avenue C will dominate Avenue B. Paying dividends is not an optimal policy. The preference between Avenues A and C, however, depends on the levels of T, T_g, and T_p. In light of these tax considerations, should the firm issue equity or debt? The following rules hold:

- If $(1 - T_p) > (1 - T)(1 - T_g)$, then debt will be optimal.
- If $(1 - T_p) < (1 - T)(1 - T_g)$, then equity will be optimal.

Equation (16.5), given further on, confirms this calculation.

VALUE OF THE FIRM AND LEVERAGE WITH TAXES

The unlevered firm's income net of all taxes is given by

$$(1 - T)\,(1 - T_g) \times \text{NOI}^{18}$$

The levered firm's cash flow to bondholders and stockholders net of all taxes is given by

$$(1 - T)\,(1 - T_g)\,(\text{NOI} - rB) + (1 - T_p)\,rB =$$
$$(1 - T)\,(1 - T_g) \times \text{NOI} \;+\; rB\,[(1 - T_p) - (1 - T)\,(1 - T_g)]$$

The first term on the right-hand side, $[(1 - T)\,(1 - T_g) \times \text{NOI}]$, is identical to the cash flow that would be obtained if the firm were unlevered. Therefore, we conclude that

$$V_L = V_U + \text{PV of the cash flow}\,\big\{rB\,[(1 - T_p) - (1 - T)\,(1 - T_g)]\big\}$$

The interest payment, the interest received by bondholders, and the interest tax shield are certain,[19] and the riskless interest rate after personal tax is $(1 - T_p) \times r$. Assuming a perpetuity and discounting by $(1 - T_p) \times r$, we obtain

$$V_L = V_U + B\left[1 - \frac{(1 - T)(1 - T_g)}{(1 - T_p)}\right] \tag{16.5}$$

A number of conclusions emerge from Equation (16.5):

1. In a world free of taxes, $V_L = V_U$.
2. In a world with a corporate income tax but no personal income tax, $T_g = T_p = 0$, and $V_L = V_U + TB$.
3. If there is no difference between capital gains tax and personal income tax, $T_p = T_g$, and, again, $V_L = V_U + TB$.
4. Many European countries impose no capital gains tax on securities ($T_g = 0$). If $T_p = T$ and $T_g = 0$, once again, $V_L = V_U$.
5. If it employs the optimal policy recommended by Equation (16.5), the firm will maximize its value.

MILLER'S ARGUMENT

Merton Miller claims that $V_U = V_L$ because, in equilibrium, the second term on the right-hand side of Equation (16.5) equals zero. Whenever that term is not zero, the firm has an incentive to change its capital structure.[20] Miller's argument assumes

---

18. We assume the firm pays no dividends, hence the lower T_g rate applies to capital gains.
19. The bondholders' cash flow, $rB(1 - T_p)$, is certain. The reduction in stockholders' net income due to the interest payment, $rB(1 - T_g)$, and the interest tax shield, $rTB(1 - T_g)$ is certain. Thus, the entire term is certain.
20. M.H. Miller, "Debt and Taxes," *Journal of Finance* (May 1977): 261–276.

marginal income tax rates increase with earnings and the maximum marginal tax rate exceeds the corporate tax rate, T. For example, if

$$(1 - T_p) > (1 - T)(1 - T_g) \qquad\qquad (16.6)$$

the firm can increase its value by issuing more debt. As more interest is paid out, the investors' taxable income will increase and T_p will increase. This process will continue until $(1 - T_p) = (1 - T)(1 - T_g)$. At that point, $V_L = V_U$ [see Equation (16.5)]. Similarly, if $(1 - T_p) < (1 - T)(1 - T_g)$, the firm can increase its value by decreasing its debt. By doing so, T_p declines and $1 - T_p$ increases until equality is restored, and the firm has no incentive to reduce its debt further. Thus, in equilibrium $V_L = V_U$.

However, the equality in tax rates as Miller implies cannot pertain, given the prevailing tax rates in the United States. For example, after the 1986 Tax Act, the maximum $T_p = T_g = 28\%$ and $T = 34\%$. Thus, the equality $(1 - T_p) = (1 - T) \times (1 - T_g)$ could not hold even if T_p attains its highest value.

In 1993 Congress changed the tax rates such that $T_g = 28\%$, $T = 35\%$, and T_p can be as high as 39.6%. Therefore, we have

$$(1 - T)(1 - T_g) = (1 - 0.35)(1 - 0.28) = 0.65 \times 0.72 = 0.468$$

This implies that for Miller's argument to be valid, $(1 - T_p) = 46.8\%$ or $T_p = 53.2\%$. This is impossible if the maximum marginal tax rate is 39.6%.

Although Miller's argument is very interesting, it remains highly controversial and raises many questions about the relationship among corporate tax, personal taxes, and optimal capital structure.

Actually, with these tax rates ($T = 0.35$, $T_p = 0.396$, and $T_g = 0.28$), we obtain $(1 - T)(1 - T_g)/(1 - T_p) = 0.65 \times 0.72/0.604 \cong 0.775$. Therefore, the firm's value increases with debt when corporate and personal taxes are considered. However, Miller's model assumes unlimited tax-deductibility of interest. To enjoy the tax benefit, the firm must first earn a profit. In reality the benefits of leverage are less than they would be under unlimited deductibility; this is particularly true if the firm has other deductible items such as depreciation and investment tax credit. When tax deductibility is limited, an optimal capital structure exists similar to the one presented in Figure 16-5 (see Section 16.2.2).[21]

---

21. More details are provided in Harry DeAngelo and Ronald Masulis, "Optimal Capital Structure Under Corporate and Personal Taxation," *Journal of Financial Economics* (March 1980): 3.

CHAPTER 17

DOES DIVIDEND POLICY MATTER?

LEARNING OBJECTIVES

After reading this chapter, you should understand:

1. The types of dividend distribution policies and the concept of an optimal dividend policy.

2. That in a perfect market, dividend and investment policies are not related and, therefore, dividend policy is irrelevant in determining a firm's value.

3. That in an imperfect market transaction costs, regulations, and taxes affect dividend policy and render it relevant.

4. How a firm uses cash dividends to signal information to stockholders.

5. Why a firm should jointly determine business risk, financial leverage, and dividend policy.

CORPORATE FINANCE IN THE NEWS

DIVIDENDS VS. BUYBACKS

Corporate dividends have failed to keep pace with surging stock prices. Dividend yields on Standard & Poor's 500 stocks hit an all-time low of 2.5 percent this summer, even as the companies' market-to-book ratios soared above the historical average of 1.9 percent to 4.3 percent . . .

The low yields indicate a combination of overvalued stock prices and companies' pessimism that earnings will stay high, making them reluctant to raise dividends . . .

At the same time, large S&P 500 companies that pay no dividends, including Microsoft Corporation, Toys "R" Us, and Tele-Communications Inc. are not big repurchasers of their own shares. Of course, many on this list are growth companies that consistently reinvest heavily in their businesses.

Source: Lyn Perlmuth, "Dividends vs. Buybacks," *Institutional Investor* (25 December 1995): 31. This copyrighted material has been reprinted with the permission of Institutional Investor (© December 1995).

17.1 INTRODUCTION

The excerpts in Corporate Finance in the News suggest three important points:

1. If a firm is not sure that earnings will stay high, it may be reluctant to raise dividends. Dividend policy and changes in dividends are very important from the firm's viewpoint.
2. Firms such as Microsoft Corporation, Toys "R" Us, and Tele-Communications, Inc.—defined as supergrowth firms in Chapter 13—may not pay dividends. They consider this the best policy, hence, for them, dividend policy matters.
3. A low dividend yield is considered an indicator of an overvalued stock. Thus, a decline in the stock price is expected when the dividend yield is low. In spite of this prediction, the stock market rally continued in 1996 and 1997 and the dividend yield on the s&p 500 index dropped to 1.63% in August 1997.

A firm mainly uses income and retained earnings to pay cash dividends to stockholders, to repurchase shares, and to pay for capital expenditures. If investors prefer to invest in a firm that pays a high dividend, relative to other similar firms, they may be willing to pay a higher price for that firm's stock. In such a case dividend policy would be relevant in determining the firm's value.

Is dividend policy relevant? Is there an optimal dividend policy—one that maximizes the firm's value? Similar to capital structure, dividend policy is a controversial issue. Let us first demonstrate the relevance of dividend policy by reviewing IBM's annual earnings per share for the period 1988–1996:

IBM

Year	Earnings Per Share (EPS, $)	Annual Dividend Per Share (DPS, $)
1988	9.20	4.40
1989	6.41	4.73
1990	10.42	4.84
1991	−1.05	4.84
1992	−12.03	4.84
1993	−14.02	1.58
1994	5.02	1.00
1995	7.23	1.00
1996	10.24	1.40

Sources: Hoovers and Microsoft Investor on the Internet, January 29, 1997; and Investment Update financial service on the Internet.

IBM experienced an upward trend in both its EPS and its dividends until 1990. In 1991 and 1992, despite heavy losses, IBM maintained its $4.84 **dividend per share (DPS)** as if to "signal" to the market that its financial stress was only a temporary setback. In general, however, a firm cannot maintain such a policy in the long run. If

Do you know how a dividend reinvestment plan works? csx Corporation has one and tells you all about it at their Web site. http://www.csx.com/docs/dividprx.html

its financial stress persists, a firm will simply not have enough cash available to continue paying a large dividend. Indeed, due to its heavy losses, IBM replaced its CEO and cut its dividend drastically in 1993. Stockholders received a mere $1.58 per share that year. This downward trend in the DPS continued into 1994. Interestingly, although IBM's holdings in cash and marketable securities amounted to more than $10 billion in early 1995, the firm continued its conservative dividend policy by announcing a stock repurchase.

From these observations, dividend policy does seem to matter to a firm's management. Changes in dividend policy are by no means arbitrary. Moreover, as can be seen in Connecting Theory to Practice 17.1, stockholders also have preferences regarding dividend policy.

CONNECTING THEORY TO PRACTICE 17.1

WHAT DO THE STOCKHOLDERS THINK?

The shareholders of Berkshire Hathaway were asked in May 1985 if they wanted to receive a dividend. Since 1969, when Warren Buffett became CEO of the company, they had never been given one. Instead, as Buffett has eloquently explained in his annual reports, all retained earnings, short of corporate taxes, have been reinvested to maximize shareholder returns. Did those same "owner-partners," as he calls them, want him to continue that policy or not?

An overwhelming 88% wisely urged him to stay the course. Says CFO Verne McKenzie: "In the last three years Berkshire's net worth has doubled. If we had paid out all that net worth as a dividend, I'm not sure our shareholders could have collectively doubled their investments."

In the past ten years, Berkshire returned an average of 32.1% per year, almost twice the return of Standard & Poor's 500-stock index. Says John Tilson, who runs the top-performing Pasadena Growth Fund: "For a company with Berkshire's high returns, and its strong franchise, paying dividends is absurd." Tilson loves Berkshire Hathaway, which at a recent price of $8,900 a share is still 5% to 10% undervalued by his estimates.

Source: Susan Kuhn, "A Tax Efficient Bonanza," *Fortune* (20 April 1992): 30. © 1992, Time Inc. All rights reserved.

MAKING THE CONNECTION

Here we see that Berkshire Hathaway's stockholders preferred not to receive dividends. The firm's dividend policy was relevant to its stockholders. Indeed, Berkshire Hathaway continued its policy and paid no dividends in 1993–1996. Its share price reached $42,700 on September 10, 1997. This does not mean that a zero dividend policy is best for all firms. Stockholders of, say, a utility firm would favor paying out most of the firm's earnings in dividends. For them, too, dividend policy is relevant.

In contrast to Berkshire Hathaway's stockholders, Bank of New York's stockholders prefer dividends. Ever since Alexander Hamilton founded it in 1784, the Bank of New York has distributed dividends every year and has the longest unbroken payment record of any New York Stock Exchange-listed firm. Since stockholders continue to invest in the bank's stock, they must like this dividend policy. From the Corporate Finance in the News excerpt, from IBM's dividend policy, and from Connecting Theory to Practice 17.1, we learn that many stockholders and managers consider the firm's dividend policy important. In fact, because they consider dividend policy so important, stockholders and management sometimes clash over it.

In this chapter we discuss and analyze the factors that affect dividend policy. Unfortunately, no formula automatically provides the optimal dividend policy; but in this chapter we will cover the various economic factors that management should consider in selecting the firm's dividend policy. In our discussion we pay special attention to how dividends, capital expenditures, transaction costs, and personal taxes are related.

17.2 DIVIDEND TYPES AND PAYMENT PROCEDURES

In distributing its wealth to shareholders, a firm must decide what type of dividend to pay and when to pay it. This section covers the types of dividends, legal restrictions on dividends, announcements of and schedule for paying dividends, and stock prices on the ex-dividend date.

17.2.1 Types of Dividends

Firms pay out their earnings to shareholders in cash or stock dividends. More common than a stock dividend, a **cash dividend** involves a cash payment to the firm's shareholders. Most firms pay **regular cash dividends** on a quarterly basis. However, in an exceptionally profitable year, a firm may accumulate a surplus of cash and decide to distribute an additional dividend, called an **extra dividend** to signify that it is an extraordinary, one-time payment.[1] When the firm pays a cash dividend, whether regular or extra, it reduces liquid assets and has fewer resources for investment. A firm does not necessarily have to earn money in the current year to pay dividends. In fact, a firm commonly uses retained earnings from previous years to pay cash dividends (as the IBM example in the Introduction demonstrated).

A **stock dividend**, the payment of shares of stock to the firm's shareholders on a pro rata basis, does not reduce the firm's liquid assets.[2] For example, a 10% stock dividend means that the stockholder receives an additional 10 shares for every 100 shares but makes no additional payment. A **stock split** is similar to the stock dividend but requires different bookkeeping. In a 2:1 split each stockholder's share is replaced by two new shares, and each share's value is generally cut in half.

---

1. Extra dividends are also called *irregular dividends* or *special dividends*.
2. It is simply a bookkeeping transfer from the firm's retained earnings to the Capital Stock (Paid-In Capital) account. There is no decrease in stockholders' equity or assets.

Although there is no economic difference between stock dividends and stock splits, the New York Stock Exchange defines any distribution of stock amounting to less than 25% of the shares investors hold as a stock dividend; any distribution of 25% or more, as a stock split. Because cash dividends involve a transfer of cash from the firm to the stockholders, they are more easily understood in economic terms. Stock dividends or stock splits involve no actual cash transfer hence the motive for distributing them is less obvious. However, a close review of the transaction costs involved reveals that stock dividends or stock splits increase the stock's liquidity and may increase the share price.

To illustrate, assume IBM's stock is priced at $600 per share.[3] To benefit from relatively low transaction costs, an investor would have to buy 100 shares (called a **round lot,** as opposed to an **odd lot** of fewer than 100 shares), which would cost $60,000 ($600 × 100 = $60,000), plus transaction costs. An investor with only, say, $31,000 to invest and who refuses to pay the relatively high transaction costs on an odd-lot purchase will decide against investing in IBM simply because she does not have sufficient funds to buy 100 shares. If it does not want to lose potential investors of this type, IBM can split its stock, say, at 2:1. This would involve a price drop[4] to about $300 per share, and our investor can then buy 100 shares (100 × $300 = $30,000), plus the transaction costs. Because the stock dividend (or stock split) causes a larger demand for the stock, the firm's equity value increases, which, as we know, is in line with the firm's goal.[5] However, if the firm prices its stock too low, stockholders and investors may be negatively affected and believe the firm is not worth as much. This is why a firm refrains from splitting its stock over and over again.

A firm may transfer cash to its shareholders with a cash dividend or a **stock repurchase**, which involves using accumulated cash to repurchase a percentage of its outstanding shares. Stock repurchase is also common when a firm wishes to change its capital structure. For instance, if management decides the proportion of equity in its capital structure is too high, it may decide to issue bonds and use the proceeds to repurchase some of its own stock.

Before turning our attention to what level of dividends a firm pays and, ultimately, how it makes that decision, let us first review the mechanical aspects of dividend payment.

17.2.2 Legal Restrictions

State laws prohibit a firm from using its capital for the purpose of paying dividends to shareholders. Indeed, the law stipulates that a firm may pay dividends only from its current or retained earnings. This provision is specifically aimed at protecting creditors. Bondholders are also protected by bond covenants that impose restrictions on the dividends a firm pays to stockholders. Moreover, an insolvent firm cannot pay dividends. Since bondholders own the firm, they have first claim to any proceeds from the liquidation process.

---

3. Although IBM's stock traded in September 1997 for about $100 per share, it did sell for as much as $600 per share in the 1960s.

4. The split creates more shares, but since the firm's total assets are unchanged, each share is worth less in comparison to shares before the split.

5. Suppose that before the split there were 1 million shares worth $1 each. After a 2:1 split, increased demand may drive the stock price higher than $0.50 per share. In such a case the firm's equity would be greater than $1 million.

17.2.3 Payment Dates

A firm announces and schedules dividend payments as follows:

1. **Declaration date**. The date on which the board of directors meets and declares the terms and timing of dividend payments.
2. **Holder record date**. The date on which the firm compiles a list of all current shareholders entitled to dividends.
3. **Ex-dividend date**. The final stock trading date for entitlement to the dividend. This date is four business days before the holder record date.

   Recall that information regarding a trade in stock should reach the firm before the holder record date. If you buy a share one day before the holder record date, your name might not reach the firm on time. To avoid this possible error due to an information flow delay, brokerage firms entitle shareholders to receive the dividends if they purchased the stock five days before the holder record date. If investors purchase stock during the four days before the holder record date, they are not entitled to that quarter's dividends.
4. **Payment date**. The date on which the firm mails the dividend by check to the stockholders listed on the holder record date.

Let us consider an example: The board of directors of Molahs, Inc. meets on October 1, 1998, and declares a quarterly dividend of $1 per share to shareholders listed on November 29, 1998, to be paid on December 2, 1998. October 1 is the declaration date; November 29 is the holder record date; November 25 (four days before November 29) is the ex-dividend date; and December 2 is the payment date. Anyone who purchases Molahs shares after the ex-dividend date will not be entitled to that quarter's dividend (but will be entitled to any dividend declared next quarter). These four dates are shown graphically in this table:

Calendar Date	Various Dividend Dates
October 1	Declaration date
November 25	Ex-dividend date
November 29	Holder record date
December 2	Payment date

Figure 17-1 illustrates how the financial media (in this case, in the European edition of the *Wall Street Journal*) presents dividend information. For example, PepsiCo declared a quarterly (Q) cash dividend of 20 cents ($0.20) on payment date March 29, 1996 for stockholders listed on holder record date March 8, 1996. The ex-dividend date, which is not reported in the paper, is four days before the record date. Semiannual dividends are denoted by the letter *S*; annual dividends, by the letter *A*. At the end of the dividends report is information on *extra (irregular)* dividends (i.e., the $0.125 per share extra dividend declared by Joachim Bancorp), and a section on cash dividends of companies that reported an increase in dividends on this date (i.e., Tri County Bancorp's cash dividend increased from $0.20 per share to $0.25 since the last semiannual payment).

U.S. DIVIDENDS

Dividends Reported February 22

Company	Period	Amt.	Payable date	Record date
		REGULAR		
Amcast Industrial	Q	.14	3-22-96	3-8
Amer Life Hldg pf	Q	.54	3-29-96	3-15
Arbor Drugs Inc	Q	.07	4-3-96	3-13
Ashland Coal Inc	Q	.11½	3-15-96	3-7
Bassett Furniture	Q	.20	3-6-96	3-4
Binks Mfg	Q	.10	4-8-96	3-8
Boston Acoustics	Q	.12½	4-19-96	3-22
Calif Bancshares	Q	.22	4-2-96	3-8
Camco Intl	Q	.05	3-19-96	3-5
CntrlMaineP3.50%pf	Q	.87½	4-1-96	3-8
ChaseManhattan pfN	–	.3214⅝	3-31-96	3-21
Citicorp ser18 dep	Q	.320¼	5-31-96	5-15
Citicorp ser19 dep	Q	.320¼	5-31-96	5-15
Citicorp adj pf2	Q	1.50	5-31-96	5-15
Citicorp adj pf3	Q	1.75	5-31-96	5-15
Coastal Corp	Q	.10	4-1-96	2-29
Coastal Corp pfA	Q	.29¾	3-15-96	2-29
Coastal Corp pfB	Q	.45¾	3-15-96	2-29
Coastal Corp pfH	Q	.53⅛	3-15-96	2-29
Conagra Cap LC pfB	M	.1247	2-29-96	2-28
Eastern Enterprise	Q	.37	4-2-96	3-4
Eldorado Bancorp	Q	.08	4-5-96	3-4
Ethyl Corp	Q	.12½	4-1-96	3-15
Farmer Brothers	Q	.55	5-6-96	4-19
Fina Inc clA	Q	.60	3-18-96	3-6
1st Empire State	Q	.70	3-29-96	3-4
1st Fint West MD	Q	.12	3-29-96	3-15
1stIntrstBcp dep F	Q	.6171⅞	3-31-96	3-15
1stIntrstBcp dep G	Q	.56¼	3-31-96	3-15
Franco-Nevada	A	bl.50	3-29-96	3-15
G&K Svcs clA	Q	.01¾	3-29-96	3-15
GeorgiaP $1.925pf	Q	.48⅛	4-1-96	3-15
GeorgiaP $1.9375pf	Q	.4844	4-1-96	3-15
GeorgiaP $2.125pf	Q	.53⅛	4-1-96	3-15

(continued)

FIGURE 17-1
(continued)

Company	Period	Amt.	Payable date	Record date
GeorgiaP $7.72pf	Q	1.93	4-1-96	3-15
GeorgiaP $7.80pf	Q	1.95	4-1-96	3-15
GeorgiaP $1.90pf	Q	.47½	4-1-96	3-15
GeoPwr $1.9875 pfA	Q	.4969	4-1-96	3-15
GeorgiaP adjpfA'93	Q	.3294	4-1-96	3-15
GeorgP adjpfA2'93	Q	.3031	4-1-96	3-15
GeorgiaP $1.9375pf	Q	.4844	4-1-96	3-15
Grey Advertising	Q	.93¾	3-15-96	3-1
GulfCanRes adjpf1	M	.023	3-12-96	2-29
Hollinger Inc	Q	b.15	6-10-96	5-24
Home Depot	Q	.05	3-22-96	3-8
Hunt Mfg Co	Q	.09½	4-3-96	3-26
Imperial Oil clA	Q	b.50	4-1-96	3-4
JLG Industries new	Q	.01	4-4-96	3-15
Kellwood Co	Q	.15	3-15-96	3-4
Laclede Gas	Q	.31½	4-1-96	3-11
Lancaster Colony	Q	.17	3-29-96	3-8
Life Partners Grp	Q	.03	3-15-96	2-28
LongIslandLighting	Q	.44½	4-1-96	3-15
LongIslandLght pfB	Q	1.25	4-1-96	3-15
LongIslandLght pfE	Q	1.08¾	4-1-96	3-15
Longs Drug Stores	Q	.28	c4-10-96	3-5
c-Revised date.				
Lufkin Industries	Q	.15	3-11-96	3-1
Northrop Grumman	Q	.40	3-16-96	3-4
Pacific Scientific	Q	.03	4-1-96	3-8
PanCanadian Petro	Q	b.20	3-29-96	3-15
Peoples Bcp OH	Q	.17	4-1-96	3-15
PeoplesBkCpIndiana	Q	c	4-22-96	4-1
c-NASDAQ correction; bank didn't declare $.14 dividend reported in 2/20 column.				
PepsiCo Inc	Q	.20	3-29-96	3-8
Pinnacle Finl Svcs	Q	.19	4-1-96	3-22
Quanex Corp	Q	.15	3-29-96	3-15
Santa Fe Gaming pf	S	p.856	3-29-96	3-8
p-Payable in shares of preferred stock.				
Seacoast Bkg Fla A	Q	.15	3-29-96	3-20
Security 1st Corp	Q	.10	3-29-96	3-15

(continued)

**FIGURE 17-1
(continued)**

Company	Period	Amt.	Payable date	Record date
Security–Conn Corp	Q	.12	4–30–96	4–10
Stant Corp	Q	.02	3–22–96	3–15
Stepan Co	Q	.11¾	3–15–96	3–1
Tennant Co	Q	.17	3–14–96	3–4
TrustCoBkCp NY	Q	.27½	3–15–96	3–1
Trustmark Corp	Q	.12	3–15–96	3–1
UJB Finl Corp	Q	.32	5–1–96	4–11
UJB Finl adjpfB	Q	.75	5–1–96	4–11
Unisys Corp pfA	Q	.93¾	4–15–96	3–15
Wendy's Intl	Q	.06	3–18–96	3–4

IRREGULAR

Company	Period	Amt.	Payable date	Record date
Guidant Corp	Q	.02½	3–29–96	3–7
Joachim Bancorp Inc	–	.12½	3–31–96	3–15
Patriot Bank Corp	–	.02	3–15–96	2–29
Westinghse Air Brk	Q	.01	3–22–96	3–7

INCREASED

Company	Period	Amounts		Payable date	Record date
		New	**Old**		
Amcore Finl	Q	.16	.15	3–13–96	3–6
American Bank CT	Q	.34	.33	3–29–96	3–15
Duracell Intl	Q	.29	.26	3–19–96	3–5
Penn-America Grp	Q	.04	.03	3–18–96	3–8
Peoples Bcp Auburn	Q	.14	.13	4–22–96	4–1
RelianceSteel&Alum	Q	.03	.02½	3–29–96	3–11
Sbarro Inc	Q	.23	.19	4–3–96	3–19
Tri-County Bancorp	S	.25	.20	3–29–96	3–5

A-Annual; b-Payable in Canadian funds; h-From Income; k-From capital gains; M-Monthly; Q-Quarterly; S-Semi-annual; t-Approximate U.S. dollar amount per American Depositary Receipt/Share.

Source: *Wall Street Journal Europe,* 26 February 1996, p.13. Reprinted by permission of The Wall Street Journal Europe, © 1996 Dow Jones & Company, Inc. All Rights Reserved Worldwide.

17.2.4 Stock Price on the Ex-Dividend Date

Would you pay more for a share of stock that was about to pay a dividend than for the same share right after the firm paid the dividend? To answer this question, let's consider an example: Suppose a firm's EPS in a given year amounts to $10. If the stock price was $100 per share at the beginning of the year, this price would likely climb to $110 to reflect the $10 EPS.[6] What will the expected stock price be on the ex-dividend date if the firm distributes a $5 per share dividend at the end of the year? The price should fall to $105, reflecting the $5 per share that the firm will transfer to the stockholders. Does this mean that the investor loses money? No, this decrease is merely a *technical* price drop, reflecting the $5 transfer from the firm to the investor. The stock price is $110 before the ex-dividend date, but the stock price drops to $105 immediately after the ex-dividend date. However, the investor's wealth is still $110 ($105 [stock price] + $5 [dividend] = $110). Immediately after the firm pays the dividend, you would be willing to pay a lower price for the stock—$105 per share, rather than $110.

Denoting the stock price just before the ex-dividend date by P_{Before}, the stock price on the ex-dividend date by $P_{Ex\text{-}dividend}$, and the dividend per share by DPS, we have the following relationship:

$$P_{Before} = P_{Ex\text{-}dividend} + DPS \qquad (17.1)$$

This relationship means: If the firm changes its DPS, the stock price on the ex-dividend date also changes but the sum of the two components, which is the stockholders' wealth, is unchanged.

Let us now focus on the important issue of how a firm chooses a dividend policy.

17.3 DIVIDEND POLICY

In establishing its policy, the firm must decide its dividend policy strategy (e.g., paying a constant dollar amount per share or a proportion of its earnings as dividends) and level of dividend (i.e., the amount of the dividend). These two decisions together comprise the firm's **dividend policy**.

17.3.1 Dividend Distribution Policy

A firm generally pays cash dividends from its earnings. Two terms related to earnings and dividends are

- **Payout ratio** = DPS/EPS
- **Retention ratio** = (EPS − DPS)/EPS

According to these definitions, we have:

$$\text{Payout ratio} + \text{Retention ratio} = 1 \qquad (17.2)$$

For example, if EPS = $10 and DPS = $4, then the dividend payout ratio is 0.4, and the retention ratio is 0.6. The payout ratio can be larger than 1. If EPS = $10 and the

6. Ignore personal taxes for now.

firm pays $15 per share as a cash dividend ($10 from current earnings and $5 from retained earnings), then the payout ratio is 1.5.

In 1979, the average payout rate for the firms in the s&p 500 Index was at an all-time low of 38%. By 1997, it had not risen much above that level.

Typically a firm adopts a policy to serve as a general guide for making dividend distributions. In this chapter we focus on the three most common dividend distri-bution policies—namely, the constant-payout-ratio dividend, the constant-dollar dividend, and the residual dividend:

1. **Constant-payout-ratio dividend**. The firm pays a fixed percentage of its earnings every year as dividends and reinvests the rest. Because earnings usually fluctuate, the dividend will also fluctuate. If, in any given year, it has negative net income, the firm pays no dividends.
2. **Constant-dollar dividend**. The firm pays a constant-dollar dividend per share, say $5 per share, regardless of the firm's earnings. In adopting this policy, the firm may also increase the dividends slightly every year to compensate for inflation. (It is still called a constant-dollar dividend policy.) For example, IBM adopted this policy for several years up to 1992, as shown earlier.
3. **Residual dividend**. The firm uses its retained earnings to fund positive NPV projects and pays whatever is left as a cash dividend. If no money is left, the firm pays no dividend. The residual dividend policy yields a variable dividend that depends on the firm's accepted projects and on its earnings.

The following problem illustrates how to determine which dividend distribu-tion policy a firm follows.

PRACTICE BOX

Problem   Ford Motor Co.'s earnings per share (EPS) and the dividend per share (DPS) are shown here:

Quarter ended	1993 IV	1994 I	1994 II	1994 III	1994 IV	1995 I	1995 II	1995 III	1995 IV	1996 I	1996 II	1996 III
EPS($)	0.65	0.83	1.63	1.04	1.47	1.44	1.45	0.28	0.49	0.53	1.56	0.56
DPS($)	0.20	0.20	0.22	0.22	0.26	0.26	0.31	0.31	0.35	0.35	0.385	0.385

Source: *Investment Update*, Internet service, 1996.

Calculate the payout ratio in each quarter. Does Ford follow a constant-payout-ratio dividend policy or a constant-dollar dividend policy with some growth over time?   *(continued)*

Solution	The payout ratio, found by dividing DPS by EPS, is as follows:											
Quarter ended	**1993 IV**	**1994 I**	**1994 II**	**1994 III**	**1994 IV**	**1995 I**	**1995 II**	**1995 III**	**1995 IV**	**1996 I**	**1996 II**	**1996 III**
Payout ratio	30.77	24.10	13.50	21.15	17.69	18.06	21.38	110.71	71.43	66.04	24.68	68.75

Because the payout ratio varies wildly—from as low as 13.5% to as high as 110.71%—Ford does not follow the constant-payout-ratio dividend policy. Instead, the firm follows a constant-dollar dividend policy with some growth over time. Like IBM, even when earnings fell sharply, Ford tried to maintain the same DPS (see the third quarter of 1995).

Having reviewed the three types of dividend distribution policies, we can now ask: Is there a "best" dividend policy from the stockholders' viewpoint?

17.3.2 The Dividend Distribution Controversy: Is There An Optimal Dividend Policy?

How does a firm determine its dividend policy? Why does one firm pay 20% of its earnings as dividends, while another firm pays 60%? Why does one firm try to maintain constant annual dividends whereas another firm tries to keep the dividend payout ratio constant? Does it matter? Is there an *optimal* dividend policy? Let us first define an optimal dividend policy:[7] An **optimal dividend policy** is one that maximizes the firm's value or its share price.

When it pays dividends, the firm transfers cash to its stockholders. The firm's stock price automatically decreases, even if stockholders desire such dividend payments and stockholders are willing to pay a higher price for the stock of a firm that pays dividends. On the ex-dividend date, the stock price is expected to be equal to the pre-dividend price minus the dividend per share. In the dividend policy analysis, we examine how the amount of dividend distribution affects the stock price or the value of the firm. In such an analysis, we refer to the pre-dividend price or to the pre-dividend value of the firm. (Alternatively, it refers to ex-dividend value plus the dividends.) In the rest of the chapter we simply call it the value of the firm or the stock price. Having this definition of the firm's value, we can assert that if an optimal dividend policy exists, dividend policy must be *relevant* because any deviation from it will decrease the firm's value. Conversely, if changes in dividend policy do not affect the firm's value, then dividend policy must be *irrelevant*.

Figure 17-2 provides a graphic description of our definition of an optimal dividend policy. The horizontal axis shows the payout ratio; the vertical axis, the firm's value. We obtain the horizontal line *aa'* if changes in the dividend payout ratio do not affect the firm's value. If dividend policy is relevant, we obtain Curve *cde* and an

7. For an interesting article on this issue, see Fischer Black, "The Dividend Puzzle," *Journal of Portfolio Management* (Winter 1976): 5–8.

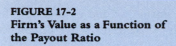

FIGURE 17-2
Firm's Value as a Function of the Payout Ratio

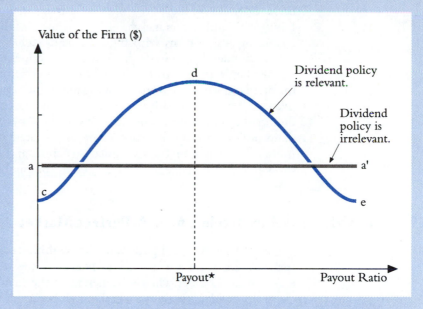

optimal payout ratio (labeled *Payout**) that maximizes the firm's value. Each firm may have a curve with a different shape, but as long as its line is not horizontal, we can identify an optimal dividend policy—one that corresponds to the firm's highest value. A similar figure can be drawn with the dividend payment on the horizontal axis, expressed in terms of dollars per share, and the optimal dividend policy expressed in dollars rather than as a payout ratio. Regardless of whether the dividend policy is measured in dollar or in percentage terms, the main issue is whether the firm's value as a function of its dividend policy is correctly described by a curve or by a horizontal line.

Dividend policy is a controversial issue among practitioners as well as among academics. Some firms pay no dividends at all. For example, since Berkshire Hathaway (see Connecting Theory to Practice 17.1), a very successful firm, neither pays stock dividends nor splits its stock, the firm's very high market price per share reflects its accumulated profit. Similarly, Microsoft, another successful firm, does not pay dividends. Some professional investors consider not paying dividends to be a drawback. For example, Smith Barney, an investment firm, recommended that its clients invest in stocks that pay a high **dividend yield** (dividend per share/current stock price). In Smith Barney's words:

. . .Without this compensation in the form of a meaningful yield, volatility is likely to be greater than would be the case if current yield were higher.[8]

There is great variability in dividend yields. This ratio is zero for many firms (for example, Microsoft) and about 9% for some utility firms. On August 4, 1997, the

8. Source: Shirley A. Lazo, "The Role of Payout in Stock Inventory," *Barron's* (23 October 1995). Reprinted by permission of *Barron's*, © 1995 Dow Jones & Company, Inc. All Rights Reserved Worldwide.

dividend yield on the Dow–Jones industrial index was 1.58% and the yield on the Dow–Jones utility average was 4.31%. Thus, Smith Barney would recommend focusing on utility firms with high dividend yields. In what follows, we discuss the role of dividend yield in determining stock values.

We begin the discussion of the dividend dilemma by presenting the arguments for dividend irrelevance and showing that these arguments are valid only in a perfect market. We then consider some market imperfections and show that, in practice, dividend policy is very relevant. We conclude by showing how business risk, dividend policy, and capital structure are interrelated and why a firm should seek a simultaneous solution for its capital structure and dividend policy. Moreover, we show that a zero dividend yield may be the best policy for supergrowth firms such as Microsoft.

17.3.3 Dividend Policy Irrelevance: A Perfect Market

Let us first see why in a perfect market with no taxes, no transaction costs, and symmetric information (the same information is known to management and stockholders), the stockholder will be indifferent to the firm's dividend policy. The principal claim for dividend irrelevance is that in a perfect market the change in stockholders' wealth is directly related to the firm's earnings, not to its dividend policy.

The intuitive explanation of this claim is straightforward. Suppose a firm's EPS is $10. The stockholder, whose income is composed of dividends and capital gains, will not care whether the firm pays $5 as a cash dividend and retains $5 or pays all of the $10 EPS as a dividend. In either case the stockholder will receive $10: $5 in a dividend and $5 in capital gains because the retained $5 per share will cause the stock price to increase by $5.

Equation (17.1) shows the result: The stock price before the ex-dividend date reflects the firm's earnings and equals the sum of $P_{\text{Ex-dividend}}$ + DPS, regardless of the dividend's size. An investor who wishes to consume $10 can sell some stock to obtain the needed funds. The investor's wealth is the stock's price before the firm pays the dividend, and the breakdown of this price between the two components, $P_{\text{Ex-dividend}}$ and DPS, does not affect that wealth. For example, $1 increase in DPS induces a $1 decrease in $P_{\text{Ex-dividend}}$ and the sum of these two terms remains unchanged. Because a perfect market has no taxes and no transaction costs, the stockholder will be indifferent between receiving income in capital gains or in dividends. This is why dividend policy does not matter. The dividend irrelevance argument is based on three assumptions:

1. No taxes on dividends or on capital gains.
2. No transaction costs.
3. Symmetric information. Since they have exactly the same information that stockholders have, managers cannot use dividend policy to disseminate new information.

INVESTMENT AND DIVIDEND POLICY

In Connecting Theory to Practice 17.1 John Tilson asserted, "For a company with Berkshire's high returns . . . paying dividends is absurd." Does this claim hold in a perfect market? No. As we will see in this section, paying dividends is not absurd in a perfect market. Berkshire can issue stocks and bonds to finance the highly profitable available projects and use these profits to pay dividends. Dividend policy is not tied to investment policy in a perfect market. In the rest of the chapter, we focus only on equity financing, e.g., financing a project either by retained earnings or by issuing stocks.

Miller and Modigliani (M & M) provide a formal argument to substantiate the claim that dividend policy is irrelevant in a perfect market, even if extremely profitable projects are available.[9] We will use data related to Fortunate Mills to demonstrate this argument (see Table 17-1). The firm has a market value of $100,000 and is an all-equity firm with 1,000 shares outstanding priced at $100 per share. Having $10,000 in cash, Fortunate Mills is considering whether to distribute some or all of

TABLE 17-1   **Financial Data on Fortunate Mills**

Part a: Basic data, December 31, 1998:

Equity	$100,000
Number of shares	1,000
Price per share	$100
Cash held	$10,000

Part b: Project NPV and stock price for various dividend policies

Project	Initial Investment ($)	NPV ($)	Firm's Value if It Accepts the Project ($)	Dividends if Project Is Financed by the Firm's Cash ($)*		Share Price Before Dividends Are Paid ($)[†]	Share Price After Dividends Are Paid ($)[‡]
				Total Dividend ($)	Dividends Per Share (DPS $)		
A	5,000	3,000	103,000	5,000	5	103	98
B	2,000	1,000	104,000	3,000	3	104	101
C	2,000	900	104,900	1,000	1	104.90	103.90
D	1,000	−500	104,400	0	0	104.40	104.40

*The dividends are equal to the $10,000 cash available minus the amount spent on projects.

†The stock price before dividend payment is

$$\text{Stock price} = \$100 + \frac{\text{NPV}}{\text{Number of shares}}$$

‡After the dividend is paid, the stock price drops by the dividend per share, as follows:

$$\text{Stock price} = \$100 + \frac{\text{NPV}}{\text{Number of shares}} - \text{Dividend per share}$$

9. M. Miller and F. Modigliani, "Dividend Policy, Growth and the Valuation of the Shares," *Journal of Business* (October 1961): 411–33.

this sum as dividends. We will see that dividend policy in a perfect market does not affect the stock price.

Fortunate Mills has four projects—A, B, C, and D—available. Let us consider the financing possibilities at the extremes first. If Fortunate Mills rejects all four projects and does not distribute the $10,000 cash as dividends, the firm's stock price will remain $100. Alternatively, if the firm distributes all of the $10,000 cash as cash dividends on December 31, 1998, its stock price will immediately drop to $90. Because for each share they hold the stockholders will now have $90 (the stock price) and $10 in cash (the dividend), their wealth will be the same with either possibility.

Now suppose management is considering the possibility of reducing the cash dividends to finance *some* of the available projects. For example, suppose management invests $5,000 of the firm's $10,000 available cash in Project A and this information is known to the stockholders. Because its NPV is $3,000, Project A creates an economic value of $3 per share ($3,000/1,000 shares), and Fortunate Mills' stock price increases to $103.[10]

Similarly, if Fortunate Mills accepts Projects A, B, and C, the firm's stock price will rise and its dividend will fall. On the other hand, if the firm accepts Project D, both its stock price and its dividend will fall because Project D has a negative NPV. As Table 17-1 shows, a dividend of $1 per share is optimal: At this level the (adjusted) share price value is maximized.

It may first appear that dividend policy is relevant. For example, if Fortunate Mills were to pay a dividend of $5 per share (accepting only Project A), rather than $1 per share (accepting Projects A, B, and C), the firm's share price before paying dividends would be lower—$103 rather than $104.90. Some might conclude that dividend policy is relevant because it apparently affects the share price. However, a closer look at this example reveals that the *projects*, not the dividend policy, increase the firm's value. In other words, Fortunate Mills can pay any dividend between zero and $10 per share, undertake Projects A, B, and C, and issue as many shares as it needs to finance these projects. For example, if the firm decides to pay $4,000 in dividends, Fortunate Mills will have $6,000 left in cash. Because it needs $9,000 for the three projects, the firm will issue $3,000 of new shares. If Fortunate Mills pays $8,000 as cash dividends, it will need to issue $7,000, and so on.

NEW STOCK ISSUE

Indeed, Miller and Modigliani claim that even if profitable projects are available, a firm's dividend policy will still be irrelevant. Their line of argument is: If profitable projects are available, the firm can issue more stock to finance the new projects and still pay its dividends as originally planned. This "new stock issue" argument destroys the link between dividend policy and investment policy. In other words, dividend policy and investment decisions involve two *separate* financial decisions. According to M & M, the projects a firm accepts, not its dividend policy, affect a firm's value.

---

10. Because we assume an efficient market, the stock price rises immediately to reflect the positive NPV. If the market is not efficient, the increase in stock price may be delayed until the information on the project becomes available to stockholders.

M & M's argument can be expressed graphically, as shown in the accompanying diagram.

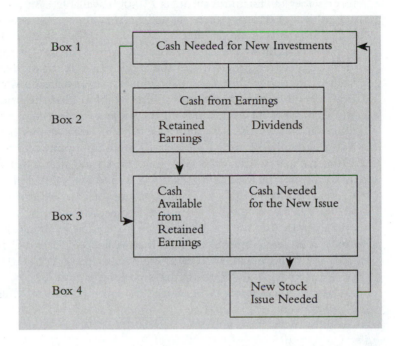

Box 1 shows the total capital needed to execute positive NPV projects. Box 2 shows the firm's available cash from earnings and its decision to divide this cash between cash dividends and retained earnings. Box 3 shows the firm's financing sources of the new projects. The size of the new issue is determined (for given dividends) to allow all projects with a positive NPV to be accepted. Box 4 shows the new issue of stock needed. Note that the total amount of cash needed for capital expenditure equals retained earnings plus the amount of the new issue. The smaller the dividend, the smaller the sum that the new stock issue will have to raise; conversely, the larger the dividend the firm pays, the greater the sum it will need from the new issue. That is, dividend policy is irrelevant as long as the firm can raise the money needed to finance positive NPV projects.

The following formula summarizes this relationship among investment, available cash, dividend policy, and new issues:

$$\text{Investment} = (\text{Earnings} - \text{Dividend}) + \text{New Issue} \qquad (17.3)$$

where

    Investment = Cash needed to execute projects with a positive NPV

      Earnings = Cash available from earnings

       Dividend = Dividend paid out

    New Issue = New issue of stock needed to finance projects with a positive NPV

If Fortunate Mills accepts Projects A, B, and C the firm's share price will rise to $104.90. The three projects require a total initial investment of $9,000. If Fortunate Mills decides to distribute all of its $10,000 available cash as dividends to existing stockholders at $10 per share, it will need a new stock issue to raise the $9,000 needed to finance these projects.

Table 17-2 illustrates the relationship among the size of the needed new stock issue, the accepted projects, and the stock price. It shows that if the $10,000 are priced as dividends, then Fortunate Mills' optimal decision is to accept Projects A, B, and C and to raise $9,000 to fund them. Note that the price at which the firm can sell the new shares depends on the projects undertaken. For example, if it undertakes Project A, the firm must raise $5,000. Because the share price is $93 ($103 − $10 dividend),[11] Fortunate Mills will issue approximately 53.76 ($5,000/$93 ≅ 53.76) new shares. After it makes the new issue and after it distributes dividends, the firm's value will be $98,000 (1,053.76 × $93 ≅ $98,000). This amount is simply the $90,000 Fortunate Mills has left after paying the $10,000 dividends, plus the $5,000 new investment and the $3,000 NPV of Project A.

In a similar way we can calculate the stock price at which the firm can issue new shares if it undertakes Projects A and B or Projects A, B, and C. If it undertakes Projects A and B, Fortunate Mills can issue new shares at $94 ($104 − $10); if it undertakes Projects A, B, and C the firm's issue price is $94.90.

Several conclusions can be drawn from the Fortunate Mills example in Tables 17-1 and 17-2:

TABLE 17-2		Fortunate Mills: Relationship Between the Size of the Stock Issue, Accepted Projects, and the Stock Price				
Dividends ($)	Size of New Stock Issue ($)	Accepted Projects	Total NPV of Projects ($)	Share Price = $100 + NPV of All Accepted Projects/Number of Old Outstanding Shares*		Stock Price on Ex-Dividend Data
10,000	5,000	A	3,000	$100 + $\dfrac{\$3,000}{1,000}$ = $103		$93
10,000	7,000	A, B	4,000	$100 + $\dfrac{\$4,000}{1,000}$ = $104		$94
10,000	9,000	A, B, and C	4,900	$100 + $\dfrac{\$4,900}{1,000}$ = $104.90		$94.90
10,000	10,000	A, B, C and D	4,400	$100 + $\dfrac{\$4,400}{1,000}$ = $104.40		$94.40

*The share price before the dividend is paid. Deduct the dividend per share to obtain the share price after the dividend is paid.

11. See the Share Price column in Table 17-2.

1. The maximum value of stockholder wealth per share is $104.90. This occurs when the firm accepts all three positive NPV projects and rejects the negative NPV project (D).
2. If Fortunate Mills finances all three positive NPV projects by retained earnings, the dividend should be $1 per share, and the share price before dividends are paid will be $104.90. If the firm totally finances the positive NPV projects by a new issue of stock, the dividend should be $10 per share, and the share price before Fortunate Mills pays dividends will be $104.90. That is, the maximum share price is $104.90, *regardless of the dividend policy.*
3. The new issue's share price depends on the projects undertaken. The higher the project's NPVs, the higher the new issue's share price because in an efficient market the stock price will adjust instantaneously to the information on the positive NPVs. The original stockholders own all the created NPV.
4. Most importantly, the available projects, not their method of financing, determine the share price. The larger the dividend, the greater the new issue, but the selected combination of new issue and dividend does not affect the share price.

In a perfect market if a firm can raise as much money as it wishes by issuing stock, dividend policy and investment policy are not linked, and dividend policy is irrelevant. A firm can adopt any dividend payout ratio it chooses and can raise the money needed to finance positive NPV projects by issuing new stock. To return to Connecting Theory to Practice 17.1, in a perfect market it would *not* be "absurd" for Berkshire to pay dividends. Berkshire would not reject projects with a high return because it can finance them by issuing more stock.

Berkshire's stockholders' and managers' preference that the firm not pay dividends only emphasizes that the market is far from perfect. In the above analysis, the main assumptions of market perfection that justified dividend policy irrelevance were as follows:

1. *Taxation of dividends and capital gains at the same rate* (or, alternatively, no personal taxes). Accordingly, the investor will be indifferent between obtaining $10 in dividends or $4 in dividends plus $6 in capital gains.
2. *No transaction costs.* The investor can sell any number of shares at no cost. For example, suppose an investor intends to spend $10 (per share held) on consumption. If she gets a $10 dividend, she will spend all of it. However, with only a $4 cash dividend, she will have to sell a portion of her stock to obtain the additional $6. This investor will be indifferent to the firm's dividend policy *only if* she can sell the shares held without transaction costs.
3. *No flotation costs.* A firm can raise the needed investment amount or any part of it with no flotation costs. The cost of a new issue is larger with flotation costs than with retained earnings, which explains why growth firms, which need large sums of money for new projects, prefer zero- or low-dividend distribution.
4. *Symmetric information.* Managers act to maximize the firm's value and managers and stockholders alike know all information regarding future projects. This condition, called **symmetric information**, excludes the possibility of managers

possessing private information about project profitability. If a firm has symmetric information, it cannot use its dividend policy to disseminate or signal information to the public, and a firm's dividend policy does not affect its stock price.

5. *Market efficiency.* Once information on the available projects' profitability is made public, the firm's stock price will jump to reflect those projects with positive NPVs.

Assumptions 4 and 5 may or may not pertain in practice. However, Assumptions 1, 2, and 3 do not pertain in most capital markets. Moreover, since the United States and most Western world countries tax dividends at a much higher rate than capital gains, investors will not be indifferent between obtaining dividends and capital gains. The exceptions are tax-exempt institutional investors such as pension funds. In the absence of transaction costs, these institutional investors would be indifferent between cash dividends or capital gains. However, for all other firms, dividend policy is far from being irrelevant.

We now show that each market imperfection is likely to overturn the case for irrelevancy. In so doing we prove that dividend policy is relevant in practice.

17.3.4 Dividend Policy Relevance: An Imperfect Market

As we have seen, the capital market is far from perfect. Transaction costs, flotation costs, taxes, and asymmetric information exist; and firms may have difficulty raising money in the capital market. Moreover, even if it can raise funds with no flotation costs, management may decide against doing so for fear of losing control of the firm by issuing stock. Market imperfections such as these render dividend policy relevant in practice. In this section we discuss how each of these factors affects dividend policy. In particular we also show that dividends can serve as a signal, conveying information to investors.

CONTROL OF THE FIRM

Suppose a firm's owners decide to finance activities by equity rather than by debt. Not wanting to lose control of the firm, the owners limit the size of the stock issue. By issuing a limited number of shares, they retain a high enough proportion of the total shares to maintain control of the firm. Mondavi Winery in Chapter 14's Corporate Finance in the News is an example.

To illustrate how this control constraint affects the stock issue size, let us return to the Fortunate Mills example. As shown in Tables 17-1 and 17-2, Fortunate Mills' optimal decision is to accept Projects A, B, and C and to reject Project D. Now we add a control constraint: To avoid losing control of the firm, management is willing to raise up to $5,000 by issuing new stock. The $5,000 raised will be sufficient to finance Project A, and the stock price will increase to $103 to reflect the project's $3,000 NPV. Fortunate Mills now faces a dilemma: How much of its $10,000 cash should it distribute as dividends? If it pays all of it as dividends, the stock price will be $103. However, if it distributes only $8,000 as dividends, Fortunate Mills will have $2,000 left to finance Project B; and the firm's stock price will rise to $104, reflecting the additional $1 per share NPV of Project B. Similarly, if Fortunate Mills pays only $6,000 as dividends, the firm will accept Projects A, B, and C and its stock price will rise to $104.90.

When it faces a constraint on the size of a stock issue, a firm may find its dividend policy to be relevant; that is, its dividend policy may affect the stock price. In our example, the firm can accept the three positive-NPV projects if it issues $5,000 new stock and limits its dividend to $6 per share, which constitutes the firm's optimal dividend policy under this control constraint. In other words, when a firm's new issue size is under constraint, dividend policy and investment are directly linked. Therefore, dividend policy is relevant.

TRANSACTION COSTS

Transaction costs affect both firms and investors. Firms incur flotation costs on new issues, and investors pay commissions to stockbrokers.

Flotation Costs on New Issues

When it places a stock issue, a firm incurs flotation costs paid to investment bankers and lawyers, as described in Chapter 14. These costs can be quite substantial, especially for small issues or for issues of firms not yet listed on an organized exchange.

Suppose our example firm, Fortunate Mills, issues $9,000 of common stock to finance Projects A, B, and C but receives only $8,000 net proceeds due to $1,000 of flotation costs. Because Projects A, B, and C require a total cash outlay of $9,000, Fortunate Mills will have to use $1,000 of accumulated cash to complement the new issue's net proceeds. That is, the firm can finance the three projects only by reducing the dividend from $10,000 to $9,000 (i.e., a dividend of $9 per share). As a result, the share price will be $103.90 rather than $104.90. The $1 per share difference reflects the flotation costs.[12]

Why is dividend policy relevant in this case? If Fortunate Mills changes its dividend policy to, say, $1 dividend per share, it will pay $1,000 as dividends and will be able to use the remaining $9,000 cash to finance Projects A, B, and C without incurring flotation costs. The share price will be $104.90. Reducing the dividend from $9 to $1 per share saves on flotation costs; and, therefore, the share price will be higher in comparison to distributing the $9 per share as dividends. In this case dividend policy *does* matter because it affects the stock price. The dividend policy is even more relevant for small firms that are sometimes refused bank loans and incur very high flotation costs of small stock issues. Small firms must rely heavily on internal funds.

As we have seen in Chapter 14, flotation costs make the cost of retained earnings lower than the cost of a new issue of equity. Suppose the cost of equity is 16% and the cost of retained earnings is 14%. An all-equity firm may either (1) pay dividends and have a new issue to finance a project whose IRR = 15%, or (2) pay no dividends and finance the project using retained earnings. If the firm pays no dividends, it should accept the project (15% > 14%); otherwise, it should reject the project. This example shows how dividend policy can affect the investment decision

---

12. Alternatively, the firm can maintain the $10 dividend per share but will need to issue more shares to raise $10,000, of which $1,000 is flotation cost and $9,000 is net proceeds. In such a case each share reflects a smaller amount of the firm's assets and profitability, the share price will be lower as compared to the case of zero flotation costs.

and, therefore, the firm's value. Investment decisions cannot be separated from financing decisions, implying that, in reality, dividend policy does matter.

Growth firms that have many positive NPV projects tend not to pay dividends and to use the retained earnings to finance new investments, which avoids the flotation costs. Connecting Theory to Practice 17.2 reveals that Berkshire Hathaway is not alone in preferring a zero-dividend policy. Microsoft, with a high rate of return on reinvestment funds, pays no dividends, and Microsoft stockholders approve of that policy.

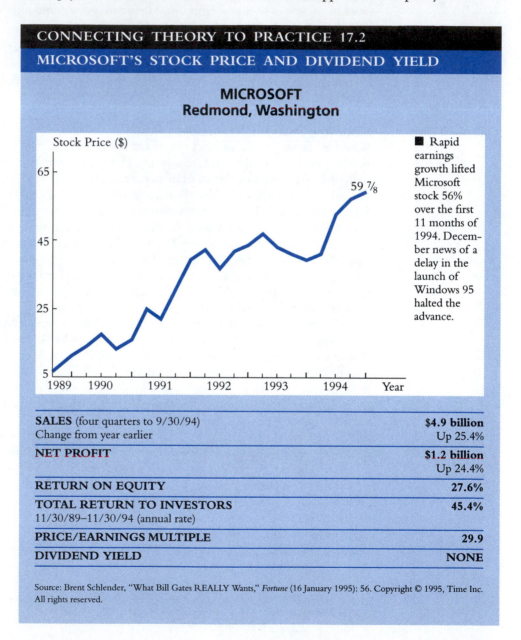

CONNECTING THEORY TO PRACTICE 17.2

MICROSOFT'S STOCK PRICE AND DIVIDEND YIELD

MICROSOFT
Redmond, Washington

Stock Price ($)

59 7/8

■ Rapid earnings growth lifted Microsoft stock 56% over the first 11 months of 1994. December news of a delay in the launch of Windows 95 halted the advance.

SALES (four quarters to 9/30/94)	**$4.9 billion**
Change from year earlier	Up 25.4%
NET PROFIT	**$1.2 billion**
	Up 24.4%
RETURN ON EQUITY	**27.6%**
TOTAL RETURN TO INVESTORS	**45.4%**
11/30/89–11/30/94 (annual rate)	
PRICE/EARNINGS MULTIPLE	**29.9**
DIVIDEND YIELD	**NONE**

Source: Brent Schlender, "What Bill Gates REALLY Wants," *Fortune* (16 January 1995): 56. Copyright © 1995, Time Inc. All rights reserved.

MAKING THE CONNECTION

Microsoft's management apparently believes that earnings are better used for reinvestment in the firm. In spite of not paying dividends at all, the firm's stock appreciated at an annual rate of 52.75% during 1989–1996. Such a policy avoids flotation costs incurred by new issues. Indeed, Microsoft continued its policy of not paying dividends, and its stock price continued to rise. Following a 2-for-1 stock split, the share price reached 135⅛ in September 10 1997, or 270¼ per old share.

The Corporate Finance in the News excerpt asserted that growth stocks are likely not to pay dividends. Why is that? A growth firm such as Microsoft has many projects with positive NPV. If it pays dividends, a growth firm will need to issue stock to finance the projects, but that involves flotation costs. A normal growth firm does not have many positive NPV projects available, and it can pay dividends without needing to raise money. This explains why a super-growth firm tends to pay relatively low or zero dividends. Indeed, Microsoft's rate of return on invested capital was 32.1% in 1996 and its sales grew by 33% that year. For the years 1992–1996, the average growth rate was 34%. Microsoft employs no debt (it is an all-equity firm); hence the best use of its earnings is reinvestment in the firm.

The Clientele Effect

When investors buy and sell stocks, they incur transaction costs that will affect their behavior and will make the firm's dividend policy relevant. Some investors may prefer higher dividends and less capital gain; others may prefer just the opposite. A firm's dividend policy may affect the number of investors who buy stock, which in turn may affect the firm's value. Let us elaborate on this assertion.

As noted, if there are no taxes and no transaction costs an investor will be indifferent between obtaining $10 per share in a cash dividend or $5 in a cash dividend and $5 in retained earnings. However, when transaction costs *are* incurred in buying and selling stock, an investor is no longer indifferent. For example, if Mike, an investor who owns 1,000 shares and wishes to spend $10,000 today, finds a cash dividend of $10 per share in his mailbox, he will be pleased because his immediate need will be met. However, if Mike receives a $5 cash dividend per share and $5 in capital gains, he will need to sell $5,000 worth of stock to accommodate his consumption need. Suppose the transaction cost is $100. After selling $5,000 worth of stock, Mike would be left with $4,900; and with the $5,000 dividend, he would have only $9,900. Mike obviously would prefer the $10 per share cash dividend. Dividend policy does matter to Mike because with the $10 cash dividend he avoids the transaction costs.

Of course, the opposite scenario is also possible: Ivy, an investor with no current consumption plans, would prefer to increase the value of her investment in the firm. She, therefore, would prefer $10 per share in capital gains through retained earnings.

If Ivy receives $10 per share in a cash dividend, she will have to incur transaction costs to buy more shares, which will leave her with an additional value of less than $10 per share.[13]

An investor who prefers annual payments will buy stocks with a high payout ratio. Another investor who prefers payment in the more distant future will buy stocks with low payout ratios.[14] The preference of various segments of investors for various types of stocks is called the **clientele effect**.[15] This means, for example, that an investor who buys zero-dividend stocks such as Berkshire Hathaway and Microsoft prefers capital gains to regular cash dividends. That Berkshire's stockholders voted overwhelmingly to continue the existing dividend policy is not surprising. Those who disliked such a policy would probably already have sold the stock.

PERSONAL TAXES

The argument for dividend policy irrelevance assumes personal taxes are either absent or are equal to the tax rate on capital gains; that is, an investor will be indifferent between obtaining a $5 dividend or a $5 capital gain. How realistic is this assumption? It accurately described the situation in the United States from 1986 to 1993 when dividends and capital gains were taxed at more or less the same rate. However, this was not the case prior to 1986, and it ceased to be the case in 1993, following the Clinton administration's income tax reform.

To see what difference the tax assumption makes, we will calculate the pretax and posttax cash flows of an investor holding one share of stock. We assume the personal income tax is 39.6% on cash dividends and 28% on capital gains. Suppose on a given date, the investor receives a dividend and sells some stocks inducing capital gain. The total pretax cash flow—dividend plus capital gain—is $10. The after-tax cash flow will vary as a function of the dividend policy. For example, if the investor receives $10 as a dividend, then after taxation at 39.6% he or she will be left with $6.04. If, on the other hand, $5 is paid as a dividend and $5 as a capital gain, the investor's after-tax cash flow will be

$$\text{After-tax cash flow} = [(1 - \text{Tax rate on dividend}) \times \text{Dividend}] \\ + [(1 - \text{Tax rate on capital gain}) \times \text{Capital gain}]$$

In our specific example, this works out to

$$\text{After-tax cash flow} = [(1 - 0.396) \times \$5] + [(1 - 0.28) \times \$5] = \$3.02 + \$3.60 = \$6.62$$

The investor will receive more after-tax cash with the 50% cash dividend–50% capital gain policy than with the 100% cash dividend policy. The firm's dividend policy affects the investor's net proceeds, because of the tax rate difference. Dividend pol-

---

13. Some firms offer **dividend reinvestment plans (DRIPs)** as a special service to their shareholders. These plans enable investors to use their cash dividends to buy additional shares of stock *without transaction costs*. Some dividend reinvestment plans also allow shareholders to make voluntary cash contributions to purchase more shares with little or no transaction costs. Ivy could benefit from a dividend reinvestment plan to buy more shares of stock without the transaction costs, in which case she would not care about the firm's dividend policy.

14. In addition, investment by institutions such as pension funds may be limited to a "legal list" of firms committed to paying dividends.

15. See, for example, R. Richardson Pettit, "Taxes, Transaction Costs and the Clientele Effect of Dividends," *Journal of Financial Economics* (December 1977): 419–436.

icy is clearly relevant. Because the tax rate on capital gains is generally lower or equal to the personal income tax rate, the investor will prefer the capital gain. As mentioned before, because institutional investors such as pension funds do not pay taxes on either dividends or capital gains, their proceeds are not affected by their firms' dividend policies.

Most European countries tax dividends but not capital gains. This, of course, further increases the advantage of capital gains. Foreign investors who invest in the United States pay zero capital gains tax and a 30% flat rate on dividends. Because these foreign investors will prefer capital gains over dividends, they will also find dividend policy relevant. Taxes, similar to transaction costs, may create a clientele effect. Foreign investors who pay a 30% tax on dividends and no tax on capital gains would prefer to invest in supergrowth firms such as Microsoft and Berkshire Hathaway because such firms provide capital gains rather than dividends.

17.3.5 The Information Content of Dividends: Signaling

If they incur no transaction costs and taxes, investors would apparently be indifferent between a $1 retained earnings per share and zero dividends or no retained earnings per share and a $1 dividend per share. They should also be indifferent as to any change in the dividend paid. However, as we shall see next, this is not the case. Asymmetrical information in the capital market may mean that a $1 dividend is worth more than $1 retained earnings. Moreover, a change in dividends may cause a change in firm value if the change in dividend policy disseminates information to stockholders.

Naturally having more information than stockholders regarding the firm's future expected earnings, management can use dividend policy to disseminate this information. Increasing dividends generally signals a rosy future. As a result, demand for the stock may increase, its price will rise, and the firm's value will increase. Similarly, if earnings are falling but the dividends remain unchanged, management signals that the firm's earnings drop is temporary. On the other hand, if management makes a large reduction in dividends, it signals that the firm's financial distress is more permanent.

Of course, the firm could simply make a prediction in its annual report concerning future earnings. However, because actions speak louder than words, the firm's actual dividend policy is more convincing than any written explanation. Therefore, the firm uses its dividend policy to convey information.

Another reason why a $1 dividend is worth more than $1 of retained earnings is that management can manipulate and distort reported earnings figures. Management cannot manipulate dividends, at least not in the long run, because they are actual cash flows. By employing a high payout ratio, the firm increases the reliability of its reported earnings. The higher the payout ratio, the more reliable the reported earnings; otherwise the firm would not have the resources needed to pay the dividends. With symmetrical information, the stockholders would know exactly what management knows about the quality of reported earnings and dividend policy does not convey any information to the stockholders. However, the market is characterized by asymmetric information, the firm uses a high payout ratio to convey information to stockholders.

Because a firm may use dividends to signal information, its dividend policy may be important even if investors incurred no taxes and transaction costs. We next discuss the signaling role of dividends.

HOW FIRMS SIGNAL WITH DIVIDENDS

A firm must have the financial resources to pay a cash dividend, and dividends convey information about the firm's profitability. Suppose the firm has had a bad year. Investors will not know whether the firm has had a temporary setback or whether it will have a series of lean years with very low earnings or even losses. If management believes the setback is only temporary and recovery is forthcoming, it will try not to cut the dividend. Stockholders could interpret the dividend cut as signaling financial distress or a more prolonged trend of decline in earnings and could rush to sell their stock, which would cause a decline in the firm's stock price.

Similarly, if it does not expect a repeat of an exceptionally good year, management may prudently not increase the dividend. If management declares an extra or irregular dividend, the firm will indicate to stockholders that this is an unusual circumstance, which they should not expect to see repeated. In this way, stockholders will not consider the next regular dividend as a dividend cut, and the stock price will not drop. On the other hand, if management privately knows future projects will likely be extraordinarily profitable, the best way it can signal that information is by increasing the regular dividend per share, rather than by paying an extra dividend. A firm with cash reserves may choose to increase its dividend, hence signaling to stockholders its potential for generating more cash. For example, in 1996 General Motors held large cash reserves. Industry analysts claimed that GM could afford to double its quarterly dividend and that the firm should distribute dividends as a signaling device.

According to the **signaling** theory, a firm with an expected decrease in earnings in the future has no motive to signal wrong positive information because such actions will be costly for it in the future. Investors believe positive information that a firm signals is generally reliable. Indeed, Offer and Siegel showed that financial analysts increased earnings forecasts of firms that increased dividends. Consequently, finance professionals believe dividends have informational content.[16]

INFORMATION THAT DIVIDENDS SIGNAL

Empirical studies have shown that dividend increases are generally followed by increases in firm value. Signals that a firm disseminates to stockholders are usually reliable. However, some firms may attempt to manipulate shareholders by sending deceptive signals. A firm that does so may succeed in its designs in the short run. However, the investing public is quite sophisticated and will not long tolerate having the wool pulled over its eyes. If the signals are misleading, stockholders will punish the firm by selling its stock.

---

16. See A. R. Offer and D. R. Siegel, "Corporate Financial Policy Information and Market Expectations: An Empirical Investigation of Dividends," *Journal of Finance* (September 1987): 889–911.

Connecting Theory to Practice 17.3 shows that reported earnings can be manipulated. This emphasizes why cash dividends have more value than retained earnings, even in the absence of taxes and transaction costs.

CONNECTING THEORY TO PRACTICE 17.3

"A BIRD IN THE HAND IS WORTH TWO IN THE BUSH"

Widespread selling of Chambers Development Co. stock last week before the company's abandonment of an unorthodox accounting method has prompted an investigation by the Securities and Exchange Commission and the American Stock Exchange.

The trading came a few days before the waste management company announced its accounting change and a $27 million write-off late Tuesday, causing its stock to plunge more than 60% in one day . . . .

On Tuesday, Chambers restated its 1991 net income to $1.5 million, or three cents a share, from the previously reported net of $49.9 million, or 83 cents a share.

One shareholder group said it filed a class-action lawsuit Wednesday against Chambers, senior executives there, and Grant Thornton, the company's auditor. The suit, filed in federal court in Pittsburgh, alleges the company and senior management artificially inflated earnings and violated generally accepted accounting rules covering deferment of costs. Plaintiffs include people who purchased stock between March 17, 1990, and March 17, 1991.

Mr. Knight, Chamber's chief financial officer who joined the company after serving as its auditor with Grant Thornton, said: "If I thought I was doing the wrong thing before, I'd be in hiding. It's a judgment call, and we made it."

Source: Gabriella Stern, "SEC Investigating Unusual Activity in Chambers Development Stock Options," *Wall Street Journal*, 20 March 1992, p. A5. Reprinted by permission of *The Wall Street Journal*, © 1992 Dow Jones & Company, Inc. All Rights Reserved Worldwide.

MAKING THE CONNECTION

Dividends are cash outflows, and a firm needs resources to pay them. A firm can use retained earnings in the short run, but in the long run it must earn the money needed to pay dividends. Had Chambers paid 83 cents per share, the firm would have increased the chances of reporting its true earnings. Because its true earnings were only 3 cents per share, Chambers probably could not have paid an 83 cent per share dividend. A high payout ratio increases the chance that a firm's reported earnings are its true earnings.

Let us elaborate on the information that dividends can convey regarding the quality of reported earnings. When a firm reports $10 earnings per share and pays a shareholder $10 per share in dividends, the investor will have $10 in hand. However, when the firm reports EPS of $10 and pays zero dividends, the $10 does not reach the investor. Are investors indifferent between obtaining a $10 dividend or seeing $10 per share reported in the firm's income statement? If the firm has correctly reported profit in its income statement, the investor should be indifferent.

However, Connecting Theory to Practice 17.3 indicates reasons why the investor may not be indifferent. First, since management can artificially and illegally inflate the firm's reported earnings, the $10 listed as retained earnings may actually be much less. In contrast, a $10 cash dividend is worth exactly $10. Second, the firm can legally change its accounting procedures, thereby inducing changes in the reported earnings. This is why the investor often perceives a $10 cash dividend as more reliable than $10 listed as retained earnings. Under such circumstances who would blame the investor for preferring "a bird in the hand over two in the bush"?

Even without systematic distortion in the EPS, the investor may prefer dividends to retained earnings. Suppose the investor believes the reported EPS is accurate *on average*, but has a 50% chance of being higher and a 50% chance of being lower than reported. Table 17-3 illustrates this scenario. One firm distributes all of its $10 EPS as dividends, and the other firm reports $10 EPS but pays no dividends. Firms tend to *smooth* their reported earnings—that is, they tend to understate EPS in a good year and overstate it in a bad year. Suppose the investor knows the firm is smoothing its reported earnings but believes that, on average, the firm has no real reason to distort the earnings systematically in one direction or the other. For example, if the investor believes that the true EPS has a 50% chance of being $12 and a 50% chance of being $8, the EPS's expected value will be $10 [(0.5 × $12) + (0.5 × $8) = $10]. The investor would receive exactly that sum if the firm were to distribute all of the $10 EPS as dividends.

Which alternative is better for the investor? Since the investor is probably risk-averse—most investors are—he or she will prefer the $10 dividend with certainty

TABLE 17-3 Reported EPS versus Certain Dividends	Dividend (Reported EPS = DPS = $10)		EPS Probability Distribution (Reported EPS = $10 and zero dividends)	
	Probability	Dividends	Probability	EPS
	1	$10	½	$8
			½	$12
Expected value		$10		$10
Variance		0		4[a]

[a]$\sigma^2 = [\frac{1}{2}(8 - 10)^2] + [\frac{1}{2}(12 - 10)^2] = 4.$

over the retained earnings (capital gain) with a $10 expected value and a nonzero variance. Recall: The higher the variability, the lower the value of the uncertain cash flow. Consequently, even without systematic distortion in the reported EPS, the uncertainty regarding the true EPS makes risk-averse investors prefer dividends. This is another reason why a $1 dividend may be worth more than $1 of retained earnings.

17.3.6 Dividend Policy and Business Risk

We have learned that stockholders assign information content to a firm's dividend and, in particular, to changes in that dividend. It is in the firm's best interest not to cut dividends and to pay annual dividends regularly. Suppose that a firm decides that it is optimal to distribute a constant dividend each year. What factors determine that firm's dividend level?

Business risk and financial leverage are two principal factors that affect dividend level. Let us first assume an all-equity firm and no taxes and focus on the business risk factor. Figure 17-3 depicts two firms, A and B. Firm B's NOI variability is much larger than Firm A's. Because both are all-equity firms, the line labeled *EPS* intersects

FIGURE 17-3
Business Risk and Optimal Dividend Policy
The left vertical axis measures the EPS and the right vertical axis measures probability.

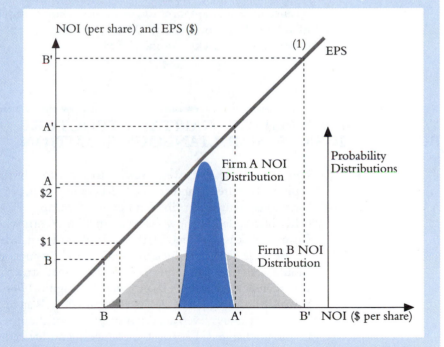

the origin. Since NOI, given on the horizontal axis, is on a per-share basis, it equals EPS (for an all-equity firm with no taxes). Line 1 in Figure 17-3 is a 45° line, and the range of possible NOI equals the range of EPS, given on the vertical axis. Firm A's NOI variability dictates that its EPS will fall in Range AA', whereas Firm B's NOI variability dictates that its EPS will fall in Range BB' on the vertical line.

Let us demonstrate the relationship between business risk and dividend policy when the firm distributes a constant-dollar dividend. We assume current earnings are the only source of funds for paying dividends. Suppose both pay a dividend of $1 per share. Because $1 is above Point B, Firm B may be forced to cut its dividend if it has no other resources for paying dividends. The shaded area under the distribution shows Firm B's probability of cutting its dividend. What about Firm A? Since its lowest possible EPS, given by Point A, is located above the $1 level, Firm A should have the cash needed to pay the $1 cash dividend per share. Moreover, Firm A can safely increase the annual dividend to $2, with no need to cut future dividends. Firm B's optimal dividend level will be lower than $2. If the level goes above $2, Firm B has a substantial probability of a future dividend cut.

NOI is not necessarily positive in practice. If EPS is negative, both Firms A and B may need to cut their dividends. However, the simple example shown in Figure 17-3 conveys the idea that the smaller the firm's business risk, the more certain the future earnings and the larger the dividend the firm will be able to pay without threat of a future dividend cut. This is precisely why utility firms (which are characterized by relatively small business risk) pay higher dividends than firms in riskier businesses (e.g., transportation or mining). For example, on August 4, 1997, the dividend yield on stocks in the Dow-Jones utility index was 4.31% while the yield on transportation stocks was only 1.58%.

17.4 DIVIDEND POLICY, CAPITAL STRUCTURE, AND BUSINESS RISK: A SIMULTANEOUS SOLUTION

Earlier in the chapter we promised to show that business risk, dividend policy, and capital structure are interrelated. To demonstrate, let us again assume the firm follows a constant-dollar dividend policy. Similar to Figure 17-3, Figure 17-4 has another line added to show EPS as a function of NOI when the firm employs leverage. Business risk is measured by the variability of NOI, which leverage does not affect.

Because leverage, dividend policy, and business risk are interrelated, the firm should seek a simultaneous solution for capital structure and dividend policy. Let us first review an all-equity firm. Line 1 in Figure 17-4 describes the unlevered firm's EPS (just as in Figure 17-3). Its EPS will fall in Range AA', which lies on Line 1. If the firm employs leverage, the distribution of the NOI reflecting the business risk remains unchanged, but the EPS changes. The levered firm's EPS is given by Range BB', which lies on Line 2. (Be sure to note, also, EPS levels A, A', B, and B' on the vertical axis.)

FIGURE 17-4
Leverage and Dividend Policy
The left vertical axis measures the EPS and the right vertical axis measures a probability function.

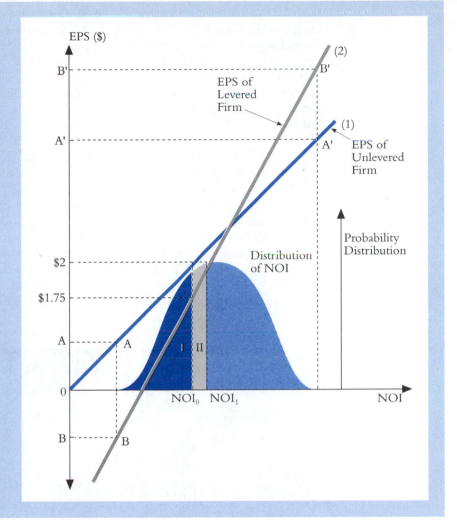

Now let's bring in dividends. Assume the all–equity firm pays a $2 per share dividend. What is the probability that EPS will fall short of $2 so the firm will have to cut its future dividend level? This probability is given by the area labeled *I* under the bell-shaped curve. If NOI is smaller than NOI_0, the all–equity firm's EPS will be less than $2, and the firm will have to cut its $2 dividend per share. Now suppose the firm decides to employ leverage and maintain its $2 per share dividend policy. What is the probability of the EPS falling short of $2? Looking again at Figure 17-4, we see that if NOI is smaller than NOI_1, the levered firm's EPS will be smaller than $2; and the probability of a dividend cut increases from Area I to the larger area, I + II.

Leverage increases the probability of a dividend cut. If the firm wishes to use leverage without the probability of dividend cuts exceeding Area I (the same probability as for the all–equity firm), it would have to pay a lower dividend. In our example the size of that lower dividend would be $1.75 per share. It is easy to show that the higher the business risk, the less the leverage the firm should employ if it does not wish the probability of a dividend cut to exceed a given critical level.

What lesson can we learn from this example? One thing is certain: Management cannot make one decision in isolation from the others. Capital structure, dividend policy, and business risk are interrelated. For any given business risk, the greater the leverage, the lower the optimal constant-dollar dividend. However, the task of identifying the optimal debt–dividend policy for a given level of business risk is not simple. The firm will have to experiment with its capital structure and dividend policy by increasing the leverage slightly and decreasing the dividends slightly and then observing the market reaction. By trying different combinations of these two factors, the firm may succeed in approaching its optimal leverage and dividend policy.

The median debt/capital ratio for utilities was 36.6% in 1996; the ratio was zero for software companies. The explanation for this marked difference can be found in the greater business risk experienced by software firms.

In Applying Theory to Practice 17.1, we show that if the dividend remains at the same level, an increase in leverage increases the probability of a dividend cut. Alternatively, for a given business risk, the more leverage that a firm uses, the lower its constant dividend per share should be—that is, if the firm wishes to maintain the probability of a dividend cut unchanged.

APPLYING THEORY TO PRACTICE 17.1

GERBER PRODUCTS' DIVIDEND POLICY

The following table presents selected data on Gerber Products:

Year	Earnings per Share ($)	Dividend per Share ($)	Dividend as a Percent of Net Profit (%)
1984	0.69	0.29	42
1985	0.56	0.33	59
1986	0.46	0.33	72
1987	0.67	0.33	49
1988	1.08	0.37	34
1989	1.42	0.46	32
1990	1.70	0.57	34
1991	1.93	0.66	34
1992	1.64	0.77	47
1993	1.70	0.80	47
1994	1.95	1.00	51

Source: *Value Line Investment Survey*, various issues.

Gerber Products had about 72 million shares outstanding in 1994 with a market value of $2 billion. The firm's long-term debt was about $120 million and the interest on this debt was $11 million per year. Gerber's short-term debt was negligible. The corporate tax rate was 35%. The firm's policy was to pay cash dividends only from current earnings, not from retained earnings. On August 24, 1994, Sandoz Ltd purchased 99.2% of Gerber Products for $53 a share.

Questions

1. Analyze Gerber's dividend policy in the period 1984–1994 as reflected by the above data. Calculate the average annual growth rate of DPS.
2. Calculate Gerber's NOI for 1994. Suppose the firm believes that any dividend cut will signal bad news to the stockholders. Management is optimistic regarding future earnings although it believes that setbacks are possible. Management estimates in 1995 that NOI has a 1% chance of falling by 40% or more from its 1994 level, a 10% chance of it falling by 30% to 40%, a 20% chance of it falling by 20% to 30%, and a 69% chance of it falling by 20% or less. Use these probabilities to calculate the probability of a mandatory dividend cut in 1995.
3. How would your answer to Question 2 change if Gerber were to repurchase half of its shares and to finance this repurchase by issuing $1 billion debt at a 9.252% interest rate? Assume Gerber carries out the stock repurchase at the current market price and has negligible flotation costs.

MAKING THE CONNECTION

1. The published data reveal that Gerber's management considers dividend policy to be very important. Dividends were not cut even in relatively bad years. Although the EPS dropped from $0.69 in 1984 to $0.46 in 1986, the dividend was not reduced; on the contrary, it rose from $0.29 in 1984 to $0.33 in 1985 and remained at that level until 1988. Gerber either kept the dividend constant or increased it, but the firm never cut it. The average compounded growth rate in its dividend across years is calculated as follows:

$$\$0.29 \times (1 + g)^{10} = \$1.00$$

The annual growth rate, g, is given by

$$g = \left(\frac{\$1.00}{\$0.29}\right)^{1/10} - 1 \cong 0.1318 \text{ or } 13.18\%$$

As a result of Gerber's dividend policy, the payout ratio varied from a low of 32% to a high of 72%. Gerber's management evidently considered the constant-dollar dividend (with annual growth) rather than the constant-payout-ratio as more important to the stockholders.

2. EPS in 1994 was $1.95. NOI can be found by the formula

$$\text{EPS} = \frac{(1 - T)(\text{NOI} - \text{Interest})}{\text{Number of shares}}$$

where $T = 0.35$ is the tax rate. Therefore, NOI in 1994 was

$$\text{NOI} = \frac{\text{EPS} \times \text{Number of shares}}{1 - T} + \text{Interest payout}$$

or

$$\text{NOI} = \frac{\$1.95 \times 72 \text{ million}}{1 - 0.35} + \$11 \text{ million} = \$227 \text{ million}$$

where $11 million is the interest on the debt. The dividend paid in 1994 amounted to $72 million ($1 × 72 million shares).

If NOI falls by 40%, Gerber's net earnings will be

$$(1 - T) \times (0.60 \times \text{NOI} - \text{Interest}) = 0.65 \times (0.60 \times \$227 \text{ million} - \$11 \text{ million})$$
$$= \$81.38 \text{ million}$$

Therefore, even with this large possible decrease in NOI, Gerber will be able to maintain the $1 dividend per share. For any decrease of less than 40% in the NOI, Gerber will have sufficient funds to cover the $72 million dividend payment. Based on management's beliefs regarding the future values of NOI, the probability of a dividend cut is very small and definitely less than 1% (because the probability of a 40% reduction or more in the NOI is only 1%).

3. The market value of Gerber's equity is $2 billion. Suppose Gerber repurchases $1 billion of its equity and finances it by debt at an interest rate of 9.252%. The number of shares will be reduced by half (to 36 million), and the interest bill will be

$$\$11 \text{ million} + (0.09252 \times \$1 \text{ billion}) = \$103.52 \text{ million}$$

With the new capital structure, the lower part of Gerber's NOI distribution and net earnings distribution will be as follows:

Decline in NOI	Probability	Maximum NOI (in million)	Maximum Earnings = $(1 - T)$ (NOI − Interest) (in million)
40% or more	1%	$227 × (0.60) = $136.2[a]	$(1 - 0.35) \times (\$136.2 - \$103.52)$ = $21.242[a]
40% to 30%	10%	$227 × (0.70) = $158.9[b]	$(1 - 0.35) \times (\$158.9 - \$103.52)$ = $35.997[b]

[a]If the NOI drops by more than 40%, the value reported in the table will be lower.

[b]If the NOI drops by more than 30%, the value reported in the table will be lower.

The firm now has 36 million shares outstanding. In order to pay a $1 dividend per share, Gerber will need net earnings amounting to $36 million. This calculation reveals that there is 11% chance of Gerber having to cut its future dividends. To be more precise, there is a probability of 11% (10% + 1%) of the net earnings being $35.997 million or less, thus necessitating a dividend cut. The other values do not need calculation because, for a decrease in the NOI of less than 30%, Gerber will have sufficient earnings to cover the $1 dividend per share. Thus, increasing the leverage increases the probability of a dividend cut. This application demonstrates how the level of dividends distributed, business risk (the variability of NOI), and financial leverage are related.

17.5 THE EMPIRICAL EVIDENCE

Testing whether an optimal dividend policy exists and whether stockholders prefer high or low dividends is quite complex. Many factors must be held constant to obtain reliable results. A positive association between the pretax average return on stocks and their dividend yield would imply that investors do not like high dividend yields: The higher the dividend yield, the higher the required average rate of return on the stock (or the lower its price for any given cash flow). Conversely, a negative association would imply preference for high dividend yields.

Empirical studies have produced inconclusive results. Brennan as well as Litzenberger and Ramaswamy found a positive association, indicating a preference for low dividend yields. On the other hand, Black and Scholes as well as Miller and Scholes did not find such an association. Thus, at this time, no unequivocal empirical evidence exists regarding preferred dividend policy.[17]

However, empirical studies have shown that a firm's stock price will generally rise when its dividends increase. For example, Asquith and Mullins[18] found a significant increase in share price when a firm initiated dividends after 10 years of not paying them or when a firm paid the first dividend in its history. The information content of dividends explains this price reaction to a dividend increase. A firm signals the stockholders good news and the share price responds positively. Indeed, financial analysts have sometimes revived their earnings forecast when dividends change, and their forecasts may affect the stock price.

17. For the empirical findings, see the following: M. Brennan, "Taxes, Market Valuation and Corporate Financial Policy," *National Tax Journal* (December 1970): 417–427; R. Litzenberger and K. Ramaswamy, "The Effect of Personal Taxes and Dividends on Capital Asset Prices: Theory and Empirical Evidence," *Journal of Financial Economics* (June 1979): 163–195; R. Litzenberger and K. Ramaswamy, "The Effects of Dividends on Common Stock Prices: Tax Effects or Information Effect?" *Journal of Finance* (May 1982): 429–443; F. Black and M. Scholes, "The Effects of Dividend Yield and Dividend Policy on Common Stock Prices and Returns," *Journal of Financial Economics* (May 1974): 1–22; and M. Miller and M. Scholes, "Dividends and Taxes: Some Empirical Evidence," *Journal of Political Economics* (December 1982): 1118–1141.
18. P. Asquith and D. Mullins, Jr., "The Impact of Initiating Dividend Payments on Shareholder Wealth," *Journal of Business* (January 1983): 77–96.

CONNECTING THEORY TO PRACTICE 17.4

DIVIDENDS REVIEW

Dividends are rising, but not fast enough to keep up with stock prices. So says Arnold Kaufman, editor of *Standard & Poor's Outlook* newsletter. Kaufman expects dividend growth of 5% to 6% in 1995. As recently as June, he was forecasting a 7% increase. During the first eight months of this year 1,278 corporations raised dividends, against 1,199 in the same period last year.

The yield on the s&p 500 fell to 2.46% in early August, its lowest level since Standard & Poor's began collecting this information in 1926. An acceleration in both corporate profits and payouts could move this relationship closer to historical levels. So could a sharp market correction.

Some of the best dividend prospects may lie overseas, for investors willing to tolerate currency risk. "An economic recovery in Europe could lead to faster dividend growth there than in the U.S.," notes Catherine Ayers-Rigsby, president of Ceros Portfolio Management Co. The table lists ten European stocks with five-year dividend growth rates over 15% that pay out no more than half their profits.

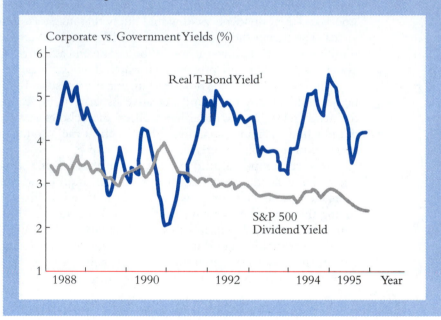

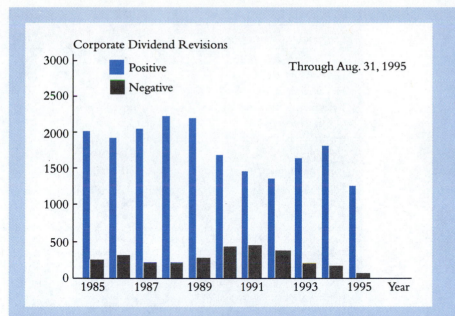

Corporate Dividend Revisions

Through Aug. 31, 1995

Representative Industry Payouts[2]

Industry	Yield	Payout Ratio	P/E
Auto & truck mfg	3.3%	22%	6.9
Banking	3.2	38	11.8
Electric utilities	6.4	81	12.6
Food processing	2.1	40	18.8
Health care svcs	0.3	5	24.1
Paper & forest prods	2.6	30	12.9
Petroleum	4.2	70	17.7
Pharmaceuticals	2.6	46	20.2
Retailing	1.5	21	18.0
Software	0.2	6	34.3

Companies with High Payout Ratios

Company/Business	Price	Yield	Payout Ratio[3]
McDermott Intl/oilfield construction	22¾	4.4%	NM
Aetna Life & Casualty/insurance	68¼	4.0	201%
Ultramar/energy	23⅝	4.7	172
Jacobson Stores/department stores	9¾	5.1	156
Niagara Mohawk Power/electric utility	12	9.3	153
Cascade Natural Gas/oil refining	14⅛	6.8	132
Piccadilly Cafeterias/restaurants	8	6.0	120
Entergy/electric utility	24⅛	7.5	119
Kuhlman/electrical equip & metal prods	11¾	5.1	113
Occidental Petroleum/energy	21¾	4.6	105

Foreign Stocks with Attractive Dividends

Company/Country	Business	Yield	Payout Ratio
CML Microsystems/UK	electronics mfg	5.1%	48%
Deveaux/France	textiles	4.3	36
Hollandia Industriele/Holland	construction	5.6	38
Kalamazoo Computer/UK	software	3.8	33
Lloyds Chemists/UK	drugstores	4.1	34
OM Gruppen/Sweden	securities brokerage	6.3	40
ONET/France	environmental svcs	3.7	46
Park Food Group/UK	food distributing	3.8	50
Quicks Group/UK	auto dealerships	4.1	45
SPIR Communication/France	publishing	3.3	50

Data as of 8/31/95. [1]Yield on 30-year Treasurys adjusted for inflation using the trailing 12 months' increase in the Consumer Price Index. [2]Capitalization-weighted. Dividends divided by net income: all extraordinary items are excluded. [3]Average during the latest four quarters. NM: Not meaningful. Sources: Market Guide Database Service and Value Line Database Service via OneSource Information Services: Standard & Poor's Dividend Record: World Equities.

Source: Ronald Boone, Jr., "The Dividend Review," *Forbes* (September 25, 1995): 220. Reprinted By Permission of FORBES Magazine © Forbes Inc., 1995.

MAKING THE CONNECTION

Since more firms make positive dividend revisions than negative ones, firms are reluctant to cut their dividends (as the IBM case at the beginning of the chapter also indicates). This means managements consider dividend policy to be very relevant. The dividends review also reveals a large difference in the payout ratio across industries. For example, the payout ratio is 81% in electric utilities, where the business risk is very low. In contrast, software firms, which probably have a much higher business risk, have a much lower 6% payout ratio. Also, some firms pay more than 100% of their earnings as dividends, and some foreign firms have "attractive" dividends.

The dividend yield on S&P 500 was 2.46 in 1995. Stock prices continued to climb, despite the investment community's anticipation of a market correction, and reached a dividend yield on S&P 500 of 1.63% in August 1997. Dividend policy remains a controversial issue. Moreover, it has no one recipe: The best policy for Niagara Mohawk could be disastrous for Microsoft. This chapter and Connecting Theory to Practice 17.4 make clear that management gives dividend policy a great deal of consideration and cannot find the best policy if it does not consider business risk and leverage. Dividend policy does matter, and different firms (and industries) adopt different dividend policies depending on their businesses and financial risks. This chapter sheds light on the factors that need to be considered when determining a firm's optimal dividend policy.

SUMMARY

In a perfect market with symmetric information, no transaction or flotation costs, and no personal taxes or the same tax rate on income and capital gains, stockholders will be indifferent between obtaining their return in cash dividends or in capital gains. Dividend policy does not matter in this case. No link exists between dividend policy and capital expenditure in a perfect market. If projects with positive NPVs are available, a firm can finance them either by using retained earnings or by issuing more stock or debt. However, in an imperfect market, dividend policy and capital expenditure *are* related, and dividend policy *does* matter.

When a firm incurs flotation costs, it will prefer financing projects with retained earnings. Personal taxes enhance stockholders' preference for capital gains rather than dividends.

Although management can manipulate accounting data over the years, it cannot manipulate dividends in the same way because the firm needs resources to pay them. The uncertainty of retained earnings (and capital gains) induces stockholders' preference for cash dividends.

Because cash dividends signal information to the market, management will be reluctant to cut dividends even if earnings have declined. A dividend cut would be a signal that the firm's financial distress is not merely temporary.

Because dividend signaling affects stock price, a firm should simultaneously determine its business risk, financial risk, and dividend policy. Various industries have different levels of business risk, and the optimal dividend policy will vary from one industry to another, as well as from one firm to another within the same industry.

CHAPTER AT A GLANCE

1. Firm's value and dividend policy:

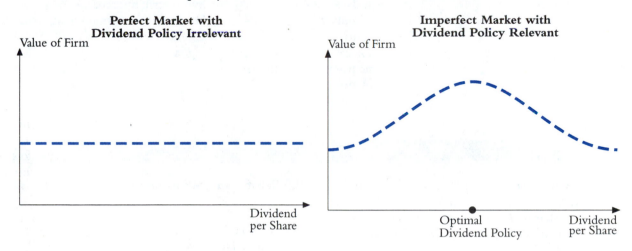

2. Dividend policy is *irrelevant* when
   a. There are no personal taxes or when tax rates on dividends and capital gains are the same.
   b. There are no transaction costs.
   c. There are no flotation costs, and the firm can issue as many shares as it wishes at the market price.
   d. There is no threat of losing control of the firm from a new stock issue.
   e. There is symmetric information: All information known to the managers is also available to the public; therefore dividends cannot be used to signal information.

3. Dividend policy is *relevant* when
   a. The tax rate on dividends is higher than that on capital gains (preference for low dividends).
   b. There are transaction costs (with the preference for dividends or capital gains depending on the stockholders' consumption preference—the clientele effect).
   c. There are flotation costs on a new stock issue (preference for low dividends to use retained earnings as a source of internal financing).
   d. There is a threat of losing control of the firm due to a new issue (preference for low dividends to conserve cash).
   e. There is asymmetric information (dividends signal private information held by management).

KEY TERMS

Dividend per share (DPS)	Declaration date	Residual dividend
Cash dividend	Holder record date	Optimal dividend policy
Regular cash dividend	Ex-dividend date	Dividend yield
Extra dividend	Payment date	Symmetric information
Stock dividend	Dividend policy	Dividend reinvestment plan (DRIP)
Stock split	Payout ratio	Clientele effect
Round lot	Retention ratio	Signaling
Odd lot	Constant-payout-ratio dividend	
Stock repurchase	Constant-dollar dividend	

REVIEW AND PRACTICE

17.1 A firm distributes a 20% stock dividend. Before distributing the stock dividend, the firm had 1 million shares. How many outstanding shares does the firm have after it makes the stock dividend distribution?

17.2 A firm had 1 million shares before splitting 2:1. How many shares does the firm have outstanding after the split?

17.3 What is an *ex-dividend date*? What is a *payment date*?

17.4 Describe the *constant-payout-ratio*, *constant-dollar*, and *residual dividend* distribution policies.

17.5 You have the following data on Lazer Corporation:

Year	EPS ($)	DPS ($)	Capital Expenditure ($ million)
1	4	1	6
2	3	1.05	2
3	2	1.1	0
4	−1	1.15	3

Lazer has 1 million shares outstanding. What dividend distribution policy does the firm follow?

17.6 Repeat Problem 17.5 but this time let the dividends be $1, $0.75, $0.50, and $0 in each respective year.

17.7 Repeat Problem 17.5 but this time let the dividends be $0, $1, $2, and $0 in each respective year.

17.8 The firm's stock price on June 15 was $200. In July the firm paid a 25% stock dividend. In September it split its stock 2:1. In October it paid cash dividends of $5 per share. What is the firm's expected stock price after all these distributions? Did investors lose money as a result of the stock price change?

17.9 An investor wishes to invest $10,000 in the stock market. To avoid large transaction costs, he or she considers buying only round lots. In 1993 Intel's stock price increased from $50 to $115 a share and then the firm split its stock 2:1. Explain how this would affect the investor's decision to purchase Intel stock and the market price of that stock.

17.10 A firm is considering whether to use its $100,000 accumulated cash to pay a cash dividend or to invest in the following projects:

Project	Initial Outlay ($)	NPV ($)
A	50,000	10,000
B	30,000	8,000
C	30,000	5,000

The firm has 100,000 shares outstanding and the share price is $10 (before the information on the projects is known).

a. Assume the firm cannot raise additional money. What will be the optimal dividend–investment decision?

b. What will be the share price before the firm pays dividends but after the stockholders have information on the projects? What will be the share price after the firm pays the dividends?

c. Repeat 17.10a and 17.10b but this time assume the firm can raise as much money as it wishes with no transaction costs.

d. Repeat 17.10a and 17.10b but this time assume there are 10% transaction costs. For instance, if the firm issues $50,000, its net proceeds will be only $45,000.

17.11 The required rate of return on a firm's equity is 20%. It earns $1 million, distributes $0.5 million in cash dividends, and reinvests the remaining $0.5 million. What should be the average rate of return on the invested retained earnings for an investor *not* to be worse off than receiving the full $1 as dividends?

17.12 The required rate of return on a firm's stock is 15%. The firm has the opportunity to reinvest at 25% (with risk kept constant). Evaluate the following assertion about this situation: "The firm should not pay dividends but should reinvest its available resources."

17.13 A firm has been paying a $10 cash dividend per share for five years, and the annual inflation rate has been 10%. Calculate the annual cash dividend in real terms. What should be the nominal dividend for a $10 annual dividend in real terms? [Hint: Real dividend = Nominal dividend/(1 + Inflation rate).]

17.14 A firm's retained earnings are $100 million, and it pays out $50 million as dividends. The capital expenditure for next year is $500 million. What should be the size of the new stock issue? Does the financing have to be a stock issue?

17.15 How would your answer to Problem 17.14 change if, instead of paying cash dividends, the firm decided to pay 20% stock dividends?

17.16 A firm earns $10 per share every year. An investor who holds 1,000 shares in the firm needs

$10,000 a year for consumption. The stock price at the beginning of the year is $100.

a. How many shares should the investor sell at the end of each year if the firm does not pay any dividends? Conduct calculations for each of the next three years. How many shares will the investor hold after three years? Assume there are no transaction costs.

b. Repeat 17.16a but this time assume transaction costs of 2% on each sale. Will the investor prefer the firm to pay cash dividends or to retain its earnings?

17.17 Repeat Problem 17.16 but this time assume the firm pays all its earnings as cash dividends. However, the investor does not need the cash and, therefore, reinvests the dividends by buying more stock. The transaction costs are 2% on each purchase. How do the results of Problems 17.16 and 17.17 relate to the *clientele effect*? Explain.

17.18 Since 1993 the top marginal personal tax rate has been 39.6%; the capital gains tax rate, 28%. An investor who pays 39.6% income tax is considering investing $1 million in Firm A or Firm B. Both firms earn $10 per share and their current stock price is $100. Firm A distributes all of its earnings as cash dividends; Firm B does not pay cash dividends at all. Calculate the before- and after-tax income on each investment.

17.19 The interest rate on debt dropped from 6% to 4%. How might this affect the firm's dividend policy?

17.20 A firm reports earnings (all of which it retains) of $20 per share. However, you believe that the true earnings are at either $15 or $25 per share with equal probability. Calculate the mean and the variance of the firm's EPS. Can the capital gain corresponding to this case be less than $20 per share? Explain. Would you prefer a $20 per share cash dividend?

17.21 A firm pays a cash dividend of $10 per share. It also distributes 10% stock dividends every year. Suppose the firm pays the stock dividends in June and pays the cash dividends in December of each year. Calculate the *effective* dividend per share for an investor who buys 100 shares in January and holds these shares for three years. What is the effective

growth rate of the dividends? (Hint: "effective" means dividend per "old" share bought in January.)

17.22 A firm increases its dividend payout ratio from 10% to 80%. As a result, many investors in high tax brackets sell the stock and other (low tax bracket) investors who have never before invested in the stock, buy it. Use personal taxation and clientele effect arguments to explain this phenomenon.

17.23 A firm's NOI can range from $6,000 to $25,000. Assume all NOI values have equal probability when the NOI changes in $1,000 units. (That is, the probability of NOI = $6,000 is $\frac{1}{20}$; the probability of NOI = $7,000 is $\frac{1}{20}$; and so on and the probability of NOI = $25,000 is $\frac{1}{20}$). The firm has 25,000 shares outstanding and plans to pay a dividend of $0.50 a share. The stock price is $10 per share. All dividends are paid out of current earnings.

a. What is the probability of a future dividend cut if the firm is an all-equity firm?

b. What is the probability of a dividend cut if the firm repurchases 15,000 of its shares at $10 each and issues $150,000 debt at 8% interest?

17.24 Repeat Problem 17.23 but this time assume the business risk is much smaller and the NOI falls in the range of $14,000 to $17,000. In this case the possible NOI values are $14,000, $15,000, $16,000, and $17,000 with equal probability.

17.25 An investor believes that beta is the correct measure of risk. He or she expects to receive an average of $5 in cash dividends and $5 in capital gains (or retained earnings) at the end of the year. The beta of the dividends is 1, and the beta of the capital gains is 2.

a. What is the beta of the firm's stock? (Hint: Recall that beta is the weighted average of the betas of the various components of income.)

b. Now suppose the firm decides to change its dividend policy: it will distribute, on average, only $2 as cash dividends and keep $8 as retained earnings. How will this change affect the firm's beta?

c. In your view, will the stock price decrease, increase, or remain unchanged as a result of the above change in dividend policy? (Hint: Use the CAPM framework.)

INTERNET   QUESTIONS

17.26 Visit the following Web site and complete the tutorial on cash dividends, stock dividends, stock splits, and reverse stock splits.

http://www.e-analytics.com/index.htm

17.27 Visit Thomson Investor's Network Stock Center and look at the dividends paid over the past few years by major "blue chip" companies such as Ford and Exxon. Then check the dividends paid by smaller, quickly growing firms such as Intel. Based on what you learned in this chapter, categorize their dividend policies (stable amount per share, etc.) and justify the policies based on the nature of the firms.

http://www.thomsoninvest.net

YOUR TURN: APPLYING THEORY TO PRACTICE

NORWEGIAN BANKS CLASH OVER DIVIDENDS

Den norske Bank and Christiania Bank, Norway's two largest commercial banks, have rejected demands by the state-backed Bank Investment Fund, their biggest shareholder, for a 1994 dividend of 50 percent of net profits.

The clash is expected to test the authority of the banks and how far the state is willing to interfere in the bourse-listed companies.

The fund was established in 1991 as a vehicle through which to channel more than NKr20bn ($3.02 billion) of state funds to rescue the banking system when it was on the verge of collapse.

The appropriations subsequently resulted in the state owning 72 percent of DnB and 68.9 percent of Christiania, share holdings which are managed by the fund on the state's behalf.

At the time of the rescue the minority Labour government stressed it would not interfere in the banks' business.

The state is now seeking to define dividend policy, in a move testing the banks' independent authority. Both DnB and Christiania have sought to play down the conflict.

In a confidential letter which the banks publicized, the fund stressed that the owners of the banks should determine dividend policy which "defines what the owners demand from the bank, and thus from the bank's directors and management."

Norway's Companies Act states that the board is responsible for proposing the dividend, which cannot be increased by the general assembly.

The state could overrule the banks by rejecting 1994 accounts in which the dividend payment is proposed, but could also exert political pressure.

The fund argues that the banks experienced exceptionally good results in 1994 and that an "extraordinary" dividend would not weaken capital adequacy for which a goal for core capital of 6 to 7 percent of risk-weighted assets has been set.[19]

The banks argue that a dividend of between 30 percent and 40 percent represents market practice, with the payout ratio being relatively low in years with a high net result and similarly high in years with low net results.

DnB is due to publish 1994 accounts on February 14 and Christiania a week later. Both are widely expected to achieve record results.

Source: *Financial Times*, 1 February 1995. © Financial Times. 1995.

Questions

1. Discuss the dividend conflict presented in the accompanying article. What might be the motive of the banks' boards of the directors not to increase the dividends to 50% of the profit? (Hint:

---

19. *Core capital* is the minimum amount of capital the bank must hold as a percent of its total assets.

Consider the effect of agency costs.) In light of this discussion, do you think Equation (17.1) in the text is valid for this case?

2. By the Norway's Companies Act, the general assembly cannot increase the dividends that the company's board proposes. What can the Bank Investment Fund do to force the desired 50% dividend payout ratio?

3. Suppose the two banks can adopt accounting rules that will decrease the reported profit. The management receives compensation by the formula $C = \$10,000 \times \text{Max} [0, (\text{EPS} - \$10)]$, where C is the compensation and EPS is the *reported* EPS. Discuss the pros and cons of an earnings-smoothing policy in light of the above dividend conflict.

4. How would your answer to Question 3 change if the compensation of the banks' managements were tied to the banks' total assets?

5. Suppose managers' compensation is tied to the banks' assets. Also assume the Bank Investment Fund's manager believes that if only 30% of the 1994 earnings are distributed as cash dividends, the bank will undertake projects with negative NPV. With a 50% dividend payout ratio, the banks will undertake projects with positive NPV. Could this be a reason for the pressure imposed on the bank to pay 50% of the earnings as dividends? Demonstrate your answer graphically. Assume each bank has $100 million available for cash dividends and reinvestment. (Plot the IRR and cost of capital on the vertical axis and the 1994 capital expenditure on the horizontal axis.) If this is indeed the case, can we say that Equation (17.1) holds and, therefore, the Fund's managers should be indifferent to the dividend policy?

CHAPTER 18

LONG-TERM FINANCIAL PLANNING

LEARNING OBJECTIVES

After reading this chapter, you should understand:

1. Why a firm needs long-term financial planning.

2. How to prepare pro forma financial statements.

3. The various ways to forecast sales.

4. How to estimate the firm's future external financial needs.

STILL SHINING

. . . One beneficiary of a Byte Christmas would be Compaq, the world's largest maker of personal computers and the No. 2 seller (after Packard Bell) of PCs in the U.S.

Many analysts see this Christmas as the last hurrah for U.S.-focused PC makers. "Nineteen ninety-six will mark a turning point," says Bose. "After more than half a decade of almost spectacular growth, the good times are going to end. U.S. sales of personal computers will grow no more than 17% in '96 and average about 12½% a year between now and 2000. That's down from over 30% a year in the first half of the decade . . ."

The company uses complex simulation software to track trends in the global marketplace. Demand, pricing, dealer inventories and other factors are examined to help set price and production targets.

Source: Jay Palmer, "Still Shining," *Barron's* (December 11, 1995): 15. Reprinted by permission of *Barron's*, © 1995 Dow Jones & Company, Inc. All Rights Reserved Worldwide.

18.1 INTRODUCTION

As the economy changes continuously, a firm needs to respond quickly to take advantage of new business opportunities as they arise. When growth rates change, a firm needs to plan production, capital expenditure, and pricing policy. As shown in Corporate Finance in the News, Compaq's growth rate is predicted to decline from 30% per year to 12%. This decline, if it occurs, will affect Compaq's cash flow, and the firm must develop a plan to face this trend.[1]

To initiate the new activities that will improve its competitive performance, a firm needs to undertake long-term planning. Indeed a Gallup Poll of 414 chief executives reveals that 22% of them said that long-term planning is their main goal. (Only profitability ranked higher.)[2] Financial planning requires decisions about issues as varied as capital expenditure, production, price setting, sales promotion, and product image. Such plans form the firm's financial blueprint. Management is responsible for elaborating the firm's strategy as well as for adjusting it to ever-changing conditions. Execution of plans may not always be successful, and achievements often fall short of goals, especially when management incorrectly interprets environmental changes that affect the firm. This is demonstrated by Kmart's "renewal program" presented in Connecting Theory to Practice 18.1.

CONNECTING THEORY TO PRACTICE 18.1

KMART: THE BEST-LAID PLANS

The telephone rings in Troy, Mich. once, twice . . . 22 times. Finally a recording cuts in, requesting the caller to phone again later since no one is picking up. Certain he must have misdialed, the caller dials again. Same result. Only on the twelfth ring of the third try is there a response: "Kmart international headquarters," says a cheerful operator at the Troy offices of Kmart Corp.

It's a small sign, but a telling one, that all's not well at the nation's second-largest retailer. Midway through Chairman Joseph Antonini's ambitious $3 billion to $3.5 billion "renewal" program, over 1,200 of Kmart's 2,435 discount stores have been modernized, expanded, relocated or built from scratch. When *Forbes* [magazine] last visited Antonini and Kmart in 1991, we were very impressed with their plans. We said, "If Antonini's right about earnings—and he makes a convincing case . . . Kmart is one of the cheapest stocks on the market."

The market capitalization of Kmart has indeed doubled since then, to $10.2 billion. But alas, Antonini is still far short of his goals. In 1991 Antonini said his goal was to reach $35 billion in discount store sales by [the end of] the

---

1. As a matter of fact, there was a decline in the growth rate of Compaq's sales in 1996, but a much smaller decline than predicted—32.7% relative to an average growth rate of 37.8% over the previous five years. The firm's management should also analyze the effects on cash flows of errors in sales forecasts.

2. Julie Androshick, "New Year's Resolutions," *Forbes* (13 January 1997): 20. Reprinted By Permission of FORBES Magazine© Forbes Inc., 1997.

year through January 1996 (*Forbes*, May 27, 1991). Kmart has been growing at less than half the rate needed to achieve its goal. . . .

Why has reality fallen so far short of expectations? No question that the new stores are a vast improvement. . . .

But if you want to know why domestic Kmart sales have risen just 6.3% in the past two fiscal years while Wal–Mart's have risen about 25%, note the levels of service. While salespeople at Wal–Mart and Dayton Hudson's Target chain seem eager to please and to help, Kmart's "associates" remain largely indifferent. For example, asked for a specific item, an associate waved in the general direction of the department. . . .

Source: Subrata N. Chakravarty, "The Best-Laid Plans . . .," *Forbes* (3 January 1994): 44–45. Reprinted By Permission of FORBES Magazine © Forbes Inc., 1994.

MAKING THE CONNECTION

Connecting Theory to Practice 18.1 indicates that Kmart's ambitious $3.5 billion "renewal" program resulted from a misdiagnosis of Kmart's illness. Customer service improvement, not just more modern stores, was needed. Therefore, Kmart sales grew at less than half of the rate planned. Failures like this do not mean that plans and forecasts are worthless. On the contrary, planning is essential. Only by analyzing the firm's plans and, in particular, any deviation of the realized figures from the planned figures can management better diagnose the firm's illness and prescribe the right treatment to improve the firm's performance. However, sometimes the firm's CEO pays for the wrong diagnosis. The board of directors may conclude that a change in the firm's leadership is needed. Indeed, in March 1995 Joe Antonini was removed as CEO of Kmart. Kmart's sales grew by only 0.4% in 1996 whereas Wal–Mart's sales grew by 12.2%. Two years after the removal of Kmart's CEO, the firm still had not recovered from the wrong diagnosis.

A firm's activities and characteristics change over time. Some changes are not under the firm's control. For instance, the firm cannot control the emergence of new competitors in the market, an aggressive marketing campaign that a rival firm initiates, a decrease in the interest rate, or new government regulations. Nonetheless, changes such as these may affect the firm's decisions and strategies. Many changes, however, are a direct result of the firm's long-term plans and the changes it initiates in response to macroeconomic needs. In this chapter we focus on changes that the firm plans, which generally involve

1. A long-term goal expressed in terms of future growth, market share, or earnings per share.
2. The actions required to achieve these goals.
3. The forecasted financial consequences of such actions.
4. A post-audit, or checking the realized figures and comparing them to the forecasted figures. This analysis is important for improving the forecasts.

For example, if Intel Corporation's goal is to be a leader in the computer chip industry, it will have to invest a certain amount of money each year in research and development. To finance capital expenditure, Intel's management will have to decide whether to raise money by issuing debt or equity or by cutting dividends, or both. The firm will then have to decide whether to invest in new production facilities. After successfully executing the projects, it will benefit from its R&D investment and enjoy the resulting cash flows. All of these actions require advance financial planning.

In this chapter we study long-term planning. We first demonstrate Boeing's long-term planning and the actions it took in response to a decline in the demand for aircraft. Then we discuss various methods of forecasting the firm's financial needs.

18.2 LONG-TERM PLANNING: BOEING'S ECONOMIC FORECAST THROUGH YEAR 2010

Long-term planning has direct implications for the firm's financial needs, the size and characteristics of its workforce, and its capital expenditure.

While the firm has control of the actions that it initiates, it has very little control of competitors' activities or of the macroeconomic factors. However, management can prepare in advance a response to any change in these two factors. In this section we present Boeing Corporation's 1993 long-term planning and compare it to what actually happened in the years 1993–1996.

Much can be learned about the firm's long-term planning by reading its financial statements. For instance, Boeing's 1992 financial statements were preceded by a letter to the stockholders in which the president wrote:

Development of the new Boeing 777 is on schedule. Major assembly has begun, and the first delivery is scheduled in 1995. We're confident that our new 777 family of wide-body aircraft will be a big factor in sustaining the company's leadership in commercial aviation well into the 21st century.

One cannot predict with certainty when the air travel industry will mount a strong recovery, but airline profitability—in concert with growth in air traffic—will drive demand for new aircraft. Our current forecast projects a total market for commercial transport aircraft of more than $800 billion (in 1993 dollars) through the year 2010. Our long-range strategy at Boeing is to keep ahead of the competition by delivering products and services that clearly represent the best value for our airline customers. The company's top priority over the next few years is to reduce overall costs while continuing to stress quality.[3]

How long is long-term planning? The time span may be only a few years, or it may be much longer. As the president's letter to stockholders indicates, Boeing's plan in the early 1990s was mainly concerned with the delivery of the 777 model in 1995, and forecasts were made for the demand for aircraft up to year 2010.

Although the firm has a long-term plan, it should be able to respond to changes in the economy, if necessary. For example, the decrease in the demand for planes

---

3. Boeing 1992 financial statements.

had a severe impact on Boeing's profit, and the firm needed to respond urgently to this change in demand. Although investment and expansion almost always accompany planning, sometimes the best plan is to incur shrinkage. Indeed, in 1992 Boeing cut its workforce substantially, and more cuts were pending in 1993. When a firm faces shrinking demand for its product, with no sign of improvement in the near future, the layoff of employees may well be the correct action. Boeing explicitly addressed this issue in its 1992 financial statement:

Company wide employment (including subsidiaries) was reduced by about 10,000 during 1992 and stood at 143,000 at the year's end. In 1993, production cutbacks will force us to eliminate approximately 23,000 jobs. Attrition and job transfers will be used to buffer the effects of this reduction, but substantial layoffs will also be necessary. This is a difficult period, and we intend to accomplish this downsizing with sensitivity to the needs of our employees.[4]

Boeing's management assumed that in the long term the market would pick up. Therefore, it continued to invest in research and development even in a year of layoffs:

To maintain its market leadership, Boeing continues to study the potential for model upgrades and new derivatives of its current product line, as well as the development of entirely new aircraft. The guiding strategy behind all the company's research efforts is to offer airline customers the most cost-efficient solution to their current and future needs. The test for any new technology is whether it can add value for airline customers by improving an aircraft's safety, operational efficiency, or economic utility. To meet the future needs of its airline customers, and to sustain the company's leadership in the 100–150 seat market, Boeing is actively studying new derivatives of the popular 737 series that would offer advanced features, while still retaining a high degree of commonality with the current 737 fleet.[5]

Boeing's financial statements spelled out the future goals of each of its branches. It was clear that management based the firm's growth rate on the world economy's recovery, using published data on macroeconomic factors:

Most economists look for world GDP [gross domestic product] to grow between 3 and 3.5 percent per year over the next 18 years. Based on that general forecast, Boeing expects that air travel will grow at an average annual rate of somewhat more than 5 percent through the year 2010 . . . . The company estimates that the total commercial jet transport market for this period will be over $800 billion in 1993 dollars. With the company's current line of jet transports, and its continuing commitment to upgrade current products and develop new ones to meet customer needs, Boeing is well positioned to sustain its historical leadership in the commercial airplane market.[6]

Did Boeing make the right decision in 1992? Did the demand for aircraft decline as predicted? As can be seen in Connecting Theory to Practice 18.2, the market for Boeing airplanes continued to decline in 1994 and 1995, which justified the decision to cut jobs.

---

4. Boeing 1992 financial statements.
5. Boeing 1992 financial statements.
6. Boeing 1992 financial statements.

CONNECTING THEORY TO PRACTICE 18.2

BOEING CUTS JOBS AS ORDERS FALL

Boeing, the U.S. aircraft maker, yesterday said it had not decided how many jobs would be cut as a result of falling orders from airlines. Boeing's statement followed a report that the company was about to announce a cut of 7,000 jobs and further fall in the production of 737 and 757 jets. Mr. Frank Shrontz, chairman, said last month the group's jet deliveries were likely to fall from 270 in 1994 to 230 this year. This compares with a 1993 delivery figure of 330.

Mr. Shrontz said: "Planned production rates will continue to be adjusted as necessary to match customer requirements. Unfavorable operation results being experienced by certain U.S. airlines may result in further selective production rate reductions." Boeing has sharply reduced employee numbers over the past few years. During 1993, they were cut by 18,000 to 125,500. By the end of last year, employee numbers had fallen further to a little over 117,000.

Source: Michael Skapinker, "Boeing to Cut Jobs as Orders Fall," *Financial Times*, 2 February 1995, p. 4. © Financial Times, 1995.

MAKING THE CONNECTION

The forecast of the jet deliveries for 1995 was almost on target: In 1995 Boeing delivered 206 jets, even less than the 230 forecast, and sales grew in 1996 by only 3%. The accurate information on the sharp decline in the demand for jets allowed the firm to plan its future activities accurately. Had it not made the drastic reduction in its labor force, Boeing would have been financially distressed. By cutting back during the recession years, Boeing managed to come out a winner when the market began to recover in early 1997. During 1997 Boeing received new orders for 559 aircraft worth $42.8 billion and claimed to hold 64 percent of the world aircraft market.[7]

The Boeing example touches on a number of the important ingredients of long-term financial planning:

1. The firm should first forecast economic trends. Any change in the economy as a whole could affect the firm's profitability.
2. Planning that looks 10 or 20 years ahead is not uncommon for a firm with a long R&D cycle such as Boeing. For instance, if Boeing did not invest in research and development, it could not compete 5 to 10 years down the road. Any decline in current demand for the firm's products could well be temporary.

For other firms that do not invest in research and development—supermarkets, for example—long-term plans may cover only 1 or 2 years.

7. See Michael Skapinker, "Boeing Wins 64% Share of Market," *Financial Times*, 8 January 1997, p. 4. © Financial Times, 1997.

3. The firm's goal is to maximize stockholders' wealth. This usually means that the firm should work to improve the product and to maintain or increase its market share. To achieve this, the firm should invest in research and development and, at the same time, should achieve a high degree of efficiency by such means as laying off unproductive employees. Although the financial implications of such plans are usually not reported in the firm's annual financial statements, they are without a doubt known in detail by the CFO.

4. Optimistic forecasts sometimes fail to materialize. Firms must be prepared for such an eventuality.

5. When a decline in sales represents a trend, the firm sometimes has no choice but to reduce investment in research and development. For example, in 1994 Boeing's outlay on research and development was $1,704 million; the corresponding figure for 1995 was $1,267 million—about a 25% reduction.

One goal of the firm's long-term financial plans is to forecast future cash flows and financial needs. When the firm has such a projection, it can make plans for the amount and timing of financing needs, as well as of expenditures. How does the firm use its financial blueprint to forecast future cash flows? The techniques it can use are discussed next.

18.3 PRO FORMA FINANCIAL STATEMENTS

A firm uses a planning tool called **pro forma** (or **projected**) **financial statements**, which show its financial needs or cash surplus in the forthcoming periods. Modeled on ex-post financial statements (published financial statements that show actual results from prior periods), pro forma financial statements are forecasted financial statements. The firm tries to estimate how its statements will look in the future. There are three pro forma statements: the pro forma balance sheet, the pro forma income statement, and the pro forma sources and uses of funds statement.

Table 18-1 summarizes Cotton Loom Corporation's 1996 ex-post financial statements (all figures are in $ thousand).[8] The main items are

1. *Depreciation.* Not a cash outflow, depreciation is recorded in the income statement as part of the cost of goods sold. Because it is not a cash payment, the $250 amount is added back as a source of funds in the sources and uses of funds statement.

2. *Fixed assets.* In the balance sheet we use fixed assets net of accumulated depreciation. As shown in the balance sheet, the investment in fixed assets (see Sources and Uses of Funds) less depreciation gives the change in fixed assets ($700 − $250 = $450). Thus, fixed assets grew from $7,550 to $8,000.

---

8. For easier explanation of underlying principles, the financial statements have been condensed.

TABLE 18-1
Cotton Loom's
1996 Financial
Statements
(in $ thousand)

Part a: Income Statement

Revenue	$8,000
Cost of goods sold	6,000
Earnings before interest	$2,000
Interest	1,000
Earnings before tax	$1,000
Tax at 35%	350
Net income	$650

Part b: Sources and Uses of Funds

Sources:	
Net income	$ 650
Depreciation	250
Operating cash flow	$ 900
Additional borrowing	1,000
Additional stock issue	0
Total sources	$1,900
Uses:	
Investment in fixed assets	$ 700
Stock repurchase	1,000
Dividends	200
Total uses	$1,900

Part c: Balance Sheet

	1996	1995	Change During the Year
Assets:			
Net working capital	$ 2,000	$2,000	0
Fixed assets (net of depreciation)	8,000	7,550	$ 450
Total assets	$10,000	$9,550	$ 450
Liabilities:			
Debt	$ 8,000	$7,000	$1,000
Equity	2,000	2,550	−550
Total liabilities	$10,000	$9,550	$ 450

Ever thought of starting your own business? British Columbia has an excellent OnLine Small Business Workshop that shows how to put together a business plan for a new venture, including cash flow forecasts, pro formas, and all the other elements of a good business plan.
http://www.sb.gov.bc.ca

3. *Debt/equity ratio.* The firm changed its debt/equity ratio during the year. It borrowed $1,000 and used the funds to repurchase $1,000 of its equity.

Let us look at how the changes in equity and retained earnings are calculated: The change in the book value of equity is given by:

$$\text{Change in the book value of equity} \tag{18.1}$$
$$= \text{Net income} + \text{Stock issue} - \text{Dividends} - \text{Stock repurchase}$$

Cotton Loom issued no new stock. Therefore, we have

$$
\begin{array}{c}
\text{Change in the}\\
\text{book value of equity}
\end{array}
= \underset{\substack{\downarrow\\ \text{Net}\\ \text{income}}}{\$650}
+ \underset{\substack{\downarrow\\ \text{Stock}\\ \text{issue}}}{\$0}
- \underset{\substack{\downarrow\\ \text{Dividend}}}{\$200}
- \underset{\substack{\downarrow\\ \text{Stock}\\ \text{repurchase}}}{\$1,000}
= -\$550
$$

Table 18-1 summarizes the financial consequences of the firm's actions during 1996. A similar framework can be used to prepare the pro forma financial statements for the next few years. To do so, the firm must include plans regarding its capital expenditure, dividend policy, and debt/equity ratio, in addition to its forecasts of sales and costs.

Let us attempt a few forecasts for Cotton Loom: Suppose sales and cost of goods sold are expected to increase by 5% in 1997. However, to take advantage of new production technology, the firm plans to invest in new machines to maintain its market share. The new fixed assets are expected to involve a $3 million capital expenditure. The firm intends to increase its dividends by 5%. Because the firm's debt/equity ratio is rather high, interest costs are also rather high; and Cotton Loom decides to finance all its needs in 1997 by issuing stock. To calculate the dollar amount of the stock issue, the firm first must prepare pro forma financial statements, listing its financial needs, as shown in Table 18-2.

The pro forma statements (with all figures in $ thousand) reveal that

1. Revenue and cost of goods sold are forecasted to grow by 5%. These two items generally grow at the same rate, as here.
2. Depreciation, which was $250 in 1996, is expected to increase to $285 in 1997 due to the additional investment made in 1996. This is not a cash outflow, and as before, it is added back as a source of funds.
3. Because the firm is planning a capital expenditure of $3,000 and dividend payments of $210, it needs an external financing source. The **external financial needs (EFN)** are defined and calculated as follows:

$$\text{External financial needs} = \text{Uses of funds} - \text{Operating cash flows} \tag{18.2}$$

In our example, EFN = $2,210 ($3,210 − $1,000 = $2,210). Since the firm plans to raise this money by issuing stock, management will have to prepare a prospectus, initiate negotiations with underwriters, and so on. The pro forma statements provide information regarding financing needs or accumulated cash.

TABLE 18-2
Cotton Loom's
1997 Pro Forma
Financial
Statements
(in $ thousand)

Part a: Income Statement

		Changes and Explanations
Revenue	$8,400	+5%
Costs of goods sold	6,300	+5%
Earnings before interest and taxes	$2,100	
Interest	1,000	
Earnings before tax	$1,100	
Tax of 35%	385	
Net income	$ 715	

Part b: Sources and Uses of Funds

Sources:	
Net income	$ 715
Depreciation	285
Operating cash flow	$1,000
Borrowing	0
New issue	2,210
Total	$3,210
Uses:	
Investment	$3,000
Stock repurchase	0
Dividends	210
Total uses	$3,210

Part c: Balance Sheet

	1997	1996	Changes
Assets:			
Net working capital	$ 2,000	$ 2,000	$ 0
Fixed assets (net of depreciation)	10,715	8,000	+ 2,715
Total assets	$12,715	$10,000	+$2,715
Liabilities:			
Debt	$ 8,000	$ 8,000	$ 0
Equity	4,715	2,000	+ 2,715
Total liabilities	$12,715	$10,000	+$2,715

4. There is no forecasted change in net working capital. On the pro forma balance sheet, fixed assets grew by $2,715, calculated as follows:

$$\$2,715 \quad = \quad \$3,000 \quad - \quad \$285$$

↓	↓	↓
Additional fixed assets	Capital expenditure	Depreciation

Because there is no forecasted change in the debt, Cotton Loom can use only the increase in equity during the year and the new level of equity at the end of 1997 to balance its pro forma balance sheet. The change in the book value of equity is obtained as follows (see Equation (18.1)):

Change in the book value of equity

= Net income – Dividends + New stock issue – Stock repurchase

In the Cotton Loom case we obtain the following net change in the equity forecasted for year 1997:

Increase in the book value of equity = $715 – $210 + $2,210 – $0 = $2,715

We see that Cotton Loom repurchased stock in 1996 and issued new shares in 1997. The firm's actions during 1996 and the pro forma statements for 1997 can be interpreted in two alternate ways: (1) The firm did not engage in long-term planning prior to 1996. Evidence for this view is Cotton Loom's stock repurchase in 1996 and its need for a stock issue just one year later. In the absence of other economic factors not known to us (i.e., the stock price may have been very low at the time of the repurchase in 1996, or the 1997 investment opportunities were not known in 1996), the stock repurchase in 1996 would seem to have been a misguided decision. Or, (2) the firm had long-term plans but made errors in the forecast of its future financial position.

The following problem projects the equity Cotton Loom will need in 1998.

PRACTICE BOX

Problem

Suppose Cotton Loom intends in 1998 to clear the debt on its balance sheet (because the interest rate is too high and the board of directors has decided on a zero–debt policy). Sales are forecasted to grow 10% by 1998. Due to improved production efficiency, the cost of goods sold will increase by only 8%. Capital expenditure will be $5,000, and dividends will remain at their 1997 level. Depreciation will be $467. Prepare Cotton Loom's pro forma financial statements for 1998. How much equity should the firm raise in 1998? (Present all figures in $ thousand.)

(continued)

Solution   **TABLE 18-3**   **Cotton Loom's 1998 Pro Forma Financial Statements (in $ thousand)**

Part a: Income Statement

		Changes and Explanations
Revenue	$ 9,240	10% growth
Cost of goods sold	6,804	8% growth
Income before interest and taxes	$ 2,436	
Interest	1,000	
Earnings before tax	$ 1,436	
Tax at 35% rate	503	(Round number—The precise number is 502.6)
Net income	$ 933	

Part b: Sources and Uses of Funds

Sources:		
Net income	$ 933	
Depreciation	467	(Mainly depreciation on the machine purchased in 1996)
Operating cash flow	1,400	
Additional stock issued	?	(We need to solve for this value)
Total	$13,210	
Uses:		
Investment	$ 5,000	
Dividends	210	
Redemption of debt	8,000	
Total	$13,210	

Part c: Balance Sheet

	1998	1997	Change
Assets:			
Net working capital	$ 2,000	$ 2,000	0
Fixed assets (net of depreciation)	15,248	10,715	4,533
Total assets	$17,248	$12,715	$4,533
Liabilities:			
Debt	$ 0	$ 8,000	−$8,000
Equity	17,248	4,715	12,533
Total	$17,248	$12,715	$4,533

Table 18-3 provides the solution. Let's examine the various items in these statements: First, revenue is forecasted to grow by 10%; cost of goods sold, by 8%. The firm will pay interest of $1,000 because the debt is redeemed at the end of the year. Thus, the pro forma net income is $933.

The firm's operating cash flow is $1,400. However, the firm needs $13,210 for capital expenditure, debt redemption, and dividend payment. Because the operating cash flow is only $1,400, the stock issue needed in 1998 will be $11,810 ($13,210 − $1,400 = $11,810). Fixed assets grow by the additional $5,000 investment less the $467 depreciation, to give $4,533.

Because the firm intends to redeem all its debt, the debt on the 1998 pro forma balance sheet is reduced by $8,000 to $0. Finally, the change in equity is obtained by Equation (18.1)

> Change in the book value of equity
> = Net income − Dividend + New stock issue − Stock repurchase

which in our example is

> Change in equity = $933 − $210 + $11,810 − $0 = $12,533

Hence, the equity on the pro forma balance sheet for 1998 is

$4,715	+	$12,533	=	$17,248
↓		↓		↓
Equity in 1997		Change in equity		Equity in 1998

18.4 FORECASTING SALES USING REGRESSION ANALYSIS

Because it provides the basis for deriving most of the other items, the sales forecast is the most crucial ingredient in the pro forma financial statement. Some of the other pro forma items are directly related to sales (i.e., cost of goods sold), and some are indirectly related to sales (i.e., additional required inventory and additional required fixed assets). Due to normal economic growth or as a result of the firm's aggressive promotional action, sales can change over time.

The normal growth of sales can be extrapolated by reviewing the firm's past record. We will demonstrate it by studying Boeing Corporation's sales record. Figure 18-1 depicts Boeing's actual sales for the years 1988–1992 and forecasted sales for years 1993–1995. Sales for 1993 were forecasted using a simple technique: Draw a straight line through the actual sales points given in Figure 18-1 for 1988–1992 sales and then continue this line to point P, to obtain projected sales in 1993. The straight line that best fits all the points is called a *regression line*.

In Figure 18-1, sales (in million $) correspond to the straight line:

$$\text{Sales in year } t = a + b \times t \tag{18.3}$$

where point *a* is the value at which the straight line intersects the vertical axis and *b* is its slope. To facilitate an easier calculation, we denote 1988 as Year 8. Thus 1989 is

FIGURE 18-1   **Boeing's Sales for 1988–1995: The Linear Regression**

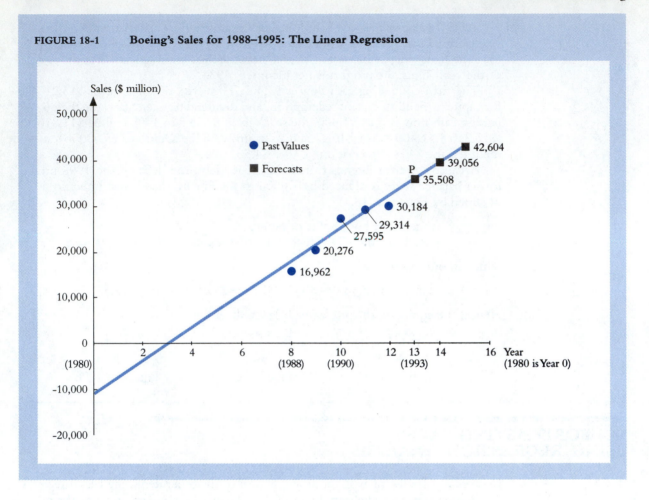

Year 9, 1990 is Year 10, and so on. If we denote the year by x_i (which is the actual year minus 1980) and sales in this year by y_i, the regression line can be written as follows:

$$y_i = a + bx_i$$

The estimates of a and b are given by

$$b = \left(\sum_{i=1}^{n} x_i y_i - n\overline{x}\,\overline{y}\right)\Big/\left(\sum_{i=1}^{n} x_i^2 - n\overline{x}^2\right)$$

$$a = \overline{y} - b\overline{x}$$

where $\overline{y}$ and $\overline{x}$ are the averages of the two variables:

$$\overline{y} = \frac{1}{n}\sum_{i=1}^{n} y_i$$

$$\bar{x} = \frac{1}{n}\sum_{i=1}^{n}x_i$$

and n is the number of observations.

We demonstrate the regression technique to estimate sales by using five years of figures for Boeing Corporation.[9] Using the Boeing example, we have $a = -10{,}616$ and $b = 3{,}548$.[10]

Plugging in the estimates for a and b, we find that Boeing's projected sales for 1993 are as follows:

$$\text{Projected sales} = a + b \times (1993 - 1980)$$

$$= -\$10{,}616 \text{ million} + \$3{,}548 \text{ million} \times 13$$

$$= \$35{,}508 \text{ million}$$

This amount equals the value shown by point P. The sales for 1994, 1995, and beyond can be estimated in the same way: Substitute $14 = 1994 - 1980$ for x_i to obtain the 1994 sales; substitute $x_i = 15 = 1995 - 1980$ to obtain the 1995 sales, and so forth. Thus, for 1994 we obtain

$$\text{Projected sales} = -\$10{,}616 \text{ million} + \$3{,}548 \text{ million} \times 14$$

$$= \$39{,}056 \text{ million}$$

For 1995 we obtain

$$\text{Projected sales} = -\$10{,}616 \text{ million} + \$3{,}548 \text{ million} \times 15$$

$$= \$42{,}604 \text{ million}$$

The regression method has two main advantages: (1) It is quick and simple, and (2) it does not depend on personal or subjective judgment that, in the case of management, may reflect overoptimism or reluctance to accept bad news.

The disadvantages of the regression technique are that it allocates the same weight to each point of time (year), and it does not reflect information known to management regarding the future (such as new orders). If we had used only data from 1990–1992 to predict future sales, we would have made much lower sales estimates. In Boeing's case it is obvious that sales in 1990–1992 were a better indicator of the firm's financial status than the entire period 1988–1993, during which a large growth in sales occurred. For example, sales jumped by over $7 billion in 1990. However, sales growth was moderate in 1991 and 1992. In Boeing's case new orders are a more reliable indicator of future sales than the regression equation gives us. Indeed, new orders were only $17.8 billion in 1992 compared to $20.6 billion in 1991. In its 1992 financial statements, Boeing's management announced:

Due to lower demand, and the growing number of requests by customer airlines to defer orders, the company will cut production rates on Boeing 737, 747, 757, and 767 jetliners. By mid-

9. For such regression analysis, one generally needs more than five years. However, to avoid cumbersome calculations here, we use only that number of years. Whatever number of years, using only the regression technique to estimate sales by a firm such as Boeing (which has a lot of information on the future deliveries of jets) can present dangers, which we'll discuss in the text. Thus, using a smaller number of years facilitates the demonstration without losing the main points that we want to emphasize.

10. The slope of the line is b. It tells us that for each one-unit change in x (years), y (sales) increases by $3,548 million.

1994, after all these rate reductions are in effect, Boeing will be producing 21 jetliners per month—compared with 32.5 at year-end 1992.[11]

This cut in production represented a drastic reduction in business (a drop of about 35%). Thus, at the end of 1992, stable revenue from sales—but certainly not growth—could be forecasted for 1993 and 1994. However, the regression technique reveals a positive growth in sales (and an estimated $35,508 million sales for the year 1993). In fact, a better estimate would have been a reduction in sales—maybe not in 1993 but certainly in 1994 and 1995.

Boeing's sales forecast clearly demonstrates that management should not rely solely on the regression technique. Actual sales dropped to around $25 billion in 1993 and continued to fall in 1994, to about $21 billion. In 1995 sales were $19.5 billion. In 1996 sales grew slightly to $20.7 billion. (At the end of 1996 it was announced that Boeing was merging with McDonnell-Douglas to create a firm with sales of about $34 billion.) In contrast, for 1994 the regression technique yielded $39.1 billion, or almost twice the actual 1994 sales, and for 1995, the regression technique forecast $42,604 million, again about twice the actual sales. We see that for accurate sales forecasts, management must also use other information at its disposal.

The regression technique is definitely misleading—and inappropriate—in Boeing's case. It produces inaccurate results because it assumes that future sales follow the same pattern as past sales did. Boeing only needed to review its order book to see that the pattern had changed.

Under what circumstances is the regression technique useful? In the case of supermarkets or in the food and drug industry, the regression technique is probably better than subjective forecasts. In such industries, long-term orders do not accumulate years in advance. The regression technique is probably the most appropriate means of predicting future sales when sales grow at a random rate corresponding, more or less, to the inflation rate and the economic growth rate, and when there is no other information regarding new competitors, innovation, and so on. In other cases, however (such as Boeing), human judgment and accumulated information regarding customer orders should be exercised in sales forecasting.

Because they determine the firm's financial needs, estimates of sales growth are crucial. Pro forma financial statements are one way of estimating those needs. In the next section, we discuss a different approach to determine the firm's financial needs.

18.5 FORECASTING A FIRM'S EXTERNAL FINANCIAL NEEDS

The firm's external financial needs for the next year are calculated on the basis of forecasted sales as follows:

$$\text{External financial needs} = \text{Required increase in assets} \tag{18.4}$$
$$- \text{Increase in "automatic" liabilities} - (\text{Next year's net income} - \text{Dividend})$$

11. Boeing 1992 financial statements.

All these variables are directly related to the sales forecast. Therefore, the key variable in estimating the EFN is the estimated growth rate of sales. Then all the other variables can be calculated by assuming that all variables change at the same rate as sales. Before we discuss the formula for the EFN calculation, let us demonstrate the calculation by means of a simple example.

The 1997 financial statements of International Electronics contain the following data (in $ millions):

Sales	$3,000
Total assets	6,000
Net income	300
Accounts payable	500
Dividends	150
Net Income – Dividends	150

The firm's management estimates that sales will grow by 20% in 1998. What is the EFN for 1998?

The **linear model** assumes that all variables grow linearly with sales—that is, all variables are assumed to grow by the same percentage as sales. To be specific, because sales are estimated to grow by 20% ($3,000 × 1.2 = $3,600), total assets will also grow by 20% ($6,000 × 1.2 = $7,200). Therefore, the firm will need $1,200 ($7,200 − $6,000 = $1,200) to finance the growth in total assets.

Automatic growth refers to funds obtained by simply maintaining the same payment policy. For example, if sales increase and the firm does not change its policy regarding payment to creditors and suppliers, accounts payable will also grow by 20%, to $600 ($500 × 1.2 = $600). An increase in accounts payable implies that the firm borrows, so to speak, from its suppliers. Hence, the $100 growth in accounts payable ($600 − $500 = $100) represents a source of funds based on "automatic" growth. Since management needs to take no special action to obtain these funds, the term "automatic" is used. The firm may also possess other **automatic liabilities**—liabilities that increase automatically as sales increase, such as state sales taxes or debt to the IRS.

The final variable in Equation (18.4) is net income less dividends, which equals the change in retained earnings. Because net income less cash dividends is an internal source of financing, it is subtracted in calculating the external financial needs. Looking at our example of International Electronics, we see the firm's net income was $300 in 1997, and that amount is assumed to grow by 20% in 1998 ($300 × 1.2 = $360). If it maintains a payout ratio of 50%, the firm will pay $180 of its net income as dividends and retain $180. We then can estimate the EFN as follows:

$$\text{EFN} = \$1,200 - \$100 - \$180 = \$920$$

Thus, the firm will need an additional $920 from external sources (debt or equity) to finance the forecasted expansion.

18.5.1 The Linear Formula

By the linear model described above, sales, assets, liabilities, net income, and dividends, all grow at the same rate, G. Therefore, the EFN formula can be written as follows:

$$\text{EFN} = (\text{Assets} \times G) - (\text{``Automatic'' liabilities} \times G)$$
$$- [(\text{Net income} - \text{Cash dividends}) \times (1 + G)]$$

Note that we multiply the final term by $(1 + G)$ and the other terms by G because all of this (net income − cash dividends) is a source of funds for the next year while only the change in assets and "automatic" liabilities will affect next year's funds. This formula can be rewritten as follows:

$$\text{EFN} = a + b \times G \qquad\qquad (18.5)$$

where

$a = -(\text{Net income} - \text{Cash dividends})$ (note the minus sign)

$b = (\text{Assets} - \text{``Automatic'' liabilities} - \text{Net Income} + \text{Cash Dividends})$

$G = \text{Growth rate}$

Note that a and b are constant and that EFN and G vary.

Applying this formula to the International Electronics example, we find that (note that in this case "automatic" liabilities are simply accounts payable)

$$a = -\$150$$

$$b = \$6{,}000 - \$500 - \$300 + \$150 = \$5{,}350$$

Because $G = 20\%$, we get

$$\text{EFN} = -\$150 + (\$5{,}350 \times 0.2) = \$920$$

This result is the same as that obtained before by our direct calculation of EFN using Equation (18.4).

Figure 18-2 illustrates the linear relationship for two firms labeled A and B. Note that when the EFN is negative, the firm is generating funds, and management should have a plan for the use of these funds. Because Firm B uses a relatively low level of investment to create its sales, its EFN is less sensitive to changes in the sales growth rate. However, by the same token, the firm generates very few funds when the growth rate is relatively low. The opposite holds for Firm A. Firm A's management should invest more effort in predicting the growth rate, G, because small errors in forecasting G will produce much sharper fluctuations in firm A's EFN. Any error in estimating sales growth will have more severe implications for Firm A than for Firm B.

You may get the impression that the more successful a firm is, the more money it needs to spend. This is the case for those years in which the firm experiences rapid growth. However, as the firm matures, sales growth slows, and EFN becomes negative. Cash inflows are then available to distribute as dividends or to repurchase stock.

It is also common to express the EFN by the following formula, which yields the same value for EFN as Equation (18.5):

$$\text{EFN} = P_A \Delta S - P_{AL} \Delta S - P_{NI} \times S_1 \times (1 - d) \qquad\qquad (18.6)$$

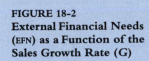

FIGURE 18-2
External Financial Needs (EFN) as a Function of the Sales Growth Rate (G)

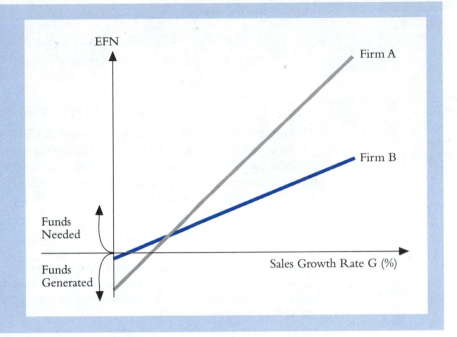

where

$$P_A = \text{Ratio of assets to sales}$$

$$P_{AL} = \text{Ratio of "automatic" liabilities to sales}$$

$$P_{NI} = \text{Ratio of net income to sales}$$

$$S_1 = \text{Forecasted sales for next year}$$

$$\Delta S = \text{Forecasted change in sales}$$

$$d = \text{Payout ratio}$$

In our International Electronics example, we have

$$P_A = \frac{\$6,000}{\$3,000} = 2$$

$$P_{AL} = \frac{\$500}{\$3,000} \cong 0.167$$

$$P_{NI} = \frac{\$300}{\$3,000} = 0.1$$

$$S_1 = \$3,000 \times 1.2 = \$3,600$$

$$\Delta S = \$3,600 - \$3,000 = \$600$$

$$d = \frac{\$150}{\$300} = 0.5$$

Using Equation (18.6) and the previous figures, we obtain

$$\text{EFN} = (P_A \times \Delta S) - (P_{AL} \times \Delta S) - [P_{NI} \times S_1 \times (1 - d)]$$

$$\text{EFN} = 2 \times \$600 - (0.167 \times \$600) - [0.1 \times \$3,600 \times (1 - 0.5)]$$

or

$$\text{EFN} = \$1,200 - \$100 - \$180 = \$920$$

This result is exactly the same as we obtained using Equation (18.5).[12]

So far we have stated the EFN formula in terms of the external financial needs for the next year. If we assume that the growth rate remains constant, we can revise the formula to determine the external financial needs in any particular year in the future. For example, the external financial needs $t + 1$ years from now will be

$$\text{EFN}_{t+1} = (\text{Assets}_t \times G) - (\text{``Automatic'' liabilities}_t \times G)$$
$$- [\text{Net income less cash dividends}]_t \times (1 + G)$$

where the subscript t indicates "t years from now."

Because we are assuming that the growth rate remains constant for each year, we can express the year-t parameters in terms of current-year parameters. This is done using the following formulas:

$$\text{Assets}_t = \text{Assets} \times (1 + G)^t$$

$$\text{``Automatic'' liabilities}_t = \text{``Automatic'' liabilities} \times (1 + G)^t$$

$$[\text{Net income less cash dividends}]_t = \text{Current net income less}$$
$$\text{Current cash dividends} \times (1 + G)^t$$

where Assets, "Automatic" liabilities, and Change in retained earnings, are the parameters of the current year.

Plugging these definitions into the formula for EFN_{t+1} we finally obtain

$$\text{EFN}_{t+1} = \text{Assets} \times (1 + G)^t \times G - \text{``Automatic'' liabilities} \times (1 + G)^t \times G$$
$$- (\text{Net Income less Dividends}) \times (1 + G)^{t+1}$$

For example, using this formula, we can estimate the external financial needs of International Electronics three years hence. Inserting the numbers, we obtain (in millions)

$$\text{EFN}_3 = \$6,000 \times (1 + 0.2)^2 \times 0.2 - \$500 \times (1 + 0.2)^2 \times 0.2 - [\$300 - \$150] \times (1 + 0.2)^3$$
$$= \$1,324.8$$

Thus, if the growth rate of 20% per year will continue for 3 years, by the third year International Electronics will require external financing of $1,324.8 million.

---

12. It is not surprising that we obtained the same result as before. The reason is that $P_A \Delta S = \dfrac{\text{Assets}}{\text{Sales}} \times \text{Change in Sales}$ is nothing but assets times the growth rate of sales. Similarly, $P_{AL} \times \Delta S = \dfrac{\text{Automatic Liabilities}}{\text{Sales}} \times \text{Change in Sales}$ equals automatic liabilities $\times G$. And finally, $P_{NI} \times S_1(1 - d) = \dfrac{\text{Net income}}{\text{Sales}} \times \text{Sales}(1 + G)(1 - d) = (\text{Net income less dividends}) \times (1 + G)$. Thus Equations (18.5) and (18.6) yield the same EFN.

18.5.2 Using a Spreadsheet for Financial Forecasting

In financial planning and in preparing pro forma financial statements, a firm must consider many variables simultaneously, and there are a range of estimates for each item appearing in the financial statements. The analysis can be quite complex. Furthermore, as time passes and more information is accumulated, the firm may have to revise its forecasts. Manually preparing a pro forma statement for each scenario is both time-consuming and inefficient. Fortunately, computer spreadsheet programs such as Lotus 1–2–3 and Excel are capable of providing pro forma statements for all possible changes and estimates. The spreadsheet technique is especially useful when pro forma statements are needed for relatively long future time spans. For example, in 1997 Microsoft published its pro forma statements as a spreadsheet file on its Internet site. Stockholders and potential investors could forecast earnings by downloading the file and inserting different estimates for future income statement items.

Table 18-4 presents the income statement of Computer Users Company for 1996. The table also presents the firm's forecasted income statements for 1997–2005, which were generated using the Excel spreadsheet program. The basic idea in generating the forecasts is to enter the formulas that allow the spreadsheet to calculate the income statement. For example, the financial analyst would enter the following formula:

$$\text{Earnings before interest and taxes} = \text{Sales} - \text{Cost of goods sold}$$

The spreadsheet then would apply that formula for all years considered. After entering all the formulas for building the income statement in each year, the analyst enters the formulas governing the changes from year to year. In our example the firm forecasts that sales and costs of goods sold will grow at an annual rate of 10% and that interest is expected to remain the same. Using these simple relationships, the spreadsheet can forecast the income statement for any number of years.

TABLE 18-4	Pro Forma Income Statement of Computer Users Company, 1996–2005 ($ million)									
Growth	10%									
Income Statement (in million $)										
Year	1996	1997	1998	1999	2000	2001	2002	2003	2004	2005
Sales	100.00	110.00	121.00	133.10	146.41	161.05	177.16	194.87	214.36	235.79
Cost of goods sold	60.00	66.00	72.60	79.86	87.85	96.63	106.29	116.92	128.62	141.48
Earnings before interest and taxes	40.00	44.00	48.40	53.24	58.56	64.42	70.86	77.95	85.74	94.32
Interest	20.00	20.00	20.00	20.00	20.00	20.00	20.00	20.00	20.00	20.00
Earnings before taxes	20.00	24.00	28.40	33.24	38.56	44.42	50.86	57.95	65.74	74.32
Taxes (35%)	7.00	8.40	9.94	11.63	13.50	15.55	17.80	20.28	23.01	26.01
Net Income	13.00	15.60	18.46	21.61	25.07	28.87	33.06	37.67	42.73	48.31

TABLE 18-5 Pro Forma Net Income of Computer Users Company for Various Estimates of the Growth Rate in Sales ($ million)	Growth Rate	Forecasted Net Income				
		1996	1997	1998	1999	2000
	0%	13.00	13.00	13.00	13.00	13.00
	5%	13.00	14.30	15.67	17.10	18.60
	10%	13.00	15.60	18.46	21.61	25.07
	15%	13.00	16.90	21.39	26.54	32.47
	20%	13.00	18.20	24.44	31.93	40.91

What if Computer Users Company is uncertain about the growth estimate of 10%? Does the analyst have to redo all the above work? Not at all. One advantage of using spreadsheets is the ease in which changes of parameters can be performed. Most modern spreadsheets can automatically create tables with ranges of estimates. For example, assume Computer Users Company is uncertain about the growth rate but estimates it to be in the range of 0% to 20%. Table 18-5, generated with an Excel spreadsheet, presents the forecasted net income in years 1996–2000 for estimates of growth rates in that range. As we can see, for a growth rate of 0%, net income will remain constant at $13 million. For a growth rate of 20%, net income will more than quadruple by the year 2000. Once it further refines its growth estimates, the firm can use the same technique to refine its net income estimates. Thus, if Computer Users Company estimates the growth rate to be between 5% and 15%, it can conclude that net income in the year 2000 will be in the range of $18.6 million to $32.47 million.

APPLYING THEORY TO PRACTICE 18.1

PACCAR, INC.'S PRO FORMA STATEMENTS

PACCAR, Inc. manufactures heavy-duty diesel trucks, as well as mining and logging vehicles, railcars, winches, and various truck replacement parts. The firm has 13 plants in the United States, Canada, Australia, Mexico, and the United Kingdom. We will use the following data to prepare pro forma financial statements:

	1992	1993
Revenues per share ($)	80.85	104.50
"Cash flow" per share ($)	3.30	5.60
Earnings per share ($)	1.93	4.00
Dividend declared per share ($)	1.30	2.00
Capital spending per share ($)	2.40	2.25
Book value per share ($)	30.70	33.00

Common shares outstanding (millions)	33.80	33.50
Revenues ($ million)	2,735.20	3,500.00
Operating margin	7.3%	8.0%
Depreciation ($ million)	47.20	53.00
Net profit ($ million)	65.20	134.00
Income tax rate	28.8%	35.0%
Net profit margin	2.4%	3.8%
Working capital ($ million)	1,225.80	1,310.00
Long-term debt ($ million)	498.60	640.00
Net worth ($ million)	1,038.40	1,105.00
Retained earnings to common equity (%)	2.7	6.0
All dividends to net profit (%)	57.0	50.0

Note: The 1993 data are based partially on realized figures; and on estimates for the latter part of 1993.

Source: *Value Line Investment Survey*, September 17, 1993.

Additional information:
1. The total value of PACCAR's assets in 1993 was $1,500 million.
2. Estimates for years 1994, 1995, 1996: Sales are expected to increase by 20% in 1994, 1995, and 1996. The ratio of cost of goods sold to revenue will be 0.89, which is about the same as in 1993. The firm's capital spending will be $55 million for each of the three years. The tax rate is 35%. Annual depreciation will be a constant $57 million. The total debt in 1993 was $1,185 million on which PACCAR paid $106 million interest; the firm does not plan to change its total debt in the next three years. In 1994 the firm plans to increase the dividend per share, and the total dividend payment will be $85 million. The firm plans to maintain this level of dividend per share in 1995 and 1996. There will be no change in net working capital. To produce the increase in sales, there will be no need to invest in more assets beyond the $55 million capital spending mentioned previously. The firm has overcapacity, and the size of its assets will be the same as in 1993. If there is a cash surplus during the next three years, the firm will repurchase some of its shares; if there is a cash deficit, the firm will issue more stock.

Questions
1. Prepare pro forma income statements and pro forma sources and uses of funds statements for 1994, 1995, and 1996. Should the firm prepare a prospectus and attempt to raise more equity in 1994–1996?
2. The firm's total assets are $1,500 million. It has no automatic liabilities. Use the EFN formula to estimate the EFN for 1994, 1995, and 1996 at a growth rate of 20%.
3. How can your answers to Questions 1 and 2 be reconciled? Which estimate is more accurate?

MAKING THE CONNECTION

1. We construct the firm's pro forma income statements and pro forma sources and uses of funds statements for years 1994–1996 on the basis of the previous data:

Income Statement (in $ million)

		1994	Explanation	1995	Explanation	1996	Explanation
(1)	Revenue	4,200.0	$(3,500 \times 1.2)$	5,040.00	$(3,500 \times 1.2^2)$	6,048.000	$(3,500 \times 1.2^3)$
(2) = (1) × 0.89	Cost of goods sold	3,738.0	$(4,200 \times 0.89)$	4485.60	$(5,040 \times 0.89)$	5,382.720	$(6,043 \times 0.89)$
(3) = (2) − (1)	Earnings before interest	462.0		554.40		665.280	
(4)	Interest	106.0		106.00		106.000	
(5) = (3) − (4)	Earnings before taxes	356.0		448.40		559.280	
(6) = (5) × 0.35	Tax (35%)	124.6		156.94		195.748	
(7) = (5) − (6)	Net income	231.4		291.46		363.532	

Sources and Uses of Funds

	1994	1995	1996	Explanation
Sources				
Net income	231.4	291.46	363.532	Because depreciation is included in the cost
Depreciation	57.0	57.00	57.000 ←	and is not a cash outflow, we add it as a source of cash.
Operating cash flow	288.4	348.46	420.532	
Stock issue or repurchase	$-x$	$-x$	$-x$ ←	We will solve for x to balance out the sources and uses. Remember that by accounting rules, sources and uses must balance.
	140	140	140	
Uses				
Capital spending	55	55	55	
Dividends	85	85	85	
Total uses	140	140	140	

Thus, for 1994 the firm has a surplus of

$$x = \$288.4 \text{ million} - \$140 \text{ million} = \$148.4 \text{ million}$$

The firm will repurchase its stocks for this amount. For the subsequent years, the surplus grows to the following amounts:

1995: $x = \$348.46 \text{ million} - \$140 \text{ million} = \$208.46 \text{ million}$

1996: $x = \$420.532 \text{ million} - \$140 \text{ million} = \$280.532 \text{ million}$

Therefore, the company will be able to repurchase its stock or reduce its debt in these years also.

2. To calculate the EFN for 1994, we will use the linear formula from Section 18.5.1. Automatic liabilities are zero. Thus, for 1994 we have

$$\text{EFN} = \text{Assets} \times G - [\text{Net income} - \text{Dividends}] \times (1 + G)$$

The net income is $134 million, and the dividend is $67 million ($2 per share $\times$ 33.5 million shares = $67 million). Therefore, Net income − dividends is $67 million ($134 million − $67 million). Assets are given as $1,500 million and G is assumed to be 20%. Plugging these numbers into the formula, we obtain

$$\text{EFN} = \$1{,}500 \text{ million} \times 0.2 - \$67 \text{ million} \times (1 + 0.2) = \$219.6 \text{ million}$$

To estimate the EFN for 1995 and 1996, we will use the multi-year EFN formula given in Section 18.5.1 of this chapter. The EFN in 1995 (two years from 1993) is

$$\text{EFN}_2 = \text{Assets} \times (1 + G) \times G - (\text{Net income less dividends}) \times (1 + G)^2$$

$$= \$1{,}500 \text{ million} \times 1.2 \times 0.2 - \$67 \text{ million} \times 1.2^2$$

$$= \$263.52 \text{ million}$$

For 1996 the EFN will be

$$\text{EFN}_3 = \text{Assets} \times (1 + G)^2 \times G - (\text{Net Income less Dividends}) \times (1 + G)^3$$

$$= \$1{,}500 \text{ million} \times 1.2^2 \times 0.2 - \$67 \times 1.2^3 \cong \$316.22 \text{ million}$$

3. According to the linear formula, the firm needs to raise $219.6 million in 1994, $263.52 million in 1995, and $316.22 million in 1996. However, according to the pro forma analysis, the firm has a surplus of funds ($148.4 million in 1994, $208.46 million in 1995, and $280.532 million in 1996) and should repurchase some of its stock. The critical item here is the 20% growth in assets that the EFN formula assumes. The firm's management believes it can increase sales by 20% with no need to increase the firm's assets. If, indeed, the firm has production overcapacity, the linear formula is wrong, and the pro forma analysis is more accurate.

    The lesson to be learned from this case is that the EFN formula assumes that all items grow at the same rate, whereas in practice this is not usually so. In this example, for instance, if the assumption of overcapacity is found to be correct, the firm's costs will not increase at the same rate as sales. Therefore, the EFN formula will not be applicable in this specific case.

SUMMARY

Most firms engage in long-term planning. The range of such planning will be related to the industry's characteristics—it could be one or two years for a grocery store or 20 years for a firm such as Boeing.

The main component in forecasting a firm's future development is its sales. Growth in sales may depend on the overall state of the economy, or it may be due to the firm's aggressive promotion action. Estimates for the growth rate provide the basis for the pro forma financial statements and the linear model by which the firm forecasts its future external financial needs (or surplus of cash). The following items generally fluctuate with sales:

1. Costs of goods sold
2. Capital expenditure
3. Accounts payable
4. Accounts receivable
5. Inventory

Once the firm has forecasts for these items, it will be able to make decisions regarding

6. Cash dividends
7. Level of debt
8. Level of equity

Even if the firm does not take any special action to change its sales figures, fluctuations will take place in the volume of sales due to fluctuations in the economy, and Items 1 through 5 will fluctuate accordingly. However, Items 6 through 8 are variables about which the firm can make choices, such as deciding on the debt/equity ratio or the dividend policy.

Finally, recall that growth does not always require external funds; a firm may be very profitable and generate its own funds.

CHAPTER AT A GLANCE

1. The pro forma financial statements include
    a. An income statement
    b. A sources and uses of funds statement
    c. A balance sheet

2. Change in the book value of equity:

    Changes in the book value of equity = Net income − Cash dividends + Stock issue − Stock repurchase

3. External financial needs (EFN):

    $$\text{EFN} = \text{Required increase in assets} - \text{Increase in ``automatic'' liabilities}$$
    $$- \text{Next year's net income less cash dividends}$$

4. Linear formula for EFN:

    $$\text{EFN} = a + (b \times G)$$

    where a and b are constants and G is the forecasted growth rate of sales

5. Linear formula is also expressed as

    $$\text{EFN} = P_A \Delta S - P_{AL} \Delta S - P_{NI} \times S_1 \times (1 - d)$$

    where

$$\textsc{efn} = \text{External financial needs}$$

$$P_A = \text{Ratio of assets to sales}$$

$$P_{AL} = \text{Ratio of ``automatic'' liabilities to sales}$$

$$P_{NI} = \text{Ratio of net income to sales}$$

$$S_1 = \text{Forecasted sales for next year}$$

$$\Delta S = \text{Change in sales}$$

$$d = \text{Payout ratio}$$

KEY TERMS

Pro forma (projected) financial statements

External financial needs (EFN)
Automatic growth

Automatic liabilities

REVIEW AND PRACTICE

18.1 What are the basic ingredients of a firm's financial blueprint?

18.2 A firm is planning to cut the number of its employees by 10% a year and to increase its capital expenditure by 15% a year. Are these two actions necessarily contradictory? Discuss.

18.3 Use the data in Table 18–2 and extend the pro forma financial statement to 1998. You have the following information: Revenues will increase by 10%. Cost of goods sold will increase by 5%. Since the firm will redeem $4,000 of its debt in mid-1998, the interest in year 1998 will be only $600. Depreciation will be $178. Investment will be $3,000. Dividends will increase by 10%. Net working capital (i.e., inventory) will increase by 50%.

The firm will obtain external financial funds by issuing equity. The equity will be issued in the middle of the year, but for simplicity assume no dividend payments on the new equity.

18.4 A firm's net income is $1,000. At midyear it issues new stock worth $500, and at year-end it issues bonds (which it uses for stock repurchase) worth

$200. The firm pays 50% of its net income as dividends. What is the total change in equity?

18.5 A firm's policy is not to issue bonds and to distribute all its net income as dividends. The firm repurchases $1,000 of its equity. What is the net change in equity?

18.6 The net change in a firm's equity is $5,000. Its net income is $4,000, and its dividends total $6,000. Determine the new stock issue's value.

18.7 A firm's total source of funds amounts to $10,000. The capital expenditure is $20,000, and dividends are $5,000. What is the EFN?

18.8 The additional fixed assets in a pro forma balance sheet are $100,000. The capital expenditure is $200,000. What is the depreciation?

18.9 "If the pro forma capital expenditure equals depreciation, there will be no change in fixed assets." Evaluate this statement.

18.10 Coneco Corporation has the following five-year sales record:

Year	Sales (in $ million)
1	300
2	310
3	320
4	330
5	340

Use a simple regression technique to estimate Year 6 sales. Do you think the estimate is reliable?

18.11 Repeat Problem 18.10 with the following data:

Year	Sales (in $ million)
1	300
2	330
3	380
4	360
5	350

Discuss the difference in the sales estimates in Problems 18.10 and 18.11. In which case is the regression technique more appropriate?

18.12 Super Electronic Corporation has the following sales record:

Year	Sales (in $ million)
1	1,000
2	1,100
3	1,200
4	1,300
5	1,500
6	900

In Year 6 a competitor in the industry emerges with a new product and manages to take a large share of the market from Super Electronics. Use the regression technique to estimate sales in Year 7. Discuss your results.

18.13 A firm forecasts that its sales and all other items in its financial statements will increase by 10% next year. This means that one of the following conclusions is correct:

a. EFN will increase by 10% of the firm's total assets.

b. EFN will increase by 10% of the firm's equity + debt.

c. EFN = 0.

d. EFN = 10% of assets − Increase in automatic liabilities − (Net income − Cash dividends).

Which of the conclusions is correct? Illustrate your answer with a numerical example.

18.14 Como Films forecasts that its sales will increase by 10% each year for the next 10 years, and that its fixed assets will increase by 50% in the first year and then remain unchanged for the following nine years. Its liabilities, which increase automatically with sales, will increase by 5% a year for the next 10 years, and its net income and dividends will increase by 10% a year.

Additional data for the current year:

Fixed assets	$100,000
Sales	500,000
Accounts payable	20,000
Net income less dividends	30,000

Calculate the EFN for each of the next 10 years. How would your answer change if the firm decided to distribute all of its net income as dividends?

18.15 You have the following data:

Assets	$1,000 million
Automatic liabilities	100 million
Sales	2,000 million
Net income	150 million
Dividends	50 million

Assume that all items increase linearly with sales.

a. Plot the EFN line as a function of the growth rate of sales.

b. What is the EFN for the following values of G: 0%, 5%, and 50%?

18.16 Use the figures in Problem 18.15 to find a formula for the EFN, but assume that: "All items increase at the same rate up to sales of $2,500 million; thereafter, assets, automatic liabilities, and net earnings and dividends increase at half the sales growth rate."

18.17 For Firms A and B we have the following EFN lines (in $ million):

Firm A: EFN = −100 + (1,000 × G)
Firm B: EFN = −5 + (100 × G)

a. Plot the two lines.
b. Calculate the growth rate that will result in each firm having a zero EFN.
c. At what growth rate will these two firms have exactly the same EFN?

18.18 A firm distributes all its net income as dividends, and it has no liabilities that increase automatically with sales. The assets-to-sales ratio is 1.
a. Write the EFN equation. Will this firm always have external financial needs? If so, would this mean that the firm is not profitable?
b. The CFO thinks it will be hard to raise money in the near future. What remedy would you suggest to solve this problem?

18.19 Suppose a firm's accounts payable and accounts receivable increase linearly with sales, and each grows at the same rate. In addition, accounts payable equal accounts receivable. Assets other than accounts receivable are unaffected by sales' changes. Write the EFN equation and draw the EFN line (EFN as a function of the growth rate in sales), assuming that net income is 10% of sales, the payout ratio is $d = 0.25$, and current sales are $100,000.

18.20 Evaluate the following two assertions for the equation EFN = $a + (b \times G)$:
a. "If $b = 0$, the EFN must be negative."
b. "If $a = 0$, the firm is distributing all its net income as dividends."

INTERNET QUESTIONS

18.21 Use the Interactive Tool Box at the following Web site to set up a cash budget for a real (if you have all the data) or a hypothetical firm. Then set up a variance budget (variance = budget amount − actual amount). Tutorials are available if you need them.
http://www.edgeonline.com

18.22 Complete the "Preparing a Cash Flow Forecast" tutorial. Then take a look at the cash flow worksheet (both designs). Prepare a summary of what you found.
http://www.sb.gov.bc.ca

YOUR TURN: APPLYING THEORY TO PRACTICE
COCA-COLA'S EXTERNAL FINANCIAL NEEDS

Coca-Cola sales for 1985–1994 (in $ million) were as follows:

Year	Sales
1985	7,904
1986	8,669
1987	7,658
1988	8,338
1989	8,966
1990	10,236
1991	11,572
1992	13,074
1993	14,600
1994[a]	16,700

[a]Estimate

Financial data for 1994 were as follows:
Net profit: $2,555 million
Income tax rate: 31.5%
Net working capital: −$1,415 million
Dividend payout ratio: 0.40
Book value of fixed assets: $10 billion

Source: *Value Line Industrial Survey*, various issues.

Additional information:
1. The firm pays 9% interest on its long-term and short-term debt; the total debt in 1995 is $3,486 million. There are 1,303 million shares of stock outstanding.

2. In every year the cost of goods sold is 76% of sales.
3. Depreciation is estimated to be $450 million in 1995.
4. By December 1995 the firm needs to have $2,150 million to invest in Eastern Europe and China.
5. The firm's dividend per share will increase to $0.90 in 1995.
6. In 1995 Coca-Cola will hold the same net working capital as in 1994.
7. In 1995 Coca-Cola's tax rate will remain at 31.5%.

Questions

Use the data to answer the following questions:

1. Apply the regression technique to estimate Coca-Cola's sales in 1995 and 1996. Actual sales were $17.6 billion in 1995 and $18.9 billion in 1996. By how much did estimated sales differ from actual sales in these two years?

2. At the end of 1996, Coca-Cola's management was planning its investment in China and Eastern Europe. Assume that Coca-Cola had hired you as a financial advisor to assess its external financial needs. Use your sales estimates for 1995 to prepare pro forma financial statements. Does the firm need to issue more stock in 1995? If so, how much equity should it raise? (Assume any additional sources needed will be raised as equity and that no additional borrowing will take place.)

3. How would your answer change if you were to use the linear formula (18.6), where G is taken as the geometric average[14] of the nine years' sales growth? Assume the net value of "automatic" liabilities will be zero in 1995 and the dividend payout ratio will be the same as in 1994. How would your results change if the growth rate was half of your estimate obtained previously?

4. How do you explain the difference between the results obtained in Question 2 using the pro forma statement and the results obtained in Question 3 using the EFN formula (18.6)? (Hint: Recall that Equation (18.6) assumes that assets grow at the same rate as sales.)

---

14. The geometric average is given by

$$\sqrt[n]{(\text{Sales in last year} \div \text{Sales in first year})} - 1$$

where n is the number of years. It represents the constant yearly growth rate that would have produced the growth of sales that actually occurred.

CHAPTER 19

SHORT-TERM FINANCIAL PLANNING

LEARNING OBJECTIVES

After reading this chapter, you should understand:

1. The importance of working capital management in ensuring the firm's financial robustness.

2. The ways to reduce net working capital.

3. Why the longer the cash flow cycle, the more money the firm will need to finance its operating cycle.

4. How to calculate the inventory period, the accounts receivable period, and the accounts payable period.

5. How carrying costs and shortage costs are used to determine the firm's optimal investment in current assets.

6. That the time gap between a firm's cash outflows and inflows generally requires short-term financing.

7. The various ways to finance current assets.

CORPORATE FINANCE IN THE NEWS

CHRYSLER'S CASH HOARD

Chrysler Corporation has made clear that it believes it has become a lean, mean fighting machine that would be hard-pressed to squeeze much more out of its $50 billion balance sheet. And it is bracing for a possible sharp recession by seeking to build up a $7.5 billion cash cushion . . .

In an interview, Mr. York [vice chairman of Tracinda Corporation, one of Chrysler's major stockholders] estimates Chrysler's cash needs in a future recession by starting with the amount it burned through in the last one—$4.4 billion, by his reckoning. He agrees with Chrysler that its larger size means it would need more working capital in a recession today—$400 million more, in his view. That would put its recessionary cash needs up to $4.8 billion.

Source: Steven Lipin and Gabriella Stern, "Chrysler's Cash Hoard Could Reach $10.7 Billion," *Wall Street Journal*, 20 October 1995, p. 1. Reprinted by permission of *The Wall Street Journal*, © 1995 Dow Jones & Company, Inc. All Rights Reserved Worldwide.

19.1 INTRODUCTION

With its $50 billion of assets, Chrysler claims to have become "a lean, mean fighting machine" by managing its assets effectively and by seeking to maintain a $7.5 billion cash cushion. However, Mr. York, who agrees that the firm needs more working capital, disagrees with the planned cash buildup. He believes that $4.8 billion would be sufficient to face a recession. If, in fact, $4.8 billion is sufficient, Chrysler could use the surplus cash for other purposes—long-term investments, dividend payments, or stock repurchases.

Thus far most of this book has been devoted to long-term financial decisions and planning. In the final three chapters we turn our attention to **short-term financial planning.** Short-term decisions are those that involve cash flows within a 12-month period. These decisions are typically related to investment in short-term assets such as inventory, cash, and accounts receivable. For example, taking out a three-month loan from a bank or extending six months' credit to customers are short-term financial decisions. Chrysler's decision to hold $7.5 billion in cash is another example.

As we can see from Corporate Finance in the News, working capital includes assets in the "cash" category. Because of its large investment in liquid assets, even a small improvement in short-term asset management can mean large savings for Chrysler.

To understand the magnitude of short-term assets relative to long-term assets, consider J.C. Penney, whose financial statements we will study throughout this chapter. In January 1997 the firm's total assets were $22.1 billion and its current assets were $11.7 billion. Thus, about 53% of the firm's assets were current assets, consisting mainly of inventory and accounts receivable.

Because J.C. Penney is a merchandising business, the bulk of its investment is in current, rather than in fixed, assets. Therefore, the firm's management needs to pay close attention to its short-term financial decisions. Connecting Theory to Practice 19.1 demonstrates the importance of good management of current assets—also called **working capital management.**

CONNECTING THEORY TO PRACTICE 19.1

AMERICAN STANDARD: THE PROPHET OF ZERO WORKING CAPITAL

Emmanuel Kampouris, the Egyptian-born CEO of American Standard, studies the Bible not just for moral lessons, but for management guidance too. His idol is the redoubtable Nehemiah, who in 445 B.C. rallied a small group of Israelites to rebuild the wall around Jerusalem in just 52 days. "It's an example of excellent leadership and smart management," marvels Kampouris. Inspired by the Old Testament, Kampouris is performing an epic feat of his own. In the past five years he has overcome the double scourge of huge debt and depressed markets to steer his company, a diversified manufacturer, from near ruin to robust health.

Kampouris's strategy is a model for managers in mature industries. He has succeeded by relentlessly reducing American Standard's appetite for working capital, especially that tied up in inventories. His ability to run a company with annual revenues of $4.2 billion on a shoestring has won the admiration of Jack Welch, the thrifty boss of General Electric. . . .

By planning for the worst, Kampouris saved the company. In the early 1990s markets soured in all three of American Standard's businesses: plumbing supplies, air conditioners, and brakes for trucks and buses. The U.S. construction slump hobbled sales of bathroom fixtures and air conditioners, while the recession in Europe—American Standard's largest automotive market—slammed production of brakes. Faced with static sales and huge interest payments, Kampouris reached for a pot of gold: American Standard's $735 million in working capital.

He set the Nehemiah-like goal of reducing it to zero by 1996. That's an amazing target; U.S. companies, on average, use more than 15 cents in working capital from each $1 of sales. To get to zero, a company must push inventories so low they can be financed without borrowing. The idea is to deliver goods—and to bill customers—more rapidly, then use the customer's money to pay for minimal stocks, without speeding up payments to suppliers.

At American Standard, Kampouris introduced a lean manufacturing system called demand flow technology. Under demand flow, plants manufacture products as customers order them. Suppliers deliver straight to the assembly line, reducing stocks of parts, and plants ship the products as soon as they're completed, thus cutting the inventory of finished goods.

Demand flow has revitalized the factory in Lexington, Kentucky, that manufactures cool- and hot-air blowers for commercial buildings. In 1990 the plant churned out huge volumes of single components in long production runs. Metal frames, fans, and other parts covered ten acres of blacktop. It took an average of 15 days to assemble a machine. Today, small workstations produce a unit's components when it is ordered. The parts can be made and assembled in no more than two days. In three years inventories at the Lexington plant have dropped from $9 million to $5.5 million, despite a 40% rise in output.

Overall, American Standard has pared its inventories more than 50%, to $326 million, since 1990. As a result, working capital now absorbs just 5 cents from each $1 of sales. By saving interest payments on supplies, the company has increased its cash flow by $60 million a year. . . .

Source: Shawn Tully, "American Standard: Prophet of Zero Working Capital," *Fortune International* 129, no. 12 (June 1994): 61. Copyright © 1994, Time Inc. All rights reserved.

MAKING THE CONNECTION

Connecting Theory to Practice 19.1 tells how Emmanuel Kampouris, CEO of American Standard, succeeded in steering his company from near ruin to a state of financial health. He did so largely by improving management of short-term assets and liabilities. Specifically, he decreased inventory, decreased receivables (by billing customers more rapidly), and used more suppliers' credit (accounts payable).[1]

Important for all firms, efficient management of current assets and liabilities is particularly so for merchandisers such as J.C. Penney, Sears, and Kmart due to their substantial investment in current assets. In our discussion of short-term financial planning, we will focus on the following issues:

- Alternative ways to reduce working capital.
- The optimal level of current assets.
- The impact that better management of current assets and liabilities can have on the firm's profitability.
- The best way to finance the optimum level of current assets, and the effect this financing decision has on the firm's working capital.

Many U.S. firms increased their profits through better management of current assets, and specifically by holding relatively low levels of inventories. To illustrate, in 1997 the inventory/sales ratio of American firms was at a 30-year low. Some economists believe better management of working capital is one main reason why earnings per share were so high in 1996.

19.2 WAYS OF REDUCING NET WORKING CAPITAL

Let's begin by defining working capital and seeing what zero working capital means. *Gross working capital* refers to the firm's current assets, while *net working capital* is the firm's current assets minus its current liabilities. Gross working capital represents that portion of the firm's resources that circulates from cash to inventory to short-term investments and back to cash in the regular course of business. As we indicated in Chapter 3, **net working capital** is the difference between current assets and current liabilities.

$$\text{Net working capital} = \text{Current assets} - \text{Current liabilities} \qquad (19.1)$$

For the sake of brevity, the word "net" is sometimes omitted in referring to net working capital. For example, in Connecting Theory to Practice 19.1, the article refers to "zero working capital," but what it really means is "zero *net* working capital." Firms generally cannot operate without current assets. To avoid confusion in this book, "working capital" will mean net working capital, while current assets will be referred to as "current assets" (not as "working capital").

J.C. Penney's 1996 financial statements, presented in Table 19-1, show the main elements of its current assets and current liabilities: The firm's main current assets are

1. On December 5, 1996 Tyco International made a $4 billion bid to acquire American Standard. American Standard's board met that same day and rejected the bid. For more details, see Harlan S. Byrne, "Watch This Space," *Barron's* (20 January 1997): 12.

TABLE 19-1   **Consolidated Balance Sheets and Additional Financial Data of J.C. Penney (in $ million)**

Assets (in $ million)

	1996	1995	1994	1993	1992
Current assets					
Cash and short term investments of $131, $173, $207, $156, and $405	$ 131	$ 173	$ 261	$ 173	$ 426
Receivables, net	5,757	5,207	5,159	4,679	3,750
Merchandise inventories	5,722	3,935	3,876	3,545	3,258
Prepaid expenses	102	94	172	168	157
Total current assets	11,712	9,409	9,468	8,565	7,591
Properties, net	5,014	4,281	3,954	3,818	3,755
Investments, primarily insurance operations	1,605	1,651	1,359	1,182	991
Deferred insurance policy acquisition costs	666	582	482	426	372
Other assets	3,091	1,179	939	797	758
	$22,088	$17,102	$16,202	$14,788	$13,467

Liabilities and Stockholders' Equity (in $ million except share data)

	1996	1995	1994	1993	1992
Current liabilities					
Accounts payable and accrued expenses	$ 3,738	$ 2,404	$ 2,274	$ 2,139	$ 2,038
Short term debt	3,950	1,509	2,092	1,284	907
Current maturities of long term debt	250	—	—	348	—
Deferred taxes	28	107	115	112	64
Total current liabilities	7,966	4,020	4,481	3,883	3,009
Long term debt	4,565	4,080	3,335	2,929	3,171
Deferred taxes	1,362	1,188	1,039	1,013	1,012
Bank deposits	724	767	702	581	538
Insurance policy and claims reserves	781	691	568	540	462
Other liabilities	659	472	462	477	570
Stockholders' equity					
Preferred stock, without par value:					
Authorized, 25 million shares–issued, 1 million shares of Series B LESOP convertible preferred	568	603	630	648	666
Guaranteed LESOP obligation	(142)	(228)	(307)	(379)	(447)
Common stock, par value 50¢:					
Authorized 1,250 million shares—issued, 224, 224, 227, 236, and 235 million shares	1,416	1,112	1,030	1,003	955
Reinvested earnings	4,110	4,397	4,262	4,093	3,531
Total stockholders' equity	5,952	5,884	5,615	5,365	4,705
	$22,088	$17,102	$16,202	$14,788	$13,467

Source: J.C. Penney, 1996 financial statements.

(continued)

TABLE 19-1	*(continued)*				
Additional Data from Other Financial Statements					
	1996	**1995**	**1994**	**1993**	**1992**
Net income	$ 565	$ 838	$ 1,057	$ 940	$ 777
Cash flow from operations	382	1,403	738	286	1,574
Sales	22,653	20,562	20,380	18,983	18,009
Cost of goods sold (total costs and expenses)	22,740	20,078	19,383	18,024	17,256

accounts receivable and inventory, and its main current liabilities are accounts payable and short-term debt payments. The investment in current assets was $11,712 million, of which J.C. Penney financed $7,966 million by short-term liabilities and financed the rest by long-term liabilities and equity. J.C. Penney's net working capital was $3,746 million ($11,712 million − $7,966 million = $3,746 million).

Connecting Theory to Practice 19.1 seems to suggest that reducing net working capital creates value. Can we say that the lower the net working capital, the better the firm fares? Absolutely not! It really depends on how the firm reduces its working capital. For example, suppose a firm holds $100 million of inventory and $40 million of accounts payable. With no other current assets or current liabilities, its net working capital is $60 million. The firm can reduce net working capital to zero by taking a short-term loan of $60 million. However, such a move may make stockholders fare worse because of the interest on the borrowed money.

While zero net working capital may be the ideal level, not all ways of attaining that goal are equally attractive. One good way of achieving it is by improving current asset and current liability management. If, for example, a firm manages its inventory more efficiently, the resulting reduction in net working capital can create value.

Connecting Theory to Practice 19.1 indicates that American Standard reduced its net working capital to near zero, thus freeing funds for other uses. If J.C. Penney had been able to reduce its net working capital to zero in 1996 by more efficient management of its current assets and liabilities, it would have freed $3,746 million for other uses. The goal sounds desirable. Why, then, don't more firms achieve it? We examine this issue in the next section.

19.3 FINANCING CURRENT ASSETS: THE OPERATING CYCLE VERSUS THE CASH FLOW CYCLE

A firm cannot operate without current assets, especially cash and inventory, which it must finance. Suppose, for example, that J.C. Penney purchases a $1 million of inventory on 30 days' credit. The inventory lies on the firm's shelves for an average of 90 days, by the end of which customers have bought the merchandise for $1.35 million.[2] On average, credit is extended to customers for 10 days. These transactions and cash flows can be summarized as follows:

Day	Transaction	Cash Flow Involved
0	J.C. Penney receives the purchased inventory.	——
30	J.C. Penney pays for the purchase.	–$1 million
90	Customers buy the inventory.	——
100	J.C. Penney collects the cash from customers.	+$1.35 million

What we have here are two different cycles: an *operating cycle* and a *cash flow cycle*. The **operating cycle** is the time between when the firm receives the inventory from suppliers and when it collects cash from customers. In our example the operating cycle is 100 days.

The operating cycle can be separated into two time segments and expressed as follows:

$$\text{Operating cycle} = \text{Inventory period} + \text{Accounts receivable period}$$

The **inventory period** is the time from the receipt of merchandise until its sale for either cash or credit—that is, the time during which the firm holds it as inventory.[3] The **accounts receivable period** (or *receivables period*) is the time between when the firm sells the merchandise and when it collects cash from customers. In our example we have

$$\text{Operating cycle} = \text{Inventory period} + \text{Accounts receivable period}$$
$$\downarrow \qquad\qquad\qquad \downarrow \qquad\qquad\qquad \downarrow$$
$$100 \text{ days} \quad = \quad 90 \text{ days} \quad + \quad 10 \text{ days}$$

The **cash flow cycle,** on the other hand, is the time between when the firm pays for merchandise and when it collects the cash from customers. This time is 70 days in our example. The cash flow cycle can also be broken into two time segments and expressed as

$$\text{Cash flow cycle} = \text{Operating cycle} - \text{Accounts payable period}$$

The **accounts payable period** (or *payables period*) is the time between when the firm receives the merchandise and when it pays for it. In our example, since the accounts payable period is 30 days, we have

$$\text{Cash flow cycle} = \text{Operating cycle} - \text{Accounts payable period}$$
$$\downarrow \qquad\qquad\qquad \downarrow \qquad\qquad\qquad \downarrow$$
$$70 \text{ days} \quad = \quad 100 \text{ days} \quad - \quad 30 \text{ days}$$

Because most firms accumulate inventory and only later sell it to customers, the typical firm's operating cycle is longer than its accounts payable period. This timing

2. For simplicity we are assuming that all inventory is purchased on a single day. In practice of course, a firm adjusts its inventory more or less continuously.

3. For a manufacturing firm, the inventory period includes the time it holds goods as raw inventory, as work-in-process, and as finished inventory.

difference creates a need for current asset financing. In our example the firm needs cash to pay $1 million to its suppliers on Day 30, but it will not receive money from its customers until Day 100. Therefore, the firm will need either to borrow money for 70 days or to finance the $1 million payment with its own resources (i.e., by its cash holdings or by selling its marketable securities). If J.C. Penney could extend the accounts payable period to 100 days, it could finance all current operations by payables and would have no need for additional funds. However, since few suppliers will wait 100 days to collect their cash payment, the firm will need additional funds to finance its inventory. If J.C. Penney can decrease its inventory and accounts receivable periods or increase its accounts payable period without affecting its day-to-day operations, we say that the firm is managing its current assets and liabilities more efficiently.

Perhaps you noticed we said that J.C. Penney must borrow $1 million—rather than $1.35 million—to pay for its inventory purchase. In planning to finance its current asset needs, the firm should use the cost of goods sold (CGS) as the relevant amount. (In our example CGS is the inventory's cost, because no other costs are assumed.) The difference between the $1.35 million revenue from sales, which the firm will collect from the customers on Day 100, and the $1 million that the firm owes its suppliers represents the firm's profit.

Finally, note that by substitution the cash flow cycle can also be written as

$$\text{Cash flow cycle} = \text{Inventory period} + \text{Accounts receivable period} - \text{Accounts payable period} \quad (19.2)$$

Using the previous example, we have

Cash flow cycle = Inventory period + Accounts receivable period − Accounts payable period

| 70 days | = | 90 days | + | 10 days | − | 30 days |

To shorten its cash flow cycle, the firm can change one or more of these inputs: It can reduce the inventory period (as American Standard did in Connecting Theory to Practice 19.1), reduce the accounts receivable period, or extend the accounts payable period. Any of these actions will reduce net working capital.

Figure 19-1 summarizes the relationship among the various cycles. Determining the various cycles seems to be quite simple. However, in practice the calculation will be more complex because a firm purchases goods more than once a year and makes sales daily. A firm also has other production costs that it needs to finance.

Analyzing the operating cycle and, in particular, the cash flow cycle is important for two main reasons. First, the breakdown of the cash flow cycle into its components can help management locate weak links in the cycle and take corrective measures. For example, if J.C. Penney discovers its inventory period is much longer than that of similar firms, it should consider ways to move its inventory faster to save some financing costs. Perhaps J.C. Penney could reduce its inventory period similar to how American Standard reduced its inventory period. American Standard's (Connecting Theory to Practice 19.1) inventory period and accounts receivable period were crucial. The CEO cut the time to assemble certain machines from 15 days to 2 days, thereby reducing the inventory period, and he also cut the accounts receivable

FIGURE 19-1   Relationships Among the Various Components of the Operating and Cash Flow Cycles

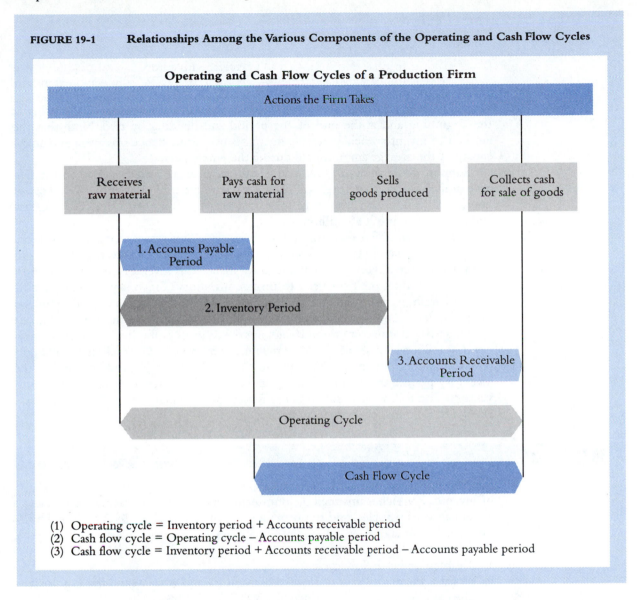

Operating and Cash Flow Cycles of a Production Firm

(1)   Operating cycle = Inventory period + Accounts receivable period
(2)   Cash flow cycle = Operating cycle − Accounts payable period
(3)   Cash flow cycle = Inventory period + Accounts receivable period − Accounts payable period

period by speeding the billing of customers. These changes reduced the cash needed to finance current assets and saved American Standard a great deal of money. Second, analyzing the cash flow cycle provides information that management can use to make accurate estimates of the firm's current asset needs.

Any variable in the operating and cash flow cycles will influence the amount needed to finance current assets. Next, we show how those variables—the inventory period, the accounts receivable period, and the accounts payable period—are calculated and how they are used in determining the firm's short-term financial needs.

19.3.1 The Inventory Period

The inventory period is given by

$$\text{Inventory period} = \frac{\text{Average inventory}}{\text{Cost of goods sold per day}}$$

where the average inventory is determined by adding the inventory and starting at the beginning and at the end of the period and dividing by two. Note that the amount of inventory held generally fluctuates over time, hence this average is an estimate of the average amount held during the whole period.

Suppose Shira Perfume Company's daily sales are 1 million units, and it sells each unit for $15; therefore, the daily sales amount to $15 million. The cost of goods sold (production costs) is $10 per unit, which amounts to $10 million per day and makes gross profit $5 million per day.

Suppose that Shira's inventory period is 50 days. This means that a unit produced (or purchased) stays in the firm's storage facilities for 50 days on average. Shira's CFO needs to arrange a short-term bank loan to finance this inventory investment. How much money does the firm need to finance inventory? Since it produces (or purchases) 1 million units every day, the firm needs to finance an inventory of 50 million units (1 million units × 50 days = 50 million units). Because the firm needs to finance only the $10 per unit cost of goods sold, not the $5 gross profit, it will need $500 million (50 million units × $10 = $500 million, or 50 days × $10 million = $500 million) to finance its inventory. With information on daily cost of goods sold and on the inventory period, the firm can determine how much money it needs to finance inventory. The following problem demonstrates how changes in the cash flow cycle affect a firm's need for short-term financing.

PRACTICE BOX

Problem

Suppose American Standard's average $735 million working capital consists solely of inventory, which is financed by long-term debt at 10%. The firm's receivables are equal to its payables, and the firm's annual sales amount to $4.2 billion. The inventory's cost is 80% of the revenue from sales. For simplicity assume there are no other costs.

a. Estimate the cash flow cycle.
b. What is the annual cost of financing inventory and what would this cost be if the cash flow cycle were reduced by 50%?
c. Suppose the firm's CFO is trying to convince its suppliers to extend their credit period.

How much would be saved if a "zero net working capital" target were met (with no extra payment to the suppliers)?

Solution

a. First note that, using Equation (19.2), because the receivables and payables are zero, we have

Cash flow cycle = Inventory period

(continued)

Therefore, we can determine the cash flow cycle by estimating the inventory period. To determine the length of the inventory period (which thus far in the chapter has been "a given"), we need to know the inventory's size and the daily cost of goods sold to plug into the following equation:

$$\text{Inventory period} = \frac{\text{Average inventory}}{\text{Cost of goods sold per day}}$$

We know that sales amount to $4.2 billion, which on an average daily basis would be

$$\frac{\$4.2 \text{ billion}}{365 \text{ days}} \cong \$11.5 \text{ million per day}$$

Since the inventory's cost is 80% of revenue from sales, the firm's daily cost of goods sold is

$$0.80 \times \$11.5 \text{ million} = \$9.2 \text{ million per day}$$

We know that the working capital, which consists solely of inventory, is $735 million, so we can plug numbers into the equation to calculate the cash flow cycle:

$$\text{Inventory period} = \frac{\text{Average inventory}}{\text{Cost of goods sold per day}}$$

$$= \frac{\$735 \text{ million}}{\$9.2 \text{ million}} \cong 79.89 \text{ days}$$

In other words, $735 million is sufficient to finance about 80 days of the firm's operations. (Note that with daily sales of $11.5 million, the firm collects on any given day more than the $9.2 million daily cost of goods sold. The firm uses the difference to finance other capital expenditures and to pay interest, dividends, and so on.)

b. American Standard's financing cost (interest expense) of maintaining its current inventory is

$$\$735 \text{ million} \times 0.1 = \$73.5 \text{ million}$$

If the firm cuts its cash flow cycle by 50%, the inventory period will be 39.945 days (79.89/2), and the firm will need the following amount to finance its inventory:

$$\$9.2 \text{ million} \times 39.945 \text{ days} \cong \$367.49 \text{ million}$$

The financing cost will be only

$$\$367.49 \text{ million} \times 0.1 = \$36.749 \text{ million}$$

By cutting its cash flow cycle in half, the firm will also cut its financing costs in half.

c. If the firm succeeded in achieving its zero working capital target, it would save *all* of its financing costs ($73.5 million).

19.3.2 The Accounts Payable Period

Shira Perfume buys raw materials from its suppliers. By not paying in cash, Shira uses its accounts payable as a source of financing. Accounts payable represent the credit the firm receives from its suppliers—a form of external financing. The accounts payable period is calculated as

$$\text{Accounts payable period} = \frac{\text{Average accounts payable}}{\text{Cost of goods sold per day}} \qquad (19.3)$$

The average payables are determined by adding the payables outstanding at the beginning and at the end of the period, then dividing by two.

Because the firm may pay its other production expenses (i.e., wages, electricity) on credit, it is common to calculate the accounts payable period by dividing average payables by daily cost of goods sold, which includes these other expenses. Assume that Shira's average accounts payable is $150 million, and its daily cost of goods sold is $10 million. Therefore, the accounts payable period is 15 days.

The accounts payable period is the length of time, on average, the firm receives credit from its suppliers. In our example, Shira receives 15 days of credit. Remember: Accounts payable are a source of external financing. The longer the accounts payable period, the less the firm relies on other sources of financing its working capital.

19.3.3 The Accounts Receivable Period

The accounts receivable period is used to calculate the working capital needed to finance the firm's receivables. To calculate the working capital needed to finance the receivables, we focus on total sales per day. Thus, we calculate the accounts receivable period as

$$\text{Accounts receivable period} = \frac{\text{Average accounts receivable}}{\text{Total sales per day}} \qquad (19.4)$$

In this calculation average receivables are determined by adding the receivables outstanding at the beginning and at the end of the period, then dividing by two.

To see how the accounts receivable period is used, suppose Shira's average accounts receivable are $150 million, total sales are $15 million per day, and the production costs (cost of goods sold) of these daily sales are $10 million. (The difference between the revenue from sales and the production costs represents the firm's gross profit—a key point we will come back to shortly.) To calculate the accounts receivable period, we divide the average accounts receivable by total daily sales: $150 million/$15 million = 10 days.

We said earlier that the accounts receivable period is used to calculate the cash needed to finance the firm's receivables. What does this number tell us about the amount of cash needed? For example, once we determine that the accounts receivable period is 10 days, to know the amount of money that the firm will need to finance these 10 days, we need to know the amount of cash needed per day. For that amount should we use the total sales per day ($15 million in our example) or the production costs per day ($10 million)? If you said the production costs, you are right: Because production costs amount to $10 million a day and because the firm has to wait 10 days until it receives the money from its customers, it will need $100 million ($10 million × 10 days = $100 million) to finance its accounts receivable.[4] (Note that the receivables include $50 million of profit that does not have to be financed.) In short, the firm has to finance 10 days of *production*—not 10 days of sales—because there is no need to finance the $5 million per day profit.

19.3.4 Uncertainty

The above calculations are simplistic and the financial needs are easy to determine. In practice all the figures (e.g. daily sales) are not known with certainty, which makes the firm's CFO work much harder. For example, because daily amount of sales is not certain, the cash flow cycle is only an estimate. There may be $2 million sales on one day, $4 million on another day, and $0.5 million the day after. Similarly, receivables invariably fluctuate from day to day. Therefore, to face these possible uncertain fluctuations, the firm will probably choose to hold more cash than the preceding calculations prescribe. The effect of uncertainty on short-term financial management is discussed in Section 19.4.

19.3.5 Seasonality

Thus far none of our calculations have taken seasonal business fluctuations into account. If there is a strong **seasonality factor** in sales, the various calculated periods may be distorted. For example, consider a firm that makes most of its sales in December

---

4. When a firm sells partly on credit, the accounts receivable period is sometimes calculated as

$$\text{Accounts receivable period}_{II} = \frac{\text{Average accounts receivable}}{\text{Credit sales per day}}$$

In determining total financial needs, this calculation yields the same result as the accounts receivable period discussed in the text (which we denote here by a subscript I to distinguish from the other version of calculation):

$$\text{Accounts receivable period}_{I} = \frac{\text{Average accounts receivable}}{\text{Total sales per day}}$$

To see this, let the ratio of credit sales to total sales be denoted by a. Then

$$\text{Receivables period}_{II} = \frac{\text{Average accounts receivable}}{a \times \text{total sales per day}} = \frac{1}{a}\text{Accounts receivables period}_{I}$$

Let total financing needs with a Type I calculation be

$$y_{I} = \text{Cost of goods sold per day} \times \text{Accounts receivable period I}$$

Let total financing needs under a Type II calculation be

$$y_{II} = \text{Cost of goods sold on credit per day} \times \text{Accounts receivable period II}$$

Because the ratio of credit sales to total sales is a, we obtain

$$y_{II} = a \times \text{Cost of goods sold per day} \times \frac{1}{a} \times \text{Accounts receivable period I} = y_{I}$$

The two methods yield the same result. While both methods can be used to analyze the firm's short-term financing needs, some analysis (and in particular, assessment of receivables policy and bad debt) can be done only with Accounts Receivable period$_{II}$.

and sells on 30 days' credit. If we divide the accounts receivable on December 31 by average daily sales, a much longer accounts receivable period than 30 days will be obtained. To see this, suppose the firm's sales are $435 million in December and $60 million in every other month. Sales are on 30-day credit. Total sales are $1,095 million ($11 \times \$60$ million + $435 million = $1,095 million). Average daily sales are therefore $3 million ($1,095 million/365 days = $3 million). Receivables as of year-end are the $435 million produced by December sales.

If receivables at the beginning of the year were also $435 million, then average receivables are $435 million. The accounts receivable period obtained is 145 days (Average receivables/Sales per day = $435 million/$3 million = 145 days). Even though the firm grants credit for only 30 days, its accounts receivable period seems much longer. Therefore, it is important to know the seasonality of sales and the firm's credit policy to identify the correct accounts receivable period.

19.4 WORKING CAPITAL: INVESTMENT AND FINANCING DECISIONS

Firms face two decisions in managing current assets: (1) how much to invest in current assets (the left-hand side of the balance sheet) and (2) whether to finance that investment by short- or long-term liabilities (the right-hand side of the balance sheet). Decision 1 determines the level of investment in current assets, while Decision 2, for a given level of current assets, determines the net working capital. Figure 19-2 depicts a typical firm's balance sheet. The firm has both current and fixed assets

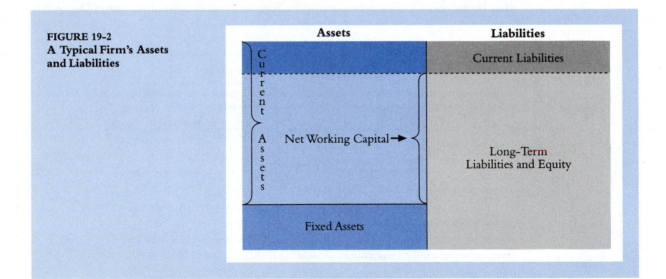

FIGURE 19-2
A Typical Firm's Assets and Liabilities

on the left side of the balance sheet. On the right side are current liabilities, long-term liabilities, and equity. Because current assets are typically larger than current liabilities, most firms hold a positive net working capital.

19.4.1 The Optimal Level of Current Assets

In principle, investment in current assets can be evaluated using the NPV rule of Chapter 5. The increase in a firm's sales and cash flow can be estimated for each additional dollar invested in current assets, and the NPV rule can be applied to determine the optimal investment in current assets—that is, the investment in current assets should be increased as long as the NPV of the additional invested dollar in current assets is positive. When the NPV due to an additional investment in current assets turns negative, the firm should stop investing in current assets. However, in practice it is more common to consider the *costs*, rather than the *revenue*, induced by holding current assets. In this case the optimal level of current assets is the level that minimizes the firm's costs. Both approaches yield the same result, but some managers prefer to focus on the costs that the firm has to incur in selecting the investment in current assets. By focusing on costs, the firm can better manage its holdings of current assets. Let us elaborate on these costs.

CARRYING COSTS

Financing a firm's inventory includes various costs—those associated with storage, handling, insurance, and damage or decay during storage. Holding receivables also involves costs. First, the firm needs to borrow or issue stock to finance the receivable. Second, the firm eventually writes off some of the receivables as bad debt. The firm also incurs an *opportunity cost* by holding cash, which yields a zero or relatively low return, rather than investing the cash in production or using it in some other productive manner. Together, all of these costs constitute the **carrying costs** of holding current assets. The larger the firm's current assets, the larger the carrying costs.

SHORTAGE COSTS

If they have carrying costs, why does the firm hold current assets at all? Simply because without them it would incur **shortage costs.** If a firm runs out of inventory, its potential customers will go to competitors. Suppose you want to buy a used car. You go to one used car dealer who has only a few cars in stock, none of which appeal to you. Just across the street is another dealer with a choice of cars of the type you wish to buy. You close a deal with the second dealer. Losing a customer because of not holding a large enough inventory represents a shortage cost for the first dealer.

Similarly, shortage costs can occur with other forms of current assets. A firm that holds a low level of receivables and sets a restrictive credit policy may lose customers who wish to buy on credit. A firm that decides to hold a low level of cash may need to borrow money at a higher interest rate than it would normally pay to cover its current obligations during periods when it has mistimed its cash flows. A firm with too low a level of raw materials may be forced to stop production, which will later result in shortage costs. Generally speaking, the smaller the amount invested in current assets, the larger the shortage costs.

Figure 19-3 depicts the relationship of carrying costs and shortage costs to the level of current assets. The carrying costs are shown by a straight line because it is assumed that for each additional dollar held, the same additional carrying costs are incurred.[5] The shortage costs are a declining function of the current assets held. With very low investment in current assets, a firm loses customers, has frequent production stops, and has high shortage costs. As the level of current assets increases, the shortage costs decrease.

Beyond some level the marginal change in shortage costs will become insignificant. For example, suppose sales of a given product are $100 million a year. By increasing the inventory of this product, the firm can reduce the shortage costs (recall the car dealers). What benefit can the firm gain from holding, say, $100 million in inventory? Because sales are about $100 million, the shortage costs with $100 mil-

FIGURE 19-3
Carrying and Shortage Costs as a Function of Current Assets

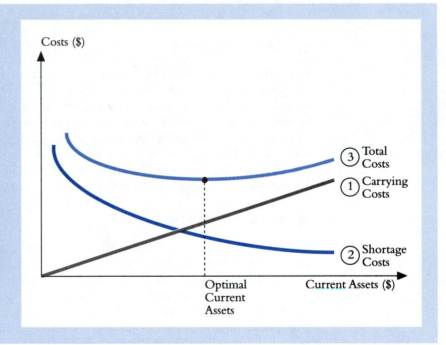

5. In practice for a high level of current assets, the carrying costs may increase at a lower rate as the amount of current assets increases (i.e., the firm receives a discount for a large volume of inventory insurance). However, the analysis remains unchanged even if carrying costs are described by a curved, rather than a straight, line.

lion of inventory will be zero or close to zero. Increasing inventory even further will not significantly reduce the shortage costs. Therefore, the shortage cost function is not linear and, beyond a certain level of current assets, does not decline any further. It levels off close to the horizontal axis. (See Figure 19-3.) The rate of the decline in the shortage cost curve may vary from one product to another, and is also affected by market competition. If competition is not very intense, customers may be willing to wait for the product to be supplied.

Total cost (see Curve 3 in Figure 19-3) is the sum of carrying costs and shortage costs. The optimal level of current assets is the one that minimizes total cost.[6] This optimal level of current assets is a function of these two types of costs: If carrying costs decrease, the minimum point of the total cost will shift to the right, and the firm should hold more current assets. Similarly, if carrying costs increase, the firm should hold fewer current assets.

Thus far we have discussed the left-hand side of the balance sheet—the current assets. We now turn to the right-hand side of the balance sheet—how to finance the current assets.

19.4.2 Financing the Current Assets

The firm first decides the level of current assets it will hold, and the decision it makes on how to finance those current assets determines its net working capital. For example, if the firm decides to finance all of its current assets by accounts payable and short-term borrowing, then current assets will equal current liabilities, and the net working capital will be zero. However, if the firm decides to finance some of its current assets by long-term liabilities or by equity, then net working capital will be positive. A firm must consider two main factors when deciding how to finance current assets: maturity matching and financing costs.

1. *Maturity matching.* A firm generally finances long-term assets with long-term liabilities and equity and finances short-term assets with short-term liabilities. This is called **maturity matching.** To see why maturity matching is important, consider a firm that is buying a machine with an economic life of 10 years. If it finances the machine by short-term borrowing, the firm will have to renew the borrowing every year. This will involve high costs due to shopping for a loan every year and to risking an increase in the interest rate. Moreover, if the firm's financial position worsens, borrowing may not be available at all, which, in turn, may induce bankruptcy.

---

6. As we can see in Figure 19-3, the minimum total cost is not necessarily at the intersection point of the other two curves. Unless we have an explicit formula for the shortage costs as a function of the level of current assets, it is impossible to pinpoint the precise point at which the total costs are minimized. In Chapter 21 we analyze the ordering and carrying costs of inventory (but not shortage costs). Because of the specific way both ordering and carrying costs depend on the inventory level, the minimum cost is obtained at the point where the two curves intersect.

Similarly, if it finances short-term assets such as receivables with long-term liabilities and equity, the firm will have excess cash at times because the value of the receivables varies seasonally. Thus, the firm must be aware of the exact timing of accrued surplus funds and how to invest them. The firm generally invests surplus funds in short-term securities, which it can sell as the need to finance receivables arises. Such maturity mismatching can lead to losses for the firm, because the rate of return on short-term securities is usually lower than the borrowing interest rate.

2. *Financing costs.* Interest rates on short-term borrowing are generally lower than those on long-term borrowing. In financing its current assets, the firm must weigh the risk of having to renew its borrowing every year at an unknown future interest rate (and the transaction involved with each borrowing) against the benefit of the generally lower interest rate on short-term borrowing.

Figure 19-4 illustrates the variability of a firm's total assets over time for various financing policies. First, note that because firms tend to grow over time, fixed assets also generally grow over time, as indicated by the general upward slope of Curve 1. The total assets needed for the firm's operations are described by Curve 2, which indicates a seasonality in the firm's total assets. For example, Toys 'R' Us needs a very substantial inventory in the period leading up to Christmas, and the firm may borrow money to invest in inventory before the holiday season. Both inventory and borrowing levels will decrease after Christmas. The difference between Curve 2 and Curve 1 represents the firm's current assets needed. See, for example, the breakdown of the assets into these two components in 1995.

Suppose a firm's level of assets demonstrates strong seasonality, and the division between current and fixed assets is as shown in Figure 19-4. How should the firm finance the assets? By short-term liabilities? By long-term liabilities and equity? By a bit of both? Curves 3, 4, and 5 in Figure 19-4 represent three possible financing strategies. In each policy, the firm finances all assets below the respective curves by long-term liabilities and equity. The differences among the three financing strategies (described in Figure 19.4) relate to how a firm finances the *seasonal current assets.* Curve 3 represents the policy that best fits the maturity matching principle. In accord with the maturity matching principle, a firm should finance all assets below the curve (fixed assets + permanent current assets, where permanent assets is the lower level of current assets needed at each time) by long-term liabilities and equity. A firm should finance all current assets above Curve 3 by short-term borrowing and payables. In this way the firm achieves the maturity matching principle.

If long-term liabilities and equity are substantially cheaper than short-term liabilities, it may pay a firm to violate the matching principle. The firm may decide to finance all its assets by long-term liabilities and equity. Curve 4 demonstrates this asset financing strategy. In such a case the firm will have extra cash whenever its current asset needs decrease due to seasonality, and the firm will convert the extra cash into short-term, marketable securities. The volume of the investment in marketable securities is shown by the difference between Curve 4 and Curve 2, which varies

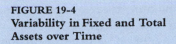

**FIGURE 19-4
Variability in Fixed and Total
Assets over Time**

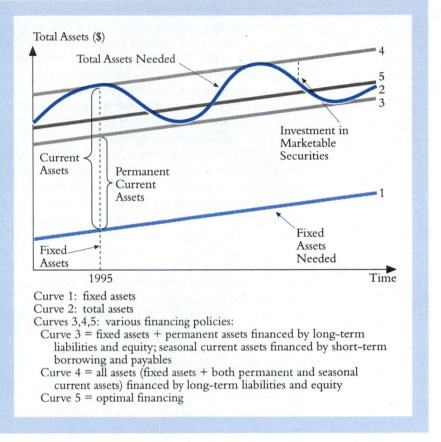

Curve 1: fixed assets
Curve 2: total assets
Curves 3,4,5: various financing policies:
   Curve 3 = fixed assets + permanent assets financed by long-term
      liabilities and equity; seasonal current assets financed by short-term
      borrowing and payables
   Curve 4 = all assets (fixed assets + both permanent and seasonal
      current assets) financed by long-term liabilities and equity
   Curve 5 = optimal financing

over time. Whenever the firm needs to purchase more inventory or other current
assets, it will simply sell some of its marketable securities. However, this policy has a
drawback: The firm may lose money because long-term debt is generally more expensive than short-term debt. For example, under this financing policy, the firm
may pay 10% interest on long-term debt but earn only 5% on its marketable securities. Thus, the firm may forgo interest—the gap between 5% and 10%. However,
the advantage of the policy represented by Curve 4 is that the firm does not need to
continually shop for borrowing—a practice that may lead the firm to financial distress if short-term interest rates rise to unexpectedly high levels. Thus, Curve 4 represents a lower-risk, but probably the most expensive, financing policy.

   Let us elaborate on the cost and risk of each financing policy by comparing
Curves 3 and 4, which demonstrate the risk-return relationship we have seen time
and again. As mentioned above, short-term interest rates are generally lower than

long-term interest rates, so the financing policy described by Curve 3 is less expensive than the one described by Curve 4 but, at the same time, riskier. The firm pays the lower short-term interest rates. However, it is exposed to the risk that when it needs more funds, it will have to borrow at a higher interest rate if that rate on borrowing has increased. On the other hand, the financing policy expressed by Curve 4 is less risky but more expensive. Although the firm would not have to worry about the availability of short-term borrowing or its rate at renewal, the cost of long-term debt would probably be greater than the interest rate the firm could earn on its investment in marketable securities.

As with portfolio selection, firms will trade between risk and return (or risk and costs) and choose a policy located between Curves 3 and 4—a policy such as that described by Curve 5. The Curve 5 policy might provide an optimal compromise. A firm finances all assets below the curve by long-term debt and equity and finances all assets above it by short-term debt and payables. Of course, Curve 5 may move closer to Curve 4 over time, if the firm expects difficulty in renewing its short-term borrowing, if the setup costs of borrowing increases, or if short-term and long-term interest rates move closer to each other. On the other hand, if the short-term rates are much lower than long-term interest rates or if it is easy to renew short-term borrowing, Curve 5 will approach Curve 3.

We cannot provide a precise recipe for finding the location of Curve 5 because it will depend on the risk-return preference of the firm's management. However, we can identify the factors affecting the decision, as covered in the preceding paragraph. Even if the risk-return preference is known, some intuition and artistry are needed to select the location of Curve 5, which, in turn, will determine the level of net working capital. Moreover, because the key decision factors—interest rates and the ease with which short-term borrowing may be renewed—vary over time, the location of Curve 5 will also vary over time.

Finally, it is interesting to note that financing policies corresponding to Curves 3, 4, and 5 all advocate financing at least the permanent portion of current assets with long-term debt and equity. This implies that current assets are larger than current liabilities, hence the networking capital is positive.

19.5 SHORT-TERM FINANCIAL PLANNING: THE CASH BUDGET AND THE FINANCING DECISION

We see from Figure 19-4 that, depending on which financing policy it adopts, the firm may face a seasonal cash shortage or surplus. If it can anticipate the shortage or surplus, the firm can manage its current assets and liabilities in an efficient way. The cash budget is a tool for predicting cash shortages and surpluses.

In Chapter 3 we learned that the annual statement of cash flows shows the beginning-of-the-year cash position plus all factors that create cash inflows and cash outflows during the year. It also shows the end result, which is the cash position at year-end. The statement of cash flows relates to the *past*, generally the latest year of the firm's activities. However, it is also a useful tool in predicting the firm's *future* cash needs. The firm can estimate its monthly sales and, given its credit policy, can predict its future cash flows from these sales. By the same token, the firm can forecast its inventory purchases and, given its payables agreements with suppliers, can predict its future cash outflows. Similarly, the firm will be able to predict other planned cash outflows such as administrative costs, investments relating to expansion, dividends, and interest.

19.5.1 The Cash Budget

By summing all these cash inflows and cash outflows, the firm can estimate the net cash deficit or surplus in every future period. This statement of a firm's cash position in future periods is a **cash budget.** For example, suppose the firm's estimated cash positions and cash flows in the coming year are as follows:

Estimated Cash Positions and Cash Flows (in $ million)

	Quarter 1	Quarter 2	Quarter 3	Quarter 4
Beginning-of-quarter cash position	100	140	200	−100
Net cash inflow/outflow	40	60	−300	250
End-of-quarter cash position	140	200	−100	150

The firm has $100 million in cash at the beginning of Quarter 1. It generates $40 million in the first quarter and, therefore, has $140 million at its disposal at the beginning of the second quarter. In the second quarter it creates an additional $60 million cash inflow, increasing its available cash to $200 million. However, in the third quarter the firm has a cash outflow of $300 million and a resulting $100 cash deficit. Then in the fourth quarter the firm has another cash surplus.

Whenever a firm has a temporary cash surplus, the financial manager will invest this surplus (or some part of it) in marketable securities. In this way the firm can earn interest on the surplus while, at the same time, maintaining liquidity.

How to handle the $100 million deficit in the third quarter is a trickier issue. Note that this deficit is not necessarily a bad sign; it may be a result of a planned expense—a capital expenditure that will create cash flows in the future. A CFO needs to take a number of steps in the case of a deficit:

Step 1. Check the source of the deficit. Is it due to a capital expenditure, a dividend payment, or some planned event? Or is it due to cash obligations to suppliers, banks, and so on?

Step 2. Check whether the cash outflows creating the deficit are necessary. Maybe the decision that led to the deficit was misguided and should be canceled (i.e., do not expand production operations, cut the dividend, etc.). However, in

http

Entrepreneurial Edge Online bills itself as the "Small Business Solution Source." Take a look at their Business Builders (e.g., preparing cash budgets and cash flow statements), Interactive Toolbox, Virtual Networks, and other handy tools available to entrepreneurs.
http://www.edgeonline.com

some cases cancellation may hurt the firm. For example, if the firm cuts the dividend, its stock will be less attractive; or if expansion is curtailed, the stock price may decline. If the firm is able to finance the deficit, it might be better not to cancel the decision that induced it. In many cases the deficit will be due to external obligations not under the firm's control (i.e., repayment of a bank loan). In such cases the firm will have no option but to finance the deficit.

Step 3. Decide whether to finance the deficit by long- or short-term liabilities, by equity, or by some combination of these financing sources. If the deficit is chronic and likely to continue into the future, the firm should finance it by long-term liabilities or equity. If it is a short-term deficit and due to a seasonal fluctuation, the firm would do better to finance it by short-term liabilities. It is common to sell short-term securities when cash is needed. Recall, however, that these securities are financed by either debt or equity.

Step 4. If the deficit is temporary and will be financed by short-term liabilities, select the specific short-term liability to be used. If the firm decides to borrow money to finance the deficit, choose the type of borrowing vehicle.

19.5.2 Short-Term Financing with Liabilities

A firm can use various current liabilities as sources of short-term financing to cover a temporary cash deficit. We will examine each liability that a firm can use to finance a cash deficit.

ACCRUALS

A firm usually pays its employees on a biweekly or monthly basis. The expenses that accumulate prior to payment of the salaries are listed on the firm's balance sheet as "Accruals" and may be held before payment as cash. The tax that accumulates prior to the firm's periodic payments to the IRS is also an accrual and can be held as cash before being paid. **Accruals,** liabilities for which payment has not yet been made, can constitute a source of short-term financing. Actually, if the firm could pay its employees once a year (at year-end), it would be glad to do so because this would constitute a source of cost-free financing. Of course, no employee would agree to such an arrangement—nor do tax authorities look kindly at the possibility of late payments and thus, at a minimum, charge hefty interest for them. The firm has little control over accruals as a source of financing, and it cannot expand them substantially to cover a cash deficit.

ACCOUNTS PAYABLE

Suppose the firm buys $20 million of inventory every day for a month from a supplier that offers the firm credit of *2/10, net 30*. This means the firm receives a 2% discount if it pays within 10 days, and it pays the net price with no discount if it pays between 11 and 30 days. If the firm has a cash surplus, it can take advantage of the discount. However, if it has a cash deficit, the firm will opt for the 30-day credit period and pay after that amount of time. If the firm delays its payment until the end of the 30 days, the total amount of short-term financing by accounts payable in this example will be $600 million ($20 million per day $\times$ 30 days = $600 million).[7]

Suppose, though, the firm convinces its supplier to extend the credit by 10 days, to 40 days. Its short-term financing from accounts payable will jump to $800 million ($20 million per day $\times$ 40 days = $800 million).

Of course, we know there are no "free lunches"; credit extension of this kind will have its cost. The effective interest rate paid on such accounts payable will be demonstrated in Chapter 21.

Accruals and accounts payable are known as **spontaneous financing** because they expand and contract as business expands and contracts. For example, if the firm's sales expand and it needs to buy $60 million (rather than $20 million) inventory a day on 30-day credit, the accounts payable financing will also expand to $1,800 million ($60 million per day $\times$ 30 days = $1,800 million).

SHORT-TERM BANK LOANS

In contrast to spontaneous sources of financing, a **short-term bank loan**—a loan for one year or less—is more under the firm's control and is based on a formal agreement with the bank. Short-term bank loans can be arranged in various ways. The firm applies for the loan; and once the bank grants the loan, both the firm and the bank sign a *promissory note* specifying the terms of the agreement—namely, the size of the loan, the interest rate, repayment terms, and so forth.

LINE OF CREDIT

A bank can also grant another source of short-term financing: a **line of credit,** which is a moral, rather than a contractual, commitment to make a loan to a particular borrower up to a specific amount and for a definite time period. According to this arrangement, the bank provides a loan up to a certain level, say $1 million, for a specified time period, generally one year. If during the first month of the year, the firm uses, say, $0.4 million, it will still have $0.6 million left to use. The stronger the firm's financial position, the larger the line of credit that the bank will grant. The advantage of having a line of credit is that money is available whenever the firm needs it. The firm pays interest on only the funds that it draws on.

Banks commonly require borrowers to hold on deposit, at a zero or very low interest rate, an amount equal to 10% of the line of credit plus 10% of any borrowing against the line of credit. Such **compensation balances** increase the effective interest rate.

---

7. The firm waits 30 days to pay each invoice. By the end of 30 days, it buys 30 $\times$ $20 million = $600 million of inventory but has not yet paid its first invoice. In effect, the firm borrows $600 million from its suppliers. On Day 31, it pays Day 1's invoice but purchases an additional $20 million inventory on credit. Total credit from suppliers remains at $600 million thereafter.

For example, suppose Seeds Inc. needs $90 million. The bank is willing to lend Seeds this sum at 9% interest as long as the firm deposits 10% of the loan's value in the bank at zero interest. Therefore, to obtain the $90 million that it needs, Seeds Inc. will have to borrow $100 million. Because the firm pays 9% on the total $100 million loan but gets to use only $90 million, the effective interest rate on the loan will be

$$\frac{0.09 \times \$100 \text{ million}}{\$90 \text{ million}} = \frac{\$9 \text{ million}}{\$90 \text{ million}} = 0.10 \text{ or } 10\%$$

REVOLVING AGREEMENT

A firm must negotiate a line of credit every year, but the bank may agree to commit itself for more than one year. Such a loan with a commitment to renew is a **revolving agreement** (or **revolver**). Unlike a line of credit, a revolver is a contractual agreement between the bank and the customer. Because it is a legal commitment, the bank usually charges a fee of about 0.25% on the unused balance as compensation for its commitment to the firm. For example, if a firm is granted $100 million credit and the prime interest rate is 9%, the bank will charge an extra 1% on top of the prime rate for the used funds plus the fee on the unused balance. If the firm uses only $40 million in the first year, it will pay the bank the following amount for the short-term financing:

KBK Capital Corporation will arrange a working capital revolver for you, from $100,000 (peanuts) to $5 million.
http://www.kbkcapital.com/screen_2_a.html

$$[(0.09 + 0.01) \times \$40 \text{ million}] + (0.0025 \times \$60 \text{ million}) = \$4.15 \text{ million}$$

$\qquad\qquad$ Interest on loan $\qquad\qquad$ Fee for unused part of loan

which is 10.4% of the $40 million borrowed.

SECURED LOANS AGREEMENT

When it takes out a long-term loan, a firm usually pledges its buildings, land, or machinery as collateral. With short-term loans, it is more difficult to find assets to serve as collateral. In such cases a firm can use its portfolio of securities, its receivables, or its inventory. A short-term loan of this type is a **secured loan.** From the bank's standpoint, the better the collateral, the less risky the secured loan and the lower the interest rate it will charge.

APPLYING THEORY TO PRACTICE 19.1

J.C. PENNEY'S WORKING CAPITAL MANAGEMENT

In our study of short-term financial planning, we have defined working capital and have covered the concept of zero working capital. In addition, we have reviewed the ways a firm can reduce its net working capital and how it can finance its current assets. Our discussion has also included the operating and cash flow cycles and the cash budget. Incorporating all that we have learned, we now continue our study, using J.C. Penney's management of its working capital as an example. We focus on 1992 and 1993, years characterized by a change in credit policy.

As we learned from reviewing J.C. Penney's 1996 financial statements (Table 19-1), approximately 53% of the firm's assets were current assets. This percentage represents a bulk of the firm's investment and needs to be managed closely. Certainly, the firm must make the right short-term financial decisions, or it could be financially distressed. This Applying Theory to Practice shows how even small improvements in managing working capital can mean substantial savings for the firm.

The following information is taken from J.C. Penney's 1993 to 1996 financial statements, the *Investment Update* financial service on the Internet, and *Barron's* online. Table 19-1 provides J.C. Penney's balance sheet and selected financial income statement data for 1994, 1995, and 1996, and selected citations from these statements.

1. **Quarterly Sales (in $ million)**

Quarter	1996	1995	1994	1993	1992	1991
1	4,688	4,367	4,350	3,964	3,793	3,433
2	4,753	4,435	4,242	3,963	3,789	3,456
3	5,788	5,128	5,149	4,735	4,342	3,937
4	8,157	6,632	6,639	6,321	6,085	5,375

2. **Net Interest Expense and Credit Costs (in $ million)**

	1995	1994	1993	1992	1991
Finance charge revenue	631	624	523	509	567
Bad debt expense	219	177	95	122	175

3. "Financial position: The Company generated $286 million in cash from operating activities in 1993, compared with $1,574 million in 1992 and $911 million in 1991. The change in 1992 was due to an increase in customer accounts receivable, particularly in the fourth quarter when the utilization of the J.C. Penney credit card increased. . . .

   In 1993, the Company established J.C. Penney Card Bank, N.A., which issues J.C. Penney credit cards to customers in five states."

4. "Committed bank credit facilities available to the Company as of January 25, 1997, amounted to $6 billion. In 1996, the Company amended its two existing syndicated revolving credit facility agreements and entered into two new syndicated revolving credit facilities."

Questions

Use the data just given and Table 19-1 in Section 19.2 to answer the following questions:

1. Draw a diagram showing the firm's division of assets and liabilities for 1996 into current and fixed categories. Does the firm have positive net working capital?

2. Determine why the firm's cash flow from operations decreased dramatically in 1993. Do the accounts receivable reflect a spontaneous response to the growth in sales, or do they reflect a new policy regarding credit sales?

3. In 1993 the firm reduced its bad debt (i.e., a debt whose chance to be collected is very small) to $95 million. What was the bad debt as a percentage of the average accounts receivable in 1993? What would be your prediction regarding bad debt in 1994, based only on the 1993 data? Do you believe J.C. Penney was heading for financial distress? Compare with the actual 1994 figures.

4. Analyze the firm's quarterly sales for the years 1991–1996. Do you think the firm needs a line of credit or a revolver? Explain why J.C. Penney should not finance all its current assets by long-term liabilities and equity. What solution did J.C. Penney adopt to finance the seasonal increase in sales?

5. After acquiring Eckerd Corporation in 1996, J.C. Penney feared future cash flow problems. Suppose it hired you as an expert on working capital management to shorten the cash flow cycle and avoid financial distress. Use the 1996 balance sheet to calculate the accounts payable period, the accounts receivable period, and the inventory period as well as the cash flow cycle. Suppose you are able to cut the receivables period by 2 days and the inventory period by 10 days without depressing the volume of sales. The firm's cost of capital is 10%. You charge 5% of the induced savings as a consulting fee. How much should J.C. Penney pay you?

MAKING THE CONNECTION

1. The following table shows the firm's fixed and current assets and liabilities for 1996 (in $ million):

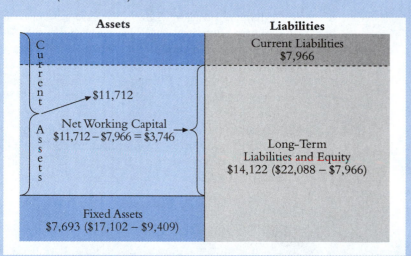

J.C. Penney's net working capital is $3,746 million.

2. In spite of the net income increase in 1993, the generated operating cash flow decreased from $1,574 million to $286 million. Most of the difference

was due to an increase in receivables, which caused a decrease in the firm's cash flow. The reported figures for receivables were $3,750 million for 1992 and $4,679 million for 1993. The firm sold more on credit in 1993, which implies that it generated less cash that year. If receivables had not changed between 1992 and 1993, the cash flow generated from operations would have been $929 million higher, or $1,215 million in 1993. It appears that J.C. Penney's new credit policy is the reason behind the reduction in cash flow.

Does the change in receivables reflect spontaneous growth due to sales growth? We shall see next that this is not the case. In 1993 sales grew by

$$\frac{\$18,983 \text{ million}}{\$18,009 \text{ million}} - 1 \cong 0.0541 \text{ or } 5.41\%$$

Accounts receivable grew by

$$\frac{\$4,679 \text{ million}}{\$3,750 \text{ million}} - 1 \cong 0.2477 \text{ or } 24.77\%$$

The growth in receivables was not simply due to an increase in sales. The firm changed its credit policy, and this change induced the sharp increase in receivables. In 1993 the firm established the J.C. Penney Card Bank, which issued J.C. Penney credit cards in five states. This boosted the accounts receivable. Although the firm was generous in extending credit to customers, no substantial growth in sales followed. Therefore, the firm should have reconsidered its credit policy.

Another possibility is that the new credit policy was not intended merely to boost sales but to enable J.C. Penney to operate as a bank and to collect interest on its credit. If so, J.C. Penney should reconsider this policy by weighing net interest income from credit sales against bad debt, collection expenses on bad debt, and the firm's cost of capital to finance these receivables. From Item 2, we see that the finance revenue in 1993 grew from $509 million to $523 million (about 2.8%), which is much less than the 24.77% growth in receivables. Thus, earning interest on receivables does not seem to be the motive for the new credit policy.

3. In 1993 bad debt amounted to $95 million. Based on the data in Table 19-1, the average accounts receivable for 1993 is given by

$$\frac{\$4,679 \text{ million} + \$3,750 \text{ million}}{2} = \$4,214.5 \text{ million}$$

Therefore, bad debt as a percentage of average receivables was

$$\frac{\$95 \text{ million}}{\$4,214.5 \text{ million}} \cong 0.0225 \text{ or } 2.25\%$$

This result is quite high and the firm should consider it when determining its credit policy. A policy that encourages cash sales will avoid bad debt and help prevent the deterioration in the firm's cash position. However, the firm should weigh the losses due to bad debt against a possible reduction in sales that might occur under a more restrictive credit policy.

Accounts receivable grew dramatically in 1993. If bad debt for J.C. Penney is typically some percentage of its receivables, then the firm could have expected to see an increase in the amount of bad debt in 1994.

Thus, a number of factors—a sharp increase in receivables, a sharp decrease in the cash generated by operations, a predicted increase in bad debt, and a modest increase in sales—indicate that unless correction measures are taken, J.C. Penney may find itself in financial distress in future years. Therefore, the firm should consider change in its credit policy.

Indeed, the 1994 figures show that bad debt almost doubled from $95 million to $177 million. It grew further in 1995 while sales continued to grow at only a modest rate.

4. Quarterly sales (in $ million):

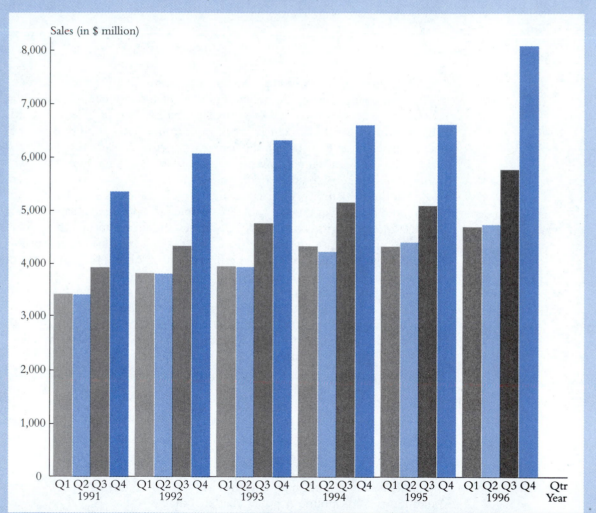

Source: J.C. Penney's Quarterly Sales, 1991–1996.

As we can see from the quarterly sales figures, a strong seasonality factor exists with sales picking up in the third and, especially, the fourth quarters. Thus, J.C. Penney needs short-term sources to finance the increases in working capital that the seasonal increases in sales require.

Indeed, we see from Item 4 that in early 1997 J.C. Penney had $6 billion committed in bank credit facilities. Because sales between the first and last quarters differ by about $2–$3.5 billion in the years 1993–1996, this revolver should be sufficient to finance J.C. Penney's seasonal cash needs.

5. As an expert on working capital management, you would first calculate the sales and production costs (cost of goods sold) per day:

$$\text{Sales per day} = \frac{\$22,653 \text{ million}}{365 \text{ days}} \cong \$62.06 \text{ million}$$

$$\text{Production costs per day} = \frac{\$22,740 \text{ million}}{365 \text{ days}} \cong \$62.30 \text{ million}$$

Using these data, we find the following:

$$\text{Inventory period} = \frac{\text{Average inventory}}{\text{Production costs per day}}$$

$$= \frac{(\$3,935 \text{ million} + \$5,722 \text{ million})/2}{\$62.30 \text{ million}} \cong 77.5 \text{ days}$$

Note that we use the average of the beginning and end-of-year inventory.

Next we calculate the accounts receivable period and accounts payable period, using average receivables and payables:

$$\text{Accounts receivables period} = \frac{\text{Average receivables}}{\text{Sales per day}}$$

$$= \frac{(\$5,207 \text{ million} + \$5,757 \text{ million})/2}{\$62.06 \text{ million}} \cong 88.3 \text{ days}$$

$$\text{Accounts payables period} = \frac{\text{Average payables}}{\text{Production costs per day}}$$

$$= \frac{(\$2,404 \text{ million} + \$3,738 \text{ million})/2}{\$62.30 \text{ million}} \cong 49.3 \text{ days}[8]$$

Therefore, the cash flow cycle is

$$\text{Cash flow cycle} = 77.5 \text{ days} + 88.3 \text{ days} - 49.3 \text{ days}$$

$$= 116.5 \text{ days}$$

8. Actually, since we assume the payables include not only inventory purchases but also other financial obligations involved with sales, we divide by $62.30 million. Therefore, in the numerator we include not only accounts payable but also other accrued expenses related to production.

J.C. Penney needs to finance 116.5 days of operation. Because the firm's production expenses amount to $62.3 million per day, the total financing it needs is

$$116.5 \text{ days} \times \$62.3 \text{ million} \cong \$7,257.95 \text{ million}$$

You succeed in cutting the cash flow cycle by a total of 12 days. This means that the firm can reduce the capital needed to finance operations by

$$12 \text{ days} \times \$62.3 \text{ million} = \$747.6 \text{ million}$$

and at 10% annual cost, this means that J.C. Penney will have annual savings of

$$0.1 \times \$747.6 \text{ million} = \$74.76 \text{ million}$$

Because your fee is 5% of the savings, you have earned $3.738 million. Not a bad day—and it's an even better one for J.C. Penney! This analysis shows the importance of current asset and liability management: Even relatively small improvements can induce substantial savings.

Your main recommendations to J.C. Penney would be as follows:

a. Examine why the liberal credit policy did not result in a larger increase in sales. To refine the analysis, examine the sales growth of other department stores in 1992, 1993, and 1994. For example, Dillard Department Stores' sales increased by 17% in 1992 and by 12% in 1993 with no substantial increases in receivables.[9] This difference should be a danger signal for J.C. Penney. However, it is possible that the liberal credit policy will boost sales and earnings in future years. It takes time for customers to become acquainted with the new policy.
b. Try to cut the cash flow cycle.
c. Assess the projected cash flows and, in particular, the risk of bad debt.
d. Reconsider the J.C. Penney credit card policy. It may be very expensive and may cause cash flow problems and financial distress in the future. If the firm decides not to change the policy, it should prepare financial resources to cover future cash deficits.

SUMMARY

A firm generally holds current assets and has current liabilities. The current assets (i.e., inventory, cash receivables) comprise the firm's gross working capital. The current assets less the current liabilities are the firm's *net* working capital. Management of current assets and liabilities involves several steps:
1. Determine the level of current assets and, in particular, the level of inventory and accounts receivable.

9. *Value Line Investment Survey*, 25 February 1994.

2. Decide whether to finance current assets by short- or long-term liabilities or by equity. In making this decision, consider several factors: (a) maturity matching, (b) financing costs, and (c) seasonality of sales. Once the financing decision is made, the net working capital is determined.

3. Shorten the cash flow cycle, which is the time between when the firm pays its suppliers and when it collects the receivables. The longer this cycle, the more resources the firm will need to finance its purchases and its production costs. Any shortening of the cash flow cycle that does not depress the firm's sales will save costs and increase profits.

4. The firm's future cash surplus or deficit can be forecasted using the cash budget. Such a forecast is important because the firm can arrange short-term financing if it expects seasonal deficits.

CHAPTER AT A GLANCE

Net working capital = Current assets − Current liabilities

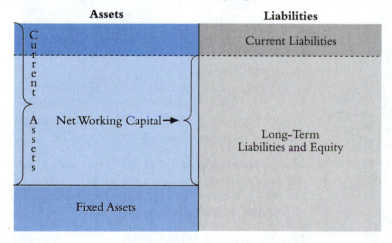

Operating cycle = Inventory period + Accounts receivable period

$$\frac{\text{Average inventory}}{\text{Cost of goods sold per day}} \qquad \frac{\text{Average receivables}}{\text{Total sales per day}}$$

Cash flow cycle = Operating cycle − Accounts payable period

$$\frac{\text{Average payables}}{\text{Cost of goods sold per day}}$$

Cash flow cycle = Inventory period + Accounts receivable period − Accounts payable period

KEY TERMS

Short-term financial planning
Working capital management
Net working capital
Operating cycle
Inventory period
Accounts receivable (receivables)
  period
Cash flow cycle

Accounts payable (payables)
  period
Seasonality factor
Carrying costs
Shortage costs
Maturity matching
Cash budget
Accruals

Spontaneous financing
Short-term bank loan
Line of credit
Revolving agreement (revolver)
Compensation balances
Secured loan

REVIEW AND PRACTICE

19.1 A firm's current assets are $100 million and its total assets are $300 million. Long-term liabilities and equity total $150 million. Calculate the firm's net working capital.

19.2 As reported in Connecting Theory to Practice 19.1, the CEO of American Standard has a goal of zero net working capital. Suppose the net working capital is positive and the firm's CFO takes on short-term debt to finance the inventory held. Does he reduce the net working capital by such a transaction?

19.3 A firm's credit payments to its suppliers are set at 2/10 net 30. By paying on the 30th day rather than the first day, the firm causes several changes in the working capital and its components. In this case which of the following statements are true and which are false?
a. The firm's net working capital decreases.
b. The firm's current liabilities increase.
c. The firm's current assets increase.
d. The firm's long-term liabilities increase.

19.4 Kaput Corporation's inventory was $100 million in 1996 and $140 million in 1997. Sales in 1997 were $400 million and the cost of goods sold was $365 million. Calculate the inventory period. What is the inventory turnover ratio? Hint: Recall from Chapter 3, Appendix 3A, that inventory turnover ratio is given by

$$\text{Inventory turnover ratio} = \frac{\text{Cost of goods sold}}{\text{Inventory}}$$

19.5 A firm makes 20% of its sales for cash, 30% on 30 days' credit, and 50% on 60 days' credit.
a. What is the average credit period the firm extends to its customers?
b. The firm's daily sales amount to $1 million. The cost of goods sold is 80% of sales. Calculate the accounts receivable period. How much cash does the firm need to finance the accounts receivable?

19.6 Suppose that, without affecting sales, a firm can either extend the accounts payable period by five days or shorten the accounts receivable period by five days. Which policy is preferable? Why?

19.7 We have the following data on Gap Stores (in $ million):

	1992	1993
Ending inventory	356.7	496.6
Ending receivables	9.9	16.7
Ending accounts payable	193.4	236.0
Sales	$2,960.4	$3,300.0

Source: *Value Line Investment Survey*, 25 February 1994.

The cost of goods sold is 70% of sales. Calculate the operating cycle and the cash flow cycle.

19.8 We have the following data on the quarterly sales of Gap Stores:

Fiscal Year Begins	Quarterly sales ($ million)				Full Fiscal Year
	April Period	July Period	October Period	January Period	
1990	402.4	405.0	501.7	624.7	1933.8
1991	490.3	523.1	702.0	803.5	2518.9
1992	588.9	614.1	827.2	930.2	2960.4
1993	643.6	693.2	898.7	1064.5	3300.0
1994	750.0	800.0	1060.0	1240.0	3850.0

Source: *Value Line Investment Survey*, 25 February 1994.

a. Draw a graph with the quarterly sales on the vertical axis and the sales period on the horizontal axis. Is there a seasonality factor in Gap's sales?
b. Would you recommend that Gap Stores negotiate a credit line or a revolving agreement with a bank? What amount of credit line, in your opinion, would be appropriate?

19.9 Use the data in Problem 19.8 plus the fact that the accounts receivable were $9.9 million in 1992 and $16.7 million in 1993 to answer the following questions:
a. What is Gap's accounts receivable period? Discuss your results.
b. In 1993 Gap considered issuing a Gap credit card, which would grant its customers 30 days credit. Estimate the maximum possible accounts receivable at the end of 1993 with such a credit card.

19.10 Nada Company's accounts payable and accounts receivable periods are zero. The firm holds an inventory of $100 million and there is an equal chance of daily sales being $20 million or $15 million. The cost of goods sold is 80% of sales.
a. Calculate the inventory period and the cash flow cycle for each sales scenario.
b. How much money does the firm need to guarantee no shortage of cash?

19.11 A new firm is just starting operations. Its cash position is $50 million at the beginning of the year. Its predicted sales are $50 million, $100 million, $50 million, and $200 million in each of the next four quarters, respectively. The firm sells on 45 days' credit. It will have to pay $40 million to its suppliers in the first quarter, and then it will have a cash outflow of $100 million in each of the next three quarters. Prepare the firm's cash budget. Will the firm need a credit line or some other short-term borrowing scheme?

19.12 We have the following financial data on Jan Bell Marketing:

Current Position ($ million)	1992	9/30/93
Cash assets	49.6	0.7
Receivables	66.9	26.2
Inventory (FIFO)	106.7	181.7
Other	8.8	53.3
Current assets	232.0	261.9
Accounts payable	25.9	8.8
Debt due	—	16.4
Other	8.0	54.9
Current liabilities	33.9	80.1

Source: *Value Line Investment Survey*, 25 February 1994.

Annual sales in 1993 were $280 million. The cost of goods sold was 70% of the sales. Assume the financial data for September 30, 1993, remain unchanged up to December 31, 1993.
a. Calculate the inventory period, the accounts receivable period, and the accounts payable period.
b. Calculate the operating and cash flow cycles and plot these two cycles on a graph.
c. Suppose the firm's cost of capital is 10%. Calculate the cost (in dollars) of financing the cash flow cycle.
d. The firm's suppliers are willing to allow the firm to increase its accounts payable period by 10 days. However, the firm would have to pay the suppliers $250,000 compensation for such an arrangement. Would you recommend that the firm accept the suppliers' offer?

19.13 You have the following data for Stanton, Ltd.:

Item	Beginning of Year	End of Year
Accounts receivable	$10,000	$20,000
Accounts payable	$ 8,000	$12,000
Inventory	$40,000	$60,000

Annual sales amount to $100,000 and the cost of goods sold is $80,000.

a. Calculate the inventory period, the accounts receivable period, and the accounts payable period as well as the cash flow cycle.

b. How much money does the firm need to finance its cash flow?

19.14 A firm's carrying costs are 10 cents per dollar of current assets held. Its shortage costs are $1 million if it holds zero current assets. For each additional dollar of current assets the firm holds, the costs drop by 5 cents until they reach zero.

a. At what level of current assets do the shortage costs reach zero?

b. What is the optimal level of current assets?

c. Plot your results on a graph.

19.15 Repeat Problem 19.14, but assume the carrying costs

a. Increase to 15 cents per dollar of current assets held.

b. Decrease to 5 cents per dollar of current assets held.

Analyze your results and compare them to those of Problem 19.14.

19.16 Juzzy Shoes' shortage costs are as follows:

Current Assets	Shortage Costs
Up to $5 million	$1 million
$5 to $10	$500,000
$10 to $20	$250,000
$20 million	$0

For up to $10 million of current assets held, carrying costs are 5 cents per dollar. Due to better rates on high volumes of insurance, for each additional dollar of current assets above $10 million, the carrying cost is 3 cents per dollar. Plot the carrying costs, the shortage costs, and the total cost functions. What is the optimal level of current assets?

19.17 Records Unlimited holds $10 million of current assets, and its annual net operating income will be $2 million. If it holds $5 million current assets, its annual net operating income will be $1.5 million. The reduction in income is due to the fact that the firm will be out of stock on some days and will lose customers. Assume the cash flows are perpetuities.

a. The firm's cost of capital is 10%. Which is the better level of current assets? (Hint: Use the NPV rule from Chapter 5.)

b. How would your answer change if the cost of capital was only 5%?

c. How does the analysis given in the problem relate to carrying costs and shortage costs?

d. Suppose the firm's only cash flows induced by its investment are those presented in the problem. What additional information do you need to calculate the PV of the firm's equity?

19.18 Your firm needs to borrow $90 million for one year. The bank requires a 10% compensation balance on which it will pay the firm 1% interest annually. The borrowing rate is 9%. Another bank offers you the loan for 9.2% with no compensation balance. Calculate the effective interest rate on each of the two loans. Which loan would you choose?

19.19 A bank offers your firm the following two alternative loans:

1. A loan of up to $100 million, but the bank does not commit itself for this sum. If you borrow only say, $20,000 today, the bank may refuse to lend you more money in the future. You pay 10% annual interest on the amount of money used.

2. A $100 million committed revolver. Your firm pays 10% annual interest on the amount used plus 0.25% on the unused portion of the $100 million. The bank is committed up to $100 million.

a. Calculate the effective interest rate if you use $1 million, $10 million, or $100 million of the credit line. What are the pros and cons of each loan?

b. Suppose the future economy and, in particular, the inflation rate are very uncertain. Which loan would you prefer? Which is riskier?

19.20 Dowin Company's cash flow cycle is 100 days, its accounts payable period is 10 days, and its inventory period is 50 days. Calculate the receivables period.

19.21 "If the accounts payable period equals the accounts receivable period, then, by definition the firm will not need cash to finance its current operations because the cash flow cycle will be zero." Evaluate this assertion.

19.22 The following data describe Reebok International's current assets and liabilities. Sales in 1993 are $2,893.5 million, and cost of goods sold is 80% of the sales.

Current Position ($ million)	1991	1992	9/30/93
Cash assets	84.7	105.4	123.1
Receivables	425.6	418.1	555.4
Inventory (FIFO)	436.6	434.2	433.3
Other	80.2	102.5	92.7
Current assets	1,027.1	1,060.2	1,204.5
Accounts payable	308.4	281.4	350.0
Debt due	40.4	8.2	40.6
Other	75.7	96.0	93.6
Current liabilities	424.5	385.6	484.2

Source: *Value Line Investment Survey*, 25 February 1994.

Assume that the figures for year-end 1993 are the same as those reported for 9/30/93.
a. Calculate the accounts receivable period, the inventory period, and the accounts payable period in 1993.
b. Calculate the cash flow cycle.
c. The marketing manager suggests that credit sales be extended to increase the accounts receivable to $800 million. She claims that in this way sales will increase by 10% and the firm's EPS will increase from $2.61 to $2.80. Suppose the CFO accepts these calculations but claims that the marketing manager forgot to account for the additional costs related to the increase in receivables that, on an annual basis, amount to 10% of the additional receivables. Reebok has 84.5 million shares outstanding. Should the CFO accept the marketing manager's suggestion after correcting for the error?

19.23 A firm is considering increasing its inventory by $100 million. The short-term interest rate is 5%, the long-term interest rate is 10%, and the cost of equity is 15%. The firm's weighted average cost of capital is 12%. There are no other carrying costs apart from the financial costs. What are the firm's carrying costs? (Hint: See Chapter 10.)

19.24 Sears pays $120 million in quarterly dividends. The firm predicts a deficit of $100 million in the next quarter. The current assets manager suggests withholding the dividend payment, thereby solving the deficit problem at no cost at all. Appraise this suggestion. Would you recommend that Sears accept it? (Hint: See Chapter 17.)

19.25 Suppose a firm reaches an agreement with its suppliers whereby payment is made whenever it cashes its sales. What is the cash flow cycle in such a case? How much current debt does the firm need to finance its operations in such a case?

INTERNET   QUESTION

19.26 Visit the Small Business Workshop and complete the tutorials on short-term and long-term financing. Prepare a business memo summarizing your findings.

http://sb.gov.gc.ca

YOUR TURN: APPLYING THEORY TO PRACTICE

FRUIT OF THE LOOM: WORKING CAPITAL, EARNINGS PER SHARE, AND STOCK PRICE

Stock price is commonly related to a firm's EPS. Although EPS analysis usually focuses on long-term investments, short-term investments sometimes determine the firm's profitability as well as its stock price. Fruit of the Loom provides an excellent example of such a case. We focus on the years 1993 and 1994. Those years are interesting because Fruit of the Loom held excess inventories, which led to firing 2,000 workers. After a short period of time sales increased and the firm needed to rehire workers. We analyze the mistakes made by management in these years.

Figure 19-5, taken from *Value Line Investment Survey*, provides financial data for Fruit of the

Loom up to 1993 as well as estimates for 1994. Use Figure 19-5 and the following information extracted from *Business Week* to answer the questions that follow.

"In gearing production to estimated demand for its products, Fruit of the Loom made a wrong move at a wrong time in late 1993. Commanding a 40% market share in men's and boys' underwear in the United States through its savvy marketing and making its popular apple-and-grape logo a hot label on casual wear in Europe, Fruit of the Loom had experienced steadily increasing sales and earnings since 1987. By early 1993 the firm had anticipated even higher demands for its

FIGURE 19-5 *Value Line*'s **Report on Fruit of the Loom**

Fruit of the Loom, Inc. is the successor to Northwest Industries, Inc., which was incorporated in Delaware in 1967. In March of 1985, Northwest was taken private by William Farley in a leveraged buyout. The company recapitalized in early 1987, exchanging its existing common for 15,294,988 shares of Class A and 15,205,012 of Class B common stock, and making a public offering of an additional 31,050,000 shares of Class A common at a price of $9.00 a share.

Capital Structure as of 9/30/93

Total Debt $1190.7 mill. Due in 5 yrs $720.0 mill.

LT Debt $1118.9 mill.   LT Interest $65.0 mill.

Incl. $104.4 mill. capitalized leases.

(LT interest earned: 3.1x; total interest
    coverage: 2.8x)   (53% of Cap'l)

Leases, Uncapitalized Annual rentals $7.4 mill.

Pension Liability None

Pfd Stock None

Common Stock 74,900,000 shs.   (47% of Cap'l)

Class A: 68,900,000 shs.

Class B: 6,000,000 shs.

Current Position ($ mill.)	1991	1992	9/30/93
Cash Assets	31.4	57.4	60.1
Receivables	198.3	233.4	311.7
Inventory (LIFO)	331.9	415.0	568.2
Other	94.7	37.8	46.6
Current Assets	656.3	743.6	986.6
Accts Payable	49.4	80.5	56.3
Debt Due	151.4	188.2	71.8
Other	169.5	164.9	174.0
Current Liab.	370.3	433.6	302.1

Annual Rates of change (per sh)	Past 10 Yrs.	Past 5 Yrs.	Est'd '90–'92 to '96–'98
Sales	—	4.5%	11.0%
"Cash Flow"	—	30.5%	17.5%
Earnings	—	—	20.5%
Dividends	—	—	Nil
Book Value	—	—	22.5%

FIGURE 19-5   *Continued*

Quarterly Sales ($ mill.)

Cal-endar	Mar.31	Jun.30	Sep.30	Dec.31	Full Year
1990	323.7	443.0	355.6	304.5	1426.8
1991	349.2	468.3	392.0	418.6	1628.1
1992	423.3	534.1	451.2	446.5	1855.1
1993	428.9	523.0	484.2	448.3	1884.4
1994	*450*	*570*	*550*	*530*	*2100*

Earnings per Share

Cal-endar	Mar.31	Jun.30	Sep.30	Dec.31	Full Year
1990	.21	.56	.36	.06	1.19
1991	.26	.51	.36	.42	1.55
1992	.48	.75	.61	.64	2.48
1993	.58	.77	.64	.26	2.25
1994	*.35*	*.75*	*.70*	*.70*	*2.50*

Fruit of the Loom's common stock has fallen significantly over the past year. From its high of $49 dollars in 1993, this issue has lost over 45% of its value. The descent mirrors the deterioration in the company's business stemming from lackluster consumer demand and bloated inventories. Specifically, the fleece wear business (sweat shirts and sweat pants) has been burdened by inflated inventories and excess capacity within the industry, which has put downward pressure on prices and operating margins. These factors have combined to dramatically squeeze profits.

The going will continue to be tough in the opening half of the year. To counter the inventory problem, the company has cut back production at its domestic operations. These plants are currently running on a shorter work week, and this should continue until inventories return to acceptable levels. In the meantime, operating expenses will remain high due to lower plant utilization. And, despite a reviving domestic economy, a cautious approach on the part of retailers is apt to keep apparel sales in check in the first six months. The aforementioned events will likely lead to a decline in year-over-year earnings in the first two quarters.

But earnings comparisons should turn positive in the latter half of 1994. A gradual increase in consumer demand for apparel should bring inventories back to normal levels. This may allow operations to return to regular work schedules, which, in turn, should allow margins to expand. All in all, we look for earnings to rebound to $2.50 a share, an 11% increase over '93's tally.

We are bullish on the company's long-term prospects. Its foray into the sports licensing business with the recent acquisition of Salem and Jostens Sportswear should make it a major force in this market. Too, the European operations have been growing nicely and there is substantial room for improvement. Moreover, a powerful *Fruit of the Loom* brand name should permit earnings to increase at a double-digit pace through 1996–98.

Although untimely for the year ahead, patient investors with a long-term horizon may find this equity of interest.

Vik Malhotra   *February 25, 1994*

Source: *Value Line Ivestment Survey.*

clothing lines and had boosted production. However, that demand did not materialize, and inventories rose to record levels. William Farley, Fruit of the Loom's CEO, took drastic action during the fourth quarter of 1993. He laid off 2,000 workers at 41 U.S. plants to cut back production. That cutback was sharp—too sharp. When demand suddenly soared in February 1994, the firm had to frantically scramble to rehire thousands of workers and to reboost production.

Farley reported in mid–May 1994 that his miscalculation had already cost Fruit of the Loom $40 million in lost sales and in costs related to firing and hiring. Analysts estimated that the firm's 1994 profits would drop by 11%, to $185 million; and Fruit of the Loom stood to lose $200 million in 1994 sales. Farley's miscalculation was especially untimely, occurring just as he was driving the $1.9 billion company on an acquisition spree into new markets. For instance, the firm had paid $100 million for the Gitano Group Inc.'s assets and had negotiated to buy the license to the Calvin Klein jeans label.

Following Fruit of the Loom's snafu, shareholders remained wary. After rising to $50 in 1993, their stock settled to $30 in 1994; and a group of shareholders, claiming that Fruit of the Loom misled investors about the weakening state of the business, filed suit in late December 1993. Kemper Financial Services Inc. also sold its 2.4% stake in early 1994 when it became concerned about the firm's outlook."

Questions

1. Calculate the inventory period, the accounts payable period, and the accounts receivable period as well as the operating and cash flow cycles for the years 1992 and 1993. In your calculations assume the cost of goods sold amounts to 82% of sales and the data for 12/31/93 and for 9/30/93 are the same.

2. Assuming it is well managed, inventory should grow at the same pace as the growth in sales. Calculate the growth rate in sales for the years 1991, 1992, and 1993 and the growth rate in inventory in 1992 and 1993. What was the excess inventory held in 1993? Now suppose the firm's management estimates the increase in sales in 1993 and use this estimate to increase the end-of-1992 inventory to meet these sales. How much inventory should the firm hold at the end of 1992 if the growth rate in sales in 1993 is the same as the average growth rate in 1991 and 1992? What was the current assets manager's main mistake? Calculate the growth rate in sales in 1993 that would justify the $568.2 million inventory held at the end of 1993.

3. Suppose the firm's optimal inventory level at the end of 1993 is the same as in 1992—namely, $415 million. The cost of financing the working capital is 10%. By how much will Fruit of the Loom's EPS increase in 1994 after reducing the

unnecessary excess inventory? Suppose this savings is the only difference between the 1993 EPS and the EPS forecasted for 1994. What would the EPS forecasted for 1994 be in such a case? Compare your result to *Value Line*'s forecast.

4. Is there a strong seasonality factor in the firm's sales that might require a large credit line (as observed in the J.C. Penney case)? Explain the difference between the sales seasonality of J.C. Penney and that of Fruit of the Loom. What differences in the nature of the products each of these two firms sells might account for differences in their seasonality?

5. Fruit of the Loom pays 20% of sales for raw materials: Most of the cost of goods sold consists of wages, electricity, and so on. Use this information to explain the large gap between the firm's receivables and payables. Can the firm finance most of its current assets by increasing its payables?

6. The firm laid off 2,000 workers in the fourth quarter of 1993. If the demand for the firm's product increases in the future, the firm will need to hire more workers. Laying off and then rehiring cost the firm a great deal of money. What other policy could the firm adopt to boost sales and to rid itself of excess inventory?

7. The following range of prices characterize the stock of Fruit of the Loom.

Year	1987	1988	1989	1990	1991	1992	1993
High $	9.8	7.6	16.0	15.4	28.0	49.6	49.3
Low $	3.9	4.5	5.3	6.1	7.6	26.6	22.9

In 1993 the stock price of Fruit of the Loom fell from $49.3 to $22.9. Can this change be attributed solely to its excess investment in inventory?

8. Based on your answers to Questions 1–7, write a report to the CEO on the firm's financial position together with suggestions on how to solve the firm's financial distress.

CHAPTER 20

MANAGING CASH ASSETS

LEARNING OBJECTIVES

After reading this chapter, you should understand:

1. Why a firm needs to hold cash assets.

2. How cash flow fluctuations may generate short-term cash deficits or surpluses.

3. How a firm uses float to minimize its cash assets holdings.

4. Ways to improve a firm's cash management efficiency.

5. How a firm decides on levels of cash and short-term marketable securities.

6. Why a firm invests its cash in repurchase agreements.

CORPORATE FINANCE IN THE NEWS

FLOAT

Next comes the insurance company "float." Float is a technical term referring to the provisions for unpaid claims and the premiums paid in advance by the insured, which are, of course, held and used by the insurance company pending the payment of claims.

This is virtually free money for the insurer, though sometimes it must be dipped into for paying out claims.

"We regard our float as a very significant asset," says (Warren) Buffett (CEO of Berkshire Hathaway). "We probably have as large an amount of float compared to our premium volume as virtually any property and casualty company there is—and that's intentional."

Had Berkshire had to borrow money at prevailing interest rates, the cost would have been close to $800 million a year.

Source: Robert Lenzner and David S. Fondiller, "The Not-So-Silent Partner," *Forbes* (22 January 1996): 78. Reprinted by Permission of FORBES Magazine © Forbes Inc., 1996.

20.1 INTRODUCTION

In Chapter 19 we learned how a firm should manage its current assets and current liabilities. We also studied the factors that determine the optimal levels of cash assets and working capital. In this chapter we focus on the management of one type of current asset—cash.

As Corporate Finance in the News relates, "float" is a significant cash asset. While an insurance firm must make provision for unpaid claims, it can also use the cash to save millions of dollars in interest. In Section 20.5.2 we define other sorts of "floats" and discuss in detail how a firm can use float as a source of financing.

Cash assets refers to cash and short-term marketable securities. The term *cash* means something slightly different for firms than what you would mean if you told a friend you didn't have enough cash to buy dinner and a movie ticket. A firm's cash is not just the currency and coins that may be in its registers or petty cash boxes; a firm's cash also includes demand deposit accounts in banks. For simplicity we refer to both currency and demand deposits as the firm's **cash.** The firm also holds short-term **marketable securities,** which are investments in assets such as short-term U.S. Trea-sury bills, certificates of deposit (CDs), and commercial paper. In our discussion of cash assets in this chapter, we distinguish between cash and marketable securities whenever such a distinction is warranted. Otherwise, we use the term **cash assets** as a whole category—that is, as the sum of cash and marketable securities. Except for the interest they provide, marketable securities are very similar to cash and are sometimes called *near-money assets* or *liquid assets*. The firm can easily sell marketable securities with no risk of significant loss.

The main feature of cash assets is their liquidity. Cash and demand deposits can be made available immediately. A firm can sell short-term securities for cash rela-tively quickly at the prevailing market price. Because such securities have very short maturities, any losses a firm sustains due to an interest rate increase are usually very small—that is, the firm can usually receive 100% of the securities' value.[1] Of course, holding cash assets has both benefits and costs. Holding cash assets not only ensures smooth-running operations, but it also means that the firm will have readily avail-able cash to take advantage of unforeseen investment opportunities. Holding cash also has an *opportunity cost*. For instance, if the firm invests its cash assets in produc-tion, it might earn 12%; whereas it might earn only 3% holding the same amount in cash assets. The 9% difference represents the opportunity cost of holding cash assets.

Most large firms have a cash manager who reports to the treasurer who reports to the firm's CFO. The cash manager has four principal tasks:

- To strike a balance between the costs and benefits of holding cash assets—that is, to determine the optimal level of cash assets.
- To determine the optimal division of cash assets between cash and marketable securities.

1. Long-term U.S. government bonds are default-free, but they cannot be considered as marketable because increases in the interest rate will cause heavy losses.

- To decide how to finance cash assets.
- To decide what to do with any surplus cash assets.

If the firm has excess cash flow from operations, it can use some of the excess to finance its cash asset needs and can reinvest the remainder in production or distribute some of it to its stockholders as a dividend or use it for a stock repurchase. If the cash flow from operations is not sufficient, the firm may have to issue stocks or bonds to finance its cash asset needs. The firm's method of financing cash assets may vary over time because sharp swings in a firm's cash situation—from deficit to surplus, and back—are not uncommon. For example, in the early 1990s IBM faced severe losses and had to cut its dividends drastically. By 1997 the tables turned, as shown by the following IBM press release:

For the full year we grew at 9 percent . . . In addition we completed the year with more than $8 billion in cash, after about $6 billion in capital expenditures, $1 billion in acquisitions and nearly $6 billion in common share repurchases.[2]

The financing of cash assets depends on the firm's success in operations, and the best financing policy for one year may become a very bad policy for another year.

This chapter covers the management of cash assets. We first discuss why a firm needs to hold cash assets and how a firm should determine the optimal level of cash assets it holds.

20.2 WHY DO FIRMS HOLD CASH ASSETS?

A firm holds cash assets for various reasons: to make routine transactions, to qualify for loans, to have cash for a "rainy day," or to take advantage of unexpected investment opportunities, as discussed next.

20.2.1 Transaction Motive

Perfect synchronization between the firm's cash inflows and outflows is virtually impossible to achieve. For example, the firm may owe $5 million in wages and rent on Friday but will not have that amount available until the following Tuesday when its accounts receivable are due. To make the routine payments associated with its ongoing activities, the firm will need to hold cash assets. Holding cash assets for such purposes is called the **transaction motive.**

A firm sometimes accumulates cash assets for a large planned transaction that has nothing to do with routine transactions. For example, in 1993 Nike held more than 22% of its current assets in cash assets, while Reebok was holding only about 10%. Was Nike holding too high a level of cash assets? Not necessarily. Nike may have been maintaining a relatively high cash assets balance to have cash readily available for a large transaction, as suggested in Connecting Theory to Practice 20.1.

2. IBM press release, January 21, 1997.

CONNECTING THEORY TO PRACTICE 20.1

WHY IS NIKE HOLDING A PILE OF CASH?

Mr. Knight [chairman and CEO of Nike] declined to confirm or deny rumors that Nike is negotiating to buy New York's Madison Square Garden sports arena, acquired by Viacom, Inc. in its takeover of Paramount Communications.[3] The move seems plausible, because Mr. Knight has said he wants to establish a business promoting entertainment events, in a way that would also promote Nike's brand name. And Mr. Knight himself seemed to think the acquisition plausible, hinting that "you wouldn't rule it out . . . but generally it would have to be a situation that . . . brings enhancement to our brand and world-wide message."

Source: *Wall Street Journal*, 8 July 1994, p. B2. Reprinted by permission of *The Wall Street Journal*, © 1994 Dow Jones & Company, Inc. All Rights Reserved Worldwide.

MAKING THE CONNECTION

Two firms in the same industry may hold very different levels of cash assets because they have different plans. In most cases if it plans a major cash transaction not associated with routine transactions, a firm will probably hold its cash assets in interest-earning marketable securities, rather than in cash, to take advantage of the return.

20.2.2 Precautionary Motive

Another reason for holding cash assets is the **precautionary motive**—the need to have a safety margin for unforeseen needs. For example, an insurance firm that is suddenly faced by a barrage of claims due to hurricane damage will have unexpectedly large cash outflows and will need extra cash to meet those unforeseen payments. However, the firm does not need to hold cash in anticipation of such needs; instead, it can hold short-term marketable securities, which it can sell as needed.

20.2.3 Speculative Motive

A firm sometimes holds cash assets to take advantage of unexpected investment opportunities. For example, a firm will need cash assets to take advantage of a bargain purchase that might suddenly become available. Holding cash assets for this purpose is called the **speculative motive.**

---

3. Eventually Nike did not buy the Madison Square Garden sports arena, but it did purchase the world's largest hockey equipment maker (Canstar Sports) and its subsidiaries in Southeast Asia.

20.2.4 Compensation Motive

A final motive for holding cash assets is that, as mentioned in Chapter 19, banks sometimes require their borrowers to maintain compensation cash balances. To obtain a loan or other banking services, the firm will be required to hold some level of cash in the bank.

20.3 THE FIRM'S OPTIMAL LEVEL OF CASH ASSETS

A firm holds cash assets for all of these reasons and may pool them because it has no need to divide the cash assets and allocate them in advance for any specific purpose. However, once the firm decides on the level of cash assets to be held, it will have to decide on how to divide these cash assets between cash and marketable securities.

Both cash and marketable securities yield a relatively small return, but the return on cash is smaller. On the other hand, cash is liquid; the firm can use it immediately with no fear of even a small capital loss. The division between cash and marketable securities depends on the relative importance of the four motives for holding cash and also depends on three additional factors:

1. *Frequency and intensity of the fluctuations in the firm's cash outflows and inflows.* The more frequent and the more intense the fluctuations, the less predictable the need for cash and, therefore, the higher the proportion of cash the firm should hold.
2. *Interest rate on short-term marketable securities.* The higher the interest rate, the larger the opportunity cost of holding cash and, therefore, the lower the proportion of cash the firm should hold.
3. *Transaction or trading costs.* A firm that holds marketable securities may need to sell them if it needs cash. Buying and selling securities involves transactions costs: The larger the transaction costs, the higher the proportion of cash the firm should hold.

Let's look at an example: J.C. Penney's division of cash assets into cash and marketable securities. In 1994 J.C. Penney held cash assets totaling $261 million, of which about 80% was in short-term securities and the rest was in cash. The following problem reveals that even if the market interest rate sharply increases, holding marketable securities is quite safe.

PRACTICE BOX

Problem   In 1994 J.C. Penney invested $207 million in government zero-coupon bonds. Each bond had a three-month maturity, a par value of $1,000, and an annual

(continued)

yield to maturity of 7%. The firm also held $54 million in cash, which earned no interest. Suppose after two months, the annual yield to maturity on the government bonds suddenly rose to 8%. At the same time J.C. Penney needed to pay $261 million in cash. Calculate how much cash was available and how much would be available if J.C. Penney held all the cash assets in cash. How much cash would J.C. Penney have if the yield to maturity drops to 6%? Assume a zero interest on cash.

Solution

If it held all the cash assets in cash, J.C. Penney would have all the cash it needs to make the payments.

The bonds' price three months before maturity is given by P_3, where $^3/_{12}$ is the portion of the year left to maturity:[4]

$$P_3 = \frac{\$1,000}{(1 + 0.07)^{3/12}} \cong \$983.23$$

This is the price J.C. Penney paid for each bond. After two months, when the firm needed the money, the yield to maturity rose to 8%. Because there was only one month left to maturity, the bond price was P_1:

$$P_1 = \frac{\$1,000}{(1.08)^{1/12}} \cong \$993.61$$

Thus, the firm earned

$$\frac{\$993.61}{\$983.23} - 1 \cong 0.0106 \text{ or } 1.06\%$$

on its investment in bonds. The value of the whole bond investment was $209.19 million ($207 million × 1.0106 ≅ $209.19 million). Thus, the firm obtained $263.19 million ($54 million + $209.19 million = $263.19 million), which was more than the $261 million needed. Therefore, J.C. Penney had all the cash it needed.

Note that the rate of return on zero-coupon bonds is composed of the bond's price appreciation as the maturity decreases plus the capital gain or loss. If the interest rate increases, the firm will face a capital loss on the bonds that it holds. In our case, in spite of the sharp rise in the interest rate, the firm still fared better by holding marketable securities than cash, because the effect of the price increase due to the decrease in time left to maturity outweighed the price decrease due to the increase in the interest rate.

What if the interest rate had decreased to, say, 6%? In that case the bond's price would have been

$$P = \frac{\$1,000}{(1.06)^{1/12}} \cong \$995.16$$

(continued)

4. For bond pricing, see Chapter 12 Equation (12.1).

and the rate of return on the investment would have been

$$\frac{\$995.16}{\$983.23} - 1 \cong 0.0121 \text{ or } 1.21\%$$

In the case of an interest rate decrease, the cash flow from selling the bonds would have been $209.5 million ($207 million $\times$ 1.0121 $\cong$ $209.5 million), and the total cash available would have been $263.5 million ($54 million + $209.5 million = $263.5 million).

Because a variety of short-term investments are available, the cash manager's role is complex. A firm can invest cash assets in marketable securities, overnight deposits, foreign currency, or demand deposits. Each investment has its own particular rate of return and liquidity characteristics. The cash manager must select the best investment strategy, taking both return and liquidity into account.

We saw that holding short-term marketable securities was profitable for J.C. Penney. We will elaborate further on the division of cash assets between cash and marketable securities in Section 20.7.

As you might expect, a low level of cash assets may force the firm to interrupt operations. Such interruption may have the effect of decreasing the firm's overall rate of return on equity and, hence, the stockholders' wealth. In addition, if the firm does not have enough cash to pay wages on time, it may face employee resignations and labor disputes.

If high levels of cash assets ensure smooth-running operations and contented employees, why doesn't the firm simply ensure these results by holding high levels of cash assets? If the firm's level of cash assets is too high, it may reduce the stockholders' wealth because the rate of return on cash assets is, on average, much lower than it is on productive projects. Moreover, the firm pays corporate income taxes on the interest earned and can avoid these taxes if stockholders invest directly in these assets. In the extreme case, consider a firm that invests only in marketable securities. It might earn, say, 6% on this investment, but only 3.9% [(1 − 0.35) × 6% = 3.9%] on an after-tax basis. If stockholders were to purchase the securities directly, they would earn 6% and avoid the corporate tax. Thus, investing all the firm's resources in cash assets will decrease the stock price. To avoid this situation, the firm will seek the **optimal level of cash assets** to maximize its value. Table 20-1 illustrates the level of cash assets that a sample of U.S. firms hold. Notice that cash assets as a percent of total current assets ranges from 0.16% for Wal-Mart Stores to 22.82% for Nike.

Because holding high levels of cash decreases the return on equity, a firm tries to keep its level of cash assets to a bare minimum that still allows operations to run smoothly. It will invest any remaining available cash in productive projects yielding a higher rate of return. What happens if cash accumulates and no profitable investments are available? Although this position is definitely better than having no cash at all, holding too high a level of cash assets is like holding an idle asset. Idle assets generate zero or very low returns, and the firm's rate of return on its assets or on its equity will fall. The firm will do all it can to avoid such a situation and will take actions to reduce

TABLE 20-1 Cash Assets Held by a Sample of U.S. Firms (October 31, 1993)	Firm	Cash Assets ($ million)	Total Current Assets ($ million)	Cash Assets as Percentage of Current Assets
	Kmart	534	12,622	4.23
	J.C. Penney	315	8,207	3.84
	Sears	2,051	28,539	7.19
	Wal-Mart Stores	22	13,897	0.16
	Nike	367	1,608	22.82
	Circuit City	41	1,266	3.24
	Toys 'R' Us	122	3,195	3.82
	Dillard Dept. Stores	42	2,698	1.56
	Reebok International	123	1,204	10.22

Source: *Value Line Investment Survey*, 25 February 1994.

its cash assets. Connecting Theory to Practice 20.2 demonstrates the predicament of "rich firms" and how they attempt to solve their cash assets problems.

CONNECTING THEORY TO PRACTICE 20.2

SOLVING CASH ASSET PROBLEMS

BUY YOURSELF[5]

After three years of economic recovery, many American firms are now flush with cash. It is proving harder to spend this money than it was to earn it. True, there has been a modest pick-up in investment. No doubt the odd corporate jet has been bought, and headquarters started up. But many firms are admitting that they cannot find anything useful to do with the cash. They are handing it back to shareholders, both by raising dividends and, increasingly, by buying back their own shares.

On June 23rd Chase Manhattan, a New York bank, said it planned to acquire around 4.5% of its outstanding shares within 18 months. This followed repurchase announcements earlier in the month by, among others, Merrill Lynch, an investment bank, Allstate, an insurer, and Philip Morris, a tobacco and foods group.

REPURCHASING JAPAN[6]

After two decades of talk, Japan is at last set to allow companies to buy back their shares. Two laws intended to make this possible were passed by the Diet

5. "Buy Yourself: Share Repurchases," *The Economist*, 2 July 1994, pp. 68–70. © 1994 The Economist Newspaper Group, Inc. Reprinted with permission. Further reproduction prohibited.

6. "Repurchasing Japan," *The Economist*, 2 July 1994, p. 71. © 1994 The Economist Newspaper Group, Inc. Reprinted with permission. Further reproduction prohibited.

[Japan's parliament] on June 22nd, just in time to avoid being caught up in Japan's latest political crisis. The new rules will probably take effect sometime next year. They should help firms cope with several big challenges.

The first is Japanese firms' poor return on equity (ROE). Jason James, an analyst at James Capel, reckons that the ROE of Tokyo-listed firms will be around 3% in the year to next March, compared with about 15% in America and Britain, and 8½% in France and Germany. Japan's Ministry of Finance reckons that low ROE is a big reason why the stock market is stuck at around half its 1989 peak. Low ROEs can be blamed in part on Japanese firms' huge financial reserves, which swell their equity capital. Since the reserves generally earn poor returns, they drag down the average return on equity. Handing part of these reserves to shareholders through share buy-backs may prove a useful way of boosting ROE. If shareholders think they can invest the cash better than a firm can, they may reward repurchasing companies with higher share prices.

MAKING THE CONNECTION

Cash-rich U.S. firms have the option of transferring their cash asset surplus to stockholders. Many Japanese firms also have excess cash, and the Japanese government has passed legislation to allow firms to dispose of their accumulated cash and, thereby, to boost the rate of return on equity.

If a firm has cash but no profitable projects, the rate of return on equity and the stock price will both decrease. Wealth is destroyed. By transferring excess cash to stockholders and by avoiding negative NPV projects, a firm creates wealth. As we see from Connecting Theory to Practice 20.2, many U.S. and Japanese firms have decided that reducing the level of cash assets by transferring cash to the stockholders is better than holding on to too much cash and reducing the firm's ROE.

Deciding on this optimal level, the firm can use its cash budget as a tool for predicting future cash shortages or surpluses. The task of the firm's CFO is to determine the optimal level of cash.

20.4 USING THE CASH BUDGET TO PREDICT CASH SHORTAGES OR SURPLUSES

As explained in Chapter 19, Section 19.5, the cash budget is the primary tool that a firm uses for short-term financial planning. The **cash budget** summarizes all the firm's cash inflows and cash outflows and helps determine the specific needed amounts of cash assets.

Once the firm has this information on its projected cash deficits and surpluses, it can plan its operations in the financial market. For example, if a temporary surplus is predicted for a particular month, the firm can buy short-term securities. If the surplus is expected to be permanent, the firm can invest it in long-term projects or can repurchase its stock.

In the case of a projected deficit, the firm can consider reducing its nonmandatory cash outflows rather than borrowing cash. For example, the firm may decide to postpone a planned capital expenditure. However, this would affect its future profitability. Similarly, the firm may decide to cut its cash dividend. However, the market might interpret this as signaling bad news. The firm's best policy is to prepare a cash budget, to forecast its cash needs, and then to prepare a credit line in case of a cash deficit or a cash investment in case of a cash surplus.

20.5 TECHNIQUES FOR MINIMIZING CASH BALANCES

The cash manager's goal is to minimize the firm's cash balances without affecting its operations. This is achieved by **cash management efficiency.** The more efficient the management of cash assets, the smaller the amount of cash the firm needs to hold without affecting its smooth operation. The main reason for keeping cash holdings to a minimum is that a firm receives no interest (or very low interest) on cash balances. The lower the cash balances, the more the firm saves on opportunity costs.

For example, in 1996 Microsoft held more than $6.9 billion in cash assets, divided between $2.6 billion in cash equivalents, yielding zero return, and $4.3 billion in marketable securities, yielding about 5% interest. Suppose due to improvement in cash management efficiency, Microsoft was able to reduce its cash balances by $500 million and to shift an additional $500 million to marketable securities yielding 5% annual interest; this would create additional annual revenue of $25 million (0.05 $\times$ $500 million = $25 million). Therefore, the 5% annual interest is the opportunity cost of cash: Microsoft could earn 5% on any amount of cash assets it held in marketable securities.

Cash management is not a simple task in large firms. Firms such as Sears, IBM, General Motors, and Intel have manufacturing plants in many different regions of the United States and the world, and they need to make cash payments and to collect cash in different currencies across a wide geographic area. Such international operations further complicate the task of cash management. The cash manager has to ensure that any surplus cash in one bank account is moved quickly to another where it is needed. Efficient coordination among the firm's bank accounts will serve the firm well in keeping its cash balances to a minimum. Whenever it has a temporary cash surplus, the firm should invest it in marketable securities.

The firm generally receives interest (albeit low) on its deposits; and the more liquid the deposit, the lower the interest. For simplicity in the rest of the chapter, we assume *zero* interest on cash deposits in the bank and a positive rate of return on marketable securities. If in practice the firm earns positive interest on bank deposits, the analyses remain unchanged as long as the rate of return on marketable securities is higher.

What actions can a firm take to minimize its cash balances and to improve cash management? The cash manager has four principal actions:

1. Synchronize cash flows. This difficult task must be coordinated with other departments, especially the credit department.

2. Accelerate cash collection.
3. Delay cash disbursements as much as possible without damaging the firm's credit rating or angering its suppliers.
4. Move funds quickly from one bank account to another to balance surpluses and deficits.

In the remainder of this section we examine the specific techniques cash managers use toward these ends.

20.5.1 Synchronizing Cash Flows

Suppose a firm pays its bills on a weekly basis but collects its payments biweekly. If so, we say the firm has a lack of cash flow **synchronization**—that is, its cash out-flows and inflows do not occur simultaneously. The firm can reduce the needed cash balances if it can move the cash disbursements and cash collections into the same cash flow cycle. Sometimes such synchronization is not possible; at other times it is accompanied by additional costs. For example, the firm may be able to pay its bills on a biweekly basis by adding some percentage to the bills to compensate the cash receivers for the week's time delay. The firm's management should consider the benefits and the costs of synchronization before deciding whether it is worthwhile to achieve.

20.5.2 Managing Float

In Corporate Finance in the News, it is claimed that float is "virtually free money." What is float? How can a firm increase it? We now turn to these questions.

One way to reduce the firm's cash balances is to speed cash collection and to slow cash payments. **Float management** describes this activity of accelerating cash collection and delaying cash disbursement, where **float** is the value of uncollected checks in a stage of transfer from one bank to another.

As a rule, the greater the distance between the paying and the deposit banks, the longer it takes for a check to clear. The greater the distance, the more uncleared checks and the larger the float. Large float is advantageous to check writers, whose money will continue earning interest until their checks clear. It is disadvantageous to check recipients who must wait for checks to clear before gaining access to the funds or earning interest on them. By slowing down its cash payments, the firm creates a *disbursement float*; by speeding up its cash collection, it creates a *collection float*. By efficient management of the float, the firm will have more cash available for operations.

Disbursement float is defined as

$$\text{Disbursement float} = \text{Payments recorded on firm's books} \quad (20.1)$$
$$- \text{Payments cleared by the bank}$$

To illustrate, suppose Xerox Corporation writes checks for $100,000 every day. When the checks are written, Xerox reduces the cash balance recorded on its books. However, the bank does not immediately clear the checks. In fact, several days are required before the bank receives and processes the checks and reduces Xerox's cash balance. This delay is called the **disbursement delay.**

The disbursement delay has three components. Assume the checks are delivered by mail, and it takes three days for the postal service to deliver them to the recipients—this is called the **mail time delay.** It takes another day for the recipients to sort, record, and deliver the checks to the bank—this delay is called the **processing delay.** Finally, the recipient's bank needs time to clear the checks through the banking system. Two more days elapse during this **availability delay** before the banking system clears the check and presents it to Xerox's bank. In this example, in total, six days pass from the date Xerox writes the checks and records the payments on its books to the time when the bank actually removes the money from Xerox's checking account.

Because the firm writes checks for $100,000 per day, the disbursement float for six days will be $600,000. Xerox earns interest on this $600,000, even though its own corporate records show that the cash has already been transferred to the recipients. Thus, the firm clearly benefits from the large disbursement float.

Corporate Finance in the News discussed a form of float that is unique to the insurance industry. An insurance firm receives premium payments and makes provisions for future claims. That provision for claims reduces the firm's equity but does not affect cash until the firm pays the claims. The time difference from when the provision is made (and equity is reduced on the firm's books) and when a claim is settled is disbursement float. Such float saves Berkshire Hathaway over $800 million of interest each year.

Parallel to the disbursement delay, a **collection delay** is created by the time lapse between when the firm receives a check and the bank credits the firm's bank account. Suppose Xerox receives $200,000 from its customers every day. When it receives the checks, Xerox records them in its books. It deposits the checks in the bank immediately, but two days elapse before the customers' banks honor the checks and credit Xerox for this sum. Thus, the **collection float** is defined as

$$\text{Collection float } = \text{Receipts recorded on the firm's books} \qquad (20.2)$$
$$- \text{ Receipts cleared by the bank}$$

In our example, Xerox's collection float is $400,000 because two processing days are required before the $200,000 deposits become available.

The firm's disbursement float minus its collection float is called the **net float:**

$$\text{Net float} = \text{Disbursement float} - \text{Collection float} \qquad (20.3)$$

In the Xerox example, we have

$$\text{Net float} = \$600,000 - \$400,000 = \$200,000$$

This $200,000 net float means that Xerox has $200,000 of free cash available for other purposes. The goals of float management are to increase the disbursement float as much as possible, to decrease the collection float as much as possible, which increases the net float, as the following problem demonstrates.

PRACTICE BOX

Problem   Suppose Dock Inc. (which starts its operations on Day 1) receives checks worth $100 million each day. The cash corresponding to the checks received on Day 1 is credited to the firm's bank account on Day 3, the cash corresponding to the checks received on Day 2 is recorded on Day 4, and so on. Describe the receipts recorded in the firm's books and the receipts cleared by the bank. Calculate the collection float for each day.

Solution   We have the following bank and cash balances (in $ million):

Day	1	2	3	4	5	. . .
Changes in the firm's books	100	200	300	400	500	. . .
Changes in the bank's cash balance	0	0	100	200	300	. . .
Collection float	−100	−200	−200	−200	−200	. . .

Note that the firm receives checks for $100 million every day; therefore, the firm's cash book value increases by $100 million daily. The bank records the cash from the first day's checks on Day 3, the cash from the second day on Day 4, and so on. On the first day, the collection float is −$100 million; but from Day 2 on, the firm has a constant collection float of −$200 million. The book balance and the bank cash balance increases at $100 million a day, leaving the float unchanged at −$200 million.

We need to make a final point about mail time delay: Note that when the firm writes checks, the mail time delay affects the disbursement float. However, when a customer writes a check, the mail time delay does not affect the collection float because the firm does not record the check's amount in its books until it receives the check. (That is, the mail time delay is already over by the time the firm receives the check.) Although technically the mail time delay does not affect the collection float, this does not mean that mail time delay is unimportant. The sooner the check is cleared and recorded in the firm's bank account, the sooner the firm's bank cash balance increases. As we know, the sooner it receives the cash flows, the better the firm fares.

20.5.3 INCREASING THE NET FLOAT

As already mentioned, the firm should try to speed cash collection to minimize the collection float and should try to slow its payments to increase the disbursement float. These two actions will maximize the net float that, in turn, provides the firm with cash balances for use in current operations. We turn now to techniques for increasing the net float.

LOCKBOXES

Using lockboxes is one of several ways to cut the mail time delay. Suppose a customer located in California sends a check to Kodak's headquarters in Rochester, New York. To shorten the mail time delay, the firm can establish a post office box, called a **lockbox,** in California. The customer will be instructed to send the check to the lockbox. A local bank will check the lockbox several times a day and will deposit the checks taken from the lockbox in the firm's local account. The California bank will send the firm a daily electronic record of the receipts. The firm will then update its cash and receivables balances. In this way the mail time and processing delay can be cut from, say, three days to only one day. Large firms have many lockboxes spread over the country.

Figure 20-1 demonstrates the collection procedure with and without lockboxes. A customer living in Berkeley, California, sends a check to Kodak, whose headquar-

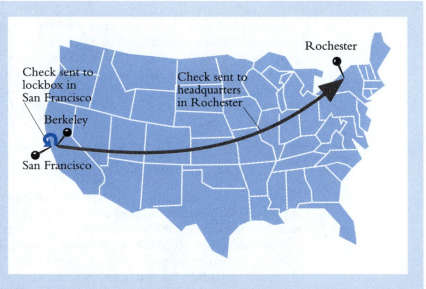

FIGURE 20-1
Accelerating Collections by Using Lockboxes

	Regular Process	Accelerated Process	Days Saved
Mail time delay	Customer in Berkeley mails the check to Rochester.	Customer sends the check to San Francisco lockbox (post office box).	2
Processing delay	Firm receives and deposits the check but cannot use the funds yet.	Local bank collects the check from the lockbox and clears it through a local clearing house.	1
Availability delay	Bank clears the check and transfers the cash to the firm's account.	Local bank notifies the firm by electronic means that the cash is available.	1
Total number of days saved			4

ters is in Rochester, New York. Sending the check directly to Rochester takes about three days. Kodak then deposits the check in its bank, and the bank sends the check to the Federal Reserve System for clearing. The Federal Reserve processes the check and transfers the money from the customer's account to Kodak's account, and the bank then notifies Kodak that the money is available. Contrast this with lockbox system: The customer sends the check to Kodak's lockbox in San Francisco, which cuts the mail time delay by two days. The local bank checks the lockbox several times a day and processes the checks through a local clearing house, cutting the processing delay by one day. The local bank notifies Kodak by electronic means that the checks are available, which cuts the availability delay by one day. Altogether, in our example, Kodak saves four days, and the money is available in Kodak's bank account four days earlier. Of course, the local bank will charge a commission for its services. Kodak should weigh the costs against the benefits of the lockbox arrangement. The following problem illustrates this issue.

PRACTICE BOX

Problem

Let us continue the previous example. Checks for an average sum of $500 are sent to Kodak. The local bank that collects and processes the checks from the lockbox charges $1 per check. The daily interest rate is 0.02%. By using the lockbox rather than direct mail to Rochester, Kodak has the cash available four days earlier. Should the firm continue to use the lockbox system? What if the average check is for $5,000?

Solution

The interest on the extra four days of cash availability is approximately

$$4 \text{ days} \times \$500 \times 0.0002 = \$0.40 \text{ per check}$$

The bank charges a $1 commission fee per check. The firm fares better with the regular, slower clearing system.

If the average check is for $5,000, the firm fares better with the lockbox system because

$$4 \text{ days} \times \$5,000 \times 0.0002 = \$4 \text{ per check}$$

The firm still pays a $1 commission per check, but in this case the lockbox system saves $3 per check.

These savings may seem small, but consider large firms such as Exxon, General Motors, and IBM, whose sales amount to $200 million per day. Assuming $5,000 per average check, these firms would receive 40,000 checks per day. Using the numbers in our example, these large firms might save $43.8 million annually (40,000 checks × $3 = $120,000 every day, or $43.8 million annually).

PREAUTHORIZED DEBIT

Funds can be automatically transferred from a customer's account to the firm's account on a certain date by a **preauthorized debit** agreement. This eliminates all time delays—which is an advantage for the firm. However, the customer forfeits his or her disbursement float and, therefore, will usually require compensation.

CONCENTRATION BANKS

Earlier we discussed the importance of moving cash from one bank to another as quickly as possible to balance deficits and surpluses. This can be achieved by having an account in a **concentration bank,** a geographically centralized bank where several of the firm's accounts are pooled.

A firm typically has a number of lockboxes that many different, local banks handle and has a cash account at each of these banks. Rather than having a cash surplus in one bank and a cash deficit in another, the firm may choose a **cash concentration** procedure, which pools the balances at each local bank into a more limited number of concentration banks. By pooling accounts in this way, the firm can keep better track of its cash. In addition, because large amounts of money are involved, the firm may be able to negotiate a better deal with the bank.

Figure 20-2 illustrates how a firm can use lockboxes and a concentration bank to increase cash management efficiency. Note that the firm receives checks directly at its headquarters as well as through lockboxes. Local banks collect the checks and deposit them in a concentration bank. By managing one account rather than many, the firm minimizes the cash balances needed, and it can invest more of its cash assets in short-term securities.

One method of transferring cash surpluses to the concentration bank is by using a **depository transfer check (DTC),** a preauthorized check that does not need a signature. A DTC is restricted to making deposits to a particular account at a particular bank. The collection bank transfers money to the concentration bank daily by writing a DTC payable to the concentration bank.

AUTOMATED CLEARING HOUSES

An **automated clearing house (ACH),** an electronic network, sends data from one bank to another. No paper checks are sent (thus avoiding mail time delay), and the ACH guarantees one-day clearing regardless of the bank's location. Because a wire transfer involves a fairly large commission per wire, a firm generally uses it only for relatively large sums.

20.5.4 Managing Cash Disbursements

The firm improves its cash management mainly by decreasing its collection float; it can do very little to increase its disbursement float. The firm can delay payments to its suppliers by sending checks from a bank branch located far from the supplier. Although the firm may succeed in increasing its disbursement float by using tactics of this kind, suppliers will not be happy with such a policy. Some may even consider such a policy unethical.

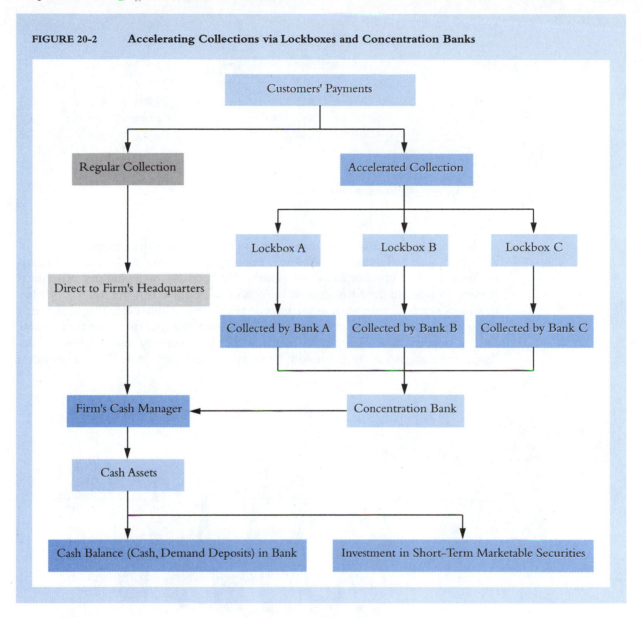

FIGURE 20-2   Accelerating Collections via Lockboxes and Concentration Banks

20.6 THE SEASONALITY FACTOR IN CASH MANAGEMENT

Seasonality in a firm's sales will lead to seasonality in its financing needs and in the cash assets that it holds. For example, consider Toys 'R' Us sales for 1991–1996 (in $ million):

Quarter	1	2	3	4
1991	1,025	1,056	1,181	2,860
1992	1,172	1,249	1,345	3,401
1993	1,286	1,317	1,449	3,997
1994	1,462	1,452	1,631	4,200
1995	1,492	1,614	1,714	4,480
1996[a]	1,625	1,750	1,875	4,950

[a]Estimates

Source: *Value Line Investment Survey*, various issues.

Sales in the fourth quarter of each year amount to more than double the sales in any other quarter. Figure 20-3 illustrates the seasonality factor in the financial needs of Toys 'R' Us. For simplicity we assume that total assets (including cash assets) needed to operate the firm amount to 50% of sales. Line 1 in the figure describes the assets needed in the various quarters of years 1991–1996. Note that as the firm expands over the years, the amount of needed assets also increases over time. However, probably due to large investment needed in inventory and receivables, the firm's financing needs are greatest in the fourth quarter each year. Thus, we notice a

**FIGURE 20-3
Seasonality Factor in
Toys 'R' Us's Financial
Needs and the
Financing Sources**

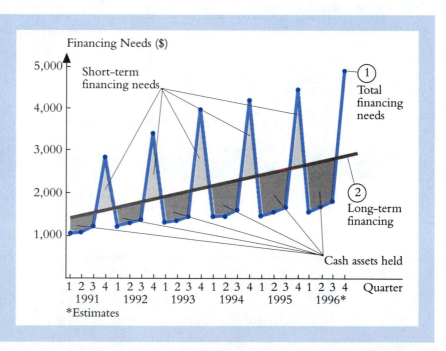

seasonal peak in the firm's total asset needs in the fourth quarter of each year. The assets held include cash assets, fixed assets, and inventory.

Figure 20-3 also shows that the firm's long-term financing policy may create an additional *seasonal surplus* of cash assets. To illustrate, suppose Toys 'R' Us employs long-term debt and equity as illustrated by Line 2 in Figure 20-3. Whenever Line 1 is above Line 2, the long-term financing sources will not be sufficient; and the firm will need to borrow from the bank or use other short-term financing sources to finance its operations. Alternatively, whenever Line 2 is above Line 1, the firm will have long-term financing sources in excess of its needs. The firm will hold its temporary surplus in cash assets in cash and short-term marketable securities.

Should the firm invest its surplus funds in long-term assets, which offer greater rates of return than short-term assets? This policy would be risky because when sales pick up in the fourth quarter, the firm will need the money. Retrieving it from the long-term investment may involve losses. For example, if it invests in 30-year, zero-coupon bonds and the yield to maturity rises from, say, 6% to 7%, the firm suffers a capital loss of almost 25% of the amount invested. To see this, let F be the face value of each bond. At a yield of 6%, the bond's price is $P_{6\%} = F/(1.06)^{30}$. If the yield changes to 7%, the new price will be $P_{7\%} = F/(1.07)^{30}$. The capital gain (or loss) is given by

$$\frac{P_{7\%} - P_{6\%}}{P_{6\%}} = \frac{\dfrac{F}{(1.07)^{30}} - \dfrac{F}{(1.06)^{30}}}{\dfrac{F}{(1.06)^{30}}} = \frac{(1.06)^{30}}{(1.07)^{30}} - 1 \cong -0.25 \text{ or } -25\%$$

It is better to invest the seasonal cash surplus in short-term marketable securities, which are almost riskless. The question that remains is how much of the cash assets should the firm hold in cash and how much should it hold in marketable securities? To this we turn next.

20.7 DIVIDING CASH ASSETS BETWEEN CASH AND MARKETABLE SECURITIES: THE BAUMOL MODEL

When the firm seeks the optimal mix of cash and marketable securities, it must consider two factors: (1) selling securities when cash is needed incurs transaction costs, and (2) cash earns no or relatively low interest. Here we discuss how the firm uses these factors to determine the optimal division of cash assets.

A firm shifts between holding cash and marketable securities depending on its cash needs over time. If the firm holds idle cash because it anticipates a need for cash in the short run, the opportunity cost of doing so will equal what it could earn on marketable securities. This cost increases as a function of the cash balance size: The more cash the firm holds, the larger the opportunity cost. Figure 20-4 illustrates the various costs involved in holding cash. The opportunity costs are described by Line 1, which is a straight line because it varies directly with the increase in the cash balance.

FIGURE 20-4
Costs of Holding Cash

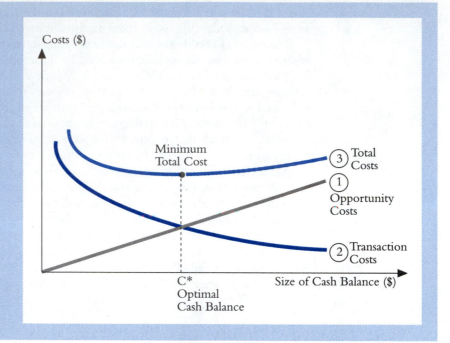

The firm sells marketable securities as it needs cash and purchases them as surplus cash accumulates. If it conducts many such transactions during the year, the firm will have large brokerage costs. These transaction costs are described by Curve 2 in Figure 20-4.[7] The more cash a firm holds, the fewer transactions it needs to conduct and the lower its transaction costs. In the extreme, if the firm holds a sufficient amount of cash, it never sells short-term securities and the transaction costs are equal to zero. The total costs, described by Curve 3, are the sum of the first two cost components (opportunity costs and transaction costs). The firm's optimal cash balance is Point C^*; where the total cost is smallest and where the curves for opportunity costs and transaction costs intersect.

Economist William Baumol devised a model to derive the *optimal starting cash level*.[8] The model uses the following notations:

F = Fixed cost paid when a transaction in the marketable securities is conducted. Each time the firm buys or sells marketable securities, it incurs transaction costs of $\$F$, regardless of the transaction's size.

T = Total amount of cash needed to conduct transactions over a given planning period, usually one year.

r = Opportunity cost of holding cash, given by the interest rate on marketable securities, or the difference between what is earned on marketable securities and cash deposits.

7. As we shall see, when there is a fixed cost per transaction, transaction costs are of the form $(T/C)F$, where F is the fixed cost, C is the amount of cash held, and T is the total amount of cash needed to conduct transactions during a year.
8. See W. J. Baumol, "The Transaction Demand for Cash: An Inventory Theoretic Approach," *Quarterly Journal of Economics* (November 1952): 545–556.

C = Cash level at the beginning of each cycle, with $C/2$ as the average cash balance. Note that if the firm decides to hold, say, $C = \$100,000$ in cash, it uses the money until the balance reaches zero. At that point, the firm sells $\$100,000$ of marketable securities to replenish its cash balance. Baumol assumes that cash balances decrease linearly over time. If it takes three months for C to drop from $\$100,000$ to zero, then each cycle is three months long.

C^* = The optimum level of C, with an average cash balance of $C^*/2$.

To illustrate the idea of the average cash balances held ($C/2$), we use two competing cash balance policies:

- Policy 1: The firm starts its operations at time zero with $C_1 = \$100,000$ in cash. Each week the firm's cash outflow exceeds the firm's cash inflows by $\$25,000$. The cash balance drops by $\$25,000$ per week and reaches zero at the end of the fourth week. Then the firm sells $\$100,000$ of its marketable securities and starts once again, at the beginning of the fifth week, with $\$100,000$. Thus, each cycle is four weeks. These cash balances are described by the Curve 1 "sawtooth" pattern in Figure 20-5.

- Policy 2: If the firm starts its operations at time zero with $C_2 = \$50,000$ in cash, the cycle lasts two weeks, and it will get the lower "sawtooth" pattern described by Curve 2.

  If the firm starts with a cash balance of $\$100,000$, the average balance during each cycle, and also during the year, will be $(\$100,000 + \$0)/2 = \$50,000$. If the firm starts with a cash balance of $\$50,000$, the average cash balance will be $(\$50,000 + \$0)/2 = \$25,000$.

FIGURE 20-5
Changes in Level of Cash Balance Over Time

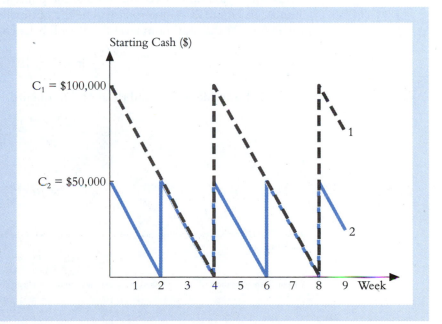

Which policy is better, $C_1 = \$100{,}000$ or $C_2 = \$50{,}000$? We can use Baumol's model to identify the optimal level, C^*, of cash balances for each cycle. This is the point at which the total cost of holding cash is minimized (as we saw in Figure 20-4). To find the optimal level of cash, we need to analyze the opportunity and transaction costs of holding cash using the notations of the model given previously:

- *Opportunity costs.* The firm holds, on average, a cash balance of $\$C/2$ on which no interest is earned. Therefore, the opportunity cost is $(\$C/2) \times r$, where r is the after-tax interest rate on marketable securities.
- *Transaction costs.* Suppose the firm sells $\$C$ of its marketable securities at the beginning of the year and holds the proceeds in cash. When it uses all the cash, the firm will need to sell more marketable securities to replenish its cash balance. For simplicity assume the firm pays a fixed transaction cost each time it trades marketable securities. How many times will the firm trade securities during the period? If the total cash needs for transaction activities during the period is $\$T$, and if the firm sells $\$C$ of marketable securities every time it needs cash, then the number of trades during the period will be T/C. Since the firm pays $\$F$ for each trade, total transaction costs will be $(T/C) \times F$.

The total costs will be

$$\text{Total costs} = \left(\frac{C}{2}\right) \times r + \left(\frac{T}{C}\right) \times F \tag{20.4}$$

For given values of T, r, and F, we seek the value of C^* that minimizes the total costs. When the total cost is minimized, the optimal values of the two cost components equal each other.[9] This means that the point at which the two curves (Curves 1 and 2 in Figure 20-4) intersect will be the optimal cash balance and the minimum total costs. At that optimum level C^* of cash balance we have

$$\left(\frac{C^*}{2}\right)r = \left(\frac{T}{C^*}\right)F$$

Multiply both sides by C^* and isolate C^* to obtain:

$$C^{*2} = \frac{(2T \times F)}{r}$$

or

$$C^* = (2T \times F/r)^{1/2} \tag{20.5}$$

9. Note that C is any arbitrary cash level held, and C^* is the optimal level of the cash held. According to Equation (20.4), the total cost equals

$$TC = \left(\frac{C}{2}\right)r + \left(\frac{T}{C}\right)F$$

We can differentiate the total cost with respect to C and equate to zero to obtain the minimum total cost:

$$\frac{r}{2} - \left(\frac{T}{C^{*2}}\right)F = 0 \quad \text{or} \quad \left(\frac{C^*}{2}\right)r = \left(\frac{T}{C^*}\right)F$$

where C^* is the optimum cash balance at the beginning of each cycle and $C^*/2$ is the average cash balance in each cycle. To find the optimum cash balance, we plug numbers into Equation (20.5).

We asked earlier whether $C_1 = \$100,000$ or $C_2 = \$50,000$ represents the optimal policy. To answer this question, we need more information. Suppose $T = \$10$ million, $F = \$50$, and $r = 0.1$. Then

$$C^* = (2T \times F/r)^{1/2} = (2 \times \$10 \text{ million} \times \$50/0.1)^{1/2} = \$100,000$$

and the firm is better off holding $100,000 at the beginning of each cycle. Indeed with $C^* = \$100,000$, the total cost is

$$\text{Total cost} = (\$100,000/2) \times 0.1 + (\$10,000,000/\$100,000) \times \$50$$
$$= \$5,000 + \$5,000 = \$10,000$$

With $C = \$50,000$, total cost is higher:

$$\text{Total cost} = (\$50,000/2) \times 0.1 + (\$10,000,000/\$50,000) \times \$50$$
$$= \$2,500 + \$10,000 = \$12,500$$

The following problem addresses the issue of calculating Sears' optimal cash holdings.

PRACTICE BOX

Problem

Sears holds $2,051 million in cash assets. The annual interest rate on marketable securities is 3%, and zero interest is earned on cash. The total amount of cash needed for transactions during the year is $2 billion. The fixed costs are $5,000 per transaction. Calculate the optimum cash balance that Sears should hold.

Solution

The optimum starting cash level C^* is given by

$$C^* = (2 \times \$2 \text{ billion} \times \$5,000/0.03)^{1/2} \cong \$25,819,889$$

Therefore the firm should hold about $25.8 million in cash and should invest the rest in marketable securities earning 3% a year.

20.8 FORECASTING THE DAILY CASH FLOWS: THE STONE AND MILLER APPROACH

Baumol's model is simplistic in that it assumes that the reduction in the cash the firm holds over time is linear. Since a firm faces daily cash inflows and cash outflows, the cash reduction may be much different from the linear pattern described in Figure 20-5.

Bernell Stone and Tom Miller suggest that the firm can forecast its daily cash flows by monitoring their scheduling and distribution, as follows:[10]

---

10. Bernell K. Stone and Tom W. Miller, "Daily Cash Forecasting with Multiplicative Models of Cash Flow Patterns," *Financial Management* (Winter 1987): 45–54.

- *Scheduling.* The firm can follow its invoices and other transactions to forecast the daily cash flows. For example, approving an invoice of $1 million for payment with terms of 2/10 net 30 implies that, given the firm's policy not to take the discount, there will be a cash outflow of $1 million 30 days after the invoice date. In a similar way the firm can keep a schedule of all its big future cash inflows and outflows. This schedule is the firm's daily cash flow forecast.
- *Distribution.* The firm can forecast the distribution of cash flows. For example, if it writes $1 million in checks on Monday, then the firm might predict cash withdrawals of that amount between seven and ten days later, depending on the disbursement delay. For example, cash withdrawals of $200,000, $300,000, and $500,000 might be made from the firm's bank account on the following Monday to Wednesday. Using these forecasted distributions of various transactions, the firm can make its aggregate daily cash flow forecast.

Miller and Stone suggested statistical methods to find the distribution of cash flows throughout a month by analyzing past months' data. These statistical methods, combined with the scheduling method, can be used for cash flow forecasting. They assume the monthly cash flow is dominated by a *day-of-the-week cycle* (mainly due to the effect of weekends) and by a *day-of-the-month cycle.* The latter is created due to company policies such as monthly payrolls, credit agreements in which the cash flows are tied to a certain day of the month, and internal company procedures. By statistically analyzing previous months' data, the firm can calculate the day-of-the-month effect, the day-of-the-week effect, and the interaction between them. These analyses enable the firm to estimate the amount of daily cash flow needed by dividing the total monthly cash flow by the appropriate day-of-the-month and day-of-the-week parameters. Using this technique dictates to the firm how much cash to hold on each day and when to sell the marketable securities.

The Stone and Miller cash flow model is more realistic than the one Baumol suggested. Stone and Miller consider the uncertainty of cash flows and do not assume that a firm uses cash at a constant rate over time. In practice, most firms use the scheduling method and some version of the distribution method, though some rely on intuition and experience.

20.9 CASH MANAGEMENT IN INTERNATIONAL FIRMS

Recall the Swiss firm Ciba, discussed in Chapter 11 in Applying Theory to Practice 11.1, which has manufacturing plants in many countries around the world. The cash manager at Ciba faces two issues: (1) what level of cash should the firm hold, and (2) in what currencies should this cash be held?

Most of Ciba's operations are conducted in Swiss francs, and all cash flows related to the activities of plants in foreign countries are conducted in local currencies (e.g., lire in Italy, dollars in the United States). Therefore, Ciba must hold some cash in local currencies, too. Suppose Ciba holds 100 million Swiss francs for one month's activities related to its plant in Italy. An adverse foreign currency fluctuation (i.e., the SF weakens relative to the lira) means that 100 million Swiss francs will be insufficient to cover the activities in Italy. Ciba has two options for handling the risk of adverse foreign currency fluctuations:

1. Hold cash balances in Italian lira.
2. Hold all cash balances in Swiss francs but also hold options (or forward contracts) to guarantee a certain predetermined exchange rate.[11]

The disadvantage of Option 1 is that the firm would have to manage many accounts in many currencies. Therefore, it would not enjoy the financial benefits of holding one big cash account, which it can manage more efficiently than many smaller accounts. The disadvantages of Option 2 are: options cost money, and experts are needed to handle these rather complicated transactions. The firm must weigh the pros and cons of each option to determine which is the better alternative. The cash manager's task in an international firm is much more difficult than a similar one in a domestic firm.

Most international firms, Ciba included, use options, forward contracts, and other derivatives to hedge foreign currency risk.

20.10 INVESTING CASH IN REPURCHASE AGREEMENTS

Firms holding cash generally do so in a bank deposit, which generally pays a relatively low interest rate. However, more and more firms are investing a large portion of their cash in instruments called **repurchase agreements (repos).** Investment in repurchase agreements works as follows:

1. A security dealer who holds Treasury bonds needs a large amount of cash for a certain period, say one week.
2. The security dealer sells the bonds to the firm for cash, with the agreement that he or she will repurchase the bonds at a predetermined price and date. For example, the security dealer may sell the Treasury bonds for $100 each and may then repurchase them one week later for $100.07 each.
3. A repo pays the same or a higher interest rate than a short-term bank deposit. The security dealer is ready to pay a higher interest rate for the needed cash because he or she is not authorized to enter the deposit market that the banking system uses. The repo market is sometimes called the *financing market* because security dealers finance their bond positions by using these transactions.

This transaction amounts to the firm lending its cash surplus to the dealer and holding the securities as collateral. Because the firm's alternative is to deposit the money in the bank (uninsured and at a lower interest rate), the firm benefits from lending the money to the security dealer. With U.S. Treasury bonds and other high-quality bonds serving as collateral, and with the interest on repos at least as high as the interest rate on bank deposits, repurchase agreements seem to defy the trade-off between risk and return. As shown in Connecting Theory to Practice 20.3, some institutional investors claim that "free lunches" occasionally exist in the market!

http

Contingency Analysis maintains a nice glossary that defines and then discusses such financial terms as repos, reverse repos, liquidity, payment netting, reinvestment risk, and much more.
http://www. contingencyanalysis. com

---

11. See Chapter 11 for a review of these instruments.

CONNECTING THEORY TO PRACTICE 20.3

REPOS: THE OCCASIONAL FREE LUNCH?

. . . What is surprising and what makes the repo market so attractive is that the investor typically receives a similar return on these very different alternative investments—and sometimes a higher return on the repo. Repos often seem to defy the trade-off between risk and return that investors have come to expect. According to investment theory, a fully secured investment should provide a lower return than the same investment unsecured. Yet, in practice, the yield on repos is highly competitive with bank deposits and, when dealers are competing for limited financing, repo rates can often be pushed even higher than deposit rates. Securities dealers are not members of the Federal Reserve and so cannot enter the wholesale deposit markets available to banks. As a result, their sources of financing are limited.

A SUPERIOR MONEY MARKET INVESTMENT

"Repo" may never become a household word—the minimum investment typically is $1 million—yet the U.S. Treasury repo market involves more daily turnover than any other financial market in the world: more than $1 trillion. Corporations, money managers, government institutions, pension funds, and banks use it as a safe haven for cash and as a flexible alternative to deposits and money market instruments such as CDS [certificates of deposit] and commercial paper. In the U.S. market, repo collateral is most typically U.S. Treasury bonds, though it may also be mortgage securities, corporate bonds, or other forms of debt as agreed by the counterparties.

The most dramatic growth over the past few years, however, has been in the international or "multi-currency" repo market . . . .

Those who enter these markets early will reap the greatest rewards. Until June of 1993, Terence Moore, European cash manager for DuPont and Conoco, had been investing most of the companies' surplus funds—20 different currencies—in bank time deposits. "After June, we started looking at the repo market," says Moore. He then started investing in multi-currency repos with many of the same banks he was depositing funds with on an unsecured basis. He accepted a wide range of collateral, including single-A Eurobonds and emerging-market debt.

"The banks were offering us considerably better rates on the repos," says Moore, "than we were getting from them on our unsecured deposits." By investing in repos, Moore figures he has improved DuPont/Conoco's annual return on its cash by an eighth of a percent. Since the average value of funds invested is $1.5 billion, that's nearly $2 million more per year than before. "And we have done this without increasing our risk," he adds. "As long as the bank or brokerage house has been assessed as creditworthy by our credit department, we don't mind what collateral they give us. We feel that we are not taking market risk on the collateral, since the bank is obliged under the repo agreement to buy it back on termination at the same price." Who says there's no such thing—occasionally—as a free lunch?

MAKING THE CONNECTION

This may be one of the few "free lunches" that exist in capital markets. Because security dealers are not allowed to enter the deposit market, they are willing to pay a relatively high interest rate for short-term borrowing with less risk to the lenders. Cash managers at DuPont and Conoco take advantage of this situation.

In managing its assets, a firm seeks its optimal level of cash assets. To maintain that optimal level, a firm minimizes its cash balance, considers the seasonality in its cash management, divides its cash assets between cash and marketable securities, forecasts its daily cash flows, and sometimes invests cash in repurchase agreements. In Applying Theory to Practice 20.1, you will analyze how one firm, Toys 'R' Us, manages its cash assets.

APPLYING THEORY TO PRACTICE 20.1

CASH ASSETS MANAGEMENT AT TOYS 'R' US

Table 20-2 provides a summary of financial and market data on Toys 'R' Us. In 1993, Toys 'R' Us initiated a $1 billion stock buyback program. We will analyze Toys 'R' Us's cash assets management in and around 1993 by answering the following questions.

TABLE 20-2   **Value Line Report on Toys 'R' Us**

Capital Structure as of 10/30/93	**Current Position ($ mill.)**	1991	1992	10/30/93
Total Debt $1254.7 mill. Due in 5 Yrs $125.0 mill.	Cash Assets	35.0	444.6	122.3
LT Debt $702.1 mill. LT Interest $60.0 mill.	Receivables	73.1	64.1	90.7
est. $85.7 mill. capitalized leases	Inventory (LIFO)	1275.2	1390.6	2898.6
(Total interest coverage: 10.6x) (20% of Cap'l)	Other	21.0	27.6	83.7
Leases, Uncapitalized Annual rentals $160.9 mill.	Current Assets	1404.3	1926.9	3195.3
Pension Liability None—No defined benefit plan	Accts Payable	484.0	858.8	1838.2
Pfd Stock None	Debt Due	388.1	293.3	552.6
Common Stock 290,438,557 shs. (80% of Cap'l)	Other	355.5	442.2	377.2
as of 11/22/93	Current Liab.	1227.6	1594.3	2768.0

(continued)

TABLE 20-2 *Continued*

Annual Rates of change (per sh)	Past 10 Yrs.	Past 5 Yrs.	Est'd '90–'92 to '95–'96
Sales	20.5%	19.5%	*16.5%*
"Cash Flow"	21.5%	19.0%	*18.0%*
Earnings	21.5%	18.0%	*17.5%*
Dividends	—	—	*Nil*
Book Value	25.0%	21.0%	*16.5%*

Fiscal Year Begins	Quarterly Sales ($ mill.)				Full Fiscal Year
	Apr.Per.	Jul.Per.	Oct.Per.	Jan.Per.	
1990	944.8	964.0	1052.6	2548.6	5510.0
1991	1025.6	1056.2	1181.7	2860.7	6124.2
1992	1172.5	1249.2	1345.8	3401.8	7169.3
1993	1286.5	1317.0	1449.1	*3997.4*	*8050*
1994	*1550*	*1600*	*1750*	*4600*	*9500*

Fiscal Year Begins	Earnings Per Share				Full Fiscal Year
	Apr.Per.	Jul.Per.	Oct.Per.	Jan.Per.	
1990	.11	.09	.10	.81	1.11
1991	.08	.08	.11	.88	1.15
1992	.10	.11	.12	1.14	1.47
1993	.12	.12	.13	*1.28*	*1.65*
1994	*.13*	*.15*	*.17*	*1.55*	*2.00*

Toys 'R' Us' holiday sales increased by 15% over year earlier levels . . . Results for this critical eight-week period ended December 25th were in line with expectations. The continued success of action figure and video soft-

Source: *Value Line Investment Survey*, 25 February 1994.

ware products, the expansion of the mail catalog, and the rollout of 170 new Books "R" Us departments were the chief reasons for the 7.4% domestic same store sales gain.

. . . but the stock price has fallen 15% over the same time frame. Unlike the three previous Christmas seasons, last year's period was preceded by relatively optimistic consumer spending forecasts. As a result, the potential for an upside sales surprise was greatly diminished. The 2.3% decline in foreign same-store sales during the holiday period also probably contributed to recent share price weakness . . .

But we expect that foreign operations will eventually provide most of the future earnings gains. The international store base has grown from 52 to 234 venues over the past five years and an additional 70 stores will be opened in 1994. International operating profits, which account for roughly 15% of the entire company's operating profits, will likely grow to 40% of the total by the end of the decade.

A share buyback program should help support the stock price while overseas results improve. With the bulk of its foreign startup expenses behind it, Toys should begin generating substantial excess cash flow. The Board of Directors has authorized a $1 billion buy back of common stock over the next several years.

This issue should outperform the market averages in the coming year and over the long haul, as well. Like many other specialty retailers, Toys has felt the pressure of increased competition from discount chains, especially since former rivals, Child World and Lionel, went into bankruptcy in 1992. And we feel this development will continue to limit margin expansion over the next few years. However, the company is well positioned to capitalize on the eventual rebound of many foreign economies, whose current weakness is constraining earnings growth. Hence, Toys should meet our 17% annual earnings growth projections through 1997 as these opportunities are fully realized.

Charles C. Moran *February 25, 1994*

Questions

1. Use the quarterly sales data corresponding to years 1991–1996 given in the Toys 'R' Us table in section 20.6 to draw a figure with time (by quarters) on the horizontal axis and with sales on the vertical axis. In which quarters does the firm need to sell marketable securities and to borrow short-term from banks to finance its operations? (See also the current assets data for Toys 'R' Us in Table 20-1.)

2. Suppose the firm sells its merchandise for cash only. (Indeed, the receivables are negligible relative to the firm's sales.) Assume the firm estimates its future quarterly sales and buys inventory accordingly. Also assume the firm pays its suppliers for each quarter's sales in the quarter before those sales are made. Payments to suppliers amount to 70% of sales. For example, if the firm sells $1 million in the *fourth* quarter, the inventory costs 70% of the sales, and the firm pays its suppliers $0.7 million in the *third* quarter. (The difference—$0.3 million in this example—is the firm's gross profit.) Use the sales figures in the table in Section 20.6 and the given assumptions to calculate the firm's cash inflows and cash outflows resulting from sales and payments to suppliers in 1993.

3. Suppose the firm now hires you as a cash management expert. Would you recommend basing a cash assets management strategy on annual sales or on quarterly sales? Explain.

4. Using the assumption regarding the payment schedule in Question 2, analyze the cash assets management for each quarter of 1993. How much cash assets does the firm need for the third quarter? Suppose the annual interest rate is 3%, and zero interest is earned on cash. The fixed trading cost is $5,000 per transaction. How much cash does the firm need to hold in the third quarter? How much should the firm hold in marketable securities in that quarter?

5. How, in practice, did Toys 'R' Us finance its short-term financial needs in 1993? In your answer, rely on the current position at the end of 1992 and in October 1993.

6. Suppose in 1993 Toys 'R' Us suppliers offered 1/10 net 30 terms of trade. In 1995 the terms changed to 2/10 net 30. Use the following data, taken from *Value Line* (February 23, 1996), to analyze Toys 'R' Us's response to the change in terms of trade.

Current Position ($ million)	1993	1994	10/28/95
Cash Assets	791.9	369.8	−220.3
Receivables	98.5	115.9	138.0
Inventory (LIFO)	1777.6	1999.2	3646.4
Other	40.4	45.8	78.3
Current Assets	2708.4	2530.7	4083.0
Accts Payable	1156.4	1339.1	2201.8
Debt Due	239.9	122.7	1483.5
Other	678.8	675.1	362.7
Current Liabilities	2075.1	2136.9	4058.0

Source: *Value Line*, 23 February 1996.

7. In view of the large cash shortage in the third quarter, how can you explain the $1 billion stock repurchase plan?

MAKING THE CONNECTION

1. The following illustration reveals a strong seasonality factor in sales. Sales are relatively stable (apart from normal growth) in the first three quarters and peak in the fourth (holiday) quarter.

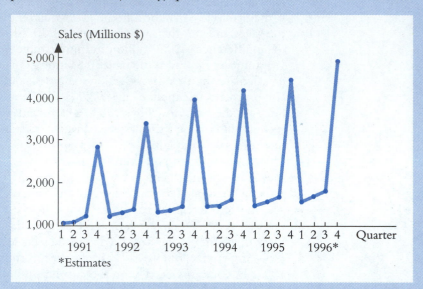

*Estimates

Most of the sales are in the fourth quarter, so the firm increases its investment in inventory in the fourth quarter. We see from the current assets position that on October 30, 1993, the firm had an inventory of $2,898.6 million, compared with a $1,390.6 million inventory at the end of the 1992 fiscal year—after the peak sales.

The firm will need short-term financing sources to finance its seasonal needs. It can use its accounts payable, sell marketable securities, use its cash holdings, or borrow short-term.

2. Using the assumptions given, the cash inflows and outflows corresponding to the four quarters of 1993 are as follows (in $ million):

Quarter	Q1 1993	Q2 1993	Q3 1993	Q4 1993	Q1 1994
Cash inflow (= sales; see Table in Section 20.6)	1,286.5	1,317.0	1,449.1	3,997.4	1,462
Cash outflow	$-0.7 \times 1,317$ $= -921.9$	$-0.7 \times 1,449.1$ $\cong -1,014.4$	$-0.7 \times 3,997.4$ $\cong -2,798.2$	$-0.7 \times 1,462$ $\cong -1,023.4$	
Net cash flow (outflow)	364.6	302.6	-1,349.1	2,974.0	

Since the cash outflow is 70% of the succeeding quarter's sales, the firm has a cash surplus in all quarters except the third, in which a $1,349.1 million cash deficit is observed.

3. The cash assets needed are a function of the firm's payments. Because sales have a strong seasonality factor (as do the payments the firm makes and the cash it receives), the cash assets needed vary across quarters. Any analysis based on annual sales does not detect the seasonality in the financing needs and will be misleading.

4. The firm holds cash assets to meet its payments. However, in Quarters 1, 2, and 4, the cash inflow is larger than the cash outflow, and the firm accumulates a cash surplus. In these quarters, the firm can invest the cash surplus in marketable securities, which it will sell in the third quarter when it needs the money.

   In the third quarter, the firm needs $1,349.1 million to finance its cash deficit. It can sell marketable securities, use its cash holdings, or borrow from the bank.

   Assume the firm holds $1,349.1 million in cash assets at the beginning of the third quarter. How should the firm divide this between cash and marketable securities? Using Baumol's model, the amount of cash that the firm should hold is

$$C^* = (2T \times F/r)^{1/2}$$

   In our case, $T = \$1,349.1$ million and $F = \$5,000$. The annual interest rate (opportunity cost) is 3%. The time period corresponding to the $1,349.1 million cash spending is one quarter, so the opportunity cost corresponding to one quarter is

$$(1.03)^{1/4} - 1 \cong 0.00742 \text{ or } 0.742\%$$

Thus, the optimum cash level, C^*, is

$$C^* = (2 \times \$1,349,100,000 \times \$5,000/0.00742)^{1/2} \cong \$42,640,287$$

   Therefore, by Baumol's model, the firm should hold about $43 million in cash and should hold the rest of its cash assets in marketable securities.

5. As we can see from the current assets report, the firm had purchased most of the inventory it needed by October 30, 1993. The firm financed this inventory by payables (which were much higher in October 1993 than in December 1992) and by short-term debt. The firm also decreased its cash assets position, probably by also using this source to finance the third-quarter operations. The firm did not pay for the fourth quarter sales in the third quarter, as assumed in Question 2, but it paid for most of its purchases for the sales of the fourth quarter in the fourth quarter itself. (See the large increase in accounts payable in October 30, 1993.) In this way the firm achieved better synchronization of its cash inflows and outflows than assumed previously and as a result, needed much fewer cash assets. Of course, the firm could have paid its suppliers within the discount period to obtain a cash discount, but it would have needed short-term financing to do so, as explained before. In making this decision, a firm

should weigh the cost of the short-term financing needed versus the discount obtained.

6. In 1993 accounts payable more than doubled from $858.8 million in December, 1992, to $1,838.2 million in October, 1993 (see Table 20.2). This was the main source of inventory financing. In 1995 the main source of inventory financing was the increase in short-term debt from $122.7 million in December, 1994, to $1,483.5 million in October, 1995. Accounts payable was a secondary source in 1995, but it was the main source in 1993.

    Because the discount for cash payment increased in 1995, the firm elected to pay cash for a large portion of its purchases and to finance its inventory mainly with debt—a very rational response to the change in the terms of trade.

7. Toys 'R' Us may have had a cash shortage in a given quarter, but over the whole year it was profitable and created a positive cash flow. The firm did not pay cash dividends but, instead, used the stock repurchase technique to pay its stockholders. A cash deficit in any one quarter is irrelevant in the stock repurchase decision. The relevant figure for such a decision is the *annual* cash surplus or deficit. On an annual basis, Toys 'R' Us had a cash surplus, which explains its repurchase decision.

SUMMARY

To ensure smooth-running operations and to take advantage of unforeseen "bargains" in the market, a firm holds cash assets consisting of cash and short-term marketable securities. The larger the seasonal fluctuations in a firm's activities, the larger the fluctuation in cash assets it holds. A firm earns no interest (or very low interest) on cash balances and earns a little interest on marketable securities. However, even this interest is low relative to the rate of return that it can earn on other investments. Thus, holding cash and marketable securities is expensive.

The firm should attempt to minimize its cost of financing cash assets. The faster the firm receives cash from its customers and the slower it pays suppliers, the lower its cost of maintaining cash balances.

If the firm has a permanent cash surplus, it can use that surplus to pay dividends, to repurchase stock, or to make capital expenditures. When the cash surplus is temporary, the firm can invest this money in marketable securities and can sell them as it needs cash.

The division of cash assets between cash and marketable securities depends on the total amount of new cash needed during the planning period (usually a year), the opportunity costs of holding cash, and the transaction costs of trading in short-term securities. Two models have been suggested to determine the optimal cash balance: Baumol's model (which assumes that cash balances decline at a constant rate, which implies certainty of cash payment) and Stone's and Miller's model (which does not assume certainty).

In practice, cash management is quite complex because the firm can hold cash in foreign currencies, use derivatives to hedge risk, and enter into repurchase agreements.

CHAPTER AT A GLANCE

1. Reasons for holding cash:
   a. Transaction motive
   b. Precautionary motive
   c. Speculative motive
   d. Compensation motive

2. Cash assets = Cash (including demand deposits) + Marketable securities

3. Disbursement float = Payments reported on firm's books − Payments cleared by the bank

4. Collection float = Receipts recorded on the firm's books − Receipts cleared by the bank

5. Net float = Disbursement float − Collection float

6. Division of total cash assets into cash and marketable securities at the beginning of each cycle:

The Baumol Model

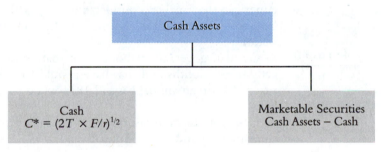

where

   T = Total cash needed to conduct transactions during a given period, usually a year
   F = Fixed transaction costs of trading in marketable securities
   r = Opportunity cost (interest rate on marketable securities) of holding cash
   C^* = Optimum starting cash level

KEY TERMS

Cash	Synchronization	Collection float
Marketable securities	Float management	Net float
Cash assets	Float	Lockbox
Transaction motive	Disbursement float	Preauthorized debit
Precautionary motive	Disbursement delay	Concentration bank
Speculative motive	Mail time delay	Cash concentration
Optimal level of cash assets	Processing delay	Depository transfer check (DTC)
Cash budget	Availability delay	Automated clearing house (ACH)
Cash management efficiency	Collection delay	Repurchase agreements (repos)

REVIEW AND PRACTICE

20.1 Define *cash assets*. Can a firm's cash assets be larger than its current assets?

20.2 What are the motives for holding cash assets? Explain each of them briefly.

20.3 Suppose a firm has a permanent cash surplus. For what purposes can the firm use the excess cash?

20.4 It is suggested that whenever a firm has a cash deficit there is no need to take on short-term debt; rather, the firm can simply cut its dividends in quarters with cash deficits and pay higher dividends in quarters with cash surpluses. Evaluate this view. (Hint: Recall what you studied about dividend policy in Chapter 17.)

20.5 Firms A and B have the following quarterly cash flows (in $ million):

Quarter	Firm A	Firm B
1	200	150
2	200	250
3	180	400
4	220	−100

Both firms hold $100 million of cash assets. In your view, which firm will hold a lower proportion of the cash assets in cash? Explain.

20.6 A firm earns 3% annually on its short-term securities. The firm can increase its marketable securities by $100 million by decreasing its cash holdings by this same amount. This can be done for three months only. Calculate the firm's earnings from such a shift in the division of its cash assets.

20.7 Elco Inc. decides to invest its cash assets (which it needs for seasonal operations) in 30-year bonds. Elsint Inc. holds its cash assets in the form of three-month bonds. Both bonds are zero-coupon bonds with a 5% yield-to-maturity and a par value of $1,000. Immediately after the firms bought these bonds for $1,000, the yield-to-maturity of both bonds rose to 6%. Calculate the loss (or gain) to

Elco and to Elsint. Which firm is likely to face a cash deficit? Why?

20.8 From the standpoint of a U.S. firm, which of the items given here are cash assets and which are not?
a. Cash.
b. A three-month bond issued by Philip Morris Incorporated.
c. A three-month U.S. government bond.
d. A three-month bond issued by the German government (in German marks).
e. A 20-year U.S. government bond.
f. IBM stock.

20.9 The cash manager at Gilboa Corporation, an American steel maker, considers investing $10 million for three months in one of the following options:
a. German government bonds that mature in exactly three months and that have a yield-to-maturity of 9% on an annual basis (2.18% on a quarterly basis).
b. U.S. short-term Treasury bills whose maturity is three months and whose annual yield is 6% (1.47% per quarter).

The current exchange rate is 1.60 German marks per dollar. Gilboa can buy a put option to sell 16,332,451 marks in three months at a striking price of 1.6 marks per dollar. The put option would cost the firm $10,000.

The cash manager strongly emphasizes the need to have a liquid investment because the firm needs the cash to pay short-term liabilities due in three months. In your view, which investment is more liquid? Which option would you recommend if put options are not available?

20.10 Fast Delivery Inc. collects $100 million a month from its receivables. It has to pay its suppliers $150 million in the first month, zero in the second month, $150 million in the third month, zero in the fourth month, and so on.
a. What cash level does the firm need to hold?

b. Suppose the firm's suppliers agree to average the cash receipts across months, provided the firm pays them $76 million a month (rather than $75 million). Before accepting the offer, the firm borrowed the extra cash it needed at an interest rate of 3% annually. Should the firm agree to the suppliers' conditions to synchronize its cash flows?

20.11 An American firm is considering whether to hold its cash assets in short-term U.S. government bonds yielding 3% annually or in German short-term government bonds yielding 5% annually.
a. Which asset is more liquid?
b. Which asset is more profitable?
c. Which asset is riskier?
d. Suppose the exchange rate is $1 = 1.60 DM at the time the German bond is bought. The three-month bond is a zero-coupon bond with a par value of 1,000 DM. After one month the yield increases to 8%, but the exchange rate remains unchanged. Calculate the loss to a firm holding the bond.
e. Calculate the loss to a U.S. firm holding the German bond if the exchange rate after one month is $1 = 2 DM and the yield is 8%, as in Problem 20.11d. Discuss your results. Is the German bond a cash asset?

20.12 U.S. Plastic Inc. writes checks for $10 million a day. The checks are sent in the mail, and it takes two days for them to arrive. It takes one more day for the checks to be processed and three more days for the recipient's bank to clear the checks and to make the money available to the recipient.
a. What are the various time delays in this case?
b. Calculate the disbursement float.

20.13 Suppose Firm A sells to Firm B. "Firm B's disbursement float equals Firm A's collection float." Do you agree? Defend your view.

20.14 Milkaway Inc. writes checks for $10 million a day. The mail time delay is three days. The firm's customers write checks to the firm amounting to $15 million a day, and the mail time delay is also three days. There are zero processing and availability delays. Calculate the following:
a. Disbursement float.

b. Collection float.
c. Net float.

20.15 Dunlop Inc. receives checks for $10 million a day. The total collection delay is five days. Prepare a table showing the firm's bank balance, its available cash balance, and the collection float for each of the next 10 days.

20.16 Exxon receives checks amounting to $200 million a day. The total collection delay is six days. The firm is considering establishing lockboxes using a local bank, which will cut the collection delay to three days. The bank charges $1 for each check processed. The daily interest rate is 0.025%.
a. Should Exxon establish the lockbox system if the average check is for $50,000?
b. How would your answer change if the average check were for $1,000?
c. Suppose Exxon establishes the lockbox system but only its mail delay is reduced. Will it affect the collection float?

20.17 Water Supply Inc. holds 10 demand-deposit bank accounts. The safety level of cash that the firm needs to hold in each account is $100,000, on which zero interest is earned. The firm is considering whether to establish a master account in which it will need to hold a safety cash level of $300,000, with all the other accounts becoming subaccounts. Establishing the master account will cost $10,000 a year. The firm earns 4% annually on marketable securities.
a. How much will the firm save annually by establishing the master account?
b. How would your answer change if there were only four subaccounts and if the other data remain unchanged?

20.18 Elron Inc. needs $500 million in cash to conduct its operations during the next six months. The fixed cost per transaction in marketable securities is $1,000, and the annual interest rate on marketable securities is 3%.
a. What is the optimum division between cash and marketable securities?
b. How many times during the half year does the firm trade in securities?

20.19 Use the data in Problem 20.18 to calculate Elron's optimum cash holding if each of the following changes takes place:

a. The interest rate increases to 5%.

b. Fixed costs per transactions in marketable securities increase to $5,000 per trade.

c. The total new cash needs are $800 million.

d. The $500 million cash is needed for one year rather than for six months.

Discuss your results in each case.

20.20 Duback Inc. holds $100 million in cash on the first day of each cycle. This cash balance decreases by $20 million a day. Draw a "sawtooth" diagram showing the cash balances. How would the diagram change if the firm held only $40 million in cash on the first day of each cycle?

20.21 Mass Brothers Inc. earns 3% annually on its marketable securities. The cost of trading in these securities is $1,000 per transaction. The firm's total cash needs for transactions during the year are $365 million. The firm's cash decreases by $1 million a day.

a. Plot the opportunity cost, transaction cost, and the total cost curves as functions of the cash balance's size.

b. What is the optimal cash balance at the beginning of each cycle?

20.22 Dayton Hudson Company operates Marshall Field's and Target department stores. The following are its quarterly sales:

Fiscal Year Begins	Quarterly Sales ($ million)				Full Fiscal Year
	Q1	Q2	Q3	Q4	
1990	3,007	3,242	3,625	4,865	14,739
1991	3,349	3,562	3,955	5,249	16,115
1992	3,719	3,967	4,340	5,901	17,927
1993	4,040	4,287	4,625	6,281	19,233
1994	4,465	4,802	5,046	6,998	21,311

Source: *Value Line Investment Survey*, 25 February 1994 and Investment Update Service on the Internet, 1996.

a. Plot the sales as a function of time (quarters).

b. Assume that the total assets needed for running operations amount to 200% of sales. Plot the total asset value as a function of time.

c. The firm decides to finance some of its total assets with long-term liabilities and equity and some by short-term borrowing. The long-term financing for the whole year amounts to 80% of total assets needed in the third quarter. Describe graphically the firm's short-term financing.

d. Suppose the cost of long-term financing is 10%, the cost of short-term borrowing is 5%, and the firm is earning 3% on marketable securities. The needed assets in each quarter are financed at the beginning of the quarter. Show the firm's quarterly net total costs in the following scenarios:

1. The financing decision is as in Problem 20.22c.

2. The firm finances assets by long-term financing.

20.23 Refer to the data in Problem 20.22. Assume the firm sells for cash and buys inventory for cash. Also assume the firm estimates its quarterly sales and prepares its inventory for each quarter's sales, one quarter in advance. Assume the sales estimates equal the actual sales reported in Problem 20.2. The inventory costs amount to 8% of the sales.

a. Calculate the cash assets needed at the beginning of each quarter.

b. The rate of return on T-bills is 3% a year. The fixed transaction cost of trading in these securities is $500. How should the firm divide its cash assets between cash and marketable securities?

I N T E R N E T   Q U E S T I O N

20.24 Nations Bank maintains a "treasury management" service for its clients. Visit its Web site and read about the service. Prepare a memo summarizing what you found.

http://www.nationsbank.com/smallbiz/html/treasury.htm

YOUR TURN: APPLYING THEORY TO PRACTICE

CASH MANAGEMENT AT LURIA & SON

Use the data from *Value Line Investment Survey* to answer the following questions.

Capital Structure as of 10/31/93

Total Debt $12.9 mill.   Due in 5 Yrs $12.3 mill.

LT Debt $1.2 mill.   LT Interest $.1 mill.

(Total interest coverage: 31.1x)

(1% of Cap'l)

Leases, Uncapitalized Annual rentals $8.4 mill.

Pension Liability None

Pfd Stock None

Common Stock 5,400,080 common shs.
(Includes 1,449,547 Class B shs.) (99% of Cap'l)

Current Position ($ mill.)

Current Position ($ mill.)	1991	1992	10/31/93
Cash Assets	17.4	24.9	1.5
Receivables	1.1	2.6	1.5
Inventory	78.1	76.6	110.0
Other	1.8	2.4	4.2
Current Assets	98.4	106.5	117.2
Accts Payable	42.4	40.3	52.3
Debt Due	.2	.2	11.7
Other	4.1	10.3	—
Current Liab.	46.7	50.8	64.0

Annual Rates of change (per sh)	Past 10 Yrs.	Past 5 Yrs.	Est'd '90–'92 to '96–'98
Sales	7.0%	5.0%	9.0%
"Cash Flow"	1.0%	−5.5%	18.0%
Earnings	−8.5%	−18.5%	34.0%
Dividends	—	—	NMF
Book Value	12.5%	5.5%	7.0%

Fiscal Year Begins	Quarterly Sales ($ mill.)				Full Fiscal Year
	Apr.Per	Jul.Per	Oct.Per	Jan.Per	
1990	47.6	45.8	40.0	80.0	213.8
1991	40.5	43.6	37.7	85.8	207.6
1992	46.7	45.3	41.3	102.3	235.6
1993	48.3	44.9	44.8	107.0	245
1994	53.0	50.0	48.0	124.0	275

Fiscal Year Begins	Earnings per Share				Full Fiscal Year
	Apr.Per	Jul.Per	Oct.Per	Jan.Per	
1990	d.05	.01	d.35	.59	.20
1991	d.02	.02	d.29	.51	.22
1992	.01	.01	d.18	.80	.64
1993	.06	.04	d.09	.84	.85
1994	.08	.08	d.06	1.00	1.10

Luria's face-lift continues. The company's outmoded catalog showrooms are being transformed into superstores featuring mass displays of self-service merchandise. So far, four locations have adopted the new 35,000–40,000-square-foot format, and management hopes to convert all of its stores within the next five years. Internal cash flow should cover the estimated annual costs of $5 million–$7 million; some existing stores will be expanded and renovated, while smaller sites, ill-suited to the conversion, will be closed and relocated. Management is encouraged by the public's initial response. We think that each superstore location should generate at least 25% greater sales volume than under the catalog showroom layout.

Meanwhile, Luria had a decent Christmas season, we believe. The company faced difficult comparisons in the recently ended holiday quarter, because strong replacement demand was stimulated by damage from Hurricane

(continued)

Andrew in the year-earlier period. Nevertheless, we expect the retailer to report higher sales figures this time around. But top-line growth likely came at the expense of gross margins; extensive discounting was required in a retailing climate marked by vigorous competition and budget conscious consumers. As a result, we have reduced our fourth-quarter earnings estimate by 13¢ to 84¢ per share. Still, Luria's bottom line grew nicely last year and . . .

We expect continued positive earnings momentum in the current fiscal year. Sales growth will likely accelerate as more locations are converted into the superstore format and economic conditions continue to im-

Source: *Value Line Investment Survey,* 25 February 1994.

prove. And, in contrast to the showrooms, the new stores should encourage impulse buying, leading to wider profit margins. We are assuming only slight gross margin improvement, however, given the highly competitive retailing environment. At any rate, we think share net will rise nearly 30%, to $1.10.

This timely stock appears to have good 3- to 5-year appreciation potential as well. Now that the company's remodeling program is well under way, plans are being considered for out-of-state expansion, all suggesting that the strong positive earnings trend will continue.

Larry S. Gendler, CFA   *February 25, 1994*

Questions

1. How does Luria finance its current assets?

2. Draw a graph for years 1990–1994 with quarterly sales on the vertical axis and time (quarters) on the horizontal axis. Do you detect a seasonality factor? If so, in which quarter?

3. How did Luria finance its current assets on October 31, 1993? How did it finance the change in the current assets from 1992 to October 31, 1993?

4. Assume Luria sells for cash and buys its inventory on 45 days' credit. The sales for each quarter are bought in the previous quarter, and the cost of the inventory is 70% of sales. To be more specific, each quarter is divided into two subperiods: Days 1–45 and Days 46–90. The sales are divided equally between these two subperiods. The sales corresponding to each subperiod are purchased two subperiods earlier. Each purchase is for 45 days' credit. Assume that during 1993 and 1994 the quarterly sales estimates equal the actual sales as reported in the table. Also assume

at the beginning of 1993 the cash balance is that reported in the table ($24.9 million) and there are $7.5 million of miscellaneous cash expenses in each subperiod. Prepare the quarterly cash budget for year 1993.

5. Assume the total payouts in each quarter reported in Question 4 represent the cash outflow the firm pays in the corresponding quarter. Also assume the firm holds cash as reported in Question 4. What amount of cash assets does the firm need in each quarter of 1993 to meet its additional forecasted cash outflow?

The firm earns 3% annually on marketable securities, and its fixed transaction cost per trade in these securities is $500. What amount of cash and what amount of marketable securities does the firm need to hold at the beginning of each of the quarters of 1993? (Hint: Use Baumol's model.)

6. Analyze the firm's cash assets holdings in 1991, 1992, and October 31, 1993. How can you explain the large drop in cash assets in 1993?

CHAPTER 21

MANAGING ACCOUNTS RECEIVABLE AND INVENTORY

LEARNING OBJECTIVES

After reading this chapter, you should understand:

1. How a firm can operate with or without accounts receivable.

2. The pros and cons of cash and credit sales and investment in receivables.

3. The pros and cons of investment in inventory.

4. How the various costs of investment in receivables and in inventory are considered when determining the optimal investment in each.

5. How a firm determines the economic order quantity.

6. The techniques a firm can use to manage its inventory.

CORPORATE FINANCE IN THE NEWS

"Another example is in inventory turnover: Chrysler estimates

that between $155 million and $260 million could be saved

through more productive turnover of inventory . . . ."*

"Net interest and credit costs for the quarter increased $24

million from 1994 due to higher bad debt expense from adverse

trends in delinquencies and consumer bankruptcies."†

Sources: *Steven Lipin and Gabriella Stern, "Chrysler's Cash Hoard Could Reach $10.7 Billion," *Wall Street Journal*, 20 October 1995, p. 1. Reprinted by permission of The Wall Street Journal, © 1995 Dow Jones & Company, Inc. All Rights Reserved Worldwide.

†J.C. Penney press statement, February 22, 1996.

21.1 INTRODUCTION

In the Corporate Finance in the News citations, we deal with two issues analyzed in this chapter: inventory (see the citation related to Chrysler) and receivables (see citation related to J.C. Penney). Most firms cannot operate without inventory. And, as Corporate Finance in the News relates, efficient turnover may save Chrysler $155–$260 million a year. Firms can operate without receivables but may lose market share to competitors who sell on credit. To compete in the retail industry with Sears, Dillards, and others, J.C. Penney decided to sell on credit, and it pays a price—cost needed to fund the receivables and money lost to bad debt when customers declare bankruptcy.

In this chapter we will discuss the management of accounts receivable and inventory. In Table 19-1 we saw that accounts receivable and inventory together accounted for over half of J.C. Penney's total assets in 1996.[1] Clearly, any improvement in the management of these two assets would likely affect the firm's value. If it could drastically reduce (or eliminate) the investment in inventory and receivables without affecting operations, J.C. Penney would be able to increase its profits. Is it possible for a firm such as J.C. Penney or Chrysler to eliminate these investments altogether? To answer that, we need to understand why a firm invests in these two categories of current assets.

Why does a firm hold inventory? The answer is quite simple: Holding inventory ensures smooth-running operations. Because perfect synchronization between production and sales is virtually impossible to achieve, a firm generally needs to hold an inventory of finished goods. A production firm such as Chrysler needs to hold an inventory of raw materials because synchronizing deliveries of raw materials with production is difficult. It also needs to hold an inventory of goods in process because achieving perfect synchronization between the various stages of production is difficult. Without adequate inventory, smooth-running operations are not feasible.

Unlike inventory, investment in receivables is not always necessary. A firm may choose to sell for cash only and not have receivables. However, most firms do invest in receivables. If management believes that the firm will not be able to compete in the market without granting credit, it will probably decide to offer credit to its customers.

Assuming, then, that most firms have inventory and receivables, the task is to determine the best management of those two assets to minimize their cost to the firm and to increase their contribution to the firm's profitability. That is the topic of this chapter.

First, we discuss the management of accounts receivable. We'll see how a firm's management of its receivables affects its profitability and its stock price, especially if these account for a sizable proportion of the firm's total assets.

21.2 ACCOUNTS RECEIVABLE, CASH FLOW, AND NPV

Selling on credit may create additional sales, which has a positive effect, but deferring the cash flow (receivables) until a future date reduces the NPV net present value

---

1. Specifically, the amounts were 26.1% ($5,757 million/$22,088 million) invested in receivables, 25.9% ($5,722 million/$22,088 million) in inventory, for a total of 52% of J.C. Penney's total assets.

of the incremental cash flows. One issue that the firm must consider when evaluating its receivables policy is the timing of the account payments. More specifically, the timing of the cash flows from receivables can affect the net present value and the investment decision. A project that seems to be very profitable according to accounting data may have a negative NPV because the firm will not receive the cash flow from the receivables until some time in the distant future.

Let's review an example. Suppose Airbus Industries agrees to sell ten planes to Delta Airlines at the end of December 1998. Each plane costs $60 million. Airbus's total production costs (not including interest costs) are $50 million per plane. Delta would like to buy the planes on credit according to the following terms: $100 million to be paid on delivery (December 1998) and $500 million to be paid at the end of 1999. Assume Airbus will pay all its production costs in cash at the *beginning* of 1998. Thus, one year would elapse between the production costs and the date of the sale. What would Airbus's accounting profit be from this transaction? What would its cash flow be? What would this deal's NPV be for Airbus? What would the receivables amount be in this transaction?

Because Airbus would transact the sale at the end of December 1998, accounting rules require it to record the sale as revenue in 1998.[2] Therefore, Airbus's gross profit on this transaction, at a production cost of $50 million per plane, would be $100 million [10 planes × ($60 million − $50 million) = $100 million]. The net accounting profit is calculated by deducting other costs such as interest and taxes. To isolate the effect of the delay in the cash flow due to the terms of the credit on the project's NPV, we assume all the other costs are zero. Airbus's accounts receivable as a result of this transaction would be $500 million [(10 planes × $60 million) − $100 million = $500 million] because it would receive $100 million in cash from Delta and the rest of the payment would be on credit.

Are the terms of the sale good for Airbus? If we review the accounting profit, it seems to be a very good deal. However, if we examine the cash flows and calculate the NPV, we obtain a different result. Airbus's cash flows are as follows:

	January 1998 Production costs	December 1998 Payment by Delta	December 1999 Payment by Delta
Airbus's cash flows	−$500 million	$100 million	$500 million
Airbus's receivables		$500 million	0

Assuming the cost of capital is 16%, the NPV of Airbus's cash flows would be

$$\text{NPV} = -\$500 \text{ million} + \frac{\$100 \text{ million}}{1.16} + \frac{\$500 \text{ million}}{(1.16)^2}$$

$$\cong -\$42.21 \text{ million}$$

Since the project's NPV is negative, Airbus should reject it. The deal is not a good one for Airbus.

---

2. Common accounting practice is to record all credit sales as revenue if credit is granted for one year or less. However, if a firm grants credit for a longer period, say five years, it records only the present value of the receivables as revenue.

Only if Airbus can put pressure on Delta to pay earlier will the transaction be worthwhile. If Airbus sold all planes for cash, its cash flows would be as follows:

January 1998	December 1998
–$500 million	$600 million

In that case the NPV of the deal would be

$$\text{NPV} = -\$500 \text{ million} + \frac{\$600 \text{ million}}{1.16} \cong \$17.24 \text{ million}$$

Selling for cash is clearly better. So why does Airbus even consider selling on credit? If Airbus were to eliminate credit sales, it would probably have fewer customers. Those customers who are unable or unwilling to pay cash will prefer one of Airbus's competitors that does sell on credit. Some customers may even decide against the purchase altogether. Selling for cash only is likely to result in reduced sales, and the main reason for extending credit is to stimulate sales. However, boosting sales has its costs; and if extending credit produces a negative NPV, the firm should not consider credit sales.

Most firms are willing to carry accounts receivable to boost sales. Because the true economic profit (project NPV) of the enhanced sales depends on the receivables eventually being collected, as well as on the length of the collection period, management must be very careful in deciding the firm's credit policy.

In contrast to Airbus's project, the project that Magic Toys considers in the following problem has a positive NPV.

PRACTICE BOX

Problem

Magic Toys is considering an investment. The investment requires an initial outlay of $5 million and has an economic life of six months. The investment is transacted at the end of January. Without extending credit to its customers, sales will be very low and the project's NPV will be negative. However, by offering three months' credit, sales will amount to $10 million a month. Production costs are $8 million a month, and this $8 million cash outflow occurs in the same month as the sales. Assume all sales and costs occur at the end of the month starting in February. The firm's cost of capital is 12.68%, which is 1% on a monthly basis. Calculate the monthly accounts receivable and the monthly cash flow. Should Magic Toys extend credit and accept the project?

Solution

The following table summarizes the project's cash flows (in $ million):

(continued)

	Jan.	Feb.	Mar.	Apr.	May	June	July	Aug.	Sept.	Oct.
Sales	0	10	10	10	10	10	10	0	0	0
Receivables	0	10	20	30	30	30	30	20	10	0
Cash flows:										
Cash inflow receivables	0	0	0	0	10	10	10	10	10	10
Cash outflow production costs	0	−8	−8	−8	−8	−8	−8	0	0	0
Initial outlay	−5									
Net cash flow	−5	−8	−8	−8	2	2	2	10	10	10
PV at 1% a month	−5	−7.92	−7.84	−7.76	1.92	1.90	1.88	9.33	9.23	9.14

Note that Magic Toys sells $10 million every month starting in February. Therefore, receivables grow by $10 million a month. Since the credit is for three months, February sales are paid in May. Therefore, receivables decrease by $10 million in May, but they also increase by $10 million due to May sales. Taking these two cash flows into account, receivables remain constant. In fact, they remain constant up to July. From August on, receivables drop by $10 million a month because Magic Toys collects the receivables but makes no new sales. (Remember: The economic life of the project is six months.)

The monthly cost of capital is 1% (12.68% annually). The last line in the table gives the PV of the various monthly cash flows. The NPV is $4.88 million (which is the sum of the PV of all monthly cash flows), and Magic Toys should extend credit and accept the project.

21.3 CREDIT POLICY AND INVESTMENT IN RECEIVABLES

We have just seen the importance of the firm's decision to extend credit. A firm can extend credit to individual customers or to other firms. Credit to customers is **consumer credit** and credit to other firms is **trade credit**. A **credit policy** has two main components: the credit period and the credit terms.

The **credit period** is the length of time for which the firm grants credit. For example, a firm may grant 45 days' credit. In some cases a firm may grant different credit periods to different customers. In such cases we calculate the firm's weighted average credit period.

The **credit terms** are specified in the credit agreement. For instance, 2/10, net 45 means that if the customer pays within 10 days of the purchase date, the firm will grant a 2% discount. However, if the customer chooses not to take advantage of the discount, he or she will pay the full price no later than 45 days from the purchase date. Such terms are also common in trade credit.

How does the firm decide its credit policy? First, it reviews its accounts receivable period and inventory period (see Chapter 19 Sections 19.3.1 and 19.3.3). If these two periods are relatively long, the firm will try to sell as much as it can for cash to avoid additional financing. Second, it will study credit practices prevailing in the industry. If competition in the industry is intense and if the firm's competitors grant, say, 60 days' credit, the firm will have difficulty selling for cash only. It may lose customers who need the credit line to synchronize their cash flows or who simply do not have cash to pay for the purchase. Third, the firm will establish credit standards based on its customers' credit risk. As a rule, the larger the customer's credit risk, the shorter the credit period that should be extended. The firm may not grant credit at all to a very high credit risk customer.

Selling for cash only is possible in principle. Such a policy reduces the need to invest in receivables, and it avoids the administrative costs involved in evaluating a customer's credit risk and collecting the receivables, as well as the costs associated with the loss from bad debt. Even when the firm offers the option of paying on credit, it will generally encourage customers to pay cash. Be that as it may, if selling for credit is a common practice in a given industry, the firm cannot force its customers to buy for cash.

Finally, discounts for cash payment are more common in trade credit than they are in consumer credit. Consumers who conduct small transactions generally pay cash; and when they buy on credit, they pay the same price as the cash price as long as they pay within the period specified in the credit agreement. Consumers who pay before the end of the credit period receive no discount. In trade credit, however, firms commonly offer cash discounts, and the firm given credit must decide whether to accept the discount—a decision that involves calculating the cost of credit. We now turn to that issue, specifically to the question of how to calculate the effective interest rate on cash discounts.

http

Visit VisionPoint's Web site to see the many ways in which accounts receivable are classified and collected, as well as the many types of reports that AR management requires.
http://www.sbt.com/sbtlib/pvp8ar.html

21.4 THE COSTS AND BENEFITS OF CREDIT

Connecting Theory to Practice 21.1 demonstrates the connections among a firm's credit policy and its sales, receivables, and cash flows.

CONNECTING THEORY TO PRACTICE 21.1

J.C. PENNEY'S RECEIVABLES POLICY

The Company generated $286 million in cash from operating activities in 1993 as compared with $1,574 million in 1992. The change in 1993 was due to an increase in customer accounts receivable, particularly in the fourth quarter when the *utilization of the J.C. Penney credit card increased to 47.5 percent* of sales from 46.6 per cent in 1992's comparable period.

Total customer receivables serviced by the Company were $4.4 billion at the end of 1993. The increase in customer receivables was due to the higher sales volume in 1993. In 1993, the Company established the *J.C. Penney Card Bank*, National Association, which issues J.C. Penney credit cards to customers in five states.

The Company's decision to accept the Discover Card in April 1993 contributed to 1993's growth in attracting new customers.

Source: J.C. Penney 1993 financial statements.

MAKING THE CONNECTION

Selling on credit has the benefits of increased sales and new customers. However, selling on credit, as we have seen in J.C. Penney's case, means that the firm will have less cash from operations. The further in the future the cash flows occur, the lower the present value of those cash flows. Worse still, some receivables are not collected at all. A policy that involves holding a high proportion of receivables has its benefits (boosted sales) and its costs (delayed cash flows and risk of default). Management must consider these factors when determining the firm's optimum policy regarding receivables.

Let us elaborate on the costs and benefits of credit sales. When credit is involved, buyers and sellers both have costs and benefits. However, the benefit to one side is not necessarily a cost to the other.

Accounts receivable involve both costs and benefits to the firm. To demonstrate the cost of credit, we begin with an example: Suppose Intel's credit policy is 2/10, net 30. If IBM buys microchips from Intel on credit, it will pay $10 million. If IBM pays cash, it will pay $9.8 (0.98 × $10 million = $9.8 million). What is IBM's rate of return on an annual basis if it decides to take the cash discount? Let us review IBM's cash flows in each case:

IBM's Cash Flows (in $ million)

Time line	10 days	30 days
(1) Cash purchase	−$9.8	0
(2) Credit purchase	0	$10
(3) Incremental cash flow = (1) − (2)	−$9.8	$10

By switching from a credit purchase to a cash purchase, IBM has an incremental cash flow, which is calculated as follows: If IBM decides to use cash, on Day 10 it will have to pay $9.8 million instead of $0 (the −$9.8 million incremental cash flow on Day 10), but on Day 30 IBM will pay nothing instead of $10 million (the $10 million incremental cash flow on Day 30). In other words, IBM pays $9.8 million on Day 10 and saves $10 million on Day 30. The cash purchase can be seen as an investment with an initial outlay of $9.8 million and a cash inflow of $10 million 20 days later. Is this incremental cash flow worthwhile to IBM? How can we tell?

Cash flows can be evaluated by examining their NPV or IRR (as in project evaluation). In order to obtain percentage figures, which can be compared to the borrowing interest rate, let us demonstrate with the IRR calculation. The IRR on the incremental cash flow is given by

$$\$9.8 \text{ million} = \frac{\$10 \text{ million}}{1 + \text{IRR}}$$

$$\text{IRR} \cong 2.04\%$$

This is the IRR for 20 days; on an annual basis, it is

$$(1.0204)^{365/20} - 1 = (1.0204)^{18.25} - 1 \cong 0.4456 \text{ or } 44.56\%$$

Since paying cash is very lucrative for IBM, the firm should take advantage of the discount offered on the cash payment. If IBM does not have the sum needed, it should take out a 20-day loan from the bank for this purpose. As long as the bank does not charge more than 2.04% for 20 days, the transaction is worthwhile.

From the above calculation, we would expect all buyers to prefer cash to credit. However, in practice, this is not the case. Why? There are two principal reasons:

1. The discount offered on cash payments may be much smaller than in this example and, therefore, less worthwhile.
2. Some buyers need the accounts receivable period to synchronize their cash flows. If these buyers cannot easily obtain short-term loans from the bank, they have no choice but to make their purchases on credit.

Let's now turn to Intel, a firm that sells on credit. If IBM can earn 44.56% annually by taking advantage of the discount on cash payments, does this mean that Intel will lose 44.56% annually by offering this discount? No. Although Intel offers a very large discount for cash payments, it obtains the following additional benefits from such payments:

1. The firm does not need additional sources of financing because cash is available.
2. The firm avoids bad debt.
3. The firm saves the administrative costs involved in the collection of receivables.

Intel should include these benefits in its calculations of the cost of a cash-only policy.

To illustrate, suppose that based on past experience Intel expects to write off 1.3% of the receivables as bad debt and expects to have administrative costs of 0.5% of its receivables. In such a case Intel's average net cash collection on a $10 million credit sale will be only $9.82 million [$10 million × (1 − 0.013 − 0.005) = $10 million × 0.982 = $9.82 million].

From Intel's viewpoint, the difference between a credit sale and a cash sale is $0.02 million ($9.82 million − $9.80 million), rather than $0.20 million ($10 million − $9.80 million). Intel's implied interest rate for the discount on cash payments is only

$$\frac{\$9.82 \text{ million}}{\$9.8 \text{ million}} - 1 \cong 0.002 \text{ or } 0.2\% \text{ for 20 days}$$

On an annual basis, the discount on cash payments is

$$(1.0020)^{18.25} - 1 \cong 0.0371 \text{ or } 3.71\%$$

This interest rate is much lower than the 44.56% obtained before in the calculation of the interest rate from IBM's viewpoint. As we can see, what seemed to be a very large and unreasonable cash discount of almost 45% on an annual basis, from Intel's viewpoint amounts to only 3.71% on an annual basis. Saving administrative costs and avoiding bad debt help explain why firms provide what seem to be very generous discounts.

21.4.1 Direct Benefits and Costs of Credit Sales

We have seen how the interest rate cost of credit is calculated. Accounts receivable also involve other costs and benefits. A *direct* benefit of credit sales from the seller's viewpoint is interest income from late payments. Customers who do not pay on time usually are allowed to extend their credit period, but they must pay interest on the outstanding credit. If you use Visa, American Express, Sears, or any other credit card, you know that the interest on delayed payments can be very high. Firms that issue cards to consumers—including credit card firms such as MasterCard and Discover and retailers like J.C. Penney and Eddie Bauer that issue cards for use in their stores—actually operate similarly to banks in that they earn interest income from the credit they offer. If the firm receives interest, is selling on credit a source of net income to the firm? Not necessarily. Credit sales also involve costs.

Costs related to receivables include the cost of credit—these costs incurred for risk evaluation, bad debt, operating expenses, administration costs, and financing the investment in receivables (which are calculated as the firm's cost of capital multiplied by average receivables). Table 21-1 demonstrates J.C. Penney's interest income and expenses on its store credit card. As you can see, after accounting for all direct income and expenses, J.C. Penney lost $247 million on its credit sales in 1991, $183 million in 1992, and $140 million in 1993.

Does this mean that J.C. Penney should have abandoned its credit policy? Not necessarily. In 1994, for the first time in its history, J.C. Penney reported a net profit of more than $1 billion. The firm's credit policy evidently stimulated sales and increased profits. We will discuss this indirect benefit in greater detail in the following section.

21.4.2 Indirect Benefits of Credit Sales

Retailers such as J.C. Penney and Sears issue their own credit cards, which give customers the option, within a certain time period, of paying the same price for purchases made on credit as they would for cash purchases. Firms such as these do

TABLE 21-1	1993	1992	1991
Pretax Cost of J.C. Penney's Credit Card (in $ million)			
Receivables	4,679	3,750	4,131
Finance charge revenue			
On receivables owned	(523)	(509)	(567)
On receivables sold	(129)	(166)	(197)
Total	(652)	(675)	(764)
Bad debt expense	128	171	240
Operating expenses (including in-store costs)	265	270	275
Cost of capital	399	417	496
Total	792	858	1,011
Pretax cost of J.C. Penney card	140	183	247

The cost of capital shown in the table represents the cost of financing both company-owned accounts receivable and securitized[a] accounts receivable. The cost of the sold receivables is the actual interest paid to certificate holders. The owned accounts receivable are financed by both debt and equity. The debt component uses the total company weighted average interest rate, whereas the equity component uses the company's minimum return on equity objective of 16 percent. On a combined basis, for both owned and sold receivables, the debt and equity components of the total capital requirements were 88% debt and 12% equity, which approximates the finance industry standard debt to equity ratio.

Source: J.C. Penney, 1993 financial statements.

[a] J.C. Penney sold a portion of its receivables to a trust that issues certificates to the public. This enables J.C. Penney to obtain cash from sales while continuing to sell on credit. This technique costs J.C. Penney money (i.e., for each $100 of receivables, J.C. Penney may receive only $92 in cash).

not usually levy a charge if customers pay the balance within the credit period, called a **grace period,** typically 25 days. However, if customers decide to extend the credit period, interest charges on the accounts can reach up to 21% on an annual basis.

This type of credit policy generally causes losses to the firm: The cash inflow from sales is deferred, administrative costs are incurred, and bad debt is common. Since this is the case, why do firms offer this type of credit? Why don't they simply sell for cash only? Because by offering credit, firms usually boost their sales and, sometimes, even their profit. The following results from a survey of retail industry executives reveal the importance of credit sales:

Two-thirds of the chains have never tried to quantify the incremental sales that credit cards generate. Of those that do, all said the incremental sales increases were over 20%.

All agreed that if they eliminated acceptance of credit cards, their sales would decrease, with 72% saying the decrease would be more than 20%, 14% saying the drop would be between 16% and 20%, and 14% saying it would be between 16% and 10%.

Almost three-quarters (72%) said the decrease would come within the first six months, 14% said between seven months to a year and 14% said between 13 and 18 months.[3]

The consensus is that credit sales stimulate sales. Note that even a 10% decrease in sales would be considered devastating. Credit boosts sales and is clearly important, even if costly. Firms simply cannot afford *not* to offer credit.[4] We'll illustrate this issue with the following problem.

PRACTICE BOX

Problem

Diamonds Inc. is planning a $900,000 investment at the beginning of next year. If all sales are for cash, the firm's revenue will be $400,000 at the end of each year. Production costs are $300,000 per year. Assume variable production costs amount to 75% of sales, regardless of sales volume. Thus, the net annual cash flow is $100,000 (ignoring taxes). The cash flow is a perpetuity. The cost of capital is 12%.
a. Is the investment worthwhile?
b. Now consider an alternative sales policy. The firm will offer six months' credit with no extra charges. Due to the credit policy, sales (and costs) are expected to double. Assume the PV of the bad debt is negligible. What is the NPV of the investment with this credit policy? Is the credit policy worthwhile?

Solution

a. For cash sales only, the firm's cash flow is as follows:

Time (year)	0	1	2	3	. . .
Cash flow (in $ thousand)	−900	100	100	100	. . .

At a 12% discount rate, we have

$$\text{NPV} = \frac{\$100,000}{0.12} - \$900,000 \cong -\$66,667$$

Diamond Inc. should reject the project.

b. Now let us see if a change in the credit policy can save this project. With six months' credit, we obtain the following cash flows:

Date (year)	0	1	1.5	2	2.5	3	3.5	. . .
Investment (in $ thousand)	−900							
Cash outflow (in $ thousand)		−600		−600		−600		. . .
Cash inflow (in $ thousand)			800		800		800	. . .

Note that both sales and costs are double with credit sales relative to cash sales. With six months' credit, the receivables of Year 1 sales are collected six

(continued)

---

3. See "The Third Annual Arthur Anderson Survey of Retail Credit Trends," *Chain Store Executive,* January 1993, sec. 3, p. 23B.
4. Credit seems to be so important in stimulating sales that, several years ago, many department stores (J.C. Penney included) began accepting non-store credit cards such as Visa, Discover, and American Express. Department stores would pay the credit card fees on the amounts charged. Of course, the stores wouldn't have to contend with the costs of credit evaluation, collection efforts, or bad debt.

months later (i.e., 1.5 years after the investment). Similarly, the cash from Year 2 sales is collected 2.5 years after the investment, and so on.

The best way to evaluate this project is to calculate the NPV of revenue and the NPV of costs separately, each as a perpetuity.

The PV of costs (in $ thousands) is

$$PV = \frac{-\$600}{1.12} + \frac{-\$600}{(1.12)^2} + \ldots = \frac{-\$600}{0.12} = -\$5,000$$

The PV of revenue (in $ thousand) is

$$\frac{\$800}{(1.12)^{1.5}} + \frac{\$800}{(1.12)^{2.5}} + \ldots = \frac{1}{(1.12)^{0.5}}\left[\frac{\$800}{1.12} + \frac{\$800}{(1.12)^2} + \ldots\right]$$

$$= \frac{1}{(1.12)^{0.5}} \times \frac{\$800}{0.12}$$

$$\cong \$6,299.41$$

With credit sales, the NPV (in $ thousand) is:

$$NPV = \$6,299.41 - \$5,000 - \$900$$

$$= \$399.41$$

Since the project is worthwhile, Diamond Inc. should accept it and should adopt the new credit policy because it will boost sales and profits.

In practice, production costs may increase more slowly than sales, which will further increase the project's NPV. On the other hand, the firm should also include collection and bad debt costs in the computation, which will reduce the NPV. Credit sales are a good idea as long as the NPV is positive and larger than the NPV with cash sales.

In Applying Theory to Practice 21.1, we analyze J.C. Penney's reported and actual "cost of capital," which it used to calculate the cost of financing the credit it provides. Here we also see the direct and indirect costs and benefits of credit sales.

APPLYING THEORY TO PRACTICE 21.1

THE COST OF J.C. PENNEY'S CREDIT CARD

In 1993 J.C. Penney introduced the J.C. Penney card, which granted credit to its customers. It is interesting to see how J.C. Penney analyzed the cost of receivables in its 1993 financial statements. To analyze J.C. Penney's receivables policy and the cost of the J.C. Penney credit card, we use the following data for that year:

1. Table 19-1, the column corresponding to 1993.
2. Table 21-1 in this chapter.
3. The following additional data. The average cost of debt (long-term and short-term) is 8.81%. The cost of equity is 16%. The firm's accounts payable consist of credit obtained from suppliers at 2/10, net 30. The stock price was, on average, $45 in 1993, and the firm has 236 million shares outstanding.

Questions
1. In 1993 J.C. Penney reported $399 million as "cost of capital" expenses. (See Table 21-1.) What is the implied cost of capital (in percent) used in this calculation?
2. Table 21-1 shows that J.C. Penney deducts the cost of capital as a financing expense when it calculates the annual cash flow due to its receivables. Assume the firm uses the same procedure in project evaluation (i.e., J.C. Penney incorporates financing costs with other cash flows). In Chapter 7 we learned that cost of capital should *not* be deducted from cash flows. There seem to be two ways of incorporating the investment in receivables in project evaluation: one *with* deduction of the cost of capital (or cost of the receivables financing) from the annual cash flows (as J.C. Penney uses) and one *without* deduction of the cost of capital from the cash flows.

   Assume the firm's annual sales amount to S starting at the end of Year 1, and the firm grants credit in the amount of R for one year. (This assumption is for simplicity only because in practice J.C. Penney's credit is for a shorter period.) J.C. Penney raises R at the end of Year 1 to finance its receivables. The sales occur at the end of each year. Write the cash flows that J.C. Penney receives by each of the two methods. Is J.C. Penney wrong in deducting the cost of capital, or are the two methods equivalent? (Assume perpetual cash flows.)
3. According to Table 21-1, J.C. Penney finances 88% of its receivables by debt, and 12% by equity.
   a. Calculate the weighted average cost of capital (WACC) in 1993 with the above financing proportions, where the cost of debt is 8.81% and the cost of equity is 16%.
   b. Calculate the WACC in 1993 using the book value of equity and debt as weights.
   c. Calculate the WACC in 1993 using the market value, rather than the book value, of equity. For debt, assume the book value equals the market value. Contrast the firm's own calculation (see Table 21-1) with what, in your view, should be the correct calculation. Ignore all other financing sources when performing your calculations.
4. In Table 21-1 we see that "cost of capital" as defined in the table is $399 million. How would you change this number in light of your answer to Question 3c?

MAKING THE CONNECTION

1. The firm's average receivables during 1993 were as follows:

    ($4,679 million + $3,750 million)/2 = $4,124.5 million

    Thus, the implied cost of capital is

    $399 million/$4,124.5 million ≅ 0.0967 or 9.67%

    where $399 million is the financial cost (reported as "cost of capital" in Table 21-1).

2. a. The PV method (without deduction of financing costs):

    Suppose J.C. Penney's sales are $S per year. Since some sales are on credit, the first year's cash flow is only $(S − R)$ where R denotes the receivables due to that year's credit sales. In the second year, the firm's cash flow is $S, composed as follows:

$S − R$	Amount from second year sales
+ R	Collection of the first year's receivables
$ S	Total cash flow

    Similarly, the cash flow for all subsequent years is $S. Using the perpetuity formula, this cash flow's PV is

    $$\frac{\$(S - R)}{1 + k} + \frac{\$S}{(1 + k)^2} + \frac{\$S}{(1 + k)^3} + \cdots = \frac{\$S}{k} - \frac{\$R}{1 + k}$$

    where k is the cost of capital and $\$S/k$ is the PV of the perpetuity $S.[5]

    b. J.C. Penney's method (with deduction of financing costs):

    Suppose J.C. Penney started its operations in Year 1. It raises $R to finance the receivables, and from Year 2 on, it pays kR as financial expenses. It deducts kR annually as cost of capital expenses. (See Table 21-1.) The method can be summarized as follows:

End of Year	1	2	3 . . .
Cash flow from sales (in $)	$S − R$	S	S . . .
Raise $R (by issuing stocks and borrowing $R at the end of Year 1) (in $)	+R		
Financing cost (at k%) (in $)		−kR	−kR . . .
Net cash flow after deducting financial costs (in $)	S	$S − kR$	$S − kR$ . . .

5. See Chapter 4 for the perpetuity formula.

Thus, the firm raises money to finance the $R receivables at the end of the first year and pays financing costs of $kR from Year 2 on. The cash flow's PV is

$$PV = \frac{\$S}{1 + k} + \frac{\$S}{(1 + k)^2} + \ldots$$

$$- \frac{\$kR}{(1 + k)^2} - \frac{\$kR}{(1 + k)^3} - \ldots$$

or

$$PV = \frac{\$S}{k} - \frac{\$kR}{k(1 + k)} = \frac{\$S}{k} - \frac{\$R}{1 + k}$$

Thus, J.C. Penney's method (with deduction of financing costs) and the discounted cash flow method (without deduction of financing costs) produce the same PV. Therefore, J.C. Penney's method is correct, and the two methods are equivalent.

3. a. According to Table 21-1, J.C. Penney finances 88% of the receivables by debt and 12% by equity. With these weights we obtain

$$(0.88 \times 8.81\%) + (0.12 \times 16\%) \cong 9.67\%$$

b. The weighted average cost of capital *should* be

$$k = \left(8.81\% \times \frac{D}{V}\right) + \left(16\% \times \frac{S}{V}\right)$$

where D/V and S/V are the proportions of debt and equity based on their market values. Assuming debt and equity are the only financing sources and that book values equal market values, for 1993 we obtain (see Table 19-1)

Debt = $1,284 million + $348 million + $2,929 million

= $4,561 million

Total equity = $5,365 million

Assuming there are no other financing sources, the total assets are $9,926 million ($4,561 million + $5,365 million = $9,926 million). The firm's weighted average cost of capital is

$$\left(\frac{\$4,561 \text{ million}}{\$9,926 \text{ million}} \times 8.81\%\right) + \left(\frac{\$5,365 \text{ million}}{\$9,926 \text{ million}} \times 16\%\right)$$

$$\cong 4.05\% + 8.65\% = 12.70\%$$

This amount is much higher than the WACC J.C. Penney uses in calculating the cost of capital given in Table 21-1.

c.   Ignoring all other financing sources, we get:

Debt value (= book value of debt) = $4,561 million

Equity value = $45 × 236 million shares = $10,620 million

Total asset value = $4,561 million + $10,620 million = $15,181 million

Therefore, the weighted cost of capital using market values is

$$k = \left(\frac{\$4,562 \text{ million}}{\$15,181 \text{ million}} \times 8.81\% \right) + \left(\frac{\$10,620 \text{ million}}{\$15,181 \text{ million}} \times 16\% \right)$$

$$\cong 2.65\% + 11.19\% = 13.84\%$$

As shown in Chapter 10, the correct calculation is as given in 3c; namely, a WACC of 13.84%. When the market values are not available, we can use the book values as estimates and rely on the cost of capital given in 3b. The calculations in 3a are irrelevant. The implication of financing 88% of the receivables by debt is that J.C. Penney financed other projects with less debt (because the average debt financing of the whole firm is less than 88%). In Chapter 10 we saw that the WACC should be calculated with optimum long-term weights, not with the weights used for the specific project under consideration.

4. Using the correct calculation for J.C. Penney's WACC, the "cost of capital" expenses should be $570.83 million:

$$0.1384 \times \text{Average receivables} = 0.1384 \times \$4,124.5 \text{ million}$$

$$\cong \$570.83 \text{ million}$$

rather than the $399 million that was actually charged. Adding the bad debt and operating expenses, the total cost is $963.83 million.

Does this mean that J.C. Penney's credit sales are not worthwhile? No. Credit sales are likely to boost sales that, in turn, will increase J.C. Penney's profits and future cash flows. Indeed, in the fiscal year ending on January 1995, J.C. Penney reported that sales climbed 7.4%. This might not be as great an increase as was hoped, but it is still a marked improvement. By 1996 J.C. Penney felt it was in a strong enough position to acquire Eckerd Corporation, the fourth largest drugstore chain in the U.S. It seems that the benefits of credit sales—increase in sales and improvement in the firm's position in the retailing market—in this case outweighed the financing costs.

21.5 THE OPTIMAL LEVEL OF INVESTMENT IN RECEIVABLES

By now you should be convinced that credit sales help increase sales and future cash flows. The next question is whether the benefit that can be gained from credit sales has a limit. In other words, is there an optimal level of investment in receivables?

Receivables involve two types of costs: carrying and opportunity. Investing in receivables incurs carrying costs; not investing in receivables incurs opportunity costs due to the loss of customers. The optimum investment in receivables is the level of receivables that minimizes the total of these two costs. Let's examine each type of cost.

21.5.1 Carrying Costs

The **carrying costs** associated with receivables are as follows:

1. Required return on the investment—that is, the firm's cost of capital.
2. Cost of bad debt.
3. Administrative costs (including the cost of credit evaluation).

If the firm sells for cash only, these three costs will be zero. If the firm sells for credit, these costs will increase as the receivables increase. Figure 21-1 shows the optimal level of investment in receivables as a function of carrying costs and opportunity costs (which will be discussed next).

Two of the three carrying costs—administrative costs and the cost of capital—tend to increase linearly with the increase in receivables. The larger the receivables, the more money the firm needs to finance them. Similarly, administrative costs tend to increase linearly with receivables: The larger the receivables, the larger the administrative costs of servicing them. However, the cost of bad debt probably increases nonlinearly, because the more liberal the credit policy, the sharper the increase in bad debt.

FIGURE 21-1
Optimal Level of Investment in Receivables as a Function of Carrying and Opportunity Costs

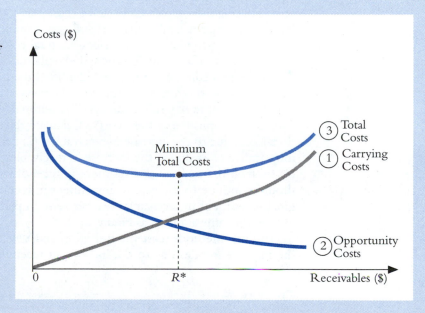

Let us elaborate: Suppose a firm increases its receivables by extending the credit period from, say, one month to two months. In such a case collection of the receivables becomes less certain: It is harder to predict a customer's economic strength two months from now (relative to one month from now). Another way the firm can increase its receivables is by granting credit to riskier customers—a policy that is likely to result in a larger proportion of bad debt. The direct carrying costs of receivables are probably linear for a low level of receivables and increase in an accelerated manner as the proportion of bad debt increases, as Curve 1 in Figure 21-1 shows.

21.5.2 Opportunity Costs

We've seen that if the firm sells for cash only, it risks losing customers. The **opportunity costs** of losing customers can be very high. Suppose if a firm has $100 million in receivables, its sales would be $1 billion. With $250 million in receivables, the firm's sales would be $1.5 billion. The opportunity cost of an additional $150 million invested in receivables is the income the firm would lose should it decide to have $100 million rather than $250 million in receivables. As the firm increases the credit that it offers to its customers, the firm attracts more customers, the receivables increase, and the opportunity costs decline—that is, the higher the receivables, the lower the opportunity costs, as Curve 2 in Figure 21-1 shows.

Note that the decline in opportunity costs tends to level off above a certain level of receivables: If the firm succeeds in capturing all (or almost all) potential customers, the additional opportunity costs from not increasing receivables any further become very small and can even reach zero. In that case Curve 2 will be flat and close to the horizontal axis. Recall that the firm can make its credit policy less restrictive in two ways: either by extending the credit period for high-quality (low-risk) customers or by offering the same credit period to customers whose credit risk is relatively high. Receivables increase, sales increase, and opportunity costs decline in both cases.

Curve 3 in Figure 21-1 describes the total costs. The optimal investment in receivables is given by Point R^* where the total cost curve reaches its minimum level.[6]

In the preceding discussion we identified the optimal investment in receivables by focusing on the total costs function. However, as in project evaluation, the firm could also use the NPV rule to analyze the optimal level of investment in receivables. This is accomplished as follows: (1) Calculate the increased cash flows from additional sales due to the increase in receivables, (2) deduct the cost of bad debt and administrative costs due to the increase in receivables, (3) discount the cash flows, and (4) subtract the additional investment in receivables. If the NPV is positive, the firm should continue to increase its investment in receivables until the NPV of the marginal investment in receivables reaches zero. In principle the NPV method produces exactly the same solution as Figure 21-1.

In both methods (cost minimization and NPV rule) the firm needs to estimate the increase in sales due to the increase in receivables. In practice neither the cost

6. Note that (unlike the similar optimal cash level illustration in Chapter 20 see Figure 20.4) the minimum total cost does not necessarily occur at the intersection of Curves 1 and 2. The reason is that no simple relationship exists between operating costs and the level of receivables.

minimization method nor the NPV rule is easy to apply because estimating the cash flows is difficult. The firm will have to use a trial-and-error method (i.e., experiment with different levels of receivables) and then observe the sales that occur in response to various credit policies. Indeed, a firm commonly experiments with the credit terms that it offers on a regional basis or on a product line to determine if and how they affect sales and payment behavior.

21.6 CREDIT POLICY IN PRACTICE

Table 21-2 provides information on the receivables and sales of a sample of firms. As we can see from the last column, receivables as a percentage of sales vary from firm to firm, even within the same industry. The receivables percentage is only 1.4% at Wal-Mart but reaches 36.1% for Sears, for example. Similarly, it is 16.1% for Nike and 27.7% for L.A. Gear. The higher this percentage, the more relaxed the firm's credit policy.

Credit policy is a function partly of the product sold and partly of the intensity of industry competition. However, even within the same industry, large differences in the receivables percentage occur. This may reflect differences in managerial philosophy regarding the importance of credit sales rather than some optimized economic model. As mentioned earlier, because quantifying all the economic factors needed to determine the optimal level of investment in receivables is very difficult, finding such wide variations in the credit firms grant is hardly surprising.

TABLE 21-2 Receivables, Sales, and Receivables as a Percentage of Sales for Selected Firms (1993)	Receivables ($ million)	Sales ($ million)	Receivables as a Percentage of Sales (Rounded)
Apparel Industry			
Fruit of the Loom	311.7	2,100.0	14.8
Russell Corp.	243.9	930.0	26.2
Retail Stores			
Kmart	1,571.0	41,025.0	3.8
Wal-Mart	969.9	67,375.0	1.4
Sears	18,365.3	50,838.0	36.1
Service Merchandise	33.3	3,814.6	0.8
Shoe Industry			
L.A. Gear	106.6	385.0	27.7
Nike	631.6	3,931.0	16.1
Reebok	555.4	2,893.9	19.2

Source: *Value Line Investment Survey,* 25 February 1994.

However, another possible explanation for the large difference in receivables is technical. In using third–party credit cards, some firms extend credit to customers through a third party. For example, Wal–Mart has for years accepted Visa, Master-Card, and Discover credit cards; whereas until a few years ago, Sears accepted only its own credit card. As a result, Sears's income statement revealed a relatively large amount of outstanding receivables, and Wal–Mart's income statement revealed a relatively low amount of receivables. Thus, comparing credit policies based on observed outstanding receivables should be done with great care.

21.7 INTEREST RATE RISK AND FOREIGN CURRENCY RISK INHERENT IN RECEIVABLES

We have mentioned the risk of bad debt. As the following excerpt from IBM's 1996 financial statements reveals, receivables also entail other risks.

Inherent in customer financing are certain risks: credit, interest rate, currency, and residual value. The company manages credit risk through comprehensive credit evaluations and pricing practices. To manage the risks associated with an uncertain interest rate environment the company pursues a funding strategy of substantially matching the terms of its debt with the terms of its assets. Currency risks are managed by denominating liabilities in the same currency as assets.

Interest rate risk arises when the receivables' maturity differs from the financing source's maturity. In such cases the firm may incur losses when the interest rate changes. To avoid such losses, IBM tries to match the maturities of its liabilities and receivables.

If receivables are for, say, six months, IBM borrows for six months—which is *maturity matching*. Recall that price differences between sales for cash and sales on credit reflect, among other things, current short-term interest rates. If a firm borrows long-term at, say, 10% interest to finance receivables, it loses if interest rates fall. When the firm renews its receivables, it can add a relatively small amount to the price of credit sales (reflecting the, say, 5% short-term interest rate). Yet, IBM continues to pay a higher long-term interest rate of 10%. The firm can avoid this interest rate risk by maturity matching.

IBM raises money to finance its receivables, which may be denominated in various currencies. If it maintains receivables in German marks, IBM borrows in marks to finance those receivables. Any change in exchange rates affects both assets (receivables) and liabilities in the same way—a hedged position. This is called *currency matching*.

Let us elaborate. IBM is exposed to foreign exchange risk because it sells its products internationally. Suppose it sells to a German customer on three months' credit and generates receivables amounting to 500 million DM. If the exchange rate at the time of the sale is $1 = 1.6 DM, the receivables will amount to $312.5 million (500 million DM/1.60 = $312.5 million). However, when the German customer pays three months later, the exchange rate may be different; and IBM cannot be sure of the dollar amount of the receivables. For example, if the exchange rate on the payment date is $1 = 2 DM, IBM will receive only $250 million (500 million DM/2 = $250 million).

To safeguard against foreign exchange risk, firms strive to match their receivables and liabilities in various currencies. Accordingly, when IBM receives the 500 million DM, it will use this sum to pay German suppliers and thereby eliminate the need to convert marks into dollars. Although this is a good way to avoid this risk exposure, it is hard to handle in practice, especially if transactions are conducted in many countries and in many different currencies.

Other ways to avoid foreign currency risk and interest rate risk are to buy forward contracts on foreign currencies and to buy options on the interest rate. (See Chapter 11 Sections 11.8.4 and 11.8.5.)

21.8 CREDIT RISK ANALYSIS: COLLECTION OF RECEIVABLES AND BAD DEBT

When a firm sells on credit, it faces **credit risk**—that is, the risk of its receivables being uncollectible and becoming bad debt. To minimize this risk, the firm may decide to evaluate its customers' credit risk before entering into a credit agreement with them. If you have ever applied for a credit card, you have been on the consumer-credit end of this process. After the firm has extended credit, it must monitor its receivables and take action if they are slow in being collected. In this section we examine the techniques firms use to do both these things.

21.8.1 Evaluating Credit Risk

A firm evaluates a customer's credit risk according to five criteria, known as the **five Cs of credit.** These are as follows:

1. *Character*. Does the customer intend to pay? This criterion, which is generally based on a past credit record, is a firm's principal consideration in deciding whether to provide credit.
2. *Capacity*. The customer's future cash flows and ability to pay.
3. *Capital*. The customer's financial reserves.
4. *Collateral*. The assets the customer pledges as collateral and their economic value in the case of default.
5. *Condition*. The general economic conditions (recession or boom) prevailing in the customer's geographical location.

The firm may assign a score from 1 to 10 on each of the five Cs (where, for example, 10 denotes very good and 1 denotes very poor) and then sum the scores on each item. Based on its past experience, the firm may decide to deny credit to any customer with a score of, say, less than 41. This method is known as **credit scoring.** Alternatively, the firm may decide to use the payment-analysis services of a company such as Dun and Bradstreet.

21.8.2 Evaluating Collection of Receivables

Making the credit decision is only the first step in managing receivables. The firm must also monitor its accounts receivable to determine whether customers are paying on time. To keep track of its receivables situation, the firm uses an **aging schedule.** Similar to the following table, an aging schedule shows the "ages" of unpaid accounts and what percentage of the total value of receivables those accounts represent:

Aging Schedule

Age of the Account	Percentage of Total Value of Accounts Receivable
0–20 days	55
21–60 days	20
61–90 days	15
90+ days	10
Total	100

Suppose the firm offers 60 days' credit. From the data in the table, it knows that 25% of the payments are late—that is, all accounts older than 60 days (15% + 10%). A firm prepares an aging schedule periodically. If the percentage of overdue accounts increases over time, the firm may take more aggressive measures to collect its receivables. It may even reconsider its credit policy to avoid financial distress.

When overdue accounts reach various ages, the firm takes the following steps to collect late receivables:

1. Send the customer a delinquency letter, sometimes with penalties attached for late payment.
2. Call the customer.
3. Hire a collection agency.
4. Take legal action against the customer.

For example, the firm whose aging schedule is shown in the table may decide to send a delinquency letter when an account reaches 65 days (5 days overdue); call the customer at 70 days; hire a collection agency at 75 days; and take legal action against the customer at 90 days.

If the firm determines that there is little or no chance of collecting the receivables, it will write them off and classify the accounts as bad debt. The following excerpt from J.C. Penney's 1996 financial statements illustrates the firm's policy regarding bad debt:

The Company's policy is to write off accounts when the scheduled minimum payment has not been received for six consecutive months, if any portion of the balance is more than 12 months past due, or if it is otherwise determined that the customer is unable to pay. Collection efforts continue subsequent to write off, and recoveries are applied as a reduction of bad debt losses.

During the period 1988 to 1990, the Company transferred portions of its customer receivables to a trust which, in turn, sold certificates representing undivided interests in the trust in public offerings. Certificates sold during this period totaled $1,400 million. As of January 25, 1997, $725 million of the certificates were outstanding and the balance of the receivables in the trust was $1,869 million. The Company owns the remaining undivided interest in the trust not represented by the certificates and will continue to service all receivables for the trust.

As we can see from the above excerpt a firm can finance its receivables by selling them to a trust or to some other financial institution. Here's how this technique works: Suppose J.C. Penney sells $1 billion of its receivables to a trust. The trust will then issue certificates to the public and use the proceeds to pay J.C. Penney some portion of the receivables. J.C. Penney thus changes its receivables to securities through a process called *asset securitization*. Suppose J.C. Penney receives 90% of its receivables in cash. When the receivables are collected, the trust uses the money to pay the certificate holders (principal and interest). Called **certificate amortization,** this practice is quite common. For example, we find the following in IBM's 1996 financial statements:

At year end 1996, the company had a net balance of $1.1 billion in assets under management from the securitization of loans, leases, and trade receivables . . . . The company received total cash proceeds of approximately $4.0 billion and $3.4 billion in 1996 and 1995, respectively, from the sale and securitization of these receivables and assets.

21.9 FINANCING RECEIVABLES: FACTORING

Aside from securitization, the firm can finance the receivables by selling them to another party. This is called **factoring,** and the buyer of the receivables is called the *factor*. Factoring can take the form of either a factoring agreement or an assignment (pledging) agreement.

The **factoring agreement** involves outright sale of the firm's receivables to a finance company *without recourse*. According to this arrangement, the factor takes on the receivables, the credit, the collection task, and the risk of bad debt. The firm selling its receivables receives the value of the receivables minus a commission charge (generally 3–4% higher than the prime interest rate) as compensation for the risks the factor assumes. Thereafter, customers make direct payments to the factor.

In an **assignment (pledging) agreement,** the *ownership* of the receivables is not transferred; the receivables are given to a finance company *with recourse*. The finance company advances some proportion of the receivables' value, generally in the range of 50–80%. The firm remains responsible for service charges, interest on the advance, and losses due to bad debt. According to this arrangement, customers make direct payments to the firm.

The following problem compares a firm's costs of a factoring agreement and an assignment agreement.

PRACTICE BOX

Problem

Hot Tub Inc.'s credit sales amount to $500,000 a month. The collection period is 30 days. A factor offers to buy, without recourse, 80% of the firm's receivables at a charge of 3% plus a handling fee of 0.5% of the total receivables.

A bank offers Hot Tub Inc. a loan to cover 80% of the receivables at 2% a month. The credit collection cost is 1% of the credit sales, and the bad debt cost is estimated to be 2% of the credit sales. Assume all costs are incurred at the end of the 30-day period.

Should Hot Tub Inc. borrow from the bank or make a deal with the factor?

Solution

Because the collection period is 30 days, all calculations are on a monthly basis.

Cost of factoring:

Handling fee (0.005 × $500,000)	$ 2,500
Factor charge (0.03 × 0.80 × $500,000)	12,000
Total cost	$14,500

Bad debt losses and handling costs are the factor's responsibility.

Cost of bank financing:

Interest (0.02 × 0.80 × $500,000)	$ 8,000
Collection costs (0.01 × $500,000)	5,000
Bad debt (0.02 × $500,000)	10,000
Total cost	$23,000

Because the total cost of the factoring agreement is less than the total cost of the bank financing, Hot Tub Inc. should close a deal with the factor.

Note that both factoring and receivables securitization provide financing sources for receivables. With factoring, the financing source is the factor; with securitization, it is the public who buys the securities.

21.10 INVENTORY MANAGEMENT

We now turn from accounts receivable to the second topic of the chapter—inventory. Corporate Finance in the News claims that Chrysler may save $155–$260 million by increasing its inventory turnover. Because inventory turnover is sales divided by average inventory held, this implies that, for a given level of sales, Chrysler must hold smaller inventories—this is Chrysler's source of savings.

The inventory manager's main task is to decide at which level (in both units and dollar value) each product should be held in inventory. It costs a firm money to hold inventory. Therefore, a firm such as Nike gives a discount to retailers if they are willing to hold the inventory of Nike shoes. Nike's aggressive inventory management is essentially aimed at saving inventory costs by pushing inventory from the firm to the retailers as quickly as possible. Connecting Theory to Practice 21.2 explains how Nike accomplishes this.

Table 21-3 provides information on the inventory and sales of a sample of firms in various industries. The last column gives inventory as a percentage of sales. As you can see, considerable variation exists across industries and even across firms within the same industry. Nike, for instance, holds only 13.40% of its annual sales as inventory, whereas L.A. Gear holds 28.36%. Due to its substantial savings on inventory costs, Nike has a financial edge over L.A. Gear.

CONNECTING THEORY TO PRACTICE 21.2

NIKE'S INVENTORY AND PRODUCTION CONTROL

As important as Nike's image-building prowess, however, was the company's often-overlooked inventory-control system. Called "Futures," it is at the core of Nike's consistent profitability. Nike forces retailers to order up to 80% of their purchases six to eight months in advance in return for guaranteed delivery times and a discount of up to 10%. The result: Nike knows exactly what its orders are early enough to plan production accordingly. That avoids excess inventory and assures better prices from its Asian plants. Retailers hate it because if they guess wrong about the market, they get stuck with the shoes.

Source: Dori Jones Yang, Michael Oneal, Charles Hoots, and Robert Neff, "Can Nike Just Do It?" *Business Week* (18 April 1994): 89.

MAKING THE CONNECTION

By soliciting orders six to eight months in advance of delivery and by passing much of the uncertainty to the retailers, Nike can hold a low level of inventory and plan its production accordingly. However, there are no "free lunches." To convince the retailers to stock its products, Nike offers them a 10% discount. Some retailers may even dislike the policy so much that they may decide not to order Nike shoes.

21.10.1 Inventory Costs

Holding inventory involves three types of costs: carrying, ordering, and shortage. The inventory manager's goal is to hold the level of inventory that minimizes these costs; this will be the firm's optimal inventory level.

CARRYING COSTS

The carrying costs of inventory include the cost of capital, storage and handling costs, insurance costs, property taxes, economic depreciation, and obsolescence costs. To illustrate the depreciation cost, consider a car dealer who holds a car in inventory

TABLE 21-3 Inventory, Sales, and Inventory as Percentage of Sales for Selected Firms (October 1993)		Inventory October 1993 ($ million)	Sales 1993 ($ million)	Inventory as a Percentage of Sales (%)
Apparel Industry				
Russell Corp.		268.8	930.8	28.88
Liz Claiborne		406.5	2,204.3	18.44
Textile Industry				
Dixi Yarn		110.3	594.6	18.55
Springs Industries		267.8	1,975.7	13.55
Retail Store				
Consol Stores		316.7	1,060.0	29.88
Dillards		1,636.6	5,300.0	30.88
Shoe Industry				
L.A. Gear		109.2	385.0	28.36
Nike		526.9	3,931.0	13.40

Source: *Value Line Investment Survey*, 25 February 1994.

for a year. When new models are released to the market, the year-old car loses about 10–15% of its value, even if it still has zero mileage on its speedometer. That loss in value is the car's economic depreciation. Depreciation costs are about 10–15% of annual inventory (depending on the product), and the cost of capital is generally in the range of 10–15% annually (depending on the industry). For most products, a firm incurs carrying costs of at least 20–30% of the inventory's value each year.

ORDERING COSTS

The **ordering costs** of inventory are the costs of placing an order, including shipment costs. Ordering costs can vary dramatically from one product to another and with the distance between seller and buyer. Most of these costs represent shipping costs.

SHORTAGE COSTS

As noted in Chapter 19, **shortage costs** are the costs of running out of stock: If the firm runs out of an inventory of finished goods, it may lose customers. For a production firm, running out of raw material interrupts production that, once again, involves costs. These are mainly the costs of paying workers for downtime and of shutting down and then restarting machinery (called *setup costs*).

21.10.2 Techniques for Managing Inventory

The more varied the products a firm holds, the more difficult the management of its inventory. However, since a firm can hold inexpensive items such as nuts, bolts, and plastic bags in large quantities, it does not need to use a complicated, quantitative inventory model to manage them. The firm can even hold many more of such items than it actually needs. Although the inventory cost of these items is relatively low, any shortage of them is likely to slow or even stop production, and the firm's "extra" investment in inexpensive items makes financial sense. Quantitative methods are recommended only for the more expensive items because they contribute most to the firm's inventory costs. The best-known model for inventory management is the economic order quantity (EOQ) model.

ECONOMIC ORDER QUANTITY (EOQ) MODEL

The **economic order quantity (EOQ) model** enables the firm to determine its optimum level of inventory—that is, the level of inventory that minimizes the total related costs. The model assumes that the firm knows the demand for its product with certainty, that the firm sells its inventory at a steady rate, and that the firm also knows how long it takes for an order of new inventory to arrive. Let's see how a firm uses the EOQ model.

Carrying costs are a function of the inventory the firm holds. Suppose the starting inventory is Q units, and the firm sells 25% of the starting inventory each week. By the end of the fourth week, the inventory is zero. On average the firm holds only $Q/2$ units. Figure 21-2 illustrates how the inventory decreases over the first four weeks. At the end of Week 4, the firm receives a new order and, once again, holds Q units. This new inventory also declines by 25% a week. On average the firm holds $Q/2$ units during the whole year. If the annual carrying costs in dollars per unit are $\$C$, the annual carrying costs, CC, are given by

$$CC = \$C \times \frac{Q}{2}$$

Suppose the firm sells T units per year. If it orders Q units at a time, it will have to place an order T/Q times during the year. Ordering costs, denoted by $\$F$, are assumed to be fixed per order and independent of the order's size. (For example, a truck delivers produce to a local store and charges $200 per trip, regardless of the number of boxes ordered.) The total ordering costs depend on the number of orders per year. The total ordering costs are therefore

$$OC = \$F \times \left(\frac{T}{Q}\right)$$

If the firm orders $Q = T$ units at a time, it makes only one order a year, and the costs are simply $\$F$. If the firm holds a very small inventory, it will need to order many

FIGURE 21-2
Changes in Inventory Level over Time

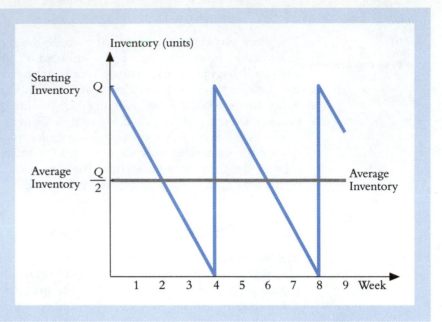

times during the year and the OC will be very large. The larger the inventory, the smaller OC. Figure 21-3 illustrates the inventory carrying costs (Curve 1), the ordering costs (Curve 2), and the total costs (Curve 3) as a function of the size of the inventory order, Q. The total costs are:[7]

$$TC = CC + OC$$

The optimum inventory order, denoted by Q, is obtained at the point where the total costs are minimized. At this point, as shown in Figure 21-3, we have:[8]

$$OC = CC$$

or

$$F\left(\frac{T}{Q^*}\right) = C\left(\frac{Q^*}{2}\right)$$

Solving for Q^*, we get the optimum inventory order:

7. Note that the EOQ model assumes that the firm knows *with certainty* (a) the rate at which it sells the inventory and (b) the time it takes a new inventory order to arrive. Thus, the model assumes that the firm will always order inventory enough time in advance and will not incur shortage costs.

8. The total cost, TC, is

$$TC = F \times \left(\frac{T}{Q}\right) + \left(\frac{Q}{2}\right) \times C$$

Differentiating with respect to Q and equating to zero, we obtain the minimum total cost:

$$-F \times \left(\frac{T}{Q^2}\right) + \frac{C}{2} = 0 \quad \text{or} \quad F \times \left(\frac{T}{Q}\right) = C \times \left(\frac{Q}{2}\right)$$

Hence, $OC = CC$.

FIGURE 21-3
Inventory Costs as a Function of the Inventory Held

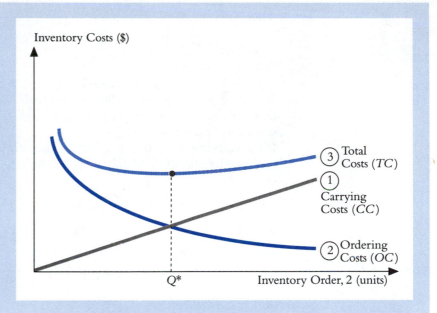

$$(Q^*)^2 = \frac{2TF}{C}$$

or

$$Q = \left(\frac{2TF}{C}\right)^{1/2} \tag{21.1}$$

The following problem demonstrates how a firm uses EOQ.

PRACTICE BOX

Problem

Barnaby's Department Store sells 52,000 units of a given product during the year. The cost of each unit is $10, and the carrying cost is 25% of the inventory value. The ordering cost is $500.
a. Calculate the optimal order that Barnaby's should place.
b. What is the average inventory?
c. How would your answer change if the carrying cost per unit were only 2.5% of the inventory value?

Solution

a. The carrying cost per unit is

$$0.25 \times \$10 = \$2.50$$

(continued)

Therefore, the optimal order is

$$Q^* = \left(\frac{2TF}{C}\right)^{1/2} = \left(\frac{2 \times 52{,}000 \times \$500}{\$2.50}\right)^{1/2} \cong 4{,}560.7 \text{ or } 4{,}561 \text{ units}$$

(Only whole units can be ordered.)

b. The average inventory is 2,280.5 units (4,561/2 = 2,280.5 units). Because the firm sells 52,000 units during the year (1,000 units a week), the inventory is sufficient for about 4.5 weeks.

c. If the carrying cost is only 2.5% of the inventory's value, the carrying cost per unit will be only $0.25 (0.025 × $10 = $0.25), and we get

$$Q^* = \left(\frac{2 \times 52{,}000 \times \$500}{\$0.25}\right)^{1/2} \cong 14{,}422 \text{ unit}$$

As expected, if the carrying cost per unit is relatively small, the firm can afford to hold much larger inventory.

SAFETY STOCK

The EOQ model assumes the firm knows the sales rate and the delivery time with certainty. However, in practice these two factors are uncertain. Therefore, to avoid shortage costs, the firm will also hold **safety stock.** Figure 21-4 demonstrates the inventory level with uncertainty and with safety stock. If all variables such as sales and delivery time are certain, the firm will never plan to hold stock below level *SS.* For example, if the firm knows the delivery time is one week, it will reorder at t_1 and the orders will be delivered at t_2. If the order is delayed, the firm will dip into its safety stock. Without its safety stock, the firm would lose customers. The firm can also use its safety stock if sales unexpectedly increase.

When uncertainty prevails, the firm should modify the EOQ model to account for shortage costs. For given carrying and shortage costs, the level of safety stock will depend on the variabilities in the delivery time or in the sales rate. The greater the variability of these two factors, the larger the safety stock that the firm should hold.

JUST-IN-TIME (JIT) INVENTORY

One inventory control method, called **just-in-time (JIT) inventory,** has become popular over the last decade, particularly among Japanese and U.S. automobile makers. The main idea is to cut the level of inventory held to reduce inventory costs. This can be done only if the suppliers of parts and raw materials cut delivery time and can supply the firm with the needed parts in a matter of hours. For example, Toyota, which is a leader in applying the JIT system, holds in inventory only the parts needed for immediate production. Since Toyota's parts suppliers are located close to its manufacturing plants, they can supply the needed parts almost on demand, and Toyota can hold a very low inventory level without danger of shortages.

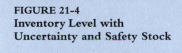

**FIGURE 21-4
Inventory Level with
Uncertainty and Safety Stock**

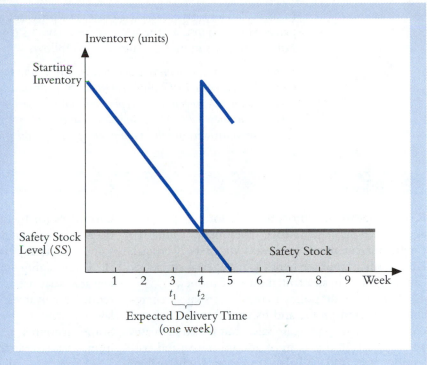

However, the suppliers themselves must hold a large inventory of parts that they can deliver in a matter of hours. Using JIT, the firm simply shifts its inventory investment to its suppliers. To truly reduce investors' costs, the suppliers of Toyota's assembly line should also use the JIT method with their suppliers, and so on. In practice the firm and its suppliers can reduce their inventory levels only if they all operate in the same location and all employ the JIT method. This can be accomplished only if they have a high degree of coordination among them.

U.S. automobile firms have also adopted the JIT inventory method. If General Motors, Ford, and Chrysler turn over their inventory 12 times a year and if the Japanese automakers turn over their inventory 50 times a year, the U.S. firms would have much larger inventory costs and would be financially unable to compete with the Japanese firms. Many large and small firms alike have adopted the JIT method. For example, this policy was one component in the "zero net working capital" goal that American Standard CEO Kampouris advocated. (See Connecting Theory to Practice 19.1.)

The JIT method is riskier due to the possible volatility of the prices of the goods the firm buys. Firms that employ the JIT method have chosen to incur greater price volatility in exchange for lower carrying costs. Holding relatively large inventories means relatively large carrying costs, but provides a hedge against price changes. If prices rise, a firm that employs JIT will have to pay a higher price for inventory. A *Barron's* article summarizes the effect as follows:

In total, then, it is incremental demand relative to the current level of supplies that will drive commodity prices in 1997. And just as in '96, companies will choose to make themselves vulnerable to the risks involved in keeping inventories low. There is always the potential for prices to skyrocket, as they did in 1996, in grains and energy, or to plunge, as they did in copper. Will investors continue to reward these companies for minimizing inventories? Earnings will tell.[9]

SUMMARY

Receivables and inventory account for high percentages of a typical firm's total investment. Therefore, careful management of these two assets is crucial. Even a small improvement in managerial efficiency can save the firm substantial sums of money.

A firm's credit policy may affect its sales, receivables, reported profit, and its cash flows. A relaxed credit policy may increase sales, but it also increases a firm's costs in the form of administrative and collection costs and bad debt increase. Each level of receivables involves two costs—carrying costs and opportunity costs. The optimal level of receivables is the level that minimizes the sum of these two costs. A firm can evaluate its investment in receivables either by a cost minimization technique or by employing the NPV method.

A firm can minimize the risks involved in credit sales (bad debt, interest rate risk, and foreign currency risk) in various ways. For instance, a firm can minimize bad debt by evaluating the customer's credit risk, using the five Cs of credit, before extending credit. By matching the maturities of liabilities and receivables (or by buying a forward contract or options on the interest rate), a firm can minimize interest rate risk. If a firm matches the maturities of liabilities and receivables in various currencies (or by buying a forward contract or options on the foreign exchange rate), it can minimize foreign currency risk.

Using aging schedules to analyze accounts receivable that are overdue, a firm can take steps to reduce receivables. The longer the customer's delayed payment, the more severe the firm's action. Some accounts receivable will be bad debt—or money that the firm will probably never collect.

A firm may sell on credit because credit sales are a common industry practice or because it needs to attract customers. If a firm does not wish to invest in receivables, it can sell them to another party called a *factor*.

In managing its inventory, a firm should focus on the most costly items. The economic order quantity (EOQ) model can help a firm determine the optimal quantity to be ordered and the average inventory held. When there is uncertainty about sales and product arrival times, the firm will hold more inventory than the model recommends. This additional inventory is called *safety stock*. In using the just-in-time methods, a firm minimizes its inventory holdings. This method requires that inventory be held in close proximity to the purchaser.

---

9. Cheryl Strauss Einhorn, "Accepting Volatility," *Barron's* (30 December 1996): MW12. Reprinted by permission of *Barron's Market Week*, © 1996 Dow Jones & Company, Inc. All Rights Reserved Worldwide.

CHAPTER AT A GLANCE

1. Accounts Receivable

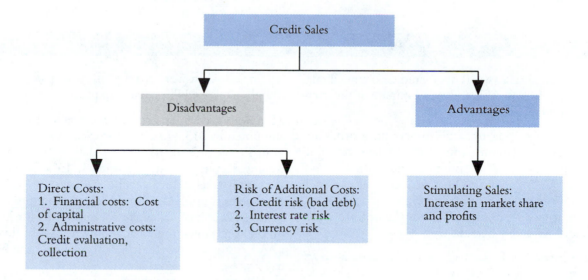

The optimum level of receivables: The firm should increase the investment in receivables as long as the NPV of the marginal investment is positive. At this point the total costs incurred by holding the receivables will be minimal.

2. Inventory
The Economic Order Quantity (EOQ) Model:
The optimum order is given by

$$Q^* = \left(\frac{2TF}{C}\right)^{1/2}$$

where
T = number of units sold during the year
F = cost per order
C = carrying cost (in dollars) per unit
Q^* = optimum number of units in each order

KEY TERMS

Consumer credit	Credit terms	Credit risk
Trade credit	Grace period	Five Cs of credit
Credit policy	Carrying costs	Credit scoring
Credit period	Opportunity costs	Aging schedule

Factoring
Factoring agreement
Assignment (pledging) agreement
Certificate amortization

Ordering costs
Shortage costs
Economic order quantity (EOQ)
  model

Safety stock
Just–in–time (JIT) inventory

REVIEW AND PRACTICE

21.1 A firm sells on 30 days' credit. Its annual sales are $200 million. What is your estimate of the average accounts receivable?

21.2 Suppose without offering credit, a firm's annual sales are $100 million. With 30 days' credit, its annual sales are $110 million; and with 60 days' credit, $115 million. The firm's cost of capital is 20%. Production costs (excluding financing costs) amount to 90% of sales. What is the optimal credit policy? Assume perpetual cash flows.

21.3 Firm A sells for cash, Firm B offers 30 days' credit, and Firm C offers 60 days' credit. The sales of each firm amount to $10 million a month. Show the three firms' cash flows from sales for each of the first six months of sales.

21.4 A firm is considering investing $100 million in a new plant. Annual sales are estimated at $20 million. The firm will pay annual costs, estimated at $6 million, in cash at the end of each year. Cash inflows from sales will occur six months later because the firm grants six months' credit. The cost of capital is 11%. Should the project be accepted? Assume a perpetuity and that these are the only cash flows involved in the investment.

21.5 Define and explain *credit period* and *credit terms*.

21.6 Sears charges 21% annual interest on its credit card. However, the credit card agreement stipulates: "You have 30 days from your billing date to repay your balance before being charged a finance charge." (These 30 days are the grace period.) Suppose you use your Sears card for purchases amounting to $1,000 and you pay 55 days later. The billing date is 10 days after you buy the product. What is the *effective* annual interest rate charged? How

would your answer change if you paid seven months after the billing date? Explain.

21.7 Sears's average accounts receivables for 1993 amounted to $13,470.2 million. Sears's charges are as in Problem 21.6. Its cost of debt is 9% and its weighted average cost of capital is 15%. Sears finances all receivables by debt. Assume the risk of receivables is similar to the risk of all other projects that Sears accepts. Calculate the net profit (or loss) on the receivables under the following assumptions:
a. All customers pay their balances during the 30-day grace period.
b. All customers repay their credit after 13 months. Which situation will Sears prefer?

21.8 Bad debt, on average, amounts to 5% of credit sales. The firm sells on credit at 1/10, net 30. Credit sales are $10 million a month. The appropriate discount rate on the receivables is 1% per month. Would the firm fare better if all customers took advantage of the discount and paid on Day 10? Illustrate your answer with PV calculations.

21.9 You buy from your supplier on credit at 1/20, net 30. What is the IRR if you take advantage of the cash discount and pay on Day 20? Suppose your cost of capital is 1% per month. Would you opt for the cash discount?

21.10 What are the costs associated with accounts receivables?

21.11 What is the principal benefit from credit sales? Will a bakery or an apparel store benefit more from credit sales? Explain.

21.12 The survey cited in the text found that retail executives believe that if they do not offer credit, on average, sales will drop as follows (figures changed slightly, for simplicity):

20% (72% of responses)
18% (14% of responses)
 8% (14% of responses)

Suppose the cost of sales is $0.80 per dollar sale. Big Ben Inc. sells for 60 days credit. Its annual sales amount to $120 million. Carrying costs are 20% of receivables. The firm is considering selling for cash only. Assume the given percentage figures represent the probabilities of decreased sales if the firm sells for cash rather than for credit.

a. What is the net annual income if the firm continues to sell for credit?

b. Calculate the mean and variance of the firm's net income without credit sales. Do credit sales dominate cash sales by the mean–variance rule?

c. How would your answer to 21.12b change if the carrying costs were 30% of receivables? Should the firm shift to cash sales?

21.13 A study cites the following costs:[10]

Percentage Carrying Cost of Receivables Dollars

	Age of Receivables			
	30 Days	60 Days	90 Days	120 Days
Administrative costs	0	0.50	1.50	2.00
Opportunity costs	0	2.50	7.50	12.50
Bad debt	1.00	4.00	6.00	10.00
Other costs	0.82	3.29	3.74	6.21
Total cost	1.82	10.29	18.74	30.71

a. Explain why the chance of bad debt increases with the age of the receivables.

b. Suppose the firm sells $100 million of receivables to a trust that, in turn, offers certificates to the public. If the receivables' age is 30 days, the public pays $95 million; if it is 120 days, the public pays $60 million. Assuming the riskless interest rate is 0.5% per month, what should the percentage risk premium be in each case? Explain.

21.14 IBM grants credit to customers in Germany at 100 million German marks (DM) for 30 days. When the credit is in U.S. dollars, the carrying cost of the receivables is 20% annually. The current exchange rate is 1.6 DM per $1. Suppose 30 days from now, the exchange rate is either 1.8 DM or 1.4 DM per $1, with equal probability. To protect itself against adverse foreign exchange fluctuations, IBM buys options to sell German marks at a cost of $2 million. Alternatively, the firm can conduct a forward transaction at a cost of $0.5 million. What are the relevant carrying costs of the 100 million DM credit?

21.15 A firm orders 100,000 units every four weeks. Plot a "sawtooth" graph showing the firm's inventory (with weeks on the horizontal axis). Calculate the firm's average inventory. What are the assumptions of the EOQ model? Which of these assumptions may not hold in practice?

21.16 A Nike retailer sells 100,000 pairs of shoes during the year. The cost of each pair is, on average, $60. The inventory carrying cost is $12 per pair of shoes held in the inventory for a year. The fixed cost per order is $1,000. Calculate the optimal order quantity Q^*. How many times during the year does the retailer place an order? Calculate the retailer's average investment in inventory.

21.17 The following data relate to L.A. Gear:

	1991	1992	1993
Inventory (average) (in $ million)	141	62	109
Sales (in $ million)	618	430	385

Source: *Value Line Investment Survey*, 25 February 1994.

Suppose L.A. Gear sells only shoes and the average price per pair is $60. Carrying costs are $10 per pair, and ordering costs are $10,000.

a. Calculate the optimal inventory for L.A. Gear in 1993.

b. Suppose the firm now sells 100 different products (including shoes). The average price of each

---

10. Edmund J. McCormick Jr., *Healthcare Financial Management* (Healthcare Financial Management Association, 1993).

unit is $60. Calculate the optimal inventory that L.A. Gear should hold. Explain the difference in your answers to 21.17a and 21.17b.

c. What is the probability of L.A. Gear experiencing financial distress in 1994 or thereafter? What recommendation would you make to the firm?

21.18 Who should hold a larger inventory, a retailer who buys all products from one manufacturer or a retailer who buys from many manufacturers located in various parts of the country? Explain your answer.

21.19 Suppose due to a change in the tax law, a firm changes its capital structure, and, as a result, its WACC decreases from 15% to 12%. What effect will this change have on the optimal inventory order size Q^*? Explain your results.

21.20 Firm A and Firm B are located in California. Firm A buys its inventory from a nearby supplier. Firm B buys its inventory from a supplier located in Europe. Which firm should hold a larger safety stock? Explain your answer.

21.21 Players' Shoes and Quality Shoes operate in the same business and are similar in size. The weekly average number of units sold by Players' Shoes is 10,000, with a standard deviation of 1,000; the weekly average number of units sold by Quality Shoes is 10,000, with a standard deviation of 100.
a. Can the inventory of these two firms be described by a "sawtooth" graph (see Figure 21-2)? Explain.
b. Which firm should hold a larger safety stock? Explain.

21.22 In 1993 Nike's average inventory was $527 million, its net profit was $365 million, and the number of outstanding shares was about 74 million.[11]
a. What was Nike's 1993 EPS?
b. Suppose due to efficient inventory management, Nike succeeds in reducing its average inventory from $527 million to $300 million without affecting sales. Nike accomplishes this by means of improved prediction of demand and better coordination of production and marketing operations. The firm's cost of capital is 15%, and the other carrying costs (insurance, storage, depreciation, and so on) amount to an additional 10% of the inventory value. What is the new EPS?

21.23 The following article appeared about Nike's inventory and sales:

Nike said its first-quarter results will fall short of expectations because sales have been better than anticipated and it can't fill orders fast enough. The weakness would be recouped in the second quarter, it said, . . . Philip H. Knights, chairman and chief executive officer, said that conservative orders from retailers six months ago led Nike to maintain its lowest inventory in five years, causing some August shipments to be delayed until September after Nike's shoes proved hotter with consumers than expected.[12]

a. Discuss Nike's inventory management error in your own words.
b. Which of the following notions are relevant to Mr. Knights's assertion: uncertainty, EOQ, safety stock, shortage costs, carrying costs, annual sales? Discuss.

21.24 A firm finances its inventory by short–term debt at a cost of 6%. The firm's cost of capital is 15%. The CFO claims, "Because the investment in inventory is riskless, the financing costs of the inventory are only 6%." Evaluate this assertion.

21.25 Read the following item:

IS A BUILDUP IN GOODS ON SHELVES A REASON TO WORRY OR AN OPTIMISTIC SIGN?

. . . Yet Wall Street analysts insist their nervousness about the inventory statistics is justified. Business executives are too prone to believe that anything making sales come in below projections is temporary, they caution. Letting inventories creep up is often easier than cutting production

---

11. *Value Line Investment Survey,* 25 February 1994.

12. *Wall Street Journal,* 19 August 1994. Reprinted by permission of *The Wall Street Journal,* © 1994 Dow Jones & Company, Inc. All Rights Reserved Worldwide.

schedules. Executives put off cutbacks by telling themselves it could cost money to catch up if they reduce output and sales rebound, or worse still, that they could lose orders to better-stocked competitors.[13]

a. What are the costs of "inventory creep up" and "cutting production schedules"?

b. If the decline in sales is temporary, are the executives right in their decision? Are they right in their decision if the decline is permanent?

c. How do the notions of safety stock and shortage costs relate to this case? Explain.

INTERNET QUESTIONS

21.26 Your boss has heard of a new firm called Vision Point that offers a complete accounts receivable system. Visit their Web site and prepare a memo summarizing the services offered.

http://www.sbt.com/product/index.html

21.27 Take a look at the inventory control system maintained by RWS Information Systems. Prepare a memo summarizing the system.

http://www.rwsinfo.com/index.htm

YOUR TURN: APPLYING THEORY TO PRACTICE
MOUNTING INVENTORIES

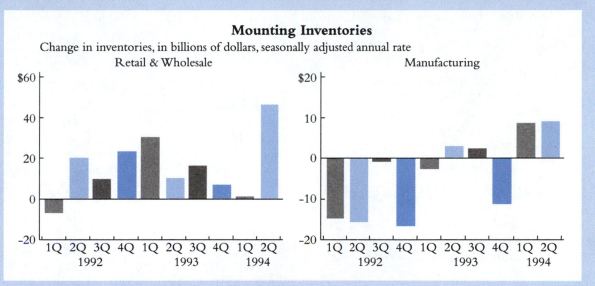

Mounting Inventories

Change in inventories, in billions of dollars, seasonally adjusted annual rate

Source: Commerce Department

"We're building inventories like crazy," says James Taylor, southern division chairman for General Parts, Inc., a Raleigh, N.C., wholesaler of automotive components to car dealers and garages. "Business is really booming—that's the main rea- son" the company's inventories are up about 5% from a year ago and up 10% in some of the fastest-growing spots, like Andalusia, Ala. "If you need a fan belt for your car, we say, 'Yes Ma'am, here it is—$6.35 plus tax,'" Mr. Taylor says.

13. "Is a Buildup in Goods on Shelves a Reason . . . ," *New York Times,* 8 August 1994. Copyright © 1994 by The New York Times Co. Reprinted by Permission.

Jos. A. Bank, a manufacturer and retailer of conservative men's and women's clothes based in Hampstead, Md., has built its inventories 5% over last year for the fall selling season. "We built up because we had to meet demand," Chairman Timothy Finley says. Vests and sport coats for men and blouses and dresses for women have been particularly popular, so Bank has stocked up a lot on these items.

INFLATION HEDGE

Some companies say they are trying to build their stockpiles to hedge against inflation. Carlson Systems Corp., a wholesaler of fasteners and packing equipment in Phoenix, has seen prices rising rapidly over the past three months on plastic strap, bags, corrugated board, and steel. "We are trying to get a lot of this in stock, but you can't do much because of the short supply," says company President Donald Carlson.

Ulrich Chemical Inc. in Indianapolis is trying to load up on methanol and liquid caustic soda because of pricing pressures in these two areas. Company officials say they worry that these two items will be more expensive in coming months.

Of course, in some pockets of the economy, inventories are building up because consumers aren't buying. Companies aren't likely to admit they misread demand and loaded up on more supply than they could sell. The fact is retail sales have slowed in recent months. Furniture sales, for example, have been sluggish, and furniture inventories have piled up.

BETTER CONTROLS

But companies are becoming better at keeping inventories in line. In nearly every sector, businesses have been burned in the past by loading up excessively. Moreover, a host of computer-driven inventory-control systems have given purchasers the means for calibrating inventories to be in line with real demand.

Manufacturers appear to be more cautious than retailers and wholesalers. The latest report on economic growth said factories increased their stockpiles at a slower pace in the quarter than they did in the first. "The building of stocks in the manufacturing sector is a defense mechanism, so that they won't get caught without goods," says Ralph Kauffman, manager of procurement and materials management at Oryx Energy Co.

A recent survey of the National Association of Purchasing Management found that only one industry category—industrial and commercial equipment and computers—reported inventory growth in July.

Source: *Wall Street Journal*, 3 August 1994, p. A2. Reprinted by permission of *The Wall Street Journal*, © 1994 Dow Jones & Company, Inc. All Rights Reserved Worldwide.

Questions

1. It is not clear whether the inventory increases are driven by optimism regarding future demand or by a drop in demand. Suppose a firm's inventory grows by 10% in the second quarter. Suggest a method to figure which of these reasons better explains the cause of the inventory increase. (Hint: Consider what you have learned on sales forecasting.)

2. Hardware Wholesaler Inc. increased its inventory from $100 million to $107 million. Suppose the inventory consists of 50 different products, with an average price of $50 per unit. The firm determines its orders by the EOQ model. The inventory carrying cost is 20% of the product price—namely, $0.20 \times \$50 \cong \$10$—and the fixed order cost is $5,000. The firm has to make a different order for each product it holds. What are the estimated annual sales with a $100 million average inventory? What is the firm's new estimate of annual sales as implied by the new average inventory of $107 million? Compare the percentage increase in sales versus the percentage increase in inventory. Plot a "sawtooth" graph (see Figure 21-2) for the $100 million inventory level.

3. Alan Greenspan, chairman of the Federal Reserve, suggested that firms "had brought inventory down to suboptimal levels and now need to replenish them."[14] Suppose that firms use the EOQ model but add a safety stock to account for uncertainty (see Section 21.10.2). Plot a "sawtooth" diagram showing why inventory stocks may be too low if the safety stock is not high enough to account for a large increase in sales during an economic recovery.

4. Mr. Taylor of General Parts, Inc., says "If you need a fan belt for your car, we say, 'Yes, Ma'am, here it is—$6.35 plus tax.'" Do you think Mr.

Taylor's shortage costs are high or low? Is Mr. Taylor's assertion relevant to certainty or uncertainty? What are the implications of such a policy regarding safety stock?

5. Carlson Systems Corp. estimates that the price of the units comprising its inventory is about to go up the next day by 10%, from $100 to $110 per unit. Discuss the following two assertions in light of this information:

a. "Because the firm gains 10% by purchasing the units immediately, it should buy a very large amount at $100 per unit."

b. "The higher the carrying cost, the smaller the additional number of units bought beyond and above the optimum value $Q^\star$."

6. What actions would you recommend to firms that "misread demand and loaded up on more supply than they could sell"?

14. *Wall Street Journal,* 3 August 1994.

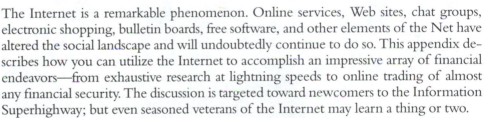

USING THE INTERNET★

The Internet is a remarkable phenomenon. Online services, Web sites, chat groups, electronic shopping, bulletin boards, free software, and other elements of the Net have altered the social landscape and will undoubtedly continue to do so. This appendix describes how you can utilize the Internet to accomplish an impressive array of financial endeavors—from exhaustive research at lightning speeds to online trading of almost any financial security. The discussion is targeted toward newcomers to the Information Superhighway; but even seasoned veterans of the Internet may learn a thing or two.

The first section of the appendix discusses the history and evolution of the Internet. Following sections describe the wealth of financial information available on the Net and how the Net can be used. The final section offers advice on getting started.

THE INTERNET: HISTORY, EVOLUTION

The Internet is a worldwide system of computers that share information electronically. More precisely, the Net is composed of millions of computers that are linked

★This section was written by Professor Russ Ray of the University of Louisville.

by cable, telephone wire, satellite signal, and other electronic means. Every day, thousands of newcomers plug into the Net and become part of this ever-expanding Information Superhighway.

Because it is largely unregulated, the Net offers no guarantee as to the validity or accuracy of its information. However, major users (government agencies, Fortune 500 firms, etc.) generally stand behind the integrity of the information they make available through the Net.

Information is shared via various conventions and standards (rules of the game, so to speak) that have evolved over the last several decades. For example, files are transferred from one computer to another by a system known as FTP (file transfer protocol). Other conventions include the Web (where various entities maintain information for others to see) and a standardized Web address format known as URL (uniform resource locator).

Anyone can access the Internet in one of three ways. A direct connection requires cable to connect to the Net and is very expensive. Generally, only major organizations, such as major universities or Fortune 500 firms, can afford a direct connection.

Service providers are a second means of tapping into the Net. These are commercial enterprises (such as AT&T, Earthlink, and MCI) that have a direct connection to the Net and sell access to others (mostly businesses) who connect to the service provider usually via standard phone wires.

Online services are the third (and most popular) avenue to the Information Superhighway. They are giant service providers that target primarily private individuals who tap into the online service via their home phones. Anyone with a personal computer, a home phone, and a modem can tap into an online service. Some of the more popular online services include America Online, Compuserve, Prodigy, and Microsoft Network.

Currently, the Internet is composed of six major segments: (1) *access providers* that build and operate the communications network (e.g., America Online and Microsoft); (2) *software providers* that design the browsers and server software needed to navigate or maintain a presence on the Web (e.g., Netscape and Sun Microsystems); (3) *security providers* that provide secure systems to transmit confidential data such as credit card numbers (e.g., Security Dynamics and Secure Computing); (4) *applications providers* that supply various kinds of value-added services such as compiling financial information on major companies (e.g., Hoovers); (5) *advertisers* who rent electronic billboards in cyberspace to advertise their goods and services; and (6) *proprietary entities* that maintain Web sites to further their own interests (corporations, government agencies, nonprofit organizations, individuals, etc.). This broad structure is likely to remain intact for the short term as the industry establishes its infrastructure.

Once you are connected to the Net, you will be able to take advantage of an incredible array of services. Besides e-mail, these services include free information and data, free software, entertainment, shopping, travel arrangements, and thousands of newspapers, journals, and magazines. Another popular online service is the *chat group,* where people from all walks of life "talk" with each other in real time.

INFORMATION/NEWS/RESEARCH

The amount of financial information available on the Net is simply staggering. Besides a vast array of current financial news, the Net provides access to hundreds of reference sources, including entire encyclopedias; thousands of financial and economic data bases; professional journals of every sort; scores of financial newspapers and magazines; electronic discussions of almost any financial topic conceivable; think tank studies; speeches; articles; announcements; reports; tutorials; and more.

Without a doubt, the Net is a researcher's dream come true. Sitting at your computer, you can research almost any financial or economic topic at lightning speed. Facilitating this process are a number of *search engines* (e.g., Yahoo, Magellan, and Alta Vista) that conduct searches in the keywords you designate.

Table I-1 lists a few of the thousands of comprehensive financial Web sites that provide financial data, information, advice, quotes, worksheets, calculators, tutorials, simulations, and links. Some are free, and some charge a monthly fee (typically, $10 to $15) for their full range of services.

The World Wide Web (WWW, or the Web) is a gold mine of financial and economic information. Thousands of organizations (and many individuals) maintain Web sites where they park mountains of information about themselves, their products, their services, and their histories. Web sites and online services provide practically any piece of financial information imaginable—stock prices, trading volume, bond ratings, and so on. Also, the Web provides a wealth of company-specific information,

TABLE I-1 Selected Financial Web Sites	Service Organization	Web Address
	Thomson Investor's Network	http://www.thomsoninvest.net
	Hoovers	http://www.hoovers.com
	PC Quote	http://www.pcquote.com
	Corporate Financials Online	http://www.cfonews.com
	CorpFiNet	http://www.corpfinet.com
	National Financial Services Network	http://www.nfsn.com
	InvestorsEdge	http://www.irnet.com
	National Corporate Services	http://www.csn.net/natcorp
	American Journalism Review News Link	http://www.newslink.org
	Financial Pipeline	http://www.finpipe.com
	Money Page	http://www.moneypage.com
	CNN Financial	http://www.cnnfn.com
	Bloomberg Personal	http://www.bloomberg.com
	bank.net	http://www.bank.net/home.rich.html
	Wall Street Directory	http://www.wsdinc.com
	BARRA	http://www.barra.com

Note that most search engines (such as Yahoo) provide excellent links to major financial Web sites.

from detailed financial statements to analysts' earnings predictions. Almost any publicly available piece of financial information can be obtained through the Internet. Currently, there are *several million* Web sites, and thousands more are being created every day.

A particularly useful Web site is maintained by the Ohio State University Finance Department (its rather lengthy URL is http://www.cob.ohiostate.edu/~fin/overview.htm). This site is a cornucopia of information on financial/economic data bases, financial services, financial links, educational resources (which include the *International Financial Encyclopedia*), electronic journals, electronic working papers, and so on. It even has a Finance Virtual Library.

Various departments and agencies of the U.S. federal government maintain Web sites, as do the governments of other major industrialized countries. These Web sites are excellent sources for instant price information, monetary data, trade statistics, and other data normally maintained by the federal government (see Table I-2).

Finally, stock exchanges, multilateral organizations, media services, and numerous private firms offer a wealth of financial information at their respective Web sites (see Table I-3).

TABLE I-2 Selected U.S. Government Web Sites	Department/Agency	Web Address
	U.S. Treasury Department	http://www.ustreas.gov
	Federal Reserve Board	http://www.bog.frb.fed.us
	Federal Deposit Insurance Corporation	http://www.fdic.gov
	Office of the Comptroller of the Currency	http://www.occ.treas.gov
	Securities and Exchange Commission	http://www.sec.gov
	Library of Congress	http://www.lcweb.loc.gov

TABLE I-3 Selected Sites of General Financial Interest	Organization	Web Address
	New York Stock Exchange	http://www.nyse.com
	American Stock Exchange	http://www.amex.com
	NASDAQ	http://www.nasdaq.com
	World Bank	http://www.worldbank.org
	Financial Executives Institute	http://www.fei.org
	Financial Economists Network	http://www.ssrn.com/FEN/index.html
	Tax Analysts	http://www.tax.org
	The Great American Web Site	http://www.uncle-sam.com
	FedWorld Information Network	http://www.fedworld.gov
	Reuters	http://www.reuters.com
	StockMaster	http://www.stockmaster.com
	Chicago Board of Trade	http://www.cbot.com
	Chicago Mercantile Exchange	http://www.cme.com
	Chicago Board Options Exchange	http://www.cboe.com

COMMUNICATION

Besides sending and receiving e-mail, you can use the Net for financial discussions on virtually any subject. You can join *newsgroups* to discuss the federal debt, the bond market, U.S.–Japanese trade, corporate mergers, electricity futures, and any other topic that at least two people want to discuss. Just park your opinion on a *bulletin board* and you will receive feedback from all over the world.

FINANCIAL SERVICES

A multitude of financial services exists on the Net, from banking and trading online to free financial software. Many major banks allow routine banking transactions to be conducted over the Net, and most online services provide real-time trading of most financial securities (after you set up an online account with their respective brokers).

Financial software is available on either a freeware or shareware basis. *Freeware* is software that is free to download; *shareware* is software that can be downloaded on a trial basis and purchased later if you like it. Online services typically offer financial software, as do many major universities and large corporations. Such software includes stock analyses (both technical and fundamental), retirement planning, loan amortizations, and even balance sheet construction. Upgrades and patches of freeware and software are also available. In order to download a particular software program (or any other data), simply choose the download option from your menu bar, and then follow instructions from there.

FINANCIAL EDUCATION

The Internet is also an excellent educational tool. A number of short courses exist on the Net, from how to pick stocks to how to analyze a company. The online services offer such courses, as do many Web sites.

Simulations too are available on the Net. Although the most popular simulation is stock trading, other simulations exist for the adventurous. Charts, graphs, and numerous graphic aids are available.

Finally, you can participate in newsgroups for various financial topics—from Medicare to the federal debt. Even if you feel you have nothing to contribute, you can at least read the bulletin boards to see what the current issues are with respect to any particular financial subject.

GETTING STARTED

Getting started on the Internet is basically a matter of getting connected. After you are connected you can "surf the Net" by pointing and clicking.

If your college or university is directly wired to the Net (the best of all worlds, due primarily to the high speed of data transmission), then your system administrator has probably set up a mechanism for accessing the Net. (An Internet icon usually appears on your main screen.) Your school may also use a Web browser, such as Netscape, that will allow you to view thousands of Web sites.

If you use a local service provider, your provider has set up a mechanism by which you can access the Net. The procedure is the same—simply point and click to explore the icons of your choice.

If you have one of the major online services (such as America Online or Microsoft Network), you will have an Internet icon as part of your main menu of choices. Again, simply point and click to open up the usual array of Internet services. A good analogy is that the Internet is a lot like being in a foreign country. No matter where you are or how lost you might become, if you keep looking and asking, you will eventually reach the place you are searching for, in addition to doing a lot of sightseeing along the way. Fortunately, the majority of the standard avenues to and through the Net are very user friendly.

Not surprisingly, there are scores of new books about the Internet, many of which are targeted toward the newcomer. Since cyberspace changes so quickly, consulting a book with the most recent copyright is generally best. After you learn the basics, one of the monthly publications devoted to the Net (such as *Netguide*) should provide you with an easy-to-read road map with which to continually navigate the Information Superhighway. A half- or full-day Internet seminar is an excellent hands-on means for learning to make use of this powerful and significant network of information.

After learning the basics, you may even want to set up your own Web page. Having your own Web page is useful for posting announcements, your résumé, and other basic information about yourself and your activities. Many how-to short courses exist on this subject, and numerous software programs are available that guide you step by step through the process. On the faster lanes of the Information Superhighway, having your own Web page has become almost a necessity.

SUMMARY

The Internet is an ever-growing electronic phenomenon, rich with potential for financial practitioners and students. Besides providing access to up-to-the-minute financial news, the Net allows users to research mountains of information at lightning speeds and with incredible convenience. Other uses include financial services, financial planning, free software, and electronic discussions of many financial topics.

Access to the Information Superhighway is easy. If you can point and click, you can surf the Net.

Chapter 1

1.1 Yes.

1.5 Bank investment is more profitable.

1.7 Return = 20 percent.

1.11 Total profit = $40 million.

Chapter 3

3.7 Net income = $13.

3.9 Incorrect

3.11 Incorrect

3.23 Both statements are true.

A.3 Inventory = $10 million.

A.5 Average collection period = 73 days.

A.7 Total asset turnover = four.

Chapter 4

4.1 For each dollar invested at 5%, we receive $1.629 in ten years.

4.3 The maximum discount with no risk is $1,818.18.

4.5 The $10,000 current payment is preferred.

4.7 The bond would be worth $13,150.13.

4.9 Cash flow B has a higher present value and higher future values.

4.11 The difference due to compounding is $31.

4.13 The implied discount rate is 16.7%.

4.15 Present value = $9,914.80 at $r = 10\%$.

4.17 $24,869 for an ordinary annuity, $27,355 for an annuity due.

4.19a pv = $18.674 million.

4.19b The athlete's wealth will be $27.86 million in ten years.

4.21 The value of Johnson Products is $56.6 million.

4.23 The present value is $10,474; the future value is $15,335.

4.25 PV = \$10,799.25; FV = \$15,092.50.

4.27 Annual rate = 16.9%.

A.1 The future value under continuous compounding is \$271.83.

A.3 The assertion is correct.

Chapter 5

5.1 NPV_A = \$23,810; NPV_B = \$31,519.

5.3. This statement is false.

5.9 NPV = \$9.09 with equity financing.

5.11 Transaction net profit = \$223.14 = NPV.

5.13 Accepting the project provides \$2,892.56 of consumption, in present value.

5.15 \$350 million > \$300 million; synergy appears to exist.

5.17 Project B will be preferred.

5.19 The NPV of the project is \$256.57.

5.21 The discount rate would be higher.

5.23 Stock price increase = \$2.60 per share.

5.25 The project NPV is zero.

Chapter 6

6.3 IRR = 23.38%.

6.5 IRR = 20%; accept the project.

6.7b IRR = 9.7%.

6.13 NPV(A) = NPV(B) when the discount rate = 8%.

6.15a NPV_A = \$11.98; IRR_A = 22.47%; NPV_B = \$8.18; IRR_B = 28%.

6.17 The NPV is positive at any discount rate; there is no IRR.

6.19 There are two solutions for IRR: 300% and 0%.

6.21 IRR = 23.4%; NPV = \$3.077.

6.23 IRR_A = 0; IRR_B = 49.98%.

6.25 As N increases, the reciprocal of the ARR approaches the payback period.

Chapter 7

7.3a Annual earnings = \$19,500.

7.3b Annual cash flow = \$69,500.

7.3c NPV = \$20,620.

7.9a NPV = \$1,149.

7.9b NPV = \$1,108.

7.11c NPV = –\$72.3 million; reject the research and development expenditure.

7.13 The NPV of hiring Shaq and broadcasting is \$502,574 (the highest NPV available).

7.15c NPV = \$1,916,582.61.

7.21 Inflation rate = 3%.

7.23a IRR of the lease is approximately 14%; NPV of the lease = –\$16,587.

7.23b NPV = \$33,413.

7.25 The nominal interest rate is 15.5%.

7.B.1 UAS_A = \$12.80; UAS_B = \$11.80.

Chapter 8

8.1 False

8.3 Expected return = 10%; risk premium = 5%.

8.5 True

8.7 Covariance can exceed one; correlation cannot.

8.9 Expected return is 8.125%.

8.11 The standard deviation is 13.7%.

8.13 The portfolio variance is always 72.22.

8.17 The portfolio standard deviation is 9.38.

8.21 Diversifying between highly correlated assets does little to reduce risk.

8.23 The statement is false.

Chapter 9

9.3a Beta = 1.07.

9.3b Market risk = 144.68; unique risk = 72.01.

9.7 IBM intercept = 1.39; beta = 0.79.

9.9 IBM expected return is 0.7498%.

9.11 Beta = 1.725.

9.15a The riskless rate is 5%.

9.15b Weight of Company A = 50%.

9.17c Portfolio beta = 3.0; expected portfolio return = 35%.

9.19 Both stocks have the same beta and the same expected return.

Chapter 10

10.3 NPV = \$3.88 million.

10.5 True

10.7 \$900,000

10.9 WACC = 11.2%.

10.11 IRR = 16.67%; NPV = –\$21,538.46.

10.17a Original after-tax cost of debt = 6.5%.

10.17b New cost of equity = 13.64%.

10.17c New WACC = 6.71%.

10.19 Total NPV = \$799 million.

10.21 WACC = 15.65%; IRR = 15%.

10.25 Project cost of capital for A = 26%; project cost for B = 9%.

Chapter 11

11.1 The provision is a call option with an exercise price of $10,000.

11.3 A put option with an exercise price of $20,000 is required.

11.7 $13.25

11.9a 7.55 options; 2.07 shares.

11.9b 24.4% on the shares and 88.7% on the options.

11.9c −37.8% on the shares and −100% on the options.

11.11 NPV = $23,110.

11.13 The value of the call is $4.92.

11.19a Discount rate = 11.1%.

11.19b Value of put option = $523.81.

11.23a $5,999

11.23b $5,000

11.A.1 The value of the call option is $10.93.

Chapter 12

12.13a The price of the bond is $57.31.

12.17 Yield-to-maturity = 16%; yield-to-call = 22.8%.

Chapter 13

13.3a Maximum price = $33.33.

13.3b Maximum price = $66.67.

13.7a $100

13.7b $57.14

13.7c $40

13.9a Growth rate = 12%.

13.9b Growth rate = 6%.

13.9c The stock price remains the same.

13.11a The current stock price is $20.

13.17 k_A = 15%; k_B = 25%; k_C = 30%.

13.23 The nominal return is 28.3%; the real return is 16.6%.

Chapter 14

14.9a Voting rights premium = 20%.

14.9b 600,000 shares at $12 each

14.13a $2

14.13b $3

14.13c $0.60 per share

14.15 $99.39 per bond

14.17 7.78%

14.19a 31%

14.19b 28%

14.23 WACC = 9.74%.

14.25a The firm must earn at least 19.1%.

Chapter 15

15.5 Average return on equity = 10, 15, and 25%, respectively.

15.7a Mean return = .09; variance = .0073.

15.7b Mean return = .13; variance = .0292.

15.13a Variance of A = Variance of (A+B) = 7,656.25; Variance of B = 30,625.

15.13b The prices cannot hold in equilibrium.

15.17 Probability = 60% for a, b, and c.

15.19 EPS = 0.00125(NOI) − $0.125.

15.23a Breakeven point = $2.5 million.

15.23c Probability = 60%.

Chapter 16

16.5a $2,702,607

16.5b $7,000,000

16.7a Borrow as much as possible.

16.7b Optimal borrowing = $358,491.

16.9a Optimal borrowing = $138.5 million.

16.9b PV of expected compensation = $6.82 million.

16.9c Agency costs = $20.9 million.

16.11a Borrow $20 million.

16.11b Borrow $10 million.

16.11c Financial distress = $1.53 million.

16.13 False

16.15a $175

16.15b $214.27

16.21 Maximum present value of tax shield = $333.33 million.

Chapter 17

17.1 1.2 million shares

17.5 Constant dollar policy

17.7 Residual dividend policy

17.11 The firm should invest in projects with returns of 20% or greater.

17.15 Issue size = $400 million.

17.21 Effective growth rate $= 10\%$.
17.23a Probability (NOI $< \$12,500$) $= 35\%$.
17.23b Probability (NOI $< \$17,000$) $= 55\%$.
17.25a Beta $= 1.5$.
17.25b Beta $= 1.8$.
17.25c As risk increases, the price must drop.

Chapter 18
18.5 Equity decreases by $\$1,000$.
18.7 EFN $= \$15,000$.
18.9 The statement is correct.
18.11 Year 6 sales $= 422$.
18.13 Statement (d) is correct.
18.15 EFN $= -\$100 + \$800G$.
18.17b For firm A, EFN $= 0$ when G $= 10\%$; for firm B, EFN $= 0$ when G $= 5\%$.
18.17c G $= 10.56\%$.
18.19 EFN $= -\$7,500 - \$7,500G$.

Chapter 19
19.1 Net working capital $= -\$50$ million.
19.3 Statements (c) and (d) are false.

19.5a 39 days
19.5b $\$31.2$ million
19.7 Operating cycle $= 68.87$ days; cash flow cycle $= 34.95$ days.
19.13a Cash flow cycle $= 237.3$ days.
19.13b $\$52,011.41$
19.17a $\$10,000$
19.21 False
19.23 $\$12$ million per year

Chapter 21
21.1 Average receivables $= \$16.44$ million.
21.7a Loss $= \$2,020.53$ million.
21.7b Gain $= \$808.21$ million.
21.9 Pay in 20 days
21.15 Average inventory $= 50,000$ units.
21.17a Optimal order $= 113,284.3$ units.
21.17b $1,132,800$ units

Table A-1   Future value of $1 at the end of T periods $= (1 + r)^T$

Table A-2   Present value of $1 to be received after T periods $= 1/(1 + r)^T$

Table A-3   Present value of an annuity of $1 per period for T periods $= [1 - 1/(1 + r)^T]/r$
(See formula (4.7) for $C = 1$)

Table A-4   Future value of an annuity of $1 per period for T periods $= [(1 + r)^T - 1]/r$

Table A-5   The value of e^{rT}: Future value of $1 invested at a *continuously compounded* rate r for T years

TABLE A-1   Future value of \$1 at the end of T periods $= (1 + r)^T$

Interest Rate

Period	1%	2%	3%	4%	5%	6%	7%	8%	9%
1	1.0100	1.0200	1.0300	1.0400	1.0500	1.0600	1.0700	1.0800	1.0900
2	1.0201	1.0404	1.0609	1.0816	1.1025	1.1236	1.1449	1.1664	1.1881
3	1.0303	1.0612	1.0927	1.1249	1.1576	1.1910	1.2250	1.2597	1.2950
4	1.0406	1.0824	1.1255	1.1699	1.2155	1.2625	1.3108	1.3605	1.4116
5	1.0510	1.1041	1.1593	1.2167	1.2763	1.3382	1.4026	1.4693	1.5386
6	1.0615	1.1262	1.1941	1.2653	1.3401	1.4185	1.5007	1.5869	1.6771
7	1.0721	1.1487	1.2299	1.3159	1.4071	1.5036	1.6058	1.7138	1.8280
8	1.0829	1.1717	1.2668	1.3686	1.4775	1.5938	1.7182	1.8509	1.9926
9	1.0937	1.1951	1.3048	1.4233	1.5513	1.6895	1.8385	1.9990	2.1719
10	1.1046	1.2190	1.3439	1.4802	1.6289	1.7908	1.9672	2.1589	2.3674
11	1.1157	1.2434	1.3842	1.5395	1.7103	1.8983	2.1049	2.3316	2.5804
12	1.1268	1.2682	1.4258	1.6010	1.7959	2.0122	2.2522	2.5182	2.8127
13	1.1381	1.2936	1.4685	1.6651	1.8856	2.1329	2.4098	2.7196	3.0658
14	1.1495	1.3195	1.5126	1.7317	1.9799	2.2609	2.5785	2.9372	3.3417
15	1.1610	1.3459	1.5580	1.8009	2.0789	2.3966	2.7590	3.1722	3.6425
16	1.1726	1.3728	1.6047	1.8730	2.1829	2.5404	2.9522	3.4259	3.9703
17	1.1843	1.4002	1.6528	1.9479	2.2920	2.6928	3.1588	3.7000	4.3276
18	1.1961	1.4282	1.7024	2.0258	2.4066	2.8543	3.3799	3.9960	4.7171
19	1.2081	1.4568	1.7535	2.1068	2.5270	3.0256	3.6165	4.3157	5.1417
20	1.2202	1.4859	1.8061	2.1911	2.6533	3.2071	3.8697	4.6610	5.6044
21	1.2324	1.5157	1.8603	2.2788	2.7860	3.3996	4.1406	5.0338	6.1088
22	1.2447	1.5460	1.9161	2.3699	2.9253	3.6035	4.4304	5.4365	6.6586
23	1.2572	1.5769	1.9736	2.4647	3.0715	3.8197	4.7405	5.8715	7.2579
24	1.2697	1.6084	2.0328	2.5633	3.2251	4.0489	5.0724	6.3412	7.9111
25	1.2824	1.6406	2.0938	2.6658	3.3864	4.2919	5.4274	6.8485	8.6231
30	1.3478	1.8114	2.4273	3.2434	4.3219	5.7435	7.6123	10.063	13.268
40	1.4889	2.2080	3.2620	4.8010	7.0400	10.286	14.974	21.725	31.409
50	1.6446	2.6916	4.3839	7.1067	11.467	18.420	29.457	46.902	74.358

(continued)

TABLE A-1 *(concluded)*

Interest Rate

10%	12%	14%	15%	16%	18%	20%	24%	28%	32%	36%
1.1000	1.1200	1.1400	1.1500	1.1600	1.1800	1.2000	1.2400	1.2800	1.3200	1.3600
1.2100	1.2544	1.2996	1.3225	1.3456	1.3924	1.4400	1.5376	1.6384	1.7424	1.8496
1.3310	1.4049	1.4815	1.5209	1.5609	1.6430	1.7280	1.9066	2.0972	2.3000	2.5155
1.4641	1.5735	1.6890	1.7490	1.8106	1.9388	2.0736	2.3642	2.6844	3.0360	3.4210
1.6105	1.7623	1.9254	2.0114	2.1003	2.2878	2.4883	2.9316	3.4360	4.0075	4.6526
1.7716	1.9738	2.1950	2.3131	2.4364	2.6996	2.9860	3.6352	4.3980	5.2899	6.3275
1.9487	2.2107	2.5023	2.6600	2.8262	3.1855	3.5832	4.5077	5.6295	6.9826	8.6054
2.1436	2.4760	2.8526	3.0590	3.2784	3.7589	4.2998	5.5895	7.2058	9.2170	11.703
2.3579	2.7731	3.2519	3.5179	3.8030	4.4355	5.1598	6.9310	9.2234	12.166	15.917
2.5937	3.1058	3.7072	4.0456	4.4114	5.2338	6.1917	8.5944	11.806	16.060	21.647
2.8531	3.4785	4.2262	4.6524	5.1173	6.1759	7.4301	10.657	15.112	21.199	29.439
3.1384	3.8960	4.8179	5.3503	5.9360	7.2876	8.9161	13.215	19.343	27.983	40.037
3.4523	4.3635	5.4924	6.1528	6.8858	8.5994	10.699	16.386	24.759	36.937	54.451
3.7975	4.8871	6.2613	7.0757	7.9875	10.147	12.839	20.319	31.691	48.757	74.053
4.1772	5.4736	7.1379	8.1371	9.2655	11.974	15.407	25.196	40.565	64.359	100.71
4.5950	6.1304	8.1372	9.3576	10.748	14.129	18.488	31.243	51.923	84.954	136.97
5.0545	6.8660	9.2765	10.761	12.468	16.672	22.186	38.741	66.461	112.14	186.28
5.5599	7.6900	10.575	12.375	14.463	19.673	26.623	48.039	85.071	148.02	253.34
6.1159	8.6128	12.056	14.232	16.777	23.214	31.948	59.568	108.89	195.39	344.54
6.7275	9.6463	13.743	16.367	19.461	27.393	38.338	73.864	139.38	257.92	468.57
7.4002	10.804	15.668	18.822	22.574	32.324	46.005	91.592	178.41	340.45	637.26
8.1403	12.100	17.861	21.645	26.186	38.142	55.206	113.57	228.36	449.39	866.67
8.9543	13.552	20.362	24.891	30.376	45.008	66.247	140.83	292.30	593.20	1178.7
9.8497	15.179	23.212	28.625	35.236	53.109	79.497	174.63	374.14	783.02	1603.0
10.835	17.000	26.462	32.919	40.874	62.669	95.396	216.54	478.90	1033.6	2180.1
17.449	29.960	50.950	66.212	85.850	143.37	237.38	634.82	1645.5	4142.1	10143.
45.259	93.051	188.88	267.86	378.72	750.38	1469.8	5455.9	19427.	66521.	★
117.39	289.00	700.23	1083.7	1670.7	3927.4	9100.4	46890.	★	★	★

★The factor is greater than 99,999.

TABLE A-2   **Present value of \$1 to be received after T periods $= 1/(1 + r)^T$**

Interest Rate

Period	1%	2%	3%	4%	5%	6%	7%	8%	9%
1	0.9901	0.9804	0.9709	0.9615	0.9524	0.9434	0.9346	0.9259	0.9174
2	0.9803	0.9612	0.9426	0.9246	0.9070	0.8900	0.8734	0.8573	0.8417
3	0.9706	0.9423	0.9151	0.8890	0.8638	0.8396	0.8163	0.7938	0.7722
4	0.9610	0.9238	0.8885	0.8548	0.8227	0.7921	0.7629	0.7350	0.7084
5	0.9515	0.9057	0.8626	0.8219	0.7835	0.7473	0.7130	0.6806	0.6499
6	0.9420	0.8880	0.8375	0.7903	0.7462	0.7050	0.6663	0.6302	0.5963
7	0.9327	0.8706	0.8131	0.7599	0.7107	0.6651	0.6227	0.5835	0.5470
8	0.9235	0.8535	0.7894	0.7307	0.6768	0.6274	0.5820	0.5403	0.5019
9	0.9143	0.8368	0.7664	0.7026	0.6446	0.5919	0.5439	0.5002	0.4604
10	0.9053	0.8203	0.7441	0.6756	0.6139	0.5584	0.5083	0.4632	0.4224
11	0.8963	0.8043	0.7224	0.6496	0.5847	0.5268	0.4751	0.4289	0.3875
12	0.8874	0.7885	0.7014	0.6246	0.5568	0.4970	0.4440	0.3971	0.3555
13	0.8787	0.7730	0.6810	0.6006	0.5303	0.4688	0.4150	0.3677	0.3262
14	0.8700	0.7579	0.6611	0.5775	0.5051	0.4423	0.3878	0.3405	0.2992
15	0.8613	0.7430	0.6419	0.5553	0.4810	0.4173	0.3624	0.3152	0.2745
16	0.8528	0.7284	0.6232	0.5339	0.4581	0.3936	0.3387	0.2919	0.2519
17	0.8444	0.7142	0.6050	0.5134	0.4363	0.3714	0.3166	0.2703	0.2311
18	0.8360	0.7002	0.5874	0.4936	0.4155	0.3503	0.2959	0.2502	0.2120
19	0.8277	0.6864	0.5703	0.4746	0.3957	0.3305	0.2765	0.2317	0.1945
20	0.8195	0.6730	0.5537	0.4564	0.3769	0.3118	0.2584	0.2145	0.1784
21	0.8114	0.6598	0.5375	0.4388	0.3589	0.2942	0.2415	0.1987	0.1637
22	0.8034	0.6468	0.5219	0.4220	0.3418	0.2775	0.2257	0.1839	0.1502
23	0.7954	0.6342	0.5067	0.4057	0.3256	0.2618	0.2109	0.1703	0.1378
24	0.7876	0.6217	0.4919	0.3901	0.3101	0.2470	0.1971	0.1577	0.1264
25	0.7798	0.6095	0.4776	0.3751	0.2953	0.2330	0.1842	0.1460	0.1160
30	0.7419	0.5521	0.4120	0.3083	0.2314	0.1741	0.1314	0.0994	0.0754
40	0.6717	0.4529	0.3066	0.2083	0.1420	0.0972	0.0668	0.0460	0.0318
50	0.6080	0.3715	0.2281	0.1407	0.0872	0.0543	0.0339	0.0213	0.0134

(continued)

TABLE A-2   *(concluded)*

Interest Rate

10%	12%	14%	15%	16%	18%	20%	24%	28%	32%	36%
0.9091	0.8929	0.8772	0.8696	0.8621	0.8475	0.8333	0.8065	0.7813	0.7576	0.7353
0.8264	0.7972	0.7695	0.7561	0.7432	0.7182	0.6944	0.6504	0.6104	0.5739	0.5407
0.7513	0.7118	0.6750	0.6575	0.6407	0.6086	0.5787	0.5245	0.4768	0.4348	0.3975
0.6830	0.6355	0.5921	0.5718	0.5523	0.5158	0.4823	0.4230	0.3725	0.3294	0.2923
0.6209	0.5674	0.5194	0.4972	0.4761	0.4371	0.4019	0.3411	0.2910	0.2495	0.2149
0.5645	0.5066	0.4556	0.4323	0.4104	0.3704	0.3349	0.2751	0.2274	0.1890	0.1580
0.5132	0.4523	0.3996	0.3759	0.3538	0.3139	0.2791	0.2218	0.1776	0.1432	0.1162
0.4665	0.4039	0.3506	0.3269	0.3050	0.2660	0.2326	0.1789	0.1388	0.1085	0.0854
0.4241	0.3606	0.3075	0.2843	0.2630	0.2255	0.1938	0.1443	0.1084	0.0822	0.0628
0.3855	0.3220	0.2697	0.2472	0.2267	0.1911	0.1615	0.1164	0.0847	0.0623	0.0462
0.3505	0.2875	0.2366	0.2149	0.1954	0.1619	0.1346	0.0938	0.0662	0.0472	0.0340
0.3186	0.2567	0.2076	0.1869	0.1685	0.1372	0.1122	0.0757	0.0517	0.0357	0.0250
0.2897	0.2292	0.1821	0.1625	0.1452	0.1163	0.0935	0.0610	0.0404	0.0271	0.0184
0.2633	0.2046	0.1597	0.1413	0.1252	0.0985	0.0779	0.0492	0.0316	0.0205	0.0135
0.2394	0.1827	0.1401	0.1229	0.1079	0.0835	0.0649	0.0397	0.0247	0.0155	0.0099
0.2176	0.1631	0.1229	0.1069	0.0930	0.0708	0.0541	0.0320	0.0193	0.0118	0.0073
0.1978	0.1456	0.1078	0.0929	0.0802	0.0600	0.0451	0.0258	0.0150	0.0089	0.0054
0.1799	0.1300	0.0946	0.0808	0.0691	0.0508	0.0376	0.0208	0.0118	0.0068	0.0039
0.1635	0.1161	0.0829	0.0703	0.0596	0.0431	0.0313	0.0168	0.0092	0.0051	0.0029
0.1486	0.1037	0.0728	0.0611	0.0514	0.0365	0.0261	0.0135	0.0072	0.0039	0.0021
0.1351	0.0926	0.0638	0.0531	0.0443	0.0309	0.0217	0.0109	0.0056	0.0029	0.0016
0.1228	0.0826	0.0560	0.0462	0.0382	0.0262	0.0181	0.0088	0.0044	0.0022	0.0012
0.1117	0.0738	0.0491	0.0402	0.0329	0.0222	0.0151	0.0071	0.0034	0.0017	0.0008
0.1015	0.0659	0.0431	0.0349	0.0284	0.0188	0.0126	0.0057	0.0027	0.0013	0.0006
0.0923	0.0588	0.0378	0.0304	0.0245	0.0160	0.0105	0.0046	0.0021	0.0010	0.0005
0.0573	0.0334	0.0196	0.0151	0.0116	0.0070	0.0042	0.0016	0.0006	0.0002	0.0001
0.0221	0.0107	0.0053	0.0037	0.0026	0.0013	0.0007	0.0002	0.0001	★	★
0.0085	0.0035	0.0014	0.0009	0.0006	0.0003	0.0001	★	★	★	★

★The factor is zero to four decimal places.

TABLE A-3   **Present value of an annuity of $1 per period for T periods $= [1 - 1/(1 + r)^T]/r$**
                         (See formula (4.7) for $C = 1$)

Number of Periods	Interest Rate								
	1%	2%	3%	4%	5%	6%	7%	8%	9%
1	0.9901	0.9804	0.9709	0.9615	0.9524	0.9434	0.9346	0.9259	0.9174
2	1.9704	1.9416	1.9135	1.8861	1.8594	1.8334	0.8080	1.7833	1.7591
3	2.9410	2.8839	2.8286	2.7751	2.7232	2.6730	2.6243	2.5771	2.5313
4	3.9020	3.8077	3.7171	3.6299	3.5460	3.4651	3.3872	3.3121	3.2397
5	4.8534	4.7135	4.5797	4.4518	4.3295	4.2124	4.1002	3.9927	3.8897
6	5.7955	5.6014	5.4172	5.2421	5.0757	4.9173	4.7665	4.6229	4.4859
7	6.7282	6.4720	6.2303	6.0021	5.7864	5.5824	5.3893	5.2064	5.0330
8	7.6517	7.3255	7.0197	6.7327	6.4632	6.2098	5.9713	5.7466	5.5348
9	8.5660	8.1622	7.7861	7.4353	7.1078	6.8017	6.5152	6.2469	5.9952
10	9.4713	8.9826	8.5302	8.1109	7.7217	7.3601	7.0236	6.7101	6.4177
11	10.3676	9.7868	9.2526	8.7605	8.3064	7.8869	7.4987	7.1390	6.8052
12	11.2551	10.5753	9.9540	9.3851	8.8633	8.3838	7.9427	7.5361	7.1607
13	12.1337	11.3484	10.6350	9.9856	9.3936	8.8527	8.3577	7.9038	7.4869
14	13.0037	12.1062	11.2961	10.5631	9.8986	9.2950	8.7455	8.2442	7.7862
15	13.8651	12.8493	11.9379	11.1184	10.3797	9.7122	9.1079	8.5595	8.0607
16	14.7179	13.5777	12.5611	11.6523	10.8378	10.1059	9.4466	8.8514	8.3126
17	15.5623	14.2919	13.1661	12.1657	11.2741	10.4773	9.7632	9.1216	8.5436
18	16.3983	14.9920	13.7535	12.6593	11.6896	10.8276	10.0591	9.3719	8.7556
19	17.2260	15.6785	14.3238	13.1339	12.0853	11.1581	10.3356	9.6036	8.9501
20	18.0456	16.3514	14.8775	13.5903	12.4622	11.4699	10.5940	9.8181	9.1285
21	18.8570	17.0112	15.4150	14.0292	12.8212	11.7641	10.8355	10.0168	9.2922
22	19.6604	17.6580	15.9369	14.4511	13.1630	12.0416	11.0612	10.2007	9.4424
23	20.4558	18.2922	16.4436	14.8568	13.4886	12.3034	11.2722	10.3741	9.5802
24	21.2434	18.9139	16.9355	15.2470	13.7986	12.5504	11.4693	10.5288	9.7066
25	22.0232	19.5235	17.4131	15.6221	14.0939	12.7834	11.6536	10.6748	9.8226
30	25.8077	22.3965	19.6004	17.2920	15.3725	13.7648	12.4090	11.2578	10.2737
40	32.8347	27.3555	23.1148	19.7928	17.1591	15.0463	13.3317	11.9246	10.7574
50	39.1961	31.4236	25.7298	21.4822	18.2559	15.7619	13.8007	12.2335	10.9617

(continued)

TABLE A-3 *(concluded)*

Interest Rate

10%	12%	14%	15%	16%	18%	20%	24%	28%	32%
0.9091	0.8929	0.8772	0.8696	0.8621	0.8475	0.8333	0.8065	0.7813	0.7576
1.7355	1.6901	1.6467	1.6257	1.6052	1.5656	1.5278	1.4568	1.3916	1.3315
2.4869	2.4018	2.3216	2.2832	2.2459	2.1743	2.1065	1.9813	1.8684	1.7663
3.1699	3.0373	2.9137	2.8550	2.7982	2.6901	2.5887	2.4043	2.2410	2.0957
3.7908	3.6048	3.4331	3.3522	3.2743	3.1272	2.9906	2.7454	2.5320	2.3452
4.3553	4.1114	3.8887	3.7845	3.6847	3.4976	3.3255	3.0205	2.7594	2.5342
4.8684	4.5638	4.2883	4.1604	4.0386	3.8115	3.6046	3.2423	2.9370	2.6775
5.3349	4.9676	4.6389	4.4873	4.3436	4.0776	3.8372	3.4212	3.0758	2.7860
5.7590	5.3282	4.9464	4.7716	4.6065	4.3030	4.0310	3.5655	3.1842	2.8681
6.1446	5.6502	5.2161	5.0188	4.8332	4.4941	4.1925	3.6819	3.2689	2.9304
6.4951	5.9377	5.4527	5.2337	5.0286	4.6560	4.3271	3.7757	3.3351	2.9776
6.8137	6.1944	5.6603	5.4206	5.1971	4.7932	4.4392	3.8514	3.3868	3.0133
7.1034	6.4235	5.8424	5.5831	5.3423	4.9095	4.5327	3.9124	3.4272	3.0404
7.3667	6.6282	6.0021	5.7245	5.4675	5.0081	4.6106	3.9616	3.4587	3.0609
7.6061	6.8109	6.1422	5.8474	5.5755	5.0916	4.6755	4.0013	3.4834	3.0764
7.8237	6.9740	6.2651	5.9542	5.6685	5.1624	4.7296	4.0333	3.5026	3.0882
8.0216	7.1196	6.3729	6.0472	5.7487	5.2223	4.7746	4.0591	3.5177	3.0971
8.2014	7.2497	6.4674	6.1280	5.8178	5.2732	4.8122	4.0799	3.5294	3.1039
8.3649	7.3658	6.5504	6.1982	5.8775	5.3162	4.8435	4.0967	3.5386	3.1090
8.5136	7.4694	6.6231	6.2593	5.9288	5.3527	4.8696	4.1103	3.5458	3.1129
8.6487	7.5620	6.6870	6.3125	5.9731	5.3837	4.8913	4.1212	3.5514	3.1158
8.7715	7.6446	6.7429	6.3587	6.0113	5.4099	4.9094	4.1300	3.5558	3.1180
8.8832	7.7184	6.7921	6.3988	6.0442	5.4321	4.9245	4.1371	3.5592	3.1197
8.9847	7.7843	6.8351	6.4338	6.0726	5.4509	4.9371	4.1428	3.5619	3.1210
9.0770	7.8431	6.8729	6.4641	6.0971	5.4669	4.9476	4.1474	3.5640	3.1220
9.4269	8.0552	7.0027	6.5660	6.1772	5.5168	4.9789	4.1601	3.5693	3.1242
9.7791	8.2438	7.1050	6.6418	6.2335	5.5482	4.9966	4.1659	3.5712	3.1250
9.9148	8.3045	7.1327	6.6605	6.2463	5.5541	4.9995	4.1666	3.5714	3.1250

TABLE A-4 Future value of an annuity of $1 per period for T periods $= [(1 + r)^T - 1]/r$

Number of Periods	Interest Rate								
	1%	2%	3%	4%	5%	6%	7%	8%	9%
1	1.0000	1.0000	1.0000	1.0000	1.0000	1.0000	1.0000	1.0000	1.0000
2	2.0100	2.0200	2.0300	2.0400	2.0500	2.0600	2.0700	2.0800	2.0900
3	3.0301	3.0604	3.0909	3.1216	3.1525	3.1836	3.2149	3.2464	3.2781
4	4.0604	4.1216	4.1836	4.2465	4.3101	4.3746	4.4399	4.5061	4.5731
5	5.1010	5.2040	5.3091	5.4163	5.5256	5.6371	5.7507	5.8666	5.9847
6	6.1520	6.3081	6.4684	6.6330	6.8019	6.9753	7.1533	7.3359	7.5233
7	7.2135	7.4343	7.6625	7.8983	8.1420	8.3938	8.6540	8.9228	9.2004
8	8.2857	8.5830	8.8932	9.2142	9.5491	9.8975	10.260	10.637	11.028
9	9.3685	9.7546	10.159	10.583	11.027	11.491	11.978	12.488	13.021
10	10.462	10.950	11.464	12.006	12.578	13.181	13.816	14.487	15.193
11	11.567	12.169	12.808	13.486	14.207	14.972	15.784	16.645	17.560
12	12.683	13.412	14.192	15.026	15.917	16.870	17.888	18.977	20.141
13	13.809	14.680	15.618	16.627	17.713	18.882	20.141	21.495	22.953
14	14.947	15.974	17.086	18.292	19.599	21.015	22.550	24.215	26.019
15	16.097	17.293	18.599	20.024	21.579	23.276	25.129	27.152	29.361
16	17.258	18.639	20.157	21.825	23.657	25.673	25.888	30.324	33.003
17	18.430	20.012	21.762	23.698	25.840	28.213	30.840	33.750	36.974
18	19.615	21.412	23.414	25.645	28.132	30.906	33.999	37.450	41.301
19	20.811	22.841	25.117	27.671	30.539	33.760	37.379	41.446	46.018
20	22.019	24.297	26.870	29.778	33.066	36.786	40.995	45.762	51.160
21	23.239	25.783	28.676	31.969	35.719	39.993	44.865	50.423	56.765
22	24.472	27.299	30.537	34.248	38.505	43.392	49.006	55.457	62.873
23	25.716	28.845	32.453	36.618	41.430	46.996	53.436	60.893	69.532
24	26.973	30.422	34.426	39.083	44.502	50.816	58.177	66.765	76.790
25	28.243	32.030	36.459	41.646	47.727	54.865	63.249	73.106	84.701
28				49.9575					
30	34.785	40.568	47.575	56.085	66.439	79.058	94.461	113.28	136.31
40	48.886	60.402	75.401	95.026	120.80	154.76	199.64	259.06	337.88
50	64.463	84.579	112.80	152.67	209.35	290.34	406.53	573.77	815.08

(continued)

TABLE A-4   *(concluded)*

Interest Rate

10%	12%	14%	15%	16%	18%	20%	24%	28%	32%	36%
1.0000	1.0000	1.0000	1.0000	1.0000	1.0000	1.0000	1.0000	1.0000	1.0000	1.0000
2.1000	2.1200	2.1400	2.1500	2.1600	2.1800	2.2000	2.2400	2.2800	2.3200	2.3600
3.3100	3.3744	3.4396	3.4725	3.5056	3.5724	3.6400	3.7776	3.9184	4.0624	4.2096
4.6410	4.7793	4.9211	4.9934	5.0665	5.2154	5.3680	5.6842	6.0156	6.3624	6.7251
6.1051	6.3528	6.6101	6.7424	6.8771	7.1542	7.4416	8.0484	8.6999	9.3983	10.146
7.7156	8.1152	8.5355	8.7537	8.9775	9.4420	9.9299	10.980	12.136	13.406	14.799
9.4872	10.089	10.730	11.067	11.414	12.142	12.916	14.615	16.534	18.696	21.126
11.436	12.300	13.233	13.727	14.240	15.327	16.499	19.123	22.163	25.678	29.732
13.579	14.776	16.085	16.786	17.519	19.086	20.799	24.712	29.369	34.895	41.435
15.937	17.549	19.337	20.304	21.321	23.521	25.959	31.643	38.593	47.062	57.352
18.531	20.655	23.045	24.349	25.733	28.755	32.150	40.238	50.398	63.122	78.998
21.384	24.133	27.271	29.002	30.850	34.931	39.581	50.895	65.510	84.320	108.44
24.523	28.029	32.089	34.352	36.786	42.219	48.497	64.110	84.853	112.30	148.47
27.975	32.393	37.581	40.505	43.672	50.818	59.196	80.496	109.61	149.24	202.93
31.772	37.280	43.842	47.580	51.660	60.965	72.035	100.82	141.30	198.00	276.98
35.950	42.753	50.980	55.717	60.925	72.939	87.442	126.01	181.87	262.36	377.69
40.545	48.884	59.118	65.075	71.673	87.068	105.93	157.25	233.79	347.31	514.66
45.599	55.750	68.394	75.836	84.141	103.74	128.12	195.99	300.25	459.45	700.94
51.159	63.440	78.969	88.212	98.603	123.41	154.74	244.03	385.32	607.47	954.28
57.275	72.052	91.025	102.44	115.38	146.63	186.69	303.60	494.21	802.86	1298.8
64.002	81.699	104.77	118.81	134.84	174.02	225.03	377.46	633.59	1060.8	1767.4
71.403	92.503	120.44	137.63	157.41	206.34	271.03	469.06	812.00	1401.2	2404.7
79.543	104.60	138.30	159.28	183.60	244.49	326.24	582.63	1040.4	1850.6	3271.3
88.497	118.16	158.66	184.17	213.98	289.49	392.48	723.46	1332.7	2443.8	4450.0
98.347	133.33	181.87	212.79	249.21	342.60	471.98	898.09	1706.8	3226.8	6053.0
164.49	241.33	356.79	434.75	530.31	790.95	1181.9	2640.9	5873.2	12941.	28172.3
442.59	767.09	1342.0	1779.1	2360.8	4163.2	7343.9	22729.	69377.	★	★
1163.9	2400.0	4994.5	7217.7	10436.	21813.	45497.	★	★	★	★

*The factor is greater than 99,999.

TABLE A-5   The value of e^{rT}: Future value of $1 invested at a *continuously compounded* rate r for T years

rT	.00	.01	.02	.03	.04	.05	.06	.07	.08	.09
.00	1.000	1.010	1.020	1.030	1.041	1.051	1.062	1.073	1.083	1.094
.10	1.105	1.116	1.127	1.139	1.150	1.162	1.174	1.185	1.197	1.209
.20	1.221	1.234	1.246	1.259	1.271	1.284	1.297	1.310	1.323	1.336
.30	1.350	1.363	1.377	1.391	1.405	1.419	1.433	1.448	1.462	1.477
.40	1.492	1.507	1.522	1.537	1.553	1.568	1.584	1.600	1.616	1.632
.50	1.649	1.665	1.682	1.699	1.716	1.733	1.751	1.768	1.786	1.804
.60	1.822	1.840	1.859	1.878	1.896	1.916	1.935	1.954	1.974	1.994
.70	2.014	2.034	2.054	2.075	2.096	2.117	2.138	2.160	2.181	2.203
.80	2.226	2.248	2.271	2.293	2.316	2.340	2.363	2.387	2.411	2.435
.90	2.460	2.484	2.509	2.535	2.560	2.586	2.612	2.638	2.664	2.691
1.00	2.718	2.746	2.773	2.801	2.829	2.858	2.886	2.915	2.945	2.974
1.10	3.004	3.034	3.065	3.096	3.127	3.158	3.190	3.222	3.254	3.287
1.20	3.320	3.353	3.387	3.421	3.456	3.490	3.525	3.561	3.597	3.633
1.30	3.669	3.706	3.743	3.781	3.819	3.857	3.896	3.935	3.975	4.015
1.40	4.055	4.096	4.137	4.179	4.221	4.263	4.306	4.349	4.393	4.437
1.50	4.482	4.527	4.572	4.618	4.665	4.711	4.759	4.807	4.855	4.904
1.60	4.953	5.003	5.053	5.104	5.155	5.207	5.259	5.312	5.366	5.419
1.70	5.474	5.529	5.585	5.641	5.697	5.755	5.812	5.871	5.930	5.989
1.80	6.050	6.110	6.172	6.234	6.297	6.360	6.424	6.488	6.553	6.619
1.90	6.686	6.753	6.821	6.890	6.959	7.029	7.099	7.171	7.243	7.316
2.00	7.389	7.463	7.538	7.614	7.691	7.768	7.846	7.925	8.004	8.085
2.10	8.166	8.248	8.331	8.415	8.499	8.585	8.671	8.758	8.846	8.935
2.20	9.025	9.116	9.207	9.300	9.393	9.488	9.583	9.679	9.777	9.875
2.30	9.974	10.07	10.18	10.28	10.38	10.49	10.59	10.70	10.80	10.91
2.40	11.02	11.13	11.25	11.36	11.47	11.59	11.70	11.82	11.94	12.06
2.50	12.18	12.30	12.43	12.55	12.68	12.81	12.94	13.07	13.20	13.33
2.60	13.46	13.60	13.74	13.87	14.01	14.15	14.30	14.44	14.59	14.73
2.70	14.88	15.03	15.18	15.33	15.49	15.64	15.80	15.96	16.12	16.28
2.80	16.44	16.61	16.78	16.95	17.12	17.29	17.46	17.64	17.81	17.99
2.90	18.17	18.36	18.54	18.73	18.92	19.11	19.30	19.49	19.69	19.89
3.00	20.09	20.29	20.49	20.70	20.91	21.12	21.33	21.54	21.76	21.98
3.10	22.20	22.42	22.65	22.87	23.10	23.34	23.57	23.81	24.05	24.29
3.20	24.53	24.78	25.03	25.28	25.53	25.79	26.05	26.31	26.58	26.84
3.30	27.11	27.39	27.66	27.94	28.22	28.50	28.79	29.08	29.37	29.67
3.40	29.96	30.27	30.57	30.88	31.19	31.50	31.82	32.14	32.46	32.79
3.50	33.12	33.45	33.78	34.12	34.47	34.81	35.16	35.52	35.87	36.23
3.60	36.60	36.97	37.34	37.71	38.09	38.47	38.86	39.25	39.65	40.04
3.70	40.45	40.85	41.26	41.68	42.10	42.52	42.95	43.38	43.82	44.26
3.80	44.70	45.15	45.60	46.06	46.53	46.99	47.47	47.94	48.42	48.91
3.90	49.40	49.90	50.40	50.91	51.42	51.94	52.46	52.98	53.52	54.05

Example: If the continuously compounded interest rate is 10% per year, the investment of $1 today will be worth $1.162, 1.5 years in the future (see value $rT = 0.1 \times 1.5 = 0.15$)

GLOSSARY

A

Accounting rate of return (ARR) rule A rule whereby a project is accepted if its accounting rate of return exceeds a predetermined critical value.

Accounts payable (payables) period The time between when a firm receives merchandise and when it pays for it.

Accounts receivable (receivables) period The time between when the firm sells merchandise and when it collects cash from customers.

Accounts receivable turnover ratio A ratio that indicates how many times a year, on average, the firm collects its receivables; it is obtained by dividing sales by accounts receivable.

Accruals Liabilities for which payment has not yet been made. Accruals can constitute a source of short-term financing.

Acquisitions The takeover of one firm by another firm.

Activities ratios Ratios that report and measure various aspects of the firm's activities. They provide information on the effectiveness of the firm's operations.

Agency costs Losses incurred when corporation managers do not act in the stockholders' best interest.

Aggressive stock Stock that is riskier than the market portfolio because it fluctuates more sharply than the market itself.

Aging schedule Used to keep track of a firm's receivables situation, the schedule shows the "ages" of unpaid accounts and what percentage of the total value of receivables these accounts represent.

Alternative/opportunity cost The value of the best alternative that is given up.

American option An option that can be exercised at any time up to and including the expiration date.

Annuity A series of equal cash flows (payments) for a given number of years.

841

Annuity due An annuity with cash payments made at the beginning of each period.

Arbitrage Buying an asset in one market at a lower price and simultaneously selling an identical asset in another market at a higher price.

Arbitrage profit When the prices of two alternative investments are not identical, a certain profit can be made by selling the investment with the higher price and buying the investment with the lower price.

ARR Accounting rate of return

Automatic liabilities Liabilities that increase automatically as sales increase.

Availability delay The time needed by the recipient's bank to clear checks through the banking system and present them to the firm's bank.

Average collection period The average number of days it takes the firm to collect its accounts; calculated by dividing the days in the year (365) by the accounts receivable turnover ratio.

Average tax rate Total tax payments divided by total income.

B

Balance sheet A list with the firm's assets on one side and the liabilities and stockholders' equity on the other; the two sides must be balanced by definition.

Bankruptcy risk Risk of losing interest or principal when investing in junk (low-grade) bonds because of the issuing firm's chance of bankruptcy.

Best-efforts arrangement One whereby the investment bank helps market a new stock issue but does not guarantee the issue or assume risk.

Beta A statistical measure of the risk of each individual asset included in a portfolio; the covariance of the individual asset's rate of return and the market portfolio's rate of return divided by the variance of the market portfolio's rate of return.

Black–Scholes option pricing formula An option pricing formula for a situation in which a stock's price can take on more than two values.

Book value The value of the equity recorded for the sale of a firm's shares of stock.

Book value per share Total common stockholders' equity divided by the number of outstanding shares.

Break-even analysis (BEA) An analysis that examines the leverage effect on earnings per share (EPS) in dollar terms.

Break-even point (BEP) The net operating income at which leverage has no effect on earnings per share. At the BEP an all-equity firm's rate of return equals the interest rate.

Business ethics The application of ethics, which encompasses society's standards of right and wrong behavior, to business practices.

C

Call option A contract that gives the holder the right to buy an asset at a predetermined price within a specified period of time.

Call provision Attached to a convertible bond, a written agreement between the firm and its bondholders that gives the firm the option to recall the bond at a specified price before the maturity date.

Callable bond A bond that is subject to being repurchased at a stated call price before maturity; most corporate bonds are callable.

Capital asset pricing model (CAPM) An equilibrium asset pricing theory that shows that equilibrium expected rates of return on all risky assets are a function of their covariances with the market portfolio.

Capital budgeting The planning and management of expenditures on long-lived assets.

Capital gains The positive change in the market value of an asset.

Capital gains tax A tax levied on capital gains.

Capital loss A negative capital gain—for example, if you buy a share of stock for $100 and sell it for $80, your capital loss is $20.

Capital market line (CML) The set of all assets, both risky and riskless, that provides the investor with the best possible opportunities; it represents the linear risk-return relationship of efficient portfolios.

Capital markets Financial markets for long-term debt and equity.

Capital rationing A firm's need to choose among acceptable projects and reject some profitable ones because funds are limited.

Capital structure A firm's mix of debt and equity, determined by its financing decisions.

Capital surplus Proceeds from the sale of stock in excess of its par value.

Carrying costs The cost of holding current assets, including inventory costs, receivables costs, and opportunity costs.

Carrying costs (receivables) The firm's cost of capital, cost of bad debt, and administrative costs associated with receivables.

Cash Currency and demand deposits.

Cash assets Cash and short-term marketable securities combined.

Cash budget A short-term financial planning tool used to forecast the firm's future cash position—surplus or deficit; it summarizes all the firm's cash inflows and cash outflows and helps determine the specific needed amounts of cash assets in future periods.

Cash concentration A procedure that pools the firm's balances into a limited number of concentration banks. By pooling accounts, the firm can keep better track of its cash.

Cash dividend A periodic cash payment to the firm's shareholders.

Cash flow cycle The time between when the firm pays its suppliers and when it collects its receivables. The longer the cycle, the more resources the firm will need to finance its purchases and production costs. Any shortening of the cycle that does not depress the firm's sales will save costs and increase profits. Analysis of the cycle helps management to locate problem areas and take corrective measures and, also, to make accurate estimates of the firm's current asset needs.

CDGM Constant dividend growth model.

Certificate amortization When a firm sells its receivables to a trust or other financial institution, the trust issues certificates to the public and uses the proceeds to pay the firm some portion of the receivables. When the receivables are collected, the trust uses the money to pay the certificate holders (principal and interest).

Characteristic line A line describing the relationship between the rate of return on an asset and the rate of return on the market portfolio.

Chief executive officer (CEO) A corporation's key decision maker.

Chief financial officer (CFO) The person responsible for the corporation's financial planning and policy, such as decisions regarding mergers and acquisitions, dividend policy, pricing of products, and timing and size of stock issues.

Chief operations officer (COO) The person responsible for the corporation's smooth operation and for coordination among its various units.

Classified common stock Stock that gives different voting rights to various classes of shareholders.

Clientele effect The preference of various categories of investors for various types of stocks.

Collection delay The time lapse between when a firm receives a check and when the bank credits the firm's bank account.

Collection float Receipts recorded on the firm's books minus receipts cleared by the bank.

Commercial paper Short-term debt issued by firms at a discount and paying no explicit interest.

Commodity swap An exchange of cash based on a specific commodity's value at specified points in the future.

Common stock A security representing part ownership in a firm.

Compound interest Interest earned on the principal and on the accumulated interest.

Concentration bank A bank where a firm's accounts are pooled.

Constant dividend growth model (CDGM) A valuation model that assumes a firm's earnings and dividends will grow every year at a constant rate. It can also be used to evaluate the firm's cost of equity.

Conventional cash flows Most projects have initial outlays followed by positive cash flows. Projects with only one change in the sign of their cash flows (for example, −, +, +, + . . .) have conventional cash flows.

Conversion price The amount of the bond's face value that is exchangeable for one share of common stock.

Conversion ratio The number of shares per convertible bond that a bondholder would receive if the bond were converted into shares of stock.

Convertible bond A bond that may be converted into shares of stock at a predetermined rate at the bondholder's discretion.

Corporate tax An income tax levied on corporations.

Corporation A legal entity formed through articles of incorporation. The owners, or stockholders, own shares of the corporation's stock.

Correlation A measure of the degree to which the rate of return on one asset moves in relation to the rate of return on another asset; a standardized statistical measure of the dependence of two variables.

Cost of debt The minimum expected rate of return that bondholders require.

Cost of equity The minimum expected rate of return that stockholders require.

Country risk Investment risk based on events or circumstances in a foreign country.

Coupon The stated periodic interest payment on a debt instrument.

Covariance A statistical measure of the degree to which two variables move together.

Credit period The length of time for which the firm grants credit.

Credit policy The terms under which a firm will extend credit to consumers and other firms.

Credit risk The risk a firm faces of its receivables being uncollectible.

Credit scoring A method used to determine the probability of default when granting customers credit.

Currency swap A swap contract that requires the exchange of different currencies.

Current ratio A measure of a firm's liquidity, calculated by dividing the current assets by the current liabilities.

D

Days in inventory A measure indicating the number of days, on average, that a firm holds inventory.

Debentures Unsecured bonds, usually long-term, that are backed by the general credit of the issuing firm.

Debt capacity A firm's ability to employ debt and reduce its tax burden because interest is tax deductible.

Debt financing Raising capital to finance new investments by means of borrowing from a bank or by selling bonds.

Debt/assets ratio A measure of a firm's long-term repayment capacity and risk; calculated by dividing long-term debt by total assets.

Debt/equity ratio A measure of a firm's long-term repayment capacity and risk; calculated by dividing long-term debt by equity.

Defensive stock A stock that fluctuates less than the market and, therefore, is considered relatively safe.

Depository transfer check (DTC) A preauthorized check that does not need a signature.

Depreciation A noncash expense charged against earnings to write off the cost of an asset during its estimated useful life.

Derivatives Financial instruments that derive their value from an underlying asset's value.

Disbursement delay The period of time before a check written and recorded on a firm's books is received by the clearing bank and processed.

Discount annuity factor A factor used to determine the present or future value of an annuity or perpetuity.

Discount bond A bond that is selling below its face value.

Discount factor (DF) A factor used to calculate the present value of an amount to be received in the future.

Discount rate Rate used to calculate the present value of future cash flows.

Discounted cash flow (DCF) principle The idea that a stock's value is the discounted value of all its future cash flows.

Discounted payback rule An investment decision rule in which cash flows are discounted at a specific interest rate and a project is accepted if its cost is recovered within a set time period.

Discounting Calculating the present value of a future amount.

Diversification Reducing risk by investing in a number of assets with different risk-return characteristics.

Dividend per share (DPS) A periodic cash payment to shareholders for each share they own.

Dividend policy A firm's decision regarding the size of dividends it will pay to its shareholders.

Dividend reinvestment plan (DRIP) A means by which investors can use their cash dividends to buy additional shares of stock without transaction costs.

Dividend yield Dividends per share as a percentage of a stock's price.

DuPont system A method of analyzing the relationship among various ratios to help pinpoint the factors affecting changes in profitability.

E

E–σ frontier The set of all portfolios such that, for a given expected rate of return, the standard deviation is minimized.

Earnings per share (EPS) Net income divided by the number of shares outstanding.

EBIT Earnings before interest and taxes.

Economic order quantity (EOQ) model A method of determining a firm's optimum level of inventory—that is, the level that minimizes the total related costs.

Economic value added (EVA) After-tax net operating profit in a given year minus a company's cost of capital in that year.

Effective annual interest rate The interest rate as if it were compounded once per time period rather than several times per period.

Efficient market hypothesis (EMH) A hypothesis that claims the stock market is efficient, so that no abnormal profit is available. In other words, the prices of securities fully reflect available information.

Equal percentage contribution rule (EPCOR) In equilibrium, the CAPM implies that each asset contributes the same percentage to the portfolio risk premium and to its risk.

Equity financing Sale of shares of stock to the public to raise money for financing new investments as well as ongoing projects.

Equity-multiple The ratio of a firm's total assets to its equity.

Eurobonds Bonds issued by corporations and governments that are traded simultaneously in a number of countries.

European option An option that can be exercised only on the expiration date.

Ex-dividend date The last date on which a stock can be sold without sacrificing the dividend.

Expected rate of return The rate of return that should be expected on average.

Expiration date The last day on which the option can be exercised.

External financial needs (EFN) Uses of funds − Operating cash flows; alternatively, the required increase in assets, minus the increase in "automatic" liabilities, minus next year's net income, less cash dividends.

F

Factoring agreement The outright sale of a firm's receivables to a finance company without recourse.

FCC Firm's cost of capital.

Financial distress Events preceding and including bankruptcy, such as violation of loan contracts.

Financial leverage The use of debt in a firm's capital structure to enhance, or "lever," the profit to stockholders.

Financial leverage ratios Ratios used to measure a firm's long-term repayment capacity and risk.

Financial markets Markets in which financial capital is traded.

Financial statement analysis Evaluation of a firm based on information contained in its financial statements.

Financial statements Reports that provide information on such items as a firm's profit (or loss), interest payments, dividends, financing (stock or bond issues, loans), debt repayments, and capital expenditures.

Financing decisions A corporation's decisions on how to provide needed resources, such as issuing stocks (equity) or bonds (debt) or borrowing short-term or long-term.

Financing mix The mix of debt and equity used by a corporation to raise the money needed to finance its projects.

Firm-commitment arrangement One whereby the investment bank underwrites a stock issue and guarantees the firm a definite amount per share regardless of market price fluctuations.

Firm's cost of capital (FCC) The risk-adjusted discount rate at which the firm's total cash flow should be discounted.

Fisher effect An adjustment in the nominal interest rate in response to changes in the inflation rate.

Fixed costs Costs that remain constant for a firm, regardless of whether it accepts a project.

Float The difference between bank cash and book cash; the value of uncollected checks being transferred from one bank to another.

Float management Accelerating cash collection and delaying cash disbursement to reduce cash balances.

Floating-rate debt Long-term bonds with interest rates subject to adjustment every few months.

Flotation cost The cost of a new issue of securities.

Foreign exchange risk The risk U.S. investors are exposed to when investing in bonds denominated in foreign currency.

Forward contract An agreement between buyer and seller to exchange goods for cash at some future date at a predetermined price.

Future value (FV) Value of a sum after it is invested over one or more periods.

Future value factor (FVF) Factor used to calculate the future value of an amount of money at the end of a certain period of time when invested at a particular rate of interest.

Futures contract An agreement between buyer and seller to exchange goods for cash at some future date at a predetermined price.

G

Grace period The period of time during which credit customers may pay the balance on their accounts without incurring an interest charge.

Gross profit margin ratio EBIT divided by sales.

Gross working capital The portion of the firm's resources that circulates from cash to inventory to short-term investments and back to cash in the regular course of business.

Growing annuity A cash flow that may grow for several years, but not forever.

Growing perpetuity A stream of cash flows that is expected to grow indefinitely.

H

Historical value The original cost of an asset minus its accumulated depreciation.

Homemade leverage The idea that if investors can borrow and lend on the same terms as firms, they can duplicate the effects of corporate leverage on their own.

I

Imperfect capital market A market that experiences transaction costs, taxes, bankruptcy, risk-varying interest rates, and agency costs.

In the money Describes a positive cash flow that can be obtained by exercising an option immediately.

Income statement A financial statement that reports a firm's earnings or losses during the reported period.

Incremental cash flow principle The idea that a firm should include variable costs and exclude fixed costs in evaluating a project's cash flows.

Indenture Written agreement between the firm and the bondholder.

Independent projects Projects are independent if accepting one of them does not rule out the possibility of accepting others.

Index analysis Tracking yearly EPS percentage changes relative to a common base year.

Indexed bonds Bonds whose coupons and principal are adjusted to the inflation rate.

Industry analysis Information obtained by comparing a firm's financial position in a given year (or over more than one year) to that firm's competitors.

Inflation A sustained increase in the general level of prices.

Inflation risk Risk that results because future inflation is uncertain and, therefore, a bond's cash flows are uncertain in real terms.

Initial public offering (IPO) The original sale of a firm's securities to the public.

Insider trading Taking advantage of information available only to insiders (such as members of the board of directors and top management) and not to the general public to gain an advantage in the securities market.

Interest coverage ratio Earnings before interest and taxes (EBIT) divided by interest expense.

Interest rate option A call option used to hedge interest rate risk.

Interest rate risk The risk of a change in a bond's price due to changes in the interest rate.

Interest rate swap A swap contract in which the counterparties agree to exchange interest payments.

Interest tax shield Tax saving due to leverage.

Internal rate of return (IRR) A discount rate at which the net present value of an investment is zero.

Intrinsic value (option) The value resulting from immediate exercise of an option.

Inventory period The time from the receipt of merchandise until its sale for either cash or credit—that is, the time during which the firm holds it as inventory.

Inventory turnover ratio The rate at which inventory is converted into sales; obtained by dividing the cost of goods sold by the year-end inventory of finished goods.

Investment schedule (IS) A curve that describes all a firm's available projects ranked by their profitability.

J

Junk bonds Speculative grade bonds, rated Ba or below by Moody's, BB or below by S&P, or unrated, that provide opportunity for large profits but at high risk.

L

Law of one price If two assets yield exactly the same distribution of future cash flows, their current market prices will be identical.

Level–coupon bond A bond that pays an identical coupon every year throughout its life.

Levered firm A firm partially financed by debt.

Line of credit A short-term source of financing granted by a bank to a particular borrower up to a specific amount and for a definite time period.

Liquidity A firm's ability to convert assets into cash on short notice and without incurring a loss.

Liquidity ratios Ratios used to measure a firm's liquidity.

Lockbox Post office boxes set up by companies to receive payments of accounts receivable.

Long position (buying) A position held by the trader who commits to purchase a security.

Lower bound (option) The lowest current value on a call option. It cannot be lower than the option's intrinsic value.

M

MACRS Modified Accelerated Cost Recovery System.

Marginal cost of capital (MCC) When a firm raises money in such a way that the cost increases with the amount of money raised, we say the firm faces an increasing MCC.

Marginal tax rate The tax rate paid on additional income.

Mark to market Daily cash settlement whenever there are changes in a futures contract price.

Market portfolio A value-weighted index of all securities. In practice, it is an index, such as the S&P 500, that describes the return of the entire value of the stock market.

Market risk (systematic risk or nondiversifiable risk) Risk stemming from general market fluctuations.

Market value The price at which willing buyers and sellers trade a firm's assets.

Market value added (MVA) The increase in a firm's value as a result of management's actions; calculated by subtracting total invested capital from the current market value of the firm's debt and equity.

Marketable securities Assets such as short-term U.S. Treasury bills, certificates of deposit (CDs), and commercial paper that are similar to cash.

Market/book value ratio The relationship between the accounting value of a firm's assets and the market price of its stock; obtained by dividing the stock price per share by the book value of equity per share.

Maturity date The date the contract between the firm and bondholder expires and the firm repays a bond's principal to the bondholder.

Maturity matching The financing of long-term assets by long-term liabilities and equity, and financing short-term assets by short-term liabilities.

Mean standard deviation (E–σ) efficient set A set of assets with the largest expected return for a given standard deviation.

Mergers Combination of two fims into one.

Modified Accelerated Cost Recovery System (MACRS) A depreciation system in which different types of assets are assigned to prespecified class life recovery periods.

Money market securities Short-term bonds usually issued for less than one year.

Money markets Financial markets for short-term debt with maturities of less than one year.

Mortgage bonds Debt obligations secured by specific assets, i.e., real property, that a firm owns.

Municipal bonds Bonds issued by state and local governments to finance their operations.

Mutually exclusive projects Projects whereby the acceptance of one means the rejection of another.

N

Net float A firm's disbursement float minus its collection float.

Net present value (NPV) The present value of all future cash flows minus the project's initial outlay.

Net profit margin ratio A ratio used to assess a firm's profitability; obtained by dividing net income by sales.

Net working capital The difference between current assets and current liabilities.

Neutral stock A stock whose price movements mimic those of the market as a whole.

Nominal cash flow A cash flow expressed in terms of the actual dollars to be received (or paid out).

Nominal interest rate Measures the annual percentage increase in a dollar amount.

Nonconventional cash flows Projects with more than one change in the signs of their cash flows (for example, $-, +, -, +, +, \ldots$).

Normal-growth firms A firm that reinvests retained earnings in projects with zero NPV.

NPV rule A rule that maintains that if the NPV of a project's cash flows is positive, the project should be accepted; otherwise, it should be rejected.

O

Odd lot Fewer than 100 shares of a stock.

Offering price The price at which the security is initially offered to the public.

Operating cycle The time between when the firm receives inventory from suppliers and when it collects cash from customers.

Opportunity cost The value of the most valuable alternative that is given up.

Optimal capital budget A budget achieved when a firm maximizes its stock price by accepting positive NPV projects and rejecting negative NPV projects.

Optimal dividend policy The dividend policy that maximizes the firm's value.

Optimal financial leverage/optimal capital structure The amount of financial leverage that maximizes a firm's market value.

Optimal level of cash assets The level of cash assets that maximizes a firm's value.

Option A contract that gives its holder the right but not the obligation to buy or sell a well-defined asset (usually a share of stock) at a predetermined price within a specified period of time.

Option premium The price paid for an option.

Ordering costs The costs of placing an order, including shipping costs.

Out of the money Describes an option whose exercise would not be profitable.

P

Par value (face value) The fixed sum transferred to the bondholder at a bond's maturity date.

Partnership A form of business with at least two owners—the partners—whose shares are determined by a partnership agreement.

Payback period (PBP) rule An investment decision rule which states that only those investment projects that have payback periods equal to or less than a particular cutoff period are accepted.

Payout ratio Proportion of a firm's net income paid out in cash dividends.

Perfect market One that has no taxes, transaction costs, bankruptcy costs, or agency costs, and where individuals and firms can borrow and lend at the same interest rate.

Perpetuity A series of equal cash flows for an unlimited period.

Poison pill provision Any measure taken by a target firm to make it less attractive to an acquirer.

Political risk Investment risk caused by political changes in a country.

Portfolio A combination of assets held by an investor.

Preauthorized debit The automatic transfer of funds from a customer's account to a firm's account on a certain date.

Precautionary motive Holding cash assets in order to have a safety margin for unforeseen cash outflows.

Preferred stock A type of equity security that has characteristics of both bonds and common stocks.

Premium bond A bond that is traded above its face value.

Present value (PV) The value today of a future cash stream.

Price/earnings (P/E) ratio The current market price per share divided by current annual earnings per share.

Principal A bond's face value; the fixed sum transferred to the bondholder at maturity.

Principle of no arbitrage profit When two investments yield exactly the same distribution of future rates of return, their current market prices will be identical.

Private placement Selling securities in large blocks to institutions, generally at some discount from the market price.

Pro forma (projected) financial statements Forecasted financial statements used by firms to project their future financial needs or cash surplus.

Probability distribution The listing of all possible outcomes of an investment together with the probability (chance) attached to each outcome.

Processing delay The time needed by the recipients of a firm's checks to sort, record, and deliver the checks to the bank.

Profitability index (PI) rule A rule that maintains that if a project's PI is greater than 1, a firm should accept the project.

Profitability ratios Used to assess a firm's profitability, these various ratios can be derived from the financial statements. The four most commonly used are the net profit margin ratio, gross profit margin ratio, return on total assets (ROA) ratio, and return on equity (ROE) ratio.

Project's cost of capital (PCC) The risk-adjusted discount rate at which a project's cash flow should be discounted.

Prospectus A summary of the information provided in the registration statement regarding a stock offering.

Proxy A stockholder's transfer of voting rights to another party who may vote as he or she wishes.

Put option A contract that gives the holder the right to sell the asset at a predetermined price within a predetermined period of time.

Put–call parity The value of a call option equals the value of buying the stock, plus buying the put, minus the discounted value of the striking price.

Q

Quick ratio A measure of a firm's liquidity calculated by subtracting inventory from current assets and dividing the resulting figure by current liabilities.

R

Rate of return The percentage change in the value of an investment over a given time period, generally one year.

Real cash flow A cash flow expressed in terms of purchasing power.

Real interest rate The percentage change in the purchasing power of an amount of money.

Registration statement A document, filed with the SEC, that provides financial and legal information about a firm that intends to make a stock offering.

Regular annuity An annuity whose cash payments are made at the end of each period.

Regular cash dividend A cash payment made by a firm to its shareholders, usually on a quarterly basis.

Replacement decision A firm's decision about the frequency of replacement for machines.

Repurchase agreement (repo) A short-term, often overnight, sale of government securities with an agreement to repurchase the securities at a slightly higher price.

Required rate of return The rate of return a firm must earn to compensate its stockholders for their risk exposure.

Residual dividend A variable dividend that depends on the firm's accepted projects and on its earnings.

Restrictive covenants Constraints placed on the firm as the issuer of bonds and written into the bonds' indentures.

Retention ratio A firm's retained earnings divided by its net income.

Return on equity (ROE) ratio Net income divided by equity.

Return on total assets (ROA) ratio Net income divided by total assets.

Rights offering An offer by a corporation to its existing shareholders giving them the opportunity to purchase additional shares of stock at special rates before the shares are offered to the public.

Risk averters Investors who dislike volatility.

Risk premium The difference between the expected rate of return on a risky asset and the riskless rate of return.

Round lot A unit of 100 shares of stock.

S

S&P 500 Standard & Poor's Composite Index

Safety stock Inventory held by a firm to avoid shortage costs.

Seasoned new issue An additional stock issue by a firm that already has stock traded in the market.

Secured loan A short-term loan obtained by pledging a firm's assets as collateral.

Securities and Exchange Commission (SEC) A government regulatory agency responsible for enforcing the rules governing the trading of securities and for approving new issues.

Security market line (SML) The linear relationship between assets' expected rates of return and their corresponding betas.

Short selling A transaction in which an investor borrows a security from a broker, sells it, and receives a cash flow. Thereafter, the investor repurchases the security and returns it to the broker.

Short-term financial management The management of short-term assets and liabilities such as cash, inventory, and short-term loans.

Shortage costs Costs a firm incurs if it does not hold enough current assets.

Sinking fund provision A bond provision whereby after a grace period the firm is required to retire some portion of its debt every year.

Sole proprietorship A form of business organization in which one person owns and controls all the business's assets and is entitled to all the profits.

Speculative motive Holding cash assets in order to take advantage of unexpected investment opportunities.

Standard deviation A standard statistical measure of the spread of a set of data.

Standby underwriting arrangement An arrangement whereby an investment bank guarantees a firm a certain price per share of stock in an issue.

Statement of cash flows Lists all of a firm's cash inflows and cash outflows from operating, investing, and financing activities during the year.

Stock dividend Payment of a dividend in shares of stock instead of cash, on a pro rata basis.

Stock options Options to buy shares of a firm's stock under favorable conditions.

Stock repurchase A firm's repurchase of its outstanding shares.

Stock split An increase in the number of outstanding shares of stock with no change in the shareholder's equity.

Straight bond A bond that pays coupon and principal, with neither the firm nor the bondholder able to change the cash flows involved.

Striking price (exercise price) The fixed, predetermined price at which an option holder can buy or sell the underlying asset.

Subordinated debentures Unsecured debt obligations whose holders' claims on a firm's assets are paid only after the claims of senior bondholders have been satisfied.

Subscription price The price at which stockholders can buy additional shares offered by a firm through a rights offering.

Sunk costs Outlays that have already been made, cannot be removed, and that should not affect future decisions.

Supergrowth firms A firm with the opportunity to invest in positive-NPV projects.

Swap contract A contract between two counterparties who agree to exchange a payment based on one asset's value for a payment based on another asset's value.

Symmetric information A condition in which managers and stockholders alike know all information regarding future projects.

Synchronization The ability to move cash disbursements and cash collections into the same cash flow cycle.

T

Time value (option) The value of a call option based on the possibility that the stock price will rise prior to the expiration date.

Time value of money A concept that holds that one dollar received today is worth more than one dollar received at some future time because today's dollar can be invested to earn interest in the interim period.

Tombstone An advertisement announcing a firm's public stock offering

Total assets turnover ratio Sales divided by total assets.

Transaction motive Holding cash assets for the purpose of making routine payments associated with ongoing activities.

Treasury bonds Long-term bonds issued by the U.S. federal government that generally pay interest semiannually.

U

Uncertainty A situation with more than one possible outcome.

Underlying asset The asset on which the option contract is written.

Underwriter An investment bank that assumes the risk of floating a firm's stock issue.

Unique risk (nonsystematic risk or diversifiable risk) The risk peculiar to a particular stock.

Unlevered firm A firm that has no debt.

V

Variable costs Costs that are likely to change if the firm accepts a project.

Variance The expected value of squared deviation of a variable from the expected return.

Volatility Fluctuation, over time, in some variable.

Voting right premium The difference between the prices of two classes of stock.

W

Warrant A security that gives the holder the right—but not the obligation—to buy shares of a firm's stock at a prespecified price and within a given time period.

Weighted average cost of capital (WACC) The average of the costs of a firm's debt and equity weighted by their proportions in a firm's capital structure.

"Window dressing" technique An attempt to show a strong financial statement for the period covering the statement's publication date.

Working capital management The management of current assets.

Y

Yield curve A curve describing the relationship between yield and the time to maturity on a bond.

Yield-to-call A bond's yield calculated on the assumption that it will be recalled.

Yield-to-maturity A bond's annual rate of return when the investor holds it until the maturity date.

Z

Zero-coupon bond A bond that pays no interim interest before its maturity date.

INDEX

G